MW00996733

ARMIES OF THE NAPOLEONIC WARS RESEARCH SERIES

"The Glory Years" of 1805—1807

Volume 1

NAPOLEON
and
AUSTERLITZ

An Unprecedentedly Detailed Combat Study of Napoleon's Epic Ulm-Austerlitz Campaigns of 1805

by

SCOTT BOWDEN

THE EMPEROR'S PRESS
Chicago, Illinois
"*Simply the Finest!*"

© 1997 Scott Bowden

All Rights Reserved. No part of this publication may be reproduced, stored in a retrieval system, or transmitted, in any form, or by any means, electronic, mechanical, photocopying, recording, or otherwise, without the prior written permission of the author.

Original Edition; Published in 1997

Printed and Bound in the United States of America

Original cartography by David L. McElhannon

Original artwork drawn by Andrew Jason Arno

ISBN 0-9626655-7-6

Books by Scott Bowden

Napoleon and Austerlitz
Napoleon's Grande Armée of 1813
Armies on the Danube 1809 (two editions)
Armies at Waterloo
Armies at Gettysburg
Armies at First Manassas

In Preparation:
Napoleon and Jena

Miniatures Rules by Scott Bowden

Chef de bataillon
Empire (five editions)
*Stars*n*Bars (two editions)*
Redcoat
Coeur de Lion
J.E.B.! (two editions)
Minuteman

For information, contact:

The Emperor's Press
5744 West Irving Park Road
Chicago, IL. 60634 U.S.A.
Telephone 773-777-7307
"Simply the Finest!"

TABLE OF CONTENTS

French Officers from Hussar and Chasseur à cheval Regiments

PREFACE

Ten years before the final Napoleonic battle fought in Belgium called Waterloo, a Great Captain led history's first modern army in two momentous campaigns that forever left their indelible mark upon history. That Great Captain was Napoleon Bonaparte, and his army was called the *Grande Armée*. Although later French armies of the Napoleonic era would take that same name, the soldiers that comprised, as a whole, those entities could in no way measure up to the experience, enthusiasm and devotion that was the collective strength of the original *Grande Armée* any more than the Roman Emperors could measure up to the man from whom they had taken their title—Caesar.

Napoleon and the *Grande Armée* of 1805 demonstrated that they waged war with unrelenting speed and fury. The three months during which these two campaigns were fought represent the zenith of Napoleon's considerable military powers, while his army was shown to be a highly-trained, professional machine—certainly one of greatest armies in history. Yet, almost 200 years after Napoleon about faced the *Grande Armée* from the English Channel, marched it across the Rhine to defeat the Austrian and Russian forces in central Europe, no detailed combat study of these battles, incorporating the combination of archival documents in France, Austria and Russia has ever been attempted prior to *Napoleon and Austerlitz*.

This daunting task was undertaken in the hope of providing a better understanding and insight into the intricacies of the Napoleonic battlefield. An additional benefit is examining the effectiveness of the rival leaders and their forces, which these archival documents, used in conjunction, offer. Employing these sources, many new and intriging findings are examined and presented in the study. Some of these are the numerical strengths of the armies and heretofore unincorporated detailed tactical battle descriptions that help us better understand the hell known as Napoleonic warfare.

For details concerning the central characters of this book, Napoleon and the *Grande Armée*, the principal source of manuscript material was the *Archives du Service historique de l'état-major de l'armée* (S.H.A.T.) at the *château de Vincennes*. The contents from 193 different cartons at S.H.A.T., totaling thousands of pieces of correspondence, after-action reports and troop returns, were utilized to bring to life the officers and men of the *Grande Armée*. Also, numerous documents from the *Archives Nationale* and the *Musée de l'Armée* were of vital importance in not only portraying Napoleon's war machine, but also the Austrian and Russian armies as well.

The main Austrian archives, the *österreichischen Kriegsarchiv* in Vienna, proved to be the principal source of information for the Austrian forces. In addition, smaller archival collections throughout Germany also yielded valuable information on the Austrian army of 1805. And while the *Kriegsarchiv* as well as S.H.A.T. held some excellent information on the Tsar's 1805 forces, most valuable were the extensive collection of regimental histories in the Russian army archives and the Russian artillery archives in Saint Petersburg.

From the study of the antagonist armies also spring numerous intriguing subplots. These range, in part, from the dynamic and often fractious personalities with which Napoleon had to deal with within this own establishment, to the importance of leadership and its role within each army, to the uneasy and distrusting alliance in which the Austrians and Russians found themselves, to the delusional Tsar Alexander I, who believed that he was on a messanic mission to expand Russian influence into central Europe while restoring the French monarchy from the clutches of the hated usurpor.

This work could have never been undertaken or completed without the kind assistance of many. In France, my sincere thanks to the General, and to the staff of the *Archives du Service historique de l'état-major de l'armée* at the *château de Vincennes* as well as to those who assisted at *Musée de l'Armée, Archives Nationale* and *Bibliothèque Nationale*. I appreciate the patience and courtesy extended me by the fine people of these distinguished institutions. Also, my thanks to Jean-Philippe Saujet and Matt DeLaMater for their assistance in helping to obtain some of the documents that related to the *Grande Armée*. In Germany, my thanks to Alfred Umhey for his research assistance.

In the United States, my heartfelt thanks go to many good friends, including: Charles Tarbox and Kip Trexel for use of their libraries; to Robert J. Holland, curator of the vast *Bibliothèque Holland*, my thanks for the use of the collection as well as his advice throughout the project. Also, I am greatly indebited to Bill Ward who was never too busy to answer my questions or to discuss the many aspects of this book. I also appreciate the efforts of John Brewster, Amy Peterson Highley, Earl Upchurch, Lynn Totten, Dana Lombardy and Fred Stovall for their valuable observations and recommendations on the manuscript. To Robert M. Epstein, Harold T. Parker and John Elting, I am humbly grateful for the views of these distinguished Napoleonic scholars and their most insightful recommendations that improved the final version of the book. Finally, I wish to thank my publisher, Todd Fisher, for his grace and ease in working with me on this project.

It is my sincere hope that you enjoy *Napoleon and Austerlitz* and that it will, in some small way, help serve to stimulate your interest and study in the period that is called of the Age of Napoleon.

Scott Bowden
Arlington, Texas

FOREWORD

Napoleon considered that a battle was best begun by careful, stubborn defensive fighting- "First, one must see... Then, the vulnerable point in the enemy's dispositions having been determined, an all-out attack was loosed against it. The secret was in the timing... The transition from the defensive to the offensive is one of the most delicate operations in war."

Of all Napoleon's battles, Austerlitz best exemplifies this maxim. Friedland came close; bad roads and bad weather, that made Davout late and Ney too late, crippled its application at Eylau. And Austerlitz remains unique for another reason—the only battle in which Napoleon deliberately lured his enemies into a "come-and-be-killed" trap. He himself regarded it as his masterpiece, thoroughly ignoring Soult's desire to be named "Duke of Austerlitz" for his share in the victory.

Scott Bowden describes the strategic and tactical aspects of this famous campaign and battle in greater detail than any other author I have encountered. Using masses of official returns from both armies, he presents a careful, sound description of events, embellished by complete orders of battle and carefully researched data on strengths and casualties. His sources are excellent (with the possible exception of Thiebault's memoirs, possibly written by a professional ghost writer). Bowden writes clearly, with obvious respect for both his subject and the historian's basic responsibility—to present the whole story as completely, accurately, and impartially as possible, maneuvering his masses of information as the Emperor did his army corps. His book should be the basic reference work on Austerlitz for years to come.

John R. Elting
Colonel, USA-Ret.

PART I

History's First Modern Army—Napoleon's Grande Armée

Élite Gendarmes of the Imperial Guard

Chapter I
"A Career Open to All Talents"— Napoleon's Grande Armée

"My motto has always been: A career open to all talents, without distinctions of birth." —Napoleon[1]

Sergeant Heuillet of the *chasseurs à pied* of the French Imperial Guard was standing his post as the Battle of Austerlitz drew to a close. Although a new member of the Guard having only joined the regiment on 17 October, Heuillet had been in uniform since the Revolution. He began his career as a drummer in the *27th demi-brigade de bataille.* At age 15, he beat the *pas de charge* as the French troops surged across the bridge of Lodi in Northern Italy on 10 May 1796.

Napoleon at Lodi

More than nine years later, during the late afternoon of 2 December 1805, Heuillet saw another sight that he would never forget. As Imperial aides-de-camp and other officers of the Imperial Guard came before Napoleon with their captured standards and stories of crushing victory, a group of Russian prisoners was close by. In this group was a young, vociferous Russian artillery officer named Major Apraxin who spoke excellent French. His outcries to be shot, preferring death to capture, drew the attention of the *chasseurs* standing guard. They told him to be quiet. The Emperor would hear him! The clamor did not escape Napoleon's attention. He ordered the Russian captive to approach. With tears streaming down his cheeks, Apraxin begged: "Sire, order your men to shoot me. I am unworthy to live for I have lost all my guns!" In a calm, conciliatory yet confident tone, the Emperor replied: "Calm yourself, young man. You should not feel dishonored to be defeated by *my* army."[2]

* *

The Embryo of a Legend
Introduction

About four kilometers (two and one-half miles) from the old encampment at Boulogne, along the high road to Paris, stands a small brick house known as the château de Pont-de-Briques. In 1804 Napoleon established his headquarters at Pont-de-Briques because it was convenient to his army, there encamped along the English Channel coast where the units were undergoing extensive training. Pont-de-Briques was close enough so that he could come and go from the château, making appearances at any one of the camps without his lieutenants having any warning. In this manner, Napoleon would conduct many of the surprise inspections for which he was famous.

Pont-de-Briques today

---

1 Charles Tristan Montholon, *Historie de la captivité de Saint-Hélène,* 2 volumes (Brussels, 1846), vol. 1, p. 112.

2 Henry Lachouque and Anne S. K. Brown, *The Anatomy of Glory—Napoleon and his Guard* (New York 1978), p. 65; Philippe de Ségur, *An Aide-de-Camp of Napoleon,* translated by H. A. Patchett-Martin (London 1895), p. 254; Claude Manceron, *Austerlitz,* translated by George Unwin (New York 1966), pp. 303-304.

The château de Pont-de-Briques is important because from this modest structure, history's first modern army was created.[3] The château itself has a distinguished façade and two prominent wings. One wing was used by Josephine, Napoleon's wife, and her attendants; in the other wing Napoleon worked in the unpretentious rooms. From these, his letters, acts and decrees poured out in voluminous proportions, shaping the instrument of war that not only was history's first modern army, and one of its greatest. Finally, there is a stone balcony overlooking the grounds, and it was from this balcony that the Emperor dictated the initial plans and orders for the immortal Ulm-Austerlitz campaign of 1805.

Before the French legions quit the region of the Boulonnais to begin their journey eastward to the Danube and their dates with destiny, the officers and men who comprised Napoleon's army spent two years in intensive training at the encampment of Boulogne.[4]

A Gathering of Eagles

Following Napoleon's victory over the Austrians in Italy at the Battle of Marengo on 14 June 1800, the Allied Second Coalition against France had collapsed. With the disintegration of that coalition, Austria made peace with France at Lunéville on 9 February 1801 and even Great Britain came to terms with the Revolutionaries by the Treaty of Amiens on 27 March 1802.[5] However, peace with France without a Bourbon king was just not acceptable to the British. Indeed, peace with France even when there was a monarch on the throne was not something Britain had embraced with any longevity since the time of Henry II (1154-1189)! Although the issue was very complex, instead of turning over Malta to the Knights of Saint John (or of Malta) as agreed at Amiens, the British retained the strategic Mediterranean island and resumed the war with France in the spring of 1803.[6]

Napoleon

With the renewal of these hostilities, Napoleon rightfully suspected that there could be no peace on the continent until Britain was defeated. To deal with the British, he ordered the concentration and training of a large army that would be organized and commanded as never before. By embracing the philosophies of French military theorists of the late 18th century, the disparate elements of the Revolutionary forces would be molded into a newly created, modern force along the coast of France near the Channel port of Boulogne,[7] there to be transported by flotillas across the narrow sea after the British navy had been lured away. Once on English soil, the French army would overwhelm British army and militia forces, then march on London where Napoleon would dictate his terms of peace.

This wasn't the first time Napoleon thought of invading Britain. On 4 floréal an VI (23 April 1798), Bonaparte declared to the Directory: "Attempting an invasion of England, without mastery of the sea, is the boldest and most difficult operation

---

[3] Fernand Émile Beaucour, *Lettres, Décisions et Actes de Napoléon à Pont-de-Briques (An VI/1798 - An XII/1804)* (Levallois 1979), pp. 16-17. Hereafter cited as *Lettres, Décisions et Actes de Napoléon* .

[4] Beaucour, *Lettres, Décisions et Actes de Napoléon,* pp. 17-18.

[5] Owen Connelly, Harold T. Parker, Peter W. Becker and June K. Burton, *Historical Dictionary of Napoleonic France, 1799-1815* (Westport 1985), p. 16. The Consulate was in power by this time, but it still seemed like the Revolution to most British.

[6] When the English did not live up to their committments made at Amiens, Napoleon said to the English ambassador: 'In this treaty I see only two names: Taranto, which I have evacuated, and Malta, which you have not.'

[7] Bonaparte to Berthier, *La Correspondance de Napoléon 1er*, 32 volumes (Paris, 1858-70), Number 6814, 25 prairial an XI (14 June 1803), hereafter referred to the *Correspondance.* For ease of reference, the author will cite the *Correspondance* document number rather than the volume and page number.

that can be imagined…"[8] In order to pull off this master stroke, a motivated army would have to be assembled and trained to the highest degree of competence. Three years after the anniversary of his famous victory at Marengo, Bonaparte issued the decree to establish various camps at which the army would be trained. The details of the First Consul's 25 prairial an XI (14 June 1803) orders to Berthier reflect Bonaparte's commitment to this project.

> I return to you, Citizen Minister, the projects that you have written for the camp of Saint-Omer. Here is the definitive base for these troops which I have decreed:
>
> Six camps will be formed, which, are destined to compose one army, and will be under the orders of six lieutenant generals, each commanding one camp. They will each have a park of artillery under the orders of an artillery general and a colonel that will act as a director of the park. The six parks will all be under the orders of the *commandant en chef* of the artillery and under the *général de brigade* in command of all the artillery parks of the six camps.
>
> The six camps will be: one in Holland, one at Gand [present day Ghent, Belgium], one at Saint-Omer, one at Compiègne, one at Saint-Malo, and one at Bayonne.
>
> The camp in Holland will be composed of 30,000 men, with 18,000 French troops and 12,000 Dutch. The 54th, 84th, 45th, 17th, 109th, 11th, 71st, 35th, and 41st *demi-brigades* [*Ligne*] will form part of this camp; forward to me the other troops destined to complete the 18,000 French troops; the 6th Hussars and the 1st *Chasseurs à cheval* will also be designated to be in this camp, along with three companies of foot artillery, one company of horse artillery, and one company of *ouvriers*.
>
> For the camp at Gand, the 6th and 13th *Légère*; 12th, 33rd, 51st, 108th, 14th, 36th, 61st, 85th *Ligne*; along with these will be the 2nd *Chasseurs à cheval*, the 7th Hussars, and the 4th, 14th, 16th and 17th Dragoons.
>
> For the camp at Saint-Omer, the 10th *Légère*, 25th, 28th, 55th, and 57th *Ligne*; the 26th *Légère*, 22nd, 43rd, 46th and 75th *Ligne*; the 8th and 11th *Chasseurs à cheval*; and the 2nd, 5th, 10th and 21st Dragoons.
>
> For the camp at Compiègne, the 9th and 24th *Légère*; the 18th, 44th, 63rd, 64th, 4th, 32nd, 96th and 111th *Ligne*; the 3rd Hussars; the 10th *Chasseurs à cheval;* and the 1st, 3rd, 8th and 9th Dragoons.
>
> Each of the *demi-brigades* mentioned above will provide only its 1st and 2nd battalions, each battalion completed to 1,000 men. It is necessary that all these regiments are notified immediately that their first two battalions will be expected by the end of the summer to perform all drill instruction, dressing ranks, etc.
>
> I am reserving the decision as to which bodies of heavy cavalry will be assigned to these three camps [Gand, Saint-Omer and Compiègne].

Berthier

[8] *Archives du Service Historique de l'État-Major de l'Armée de Terre,* (hereafter abbreviated and referred to as S.H.A.T.), Bonaparte to the Directory, 4 floréal an VI.

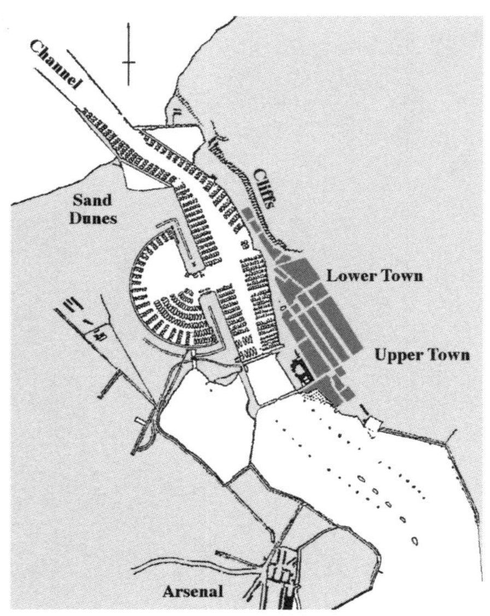

General Plan of the port of Boulogne in 1805

> The personnel of the artillery will be composed: 1) of six companies from each of the four following regiments of *artillerie à pied*—the 1st, 5th, 7th and 3rd—and all six companies from each regiment will be completed and placed on a war footing; 2) of two squadrons from each of the 2nd, 5th and 6th regiments of *artillerie à cheval,* completed and placed on a war footing; these will make 24 companies of foot artillery and 12 companies of horse artillery; 3) a *demi-brigade* of pontoniers.
>
> The first inspector of engineers will designate two companies of miners and one battalion of sappers to be placed on a war footing.
>
> The first inspector of artillery will designate the number of artillery companies necessary at each of the six camps.
>
> General Marmont, first inspector general of artillery, will be the commander-in-chief of all the artillery of the six camps.
>
> General Faultrier will be the director general of the parks of the six camps.
>
> Headquarters counselor of state Petiet will act as commissary *ordonnateur* in chief of all six camps.[9]

Following an inspection one month later, Napoleon decided to move the Belgium camp from Gand to a much more favorable and spacious location at Bruges, near the port of Ostend.[10]

By the late summer of 1803, the nucleus of the new army began arriving at the port of Boulogne. On the chalk hills around the town the formations pitched their tents in four camps where they would spend the next two years. The 'right camp' was to the right of Boulogne on the Odre Plateau; the 'left camp' was to the left of the port town on the Outreau Plateau, with the other camps at Wimeraux and Ambleteuse. All camps were within 10 kilometers of Boulogne with the right and left camps the two largest, stretching for four kilometers along the coast. The right camp on the Odre Plateau was the biggest of all as well as the one nearest to Napoleon's headquarters at château de Pont-de-Briques. On the summit of the Odre Cliff above the town, pavilions were erected from which Napoleon, Nicholas Soult and other dignitaries watched the progress of the troops. The Imperial pavilion was the grandest, measuring 100 feet long and almost 23 feet in width, with the part nearest the harbor shaped like a rotunda of 30 feet in diameter. Painted light gray, the structure was positioned so that with a single glance Napoleon could see all the camps, the town and harbor of Boulogne.[11]

Napoleon's hut above the Odre cliff

Once in their respective camps and with volunteer help from the local populace, the troops constructed wooden huts for their permanent home. Timber was collected from the woods near Boulogne, the turf for the floors raised from the plains, the mud for the walls procured from the harbor floor and the stones for the foundation gleaned from the beaches and cliffs. Modeling their camps after the Romans, the French organized the vast array of structures. Each hut housed 15 soldiers and was placed at precise distances from the others, aligned in three rows with officers' quarters separate and kitchens placed to serve each battalion. Crossroads served as boundaries for each battalion with every road bearing a sign with the name of a celebrated victory or memorable event. The Rue de Valmy, de Jemmapes, de Fleurus, de Campo-Formio, de Zürich, and du Saint-Bernard crossed with the Avenues des États-Généraux, de la Constituante, du Jeu-de-Paume, de la

---

[9] Bonaparte to Berthier, *Correspondance,* number 6814.

[10] Bonaparte to Berthier, *Correspondance*, number 6912.

[11] Fernand Nicolay, translated by Georgina L. Davis, *Napoleon at the Boulogne Camp* (New York, 1907), pp. 16-18.

Federation, de la Convention, des Pyramides, de Marengo and so on.[12] The symbols and reminders of the Revolutionary experience were just a small part of the training that the soldiers undertook in preparation for the upcoming campaigns.

Organizing and Training of an Army—Background

In order to fully understand the vast host that gathered along the Channel port of Boulogne and neighboring ports, some background is necessary. The troops that comprised Napoleon's new army were, of course, the old revolutionary formations that had been shaped by the first *amalgame*, or *embrigadement,* of 1793 and by the second *amalgame,* or *embrigadement,* in 1796. Following the overthrow of the Bourbon monarchy on 10 August 1792, by 1793 the young French Republic was under attack from the First Coalition—an alliance of European nations bent on the restoration of the French monarchy, the destruction of the Revolution, the preservation of the European civilization as known to the *ancien régime* and the partitioning of Poland. Not surprisingly, the coalition was primarily the work of England who allied itself with Austria, Prussia, Russia, Sardinia, Spain, the Kingdom of the Two Sicilies, Portugal, Baden, Hanover, and the two Hesses. While the coalition could have overwhelmed France in 1793 and early 1794 with a unity of purpose and command, the major continental powers were so consumed with their greed to partition Poland that they gave the Revolutionary government time to reorganize its forces into an effective national army.

Drilling in the camp of Boulogne

This historic reorganization was known as the first *embrigadement*—the combining of the old Royal army line units with the new volunteer battalions into a single, uniform fighting force. Before this first *amalgame,* the Republic possessed two distinctly different armies—the old Royalist army of the Bourbons and the new battalions of Revolutionary national volunteers (some historians consider that there were three armies—the former Royalists and two Republican armies, one drawn from the volunteers of 1791, and the other being the *Sans-culottes* formations raised in 1792). These formations were separated by a wide gulf of social order, pay, discipline, promotion, training and professionalism. In order to standardize the army, to increase the effectiveness of the larger volunteer battalions by having them stand beside the regulars in order to better learn the profession of arms, and to convey the Revolutionary spirit to the soldiers of the old aristocratic army units, the *embrigadement* brought these armies together by forming new units called *demi-brigades*. The forerunner of the Napoleonic regiment, each *demi-brigade* consisted of three field battalions with no depot battalion to maintain the field battalions' strength while on campaign. The three field battalions of line infantry carried a number and title *demi-brigade de bataille* whereas three light infantry battalions also carried a numeric designation and titled *demi-brigade légère*. The 1st and 3rd battalions in each *demi-brigade* were volunteers who had joined the tricolor as early as 1791 or 1792 whereas the second battalion of each *demi-brigade* was from the old Royalist army.[13]

Troops at break in the camp of Boulogne

To standardize the military symbolism throughout the national army, new flags were presented to every battalion. The 1st and 3rd battalions of each *demi-brigade* (the volunteers) had identical flags of red, white and blue in a design unique to that *demi-brigade*. The pattern of the 1st and 3rd battalion flags varied from one *demi-brigade* to another by the arrangement of the national colors. In

---

[12] G. de Lhomel, *Documents pour servir à l'Histoire de Montreuil-sur-Mer de 1789 à 1830*, 2 parts (Paris, 1965), vol. 2, p. 424; Nicolay, p. 242.

[13] Jean-Paul Bertraud, translated by R. R. Palmer, *The Army of the French Revolution* (Princeton, 1988), pp. 151-52, 163-165 and 170-171; John A. Lynn, *The Bayonets of the Republic* (Chicago, 1984), pp. 57-60 and 181.

Republican Flag, this one of the 2nd Battalion of the 23rd demi-brigade de bataille

contrast, the flag carried by the 2nd battalion of each *demi-brigade* (the old Royalists) was identical throughout the army. Since the 2nd battalion was the senior formation in each *demi-brigade*, the standardizing of the 2nd battalion's flag was a substitute for the old colonel's flag of the *ancien régime.* This flag was white, with the national colors in the upper flagpole corner. Around the edges was a repeating trim pattern of red, white and blue. Finally, the center of the flags of the 2nd battalions bore the Republican fasces topped by a tricolor Phrygian cap (called the 'bonnet of liberty') surrounded by a wreath.[14] While the 2nd battalion's flag might have been a substitute for the old colonel's flag, no other symbol could be construed as linking the Republican army with that of the Bourbons. Revolutionary symbolism was further extended by the total eradication of all ornamentation associated with the Bourbons. The new citizen army, totally committed to the ideas of *Liberté, Egalité et Fraternité*, the dictums of Rousseau and Diderot, reflected the total upheaval in French society and the hatred among the people for the corrupt *ancien régime.* Symbols and reminders of the Bourbons were replaced with slogans and pictures of republicanism, as well as the wearing of the tricolor cockade and tricolor tassels.[15]

Although the amalgamation was not uniformly implemented during 1793, the process was ordered to begin in earnest in early 1794 and was completed by the following year. When finished, the first *embrigadement* included the melding of volunteers, conscripts and old soldiers down to the company level in over 230 *demi-brigades de bataille* and *légère*.[16] This historic amalgamation helped create a formidable war machine because it provided, under the aegis of the Jacobins who politicized the army, the means of unifying the different battalions of the French people, who until then had been divided by politics and custom.[17]

The first *embrigadement,* or *amalgame,* had hardly finished when a second was needed. Hard campaigning for two years had reduced many *demi-brigades* to mere skeletons of their former, established strengths. To consolidate the veterans and to bring the battalions up to strength, the second *amalgame* was initiated in January of 1796. The number of *demi-brigades* was reduced some 40% to 140, consisting of 110 *demi-brigades de bataille* and 30 *demi-brigades légère.*[18] This amalgamation had a second monumental effect in that it also opened the door for a new selectivity in the appointment of officers.[19] By rewarding with promotions the bravest and most effective officers who had at least four years of service, the slogan *carrière ouverte aux talents* (career open to talents) became a meaningful phrase within the army. No matter what one's background or social standing was before entering the service, everyone was on equal ground under the tricolor. Here, in service to *la Patrie*, any man could prove himself and be recognized and rewarded accordingly. It cannot be overstated how motivation of this sort captivated the imagination and sparked its *élan* of every man in uniform.

Republican Emblem

Revolutionary fervor was further enhanced by an explosion of Republican music composed by a host of talented composers who saw the Revolution as the means to further musical careers that had been stifled by the *ancien régime.* The number of musicians within the army greatly increased as well, and whether on the march or in camp the *demi-brigade* bands lightened the mood of the army by

---

[14] O. Hollander, *Les Drapeaux des Demi-Brigades d'Infanterie de 1794 à 1804* (Paris, 1913), pp. 1-52 and p. 77; Pierre Charrié, *Drapeaux & Étendards de la Révolution et de l'Empire* (Paris, 1982), pp. 12-34.

[15] Bertraud and Palmer, *The Army of the French Revolution*, p. 214.

[16] Lynn, *The Bayonets of the Republic*, pp. 57-60.

[17] Bertraud and Palmer, *The Army of the French Revolution*, p. 170.

[18] Camille Rousset, *Les volontaires, 1791-1794* (Paris, 1892), pp. 336-399.

[19] Bertraud and Palmer, *The Army of the French Revolution*, p. 280.

playing the new popular marches and airs. The music, along with each battalion's flag, symbolized the unity of the army and the reborn Nation.[20]

As foreign governments continued to prosecute war against the Revolution, the French army was charged with the safeguarding of the country, which meant that the bayonets of the republic were protecting the political gains of the bourgeoisie and the peasantry. Motivated to defend *la Patrie* against all enemies, foreign and domestic, the army's power and influence grew exponentially. New tactical doctrines embracing more flexible combat formations as well as extensive use of *tirailleurs* were developed. Division and brigade commanders established drills and tactics for multi-unit evolution as well as close collaboration between the infantry and artillery. This training produced the capacity to change flexibly from offensive to defensive, to move quickly about the battlefield in order to exploit enemy weaknesses, to detach hundreds of *tirailleurs* from each battalion and have them rejoin their companies, and to increase the firepower and mobility of the already technically excellent artillery.[21] Also, with the second *embrigadement,* a new system of brigades combined on a permanent basis the various *demi-brigades* within each division.

French Republican infantry acting as tirailleurs

All these factors were an antecedent to improved French military professionalism that truly became evident in the battles from 1796 through 1800, and showed the Republican army as being extremely adept:

> in luring the enemy by apparent weakness, and firmly withstanding his assault while awaiting the moment for all factors to come together for a counteroffensive, leading to the destruction of the enemy troops. The French knew how to feel out the adversary's position, judge its components, attack in columns, and deploy in line or in a square.[22]

The majority of troops that encamped at Boulogne were these battle-hardened veterans of the Revolution. To these were added the conscripts of the annual levies who were funneled into the established regiments, there to learn from the older soldiers the art of war. All these officers and men sensed that their gathering along the English Channel was something of portent never before experienced.

Forging the Army at Boulogne

Napoleon's immortal *Grande Armée* could trace its beginning back to 6 brumaire an VI (27 October 1797), when France's then Revolutionary government, the Directory, ordered a large host to assemble along the English Channel. It was to be called the Army of England and commanded by Citizen-General Napoleon Bonaparte.[23] On 16 nivôse an VI (5 January 1798), a national loan of 80 million francs was raised to meet expenses for the invasion of the arch-enemy's homeland. Bonaparte inspected the Boulogne area in February and reported back to the Directory that the scheme must wait at least one year in order to make the proper preparations.[24] The Directory, fearful of the growing popularity of the young Corsican general and therefore eager to ruin Bonaparte's reputation established by his victories in Italy in 1796 and 1797, ordered him out of the country with the Egyptian expedition.[25] When the 30-year-old general returned from Egypt with

Bonaparte as First Consul, by Isabey

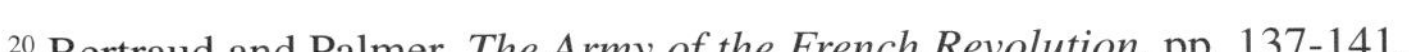

[20] Bertraud and Palmer, *The Army of the French Revolution*, pp. 137-141.
[21] Lynn, *The Bayonets of the Republic*, pp. 281-282.
[22] Bertraud and Palmer, *The Army of the French Revolution*, p. 279.
[23] Beaucour, *Lettres, Décisions et Actes de Napoléon,* p. 43.
[24] Bonaparte to The Directory, *Correspondance,* number 2419.
[25] A good, short summary of how the Directory came to this conclusion can be found in Felix Markham, *Napoleon* (New York, 1963), pp. 58-59.

his reputation still intact rather than buried with the Pharaohs, he joined in the plot to establish a new government—a plot that was already initiated by the abbé Sieyès. The coup d'état of 18 brumaire an VIII (9 November 1799) brought Napoleon to power, and when England broke the peace of Amiens in 1803, the First Consul resurrected the plan to concentrate an army and invade England.[26]

By early fall 1804, the numbers of troops in the Channel camps had reached more than 150,000 infantry, 16,000 artillerists and technical personnel, and 9,300 cavalry with more troops scheduled to arrive soon.[27] Intensive drills, begun at the company level, were steadily increased in size until the division commanders maneuvered their brigades across the countryside. Battalion drill practiced daily included forming and maneuvering in column by companies at full distance, attack column and various columns of divisions, changing from column to line and vice-versa, as well as forming into and out of square from all formations. Every other day the troops would have firing exercises in the morning with the afternoons devoted to regimental drill followed by the brigade drills. Divisional maneuvers were done every third day with ever increasing complexity under mock battle conditions. When these large mock battles took place, the Channel coastline would shake from the deafening roar of scores of cannon and tens of thousands of muskets. French soldiers refined their art of war in the hellish noise environment of the battlefield. Changes of formation while under fire (participants firing blanks) were an invaluable lesson that would be put to use on the actual battlefield.[28]

Organization of a typical French Ligne *brigade 1805-1807*

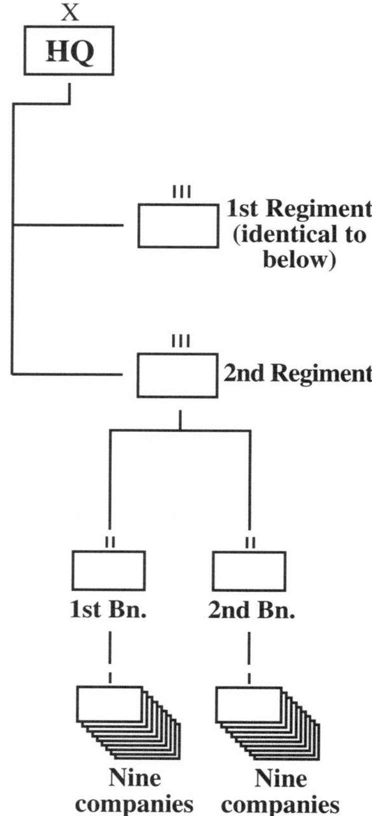

It was in these war games that regimental, brigade and division esprit de corps became more evident than that which was already in place with the old Revolutionary armies. The officers and men, under the watchful eye of their brigade and divisional commanders, living and working together in the camps for a long period of time, combined to nurture the spirit of the French army to a new level.[29] No longer just members of a regiment, soldiers and officers alike also grasped the concept of permanent brigade and divisional *élan*. This spirit was jealously preserved by the superior officers in the army who wished to retain the integrity of the working relationships of the regiments that had established a familiarity with each other while in the camps. This practice was carried over through the campaigns of The Glory Years (1805-1807). Regiments of line and light infantry that were assigned to a brigade and division usually remained with that command. While not all regiments that formed the same brigade remained together indefinitely, probably no two regiments outside the French Imperial Guard were as inseparable as the 13th *Légère* and the 17th *Ligne*. From before the 1805 campaign to Waterloo in 1815, these élite regiments served side-by-side in the same division.[30] Other combinations are almost as noteworthy, such as the famous 34th and 88th *Ligne* who drilled with each other on the chalk hills of Boulogne and were still together in 1815 in Napoleon's *Armée du Nord*.[31]

The troops established in each individual camp invariably became members of a *corps d'armée*—arguably Napoleon greatest organizational innovation.[32] From his headquarters at château de Pont-de-Briques, the Emperor designed the corps as

---

[26] J. Dechamps, "La rupture de la Paix d'Amiens: Comment elle fut préparée," in the *Revue des Études napoléoniennes*, May-June 1939, pp. 172-207.
[27] S.H.A.T., C^2 597.
[28] S.H.A.T., C^2 192.
[29] A. d'Hautpoul, *Souvenirs sur la Révolution, l'Empire et la Restauration* (Paris, 1904), pp. 285-292.
[30] S.H.A.T., C^2 476, C^2 506, C^2 525, C^2 546, C^{15} 34 and C^{15} 35.
[31] S.H.A.T., C^2 481, C^2 568, C^8 360, C^{15} 34 and C^{15} 35.
[32] Napoleon in the Marengo campaign of 1800 had experimented with the corps system, as had other French generals, but he perfected it in 1805 in the same form he used for the remainder of the Napoleonic wars.

the basic unit-of-all-arms within the Napoleonic system of command. For all practical purposes, the corps was a miniature army consisting of two or more infantry divisions, each numbering between 8,000 to 12,000 men, plus a brigade of light cavalry of 1,000 to 1,250 combatants. These troops were supported by artillery, engineers, commissariat, medical, train personnel and headquarters staff. In 1805, almost every corps was entrusted to the command of a Marshal of France. The 1st Corps, commanded by Marshal Jean-Baptiste-Jules Bernadotte, was organized in Hanover. General Auguste-Frederic-Louis Marmont's 2nd Corps encamped at Utrecht near Amsterdam, was the northern most of the Channel drill fields. Marshal Louis-Nicholas Davout's 3rd Corps encamped at Bruges, while Marshal Nicolas-Jean de Dieu Soult's 4th Corps and Marshal Jean Lannes' 5th Corps were at Boulogne. Montreuil, site of Marshal Michel Ney's 6th Corps, represented the southernmost of the Channel encampments in the Boulogne area. Further south, Marshal Pierre-François-Charles Augereau's 7th Corps conducted their training at Bayonne.[33]

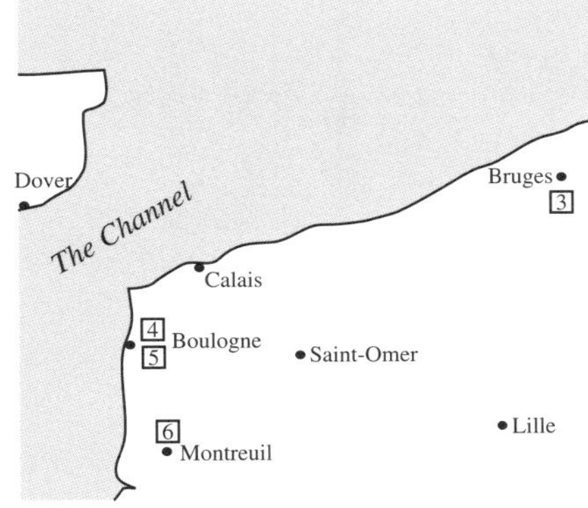

The location of the corps in the Pas-de-Calais

Equally important as the creation of the line corps, Napoleon's fertile mind yielded another of his organizational feats—the cavalry reserve. Consisting of divisions of heavy cavalry—*cuirassiers*, *carabiniers* and dragoons—the reserve cavalry corps under Marshal Joachim Murat represented a first-ever permanent concentration of masses of horse and horse artillery whose command and control could be coordinated by knowledgeable cavalry generals.[34]

The cavalry reserve was forged in a similar manner to the infantry. While the foot soldiers of several corps drilled in and around the Channel camps, joined on those grounds by many of the brigades of cavalry that shared those camps, there were also many other cavalry camps throughout France and Holland. A few kilometers inland from the port of Boulogne at the camp of Saint-Omer where the 1st Infantry Division of Soult's 4th Corps was being fashioned into a smart fighting machine under *général de division* Louis-Vincent-Joseph Saint-Hilaire, a large number of light cavalry under *général de division* François-Antoine-Louis Bourcier were also being trained.[35] At the camp at Bruges, cavalry *général de division* Frédéric-Henri Walther so greatly impressed the demanding Louis Davout, that the "Iron Marshal" made repeated mentions to Napoleon of Walther's superb handling of horsemen.[36] Particularly impressive in their appearance, horsemanship and swordsmanship were Colonel Marx's 7th Hussars.[37] As a result, Napoleon summoned Walther for a new command. Before the start of the 1805 campaign, Walther was transferred to the head of the division of dragoons that was supposed to be the most advanced in their training—the 2nd Dragoon Division.[38]

Walther

Regardless of the cavalry camp, each colonel exercised his regiment in multiple squadron evolution drill. Attacks in squadron or company echelon, envelopment by squadrons or companies to the right or left echelon, as well as squadrons abreast drills were repeated over and over, week after week, month after month until the various combinations were perfected. To make these maneuvers totally comprehensive, the cavalry brigade and division commanders took turns wielding their commands under mock battle conditions. The sound of

[33] Napoléon to Berthier, *Correspondance*, number 9158.

[34] S.H.A.T., C^2 240.

[35] S.H.A.T., C^{17} 160.

[36] S.H.A.T., C^2 201, K^1 49.

[37] S.H.A.T., C^2 213.

[38] S.H.A.T., C^2 240; this was the considered opinion of *général de division* Auguste-Daniel Belliard, chief of staff to Marshal Murat, as expressed in his inspection notes dated 28 fructidor an XIII (15 September 1805).

the trumpets and the following coordinated responses from so many mounted warriors were something very special indeed.[39]

This higher art form of cavalry deployment and evolution by the brigade and division was practiced throughout 1804 and until August 1805 at all cavalry camps, including Bruges, Montreuil, Compiègne, Amiens, Bayonne, and Nijmegen.[40] The training at these camps laid the foundation for mounted maneuvers and coordination between regiments and brigades that the French cavalry generals thought to be invaluable,[41] and were the envy of Napoleon's adversaries for the next 10 years.[42] The men and officers of the French cavalry arm worked hard to develop a familiarity among regiments and brigades which significantly increased combat efficiency beyond their numbers.

The other corps and cavalry camps were spread along the coast

In addition to the cavalry reserve, the Emperor also established an army artillery reserve, the *Grand Parc et Réserve Général de l'Artillerie.* This large pool of artillerists and associated technical personnel performed functions from bridge construction to providing additional guns and artillerists to an area within the army's zone of operation. When the *Grande Armée* was crossing the Rhine in late September 1805, the *Grand Parc et Réserve Général de l'Artillerie* consisted of 56 pieces of ordnance and the following personnel:

Grand Parc et Réserve Général de l'Artillerie
26 September 1805[43]

Designation of companies	# of companies	Present and Under Arms Officers & Men	Horses
Foot artillerists	12	1,145	—
Horse Artillerists	3	221	91
Ouvriers of Artillery	2	188	
Pontonniers	3	280	
Armorers	½	45	
Train of Artillery	18	1,418	1,874
Ouvriers of the Train	½	52	
Total	39	3,349	1,965

Soldier of the artillery train

While the number of ordnance and personnel in the *Grand Parc et Réserve Général de l'Artillerie* would increase later in the campaign as well as vary in size for each campaign, it was an important part of the *Grande Armée* to which Napoleon paid particular attention. With the establishment of the army artillery reserve, the Emperor surrounded himself with a host of hand-picked, highly trained specialists whom he could direct to assist the various corps in a wide variety of activities from building bridges to providing extra artillery or train personnel.

---

[39] S.H.A.T., C² 212.

[40] S.H.A.T., C² 192, C² 212 and C² 213.

[41] S.H.A.T., C² 246. Reports by numerous French cavalry generals during the 1806 and 1807 period repeated confirm the value of the training of the Channel encampments.

[42] S.H.A.T., C² 13. Many Austrian and Russian officers captured in 1805 stated this, which was the beginning of many such observations repeated by enemy officers throughout the Napoleonic wars. One of the most famous and compelling observations about the discipline and control the French cavalry exhibited on the battlefield was that made by the Duke of Wellington. In a letter to Lord John Russell, dated 31 July 1826, Wellington wrote: "I considered our cavalry so inferior to the French from want of order, that although I considered one of our squadrons a match for two French, yet I did not care to see four British opposed to four French, and still more so as the numbers increased, and order (of course) became necessary."

[43] S.H.A.T., C² 470.

Grenadier

Napoleon also transformed the Consular Guard into the Imperial Guard as a separate corps to serve, at least initially, under his direct control.[44] Finally, in order to administer the newly conceived army, Napoleon hand crafted a large Imperial headquarters and staff so that he could run his army as he wished.[45] The large numbers of personally selected, efficient and high-motivated officers at army headquarters played a large part in the Napoleonic success story.

It was, therefore, with seven line *corps d'armée,* a large cavalry reserve and the Imperial Guard that Napoleon created his new army. Before the troops broke camp to begin the march eastward to the Rhine and the beginning of the 1805 campaign, Napoleon gave his highly trained army a new name—*La Grande Armée*.[46] The Emperor thought the new title would befit the characteristics of the men and officers he had scrutinized for so long on the chalk hills of the Channel coast. To better understand the army, a look at its components is necessary.

The Organization of a Legend

French Infantry Organization of 1805

Napoleon's infantry were broadly classified into four categories—infantry of the line, grenadiers of the reserve, foreign regiments and the Imperial Guard. Infantry of the line were the most numerous and included both line (*ligne*) regiments and light (*légère*) regiments. Each regiment of line or light infantry would consist of two, three and sometimes four field battalions—also known as war battalions. All French line and light infantry battalions during the 1805 through 1807 period were composed of nine companies.[47]

A decree dating 2e jour complémentaire an XIII (19 September 1805) ordered that the 2nd company of fusiliers in every line battalion be converted to *voltigeurs*.[48] Full implementation of Napoleon's directive was not fulfilled until the spring of 1806, but it is clear that the change had begun to be made by the time of Austerlitz. Not surprisingly, the first regiments to comply with the Imperial change were those belonging to Marshal Davout's 3rd Corps and Marshal Soult's 4th Corps. Both Davout and Soult had already proved themselves to be the most efficient administrators among the army's corps commanders, and when the line infantry of their divisions went into action at Austerlitz, they did so with one company of *voltigeurs*, seven companies of fusiliers and one company of grenadiers.[49]

Fusilier

The line regiments that did not readily convert the 2nd company of fusiliers from every battalion into *voltigeurs* went into action in 1805 with each battalion consisting of eight companies of fusiliers and one company of grenadiers. Therefore, this was the organization which the overwhelming majority of line infantry battalions fought the Ulm-Austerlitz campaigns. At full strength, each company of fusiliers or *voltigeurs* numbered 123 officers and men, whereas the grenadiers—an élite company of hand-picked men wearing tall bearskin caps—fielded 83 combatants. When at full establishment, an 1805 French line battalion numbered

---

[44] Napoléon to Bessières, *Correspondance*, numbers 9151, 9152 and 9169.

[45] The author hopes to present a detailed look at Imperial headquarters, its departments and workings, in the forthcoming sequel entitled *Napoleon and Jena.*

[46] S.H.A.T., C^2 1.

[47] S.H.A.T., C^2 470.

[48] S.H.A.T., C^2 2, C^2 12 and C^2 470. Also, see Alain Pigeard, *L'Armée Napoléonienne 1804-1815* (Paris, 1993), p. 495.

[49] S.H.A.T., C^2 8-10; Numerous after-action reports in the *Journal des opérations du 4e corps;* Friant's and Davout's after-action reports from Austerlitz; Bourgue's *Historique du 3e régiment d'infanterie* (Paris, 1894) and Simond's *Historique du 28e régiment d'infanterie* (Rouen, 1889).

1,078 total combatants, of which 11 were the battalion staff and 1,067 officers and men belonging to the nine companies.[50]

Légère Carabinier

The organization of the light infantry *(légère)* was similar to that of the line in that there were nine companies in each battalion. Seven companies were designated as *chasseurs*—the equivalent of the line infantry's fusiliers. Wearing blue coats and breeches, plumed shakos with cords and racquets, the *chasseurs* were far more intensively trained at light infantry duties than the fusiliers of the line infantry. The *carabiniers* were the light infantry's élite shock troops. Like the grenadiers of the line, the *carabiniers* sported bearskin headgear with red plumes. Also within each *légère* battalion was another élite body of men called the *voltigeurs.* Created by decrees of 22 ventôse and 23 thermidor an XII (13 March and 13 August 1804)[51] and selected for their exceptional marksmanship, the *légère voltigeurs* were arguably the best shots in the army. When operating in open order as *tirailleurs,* the *légère voltigeurs* could seriously damage opposing enemy formed units as they picked off ranking officers and NCOs. When at full strength, every company of *chasseurs* and *voltigeurs* numbered 123 officers and men, whereas the *carabiniers* fielded 83 combatants. Therefore, an 1805 French light battalion theoretically numbered 1,078 total combatants, of which 11 were the battalion staff and 1,067 officers and men belonging to the nine companies.[52] Like the regiments of the line two, three and sometimes four field battalions—also known as war battalions—combined to form a regiment during the 1805-07 period. In 1805, however, most *légère* regiments took the field with only two war battalions. There were a total of 26 regiments of light infantry with the last being numbered 31st. However, five numbers were vacant during this campaign year, specifically the 11th, 19th, 20th, 29th and 30th.[53]

Each battalion of line and light infantry carried an 1804 lozenge-pattern national flag surmounted by an 1804 model Imperial eagle.[54] Although these flags were small, measuring only 80 centimeters (32 inches) square,[55] they were—along with the eagles—the sacred emblems of the unit. These symbols were similar in importance to the eagles and other images carried by the legionaries of Imperial Rome. They served as the rallying point for the battalion in time of crisis, as well as the focal point in the attack. The eagle and standard bearer, along with the rest of the color guard, were found in the middle of the front rank in the battalion's 4th company.

The 1804 National Color with the lozenge-pattern designed by Challiot

One or two regiments of line and/or light infantry were organized into brigades and commanded by a *général de brigade.* Two or three such brigades were organized into a division commanded by a *général de division.*

On 30 brumaire an XII (22 November 1803), First Consul Bonaparte decided to create a new division of élite troops for the invasion of England. Two months later, in January 1804, Bonaparte fixed the division's establishment at 12 battalions formed into six regiments, each regiment of two battalions. Each of these battalions was composed of six companies, three of which were grenadiers or *carabiniers,* and three companies of fusiliers or *chasseurs*—the designation depending on whether the companies were drawn from line or light regiments.[56]

In March of 1805, Napoleon revised the organization of this special division now known as the *Grenadiers de la Réserve.* Two battalions, consisting of

---

50 S.H.A.T., C^2 470.

51 Arrêtê, *Correspondance*, number 7617; *Journal Militaire* an XII/2, p. 58.

52 S.H.A.T., C^2 470.

53 Pigeard, *L'Armée Napoléonienne,* pp. 448-449.

54 Napoléon to Berthier, *Correspondance*, number 7876.

55 Charrié, *Drapeaux & Étendards de la Révolution et de l'Empire*, p. 126.

56 S.H.A.T., Xk 32.

grenadiers and fusiliers drawn from the 28th and 30th Regiments of the Line, were broken up and the companies that comprised these battalions were returned to their parent regiments. The remaining five regiments were organized into three brigades. The first and second brigade each consisted of two regiments while the third brigade had only one regiment. Each regiment was composed of two battalions of six companies per battalion. If the companies that formed the battalion were drawn from a line regiment, then three companies were grenadiers and three companies were fusiliers. If the battalion's companies were drawn from regiments of *légère*, three companies were *carabiniers* and three were *chasseurs*. Company organizations were unchanged from those established by the line and light infantry. The permanent battalions from which these companies were drawn did not replace the detached men, but rather operated in the field at a reduced establishment of only seven companies instead of the normal nine. This will explain the weaker strengths of the designated regular regiments that contributed companies to the *Grenadiers de la Réserve*. The grenadier regiments in 1805 were organized as follows:[57]

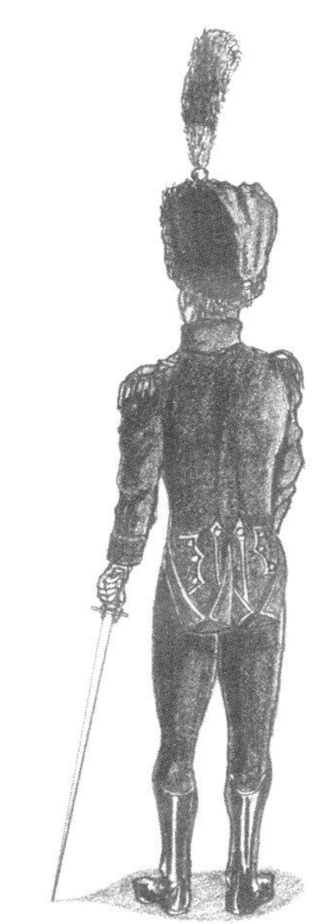

Légère Voltigeur Officer

1st Regiment:	1st *bataillon d'élite* from the 13th *Ligne*
	2nd *bataillon d'élite* from the 58th *Ligne*;
2nd Regiment:	1st *bataillon d'élite* from the 9th *Ligne*
	2nd *bataillon d'élite* from the 81st *Ligne*;
3rd Regiment:	1st *bataillon d'élite* from the 2nd *Légère*
	2nd *bataillon d'élite* from the 3rd *Légère*;
4th Regiment:	1st *bataillon d'élite* from the 28th *Légère*
	2nd *bataillon d'élite* from the 31st *Légère;*
5th Regiment:	1st *bataillon d'élite* from the 12th *Légère*
	2nd *bataillon d'élite* from the 15th *Légère.*

While the French line and light infantry of the 1808 through 1815 era would be organized into battalions of six companies each, the *Grenadiers de la Réserve* were the only French infantry battalions of the 1805-1807 period to be organized on a six-company establishment. Every battalion carried a small, silk white fanion measuring just under a half meter square with an Imperial eagle displayed in the center and brown letters along the top and bottom. At the top was the inscription "*Grenadiers de la Réserve*" while under the eagle was the designation of the regiment, abbreviated such as "4me Régt." Therefore, these battalions did not have national colors or eagles with them. For the 1805 campaign the grenadiers were placed under the command of *général de division* Nicolas-Charles Oudinot and formed part of Marshal Lannes' 5th Corps. After Oudinot was wounded at Schöngrabern near Hollabrunn, the grenadiers were jointly commanded by Oudinot and Duroc.

A Flag of Oudinot's 4th Grenadier Regiment

Finally, the 1805 *Grenadiers de la Réserve* should never be confused with the similarly named divisions commanded by Oudinot that appear with Napoleon's armies during the 1806, 1807 and 1809 campaigns. The troops and composition of the 1805 battalions were vastly different from that of the 1806 and 1807 campaigns,[58] and nothing but a distant relative of the 1809 conscript formations that were known as *demi-brigades d'élite*.[59] The 1804-1805 *bataillons d'élite* were brought together, drilled and campaigned as the same formations for two years and were the best of the so-called "Oudinot's Grenadiers." Because of these

[57] S.H.A.T., Xk 32.
[58] S.H.A.T., Xk 32.
[59] Scott Bowden and Charles Tarbox, *Armies on the Danube 1809* (Arlington, 1980 and second edition, Chicago, 1989), pp. 44-45.

distinctively different formations, Oudinot's command of the 1806, 1807 and 1809 period should be studied in detail in connection with those respective campaigns.

The 1803-1805 *Grenadiers de la Réserve* are also significant in the respect that these battalions were the first to be formed by Napoleon using the six-company establishment. Was Napoleon laying the foundation for the future line and light infantry battalion organization when he formed these battalions? If he was not experimenting, then why was the number of companies in these battalions significantly less than the line or the Guard? Regardless of the answers to these questions, one thing is certain: the six-company establishment of the *Grenadiers de la Réserve* was the forerunner to the line and light infantry establishment of the middle and late periods of the First Empire.[60]

Although the numbers of foreign regiments in French service were very few in 1805, two such formations—the *Tirailleurs du Pô* and the *Tirailleurs corses*—were élite bodies of troops and prominent members of the *Grande Armée*. Both battalions were formed by decrees of First Consul Bonaparte—the *Tirailleurs corses* in 1802 and the *Tirailleurs du Pô* in 1803. Their ranks were to be filled only with enthusiastic volunteers.[61] Manpower for the *Tirailleurs corses* came from the departments of Golo and of Liamone whereas the men who volunteered for the *Tirailleurs du Pô* came from Turin in the Po River Valley of Northern Italy. Each battalion's internal organization was the same as French light infantry, with the exception that each company consisted of 100 combatants. Therefore, at full strength, each of these battalions fielded 900 officers and other ranks in the companies, plus a staff.[62]

Reporting to the Camp of Boulogne in 1804, the *Tirailleurs corses* and *Tirailleurs du Pô* served together for more than 10 years from 1804 through the Hundred Days Campaign in 1815! From 1804 until 1811, each battalion carried an 1804 lozenge-pattern national flag and an 1804 model Imperial eagle.[63] From 1804 through 1808, these two battalions were members of Soult's 4th Corps. For the famous Danube campaign in 1809, the *Tirailleurs corses* and *Tirailleurs du Pô* were the only true veteran formations around which the newly created 2nd Corps of Napoleon's Army of Germany was built.[64] The two battalions greatly distinguished themselves at Austerlitz (1805), Eylau (1807), Ebelsberg, Aspern-Essling and Wagram (1809). However, the trend of eliminating special battalions finally caught up with them in 1811 when they and two other battalions—the Swiss Battalion Valaisan and the Hanoverian Legion—were combined to form a new light infantry regiment of four battalions, the 11th *Légère*. As senior battalion, the Corsicans made up the 1st Battalion while the *Tirailleurs du Pô* were the 2nd Battalion.[65] The new regiment was not considered a success during the 1812 Russian campaign,[66] and when the *Grande Armée* was rebuilt in 1813, only the 1st and 2nd Battalions consisting of the Corsicans and the Italians from the Po River Valley were permanently reconstituted.[67] The heroics of the Corsicans and Italians continued until the end of the Empire, with these battalions last seen in 1815 fighting under the eyes of the Emperor for whom they fought so courageously for over a

Grenadier of the Imperial Guard

[60] For the organizational details of the French six-company battalion, see Scott Bowden and Charles Tarbox, *Armies on the Danube 1809*, pp. 41-43.

[61] Napoléon to Berthier, *Correspondance*, number 7875.

[62] S.H.A.T., Xk 15 and 18.

[63] Charrié, *Drapeaux & Étendards de la Révolution et de l'Empire*, p. 171, 216 and the plate opposite p. 209.

[64] Scott Bowden and Charles Tarbox, *Armies on the Danube 1809*, p. 45.

[65] S.H.A.T., C^2 526.

[66] John R. Elting, *Swords Around a Throne* (New York, 1988), p. 370. Elting's assessment is correct with respect to the 1812 campaign.

[67] Scott Bowden, *Napoleon's Grande Armée of 1813* (Chicago, 1990), p. 245 and 301. The 4th battalion that was reconstituted in 1813 did not survive the end of year.

decade. In their last major battle, the two battalions of the 11th *Légère*—battalions the army still called the *Tirailleurs corses* and *Tirailleurs du Pô*—stormed into and captured the village of Saint-Amand during the Battle of Ligny on 16 June, then held that place against repeated Prussian counterattacks whose numbers were six times their own![68] Considering their long and distinguished record, it can be argued that the *Tirailleurs corses* and *Tirailleurs du Pô* were as good as any unit in Napoleonic service outside the Imperial Guard.

Without a doubt, the premier combat infantry of *La Grande Armée* was the French Imperial Guard. Much more than a bodyguard for the Emperor, the Imperial Guard was a miniature army composed of the French nation's best fighting men. Unlike the Russian Imperial Guard that sought members based on physical size or their status in Romanov society, only the bravest and ablest officers and men who met minimum height and service requirements were eligible for entry into the French Imperial Guard.[69]

Officer of Grenadiers à pied of the Imperial Guard

While this section deals with the infantry organization of the Guard, the origin of both the infantry and cavalry of the Guard are inseparable and deeply rooted in the Revolution. On 10 brumaire an IV (1 November 1795), in compliance with Article 133 of the Constitution of Year III, two companies—one of 120 infantry and 120 cavalry—were established to guard the members of the Directory. On 13 vendémiaire an V (4 October 1796), these troops became the *Garde du Directoire*. The members of the Guard were hand-picked, distinguished soldiers and were fanatically devoted to the Revolution. On 9 ventôse an V (27 February 1797) the foot guards were given the designation *Grenadiers à pied de la Garde* and the cavalry titled *Grenadiers à cheval de la Garde.* Following Napoleon's rise to power through the coup d'état of 18 brumaire an VIII (9 November 1799), the Guard was renamed *Garde des Consuls* (Consular Guard). Shortly thereafter, on 7 frimaire an VIII (28 November 1799), First Consul Bonaparte greatly expanded the Guard to 2,089 officers and men by calling for two battalions of grenadiers, one company of *chasseurs*, two squadrons of *grenadiers à cheval,* one company of *chasseurs à cheval* (his Guides from the Italian campaigns of 1796 and 1797), plus artillery and headquarters personnel.

Marin *of the Imperial Guard*

The Consular Guard was further expanded on 17 ventôse an X (8 March 1802) when Bonaparte formalized the two battalions of *grenadiers à pied* into a regiment and increased the *chasseurs à pied* to a regiment also consisting of two battalions. The *Grenadiers à cheval de la Garde* were increased to four squadrons, to which were also added the Guard train of artillery and hospital corps. With this expansion the Guard numbered 7,266 officers and men. Further increases to the Guard were made throughout 1803, the most famous of which was that of 30 fructidor (17 September) in which Bonaparte, in preparation for the anticipated invasion of England, called for the establishment of a *Bataillon des matelots de la Garde* (Battalion of Sailors of the Guard). Finally, on 10 thermidor an XII (29 July 1804) the transformation of the Consular Guard was completed by Napoleon through an extensive decree in which the organization was further expanded and renamed the Imperial Guard.

In 1805, the combat infantry of the Imperial Guard consisted of one regiment of *grenadiers à pied*, one regiment of *chasseurs à pied* and one battalion of *matelots.* These units—the original nucleus of the Guard infantry for the Napoleonic period—were the "Old Guard." Nicknamed "The Grumblers," the organization of the

---

[68] Scott Bowden, *Armies at Waterloo* (Arlington, 1983), p. 276. The heroics of the 11th *Légère* and the other regiments of Girard's 7th Infantry Division in the *Armée du Nord* during the Battle of Ligny can be read in A. F. Becke, *Napoleon and Waterloo*, 2 volumes (New York, 1971 reprint), vol. 1, pp. 240-241 and 253.

[69] S.H.A.T., Xab Garde impériale series; the following organizational details are from the Xab series at S.H.A.T. One of the most detailed secondary source on the organization of the Imperial Guard is: L. Fallou, *La Garde Impériale 1804-1815* (Paris, 1901).

grenadiers and *chasseurs à pied* was identical. Each regiment of grenadiers and *chasseurs* fielded 1,707 combatants. These were divided into the regimental headquarters, two war battalions of eight companies each, with each company numbering 102 officers and men.[70] The particulars of their organization are found at the end of this chapter.

As with all French infantry, each Old Guard regiment had depot personnel, although the Guard's was smaller than the battalion-size depot establishments of line and light infantry. A company of vélites totaling 190 people served as the depot for each respective Guard regiment.

From 1804 through 1808, the single *Bataillon des matelots de la Garde* was comprised of five 'crews' (their company equivalent) and a battalion headquarters for a total theoretical strength of 739 officers and other ranks. Sporting one of the most colorful uniforms in Napoleon's army, this battalion also known as the *Marins de la Garde*,[71] saw service in virtually every campaign in which Napoleon was present. In 1805, a crew of 120 helped the army cross the Rhine in late September, and then later manned a flotilla of boats on the Danube.[72] Every battalion of Imperial Guard infantry carried an 1804 lozenge-pattern national flag of 80 centimeters square on a flag pole surmounted by an 1804 model Imperial eagle.[73]

Serving alongside the infantry units of the French Imperial Guard was the Kingdom of Italy's composite regiment of Grenadiers and *Chasseurs* of the Royal Italian Guard. These grenadiers and *chasseurs*, clad in a dark green coat and wearing bearskin bonnets of a similar pattern to those of the French Imperial Guard, represented the senior infantry battalions of the Kingdom of Italy. In 1805, the Grenadiers and *Chasseurs* of the Royal Italian Guard consisted of two battalions—one battalion of grenadiers and one battalion of *chasseurs*. Unlike their French Guard counterparts, however, the Italians had a battalion organization of six companies of 75 combatants per company, plus a large headquarters staff for a theoretical regimental strength of almost 1,080 combatants.[74]

Bavarian Infantrymen

Other troops fought along side the *Grande Armée* in 1805. The majority of these were Germanic troops, the most numerous of which were the Bavarians. As of 2 October 1805, the Bavarian army theoretically numbered 24,405 combatants present and under arms. However, the actual number of combatants present and under arms was less (see Appendix B).[75] These combatants were divided among 12 regiments of infantry numbered 1st through 10th, 12th and 13th. The 1st Regiment, or Leib Regiment, was designated as 'Gardes' and the remaining 11 regiments were designated as line regiments. Every regiment of infantry consisted of two battalions, each battalion of four companies. Three companies of each battalion were designated as fusiliers and one company were grenadiers. Including headquarters personnel, a full strength Bavarian infantry regiment numbered 1,398 combatants.[76]

Supporting these regiments of infantry were also six battalions of light infantry, two regiments of dragoons, four regiments of light horse (*chevau-légères*) and a regiment of artillerists. As with the line battalions, each Bavarian light infantry battalion consisted of four companies. At full strength, each one of these light battalions fielded 706 officers and other ranks. All Bavarian cavalry regiments numbered four squadrons, each with a full strength of 479 persons.[77]

---

[70] S.H.A.T., Xab Garde impériale series and C^2 470.
[71] The terms *Matelots* and *Marins* were interchangable.
[72] D. Lomier, *Le Bataillon des Marins de la Garde 1803-1815* (Paris, 1991), pp. 82-83.
[73] Charrié, *Drapeaux & Étendards de la Révolution et de l'Empire*, p. 173.
[74] S.H.A.T., Xab Garde impériale series.
[75] S.H.A.T., C^2 470.
[76] S.H.A.T., C^2 470.
[77] S.H.A.T., C^2 470.

Supporting the Bavarian infantry and cavalry was the Bavarian artillery which, at full strength, consisted of 48 pieces of ordnance divided equally among 24 pieces in the mobile field companies and 24 regimental guns. The Bavarian artillery regiment consisted of four companies with a total strength of 609 combatants. Two companies were foot artillerists, each company consisting of six pieces of ordnance of which four were 12-pounder cannon and two were 7-pounder howitzers. The other two companies were light, or horse, artillerists. Each horse artillery company fielded six pieces consisting of four 6-pounder cannon and two 7-pounder howitzers. In addition to these pieces, each regiment of infantry had two 6-pounder guns attached that served as regimental artillery.[78]

The Bavarian ordnance was produced according to the system developed in 1800 by *Generallieutenant* Jakob von Manson. Manson had seen extensive service in both the French and Russian armies, and drew upon his experience to develop the new pieces. Known as either the 'Manson System,' or 'System 1800,' Bavarian field cannon consisted of either 6- or 12-pounders. To complement the cannon, the Manson System called for only one howitzer, the 7-pounder, which had a caliber of about 5.3 inches. In addition to these pieces, Manson designed siege pieces consisting of 6-, 12-, 18- and 24-pounder guns, a 10-pounder howitzer, plus 30- and 60-pounder mortars.[79]

A Württemberg Infantryman

In 1805, the territory that later became known as the Grand Duchy of Kleve-Berg was part of the hereditary lands belonging to Bavaria. These troops formed a separate brigade in the *Grande Armée*. Under the command of Major General Kinkel, the Berg brigade included the Kinkel Infantry Regiment and one regiment of dragoons.[80]

The Elector of Württemberg also contributed a small division of troops to the *Grande Armée*. Counting only the personnel present and under arms, the division numbered only 2,549 on 15 brumaire an XIV (6 November 1805) and 2,099 on 1 frimaire (22 November). One month later, on 1 nivose (22 December), the division's ranks had swollen to a total of 3,826 combatants present and under arms.[81]

The Württembergers were divided between three battalions of line, two battalions of *chasseurs*, one battalion of foot jägers, one squadron (later three) of chevaulegers and, until December, two half-companies of artillery—one half-company were foot artillerists while the other half-company were horse artillerists. Each half-company of artillery consisted of three 6-pounder guns and one 7-pounder howitzer, for a total of eight pieces of ordnance. In December, both the foot and horse artillery contingents were increased to a full company. At full strength, each Württemberg artillery company employed six 6-pounder cannon and two 7-pounder howitzers.[82]

Other German troops that joined Napoleon's army were brigades from Hesse-Darmstädt and Baden. These men were organized during the campaign and took no part in the fighting.

As part of General Marmont's 2nd Corps, a division of troops belonging to the Batavian Republic (future Kingdom of Holland) took an active part in the 1805 campaign. On 6 brumaire (28 October), the division numbered 257 officers and 4,784 other ranks present and under arms. These men were formed into two brigades of infantry, plus a cavalry brigade and supporting artillery. Each brigade of infantry consisted of one regiment of light infantry and two regiments of line with each regiment fielding two battalions organized on the French model. A company of

A Batavian Light Infantryman

[78] S.H.A.T., C^2 470.
[79] Müller-Brünn, *Geschichte der Bayern Armee* (Munich, 1903), pp. 180-181.
[80] S.H.A.T., C^2 470.
[81] S.H.A.T., C^2 470.
[82] S.H.A.T., C^2 470.

Cavalry of Revolutionary France

Batavian foot artillery was part of the division. The gunners served six pieces of ordnance, consisting of one 4-pounder, three 8-pounders and two 5½-inch howitzers.[83]

French Cavalry Organization of 1805

It was the French cavalry that suffered the most from the effects of the Revolution. The combat arm most favored by aristocrats, the Royal cavalry had been the portion of the army considered to be the weakest by those in the French military establishment as well as by its *ancien régime* adversaries.[84] Not surprisingly, the exodus of Royal officers from France resulted in the French cavalry being completely gutted in the early 1790s. Therefore, the French cavalry had to be more than merely restored. It needed complete rebuilding, both in spirit and organization.[85] The majority of regiments' poor performance throughout the entire 18th century indicated to the most casual observer that the ésprit de corps as well as many of the units themselves had to be completely reinvented. Because reorganization was only part of the job, the spirit of conservatism or avarice had to be replaced by discipline and audacity. To rebuild a combat arm that was a patent disgrace until late in the wars of the Revolution, Napoleon's organizational genius was put to the test.

The Emperor decided to group all his cavalry in a new but rational way, based on its roles both on and off the battlefield. Some regiments of light cavalry were grouped together into brigades and attached at the infantry corps level, there to screen and scout for their parent corps as well as to provide some combined arms battlefield support. Other regiments of light cavalry were brought together into divisions to serve essentially the same mission but for the large formations of heavy cavalry. At his resounding victory at the Battle of Marengo on 14 June 1800, Napoleon's career was saved by less than 200 French heavy cavalry expertly led by Kellermann (the younger) who compelled more than 5,000 Austrian grenadiers to put down their arms. This inspired Napoleon to organize all such heavy cavalry regiments into homogenous divisions and to combine these with divisions of dragoons thereby forming a large, coordinated command called the *Corps des Réserves de Cavalerie*.[86] The effective command and coordination of many brigades and divisions of cavalry would prove devastating to many opponents of Napoleonic France.

Carabinier

The most important formations in the reserve cavalry corps were the regiments of heavy cavalry known as *carabiniers* and *cuirassiers*. In 1805, there were 14 of these superb regiments, two of which were *carabiniers* and 12 were *cuirassiers*. The best of these were undoubtedly the *carabiniers*. They had a long, illustrious history dating back to the "Sun King," Louis XIV. In 1693 the first "Royal Regiment of *Carabiniers*" was formed, followed by the second in 1788. Composed of picked men, they survived a name change during the height of the Revolution, but their élite status was confirmed by the Consulate and Napoleon was quick to recognize their worth.[87] With towering grenadier-style bearskin caps without a brass front plate, wearing blue coats without armor and riding large black horses of

---

[83] S.H.A.T., C^2 470 and 475.

[84] Lee Kennett, *The French Armies in the Seven Years' War* (Durham, 1967), p. 49; Lynn, *Bayonets of the Republic*, pp. 199-201.

[85] David Johnson, *Napoleon's Cavalry and its Leaders* (New York, 1978), pp.11-16.

[86] S.H.A.T., C^2 1; Napoléon to Berthier, *Correspondance*, number 9151; Commandant L. Picard, *La Cavalerie dans Les Guerres de la Révolution et de l'Empire,* 2 volumes (Saumur, 1895), vol. 1, p. 254.

[87] S.H.A.T., Xc 90 through 93.

Carabiniers *on campaign*

approximately 16 hands high which added to their imposing appearance (the musicians in all regiments rode whites or grays),[88] the 1st and 2nd *Carabiniers* considered themselves special and were always brought together into one brigade, usually as the 1st Brigade of the 1st Heavy Cavalry Division. The *carabiniers'* élite reputation was upheld on numerous fields of battle throughout the Napoleonic era, and in early stages of the 1809 Danube campaign when the Guard cavalry was not present, being on the road from Spain, the Emperor relied on the *carabiniers* as his 'duty squadrons.'[89]

During the early years of the Empire, the *carabiniers* had an establishment of only two squadrons plus a regimental headquarters of 20 personnel. Each squadron was sub-divided into two companies, each company numbering 90 officers and other ranks. Therefore, the full strength roster of each *carabinier* regiment in 1805 numbered 380 people.[90] Pleased with their impressive performance during the 1805 campaign, Napoleon's decree of 31 August 1806 authorized the *carabiniers* to increase each regiment to four war squadrons of two companies per squadron.[91] Regardless of the number of squadrons that were present in the field, each carried an 1804 lozenge-pattern national standard measuring 60 centimeters (approximately 23 inches) square with an 1804 model Imperial eagle on top of the flagpole.[92]

The *cuirassiers* also considered themselves to be élite regiments. When Bonaparte was confirmed as First Consul, he inherited 25 regiments known as *cavalerie de bataille*, the forerunners of the *cuirassiers*.[93] The Revolutionary government had not known how to properly finance, equip and maintain so many regiments of heavy cavalry and these formations suffered accordingly. In his first step to restore the heavy cavalry, Napoleon abolished seven of the *cavalerie* regiments, transferring the tallest men and biggest horses into the first 12 regiments. The other six regiments with lighter men and smaller horses were converted to dragoons. Then Napoleon renamed the *cavalerie de bataille* regiments as *cuirassiers*. Further, two regiments were formed into permanent brigades with two or three brigades forming a division.[94] The *cuirassiers* were formally brought into being by the Decree of 1 vendémiare an XII (24 September 1803). By 1804, all 12 of the *cuirassier* regiments were filled out.[95] The glittering ranks of horsemen with polished steel breastplates and helmets, sitting on large horses of various shades of brown (musicians on whites or greys) of approximately 16 hands high, gave a striking impression of troops that meant business.

While the formal organization of each regiment of *cuirassiers* called for four war squadrons, the 1805 regiments managed to field only two or three squadrons of troopers per regiment,[96] each squadron carrying an 1804 lozenge-

Cuirassier

---

[88] Before the advent of practical, portable measuring devices, the size of the horse would be measured by placing one's hand horizontally next to top of the horse's front shoulder, then continuing down the animal's leg to the ground. The number of widths of 'hands' it took from the top of the front shoulder to the ground was the horse's height. It is now easier to take a measuring device and measure from the top of the horse's shoulder to the ground. Once the height is determined in inches, simply divide by four to arrive at the horse's height in 'hands.'

[89] S.H.A.T., C² 271; Picard, *La Cavalerie dans Les Guerres,* vol. 2, p. 16. The highly regarded 1st Hussars were also part of the 1809 improvised duty squadrons for Napoleon until the cavalry of the Imperial Guard arrived from Spain.

[90] S.H.A.T., C² 470; Xc 91.

[91] S.H.A.T., C² 240; Xc 91.

[92] Charrié, *Drapeaux & Étendards de la Révolution et de l'Empire*, p. 126 and 221; Pigeard, *L'Armée Napoléonienne,* pp. 514-515.

[93] S.H.A.T., Xc 95.

[94] Napoléon to Berthier, *Correspondance*, number 9151.

[95] S.H.A.T., Xc 95 through 97.

[96] S.H.A.T., C² 470.

pattern national standard measuring 60 centimeters square with an 1804 model Imperial eagle surmounting the flag pole.[97] Each squadron was sub-divided into two companies, each company numbering at full strength some 90 officers and troopers. Therefore, at full strength some 180 combatants comprised a squadron of *cuirassiers*. Another squadron acting as the regimental depot remained in the rear areas, forwarding replacement men and horses to their respective regiment. Each regiment of heavy cavalry was headed by a headquarters staff of 20 personnel.[98]

Napoleon also added to the cavalry reserve the brigades and divisions of numerous regiments of green coated dragoons. From the time of the Danube campaign of 1809 until the end of the Napoleonic era, French dragoon regiments had a reputation of battle-hardened, well-handled cavalry. Also, specific brigades or regiments in the 1805, 1806 and 1807 campaigns also distinguished themselves. It had not always been that way, however. With Napoleon's ascent to power, the dragoons were a poorly officered and incompletely organized lot. There were not enough horses to mount all the regiments and many troopers lacked the knowledge to properly care for their mounts.[99] The solution of what to do with these dismounted troopers was put forth by *général de division* Louis Baraguey d'Hilliers, whom Bonaparte had first met when he took command of the Republican Army of Italy in 1796. Baraguey argued that he could train dragoons to be not only good cavalrymen, but also adequate infantrymen as well. The Emperor agreed to the experiment. Beginning his new assignment on 6 vendémiaire an XII (29 September 1803), Baraguey took command of the 2nd Dragoon Division at their camp at Compiègne[100] and spent the next two years forging the six mounted regiments of the division into the finest dragoons in the 1805 *Grande Armée*.[101]

The dismounted dragoons were another matter. Baraguey believed that he could usefully employ the numerous dismounted squadrons of dragoons in combat roles. Therefore, when war with Austria was eminent he was assigned to command the *ad hoc* division of *dragons à pied*. Since only two or three squadrons from each dragoon regiment was mounted in 1805, the remaining one or two squadrons from each regiment were grouped into four huge provisional regiments of *dragons à pied* who, in turn, formed the division commanded by Baraguey.[102] The combats of 1805 would prove that Baraguey had been overly optimistic in his claims as to what could be accomplished with the dismounted dragoons.

Dragoon Officer and trooper of the élite company

At full strength, every dragoon regiment was supposed to have four war squadrons, each squadron of two companies. The mounted strength of each dragoon company was set at 88 officers and other ranks—or 176 combatants per squadron—all commanded by a regimental staff of 21 people.[103] Each squadron carried an 1804 lozenge-pattern national guidon measuring 60 centimeters on the pole by 80 centimeters on the fly and surmounted by an 1804 model Imperial eagle.[104]

In the dragoons and light cavalry regiments of the line, the 1st Company of each regiment's 1st Squadron was designated as the Élite Company. The élite companies were created by Decree of 18 vendémiaire an X (10 October 1801) and were organized the following year. Article 13 of the Decree stipulated that "the 1st Company of the 1st Squadron of each cavalry regiment of dragoons, *chasseurs*

[97] Charrié, *Drapeaux & Étendards de la Révolution et de l'Empire*, p. 126, 217-218.

[98] S.H.A.T., C² 470.

[99] S.H.A.T., Xc 132 through 161.

[100] S.H.A.T., C² 212.

[101] S.H.A.T., C² 240.

[102] S.H.A.T., C² 470 and 473; Napoléon to Berthier, *Correspondance*, number 9128.

[103] S.H.A.T., C² 470.

[104] Charrié, *Drapeaux & Étendards de la Révolution et de l'Empire*, pp. 126-127.

and hussars will take the name of Élite Company. The Élite Company will be formed of picked men from the [regiment], conforming to the instructions which will be given by the Minister of War."[105] In the dragoons, the *compagnie d'élite* was distinguishable by their tall bearskin caps, red plumes and fringed epaulettes. While the remainder of the dragoon regiments rode an assortment of brown horses (the musicians on whites or greys), the Élite companies tried to restrict the color of their mounts to blacks if at all possible, or dark browns. As in the infantry, the Élite Company of the cavalry regiment took its place at the head of the column or, if the horsemen were drawn up in squadrons abreast, on the right of the line.

Dragons à pied

When a dragoon regiment rode past in column, it was preceded by a small group of mounted sappers led by a sergeant. These riders carried an ax, and it was their task to clear a way through difficult terrain for the squadrons. When not engaged in a combat task, these mounted sappers served as the regimental colonel's personal escort. According to the *Ordonnance provisoire du 1er vendémiaire an XIII* (23 September 1804), each dragoon regiment was to have 10 sappers, of which one was a sergeant and one was a corporal.[106] The sappers wore the uniform and headdress of the Élite Company and often had their uniforms decorated with brass scales or distinctive embroidery on the sleeves showing crossed axes. Because the 1804 tables of organization do not show these sappers as separate or additional personnel, it is believed that they were drawn from the Élite Company.

During this period, it is noteworthy that each company of dragoons had a contingent of dismounted combatants consisting of one *sous-lieutenant* and 51 other ranks. These dismounted personnel were the ones who formed the *ad hoc* regiments of *dragons à pied*. Therefore, if a dragoon regiment was put in the field at full strength, it would have had a regimental headquarters of 21, four mounted squadrons totaling 704 people, and a dismounted contingent of 416 more (these *dragons à pied* were always detached from the parent regiment), for a total strength of 1,141 persons of all ranks.[107] With such an ambitious theoretical establishment, and with limited horseflesh available to the French cavalry arm in 1805, it is little wonder that the mounted contingents of dragoons were not realized. The dragoons strove to obtain the largest horses possible, but were typically astride animals about 14 hands high.

The French line light cavalry consisted of regiments of *chasseurs à cheval* and hussars, both of which had identical regimental organization. In addition to the regimental headquarters of 19 personnel, each regiment of *chasseurs à cheval* and hussars usually put into the field three war squadrons, although in some rare instances four war squadrons were seen. As with all French cavalry, each squadron consisted of two companies. At full strength, each company comprised four officers and 112 other ranks, for a theoretical regimental strength of 947 combatants.[108] However, the line light cavalry suffered a common ailment as did most French cavalry regiments of this era—the shortage of horseflesh prevented the *chasseurs à cheval* and hussars from fielding all their personnel.

Chasseur à cheval *officer*

From 1805 through 1807, the army counted 24 regiments of *chasseurs à cheval* numbered 1st through 26th, with the 16th and 17th vacant.[109] As with the regiments of dragoons, the 1st Company of the 1st Squadron of every regiment of *chasseurs à cheval* was named the Élite Company. Its personnel wore distinctive fur busbys with plumes and rode blacks or dark brown horses while the other companies rode an assortment of brown horses and the musicians rode whites or greys.

---

[105] S.H.A.T., Xc 143.
[106] S.H.A.T., Xc series Dragons, and C² 470.
[107] S.H.A.T., C² 470.
[108] S.H.A.T., C² 470.
[109] S.H.A.T., Xc 185 through 201, and C² 470.

Grenadier à cheval
of the Imperial Guard

Chasseur à cheval
of the Imperial Guard

Fielding considerably fewer formations than the *chasseurs à cheval,* the 10 regiments of hussars sported splendid uniforms that served as virtually the only true distinction between these two-types of cavalry. Like the *chasseurs à cheval,* the 1st Company of the 1st Squadron in every hussar regiment was the Élite Company, wearing fur busbys and plumes, and tried to restrict the color of their horses to blacks or dark browns while the remainder of each regiment rode assorted browns.

As with all French cavalry within the *Grande Armée*, the regiments of line light cavalry were entrusted with standards and eagles. Each squadron of *chasseurs à cheval* and hussars carried an 1804 lozenge-pattern national standard with an 1804 model Imperial eagle on top of the flagpole.[110] Typically, both the *chasseurs à cheval* and hussars consisted of men of smaller stature who rode an assortment of brown horses that were between 13 to 14 hands high. As with all regiments of cavalry, regimental musicians rode gray or white horses.

Perhaps the most famous cavalry within the *Grande Armée*, and certainly the best, was that belonging to the Imperial Guard. The senior regiment was the *Grenadiers à cheval de la Garde.* This impressive body of horsemen consisted of the most distinguished heavy cavalrymen and regimental officers in the mounted service. Wearing tall bearskin caps and sitting astride huge magnificent black horses that had a minimum height of 16 hands, the *Grenadiers à cheval de la Garde* were most often referred to by a nickname that seemed to befit their appearance as well as their performance in battle—the "Gods."[111] In 1805, the regiment consisted of a headquarters of 32 personnel and four squadrons, each of two companies. At full strength, each company fielded five officers and 118 other ranks, resulting in the "Gods" numbering 1,016 combatants at full strength.[112]

Insofar as seniority was concerned, the sister cavalry regiment of the *Grenadiers à cheval de la Garde* was the *Chasseurs à cheval de la Garde.* Organized identically as the *Grenadiers à cheval de la Garde,*[113] the *Chasseurs à cheval de la Garde* were hand-picked light cavalrymen sporting fur busbys and resplendent hussar-type pelisse, dolman and breeches. The *Chasseurs à cheval de la Garde* rode picturesque bays that were a minimum of 15 hands high. The *Chasseurs à cheval de la Garde* were known by two nicknames—the "Favored (or Cherished) Children" or the "Invincibles." Having the same regimental organization as the *Grenadiers à cheval de la Garde,* both the "Invincibles" and the "Gods" carried one 1804 lozenge-pattern national standard or guidon and 1804 pattern Imperial eagle per squadron. The standard for the *Grenadiers à cheval de la Garde* measured 60 centimeters square whereas the guidon for the *Chasseurs à cheval de la Garde* measured 60 centimeters along the flagpole by 70 centimeters on the fly.[114]

Attached to the regiment of *Chasseurs à cheval de la Garde* was the company of *Mameluks* recruited from Egypt. If the company was at full strength as decreed in the organization of the Imperial Guard on 10 thermidor an XII (29 July 1804), it mounted 17 officers and 107 other ranks.[115] The *Mameluks* were ferocious fighters, clothed in exotic dress and riding splendid Arabian horses. Officered by Frenchmen, from 1802 until 1815 the *Mameluks* were in every sense part of the *Chasseurs à*

[110] Charrié, *Drapeaux & Étendards de la Révolution et de l'Empire*, pp. 126-127. The standards carried by the hussards was different from the standards carried by the *chasseurs à cheval* and dragoons.

[111] The regiment had several nicknames, including the 'Big Boots' and the 'Giants.' However, their favorite nickname, and the one they were most commonly referred to, was the 'Gods.'

[112] S.H.A.T., Xab 33; Fallou, *La Garde Impériale 1804-1815,* pp. 195-196.

[113] Fallou, *La Garde Impériale 1804-1815,* p. 212.

[114] Charrié, *Drapeaux & Étendards de la Révolution et de l'Empire*, p. 173.

[115] S.H.A.T., Xab 35; Fallou, *La Garde Impériale 1804-1815,* p. 32.

cheval de la Garde. Prior to the 1805 campaign, Napoleon's Imperial aide-de-camp, General Jean Rapp, ordered a company symbol or guidon be designed for the *Mameluks*. What evolved for the 1805 campaign was a tall pole measuring 270 centimeters high with horsehair braids attached to the top. Following their brilliant conduct at the Battle of Austerlitz, the *Mameluks* were awarded an 1804 lozenge-pattern national guidon and Imperial eagle that they carried in the campaigns of 1806 and 1807.[116]

Mameluk

Completing the cavalry of the Guard was the *Gendarmerie d'élite*. Ranked as equals to the *Grenadiers à cheval de la Garde*, they wore tall bearskin caps and rode black horses of at least 16 hands in height. In 1805, the *Gendarmerie d'élite* was composed of a headquarters staff of 31 people and two squadrons of two companies each, with every company consisting of two officers and 86 other ranks. Therefore, at full strength the mounted *Gendarmerie d'élite* numbered 383 combatants.[117]

According to the decree of 28 ventôse an X (19 March 1802), the *Gendarmerie d'élite* also formed a *demibataillon* of two foot companies, each company numbering three officers and 119 other ranks. These foot companies disappeared, however, when the Imperial Guard was reorganized on 15 April 1806, and the members of the foot companies were transferred into the mounted companies, whose company strength was increased to that of the *Grenadiers à cheval de la Garde*.[118] Nicknamed the "Immortals," the *Gendarmerie d'élite* carried two 1804 lozenge-pattern national standards measuring 60 centimeters square and two 1804 Imperial eagles—one such standard and eagle for each mounted squadron.[119]

Every regiment of Guard cavalry formed its own brigade. Ideally commanded by a *général de brigade*, the 1805 Guard cavalry sometimes had only a colonel at the head of a regiment. However, when committed to battle, the Emperor would often select an Imperial aide-de-camp to lead these most valuable regiments of horse. Also, every Guard cavalry regiment usually contributed one squadron daily to form the duty squadrons for the Emperor. These duty squadrons would be commanded by another general—usually one of the Imperial aides-de-camp—and acted as Napoleon's mounted bodyguard, being committed to battle if circumstances dictated. One of the most dramatic and decisive charges ever made by the duty squadrons of the Imperial Guard was their charge at Austerlitz (please see Chapter VIII for details).

French Artillery Organization of 1805 through 1807

Gendarme d'élite
of the Imperial Guard

The artillery organization of the *Grande Armée* during the early years of the Empire was truly unique. Unlike the 1808 through 1815 period in which artillerists were permanently fused with ordnance assigned to their company, the early Empire separated personnel from guns. Ordnance was grouped into what was called 'artillery divisions.' Each artillery division consisted of two 12-pounder cannon, six 8-pounder cannon, two 4-pounder cannon and two 6 pouce howitzers, for a total of 12 pieces. One artillery division would be allocated to a corps for every division of infantry permanently assigned to that corps. For example, a corps was assigned two artillery divisions, or 24 pieces of ordnance, if it had two infantry divisions. A corps with three infantry divisions would have three artillery divisions, or 36 pieces of ordnance. Line foot and horse artillerists and artillery train personnel were assigned to the corps commander, who along with the corps artillery chief,

[116] Charrié, *Drapeaux & Étendards de la Révolution et de l'Empire*, pp. 183-184.
[117] S.H.A.T., Xab 37; Fallou, *La Garde Impériale 1804-1815*, pp. 304-305.
[118] S.H.A.T., Xab 37.
[119] Charrié, *Drapeaux & Étendards de la Révolution et de l'Empire*, p. 185.

Line Horse Artillerymen

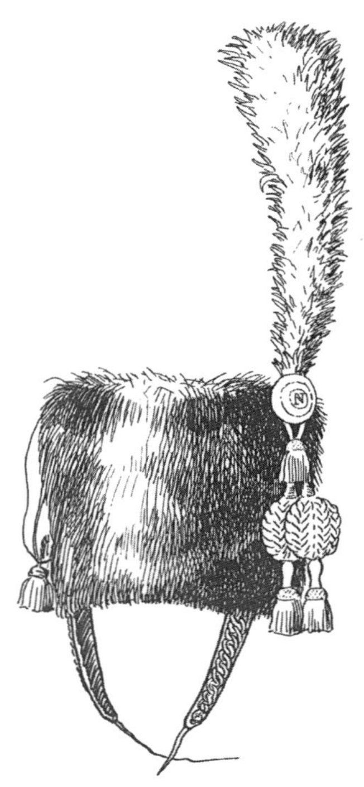

Colpack of a Horse Artilleryman of the Imperial Guard

would decide which pieces of ordnance would be dedicated to what artillery company personnel.[120]

Invariably, each *corps d'armée* had at least one company of line horse artillerists, plus two or three companies of line foot artillerists, all of which would be supported by the appropriate artillery train personnel. Artillerists would be matched-up with ordnance to fulfill specific roles. One company of line foot artillerists would operate the 12-pounder cannon assigned to the corps. This company of 12-pounders would be used as corps reserve artillery, committed to action in support of a key attack or placed in position vital to the corps' defense. Except for units serving in Bernadotte's 1st Corps, the élite horse artillerists of the line *almost always* received the mobile, yet heavy-hitting 8-pounder cannons and howitzers, while the remaining 8-pounders and all the 4-pounder cannons would be assigned to the foot artillerists with the corps.[121]

The artillery for the *Corps des Réserves de Cavalerie* had a similar but separate organization. Every two divisions of reserve cavalry—*carabiniers, cuirassiers* and dragoons—would have one company of horse artillerists, complete with six pieces of ordnance consisting of four 8-pounder guns and two 6-pouce howitzers. These line horse artillery companies would then be sub-divided into half-companies of two 8-pounders and one howitzer, with one half-company serving with each division of heavy cavalry or mounted dragoons. Therefore, all six divisions of heavy cavalry and dragoons would have a total of 18 pieces of horse artillery served by three companies of horse artillerists and accompanying train personnel that were sub-divided into half-companies for tactical employment. If a heavy cavalry division was detached from the cavalry reserve and sent to support an infantry corps, the cavalry division would take with them the half-company of horse artillerists and the three horse guns that were assigned to that division.[122]

In 1805, the horse artillery of the line consisted of six regiments numbered 1st through 6th, each regiment consisting of six consecutively numbered companies.[123] The horse artillerists wore hussar-type dark blue uniforms trimmed in red with a variety of headgear, including plumed shakos and fur busbys. Each regiment of line horse artillery was entrusted with three 1804 lozenge pattern national guidons and three 1804 pattern eagles.[124] Meanwhile, the line foot artillery comprised eight regiments numbered 1st through 8th, each regiment consisting of 22 companies.[125]

More modestly dressed than their horse artillerists counterparts, the members of the line foot artillery wore bicorne hats and dark blue uniforms with red trim. Each of the eight regiments of line foot artillerists carried two 1804 lozenge pattern national flags and 1804 pattern Imperial eagles.[126]

The artillery organization of the Imperial Guard was different from any other entity. The birth of the Imperial Guard artillery dates from a decree dated 7 frimaire an VIII (8 November 1799) which established a company of horse artillery attached to the *Garde des Consuls*. The organization was revised on 17 ventôse an X (8 March 1802) when the horse artillery of the Guard was expanded into a full squadron of two companies plus a headquarters staff.[127]

The artillery of the 1805 French Imperial Guard conformed to Napoleon's decree of 10 thermidor an XII (29 July 1804) and consisted of only horse artillerists,

[120] S.H.A.T., 4w 68 and 2w 84.; also, Archives Nationales (hereafter reffered to as A.N.), AF IV 1162.

[121] S.H.A.T., C^2 470, 474 throug 477, 479, and 481 through 485; also, see C^2 600.

[122] *Journal Militaire* an XI/1; S.H.A.T., C^2 470 and 472.

[123] *Journal Militaire* an XIII/1.

[124] Charrié, *Drapeaux & Étendards de la Révolution et de l'Empire*, p. 129.

[125] *Journal Militaire* an XIII/1.

[126] Charrié, *Drapeaux & Étendards de la Révolution et de l'Empire*, p. 129.

[127] *Journal Militaire* an XII/1; Fallou, *La Garde Impériale 1804-1815,* p. 328.

the foot artillerists of the Guard not being formed until 1808.[128] Every squadron of French Imperial Guard horse artillerists, called *Volante*, was sub-divided into two companies. Up until 1 nivose an XIV (22 December 1805), each company of *Volante* had permanently assigned to them eight pieces (the familiar arrangement of six pieces of ordnance per company being decreed after Austerlitz).[129] Of these eight pieces, four were 8-pounders, two were 4-pounders and two were howitzers. In addition, the Royal Italian Guard also had a company of horse artillerists with eight pieces of ordnance exactly like their French Guard counterparts.[130] The personnel manning the *Volante* pieces were the most distinguished artillery officers and the best gunlayers in the army. In 1805, the *Volante* boasted veteran artillerists with an average experience of 12 years. They were dressed in splendid hussar-type dark blue uniforms with red trim and fur busbys. As with the horse artillerists of the line, the Guard *Volante* carried the 1804 lozenge pattern guidon and 1804 pattern Imperial eagle, but these sacred emblems were not issued until 1806.[131]

Eagle on the Sabretache of the Horse Artillery of the Imperial Guard

It took many horses to field an artillery company. Six horses were needed to pull every 12- or 8-pounder gun assigned to a company of line foot artillerists. Howitzers and 4-pounder cannon served by line foot artillerists were invariably pulled by a team of only four horses. All horse artillery pieces, as well as any piece belonging to the French Imperial Guard or Italian Royal Guard were pulled with teams of six horses.[132]

To provide immediate ammunition for the pieces, there were trail chests on the Gribeauval guns as well as ammunition caissons traveling with the pieces. In the artillery of the line, every 4-pounder was allocated one caisson whereas each 8-pounder had two caissons, while every 12-pounder and howitzer had either three or four caissons, depending upon the availability of horses.[133] Including the ready ammunition in the trail chest, this translated into some 168 projectiles per piece of 4-pounder ordnance, 199 projectiles per every 8-pounder, 213 projectiles for each 12-pounder and 160 projectiles for each 6-pouce (or 6-inch) howitzer.[134] In the line foot artillery, caissons were drawn by either six or four horse teams. Line horse artillery caissons had teams of six horses for every vehicle. When the spare ordnance, wagons and forges are added with the guns, caissons and other vehicles associated with the artillery, a single company of line horse artillerists and accompanying train personnel serving six pieces of ordnance—four 8-pounders

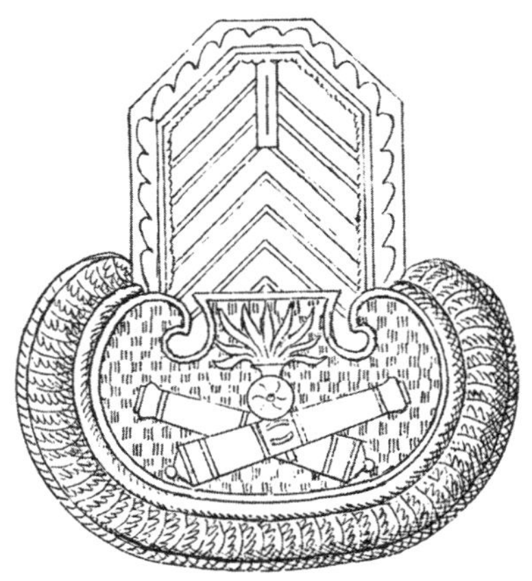

Officer's epaulette of the Horse Artillery of the Imperial Guard

[128] *Journal Militaire* an XII/1; Fallou, *La Garde Impériale 1804-1815,* p. 343.

[129] S.H.A.T., C² 470.

[130] S.H.A.T., C² 470; *Journal Militaire* an XIV.

[131] Charrié, *Drapeaux & Étendards de la Révolution et de l'Empire*, p. 173 and 227.

[132] Pigeard, *L'Armée Napoléonienne,* p. 723 lists the horses required to field a unit of line horse artillery.

[133] S.H.A.T., 2w 84. Pigeard, *L'Armée Napoléonienne,* p. 728, gives different totals.

[134] S.H.A.T., 2w 84. *Général de division* Ruty, writing his "Observations sur la partie du systèm de l'an XI" in 1814, was very specific in comparing the available ammunition capablities of the caissons and ammo boxes for the 6- and 12-pounders as well as the howitzers of the System Year XI against the old Gribeauval 4-, 8-, and 12-pounders, along with the 6-pouce howitzer. Henry Lachouque and Anne S. K. Brown, *The Anatomy of Glory*, p. 515, and Pigeard, *L'Armée Napoléonienne,* pp. 727-728 give different number of caissons and ammunition allottment. However, Pigeard's number of caissons shown on p. 728 does not agree with his horse artillery unit details as shown on page 723. Moreover, Lachouque and Brown do not list any of the System Year XI ordnance. These differences led to a lengthy study of the artillery documents in S.H.A.T., 4w 68 and 2w 84, as well as A.N., AF IV 1161 through 1165, and dozens of situation cartons at S.H.A.T., C², C⁷, C⁸ and C¹⁵ series. While the author noted that there were variations in the number of caissons taken into the field, especially in the Peninsula where there were shortage of animals was acute, he comfirms that there is no reason to doubt Ruty's "Observations," which are detailed here, in favor of any secondary source. The projectile totals given here for the 12-pounder and the howitzer assumes that each has four caissons full of ammunition.

French foot artillery in action

and two howitzers—would total 27 to 29 vehicles and 156 to 168 horses.[135] With the additional horses ridden by the artillerists themselves, the number needed to field a single company of line horse artillerists jumps to more than 225 animals.

Typical Composition of French Artillery Companies in 1805
(Consult Orders of Battle in Appendices for Specifics)

	Poundage of Guns and Number per Company				
Company Designation	3*/ 4 pdrs.	6 pdrs.*	8 pdrs.	12 pdrs.	Howitzer
Line Ft, 1 Corps, reserve co	- / -	-	-	5	1
Line Ft, 1 Corps, not reserve	5 / -	-	-	-	1*
Line Horse, 1st Corps	- / -	5	-	-	1*
Line Ft, other than 1st Corps, reserve company	- / -	-	-	6	-
Line Ft, other than 1st Corps, not reserve	- / 2	-	2	-	2
Line Horse, not 1st Corps	- / -	-	4	-	2
Imperial Guard *Volante*	- / 2	-	4	-	2
Italian Royal Guard Horse	- / 2	-	4	-	2

*The 3- and 6-pounders were Hanoverian ordnance, as were the 5.3-inch howitzers that were part of these companies of 1st Corps.

A full company of artillery as previously described carried into action the following number of pieces, vehicles and horse as detailed in the following:

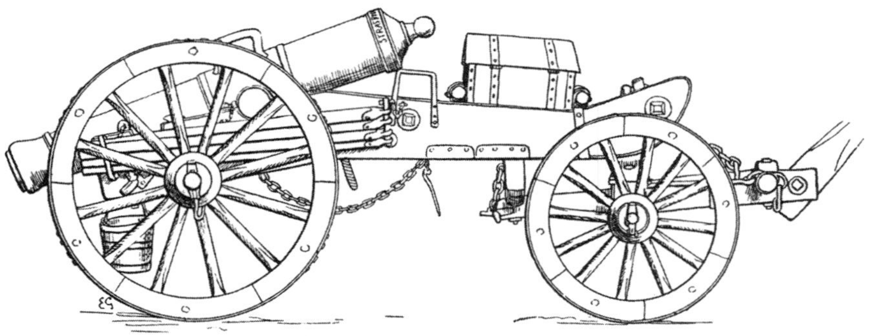

French 12-pounder (Gribeauval system) in travelling position

[135] If each howitzer has three caissons as in Pigeard, *L'Armée Napoléonienne,* p. 723, the numbers are 27 vehicles and 156 horses. If each howitzer has four caissons of ammunition as detailed by General Ruty, the total would be 29 vehicles and 168 horses.

Mobile Vehicles of a Typical French Artillery Company and Corresponding Number of Horses[136]

Company Designation	Vehicles	Horses
Line Foot—reserve company		
12-pounder guns	6	36
Replacement guns	2	8
Caissons	24	96
Wagons	3	12
Forge for the artillery	1	6
Forge for the train	1	4
Totals:	37	162
Line Foot—not reserve company		
4-pounder guns	2	8
8-pounder guns	2	12
6-inch howitzers	2	8
Replacement 8-pounder gun	1	4
Replacement howitzer	1	4
Caissons for 4-pounders	2	8
Caissons for 8-pounders	4	16
Caissons for howitzers	8	32
Wagons	3	12
Forge for the artillery	1	4
Forge for the train	1	4
Totals:	26	112
Line Horse Company		
8-pounder guns	4	24
6-inch howitzers	2	12
Replacement 8-pounder gun	1	4
Replacement howitzer	1	4
Caissons for 8-pounders	8	48
Caissons for howitzers	8	48
Wagon for the artillery	1	6
Wagon for the replacement gun/howitzer	1	6
Wagon for the train	1	6
Forge for the artillery	1	6
Forge for the train	1	4
Totals:	29	168
Imperial Guard *Volante* Company or Royal Italian Guard Horse Artillery		
4-pounder guns	2	12
8-pounder guns	4	24
6-inch howitzers	2	12
Replacement 4-pounder gun	1	4
Replacement 8-pounder gun	1	4
Replacement howitzer	1	4
Caissons for 4-pounders	4	24
Caissons for 8-pounders	12	72
Caissons for howitzers	10	60
Wagons for the artillery	2	12
Wagons for the replacement guns/howitzer	2	12
Wagon for the train	2	12
Forge for the artillery	1	6
Forge for the train	1	6
Totals:	45	264

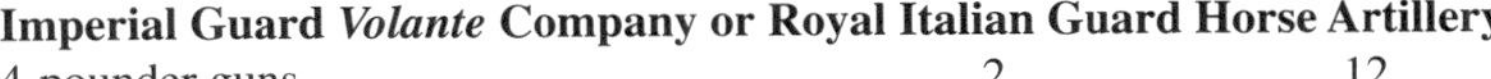

Two images of caissons used by French artillerists

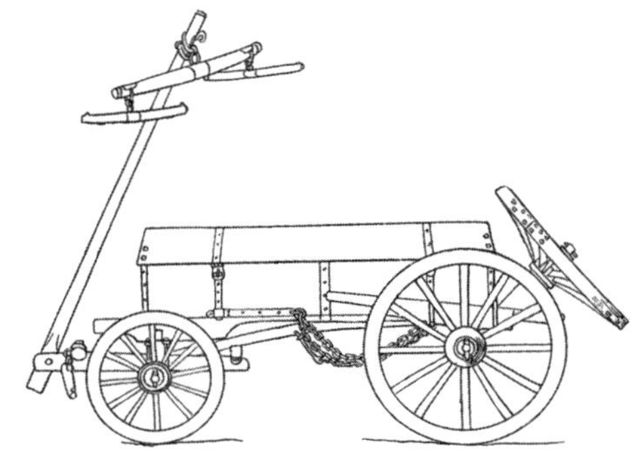

[136] Although there was an overall shortage of horses in 1805, the author has assumed that each 12-pounder and howitzer manned by line foot or horse artillerists have four caissons for each piece. To arrive at the total for three caissons per each of these pieces, simply subtract the appropriate number of vehicles and horses. These totals for horses do not include any ridden by the artillerists.

Soldier of the Artillery Train

The artillerists of the French Imperial Guard and Italian Royal Guard were supported by additional numbers of artillery train personnel when compared to line artillerists. One reason for this was that they carried into the field extra ammunition provisions.[137] By 1806, this extra ammunition was supposed to always be double the normal allotment for the guns of the line. However, this double allotment was not fully in place for the 1805 campaign. Including the ready ammunition in the trail chest of every piece, the 1805 Guard carried into the field two caissons for every 4-pounder, three caissons for every 8-pounder, and five caissons for every howitzer. This translates into 318 rounds for every Guard 4-pounder, 291 rounds for every Guard 8-pounder and 352 rounds for each Guard howitzer.[138] In later years, triple ammunition was procured if at all possible and taken along with each company. This was accomplished during the fall campaign of 1813 (Battles of Dresden and Leipzig). However, owing to the limitations in the availability of horseflesh, triple ammunition provisions were an exception.[139]

Speed in maneuvers was of the utmost importance for the Guard horse artillery. As a result, it is not surprising that all French Imperial Guard or Italian Royal Guard caissons were drawn by teams of six horses. Including the artillerists and train of artillery personnel, every 1805 Imperial Guard horse artillery company fielding eight pieces of ordnance needed a minimum of more than 350 horses![140]

Not only was the quantity of horses a requirement, the color of the animals was just as important. Black horses had the highest priority for completing the companies of the French Imperial Guard and Italian Royal Guard while assorted browns were used in the numerous companies of line foot and horse artillery. The color restriction was far from a theoretical issue—Napoleon took the matter *very* seriously. The Emperor considered the companies of *Volante* as the most important units in the army and he went to every length to insure not only the quality of their personnel, but their 'look' as well. With regard to black horses, it was decreed that the purchasing agents make available for the companies of *Volante* the first choice of any black horses, thereby maintaining both the strength and color of the animals serving in these prize units.[141] Napoleon's covenant with the black horse 'look' of the *Volante* bears no greater witness than his letter dated 1 June 1815 to General Antoine Drouot, acting commander of the Imperial Guard. At a time when horseflesh prior to the beginning of a campaign was seemingly at its scarcest, the Emperor wrote:

> I see that the *Volante* is short of horses. It is more important to have batteries of artillery than it is to have eighty horses in the [cavalry] ranks. Dismount however many *Grenadiers à cheval* you must and immediately forward their horses to the horse artillery. Four batteries that arrive late to me will cause me to lose the battle.[142]

Horse Artillerist of the Imperial Guard

As the artillery for the army began to take shape in the spring of 1805, Napoleon realized that more ordnance than what was already on hand from French manufacturers was going to be needed for any upcoming campaign. On 15 germinal an XIII (5 April 1805), Berthier announced to Marshal Bernadotte, commander-in-chief of the Army of Hanover—the future 1st Corps of the 1805 *Grande Armée*—

---

137 Arrêté, *Correspondance*, number 4967, dated 15 messidor an VIII (4 July 1800).
138 See comments in footnote 134. These numbers are based on Général Ruty's findings.
139 Drouot to Berthier, 6 August 1813, S.H.A.T; see Scott Bowden, *Napoleon's Grande Armée of 1813*, p. 124.
140 This total includes the horses for the gunners.
141 S.H.A.T., 2w 84.
142 S.H.A.T., C^{15} 5; Scott Bowden, *Armies at Waterloo*, p. 53.

that the Emperor wanted it "clearly understood that all these [Hanoverian ordnance] will make part of the campaign equipment."[143] That is why that the 1st Corps fought the 1805 campaigns using Hanoverian 3- and 6-pounder guns rather than French 4- or 8-pounder ordnance. Likewise, the Hanoverian howitzers employed by 1st Corps were 5.3-inch howitzers instead of the 6-inch French Gribeauval howitzers.[144]

The Hanoverian ordnance system of 3-, 6- and 12-pounder cannon, complemented by 5.3-inch howitzers, had been in use since before the wars of the French Revolution. It was during the last decade of the 18th century that the pieces were discovered to be far too heavy. Consequently, they were redesigned and lightened during 1800 and 1801.[145]

In addition to more guns, Napoleon also increased the size of the army's specialist troops, such as engineers and *pontonniers*. Companies of these specialists were attached at the corps level while the remainder were held at army artillery reserve headquarters, there to be held in readiness until needed.[146]

A pontoon on its carriage (Gribeauval system)

Deployments and Combined Arms Tactics in Napoleon's *Grande Armée*

Overview

From their considerable experiences in the Revolutionary wars, and from two additional years of lengthy sessions conducted by tough drillmasters in the mock battles of the Camp of Boulogne, the officers and men of the *Grande Armée* brought forth tactical flexibility and a philosophy of combined arms tactics previously unknown among the other armies of the earth. This new system and army, wielded by one of history's greatest captains, burst upon Europe in 1805. After Austria and Russia joined forces with Great Britain to form the alliance known as The Third Coalition, Napoleon was forced to turn the *Grande Armée* around from its camps along the Channel, and face the Austro-Russian armies gathering east of the Rhine River. Leaving their encampments, Napoleon's army conducted a series of lightning marches to the Rhine and beyond where they met and destroyed the Allied forces in battle. The victors of the 1805 campaigns emphasized coordination between combat arms and flexible deployments in order to maximize the assets of each combat arm. In order to understand the French system, it is imperative that the deployments of the individual arms and their interrelation be studied.

First and foremost, the three combat arms within the *Grande Armée* were viewed by Napoleon as equal partners working towards a common goal—the destruction of the enemy's armed forces. "Infantry, cavalry, and artillery are nothing without each other," the Emperor wrote.[147] The spirit of *Liberté, Egalité et Fraternité* did more than just reflect the Revolution; it carried into the new army the utmost enthusiasm among all combat arms. Cavalry supported the movements

---

[143] S.H.A.T., C^2 193; Berthier to Bernadotte, *Unpublished Correspondence of Napoleon I*, 5 volumes (New York, 1913), vol. 1, number 82; J. Freiherr von Reitzenstein, *Das Geschützwesen und die Artillerie in den Landen Braunschweig und Hannover* (Leipzig, 1900), pp. 389-391 and pp. 421-425.

[144] S.H.A.T., C^2 470 and 474. On 15 thermidor an XIII (3 August 1805), there were only four pieces of ordnance present with the 1st Corps that were of French origin, those being four 12-pounders.

[145] S.H.A.T., C^1 32. Also, see von Reitzenstein, *Das Geschützwesen und die Artillerie*, pp. 420-421.

[146] S.H.A.T., C^2 470.

[147] *The Military Maxims of Napoleon*, translated by Lt.-Gen. Sir George C d'Aguilar, (London, 1901—reprinted in 1987), p. 187.

of the infantry; both cavalry and infantry were supported by the artillery. As the guns were Napoleon's specialty, he realized that "artillery is more essential to cavalry than to infantry, because cavalry has no fire for its defense, but depends on the saber..." [148] Napoleon held the belief that a modern army should not mix infantry and cavalry into the same organizational brigade or division. "The habit of mixing small bodies of infantry and cavalry together is a bad one," Napoleon wrote, "and attended with many inconveniences. The cavalry loses its power of action. It becomes fettered in all its movements. Its energy is paralyzed..." [149]

What these three maxims translate into was as simple as it was sublime. The movements of divisions of infantry were supported by equally large formations of cavalry, and the guns assigned to the parent formations would provide necessary firepower. By committing to battle these large formations of infantry and cavalry, each combat arm would cover the weaknesses of the other and make possible opportunities that were difficult to achieve if one was not seconded by the other two.

Ideally, infantry was to be closely supported by large bodies of cavalry, thereby giving the French foot soldiers—the *fantassins*—the flexibility to deploy into whatever formation was needed to deal with the enemy's forces. If the foe was deployed to meet the infantry, then brigades or divisions of French cavalry would be brought forward, maneuvering in the gaps between the divisions of infantry. Since there was not an all-powerful formation in which infantry could equally defeat infantry as well as fend off opposing cavalry, the enemy officers would then be forced to make a choice to either defend themselves against the threatening cavalry or the nearby infantry. If enemy infantry chose to form squares or closed columns to defend against French cavalry, the enemy formations would make prime targets and be blown apart by nearby French artillery or infantry fire. Enemy infantry that refused to hunker down into defensive formations from the threat of cavalry were inviting disaster. French cavalry generals, through their extensive use of a large cloud of mounted scouts and staff officers, would locate vulnerable enemy formations. Orders quickly relayed to the cavalry command would be followed by the trumpets sounding the charge! Even if the enemy infantry then managed to transform themselves into square or closed column to face the onrushing horsemen, and even if the cavalry was unsuccessful in its attempt to break the infantry, once the cavalry receded the nearby French infantry or artillery would hustle up into close range and introduce themselves with flames of erupting muskets and cannon. Under a hail of lead and unable to effectively reply, the enemy would be forced to either commit reserves to maintain their positions or to order a withdrawal.

French infantry pack, usually taken off by the soldier before going into battle

Working in partnership with infantry as well as their own horse artillery, French cavalry generals became masters in the threatened use of force as well as in the actual commitment of their troopers. In many instances, the threat of a charge by cavalry was more effective than a charge itself. This was especially true if the enemy was prepared to meet a mounted threat. Rather than order a charge that had little chance of success, French cavalry leaders would elect to bring up their own horse artillery and work in concert with other friendly formations to inflict grievous losses on the opposition. Cavalry also had the effect of pinning an infantry foe to the ground (squares often moved more slowly than other formations). The threat of launching a cavalry charge could cost the enemy dearly as their movement would be significantly reduced. Forced to maintain a defensive posture in case the French cavalry attacked, the enemy infantry was hopelessly compromised vis-à-vis nearby French infantry and artillery. Each blast from the French cannon or

[148] *The Military Maxims of Napoleon,* p. 195.
[149] *The Military Maxims of Napoleon,* p. 190.

infantry would further reduce their ranks. Once it could be ascertained that the opposing formations were coming apart from a combination of casualties and fatigue, the cavalry would be ordered forward to do their work with the cold steel. If the enemy infantry maintained their formation, a fierce struggle would ensue. Combat was reduced to personal duels. Small numbers of horsemen might breakthrough one or more corners of a square, gain access inside the formation, kill the color guard and capture the infantry standards before fleeing with their prizes without the infantry being 'broken.' Even if the French cavalry were repulsed, the ever-present French artillery and nearby infantry kept up the pressure with firepower. If the infantry's formation was broken by the cavalry, total destruction would be swift and deadly.

The constant pressure applied by the three Napoleonic combat arms would eventually cause the toughest veteran outfit to buckle. Whether the break came from attrition caused by artillery, *tirailleurs* or formed infantry, or if the troops gave way in front of a charge that had been carefully setup, the opposing side would find it difficult to maintain themselves against these combined arms tactics over a prolonged period of several hours.[150]

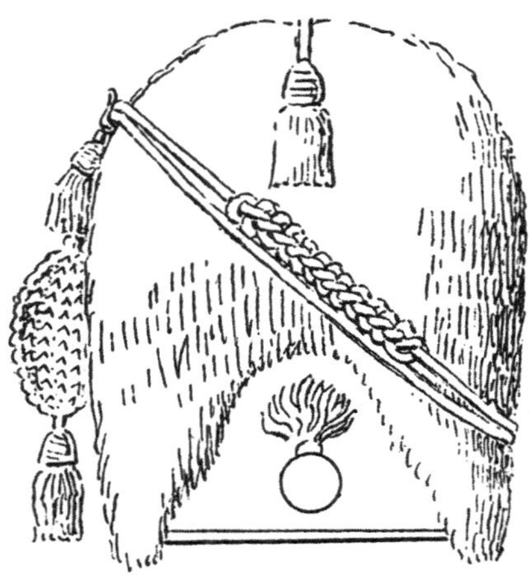

Bearskin headgear of French ligne *grenadiers*

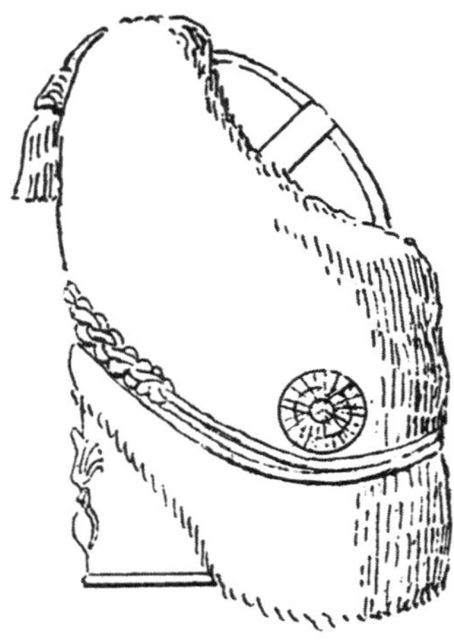

Combined arms tactics were not only preached to all combat arms, but the philosophy of inter-arms cooperation was totally indoctrinated in the *Grande Armée*. As a result, rash charges by infantry against an unshaken opponent were an exception rather than the rule, and naturally, there were sometimes good reasons to take such a risk. Battalions and regiments were part of brigades whose formations interconnected with one another to form a division. A risky or senseless charge resulting in the loss of a battalion or regiment would force tactical reserves to be committed to the front line. The preferred method of wearing down the opponent through firepower would eventually signal the opportune time to commit the *fantassins* to charge. When ordered, these were often conducted at either the regimental or the brigade level. In any charge, a combination of favorable factors would have to be present in order to tempt a Napoleonic officer into such action. The least of these would include a visible deterioration of the enemy troops that usually came after a quarter-to-half-hour of combat.

The French tactical system, as with any tactical system, had exceptions to the norm. This especially held true with regard to the better formations of the army. Élite units, if kept in reserve for most of the day, usually wasted no time with firepower tactics once introduced into the line of battle. Instead, these élite units would go straight at the enemy with the cold steel. Committed to an attack in this manner, with many of the higher ranking officers leading the way, the élite troops had an excellent chance of driving in the tiring enemy and rupturing the foe's battle line. On rare occasions, French army commanders would open a battle by launching a fierce attack spearheaded by their best troops, the idea of which was to surprise the opposition and create an opportunity whereby the enemy was initially knocked off-balance and constantly reacting to French movements. This was especially effective against portions of an enemy's line that were not supported by large numbers of cannon. This aggressive opening style included Marshal Masséna's initial attack on Fuentes de Oñono (5 May 1811) with battalions of converged grenadiers, and Napoleon's opening move at Montmirail (11 February 1814) with the battalions of the Old and Middle Guard.

Naturally, things did not always go as planned. For example, if a division of cavalry designated to support two divisions of infantry were committed prematurely

[150] Possibly the best books on the system of combat used by Napoleon and the *Grande Armée* are by General H. Camon, *Quand et comment Napoléon a conçu son système de bataille* (Paris, 1935), and *La guerre Napoléonienne—Précis des campagnes,* 2 volumes (Paris, 1925).

to a charge and subsequently broken upon the squares of the opposing infantry, or did not arrive in sufficient strength or time to coordinate their efforts with the infantry, the cavalry's absence would leave the friendly infantry and artillery to deal with whatever the enemy's forces were—all without the threatened or real use of a friendly mounted arm. If such were the case, they would continue to maintain pressure as best they could, ideally through the method of long-range fire fights and artillery fire. This style of fighting would continue until the horsemen were rallied and returned, or until fresh cavalry formations arrived.

Whether at the divisional level, corps level, or army level, reserves were valued assets that were to be saved for the right moment, their timely introduction into the line of battle affecting the outcome of the engagement commensurate with the level of the reserve. At the division level, the reserves would typically consist of a brigade. At the corps level, reserves were usually measured by the division, although smaller formations were also used, such as battalions of grenadiers and *carabiniers* that were converged from the corps' line and *légère* regiments. At the army level, reserves were thought of in division or corps-size formations. Therefore, the army had in reserve one or more corps (usually many) whereas the corps commander started out with at least one of his divisions in reserve and the division commanders in turn had at least one of their brigades as tactical reserves. Regardless of the level at which reserves were forwarded to the front lines, commitment of these troops could best be described as what happened when preparation met opportunity. If the commander was prepared, he could take advantage of any opportunity presented to him by the enemy.

The School of the Infantry—The Offensive

From the Channel Camp of Montreuil where the soldiers of the future 6th Corps of the *Grande Armée* were being put through their paces, Marshal Michel Ney wrote his views of tactical warfare in the manuscript *Étude militaire.* Written for the use of his officers, one of Ney's statements seems to characterize the French army of the Napoleonic era.

> In offensive warfare the French soldier has inexhaustible resources; his active genius, and his bravery in storming, double his energy; and a French commander ought never to hesitate in marching against the enemy with the bayonet, if the ground is at all adapted to a charge *in line* with one or more battalions at a time. It is by attacking that the French soldier has become accustomed to warfare.[151]

When looking closely, Ney's military opinions were colored by centuries of French history.

Faith in offensive warfare was imbued in French society and in their military long before the Napoleonic era. Notoriety of the French in the attack went back to the days of Hannibal and the Second Punic War of 219—202 B. C. Gallic swordsmen played important roles in Hannibal's biggest victories at Lake Trasimene and Cannae, as the Carthaginian general cunningly employed these ferocious 'barbarians' against the legions of Rome.[152] One hundred fifty years later, the Gauls were known for their dashing, yet uneven, performance against Julius Caesar and the Romans during the campaigns in Gaul (modern day France) in 58 B. C.

---

[151] Marshal Ney, *Military Studies*, translated by G. H. Caunter (London, 1833), p. 101.
[152] Theodore Ayrault Dodge, *Hannibal,* 2 volumes (New York, 1891), I, p. 140, pp. 298-305; vol. 2, pp. 360-377 and 409.

and 52 B. C.[153] The reputation of Gallic ferocity continued through Merovingian times (A. D. 500 to 751) and was still in wide acceptance during the *ancien régime.* Therefore, for more than 2,000 years—from the time before Vercingetorix led the Gallic tribes against Caesar until the soldiers of Napoleon's army were encamped at Boulogne—the military prowess of the French was their unusual spirit and energy on the offensive coupled with their difficulty to be disciplined while on the defensive. In his study of the Republican *Armée du Nord* of the early 1790's, John A. Lynn maintained that "these characteristics made the French formidable in the charge and particularly weak in controlled volley fire."[154] Improvement of this second aspect within the French infantry was one of the major focuses by Napoleon's officers during the intensive training at Boulogne.[155] However, the Emperor's officers were attempting to overcome generations of tradition.

The French spirit of the offensive surfaces in the writings of many soldiers, authors and philosophers. In his *Dictionnaire philosophique*, the great writer François Voltaire was of the opinion that:

> French artillery is very good, but the fire of French infantry is rarely superior and usually inferior to that of other nations. It can be said with as much truth that the French nation attacks with the greatest impetuosity and that it is very difficult to resist its shock.[156]

One of the most prominent soldiers of the 18th century, Marshal de Saxe, wrote in 1732 about the French in his *Mes réveries*. While the work was published posthumously, it was widely read as a valued treatise from someone who had served both with as well as against the French army. Saxe stressed the influence of national character on French tactics when he stated: "It is the distinctive characteristic of the French nation to attack."[157] Writing after Saxe, the most prominent tactical writer and theoretician of the 18th century, the comte de Guibert, was much more detailed in his observations of the French army of the *ancien régime.* In his 1772 publication *Essai général de tactique,* Guibert thought that:

> the French were without discipline, hardly suited to fire fights..., redoubtable in all attacks with cold steel and assaults on outposts. They had then, as today, that initial moment of vigor and impetuosity, that shock which one day nothing can stop, and which the next day, a slight obstacle throws back, that incredible combination of a courage sometimes above everything and a consternation sometimes carried on to a weakness.[158]

It was stated many times during the Revolution by soldiers and politicians that offensive warfare was the only option for French arms. One of the Jacobin

---

[153] Napoleon III, *History of Julius Caesar,* 2 volumes (New York, 1866). Napoleon III gives an excellent description of the Gauls of this period in volume 1, pp. 33-48, as well as a detailed battle narrative of Caesar's conquest of Gaul in volume 1.
[154] Lynn, *Bayonets of the Republic*, gives an excellent study of the French 'Cult of the Bayonet' in Chapter 8, pp. 185-193.
[155] S.H.A.T., C^2 192.
[156] Voltaire, as qouted in Emile G. Léonard, *L'armée et ses problèmes au XVIIIe siècle* (Paris, 1958), p. 235.
[157] Marshal Maurice de Saxe, translated by T. R. Phillips, *My Reveries on the Art of War* (Harrisburg, 1940).
[158] Jacques-Antoine-Hypolite de Guibert, *Essai général de tactique*, 2 volumes (London, 1773), vol. 1, p. 7.

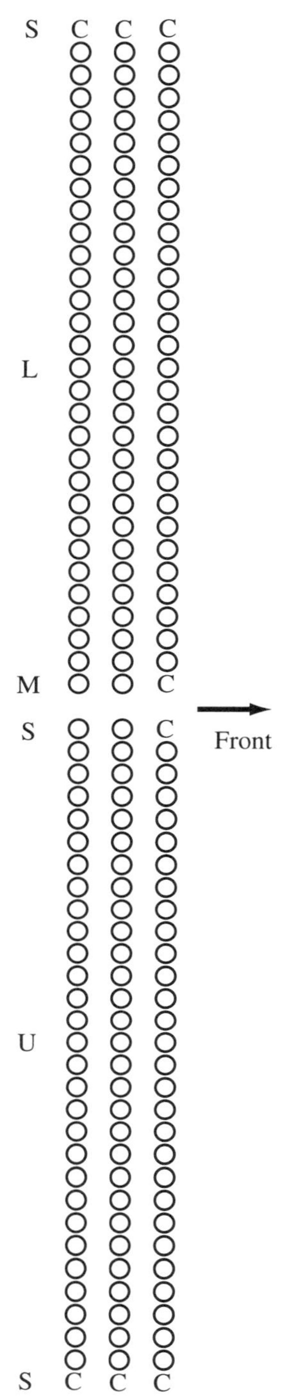

An infantry company arrayed in line—C represents corporals, S sergeants, M the sergeant major, U the sous-lieutenant, L the lieutenant, and the star the Captain

Representatives on Mission reported to Paris in 1793 that: "Every time we have attacked we have won, and ... every time we have been attacked we have almost always been defeated."[159] One of Napoleon's future corps commanders, *général de division* Joseph Souham, agreed that in the battles involving Revolutionary armies "we have few examples where the French have been beaten when they have attacked."[160] Lazare Carnot, acting as a Representative on Mission with the *Armée du Nord*, drafted a tactical directive in 1794 with a Gallic battle cry to "engage in combat with the bayonet on every occasion."[161]

Napoleonic officers realized that the army had to be extensively trained to attack either by fire or by cold steel. While the Revolutionaries of the early 1790's had been forced to employ extensive use of column formations to compensate for the lack of training among many large numbers of volunteer soldiers, the drillmasters of the Camp of Boulogne refined the already developed Republican offensive tactics for either fire or close assault using line, column or square, or any combination thereof. The French spirit of the offensive was to be usefully harnessed with a new tactical discipline.

To grasp the fundamentals of either offensive or defensive tactics, the basic building blocks of the *Grande Armée* must be understood. The battalion was the basic maneuver element—or building block—of infantry in the Napoleonic army. As previously detailed, most 1805 battalions consisted of nine companies. When formed for battle, one company was almost always detached to act as *tirailleurs* and form a screen for the remainder of the parent unit. Each battalion could perform a multitude of drill evolutions based on a host of formations. Before any further details are discussed, it is important to realize that French military terminology had two distinct meanings for the word 'division.' In one sense, division meant a large body of thousands of troops consisting of several regiments organized into two or more brigades. On the other hand, the French use of division also referred to an intra-battalion organization in which two companies comprised a division. While most of the maneuver formations had frontage widths of one company or two companies, battalions that were formed with a two-company front were known as either attack column, or column of divisions. The attack column (also known as column of attack) and column of divisions had the same frontage—two companies. However, there were many important distinctions between the two.

The overwhelmingly preferred formation of maneuver was the attack column. Listed in the *Règlement du 1er août 1791*, the attack column consisted of a two-company frontage with the middle division comprising the 4th and 5th numbered companies *always in front.* All formation changes would center off these companies. If the attack column changed formation into line, the 4th and 5th companies would end up the middle of the formation after the other companies came abreast. This is why the attack column is also known as a column that is formed on the middle, referring to the middle division being the focal point of all battalion evolutions.[162]

The attack column had a depth of one section—half the front of a *peloton*, or company—between each division. With four divisions (eight companies) in ranks, and with one company acting as *tirailleurs*, the depth of the attack column was 32 yards.

The method of deployment by attack column was further refined in the drill *Ordonnance du 12e pluviôse an XIII* (also referred to as the *Ordonnance du 1er*

---

[159] Representative Delbrel, as quoted in Lynn, *Bayonets of the Republic*, p. 188.

[160] *Général de division* Souham, as quoted in H. Coutanceau, H. Lepus and Clément La Jonquière, *La campagne de 1794 à l'armée du Nord*, 2 parts, each of 2 volumes (Paris, 1903-1908), vol. 2, 2, pp. 5-6.

[161] Lazare Carnot, as quoted in Lynn, *Bayonets of the Republic*, p. 189.

[162] S.H.A.T., *Règlement concernant l'exercise et manœuvres de l'infanterie du 1er auôt 1791.* Hereafter referred to as the *Règlement du 1er auôt 1791.*

février 1805) practiced extensively at the Camp of Boulogne.[163] If *all* companies of the battalion were formed, the attack column would show four divisions deployed as usual with the grenadier company (*carabiniers* in the light infantry) swung out to the right of the battalion as a 'wing.' In this configuration, the frontage of the attack column was three companies—the 4th and 5th numbered companies and the grenadiers (or *carabiniers*) on the right flank, or wing, of the 4th company—while the depth was four divisions, or 32 yards.[164] This size interval between the divisions allowed ample space for the rear divisions to rapidly come forward and deploy into line. When this evolution was being carried out, the *Règlement* specified that the center division (the 4th and 5th companies) were to open fire while the other companies swung into position.[165]

All formation changes out from as well as back into the attack column always followed the same method. The 4th and 5th companies were the front division, with the 6th and 3rd companies formed behind the front division, followed by the 7th and 2nd, followed by the 8th and 1st. Detaching of companies to act as *tirailleurs* also followed a pattern. The battalion commander (*chef de bataillon*) decided how many companies of *tirailleurs* were necessary for any given situation. If only *one* company of *tirailleurs* (never, ever the 4th or 5th company) was needed, the grenadier company (*carabiniers* in the light infantry) would take that company's place in column. If two companies were detached to act as *tirailleurs* for the rest of the battalion in attack column, the two companies so detached would *always* be one of the matched divisions (the 7th and 2nd companies, or the 8th and 1st companies, etc.). If four companies were detached as *tirailleurs*, then two matched divisions excluding the one with companies numbered 4th and 5th would be ordered to act as skirmishers. If six companies were needed for skirmishing activity, the remaining division with the 4th and 5th numbered companies would still act as the formed base for the battalion. Only when the entire battalion was deployed *en tirailleurs* did the 4th and 5th companies act as skirmishers. Also, the grenadier (or *carabinier* in the light infantry) company could be used to reinforce a line of *tirailleurs*.[166]

The intervals between the divisions in the attack column, and the fire methods designed to cover the deployment of the rear divisions as they came forward to form a line, leave little doubt that the attack column was not intended for shock combat, but a formation designed for rapid movement around the battlefield, easily transformed into line for fire combat, or into square to fend off enemy horsemen. It is noteworthy that nowhere in the pages of the *Règlement* is there any details for employing the attack column for combat *à la baionette*. It is given brief treatment in the 1805 *Ordonnance,* to wit: "Shock assault by the infantry is to be used as a *coup de grâce* against an opponent that is disorganized, or worn down by fatigue and fire casualties that has been skillfully applied by combined arms."[167]

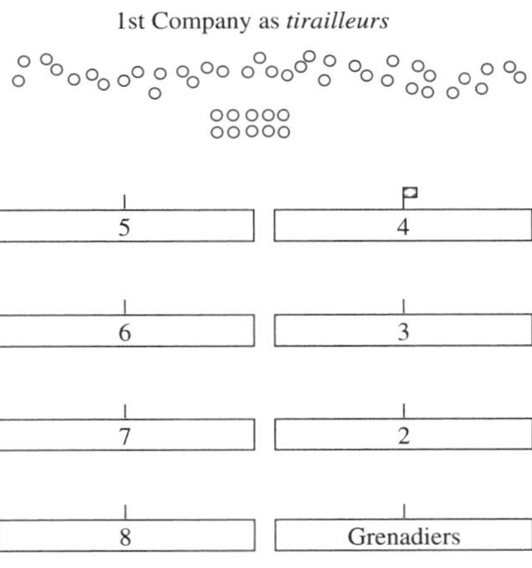

Battalion in Column of Attack

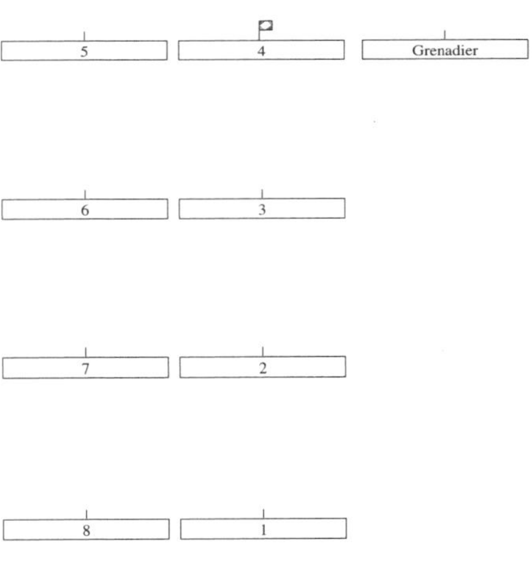

Battalion in Column of Attack, with Grenadiers on the wing—all companies are formed

[163] S.H.A.T., *Ordonnance concernant l'exercise et manœuvres de l'infanterie du 12e pluviôse an XIII.* Hereafter referred to as *Ordonnance du 12e pluviôse an XIII* or the *1805 Ordonnance.* A much simplified version of this Ordonnance was renamed *Le Système de discipline et manoeuvres d'infanterie formant les bases de tactiques modernes* and adopted throughout the Empire for drill use by the National Guard formations.

[164] S.H.A.T., *Ordonnance du 12e pluviôse an XIII.*

[165] Napoleon made reference to the 1805 *Ordonnance* on numerous occasions. Many of these came in 1813 when the Emperor offered advice to his corps commanders on the training of the young conscripts. Two such examples can be seen in: Napoléon to Lauriston, *Correspondance*, number 19553, 8 February 1813, and Napoléon to Bertrand, *Correspondance,* number 19775, 27 March 1813. To read excerpts from these and others, please consult Scott Bowden, *Napoleon's Grande Armée of 1813*, pp. 61-64.

[166] S.H.A.T., *Ordonnance du 12e pluviôse an XIII.*

[167] S.H.A.T., *Ordonnance du 12e pluviôse an XIII.*

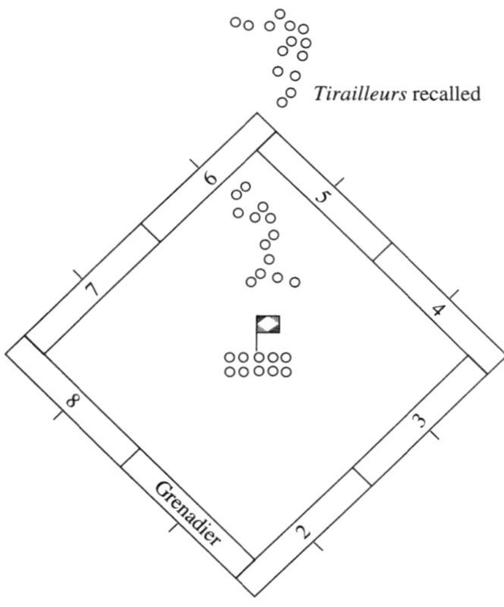

Square formed from attack column— ligne *infantry company numbers shown*

The attack column had one other trademark—the positioning of the battalion eagle and flag. Since the eagle-flag bearer and the remainder of the color guard were always formed in the front rank of the 4th company, the attack column would display the battalion's sacred symbols at the forefront or in the middle of the battalion, depending on whether the unit was in column or in line. The presence of the eagle and flag in the 4th company is why they were always the last to be deployed as *tirailleurs*. It was believed that companies acting as *tirailleurs* could not adequately protect the symbols of Napoleonic glory.

Since an attack column had the same companies always in the same place for each specific formation, drill evolution was easy to teach as well as simple to learn and perform. Special emphasis was placed on quickly forming square from attack column whenever cavalry attacked. These aspects are clearly born out in the spring of 1813, when Napoleon and his generals were trying to mold a new army following the Russian debâcle of 1812. The majority of troops that formed the 1813 *Grande Armée* were new to infantry drill and subsequently taught only two formations—the attack column and the square.[168] How different it was eight years earlier, as the superbly drilled, veteran formations of the 1805 *Grande Armée* utilized the attack column whenever possible, and if the situation called for different kinds of two-company front evolution, they could perform these from the formation known as column of divisions.

At first glance, a column of divisions might look identical to an attack column insofar as the battalion's frontage was concerned. The column of divisions also presented a two-company front, but that is where the similarities ended. Whereas the attack column always formed on the center division of companies numbered 4th and 5th, a column of divisions could form its two-company front with any companies of the battalion. The particular division of companies that was in front, and the change of formation that was desired, indicated how the formation change was to evolve. Therefore, if a battalion was deployed with a two-company front and the eagle-flag bearer and color guard were not in the front rank in the company on the right side of the battalion, then the column could not be an attack column, but rather one of the various combinations of column of divisions.

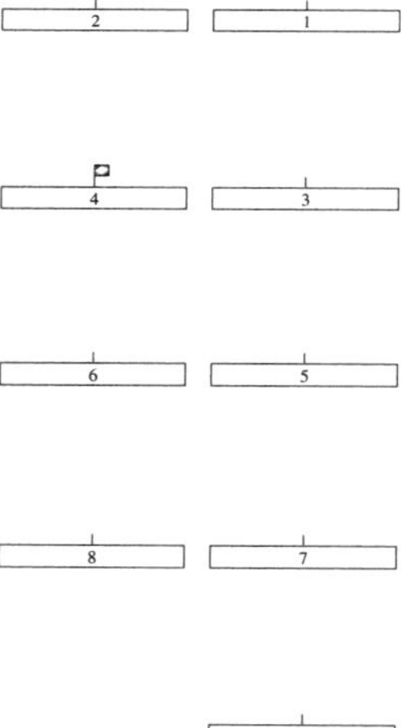

Ligne *infantry in one of many possible column of divisions at full interval*

Column of divisions could either be at full interval (two companies), at the distance of a *peloton* (company), at half-interval (like an attack column) or closed interval. Because of the four possible deployments, the column of divisions was a more flexible formation but required considerably more drill practice in order to execute. The additional skill required to perform drill in a column of divisions restricted its use to those formations whose officers and men had been able to work together for a significant period of time. Such were the units that comprised the majority of the *Grande Armée* of 1805.[169]

The extensive drill sessions practiced by the infantry battalions of Napoleon's army reflected impressive flexibility in the use of either attack column or column of divisions. To implement the desired formations, Marshal Ney went into great detail concerning all aspects of drill while in these column formations. In summarizing, the Marshal concluded that "marches and evolutions executed in column form the essential parts of military tactics."[170]

[168] Napoléon to Lauriston, *Correspondance,* number 19553; Napoléon to Bertrand, Correspondance, number 19643 (with copies of this letter to Lauriston and Kellermann (the elder), Napoléon to Bertrand, *Correspondance*, number 19775, Napoléon to Ney, *Correspondance*, number 19714, Napoleon to Marmont, *Correspondance*, number 19868.
[169] An excellent discussion of the form and function of divisional and attack columns used by the French infantry during the Revolutionary as well as the Napoleonic eras can be found in Lynn, *Bayonets of the Republic*, pp. 252-254.
[170] Marshal Ney, *Military Studies*, p. 24.

To offer greater protection against hostile cavalry who might suddenly appear through the smoke of battle, the various columns could easily be 'closed,' usually called *colonne serrée.* Closed columns meant that the interval between the companies in column had been closed to only three paces between divisions—about two and a half yards—and that supernumerary officers and NCOs who normally stood behind the third rank of each company were moved to the flank thereby connecting the companies in column and presenting to a foe a look of a block of personnel unbroken by interval. If enemy cavalry should attack, the rear company would face about and the three files on each flank would simply face outward.[171] Ney described this transformation by a closed column as a battalion "in mass, the three files on the proper flank [it is supposed that the columns have their right in front] should face to the left flank; and those on the reverse flank should face to the right; the last division would go about."[172] The *colonne serrée* was not as solid as a square that was ready to receive a cavalry charge, but it did provide most of the advantages of square while offering a more maneuverable and flexible formation. Since all but the most experienced infantry could maneuver more rapidly in closed column than in square, the *colonne serrée* was the preferred formation when enemy cavalry threatened, but were not actually attacking. If cavalry attacked and if time permitted, square was formed to repulse the horsemen.

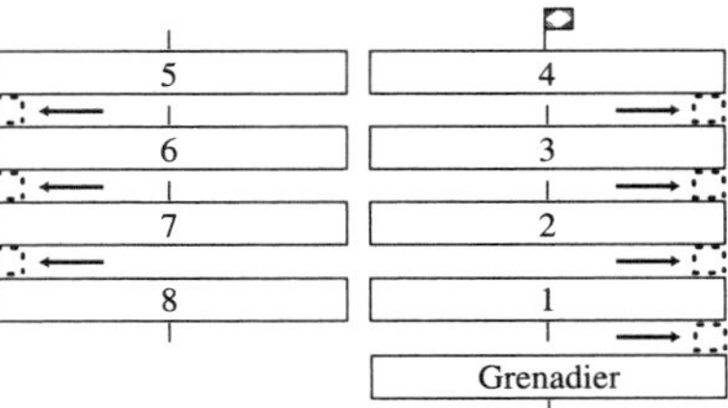

Closed column or colonne serrée: *the file closers moved to the flanks and the rear companies turned around to form an extempore square against cavalry attack*

"Squares are formed three deep, in conformity to the Emperor's instructions," Marshal Ney told his officers, "and sometimes also by doubling up the interior sections [six ranks deep], according to the principle laid down in the *Règlement* of 1791."[173] Squares could be used by infantry in a limited offensive role. In order to protect themselves against hostile cavalry while attacking, French infantry could form square and advance, all men of the square facing the same direction. If suddenly beset by cavalry, the formation simply halted and the men faced out, thereby presenting an unbroken front of bayonets. The strengths of square against cavalry were as obvious as its disadvantages against artillery and infantry. The square's compactness made it a vulnerable target and its firepower was very limited. For those reasons, the use of squares in the attack was not desired and was limited to the most specific situations when French infantry was advancing unsupported in the face of enemy cavalry.

The flexibility of Napoleon's *fantassins* is further illustrated by their use of the "column of half battalion" as specified in the 1805 *Ordonnance.* Employed at the Battle of Austerlitz as well as other Napoleonic battlefields of the 1805-1807 era, the column of half battalion was a flexible formation offering significant firepower for a column formation. The formation utilized eight companies in formed order, with a two division [four companies] frontage by two companies [six files] deep, and was intended to be used when the infantrymen were maneuvering over relatively gentle terrain and needed to occupy a wide frontage while retaining the ability to rapidly form square. Like the other columns employed by the infantry of the *Grande Armée*, the column by half battalion could easily form square by the ends of the companies on each flank advancing or falling back while the interior flanks of each company remained stationary.[174]

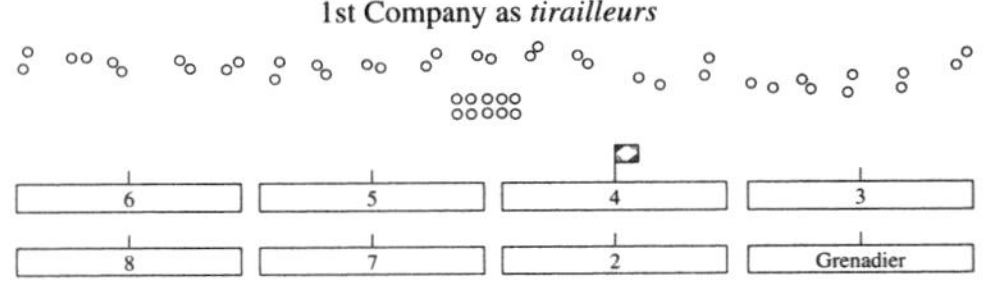

Column of half battalion, utilized by the infantry of 1st Corps at Austerlitz

The formations used in attacking an enemy position were not randomly selected. Undertaking the offensive role in battle required thoughtful infantry deployments, proper execution of formation changes given changing battle conditions and coordination with other combat arms. If sufficient supporting cavalry where nearby, the typical battlefield maneuver formation outside effective enemy

[171] S.H.A.T., *Règlement du 1er auôt 1791; Ordonnance du 12e pluviôse an XIII.*

[172] Marshal Ney, *Military Studies*, p. 32.

[173] Marshal Ney, *Military Studies*, p. 51.

[174] S.H.A.T., *Ordonnance du 12e pluviôse an XIII.*

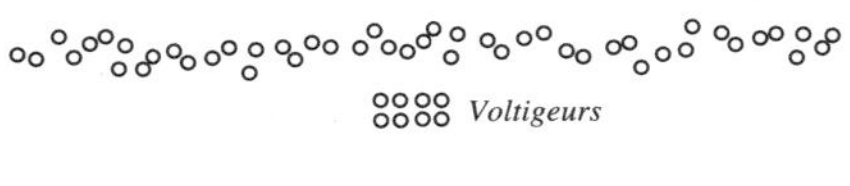

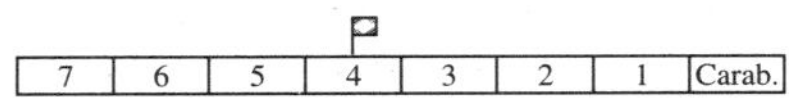

French légère *battalion in line with the* voltigeur *company deployed in front as* tirailleurs

artillery canister fire range was the attack column. Once the enemy line had been discovered by either cavalry scouts or *tirailleurs* and the enemy's whereabouts communicated, the infantry would deploy into line for the final advance. "The principles of the march in line are clearly enough indicated in the *Règlement* of 1791," Ney instructed his lieutenants. "The men and the battalions are placed facing to the front on the ground they occupy, and in perfect alignment; the colors are generally carried six paces in front when the line is to march, for the purpose of giving the cadence of the step, serving as a point of intermediate direction, and preventing the battalions from bulging out beyond the one appointed to direct the movement."[175] During these last few hundred yards, the line would present a less vulnerable target for artillery fire and would deliver volleys whenever the *tirailleurs* were withdrawn from covering the battalion's front. The firepower from these well officered, disciplined formed troops deployed in line formation, coupled with the threats from French cavalry and artillery, often spelled doom for an opponent who could not coordinate all the combat arms of his own side.

Depth was also important to any attacking infantry. Division commanders would always strive to deploy their respective commands in two or three lines of battalions, each line consisting of at least one brigade. If the division consisted of three brigades and was deployed in three lines, each brigade would typically form one of the lines with the light infantry almost always forming the first line. If the division had a regiment of light infantry (light infantry always served as a separate brigade during the 1805 through 1807 period) and was deployed in two lines, invariably the first line would consist of two brigades—one brigade of line and the other brigade light infantry. The second line would consist of another brigade of line troops. It is important to note that the brigade would almost always be deployed by battalions abreast across the division's horizontal front rather than any vertical arrangement.

By deploying in depth, division commanders allowed each one of their brigade commanders to coordinate the maneuvers and formation changes of their units. This also gave the rear brigade(s) added flexibility in being able to maneuver once the front line became hotly engaged. If all units were in column, battalions in the second or third line would *not* be positioned directly behind the battalions in the line in front of them. Rather, they would be positioned in an alternating fashion so that gave the appearance of a giant checkerboard. This checkerboard deployment accomplished several goals. First, it allowed the battalions to deploy into line quickly and evenly across each entire brigade front. Second, the battalions in the rear line could cover the flanks of the front line units, as well as move through the intervals in the front line if those battalions remained in column or square. Finally, deployment in checkerboard allowed the division and brigade commanders to perform a 'passage of lines' whereby the battalions in a second line would relieve the battalions in the first line without interpenetrating the units being passed through.

French generals tried to make sure that brigades in the second or third line were not brought so far forward as to interfere with any slight retrograde movements conducted by the front brigade. From a practical standpoint, brigades were deployed and operated so that they would not interpenetrate other friendly brigades within canister range of the enemy. Any passage of lines from one brigade to the next would normally occur while battalions were in column formation. The second line would pass through the first without any formed troops having to interpenetrate friendly battalions. This was typically accomplished by commands from the division commander that went to each brigade, and the brigade commanders, in turn, coordinated their regiments.

---

[175] Marshal Ney, *Military Studies*, pp. 35-36. Upon a cautionary command: 'Battalions will advance!' the colors remained with the ranks, rather than be carried six paces in front.

Once the location of the enemy line had been firmly established, the final advance into close range might consist of a mixed order of line and column—the famous *l'ordre mixte.*[176] While various adaptations of *l'ordre mixte* were utilized, the lowest level being a regiment of three battalions, one of the most favored combination during the 1805 through 1807 era was clearly the mixed order by brigade. Since most line or light infantry regiments of this era fielded only two war battalions, the mixed order by brigade was a common deployment. Assuming that the brigade consisted of two regiments, each of two battalions, *l'ordre mixte* by brigade consisted of all four battalions with the battalions on each flank in attack column and the center battalions deployed in line.

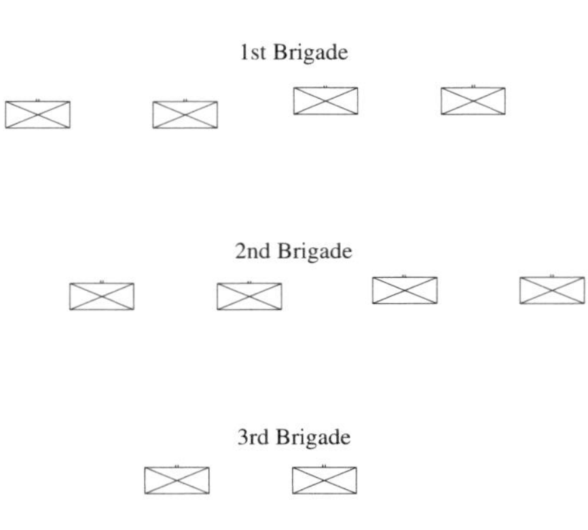

French division using checkerboard formation to deploy in depth. Each block represents an infantry battalion

French corps and division generals had the added flexibility of being able to form *ad hoc* commands on the battlefield in order to accomplish specific goals. For example, a division commander might order a *chef de bataillon* from his staff to take selected élite companies from certain regiments or brigades and form a task force with the specific purpose of silencing an enemy battery or seizing some tactical objective.[177] The flexibility of forming these *ad hoc* task force commands was made possible by the number and generally excellent quality of staff officers both at corps and division level. To assist in the implementing of orders on a day of battle, French corps and division commanders would supplement their staffs with personnel from the cavalry regiments of the corps. For example, an infantry corps commander often increased his staff on the day of a battle by adding two officers from each regiment of light cavalry in his corps. These officers would supplement the corps chief's aides-de-camp in expediting orders.[178]

If the French infantry were advancing without proper cavalry support, or if enemy cavalry were known or believed to be within striking distance, the typical battlefield maneuver formation was the attack column or closed column of divisions, the *colonne serrée*. It was rare that French generals of the 1805 through 1807 period pushed their superb infantry formed in close columns into the jaws of an enemy's defense that was ready and waiting with combined arms. Instead of plowing headlong into a prepared enemy, the advance would be temporarily suspended until the artillery crews had time to work their pieces and rain a hail of iron upon the enemy. Meanwhile, the *tirailleurs* worked their way into close range with the opposing infantry, picking off officers, NCOs and generally tormenting the enemy battle line. After a deadly dose of ordnance and *tirailleurs*, French cavalry would be summoned to breakup the opposition's horse and send the enemy squadrons packing. Defeating the enemy's cavalry would, in turn, expose their infantry to threat of a mounted attack. Forced to defend against a potential French cavalry attack, the enemy would have to react, and based on the reaction, the French infantry would deploy into line and resume the advance, or perhaps continue a more rapid advance in attack column if the enemy artillery fire was not intense.

---

[176] Brent Nosworthy, *With Musket, Cannon and Sword: Battle Tactics of Napoleon and His Enemies* (New York, 1996), pp. 131-138 has an informative discussion on the development of the mixed order.

[177] S.H.A.T., *Journal des opérations du 3e corps, Journal des opérations du 4e corps* and *Journal des opérations du 6e corps* have numerous examples of these task forces being formed throughout the campaigns of the 1805, 1806 and 1807 era. While the 1805 campaigns illustrated many such examples, as detailed at Haslach-Jungingen and at Dürenstein in Chapters V and VI, some of the most spectacular accomplishments come in the 1806 campaign, especially Davout's use of these at his triumph at Auerstädt. The use of these task forces was still in use in 1815 at Waterloo.

[178] S.H.A.T., *Journal des opérations du 3e corps, Journal des opérations du 4e corps* and *Journal des opérations du 6e corps.* Marshal Ney, *Military Studies*, p. 85. Ney states that each general of the corps (either *général de division* or *général de brigade*) may increase his staff by adding one officer and one NCO from each cavalry regiment attached to the corps.

While *tirailleurs* could have a demoralizing effect on enemy infantry while thinning their ranks, skirmishers alone could not decide an infantry fight. Eventually, the formed troops would be brought forward to resolve the issue. An advance by line or column, combined with firepower and eventually shock action, usually drove in the enemy infantry suffering from hours of fatigue and significant attrition.

It was difficult for most infantry officers to get their men moving forward once they stopped and began firing a series of volleys. For that reason, fire fights were, at least ideally, calculated rather than spontaneous. After witnessing General Friant's regiments on the defensive, followed by them going over to the offensive at the Battle of Austerlitz, Marshal Louis Davout remarked: "The division maneuvered during the entire day in perfect order, like on the practice field, firing from two ranks with admirable calm when close to the enemy."[179] Marshal Ney saw prolonged fire fights as something to be avoided.

Marshal Ney

> Most infantry officers have remarked on the almost insurmountable difficulty they find in stopping file-firing during battle after it has once begun, especially when the enemy is well within range. In spite of the commands given by field officers, this firing resembles general discharges. If the troops are to attack, it would be better, therefore, after the first two ranks have fired, to charge boldly with the bayonet and by an act of élan force the enemy to retreat.[180]

While French offensive doctrine called for a marriage of all arms working together to disrupt and dislodge the enemy, it also provided for measures to sustain the infantry if their own cavalry were not present. Regardless of the presence of friendly cavalry, there were a wide array of offensive variations from 'pinning' attacks to an all-out push—*le coup de force.* Infantry pinning attacks were designed to keep an opponent pinned to his present position. These were usually accomplished through heavy use of *tirailleurs* and artillery, as the formed infantry of the brigades conducting the pinning attack were usually deployed in dead ground as to not exposed them to enemy fire unless absolutely necessary. That certainly wasn't the case at the other end of the offensive spectrum, as the all-out assault held nothing back. Fresh troops previously held in reserve would be brought forward. Together with the other troops, all possible pressure would be brought against the enemy line. *Le coup de force* combined firepower and close assaults as French generals sought to break the enemy's physical and psychological will to resist. As Marshal Ney saw it, the "colonels of the infantry regiments are urged to drill their men in attacks peculiarly adapted to the vivacity and temperament that distinguish the French soldier from that of other nations."[181]

The School of the Infantry—Open Order Combat

What Marshal Ney referred to as "the vivacity and temperament" of the French soldier was also the foundation of their most celebrated prowess—skirmish ability. From the wars of the French Revolution, a certain mythology developed around the extensive and very effective use of open order combat by French armies. In his book *Précis historique de l'infanterie légère* published in 1806, France's leading light infantry expert, *général de division* Philibert-Guillaume Duhèsme,

[179] S.H.A.T., *Journal des opérations du 3e corps.*
[180] Marshal Ney, *Military Studies*, pp. 99-100.
[181] Marshal Ney, *Military Studies*, pp. 99-100.

wrote: "It is in this genre of combat, that the French genius shines with the greatest brilliance."[182] It was more than just patriotic rhetoric that influenced Duhèsme's writing. Emphasis on open order combat and tactics was a style of warfare to which French generals had devoted considerable time and energy since before the *Règlement* of 1791. After gaining valuable experience in the campaigns of the American Revolution, the Marquis de Lafayette claimed that he introduced to the French army the concept and use of *tirailleurs* in support of formed infantry. Before the new *Règlement* was published, Lafayette wrote in 1791 that it was he who:

> introduced... the principle, which is particularly favorable to French ardor, quickness, and intelligence, and which has since then been generally adopted; it is that of covering the active mass with a curtain of *tirailleurs,* ready to return to their units or pursue their advantages.[183]

Duhèsme

While some historians doubt that Lafayette was the father of *tirailleur* tactics in the French army, it is certain that the wars of the Revolution saw a considerable increase in the frequency and scale of open order combat within the Republican ranks.

The French grouped skirmishers into two distinct categories: *tirailleurs de marche et de combat* (march and combat *tirailleurs*) and *tirailleurs en grande bande* (*tirailleurs* in a large group).[184] The march and combat *tirailleurs* were men from their parent battalions who covered the front and flanks of the formed troops, always acting in support of the formed parent unit. These skirmishers scouted for the parent battalions, driving in enemy outposts, establishing the precise whereabouts of the opposition and bringing fire onto the enemy's front-line formations. If the enemy had no significant numbers of light troops, the *tirailleurs de marche et de combat* were usually more than enough to force back the opposing screen of skirmishers and bring havoc onto the opposing line. If the enemy had well-trained and sufficient numbers of their own skirmishers (which was very rare in the 1805 through 1807 era), then the light troops of both sides would fight each other, resulting in low casualties on the light troops and nothing significant taking place until the formed troops of one side came forward, forcing the enemy light troops to fall back on their own formed parent battalions. Then, the battle lines of formed infantry, cavalry and supporting artillery would get down to the serious business at hand.

On the other hand, *tirailleurs en grande bande* were entire battalions of troops whose goals were to either take or defend some difficult piece of terrain, or to surround the enemy's flanks. *Tirailleurs en grande bande* were a vital part of the strong-point defensive scheme. They would swarm in and around a village area, taking advantage of every possible piece of cover, shooting at the enemy as he advanced, falling back as the enemy approached the strong point during which time the attack became more and more disorganized, thereby ripening the situation for a counter-attack by French reserves. *Tirailleurs en grande bande* were also used in the offensive. They attacked up steep cliffs, through large woods and other terrain where formed battalions would find the going too difficult to negotiate. Hard to traverse terrain usually meant that enemy cavalry could not interfere with movements of the *tirailleurs*. If not utilized in difficult terrain where enemy cavalry

Légère *infantry—a* chasseur *on the left and a* carabinier *on the right*

[182] Philibert-Guillaume Duhèsmes, *Précis historique de l'infanterie légère* (Lyon, 1806), p. 152.

[183] Lafayette, as quoted in Lynn, *Bayonets of the Republic*, p. 269.

[184] Pascal Bressonnet, *Études Tactiques sur la Campagne de 1806* (Paris, 1909), pp. 370-371. Hereafter referred to as *Études Tactiques.*

could not get at them, *tirailleurs en grande bande* would be easily ridden down by a determined group of well-trained horsemen.

Another notable use of *tirailleurs de marche et de combat* or *tirailleurs en grande bande* was the attempted silencing, or at least neutralizing, of enemy artillery. The *Règlement provisoire* of 1792 was specific on how the *tirailleurs* were to conduct themselves in this-type operation:

> While battle lines are being formed and batteries placed, the commanding officers order the light infantry to advance ahead of the line infantry, so as to discover the positions of the enemy's guns and to diminish their effect. The light troops are placed in small thickets behind hedges, ditches, or small rises, according to the nature of the ground. They are commanded to fire at the enemy batteries, and to try to kill the gunners. These men do not form ranks, so as not to draw artillery fire, but separate, profiting from features that may afford them cover, and remain attentive so that they can quickly reassemble at the first signal from their officers.[185]

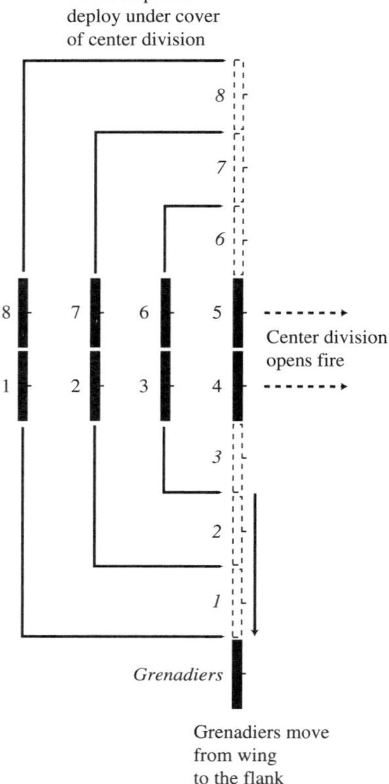

Method used to change from column of attack into line under cover of the center division

This technique was used very often by the soldiers of Napoleon's armies throughout the wars of the First Empire. *Tirailleurs de combat* from Marshal Louis Davout's 3rd Corps shot up several Prussian artillery crews at the Battle of Auerstädt on 14 October 1806.[186] At the Battle of Aspern-Essling on 21 April 1809, Marshal Jean-Baptiste Bessières led forward the *tirailleurs de combat* of the Old Guard against a grand battery of 50 Austrian guns. At that battle, the Guard *tirailleurs* took advantage of numerous canals and ditches, advanced upon the enemy artillery and poured a deadly fire into the Austrian gunners, forcing them to withdraw the grand battery to a position that could be covered by Austrian cavalry.[187]

Such tactics against enemy artillery were not limited to *tirailleurs* of the infantry. All French cavalry regiments employed mounted *tirailleurs de marche et de combat,* or skirmishers. While the formed squadrons of the regiment sought cover in some dead ground within close supporting distance, the mounted *tirailleurs* of the regiment would ride forward to bring fire onto the enemy's gun crews. With mounted sharpshooters swarming about them, the gunners had to deal with their tormentors. If the battery commander ordered his entire company to fire on the mounted *tirailleurs*, such fire would be the signal for the regimental colonel to order a charge before the gunners could reload.

There was another aspect to the impact of the fire from open order troops. *Tirailleurs* could, if given enough time and the proper cover to work over an enemy line, drain the opposition's supply of small arms ammunition. This is no better illustrated than the 24th *Légère* from Vandamme's Division at the Battle of Austerlitz. Able to deploy the majority of their two battalions as *tirailleurs*, Colonel PouRailly's officers and men shot to pieces the six battalions of the Austrian Salzburg IR#23 atop the Staré Vinohrady. The continual but mostly ineffective return fire by the Austrians against a irregular line of targets fully utilizing the cover of the topography, caused the Austrians to run seriously low on ammunition when a concerted French attack was put in by Vandamme.[188]

---

[185] S.H.A.T., *Règlement provisoire sur le service de l'infanterie en campagne du 5 avril 1792.*

[186] S.H.A.T., *Journal des opérations du 3e corps.*

[187] Jean-Roch Coignet, *Les Cashiers du Capitaine Coignet* (Paris, 1908), pp. 171-174.

[188] S.H.A.T., *Journal des opérations du 4e corps.* Details are in Chapter VIII.

The School of the Infantry—The Defensive

Marshal Ney felt that "the defensive system is ill calculated for the French soldier."[189] Nevertheless, the tactical defensive was an inescapable reality of Napoleonic combat. Troops that were assaulting would themselves be attacked on numerous occasions as attackers became defenders in the ebb-and-flow of battle. For that reason, formations had to be flexible in order to meet changing battle circumstances.

Perhaps the French aversion to defensive warfare was their firm belief in gaining and maintaining the tactical initiative. The inherent problems in sitting permanently on the defensive as opposed to a foe who was on the move, as well as relying on firepower to keep an enemy at bay, was that it all too often surrendered the initiative to the foe. When French infantry used firepower in an offensive role, they gradually wore down an enemy or to pinned him to the ground. In either case, after the enemy line was so engaged, an attack would usually be made by fresh troops introduced into the line of battle at the most opportune time. Ney asserted that infantry fire "offers real advantages only when troops are acting on the defensive."[190] The danger of standing on the defensive and relying on firepower was summed up by the red headed marshal, who warned that "ammunition always fails in the end, and this diminishes the men's confidence; each then finds some excuse, either in the condition of his musket, or even in his own impatience and vivacity, for hastening his retreat, unless the movement becomes offensive."[191]

The French, therefore, designed their various defenses and defensive schemes as disguised counterattacks in waiting. Local counterattacks were designed to take full advantage of a foe who was off-balance, thereby inflicting maximum damage on him. In the open field, the favorite defensive formation was *l'ordre mixte*. Line formations of the mixed order provided firepower while the nearby columns protected the line's flank. If threatened by cavalry, the columns would form square or closed column. By doing so, the squares or columns would anchor the flanks of the battalions deployed in line. With their flanks secure, the infantry in line presented a formidable front to mounted adversaries and could rapidly pour the volleys into advancing enemy infantry. Whether advanced upon by hostile infantry or cavalry, the French *l'ordre mixte* would have front and flanks covered by *tirailleurs*, giving way only when the advance of a formed enemy so dictated. When the opportunity presented itself, through either repulse of an enemy attack or by an enemy becoming visibly disorganized, French officers would quickly seize the moment, switch the columns into an offensive mode, and pounce on the retreating or disorganized foe. Beset in such a manner, a shaken or retreating enemy would rarely stand and their formations would come apart as they instinctively hastened their movement away from the counterattack.

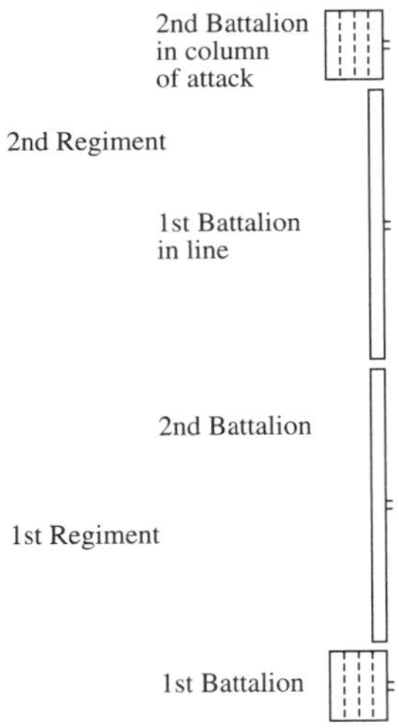

Defensive use of the mixed order in the open field was a favorite formation employed by experienced troops throughout the Empire. The *ordre mixte* was not seen often during the 1813 and 1814 campaigns because most regiments and brigades outside the Imperial Guard had not established an advanced level of regimental and brigade-level drill.[192] However, *l'ordre mixte* was employed very effectively by the superb infantry of the *Grande Armée* of 1805 and 1806 as well as by the crack troops of Napoleon's *Armée du Nord* in 1815.[193]

Without a doubt, the most deceptive and deadly defensive ploy utilized by French infantry was the 'strong point defensive scheme.' Whenever there was a

2nd Battalion in column of attack
2nd Regiment
1st Battalion in line
2nd Battalion
1st Regiment
1st Battalion

French ligne *brigade of 1805 in mixed order*

---

[189] Marshal Ney, *Military Studies*, p. 101.
[190] Marshal Ney, *Military Studies*, p. 101.
[191] Marshal Ney, *Military Studies*, p. 100.
[192] Scott Bowden, *Napoleon's Grande Armée of 1813*, p. 64.
[193] Scott Bowden, *Armies at Waterloo*, p. 32.

The French strongpoint defensive scheme

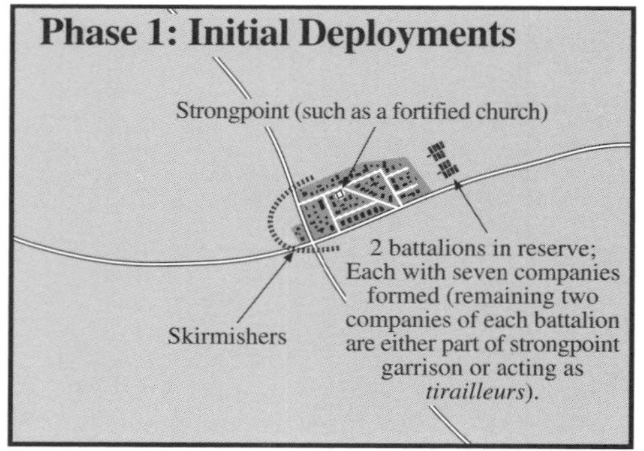

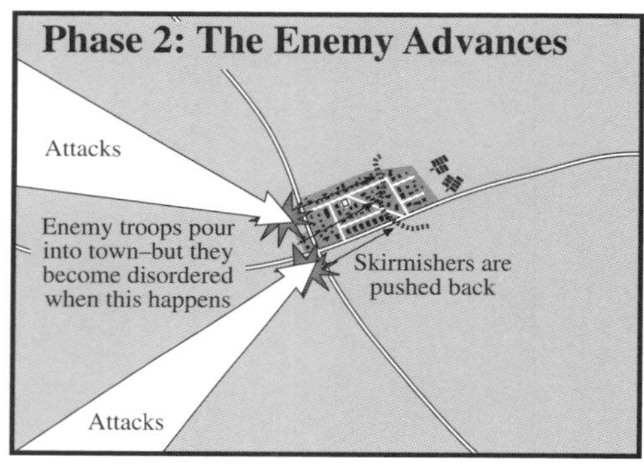

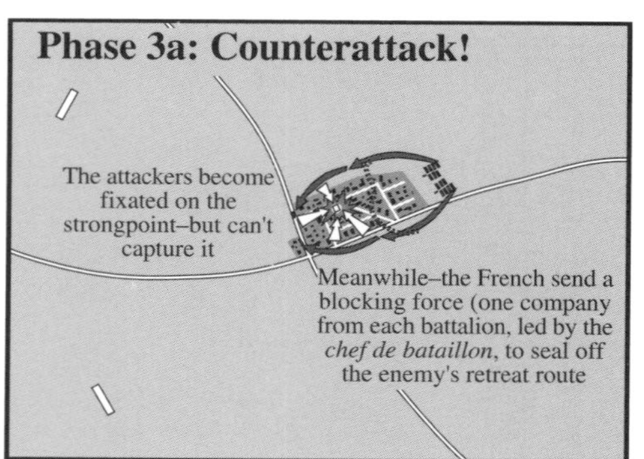

village or some other significant number of built-up structures in an important area of the battlefield, French doctrine called for those villages or built-up areas to be occupied on a very limited basis and used as pivots around which their battle line would maneuver or counterattack. This was contrary to conventional military wisdom as other armies would occupy entire built-up areas by packing battalions of men into many structures. While the allied method made it difficult for an enemy to capture a village, such doctrine consumed large numbers of men and eliminated any flexibility of those tied down in garrison.

In contrast, the French viewed a village as a way of luring an adversary into a killing ground where his formations would become disorganized, then be cut to pieces by a well designed counteroffensive. In letters sent on 30 thermidor an XII (18 August 1804) to Soult at Saint-Omer, to Davout at Bruges and to Ney at Montreuil, Marshal Berthier, writing as the Minister of War on order from the First Consul, gave instructions to the marshals for them and their subordinate generals to practice the system of the strong point defensive scheme. In these instructions, the marshals and their generals were to "utilize the inherent strengths of the French soldier" by "holding a strongpoint and launching counterattacks once the enemy had become disorganized."[194] The officers at all the other Channel camps were ordered to develop and practice this system of defense.

The strong point defensive scheme began by presenting a facade to the opposition by what appeared to be a village weakly held with only some *tirailleurs* visible along the outskirts of town. Wanting to wrest this position from the French, the enemy committed themselves to the attack. Once his troops reached the town and advanced down the streets amongst the structures, the enemy's hopes would be fanned by impressive gains as the covering *tirailleurs* would give way before the onslaught. Moving further into the village, enemy formations would be broken up by the very nature of the built-up terrain. As the French *tirailleurs* withdrew, they continued to fire into the foe until the enemy formations ran into the strong point of the defense. The strong point was almost always the most impressive structure in the village that was often sheltered from enemy artillery fire. Inevitably, this was usually a church, a tavern or a granary, and was preferably of masonry construction. Ideally, the building was fortified by French engineers, whom would loophole the walls (usually an upper floor) so that more firepower could be brought to bear on the assailants. The division commander charged with the defense of this village would select a battalion of his command to occupy the strong point. If the defense of the village was critical to the line of battle, it was not unusual for a division commander to converge his élites and commit them to hold the place. Command of such a converged élite battalion would be entrusted to a capable officer, usually a *chef de bataillon*, from the division commander's staff. Converged companies of grenadiers from the regiments of the line and *carabiniers* from the light infantry regiments of the division were ideal for such a mission as these companies brought with them their own engineers.[195]

Resuming the scenario, with most of the village now in hand and the strong point discovered, the foe would invariably assault the miniature fortress. When it was determined that the enemy's formations were sufficiently disorganized either by terrain and fatigue, or that the tactical situation called for an immediate counterattack, French reserves poised and waiting behind the village hustled forward to close the trap. Main streets or lanes leading out of the village would be closed by individual companies selected and personally led by *chefs de bataillon*. Once these troops had time to move into position, the remaining reserves, brought forward by a regimental colonel, a *général de brigade*, or perhaps the *général de division* himself, would charge into the village—usually with muskets plugged to prevent

[194] S.H.A.T., C^2 192, Berthier to Soult, with copies to Davout and Ney.
[195] S.H.A.T., C^2 470.

anyone from stopping and firing. Assailed by fresh troops, their retreat routes cut off by well led and resolute men, the enemy's formations would virtually come apart. Those who were not killed or captured fled as best they could back to friendly lines. Meanwhile, the prisoners were led away and the position was reestablished to await the enemy's next try.

As with any tactical scheme, the strong point defense did not always work perfectly. Avenues available for the enemy's withdrawal might be covered by his artillery or cavalry, thereby making it impractical for French troops to totally seal off all major retreat routes before the counterattack began. In other situations, the village terrain could be so broken up that any counterattack would be almost as disorganized as were the battalions of the enemy. In either case, it was important that the counterattack not go past the village, regardless of the enemy's flight, lest the French troops themselves be caught in a disorganized state and attacked by other enemy forces being held in reserve. However, the French strong point defense worked time and time again throughout the Napoleonic period. Just a few examples of this devastatingly effective defensive scheme include the village of Jungingen at the Battle of Haslach-Jungingen (11 October 1805), the village of Unter Loiben at the Battle of Dürenstein (11 November 1805), the village of Hassenhausen at the Battle of Auerstädt (14 October 1806), as well as the village of Essling at the Battle of Aspern-Essling in 1809, the village of Möckern at the Battle of Leipzig in 1813 and one of the greatest killing ground strong point defenses of all the Napoleonic wars being the village of Plancenoit at the Battle of Waterloo in 1815.

The French strongpoint defensive scheme, continued

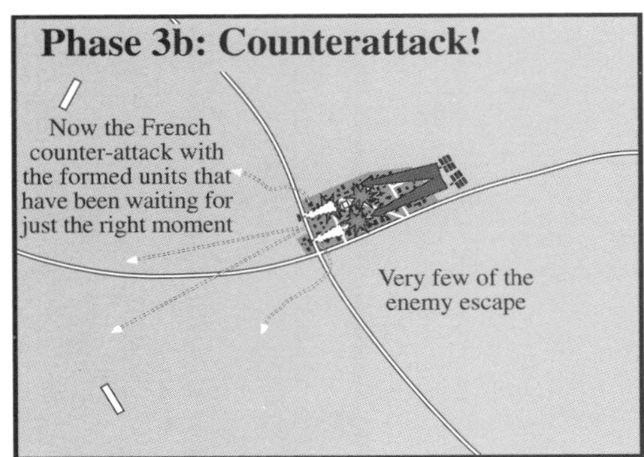

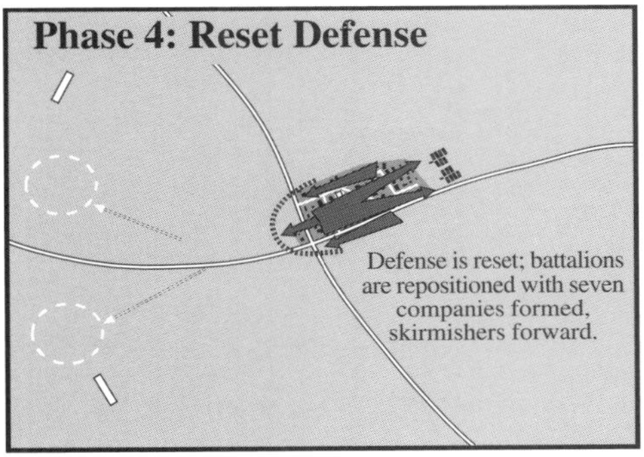

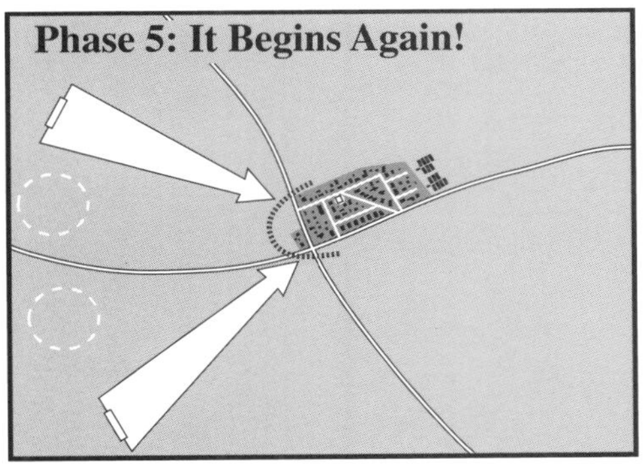

The School of the Cavalry

It may appear to be a perverse sort of logic, but one positive effect the blood-letting of the Revolution had on the French military was that it finally cleansed the cavalry arm of the lazy, aristocratic officers that stifled the tactical growth and spirit of the arm, and replaced them with energetic and aggressive volunteer officers. As with any tumult, the short term effect was not good for the Republican armies. French cavalry—always the worst combat arm under the Bourbons—passed into the hands of people who, at first, had no knowledge of the trade. The result was that Revolutionary cavalry virtually learned their trade anew and for several years suffered stern lessons at the hands of Allied regiments. Ironically, this rebirth was also the strength of the French cavalry arm during the Empire. The waves of new, aggressive officers transferring into the French cavalry in the early 1790's, were determined to elevate the combat performance of the arm. Since these men brought with them no preconceived notions of how things used to be, they were able to begin a school of the cavalry that would become the envy of Europe.[196]

Since the care, coordination and "command of a mounted unit was far more complex and demanding than that of a comparable infantry outfit,"[197] improvement in all aspects of equitation demanded thorough training as well as quality horseflesh. Authorities varied in their estimations as to how long it took before a recruit could take his place in the line of battle; the most optimistic estimate was two years whereas the most conservative estimate on record was three to four years. By any measure, rebuilding the mounted arm was a task that demanded time and talent.

Revolutionary enemies used to having their way with feeble French cavalry regiments perhaps got their first inkling of how things were going to change as early as 26 June 1794 at the Battle of Fleurus. In their work *La cavalerie pendant*

---

[196] For possibly the best story concerning the transformation of the French cavalry from the beginning of the Revolution to 1805, see: Picard, *La Cavalerie dans les Guerres*, vol. 1, pp. 1-320.

[197] Elting, *Swords Around a Throne*, p. 227.

la Révolution du 14 juillet 1789 au 26 juin 1794: La crise, French historians Edouard Desbrière and Maurice Sautai mark Fleurus as the watershed of the Revolutionary era; with that decisive battle, the French cavalry arm began to flourish. Once Napoleon appeared on the scene in Italy in 1796, he reorganized his army's cavalry into homogeneous brigades and divisions.[198] This organization was maintained and it was in these formations that the French horse trained intensively at the various Channel camps from 1803 until the beginning of the 1805 campaign.

The French cavalry generals were able to drill their brigades and divisions in large-scale maneuvers not possible by other countries. This was accomplished by many arduous years of drill, simulated combat as well as actual battle. By being able to coordinate large bodies of horse in a disciplined and orderly fashion, French cavalry generals were able to rapidly exploit opportunities as well as minimize enemy pursuit of any defeated French formations. Perhaps there was no better tribute to the French cavalry than that uttered by the Duke of Wellington, who stated: "I considered our cavalry so inferior to the French from want of order, that although I considered one of our squadrons a match for two French, yet I did not care to see four British opposed to four French, and still more so as the numbers increased, and order became more necessary."[199]

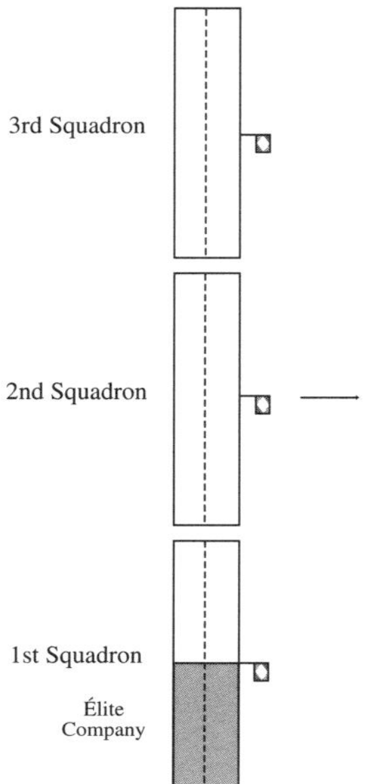

French Cavalry Regiment in three squadrons deployed abreast

The drill school of the French cavalry dated back to the cavalry regulations of Magimel. While more complete than its predecessors, Magimel's *Ordonnance de 1788* did not cover all the evolutions needed. Therefore, to improve the school of the cavalry and to regularize Magimel's work, Napoleon called for a special commission to update drill. The result of this work was called the *Ordonnance provisoire du 1er vendémiaire au XIII* (24 September 1804), and was submitted to Marshal Berthier on 6 prairial an XIII (26 May 1805).[200] The new cavalry *Ordonnance* included an extensive list of 18 possible formations and changes of formation based on the situation and the type of cavalry executing the drill. It proved so successful, that it was used as the drill guide for the cavalry until 1829.[201] The 18 drills which all cavalry were supposed to perform were:

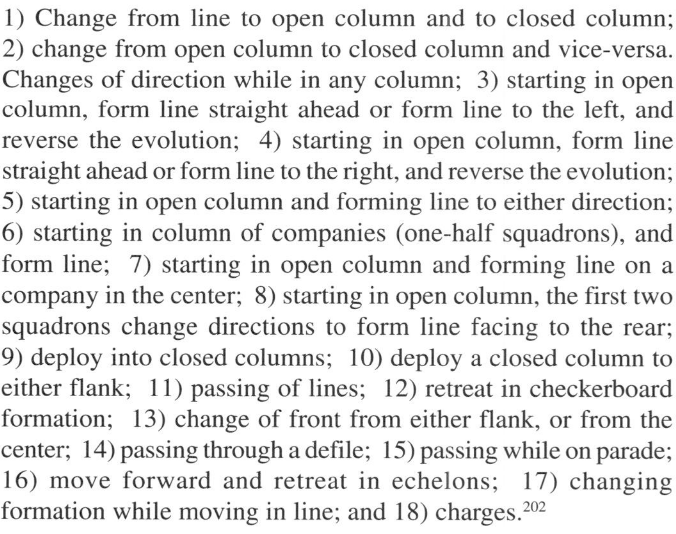

1) Change from line to open column and to closed column; 2) change from open column to closed column and vice-versa. Changes of direction while in any column; 3) starting in open column, form line straight ahead or form line to the left, and reverse the evolution; 4) starting in open column, form line straight ahead or form line to the right, and reverse the evolution; 5) starting in open column and forming line to either direction; 6) starting in column of companies (one-half squadrons), and form line; 7) starting in open column and forming line on a company in the center; 8) starting in open column, the first two squadrons change directions to form line facing to the rear; 9) deploy into closed columns; 10) deploy a closed column to either flank; 11) passing of lines; 12) retreat in checkerboard formation; 13) change of front from either flank, or from the center; 14) passing through a defile; 15) passing while on parade; 16) move forward and retreat in echelons; 17) changing formation while moving in line; and 18) charges.[202]

---

[198] Bonaparte to Berthier, *Correspondance*, number 99, 9 germinal an IV (29 March 1796).
[199] Letter from Wellington to Lord John Russell, dated 31 July 1826, as quoted in Sir Charles Oman, *Wellington's Army* (London, 1913), p. 104.
[200] S.H.A.T., *Ordonnance provisoire du 1er vendémiaire au XIII* and C^2 216.
[201] Picard, *La Cavalerie dans les Guerres*, vol. 1, p. 246.
[202] S.H.A.T., *Règlement concernant le service intérieur des troupes à cheval du 24 juin 1792.*

Charges were initiated in a host of different ways, all dependent upon the tactical situation including echelon by companies or squadrons up to an entire brigade. Regardless of the method of attack, the object was to gain the maximum frontage advantage against the opponent. This was usually accomplished by flanking the opposition's line, or by piercing the enemy line and rolling up in both directions the remainder of the line. Specific recommendations for charges included that if an officer had his command in two lines, the second line was to be held far enough in reserve as to not have it become interpenetrated by the first line should the first line be repulsed. Since frontage was often the deciding factor in cavalry fights, careful and intensive training was conducted by French cavalry officers in gaining an enemy's flank. When the cavalry had superior frontage in comparison to an enemy, a commander would want to deploy his formations in such ways as to deceive the enemy as to his actual frontage. Terrain was often used to accomplish this as squadrons would be held in defiles or other dead ground that made it difficult for the enemy to detect. If terrain did not allow deployment as to gain this deception, then the cavalry formation would deploy with its flank companies or squadrons in one or two wings behind the leading squadrons. When the time was right, the wings would move out to the flanks of the front squadrons at a faster pace than the rest of the formation, expanding the frontage of the command while on the move and making it possible for the flanking companies or squadrons to wheel in on the enemy flanks, thereby enveloping their formation. Whenever possible, squadron commanders were trained that when their command was stationed on the flank of the regiment, they were to direct the movements of their squadron as to attack an enemy's flank. These tactics were consistent with Napoleon's maxim that: "Charges of cavalry are equally useful at the beginning, the middle, and the end of a battle. They should be made always, if possible, on the flanks of the infantry, especially when this last is engaged in front."[203]

By maneuvering through the gaps between infantry divisions and corps, French cavalry usually moved in column of squadrons, being able to rapidly deploy into squadrons abreast if presenting a wider regimental front was needed. By deploying in the gaps between infantry maneuver elements, French cavalry were positioned to pursue a beaten enemy, or counterattack a foe. In either case, the positioning of cavalry regiments and their use was to prepare them for the role that they were intended—closing with the enemy.

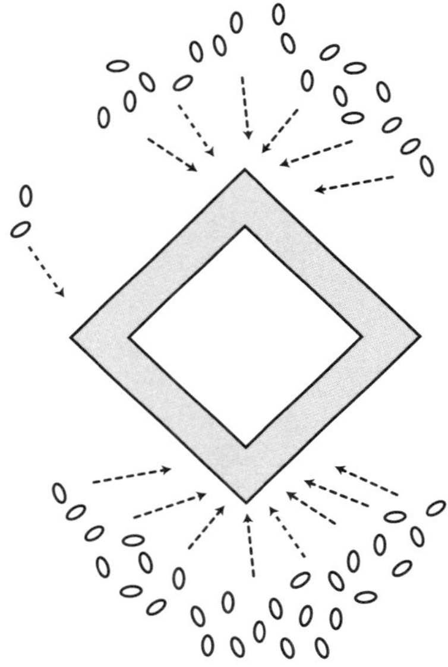

Mounted tirailleurs *concentrated their firepower on the corners of enemy squares*

If facing an enemy in square, the French cavalry's favorite method of attack was to concentrate all possible fire from the mounted skirmishers of the regiment onto one or more of the square's corners and then to mount an attack against the same corners. If nearby friendly artillery or infantry *tirailleurs* provided the firepower, the job could be made substantially easier. Once the desired corner(s) began to visibly thin out, a company or squadron would charge and try to gain entry into the square and breakup the formation. Sometimes only a few cavalrymen managed to fight their way into the square where they would battle the infantry's color guard over possession of their flag(s). This style of combat by small numbers of men often times resulted in the horsemen carrying away one or more of the enemy infantry's flags but failing to break the square. This is how the French cavalry, during their magnificent and virtually unsupported charges against the Anglo-Dutch squares at Waterloo, were able to come away with no less than five British colors.[204]

If the enemy had ordnance in the front line and a direct attack had initially failed, mounted *tirailleurs* would be brought forward to fire on the enemy artillerists while the formed squadrons would retire to some dead ground or back off far enough so that the enemy had to deal with the mounted *tirailleurs* rather than fire

[203] *The Military Maxims of Napoleon,* pp. 191-192.

[204] S.H.A.T., C^{16} 46; see Scott Bowden, *Armies at Waterloo,* p. 62, p. 347n211.

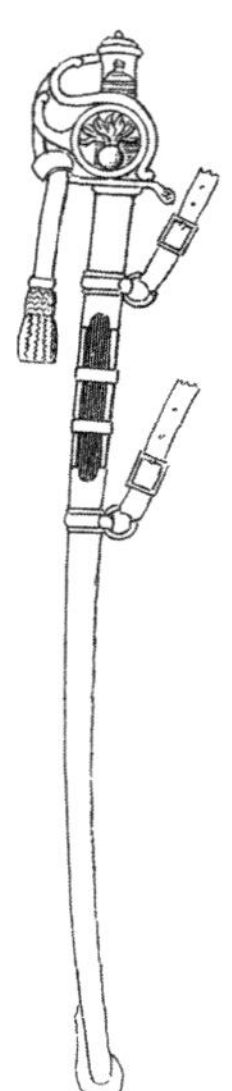

Saber of a Grenadier à cheval *of the Imperial Guard*

on the formed squadrons. If the opposing artillery commander grew impatient of the menacing mounted *tirailleurs* and ordered the entire battery to fire, that discharge cued the formed French cavalry to charge *à l'outrance*. Enemy crews would have little chance in reloading the guns before the swiftly moving French squadrons were sabering their way through the gunners. This proven, successful method of taking enemy cannon was one of the French cavalry's most renowned tactics, repeated time and again throughout the Empire. Readers familiar with the Battle of Waterloo literature will recall the incident between Cavalié Mercer's Royal Horse Artillery Troop and the *Grenadiers à cheval* of the French Imperial Guard. After failing initially to close with Mercer's guns, the "Gods" sent forward their mounted *tirailleurs* while the formed squadrons took cover in dead ground about 200 yards in front of the artillery troop. As the carbine fire from the skirmishing cavalrymen at a range of less than 40 yards took its toll on the troop's members, Mercer ordered his men not to fire but rather to stand to their pieces "with port-fires lighted."[205] Mercer realized that an order to fire in an attempt to clear his front of the mounted skirmishers would be tantamount to a death sentence for his command. He therefore had no choice but to wait and take the casualties from the enemy *tirailleurs* and hope that the "Gods" would grow impatient and order another mounted attack.

The use of mounted *tirailleurs* against the enemy's line was also an integral part of the French cavalry's threatened use of force, or pinning action. Since cavalry was ill-suited to occupying terrain or conducting fire fights, and if they were not going to charge but had to hold the enemy's attention, the French would accomplish this by positioning their formed squadrons for a charge and by use of a covering force of mounted *tirailleurs*. This did, of course, call for a keen eye for terrain. French cavalry generals had little desire to see their precious squadrons hold static positions while being blown apart by enemy artillery fire. Therefore, the regiments ordered to pin a foe had to accomplish this through the use of mounted *tirailleurs* while protecting the formed squadrons as best afforded by the undulating terrain.

The School of the Artillery and the Ordnance System of the Year XI

The Napoleonic epic offers many undeniable conclusions. One of them is that the cannon and crews of France surpassed those of all other nations. It was not by chance that the long arm of the French army established its supremacy over rival artillery. While the groundwork for the success of Napoleonic artillery was laid well before the birth of the Emperor, it was Napoleon's passion for the guns, coupled with his incomparable organizational powers and a wealth of other talented officers, that elevated the French artillery arm to a position of dominance. The artillery arm created by the Emperor was so strong that its organizational breadth and depth withstood the devastating attrition caused by the campaigns of 1812 and 1813, and proved time and again throughout the 1805 through 1815 era that it was the best on the face of the earth.

Officer's saber for the Chasseurs à cheval *of the Imperial Guard*

Just how did the French artillery of the late 18th century excel that of other nationalities, and what did Napoleon do to improve it into the killing machine of the early 1800s? To answer these questions, one must look at the 17th and 18th centuries and realize that a technological race ebbed back and forth in a similar manner as it does today. When the 1700s dawned, the armies of Europe were relatively small, professional and expensive possessions of kings. When at war, the monarchs would maneuver their armies in such a manner as to avoid major

[205] Cavalie Mercer, *Journal of the Waterloo Campaign* (New York, 1969 reprint from the London, 1870 edition), p. 173.

battles because major battles would wreck their treasured, expensive armies. Instead, the preferred method of warfare was laying sieges to desired cities, repeating the process until one side or the other sued for peace. This is no better illustrated than the career of John Churchill, 1st Duke of Marlborough (1650-1722). Recognized as the premier soldier of his age, Marlborough was considered an extremely aggressive general in the business of 'warfare of kings.' During the War of Spanish Succession (1701-1714), Marlborough fought four major battles—Blenheim (1704), Ramillies (1706), Oudenarde (1708) and Malplaquet (1709). One hundred years later from December 1805 to June 1807, Napoleon would personally command at four major battles in only 19 months. Compare this short period of time to the years that it took Marlborough to fight the same number of principal battles, and one begins to see part of the changing nature of warfare from the early 18th century to the early 19th century.

As the 1700s progressed, field artillery was in the process of rapid evolution as lighter and more maneuverable pieces were in demand as armies fought more battles while conducting fewer sieges. The Austrian and Prussian armies were first to develop improved and lighter pieces to go with this evolving style of warfare. They introduced standardized carriages with interchangeable parts, iron axles, limber boxes and aiming devices. By the beginning of the Seven Years War in 1756, the new Austrian field pieces were introduced on the European battleground, weighing less than half that of the obsolete guns of the Vallière system still employed by the French Bourbons. The lighter pieces, coupled with the many other improvements previously mentioned, made the Austrian Feurstein model guns the envy of European artillerists.[206]

While the Austrians led in the technological war of the mid-18th century, the Prussians soon followed with a new series of guns that copied the Austrian pieces. Meanwhile, the French—who had the state-of-the-art guns in the 1730s and 1740s—suddenly found themselves clinging to an ordnance system predicated on siege warfare and ill-suited to modern battles of maneuver. When introduced in 1732, the French guns of the Vallière system were the hardest hitting and longest ranged pieces in the world—an excellent combination for counter battery fire and knocking down fortress walls. Therefore, Vallière system, profoundly influenced by the views of Vauban, "rested on the assumption that a cannon's ultimate targets were the walls of enemy fortresses, not the battalions."[207] Furthermore the pieces were so heavy that any movement required horses and significant time to limber and maneuver them, especially since civilian contractors were hired to be the movers for the artillery. As a result, once deployed for battle it was very difficult to move the Vallière guns, which meant that if the army lost the battle, its guns were lost as well.

With the arrival of the Seven Years War and the repeated disasters suffered by French arms, it became apparent to many in France that a new ordnance system and a new philosophy of tactical employment were needed badly. However, the dean of the French artillery school did not see it that way. He was Joseph-Florent de Vallière, whose father had designed the 1732 ordnance system. Vallière refused to let any amount of criticism shake his filial respect. What resulted was a considerable and lengthy controversy between two factions of the French military that lasted for 20 years! Artillery officers who believed in the Vallière system and the preeminence of siege warfare and counter battery fire became known as "Reds." Officers who favored abandonment of the Vallière system, desiring instead a lighter, standardized and more mobile ordnance system, and who identified the enemy's troops as the prime targets for artillery were known as "Blues." The issue was finally settled in the 1770s when the evidence of the changing nature of warfare

[206] See Chapter III for details.

[207] Lynn, *Bayonets of the Republic*, p. 205.

demanded acceptance of the "Blues" school. The new ordnance system finally won approval in 1774. Even then, implementation was not begun until Vallière's death in 1776.[208]

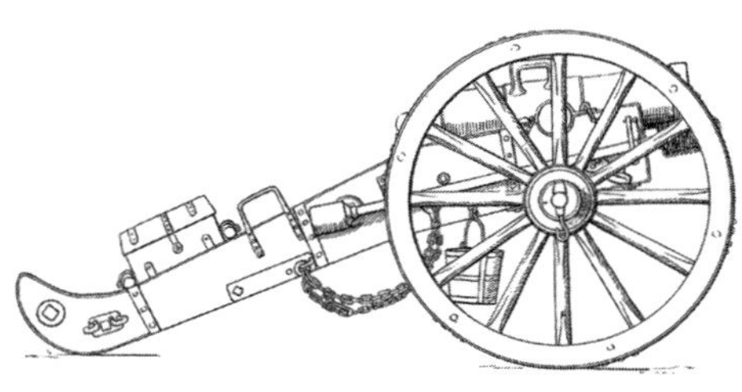

Gribeauval 6-inch howitzer

As with the preceding ordnance system, the new French guns and howitzers were known by their designer, Jean Baptiste Vaquette de Gribeauval. Certainly one of the most famous and influential artillery officers in history, Gribeauval joined the French army in 1732, the year that the Vallière system was introduced. During the Seven Years War, he was attached to the Austrian army as a general of artillery, and observed first-hand the new Feurstein ordnance. With his personal observations of the war, Gribeauval believed that France had to rethink its battlefield philosophy vis-à-vis the artillery. He argued that a completely redesigned ordnance system had to incorporate the improvements introduced since the middle of the century, as well as go much further by implementing many new, improved and modernized features.

Gribeauval began designing his new system in the early 1760s, and the field pieces were officially titled *artillerie modèle 1765, système Gribeauval.*[209] While Gribeauval continued with the pattern of 12-, 8- and 4-pounder cannon established by Vallière, the drastic improvements in weight of the Gribeauval guns were matched by standardization of carriages and limbers.[210] Gribeauval's cannon were designed with specific battlefield roles in mind, and were to be complemented by a standard 6-inch field howitzer. The light 4-pounders were designed for close infantry support as they lacked the lethality needed to crush an enemy formation. Accordingly, they saw service in the foot artillery. French battalion artillery, abandoned after the Seven Years' War, reappeared during the wars of the Revolution and it was the 4-pounders that served as battalion guns. The versatile and hard-hitting 8-pounder was ideal for either foot or horse artillery; it was light enough that it be moved swiftly around the battlefield by highly-trained crews with good, strong horse teams, and its firepower would brutalize enemy troops at ranges under 500 yards. The 12-pounders were supposed to be used in reserve roles, capable of effective counter battery fire or long-range bombardment against enemy troop formations. If employed at close ranges, the 12-pounders could cut an enormous swath through opposing flesh and bone. Siege guns of the Gribeauval system were developed 10 years after the field guns were drawn. Despite the delay in their development, the 24-, 16-, 12- and 8-pounder siege cannon, along with the 8-pouce siege howitzer were also known as the *artillerie modèle 1765, système Gribeauval,*[211] although some modern scholars often refer to the Gribeauval siege pieces as *artillerie modèle 1775, système Gribeauval.*[212]

In addition to their designated roles and lighter weights, the Gribeauval guns and howitzers had their maneuverability further aided by horses harnessed in pairs instead of in tandem. Moreover, Gribeauval believed that all vehicles should be driven by soldiers rather than unreliable civilian contractors, although that transformation would not be completed until Napoleon organized the drivers as artillery train battalions in 1800.[213] All field pieces went into action with ready ammunition available in the trail chest that nestled between the gun trails while the

---

[208] Robert S. Quimby, *The Background of Napoleonic Warfare* (New York, 1957), pp. 88-89 and 145-147.

[209] S.H.A.T., 4w 68 and 2w 84. Some writers refer to the ordnance system as the model 1764. See: Paul Willing, *Napoléon et ses Soldats l'Apogée de la Gloire 1804-1809* (Paris, 1977), pp. 90-94.

[210] See chart at the end of this chapter for a comparison of weights between the guns of the various French ordnance systems.

[211] S.H.A.T., 4w 68 and 2w 84.

[212] Willing, *Napoléon et ses Soldats l'Apogée de la Gloire 1804-1809,* p. 93.

[213] See related subject matters in Arrêté, *Correspondance,* number 4766; Bonaparte to Lacuée, number 4771 and Bonaparte to Petiet, number 4779.

piece was in motion. With ready ammunition available for the gunners in the trail chest rather than having to wait for relays from caissons, the pieces could open fire more quickly once they were unlimbered for action. Another of Gribeauval's innovations was that all his ordnance included elevating screws that improved the accuracy of the pieces. The gun laying proficiency was even more markedly advanced with the inclusion of tangent scales.

By the beginning of the French Revolutionary wars the Gribeauval pieces were the best in the world. Together with officers and crews, most of who learned their trade after the storming of the Bastille, the French artillery became legendary at the Battle of Valmy in 1792 as the guns hammered the Prussian army into defeat. It was also that year that the French horse artillery (also known as 'light artillery' or *artillerie à cheval)* was born.[214] With all its personnel mounted, horse artillery was promoted by the well-known military theorist Joseph du Teil who, along with other reformers, believed that the light artillery should be aggressively employed to support the cavalry as well as quickly moving infantry reserves. By its nature, therefore, horse artillery had to include officers and men with better than average skills. To obtain motivated personnel, the horse artillery filled its ranks with volunteers from the foot artillery and the cavalry. The men excelled in their profession—the gunlayers and officers were unquestionably the best in France outside the Imperial Guard.

Actively employed in a mobile role, including advance guard action in support of *tirailleurs* and cavalry, the horse artillery developed its expectations as an élite force of unquestioned value, able to exert an influence on the course of battle. This aggressive spirit was nurtured by the Revolutionary fervor of the country. Before Napoleon was appointed to the head of the Army of Italy in 1796, the self-confident horse artillerists were characterized by Séruzier: "They were renowned for their courage, and no less for their contentious spirit. They pushed esprit de corps far beyond the point of virtue and believed themselves infinitely superior to their comrades in the foot artillery."[215]

Since the horse artillerists were the best in the French army outside the Guard, they were almost always awarded the deadly yet mobile 8-pounders. A perfect gun for horse artillery, the French 8-pounder was substantially heavier than other nations' principal piece of ordnance—the 6-pounder. When considering that the 6-pounders for some nationalities was a small caliber piece—often referred to by French artillerists as 5-pounders—the 8-pounder compared very favorably in its range and hitting power.[216] At full strength, a company of French horse artillery consisted of six pieces—four 8-pounder guns and two 6-inch howitzers. A common practice in the Revolutionary armies, as well as during the Consulate and the early years of the Empire, was to employ the horse artillery in sections or in half-batteries. This was done so that their mobile and aggressive presence would be a force multiplier in as many places as possible on the battlefield. If deployed by sections, each section consisted of two pieces of ordnance with two sections composed of guns and one section of howitzers. If deployed by half-companies, each half-company of *artillerie à cheval* would consist of two 8-pounders and one howitzer.[217]

While the French horse artillerists of the Revolution were a select group of truly motivated and élite specialists who carried their tradition forward into the 19th century, it took an artillerist the likes of which the world had never seen

A model of a System Year XI 6-pounder on display in the Musée d'Armée in Paris. It is shown limbered with the coffret mounted on the limber. Put into production in 1805, though the piece was significantly lighter the French Gribeauval 8-pounder or other countries' 6-pounders, it had its drawbacks. Perhaps the most important of these was that when a System Year XI caisson was fully loaded, it weighed more than a fully loaded caisson for an 8-pounder. Nevertheless, it slowly replaced the older Gribeauval guns, including the army's favorite piece, the 8-pounder.

---

[214] Lynn, *Bayonets of the Republic*, p. 204.

[215] Séruzier, as qouted in Matti Lauerma, *L'artillerie de campagne française pendant les guerres de la Révolution* (Helsinki, 1956), p. 127.

[216] Due to their small caliber, some 6-pounders were referred to by Napoleon as 5-pounders, as seen in *Correspondance,* number 464. The reason for different caliber sizes was simply that nations measured pounds differently.

[217] S.H.A.T., C^2 470 and 472.

before to bring to France a complete force structure. Napoleon broadened the already excellent artillery schools so that more young men could learn the trade and receive the best training possible. And as previously mentioned, the anachronistic system of employing civilian drivers was replaced by Napoleon in 1800 with a permanent, military train of artillery. Finally, in order to come up with an organization consistent with the resources of the country, Napoleon utilized what was known as the 'artillery division'—12 pieces of ordnance consisting of two 12-pounders, six 8-pounders, two 4-pounders and two howitzers—to be the allocation basis for his newly created *corps d'armée* system (see page 91 for complete details on the artillery division organization).

Napoleon further sought to improve his artillery by updating its design and tactical employment. While the Gribeauval model pieces were still the world's standard, many officers within the French military wanted the Gribeauval pieces replaced. The dissatisfaction with either the 4- or 8-pounders started an unofficial series of experiments in manufacturing 6-pounder cannons in Milan shortly after the conclusion of the Marengo campaign of 1800. Within two months, some 60 new 6-pounder cannons and 40 new howitzers were cast in the Northern Italian city, marking the unofficial beginning of the *système an XI* ordnance.[218]

First Consul Bonaparte recognized that the design of the 35 year-old Gribeauval pieces could be improved. Besides, French intelligence sources from almost every court in Europe confirmed that Gribeauval pieces were being used as models by which other nations were either experimenting or already manufacturing improved versions of their own ordnance. Bonaparte understandably wanted to stay ahead in the technological war as well as to further develop the already excellent French school of tactical artillery thought by improving the employment of the artillery at divisional level. To accomplish these ambitious goals, the First Consul hand-picked a man he believed to be best suited for the task—Auguste Frederic Louis Viesse de Marmont.

Marmont

The son of a retired Bourbon officer who owned and operated an iron works, Marmont was born 20 July 1774 and grew up studying metallurgy and mathematics, both of which he was remarkably adept. These interests led him to enroll at the Châlons artillery school, receiving his commission in 1792. After service in the *Armée de la Moselle* and *Armée des Alpes,* Marmont was transferred to the *Armée des Pyrénées*, where during the 1793 siege of Toulon he first met a fellow artillery officer from Corsica named Napoleone di Buonaparte.[219] Following the siege of Toulon, Marmont saw duty with the *Armée du Rhin*, serving under one of the best generals of the Revolution, Louis-Charles-Antoine Desaix de Veygoux. Once Buonaparte (changed to Bonaparte) was named as commander of the *Armée d'Italie* in 1796, he appointed the young, able artillerist friend from the siege of Toulon as his aide-de-camp.

During the 1796 Italian campaign, Marmont distinguished himself at the Battle of Lodi and laid the guns that helped win the Battle of Castiglione. He established himself as a calm, skillful gunner, and returned to Paris in October with the Austrian colors captured at Rovereto, Bassano and San Giorgio. Serving with Napoleon in the *Armée d'Orient,* at Malta Marmont personally captured the flag of the fabled Knights of St. John for which he was promoted to *général de brigade.* He fought with the army at Alexandria and at the Battle of the Pyramids during the month of July 1798. As one of Bonaparte's inner circle, Marmont returned to France with Napoleon and participated in the coup of 18th brumaire. Marmont further solidified his reputation in 1800 with his timely and expert artillery

---

[218] Général L. Griois, *Mémoires*, 2 volumes (Paris, 1909), vol. 1, pp. 128-130.
[219] John L. Pimlott, "Friendship's Choice," in *Napoleon's Marshals,* edited by David Chandler (New York, 1987).

support of what was arguably the most famous cavalry action of the Napoleonic era—Kellermann's (the younger) charge at the Battle of Marengo on 25 prairial an VII (14 June 1800). Promoted to *général de division* on 22 fructidor an VIII (9 September 1800), Marmont's meteoric rise continued in 1802 when Bonaparte named him as first inspector general of artillery on 29 fructidor an X (16 September 1802), followed on 25 prairial an XI (14 June 1803) as the commander of all artillery in the various encampments of Boulogne.[220]

Marmont's appointment as Bonaparte's chief artillery advisor is testimony to Marmont's overall knowledge of the arm, exceptional artillerist skills, personal bravery and devotion to Napoleon. These were rewarded by the Emperor's trust, which lasted until 1814. Even though this long-time friendship ended when Marmont—for reasons only known to him—conspired with other French officers to commit treason and lead their army into captivity, thus sealing Napoleon's fate in the Campaign of France, there can be no doubt that Napoleon looked to Marmont for his expertise in manufacturing, organization and tactics.

On 8 nivôse an X (29 December 1801), some 18 months before Marmont received his appointment as first inspector general of artillery, the First Consul Bonaparte formed a commission "to arrive by making close-cropped tables, new materiel of artillery that would be the most advantageous for us."[221] Presiding over the commission was then *Premier Inspecteur général de l'Artillerie* d'Aboville, with commission members consisting of generals Lamartillère, Andréossy, Elbé, Songis, Faultrier, Gassendi and Marmont. These men were not only charged with developing a new ordnance system by improving upon the Gribeauval design, but also refining the tactical doctrine for France's artillery.[222] It was a daunting assignment, the undertaking of which split the commission over its feasibility. In a similar division of opinion that highlighted the two decade-long debate over whether or not the Gribeauval ordnance should replace the Vallière system, commission members took sides over whether or not the 4- and 8-pounder Gribeauval guns should be replaced with a newly-designed, single piece—the 6-pounder. Jean-Jacques-Basilien Gassendi, the 53-year-old *général de brigade* who had authored the artillery manual for the Gribeauval pieces, was the head of the group that wanted to retain the existing ordnance system. Marmont led the reform faction that pushed for the 6-pounder. Perhaps the enormity of the project was best appreciated by *chef de brigade* Chrétien-François-Antoine Favé, commander of the 4th Regiment of *Artillerie à cheval:*

d'Aboville

> It is well that the decree to study the feasibility of a new artillery system was made in Year XI, so that comparative tests with the materiel proposed to be abandoned could be completed. A good research program must be able to serve as a point of departure before being transformed into a definitive resolution.[223]

It was Marmont's reform group that convinced Bonaparte. By 12 floréal an XI (2 May 1803), it was officially determined that a new system of artillery would replace that of the Gribeauval system.[224] "The First Consul has charged me with the development of a new ordnance system," Marmont wrote on 25 fructidor an XI (12 September 1803) to *général de division* Nicolas-Jean de Dieu Soult,

---

[220] George Six, *Dictionnaire biographique des généraux et amiraux français de la Révolution et de l'Empire 1792-1814*, edited by George Saffroy, 2 volumes (Paris, 1934), vol. 2, p. 158. Hereafter referred to as *Dictionnaire biographique.*

[221] Arrêté, *Correspondance*, number 5903.

[222] S.H.A.T., 2w 84.

[223] Général Favé, *Études sur le passé et l'avenir de l'artillerie,* Volume 5 (Paris, 1871).

[224] S.H.A.T., 2w 84.

commandant of the Camp of Saint-Omer at Boulogne. "Instruct all officers of the rank of colonel or higher to submit any observations on this subject to me."[225]

The "observations" which Marmont was soliciting were those of the tactical employment roles for foot and horse artillery attached to the infantry divisions. Instead of feedback on the intended subject matter, the French officers responded vociferously about the guns themselves. Like the commission that was originally appointed to study the issue, the newly proposed ordnance system suddenly erupted into a hotly debated issue. It seemed as though everyone had an opinion. Many infantry generals and foot artillery officers were unhappy with the firepower provided by diminutive 4-pounder guns that always found their way into the companies of foot artillery. As a result, they sought to increase the poundage of the cannons allocated to the foot artillery. Ideally, the infantry wished to have the horse artillery 8-pounders close to them, or have 8-pounders present in the foot artillery companies. The loud crashes from the mouths of 8-pounder cannon served as reassuring morale boosters to even the most veteran infantry. Therefore, the infantry generals and foot artillerists wanted heavier support from guns larger than 4-pounders.

These views are evidenced in many letters. "It is important that the 4-pounders be replaced," General Louis-Vincent-Joseph Le Blond Saint-Hilaire wrote to Marmont on 29 fructidor an XI (16 September 1803). "These pieces do not have sufficient firepower and range when compared to heavier guns of the enemy. It would be preferable to have either 8-pounders or 6-pounders present in the companies of foot artillery."[226] General Soult concurred on the subject of upgrading the companies of foot artillery with heavier pieces, but went further in his observations to defend the firepower of the horse artillery. "The 8-pounders give the troops confidence that was impossible to have in the old army with only battalion guns [4-pounders]," the future marshal wrote on 4e jour complémentaire an XI (21 September 1803). "I have previously written the Minister of War [Berthier] on this matter. I am of the opinion that the infantry need heavier guns in place of the 4-pounders, although these pieces must not find their way into the horse artillery before the new ones [6-pounders] arrive."[227]

Another view was that of General Jean-Barthélemot Sorbier, one of the most highly regarded artillerists in the army. As chief of artillery of the Camp of Bruges where Davout and his officers were forging the future 3rd Corps of the *Grande Armée*, the 41-year-old horse artillery specialist Sorbier offered Marmont, with a copy to Berthier, his opinions on 6 vendémiaire an XI (29 September 1803).

> Several issues must be resolved before making any changes in tactical considerations. The center of any discussions on this subject is always the 4-pounders and what to do with them. To continue to employ these pieces is bad. I would melt them all down and make 8-pounders. Also in question is the extent of employing horse artillery. I would prefer to see the establishment expanded so that every infantry division would have horse artillery supporting its maneuvers.[228]

Lariboisère

General Jean-Ambroise Lariboisère, the 44-year-old commander of the artillery school at Strasbourg, offered his controversial views to Alexandre Berthier, the Minister of War. "Improving the firepower of the guns supporting the infantry

---

[225] S.H.A.T., 2w 84. Soult, in turn, instructed his officers to respond, C[2] 223.
[226] S.H.A.T., 2w 84.
[227] S.H.A.T., C[2] 12.
[228] S.H.A.T., C[2] 213.

is the most important issue," Lariboisère wrote on 12 vendémiaire an XII (5 October 1803). "This must be accomplished even if it means taking the 8-pounders from the light [horse] artillery and providing them with the new 6-pounders."[229]

Desvaux de Saint-Maurice

One does not have to imagine how the cavalry generals and the élite horse artillerists responded to these calls to give up their 8-pounders. One such officer was Jean-Jacques Desvaux de Saint-Maurice, the newly appointed colonel of the 6th Regiment of *Artillerie à cheval* in the fall of 1803. Destined to prove himself the premier horse artillery officer in France during the later years of the Empire, Desvaux de Saint-Maurice was one of the most vocal advocates of the 8-pounder gun. Writing to Marmont on 29 brumaire an XII (21 November 1803), the 28-year-old Desvaux de Saint-Maurice voiced the concern of many fellow horse artillery officers. "The rumors of smaller guns for the light artillery must not come to pass. The 8-pounders need to remain in the hands of our best troops. If they are taken away, it will compromise the arm. If the infantry require heavier guns, then make more 8-pounders, or give them the new 6-pounders."[230] General Antoine-Alexandre Hanicque, arguably the most distinguished horse artillery officer in France from its creation in 1792 up through the early years of the Empire, left no doubt as to his feelings on the subject. "Take the 8-pounders from the light artillery," Hanicque wrote Marmont on 12 frimaire an XII (4 December 1803), "and you take their soul from them. The light artillery must maintain its ability to strike hard, which is something that cannot be accomplished with smaller-caliber cannon."[231] General Etienne-Marie-Antoine Nansouty, the excellent heavy cavalry general, agreed. "The importance of the light artillery and its support in the movements of the cavalry are known," Nansouty told Berthier on 16 frimaire an XII (8 December 1803). "What would happen with lighter guns is not known, although the cavalry officers believe that the light artillery should never employ 4-pounder cannon or guns like the small caliber [3- or 6-pounders] pieces used by the enemy."[232]

While the cavalry generals and horse artillerists wanted nothing to do with a new system of ordnance that lightened the deadly punches thrown by their prized 8-pounders, both sides did agree on three issues. First, no one wanted to dilute the long-range, deadly 12-pounder guns assigned to foot artillery companies that were utilized in reserve roles. While improvements in the 12-pounder design were possible that would lighten the weight of the piece and slightly improve range, these valued cannon would remain the heavy field gun of the army. Second, in spite of its deployment by the horse artillery, the 6-pouce (inch) howitzer was too heavy a piece for that arm. Marmont believed that improvements in design and manufacture could significantly lighten a new howitzer for use with the horse artillery. With these points settled, Marmont set to work to resolve the dilemma of increasing the firepower of the cannon in most companies of foot artillery while not compromising the hitting power of the horse artillery. Finally, everyone agreed that employment of 4-pounders was an evil that had to be corrected. Marmont himself recognized that the 4-pounders did not have the firepower needed for the foot artillery, and that they were "inadequate when matched up against the enemy [6-pounder] guns."[233] The only question was *how* to replace them. Sorbier's idea of immediately melting down all the 4-pounders into 8-pounders was impractical from economic and weight standpoints. While the 8-pounder was already the most numerous piece in the army, it could not be a universal gun in all theaters because it consumed a lot of powder and required more caissons for ammunition, which in turn meant more horses and non-technical personnel, all of which translated

[229] S.H.A.T., C² 210.
[230] S.H.A.T., 2w 84.
[231] S.H.A.T., 2w 84.
[232] S.H.A.T., C² 212.
[233] S.H.A.T., 4w 68.

into higher costs for the French treasury and more demands on the already taxed horseflesh requirements of the army. In addition, quality saltpeter—a vital ingredient in the making of gunpowder—was already a difficult commodity for the French to obtain and replacing the 4-pounder with more 8-pounders would only exacerbate the problem. Therefore, the 8-pounder was considered to be a prohibitively expensive piece to operate *en masse* if it was to replace all of the 4-pounders throughout the entire French military establishment. Finally, the weight of the 8-pounder was a consideration. While not a problem over most European ground, the 8-pounder—total weight including carriage—was about 500 pounds heavier than a 4-pounder. This precluded the heavier piece from operating in difficult terrain that the lighter 4-pounder gun could traverse.[234]

There were other reasons to develop new ordnance. As previously mentioned, the Gribeauval pattern 6-pouce field howitzers were too heavy to suit most horse artillerists. It had been designed as a foot artillery weapon, and the light artillery employed the 6-pouce howitzer out of necessity. Recognizing the need for a lighter howitzer for the horse artillery, it was the consensus that a slightly larger caliber howitzer than the 6-pouce could be developed for use in partnership with the heavier 12-pounders while a smaller caliber, lighter howitzer could be used with horse artillery companies as well as foot companies operating cannon other than 12-pounders. This line of thinking, of course, meant replacing one howitzer with two new ones. Also, there were several aspects of the Gribeauval system limbers, trail chests, and more that were in need of improvement and updating.

Balancing all the considerations—firepower, cost of operation, number of horses and men required, and most importantly, Napoleon himself who was the advocate of a universal foot and horse artillery gun—Marmont came to the conclusion that the replacement for the Gribeauval 4-pounders could not be accomplished by manufacturing more Gribeauval 8-pounders. Due to concerns in streamlining logistics and equipment for the branch of service, and since two new howitzers were going to replace a single model of the old system, it was thought that one new gun could replace both the Gribeauval 4-pounder and the Gribeauval 8-pounder. Also, if a new ordnance system used two different caliber howitzers rather than one, the net difference in the total number of field pieces would remain unchanged. The Gribeauval system employed four field pieces—three guns and one howitzer—while the System Year XI had the same number of field pieces consisting of two cannons and two howitzers. Realizing that any plans to replace the 8-pounders would be an unpopular decision in some quarters of the army, most especially with the horse artillery officers, Marmont sought to develop his new system with the utmost forethought so as to defuse as much criticism as possible.

System Year XI limber: the coffert is visible to right

Since the infantry needed a heavier gun than the 4-pounder for support, and because the cavalry and horse artillery did not want a gun as light as the 4-pounder, Marmont sought a compromise. The solution, not surprisingly, was one which Marmont had been pushing since before he had been named *Premier Inspecteur général de l'Artillerie*. The two field guns for the new ordnance system would be an improved, larger caliber 12-pounder model and a new, very large caliber 6-pounder piece—larger than any 6-pounder previously made. Since almost every other country used a 6-pounder cannon, the appeal of this large-caliber 6-pounder had the added bonus of the French being able to cannibalize captured enemy ammunition.[235]

Also important was that all the new French ordnance would be significantly lighter than comparable sized pieces. Marmont was intent on putting to use improved metallurgy, along with better casting techniques, as well as his own

[234] The 1800 Marengo campaign was illustrative of the difficulty with the 8-pounder operating in some areas of Northern Italy.
[235] S.H.A.T., 2w 84.

understanding of the force dynamics of the barrel to thin out the cross sections where possible. In addition to these three factors, what was believed to be improved carriage design would contribute to further lighten the pieces of the System Year XI.

To go with the new System Year XI ordnance were newly designed, lighter limbers and ammunition caissons that had been drawn up by the 1801 commission headed by d'Aboville. The main visible difference in the new limbers was the presence of a small ammunition box, or *coffert,* that was manufactured as part of the limber. The *coffert* held more ready ammunition than what was previously made available in the trail chest of Gribeauval system ordnance. By designing the *coffert* above the axle in the middle of the limber, System Year XI ordnance no longer utilized ammunition trail chests. This improvement in limber and ready ammunition design was intended to provide better balance and weight considerations for movement, minimize gun breakage, all while making it possible for the crews to bring the pieces into action more rapidly and sustaining fire longer before needing ammunition from the caissons. This aspect was especially important in the horse artillery, which sometimes went into action while keeping the piece in its traces. Therefore crews operating System Year XI ordnance did not have to deal with a trail chest. That meant that they could unlimber the piece, load, fire, limber again and move quickly without first having to remove then put back the trail chest. Instead, the ammunition was available in the *coffert* on the limber.[236]

The newly-designed caisson for the System Year XI 6-pounder cannon had the advantage of carrying more ammunition than previously thought possible. For example, the Gribeauval-designed caisson carrying 8-pounder ammunition had a total of 92 projectiles in a combination of 62 ball and 30 canister rounds. Since every 8-pounder outside the Imperial Guard was supported by two caissons, this meant that there were 184 rounds in the caissons for each of these caliber guns. Add to this figure the 15 rounds stored in the trail chest, and every Gribeauval 8-pounder had a minimum of 199 rounds. Meanwhile, the Gribeauval 4-pounders outside the Imperial Guard were supported by one caisson per gun, and each caisson carried 150 projectiles. Add to these the 18 projectiles in the trail chest, and every 4-pounder had at least 168 rounds available at the beginning of a battle. In comparison, the reconfigured caisson for the System Year XI 6-pounder housed 140 projectiles and the *coffret* on the limber offered another 21 rounds of readily-available ammunition. Since each 6-pounder had one and one-half caissons assigned to it (or, three caissons for every two-gun section) the 6-pounder of the System Year XI had 231 rounds available—32 more rounds than a Gribeauval 8-pounder.[237]

System Year XI gun

When empty, the new caissons were lighter weight, though more sturdily constructed than the old Gribeauval vehicles. However, when the caisson for the 6-pounder was fully loaded, the increased ammunition available also meant a heavier vehicle to pull. For example, fully loaded caissons for the Gribeauval 8- and 4-pounders weighed 1,295 and 1,079 pounds respectively. A System Year XI caisson fully loaded with 6-pounder ammunition weighed 1,468 pounds.[238]

Another important difference in the System Year XI limber was the pole which extended out the front and to which the first two horses of the artillery team were hitched. Unlike the Gribeauval limber pole that was rigidly kept in place at all times while the guns were in action, the System Year XI limber pole hinged where it joined the limber. This had the important consideration of taking the weight off the horses shoulders when the gun was not in motion. Therefore, the animals pulling the System Year XI pieces could stay fresher for a longer period of

[236] S.H.A.T., 2w 84 and 4w 68.

[237] S.H.A.T., 2w 84.

[238] S.H.A.T., 2w 84.

time, which in turn meant guns moving faster around the battlefield.

While the number of service vehicles in support of the artillery company were essentially the same throughout the Napoleonic period as according to regulations set forth by Gribeauval, the improved caisson design for the new 6-pounder brought forth in the System Year XI had the important consideration of reducing the number of animals needed to support a company of 6-pounders when compared to an 8-pounder company. Therefore, the new 6-pounders would be harder-hitting and longer-ranged than enemy 6-pounders, provide significantly better firepower than the old 4-pounders, but would not require the number of caissons or animals as needed to support the 8-pounders. Equally important was the favorable weight consideration for the new 6-pounder. The 6-pounder gun of the System Year XI had a total weight of 2,008 pounds compared to 1,940 for the old 4-pounder and 2,456 for the 8-pounder. Improved manufacturing methods resulted in the System Year XI 12-pounder being significantly lighter than the comparable Gribeauval piece. Marmont's new 12-pounder barrel weighed 1,530 livres, or 749 kilograms, or 1,651 pounds. The entire System Year XI 12-pounder gun—barrel and carriage—weighed 1,275 kilograms, or 2,811 pounds.[239] Therefore, including the carriage, the System Year XI 12-pounder was more than 12 percent lighter than the Gribeauval 12-pounder! When one considers that in the days of 'real' horsepower and muddy roads, a 12% lighter 12-pounder piece made a big significant difference—a difference which becomes more pronounced when the weight of the French ordnance is compared to the heavier Allied pieces. When considering that the System Year XI 12-pounder had a slightly larger caliber, longer barrel and longer effective range than the Gribeauval 12-pounder—all while being significantly lighter in weight—one can appreciate the improvement that this piece offered. Obviously, these technical improvements made it easier for Napoleon to move his guns around the battlefield, a characteristic for which the Emperor's armies were famous. Also, the new System Year XI 6-pounder and 12-pounder pieces were larger caliber guns than comparable enemy pieces which meant that the French could cannibalize captured enemy ammunition if they were absolutely desperate, whereas captured French ammunition could not be used by the Russians or Austrians.

Train of Artillery of the Imperial Guard

Marmont also redesigned the siege guns, the iron coastal pieces, as well as added two mountain guns of 3- and 6-pound caliber to the French arsenal.[240]

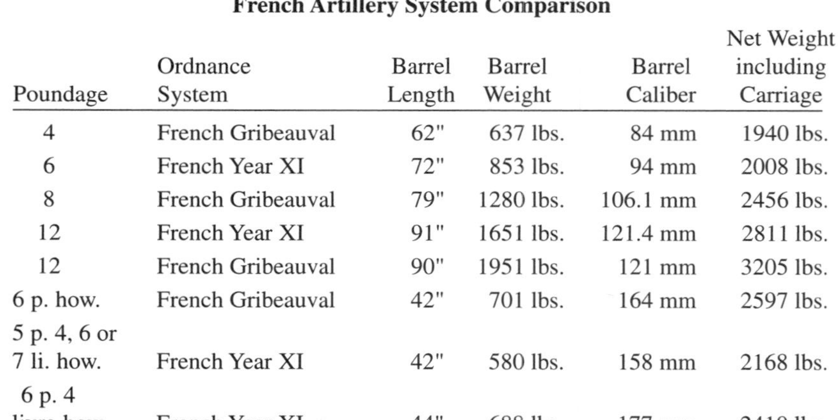

French Artillery System Comparison

Poundage	Ordnance System	Barrel Length	Barrel Weight	Barrel Caliber	Net Weight including Carriage
4	French Gribeauval	62"	637 lbs.	84 mm	1940 lbs.
6	French Year XI	72"	853 lbs.	94 mm	2008 lbs.
8	French Gribeauval	79"	1280 lbs.	106.1 mm	2456 lbs.
12	French Year XI	91"	1651 lbs.	121.4 mm	2811 lbs.
12	French Gribeauval	90"	1951 lbs.	121 mm	3205 lbs.
6 p. how.	French Gribeauval	42"	701 lbs.	164 mm	2597 lbs.
5 p. 4, 6 or 7 li. how.	French Year XI	42"	580 lbs.	158 mm	2168 lbs.
6 p. 4 livre how.	French Year XI	44"	688 lbs.	177 mm	2410 lbs.

[239] S.H.A.T., 2w 84 and 4w 68.

[240] S.H.A.T., 2w 84.

Comparison of French Gribeauval and System Year XI Ordnance

Ranges in Meters

Ordnance Poundage	System	Canister	Round-Shot (Practical)	Round-Shot (Max)	Shell
4	French Gribeauval	400	800	1250	—
6	French Year XI	500	1200	1850	—
8	French Gribeauval	550	1500	2400	—
12	French Year XI	600	1850	2700	—
12	French Gribeauval	600	1800	2600	—
6 p. how.	French Gribeauval	250	—	—	1300
5 p. 4, 6 or 7 li. how.	French Year XI	250	—	—	1200
6 p. 4 livre how.	French Year XI	300	—	—	1500

Like the cannon of the System Year XI, Marmont's new howitzers incorporated advances in manufacturing and design. The bore size for the new howitzers would be one of two dimensions— the 6 pouce 4 lignes howitzer for use with the 12-pounders, or the 5 *pouce*, 6 *lignes* howitzer for use alongside the 6-pounders. Because different manufacturers had different sized calibers, the smaller, lighter howitzers were listed as *obusier de 5 pouces, 4 lignes,* or as *obusier de 5 pouces, 6 lignes,* or as *obusier de 5 pouces, 7 lignes.* In the later years of the Empire, all of these different lighter howitzers would simply be referred to as *obusiers de 24,* which described the howitzer by the weight of its projectile, that being 24 livres (pounds).[241] The new heavy field howitzer that served along side the 12-pounder guns had a larger caliber and a longer barrel than the old Gribeauval model and was officially listed as *obusier de 6 pouces, 4 lignes.* With their redesign, both howitzers were lighter than the 6-inch howitzer designed by Gribeauval, which improved mobility but increased recoil. Marmont named the newly proposed pieces *Bouches à feu du systèm de l'an XI* (Ordnance of the System Year XI) in honor of the Revolutionary year in which the call for the new system was made.

Train of Equipment

"I intend to announce to the manufacturers that submissions for design of the new ordnance system must include all proportions of metals which are peculiar to themselves," Marmont informed Berthier on 15 ventôse an XI (6 March 1803). "Designs meeting minimum caliber specifications will then be proven on sleds [proving ground carriages]. Each piece will undergo four proof firings using large charges. Twelve-pounders will have four test shots, two with four pounds of powder and two with five pounds. Six-pounders will have two shots with two pounds of powder and two with two and one-half pounds. All howitzers will fire five proof shots will full charges."[242]

In response to Marmont's call for new ordnance, dozens of submissions were received, each with slight variations in caliber size and tube weight. Testing had already been completed and the new ordnance was already coming out of the factories when the campaign of 1805 opened. The new 6-pounders were thought to be perfect for the terrain found in Northern Italy, and Napoleon was so eager to employ the System Year XI ordnance, that he ordered artillery companies in the 27th Military Division (Northern Italy) to exchange their old Gribeauval pieces for new ones as early as June 1803, even while the ongoing debate over the new system was still hot and heavy! The First Consul declared on 3 Messidor an XI (22 June 1803):

---

[241] S.H.A.T., C^2 , C^8 and C^{15} series confirms these designations.

[242] S.H.A.T., 4w 68.

> All pieces of 4- and 8-calibers that are found in the 27th Military Division in the Italian Republic, belonging to the crews stationed there, will be melted down and recast to the caliber of 6- and 12-pounders of the new models. The new system of artillery will be in place immediately as possible for Italy and in the 27th Military Division.[243]

This order concerning the new system of ordnance clearly indicates that Bonaparte had already made his decision to replace the 4- and 8-pounders with new 6-pounders before Marmont called for opinions from other officers concerning their tactical employment. However, it would be five more years before the System Year XI ordnance began showing up in substantial numbers in Napoleon's main army. Even when the new 6- and 12-pounder guns along with the new howitzers began making their appearance in central Europe during the Danube campaign of 1809, the horse artillery companies of the cavalry reserve still held onto their beloved 8-pounders; they would be the last to give them up.[244] Even though the new System Year XI 6-pounder gun had a larger caliber than the other 6-pounders in Europe, many horse artillerists in the later years of the Empire would miss their heavier hitting 8-pounder pieces.

Due to the secondary nature of the Peninsular war and with new equipment first going to Napoleon's main army, Gribeauval ordnance continued to be the primary system employed by the Peninsular French armies from 1807 through 1814. This is clearly illustrated by two artillery orders of battle dating from the mid-to-late Empire period. One week prior to the Battle of Salamanca fought on 22 July 1812, Marmont's *Armée de Portugal* had a total of 76 mobile pieces of ordnance. Only one gun—a diminutive 3-pounder mountain cannon—was the only System Year XI piece in an army whose commander-in-chief was the architect of the new system. Over one year later on 1 October 1813, as Marshal Soult's *Armée Impériale d'Espagne* prepared to contest Wellington's forces at the Bidassoa, the ordnance present in Soult's army gives an unmistakable picture of how few System Year XI pieces were in Spain. Of the 125 pieces of ordnance which Soult possessed, only 26 were of the System Year XI, the remaining 99 consisting of the old Gribeauval pattern.[245]

Train of Artillery personnel shoeing a horse on campaign

It was much different in central Europe, however. Except for less than a handful of scattered pieces found in Germany during the opening of the 1813 campaign and in France at the very end of the 1814 campaign, the Gribeauval pattern ordnance passed into history when the *Grande Armée* crossed the Niemen River, signaling the beginning of the 1812 Russian campaign.[246] Therefore, the System Year XI guns and howitzers were the pieces exclusively in use within the Napoleon's armies that fought from Borodino to Waterloo. How the new system held up under campaign conditions, and what the officers thought of the new ordnance, is best left to be discussed in a later work.

In addition to presiding over the development of a new and improved ordnance system, Marmont was also charged by Bonaparte with updating the tactical employment philosophy of the artillery and to improve upon the artillery division organization that had been in use for years. On the eve of the 1805 campaigns, Marmont wrote Berthier on 20 thermidor an XII (8 August) with some insight on what changes would later be in store.

> The current [artillery division] system does not allow sufficient employment of horse artillery. Since these companies are the

[243] Ordre, *Correspondance,* number 6845.
[244] S.H.A.T., C^2 675.
[245] S.H.A.T., C^7 29, C^8 369 and C^8 374.
[246] S.H.A.T., C^2 698 through 702.

> most valuable and will have a smaller caliber gun in the future, their employment must be multiplied by deploying a full company with each infantry and cavalry division. With the new guns [6- or 12-pounders], I am proposing that each company of artillerists be assigned ordnance with the large howitzers [*6 pouces, 4 lignes*] going to the companies of 12-pounders and the smaller ones [*5 pouces, 6 lignes*] with the 6-pounders. In this manner, the gunners will get the best use from each piece as they will know its peculiarity.[247]

In another letter to Berthier dated 2 fructidor an XII (20 August 1805), Marmont envisioned that "each infantry division should have supporting its movement one or two companies of foot artillery and one company of horse artillery."[248] Like the guns of the System Year XI, the new tactical employment proposed by Marmont would take years before first seeing action in the Danube campaign of 1809. In the meantime, the artillery division organization deployment was used by the *Grande Armée* in the 1805, 1806 and 1807 campaigns.

The officers and men who manned the French ordnance were arguably the best artillerists in the world, and certainly the finest on the European continent. They attained their expertise through a combination of training and combat. The wars of the French Revolution had help elevate French artillery from its already proud tradition to a stature past "the previously acknowledged supremacy of the Austrian service."[249] Once Bonaparte became First Consul, he established a large artillery staff under his personal control that would oversee everything connected with the service. Artillery officers were everywhere, supervising production of ordnance and munitions, arming fortresses, as well as being permanently attached to army, corps and division headquarters staffs. One did not have to go far into the French chain of command before finding an artillery expert to solve any related problems.

Artillery officer serving as aide-de-camp

With the driving personality of Napoleon behind it, the expanding French artillery arm attracted hard-working intellectuals of the poor nobility and the middle class—and there was plenty of room for them. While many scholars have suggested that the French artillery arm was less affected by the ravages of desertion and emigration brought on by the Revolution, the facts prove otherwise. Samuel F. Scott's analysis of both officers and men in the French artillery provide an interesting study of the median length of service in the different branches of the army during the Revolution. When the Revolution began, the enlisted men in all three branches had a median length of service of four to six years. By 1793, the median was only one to three years' service. Also, while the cavalry—notorious for its desertions by the nobles of French society—had 37 percent of its enlisted men with less than a year's service in 1793, the artillery was only slightly better off since 29 percent of its enlisted men had the same length of service.[250]

The artillery officer corps fared little better. By April 1794, when the French infantry arm had 95 percent new officers when compared to July 1789 and the French cavalry had 96 percent new officers since that date, the French artillery had 81 percent new officers. If this is the stability referred to by many historians, it is an unusual way to describe history. Therefore, it can be fairly stated that the officers and men of Napoleon's artillery entered the service after the storming of the Bastille and learned their trade during the Revolutionary wars, at the superb artillery schools of Châlons, La Fère and Strasbourg, and at the camps of Boulogne.

---

[247] S.H.A.T., C^2 193.

[248] S.H.A.T., C^2 193.

[249] Elting, *Swords Around a Throne,* p. 250.

[250] Samuel F. Scott, as quoted in Lynn, *Bayonets of the Republic*, p. 208.

It was at the Channel camps that the grenadiers and *carabiniers* of the line and light infantry were trained to operate the cannon, thus joining the members of the Imperial Guard with the additional knowledge of operating ordnance.[251] The idea behind this training was connected to the proposed invasion of England as these people practiced firing cannon from the decks of small transport boats. With the start of the 1805 campaign and the march to the Danube, waterborne activity was forgotten, and the line infantry grenadiers, light infantry *carabiniers* and Guardsmen were earmarked to be called upon to assist the gunners if the artillery crews got thinned out by enemy fire.

Assignment of which pieces of ordnance went to which artillery company personnel and how they were employed was the decision of the corps commander and his artillery chief. For example, if the corps had three infantry divisions, its three artillery divisions assigned for support would consist of 36 pieces of ordnance divided among the artillery personnel. Invariably, one company of foot artillerists would receive the six 12-pounder guns and act as the corps reserve artillery. Every company of horse artillerists would be assigned four 8-pounders and two howitzers. If there was a full company of horse artillerists, plus a detachment from another company of horse artillerists, the detachment would always have a section of 8-pounders. Any other 8- and 4-pounder guns and howitzers were then assigned for service with any remaining foot artillerists.

An Artillery Général de brigade *serving as a corps artillery chief*

The guns and artillerists were assigned to divisions, or as part of a corps reserve under the command of the corps artillery chief, who usually carried a rank of *général de brigade.* Horse artillery companies were broken into sections (two pieces per section) or half-batteries (three pieces, consisting of two 8-pounders and one howitzer). Foot companies handling the 12-pounders were never broken up, but were always employed by entire company. Foot artillerists with 8- or 4-pounders and howitzers could be employed by full company, by half-battery or by section.

Artillerists manning 12-, 8-, 6- or 4-pounder cannon had three different types of projectiles they could fire—round shot, heavy case and canister. Round shot was a solid, cast iron ball about 2mm less in diameter than the caliber of the gun. For example, the System Year XI 12-pounder cannon had a bore caliber of 121.4 mm; the ball ammunition for this piece measured 119.1 mm. The effective and a maximum range depended upon the caliber of the piece. Both the Gribeauval and System Year XI 12-pounders effective round shot range around 1,800 meters, and a maximum range under ideal terrain conditions of almost 2,700 meters. An 8-pounder's effective round shot range was 1,500 meters with a maximum range under ideal conditions of approximately 2,400 meters. The new, large-caliber 6-pounder of the System Year XI had an effective round shot range of 1,200 meters with a maximum range of 1,850 meters. Finally, the small 4-pounder had an effective round shot range of 800 meters and a maximum range of 1,250. All French cannon out-ranged similar-caliber enemy pieces as illustrated in Chapters II and III.

Referred to in later years as grapeshot, heavy case was a form of canister used at distances of 400 to 550 meters depending upon the gun caliber. Heavy case was a container of large lead balls that was usually more lethal than solid shot at targets within the range of the heavy case. Once targets were within 200 to 300 meters, the artillerists would switch to using canister, or light case. Canister ammunition was made up of small lead balls, numbering 60 per discharge for a 4-pounder, 75 per discharge for the System Year XI 6-pounder, 80 per discharge for the 8-pounder, and 100 per discharge for the 12-pounder. The discharges from an entire company of ordnance loaded with canister could cripple many formations.

---

[251] S.H.A.T., C^2 192, 212, 213 and 214.

Howitzers could also fire canister, but not heavy case. When firing canister, the larger bores of the howitzers had the effect of giant sawed-off shotguns cutting a deadly swath through the enemy. At longer ranges of 750 to 1500 meters, the howitzers fired a high trajectory, spherical shell filled with powder and equipped with a fuse that detonated the explosive depending upon the length at which the fuse was cut. Ideally, the shell was supposed to burst in the air over the target, bringing possible death or injury to men and animals within 20 to 25 meters of the explosion. The exploding shells could wreak havoc on stationary targets as it didn't take the gunners long to cut the fuses to achieve air bursts. Even when the gunners cut the fuses the correct length, the faulty nature of the primitive fuses would conspire to give either premature or late explosions. If the fuse did not detonate the shell in the air, but the shell hit the ground, then exploded, the results were usually far less lethal, except for those standing beside the shell! Exploding shells could set roofs and structures on fire, as well as detonate caissons and ammunition wagons.

Howitzers were very deadly firing canister at short range, and dangerous at longer ranges when firing shell. However, their main shortcoming was the 'dead zone' in between canister and shell range. From the maximum range of a howitzer's canister range, some 250 to 300 meters, to the minimum range of a shell—approximately 750 meters—the only fire the gunners could put on an enemy was direct firing of shells, which was usually less effective than normal indirect shell fire, owing to the difficulty of properly cutting the fuses to explode when desired.

Horse artillerymen of the Imperial Guard

Rates of fire depending upon many factors, including the size of the piece and the quality of the crew attending the ordnance. Generally speaking, maximum rates of fire was two rounds per minute for 4- and 6-pounder guns, as well as for howitzers. Inspection reports from the later Empire state that Imperial Guard *Volante* crews working a maximum speed could fire off three rounds per minute from their 6-pounder guns.[252] However, 1805 Imperial Guard *Volante* crews could probably fire their 8-pounders up to twice per minute, while other artillerists could do between two and one round per minute. The 12-pounder crews could usually fire a single round between every one-to-two minutes. Maximum fire rates does not mean that the crews were capable of this-type performance for an indeterminable length of time. Blinding, black powder smoke which reduced the visibility of the gun-layers and crew, coupled with fatigue, slowed rates of fire except when needed.

The favorite target type for all artillery was formed enemy troops, with the artillerists choosing the most effective ammunition for the circumstances. If counter battery fire was called for, it was usually the 12-pounders that performed the task, although other guns would also fire counter battery if the situation demanded. Concentration of firepower was essential. Working in close coordination with infantry and cavalry, one or more artillery units would often prepare the way for friendly troops to successively defeat enemy forces. One of the favorite artillery deployments was for the foot artillery to be operating in the first line of a division while any attached horse artillery would remain (often limbered) with the second line. Once the front line had become closely engaged with the enemy, the horse artillery would be ordered forward to unlimber on an enemy's flank. The devastating effect of 8-pounders or howitzers firing canister into the flank of formed troops was often enough to decide the immediate tactical issue. When more firepower was needed with the front line, the horse artillery would start their tactical deployments accordingly. Regardless of how the artillery was deployed, the goal was that all arms would work together, complementing the strengths of each other in order to achieve victory.

---

[252] S.H.A.T., C^2 160.

Ligne *fusilier drummers*

Drum Major

Beyond Tactics and Organization

Combat Motivation, Officers, NCOs and the Ordinaire

There were many forms of motivation in Napoleon's *Grande Armée*. For starters, the popularity of music and song with soldiers is almost ageless. Martial music was one of the most popular motivations in Napoleon's *Grande Armée*. The French Revolution engendered the Paris Conservatoire, which opened in 1795, and inspired numerous songwriters and musicians, who suddenly had a large demand for their talents. Patriotic free-spirits such as Gossec, Le Sueur, Méhul, Buhl, Gebauer and Cherubini poured forth a voluminous amount of music and hymns that inspired the nation and the army, enhancing the ardor and commitment of the troops. By the time of the Napoleonic wars, French military music—like France itself—was at the zenith of its European influence, and was a vital factor in maintaining the morale of the troops. "Among all the fine arts," Bonaparte wrote to the Conservatoire in 1797, "music is the one that exercises the greatest influence upon the passions..."[253]

Napoleon enjoyed listening to music, often sang to himself and had full appreciation of its effect upon his soldiers. Consequently, music played a significant role during the Empire. The Emperor made sure that all regiments of *ligne* and *légère*, as well as the Imperial Guard, had impressive-looking and numerous bands. These bands were usually concentrated with their respective division or corps, whereas the massed bands of the Imperial Guard were typically brought together on the battlefield into a central position from where they could accompany Guard troop movements. Their triumphant-sounding marches were designed to electrify the French and demoralize the enemy. The Guard bands were heard in action at Austerlitz, Eylau, Aspern-Essling, Wagram, Dresden, Leipzig, Montmirail, Ligny and Waterloo to mention but a few.

One of the most dramatic employment of the massed Guard bands was at the Battle of Ligny on 16 June 1815. Marching behind the regiments of the Old and Middle Guard infantry, the combined bands from all Guard units and heavy cavalry regiments—over 200 strong—struck up Napoleonic France's most popular and awe-inspiring tune, David Buhl's immortal *"La Victoire est à nous"* ("The Victory is Ours"). According to eye-witnesses watching the attack go in, the music of the massed bands was heard above the noise of the battle. In a scene that would have made spectacular cinematography, the crisis and dénouement of the Battle of Ligny played out with the massed bands of the Imperial Guard in the middle of the action. After taking a pounding for six hours from French artillery and infantry, with rain falling on them while the remaining moments of daylight were obscured from their positions by cloud cover, Blücher's fatigued Prussians witnessed something that was simply was too much for their psyche. South and west of the Prussian positions in and around the village of Ligny, a large formation of Imperial Guard infantry and horse, supported by numerous companies of horse artillery plus the entirety of a full corps of *cuirassiers*, was advancing upon them. As if the heavens wanted to get a clear picture of the French attack, the clouds parted and the bright rays of the evening sun shone through onto the Napoleonic forces, reflecting off the ranks of smartly aligned bayonets, plumed bearskins and shakos and glittering armored breastplates. In the middle and behind these formations were the massed bands of the units participating in the attack, the strides in their advance keeping in cadence with the strains of *"La Victoire est à nous."* Already demoralized by what they saw, the Prussians caved in to the onslaught of these élite troops.

Every regiment outside the Guard also had its own band, which during the early Empire was exotically dressed according to the specifications set by the regimental colonel. On days of battle, regimental bands were often grouped to

[253] Bonaparte to the Inspectors of the Paris Conservatory, *Correspondance*, number 2042.

form massed brigade, division or even corps sized bands. These musicians played marches and airs to inspire the troops and to reflect battlefield events.[254] Beginning in 1805, it was customary for the entire army's bands to play prior to the commencement of hostilities what was considered the anthem of Napoleonic France—*"Veillons au Salut de l'Empire."* The playing of this piece before a battle, with which the army sang its refrains, was a tradition that was kept throughout the years; its last documented battlefield playing was prior to the commencement of the Battle of Waterloo in 1815. *"Veillons"* was a lovely melody that carried couplets that were unmistakably Republican. What specifically caused Napoleon to choose this piece as his anthem was a combination of several things. The Revolution's most identifiable theme, *"La Marseillaise,"* had vividly attached to it the senseless slaughter of The Terror. A man of order who detested everything connected with chaos and The Terror, Napoleon's blood curdled at the sound of *"La Marseillaise,"* and it was rare that he allowed that melody to be played.

In search of another popular hymn, the Emperor could not use the popular *"Chant du départ"* because Chénier's words were not suited to an Imperial presence. However, the beloved *"Veillons au Salut de l'Empire"* was perfect. The music was originally scored by Dalayrac in 1787 and orchestrated by the great Gossec in 1792, with the verses added that year by Boy. The word 'Empire' in the first line was inserted simply for the sake of rhyme, as it was a synonym for Nation. Nevertheless, the first line suited the circumstances surrounding its selection, and the lines that followed retained the Republican ideals important to the army's motivation.

Drum major

Let us watch over the safety of the Empire
Let us watch over the preservation of our Rights!
If despotism conspires against us,
We will plot the destruction of Kings!
Liberty, Liberty, all mortals must bow to thee
Tyrants tremble! You will soon atone for your crimes!
Death rather than slavery,
This is the motto for Frenchmen.

On the safety of our Country
The fate of the world depends,
Should she be enslaved,
All the nations will be slaves,
Liberty, Liberty, all mortals must bow to thee
Tyrants tremble! You will soon atone for your crimes!
Death rather than slavery,
This is the motto for Frenchmen.

There was much more than music that inspired and motivated Napoleon's troops. In 1805, the Revolutionary spirit of *carrière ouverte aux talents* (careers open to talents) was very much alive with all the officers and soldiers of the *Grande Armée*. Distinguished service by any individual was rewarded handsomely. Napoleon often personally witnessed some heroic deed, or called on a colonel to nominate the most deserving in a unit that had accomplished a Herculean task, and the individuals received the reward from the hand of the Emperor himself. The recognition was in itself prestigious. Regardless of birth or social status, anyone

[254] In his instructions to his officers, Marshal Ney said: "During battle, the regimental band shall assemble in the rear of the regiment, and play warlike airs." See *Military Studies*, pp. 88-89.

could be recognized based on talent and devotion, and this spirit motivated many within the army.

Serving to excite the zeal of the soldiers, the material rewards for such recognition might be a raise in rank and money. The most prestigious reward was a new, small medal designed by Napoleon. The medal consisted of a star with five double rays. At the center of the star, was a wreath of oak and laurel leaves surrounding, on one side, the head of the Emperor with the inscription *"Napoléon, Empereur des Français"* and on the other, the Imperial Eagle holding a thunderbolt with the inscription *"Honneur et Patrie."* The badge was enameled in white and had gold trim for the top three levels of recipients, named the grand officers, commanders and officers, and silver trim for the lowest level of recipient, called legionaries. Regardless of the level of the decoration, it was worn on a buttonhole towards the top of the tunic, attached by a red moiré ribbon. Napoleon named the medal the *Légion d'Honneur* and to be the recipient of the highest award France could bestow was more important than any monetary reward or rise in rank.

When the Legion was first proposed by the First Consul for both military and civil services "inasmuch as they have an equal claim to the gratitude of the nation," Napoleon met with substantial vocal opposition, who contended that the ribbons and crosses were nothing more than baubles of sovereignty, a precursor to a renewal of the hated aristocracy. "I defy you," Bonaparte replied, "to point out one single Republic, either ancient or modern, where there have not been awards of distinction. They call them baubles? Well, it is by such baubles that men are led."[255]

As important as music and rewards were, the central discussion of troop motivation within the *Grande Armée* must focus on two factors: the quality of leadership, namely officers and non-commissioned officers; and the primary group cohesion that bound an individual to his duty. Revolutionary France:

Legion d'Honneur

> redefined the man in the ranks. He became a citizen-in-arms, a defender of his people, and a paragon of Revolutionary morality... [and brought forth] an entire generation of young men who possessed the full range of skill and confidence characteristic of the French people.[256]

The high standards set by the officers and NCOs became the standards for the men as well. This was made possible due to the social background and character of the officers and NCOs being the same as that of the rank and file. Whereas social standing in the *ancien régime* separated the commanders from the men, the officers and NCOs of the Revolution and Empire came from every possible social background. Due to the understanding of *carrière ouverte aux talents,* many officers that had, at one time, been common soldiers, rising in rank through devotion to duty, and were therefore living success stories to their men. These officers and NCOs forged a close relationship with their men, encouraging them through their own actions. This, in turn, increased individual initiative that permeated the army down to the lowest levels.

This type of patriotism fostered a discipline that was very different from the coercion and repression commonplace in the other armies of Europe. Though hardly faultless, the French style of discipline was designed not to humiliate the common soldier, regardless of how severe the punishment. This pragmatic approach to discipline suffered the most whenever the army was on the march, leaving the primary group as the principal means of keeping the men together.

---

[255] Nicolay and Davis, *Napoleon at the Boulogne Camp,* pp. 295-296.
[256] Lynn, *Bayonets of the Republic*, p. 63.

The French soldiers' primary group, known as the *ordinaire*, was a mess group the size of a squad headed in the infantry and artillery by a corporal, and in the cavalry by a *brigadier.* Its origins dating back to the middle of the 18th century, the structure and practice of the *ordinaire* resulted in many influences flowing through this small body of men. Whereas the officers and environment of the *ancien régime* failed to motivate the *ordinaire,* the Revolution brought about a dramatically changed relationships between officers, NCOs and the men of the *ordinaire* that carried over into the Empire. The dedication of the officers and NCOs, which fostered patriotism and an enlightened form of discipline, helped forge a new sense of commitment and enthusiasm among the *ordinaire*.[257]

According to the 24 June 1792 *Règlement concernant le service intérieur de l'infanterie,* all soldiers would live and fight in their primary group—the *ordinaire*. In the line infantry and artillery, the *ordinaire* was a squad of 16 when at full strength; the size of the Imperial Guard infantry squad was 10 and the Guard artillery squad was 13. All infantry and artillery squads were led by a corporal. In the cavalry, the size of the squads varied between 11 and 19, depending upon the type of regiment. In regiments of the Imperial Guard as well as those of the line light cavalry, squads were the smallest, numbering 10 troopers and a *brigadier.* At full-strength, a dragoon squad numbered 13, including one *brigadier*; heavy cavalry such as *cuirassiers* and *carabiniers* had large squads of 19, of which one was a *brigadier.*[258]

Soldiers of the *ordinaire* lived, ate, slept, marched and fought as a unit. Being in such proximity to the others, there was no room in the *ordinaire* for animosity on any level. They "depended on each other for almost every aspect of their welfare" well before they smelled the powder smoke. When meals were prepared, the individual rations that were either distributed by the army's bakeries or procured through foraging were contributed to the *ordinaire* cooking pot and bread bag from which all shared. They slept and marched together, helping each other with any problems that would arise during campaigning.

Since the corporals were the highest ranking NCO constantly with the other members of the *ordinaire,* they were the ones who exerted considerable influence and set a constant example for the other members of the squad. In August 1805, 91 percent of the corporals in the *Grande Armée* had been in uniform at least 12 years.[259] In other words, these men were either Volunteers of 1791 or 1792, had survived the wars of the Revolution, and were able to teach their squad members the lessons of drill and combat at the Camp of Boulogne. Compare this figure to the mere 28 percent of the corporals who claimed at least seven years of service in the *Grande Armée* in August 1813, and one begins to see one of the many underlying problems with the 1813 army and why it came apart through strategic consumption.[260]

In combat, the men of the *ordinaire* would form part of their parent company. In all cases within the infantry and cavalry, men of the *ordinaire* formed part of one file of the parent company. That means that the men of the same squad fought side-by-side where they could see their comrades and shout encouragement to the other members of the squad. When dispersed to fight as *tirailleurs*, the squad acted as the lowest form of organization in the skirmish line. In the artillery, men of the same *ordinaire* served as crews for the same piece(s) of ordnance. They knew everything about those piece(s), including any peculiarities in the performance

[257] Lynn, *Bayonets of the Republic*, pp. 163-177.

[258] Lynn, *Bayonets of the Republic*, p. 164.

[259] S.H.A.T., C^2 1.

[260] S.H.A.T., C^2 536. The extensive study of the strategic consumption in the 1813 French army can be found in: Scott Bowden, *Napoleon's Grande Armée of 1813*.

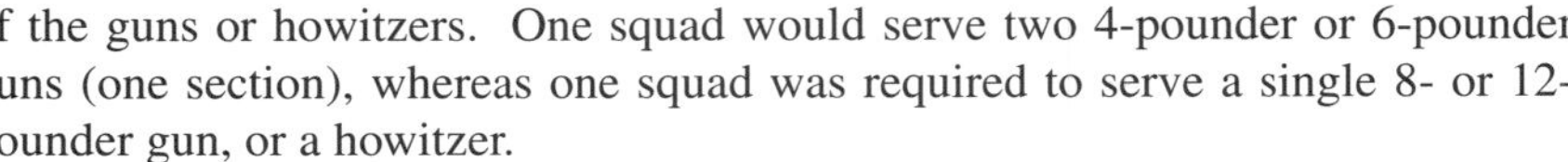

of the guns or howitzers. One squad would serve two 4-pounder or 6-pounder guns (one section), whereas one squad was required to serve a single 8- or 12-pounder gun, or a howitzer.

History's First Modern Army—Summary

The organization, training and motivation of Napoleon's *Grande Armée* stands as the forerunner of the modern army. Commanded by a mass of roughhewn but experienced officers and NCOs who had earned their rank and learned their trade in the dangerous forge known as the wars of the French Revolution, every member of the *Grande Armée* realized that promotions awaited those devoted to *"Honneur et Patrie."* This fusion of innovative organization based on permanent large formations with highly competent and staffed headquarters personnel, expert training by experienced officers and NCOs, and motivation to serve the Nation, resulted in history's first modern army.

The heart of Napoleon's organization, the corps, is still in use 200 years later. Further, the Emperor's creation of the massive cavalry reserve corps was one of the most effective organizational innovations of the 19th century and its effective employment was used to great advantage in 1805 as well as throughout the Napoleonic era. Napoleon's cavalry reserve was the forerunner of the tank divisions and corps of World War II.

Permanent brigade and division organization was another first. Units developed a familiarity with one another in the Camp of Boulogne. This translated into precision battlefield drill up to and including the brigade level, whereas other armies could not perform such evolution above the regiment. The battlefield flexibility of the *Grande Armée* boasted a liberal tactical doctrine of effective deployment of *tirailleurs*. Generals and marshals of France used combined arms tactics to great effect. The *Grande Armée* of 1805 featured coordination of the combat arms as well as a large and superb artillery organization, supported by a splendid staff commanded by a man who was arguably history's greatest soldier. Preparation for war was thorough. When the Third Coalition declared war on France, Napoleon's *Grande Armée* uncoiled upon Europe in the memorable Ulm and Austerlitz campaigns of 1805—the first two campaigns of "The Glory Years."

Tables of Organization
La Grande Armée

Source: *Tableaux les composition des corps*
Carton C^2 470
Archives du Service Historique de l'État-Major de l'Armée de Terre,
château de Vincennes

Inspector of Reviews

The Infantry

The organizations of the line infantry companies were as follows:

War-Time Company Organization
Ligne Infantry—1805

Rank	Grenadiers	Fusiliers* or *Voltigeurs*
Captain	1	1
Lieutenant	1	1
Sub-lieutenant	1	1
Sergeant-major	1	1
Sergeants	4	4
Fourrier	1	1
Corporals	8	8
Privates	64	104
Drummers	2	2
Company Totals—Full Strength	83	123

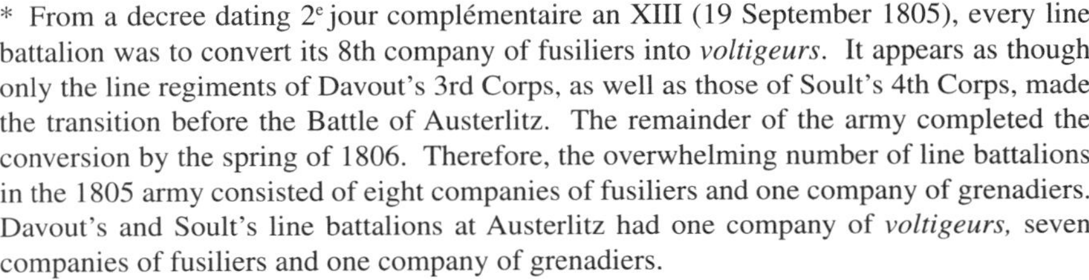

* From a decree dating 2e jour complémentaire an XIII (19 September 1805), every line battalion was to convert its 8th company of fusiliers into *voltigeurs*. It appears as though only the line regiments of Davout's 3rd Corps, as well as those of Soult's 4th Corps, made the transition before the Battle of Austerlitz. The remainder of the army completed the conversion by the spring of 1806. Therefore, the overwhelming number of line battalions in the 1805 army consisted of eight companies of fusiliers and one company of grenadiers. Davout's and Soult's line battalions at Austerlitz had one company of *voltigeurs,* seven companies of fusiliers and one company of grenadiers.

The organization of the light companies and battalion headquarters staff for both the light and line battalions were as follows:

War-Time Company Organization
Light (*Légère*) Infantry—1805 through 1807

Rank	*Carabiniers*	*Chasseurs* or *Voltigeurs*
Captain	1	1
Lieutenant	1	1
Sub-lieutenant	1	1
Sergeant-major	1	1
Sergeants	4	4
Fourrier	1	1
Corporals	8	8
Privates	64	104
Drummers or Trumpeters	2	2
Company Totals—Full Strength	83	123

Light Infantry Voltigeur

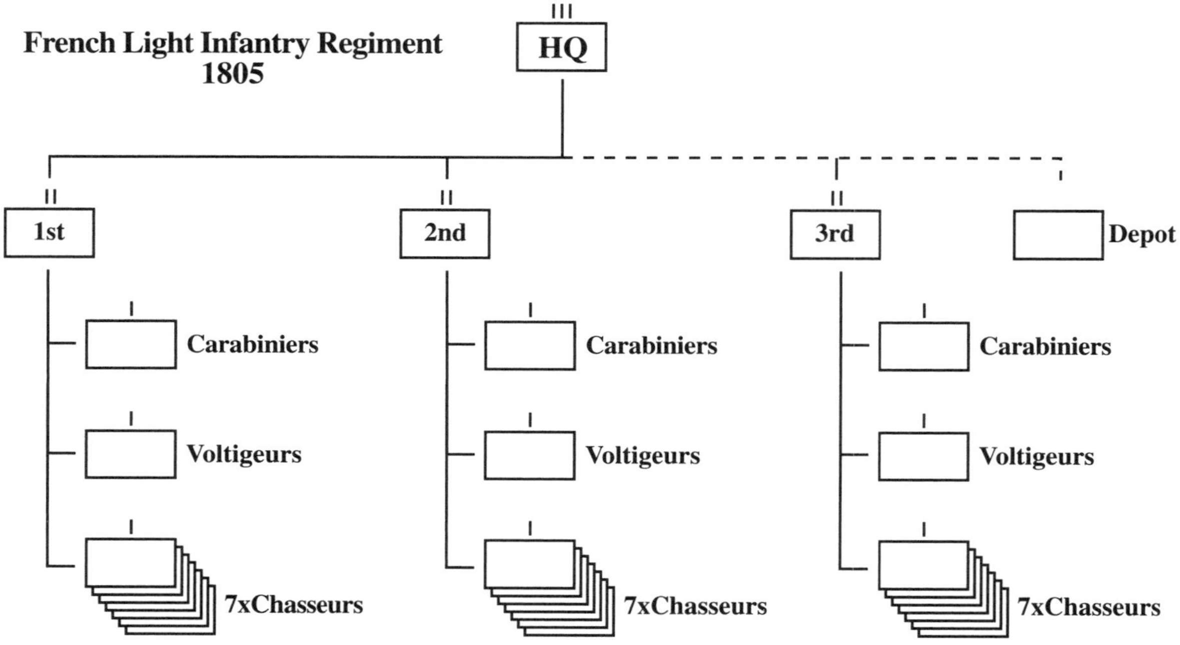

Theoretical establishment was *approximately* 90 carabiniers in that company and 120 in the *voltigeur* and *chasseur* companies. Total of 27 companies if all three battalions are present.

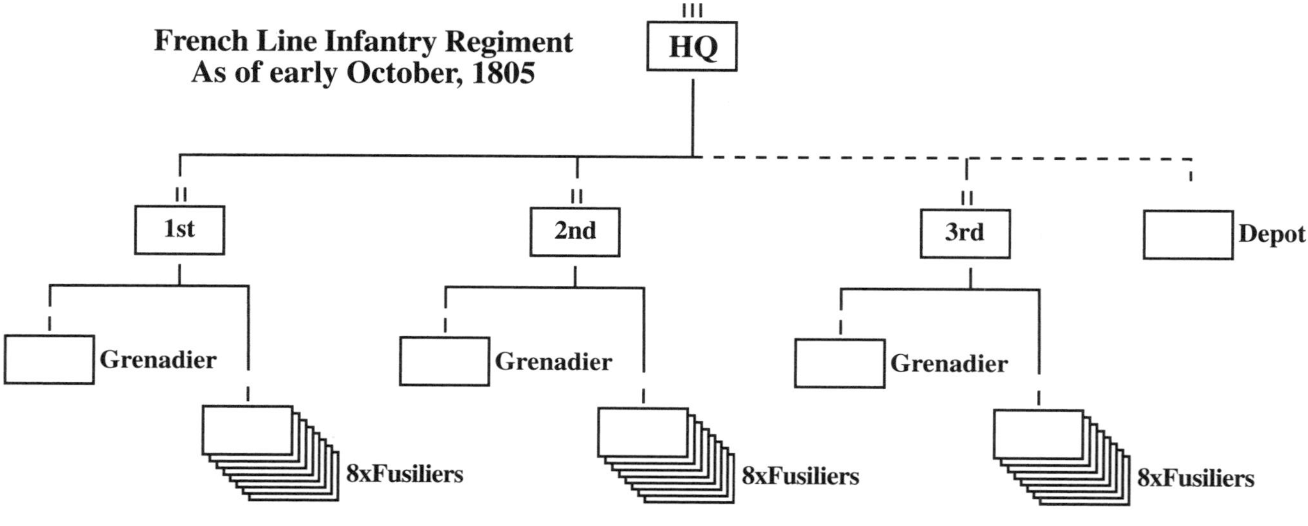

The decree changing one company of fusiliers to *voltiguers* had not yet been implemented. Theoretical establishment was *approximately* 90 grenadiers in that company and 120 in each of the fusilier companies. Total of 27 companies if all three battalions present.

Organization of Battalion Headquarters
***Ligne* and *Légère* Infantry—1805 through 1807**

Rank	Number of personnel
Chefs de bataillon (Battalion C.O.)	1
Adjudant-major	1
Quartier-maître	1
Surgeon-major	1
Sous-aide surgeon	1
Adjudant sous-officier	1
Corporal (lead) drummer	1
Master tailor	1
Master shoe maker	1
Master gaiter maker	1
Master gunsmith	1
Battalion Headquarters Total	11

Chasseur à pied
of the Imperial Guard

(All regimental headquarters personnel are in addition to the company personnel).

Organization of Regimental Headquarters
***Ligne* and *Légère* Infantry—1805 through 1807**

Rank	with 2	with 3	with 4 Battalions
Colonel	1	1	1
Major	1	1	1
Chefs de bataillon	2	3	4
Adjudants-majors	2	3	4
Treasurer	1	1	1
Surgeon major	1	1	1
Surgeon aide-majors	1	2	3
Surgeon sous-aides	2	3	4
Eagle-flag bearers	2	3	4
Adjudants sous officiers	2	3	4
Vaguemestre	1	1	1
Drum-major	1	1	1
Corporal (lead) drummer	1	1	1
Musicians	8	8	8
Master tailor	1	1	1
Master shoe maker	1	1	1
Master gaiter maker	1	2	3
Master gunsmith	1	1	1
Regimental Headquarters Totals	32	36	42

The particulars of the Imperial Guard organization were as follows:

War-Time Company Organization
Grenadiers and *Chasseurs à pied* of the Imperial Guard—1805

Rank	Grenadiers	*Chasseurs*
Captain	1	1
1st Lieutenant	1	1
2nd Lieutenants	2	2
Sergeant-major	1	1
Sergeants	4	4
Fourrier	1	1
Corporals	8	8
Sappers (rank of corporal)	2	2
Privates	80	80
Drummers	2	2
Company Totals—Full Strength	102	102

Eagle Bearer of the Grenadiers à pied *of the Imperial Guard*

Shako plate of the Marins *of the Imperial Guard*

Organization of Regimental Headquarters
Grenadiers and *Chasseurs à pied* of the Imperial Guard—1805

Rank	
Colonel	1
Major	1
Chefs de bataillon	3
Quarter-master treasurer	1
Adjudants-majors	3
Sous-adjudant-majors	3
Eagle-flag bearers	2
Health officers	3
Apprentice Surgeon*	1
Vaguemestre sergeant-major	1
Drum-major	1
Corporal (lead) drummers	3
Chief of Music	1
Musicians	46
Master tailor	1
Master shoe maker	1
Master gaiter maker	1
Gunsmiths	2
Regimental Headquarters Totals	75

*The Guard had an entire hospital staff numbering 62 surgeons, pharmacists and medical officers.

Each crew of sailors was as follows:

War-Time "Crew" (Company) Organization
Sailors (*Matelots*) of the Guard—1805 through 1808

Rank	
Capitaine de frégate, or commandant de vaisseau	1
Lieutenants or ensigns	5
Chief petty officers	5
Vice petty officers	5
Quartiers-maîtres (corporals)	5
Seamen of 1st, 2nd, 3rd and 4th classes	125
Trumpeter or Drummer	1
Crew Totals—Full Strength	147

Shako of the Marins *of the Imperial Guard*

Organization of Battalion Headquarters
Sailors (*Matelots* or *Marins*) of the Guard—1805 through 1808

Rank	
Capitaine de vaisseau, commanding the battalion	1
Adjudant-major	1
Eagle-flag bearer	1
Leading seaman treasurer	1
Health officer	1
Battalion Headquarters Total—Full Strength	5

The Cavalry

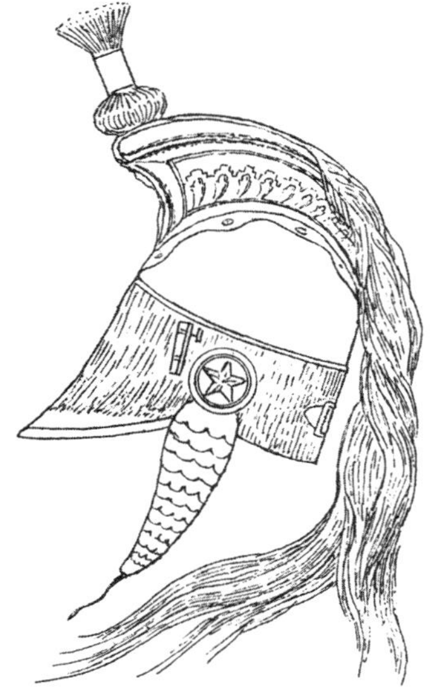

The organization of the *carabiniers* and *cuirassiers* companies and regimental headquarters staff for both were as follows:

War-Time Company Organization
***Carabiniers* and *Cuirassiers*—1805 through 1807**

Rank	Personnel	Horses
Captain	1	3
Lieutenant	1	2
Sub-lieutenant	1	2
Sergeant-major	1	1
Sergeants	2	2
Fourrier	1	1
Brigadiers (Corporals)	4	4
Privates	74	74
Trumpeter	1	1
Company Totals—Full Strength	86	90

There were two companies per every squadron present in the field.

Organization of Regimental Headquarters
***Carabiniers* and *Cuirassiers*—1805 through 1807**

Rank	Personnel	Horses
Colonel	1	4
Major	1	4
Chefs d'escadron	2	6
Adjudants-majors	2	6
Eagle-standard bearers	1 per squadron	1 per man
Quartier-maître	1	2
Surgeon major	1	1
Surgeon Aide-major	1	1
Surgeon Sous-aide	2	2
Adjudants-sous-officiers	2	2
Brigadier trumpeter	1	1
Veterinarian	1	1
Master tailor	1	—
Master saddle maker	1	—
Master boot maker	1	—
Master breeches maker	1	—
Master armorer-sword maker	1	—
Regimental Headquarters Total (*Excluding eagle-standard bearers)	20 *	30 *

Cuirassier's *Helmet*

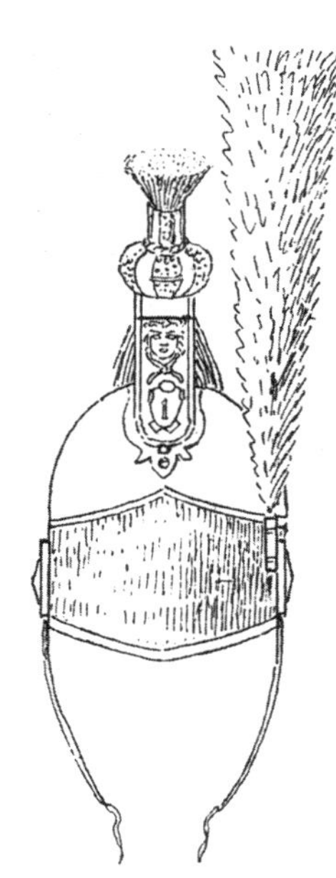

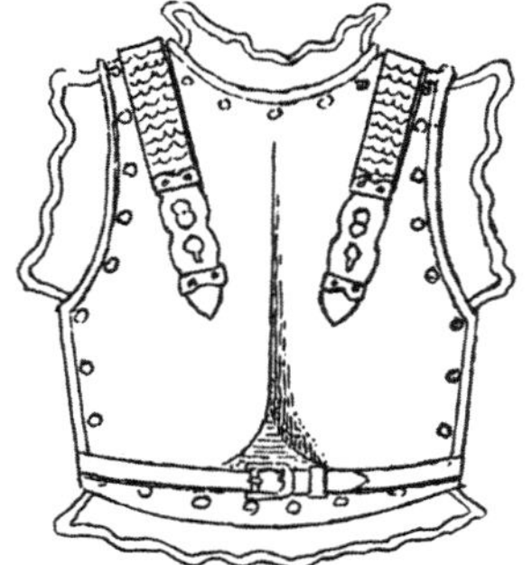

The organization of the dragoon companies and regimental headquarters staff were as follows:

War-Time Company Organization
Mounted Dragoons—1805 through 1807

Rank	Personnel	Horses
Captain	1	3
Lieutenant	1	2
Sub-lieutenant	1	2
Sergeant-major	1	1
Sergeants	3	3
Fourrier	1	1
Brigadiers (Corporals)	6	6
Privates	72	72
Horseshoe smith	1	1
Trumpeter	1	1
Company Totals—Mounted	88	92

In each company, there was also a dismounted contingent of dragoons, consisting of 1 sous-lieutenant (mounted with 2 horses available), 1 sergeant, 2 brigadiers, 46 privates and 2 drummers.
There were two companies per every squadron present in the field.

Dragoon Officer's Helmet

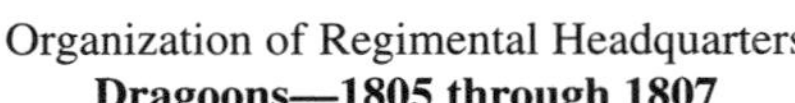

Organization of Regimental Headquarters
Dragoons—1805 through 1807

Rank	Personnel	Horses
Colonel	1	4
Major	1	4
Chefs d'escadron	2	6
Adjudants-majors	2	6
Eagle-standard bearers	1 per squadron	1 per man
Quartier-maître	1	2
Surgeon major	1	1
Surgeon Aide-major	1	1
Surgeon Sous-aide	2	2
Adjudants-sous-officiers	2	2
Brigadier trumpeter	1	1
Veterinarian	1	1
Brigadier drummer	1	—
Master tailor	1	—
Master saddle maker	1	—
Master boot maker	1	—
Master breeches maker	1	—
Master armorer-sword maker	1	—
Regimental Headquarters Total	21 *	30 *
(*Excluding eagle-standard bearers)		

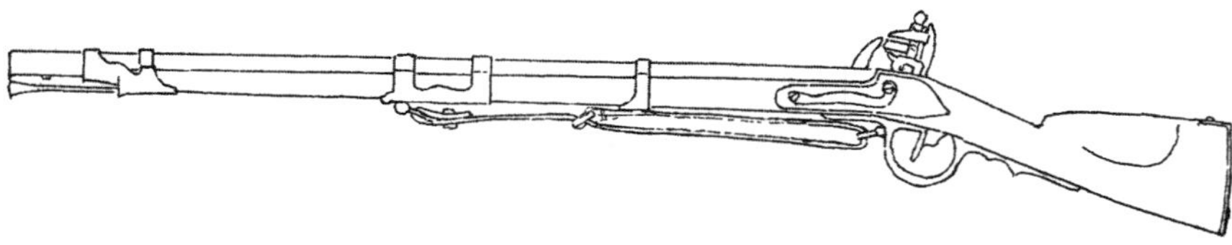

Dragoon carbine

The organization of the line light cavalry—the *chasseurs à cheval* and hussars—companies and regimental headquarters staff were as follows:

War-Time Company Organization
***Chasseurs à cheval* and Hussars—1805 through 1807**

Rank	Personnel	Horses
Captain	1	3
Lieutenant	1	2
Sub-lieutenant	2	4
Sergeant-major	1	1
Sergeants	4	4
Fourrier	1	1
Brigadiers (Corporals)	8	8
Privates—mounted	86	86
Privates—not mounted	10	—
Trumpeters	2	2
Company Totals—Mounted	116	111

There were two companies per every squadron present in the field.

Organization of Regimental Headquarters
***Chasseurs à cheval* and Hussars—1805 through 1807**

Rank	Personnel	Horses
Colonel	1	4
Major	1	4
Chefs d'escadron	2	6
Adjudants-majors	2	6
Eagle-standard bearers	1 per squadron	1 per man
Quartier-maître	1	2
Surgeon major	1	1
Surgeon Aide-major	1	1
Surgeon Sous-aide	2	2
Adjudants-sous-officiers	2	2
Brigadier trumpeter	1	1
Veterinarian	1	1
Master tailor	1	—
Master saddle maker	1	—
Master boot maker	1	—
Master armorer-sword maker	1	—
Regimental Headquarters Total (*Excluding eagle-standard bearers)	19 *	30 *

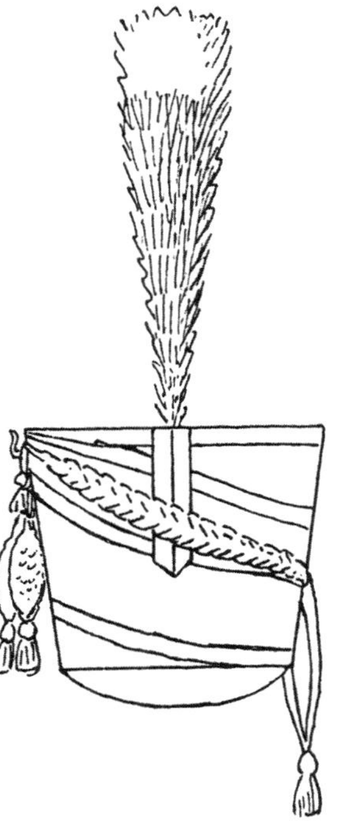

Hussar shako

The organization of the Imperial Guard grenadier and *chasseurs à cheval* regimental headquarters staff and companies were as follows:

War-Time Company Organization
Imperial Guard *Grenadiers à cheval* and *Chasseurs à cheval*—1805

Rank	Personnel	Horses
Captain	1	3
Lieutenant	2	4
Sub-lieutenant	2	4
Sergeant-major	1	1
Sergeants	6	6
Fourrier	1	1
Brigadiers (Corporals)	10	10
Privates	96	96
Horseshoe smith	1	1
Trumpeters	3	3
Company Totals—Mounted	123	129

There were two companies per every squadron present in the field.

Organization of Regimental Headquarters
Imperial Guard *Grenadiers à cheval* and *Chasseurs à cheval*—1805

Rank	Personnel	Horses
Colonel	1	4
Major	1	4
Chefs d'escadron	4	12
Adjudant-major	1	3
Adjudants-sous-majors	2	2
Captain-instructor	1	3
Sous-instructor (sergeant)	1	2
Eagle-standard bearers	4	8
Quartier-maître treasurer	1	2
Trumpet-major	1	2
Brigadier trumpeters	2	2
Kettle-drummer	1	1
Veterinarian	1	1
Veterinarian aide	1	1
Sanitary Officers	3	3
Vaguemestre	1	1
Master tailor	1	—
Master saddle maker	1	—
Master boot maker	1	—
Master breeches maker	1	—
Master armorer	1	—
Master sword maker	1	—
Master horseshoe smith	1	—
Regimental Headquarters Total	33	51

The organizations of the Imperial Guard company of *Mameluks* and their headquarters staff were as follows:

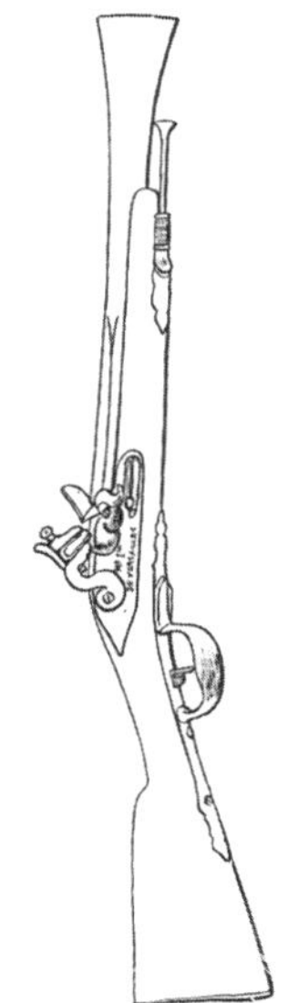
Mameluk sidearm

War-Time Company Organization
***Mameluks*—1805**

Rank	Personnel	Horses	
Captain	2	6	
1st Lieutenants	2	4	
2nd Lieutenants	2	4	
Sous-lieutenants	2	4	
Sergeants	8	*	8
Brigadiers (Corporals)	10	*	10
Privates	85	85	
Horse shoe smith	2	2	
Trumpeters	2	2	
Company Totals—Mounted	115	125	

*Two each of these were French personnel.

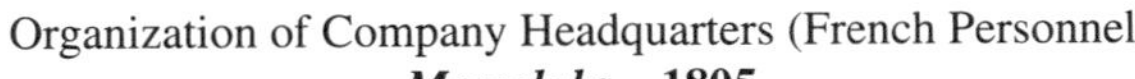
Organization of Company Headquarters (French Personnel)
***Mameluks*—1805**

Rank	Personnel	Horses
Captain, commanding	1	3
Sanitary officer	1	3
Adjudant sous-lieutenant	1	3
Sergeant major	1	3
Fourrier	1	1
Veterinarian	1	1
Master saddle maker	1	—
Master tailor	1	—
Master shoe maker	1	—
Company Headquarters Total	9	14

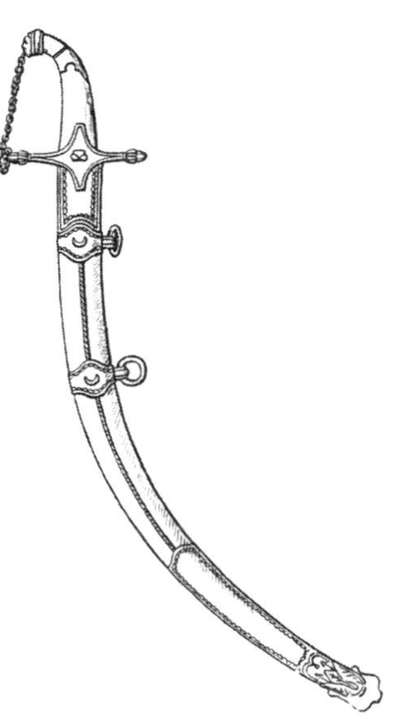
Saber of a Mameluk Officer

The Artillery & Technical Troops

The organization of each line artillery company was as follows:

War-Time Company Organization
Line Artillery—1805 through 1807

Rank	Foot Artillery	Horse Artillery
1st Captain	1	1
2nd Captain	1	1
1st Lieutenant	1	1
2nd Lieutenant	1	1
Sergeant-major	1	1
Sergeants	4	4
Fourrier	1	1
Corporals	4	4
Artificers	4	4
Cannoniers	80	80
Drummers	2	2
Company Totals—Full Strength	100	100

Organization of Regimental Headquarters
Line Artillery—1805 through 1807

Rank	Foot Artillery	Horse Artillery
Colonel	1	1
Major	1	1
Chefs de bataillon/ d'escadron	5	2
Adjudants-majors	2	1
Quartier-maître	1	1
Sanitary officer	2	1
Adjudants sous-officiers	4	2
Drum Major	1	—
Corporal drummer	1	—
Artificer chief	1	—
Brigadier trumpeter	—	1
Veterinarian	—	1
Musicians	8	—
Chief tailor	1	1
Chief saddle maker	—	1
Chief shoe/boot maker	1	1
Chief armorer-sword maker	1	1
Regimental Headquarters Total	30	15

Remember that the number of companies in each foot artillery regiment was 22, and that each horse artillery regiment had only six companies.

There was one battalion of engineers (sappers) consisting of nine companies. There was one battalion of *pontonniers* comprising eight companies. In addition, there was one company of miners. These troops were organized as follows:

War-Time Company Organization
Line Engineers (Sappers)—1805 through 1807

Rank	Engineers	*Pontoniners*	Miners
Captain en premier	1	1	1
Captain en second	1	1	1
1st Lieutenant	1	1	1
2nd Lieutenant	1	1	1
Sergeant-major	1	1	1
Sergeants	4	4	4
Fourrier	1	1	1
Corporals	4	4	4
Master worker	4	—	—
Engineers 1st class	24	—	—
Engineers 2nd class	36	—	—
Specialist workers	—	4	—
Boat handlers	—	40	—
Boat workers	—	40	—
Artificers	—	—	4
Miners 1st class	—	—	24
Miners 2nd class	—	—	56
Drummers	2	2	2
Company Totals—Full Strength	80	100	100

Organization of Battalion Headquarters
Line Engineers (Sappers) and *Pontonniers*—1805 through 1807

Rank	Engineers	*Pontonniers*
Chef de bataillon	1	1
Quarter-master treasurer	1	1
Adjudants-majors	1	1
Health officer	—	1
Surgeon major	1	—
Adjudant sous-officer	1	1
Sergeant-major, master builder	—	1
Corporal (lead) drummer	1	1
Master tailor	1	1
Master shoe maker	1	1
Master boot maker	1	—
Master armorer	—	1
Regimental Headquarters Totals	9	10

To pull the guns there was one company of train personnel assigned to every company of artillery personnel. There were six companies per battalion with each company of train personnel organized as follows:

War-Time Company Organization
Train of Artillery of the Line—1805 through 1807

Rank	
Lieutenant	1
Sergeant-major	1
Sergeants	2
Fourrier	1
Corporals	4
Privates	84
Horseshoe smiths	2
Harness makers	2
Trumpeters	2
Company Totals—Full Strength	99

Organization of Battalion Headquarters
Train of Artillery of the Line—1805 through 1807

Rank	
Captain, commanding	1
Lieutenant adjudant-major	1
Quartier-maître sous-lieutenant	1
Health officer	1
Adjudant sous-officer	1
Veterinarian	1
Forge chief	1
Master tailor	1
Master shoe maker	1
Master boot maker	1
Master armorer	1
Battalion Headquarters Totals	11

There was one squadron of two companies of Imperial Guard Horse Artillery in 1805. The organization of each Imperial Guard Horse Artillery (*Volante*) company was as follows:

War-Time Company Organization
Imperial Guard Horse Artillery—1805

Rank	Personnel	Horses
Chef d'escadron	1	3
Capitaine en second	1	2
1st Lieutenant	1	2
2nd Lieutenant	1	2
Sergeant-major	1	1
Sergeants	6	6
Fourrier	1	1
Corporals	6	6
Artificers	4	4
Cannoniers, 1st class	34	34
Cannoniers, 2nd class	38	38
Musicians	3	3
Horseshoe smith	1	1
Company Totals—Full Strength	98	103

Organization of Squadron Headquarters
Imperial Guard Horse Artillery—1805

Rank	Personnel	Horses
Colonel	1	4
Chefs d'escadron	2	6
Adjudants-major	1	2
Quartier-maître	1	2
Sanitary officers	2	2
Adjudants sous-officer	1	1
Lieutenant instructor	1	1
Eagle-standard bearer	1	1
Professor of mathematics	1	1
Vaguemestre	1	1
Brigadier trumpeter	1	1
Veterinarian	1	1
Veterinarian aide	1	1
Chief tailor	1	—
Chief breeches maker	1	—
Chief saddle/harness maker	1	—
Chief boot maker	1	—
Chief armorer-sword maker	1	—
Squadron Headquarters Total	20	14

To pull the guns of the Imperial Guard there were two companies of train personnel assigned to every company of artillery personnel. In 1805 there were a total of four companies of Imperial Guard train personnel, each company organized as follows:

War-Time Company Organization
Train of Artillery of the Guard—1805 through 1807

Rank	Personnel	Horses
Lieutenant	1	
Sergeant-major	1	
Sergeants	4	
Fourrier	1	
Corporals	6	
Privates, 1st class	26	
Privates, 2nd class	72	
Horseshoe smiths	2	
Harness makers	2	
Trumpeters	2	
Company Totals—Full Strength	117	125

Organization of French Artillery
'Division' Organization—1805 through 1807

Designation	Poundage of Guns 4-pdrs.	8 pdrs.*	12 pdrs.	Howitzers
For each line infantry division present in a *corps d'armée*, one 'artillery division' was assigned to that corps, consisting of:	2	6	2	2 = 12

*The 1st Corps of the *Grande Armée* formed in Hanover and used Hanoverian 6-pounder guns as substitutes for the 8-pounders and Hanoverian 3-pounders as substitutes for the 4-pounders.

French mobile artillery forge

Evolution of French Cannon 1732 to 1803—
Vallière, to Gribeauval, to System Year XI

System	Ordnance Description	Barrel Length	Barrel Weight	Net Weight including Carriage
Siege guns (*Canons de siege et de place*):				
Vallière	24-pounder	138"	5828 lbs.	na
(1732)	16-pounder	134"	4533 lbs.	na
	12-pounder	127"	3454 lbs.	na
	8-pounder	117"	2266 lbs.	na
	4-pounder	95"	1241 lbs.	na
Gribeauval	24-pounder (1st model)	138"	6074 lbs.	na
	24-pounder (later version)	138"	5445 lbs.	8175 lbs.
(1765)	16-pounder	134"	4437 lbs.	6559 lbs.
	12-pounder	126"	3436 lbs.	5448 lbs.
	8-pounder	114"	2347 lbs.	4232 lbs.
Year XI	24-pounder "long"	135"	4867 lbs.	7112 lbs.
(1803)	24-pounder "short"	108"	3076 lbs.	4104 lbs.
	12-pounder "long"	121"	2202 lbs.	3796 lbs.
	6-pounder "long"	91"	1250 lbs.	2828 lbs.
Field guns (*Canons de campagne*):				
Vallière	12-pounder	127"	3454 lbs.	na
(1732)	8-pounder	117"	2266 lbs.	na
	4-pounder	95"	1241 lbs.	na
Gribeauval	12-pounder	90"	1951 lbs.	3205 lbs.
(1765)	8-pounder	79"	1280 lbs.	2456 lbs.
	4-pounder	62"	637 lbs.	1940 lbs.
Year XI	12-pounder	91"	1651 lbs.	2811 lbs.
(1803)	6-pounder	72"	853 lbs.	2008 lbs.
Mountain guns (*Canons de montagne*):				
Year XI	6-pounder	47"	496 lbs.	na
(1803)	3-pounder	36"	173 lbs.	na
Coastal guns (*Canons de côtes*):				
"ancien	36-pounder	na	7760 lbs.	na
système"	24-pounder	na	5521 lbs.	na
	16-pounder	na	4187 lbs.	na
	12-pounder	na	3531 lbs.	na
Year XI	36-pounder	na	7760 lbs.	na
(1803)	24-pounder	na	5521 lbs.	na

na = data not available

PART II

Armies of the Ancien Régime

Chapter II
"Cold Steel—Bayonets and Sabers!"
The Russian Army of 1805

Late in the afternoon of 2 December 1805, Russian foreign adviser Prince Adam George Czartoryski solemnly stood at Allied army headquarters along the south bank of the Littawa stream about 70 miles northeast of Vienna on the battlefield known as Austerlitz. Although not a military man by trade, the 35-year-old Polish born Czartoryski had accompanied his master, Tsar Alexander I of Russia, to Austerlitz in order to observe the anticipated victory over the French army and its leader, Napoleon. As the wreckage of the broken Russian regiments passed by in an agonizing, slow trudge following their bloody and disastrous engagement against the enemy, Czartoryski gazed long and hard at his adopted countrymen. Their anguished faces reflected nothing of the glory and triumph that was heralded on 25 August when the army marched west from its encampments at Radziwilow, on the borders of Russia and Austrian Galicia. Instead, he saw only blood, despair and defeat. The wounded along with the exhausted survivors, most without weapons, their faces and greatcoats blackened by powder stains, moved slowly by the nobleman. Horses without riders, displaying shabraques from the most famous and noblest cavalry regiments in Russian and Austrian service, meandered aimlessly by at varying speeds and direction, adding to the kaleidoscopic scene of a confused and beaten host. As the fading rays of sunlight began to sink beneath the dense clouds of smoke, snow began to fall, outlining the retreating soldiers as if a curtain was "descending in a theater at the close of the last act."[1]

Czartoryski

Soon Czartoryski recognized some uniforms of infantry units which early that morning had comprised the army's powerful First, Second and Third Columns under 55-year-old Lieutenant-General Friedrich Wilhelm Buxhöwden. As they passed, Czartoryski counted the number of formed bodies of troops. One battalion, two... that's all of the formations that still remained intact of the more than 55 infantry battalions, five cavalry squadrons and 84 guns that had earlier that day comprised Buxhöwden's proud, powerful command. Some units had not only lost all cohesion, but all their flags as well. Not a single standard was seen of the 18 battalions belonging to Lieutenant General Presbyshevsky's Third Column. Had the French captured all these sacred emblems? Soon a bareheaded Russian officer stopped in front of Czartoryski. Earlier that day this officer's dress was an immaculate uniform of white trimmed in red and gold. Now blackened by powder stains with the gold epaulettes all but blown off, no longer sporting his white-plumed chapeau, the officer's uniform was barely recognizable as that worn by a Russian lieutenant general; it was Buxhöwden himself! Catching sight of Czartoryski, the defeated general cried out: "I have been abandoned! I have been sacrificed!"[2]

* *

[1] *Memoirs of Baron Lejeune,* translated and edited from the original French by Mrs Arthur Bell (N. d'Anvers), 2 volumes (New York and Bombay 1897), vol. 1, p.33.

[2] *Mémoirs du Prince Czartoryski,* 2 volumes (Paris 1887), vol. 1, p. 410.

Tsar Alexander I

Russian Infantry

Its Background and Makeup

At the turn of the 19th century, Russia was little advanced from a feudal state wherein serfs were still the property of the landowners, and the landowners owed their allegiance to the nobles of the ruling class.[3] By 1805, Russia's ruling family—the Romanovs—already had more than a century of despotism under its belt. Since Peter the Great's accession to the throne, Russian "peasants lost more and more of their freedom with almost every decade of the 18th century, and the lords rightly feared that the serfs would desert them in droves for the relative attractions of the army, if they were ever given the chance."[4] Thus, to secure its borders against outsiders and to keep a tight grip on its subjects, Romanov doctrine called for four *conscripted*, standing armies. These were: 1) a coastal army in the Baltic provinces and Finland; 2) a Ukrainian army; 3) an army on the Volga River to keep a watch on the Turks; and 4) an army of the reserve in and around the Smolensk-Moscow area.[5] The majority of these armies were infantry.

It is important to remember the term conscripted with relation to the Tsar's infantry. In an effort to solidify their power, the Romanovs placated the Russian nobility by allowing the erosion of serf freedoms, which made it virtually impossible for a peasant to enlist in the army. The Romanovs thus maintained their power and could conscript an almost unlimited supply of manpower into the Motherland's armies. Prior to the campaign of 1805, a levy brought at least 110,000 recruits into the service. Discounting Cossacks and auxiliary troops, the conscript class of 1805 represented almost 25% of all the men in uniform.[6]

At the head of all the Russias was Tsar Alexander I, son of Paul I and Sophia Dorothea of Württemberg. Born Alexander Pavolich on 12 December 1777, young Alexander was the first grandson and apple of his grandmother's eye, the strong-willed Russian Empress, Catherine the Great.[7] Catherine constantly feared that her son, Paul, might plot against her. As a result, Catherine went to great lengths to discredit him among the court nobles.[8] In doing so, she also took control of young Alexander's life, arranged his education by the famous Swiss philosopher and patriot, Frederic-Cesar de LaHarpe, and named Frederick the Great of Prussia as his godfather. The impressionable boy grew up under Catherine's ever-watchful presence, and was subjected to her constant criticism of his mother and father. By the time Alexander was a teenager, many within the Russian court knew that Catherine opposed Paul succeeding her. Catherine's close ties with Alexander supposedly led to his feigned agreement with her in barring Paul from the throne. When Catherine passed away on 5 November 1796, Paul supposedly destroyed her last will and testament and proclaimed himself Tsar.[9] Alexander, still only 18 years of age, watched his father's accession to the throne some two days later.

LaHarpe: once Alexander's tutor, by 1805 he was a Swiss statesman supporting French intervention

In less than five years, Paul was dead. The court nobles, eager to insure their status through constitutional guarantees and wishing to expand their power through a new predictable order, used Russia's military misfortunes against Revolutionary France at the Battle of Zürich in Switzerland, and the failed Anglo-Russian invasion in Holland, to persuade Alexander to assent to a coup against his father. Supposedly, Alexander did not want his father injured, but simply removed from power. However, the offenders did not want to see an ousted head of state returning later

[3] Hugh Seton-Watson, *The Russian Empire 1801-1917* (Oxford 1967), p. 21-22.
[4] Christopher Duffy, *Russia's Military Way to the West* (London 1981), pp. 126-127.
[5] Duffy, *Russia's Military Way to the West,* p. 126.
[6] Christopher Duffy, *Austerlitz* (London and Hamden 1977), p. 31.
[7] Connelly, et al, Historical Dictionary of Napoleonic France, 1*799-1815*, p.14
[8] John T. Alexander, *Catherine the Great* (Oxford 1989), pp. 137-138 and 234.
[9] Alexander, *Catherine the Great,* p. 326.

for revenge. Paul was murdered on 23 March 1801, and the 23-year-old Alexander became Tsar. Overcoming his initial fear of court politics, Alexander I disappointed the nobles who had done his dirty work by refusing to surrender any of his power.[10] Like his grandmother, the young Tsar was determined to rule Russia with a Romanov iron hand.

Across the vast geographical expanse of his empire, Tsar Alexander I had almost 44 million subjects.[11] Of this number, some eight million males resided in the historic heartland of Great Russia—the triangular area from its western border next to Poland, north to Saint Petersburg and then to Moscow in the east.[12] It was these White Russians who traditionally comprised the bulk of the Tsar's forces.

Russian infantry of the 1799 campaign

Since priests were exempt from military service, they joined a group of privileged merchants, manufacturers, and free landowners (*odnodvortsy*) who could avoid the army by furnishing a substitute or buying an exemption.[13] This left the serfs as the primary source of personnel for the army. The peasants were summoned for service by a series of levies. Almost every year, the government would calculate the deficiencies in personnel from the army returns and order a conscription to bring the numbers back in line. Regimental officers were given recruiting areas and they worked with local officials and landowners to attain the desired number of conscripts for their commands.

Obviously, the officers of the regiments wanted only the strongest and most intelligent men, while the landowners certainly did not want to part company with their best human assets. The serfs selected for military service were supposed to be at least five feet two inches in height and be between 17 to 35 years of age. From virtually all eyewitness accounts, it would seem that the regimental officers did an excellent job of selecting the best physical specimens available *after* the undesirables had first been given up by the landowners! Thus, if there were drunkards, thieves or idlers among the landowners' serfs, these were the first handed over to the military. Langeron summarized the entire selection process by a landowner in a succinct manner:

> If among his peasants or servants there is an incorrigible thief, then he will send him. In the absence of a thief, he will dispatch a drunkard or an idler. Finally, if his peasants are made up only of honorable men (which is almost impossible), he will consign the feeblest person he can find.[14]

Once selected, the recruit was shaved, shackled and led away for an enlistment term of 25 years. If there were any relatives, they saw him off "as if it was his funeral, with tears, lamentations and songs, the purport of which is that they shall never see him more."[15]

The entire process begs several questions: If, as Russian noblemen believed, prospects of military service were so enticing that, if left open for volunteers, the serfs would run away *en masse* and enlist, then why did the families of those serfs selected see their loved-one's departure to the army tantamount to a sentence of exile or death? On the other hand, were the noblemen looking at military prospects only from their privileged positions rather than as a life of an ordinary infantryman? Alternatively, one must wonder if, since rural Russian peasant life was nothing

---

[10] Connelly, et al, *Historical Dictionary of Napoleonic France, 1799-1815*. p. 14.
[11] Duffy, *Austerlitz*, p. 31.
[12] Duffy, *Russia's Military Way to the West*, p. 3.
[13] Duffy, *Russia's Military Way to the West*, p. 128.
[14] Langeron, as quoted in Duffy, *Russia's Military Way to the West*, p. 129
[15] J. Parkinson, *A Tour of Russia, Siberia and the Crimea 1792-1794* (London 1971), p. 103.

Pavlov Grenadiers

more than a state of enslaved, brutish misery, could the peasants figure out the best way to be earmarked for the army while, at the mean time, being able to pacify their taskmaster? The answers are, no doubt, blurred by the difference of time and culture. One thing we can be sure of, however: most people today cannot fathom the cruel conditions of life as either a serf or as a Russian infantryman during the Napoleonic period. Furthermore, the sufferings as a serf prepared them well for the life of deprivation in the ranks. Perhaps historian A. M. Turgenev best summed up the plight of the Russian serf when he wrote: "Peasants are not soldiers, and so in Russia they are not accounted human beings."[16]

One of the most renowned aspects of the Russian infantryman was his virtual unwillingness to be captured. In 1805 alone, there are almost countless instances of wounded Tsarist soldiers that had fallen into French hands who would continue to resist when other European troops would have surrendered. Such actions prompted the French saying that "it is easier to kill six Russian soldiers than to capture one."[17] This tough mind set was no doubt due to the fact that the Russian soldier of the early 19th century, even though a western European by modern standards, had more in common with the eastern Mongols than he did with any Frenchman. In fact, it can be strongly argued that no population was more radically transmuted by the Mongols than that of Great Russia. "The princes of Muscovy became the most enthusiastic and shameless of the Mongol surrogates, and much that was distinctive and unattractive about the Russian character and Russian institutions has been attributed to this experience."[18] The Mongols and their deputies destroyed the Russian middle class, brutalized the peasantry, stripped people of their human dignity and installed unmerciful ferocity coupled with absolute tyranny. Centuries later, these traits were very much alive and transferred by the Russian soldier into the savage, take-no-prisoners nature of the warfare against the Turks, themselves no genteel warriors. The Turkish campaigns of 1736-39 and 1787-91 clearly illustrate the horrific brutality of the combats between the Russians and their southern neighbors.[19] Quarter was rarely asked or granted. Even when a besieged garrison of a town negotiated a surrender, the victor would ruthlessly cut down in cold blood not only the captives but the innocent townsfolk as well.[20]

Organization of a typical Russian Musketeer Regiment

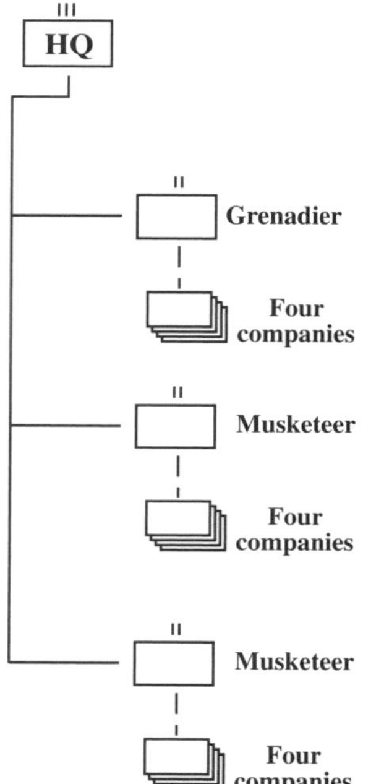

Regimental Organization

The Tsar's greencoated infantry were organized into companies, battalions and regiments. In all formations, four equal status companies comprised a battalion, and when at full strength all companies other than *jaeger* numbered approximately 180 officers and men.[21] Each *jaeger* company, if at maximum strength, totaled 120 officers and other ranks. Including staff, the theoretical establishment of all battalions other than *jaeger* was 738 combatants, whereas the *jaeger* (light infantry) battalions at full strength mustered just over 500 combatants.[22]

When combined with the headquarters, a full strength regiment other than *jaeger* boasted of three battalions numbering some 2,451 of all ranks.[23] Including

---

[16] Turgenev as quoted in Duffy, *Russia's Military Way to the West,* p. 236.
[17] *The Memoirs of Baron Thiébault,* translated and condensed by Arthur John Butler, 2 volumes (New York 1896), vol. 2, p. 167.
[18] Duffy, *Russia's Military Way to the West,* p. 2.
[19] Duffy, *Russia's Military Way to the West,* pp. 185-188.
[20] Duffy, *Russia's Military Way to the West,* p. 188.
[21] F. von Stein, *Geschichte des Russischen Heeres vom Ursprunge desselben bis zur Thronbesteigung des Kaisers Nikolai I. Pavlovich,* 2 volumes (Hanover 1885), vol. 1, p. 245.
[22] Stein, *Geschichte des Russischen Heeres,* vol. 1, p. 245.
[23] Stein, *Geschichte des Russischen Heeres,* vol. 1, p. 245.

all personnel at regimental headquarters, the weaker *jaeger* regiments numbered at full strength only 1,584 officers and men.[24] As with all nationalities, regimental headquarters consisted of the personnel necessary to administer the battalions of the regiment. In Russian regiments other than *jaeger*, these headquarters were a sanctioned haven for every type of sycophant known. Gaggles of these hangers-on—more than were needed to administer three battalions—crowded regimental headquarters and gave very little in return. *Jaeger* regiments, considered the scum of the army, had fewer people required at regimental headquarters and certainly fewer found *jaeger* regimental headquarters a desirable place to socialize.

Russian Imperial Guards

Owing to disease, straggling and previous casualties in the same campaign, few formations, if any, could ever maintain exact paper strength establishments in the field. Strengths fluctuated primarily due to the formation's march activity and combat casualties. Formations that had marched long and hard, or had sustained combat casualties, would often have far fewer men than the prescribed establishment. On the other hand, if the formation had been able to rest and recover its march stragglers as well as make up its prior combat losses with replacements newly arrived from the regimental depot battalion, then the field strength would be much closer to full strength. Therefore, owing to campaign circumstances, it was not unusual to see musketeer, fusilier and grenadier battalions with four full strength companies approaching 180 combatants early in a campaign as well as company strengths of only 120 or fewer combatants, especially after the battalions had been in the field for several weeks. *Jaeger* battalions typically fielded companies of 90 combatants or less as their administration was far less efficient, as well as the desertion and straggling rate being higher than other formations. Hence, Tsarist battalions in the 1805 through 1807 era ranged in strength from close to 700 to less than 300, with the average field strength being slightly below 500. Meanwhile, the lower quality *jaeger* battalions often numbered 500 or less. Langeron best summed up the differences between the theoretical strengths of the army and the actual number of men under arms when he wrote:

> In all the armies of Europe, there obtains a huge difference between the forces which exist on paper and those which actually appear under arms. But nowhere does this discrepancy reach such proportions as in Russia.[25]

Organization of a typical Russian Grenadier Regiment

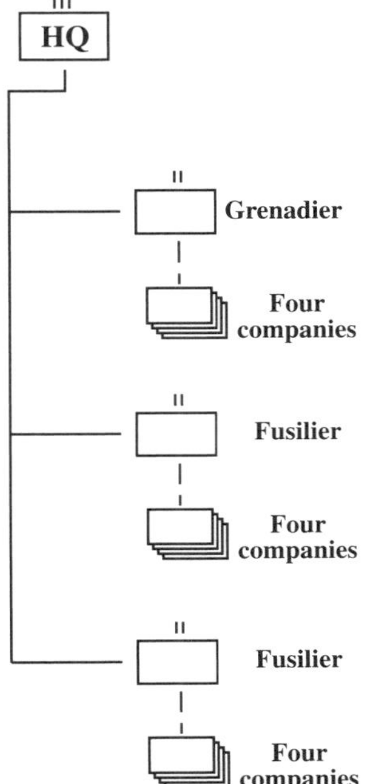

In 1805, the Tsar's armies numbered 77 regiments of infantry known as musketeers, 20 regiments of *jaeger*, 13 regiments of grenadiers and the Russian Imperial Guard. Every musketeer, *jaeger* and grenadier regiment possessed three field battalions.[26] In the musketeer regiments, two battalions were designated as musketeers and one battalion were grenadiers. Each grenadier regiment had two battalions called fusiliers and a single battalion of grenadiers. The *jaeger* regiments fielded three battalions of equal status troops—all known as *jaeger*.[27]

The infantry complement of the Russian Imperial Guard consisted of three regiments of 'heavy' infantry, of which two regiments—Semenovsky and Izmailovsky—had three field battalions whereas the Preobrazhensky Guard Regiment fielded four war battalions, although all four were not always present on campaign. Each of these regiments had one battalion of Guard Grenadiers while

---

[24] Stein, *Geschichte des Russischen Heeres,* vol. 1, p. 245.

[25] Langeron, as quoted in Duffy, *Russia's Military Way to the West,* p. 125.

[26] Stein, *Geschichte des Russischen Heeres,* vol. 1, see pp. 204-258.

[27] Duffy, *Austerlitz*, pp. 32-33; Stein, vol. 1, p. 214.

the remaining two battalions were Guard Fusiliers.[28] Completing the field formations of this élite body was the single battalion of Guard *Jaeger*. As with all *jaeger* formations of this period, the Guard *Jaeger* Battalion possessed a smaller establishment than the other Guard battalions. At full strength, the four companies of the Guard *Jaeger* fielded only 569 officers and other ranks.[29]

Every regiment possessed a single garrison battalion that was used to train recruits and feed replacements as needed into the field battalions. If a garrison battalion was filled up, it numbered some 866 people.[30] Garrison units did not accompany the army into the field, but remained in the Motherland and forwarded the replacements to the parent regiment.

Categories of Infantry

Four distinct categories of infantry were present in the Tsar's army in the 1805—1807 period. These were: 1) guard regiments; 2) grenadier regiments; 3) musketeer regiments; and 4) *jaeger* regiments.[31]

Numerically the smallest of the categories was also the most élite—the Russian Imperial Guard. Selection of rank and file Guardsmen was based almost solely on their imposing physique. Standing shoulder-to-shoulder in ranks sporting tall, distinctive headgear, the Guard gave a striking impression of a gargantuan phalanx.[32] Their officers were among the most privileged in Russian society.

Russian Grenadiers

Also considered élite troops were the grenadier regiments. Like the battalions of the Imperial Guard, these rough-and-ready formations were easily identifiable by their headgear—the mitre. Although only one of three battalions in each regiment was true grenadiers and wore the distinctive mitre caps, the two battalions of fusiliers also sported metal headgear—a shorter version of the mitre.[33] Although their education was uneven, the majority of grenadier regimental officers were combat-hardened and arguably the best infantry officers in Russian service. Non-commissioned officers of the grenadier regiments were proven veterans of many campaigns and helped shape the fighting legacy of these formations.

The most numerous infantry regiments in the army were the musketeers. While one of the three battalions within each regiment was designated as grenadier, Russia's foes did not consider the grenadiers of the musketeer regiments as the ferocious adversaries like their grenadier regiment namesakes. Further, the

---

[28] Stein, *Geschichte des Russischen Heeres,* vol. 1, p. 223; S.H.A.T., C^2 13. In March, 1800, the nomenclature of all the battalions within these three Guard regiments was officially changed to 'Grenadier.' Prior to this change, two battalions of each regiment had carried the title 'Musketeer' (Stein, p. 214), with one of the battalions designated as 'Grenadier.' The grenadier battalions of each Guard regiment would then be grouped together in the field to form the 'Guard Grenadiers,' as they were in 1805. However, despite the official nomenclature change five years earlier whereby all battalions of the Guard regiments were supposed to be called 'Grenadier,' the Russian Imperial Guard officers continued in 1805 to deploy the three battalions of the 'Guard Grenadiers' in a separate combat formation and referred to the other two battalions of each regiment as 'Fusilier'—the same name which two battalions of every the regular Grenadier Regiment carried—which was meant to be a higher designation than 'Musketeer.' Therefore, what might have been officially decreed (all battalions to be called 'Grenadier') was instead called something different ('Fusilier')—proof that decrees sometimes had a way of being changed.

[29] Stein, *Geschichte des Russischen Heeres,* vol. 1, p. 245.

[30] Stein, *Geschichte des Russischen Heeres,* vol. 1, p. 245.

[31] Duffy, *Austerlitz,* pp. 32-33; Stein, vol. 1, p. 245.

[32] W. Zweguintzow, *L'Armée Russe,* Part 4 (Paris 1973), p. 284; pp. 298-299 and uniform charts.

[33] Zweguintzow, p. 282 and uniform charts.

performance of musketeer battalions, wearing their bicorne hats,[34] was generally inferior to the fusilier battalions of the grenadier regiments. Naturally, there were notable exceptions, such as the Ryazan Musketeers; but the plain fact was that the most crucial underlying cause of poorer performances by many of the musketeer regiments was the scarcity of good officers. Most were uneducated and not motivated to excel in their positions. This is perhaps why one observer found that "the want of regimental officers is more felt in this army than in any other in Europe."[35]

Suvórov, who said: "To me, death is better than the defensive."

However, as poor as the officers were in the regiments of musketeers, they were not as bad as those dumped into the *jaeger* regiments. These officers, "disqualified by the neglect of education, and by the absence of accomplishments"[36] were either refused or turned out of all other infantry formations in the army and placed in the only regiments remaining—the *jaeger*. The discarding of the poorest officers in the service into the *jaeger* regiments, there to command the lowliest soldiers in Russian service, was further evidence of how these troops were considered to be the least trusted in an army defined by social classes. Steeped in all the trappings of 18th century military traditions, Russian tactical doctrine of this period still looked upon light infantry as a worthless and weak complement to formed battalions. So distrusted were the formations of *jaeger*, that they were not entrusted with flags unless they had distinguished themselves in battle.[37] As a result, the combat performances of the *jaeger* in the 1805 through 1807 era would rarely exceed the army's expectations.

Training

"The bayonet is a friend... the bullet is a fool."[38] From the first day of basic training, the words of Generalissimo Aleksandr Vasil'evich Suvórov (1729—1800) rang in the recruits' ears. Russian infantrymen were indoctrinated by drillmasters of the Suvórov school who sought to impress upon the young minds the total philosophy of the bayonet. Calling a musket ball that "crazy bitch,"[39] Suvórov wrote to the Austrians in 1799 that: "We must attack!!! Cold steel—bayonets and sabers! Push the enemy over, hammer them down, don't lose a moment!"[40] Such bloodthirsty exhortations were designed, no doubt, to carry Russian infantry through the defensive fire of the enemy, causing the enemy to collapse in front of the advancing ranks of bayonets. Not only was the superiority of cold steel preached

The storm of the Turkish fortress of Ochakov, 6 December 1788— one of Suvórov's victories

---

[34] There is absolutely no way that the Russian uniform changes decreed in 1805—some not decreed until late December 1805—could have ever been implemented in time for the Russian forces to use them in the Ulm-Austerlitz campaigns. Therefore, the musketeer battalions that marched into central Europe were still wearing their old bicorne headgear and not the new shako that was decreed in 1805 and appeared later. To get an appreciation of how long it took for new uniforms to appear in the field from the time they were decreed, please see Scott Bowden's "The 1812 French Uniform Myth," in *Empires Eagles & Lions,* July/August 1993. Also, refer to Zweguintzow's discussion of the musketeers headgear and his uniform charts.

[35] Sir Robert Wilson, *Brief Remarks on the Character and Composition of the Russian Army and a Sketch of the Campaigns in Poland in the Years 1806 and 1807* (London 1810), p. 44.

[36] Wilson, *Brief Remarks,* p. 43.

[37] Zweguintzow, *L'Armée Russe,* p. 329.

[38] Generalissimo Aleksandr Vasil'evich Suvórov, *Art of Victory* (Moscow 1806).

[39] Suvórov, *Art of Victory.*

[40] Generalissimo Aleksandr Vasil'evich Suvórov, *Dokumenty,* 4 volumes (Moscow 1949-1953), vol. 4, p. 13.

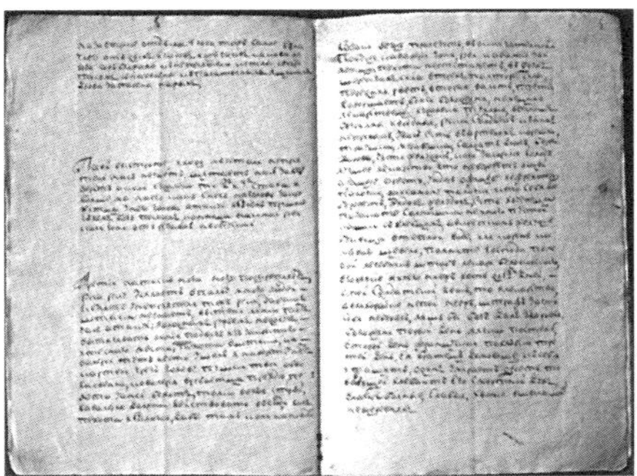

A copy of Suvórov's Art of Victory

to those new to the green uniform; the greatest possible emphasis on military bearing and appearance was also stressed to the men.[41]

According to the *Military Code Concerning the Field Service of Infantry* introduced on 29 November 1796 and for the most part faithfully adhered to until 1808,[42] the Russian soldier marched in the most martinet fashion. With his chest out and stomach in (considering the horrendously poor and scant diet of these men, the fact that his stomach was 'in' seems to be a given), the Russian infantryman marched with his right arm stiff and motionless down his side. Meanwhile, he held his left arm fully extended to hold the heavy 13-pound musket upright and 'goose-stepped'—no bending of the knees and slamming the toes to the ground—across the battlefield. Under ideal conditions, a Russian battalion in motion looked like a phalanx of automatons, their boots striking hard the ground at every beat of the drum cadence that paced out the slow 75 steps per minute march rate. At the urging of some generals, a 'quick' step of 120 paces per minute was added in 1803. However, the rigid, martial look so desired by Russian generals was too hard to keep at the faster pace for very long, causing the 'quick' pace to be reduced to a more manageable 90 steps per minute.

Paul's *Code* of 1796 "spoke of the importance of spurring on the troops by encouraging words, instead of belaboring them with the stick."[43] The following year Paul introduced his *Tactical Rules for Military Evolutions* that preached to the officers that: "The soldier must always be regarded as a human being... soldiers will do more for an officer who treats them well, and receives their trust, than for one whom they merely fear."[44] Suvórov was not amused to hear and read about Tsar Paul I's new-found sensitivity concerning the treatment of the men. While Suvórov was far ahead of other Russian officers in his bold and audacious approach to warfare, he had little use for Paul's *Code* of 1796, describing it as nothing more than "a rat-chewed parchment, found in a castle."[45]

Not surprisingly, the commander of the Russian army in 1805 was a Suvórov disciple. The 60-year-old Mikhail Ilariónovich Goleníchtchev Kutuzov reemphasized the philosophy of the attack with cold steel when on 18 October, he issued the following order:

> We shall often have to exploit the peculiar prowess of the Russians in bayonet attacks... during the attack with the bayonet the front of the formation is to be held as straight as possible, so that nobody will run ahead...[46]

Kutuzov poses before a portrait of Suvórov

Kutuzov was a consummate courtier among the Tsar and his young, impressionable sycophants. By the 1760's, Kutuzov had established his reputation for broad knowledge of infantry tactics. In 1782 as commander of the Bugskii *Jaeger* Corps, Kutuzov wrote a set of *Notes on Infantry Service in General, and that of Jaegers in Particular.* While he believed that the *jaeger* were better able to operate in areas of difficult terrain that were impractical for formed troops, Kutuzov's notes leave little doubt that the purpose of the Russian *jaegers'* life was secondary to the work of the cold steel by the troops of the main battle line.[47]

---

[41] Tsar Paul I was obsessed with the Frederician drill style of the mid-1700s, and his views filtered down the chain of command.
[42] Duffy, *Russia's Military Way to the West,* p. 205.
[43] Tsar Paul's *Code* as quoted in Duffy, *Russia's Military Way to the West,* p. 207.
[44] Tsar Paul's *Tactical Rules* as quoted in Duffy, *Russia's Military Way to the West,* p. 207.
[45] Duffy, *Russia's Military Way to the West,* p. 206.
[46] Mikhail Ilariónovich Goleníchtchev Kutuzov, *Sbornik Dokumentov,* 5 volumes (Moscow 1950-56), vol. 2, p. 96.
[47] Duffy, *Russia's Military Way to the West,* p. 184.

Immersed in the Suvórov school of the bayonet, Russian infantry up until 1807 spent little time on firepower exercises. Perhaps it was due, in part, to the multitude of different caliber small arms that were in use within the branch of service that made supply an unknown quantity. Other officers argued that the notoriously poor quality Russian powder further influenced the infantry tactics and minimized the fire power training for which a musket was most often used. Because of this philosophy it is therefore not surprising that when an attack could not be pressed home with the bayonet, or when enemy troops moved to within 80 to 150 yards and started a fire fight, Russian infantry were usually at a disadvantage.

Russian grenadiers assaulting

Russian reluctance to become proficient with small arms fire was also connected to the absence of light infantry training. Although the battalions of *jaeger* had shown substantial improvement in the campaigns of the 1770's against the Turks and Poles, the impetus of this new style warfare was dramatically reversed by Tsar Paul I, who had no use for light troops, and in 1799 reduced the number of *jaeger* to only a few companies.[48] When Alexander reconstituted the *jaeger*, they started anew and suffered from all the ills associated with regiments that were the least prestigious in the army. By 1805, no battalion—from Guard status to the lowly *jaeger*—were extensively trained in light infantry duties, which was combat in dispersed order and theoretically the special duty of the *jaeger*. In reality, Russian infantry were rarely allowed to deploy in open order, such as when infantry had to pass through thick woods or other type of formidable obstacles. Russian generals, however, would try to avoid maneuver near woods as it was thought that the cover would tempt too many to use the trees and underbrush as their avenue for desertion. The thought of placing in or near woods the regular *jaeger*—with the most negligent officers in the service commanding the most distrusted soldiers in the Tsar's uniform—was not even a consideration in 1805 unless a vigilant superior officer was present.

The absence of light infantry training was another trademark in which the Russian military leaders who clung to the traditions of the *ancien régime* could take pride. As part of the 18th century mentality that permeated the armies of old Europe, Russian light infantry were looked on as unnecessary and often unwelcome comrades to the shoulder-to-shoulder formed infantry that comprised the main battle line. The Russian officers reasoned the following: how could the *jaeger* fighting in dispersed order affect a battle decided by the courage and resolve of disciplined formed infantry who would advance invincibly, dispatching the enemy with cold steel? This philosophy, when confronted by a progressive-thinking and modern-trained adversary, rebounded on the Tsar's 1805 infantry with profound and unfavorable results.

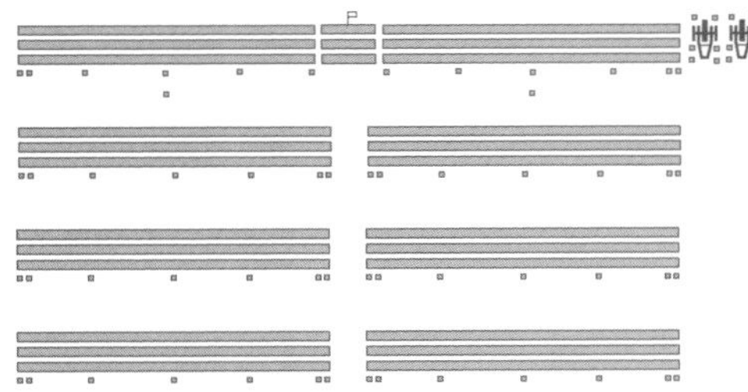

Russian battalion deployed in column. Note that each company was sub-divided into two half-companies. The two battalion guns are shown on the far right.

Infantry Deployments and Tactics

There were only three formations that Russian battalions would habitually use for battle—column by companies, line and square. A fourth formation—column of half-companies, was used in rare instances. The column of companies was the preferred formation for maneuver and attacks as it could most easily traverse terrain encountered on the majority of battlefields, as well as be transformed into square if threatened by enemy cavalry.[49] Therefore, a Russian battalion in column of companies would be 12 ranks deep (four companies, each company of three ranks) by however many files wide, which would of course depend on the strength of the companies. For example, a full-strength Russian infantry company of 180 officers and men would be arrayed three files (men) deep by almost 60 files wide (file closers not part of the file count). As in the armies of other countries, the Russian

[48] Stein, *Geschichte des Russischen Heeres,* vol. 1, pp. 204-228.

[49] Kutuzov, *Sbornik*, vol. 2, p. 95-97.

Russian battalion in line, facing left, with the battalion guns on the right flank

infantryman was deployed in ranks, shoulder-to-shoulder with his comrades on either side. Considering that the standard width of a single file (or man) was 20 inches, a full-strength Russian battalion of 738 combatants deployed in column of companies would be slightly more than 30 yards wide. Weaker battalions fielding approximately 500 combatants would have a frontage of approximately 23 yards when deployed in column of companies.

The combats of 1805 would show that deployment into line was not a preferred practice by the Tsar's officers. Undoubtedly, the main concern with these officers interested in offensive action was the restrictions imposed by low-quality troops and a wide infantry formation that had been deployed in line formation. Simply stated, when deployed in line, a battalion's width meant inevitable delays in traversing more difficult terrain that could be avoided by the battalion maneuvering in column. Furthermore, those delays would be exacerbated by the lower quality of the unit's men and training. When faced by an adversary drawn up in static positions such as a village, and with no threat of enemy cavalry interfering with their movements, Russian units would shake out into line.[50] A Russian battalion at full strength and deployed in line would be almost 240 files wide by three files deep, for a frontage of slightly less than 130 yards. A more typical example was a battalion approximately 500 strong; deployed in line, the unit would have a frontage of about 90 yards.

From their many years of fighting the wild, ferocious Turkish cavalry, veteran Russian officers and men knew well the drill of forming square and its value against mounted adversaries. The Russian infantry square formed either on a half-company front, which meant that each side of the square was six ranks deep, or on a full company front, reducing the square's depth to only three ranks. While such a formation held obvious advantages when pitted against enemy cavalry, the square certainly did not guarantee that the infantry who employed it would be impervious to a mounted attack. During several instances in the 1805 war, infantry battalions formed in square were broken by opposing cavalry. Also, infantry in square were at an obvious disadvantages when enemy infantry and artillery were nearby. A splendidly compact target, a square could be cut to pieces in no time by a well-served artillery company, or steadily whittled down by volleys of formed enemy troops, or tormented no end by sharpshooting skirmishers.

Russian battalion in square

Due to the nature of their drill system, the Tsar's infantry did not deploy into, nor could it perform maneuvers from, a two-company battalion front known in some other countries as a 'column of divisions.'[51] In theory, Russian companies were so strong that a single company could occupy the frontage of two weaker enemy companies, thereby occupying virtually the same frontage with a single company as other nationalities could with a column of divisions. This thinking ran into trouble when casualties or strategic consumption reduced the numbers within the battalion, thereby resulting in weaker companies and smaller battalion frontages.

Because of their commitment to the school of the bayonet and therefore to offensive warfare, Russian generals sought gently rolling terrain over which their battalions could attack. Rough ground, woods, marshes, swamps and other unfavorable terrain over which formed troops would have difficulty moving was avoided if at all possible. If such unfavorable terrain could not be avoided, tactical deployments would reflect the philosophy of an army still cemented in the *ancien régime.* For instance, woods that could provide useful cover were not used. Rather, Russian generals preferred to deploy their battalions forward of such undesirable terrain on ground suitable for offensive action. This preference was undoubtedly

[50] A good example of this is Langeron's combat management when attacking the village of Sokolnitz during the Battle of Austerlitz. Please see Chapter VIII.

[51] Curt Jany, "Der Russische Soldat im Felde 1806," in *Das Kasket,* Number 5 of 12 (Berlin and Vienna 1925). The Prussians had a similar drill system as well.

influenced by the fact that every Russian battalion of this era had two field pieces attached as battalion artillery. After 1805, the line *jaeger* battalions often were seen with two small 2-pounder licornes attached. However, in 1805, all infantry battalions other than the line jaeger ideally had either two 6-pounder cannon or 10-pounder licornes attached as battalion artillery.[52]

Also, every battalion other than *jaeger* were entrusted with two flags of the 1803 pattern, the colors of which varied by the recruiting area, or Inspection, of the regiment. What was consistent, however, was that each regiment had one flag with a 'white' field, while the remaining five flags had 'colored' fields. Therefore, each musketeer, grenadier and Guard regiment had a total of six flags.[53]

Ad hoc Brigades and Columns

In the finest traditions of *ancien régime* armies, there existed no permanent command structure in the Russian army above the regiment. Several regiments, however, were assigned to brigades that were nothing more than *ad hoc* commands in which the composition would change whenever there was a battle.[54] Two or more brigades were combined to form a column. Also an *ad hoc* formation was the column's composition which would change as frequently as did the makeup of the brigades that comprised the column. Each brigade and column were commanded by one of the army's general officers, and these officers would receive revised regimental and brigade assignments from army headquarters without any advance warning.

The rationale behind this seemingly capricious and arbitrary way of grouping regiments was an attempt to allow complete flexibility in the assigning of the army's assets based on the daily situation. Column deployments, which determined where the brigades and regiments were to occupy what portion of the line and their relative positions to the other units, were usually determined the night before the battle. Any changes to the deployment had to be made on an as-needed basis at the regimental level.

The weaknesses of this *ad hoc* system of command became evident once the column became engaged with the enemy and the regiments began interacting with their adversaries. Response to any crisis, or exploitation of any gain, was limited to the regiment. Therefore, the very nature of the brigade's and the column's command structure was its greatest weakness. What's more, Russian officers were victims of their own social order. Unwilling to establish a routine working relationship with other officers of outside commands who were of lesser social stature than themselves, they could do little to coordinate units from different regiments. What's more, brigades often consisted of mixed troop-types (infantry and cavalry), rather than just infantry or exclusively cavalry. Mixed brigades often restricted cavalry, or placed the horsemen under command of an infantry general who compromised rather than complemented the qualities of the cavalry. The ultimate result of the *ad hoc* command structure, coupled with the mind-set of the regimental army system, was that generals commanding the brigades and columns could not effect most coordinated maneuvers between their own combat formations while in the face of the enemy.

---

[52] Consult the Appendices for Orders of Battle details concerning these battalion pieces.

[53] General C. R. Andolenko, *Aigles de Napoléon Contre Drapeaux du Tsar 1799, 1805-1807, 1812-1814* (Paris 1969), p. 18.

[54] An excellent example of this can be seen in Chapter VI when Kutuzov changes the composition of his various columns for the Battle of Dürenstein.

The Cavalry

Its Background and Makeup

Throughout the 18th century, the Russian mounted arm suffered from a combination of poor quality of horseflesh as well as the indifference and criminality of its colonels. To make matters worse, "the stock of native horses was not only small in numbers, but poor in quality, which had far reaching consequences for the tactical efficiency, security and logistic support of the army."[55] Furthermore, the horses that were supplied to the army suffered from malnourishment and lack of exercise, which resulted in completely feeble mounts and inexperienced riders. If not on campaign, the indolent colonels—privileged nobles of Romanov society—made their regiments mount up only five or six times a year! Count Alexandre Langeron, a French *émigré* serving in the Russian army, was so unimpressed with the Tsar's cavalry that he could name only four regimental commanders who were actually capable of staying in the saddle.[56]

The Russian Imperial Eagle

The troopers who comprised the regiments of the line came from backgrounds similar to that of the infantry, although most already with some knowledge of horses and their care. Conscripted serfs were screened for any horsemanship abilities, and those who possessed knowledge about animals were sent into that branch of service. The size of the men also determined into which regiments of line cavalry they would serve. The biggest and strongest of the men who were judged to be good candidates for the cavalry were sent into the regiments of *cuirassiers*. Big men on big horses, the *cuirassier* regiments were trained for heavy fighting and took their place in the battle line beside other regiments of the line. Men of medium build with better than average horsemanship skills were candidates for the regiments of hussars and uhlans. Although specifically trained for outpost, reconnaissance and screening duties, the hussars and uhlans were needed and, for the most part, very useful on the battlefield. The smallest men, as well as those of medium build with the least amount of mounted skills, were sent into the line regiments that were the lowest in the pecking order—the dragoons. In keeping with armies tied to the philosophies of the *ancien régime*, Russian dragoons not only possessed the least desirable troopers, but also the smallest animals, all of which were commanded by the least experienced officers of the line.[57]

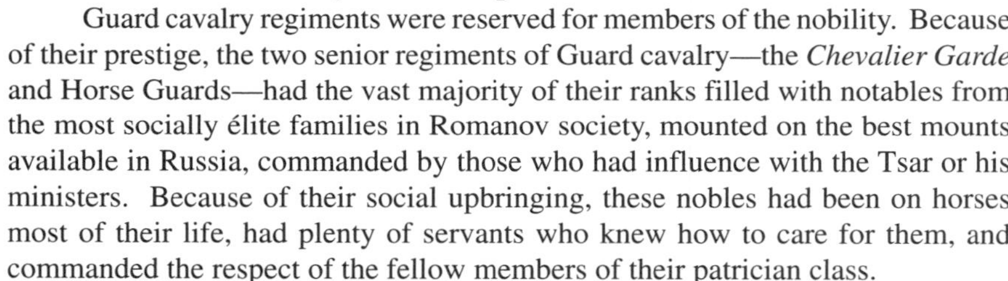

Guard cavalry regiments were reserved for members of the nobility. Because of their prestige, the two senior regiments of Guard cavalry—the *Chevalier Garde* and Horse Guards—had the vast majority of their ranks filled with notables from the most socially élite families in Romanov society, mounted on the best mounts available in Russia, commanded by those who had influence with the Tsar or his ministers. Because of their social upbringing, these nobles had been on horses most of their life, had plenty of servants who knew how to care for them, and commanded the respect of the fellow members of their patrician class.

While the regiments of the Guard and line constituted the regular cavalry forces of the Russian army, they were augmented by many regiments of peasant irregulars from the steppe—the Cossacks. Swarms of these natural horsemen were a concern to any foe due to their disregard for the rules of war as understood by most Europeans. The Cossacks were happiest when on outpost duty and therefore removed from the watchful eye of army regulars;[58] guarding the flanks of the

---

[55] Duffy, *Russia's Military Way to the West,* p. 235. The Russians had long suffered from a lack of quality as well as quanity of mounts. From Zorndorf to Zürich during the 18th century, and continuing throughout the Napoleonic wars, the size and strength of the Russian horses were constant problems facing the Tsar's commanders.

[56] Duffy, *Russia's Military Way to the West,* p. 198.

[57] S.H.A.T., C^2 13.

[58] Duffy, *Austerlitz,* p. 35.

army while marauding the countryside, terrorizing the local populace, and capturing and torturing enemy stragglers were their specialties. If they were on the battlefield, Cossacks preferred opportunistic charges against the flanks or rear of enemy troops, usually running from any enemy cavalry who presented an ordered front. The Cossacks' dislike for a formed cavalry's front would only be exceeded by their utter distaste for receiving enemy artillery fire. As a result, it was difficult to employ them for any frontline battlefield duty. Instead, they were most often seen on the far flanks or in the rear.

Regimental Organization

All formations of Russian cavalry were organized into regiments, squadrons and companies. The *cuirassiers* and most dragoons were regiments of the line that were organized into five squadrons, each squadron consisting of two companies.[59] When at full strength and including the regimental headquarters, a *cuirassier* regiment fielded 1,054 officers and men, while all but three dragoon regiments could boast 1,062 combatants.[60] Three dragoon regiments possessed a larger establishment of 10 squadrons, each with regimental strengths of 1,897.[61] Therefore, each squadron of *cuirassiers* or dragoons was supposed to consist of approximately 180 combatants, with company strengths of approximately 90. Hussar regiments fielded 10 two-company squadrons of about 180 officers and men per squadron with each company of 90 combatants. Including regimental headquarters, each hussar regiment had a theoretical establishment of 1,889 of all ranks.[62] There was also a regiment of Lithuanian Tartars totaling 1,898 and a regiment of Polish uhlans (lancers) which at full strength numbered 1,513 officers and other ranks.[63] Both the Lithuanians and Poles had 10-squadron regimental establishments, but the Poles had a much harder time finding personnel for the Tsar's service and therefore had smaller squadrons. A third regiment of uhlans was raised in 1803 and named for the Tsar's brother, Grand Duke Constantine, and consisted of 10 squadrons.

Russian Infantry Standards— the first battalion (the Grenadier Battalion in the Grenadier and in the Musketeer Regiments) carried one of the 'white' flags above as well as one the colored ones below; other battalions carried two colored flags

In 1803, Tsar Alexander decided to reorganize his heavy cavalry. There simply weren't enough large horses to adequately mount all the regiments of *cuirassiers*, and these regiments proved a burden on the government's treasury. Therefore, Alexander sought to lessen the strain of the mounted arm on the government's purse strings by reducing the number of expensive cuirassier regiments from 13 to six while increasing the number of dragoon regiments from 12 to 22. All seven of the regiments that were no longer to be kept as *cuirassiers* were converted to dragoon regiments.[64] The sum of these changes increased the number of heavy cavalry regiments from 25 to 28, while lowering the cost to field the increased number of horsemen. Because *cuirassier* regiments demanded the largest and most expensive horses possible, it was reasoned that whatever was lost in quality by the reduction in the number of *cuirassier* regiments, the overall effectiveness of the arm would be improved by the increased number of dragoon regiments.

It was also before the end of 1803 that depot squadrons were established for the regiments of the line. Each regiment of dragoons and *cuirassier* had a depot company, numbering 89 for the *cuirassiers* and 93 for the dragoons. Each hussar regiment had established a depot squadron of 150.[65] As in other countries, these

---

[59] Stein, *Geschichte des Russischen Heeres,* vol. 1, pp.229-245.
[60] Stein, *Geschichte des Russischen Heeres,* vol. 1, p. 245.
[61] Stein, *Geschichte des Russischen Heeres,* vol. 1, p. 245.
[62] Stein, *Geschichte des Russischen Heeres,* vol. 1, p. 245.
[63] Stein, *Geschichte des Russischen Heeres,* vol. 1, p. 245.
[64] Stein, *Geschichte des Russischen Heeres,* vol. 1, pp. 252-253.
[65] Stein, *Geschichte des Russischen Heeres,* vol. 1, p. 245 and 252.

Pistols and sabretache of the Russian hussars

depot formations existed for the purpose of forwarding replacements to their respective regiments during campaigns.

Guard cavalry regiments had five squadrons, each squadron of two companies. At full strength, the *Chevalier Garde* regiment fielded 991 of all ranks, the Horse Guards numbered 1,000, the Guard Hussars had 990 and the Guard Cossacks had 560.[66]

Regiments of Cossacks had varying numbers of squadrons and squadron strengths, although it was most common to see Cossack regiments take the field with five squadrons. At full strength, each Cossack squadron was supposed to field between 90 to 100 combatants. However, the realities of campaigning resulted in the Cossacks having squadron strengths much closer to 40 to 50 people.

Like the Cossacks, almost all cavalry formations rarely maintained their theoretical establishments while on campaign. Their field strengths fluctuated widely based on a variety of factors, including quality of officers and NCOs, the distances and the rapidity of marches which the unit had conducted, and much more.

Categories of Cavalry

Four distinct categories of cavalry were present in the Tsar's army in the 1805—1807 period. These were: 1) guard regiments; 2) line heavy regiments; 3) line light regiments; and 4) Cossack regiments.

As in the infantry, numerically the smallest of the categories was also the most élite—the Russian Imperial Guard. The Tsar's Guard cavalry—the noblest regiments of horse in Europe—were the social register of Romanov society. The most prominent families of Saint Petersburg served in the regiments of *Chevalier Garde* and Horse Guards. Noblemen of lesser stature, as well as some officers of low birth, served in the regiment of Guard Hussars and Guard Cossacks. As the *Chevalier Garde* and Horse Guards officers were arguably *the* most privileged in Russian society, they afforded themselves of every luxury, even while on campaign. These officers would bring servants of every kind in addition to whatever female companionship they had arranged.

Cossacks

Among the line heavy regiments, the *cuirassiers* were considered a genuine body of élite cavalry, generally better officered and mounted in 1805 than they were at any time during the 18th century. Undoubtedly, the finest *cuirassier* regiment in the 1805 Russian army was the Leib-*Cuirassier* ("Tsar's") which was recruited in the Saint Petersburg area. As improved as the *cuirassiers* were, the numerous dragoon regiments were still feeble regiments, bearing the designation of heavy cavalry in name only. Possessing smaller, weaker animals ridden by the smallest cavalrymen in the service, the dragoons were officered by men of lower social class. As a result, the dragoon regiments were the dregs of the Russian line cavalry and very few had good reputations.[67] Instead, the dragoons suffered from the class-bound barriers of society that were ever present in the Tsar's army.

Possibly the most valuable of the Tsar's line cavalry were the excellent regiments of hussars. Vastly improving since the late 18th century, the Russian hussars were, by 1805, as good as any light cavalry in Europe when it came to screening and scouting. However, it was their battlefield performance that *could* impress friend and foe alike, depending upon the quality of the unit's officers and NCOs. Russian generals had little choice but to employ their precious hussars as battle cavalry. This was brought about since the dragoons were only marginally effective and the numbers of *cuirassier* regiments and Guard cavalry were few.

---

[66] Stein, *Geschichte des Russischen Heeres,* vol. 1, p. 245.

[67] S.H.A.T., C^2 13.

Also considered line light cavalry were three regiments of uhlans. One of these regiments—the Grand Duke Constantine Uhlans—had been converted in 1803 from a hussar regiment. Additionally, there were the Lithuanian Tartars (five squadrons of this regiment were defined as Tartars and carried the lance, while five other squadrons without the lance were designated as light horse) and the Polish Uhlan Regiment.

On paper, the Russian army could call upon a vast population of Cossacks for service with the army. In 1805, there were 100,000 of these mounted men on the army's registers. They were divided into two groups: the irregular, nomadic Cossacks of Asiatic and Mongol descent; and settled, Caucasian Cossack regiments.[68] The irregular, nomadic Cossacks could number as many as 55,000 men in service to the Tsar. The most famous of these regiments came from the Don, with others recruited from Siberia, the Bug, Orenburg, the Urals and Astrakhan. A Cossack group considered more civilized was called 'settled Caucasians.'[69] Numbering on paper some 45,000, this group came from the Volga and Mosdok regions, and included Christianized Kalmucks.[70] Despite the vast number of Cossacks supposedly available, only a relative few were brought westward with the army in 1805.

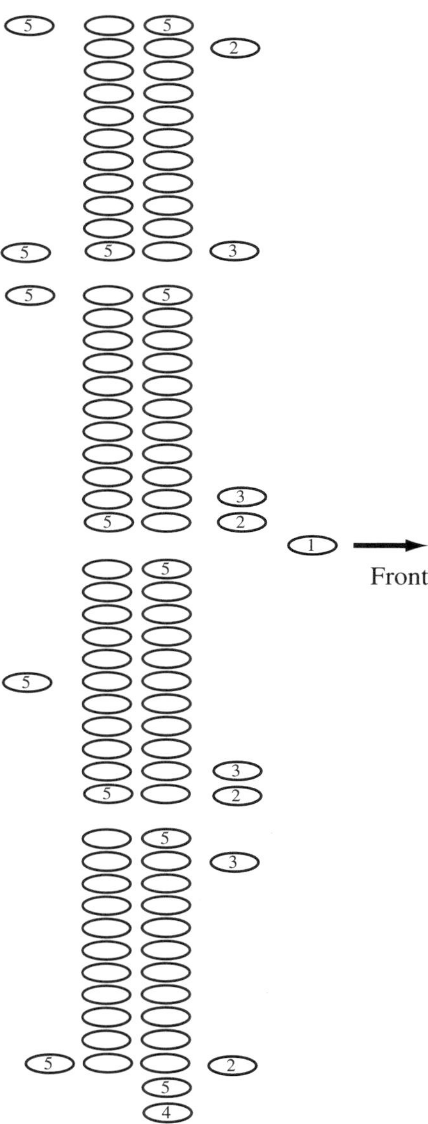

Russian Cavalry Squadron in line

1—Squadron commander
2—Platoon Commander
3—2nd in command of platoon
4—Trumpeter
5—Under Officers

Cavalry Deployment and Tactics

Russian cavalry deployed their formations according to the 1796 *Code of Field Cavalry Service* in which Tsar Paul I decreed that "the company or squadron is always arranged in two ranks, for experience shows that the third rank is useless—it impedes nearly all movements, and when anybody falls it proves dangerous to rider and horse."[71] All regiments were to be on the move when they met the enemy, never to receive a charge while standing. If attacking, the heavy cavalry gradually built up speed with a number of gaits. A walk was increased to a trot, then to a slow gallop, increasing to a 'course' (canter), and then to a full gallop. Inside 100 yards from the enemy, the commander ordered the trumpeter to sound the charge and the troopers raised their swords to fall upon the foe.[72] Depending upon the tactical situation, charge gaits were modified by a number of factors, including condition of the troops designated to charge, distance to cover during the charge, position of the enemy and their quality (if known). Smoke and the noise of battle also affected how the charge was executed. In any case, actual combat rarely reflected parade-ground style maneuvers. Nevertheless, when formed boot-to-boot, a cavalry formation's frontage would typically be 36 to 40-inches frontage per file (in this case, a man on horseback).

Starting in 1799, colonels who used to discharge their duties with indifference were slowly weeded out of service and replaced with more competent, aggressive commanders. These new commanding officers routinely put their charges through mock battles, improving the mettle of their regiments.[73]

Maneuvers were executed by company, squadron or regiment. Company and squadron sized maneuvers were especially favored when opposed to enemy infantry, as these smaller units were used to move against any exposed flanks.[74] Due to the nature of the army, coordination above the regimental level was virtually unknown. Even the splendid looking regiments of the Russian Imperial Guard,

---

[68] Duffy, *Austerlitz,* p. 35; Stein, vol. 1, p. 230.
[69] An excellent overview of the Cossacks can be found in Duffy, *Russia's Military Way to the West,* pp. 157-164; Seton-Watson, p. 57.
[70] Stein, *Geschichte des Russischen Heeres,* vol. 1, p. 230.
[71] Russian General Staff, Part 4, Book 1, Section 3, iii, as quoted in Duffy, *Austerlitz,* p. 34.
[72] Russian General Staff, Pt 4, Bk 1, Sec 3, iii, described in Duffy, *Austerlitz,* pp. 34-35.
[73] S.H.A.T., C^2 13.
[74] Russian General Staff, Pt 4, Bk 1, Sect 3, iii, as described in Duffy, *Austerlitz,* p. 35.

who enjoyed a permanency of brigade assignment unknown to the other regiments of cavalry, did little to conduct joint maneuvers.

Regiments of Russian horse were often grouped into columns and brigades alongside infantry regiments. The theory of combining infantry and cavalry under a single tactical command was as old as the *cohors equitatae* of the Imperial Roman army. However, logistical considerations as well as the battlefield environment in the horse and musket era made such arrangements impractical. For starters, regimental commanders had no experience in working with one another. This was compounded by the different supply needs for the cavalry and infantry regiments. *Ancien régime* armies also were saddled with class differences that existed between the cavalry arm and the infantry officer corps, exacerbated by a hostile battlefield environment that was clouded by and choked with smoke. Even when brigades were composed entirely of cavalry, there still existed the problems inherent in the lack of inter-regimental coordination. It is therefore little wonder that the Russian army of this era had difficulty coordinating movements between regiments once the action was joined.

The Artillery
Its Background, Makeup and Command

Arakcheev

Although the Russian artillery suffered throughout the 18th century from the lack of consistent direction and care, by 1802 those empowered to oversee the service were committed to its improvement. The massive reform began with Alexander's ascent to the throne when he named General Alexei A. Arakcheev as the new Inspector General of Artillery.[75] Arakcheev immediately went to work redesigning the antiquated Russian guns with improved, lighter gun carriages and caissons that were inspired by the French Gribeauval system. He also redesigned the tubes of ordnance with light and medium versions of the 6- and 12-pounder cannon, and reduced the number of unicorns (hereafter referred to as licornes, which were long barreled howitzers) to 2-, 10- and 18-pounders.[76]

By 1805, the ordnance of Arakcheev's new artillery system was in place with the Russian forces that saw action in Europe. The newly manufactured pieces, well designed and solidly built, were significantly heavier than French guns of similar caliber.[77] Despite this shortcoming, the system of 1805 reflected definite improvements over the previous Russian ordnance. However, beyond the close-in

---

[75] This was Arakcheev's second time to hold the title of Inspector General of Artillery. His first was from 4 January to 1 October, 1799. Grotesque and barbaric, Aracheev was infamous for his horrendously brutal treatment of officers and men of the artillery arm, examples of which are detailed in Chapter VI. His ouster in 1799 occurred when he tried to cover up the incompetence of one of his brothers.

[76] The licornes are given these designations based on the weight of the projectile that they threw. The official designation for the heaviest Russian licorne was 'half pud,' while the medium weight licorne was slightly more than a 'quarter pud.' To be precise, the Germans state that the medium Russian licorne was a 12-pfund piece. To convert the weight, one pud was equal to 40 German pfunds, which was also equal to 16.38 kilograms. Since one kilogram is equal to 2.2046 pounds, the conversion goes like this: One pud = 16.38 kg; Thus, 16.38 kg x 2.2046 = 36.111 pounds. Therefore, if one pud is 36.111 pounds, the half pud, or heaviest, licorne is an 18-pounder.

To convert the weight for the medium licorne—which threw a projectile weighing 12 pfund—goes like this: 40 pfund is 16.38 kilograms, therefore 12 pfund is the same as 4.914 kilograms. Thus, 4.914 kg x 2.2046 = 10.833 pounds, or a 10-pounder. The smallest licorne, which the Germans detail as throwing a three pfund weight projectile, converts thusly: since 40 pfund is 16.38 kilograms, three pfund is 1.228 kg; therefore, 1.228 x 2.2046 = 2.70 pounds, called in this text a 2-pounder.

[77] S.H.A.T., 2w 84 and 4w 68 compare the Russian 1805 ordnance with the System Year XI pieces.

canister range, the new cannon and licornes were still no match for comparable French pieces. While the medium 6- and 12-pounder guns had range shorter than the French, the lighter models of 6- and 12-pounders—with shorter barrels—had a woefully shorter striking distance than Napoleon's 6-, 8- and 12-pounder cannon. Similarly, the new licornes were a disappointment insofar as their range was concerned, but did impress everyone when the crews were close enough to fire canister. Without a doubt, part of the problem with the range of the Russian ordnance was attributed to the inferior quality of gunpowder that had long plagued Tsarist gunners.[78] The root of the problem stemmed from the Russian's poor quality of saltpeter, or potassium nitrate. The choices of the earth selected and the artificial means employed to obtain the saltpeter—coupled with the nitrate production works themselves—combined to produce a very dirty, inferior gunpowder.[79] A comparison of Russian and French ordnance used during the 1805—1807 period is detailed on the following chart.

Models of Russian Ordnance

Comparison of Russian and French Ordnance in 1805[80]
Ranges Shown are in Meters

Poundage	Ordnance System	Canister	Round-Shot (Practical)	Round-Shot (Maximum)	Shell
2 Lic	Russian 1805	200	—	—	700
4	French Gribeauval	400	800	1250	—
6 Lt	Russian 1805	350	850	1300	—
6 Med	Russian 1805	450	1000	1600	—
6	French Year XI	500	1200	1850	—
8	French Gribeauval	550	1500	2400	—
10 Lic	Russian 1805	300	—	—	1300
12 Lt	Russian 1805	500	1200	1800	—
12 Med	Russian 1805	550	1600	2000	—
12	French Year XI	600	1850	2700	—
12	French Gribeauval	600	1800	2600	—
18 Lic	Russian 1805	400	—	—	1500
6 p. how.	French Gribeauval	250	—	—	1300
5 p. 4, 6 or 7 liv. how.	French Year XI	250	—	—	1200
6 p. 4 liv how	French Year XI	300	—	—	1500

The men who manned the Russian pieces were selected from the strongest of the annual recruits. Big men with strong physiques, they were naturals for service in the artillery. These striking figures cut a distinctly martial look that

[78] Voenno-Istoritjeskij Musej Artillerij, Insjenernich Woisk i Woisk Swjasi (Military Museum of Artillery, Pioneers and Signal troops), Saint Petersburg.

[79] Semen R. Vorontsov, 'Zapiski S. R. Vorontsov o Russkom Voiske, Predstavlennaya Imperatoru Aleksandru Palvlovichu v 1802 godu,' *Arkiv Knyazya Vorontsova,* 40 Volumes (Moscow 1870-1895), X, pp. 449-456. Hereafter referred to as 'Zapiski.'

[80] As might be expected, the French did extensive testing with the captured ordnance of the new Russian 1805 system. General Ruty found the Russian carriages to be "exceptionally sturdy," but their range "is decidedly inferior to our pieces." See S.H.A.T., 2w 84 and 4w 68. Note that the listed maximum ranges are for direct firing, including ricochet distance. If favorable, the slope of the ground could increase the ricochet distance, as it did for the Russians at Schöngrabern.

Cut-away view of a Russian 18-pounder licorne

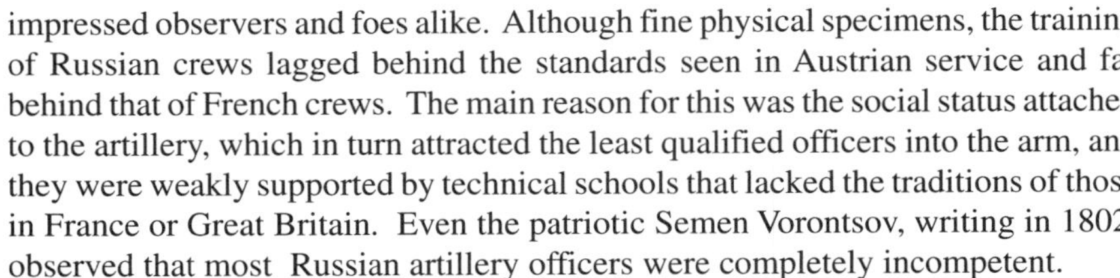

impressed observers and foes alike. Although fine physical specimens, the training of Russian crews lagged behind the standards seen in Austrian service and far behind that of French crews. The main reason for this was the social status attached to the artillery, which in turn attracted the least qualified officers into the arm, and they were weakly supported by technical schools that lacked the traditions of those in France or Great Britain. Even the patriotic Semen Vorontsov, writing in 1802, observed that most Russian artillery officers were completely incompetent.

> I have known some officers who were totally ignorant of what elevation to give their cannon for ricochet fire. As for the science of higher mathematics—so indispensable for mortar fire, where you have to calculate the trajectory of the bombs—it is something totally unknown to us.[81]

The best of the Russian artillery officers were found in the Imperial Guard Horse Artillery, with the companies of line horse artillery possessing mostly competent officers. The officers commanding the mobile companies fought their commands as one unit as well as in half-batteries, which required more know-how than the officers of the same rank in the foot artillery companies, most of which were broken up into sections to serve as battalion artillery.

To command technical troops such as the artillery was considered a bourgeois, dirty job that held little attraction for most Romanov nobles. Artillery, it was reasoned, was nothing more than support for the glittering ranks of advancing bayonets and sabers. Consequently, artillery and other technical officer positions garnered those with the least education and status in Russian society. Tolstoy's Captain Tushin, who was blamed for having fought too long at Schöngrabern during the 1805 campaign, serves as a splendid prototype of the low esteem in which artillery officers were held by the generals throughout the army.[82]

Organization and Categories of Artillery

Russian artillery was organized into regiments, battalions and companies.[83] In 1805, there were nine regiments of line foot artillery, numbered one through nine, each of two battalions. Every line foot battalion consisted of four companies of which two were designated as heavy companies and two were light companies.[84] In each heavy company there were four 18-pounder licornes, two 2-pounder licornes and eight 12-pounder cannon, four of which were called medium and four were called light. Therefore, each heavy company had a total of 14 pieces of ordnance, although the 2-pounder licornes *never* served alongside the rest of the company.[85] Each light company had 12 pieces of ordnance consisting of four 10-pounder licornes and eight 6-pounder cannon of which four were called medium and four were called light. In sum, the Tsar's entire line foot artillery establishment numbered 72 companies; half of these were 12-pounder companies and half of were 6-pounder companies, for a total of 936 pieces of ordnance.[86]

Russian 18-pounder licorne

During the wars against Revolutionary France, the Russians were greatly impressed by the performance of the French horse artillery.[87] In response, the Tsar's ministers decided to double the strength of their own line horse artillery by

---

[81] Vorontsov, 'Zapiski,' *Arkiv Knyazya Vorontsova,* X, 483-484.
[82] Leo Tolstoy, *War and Peace,* Penguin Classics Series (New York 1978), pp. 219-229.
[83] Stein, *Geschichte des Russischen Heeres,* vol. 1, p. 249.
[84] Stein, *Geschichte des Russischen Heeres,* vol. 1, p.249.
[85] This is born out in after-action reports and regimental histories as well as the report of captured Russian ordnance during the 1805 campaign.
[86] Stein, *Geschichte des Russischen Heeres,* vol. 1, p. 249.
[87] S.H.A.T., C^2 13.

increasing the establishment from a single battalion to two battalions. Each battalion consisted of five companies, each company with 12 pieces of ordnance. In all companies of line horse artillery, half the company consisted of 10-pounder licornes, the remaining six pieces were the light 6-pounder cannon. Therefore, the Russian army's entire compliment of line horse artillery numbered ten companies with a total of 120 pieces of ordnance.[88]

Cut-away view of a Russian 12-pounder

The artillery of the Russian Imperial Guard consisted of a single battalion of five companies. Two of these companies were heavy foot; two companies were light foot and one was a horse company. In 1805, there were 11 pieces in every Guard heavy company. Four pieces were 18-pounder licornes, one was a 2-pounder licorne and six were 12-pounder cannon—four medium and two light. As with the companies of the line, the 2-pounder licornes in the Guard heavy companies did not unlimber for action alongside the other pieces of their parent company, but were relegated to protect the massive baggage trains. In 1805, the two Guard light foot companies as well as the horse artillery company each consisted of 10 pieces, of which five were 10-pounder licornes and five were 6-pounder cannon, the foot companies having the medium version and the horse artillery having the light version of that gun. Therefore, all five companies of the Guard artillery fielded a total of 52 pieces of ordnance.[89]

Organization of Russian Artillery—1805[90]

	Poundage of Guns					
Unit Designation	2-pdr. Lic	6-pr Lt/Md	10-pdr. Lic	12-pdr. Lt	12-pdr. Med	18-pdr. Lic
Guard Hvy Foot Company	1	-	-	2	4	4
Guard Light Foot Company	-	0 / 5	5	-	-	-
Guard Horse Company	-	5 / 0	5	-	-	-
Line Heavy Foot Company	2	-	-	4	4	4
Line Light Foot Company	-	4 / 4	4	-	-	-
Line Horse Company	-	6 / 0	6	-	-	-

With all companies at full strength, the Tsar's artillery arm numbered a total of 1,108 pieces of ordnance[91] of which 152 were 18-pounder licornes, 219 were 10-pounder licornes, 74 were 2-pounder licornes, 152 were medium 12-pounder cannon, 148 were light 12-pounder cannon, 154 were medium 6-pounder cannon and 209 were light 6-pounder cannon. If converted into percentages, 41% of the army's ordnance were licornes while the remaining 59% were cannon. Specifically, almost 14% of the Tsar's ordnance were 18-pounder licornes, 20% were 10-pounder licornes, 7% were 2-pounder licornes, 14% were medium 12-pounder cannon, 13% were light 12-pounder cannon, 14% were medium 6-pounder cannon and 18% light 6-pounder cannon.

Russian 12-pounder

Artillery Deployment and Tactics

The deployment of Russian artillery was typical for that of armies tied to the philosophies of the 18th century. Heavy companies, as well as 6-pounder foot companies operating as a single unit, were usually batteries of position because

[88] Stein, *Geschichte des Russischen Heeres,* vol. 1, pp. 249-250.
[89] Stein, *Geschichte des Russischen Heeres,* vol. 1, p. 250.
[90] Stein, *Geschichte des Russischen Heeres,* vol. 1, pp. 249-250. Also, please consult the Orders of Battle in the Appendices.
[91] Stein, *Geschichte des Russischen Heeres,* vol. 1, p. 250.

their mobility was severely limited due to the weight of the pieces. When used in a mobile capacity, there were often significant difficulties for the drivers of the 18-pounder licornes and 12-pounder cannon to keep up with the march pace of the infantry while traveling cross-country. Faced with the choice of moving on without the heavy guns or slowing the march pace, column commanders would usually slow the other troops under their command so as not to leave the precious heavy guns behind. When in action, the heavy companies were used in various roles from counter battery suppression to direct fire support. Whether employed as a position battery or in a mobile role, only the 12-pounder cannons and 18-pounder licornes served as part of the homogeneous heavy company. The 2-pounder licornes that were, on paper, part of these heavy companies were *always* detached for separate service, usually to protect the numerous baggage trains. By 1807, at the suggestion of Prince Bagration, two such licornes were usually attached to a *jaeger* battalion as its artillery.[92]

The Russians had been totally committed to the idea of battalion artillery long before the 1805 campaign. It was believed that two pieces directly supporting each battalion significantly augmented the battalion's firepower and improved the men's morale. While it is debatable if the artillery actually improved battalion morale, there can be no doubt that the two pieces attached to each battalion did improve the formation's volume of fire.[93] However, such an arrangement made it impossible to concentrate the firepower of these various battalion pieces.

The ribbon and cross of the Order of St.George, 1st Class, instituted in 1769

In order to provide the infantry battalions with ordnance, the light foot companies designated to support the units of foot were broken into six sections, two pieces serving in each section and attached to a designated battalion. Therefore, a line light foot company with its 12 total pieces—four 10-pounder licornes and eight 6-pounder cannon—supplied six battalions, or two regiments of musketeers and/or grenadiers, with their direct artillery support. This meant that of the six battalions within two such regiments, four battalions would each have two 6-pounder guns while the remaining two battalions would each have two 10-pounder licornes in support. The two companies of Guard light foot, totaling 20 pieces of ordnance, supplied the battalion artillery for the 10 battalions of infantry in the Russian Imperial Guard. As previously mentioned, the 2-pounder licornes were, by 1807, the battalion artillery for the line *jaeger,* no doubt because their diminutive caliber being of little value and to use them with the *jaeger* was better than relegating them to the baggage trains. However, there is no indication that such an accommodation was made in 1805. Thus, the Russian generals completed their philosophical position vis-à-vis the *jaeger* and their status and importance in the army—they would have the weakest guns available as their battalion artillery.

Horse artillery was deployed by either half-companies or by the entire company. Invariably, Russian line horse artillery companies were assigned to brigades within the army's Advance Guard or some other formation in which cavalry were present.

As with all artillerists, the Russians took pride in their pieces and did not wish to see them fall into enemy hands. In this respect, Russian gunners had an almost fanatical doctrine of remaining with their pieces to contest any charging enemy rather than withdrawing to the protection of nearby infantry. Russian artillery officers were so deeply indoctrinated with a tenacity for holding their guns at all costs that they felt dishonored if any fell into enemy hands, even for a moment. There can be no doubt that the main reason the Russian officers and men possessed such fanaticism for defending their pieces to the death was because of the

[92] Voenno-Istoritjeskij Musej Artillerij, Insjenernich Woisk i Woisk Swjasi, Saint Petersburg.

[93] The fighting around Sokolnitz during the Battle of Austerlitz is evidence of the increased firepower lent by the Russian battalion pieces. Please see Chapter VIII.

consequences should they fail. The simian Inspector General of Artillery, Alexei Andreevich Arakcheev, took a perverse enjoyment in the punishment and death of any officer or gunner whom he felt was negligent in losing his guns. The 1805 campaign provides grisly examples of Arakcheev's Mongol-like barbarity, which helps the modern reader to grasp why it was that Russian artillerists preferred to die at the hands of the French rather than to survive the battle without their ordnance and then have to face Arakcheev.[94]

When Russian artillery officers unlimbered their pieces, they positioned the ordnance on the same frontage per piece observed by most European artillerists. Including the intervals to each side of the guns, every cannon or licorne occupied about 14 yards. This distance between each piece was necessary to allow proper observation through the dense, black smoke. When firing, the Russians could fire by piece, by section (two pieces), by detachment (four pieces), by half battery or by entire battery.

Finally, any discussion of the Russian army of the Napoleonic wars must include mention of their virtual non-existence of a commissariat system, as well as their massive and cumbersome baggage trains. The lack of a commissariat system was an extension of their poor staff system. Meanwhile, the numerous baggage trains were a product of the Russian officers being allowed to bring with them as many comforts as possible, which had an effect of slowing the march pace of the army.[95]

Tsar Alexander's favorite uniform—Artillery General of the Russian Imperial Guard

The Tsarist Officer Corps

Command and Control of the Army

The old-style Russian army that took the field in 1805 lacked many important features necessary to be successful. As previously discussed, the lack of tactical coordination between regiments limited what the brigade and column commanders could accomplish at their respective local levels. The practice of breaking up the light foot artillery companies in order to provide battalion artillery greatly reduced the chances of concentrating large numbers of ordnance at desired locations. Further, column commanders did not cooperate with one another due to a combination of factors, the most important of which was simply the absence of any staff training among the Tsarist officer corps.[96] Without this training, it was impossible for the Russian generals to give direction and cohesion to the individual combat arms. Further, an absence of a trained staff made it virtually impossible to give new orders to a column once the battle began other than by the commanding general's personal presence at the head of those troops. This lack of a trained staff, which made it impractical to attempt to conduct a battle by reacting to enemy movements, forced the armies of the *ancien régime* to commit themselves to offensive battle plans, except in the most obvious defensive situations. With an understanding of the Russian army's dearth of trained staff officers, Buxhöwden's exasperated remarks to Czartoryski at the close of the Battle of Austerlitz come into focus. The generals themselves were at wits end with their command system.

If the lack of a trained staff hindered the army while on the battlefield, the same absence of skilled administrators affected the army on a strategic level. That is why the army's commissariat was merely an afterthought, which resulted in a

[94] Please see Chapter VI for the gruesome details.

[95] Please see Chapters V and VI concerning the march speed of Kutuzov's army.

[96] Public Records Office (PRO), Foreign Office Papers (FOP), "Reports of the Earl of Harrington, Sir Arthur Paget, and Brigadier-Generals Ramsay and Clinton." 7/75-78. The quality of the reports is very uneven. Whereas Paget's reports seemed to be, for the most part, level-headed, Ramsey's are laughable. This report from Sir Arthur Paget is his communiqué dated 8 November 1805 in 7/75.

higher rate of strategic consumption than any other army in Europe.[97] Furthermore, there were so few Russian officers skilled enough to read a map that they habitually borrowed Austrian staff officers for a variety of duties. The two countries' officers, communicating in French, would try to coordinate movements for the Russian army, as well as arrange for supplies and converse with the local populace.

If the Tsar's officer corps gave a singular impression it was one of stupidity, which seemed to one Austrian to be:

> beyond anything you could believe possible. They are absolutely useless for anything that has to do with maneuver, and in this respect an ordinary French soldier is worth more than all the officers of the Russian army put together. The Russians are brave enough in combat, but their gallantry goes for nothing because they do not know how to direct it or use it to strike home. They charge with the bayonet... but they are so clumsy that they never manage to catch anyone.[98]

The Russians desperately needed an ally who could augment the strengths of their brave men. That ally was an old, familiar one whose traditions were also inextricably linked to the *ancien régime*.

[97] Duffy, *Austerlitz,* p. 36; also, see the table "Comparison of Strengths for Kutuzov's Army for the Period 25 August to 25 November 1805" in Chapter VI.
[98] PRO, FOP, Paget's report of 8 November 1805 in 7/75.

Russian Infantry Regiments in 1805[99]

Regiment Number in 1805	Name	Inspection (Territory)
Guard Grenadier Regiments:		
1	Preobrazhensky	Imperial Guard
2	Semenovsky	Imperial Guard
3	Izmailovsky	Imperial Guard
-	Guard *Jaeger* Battalion	Imperial Guard
Grenadier Regiments:		
1	Leib-Grenadier	Saint Petersburg
2	Pavlov	Saint Petersburg
3	Saint Petersburg	Livonia
4	Tavrick	Livonia
5	Ekaterinoslav	Lithuania
6	Little Russia	Ukraine
7	Kiev	Ukraine
8	Chersson	Dniester
9	Siberia	Dniester
10	Caucasus	Caucasus
11	Moscow	Smolensk
12	Fanagoria	Smolensk
13	Astrakhan	Moscow
Musketeer Regiments:		
1	Veliki-Lutzk	Finland
2	Neva	Finland
3	Riazan	Finland
4	Ieletsk	Saint Petersburg
5	Kexholm	Saint Petersburg
6	Bieloserk	Saint Petersburg
7	Tenguinsk	Saint Petersburg
8	Lithuania	Saint Petersburg
9	Sievia	Livonia
10	Sofia	Livonia
11	Revel	Livonia
12	Tobol	Livonia
13	Dnieper	Livonia
14	Tenguin	Livonia
15	Tula	Lithuania
16	Piskov	Lithuania
17	Mouromia	Lithuania
18	Rostov	Lithuania
19	Nysoy	Lithuania
20	Arkhangelgorod	Lithuania
21	Old Ingermanland (Galicia)	Breste
22	Ryazan	Breste
23	Viborg	Breste
24	Apsheron	Breste
25	Azov	Breste
26	Smolensk	Ukraine
27	Bryansk	Ukraine
28	Ladoga	Dniester
29	Vladimir	Dniester
30	New Ingermanland	Dniester

[99] Also see the table in Stein, *Geschichte des Russischen Heeres,* vol. 1, pp. 233-236.

31	Alexopol	Dniester
32	Koslov	Dniester
33	Yaroslav	Dniester
34	Nijegorod	Dniester
35	Bieloserk	Crimea
36	Sebastopol	Crimea
37	Troit	Crimea
38	Vytebsk	Crimea
39	Suzdal	Caucasus
40	Tiflis	Caucasus
41	Kabardinia	Caucasus
42	Caucasus	Caucasus
43	Podolia	Smolensk
44	Perm	Smolensk
45	Oglitche	Smolensk
46	Kursk	Smolensk
47	Voronejz	Smolensk
48	Moscow	Kiev
49	Butyrsk	Kiev
50	Kolyvan	Kiev
51	Novgorod	Kiev
52	Vyatka	Kiev
53	Narva	Kiev
54	Poltava	Kiev
55	Navajinia	Moscow
56	Tambov	Moscow
57	Ukraine	Moscow
58	Schlüsselburg	Moscow
59	Nacheburg	Moscow
60	Orlov	Moscow
61	Sharatov	Moscow
62	Staroskol	Moscow
63	Olonetzk	Moscow
64	Riazk	Orenburg
65	Ouf	Orenburg
66	Katerinborg	Orenburg
67	Chirvania	Siberia
68	Tomsk	Siberia
69	Seleguinia	Siberia
70	Catherine the Great	Saint Petersburg
71	Kaluga	Livonia, raised 1805
72	Mohilev	Lithuania, raised 1805
73	Kostroma	Lithuania raised 1805
74	Estonia	Ukraine, raised 1805
75	Odessa	Dniester raised 1805
76	Penza	Crimea, raised 1805
77	Vilno	Crimea, raised 1805

Grenadier

Jaeger Regiments: (*Jaeger* regiments had only numbers—no names)

1 and 2	Finland
3 and 4	Livonia
5, 6 and 7	Lithuania
8	Breste
9 through 13	Dniester
14 and 15	Crimea
16 and 17	Caucasus
18 through 20	Siberia

Russian Cavalry Regiments in 1805[100]

Regiment Number	Name	Inspection (Territory)
Guard Regiments:		
1	*Chevalier Garde*	Imperial Guard
2	Garde du Corps (Horse Guards)	Imperial Guard
3	Guard Hussars	Imperial Guard
4	Guard Cossacks	Imperial Guard
Cuirassier Regiments:		
1	Leib-*Cuirassier* "Tsar's" (Kaiser)	Saint Petersburg
2	"Tsarina's" (Empress)	Breste
3	Glukov	Dniester
4	Little Russian	Kiev
5	Ekaterino	Moscow
6	Military Order	Moscow
Dragoon Regiments:		
1	Moscow	Lithuania
2	Kharkov	Breste
3	Chernigov	Breste
4	Tver	Ukraine
5	Sjewersky	Dniester
6	Smolensk	Crimea
7	Vladimir	Caucasus
8	Tanganrok	Caucasus
9	Narva	Caucasus
10	Nischegorod	Caucasus
11	Piskov	Smolensk
12	Kargopol	Smolensk
13	Saint Petersburg	Smolensk
14	Starodub	Kiev
15	Kiev	Kiev
16	Kinburn	Kiev
17	Ingermanland	Kiev
18	Orenburg	Orenburg
19	Siberian	Siberia
20	Irkutsky	Siberia
21	Jitomir	raised August, 1805
22	Livonia	raised August, 1805
Hussar Regiments:		
1	Alexandria	Lithuania
2	Pavlograd	Breste
3	Mariupol	Breste
4	Alexandria	Dniester
5	Elisabetgrad	Dniester
6	Sumsk	Kiev
7	Isumy	Kiev
8	Achtirsk	Kiev
Uhlan Regiments:		
1	Lithuania	Lithuania
2	Polish	Breste
3	Grand Duke Constantine	Smolensk

Cossacks

[100] Also see the table in Stein, *Geschichte des Russischen Heeres,* vol. 1, pp. 233-236.

Austrian Staff Officers

Chapter III
"We Exist in Gloomy Apathy" *The Austrian Army of 1805*

The Austrian Army of Swabia was encamped around Ulm and waiting for Napoleon's forces to approach. As the days passed, the nominal commander of the army, Archduke Ferdinand d'Este, noticed that his infantry regiments were in shockingly bad condition. Most contained large numbers of unconditioned troops that had recently returned to the ranks from leave. There were also many raw conscripts that were not being properly trained due to the negligence of many officers and NCOs, as well as crippling shortages of supplies. Trying to help whip his foot soldiers into shape, the young princeling ordered firing practice for his men. Soon his aides reported back that army's scarcity of small arms ammunition was so severe that such a request was virtually impossible. Archduke Ferdinand then responded by issuing the following order dated 1 October 1805: "Since many of the newly-arrived troops have still to be trained in musketry, I approved the issue of six live rounds to be fired by every such man."[1] Therefore, it was with very little firing practice that the Austrian recruits which had never tasted battle would soon be pitted against Napoleon's highly-trained crack troops.

* *

The Infantry
Its Background and Makeup

The consecutive defeats suffered by Austria at the hands of Revolutionary France in the Wars of the First Coalition (1792-1798) and Second Coalition (1798-1800) should have sent a signal to even the most unchanging elements in the Austrian military that reform throughout the system was needed, and needed badly. It was only after the disastrous Ulm-Austerlitz campaigns of 1805 that some sensible modifications emerged from the ultra-conservative Austrian Habsburg military establishment.

The Austrian army that fought Napoleon in 1805 was still an army steeped in the traditions and trappings of prior centuries. In the early middle ages, before national defense was solely a responsibility of the state, wealthy noblemen would raise a body of men, arm and equip them for war, and contract their services with a sovereign or state. Each of these wealthy noblemen was known in Austria as *Obersten*, or *Oberst*—the most senior officer of the regiment. The *Oberst* was also the owner, or *Inhaber*, of the regiment. As the owner, he attempted to derive as much profit as practical by managing the economics of his outfit as well as the personal affairs of those within the regiment. By doing so, the *Inhaber* would make considerable money by selling commissions and promotions within his unit. Since it was the noble who paid and cared for the men, fealty was sworn not to the sovereign or state but to the *Inhaber*.[2]

Austrian Flag

In the late 17th century, the state began financing the recruitment of troops, and the men new to the uniform would swear allegiance to the sovereign instead of the *Inhaber*. It was about this time that it became the practice that the regimental

---

[1] Generalmajor Alfred Krauss, *1805. Der Feldzug von Ulm* (Vienna 1912), p. 83.

[2] Christopher Duffy, *The Army of Maria Theresa* (New York 1977), p.32.

Inhaber was not always the regimental commander in the field. Gradually, throughout the late 1600s and the 1700s, the *Inhaber* became a titular head and the actual field commander was given the title *Oberst-Leutnant*.[3]

Over several decades spanning the 18th century, the idea of numbering the regiments seemed to gain support among some of those who made policy. Finally, in 1769, numbers were awarded to the regiments that previously had been known only by the name of their *Inhaber*. Initially, the system of numbering regiments was to supplement the name of the regiment rather than replace it. Even so, the numbering of regiments did not find legions of supporters. To many conservatives within the Austrian military establishment—and there were no shortage of these—the numeric regimental designations was nothing other than a lessening of the purity of name found in the title of a regiment's *Inhaber*. Thus, it is common to read Napoleonic period references in which the Austrians mention their regiments only by the names of their *Inhabers*.[4]

Even with the introduction of numeric designations, and with specific controls on the regiment's recruiting set forth by the state, and with the actual field command of the regiment in the hands of the *Oberst-Leutnant*, the *Inhaber* of a Napoleonic era regiment still wielded considerable administrative power. He controlled promotions through the fine art of being totally capricious and arbitrary—as well as greedy! Most *Inhabers* generally favored promotions for those willing to back up their enthusiasm with lots of cash. Other *Inhabers* might favor officer appointments and promotions based on family or social connections. Matters of discipline and even personal affairs of the officer's men were often handled by the whim of the *Inhaber*. Any member of the regiment wishing to marry had to first secure the permission of the *Inhaber*, and when asking for permission one better have some money ready to back up his request![5]

Austrian Generals

The officers who formed the field command teams for each of the regiments came from different backgrounds, but shared two important traits—they were either aristocrats or from the gentry, and almost all were Catholic. Princely houses from the Netherlands, Spain, Württemberg, and Saxony sent their sons to the Austrian army. Some 70 years before the Napoleonic wars, Prague was a magnet for large numbers of the displaced Irish nobility who had fled their homeland because of religious discrimination practiced by England's monarchy.[6] Vienna held the same attraction for the newly arrived Bourbon *émigrés* fleeing Revolutionary France. An army career was a natural choice for these newcomers. The rough-and-ready Irish and many French *émigrés* proved to be excellent officers who were not afraid to 'lead from the front'—a trait that was not shared by most other Austrian generals, who had nothing to gain by recklessly exposing themselves to enemy fire.

The infantrymen the officers led—the non-commissioned ranks—were usually the most underprivileged and uneducated members of the Austrian society.[7] As the monarchy exempted most of the middle-class—landowners, professionals and merchants—from all military service, it was rare that someone from other than the lower socio-economic class would be in the infantry. Each regiment was assigned a fixed recruiting district (*Rayon*) within a territory of the Empire. Regimental officers, with authority from the state, were charged with bringing enough manpower into the ranks. In the infantry, this was accomplished by any

[3] Duffy, *The Army of Maria Theresa,* p.32.

[4] Kriegsgeschichtliche Abteilung des k.u.k. Kriegsarchiv, *Krieg gegen die französische Revolution 1792-1797* (Vienna 1905), Volume I, p. 107-109. (Kriegsarchiv documents hereafter cited as K. k. Kriegsarchiv, and in keeping consistent with the Kriegsarchiv, those volumes are designated by Roman numerals).

[5] Duffy, *The Army of Maria Theresa,* p. 32.

[6] Duffy, *The Army of Maria Theresa,* p. 28.

[7] Gunther E. Rothenberg, *Napoleon's Great Adversaries* (London 1982), p. 23.

means, regardless of morality. Besides financial inducements for volunteers, the officers ran confidence schemes to trick the unsophisticated into joining the army, as well as forming roving drunk patrols which nabbed unsuspecting intoxicated patrons from local taverns.[8]

Organization

With the exception of the 1798-1801 era, Austrian infantry regiments from 1792 to mid-1805 were composed of three field battalions of six fusilier companies per battalion, one depot battalion of four companies and one grenadier 'division' of two companies, for a total regimental strength of 24 companies. The two grenadier companies of each regiment always served on detached duty and were converged with other grenadiers to form grenadier battalions of four or six companies. The depot battalion would forward replacements to the field battalions as needed.[9]

On 14 June 1805, General Mack secured Emperor Francis' permission to begin a series of reorganizations in which the infantry would march to war in the upcoming campaign. By retaining the same 24 companies, Mack rearranged the regimental configuration into four field battalions of four companies per battalion, one depot battalion of four companies, and a grenadier battalion consisting of two companies of 'old' grenadiers (the regiment's original grenadiers) and two companies of 'young' grenadiers (*Jung-Grenadiere*). The 'young' grenadiers kept their fusilier helmets but were supposed to receive grenadier sabers. The four field battalions were numbered 1 through 4. The 4th battalion—a newly created formation—was formed by taking two companies each from the 2nd and 3rd battalions. The 1st battalion gave up two companies (these were the 'young' grenadiers) to help form the new grenadier battalion, which was numbered the 5th battalion. The depot battalion, designated as the regiment's 6th battalion, retained its four companies.[10]

The 1805 war strengths of the infantry companies are detailed in the following table:[11]

	Fusilier company	Grenadier company	Depot co.
German	201	201	215
Hungarian	201	201	212

Thus, the four fusilier battalions and the grenadier battalion each fielded, at maximum paper strength, 804 officers and other ranks per battalion. Including the regimental staff of 51 combatants, plus the four companies of the depot battalion, the full strength war footing of an Austrian infantry regiment numbered 4,931 officers and men.[12] A Hungarian infantry regiment at its full strength, war-time establishment, was 4,919.[13] Naturally, the actual field strength was often much

German Officer

---

[8] J. Cognazzo, *Freymüthige Beytrag zur Geschichte des österreichischen Militairdienstes* (Frankfort and Leipzig 1789), p. 90.

[9] K. k. Kriegsarchiv, *Krieg 1792-1797*, I, p. 231-237. Moritz Edler von Angeli, 'Die Heere des Kaisers und der französischen Revolution im Beginn des Jahres 1792,' *Mitteilungen des k und k. Kriegsarchiv*, 2nd Ser., IV (1889), p. 21-29; Moritz Edler von Angeli, 'Ulm und Austerlitz' in *Österreichische Militärische Zeitschrift* (Vienna 1877-78), p. 42.

[10] W. Rüstow, *Der Krieg von 1805 in Deutschland und Italien* (Frauenfeld 1853), pp. 57-58; Carl von Schönhals, *Der Krieg in Deutschland* (Vienna 1873), pp. 45-47; Duffy, *Austerlitz*, p. 26.

[11] Major Alphons Freiherrn von Wrede, *Geschichte der k. und k. Wehrmacht. Die Regimenter, Corps, Branchen und Anstalten von 1618 bis Ende des XIX. Jahrhunderts*, 5 volumes (Vienna 1898-1905), Volume 1, Beilage (hereafter referred to as Table) II, between pages 34 and 35.

[12] Wrede, *Geschichte der k. und k. Wehrmacht.*, vol. 1, Table II.

[13] Wrede, *Geschichte der k. und k. Wehrmacht.*, vol. 1, Table II.

Hungarian Grenadiers

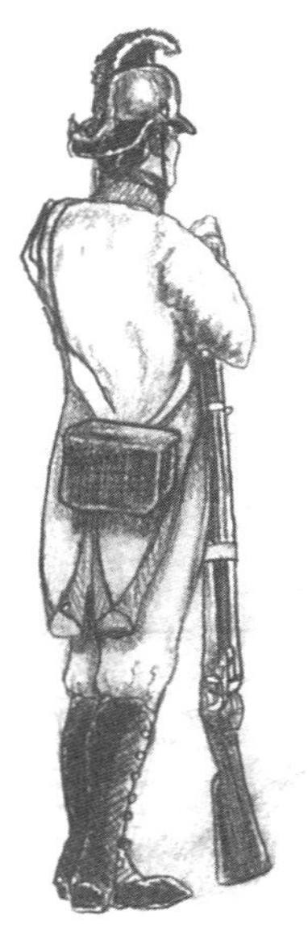

German Fusilier

weaker than the establishment. Battalions that were to number 804 usually mustered 500 to 600 men of all ranks.[14] What is more important, the numbers of officers and NCOs present in each company was less than the smaller French companies, making the larger Austrian companies harder to control under battlefield as well as marching conditions.[15]

A total of 64 line infantry regiments were in Imperial service. Two regiments—the 5th and 6th—were garrison formations and did not see action in the field. Of the remaining 62 regiments, 46 were German in origin, one a Tyrolean *jaeger* regiment, while the remaining 15 were recruited in Hungarian provinces. In addition to the line infantry were 17 *Grenzer* regiments raised from the Austrian military border. These units, initially raised during the 16th century to serve along the Hungarian borders to guard against Turkish raids, consisted of three field battalions per regiment.

Prior to the Mack reforms, each *Grenzer* regiment consisted of a total of 16 companies, each with a war-time establishment of 200 officers and men. Twelve of these companies served in two war battalions, each battalion of six companies, with the remaining four companies acting as the regimental depot. Including the headquarters staff of 28 personnel plus 150 artillerists to man the battalion guns, each *Grenzer* regiment was supposed to field 3,378 people.[16] As with the regular infantry regiments, Mack's reorganization of 1805 allowed the *Grenzer* the same number of war companies. However, the 12 companies were now divided into three, rather than two, battalions.[17]

As it was during the 18th century, the Austrian army of 1805 was a 'regimental' army, meaning that the regiment was the highest permanent organization in the army. While the designation of brigades and columns appeared in orders of battle, these were nothing more than *ad hoc* groupings of regiments or battalions made by the army commander.[18] This fact alone contributed significantly to a lack of higher command coordination that was exacerbated by the regiments being transferred almost on a daily basis from one organizational entity to another. Regiments so grouped had no chance to execute coordinated battlefield maneuvers. Further, commanders of brigades or columns had no idea from one day to the next which regiments the army commander would assign to their command, and could not therefore get to know the strengths and weaknesses of the units they were expected to lead. Like their Russian allies, these vital shortcomings were among the most telling flaws within 'regimental' armies.

Categories of Infantry

By the time of the Seven Years War (1756—1763), Austrian grenadiers were already established as the élite infantry of the army. Distinguished by their stature, strength, bearskin caps, and large mustaches, the grenadiers served on detached duty from the parent regiment, merged with grenadiers from other regiments to form converged battalions. Typically, a grenadier battalion before 1805, as well as after that year, consisted of four or six companies of grenadiers. Since every line

[14] Rothenberg, *Napoleon's Great Adversaries,* p.85; Rüstow pp.57-58; Schönhals pp. 45-47.

[15] This is clearly brought to light in General der Cavalerie Heinrich von Bellegarde's published study on the Austrian Army's field maneuvers of May 1805, *Erstes Feld-Manoeuvre bei Aviano den May 1805. Annahme, Wechselseitige Lagen Beyder Armeen, und Ihre Absichten* (Vienna 1805); Also, see J. Gallina, 'Suggestions for the Drill and Evolutions of Foot,' *Beiträge zur Geschichte des österreichischen Heerwesens.* Volume 1, *Der Zeitraum von 1757-1814* (Vienna 1872), B/573-579.

[16] Wrede, *Geschichte der k. und k. Wehrmacht.,* vol. 5, p. 232.

[17] Wrede, *Geschichte der k. und k. Wehrmacht.,* vol. 5, p. 232.

[18] Duffy, *Austerlitz,* p. 25.

regiment had two companies of grenadiers as part of its establishment, two or three regiments would contribute their grenadiers to form a battalion. These battalions were in turn grouped into reserve brigades usually numbering four to six grenadier battalions per brigade.[19]

In 1805, General Mack wanted to change this long-standing practice of converging grenadiers when he reorganized the infantry regiments. Mack sought to enhance regimental esprit de corps while increasing the number of grenadier battalions threefold by keeping the grenadiers an integral part of each regiment. In order to accomplish this, the grenadiers would have to form an entire battalion. Thus, two companies of fusiliers from the each regiment—designated as 'young' grenadiers—were merged with the 'old' two companies of grenadiers to form a new grenadier battalion.[20] Even with the new organization, many grenadier battalions continued to be taken from the parent regiments to form grenadier brigades as Austrian generals sought to create brigades of hard-hitting shock troops. However, the 1805 combat performance of the new grenadier battalions did not impress many Austrian officers; the Mack reform of diluting the grenadiers with fusiliers was abolished when Archduke Charles again reorganized the army in 1806 and the familiar converged grenadier battalions reappeared for the remainder of the Napoleonic wars.[21]

Hungarian Grenadier, with German Grenadiers in background

Of the 46 German infantry regiments, some 34 were from Inner Austria, Moravia and Bohemia. Of this number, in 1805 some 11 German regiments originated from Inner Austria while 12 came from Moravia and 11 from Bohemia.[22] The German regiments sported white coats, trimmed in regimental colors, white pants and black boots.[23]

Besides this mass of German infantry, there were regiments from other parts of the Austrian Empire. Hungarian regiments, distinguished by their black half-boots and tight-fitting blue pants, proved their worth in the War of Austrian Succession (1740-1748) and Seven Years War. Some 15 Hungarian regiments were in service in 1805.[24]

When Austria lost its possessions in the Netherlands and in Northern Italy as a result of the wars of the French Revolution, it also lost the recruiting grounds for seven regiments. Forced to change recruiting areas into Galicia (modern-day Poland) where the population had little love for the Austrian monarchy, the quality of these regiments (IRs #9, 30, 38, 44, 55, 58 and 63) dropped accordingly. The Galician regiments wore the same-style uniforms as the Germans.

The Empire had a line regiment (IR#46) recruited from the Tyrol. This regiment should not to be confused with the *jaeger* battalions raised later in the Napoleonic wars when IR#64 was disbanded. Though excellent individual warriors, the fiercely independent Tyroleans disliked outsiders. The stuffy style of combat featured in the line infantry did not grab the imagination of Tyroleans, and as a result, many officers and more than half the regiment were recruited from outside the province.

In addition to the line infantry were 17 *Grenzer* regiments hailing from the south-eastern borders of the Empire. In June 1800, several *Grenzer* units had mutinied, which spawned a Austrian reaction of looking upon the *Grenzer* as

German Fusilier

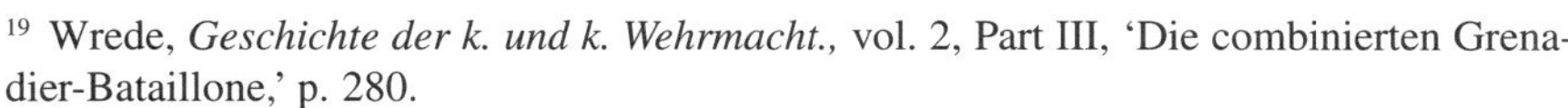

[19] Wrede, *Geschichte der k. und k. Wehrmacht.,* vol. 2, Part III, 'Die combinierten Grenadier-Bataillone,' p. 280.

[20] Wrede, *Geschichte der k. und k. Wehrmacht.,* vol. 2, p. 272; p. 329; Also, consult Table II in Volume 2 which also confirms that the Mack reforms were implemented for the 1805 campaign.

[21] Wrede, *Geschichte der k. und k. Wehrmacht.,* vol. 2, pp. 330-374; also, see Table II.

[22] Wrede, *Geschichte der k. und k. Wehrmacht.,* vol. 1, Table II.

[23] K. k. Kriegsarchiv, *Schema der kaiserl. königl. Kriegsvölker* (Vienna 1792).

[24] Wrede, *Geschichte der k. und k. Wehrmacht.,* vol. 1, Table II.

"shiftless, false and totally undisciplined."[25] By the time of 1805, the *Grenzer* regiments gave Napoleon's spies "a more military and healthy impression"[26] than did the regular army units. However, to the members of the Austrian military establishment, the 1805 Grenzer battalions lacked training, clothing and equipment. Moreover, to Carl Ritter von Schönhals, then junior officer in Mack's Swabian Army, the *Grenzer* were second-class troops. "Every report," Schönhals wrote, "complained about their [*Grenzer*] unreliability and lack of courage in battle."[27] While the *Grenzer* performance at Austerlitz would prove Schönhals wrong, it is clear that the *Grenzer* battalions had no special training and were used as just another form of line infantry.[28]

Training, Command and Deployment

'Regular, well drilled and steady'[29] were the watch words for Austrian infantry. Throughout the 18th century, tactics were unnecessarily complicated, formal and rigid—all designed to emphasize the power of the formed battalions. Each 1805 battalion would form its companies three-ranks deep. The frontage was based on the men (also known as files) being shoulder-to-shoulder, or about 20 inches of frontage per file. The formation would dress off the battalion's colors that would *always* be found on the extreme right and in the front rank.[30]

Hungarian Infantry wearing blue breeches in back, with German Infantry wearing white pants in front

Ideally, infantry would maneuver out of cannon range in column, deploy into line and then advance to close range where firepower and the bayonet would decide the issue. The bayonets were on the end of two different infantry smoothbore muskets, the older Model 1784 and the newer Model 1798. The newer model, a .69 caliber piece that could fire captured French cartridges, was a pound lighter than the older piece.[31] Despite its advantages, the new musket's acceptance was resisted by conservative elements in the Austrian military, most notably Archduke Charles, who believed it was wasteful to build new muskets when there already existed 20 million cartridges for the older, larger caliber piece. It wasn't until 1809—eleven years after its introduction—that the new piece was found throughout the entire army.[32]

Regardless of the model of small arm carried into combat, the formalized, linear tactical code employed by the Austrians failed repeatedly against the French throughout the Revolutionary wars. Although this was not due entirely to the French use of skirmishers—formed bodies of infantry decided most battles—the numerous French *tirailleurs* prompted General Mack to draft a revised infantry manual, the origins of which can be traced back to his army instructions of 1794,[33] and the various commissions that deliberated tactics and training throughout the years 1801-1804.[34] It is Mack's 1804 manuscript that suggests that the men

---

25 Rothenberg, *Napoleon's Great Adversaries,* p. 73.

26 P. Muller, *L'Espionnage Militaire sous Napoleon 1er* (Paris 1896), p. 84.

27 Schönhals, *Der Krieg in Deutschland ,* p. 69.

28 Duffy, *Austerlitz,* p. 27.

29 Duffy, Austerlitz, p. 27.

30 K. k. Kriegsarchiv, *Kriegschronik Österreich-Ungarns. Militärischer Gührer auf den Kriegsschauplätzen der Monarchie* (Vienna 1886), Volume I, pp. 11-19. The official distance was 24-inches for each file, but the formations invariably 'shrank' to 20-inches per file whenever under fire. Also, see Scott Bowden and Charles Tarbox, *Armies on the Danube 1809,* second edition (Chicago 1989), pp. 21-23.

31 A. Dolleczek, *Monographie der k. und k. österrung blanken und Handfeuerwaffen* (Vienna 1896), pp. 79-81.

32 O. Criste, *Erzherzog Carl von Österreich,* 3 volumes (Vienna-Leipzig 1912), vol. 2, 11, 50.

33 *Instructionspunkte für gesammte Herren Generals der K. K. Armee* (Frankfurt 1795). These were Mack's 1794 army instructions.

34 Rothenberg, *Napoleon's Great Adversaries,* p. 85.

comprising the third rank of each battalion might be used to extend the frontage or provide *tirailleur* cover for the parent formation. This made perfect sense, and was one of many changes incorporated into the new infantry regulations of 1807.[35] However, breaking with tradition and suddenly implementing new doctrine in 1805 was simply too radical an idea for most Austrian officers. The very fabric of the Austrian nobility resisted change at every level—something that even the conservative Archduke Charles would discover to his chagrin in 1809.[36]

Contributing in no short measure to the difficulty in command and aiding in the resistance to changes in tactical philosophy was the very makeup of the army. The Austrian army had officers and other ranks from all over Europe and control of such a multinational army was difficult. Mack declared: "No other army in Europe has the problem of a rank and file differing totally not only in language but also in custom from its officers."[37] This single fact meant that the Austrian officers had to converse in the universal language—French—and that the Imperial troops required "longer periods of training as well as a larger complement of officers and non-commissioned officers than the French."[38] Unfortunately, Austrian training was not as thorough as that of the enemy and all units, especially the *Grenzer* regiments, contained substantial numbers of "ill-trained and poorly equipped recruits."[39] The lower standard of training was no doubt partially the result of Austrian companies possessing a significantly inferior ratio of officers and NCOs when compared to the French. It is therefore not surprising to note Archduke Charles' 1804 assessments of the infantry after witnessing maneuvers at the exercise camps at Austerlitz, Pest and Wagram was that the maneuvers of the regiments were "disorderly, labored and slow."[40]

Austrian Officers

These difficulties notwithstanding, Mack sought to improve the army by introducing in the infantry a simplified arms drill, abolishing fire by the third rank, promoting a 'maneuver' step of 90 steps per minute and a 'double step' of 120 steps per minute for quick movements (normal pace of 75 steps per minute was retained), and championed the two-company 'division' front as a standard combat column formation.[41] Many drill changes sought by Mack were ignored in 1805. However, it is noteworthy that they were incorporated into the famous *Reglement* of 1807.[42]

None of the alterations, however, did anything to address the all-important issue of morale and esprit de corps above the regimental level. Without permanent brigades, divisions and corps, there was no way for the regiments to increase the army's combat effectiveness. It was an inescapable fact that the Austrian infantry of 1805 was still a relic of the *ancien régime*.

The Cavalry
Its Background and Makeup

Because the mounted service was far more attractive than the infantry, the cavalry could afford to be much more selective about its recruits. Cavalry regiments wanted men who were used to horses and knew how to care for them. Farmers, drivers and blacksmiths—men accustomed to hard work—formed the excellent core of the non-commissioned ranks of the Austrian mounted arm.

[35] *Exercier-Reglement für die Kaiserlich-Konigliche Infanterie* (Vienna 1807).
[36] Scott Bowden and Charles Tarbox, *Armies on the Danube 1809*, pp. 21 and 25.
[37] *Instructionspunkte für gesammte Herren Generals der K. K. Armee.*
[38] Rothenberg, *Napoleon's Great Adversaries,* p. 87.
[39] Rothenberg, *Napoleon's Great Adversaries,* p. 87.
[40] Duffy, *Austerlitz,* p. 27.
[41] *Vorschrift welche Gegenstände des Exercitiums und der Evolutionen der Infanterie abzuschaffen oder zu vereinfachen sind* (Vienna 1805), p. 14.
[42] K. k. Kriegsarchiv, *Exercier-Reglement für die Kaiserlich-Konigliche Infanterie.*

In many respects, much of the cavalry's background was similar to that of the infantry. *Inhabers* of a cavalry regiment wielded the same power and influence as *Inhabers* of infantry regiments. Like the infantry, when numbers were assigned to the cavalry regiments, they were still referred to in the army by the regiment's titular head.[43]

While senior commanders in the cavalry were among the most powerful and influential members of Habsburg society, most cavalry officers tended to come from Austria's parvenu nobility rather than from the great families of the Empire. This resulted in the cavalry being led by ambitious officers where "nobility enjoys no preference . . . for all the things are determined by rank. The higher a man rises in rank, the more it is up to him to distinguish himself and win merit."[44] This spirit, coupled with excellent recruits and superior horseflesh, would, on the surface, lead one to believe that the Austrian mounted arm was a consistent, dangerous and most battle worthy opponent. However, throughout the wars of the French Revolution, combat performance of the Austrian horse was disappointing.[45] In 1805, General Mack was intent on improving the cavalry's performance.

Organization

Austrian cüirassiers in rear, with dragoons in front

For the campaign of 1805, the established strength for all regiments was eight squadrons, each of two companies. For the heavy cavalry regiments—*cuirassier* and dragoons—each squadron was to number 131 combatants and 125 horses. Including a regimental staff of 53 personnel, each heavy cavalry regiment was to take the field with 1,101 officers and other ranks, plus a reserve squadron in depot numbering 133 men and 123 horses. The light cavalry—hussars, chevaulegers and uhlans—called for squadrons of 151 persons and 145 horses, bringing each regiment's paper strength with the regimental staff to 1,261 combatants, plus a reserve squadron in depot of some 180 men and 171 horses.[46] Regardless of the type of regiment, Austrian cavalry squadrons of 1805 virtually never attained regulation strength.[47]

Like the infantry, the Austrian cavalry had no permanent higher organization. Two or three regiments—or in some instances portions of two or three regiments—formed a brigade. Regiments assigned to a brigade one day might be reassigned to another the next, remain with that brigade for a week and then receive orders to serve elsewhere, and so on. Invariably, heavy cavalry were grouped together to form brigades, and light cavalry regiments were grouped with other light cavalry. Thus, all brigade organization was *ad hoc*, preventing the cavalry regiments from ever achieving command coordination with one another.[48] If a sizable Austrian

---

[43] Wrede, *Geschichte der k. und k. Wehrmacht.*, III, p. 48. The 1769 numbering system for the Austrian cavalry did not differentiate between the types of cavalry, but simply gave every regiment a number, regardless of type. In 1798, a new and improved system was introduced that numbered each regiment within its respective type. The 1798 numbering system was in use in 1805.

[44] J. Esterházy de Gallantha, *Regulament und unumänderlich-gebräuchliche Observations-Puncten* (Gavi 1747), p. 410. Esterházy's comments in his superb private regimental regulations still held true in 1805.

[45] K. k. Kriegsarchiv, *Krieg 1792-1797.*

[46] Wrede, *Geschichte der k. und k. Wehrmacht.*, vol. 3, Table I; Rothenberg, *Napoleon's Great Adversaries,* p. 85.

[47] At the Battle of Haslach-Jungingen, 11 October 1805, the Austrian squadrons, several of which had suffered losses a few days earlier at Wertingen, averaged only 70 combatants. The Austrian squadrons that participated in the Battle of Elchingen on 14 October averaged only 100 combatants. Further proof of this is seen in the squadron strengths at Austerlitz, which averaged between 60 to 75. Please consult the Orders of Battle in the Appendices.

[48] Duffy, *Austerlitz,* p. 25; Rothenberg, *Napoleon's Great Adversaries,* p. 85.

cavalry regiment was kept together, rather than be split into smaller two-squadron operating formations, the large regimental establishment would partially compensate for the lack of higher operational coordination.

Austrian Dragoon

Categories of Cavalry

There were 35 regiments of Austrian horse in 1805,[49] subdivided into categories based on size of its mounts and the nature of its mission. The largest and strongest men and horses went into the cüirassiers—armored regiments who traced their origin in Austrian service back to 1550.[50] There were eight of these imposing formations, and these were employed as the shock cavalry of the army, bearing the brunt of fighting in pitched battles. Although the six regiments of dragoons were considered heavy horse whose lineage came from the arquebusiers of the late 1500s, they were, by 1805, a lighter, more versatile breed of cavalry, capable of doing anything on and off the field of honor. It was not unusual to see dragoons taking their place in the line of battle as well as performing screening and scouting missions. Twelve hussar regiments owed their origin to the wild, swift moving bodies of horsemen from Hungary. Originally used for duties off the battlefield, by the time of the Napoleonic wars the hussars had a better combat record than did most dragoon regiments in Austrian service. A newer type of cavalry in Austrian service, the chevaulegers, combined the best virtues of the quick-moving hussars and the steady combat abilities of the heavier class of cavalry. Making their first appearance in the Seven Years War, the chevauleger regiments proved to be some of the finest bodies of horse in the army.[51] At the time of the 1805 campaign, there were six regiments of chevaulegers. Finally, there were three regiments of uhlans, or light lancers. Two uhlan regiments were raised in 1798 with the third formed in 1801.[52]

Not surprisingly, the national origin and recruiting area of the cavalry regiments was along category lines. Of the 35 Austrian cavalry formations, the *cuirassiers,* dragoons and chevaulegers—some 20 regiments—were German. The 12 flamboyant hussar regiments were unmistakably Hungarian, while the three uhlans regiments found their recruits primarily in Galicia, where men had a preference for the lance.[53]

Austrian Uhlan

Cavalry Tactics

Austria's conservative military never made changes hastily. By the time of the French Revolution, most other countries had converted their cavalry from a three-rank to a two-rank deep squadron formation. Austrian leaders, however, still insisted that their regiments cling to the three-deep files of horsemen. Throughout the wars of the French Revolution, it became apparent to many that the deeper Austrian cavalry formations were at a distinct disadvantage against the two-rank regiments of French horse.[54] All too often, the French would employ their wider frontage to overlap and envelope their Austrian adversaries. One of Mack's 1805

[49] There had been 42 regiments in Austrian service, but the expense to maintain these caused, in part, a reduction to 35 regiments in 1799. See Wrede, *Geschichte der k. und k. Wehrmacht.,* vol. 3, Table II between pages 12 and 13.

[50] Wrede, *Geschichte der k. und k. Wehrmacht.,* see extensive regimental histories in Volume 3.

[51] Duffy, *The Army of Maria Theresa,* p. 92.

[52] Rothenberg, *Napoleon's Great Adversaries,* p. 74.

[53] Wrede, *Geschichte der k. und k. Wehrmacht.,* see extensive regimental histories in Volumes 3 and 4.

[54] K. k. Kriegsarchiv, *Krieg 1792-1797.*

Austrian Dragoons at rest

Masses of Austrian Cavalry in action

reforms—and possibly his best—was to officially reduce the cavalry's line of battle from three to two ranks.[55]

Like most countries, Austrian cavalry rode virtually stirrup to stirrup. Depending on the size of the mount and rider, file frontage varied from 36 to 45 inches with a five pace interval between ranks, and a 12 pace interval between divisions (two-squadron formations).[56] Therefore, at full strength, a squadron of 150 would be 75 files wide by two ranks deep, for a frontage ranging from 75 yards to 95 yards with about 12 yards of depth.

Each squadron was subdivided into two companies, each of two *Züge*. At the head of each squadron were two captains. Deployed in line of battle, the senior captain of the squadron, the *Erster Rittmeister*, placed himself at the center of his command (between the companies of the squadron) along with the squadron standard-bearer, the *Estandarten-Führer*. The squadron's second captain, the *Rittmeister en second*, either joined them or rode behind the second rank.[57]

According to the long-standing tradition,[58] cavalry were forbidden to receive an enemy charge at the halt. When delivering a charge, Austrian cavalry regulations of 1784, which were nothing more than slightly updated version of the 1769 regulations, mandated that the squadrons must remain well closed up in their ranks and maintain a common frontage with the rest of the regiment. The charge was to be executed with gradually building speed. At a distance of about 80 paces from the enemy, the horsemen were to attack at a full gallop. Every cavalry officer was to be firmly committed to two things of fundamental importance: the first was to assail the enemy with the greatest speed and force, and the other was to seek to take them in the flank. The regulations emphasized deployment by, and tactics evolving from, the two-squadron division formation.[59] Furthermore, there were complex regulations for the horsemen using their carbines, although mounted fire fights were not preferred over shock action. Nevertheless, issuing small arms fire while in the saddle was still very much an option.[60]

The 1784 manuscript regulations also mention a 'massed charge by several mounted regiments,' though absolutely no details were provided on how the regiments were to be coordinated.[61] The unfamiliarity between regiments, owing in part to their frequent transfers between brigades as well as the mind-set of the officers to employ the cavalry in two-squadron formations, prevented any practical coordination between tactical formations of the same regiment, much less coordinating different regiments of the same brigade. Similarly, there was virtually no way for the cavalry and infantry commanders to coordinate attacks. As a result, cavalry actions in the 1805 Austrian army were definitely regimental affairs.

Probably the most damaging of the 'regimental army' mentality was the typical Austrian cavalry deployment mind-set—sub-dividing the regiments into two-squadron, or division, operating formations. This was especially true in the Ulm campaign in which eight squadrons belonging to one regiment would usually not be seen together.[62] They would instead be distributed into four tactical operating

---

[55] K. k. Kriegsarchiv, *Instructionspunkte für gesammte Herren Generals der K. K. Armee.*
[56] K. k. Kriegsarchiv, *Instructionspunkte für gesammte Herren Generals der K. K. Armee.*
[57] K. k. Kriegsarchiv, *Instructionspunkte für gesammte Herren Generals der K. K. Armee.*
[58] K. k. Kriegsarchiv, *Regulament und Ordnung für gesammte Kaiserl. Königl. Cuirassier und Dragoner Regimenter,* 2 parts (Vienna 1749), II, 320-322. These were the 1751 cavalry regulations that were virtually unaltered in the *Reglements* of 1769 and 1772.
[59] K. k. Kriegsarchiv, *Exercitii Regelement für die gesammte Kaiserl. Königl. Kavallerieregimenter* (Vienna 1769). Slightly updated in the *Neuabgeändertes Exerzierreglement für die gesammte Kaiserl. Königl. Kavallerieregimenter* (Vienna 1772), then updated in the 1784 Kriegsarchiv manuscript entitled 'Reglement für die k. k. Cavallerie.'
[60] K. k. Kriegsarchiv, 'Reglement für die k. k. Cavallerie.'
[61] K. k. Kriegsarchiv, 'Reglement für die k. k. Cavallerie.'
[62] Please see Chapter V for details, as well as the Orders of Battle in the Appendices.

units with two squadrons serving with one division while two squadrons would be present with another division, and so on. This habitual penny-packeting of horse would show its glaring shortcomings in 1805 as two squadrons of any Austrian regiment would have almost no chance against entire regiments or brigades of highly coordinated French cavalry.

The Artillery

Its Background and Makeup

Austrian artillery came into prominence during the Seven Years War (1756-1763), influencing the European balance of power and contributing significantly to the art of war during the mid-18th century.[63] During this time—from 1744 until 1772—the guiding light of Austria's artillery was Prince Joseph Wenzel Liechtenstein. Liechtenstein was largely responsible for quickly transforming the Austrian artillery from an antiquated, inefficient service during the War of Austrian Succession (1740-1748), to a modern and deadly arm by the latter half of the Seven Years War.

The entire branch of service, complete with all supporting organizations, was revamped during this period. One of the more important changes instituted by Liechtenstein was the creation of the *Artillerie-Füselier* Regiment. Rather than relying on the long-established practice of borrowing infantrymen to provide muscle in handling the pieces, the artillery fusiliers consisted of trained personnel whose duty was to assist the gunners. In Liechtenstein's opinion, the artillery fusiliers proved so effective during the campaigns of 1757 that their establishment was increased the next year. Also of note was Liechtenstein's departure from relying on *ad hoc* civilian transport for the guns and creating a permanent artillery transport organization, the *Ross-Partei*. Thus, by the establishment of the artillery fusilier and the artillery transport, all functions related to the artillery were handled by that branch.[64]

Austrian artillerists

With Liechtenstein's death in 1772, the new director of artillery, General Franz Ulrich Kinsky, imposed wide-ranging changes that unraveled much of his predecessor's accomplishments. Kinsky removed the *Ross-Partei* from established army jurisdiction and placed it under control of a new state transport organization. Without a permanent organization to pull the guns, the teams and drivers had to be created from scratch every time war broke out.[65] This lack of draft horses and drivers severely compromised the mobility of the Austrian artillery, a painful shortcoming vividly shown during the campaigns of 1805, when only slightly more than half the needed animals and drivers were in the field.[66] Even worse was Kinsky's decision to abolish the *Artillerie-Füselier* Regiment. The elimination of the artillery fusiliers forced gunners to conscript "unskillful, unwilling and negligent"[67] infantrymen to assist them while on campaign. Such was the practice of the Austrian artillery as it marched off to face Napoleon's *Grande Armée*.

Organization and Categories of Artillery

The theoretical establishment of the Austrian artillery was four regiments of artillerists of 16 companies apiece totaling 11,260 gunners.[68] These gunners, together with the volunteer laborers from the infantry and the grossly under strength

[63] Duffy, *The Army of Maria Theresa,* p. 105.
[64] Duffy, *The Army of Maria Theresa,* p. 107.
[65] Rothenberg, *Napoleon's Great Adversaries,* p. 26.
[66] Duffy, *Austerlitz,* p. 28.
[67] K. k. Kriegsarchiv, *Artillerie Systeme ab Anno 1753* (Vienna 1753); Rothenberg, *Napoleon's Great Adversaries,* , p. 26.
[68] Rothenberg, *Napoleon's Great Adversaries,* p. 87.

polyglot of drivers and teams, were assigned to either foot or cavalry artillery units.

Foot artillery was attached to infantry formations with the gunners walking or running behind the horse-drawn pieces. There were two different types of Austrian foot artillery in 1805: battalion guns and position batteries. Except when terrain prohibited, battalion guns were virtually married to the movements of their parent formation. In the Danube theater of operations, there were *usually* two 6-pounder battalion guns for every infantry battalion, although Mack's Army of Swabia also took the field with 3-pounder battalion guns. The same number of pieces were allocated in the Italian theater, but due to the more difficult terrain they were invariably 3-pounder pieces instead of the heavier 6-pounders. Position batteries, as the name implies, were foot artillery units designed to fire from advantageous positions—a form of reserve artillery that supported a large body of troops such as brigades or several brigades known as a 'column.' Each position battery consisted of six pieces of ordnance of which two were 7-pounder howitzers and four were either 6-pounder or 12-pounder cannon.

Cavalry batteries—*Cavallerie Batterien*—were the Austrian version of horse artillery and were attached to cavalry brigades. Whereas true horse artillery units had all personnel mounted on horseback, Austrian cavalry batteries had the officers and NCOs mounted on horses while the crews rode on the specially designed elongated trails of cavalry guns, howitzers and caissons. One can only imagine the discomfort experienced by the men who were unfortunate enough to have to straddle the sausage-like contraption! Cavalry batteries were designated as either 3-pounder or 6-pounder batteries. Typically, the 3-pounder cavalry batteries were deployed in Italy, while the 6-pounder cavalry batteries used in the Danube theater of operations.[69] Regardless of designation, every cavalry battery consisted of six pieces of ordnance of which two were 7-pounder cavalry howitzers and four were 3- or 6-pounder cavalry guns. The following table will help illustrate the organization of these various units:

Austrian 3-pounder gun

Organization of Austrian Artillery[70]

Battery Designation	Poundage of Guns 3 pdr	6 pdr	12 pdr	Ft.How	Cav Hw
3 pdr. Battalion Guns	2	-	-	-	-
6 pdr. Battalion Guns	-	2	-	-	-
6 pdr. Position Battery	-	4	-	2	-
12 pdr. Position Battery	-	-	4	2	-
3 pdr. Cavalry Battery	4	-	-	-	2
6 pdr. Cavalry Battery	-	4	-	-	2

The ammunition that was carried into action consisted of the following:

[69] All the cavalry batteries to see action in Mack's army in front of Ulm, as well as the cavalry batteries engaged at Austerlitz, were the 6-pounder variety. Please see Orders of Battle in Appendices.

[70] Wrede, *Geschichte der k. und k. Wehrmacht.*, vol. 4, p. 140; also see Kriegsgeschichtliche Abteilung des K. k. Kriegsarchiv, *Krieg 1809,* 6 volumes (Vienna 1907-1910), Vol. 1, p. 79. Hereafter referred to as *Krieg 1809.* The battalion guns disappeared from Austrian service after the 1805 war.

Rounds of Ammunition per gun carried into battle[71]

Kind of Ordnance	Ball	Grape	*"Buck Shot"*	Shell	Flare
3 pdr.	132	36	8	-	-
6 pdr.	160	28	-	-	-
12 pdr.	70	32	-	-	-
Ft. Howitzer	-	-	10	80	3
6 pdr. Cav. gun	124	24	-	-	-
Cav. Howitzer	-	-	13	62	1

"Buckshot" light case was officially designated to be used only against friendly troops attempting to desert.

Further ammunition was available in the reserve ammunition train that was always stationed one to two miles behind the front lines. When a battery's ammunition needed replenishing, the non-technical personnel of the battery would travel back to the reserve ammunition train to procure additional rounds. The table below details the additional ammunition carried in the reserve ammunition train.

Austrian gunners in action

Each piece of ordnance — **Additional available rounds**[72]

Kind of Ordnance	Ball	Grape	*"Buck Shot"*	Counter Battery Rounds	Shell
3 pdr.	90	12	2	-	-
6 pdr.	94	26	-	-	-
12 pdr.	123	40	-	22	-
6 pdr. Cav. gun	94	26	-	-	-
all Howitzers	-	-	12	-	72

Special note should be given the 'Counter Battery Rounds' designation listed on the above table. Austrian doctrine stipulated that 12-pounder 'position batteries' were the only pieces capable of engaging enemy artillery at longer ranges with any chance to inflict noticeable damage.[73]

By 1805, Austrian guns and howitzers, once the most feared ordnance in Europe, were nothing more than a collection of antiques from the 18th century.[74] When Major-General Anton Feuerstein introduced his ordnance system in 1753, Austrian pieces were the most advanced in the world. So impressive was the Feuerstein mobile and hard-hitting 12-pounder, it inspired the 'Austrian' 12-pounder model of Frederick the Great's army,[75] also served as a basis for Gribeauval's improvements to French ordnance later in the 18th century as well as the French System Year XI ordnance of early in the 19th century,[76] and can even be considered

[71] Wrede, *Geschichte der k. und k. Wehrmacht.*, vol. 4. Still unchanged in 1809, see *Krieg 1809,* p. 80.

[72] Wrede, *Geschichte der k. und k. Wehrmacht.*, vol. 4 ; unchanged in 1809. See *Krieg 1809,* p. 91.

[73] *Instructionspunkte für gesammte Herren Generals der K. K. Armee.*

[74] A. Dolleczek, *Geschichte des österreichischen Artillerie* (Vienna 1887), see ranges for weapons on pp. 362-363 and 440-441; Rothenberg, *Napoleon's Great Adversaries,* p. 26; Duffy, *Austerlitz,* p. 27.

[75] Christopher Duffy, *The Army of Frederick the Great* (New York 1974), pp. 113-14.

[76] S.H.A.T., 2w84 and 4w68.

the grandfather of the famous 12-pounder 'Napoleon' gun of the American Civil War. However, the wars of the French Revolution showed that the Austrians had fallen seriously behind in the technological war. Not only were their guns significantly heavier than the French pieces, they were outmatched in range as well.

Comparison of Austrian and French Ordnance in 1805[77]
Ranges Shown are in Meters

Poundage	Ordnance System	Canister	Round-Shot (Practical)	Round-Shot (Maximum)	Shell
3	Austrian Feuerstein	300	450	900	—
4	French Gribeauval	400	800	1250	—
6	Austrian Feuerstein	400	700	1200	—
6	French Year XI	500	1200	1850	—
8	French Gribeauval	550	1500	2400	—
12	Austrian Feuerstein	500	1000	1800	—
12	French Year XI	600	1850	2700	—
12	French Gribeauval	600	1800	2600	—
7 how	Austrian Feuerstein	250	—	—	1200
6 p. how.	French Gribeauval	250	—	—	1300
5 p. 4, 6 or 7 liv. how.	French Year XI	250	—	—	1200
6 p. 4 liv how	French Year XI	300	—	—	1500

Austrian ordnance and supporting equipment was usually painted in ochre with black metal fittings. However, battalion guns and ammunition wagons were often more easily recognized as *Inhabers* ordered their regimental facing colors striped across the trail and wheels of the regiment's ordnance and other mobile equipment.[78]

Command and Deployment

The organization of the Austrian artillery, most notably the long-standing practice of distributing two pieces of ordnance to each battalion, had a substantial impact on deployment and tactics. Some Austrian generals had experimented as early as 1798 with taking the battalion guns from the parent infantry units and organizing them into *ad hoc* brigade batteries of 6 to 8 pieces. However, the outmoded practice of keeping battalion guns with the infantry was adhered to during the campaigns of 1805. Against Napoleon's forces in the Danube theater, Austrian fusilier and grenadier battalions were supported by 6-pounder battalion guns, while *Grenzer* battalions were allocated 3-pounder guns or none at all. The majority of pieces were therefore distributed in penny packets with the remaining guns organized as either position batteries or cavalry batteries with minimal command control over these different units. As a result, it was rare indeed when two or more batteries were coordinated in movements or fire.

---

[77] Dolleczek, pp. 362-363 and 440-441; Wrede, vol. 4, p. 140; S.H.A.T., 2w84, 4w68; *Archives nationales,* AF IV 1161-1165 and 1378, hereafter referred to as A.N.
[78] Castle Förchtenstein, Esterházy Estate Museum, Eisenstadt.

The Austrian Officer Corps
Command and Control of the Army

Like its Russian ally, the Austrian army of 1805 was prepared only to fight another war of the 18th century. The concept of coordination between regiments was limited at best, while coordinated brigade movements in the face of the enemy were unthinkable. The practice of providing battalion artillery to the infantry, while bolstering individual firepower of each battalion, significantly diminished the opportunities to concentrate large numbers of artillery batteries. While the Austrians possessed far more capable staff officers than the Russians, their staff and administrative personnel were too few. This, plus the still-enormous baggage train of the army (despite Mack having curtailed the number of regimental and individual transport), coupled with an acute shortage of horses, affected the speed with which the Austrians could maneuver. As a result, the Austrians moved at 18th century-style daily march rates of an average of five to seven miles when the French would be routinely conducting comparatively lightning movements three times as fast.

On the battlefield, non-*émigré* Austrian officers had long had a reputation of not leading from the front. Perhaps these men of title and property had too much to lose by exposing themselves to fire. Regardless of the reasons, the *ancien régime* attitude by the officer corps failed to motivate the greater body of men. Perhaps this is why Archduke Ferdinand confided in his dairy that "we exist in gloomy apathy."[79]

It was, therefore, with an outmoded 'regimental' army and mostly uninspiring leaders that the Austrian army marched off to war to meet Napoleon Bonaparte and his personally crafted instrument of war.

[79] O. Regele, "Karl Freiherr von Mack und Johann Ludwig Graf Cobenzl. Ihre Rolleim Kriegsjahr 1805," in the *Mittheilungen des Österreichischen Staatsarchivs,* XXI (Vienna 1968). Hereafter referred to as *Mittheilungen.*

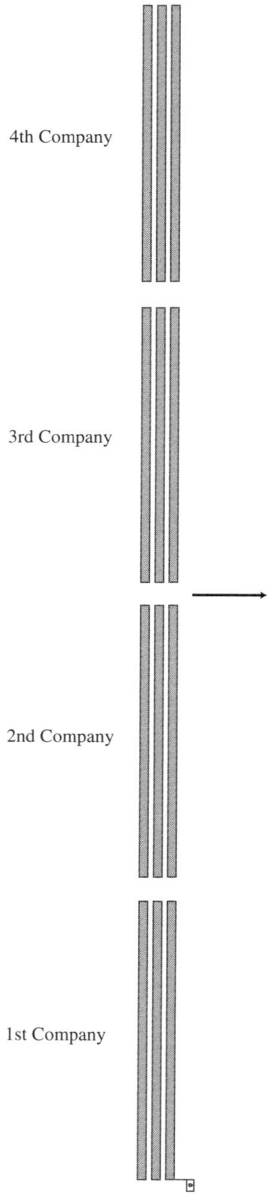

4th Company

3rd Company

2nd Company

1st Company

Austrian 1805 battalion deployed in line

Austrian Line Infantry Regiments in 1805

Regiment Number	Name	Recruitment	Territory
1	Kaiser Franz II	German	Moravia
2	Erzherzog Ferdinand	Hungarian	
3	Erzherzog Karl	German	Austria
4	Hoch-und-Deutchmeister	German	Austria
5	1st Garrison Regiment		
6	2nd Garrison Regiment		
7	Karl Schröder	German	Moravia
8	Erzherzog Ludwig Josef	German	Moravia
9	Czartorisky-Saggusco	Galician	
10	Anspach-Bayreuth	German	Bohemia
11	Erzherzog Rainer	German	Bohemia
12	Manfredini	German	Moravia
13	Reisky	German	Austria
14	Klebek	German	Austria
15	Karl Riese	German	Bohemia
16	Erzherzog Johann Joseph	German	Styria
17	Reuss-Plauen	German	Bohemia
18	Stuart	German	Bohemia
19	Alvinczy	Hungarian	
20	Kaunitz-Rietberg	German	Moravia
21	Gemmingas-Hornberg	German	Bohemia
22	Koburg	German	Moravia
23	Salzburg	German	Austria
24	Auersperg	Galician	
25	Spork	German	Bohemia
26	Hohenlohe-Bartenstein	German	Austria
27	Strassoldo	German	Austria
28	Fröhlich	German	Bohemia
29	Lindenau	German	Moravia
30	de Ligne	Galician	
31	Benjowsky	Hungarian	
32	Esterházy	Hungarian	
33	Sztarrai	Hungarian	
34	Davidovich	Hungarian	
35	Erzherzog Maximilien	German	Bohemia
36	Kolowrat-Krakowsky	German	Bohemia
37	de Vins/Auffenberg	Hungarian	
38	Württemberg	Galician	
39	Duka	Hungarian	
40	Josef Mittrowsky	German	Moravia
41	Sachsen-Hildburghausen	Galician	
42	Erbach	German	Bohemia
43	Valsassina	German	Austria
44	Bellegarde	Galician	
45	Lattermann	German	Styria
46	Neugebauer	German	Tyrol
47	Vogelsang (aka Kinsky)	German	Bohemia
48	Vukassovich	Hungarian	
49	Kerpen	German	Austria
50	Stain	German	Austria
51	Splényi	Hungarian	
52	Erzherzog Franz Karl	Hungarian	
53	Johann-Jellacíc	Hungarian	

54	Froon	German	Bohemia
55	Reuss-Greitz	Galician	
56	Wenzel Coloredo	German	Moravia
57	Josef Coloredo	German	Bohemia
58	Beaulieu	Galician	
59	Jordis	German	Austria
60	Gyulai	Hungarian	
61	St. Julien	Hungarian	
62	Franz Jellacíc	Hungarian	
63	Erzherzog Josef Franz	Galician	
64	Tyrolian Jäger	German	Tyrol

Grenadier Battalions in 1805

Under the 1805 Mack reforms, grenadier battalions were designated as the 5th Battalion of each regiment. The new grenadier battalion that saw action in 1805 consisted of a total of four companies of which two were its original, or so-called 'old' grenadiers, and two companies were fusiliers of the same regiment designated as 'young' grenadiers.

Austrian 1805 battalion in column of companies

National Grenz Infantry in 1805

Regiment Number	Name	Recruitment	Coat Color	Facing Color
1	Liccaner	Carlstadt	White	Yellow
2	Otocaner	Carlstadt	Brown	Yellow
3	Oguliner	Carlstadt	White	Orange
4	Szluiner	Carlstadt	Brown	Orange
5	Warasdiner Kreuzer	Warasdin	White	Red
6	Warasdiner St. George	Warasdin	Brown	Red
7	Broder	Slavonia	White	Pink
8	Gradiskaner	Slavonia	White	Pink
9	Peterwardeiner	Slavonia	White	Lt Blue-Gray
10	1st Banal	Banal	Brown	Dark Red
11	2nd Banal	Banal	Brown	Dark Red
12	Deutsch-Banater	West Banat	Brown	Sky Blue
13	Walachisch-Illyrische	East Banat	White	Sky Blue
14	1st Székler	Siebenburg	White	Crimson
15	2nd Székler	Siebenburg	Brown	Crimson
16	1st Walachen	Siebenburg	White	Green
17	2nd Walachen	Siebenburg	White	Green

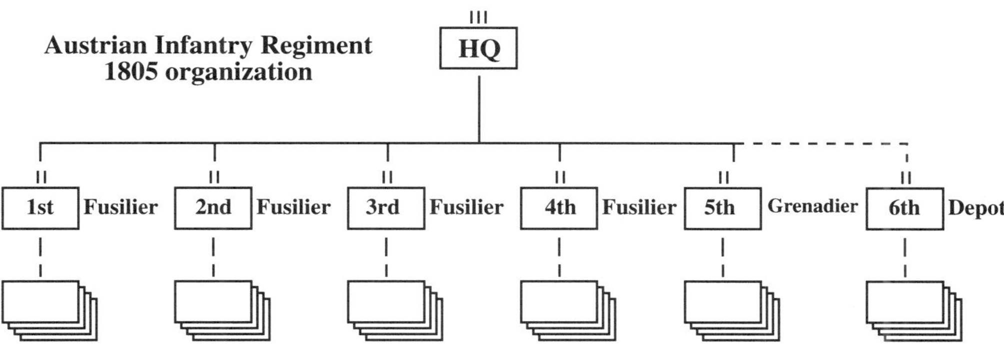

Each regiment had a total of 24 companies, each battalion having four companies.
The theoretical strength of each company was 201 officers and other ranks, but these strengths were rarely attained. Once the campaign began, the strengths shrank to a point where the average company strength at Haslach-Jungingen was only 135. Of note is the fact that 1805 was the only campaign of the Napoleonic Wars where Austrian Infantry battalions had only 4 companies (the "Mack Reforms" of 1805).

An Austrian hussar leading a spare mount

Austrian Cavalry in 1805

CÜIRASSIER REGIMENTS IN 1805
Cüirassier-Regiment Kaiser #1
Cüirassier-Regiment Erzherzog Franz #2
Cüirassier-Regiment Erzherzog Albert #3
Cüirassier-Regiment Erzherzog Ferdinand #4
Cüirassier-Regiment Nassau-Usingen #5
Cüirassier-Regiment Mack #6
Cüirassier-Regiment Lothringen #7
Cüirassier-Regiment Hohenzollern #8

DRAGOON REGIMENTS IN 1805
Dragoons-Regiment Erzherzog Johann #1
Dragoons-Regiment Hohenlohe #2
Dragoons-Regiment Württemberg #3
Dragoons-Regiment Levenehr #4
Dragoons-Regiment Savoyen #5
Dragoons-Regiment Melas #6

CHEVAULEGER REGIMENTS IN 1805
Chevaulegers-Regiment Kaiser #1
Chevaulegers-Regiment Hohenzollern #2
Chevaulegers-Regiment O'Reilly #3
Chevaulegers-Regiment Latour #4
Chevaulegers-Regiment Klenau #5
Chevaulegers-Regiment Rosenberg #6

HUSSAR REGIMENTS IN 1805
Hussar-Regiment Kaiser #1
Hussar-Regiment Erzherzog Josef #2
Hussar-Regiment Erzherzog Ferdinand #3
Hussar-Regiment Hessen-Homburg #4
Hussar-Regiment Ott #5
Hussar-Regiment Blankenstein #6
Hussar-Regiment Liechtenstein #7
Hussar-Regiment Kienmayer #8
Hussar-Regiment Erdödy #9
Hussar-Regiment Stipsicz #10
Székler *Grenz*-Hussaren-Regiment #11
Palatinal-Hussaren-Regiment #12

UHLAN REGIMENTS IN 1805
Uhlanen-Regiment Merveldt #1
Uhlanen-Regiment Schwarzenberg #2
Uhlanen-Regiment Erzherzog Karl #3

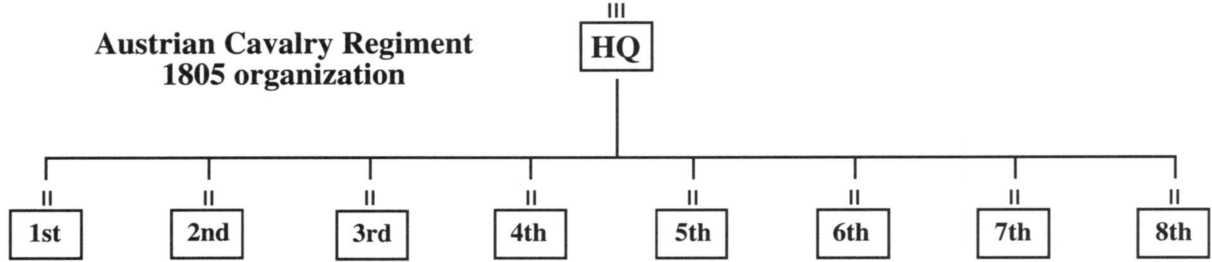

Total of 8 squadrons, each with two companies for a total of 16 companies, and each pair of squadrons often operating together tactically to form a "division".

Full Strength Standings of Austrian Field Troops as of 1 September 1805

Description	Men	Horses	TOTAL Men	TOTAL Horses
INFANTRY				
46 German Line Infantry Regiments of 6 battalions each. Each regiment had 2 Grenadier and 18 Fusilier companies, with 4 depot companies. At full strength, each regiment numbered approximately 4,931 combatants	226,826			
15 Hungarian Line Infantry Regiments of 6 battalions each. Each regiment had 2 Grenadier and 18 Fusilier companies, with 4 depot companies. At full strength, each regiment numbered approximately 4,913 combatants	73,695			
1 Tyrolian *Jaeger* Regiment (IR#64) of 6 battalions, totaling 20 companies, with 4 depot companies. At full strength, the regiment numbered approximately 4,931 combatants	4,931		305,452	
EXTRA CORPS				
9 Pioneer divisions at 398 men per division	3,582			
1 Miner corps of 5 companies	637			
1 Sapper corps of 6 companies	760			
1 Pontonier battalion of 6 companies	770		5,749	
ARTILLERY				
1 Bombardier corps of 5 companies	1,075			
4 Artillery Regiments of 16 companies each	11,260		12,335	
Total for these categories			323,536	
GRENZ TROOPS				
13 Croatian *Grenz* Regiments, each regiment consisting of 3 field battalions and 1 reserve battalion (16 total companies)	43,914			
4 Siebenburger *Grenz* Regiments, each regiment consisting of 3 field battalions and 1 reserve battalion (16 total companies)	13,512			
1 Boat Handler battalion of 6 companies and 1 reserve division	1,719			
1 Szekler *Grenz* Hussar Regiment of 8 field squadrons and reserve squadron	1,441	1,331 *		
Total for the *Grenzer*			60,586	1,331
CAVALRY				
8 Cüirassier Regiments, each regiment consisting of 8 field squadrons and 1 reserve squadron with a paper strength of 1,234 combatants and 1,123 horses per regiment	9,872	8,984 *		
6 Dragoon Regiments, composition identical to that of the cüirassier regiments	7,404	6,738 *		
6 Chevauleger Regiments, each regiment consisting of 8 field squadrons and 1 reserve squadron with a paper strength of 1,441 men and 1,331 horses	8,646	7,986 *		
11 Hussar Regiments, each regiment consisting of 8 field squadrons and 1 reserve squadron, with a paper strength of 1,441 men and 1,331 horses per regiment	15,851	14,641 *		
3 Uhlan Regiments, each regiment consisting of 8 field squadrons and 1 reserve squadron, with a paper strength of 1,441 men and 1,331 horses per regiment	4,323	3,993 *		
Total for these cavalry			46,096	42,342
STAFF TROOPS				
Staff infantry division of 2 companies and 10 other independent companies	2,856			
Staff dragoon squadron and 10 other independent flügels (Flügels were half-squadron strength organizations)	898	873		
Total for these categories			3,754	873
Theoretical Army Totals (not actual combatants, but only paper strength establishment)			**437,726**	**44,546**

* excludes staff horses

Combat Efficiency Profile of the Austrian Armies in 1805

The following chart is designed to aid the reader's appreciation of the better combat troops within the Austrian army. Please remember that while column composition may have changed several times during the campaign, the organization relating to theater or battle has been used for this analysis.

Column Designation	Best Unit(s) in Column
in Tyrol (Chasteler)—	Klebek IR#14
in Tyrol (Jellachich)—	Rosenberg Chevaulegers #6
in Italy (Bellegarde)—	Karl Schröder IR#7 Hohenlohe-Bartenstein IR#26 Splényi IR#51 Kaiser Dragoons #1; Kienmayer Hussars #8
in Italy (Argenteau)—	Erzherzog Karl Uhlans #3
in Italy (Davidovich)—	Ott Hussars #5
around Ulm—	Latour Chevaulegers #4 and Erzherzog Albert Cuirassiers #3
Danube (Kienmayer/Merveldt)—	Hoch-und-Deutchmeister IR#4 Liechtenstein Hussars #7 Merveldt Uhlans #1
Austerlitz (Kienmayer)—	O'Reilly Chevaulegers #3 Hessen-Homburg Hussars #4 Székler-Grenz Hussars #11

Special note: Probably the finest of all the line infantry regiments was Hoch-und-Deutchmeister IR#4. The officers and many men were members of the Teutonic Order and the regimental proprietor, or *Inhaber*, was the current head of the Order. The regiment was wrecked on 8 November when Davout's men trapped the main body of Merveldt's Austrian column at Mariazell.

Austrian Officer Rankings and Designations

Rank	Equivalent
Generalissimus	Commander-in-chief of all armies in the field
Feldmarschall or FM	Field-Marshal
Feldzeugmeister, or FZM in the infantry, and *General der Cavalerie*, or GdC (GdK) in the cavalry	Full General
Feldmarschall-Leutnant, or FML	Lieutenant General
General-Feldwachtmeister, or GM	Major General
Inhaber	The proprietor, or owner of the regiment, often generals or a wealthy officer. For example, the *Inhaber* of Erzherzog Karl IR#3 was Archduke Charles himself.
Oberst	Colonel in charge of the regiment in the absence of the *Inhaber*.
Oberst-Leutnant	Lieutenant Colonel
Major	Major
Hauptmann (infantry), or *Rittmeister* (cavalry)	Captain
Ober-Leutnant	1st Lieutenant
Unter-Leutnant	2nd Lieutenant

PART III

The First Blitzkrieg
The Ulm Campaign of 1805

Marshal Lannes (left) leads his corps into Germany

Chapter IV
"Our Government Have So Contrived Things"
The Allied Third Coalition

"The English want war, but if they are the first to draw the sword I will be the last to sheath it."—Napoleon, 1803[1]

England Against Napoleon

Above, a British medallion celebrating the Peace of Amiens. Below, a French one doing the same.

Napoleon's men along the Channel were training for a war that England had already started. It began on 18 May 1803 when two British frigates seized two French merchantmen in the Bay of Audierne, signaling the opening of hostilities. This incident came two days after George III, King of England—formerly the self-styled King of France—held a Council at which "letters of marque and reprisals against France"[2] were ordered. This action had come less than 14 months after the Treaty of Amiens, which had established peace between France and Great Britain for the first time since 1793.

Like the other oligarchs of Europe, George III had never reconciled himself to Amiens. The wars of the French Revolution were supposed to have been conflicts "of extermination"[3] to those who dared throw off the rule of kings. The English hatred for the Revolution was grounded in fear that the idea of freedom might spread to their own countrymen and to the slaves of their far-flung Empire. To put it simply, the English held in contempt anyone with red instead of blue blood in his veins. This abhorrence especially applied to Napoleon Bonaparte, the man who dared to supplant 14 centuries of kings.

Those in power in England sought war with France as further means to topple the insecure Consular Government that was not yet three years old. It must be remembered that Napoleon's was a middle-of-the-road government—one that brought moderation to a country that had swung from the feudal system of the Bourbons to the Terror of the Jacobins. Napoleon's new Civil Code (the *Code Napoléon*) was as massively comprehensive as it was monumental. Of all the important aspects of Napoleon's new civil code, none were more important than the landmark rights for property owners which enumerated and guaranteed for all persons equality in the eyes of the law. In addition, Napoleon brought forth new financial order by founding the now venerable Bank of France. He also improved public works and education, as well as instituted a policy that refrained from subordinating the State to the Church and vice-versa. So enduring were these hallmarks of Napoleonic rule, that the *Code Napoléon* has been adopted, or has influenced the codes of law, in all other European countries as well as those under European control since that time. In short, Napoleon's laws are today still the

[1] Harold C. Deutsch, *The Genesis of Napoleonic Imperialism* (Philadelphia, 1975), p. 129.
[2] Duke of Buckingham and Chandos, *Memoirs of the Courts and Cabinets of George III* (London, 1835).
[3] William Pitt to the House of Commons, 31 January 1793; and John W. Fortescue, *British Statesmen of the Great War 1793-1814* (Oxford, 1911).

CODE CIVIL

DES

FRANÇAIS.

ÉDITION ORIGINALE ET SEULE OFFICIELLE.

À PARIS,

DE L'IMPRIMERIE DE LA RÉPUBLIQUE.

AN XII. 1804.

The title page to the Code Napoléon

Lord Whitworth

cornerstone of French and European society.[4]

These advances were seen in a different light on the other side of the Channel. By refusing to implement the terms of the Treaty of Amiens, Britain gave hope to all enemies of Napoleon's Consular Government. The Royalist *émigrés* and the other courts throughout Europe, as well as other Royalists and the Jacobins still in France, all welcomed a new war that would cause the downfall of Napoleon and the appearance of a new governing body. Exactly what type of new government was desired depended on one's point of view. The Royalists sought the restoration of the *ancien régime*. The Jacobins called again for the blood of those who were not convinced Revolutionaries. Therefore, in a strange twist of fate, Royalists and Jacobins found themselves allied against a common enemy—Napoleon Bonaparte.

To help agitate against Napoleon's Consular Government, the English press was in the forefront in representing Napoleon as a monster of unspeakable evil—the anti-Christ. Caricatures of Napoleon beginning in 1797 continually reinforce the image of Napoleon as "a clever, desperate Jacobin—even terrorist."[5] The earliest English caricature appearing 14 April 1797 entitled 'The French Bugaboo frightening the Royal Commanders,' shows Napoleon seated on the back of the devil vomiting armies and cannon. Other caricatures repeatedly show a yellow-skinned pygmy dubbed the 'Corsican Ogre' or 'Corsican Tyrant' threatening the stability of Europe and the world. On 1 February 1803, the *Morning Post* described the First Consul as "an unclassifiable being, half-African, half-European, a Mediterranean mulatto."[6]

The English obsession of what Napoleon and a new France might export to the rest of the world was consistent with the views of most reactionaries. When Napoleon "spoke a good deal of the possibility of doing away with all differences between the inhabitants of the two worlds—of blending the black and the white, and having universal peace," Lord Whitworth reacted that Napoleon was "ambitious of universal empire and to convince the world that everything must bend to his will."[7] However, Napoleon did more than just talk about equality between people, regardless of skin pigmentation; he also proclaimed freedom to the people of color who lived in French colonies in the Caribbean. In a Proclamation to the Citizens of Santo Domingo (Haiti) issued on Christmas Day in 1799, Bonaparte declared:

> The Consuls of the Republic, in announcing to you the new social order [the Creation of the Consulate in France], declare to you that these sacred principles, the liberty and equality of the blacks, shall remain forever inviolate and immutable in your country. If there are men in the colony of Santo Domingo who bear us ill will, if there are any who remain in communication with the enemy, remember, brave Negroes, that France alone recognizes your liberty and your equal rights.[8]

---

[4] The French Revolutionaries had been interested in replacing the 400 different code used in France during the *ancien régime* with a uniform laws. They had made little progress, however, before Bonaparte came to power. The First Consul was intent on bring uniformity and order to France, and therefore became personally involved in the project. What emerged was Napoleon's Civil Code, also known as the *Code Napoléon,* and was more important than his subsequent laws, which were: the Code of Civil Procedure (1806), the Commercial Code (1807), the Criminal Code and Code of Criminal Procedure (1808) and the Penal Code (1810). Napoleon, looking back from his exile on Saint Helena, considered these collective codes of law as a greater victory than any he had won on the battlefield.

[5] The Earl of Malmesbury, *Diaries and Correspondence* (London, 1844), p. 49.

[6] The *Morning Post,* 1 February 1803; also see: F. J. Maccunn, *The Contemporary English View of Napoleon* (London, 1914).

[7] O. Browning, *England and Napoleon in 1803* (London, 1887), in the Liverpool Papers, British Museum, London.

[8] Bonaparte to the Citizens of Santo-Domingo, *Correspondance*, number 4455.

Almost two years later, in another Proclamation issued on 17 brumaire an X (8 November 1801), the First Consul declared to the inhabitants in the Caribbean under the French flag that: "Regardless of your origin and color, you are all Frenchmen. All of you are free and equal before God and the Republic."[9] To the English Government, a governing body that controlled more people than any other in the world, Napoleon's words of freedom and equality threatened the very foundation on which their power was built.[10]

King George III

English hysteria was further heightened by their own propaganda in connection with three important incidents. The first, in late 1802, dealt with Piedmont, the country south of Switzerland abutting the southeast corner of France. In the campaigns against the Austrians in 1796-97 and 1800, Napoleon had twice conquered that country. After Amiens, Napoleon invited Piedmont's King Charles Emmanuel to return to the throne that he had left, having fled to Rome during the campaign of 1800. However, Charles Emmanuel, who was "exceedingly weak and ruled by [Catholic] priests, declined to do so."[11] This declination was the opportunity Napoleon needed. Piedmont's status was not addressed at Amiens, nor at Lunéville. This was, no doubt, by Napoleon's design. He realized the vital importance of the Alpine passes from his Italian campaigns, and correctly identified the potential problem of leaving a vacuum between France and the Cisalpine Republic that the Austrians could exploit at a later date. Further, the Piedmontese had little love for the Austrian Habsburgs, and Piedmontese envoys to France signaled their desire for a democratic government and religious tolerance. As a result of all these factors, Napoleon annexed Piedmont—a move that the Piedmontese preferred to the rule of Charles Emmanuel—and also renamed the Cisalpine Republic the Italian Republic with himself as President.[12]

The English Government, however, used the Piedmont's change in status to rise up in righteous indignation against alleged French imperialism. Even though the Piedmontese were agreeable with the annexation, the British labeled this act as new proof of Napoleon's unquenchable thirst for more territory and power. What totally impeaches the self-righteousness of the English was their Act of Union of 1801 that 'united' Ireland to the crown against the wishes of the Irish people. Going hand-in-hand with this Act of Union was the suppression of the Irish Parliament. Catholic emancipation was not allowed. As anywhere else in places where the English ruled, Catholics in Ireland were forbidden to hold office or vote.

The second incident dealt with Egypt. In January 1803, the English still had not evacuated Alexandria as they had promised to do by the preceding September in accordance with the Treaty of Amiens. While this irritated Napoleon and the Consular Government, the situation worsened significantly on 18 January. *The Times* newspaper gave a glowing review of Sir Robert Wilson's *History of the British Expedition to Egypt.* Wilson, never one to give a balanced view of any situation, offered only contempt for the French army and its leader. Wilson described Napoleon as a "man of… Machiavellian principles" who murdered 580 of his own sick men at Jaffa while under the influence of an overdose of opium.[13] Wilson's

British cartoonists ridiculed Napoleon

---

[9] Proclamation, *Correspondance,* number 5859.

[10] Napoleon, however, was later convinced of the need to reinstate slavery in the West Indies, a move which he later admitted as "the greatest mistake I ever made." See Gaspard Gourgaud, *Sainte Hélène: Journal inédit de 1815 à 1818,* 2 volumes (Paris, no date), vol. 1, p. 402, and Napoléon's "Notes sur Saint-Domingue," *Correspondance*, Volume 30, p. 525-536.

[11] Vincent Cronin, *Napoleon Bonaparte: An Intimate Biography* (New York, 1972), p. 229.

[12] Octave Aubry, *Napoleon: Soldier and Emperor*, translated by Arthur Livingston (New York, 1938), p. 130.

[13] Review of Sir Robert Wilson, *History of the British Expedition to Egypt* in the 18 January 1803 edition of *The Times.*

Sébastiani in Turkey

diatribe was readily swallowed by most English people as well as the other courts of Europe that had no tolerance of a usurper sitting on the throne of France. Accordingly, Wilson's lie was echoed in subsequent articles and in numerous halls of State.

Napoleon was incensed by this slander in a newspaper that was the most influential publication in England. In a response designed to answer Wilson's falsehoods and prod the British into making good on their promises given at Amiens, the First Consul decided to published a report in *Le Moniteur* from Horace-François-Bastien Sébastiani, a *comme-chef de brigade* of the 9th Dragoons, who had recently returned to France from a mission to Turkey and Egypt. While Napoleon toned down some of Sébastiani's gasconade, he did not edit the verbiage that "six thousand men would suffice to reconquer Egypt"[14] if the British failed to honor their obligations as set forth by the Treaty of Amiens. The English Government was only too happy to use Sébastiani's published report as further evidence of Napoleon's unquenchable thirst for conquest. Furthermore, the British circulated that issue of *Le Moniteur* to sow seeds of discontent in Russia as well, which was sensitive to her Mediterranean island prize of Corfu. French aggression in the Mediterranean, argued the English Government, would threaten Corfu. As a result of this line of thinking, the court in Saint Petersburg supported a tougher British policy against Napoleon.

The third incident had to do with Switzerland. In the late 18th century, the Swiss Confederation was a loose organization of 13 virtually sovereign cantons, plus other allied and independent states that together totalled 22 cantons. Each canton had its own form of government, but the people who lived in these cantons shared a growing sense of solidarity fueled by the Revolutionary enthusiasm sweeping many countries bordering France. However, the few aristocrats who ruled the Confederation had no intent of foregoing their wealth and feudal rights. Further, these privileged few had their money tied closely with English banks as well as Swiss ones. The aristocracy's intent to maintain the status quo clashed sharply with the prevailing public sentiment which cried out for a unified state and a constitution modeled after the French.

From Paris, at the urging of expatriate Swiss liberals Peter Ochs and Frederick Laharpe, the Directory instructed General Bonaparte to visit Switzerland to test public opinion. This Napoleon did following the Congress of Rastadt in November 1797. He was welcomed as a hero—a sign that the Directory used to order French troops into the cantons in January of 1798 to aid in the popular movement to liberate themselves and to seize the financial center in Berne. As the *ancien régime* in the cantons dissolved, the Helvetic Republic was proclaimed.[15]

William Wickham

As a new, liberal constitution modeled on that of the French was being established in Switzerland, the English, Austrians and Russians were planning to turn back the clock. Funded by plenty of English gold, Austrian and Russian armies commanded by Suvórov launched a campaign into Switzerland in 1799 aimed at defeating the French forces there and restoring aristocratic rule. Once this happened, it would be banking business as before. William Wickham, England's emissary in Switzerland, found that public sentiment rested decidedly on the side of the French. On 20 July 1799, Wickham wrote from the canton of Schwyz that:

> The magistrates and ancient families … have not only entirely lost the public confidence and esteem, but they are become so much the object of hatred to the peasants that were it not for the

[14] Horace-François-Bastien Sébastiani, *Le Moniteur,* 10 pluviôse an XI (30 January 1803).
[15] For a complete history of the Swiss during the French Revolution, consult: E. Chapuisat, *La Suisse et la Révolution française* (Geneva, 1945).

> presence of the Austrians I am persuaded that many of them would be made an immediate sacrifice to the popular fury.[16]

The Battle of Zürich

In Zürich, Wickham found the people "contented with nothing but a republic formed after the example of France."[17]

Militarily, the situation was decided at the Battle of Zürich (25 September through 5 October 1799) when the French *Armée d'Helvétie* under Andre Masséna first cut to pieces the Austro-Russian forces under Russian General I. Rimski-Korsakov, then turned on a Russian relief army under Suvórov, routing it in turn.[18]

The Swiss political environment was more involved. Following Masséna's crushing military victories against the allied forces in Switzerland, Napoleon ordered the French army to disengage from the country as promised by the Peace of Amiens. As the French withdrew, the country was governed by the Swiss with their new constitution that established equality before the law and set up a modern, united administrative state. Into this delicate political sphere reentered the English, who were intent on destablizing the country's new government and causing further agitation on the continent. Aided by a flood of English gold funneled through the old Confederation aristocrats, the Swiss were soon at each other's throats, the old establishment against the new. Civil war erupted and the country was plunged in chaos.

The tumult in Switzerland was intolerable for France. Disgusted that Britain had once again used Switzerland "as a second Jersey from which to encourage agitation,"[19] Napoleon sent in French troops in response to the Swiss' request in order to put an end to the fighting, and summoned to Paris the leading Swiss citizens in order to establish another constitution with which everyone could live. After listening to all sides, Napoleon astutely chose a middle course. Fusing political ideas new and old, Napoleon created his historic Act of Mediation.[20] This Napoleonic instrument still stands today as the basis of the Swiss government. In addition to the new constitution, Switzerland was also bound by a defensive alliance to France.

A British cartoonist recognized why the Peace of Amiens was doomed: the world was too small for the two sides to share.

When the English Government caught wind of the Paris meetings with the Swiss dignitaries, Under-Secretary of State Moore was sent to Switzerland "to encourage and stimulate the oligarchic party."[21] Moore arrived only to find the frontier closed. With their upper-class Swiss friends no longer in power nor controlling Swiss finances, the English Government and English bankers were big losers. Castigation followed with English newspaper editors and speakers in Parliament taking turns vilifying Napoleon who, according to them, was "audaciously interfering to deprive the gallant Swiss of the right of establishing their liberties."[22] The British called Napoleon's Act of Mediation further proof of his intention to extend French influence, and seized the event as a pretext to harden their stances against France and to pin everything on Napoleon and his ambitious career. King George III, described as "extremely eager"[23] for a resumption of hostilities, recommended that the militia be called out and 10,000 more men levied for the Royal Navy. He also announced that Malta would not be given up as

---

[16] P.R.O., F.O. 74, Volume 38.
[17] P.R.O., F.O. 74, Volume 38.
[18] Duffy, *Russia's Military Way to the West,* pp. 212-232, gives an excellent account of the campaign.
[19] Napoleon, as quoted in J. Dechamps, "La rupture de la Paix d'Amiens: Comment elle fut préparée," in the *Revue des Études napoléoniennes*, May-June 1939, p. 182.
[20] Bonaparte's Exposé of the Situation of the Republic, *Correspondance,* number 6591.
[21] P.R.O., F.O. 74, Volume 36.
[22] P.R.O., F.O. 74, Volume 38.
[23] Buckingham and Chandos, *Memoirs of the Courts and Cabinets of George III,* p. 218.

promised by England in the Treaty of Amiens, and demanded that France remove all her troops from Holland and Switzerland.

The double standard of British foreign policy could be seen through by many, including William Grenville, former Foreign Minister in the Pitt Government. After witnessing the course of events for the past several years, and hearing that Britain would not honor her commitments made at Amiens, Grenville told his brother, the Marquess of Buckingham on 22 March 1803:

The Bourbon agents infiltrate France at a lonely landing place on the coast

> Our government have so contrived things, that it is hardly possible for Bonaparte himself to recede, had he the wish to do so... If he now suffers himself to be intimidated by our preparations [for war], he must lose all consideration both at home and abroad.[24]

With the seizure of the two French merchantmen on 18 May 1803, France and Britain were plunged back into another war that would last 12 long, bloody years. There is ample evidence that all the other European courts realized that war was forced on Napoleon. Prussian Foreign Minister Karl August von Hardenberg, no lover of Napoleonic France, wrote to the comte de Provence in England: "It would have been desirable for England to show as much good will for peace as Bonaparte."[25] A Bourbon agent writing from Paris conceded that: "It seems certain that Bonaparte has decided on war with extreme reluctance."[26] Perhaps this reluctance—at least during this time in his career—is what Napoleon had in mind when he later declared: "I have never really been my own master; I have always been governed by circumstances."[27]

The Third Coalition Takes Shape

Royalist Plots Against Napoleon

Long before England broke the Peace of Amiens, the English Government decided that Napoleon would be the issue that they would use to bring together the other countries of Europe in order to oppose France. What's more, the English committed themselves to help finance any person or group intent on eliminating the usurper. With English guineas, a training camp at Romsey was set up for the express purpose of training Bourbon *émigré* conspirators and assassins who wished to return to France to get rid of Napoleon and his family. An underground army of Bourbon faithful, generously financed and trained in England, was dedicated to the restoration of the Bourbons and Louis XVIII to the throne of France, which they believed could be accomplished by the assassination of the Corsican.[28]

The Infernal Machine

The Bourbons' murderous plots began on Christmas Eve 1800 with the explosion of a bomb known as the "Infernal Machine." This attempt to assassinate Napoleon was masterminded by the reactionaries George Cadoudal and the comte d'Artois, brother of Louis XVI. The comte d'Artois was an ultraroyalist whose extravagance and irresponsible indulgences made him archetypical of the leadership that provoked the French Revolution and, not surprisingly, a failure as king of France as Charles X (1824-1830). Under d'Artois' direction, the Royalist conspirators met in Paris and ignited a crudely made bomb near the coach that was

---

[24] Grenville, as quoted in Buckingham and Chandos, *Memoirs of the Courts and Cabinets of George III,* p. 220.
[25] S.H.A.T., C^2 13.
[26] *Relations secrétes des agents de Louis XVIII à Paris sous le consulat* (Paris, 1899).
[27] Emmanuel Las Cases, *Mémorial de Saint Hélène,* 9 volumes (Paris, 1897), Napoleon's conversation of 11 November 1816.
[28] A.N., F^7 6271.

carrying the First Consul to the Opéra. The explosion killed nine and injured 26 innocent people while failing to hurt Bonaparte.[29]

Having his agents fail to dispose of Napoleon with the "Infernal Machine," d'Artois decided that Cadoudal himself should cross the Channel to personally see that the next attempt did not fail. Ideas for the succeeding plot took shape over the next three springs. Then, in August 1803 Cadoudal slipped into Paris. During the six months that followed, he gathered around him 60 conspirators who committed to a scheme of assassinating Napoleon during a review. Once Napoleon was dead, Cadoudal would be joined in France by the comte d'Artois, who would open the frontiers to *émigrés* and invading allied armies, place Louis XVIII on the throne, and turn the clock back to the good old days of the *ancien régime* by destroying the Napoleonic Code and the gains of the Revolution. Among those involved with this plot were Generals Charles Pichegru along with Jean Victor Moreau, one of the most popular generals of the Revolution. According to Cadoudal's second-in-command, Bouvet de Lozier, the conspirators had several meetings that included Bouvet, Cadoudal, Pichegru and Moreau. However, these gatherings accomplished little because those involved could not agree about the type of government that should be set up after Bonaparte's death. Everyone wanted a Bourbon king, except Moreau, who was willing to join the conspirators only if he was to be named as military dictator. The Royalists argued with him unsuccessfully, but Moreau's open opposition to the Consular Government and his consorting with traitors would finish his career in French uniform.[30] The impasse could only be solved by the arrival of a prince of the House of Bourbon who would lead the coup.

Cadoudal

Louis-Antoine de Bourbon Condé, the duc d'Enghien, was the last of the famous Condés, a family long known for their military stature dating from the 1500s. The 31-year-old *émigré* lived on the political edge in a turbulent political time. From his estate in the Baden town of Ettelheim—about 10 miles from the French border—the duc d'Enghien was planning to lead an *émigré* force into Alsace in the event of a continental war. While Enghien bided his time, his agents were sowing seeds of insurrection in eastern France. The duc d'Enghien's efforts were financed by the English Government that granted him 4,200 guineas a year to recruit and train a network of Royalist spies and agitators. With this manpower and money, Enghien pledged to "combat not France, but a government to which his birth made him hostile."[31] When the Paris police nabbed Cadoudal after following him for weeks, he cracked under questioning and the conspiracy unraveled. All the prominent participants were uncovered and taken into custody. Pichegru died in prison and Moreau was exiled from France. Before he was executed for his part in the plot, Cadoudal confessed that his men were to murder the First Consul only when a Bourbon prince came to Paris and that he was expected to arrive soon. Subsequent police reports from Brittany stated that Royalists in the Vendée believed that the duc d'Enghien would soon be returning to Paris, from which he would lead France into an anti-Bonapartist paradise. Making these reports believable was the information provided by double agent Mehée de la Touche, who met with an English agent named Francis Drake in Münich. Drake confided to Mehée that Enghien was to lead an *émigré* force as his grandfather, the Prince of Condé, had done in the Prussian invasion of France during the Valmy campaign of 1792. Drake also paid £10,000 to Enghien to help finance an insurrection in eastern France that was to flare up the same time a continental war began.[32] Finalizing the

the duc d'Enghien

[29] A.N., F^7 6272.

[30] Jean-Victor Moreau, a 40-year old distinguished general of the Revolution, had commanded the *Armée du Nord* in 1795 and the *Armée du Rhin-et-Moselle* in 1796 before defeating the Austrians at the Battle of Hohenlinden in December, 1800.

[31] A. Boulay de la Meurthe, *Les dernières années du duc d'Enghien* (Paris, 1886), p. 4.

[32] Letter from Drake in the Liverpool Papers, British Museum.

compelling case against Enghien was another report Napoleon received from Joseph Fouché, the Minister of General Police. Fouché related that his agents had discovered that the exiled traitor General Charles-François du Perier Dumouriez and an English Colonel Smith were with the duc d'Enghien.

Whether or not all the reports were true, Napoleon had heard enough. The incessant Bourbon plots aimed to murder him and his family had, in his mind, reached the point of a Corsican blood feud. He had to put a stop to these assassination attempts. Cadoudal's confession, coupled with police reports about rumors from the Vendée, the Royalist enlistment of the treasonous Dumouriez, the English attempt to finance open rebellion and the admission that Enghien was to lead *émigrés* against *La Patrie,* was enough to present in Napoleon's mind a *prima facie* case against the duc d'Enghien. He was still a Frenchman and subject to French law, regardless of his place of residence. On Napoleon's order, 300 troopers of the 26th Dragoons under *général de brigade* Michel Ordener, ironically a former dragoon in the old legion of the Condé and now commander of the *Grenadiers à cheval* of the Imperial Guard, crossed the border into Baden on the night of 14 March 1804.[33] These French cavalrymen, along with some troopers of the 22nd Dragoons, encircled the timbered house in Ettelheim where the last member of the Condé family was awakened from his slumbers. Before he knew what had happened, the duc d'Enghien was whisked back to his native country and incarcerated at the military prison at the château de Vincennes on the outskirts of Paris.

One of the conspirators, Pichegru died in prison

Charged with conspiracy in the time of war, the duc d'Enghien was subject to military law. In accordance with the statutes, a tribunal of seven colonels sat in judgment. During the proceeding, Enghien admitted to the court that: "I asked England if I might serve in her armies, but she replied that was impossible: I must wait on the Rhine, where I would have a part to play immediately, and I was in fact waiting."[34] When questioned, the duc d'Enghien also confirmed that England was subsidizing his efforts to combat the French Government. While the questioning was going on, Napoleon examined Enghien's papers. From his inspection of these documents, the First Consul learned that Dumouriez had been confused by Fouché's police with a harmless *émigré,* the Marquis de Thuméry, and Colonel Smith had likewise been mistaken for a German called Schmidt. It became clear at that point that the Bourbon prince that was involved in the Cadoudal plot was still an enigma, and that Enghien was not directly connected with this specific intrigue hatched by the comte d'Artois. Nevertheless, the young Condé *was* plotting the downfall of the Consular Government with enemies of France. The tribunal unanimously found the duc d'Enghien guilty accordingly to Article 2 of the law of 6 October 1791, to wit: "Any conspiracy and plot aimed at disturbing the State by civil war, and arming the citizens against one another, or against lawful authority, will be punished by death."[35]

Until this time, failed Bourbon assassination attempts had resulted in their operatives being caught, and perhaps punished, without any direct consequences against one of the family's nobles. In the past, Napoleon had stepped in and showed mercy when he chose. Among these examples would be the Concordat of 1801 which gave amnesty to all royalists. As a result some 40,000 *émigrés* returned to France.[36] On another occasion he yielded to the Bourbon Princess Hatzfeld when she pleaded for her husband's life after he had been caught spying. Of the Cadoudal

---

[33] Bonaparte to Berthier, *Correspondance*, number 7608.

[34] A. Boulay de la Meurthe, *Les dernières années du duc d'Enghien* (Paris, 1886).

[35] Cronin, *Napoleon Bonaparte*, p. 244.

[36] Martyn Lyons, *Napoleon Bonaparte and the Legacy of the French Revolution* (New York, 1994), pp.77-93; Connelly, Parker, Becker and Burton, *Historical Dictionary of Napoleonic France, 1799-1815*, p. 124.

accomplices, the First Consul had intervened and saved eight of the 20 *noblesse* who had been condemned to death. However, his repeated mercy had been rewarded with only repeated attempts on his person, members of his family and government. The Enghien incident was the final straw. "Let them [Bourbons] lead all Europe against me in arms, and I'll defend myself," Napoleon declared. "An attack like that is legitimate ... I'll teach them to legalize murder!"[37] The First Consul reasoned that the Bourbons' long-standing vendetta against him needed a sufficiently strong countermeasure. The duc d'Enghien was to be shown no mercy. All Europe would get the message: further assassination attempts would invoke the strongest possible course of French justice. Therefore, following the end of his trial and sentencing which lasted from 1 A.M. to 2:30 A.M. on 21 March 1804, the duc d'Enghien was led out of the cold, high walls of the prison and by torchlight was summarily executed by a firing squad. His spot of execution is still marked today by a small white cross backed against the outer wall of the château de Vincennes.

The Allies Fall in With England

In his biography of Napoleon, the renowned French artist Job illustrates the Enghien incident with remarkable simplicity and clarity. Shown backed up against the outer wall at Vincennes facing a firing squad is the duc d'Enghien. From a lantern resting on the ground several feet in front of him, there is cast upon the château's wall an enormous shadow that dwarfs the Condé.[38] Indeed, the long shadow of the duc d'Enghien was forever cast against Napoleon.

Job's view of Enghien's execution

The Enghien incident would dog Napoleon the rest of his life, even though he reacted the only way he knew how. When Cadoudal confirmed that, through the efforts of the comte d'Artois, there were 60 paid assassins in Paris, and that the previous Bourbon plots were openly admitted to as well, Napoleon responded according to the code of the Corsican vendetta. Attacks by members of one clan (the comte d'Artois) against another clan (the Bonapartes) could only be avenged by the death of another member of the clan (the duc d'Enghien) which initiated the attempted murders.

European monarchs considered the plots to assassinate Napoleon as an extension of the Bourbons' legitimate right to recover their throne. On the other hand, Napoleon's dealing with the duc d'Enghien was, in the eyes of these sovereigns, nothing less than a lawless kidnapping and murder by a ruthless thug. The Enghien incident gave the courts in London, Vienna, Saint Petersburg and elsewhere a reason to renew hostilities and settle old scores. Therefore, like the wars of the French Revolution, the Napoleonic wars were ideological conflicts whereby 'legitimate' kings operated by a code of conduct which no one else was allowed to employ, especially Napoleon Bonaparte. The cries of righteous indignation that arose from Bourbon sympathizers over the Enghien incident were totally impeached by the blood on their own hands. When Louis XVIII gained the throne in the Restoration, he refused to allow any inquiry into the death of the duc d'Enghien. This is, no doubt, because the complicity of the comte d'Artois and of the English officials in the Cadoudal plot would have proven too embarrassing. However, Napoleon's example of Enghien did have the desired effect. Bourbon plots against him and his family ceased. If European monarchs wanted to get rid of the usurper they would have to accomplish that on the field of battle.

The English wanted to fan the continental fires of war for good reason. It was no secret that an enormous French army had been encamped and training along the Channel since the fall of 1803. Bourbon agents discovered that a portion of the French training included disembarkation drills from small boats. Add to

[37] Napoleon, as quoted in Cronin, *Napoleon Bonaparte*, p. 243.
[38] Job, *Bonaparte* (Paris, 1975).

this the substantial combined Franco-Spanish fleet that could set sail and threaten any number of the far-flung possessions of the English Empire, drawing the English fleet away from their homeland. Therefore, to remove the threat of invasion from their island nation, the English Government considered it a top priority to stir into action the continental armies of Russia and Austria.

The first country to join England was Russia, whose foreign trade was largely controlled by 4,000 English merchants based in Saint Petersburg. Since Russia's economy so heavily depended upon English trade and gold, Tsar Alexander was most enthusiastic about a new coalition against the usurper. The duc d'Enghien's arrest in Baden, the home of Alexander's wife, gave what the Tsar considered to be a good reason for war. He sent to Paris a note in protest of the French Government's violation of Baden as a neutral country when the duc d'Enghien was arrested. At Napoleon's direction, Foreign Minister Talleyrand responded with a note inquiring as to why Alexander failed to prosecute the murderers of his father, Tsar Paul. Insofar as Alexander was concerned, legitimate monarchs could question rogues, but Napoleon's reply along the same line was simply a tactless insult. A commoner could not question the dealings of a rightful king. Alexander, who "had elected himself the conscience of Europe," [39] therefore became anxious for war.

The Tsar was no doubt further influenced by his Anglophile chief advisor on foreign affairs, Prince Adam George Czartoryski, who suggested that Russia adopt the strongest possible expansionist policies in connection with central Europe. Under the guise of founding a vast Pan-Slavic state west of his current borders, Alexander was eager to expand Russia's influence by putting Russian troops into the field. The English Government agreed to compensate Alexander and the other allied heads of state some £1.25 million for every 100,000 troops to march against Napoleon.[40]

Emperor Francis II

The Emperor of Austria was less decisive. Emperor Francis II was the "sovereign of a ramshackle congeries of provinces"[41] known as the Habsburg Empire. What is more important, he was diametrically opposed to the ideas of the French Revolution while being committed to preserving the status quo of the *ancien régime* within Austrian territory and throughout the remainder of Europe. As a consequence, he listened intently to any recommendations that would throw France back to their old pre-Revolutionary boundaries. There were many of his cabinet ministers like Count Colloredo, who were champing at the bit to form a new alliance against Napoleon. On the other hand, there were experienced soldiers, such as his brother Archduke Charles, who warned Francis of the untrustworthy nature of Russia as an ally, which could result in Austrian forces suffering the most from the upcoming fight. Furthermore, the history of the last 150 years clearly showed that the English could send money, but were unlikely to risk their small army against a powerful European host. This policy led historian M. von Angeli to conclude: "Apart from Marlborough, no Englishman has believed that Britain could strive for the dominion of the seas by fighting on the Danube."[42]

When Francis received word that the Tsar and King George had concluded a new coalition on 11 April 1805, the Austrian Emperor agreed on a joint military operation with the Russian army. In addition to the Austrians, Russians and English, the Swedes joined the coalition, thanks to the English propaganda campaign surrounding the Enghien incident. Once all the treaties of alliance were ratified, serious military plans for the coalition forces were laid out by Tsar Alexander.

[39] Brigadier General Vincent J. Esposito and Colonel John Robert Elting, *A Military History and Atlas of the Napoleonic Wars* (New York, 1963), Introduction to the Ulm-Austerlitz Campaign.

[40] M. A. Thiers, *The History of the Consulate & the Empire of France under Napoleon*, 2 volumes (London, 1875), vol. 1, p. 641; Cronin, *Napoleon Bonaparte*, p. 256.

[41] Duffy, *Austerlitz*, p. 4.

[42] Angeli, *Mitteilungen des k und k. Kriegsarchiv*, p. 384.

This convention, formalized on 9 August 1805, set the forces of the Third Coalition in motion.[43]

The Allies Formulate Their Strategy

To Tsar Alexander, there was never any doubt as to his purpose for war. The glories of being the one to defeat Napoleon and restore the Bourbons to their righteous throne was foremost in the mind of the 28-year-old Russian monarch. Alexander saw himself as a modern messiah of royalty, returning Europe to the 'glory' of the *ancien régime.* His purpose in the upcoming 1805 campaign would be to lead his army westward and, somewhere in central Europe, with the aid of Austria and other allies, Alexander and the Russian army would engage and destroy the forces of the usurper. Once the military situation was settled, Alexander envisioned his procession into Paris where he would be hailed as the savior of Europe.

In order to accomplish Alexander's messianic mission, a vast offensive across the breadth of the continent was designed in order to sweep away France and all her allies. Coalition forces were to liberate Hanover and the other German states along the Rhine River, as well as Switzerland, Holland and Northern Italy. Alexander's original plan called for the continental allies to put no less than 400,000 men into the field. This number was later revised downward, but could swell to more than 500,000 if Prussia threw in her lot with the coalition. Whether or not the Prussians joined the alliance, there were to be five Russian armies involved. Under the most optimistic estimates, the Tsarist forces would total some 165,000 men. The primary focus was on central Europe, thus on the surface encompassing Czartoryski's pipedream of establishing a new Pan-Slavic utopia. Four Russian armies and another combined allied force were to be committed to this theater of war. General Bennigsen, at the head of a small army hoped to be 20,000 men strong, was to move through Bohemia towards Franconia where he would be able to cover the strategic northern flank of the forces operating on the Danube. Meanwhile, another army consisting of 16,000 Russians under General Tolstoy would march to Stralsund in Swedish Pomerania. There they would combine with 12,000 Swedes and move overland and strike into Hanover where they would be reinforced by 15,000 British that would disembark at Cuxhaven. This army would then threaten Holland, consequentially encouraging Prussia to join the coalition. Two more Russian armies, each *hoped* to be as strong as 50,000 combatants under Generals Kutuzov and Buxhöwden, would move from the Motherland southwest towards the Danube. These forces could either join up with Austrian forces on the Danube or support Bennigsen's southern flank, depending upon whether Prussia remained neutral. The fifth Russian force numbering 12,000 men was already at their Mediterranean island of Corfu while another 13,000 were in reserve at the Black Sea port of Odessa. These troops were to team up with a British expeditionary force of 5,500 troops from Malta, and using Corfu and Malta as bases, would move by sea and disembark in Naples where Russian General Lacy was making preparations for their arrival. Once the Russian and British forces joined with the Neapolitan army of 36,000, the allied force of 66,500 combatants would march up the Italian boot, liberate the minor Italian Papal States, defeat France's strongest ally in the form of Kingdom of Italy, and hook up with Austrian forces, putting the squeeze on this Napoleonic ally from the east and north.[44]

Theoretical strength of the planned Allied Forces for the defeat of Napoleon

North Germany
16,000 Russians (Tolstoy)
12,000 Swedes
15,000 Britsih

Franconia
20,000 Russians (Bennigsen)

Bavaria
72,000 Austrians (Ferdinand)
supported by
50,000 Russians (Kutusov) &
50,000 Russians (Buxhöwden)

Tyrol
22,000 Austrians (John)

Northern Italy
94,000 Austrians (Charles)

Southern Italy
36,000 Neapolitans
25,000 Russians (Lacy)
5,500 British

---

[43] Angeli, *Mitteilungen des k und k. Kriegsarchiv*, p. 422, states that the signing Coalition members agreed that they were "trusting in the loyality of its partners."

[44] Duffy, *Austerlitz*, p. 6; Esposito and Elting, *A Military History and Atlas of the Napoleonic War,* text to Map 46; Thiers, *The History of the Consulate & the Empire of France under Napoleon*, vol. 2, p. 2 and 13.

The English had little respect for their parvenu opponent—in this cartoon a lilliputian Bonaparte is inspected by George III

Insofar as the Italian theater was concerned, Tsar Alexander had a special form of treachery in store for Napoleon. If Napoleon was somehow forewarned of the allied plans, Alexander feared that the 18,600 man French army under the command of General Gouvion Saint-Cyr stationed in the Papal States around Rome to the north of Naples could utterly crush the Neapolitans before the Russians and British arrived. Therefore, Alexander and his counselors suggested to the Neapolitan Bourbons that they approach Napoleon about a treaty of neutrality. This document, which was presented to Napoleon in September, stipulated that Saint-Cyr's army at Tarentum be withdrawn from the Papal States, in exchange for Neapolitan neutrality, coupled with the condition that no Russians or British would set foot on southern Italian soil. Of course, the Neapolitan Bourbons, nor the Russians, nor the British had any intention of honoring the treaty. It was simply a ruse to buy time for the disparate elements of the fifth allied army to land in Naples and begin their conquest of the Papal States and the Kingdom of Italy.

Napoleon agreed to this treaty. It was signed in Paris on the morning of 24 September 1805 before the Emperor mounted his carriage to begin his journey to join the *Grande Armée* on the Rhine. The reasons for Napoleon accepting such a proposition were numerous. First, Napoleon believed that the morally weak Neapolitan Bourbons were only interested in maintaining their throne and would not dare commit themselves to the Third Coalition. Accepting this as true, Napoleon could not dream that the court in Naples was preparing to commit the worst form of treachery against him. He was convinced that the example he had made of Venice in 1797 was sufficient deterrence against any Italian state that dared to deliberately deceive him. Finally, Napoleon believed that the treaty of neutrality with Naples provided a golden opportunity. By securing the southern flank of the *Armée d'Italie* and releasing Saint-Cyr's 18,600 men from central Italy to march to Masséna's assistance, the Emperor reasoned that it was possible to prevent Archduke Charles' Austrians from ever crossing the Adige River.

The Austrians were to field three armies totaling an estimated 178,000 combatants, but the Austrians saw the main theater as Northern Italy rather than central Europe. Allied grand strategy attempted to accommodate Austrian wishes. This was especially ill-advised since Allied intelligence sources knew that Napoleon had at least 150,000 men encamped along the Channel and that the only logical course of action for him would be to move this host into Germany. Archduke Ferdinand (with General Mack as acting army commander) with 72,000 men was to move into Bavaria, where he was to then wait on the Danube for the Russians. Once combined, the Austro-Russian forces would march west towards the Rhine where they would engage and destroy any French opposition. Meanwhile, Archduke John's 22,000 men in the Tyrol would remain on the defensive, acting as a strategic link between the forces on the Danube and largest Austrian army operating in Northern Italy. The Tyrolian army was to join in offensive movements *only* when the main Austrian army in Italy crossed the Adda River. It was Italy where the Austrians wished to make their major effort, thereby recovering many of the territories lost during the wars of the French Revolution. Numbering 94,000 combatants commanded by the country's most capable general, Archduke Charles, the Austrian Army of Italy was to drive westward across Northern Italy, destroy the Franco-Italian forces and capture Milan in the process.[45]

The final act of Alexander's plan of campaign predicted that the Prussians as well as the Bavarians, Saxons, Hessians, Brunswickers and Danes would join in the advancing coalition host. Then with at least 500,000 men marching with them, Alexander hoped that the French, Swiss and Italians—driven back on all fronts

[45] Esposito and Elting, *A Military History and Atlas of the Napoleonic War,* see Map 46; Thiers, *The History of the Consulate & the Empire of France under Napoleon*, vol. 2, p. 15

with their armies in defeat and Napoleon humiliated—would rise up against the anti-Christ and welcome back the rule of kings. Such was Alexander's dream of conquest—a dream whose most glaring flaw was that it failed to grasp the enormity of the undertaking as well as the quality of the opposition. As Alexander himself would soon find out, the French army he was about to face was like nothing like he or his generals had ever been seen before, and led by a man who was arguably history's greatest soldier.

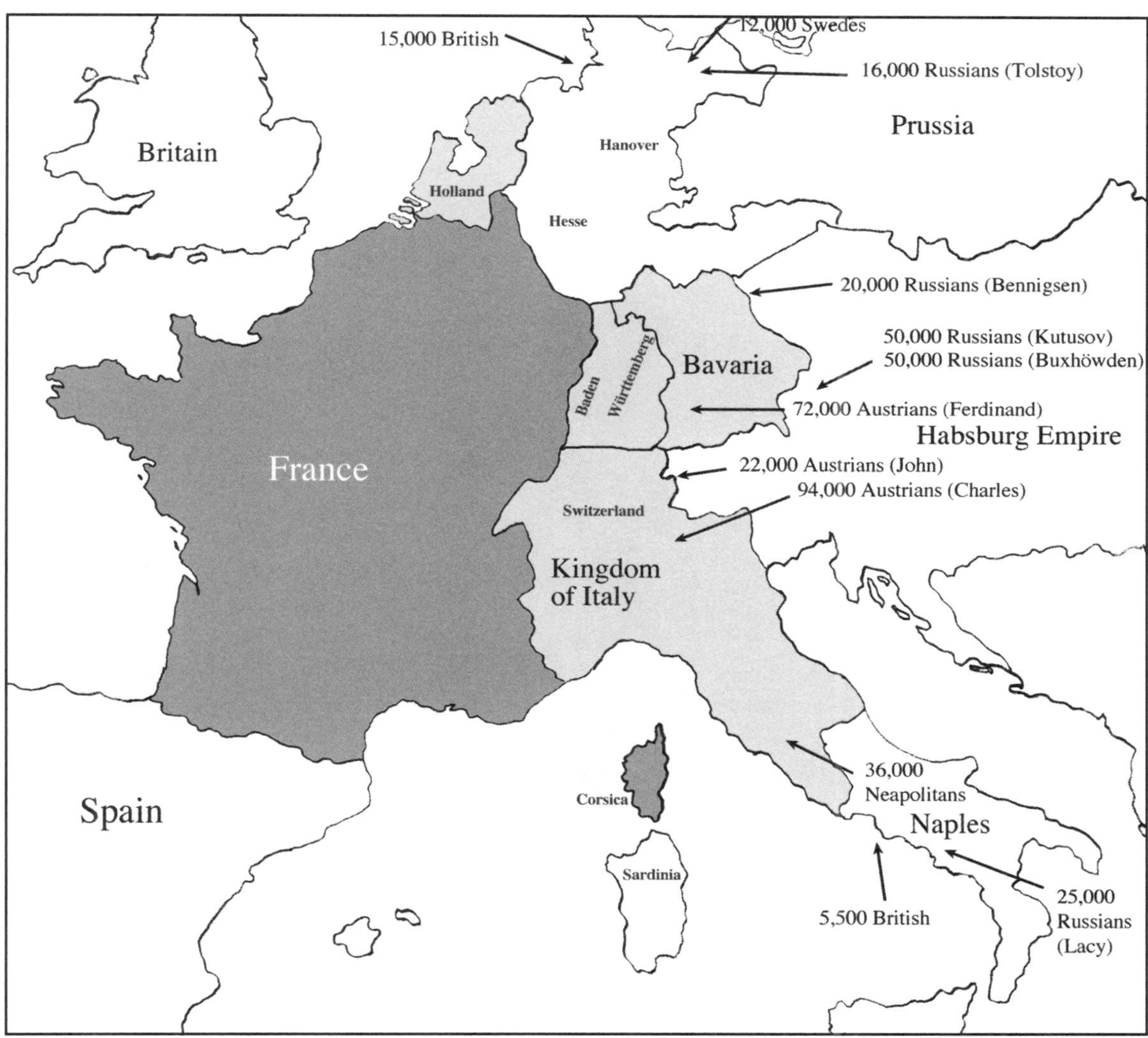

Allied Grand Strategy in 1805; strengths are theoretical

Chapter V
"The Débris of Some Wrecked Vessel" *The Ruination of General Mack at Ulm*

The weather had been miserable for two weeks. The depressingly endless autumn rain and snowfall seemed to reflect the morale of the Austrian army around Ulm which had sunk as low as the muddy boots worn by her soldiers. Outmarched, outgeneraled and outfought at every engagement since the start of the 1805 campaign, "the morale of the Austrian army was beyond all repair."[1] With no other troops coming to their rescue, unable to escape the ring of French soldiers that had been masterfully placed around Ulm by Napoleon, the Austrian generals saw no other alternative but to capitulate. It was agreed that the Austrians were to deliver Ulm on 20 October.

As the rains continued into the morning of that day, Napoleon drew up the *Grande Armée* before the Danube fortress in readiness to accept the Austrian surrender. At two in the afternoon, the rains suddenly stopped and the clouds parted as if the heavens wished to see the spectacle clearly. With the warming rays of a brilliant sun reflecting off the stunning dress uniforms, glittering bayonets and muskets of Napoleon's host, the Austrian army marched out of Ulm and into captivity. To most of Napoleon's soldiers, veterans of a decade of wars against the Austrians, this triumph had a very special meaning: a longtime adversary who opposed the French Revolution and anything to come from it had been completely humiliated in a lightning campaign. Unable to contain themselves at the sight that was unfolding before their eyes, Napoleon's soldiers celebrated while in ranks with "a joy that was almost indecent."[2]

The Surrender of Ulm, by Berthon

Meanwhile, as Napoleon watched the procession of tens of thousands of prisoners pass by, he engaged in conversation with a party of 15 Austrian generals who were around him. The Emperor spoke sympathetically to these captive officers, who seemed moved by Napoleon's civility, grace and unpretentious bearing. The Emperor's courtesy was also reflected by a curious Imperial staff officer, who politely asked one of the older Austrian generals to be so kind as to point out their commanding officer. The whitecoated gentleman replied: "The man standing before you is the unfortunate General Mack."[3]

* *

The 1805 Campaign Begins
Napoleon

Napoleon Bonaparte, the five-foot six-inch Corsican artillerist, rose to power in France through the combination of his determined personality and the turbulent political environment of the late 18th and early 19th centuries. This man, who left a remarkable series of lasting contributions to modern society, would also fight and win more major battles under varying climatic conditions than any other military

---

[1] Duffy, *Austerlitz,* p. 50.

[2] *Mémoirs de Duc de Raguse (Marmont) de 1792 à 1832*, 9 volumes (Paris, 1857), vol. 2, p. 320.

[3] *An Aide-de-Camp of Napoleon: Memoirs of General Count de Ségur,* translated by H.A. Patchett-Martin (London, 1895), p. 206. Hereafter referred to as *Memoirs of Ségur.*

Carrying Napoleon, a pregnant Letizia flees over mountain trails

leader of any age. To accomplish awe-inspiring military feats as well as bring order and prodigious change into the world, Napoleon had to be a fighter, as he was beginning with his in utero life.

Unlike his elder brother, Joseph, who was "the outcome of a relatively tranquil pregnancy" and was a *joli enfant*—a smiling, happy, gurgling baby—"who automatically charmed everyone who approached him,"[4] Napoleon was markedly different. His mother, Letizia, had a very difficult pregnancy with Napoleon. While she was in her second trimester, Letizia had to flee from enemy troops by riding on a mule over remote and rocky Corsican mountain trails. Food was scarce in those chaotic months of early 1769, but there was no shortage of emotional tension and physical demands caused by bumpy rides on mule back. When Letizia delivered her second child on 15 August 1769, "a scrawny baby with spindly legs and an abnormally large head"[5] appeared. As an infant, Napoleon's physical appearance did not win the hearts of those coming to see the new 'baby Buonaparte.' Then, due perhaps to malnutrition or to stress, Letizia's milk failed her. Napoleon was removed to a back room where a wet nurse cared for him. Only when the third child, Maria-Anna, arrived two years later did Napoleon actually come out of the back room and rejoin the family unit. No doubt the toddler could sense that he was excluded from the family's more loving relationships.

The two-year-old emerging from the back room viewed his family situation as one to be handled in a competitive and combative manner. As a result, the young child turned to picking fights with his older brother to gain attention. Eventually, Napoleon's method turned into habit, and habit became a script in determining his behavior. There is no better testament to this behavior than Napoleon's own words to his son in 1813. "Lazybones," Napoleon playfully admonished the two-year-old King of Rome, "when I was your age I was already beating up Joseph."[6] However, it was Letizia that constantly reminded her scrappy second son that respect and attention would only be gained through achievement. Napoleon took his mother's advice to heart and strove to achieve in every situation. He was never satisfied at being anything but the best, and he would use every opportunity to prove his superiority.

A snowfight at Brienne, the school where Napoleon's leadership capabilities first surfaced

With this type of attitude, the irrepressible climber defiantly met life's demands. Every time an obstacle was placed in his path, Napoleon accepted and met the challenge. Perhaps no three incidents bear greater witness to Napoleon's moral strength in accepting challenges than when he was a nine-year-old entering the college of Brienne, followed years later as First Consul of France and later still as Emperor. The first of these incidents took place in 1778 when Napoleon entered Brienne. While his looks had improved since he was an infant, the new kid in school had a massive Corsican chip on his shoulder, which provoked the strongest possible hazing by the contemptuous young sons of the petty nobility. To eclipse his tormentors, Napoleon responded with hard work to become the star pupil. He especially excelled in mathematics, uncovering his almost unbelievable analytical powers. He could read or be told something only once and instantly recall it for use at a later time, astonishing teachers and classmates alike. The second occurrence in this illustration happened more than 20 years later in the early 1800s. The scenario was analogous to the first, but on a much larger stage. As First Consul of France, Napoleon was treated with nothing but contempt by the other ruling

---

[4] Harold T. Parker, "Why did Napoleon Invade Russia? A Study in Motivation, Personality & Social Structure," in *Proceedings 1989, Consortium on Revolutionary Europe 1750-1850,* edited by Donald D. Horward and John C. Horgan (Tallahassee, 1990), p. 88.

[5] Parker, "Why did Napoleon Invade Russia? A Study in Motivation, Personality & Social Structure," in *Proceedings 1989,* p. 88.

[6] Parker, "Why did Napoleon Invade Russia? A Study in Motivation, Personality & Social Structure," in *Proceedings 1989,* p. 88.

monarchs of Europe. As a new arrival among rulers, he felt that he must excel in both competitive and combative manners. His competitive drive resulted in hard work from which emerged the *Code Napoléon* and the creation of modern Europe. Meanwhile, his combative nature called for the training of a large army along the Channel, thus threatening arch-enemy England. Years later, following the loss of an entire army in Russia during 1812, and with all Europe rising up against him, Napoleon again met the challenge according to the creed by which he had lived his whole life—he responded competitively and combatively. Napoleon performed his most remarkable military organizational feat by creating a new *Grande Armée* in weeks. The Emperor then led his men to victory after victory in the spring campaign of 1813. The following year, during the Campaign of France when things looked their bleakest, Napoleon continued to meet his challenges the only way he knew from the time he was in his mother's womb—he fought!

Napoleon, by Gros

With this brief introduction into his personality, it is not surprising that Napoleon responded to the continuous Bourbon assassination plots in both combative and competitive ways. Napoleon's combative response to the Bourbon plots as discussed in the preceding chapter was the death of the duc d'Enghien as well as the bringing together of an army along the Channel. His competitive response was to accept numerous requests to legitimize his position as head of France with the title 'Emperor.' The French legislative body agreed that "the Government of the Republic [be] entrusted to a hereditary Emperor."[7] The final decision was presented to the electorate, and was overwhelmingly approved by the French people on 18 May 1804. If the French people's decision to have Napoleon become Emperor was not enough to drive the Bourbons out of their collective minds, then certainly the Pope's acceptance of an invitation to travel to Paris and assist in the coronation at the cathedral of Notre Dame on 2 December 1804 was sufficient fodder to keep the fire of their hatred burning for years to come. Like the Bourbons, the other monarchs of Europe saw Napoleon's coronation as an affront of equally unforgivable magnitude as what they considered to be the judicial murder of the duc d'Enghien.

Napoleon's decision to take the title as Emperor was a popular one among most men and officers in the French army. Louis Davout's response was typical among the senior officers. On 1 May 1804, the commanding general at the camp of Bruges and the soon-to-be Marshal wrote the following to Napoleon:

> Citizen First Consul, I have the honor of addressing to you the spontaneous expression of the generals, officers, soldiers, inspectors of the services and the administrators of the camp of Bruges. They demand, along with all Frenchmen, to be assured, by an order of unvarying succession in your family, of the heredity of the supreme Magistracy. The army also desires for you to take the title of Emperor of the French. This is less an honor for you than a guarantee of our happiness to come. Your name alone surpasses all the titles which are given to those who govern. But as you command a grand and brave nation, you must take a title as is assigned to sovereigns of the most powerful nations... You will remove all hope of the Bourbons who are without virtue or glory.[8]

Napoleon in his coronation robes

---

[7] A.N., BII. 722.

[8] Louis N. Davout, *Correspondance du maréchal Davout prince d'Ekmühl: ses commandements, son ministère, 1801-15,* edited by Charles de Mazade, 4 volumes (Paris, 1885), vol. 1, pp. 79-80. Hereafter referred to as *Correspondance Davout.*

Napoleon's Imperial Crest

The day after the Empire became a reality, Napoleon announced his decision to name 18 generals as Marshals of France. The decree dated 19 May 1804 was designed to recognize men for various reasons, and to forever tie them to Napoleon. In remembering the heroes of the Revolution, and to keep intact the lineage from the Republic to the Consulate to the Empire, four men were given the title 'honorary' marshals. These were Kellermann (the elder), Lefebvre, Pérignon and Serurier. Not intended to be active campaigners, these honorary marshals mostly held administrative posts.

The remaining 14 marshals were selected through a combination of faithful service and personal loyalty, as well as winning over those important generals who were outspoken opponents of the Consulate. Those nominated based on personal loyalty to Napoleon included Berthier, Bessières, Davout, Lannes, Mortier, Murat and Ney. The men nominated to be marshals based on distinguished past battlefield services were Brune, Jourdan, Masséna, Moncey and Soult. Among the opponents of the Consulate to be given the title of marshal were Augereau (a staunch Republican) and Bernadotte.

Many of these marshals would have prominent roles in the campaign of 1805. As the French forces on the Channel were reorganized in the summer of 1805, Napoleon employed his marshals as corps commanders of the *Grande Armée*. Only the 2nd Corps, commanded by Marmont, took the field without a Marshal of France at its head. Everyone in the *Grande Armée* was animated with excitement about the upcoming war. One Frenchman described the feeling of the army as a whole:

> All the ambitious young men were galvanized by the idea of the coming campaign. Every one of them was dreaming of the prospects of glory and rapid promotion, and they hoped to distinguish themselves in the eyes of their leader. He was the idol of his army, and he had the secret of involving his men with him in the unbelievable activity of his affairs.[9]

Therefore, with capable men in command of his experienced troops and a nation solidly behind him, Napoleon readied his instrument of war for its first epic campaign.

The Best Laid Plans...

Napoleon at the Camp of Boulogne

The Camp of Boulogne had been set up to prepare Napoleon's military machine for an invasion of England. Even with war clouds gathering in central Europe, Napoleon remained focused on his enemy across the Channel rather than on the continental foes of Russia and Austria. For years, Napoleon had refined his elaborate plans for the invasion of England, which he and the army were now prepared to implement. In preparation to accomplish this goal, the army had conducted comprehensive drills and mock battles along the Channel for almost two years, as well as trained for amphibious maneuver and shore-to-shore operations in small boats. (The grenadiers of the line infantry regiments and the *carabiniers* of the light infantry had received their dual training as artillerists by operating the cannon on board the small invasion craft.) By the summer of 1805, with more than 195,000 troops and 3,000 light craft assembled along the Channel, Napoleon's army was ready to invade England.[10] There was only one problem: England's

---

[9] *Mémoirs de Bourrienne,* 10 volumes (Paris, 1829), vol. 7, p. 10.

[10] S.H.A.T., C^2 200 and 201.

powerful fleet was in home waters and it was commanded and crewed by some of the finest sailors in the world. What's more, England's premier admiral, Lord Nelson, would have to be neutralized so as not to interfere with French plans.

Decrès

In order to invade England, Napoleon would have to have complete mastery of the English Channel for a minimum of three days. To accomplish this, Nelson's squadrons (there were several blockading squadrons, but Nelson's was the biggest threat to French plans) would have to be eliminated from the equation. Napoleon's original plan called for Vice-Admiral Louis Latouche-Tréville—the man who repulsed Nelson at Boulogne on 15 August 1801—to set sail from Toulon in the south of France, slip past Nelson's squadrons patrolling that Mediterranean port, make for Rochefort in the Bay of Biscay. There he would join up with another French squadron, then swing west around Brest and head into the Channel. Once in the Channel, Latouche-Tréville would keep the English ships at bay long enough for the invasion craft to cross the narrow sea.

Unfortunately for Napoleon, Latouche-Tréville died suddenly on 20 August 1804 thus depriving "France of her ablest admiral, and the British fleet an opponent worthy of its steel."[11] Napoleon's next three ablest admirals were already employed. These were Bruix, Ganteaume and Missiessy, who were in command of the invasion flotillas and with the fleets at Boulogne, Brest and Rochefort, respectively. To replace the talented Latouche-Tréville, Napoleon listened to the recommendation of his Minister of Marine, Denis Decrès, who suggested that Pierre Charles Jean Baptiste Silvestre de Villeneuve take command. Although there was nothing in Villeneuve's résumé to suggest that he was fitted to succeed Latouche-Tréville, there were no other candidates with better records. With justifiable misgivings, Napoleon approved Villeneuve's appointment to the important Toulon fleet.

Soon after Villeneuve took command at the southern French port, the war suddenly took on a different look. The English were expecting a declaration of war from Spain, and suspected that only the safe arrival of Spain's latest treasure fleet delayed its announcement. On that perhaps unprincipled but not inexplicable reason—excepting maybe greed—the English seized the Spanish treasure fleet in October 1804. This unprovoked act suddenly brought Spain and her sizable fleet in on the side of France. Even with his naval strength increased, Napoleon and his ministers did not believe that the superb English crews could be defeated in a standup fight against a combined Franco-Spanish fleet. Therefore, the new Emperor devised a theoretically excellent ruse meant to draw Nelson and his squadrons away from the Channel.[12] Napoleon was unaware, however, of standing Admiralty orders: if any French ships under blockade put to sea and escaped the blockading squadrons, the admiral in command of those ships would sail immediately for the Channel in order to thwart any invasion.

Bruix

Napoleon's original Franco-Spanish Combined Fleet plan called for Villeneuve to set sail from Toulon with 11 ships-of-the-line and numerous frigates. With 6,500 army troops on board, Villeneuve would slip by Nelson's blockading ships and head for Spain. He would stop briefly at Cartagena and Cadiz, picking up the Spanish squadrons in those ports, then head for the West Indies with all speed. Once in those waters, he would rendezvous with the Rochefort squadron under Missiessy, who was also carrying invasion troops for the West Indies, disembark the army and raise havoc with England's valuable Caribbean colonies. In the meantime, Ganteaume would put to sea from Brest, break the blockade and sail south to Ferrol, Spain. Once at that port, Ganteaume would be reinforced by

[11] Geoffrey Bennett, *The Battle of Trafalgar* (Annapolis, 1977), p. 86.

[12] Napoleon's elaborate instructions for the movements of the French fleet can be seen in: Bennett, *The Battle of Trafalgar,* pp. 89-90.

Villeneuve

additional Spanish ships-of-the-line stationed there and those sailing up from Cadiz, then return to sea to meet up with Villeneuve. It was reasoned by Napoleon that the aggressive Nelson would follow Villeneuve, thus removing this preeminent English fleet from European waters. Once in the West Indies and with Nelson in hot pursuit, Villeneuve was to double back to the Bay of Biscay, collect Ganteaume's numerous ships and together they would sail into the Channel and protect the invasion craft while the army invaded England. Once on English soil, Napoleon would play the modern role of William the Conqueror and suppress the country that, according to Napoleon, "has oppressed France for six centuries."[13]

"Napoleon's final plan was theoretically excellent,"[14] but with the luxury of hindsight, it could have only worked if there were Franco-Spanish admirals who had the moral courage to rise to the Emperor's demands. As it was, the plan ran into trouble almost immediately. Missiessy, with five ships-of-the-line, left Rochefort according to schedule on 11 January 1805, slipped past Vice-Admiral Sir Thomas Graves' blockading squadron as planned and headed for the West Indies, arriving there on 21 February. Villeneuve, with 11 ships-of-the-line and seven accompanying frigates, left Toulon on 17 January only to run into a three-day-long gale in the Gulf of Lions. With his ships suffering only minor damage, Villeneuve lost his nerve and put back to port, arriving in Toulon on 20 February.

When news of Villeneuve's return reached Napoleon, he could hardly believe his ears. "What is to be done with admirals who... hasten home at the first damage they receive?" the Emperor asked. Napoleon went on to add: "The damage should have been repaired *en route*... A few topmasts carried away... [are] everyday occurrences. The great evil of our navy is that the men who command it are unused to all the risks of command."[15]

While Villeneuve was back in port, the French squadron under Missiessy was conducting "a brilliant campaign"[16] in the West Indies. Missiessy landed troops on Dominica on 22 February, appeared off St. Kitts on 5 March, and off Montserrat on 9 March. Due to Villeneuve's failure to escape the Mediterranean, and because it would be two months before Villeneuve arrived in the West Indies, the naval ministry in Paris ordered Missiessy to return home to Rochefort to refit his ships in order to join Villeneuve's return trip to the Channel. Before leaving, Missiessy reinforced the French garrison at San Domingo by dropping off his troops.

With repairs finished on the Toulon fleet, Villeneuve ordered his ships to weigh anchor on 30 March. By 6 April, Villeneuve's 10 ships-of-the-line arrived at Cartagena only to find that Spanish Rear-Admiral Salcedo's six ships-of-the-line were not ready for sea. Moving past Gibraltar, Villeneuve picked up his other ship-of-the-line, the 74-gun *Aigle,* outside Cadiz where he was joined by five Spanish ships-of-the-line under Vice-Admiral Frederico Carlos Gravina. Together, these ships headed for the West Indies, arriving off Martinique at Fort-de-France on 14 May.

Missiessy

Napoleon then decided to dispatch fresh orders to Missiessy. His recall was canceled and Missiessy was to return to the West Indies. Once back in the Caribbean, Missiessy was to meet up with Villeneuve's ships as well as those from Brest and Ferrol. The Combined Fleets, estimated to be at least 50 ships-of-the-line, were to be under the command of the more experienced Vice-Admiral Ganteaume and were then to make for the Channel, destroy the smaller English fleet in those waters, and appear off Boulogne between 10 June and 10 July. However, Ganteaume

[13] S.H.A.T., C^2 201.
[14] Esposito and Elting, *A Military History and Atlas of the Napoleonic Wars*, text to Map number 45.
[15] Bennett, *The Battle of Trafalgar,* p. 104.
[16] Esposito and Elting, *A Military History and Atlas of the Napoleonic Wars*, text to Map number 45.

failed to sortie from Brest, stirring up a new set of orders. While Villeneuve was making his westward trek across the Atlantic as Missiessy was heading east, one messenger missed Missiessey's force and they dropped anchor in Rochefort on 20 May. Once that mischance was recognized, another messenger was sent to find Villeneuve with Napoleon's fresh instructions to remain in the Caribbean for 35 days, laying waste to numerous English ports before returning to European waters.[17]

Gravina

Reinforced by two ships-of-the-line under Rear-Admiral Magon de Medine that had slipped out of Rochefort on 1 May, Villeneuve started immediately to menace English interests. The first target was the fortress of Diamond Rock on Martinique, which surrendered to the Combined Fleet after a three day bombardment. Villeneuve then learned from a friendly passing American schooner of a heavily laden English convoy bound for home off Barbuda. He pursued this lead, found the convoy and captured 15 ships. At this time, Villeneuve was also informed by his scouting frigates that Nelson had arrived in the Caribbean. Not wishing to risk an engagement while laden with 15 captured ships, Villeneuve burned all but one of the prizes and decided to abandon all further operations in those warm waters.[18] He reasoned that he had accomplished this leg of his mission by having lured Nelson away from the Channel.

Nelson, who saw his primary duty as protecting Sicily and Egypt, reached Gibraltar on 8 May to learn of Villeneuve's direction of sail. Nelson decided to ignore his standing orders, and with only 10 ships-of-the-line, followed Villeneuve to the West Indies. He remained in the West Indies until 12 July—more than a month after Villeneuve's departure—and then sailed back to The Rock. Before leaving Barbados for Gibraltar, Nelson dispatched the fast brig *Curieux* to report to the Admiralty that the Combined Fleets must be returning to European waters. Nelson guessed that the enemy was heading for Toulon and therefore decided to return to the Mediterranean. By sheer luck, the *Curieux* sighted Villeneuve's ships north of the Azores in the mid-Atlantic on 19 June heading eastward for the Bay of Biscay. When the English brig anchored in Plymouth Sound on 7 July, the alarm was sounded.

The Admiralty responded by ordering the squadrons off Brest and Ferrol to immediately lift their blockades and take up positions to intercept Villeneuve's ships. One fleet numbering 14 ships-of-the-line under Admiral Sir William Cornwallis took a position off Ushant Island near Brest, while another fleet consisting of 15 ships-of-the-line under command of Vice-Admiral Sir Robert Calder waited to the west of Cape Finisterre off Ferrol. In the meantime, Ganteaume was still at Brest, as he had been unable to slip out of port without a fight, thanks to the nearby ships under Cornwallis. With Villeneuve approaching from the west, Ganteaume once again received new orders to weigh anchor, take his 21 ships-of-the-line to sea, join up with the Rochefort squadron, rendezvous with the Combined Fleet and then lead the fleet back into the Channel. Cornwallis' ships, however, prevented Ganteaume's escape.

Nelson

Villeneuve could have used the additional ships from Brest to fortify his courage. On the foggy morning of 22 July 1805, the Combined Fleet was discovered by Calder off Cape Finisterre. In that chance encounter, two of Gravina's worn-down Spanish ships were taken by the English while two other Spanish ships were mauled. Instead of accepting these losses and pushing on towards the Channel, Villeneuve chose to retire to the south, reaching Vigo Bay on 26 July. After receiving reinforcements in the form of the Rochefort squadron plus other Spanish ships, Villeneuve's strength was up to 35 ships-of-the-line. The Combined Fleet relocated to Ferrol and dropped anchor on 2 August. Calder, with his two prizes in tow and

---

[17] Napoléon to Vice-Admiral Decrès, *Correspondance*, numbers 8654, 8655 and 8659.

[18] Bennett, *The Battle of Trafalgar,* pp. 109-110; Thiers, *The History of the Consulate & the Empire of France*, vol. 1, pp. 644-646.

Ganteaume

the enemy fleet held in check from reaching the English Channel, had initially retired to the north, then resumed his blockade of Ferrol with only 18 ships, where Villeneuve's much larger fleet had anchored.[19]

According to Ségur, when on the morning of 13 August the Emperor heard of Villeneuve's action off Cape Finisterre and his subsequent decision to fall back on Ferrol, he realized that his diversionary plan had failed and paced the floor at a furious pace for an hour. The man whose normal composure was unflappable suddenly erupted like a volcano. The Corsican's eyes blazed with fire as he talked to Daru.

> Do you know where that bloody fool Villeneuve has gone? He's at Ferrol! At Ferrol, for heaven's sake! Do you know what that means—at Ferrol? He has been beaten; he has gone to hide himself at Ferrol. That is the end of it, he will be blocked up there. What a navy! What an admiral! What useless sacrifices![20]

With his two-year plan at risk of being scrapped, the Emperor once again sent dispatches to his admirals, imploring them to take action. Villeneuve was urged to break out of Ferrol and destroy the much smaller covering fleet if they were foolish enough to offer battle. Once at sea, Villeneuve was to meet up with Rear-Admiral Allemand's [who had replaced Missiessy] five ships-of-the-line sailing from Rochefort and sail for the Channel. Meanwhile, Ganteaume was to take his superior numbers and break the blockade at Brest. Taking into account losses in battle breaking the blockades, Napoleon reasoned that the fleets combined would have a strength of more than 50 ships-of-the-line. With this force, the French navy would sail toward the Channel and into history.[21]

Ganteaume weighed anchor, but could not muster the courage to close with the blockading squadrons that counted roughly the same number of ships-of-the-line as he. The Brest fleet put back into port. Meanwhile Villeneuve left Ferrol on 9 August and headed northwesterly. When Allemand's squadron from Rochefort could not be found, Villeneuve once again lost his nerve, turned south on 15 August and made for Cadiz where he knew there was a sizable Spanish fleet at anchor. With Villeneuve's decision to leave French waters, all hope was lost for an invasion of England in 1805.

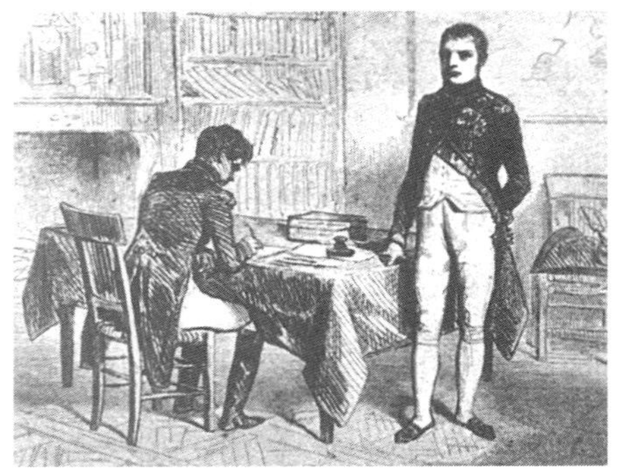

Napoleon dictates the plan for the Ulm Campaign

Pirouette From the Coast

"Where," Napoleon complained from his headquarters at château de Pont-de-Briques, "did my admirals learn that they can make war without taking risks?"[22] Within days of asking that rhetorical question, the Emperor received news that would forever turn his head eastward. On 13 August, after news came to the Emperor about the growing Austrian troop concentrations in Italy and the Tyrol, Napoleon first uttered his verbal plans for the 1805 campaign when he got the word about Villeneuve retiring on Ferrol. Following his outburst as previously detailed, Napoleon pointed to a desk and told Daru, the future Intendant General of the army: "Sit down there! Write!" Unrolling a vast, detailed seven by ten foot map of Europe placed it down over the maps of the Channel and the coasts which for the past two years had occupied his mind, Napoleon, without hesitation, and:

---

[19] Bennett, *The Battle of Trafalgar,* pp. 112-119; *Memoirs of Ségur,* p. 148.

[20] *Memoirs of Ségur,* p. 152.

[21] Napoléon to Vice-Admiral Villeneuve, *Correspondance*, number 9022; Napoléon to Vice-Admiral Decrès, *Correspondance*, number 9026; and Napoléon to Rear-Admiral Gourdon, *Correspondance,* number 9027.

[22] Bennett, *The Battle of Trafalgar,* p. 127.

> without any apparent meditation, and in his brief, concise, and imperious tones... dictated to him without a moment's hesitation the whole plan of the campaign of Ulm as far as Vienna... His foresight which was as much to be depended upon his memory, could already predict, starting from Boulogne, the principal events of this projected war, their dates and their decisive results; and he dictated these to Daru with such certainty that a month after they had been fulfilled, he was able to remember them.[23]

The formations that would be assigned to the secondary theaters were also set forth by Napoleon. Marshal Brune with 21 '3rd Battalions' of the regiments that had departed for Germany, 15 battalions of naval artillerists and selected Italian troops that had been trained in the Boulogne camp would remain on the Channel coast to watch the English who were likely to repeat something similar to the 1799 Helder Expedition.[24] General Gouvion Saint-Cyr with 18,600 combatants would guard the Papal States in central Italy while also protecting Marshal Masséna's southern flank. Masséna, with a paper strength of 50,000 troops in Northern Italy, would keep the larger Austrian army in check while Napoleon crushed the opposition on the Danube. Masséna's role was far from a minor one, however. He began the 1805 campaign as Napoleon's most proven independent commander and would no doubt have his hands full with the main Austrian army, estimated to be twice the strength of the *Armée d'Italie*. To increase the effectiveness of the Army of Italy—in December 1805 officially titled the *8e corps de la Grande Armée*[25]—the Emperor wished for Masséna to be extremely active in his maneuvers, thereby "multiplying the mass by the rapidity"[26] of march that would also prevent the Austrians from transferring troops to Germany. It was a tall order, but the Emperor had complete confidence in his old troops if properly led. This cannot be better illustrated than by the Emperor's following advice to his marshal. "I recommend my brave Army of Italy to you, but do not allow them to fight in detachments. Eighty thousand Austrians, drawn up as they are, are no match for 50,000 of our soldiers provided they stay close together."[27]

Masséna

With preparations completed to secure his flanks and rear,[28] Napoleon had decided on 23 August to authorize the marching orders for the troops that had spent the last two years honing their combat skills in the Channel encampments. These men, who officially had been designated as the *Armée des côtes de l'Océan*,[29] needed a new name. The Emperor decided that because the new army was to be committed to operations in central Europe, it would be called the *Grande Armée*.[30] Since the Austrians were already making for the Black Forest, no doubt wishing to control the narrow defiles through which any adversary would have to debouch if approaching from the west, Napoleon decided to use that Austrian fixation to his advantage. The cavalry reserve commanded by Marshal Joachim Murat would

---

[23] *Memoirs of Ségur*, p. 153. This is a popular story, retold often by various Napoleonic writers. However, Claude-François de Méneval, who was one of Napoleon's private secretaries from 1802 to 1815, doubts that Napoleon would have taken Daru into his confidence at this point in time. See: *Memoirs of the Baron de Méneval*, 2 volumes (New York, 1894), vol. 1, pp. 362-365.

[24] S.H.A.T., C^2 486.; Napoléon to Brune, *Correspondance*, number 9228.

[25] S.H.A.T., C^2 12 and 484; Order of the Day, 26 frimaire an XIV (17 December 1805), *Unpublished Correspondence of Napoleon I*, vol. 1, number 234.

[26] *Military Maxims of Napoleon*, p. 111.

[27] Napoléon to Masséna, *Correspondance*, number 9286.

[28] Napoléon to Berthier, *Correspondance*, number 9159; Note, *Correspondance*, number 9214 and Instruction for the Defense of Boulogne, *Corressponance*, number 9252.

[29] S.H.A.T., C^2 201.

[30] Napoléon to Berthier, *Correspondance*, number 9158.

form an impenetrable screen along the middle Rhine and into the Black Forest. Once in front of that vast woodland, Murat would conduct active demonstrations in this area thereby further drawing Austrian attention away from the decisive flank where Napoleon wished to attack.[31] Meanwhile, seven army corps would break camp, about face from the Channel, march swiftly to the Rhine and beyond, and conduct a vast wheel into Swabia, thereby totally compromising the Austrian strategic right flank and rear.[32]

Although Napoleon had already proved the value of the corps system during the Marengo campaign of 1800 when he strategically moved large bodies of troops swiftly and effectively, the 1805 campaign stands as a testament to Napoleon's perfected system. At the center of his *modus operandi* stands one of Napoleon's organizational masterpieces—the *commissaire général* (intendant general). As with any army, one of the biggest factors in an army's rate of march was the 'logistical tail'—trains of wagons, cattle, camp followers, and more. March rates of the armies of the *ancien régime* went hand-in-hand with the size of their logistical trains: it was rare to see an old army march more than 10 miles a day. The French broke from this tradition during the wars of the French Revolution almost by necessity, since their administrative branch collapsed in total shambles when it attempted to feed an army establishment that had grown dramatically in size. As a result, Republican armies were forced to 'live off the countryside,' and suffered enormous strategic consumption (loss of manpower) as a result.

Daru

Napoleon's secret in moving large numbers of troops swiftly and with minimal wastage was two-fold. First, every army corps was kept together by assigning each an independent line of march. As such, they were separated from other corps for the purpose of order and obtaining food, yet close enough to march to another corps' assistance within a day if the need arose. Second, along each line, the different corps would halt at the end of every day's march to eat the foodstuffs that had been requisitioned from the local population by the *ordonnateurs* of the intendant general's staff. The Emperor's *ordonnateurs* paid for the requisitioned goods with hard currency, and Napoleon saw to it that his supply officers were well financed with currency that would be honored wherever the army was traveling.[33] In addition to the requisitions, the troops would be given a daily ration of 24 ounces of bread baked by the corps' traveling bakeries. As with the other foodstuffs, the grain necessary to bake the bread was a requisitioned item as well, thereby eliminating the need to transport this bulky material.

As a result, Napoleon's innovations dramatically increased the speed of the army's movement as well as reduced the logistical tail of its administrative units. Rather than totally 'living off the countryside' as French armies did during the Revolutionary wars, or depending completely upon the army's supply trains for all food stuffs as did the Austrians and Russians, Napoleon wanted the *Grande Armée* to subsist from the bread of the army's bakeries as well the requisitions made by the staff of Napoleon's ablest administrator, Daru. This unconventional system of supply was described by Octave Levasseur thusly:

> The Emperor's energetic way of warfare demanded that his forces be free of those numerous supply columns which [old] armies used to drag about with them, and which so delayed their movements. He knew that he had to begin the campaign in

---

[31] Napoléon to Murat, *Correspondance,* numbers 9205, 9206, 9231, 9238 and 9244.

[32] Napoléon to Berthier, *Correspondance,* number 9137; Napoléon to Bernadotte *Correspondance,* number 9184; Napoléon to Ney, Napoléon to Lannes, Napoléon to Davout, *Unpublished Correspondence of Napoleon I*, vol. 1, numbers 182, 183 and 184.

[33] Napoléon to Daru *Correspondance,* number 9161; and Napoléon to Daru, *Unpublished Correspondence of Napoleon I*, vol. 1, number 186.

> September, and by that time of the year every village, every house even, offered him a ready-stocked magazine of victuals and fodder.[34]

As with any system, all was not perfect. When the *ordonnateurs* were unable to procure the requisitioned food for whatever reason, the men resorted to foraging, which in turn led to strategic consumption. Nevertheless, Napoleon would use this new supply system along with his *corps d'armée* system to create a new weapon of war—his men's feet.

On 27 August 1805, the *Grande Armée* broke camp and began its historic march to the Rhine, the beginning of one of the most celebrated campaigns in history.

A Tornado Descends on the Danube while a Tortoise Approaches From the East

Napoleon was anxious for his army to conduct a series of lightning marches to the Rhine and beyond in order to wrest the strategic initiative away from the Austrian forces already mobilizing to move up the Danube. Bernadotte's 1st Corps and Marmont's 2nd Corps, marching from Hanover and Holland respectively, had well-stocked routes to the Danube theater of operations. As such, food requisitions were easily met and those corps arrived well-fed and ready for action. Meanwhile, Davout's 3rd Corps, Soult's 4th, Lannes' 5th and Ney's 6th moved quickly from the Channel across modern-day Belgium and northeastern France to reach the middle Rhine between Mainz and Strasbourg. Joining the army were the French and Royal Italian Imperial Guard units which left Paris on 29 August.[35] These corps, having marched across France or Belgium at an average rate of just over 30 kilometers (20 miles) per day, were well supplied with several extra pairs of shoes per man, adequate transports and requisitioned supplies. Meanwhile, Augereau's 7th Corps moved across the entire breadth of France, traveling 800 miles from Brest to the Rhine. Marcellin de Marbot, a lieutenant serving as an aide-de-camp on Marshal Augereau's 7th Corps staff, described the marching weather for 7th Corps as "magnificent."[36]

Augereau

The troops that moved across France and Belgium did so on a series of forced marches. Coignet of the *Grenadiers à pied de la Garde* recalled the regiment's march from Paris to Strasbourg. "We marched by platoons day and night, without being given an hour of sleep," Coignet wrote. "We clung together in ranks to prevent ourselves from falling. Whenever a grenadier did collapse nothing could awaken him, even if he fell into a ditch and was belabored with the flat of a sword."[37] Marshal Soult's superbly drilled 4th Corps marched from Boulogne to Speyer on the Rhine with "scarcely a man lost."[38] On 8 September 1805, after 13 days of marching, Marshal Lannes' 5th Corps had lost only 10 men.[39] According to parade states taken on or about 26 September when most of the *Grande Armée* crossed the Rhine, Napoleon had 177,613 officers and men present and under arms (excluding staff personnel, the allied Bavarian troops, and other auxiliary forces in the theater). These men consisted of 138,194 combatants in 186 infantry battalions, 25,326 cavalrymen and 24,464 horses in 184½ squadrons, plus an additional 14,093

[34] *Souvenirs Militaires d'Octave Levasseur* (Paris, 1914), p. 31.
[35] Napoléon to Bessières,*Correspondance,* numbers 9151 and 9152.
[36] *Memoirs of Baron de Marbot,* translated by A. J. Butler, 2 volumes (London, 1892), vol. 1, p. 161.
[37] *Les Cahiers du Capitaine Coignet (1799-1815),* (Paris, 1883), pp. 164-165.
[38] Duffy, *Austerlitz,* p. 41; S.H.A.T., C^2 477.
[39] S.H.A.T., C^2 481.

Napoleon seals his alliance with Württemberg with a meeting at Stuttgart

artillerists and support personnel with another 1,256 horses for the horse artillerists and 7,850 horses pulling 350 of the various-caliber pieces of ordnance and other vehicles (please see Appendix A).[40] In addition to his own army, the Emperor had at his disposal some 20,252 Bavarian infantry, 1,708 Bavarian cavalry and 48 pieces of Bavarian ordnance (these Bavarians are detailed in Appendix B). An additional brigade of Baden troops numbering some 2,000 effectives, plus a small division of more than 2,500 Württembergers were added to the *Grande Armée* the first two days of October. Another brigade of 2,300 men from Hesse-Darmstädt soon joined Napoleon's forces, as did a regiment of infantry and a regiment of cavalry from the hereditary lands controlled by Bavaria that in 1806 became known as the Grand Duchy of Kleve-Berg.[41]

While the French were pushing their corps eastward towards the Rhine, Archduke Ferdinand's Austrians were moving in the opposite direction. While some Austrian units had begun the offensive on 2 September, most of the 72,000-man Habsburg army broke camp at Wels on 5 September. Marching westward, the Austrians poured across the Inn River and into Bavaria. They did so under the assumption that Bavaria's Elector, Maximilian-Joseph, would ally his country with the Third Coalition and therefore place his 22,000-man army and well-stocked depots at the disposal of Archduke Ferdinand. This presumption was grounded in wishful thinking rather than in fact. Simply, the Austrians were entranced with the strength of the Ulm position, which as recently as 1800 had been held for a long time by Marshal Kray against the French *Armée du Rhin* under Moreau. The Austrian line of thinking was this—Ferdinand's 72,000 men, reinforced by Bavaria's 22,000 men, could effectively block any French advance from the Rhine until Kutuzov's Russian army arrived. Then, with approximately 140,000 combatants, the Allied forces would crush Napoleon's forces. Since the lead elements of the Austrian army arrived on the Bavarian border on 7 September, and with Napoleon far away, the Austrians believed that their presence would be sufficient to force the Bavarian Elector to join the Third Coalition.[42]

Maximilian-Joseph of Bavaria

To assist Maximilian-Joseph in his decision, the Austrians first sent to the Elector on 24 August a treaty of alliance, promising that Bavaria's entry into the Coalition would be treated with the utmost secrecy. This was followed on 7 September by a visit to Munich from Austrian envoy General Karl von Schwarzenberg, whose presence was intended to finally convince Maximilian-Joseph to make up his mind.

For Bavaria's Elector, decision making did not come easily. The 49-year-old Maximilian-Joseph was unhappy at the prospects of attaching himself and his country to either France or Austria. Positioned squarely between the major antagonists, Bavaria had long been a battleground over which France and Austria fought, only to be forgotten whenever one side made peace with the other. Napoleon realized Maximilian-Joseph's concerns and his distrust of the court in Vienna. In an attempt to convince Maximilian-Joseph to ally with France, Napoleon wrote to the Elector that an alliance with Austria would be disastrous for his country. Announcing that the *Grande Armée* would soon be marching to Germany, Napoleon wrote to Maximilian-Joseph: "You will be succoured in time," the Emperor advised on 7 fructidor (25 August), "and the house of Austria vanquished shall be forced to cede to you a considerable amount of territory with the wrecks of its own patrimony."[43]

Although Napoleon realized the proximity of the Austrian army would cause Maximilian-Joseph some initial concerns, the Emperor had no idea of the pressure

---

[40] S.H.A.T., C^2 470.

[41] S.H.A.T., C^2 470.

[42] Thiers, *The History of the Consulate & the Empire of France*, vol. 2, p. 15.

[43] Napoléon to the Elector of Bavaria, *Correspondance,* number 9134.

being applied to the Elector by his much younger spouse! The Electress of Bavaria was one of three attractive Baden princesses whom were on the thrones of Europe. One of her sisters was the queen of Sweden while her youngest sister was the Tsarina of Russia. These sisters, raised in the school of the *ancien régime*, had nothing but animosity for the ideals of the French Revolution, and were therefore contemptuous of Napoleonic France. With her other sisters already aligned against Napoleon, the Electress went to every contrivance to persuade her husband not to ally with the usurper. She threw temper tantrums; she wept; she did everything a woman could do to make her husband's life miserable. Regardless of Maximilian-Joseph's well grounded concepts of the Enlightenment, the realization that Austria had never been a friend, and despite the Elector's verbal intentions to the French minister in Munich to join Napoleon, the tactics of the Electress were working their magic when Schwarzenberg made his appearance in Munich on 7 September to secure the alliance of Bavaria with the Third Coalition.

The Austrians advance into Bavaria

There seems little doubt that Maximilian-Joseph was about to throw in his lot with the Allies when several events unfolded almost at the same time. The first was the unannounced advance of the Austrian army over the Bavarian border about the time Schwarzenberg arrived in Munich. Passing over the Inn before a treaty had been concluded was viewed by many influential and outraged Bavarians as an act of territorial violation. Second, with the advance of the Austrians came their supply officers with wagon loads of out-of-date, and almost valueless, paper money that Vienna had replaced with a new currency. The only possible reason that the Austrians carried with them an old currency was that they intended to pay the Bavarians for requisitioned supplies with monies that they *knew* were worthless. It did not take long for the Bavarians to figure out this ruse, and word spread like wildfire before the Austrian advance. This served to further incense the Bavarian public against the Austrians. Finally, this sentiment was also reflected in a straw opinion poll among the Bavarian officers in Munich, the results of which reached the Elector on 8 September and reported that they overwhelmingly favored serving alongside France. This poll was undoubtedly influenced by Schwarzenberg's announcement the day before that the Bavarian units were to be interspersed within Austrian columns rather than serving together in homogeneous Bavarian divisions.[44]

With public and army opinion overwhelmingly against an alliance with Austria, the pressures exerted by the Electress were no longer sufficient to bring Bavaria into the Third Coalition. Her husband was left with no alternative. Maximilian-Joseph backed out of negotiations and ordered the army to retire north to Würzburg on the upper Main River. He fled with his court on the night of 8 September, arriving in Würzburg on the 12th where he declared his alliance with Napoleon and awaited the arrival of the French army.[45]

Bavarian troops on the march

Meanwhile, the westward march by the Austrians across Bavaria was an unpleasant experience for this dynastic army. The Austrian's massive and bulky supply trains were unable to fully mobilize an adequate number of horses prior to the outbreak of hostilities. When the Austrians began pushing westward, the logistical tail of the army broke down almost immediately, resulting in many of the troops not receiving their accustomed cooked rations. With the Bavarians unwilling to accept the outdated Austrian currency as payment, requisitions were understandably slow in materializing. As this problem grew in magnitude and requisitioned supplies became scarce, the march rate of the army slowed to a crawl.

Another problem facing the Austrians was the new regimental organization prescribed earlier in the year by General Mack. The reorganization had only recently been implemented when the army was forced to move out. The new 4th Battalions,

[44] Marcus Junkelmann, *Napoleon und Bayern* (Regensburg, 1985), pp. 88-96. Thiers, *The History of the Consulate & the Empire of France*, vol. 2, pp. 15-16.
[45] Junkelmann, *Napoleon und Bayern*, p. 96.

as well as the newly configured grenadier battalions, had barely been formed when the Austrian offensive began. Moreover, many battalions were without all their ammunition and equipment! As late as 1 October 1805, Archduke Ferdinand wrote what must have been characteristic of his command: "Since many of the newly arrived troops have still to be trained in musketry, I approve the issue of six live rounds to be fired by every such man."[46] With only this limited experience, Austrian recruits would soon be pitted against French troops who were not only seasoned campaigners of the Revolutionary wars, but also veterans of the two-year camp of Boulogne.

In addition to these shortcomings, there was a serious rift at army headquarters that threatened to cripple the already fragile stability of the army. Archduke Ferdinand had been given the titular command of the Danube army for one reason—an army commanded by a high-born Habsburg would prevent it from coming under the orders of any Russian. Since Tsar Alexander and his armies were on the move to the theater of war, and because Austrians considered their allied Russian officers to be valueless when it came to staff work, the last thing Vienna wanted was for their army operating in the Danube theater to fall into the clutches of clumsy Muscovite generals. The Austrians only had to think back a few years to the campaigns they shared under the command of Suvórov; those were not fond memories. That is why the war council in Vienna selected Archduke Ferdinand to head the Swabian army. Ferdinand was an energetic 24-year-old Italian princeling who took his soldiering seriously. The young archduke saw no reason why he should be denied command of his army as he was familiar with the theater of war and believed that the strategic situation was fraught with danger. Ferdinand feared that a French army of no less that 150,000 commanded by Napoleon *could* erupt from the Rhine across Ansbach towards the Danube before the Russians could effect a junction with his army. Since a march along those lines would totally compromise the strategic right flank of the Austrian army in Bavaria, Ferdinand cautioned that Austrian troops move no further west than the Isar River and Munich to await the Russians.[47]

Archduke Ferdinand

Deciding against Archduke Ferdinand's plan was the army's second-in-command, *Feldmarschall-Leutnant* (FML) Freiherr Karl Mack von Leiberich. The author of numerous army reforms, the 53-year-old Mack had the support of Foreign Minister Count Ludwig Cobenzl and the *Hofkriegsrat*—an amazing feat considering the fact that he was a Protestant! How this man could rate such pull with his superiors was the result of a long army career that had begun in 1769 when he was 17 years old. He proved himself to be a skilled writer, was taken under the protective wing of Field-Marshal Lacy, and was attached to the Emperor's staff for frontier inspection in 1778. He distinguished himself in action against the Turks during the campaigns of 1787 through 1790. By 1790, Mack, now a colonel, was chief of staff of the Moravian Army of Observation. Gaining further attention for his *Instructionspuncte für Generals* that advocated the spirit of the offensive, Mack was promoted to *General-Feldwachtmeister* (GM), then transferred to the Army of the Netherlands in 1794. Chief of staff to Prince Josias von Coburg, Mack was entrusted to draw up plans of operation to defeat the French Revolutionary *Armée du Nord.* Mack proposed that six widely separated columns converge on and annihilate the invading French. Far too ambitious and complex a plan to coordinate, the Austrians were defeated badly in a series of engagements fought on 18 August 1794 known as the Battle of Tourcoing. Following this debâcle, Mack was relieved of duties on the Rhine and then loaned to the Bourbons as commander of the Neapolitan army from November 1798 to January 1799. During this brief stint as

---

[46] Krauss, *1805. Der Feldzug von Ulm*, p. 83.

[47] Regele, *Mittheilungen*, pp. 146-149.

leader of these forces Mack demonstrated only mediocre ability, and it is fair to state that Mack's capacity for command was rivaled only by the quality of his troops. His poorly-equipped and poorly-officered Neapolitan forces were defeated at the Battle of Civita Castellana by French General Jean-Etienne Championnet on 4 December 1798. Captured the following month by enemy troops and taken to France, Mack slipped back to Austria in 1800 in breach of his parole. During the next four years, Mack lived in semi-retirement on his Bohemian estate, writing numerous articles on offensive warfare and proposed army reorganization.

Mack

In 1805, Foreign Minister Count Ludwig Cobenzl believed that Mack was the man to lead Austria back to military supremacy. Even though Archduke Charles was the nominal minister of war and considered by many to be the premier soldier in Austria, Cobenzl persuaded the *Hofkriegsrat* to name Mack as *Generalquartiermeister*—or chief of staff of all the Austrian armies, which was arguably the most powerful military position in the country. Following a reading of Mack's optimistic report on Austria's ability to mobilize for war, the Aulic Council agreed to Cobenzl's scheme. Eager to strike back at France for the humiliating defeats in 1796-97 and 1800, the *Hofkriegsrat* promoted Mack on 22 April 1805. Mack wasted no time ingratiating himself with the court nobles, promising a vastly improved army that he would reorganize and lead to victory over the hated usurper.[48]

Mack told the Vienna court that the army should move with greatest speed towards the Iller and the city of Ulm, which Mack described as "the queen of the Danube and the Iller, the bulwark of the Tyrol, and the key to half of Germany."[49] The city had proved important during every campaign for Germany since the age of Gustavus Adolphus in the first half of the 1600s. Mack convinced the nobles in Vienna that the army should not delay in moving towards Ulm. So ordered, the army marched across Bavaria, arriving at the juncture of the Iller River and the Danube as agreed. Once in this position, Ferdinand wanted to deploy the army to meet any anticipated French offensive from the northwest through the Prussian enclave of Ansbach. Mack rejected this line of reasoning based on his preconceived notion that Napoleon would never violate what Mack considered to be neutral Prussian territory. Instead, Mack wanted to issue orders for fortifying the cities of Ulm and Memmingen so that they could be used as bases from which his army would leap out and attack the French as they emerged from the Black Forest—the only route of attack into Bavaria deemed by Mack to be available. The impasse was resolved when Emperor Francis sent a letter to Ferdinand explaining that Mack was the *de facto* commander of the army, and would report directly to Vienna. This letter served to exacerbate the already existing tension of jealousy and mistrust between Ferdinand and Mack. As a result, the two would only communicate in writing, and "no general officer would attend General Mack unless accompanied by another general officer to bear witness of what passed."[50]

The Austrians used forced labor to fortify Ulm

Marching to join this unsettled Austrian army was Kutuzov's Russians. These 46,405 troops, divided into six 'columns,' together with their massive supply trains, had broken camp at Radziwilow, southwest of Warsaw on the borders of Russia and Austrian Galicia, on 25 August 1805.[51] The fact that Kutuzov was leaving Radziwilow some 10 days behind schedule did not dim the general's confidence. "Our army marches to chastise the forces of an evil and corrupt government,"[52]

[48] Connelly, Parker, Becker and Burton, *Historical Dictionary of Napolenic France, 1799-1815*, pp. 317-318.

[49] Angeli, 'Ulm und Austerlitz' in *Österreichische Militärische Zeitschrift,* p. 463.

[50] PRO, FOP, Paget's report of 1 November 1805 in 7/75.

[51] *M. I. Kutuzov. Sbornik Dokumentov*, 5 volumes (Moscow, 1950-1956), vol. 2, p. 41; Duffy, *Austerlitz,* p. 52.

[52] T. Bernhardi, *Denkwürdigkeiten aus dem Leben des Kaisel. Russ. Generals... von Toll*, 4 parts (Leipzig, 1865)., part 1, p. 102.

the general declared to his troops prior to their departure. Likewise, while the army was marching southwesterly, Kutuzov was ordered by Tsar Alexander to detach the army's VI Column under Lieutenant General Rosen, which consisted of nine battalions and 10 squadrons towards the Turkish frontier. When General Kutuzov advised Emperor Francis of this development with an added air of optimism "that where the Russian army was concerned, courage was more important than numbers,"[53] Emperor Francis took exception to the weakening of the Russian army. An immediate appeal to the Tsar resulted in Rosen's 7,500-man column being recalled for duty on the Danube.[54]

The 175-mile march route of Kutuzov's Russian army from Radziwilow to Teschen, at the border of the Austrian provinces of Galicia and Moravia, was finally accomplished in 29 days—a typically labored pace of an *ancien régime* army of a mere six miles a day! Upon arrival in Teschen on 22 September, Kutuzov noted to Austrian authorities that his "soldiers [had] already endured much fatigue, and they [were] suffering badly."[55] This was due, in part, to the rains that had contributed to the slow pace of the army. However, the Austrians had news of Napoleon's army—it had left the Channel encampments and was marching to Germany. If Kutuzov's Russians were to reach General Mack's army before the Austrians confronted the usurper, more speed—and lots of it— was needed. To assist the Russians in their movement westward, Austrian authorities in Teschen had ready some 2,233 two-horse carts which could help carry Kutuzov's foot soldiers. Correctly sensing the urgency in the developing strategic picture, Kutuzov took what amounted to be a drastic step for any army still operating by the rules of 18th century warfare—he ordered the officers and men alike to leave their baggage behind at Teschen. The army was to move as rapidly as it could on a southwesterly march towards Bavaria.

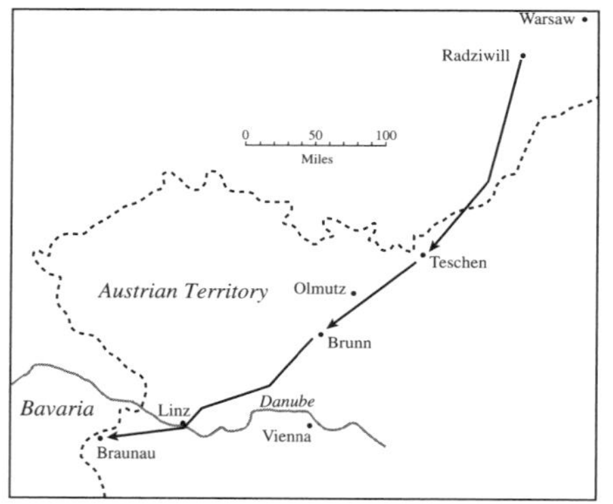

Kutuzov's route to Braunau

Urging his men on with a reduced 'logistical tail,' Kutuzov was able to more than double the army's average march rate to just over 16 and one-half miles a day. This was accomplished by Kutuzov's decree which set forth the forced march order for each column. "The first part of each column must always go ahead on the vehicles," the general instructed his column commanders, "so that it can complete the first half of the march before the rearward part of the column, which comes up on foot."[56] The columns made a respectable 16 miles the first day out of Teschen, but it was immediately apparent that the heavy Russian ordnance and accompanying trains could not keep up the pace. More and more overworked draft horses, which had become fatigued during the march from Radziwilow to Teschen, began coming up lame. As a result, Kutuzov ordered one day of rest after every four of marching. Still, the new guns of the Arakcheev 1805 ordnance system—especially the medium 6- and medium 12-pounders—were too heavy for the number of available Russian draft horses to consistently pull 16 miles a day. "It would do the service no good to see this important element of the army so exhausted on the way," Kutuzov wrote Czartoryski on 23 September, "that it did not have the wherewithal to act when it reached its destination."[57] Therefore it was decided that the artillery would not try to stay up with the other combat arms. The infantry, cavalry and artillery would maintain their fastest speed practical. This had the almost instantaneous result of the columns becoming elongated much more than normal. This meant that while the infantry might move 16 miles a day, the artillery lagged behind, doing no more mileage than its animals could manage. Even the teams that pulled the light 6-pounder guns that served as battalion artillery

[53] S.H.A.T., C² 13.
[54] Duffy, *Austerlitz,* p. 52.
[55] *Kutuzov. Sbornik*, vol. 2, p. 53.
[56] *Kutuzov. Sbornik*, vol. 2, p. 68.
[57] *Kutuzov. Sbornik*, vol. 2, p. 53.

were soon unable to keep up with their parent infantry unit. The cavalry was also affected. Most Russian dragoons—the regiments that commanded the least respect in that arm and were mounted on the animals that had been picked over by the army's other regiments—were forced to walk alongside their horses, which were not strong enough to maintain the daily rigors of campaign.

Strung out along an ever lengthening line of march, Kutuzov's army trudged towards the Danube. For an army used to moving between five to 10 miles a day, the new daily march pace seemed to be torturous. Falling behind the formations of infantry within each column would be the sick and the stragglers whose numbers increased daily. These delinquents were kept moving by cavalrymen that led their horses while on foot. All of these preceded the companies of artillery and the battalion guns whose exhausted draft horses struggled to pull their loads. On 1 October, Kutuzov reported that "the shoes of most of the troops have broken down in the prevailing wet weather. They have had to march barefoot, and their feet have suffered so badly on the sharp stones of the highways that the men are incapable of service."[58] The condition of the army became so alarming to Kutuzov that he decided to allow the army one day's rest after every three of grueling marching.

By 12 October, the first elements of the Russian army reached the fortress of Braunau on the Inn River that feeds into the Danube along the Austro-Bavarian border. These initial arrivals had made the 265-mile trek from Teschen in 20 days. After deducting the four days of rest along the way, the distance that had been covered by the fastest of Russian units in 16 actual days of marching was accomplished at an average of slightly more than 16 and one-half miles per day. Over the next two weeks, regiments, battalion guns and artillery companies slowly arrived along the Inn, all their ranks depleted by stragglers and the sick.

When excluding Rosen's detached VI Column numbering approximately 7,500 (including artillerists), the units remaining with Kutuzov numbered 38,905 when they left Radziwilow. More than 11,000 of these young Russian soldiers fell out of ranks on the way to the Bavarian border and never rejoined their units. Therefore, Kutuzov's army suffered an astounding strategic consumption rate of 30% on its march to Braunau! As of 23 October, Kutuzov's Russians numbered only 27,092, to which 20,000 Austrians were added from the outer columns of Mack's army positioned east of Ulm.[59] These Austrian forces were reeling back to the Inn River as the result of one of the greatest strategic triumphs in history.

When Napoleon arrived at Strasbourg on the Rhine River on 26 September 1805, the popular Emperor and his staff were welcomed in a way that became a familiar one during the Napoleonic wars.

> [Napoleon's] arrival was announced by salvoes of artillery and the ringing of bells. The Guard, resplendent in its youth and its uniforms, led the majestic procession. It was welcomed by exclamations a thousand times repeated. The inhabitants of Alsace flowed after it like a torrent.[60]

Napoleon watches his army cross the Rhine

Napoleon remained in Strasbourg for the next several days, overseeing all details of the nation and army.

"My brother," Napoleon wrote to Joseph on 4 vendémiaire (26 September), "I have arrived in Strasbourg. All the army has crossed the Rhine. The enemy occupies the outskirts of the Black Forest. Our maneuvers will begin soon. I am

---

[58] *Kutuzov. Sbornik*, vol. 2, p. 68.

[59] S.H.A.T., C^2 13. Also, please see chart in Chapter VI, "Comparison of Strengths for Kutuzov's Army for the Period 25 August to 25 November 1805."

[60] *Memoirs of a French Napoleonic Officer: Jean-Baptiste Barrès, Chasseur of the Imperial Guard,* translated by Bernard Miall (London, 1925), pp. 56-57.

very satisfied with the departments that I have crossed. Whereupon I pray God to keep you in his holy and worthy protection."[61] The following day, the Emperor advised his foreign minister, Talleyrand, that: "All goes well here. The Austrians are in the defiles of the Black Forest; God will it that they stay there. My only fear is that we might scare them too much. The next 20 days will see many things happen."[62]

Contrary to these feelings was the Emperor's displeasure in the army's supply system. To General Jean-François-Aimé Dejean, Minister of Administration of War, Napoleon dictated the following on 4 vendémiaire (26 September):

> I have arrived at Strasbourg. The biscuits that I have demanded are not made. The caissons destined to go through Sampigny have not arrived, and even the 150 that I had at Boulogne are not here. Also, the shoes have not arrived. Press with all possible speed the execution of the orders that I have given. The army is today over the Rhine, especially the cavalry.[63]

The march of the army had been so fast that the *ordonnateurs* were unable to secure requisitions before the troops passed. Corporal Jean-Pierre Blaise of the 108th *Ligne*, Friant's Division, Davout's 3rd Corps, lucidly recalled the progress of his regiment:

> The speed of our march made it impossible for suppliers [*ordonnateurs*] to keep pace with us, and so we were often short of bread in spite of all the efforts of our commanding general, Marshal Davout... Fortunately, it was the height of the potato season, and they were plentiful in our area. How many times did we ruin the hopes of the villagers! We pillaged from them the fruits of an entire year's work. However we were, as you might say, forced to do so.[64]

Napoleon watches his troops crossing the Rhine

Despite these problems, the *Grande Armée* had very few stragglers at this point in the campaign. This is no better illustrated than Marmont's 2nd Corps. When these troops arrived at Mayence, completing their 205 mile march from Utrecht without a single day of rest, only nine men had dropped out of ranks![65]

Even with logistical matters in less than satisfactory shape, the Emperor would not delay pushing his troops across the Rhine. Napoleon wanted the *Grande Armée* to be concentrated east of that great river, yet far enough outside the enemy's reach before finalizing his plan of operation. He reasoned that by the time the army had advanced along a line from Würzburg southwest to Heilbronn to Oberkirch near Strasbourg, more precise information concerning the whereabouts of the enemy would be received and orders could be given at that time. The Emperor did not have to wait long.

Beginning on 13 September—a week before he left Paris for Strasbourg—Napoleon began receiving reports from Marshal Joachim Murat, commander-in-chief of the cavalry reserve, describing the Austrian invasion of Bavaria and subsequent advance up the Danube to the Inn River and the city of Ulm. By the

---

[61] Napoléon to Joseph, *Correspondance*, number 9266; *The Confidential Correspondence of Napoleon Bonaparte with His Brother Joseph*, 2 volumes (London, 1855), vol. 1, number 85.
[62] Napoléon to Talleyrand, *Correspondance*, number 9270.
[63] Napoléon to Dejean, *Correspondance*, number 9267.
[64] E. Fairon and H. Heusse, *Lettres des grognards* (Paris, 1936), p. 98.
[65] S.H.A.T., $C^2$475.

time the *Grande Armée* crossed the Rhine, Murat's reports of 25 and 26 September gave Napoleon a good picture of the positions of the Austrian army, which seemed to be concentrated around Ulm, not maneuvering in any direction, and seemingly content to limit activity to conducting patrols as far west as the Black Forest. Furthermore, Murat's reports conspicuously omitted information on the Russians, which meant that they had yet to enter the immediate theater of operations.[66] All this convinced the Emperor that he should march his army immediately against Mack's Austrians.

Writing to his stepson, Prince Eugène, on 7 vendémiaire (29 September), Napoleon said:

> My Cousin, hostilities have commenced. The army corps of Marshal Bernadotte and General Marmont are at Würzburg, joined there by the Bavarian army of 25,000 [*sic*] men. The corps of Marshal Davout has crossed the Rhine at Manheim; it is this day at Neckar. The corps of Marshal Soult has crossed the Rhine at Speyer and today will be at Heilbronn. The corps of Marshal Ney has crossed the Rhine vis-à-vis Durlach, and will today be at Stuttgart. The corps of Marshal Lannes has crossed the Rhine at Kehl, and is today at Ludwigsburg. My Guard has just arrived; it is 8,000 men strong. The artillery park is next in line to arrive.[67]

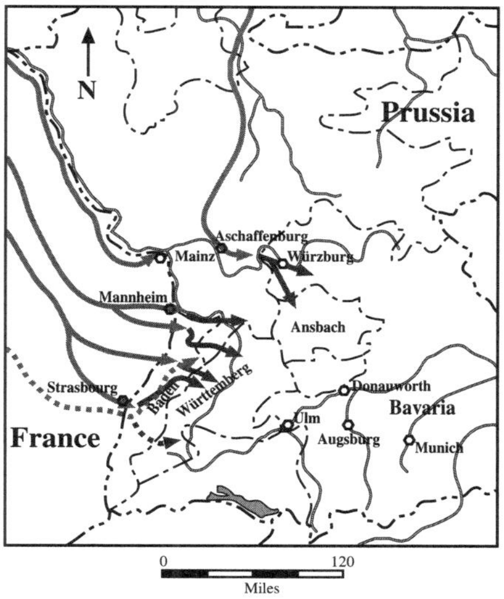

The French columns close in on Ulm

The following day, on 8 vendémiaire an XIII (30 September 1805), Napoleon issued the following proclamation to the *Grande Armée*:

> Soldiers, the war of the Third Coalition has begun. The Austrian army has crossed the Inn, violated treaties, attacked and chased our ally from his capital. You have force marched to the defense of our frontiers. Already you have crossed the Rhine. We will not stop until we have insured the independence of the German states, helped our allies and smashed the pride of the unjust assailants. Our generosity will no longer deceive our policy.
>
> Soldiers, your Emperor is among you! As the advance guard of a great people, it may be necessary for you to completely lift up my voice to confuse and dissolve this new league that has been spawn by the hatred and gold of the English. But, Soldiers, we will have forced marches to make, fatigues and deprivations of all kinds to endure. Some obstacles will oppose us, but we will conquer them, and we will not rest until we have planted our eagles in the territory of our enemies![68]

The following day, Napoleon wrote his brother Joseph:

> The army is advancing rapidly. The 1st and 2nd Corps have joined the Bavarians, and left Würzburg; the 3rd, 4th, and 6th Corps are beyond the Neckar River. The enemy marches and countermarches, and seems to be very puzzled. In a few days we shall be fighting. The army has not one loss, either from desertion or sickness. I shall be at Stuttgart this evening. As we

[66] S.H.A.T., C^2 1.
[67] Napoléon to Eugène, *Correspondance*, number 9290.
[68] Proclamation to the Army, *Correspondance*, number 9293.

> shall move very quickly, you must not be astonished if you hear nothing from me for some days... all the Germans are well disposed towards us.[69]

As the *Grande Armée* moved swiftly from the Rhine towards the Danube and confrontation with the Austrian army, its march path and converging columns left an impression of a giant tornado, "twisting its way out of the sky, and curling downwards to work chaos and destruction on the earth."[70] When the maneuver began on 25 September, the army was spread out along a line 160 miles long from Strasbourg to Würzburg. At the center of the tornado, or funnel, were the inner columns of Lannes' 5th Corps, Ney's 6th, the Imperial Guard, Artillery Park, and Murat's Reserve Cavalry. This innermost portion of the funnel crossed the Rhine between Strasbourg and Pforz, then weaved easterly to Stuttgart. The middle of the funnel consisted of Soult's 4th Corps with Davout's 3rd to its' left. These corps crossed the Rhine at Speyer and Mannheim, respectively. Meanwhile, the outer portions of the funnel was formed by Marmont's 2nd Corps and Bernadotte's 1st Corps as they churned past Würzburg. As the corps marched further eastward, they drew closer together until the funnel compressed along a 70-mile sector west and north of the Danube from Geislingen (opposite Ulm) to Eichstädt on the Altmühl River.

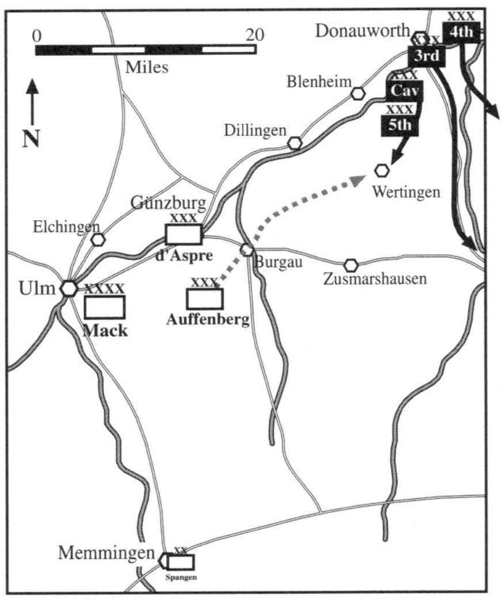

The armies move to contact at Wertingen

The positioning of the *Grande Armée* north and east of Ulm gave Napoleon the flexibility to be able to react to three of the four options that General Mack might choose. If the Austrian general marched northwest to meet the *Grande Armée*, the French corps could react swiftly to rapidly concentrate for battle. If Mack decided to stay along the Danube and fight—an option Napoleon did not seriously consider that the Austrian general would chose—the Emperor could redirect his army's march in order to cut the Austrians off from Vienna and annihilate the Habsburg army around Ulm. If the Austrians cut and ran for Vienna, the *Grande Armée* was in position to readily pursue and run down the slower moving adversary. However, if Mack chose to immediately retreat into the Tyrol, there could be little that Napoleon could do to prevent that from taking place. To eliminate that option, the Emperor knew that his army would have to continue to move swiftly.

The Combat at Wertingen

While French forces were descending on the Danube, General Mack was busying himself by issuing orders that further concentrated his army around Ulm. One reason Mack was doing this was due to the fact that the vaunted Austrian light cavalry "had bungled its security mission."[71] Until 3 October, Mack believed that the French would approach his position around Ulm through the eastern exits of the Black Forest and not violate what he believed to be the neutrality of Ansbach. However, from the Black Forest to the border of Ansbach, there was a 60-mile front that the Austrian light cavalry was supposed to picket in order to warn Mack of any approaching enemy. When Murat's cavalry withdrew from the Black Forest and there was no French infantry behind them, Mack realized that Napoleon's army could only be descending upon him from the north and northwest, despite the fact that he had received no information from his cavalry about these presumed enemy movements. To put this into perspective, the Austrian light cavalry failed to penetrate the French light cavalry screen and detect Ney's 6th Corps before

---

[69] Napoléon to Joseph, *Correspondance*, number 9305.

[70] Duffy, *Austerlitz*, p. 42.

[71] Esposito and Elting, *A Military History and Atlas of the Napoleonic Wars*, text to Map 47.

Above a view of the hill, seen from the south, where Murat placed his horse artillery. To the extreme left the church at Gottmannshofen is just visible. Below is a map of the Wertingen area

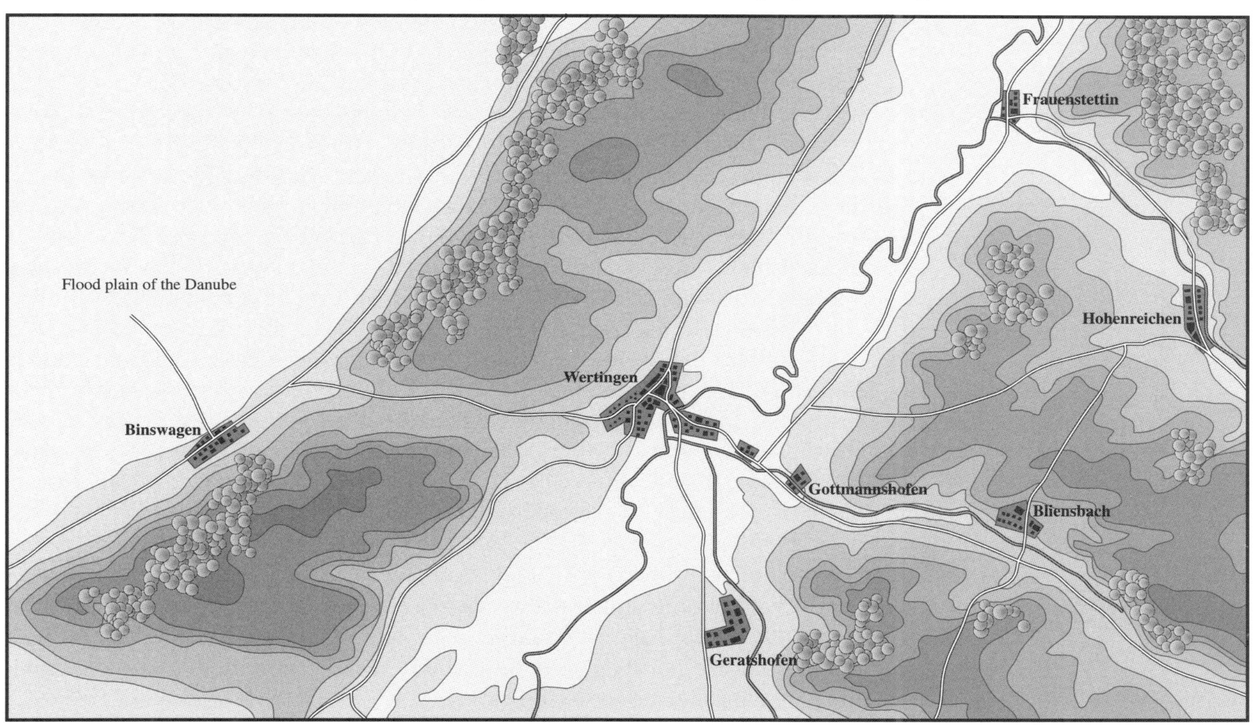

Wertingen as seen from the ridge south of town where the Austrians made their final stand.

Austrian Hussars

Austrian Jäger

Stuttgart, some 60 miles northwest of Ulm, four days earlier on 29 September!

Faced with the first of several critical decisions, Mack issued a series of orders in which he expressed his desire to counterattack the French army as it crossed over to the southern bank of the Danube. This decision did not sit well with Mack's aristocratic colleagues who served as column and division commanders. These noblemen wanted nothing to do with fighting a French army that could possibly get between them and their capital. Instead, these officers called for an escape to Vienna posthaste. This view was also echoed by Archduke Ferdinand, who thought it best to accept whatever losses the army might take, and save the rest by making a beeline for Munich before the French crossed the Danube *en masse*. If necessary, the army could continue its retrograde movement and fall back to Braunau, or to Vienna. Somewhere along the way, the Austrian army would meet up with the Russians, turn and defeat the pursuing French.[72]

Despite these protestations, the unpopular Protestant stood alone against the opinion of his officers. Mack believed that a retreat would be disastrous, owing to the worsening weather and the horrible condition of the horses that were assigned to the army's train of artillery and 'logistical tail.' Besides, Mack knew that the position of Ulm had historically proven itself to be unassailable. He instead called for an active defense around Ulm in order to hold out long enough for Kutuzov's Russians to come to the rescue. To accomplish this, Mack ordered General d'Aspre with a column consisting of three fusilier battalions of Württemberg IR#38, three fusilier battalions of Erzherzog Karl IR#3, four fusilier battalions of Kaunitz-Rietberg IR#20, supported by 20 6- and 3-pounder battalion guns attached to these infantry formations, two companies of Tyrolian jägers, two squadrons each from Cüirassier-Regiment Hohenzollern #8, Chevaulegers-Regiment Rosenberg #6 and Uhlanen-Regiment Schwarzenberg #2 to hold the bridgeheads at Günzburg in order to prevent the French from crossing the Danube at that point.[73]

Meanwhile, a force of 5,000 infantry and 400 cavalry under the command of FML Auffenberg was sent out from Ulm to scout in the direction of Donauwörth in response to a vague report that the French were approaching the Danube from the northwest. The infantry contingent of Auffenberg's Column consisted of nine battalions, of which six were grenadiers and three were fusiliers. The grenadier battalions were from Stuart IR#18, Spork IR#25, Württemberg IR#38, Erbach IR#42, Reuss-Greitz IR#55 and Colloredo IR#57, while the three fusilier battalions came from Reuss-Greitz IR#55. Auffenberg's mounted contingent consisted of two squadrons of Cüirassier-Regiment Erzherzog Albert #3 and two squadrons of the Chevaulegers-Regiment Latour #4. Normally, a contingent of nine battalions of infantry would have 18 battalion guns accompanying it. However, the poor condition of the horses pulling the artillery resulted in only nine battalion guns were able to make the sortie.[74]

The far right flank of the army was entrusted to FML Kienmayer with a column numbering 10,000 men in 10 battalions of infantry and 30 squadrons of horse. From his position around the Neuberg-Ingolstadt area, Kienmayer was to fulfill two important missions. As the strategic right flank of the army, Kienmayer's cavalry had to keep an eye on the Bavarians in the Upper Palatinate around Nuremberg. Also, the Austrian horse was to watch for the arrival of Kutuzov's Russian army.[75] Believing that his army was securely positioned where it could fall back on the fortified positions on the Michelsberg plateau above Ulm and sustain itself until help arrived, Mack waited for Napoleon's next move. He would not have to wait long.

---

[72] Angeli, 'Ulm und Austerlitz' in *Österreichische Militärische Zeitschrift,* p. 462-464.

[73] *K. k. Kriegsarchiv*, *Feldacten* for 1805, Vienna.

[74] *K. k. Kriegsarchiv*, *Feldacten* for 1805.

[75] *K. k. Kriegsarchiv*, *Feldacten* for 1805. Also, see: Krauss, *1805. Der Feldzug von Ulm.*

By 7 October, the *Grande Armée* was already pouring across the Danube at Münster, Donauwörth and Neuberg. Acting on the information confirmed by several hundred prisoners taken in the capture of the bridges over the Danube, Napoleon realized that his prey had not tried to cut and run for Vienna, but was still massed around the Danube and Iller Rivers at Ulm. Assuming that the Austrians would now certainly try to escape to Vienna, the Emperor gave urgent orders to Murat's *Corps des Réserves de Cavalerie* (less Walther's and Bourcier's divisions of dragoons and d'Hautpoul's *cuirassiers*) and Lannes' 5th Corps (less Gazan's 2nd Infantry Division)—both of which had already passed the Danube at Münster and Donauwörth—to march southward from the Danube and position themselves between Ulm and Augsburg. The purpose of this maneuver was to position a strong combined arms force that would cut the main Ulm-Augsburg-Munich highway along which Mack was expected to retreat his army eastward. "You are authorized," the Emperor told Murat on 15 vendémiaire (7 October), "to take two regiments from the corps of Lannes to support the movements of your heavy cavalry. You will have strong bodies of enemy on the road from Augsburg to Ulm."[76] Meanwhile, Soult's 4th Corps, reinforced by Walther's 2nd Dragoon Division and d'Hautpoul's 2nd Heavy Cavalry Division from Murat's cavalry reserve, and Davout's 3rd Corps were ordered to cross the Danube and march southward, pursuing Kienmayer's Column and occupying the countryside between Augsburg and Aichach. Although Napoleon did not anticipate that the Austrians would do so, in order to block any possible advance along the north bank of the Danube, the Emperor placed Ney's 6th Corps, reinforced by Gazan's 2nd Infantry Division from Lannes' 5th Corps, Bourcier's 4th Dragoon Division and Baraguey d'Hilliers Dismounted Dragoon Division.

Austrian Dragoons

Unknowingly marching to meet the French onslaught were the Austrians under FML Auffenberg. Following a forced march on the night of 7-8 October, Auffenberg's fatigued troops reached the village of Wertingen after sunrise on the 8th. Not anticipating any chance meetings with Napoleon's forces when ending his movement, Auffenberg had dispersed his infantry and heavy cavalry in and around Wertingen while the chevaulegers were posted in a nearby hamlet called Hohenreichen. As his troops rested during the morning hours, Auffenberg held an officers call. This conference was suddenly interrupted after noon by a trooper of the Latour Chevaulegers with word that masses of French cavalry were in sight and advancing rapidly. Scoffing at a report from a common soldier, Auffenberg did nothing. After all, the Austrian general had been told by army headquarters the day before that the closest French were probably Bernadotte's 1st Corps, and their last reported position was at Würzburg, where only a few days prior they had been joined by the Bavarians. The trooper's return to his regiment and subsequent story to his superiors prompted an officer of the Latour regiment to ride to Auffenberg's headquarters insisting that the story was true. Not able to ignore the presentation of a member of the noble class, Auffenberg barely had time to call his troops to arms when the scouts of Murat's cavalry galloped within cannon range of the outskirts of Hohenreichen.[77]

These mounted scouts preceded the advance of the *Corps des Réserves de Cavalerie* under the Emperor's brother-in-law. Prince Joachim Murat had set out from Donauwörth with three divisions of his corps around 8:00 A.M. on 8 October 1805. With Murat were the 1st Heavy Cavalry Division under Nansouty, with the 1st Dragoon Division under Klein and Beaumont's 3rd Dragoon Division in the lead. Moving south towards Wertingen with almost 8,000 horsemen and three half-companies of horse artillery totaling nine guns, Murat was soon joined by Fauconnet's light cavalry brigade from Lannes' 5th Corps. Fauconnet brought

---

[76] S.H.A.T., C^2 201.

[77] *K. k. Kriegsarchiv*, *Feldacten* for 1805, Vienna.

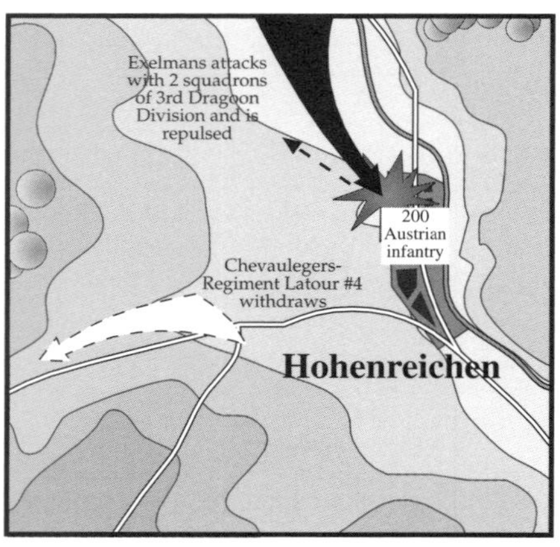

Exelmans' first attack at Hohenreichen

with him 600 eager troopers of the 9th and 10th Hussars as well as another half-company of horse artillery, boosting Murat's command total to some 8,600 combatants supported by 12 pieces of ordnance.[78]

Sending the light cavalry in advance of the heavy cavalry and dragoons, Murat soon received word back from a scout of the 10th Hussars that an Austrian force was around Hohenreichen and Wertingen, believed to be about 12,000 strong. After dispatching messengers to Marshal Lannes about the location of the enemy, Murat sent forward one of his aides-de-camp, *chef d'escadron* Rémy-Joseph-Isidore Exelmans to ride to the head of the corps. Exelmans was a proven officer with a reputation of knowing how to act decisively. He had answered the call to save *La Patrie* by joining the Republican army as a member of the Volunteers of 1791. As an infantryman, he served under Oudinot in the *Armée de la Moselle* in 1792-1794. Transferring to the artillery, he saw service in the *Armée de Sambre-et-Meuse* from 1794 to 1797. Rising in rank to *sous-lieutenant* in 1796 and considered to be a highly intelligent officer, Exelmans was recommended and approved for transfer to General Elbé's staff in 1798, after which he was sent to Italy and served under Macdonald as a captain of the 16th Dragoons. Following the campaigns of 1799 and 1800, Exelmans was selected as one of Murat's aides-de-camp in 1801. He was present during the two-year encampment of Boulogne where he paid considerable attention to the training of the dragoons. Dressed in the scarlet-plumed fur busby and uniform of the Élite Company of the 15th *Chasseurs à cheval*, Exelmans was 29-year-old *chef d'escadron* when Murat ordered him to the head of the corps of cavalry riding towards the Austrians and the first battle of the 1805 campaign.[79]

When Exelmans arrived on the scene outside Hohenreichen, he carried with him, like any other French aide-de-camp, the command authority of his superior officer. So empowered, the *chef d'escadron* was in command of the battle until Murat arrived. Exelmans saw what he believed to be about 200 Austrian infantry interspersed between the houses of the small hamlet while the mounted squadrons of Chevaulegers-Regiment Latour #4 were withdrawing towards a ridge that separated Hohenreichen and Wertingen. The main Austrian body was further south, behind the village of Wertingen. These infantry were already forming squares on the level, elevated plain beyond the village of Wertingen, and their battalion guns were unlimbered for action, with formed squadrons of Austrian cavalry protecting both flanks of the division. However, feeling threatened by so many French cavalry, the Latour Chevaulegers abandoned the ridge between Hohenreichen and Wertingen. Therefore, with no enemy cavalry in position to threaten his movements towards Hohenreichen, and because the ridge between Hohenreichen and Wertingen was needed for the French artillery to fire on the main Austrian body beyond Wertingen, Exelmans ordered that Hohenreichen be cleared of Austrian infantry. Two squadrons of General Boyé's 1st Brigade from Beaumont's 3rd Dragoon Division dismounted and were soon moving forward to take the hamlet by storm. Remaining on horseback while leading forward the two squadrons of dismounted dragoons, Exelmans attacked the hamlet. From the cover of the wooden houses, the Austrians easily repulsed the initial attack from these reluctant infantrymen. Exelmans called for reinforcements and soon four dismounted squadrons from the 5th and 8th Dragoons attacked with Exelmans at their head. Like the first attack, this too failed. Infuriated with his dragoons by these setbacks, Exelmans was determined that the third attack would succeed. The remaining regiment of Boyé's brigade, the 12th, was ordered to join in the attack along with General Scalfort and his 9th Dragoons. Leaving their horse-holders behind with the mounts, Exelmans was soon leading four entire regiments of dismounted dragoons with muskets in hand.

Dismounted French dragoons storm Hohenreichen

---

78 S.H.A.T., C² 240, 470 and 472.

79 Six, *Dictionnaire biographique*, vol. 1, p. 434.

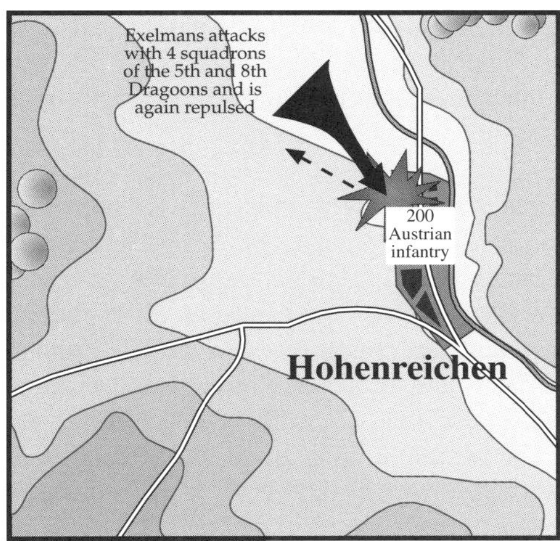

Exelmans' second attack at Hohenreichen

Exelmans, shown here in his later rank of général de division

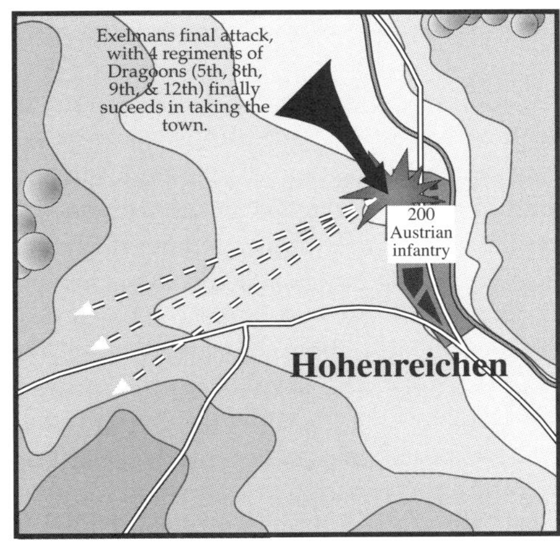

Exelmans' final attack at Hohenreichen

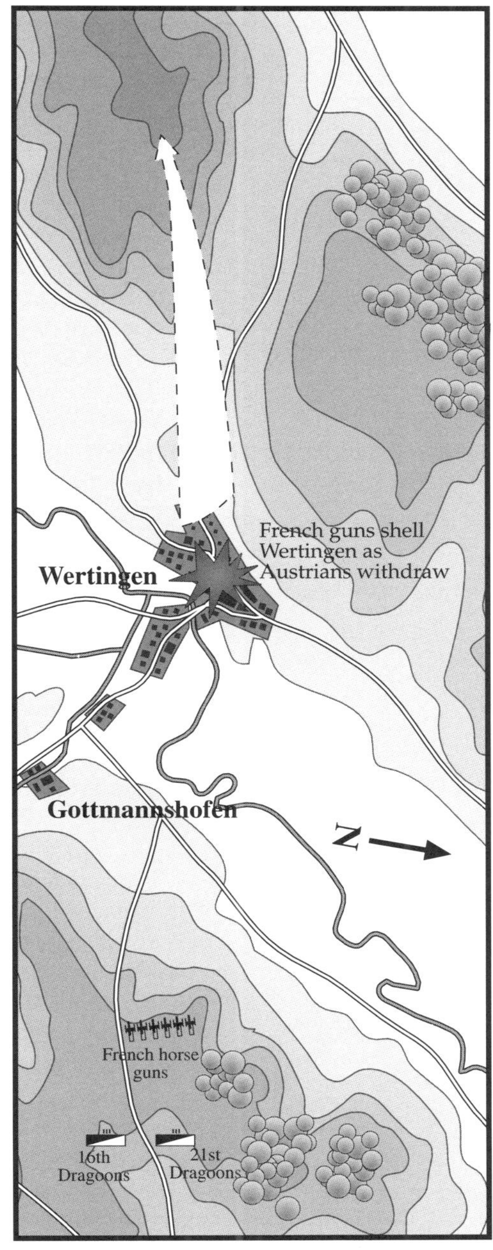

The Austrians fall back beyond Wertingen

Trumpeter and officer of chasseurs à cheval

Exelmans, shown here in the uniform he wore in 1805, finds a remount during the action at Wertingen

These men swarmed over the heroic but hopelessly outnumbered Austrians in Hohenreichen. The whitecoated infantry that were not killed, wounded or captured in the hamlet fled as best they could some 1,000 yards back over the ridge, through Wertingen, and towards Auffenberg's main body which was ready and waiting for the French cavalry.

Having finally cleared Hohenreichen, Exelmans acted quickly. Not wanting to give the Austrians any time to organize a counterattack against his dismounted squadrons, he decided to continue the battle without pausing by applying pressure on the enemy with a mounted attack. While two brigades of Beaumont's command were finding their way back to their mounts, and with the head of 1st Dragoon Division just beginning to come onto the field, Exelmans brought forward the three horse guns of Beaumont's Division as well as the three horse guns with Fauconnet's 5th Corps light cavalry. The pieces unlimbered on the ridge north of Wertingen, their crews having a splendid view of Auffenberg's entire command only 1,100 yards away. Under the cover of these guns the dismounted dragoons remounted and reformed for action. To protect all these friendlies, the remainder of Scalfort's command consisting of the 16th and 21st Dragoons, remained mounted on the reverse slope of the ridge, close to the guns to serve as protection should the Austrian cavalry decide to attack. Meanwhile, the élite crews of these four 8-pounder guns and two 6-inch howitzers quickly settled to their work. Ball and shell fell into the densely packed squares of Austrians, and these projectiles exacted a terrible price each time one found its mark. Replying to the French artillery fire were the 6-pounder battalion guns in Auffenberg's command. The Austrian fire was ineffective, however, owing to the combination of distance and the fact that the French pieces were uphill. Realizing that they enjoyed a distinct advantage, rather than attempting to fire counter battery and silence the Austrian smaller pieces, the French horse artillerists kept their devastating fire concentrated onto the compact infantry targets.

Meanwhile, after directing General Fauconnet to send his hussars on a wide flanking movement, Exelmans ordered Generals Boyé and Scalfort to prepare their recently remounted units for an attack. The 5th and 8th Dragoons remained in reserve after detaching men to escort the prisoners to the rear. Meanwhile, deploying into squadrons abreast, soon the 9th and 12th Dragoons, preceded by *généraux de brigade* Boyé and Scalfort along with Colonels Maupetit and Pagès, were moving to the attack at the orders of a *chef d'escadron.* As the French passed over the Wertingen ridge, into the shallow valley and gently rising plateau beyond, they pressed home their assault. Austrian grenadiers were ready and waiting in square, and soon Exelmans' horse was shot out from under him. Close by, Colonel Maupetit of the 9th Dragoons charged into the whitecoated ranks where he was wounded and unhorsed by an Austrian bayonet. In the confusion of combat, Maupetit miraculously escaped further harm.

Dragoon élite company ready for action

The élan of Boyé's and Scalfort's dragoons was not enough to break any of the Austrian squares. As the tide of the French attacking squadrons receded, Exelmans mounted another horse and called for the dragoons to renew their efforts. Covered by the fire of the French horse artillery, the 9th and 12th Dragoons reformed in the shallow valley. For this attack, the *compagnies d'élite* of both regiments were grouped directly under Exelmans. The signal for the attack being given, the French horse artillery fire slackened as the cavalry once again pressed home their charge. Squadrons of greencoated dragoons on brown horses swarmed around the bastions of whitecoated infantry. The Frenchmen cut and sabered the Austrian grenadiers, who fought back with point-blank musket fire and thrusts of bayonets. Meanwhile, Exelmans, at the head of the two bearskinned *compagnies d'élite* from the 9th and 12th, was working over one square of Austrian grenadiers that did not have the protection of battalion artillery. By concentrating their mounted fire at two of the corners, the dragoons began seeing the effect of their fire with the thinning

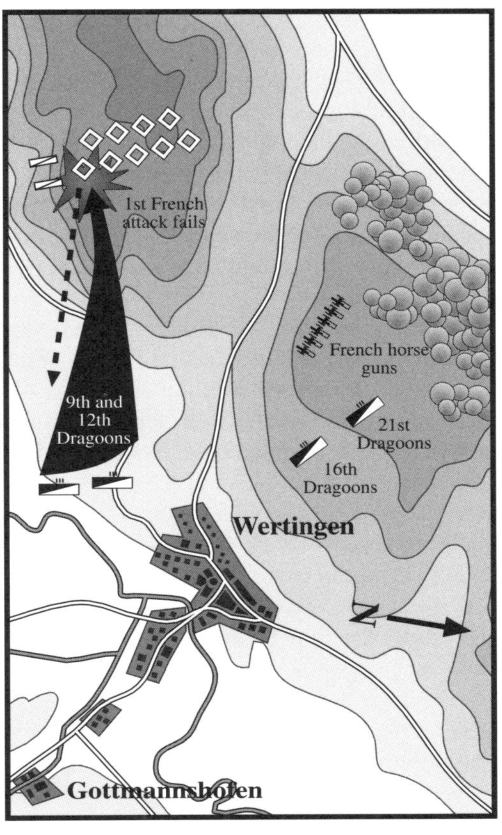

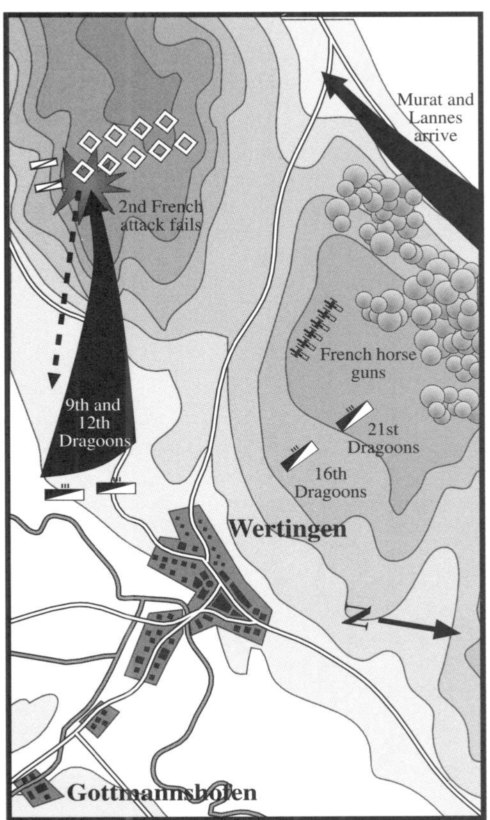

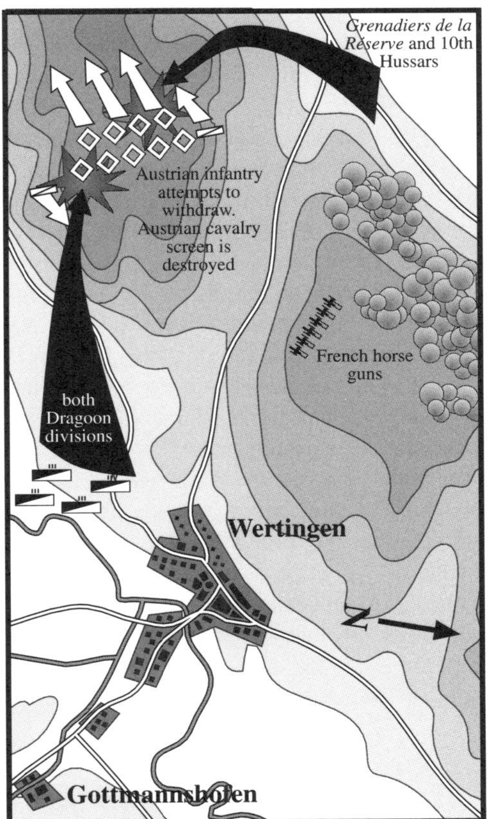

Top left, the first French cavalry attack on the Austrian squares.

Top right, Lannes and Oudinot arrive while the French cavalry continue their attacks.

Bottom left, .the final phase of the battle.

Dragoon élite company charging

of the enemy's ranks. Moving in front of the Élite Company of the 9th, Exelmans gave the order for both élite companies to charge. Striking the Austrian square at two points, the dragoons battled to gain entry. They had momentarily broken into the square when the grenadiers shifted troops from other sides of the square, successfully closing the breach and repelling the mounted troopers. During this charge, Exelmans had his second horse shot out from under him, remounted another and returned to French lines. With the Austrians holding their own, the second mounted attack receded. The dragoons withdrew over the ridge and reformed on the reverse slope where the dismounted brigades of the division had remounted their horses following the capture of Hohenreichen.

As Exelmans was making this second attack, Marshal Murat arrived on the field with the remainder of his corps, followed closely by Marshal Lannes at the head of Oudinot's *Grenadiers de la Réserve*. With the increasing noise of battle coming from enemy fire as Exelmans' dragoons pressed home their charges, Murat and Lannes met about 4:00 P.M. near one of the half-companies of horse artillery on a small hillock that formed the southern end of the crescent-shaped ridge above Wertingen. From their vantage point on this low ridge, and with the French ordnance temporarily suspending its fire during the dragoons' attack, both marshals had the opportunity to witness Exelmans' daring attempt to break the enemy squares.

A portrait of Murat in action at Wertingen

Prince Murat's arrival on the field was delayed because he had not anticipated the action fully developing until Lannes arrived with the infantry. As Murat made his appearance at the head of Nansouty's heavy cavalry, he was pleasantly surprised that Lannes had arrived sooner than expected. Before receiving any messengers concerning the fight around Wertingen, Lannes had heard the gunfire and ordered the 5th Corps infantry to march to the sound of the guns. Therefore, the battle's direction on the French side shifted from the shoulders of a *chef d'escadron* to two marshals of France. While Oudinot's grenadiers halted their march long enough to drop their packs and ready their battalions for action, Lannes and Murat held a quick conference of war. Only two hours of daylight remained; a plan would have to be formulated quickly and troops moved swiftly.

A quick glance of the ground revealed both the strength and weakness of the Austrian position. The plateau on which Auffenberg's command was deployed was a secure and strong enough position if attacked head on from the north. However, to the northwest, or the Austrian left flank, the plateau fell off at a steep 37 degree grade, and the sloping terrain was covered by woods. At the bottom of the slope was the Old Roman Road that led around the plateau to the southern end of the Austrian position. Lannes suggested that he and Oudinot lead the division of *Grenadiers de la Réserve* under the cover of the woods along the edge of the plateau, along the Old Roman Road, and towards the enemy's rear. Acting in concert with Fauconnet's hussars, the infantry would position itself to block any retreat that might be attempted. While this maneuver was taking place, the French horse artillery would bombard the enemy positions in preparation for the final attack. Once Lannes, Oudinot and Fauconnet were in position, Murat would unleash his squadrons while Oudinot's grenadiers attacked from the rear.[80]

These preparations were not being made against a foe who was idly waiting for the next attack. With the surprising and sudden appearance of Lannes, Auffenberg recognized his impossible position. He rode from square to square giving the order for the infantry to withdraw while the cavalry was to cover the infantry's flanks as best it could.[81] The retrograde movement of the Austrian squares was not nearly fast enough to escape the quick advance of the Oudinot's columns. In an attempt to buy some time for the infantry to escape, Auffenberg's outnumbered cavalry tried to cover the movements of the squares by charging Oudinot's

---

[80] S.H.A.T., C^2 240; *Journal des opérations du 5e corps.*

[81] Picard, *La Cavalerie dans Les Guerres de la Révolution et de l'Empire*, vol. 1, p. 265.

Napoleon rewards a dragoon

grenadiers once they had emerged from their circuitous route around the plateau. The advance of the Cüirassier-Regiment Erzherzog Albert #3 succeeded in temporarily halting the French infantry which had to change from column into square. However, the desired effect was short-lived as the 10th Hussars moved against the Austrian horse. In the brief fight that followed, the 10th used its superior frontage to outflank the Austrian heavy cavalry. While one squadron of hussars broke up the Austrian heavies from the flank, two others assailed the Albert Cüirassiers from the front. The coordinated French squadrons were too much for the Austrian horse; they were routed in minutes. On the other flank, Murat sent in both divisions of dragoons, spearheaded by the 1st Dragoons led by Napoleon's nephew, Colonel Arrighi de Casanova, and Colonel Privé's 2nd Dragoons. With vastly superior frontage, the French horse blew through the two squadrons of the Chevaulegers-Regiment Latour #4, then tried overpowering one line of Auffenberg's squares. French audacity seemed to work. With his cavalry support gone, Auffenberg's ordered retreat soon fell into disorder, and disorder turned into panic as the squares began to also be assaulted and broken by both French grenadiers and dragoons. Auffenberg's entire line soon became engulfed in a sea of blue infantry and greencoated cavalry, and after 6:00 P.M. when the last rays of daylight were leaving the western sky, those who could escape turned and ran.

Austrian survivors were few. Auffenberg, along with the other general officers, managed to escape along with only 1,400 of the 5,000 Austrian infantry that went into action. The Austrian cavalry, which under normal circumstances would have suffered lighter casualties than the infantry, had been butchered by the highly coordinated French squadrons. The Austrian horse could barely count 100 survivors of the 400 that started the battle. In Colonel Gingen's two squadrons of Cüirassier-Regiment Erzherzog Albert #3, five officers and 65 men were either killed or wounded while another seven officers and 28 troopers were captured. The Austrian dead numbered 130 with another 850 wounded. In addition to these casualties, Auffenberg's command lost more than 2,900 as prisoners of war. The majority of all casualties were suffered by the Reuss-Greitz IR#55. All three of the fusilier battalions, along with the grenadier battalion of this Galician-based regiment were either killed, wounded or captured. In addition to the total destruction or capture of Reuss-Greitz IR#55, the grenadiers from Spork IR#25 were also taken captive. Another two lieutenant-colonels, six majors plus 60 other officers were captured by the French. In the hands of the victors were also eight stands of colors, five 6-pounder battalion guns and four 3-pounder battalion guns.[82] One more 6-pounder fell into Murat's hands that evening, as Auffenberg's command had all but ceased to exist.[83]

A French dragoon on reconnaissance

In stark contrast to the more than 3,900 killed, wounded and captured suffered by the Austrians, French casualties were very light. General Dupas' 2nd Brigade of Oudinot's *Grenadiers de la Réserve* suffered the most infantry casualties—they lost 42 men killed and wounded. The other two brigades of Oudinot's Division counted only 21 men down. Including Murat's dragoons that suffered almost 250 casualties (Nansouty's 1st Heavy Cavalry Division was not engaged), the losses for the entire French force at Wertingen came to a total of 319 *hors de combat.*[84]

To send word of the victory to Imperial headquarters, Lannes and Murat both agreed that Exelmans should ride to Donauwörth. With the captured Austrian standards in hand, Exelmans reported to the Emperor. After Napoleon received Exelmans and his report, which was followed by numerous questions about the conduct of the troops involved, the Emperor awarded Exelmans with the cross of an officer of the *Légion d'Honneur,* proclaiming that it was the first medal earned

---

[82] S.H.A.T., C^2 470.

[83] S.H.A.T., C^2 13; *K. k. Kriegsarchiv*, *Feldacten* for 1805, Vienna.

[84] S.H.A.T., C^2 470 and 472.

in the new war.[85] To Marshal Murat, the Emperor wrote on 17 vendémiaire (9 October): "My Cousin, I am extremely satisfied with the report made to me [by Exelmans] of the good conduct of the cavalry and especially the dragoons in the battle yesterday."[86] Sending his congratulations to Marshal Lannes that same evening, Napoleon stated:

> My Cousin, I have seen with pleasure in your report [through Exelmans] the good conduct of the *Grenadiers de la Réserve.* It is unfortunate that you had only two hours of daylight in which to fight your battle. Otherwise, not a man would have escaped you. Post an order to the grenadiers that I am happy with their conduct in the combat of Wertingen.[87]

News of the French victory at Wertingen electrified the footsore soldiers of the *Grande Armée.* Napoleon's troops had been in constant motion for almost six weeks. During this time, they had moved from their Channel encampments, crossed the Rhine and arrived on the Danube. They were becoming eager to begin realizing some fruition of their labors and this small battle gave an important boost in morale at a time when the weather was worsening. "The action of Wertingen does great credit to the dragoons and to the cavalry," Napoleon wrote to Joseph on 18 vendémiaire (10 October). "It was a pleasant little success for Murat, who was in command."[88] In the Order of the Day posted on 21 vendémiaire (13 October), Napoleon declared: "The Emperor expresses his satisfaction to the divisions of dragoons, the 10th Regiment of Hussars, and other troops who took part in the Battle of Wertingen."[89] For Napoleon and the *Grande Armée,* Wertingen heralded an auspicious start to a momentous campaign.

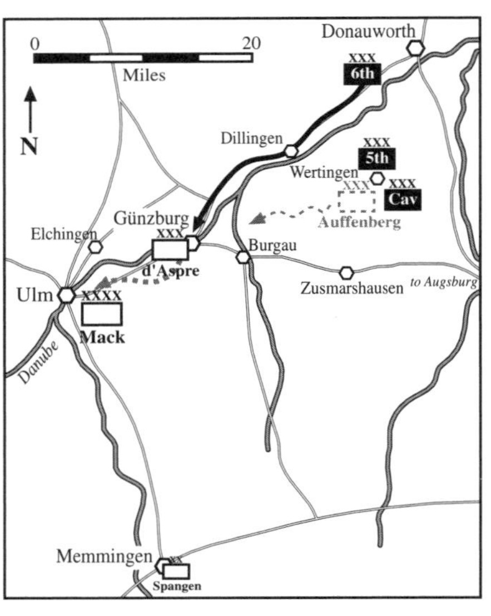

Malher reaches Günzburg with the 3rd Infantry Division of Ney's Corps

The Combat at Günzburg

The day that Murat and Lannes were annihilating Auffenberg's command at Wertingen, Marshal Soult's 4th Corps, along with the Imperial Guard, d'Hautpoul's 2nd Heavy Cavalry Division and Walther's 2nd Dragoon Division, were approaching Augsburg. Once at this city, the French cut the highway that General Mack's army in and around Ulm used for its line of communications with Vienna. Marshal Davout's 3rd Corps, having crossed the Danube at Neuberg, was ordered to push south to Aichach to take an intermediate position between Soult and Marmont's 2nd Corps that was also crossing at Neuberg. Marmont was to head for Augsburg to join Soult, the Imperial Guard and other forces gathering at this point on the Lech River. Meanwhile, Bernadotte's 1st Corps, the outermost corps of the army, was at Ingolstadt. Once across the Danube, this corps was to head for Munich and serve as a covering force should the Russians show. Finally, Marshal Ney was ordered to take control of General Gazan's 2nd Infantry Division from Lannes' 5th Corps and Baraguey d'Hilliers Dismounted Dragoon Division so that he could either reach Augsburg by the 10th, or fall upon the Austrian flank. Ney was also instructed by Berthier to capture Günzburg, thus severing the Ulm-Augsburg road.[90]

---

[85] S.H.A.T., C^2 2.
[86] Napoléon to Murat, *Correspondance*, number 9356.
[87] Napoléon to Lannes, *Correspondance*, number 9357.
[88] Napoléon to Joseph, *Correspondance*, number 9359; *The Confidential Correspondence of Napoleon Bonaparte with His Brother Joseph*, vol. 1, number 91.
[89] S.H.A.T., C^2 12; and Order of the Day, *Unpublished Correspondence of Napoleon I*, vol. 1, number 199. Also, see: Proclamation to the Army, *Correspondance,* number 9381.
[90] S.H.A.T., C^2 2.

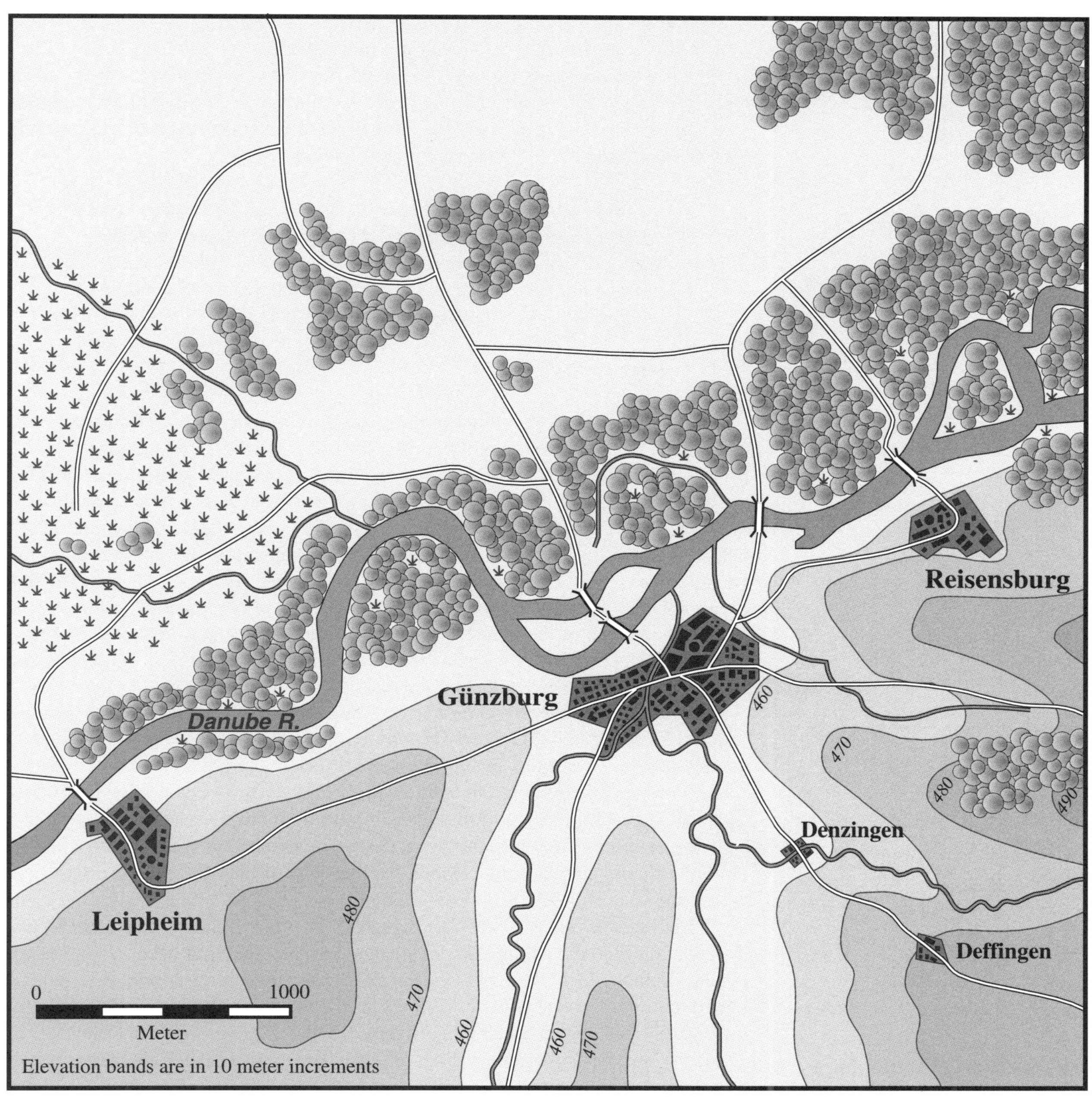

The Battlefield of Günzburg

d'Aspre

These maneuvers ordered by Napoleon were based on two assumptions: 1) that Mack had realized the hopelessness of his fortified positions around Ulm. As a result, Mack was sure to abandon Ulm, attempting to run for Vienna and for the Russian army approaching from the east; and 2) that the anticipated Austrian retreat route towards Augsburg would result in a major battle along the Lech River on 9 or 10 October. However, before the 9th ended, Napoleon realized what the prisoner reports had been telling him: Mack's army was not moving eastward, but remained at the juncture of the Danube and Iller Rivers at Ulm. Writing to his brother Joseph, Napoleon advised on 18 vendémiaire (10 October):

> The army is in good spirits, their wish to be seriously engaged, and their patience under fatigue, are good omens. My headquarters are today at Zusmarshaussen. I have neither carriage nor secretaries, nor anything else here, but I intend this evening to join the headquarters at Augsburg.
>
> I have the enemy surrounded in Ulm; they were defeated yesterday by Ney.[91]

The combat of which the Emperor was speaking occurred at Günzburg on 9 October. The battle was fought between the 3rd Infantry Division under General Malher of Ney's 6th Corps and Baron d'Aspre's Austrian Column guarding the bridge approaches to the village overlooking the Danube. It will be remembered that d'Aspre's command was holding Günzburg on the orders of General Mack who was operating under the assumption that the French would have to cross the Danube near Ulm. However, following the crossing down river by most of the *Grande Armée*, Napoleon ordered Ney—whose entire command was at that time on the north bank of the Danube—to take all the bridges between Günzburg and Ulm and establish contact with Lannes and Murat who were on the south bank and moving their corps westward from Zusmarshaussen in order to link-up with Ney.[92]

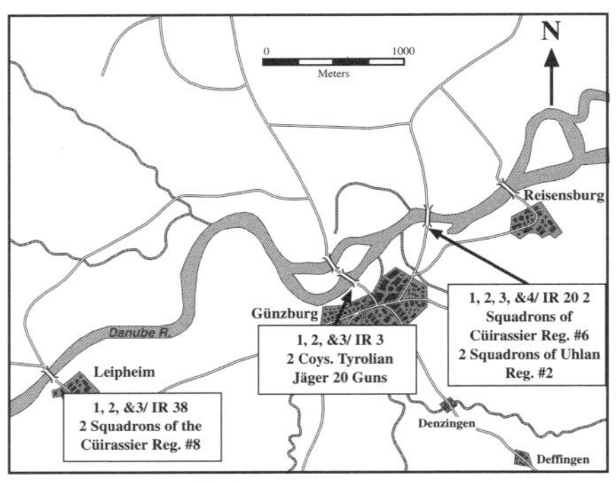

D'Aspre's deployment at Günzburg

Marshal Ney wasted no time in ordering the 6th Corps into motion. The 1st Infantry Division under General Dupont, with the Dismounted Dragoon Division under Baraguey d'Hilliers in support, were directed to advance on Ulm. General Loison and the 2nd Infantry Division, along with the Corps Cavalry Brigade under General Auguste de Colbert (which was scouting in advance of both Dupont and Loison), were to move on Elchingen and capture the bridge at that point. Finally, the 3rd Infantry Division of General Malher was to take the three bridges near Günzburg.

Malher was closer to his objective than the other division commanders, and the general ordered his *fantassins* to assault Günzburg without delay. Jean-Pierre-Firmin Malher, the 44-year-old *général de division*, had come a long way since he joined the infantry *régiment de Neustrie* at age 16. Rising to the rank of sergeant in 1780, he obtained an honorable discharge from the Royal Army in December of 1784. When the Revolution came, Malher declared for the Republic and was named as a corporal in the *Garde Nationale* in Paris, rising to a *sous-officier* with the 14th battalion of light infantry in early 1792. A confirmed Republican whose political zeal was also matched by his good administrative skills, Malher rose rapidly in rank in the politically turbulent *Armée du Nord*, being named as *adjudant général chef de brigade* in June 1795. Named as chief of staff under the stern General Vandamme for several years, Malher was a *général de brigade* by 1799 and assigned to Bonaparte's *Armée de Réserve* in 1800. Present at several battles during the 1800 Italian campaign, Malher was wounded at Marengo. During the next several years, Malher served very capably in various capacities, being promoted to *général*

[91] Napoléon to Joseph, *Correspondance*, number 9359.

[92] Napoléon to Lannes, *Correspondance*, number 9352.

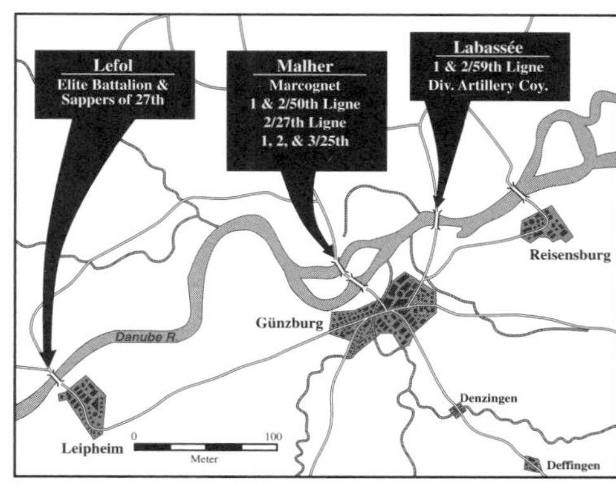

Malher's plan of attack at Günzberg

de division in August of 1803. By October the following year, Malher was named as commander of the 3rd Infantry Division at Marshal Ney's camp at Montreuil. Not having seen combat for more than five years, Malher eagerly led his troops forward on the cold, snow-driven morning of 9 October 1805.[93]

Patrols from Colbert's cavalry reported that the Austrians were in strong positions opposite Günzburg. Upon hearing these reports, Malher decided to spur his horse forward to personally reconnoiter the ground. From a hill almost two miles from Günzburg, Malher saw the rolling countryside and trees dusted with snow, reflecting off the clear waters of the Danube. As Malher looked over the Austrian dispositions, he must have had no illusions about the difficult task ahead for him and his men.

The general saw the three bridges over which his infantry could gain a foothold on the Austrian side of the river. The largest bridge was opposite the town of Günzburg, while a second was two miles above Günzburg at the village of Leipheim, and the third was 1,000 yards below Günzburg bridge at the little hamlet of Reisensburg. On this part of the river, the south bank that the Austrians occupied dominated all the bridges as well as the lower elevations on the northern bank of the Danube. In this area, the Danube was between 100 to 150 yards wide and not regularly formed. Instead, it meandered along, splitting into two or more smaller branches of water and forming in its course a multitude of small islands between the narrow branches. Covering these islets and the northern bank of the river were numerous marshes interspersed with willows and poplars. These trees could provide cover for the troops moving against the Günzburg and Reisensburg bridges, but there was no such cover available for those advancing against the Leipheim bridge. This was just one of the problems for any troops attempting to carry the upper bridge at Leipheim. Any approach was in full view of the Austrians, and the only road to the bridge was parallel to the Austrian positions, thereby exposing French troops to enfilading artillery fire. If the road was not used, attacking troops would have a difficult march to cross a series of marshes in order to reach the bridge. Awaiting any French movements, Austrian infantry could be seen already deployed and ready to resist attempted crossings at any of the bridges. However, the center bridge at Günzburg was the only one where the Austrian artillery could be seen on the elevations above the bridge.

The main bridge at Günzburg today, as seen from the east

Malher decided that his best chance for success was a simultaneous attack against all three bridges. By assaulting all the enemy held positions at the same time, Malher reasoned that the Austrians would probably be unlikely to shift troops from any one area in order to reinforce another. On the other hand, if any of the attacking groups was successful in storming the bridges, additional troops had to be available to reinforce success. Malher therefore divided his division—which consisted of two brigades totaling four regiments totaling nine battalions—into three attacking groups. The northern attack group was under the command of *général de brigade* de Labassée and assigned the capture of the Reisensburg bridge. Although de Labassée had two regiments under his command, only Colonel Lacuée and the two battalions of the 59th *Ligne*, supported by all the division's artillery company consisting of two 4-pounders, four 8-pounders, one 12-pounder and one 6-inch howitzer, were allocated by Malher for this sortie. In contrast, the Austrian troops guarding the Reisensburg bridge had no artillery in support. Nevertheless, Malher did not want to stack up additional strength behind the attacking battalions of the 59th if they were unsuccessful. The other regiment of de Labassée's brigade, Colonel de Lamartinière's 50th *Ligne* consisting of two battalions, was temporarily brigaded with the three battalions of the 25th *Légère* and the two battalions of the 27th *Ligne* which combined to form the command under *général de brigade* Marcognet. This reinforced brigade was personally led by Malher who earmarked

[93] Six, *Dictionnaire biographique*, vol. 2, p. 144.

for himself the most difficult mission—the assault over the main bridge at Günzburg opposed by numerous enemy backed up by 20 pieces of ordnance. Leaving the 1st battalion of the 27th *Ligne* in reserve to act as an available source of troops for either de Labassée or the main assault group in the center, Malher and Marcognet had six battalions with which they could storm Günzburg.[94]

With two battalions comprising the northern attack group, six battalions in the center and one in reserve, all nine of Malher's battalions were committed to assaulting just two bridges. Therefore, with what troops did Malher compose the southern attack group that had the difficult assignment of capturing the Leipheim bridge? The answer is that the general created another formation using a standard French tactical doctrine of converging élites within his command to form an *ad hoc* battalion(s). In this case, Malher ordered his division chief-of-staff, *adjudant-commandant* Lefol, to take the élite companies from the division's nine battalions and form an *ad hoc* converged battalion with which he would assault the bridge at Leipheim. Six grenadier companies of the 27th, 50th and 59th *Ligne* Regiments, as well as the three *carabinier* companies from the 25th *Légère*, combined to form this converged élite battalion. Therefore, when the parent battalions of the division went into action they did so with only eight companies instead of the usual nine. Furthermore, the converged élite battalion took with it the sappers of the 27th *Ligne*, leaving the sappers of seven élite companies from the 50th and 59th *Ligne* and 25th *Légère* with their parent battalions as a precautionary measure.[95]

Adjudant-commandant *Lefol, chief of staff of Malher's 3rd Infantry Division*

While these French preparations were being made, *General-Feldwachtmeister* Baron d'Aspre, the Austrian column commander, reviewed his deployments from his observation point above the hamlet of Reisensburg. To cover the Reisensburg bridge, GM Baron d'Aspre had deployed the four fusilier battalions of Kaunitz-Rietberg IR#20. Since these Galicians were his most unreliable troops, he backed them with good quality cavalry consisting of two squadrons from Chevaulegers-Regiment Rosenberg #6 and two more squadrons from Uhlanen-Regiment Schwarzenberg #2. Opposite the bridge at Leipheim were three fusilier battalions of the steady Württemberg IR#38 and two squadrons of the rough-and-ready Cüirassier-Regiment Hohenzollern #8. Opposite the main bridge at Günzburg were his best troops—the three fusilier battalions of the excellent Erzherzog Karl IR#3, plus two companies of élite Tyrolian jägers and all 20 of the 6- and 3-pounder battalion guns from his command.[96]

About 9:00 A.M., d'Aspre observed Malher's columns of bluecoated infantry approaching his positions opposite Reisensburg and Günzburg. A French *émigré* officer in Austrian service, d'Aspre watched with a professional's appreciation the celerity in which his former countrymen moved to the attack. In d'Aspre's mind, there could be no mistake as to the French objectives—they wanted the Danube bridges and a foothold across on the southern bank. Not seeing any threatening movements towards the bridge at Leipheim, d'Aspre sent orders to the regimental commander at Reisensburg to destroy that bridge. Baron d'Aspre then galloped to the troops positioned in front of Günzburg. The Austrian general ordered his two companies of Tyrolians to follow him at once across the river in order to buy time for the engineers to destroy the Günzburg bridge. Double-timing across the 100 yard-wide structure, d'Aspre ordered his Tyrolians into line on the island that separated the north from the south bank.

Baron d'Aspre had barely accomplished his deployments when the three battalions of Colonel Morel's 25th *Légère* came pouring across another bridge that

---

[94] S.H.A.T., *Journal des opérations du 6e corps.*

[95] S.H.A.T., *Journal des opérations du 6e corps.*

[96] Franz Willbold, *Napoleons Feldzug um Ulm Die Schlacht von Elchingen 14 Oktober 1805* (Ulm, 1987), pp. 27-28.

connected the island to the north bank with *général de brigade* Marcognet at their head. Pierre-Louis Binet de Marcognet was an aggressive officer, of which his combat record and numerous wounds bore incontestable proof. As a member of the infantry *régiment de Bourbonnais*, Marcognet was 15 years old when he served under Rochambeau in America during the decisive Yorktown campaign in 1781. Rising to the rank of captain in the infantry by the time the French Revolution began, Marcognet continued with his army career. From 1793 to 1800, he was wounded six times in battles against the Austrians. As commander of the 108th *demi-brigade de bataille* in Grandjean's Division, Marcognet was wounded and taken prisoner at the Battle of Hohenlinden on 3 December 1800. Returning from captivity two months later, he assumed his command as commander of the 108th. Two years later, Marcognet was promoted to *général de brigade* and assigned to command the 1st Brigade of the 3rd Infantry Division in Ney's camp at Montreuil.[97]

Marcognet

When the 39-year-old Marcognet led forward the 25th *Légère* on the morning of 9 October, he saw opposite his men d'Aspre's Austrians. Wasting no time, Marcognet ordered Colonel Morel to deploy his battalions into line. That done, the signal was given and some 1,800 French light infantrymen moved forward (the *carabiniers* of these battalions were not present with their parent units, and therefore not included in this total), sweeping before them the outnumbered and enveloped companies of Tyrolians. Within minutes, more than 200 Tyrolians were captured along with their commanding general, GM Baron d'Aspre. After rounding up these prisoners, Marcognet and the 25th *Légère* pressed forward to the Günzburg bridge. As they approached the structure, the French witnessed the Tyrolian survivors fleeing across the prize as Austrian engineers were demolishing sections of the bridge's wooden flooring. The sacrifice by d'Aspre and the Tyrolians had not been in vain. They had bought enough time to allow their comrades to sufficiently damage the Günzburg bridge so that formed troops could not pass over it before repairing the flooring. When the 25th *Légère* appeared near the bridge, the Austrian engineers withdrew to the opposite bank as Austrian infantry and artillery opened a covering fire.

As the French came upon the Günzburg bridge, they left the cover of the wooded island and stood exposed in the open on the gravel banks of the river. Unable to ford the deep current, the French had to choose whether to withdraw or repair the bridge under fire. Malher and Marcognet wasted little time in choosing the bold approach. To attempt repairs, volunteers were called to assist the sappers of the grenadier and *carabinier* companies from the 50th *Ligne* and 25th *Légère*. These men were led forward by Colonel Louis-Joseph-Elisabeth Cazals, commanding officer of the engineers in 6th Corps, who was present with Malher. With Cazals directing, the volunteers climbed the piers of the damaged section of the bridge to effect repairs by means of joists. To provide cover for these brave souls, the three battalions of the 25th *Légère* and the 1st Battalion of the 50th *Ligne* were brought into line to fire at the enemy on the other bank who were about 100 yards distant. The Austrians returned fire with the three fusilier battalions of Erzherzog Karl IR#3, as well as with a hail of canister fire from their 20 cannon that had been concentrated above the bridge. With each passing minute, Austrian bullets found their mark. French workmen were hit and their place was taken by other volunteers. Colonel Cazals went down, taking a wound to the upper leg. Two battalion commanders of the 25th *Légère* were put out of action with wounds. Volleys from the French infantry could not come close to equaling the firepower put forth by roughly the same number of veteran infantrymen and so many 6-pounder guns. For an hour, this uneven contest continued. The French work parties were just too close to the enemy. Recognizing that in this situation discretion was

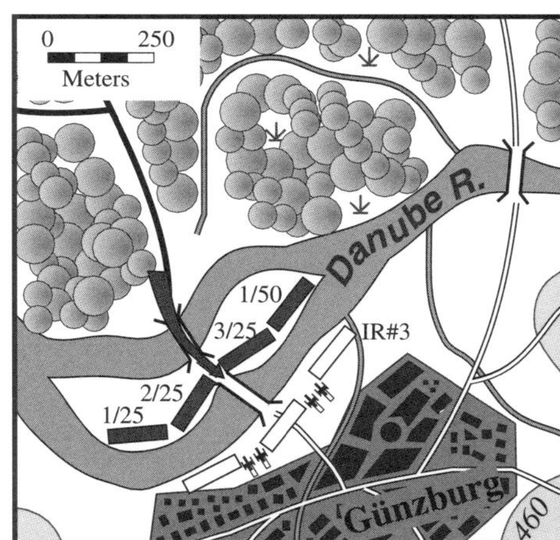

The French try to force the bridge at Günzburg

---

[97] Six, *Dictionnaire biographique*, vol. 2, p. 153.

the better part of valor, Malher and Marcognet had no choice but to call off the attempted crossing. As the French infantry withdrew to the cover of the willows and poplars, it was very evident that the normally clear waters of the Danube had been colored with the price of Gallic gallantry. The ranks of the 25th *Légère* had been thinned by several hundred men. In addition to *chef de bataillon* Arné and *chef de bataillon* Frapart being wounded, the 25th had six company commanders down along with a dozen lieutenants and sub-lieutenants either killed or wounded.[98]

As the troops under Malher and Marcognet were attempting to repair the Günzburg bridge, the other French attacks were also underway. Opposite Leipheim, the converged élite battalion under Lefol became hopelessly bogged down in the marshes. Unable to extricate his men from the bottoms, Lefol called off the attack; his battalion had failed to come within 1,000 yards of the Leipheim bridge.

While two of the French assault groups had failed to take their objectives, *général de brigade* de Labassée, Colonel Lacuée and the 59th *Ligne* were making one of the more impressive bridge assaults of the Napoleonic period. General Mathieu de Labassée was an experienced light infantryman from the *ancien régime*, Revolution and Consulate eras. His connection with Napoleon dated from the campaign of 1800, as de Labassée served as *chef de brigade* of the 9th *demi-brigade légère* at the Battle of Marengo. The fame won by de Labassée at Marengo earned him a promotion to *général de brigade* in September 1803. For the next 18 months, de Labassée was in Ney's camp at Montreuil putting the 50th and 59th *Ligne* through their paces. When he called for the 59th *Ligne* to follow him across the Reisensburg bridge at Günzburg the 41-year-old general had been in military service for 30 years.[99]

Baron d'Aspre's order to destroy the Reisensburg bridge had only been partially carried out when de Labassée and Colonel Lacuée began their attack. Repairing the bridge while under small arms fire, the 59th *Ligne* soon passed over the Danube. The troops destined to be first to resist the onslaught of the two French battalions were the four fusilier battalions of Kaunitz-Rietberg IR#20. This Austrian regiment, with its whitecoats and lobster-red facings, had not been distinguished in combat since the Battles of Lobositz (1756) and Hochkirch (1758) during the Seven Years War.[100] Those glory days had long since past when, in 1805, Kaunitz-Rietberg IR#20 ranks were filled from men drawn from recruiting areas in lower Galicia. The people of this area had no love for the Austrians, and the combat record of the regiment during the wars of the Empire seemed to reflect that lack of enthusiasm.

Preparing to meet the assault of the French 59th *Ligne*, the colonel of Kaunitz-Rietberg IR#20 deployed his battalions very poorly. The Austrian officer placed his formations in line *one behind the other* so that the regiment was one battalion wide by four battalions deep. Perhaps the Austrian battalions were placed in this formation after being raked by the supporting French artillery fire. If this was the case, the Austrian commander only made matters worse. Regardless of the reason for such deployment, when de Labassée, Colonel Lacuée and the 1st Battalion of the 59th *Ligne* rushed across the bridge, the French were opposed by only the 1st Battalion of IR#20. Even though the Austrians enjoyed advantages of position and frontage, French leadership and élan were too much. The steady advance of the 59th caused the lead battalion of IR#20 to break. As the Austrians fled, their retreat path carried them into the ranks of the rear battalions of the regiment,

---

[98] S.H.A.T., C[2] 482; *Journal des opérations du 6e corps;* A. Martinien, *Tableaux par Corps et par Batailles des Officiers Tués et Blessés Pendant les Guerres de l'Empire (1805-1815)* (Paris, 1899), p. 445. Hereafter referred to as *Tableaux des Officiers Tués et Blessés.*
[99] Six, *Dictionnaire biographique*, vol. 1, p. 312.
[100] Duffy, *The Army of Maria Theresa,* p. 224.

throwing each one of these formations into disorder. Seeing the first Austrian battalion dissolve before them, de Labassée and Lacuée immediately ordered the pursuit of these fugitives. The flight of these soldiers caused disruption in the rear units. This confusion, coupled with the vigorous pursuit by the victorious French, caused the collapse of the entire Austrian regiment. One by one, the Austrian battalions were carried away by the audacious French attack until all four Austrian battalions were reduced to mobs fleeing southeasterly towards Günzburg.[101] Despite the fact that the Austrians outnumbered their opponents by a two to one margin, the faulty deployment of IR#20 meant that any defeat suffered by the lead battalion would virtually guarantee the disruption of the remaining three. In addition, the 59th *Ligne* were crack troops led by tactically expert officers who did not waste a moment in seizing the good fortune presented to them.

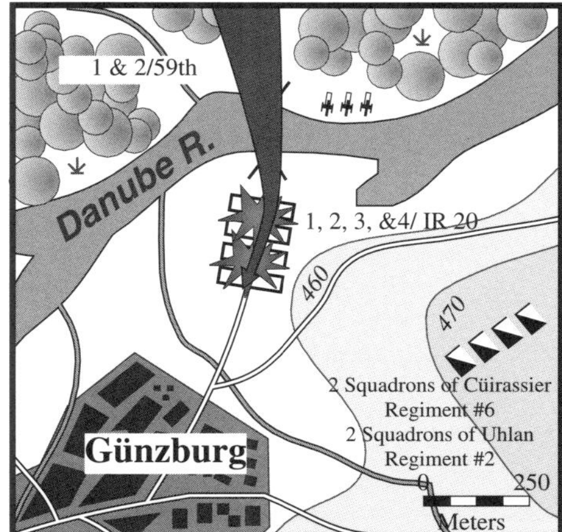

Lacuée and de Labassée break through IR#20

As the powder smoke cleared from this attack, Colonel Lacuée was found lying dead from a bullet to the heart. However, de Labassée had no time to mourn his fallen comrade. Seeing the Austrian cavalry moving forward to counterattack his men, de Labassée positioned both battalions of the 59th *Ligne* abreast and ordered them to form square. The drill evolution into square was quickly accomplished by the 59th, which was charged three times by the two squadrons of the Chevaulegers-Regiment Rosenberg #6 and two times by two other squadrons from Uhlanen-Regiment Schwarzenberg #2. Each charge by the Austrian cavalry was repulsed by volleys from the French squares.[102]

Having gained a toehold across the river, de Labassée sent word to Malher. The division commander ordered the 1st Battalion of the 27th *Ligne* quickly across the Danube, followed by Malher, Marcognet's brigade and finally Lefol's converged élites. Deploying the entire division south of Reisensburg before dark, Malher resumed the advance, capturing six Austrian cannon as his men penetrated to the outskirts of Günzburg. Following the repulse of the Austrian cavalry, no further counterattacks against Malher were attempted. Perhaps the Austrian chain of command was in disarray owing to the capture of d'Aspre. However, a more likely answer was that Archduke Ferdinand, who had appeared on the scene during mid-morning with 14 additional squadrons from five different cavalry regiments, had chosen not to mount any more efforts to expel the French from the Günzburg vicinity, choosing instead to deploy what infantry he had at his disposal to resist any further advance by Malher. This decision was no doubt due to the Archduke's knowledge of the combat the day before at Wertingen and that the French were already across the Danube in strength and approaching Günzburg from the east.

Therefore, Ferdinand ordered the troops around Günzburg to fall back on Ulm. They did so after dark, leaving behind 150 dead on the field, with another 300 wounded. As happens in war, many of the Austrian injured were in no shape to be moved and had to be left to the clemency of the French. Add to these another 200 Tyrolians and Baron GM d'Aspre captured by center assault group under Malher and Marcognet, plus more than 1,000 men of IR#20 that were taken by the 59th *Ligne*, and the casualties suffered by the Austrians at Günzburg total at least 1,650 of all ranks and six pieces of ordnance, of which two were 6-pounders and four were 3-pounders.[103] Malher's losses were only 519 of his total division strength of 6,469, with almost 400 of the casualties being suffered by the 25th *Légère*. Fortunately for Malher, many of the wounded had suffered only minor injuries; they would return to ranks within a few days.[104]

[101] S.H.A.T., *Journal des opérations du 6e corps.*
[102] S.H.A.T., *Journal des opérations du 6e corps.*
[103] S.H.A.T., C² 13 and 470; *Journal des opérations du 6e corps.*
[104] S.H.A.T., C² 16 and 482.

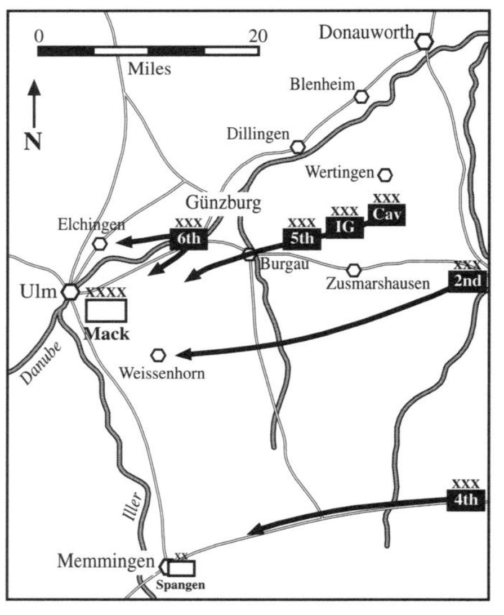

Operational situation
10 October 1805

Napoleon Draws the Noose Tighter

The day after the combat at Günzburg, Napoleon moved his headquarters to Augsburg in order to be at the center of the operational area of the *Grande Armée*. Having arrived at this city on the Lech River, the Emperor had once again pulled off his favorite strategic maneuver—the advance of envelopment, or *la manoeuvre sur les derrières*. This maneuver, which was employed no less than 30 times during his career, gave Napoleon enormous advantages if successful. The most obvious and important advantage was that by marching his army onto the enemy's line of communication, Napoleon could achieve favorable battle conditions and force the enemy to fight on ground not of the enemy's choosing. In this case, the Austrians wanted to give battle against an opponent approaching the Ulm position from the west. It was not to be. By 10 October, the center of French army operations was due east of Ulm and Napoleon was about to set into motion the next phase of the campaign.

After realizing that the numerous reports from prisoners were saying that Mack's army remained in and around the juncture of the Danube and Iller Rivers, the Emperor came to the conclusion that the Austrian general had only one reasonable choice remaining—leave Ulm immediately by running southward for the Tyrol and the Alps by way of Memmingen and Kempten. Once under the cover of that mountainous terrain, Mack could join up with Archduke John's army. The combined forces of Mack and John could then fall back to Italy, unite with Charles' main army, and continue the campaign while the Russians maintained their presence on the Danube nearer Vienna.

Napoleon therefore ordered his brother-in-law, Marshal Joachim Murat, to act an army wing commander by giving orders not only to his own cavalry corps, but to Lannes' 5th and Ney's 6th Corps as well. Because Napoleon believed that Mack would not stay at Ulm, choosing instead to flee for the Tyrol, the Emperor hoped that Murat could easily direct these corps to mop up around Ulm and prepare to march south towards Memmingen, there joining the rest of the *Grande Armée* in the anticipated destruction of the Austrian army.

The lightning march of the *Grande Armée* from the Rhine past the Danube, which cut the Austrian army off from Vienna, had stunned many officers in Austrian uniform. Their psyche was further damaged by the Austrian defeats at Wertingen and Günzburg, resulting in the majority of the officers of Mack's army being thoroughly disheartened. Archduke Ferdinand led the dissenting officers in urging an immediate retreat to the Tyrol. However, Mack was convinced about two points: 1) he believed in the strength of the fortified Ulm position and because of that strength, he could hold out until help arrived; and 2) the Austrian army could act as Napoleon's had done by maneuvering across the enemy army's lines of communication by crossing over onto the north bank of the Danube and raiding the Emperor's rear areas. On the 9th, Mack had ordered his army to cross the river over the bridges at Günzburg in preparation to move against Napoleon's lines of communication. However, Malher's successful attack aborted that plan. With news of Malher's capture of the Reisensburg bridge at Günzburg, the fighting spirit of the Austrian army seemed to deflate almost overnight.

Clearly, Mack did not prefer to fight the French by marching his army eastward and giving up his position at Ulm. However, he was not afraid to face the French army by using the fortress of Ulm as his base. This attitude, however, was not shared by the majority of those in Mack's army, whose collective morale had been substantial damaged by Napoleon's *la manoeuvre sur les derrières*. In an attempt to breathe new life into his command, Mack reorganized the columns by concentrating the best troops under his best, most confident commanders, and decided to commit his command on a course of extraordinary audacity. Since his generals had no confidence in remaining at Ulm, and estimating that Napoleon was already on the move towards Memmingen to block any retreat movement to the Tyrol, Mack decided to lead the army along the north bank of the Danube, cut across the route that the French had covered with their equipages and their depôts, then keep moving northeastward until they reached Bohemia.

Napoleon could not have dreamed that an adversary that had remained virtually motionless for so long would suddenly embark on such a bold course. However, this perception changed on 10 October when the Emperor received the interrogation reports of the captured d'Aspre and other Austrian officers following Malher's action at Günzburg. From those captives, it was learned that Mack was still at Ulm with his army and that he now intended to lead his men across the Danube and operate on the north bank. "The enemy is at Ulm," Ney wrote Napoleon, "and is much stronger than the estimated 15,000 men encountered at Günzburg. It appears as though they will form a line of battle with Ulm on their left flank and the main line facing east."[105] A second message from Ney further clarified the situation.

> The Austrians had at least 30,000 men at Günzburg and were led by Archduke Ferdinand. Mack was likewise there along with 14 other generals. From the statements of General d'Aspre, the Austrians intended a large blow against my corps, but the attack on Günzburg has frustrated everything. The retreat of the Austrians is towards Biberach [to the southwest].[106]

Although Ney's second message overestimated the enemy strength at Günzburg, it was clear to the marshal that the main Austrian force remained in and around Ulm. Based on this information, Napoleon therefore sent the following orders to his corps commanders. Bernadotte and the 1st Corps—with a division of Bavarians attached—were to continue to Munich where the Elector Maximilian-Joseph would re-enter his capital. The Bavarians would then be used as reconnaissance forces in order to give the best possible intelligence concerning the approach of the Russians.[107] Davout and the 3rd Corps with d'Hautpoul's heavy cavalry attached would stop along the Ammer River to be in a position to support Bernadotte if the Russians should suddenly make an appearance.[108] Soult and the 4th Corps had already left Augsburg and were heading south to Landsberg. Once the 4th Corps reached Landsberg, they were directed to turn west and make for Memmingen. Marmont and the 2nd Corps were to march southwesterly from Augsburg to Weissenhorn to serve as the link between Soult and Lannes. Lannes and the 5th Corps, followed by Bessières' Imperial Guard, were to move with Murat to Burgau and then further west to the Rathbach River, linking up with Ney. Ney's 6th Corps was to join with Lannes and Murat to draw the noose tighter around Ulm from the east and northeast. Blocking the Austrians from the west was Marshal Augereau's 7th Corps. "My Cousin," the Emperor wrote Augereau on 19 vendémiaire (11 October), "I am writing you from Augsburg. Movements continue to unfold with great rapidity. The army of Prince Ferdinand is cut off and entirely separated from the Russians."[109] Napoleon therefore ordered Marshal Augereau, whose 7th Corps had marched across France from Brest and was the last to cross the Rhine, to base his corps at Freiburg in order to intercept any Austrians attempting to escape from Ulm to the southwest into Switzerland.

---

[105] S.H.A.T., C[2] 3; *Journal des opérations du 6e corps.*
[106] S.H.A.T., *Journal des opérations du 6e corps.*
[107] Napoléon to Bernadotte, *Correspondance*, number 9363.
[108] Napoléon to Davout, *Correspondance*, number 9367.
[109] Napoléon to Augereau, *Correspondance*, number 9368.

Napoleon addresses the troops of 2nd Corps on the march to Weissenhorn, by Gautherot

The French Army enters Munich as liberators on 24 October, by Taunay

With these dispositions, Napoleon was concentrating the bulk of the *Grande Armée* between Memmingen and Ulm. This meant that the Emperor had at his disposal within one day's march of Ulm more than 100,000 combatants of the Imperial Guard, 2nd, 4th, 5th, 6th Corps and the Cavalry Reserve. On the other hand, if Mack's army had not been dispatched before Kutuzov's Russians arrived in the theater, Davout's reinforced 3rd Corps, plus Bernadotte's 1st Corps and the Bavarians would combine forces to total more than 60,000 combatants along the Isar River to oppose and delay the march of an enemy whose army was estimated to be no larger than these Napoleonic covering forces.

Once these orders were completed, Napoleon left Augsburg at 11:00 P.M. on the night of 12 October. The Emperor's destination was Weissenhorn, 35 miles west from Augsburg and 10 miles southeast of Ulm. In route to that town, the Imperial entourage came across Marmont's 2nd Corps which was traversing the same course. Closely observing the French and Dutch troops as he passed by, Napoleon saw etched in the faces of his men the fatigue that had been exacerbated by the frightful weather. The thick snows that had fallen for days had thawed, transforming the countryside into a quagmire and rendering the roads all but impassable. The Emperor watched his men struggle to assist teams of horses in moving artillery and other vehicles that had sunk deep into the Bavarian mud. Napoleon stopped his carriage and got out to be with these men. Marmont's soldiers flocked around the Emperor who then conducted an impromptu conference. Napoleon clearly explained to the troops the overall situation in the theater of war, the maneuver from the Rhine across the Danube that they had conducted, and the purpose for the current march being undertaken back towards Ulm. The Emperor impressed upon these men the importance of their toils and promised them a triumph "as glorious as that of Marengo."[110] Napoleon then departed to the shouts of *"Vive l'Empereur!"* With this speech, the spirits of Marmont's men had been electrified. Those who heard Napoleon's words repeated them to those who had not been within earshot. The march pace of 2nd Corps quickened as the men hastened to take part in the destruction of the cornered Austrian army.

The Thrashing of the Austrians at Haslach—Jungingen

As Marmont and the other Napoleonic troops were closing fast on Ulm and the southern side of the Danube, remarkable developments were underway on the northern bank. When Napoleon gave authorization to his brother-in-law, Marshal Murat, to coordinate the movements of not only his own cavalry reserve, but also the 5th and 6th Corps, the Emperor did so under the assumption that Mack would not remain at Ulm. "I am writing to Prince Murat," the Emperor informed Marshal Lannes on 17 vendémiaire (9 October), "to give him authority over your body of troops. If new circumstances do not change anything, you will soon be in a position to be near Augsburg by sometime tomorrow in order to complete operations that are judged to be necessary."[111]

The operation that the Emperor was referring to was the anticipated movement of Mack either east towards Augsburg or south to the Tyrol to escape the *Grande Armée.* This opinion was conveyed to Murat, who saw no need for Ney to maintain any of his troops on the north bank of the Danube. Following the victory at Günzburg, the reinforced 6th Corps had approximately 11,000 men still remaining on the north bank. These were composed of the 1st Infantry Division under General Dupont, the 1st Hussars of Colbert's 6th Corps light cavalry, plus General Bourcier's

---

[110] Thiers, *The History of the Consulate & the Empire of France*, vol. 2, p. 25.
[111] Napoléon to Lannes, *Correspondance*, number 9357.

Murat

4th Dragoon Division and General Baraguey d'Hilliers Dismounted Dragoon Division. The remainder of Ney's command—two regiments of Colbert's light cavalry, plus the 2nd and 3rd Infantry Divisions under Loison and Malher, respectively—were on the southern bank. Murat therefore ordered Ney to bring all of his command except the attached dragoon division over to the south bank so that all divisions could participate in the anticipated action on the south side of the Danube. Bourcier's horsemen would cover the north bank.[112]

Ney had a different opinion. Prisoners taken at Günzburg confirmed three things: 1) Austrian morale was plummeting; 2) the dispirited troops were retreating towards Biberach and Ulm; and 3) a portion of Mack's army was still at Ulm, which meant that the Austrians were already on the north bank of the Danube. The commander of the artillery of 6th Corps, *général de brigade* Seroux, remembered Marshal Ney asking his staff: "Why don't the Austrians seize the opportunity to escape by the left [north] bank of the Danube, trampling under their feet all our baggage and artillery, which certainly cannot give them much opposition?"[113] The redheaded marshal therefore believed that his entire corps was needed on the north bank in order to prevent the Austrians from escaping towards the northeast.

This seemingly reasonable request fell on deaf ears. Murat would hear none of these arguments. The Emperor had expressed the opinion that the Austrians would be abandoning Ulm in order to flee southward. Armed with this Imperial insight, Murat was unswerving in his belief that Napoleon knew best. Numerous exchanges flew between the marshals. Verbal requests by Ney to move his entire corps onto the north bank were countered with verbal instructions from Murat to do the exact opposite. This bickering went on for hours, consuming most of the daylight hours of 10 October. Finally, Murat had had enough. He sent written instructions to Ney which made it impossible to change the positions of the divisions of 6th Corps. "It remains understood," Murat had his chief of staff, Belliard, write to Ney at 6:00 P.M. on 18 vendémiaire (10 October), "to take Ulm and the important surrounding points. His Majesty gives you a free hand to achieve this goal during tomorrow morning [11 October]. The Dismounted Dragoon Division will accompany you..."[114] A quick-tempered Ney took this imperious response personally. He considered that the inexperienced Murat had no business speaking for the Emperor.

Belliard

Mounting his horse, Ney decided to ride to Murat's headquarters to settle the matter. Along the way, Ney met up with Lannes. In Lannes' entourage was *chef d'escadron* Subervie, who remembered that the commander of 6th Corps was livid.

"It is a ridiculous order, " Ney declared to Lannes. "If the Austrians come out that way, Bourcier cannot stop them. And once they get through, they can turn and roll up every supply wagon and ammunition cart in the whole army. Then we will be cut off from France. I cannot understand what Murat means."

"The trouble with Murat," Lannes responded, "is that he cannot see anything on a grand scale. He's an able cavalry leader in battle, but he's no grand-tactician, and the Emperor ought to know it."

"It's too much of a family affair," Ney concluded. "Even though Murat is his brother-in-law, there is no reason why the Emperor should entrust him with so much authority. If he does not stop listening so much to his damned sisters, they will ruin him."[115]

Arriving at Murat's headquarters, Ney argued his case. *Général de division* Belliard, Murat's chief of staff, remembered Ney spreading a map over a table, and attempted to point out the dangers of Murat's proposed order. Heated words

---

[112] S.H.A.T., C^2 240.

[113] S.H.A.T., *Journal des opérations du 6e corps.*

[114] S.H.A.T., C^2 240.

[115] S.H.A.T., *Journal des opérations du 5e corps.*

flew between the two marshals until the tension grew to break point as Murat pointedly told Ney: "You understood nothing of the plans of the army." Furthermore, Murat haughtily added that: "It is my way to make my plans in the face of the enemy!" Ney put his hand to his sword hilt and the two might have settled the matter right then and there had it not been for the intervention of other officers. Finally resigning himself to the situation, Ney chose to defuse the matter and concluded the confrontation with these words. "You are making a mistake, Murat, but today you are in command. Your orders will be obeyed." With that, Ney turned and departed.[116]

The significance of this disagreement was that the position of Ney's command remained unchanged during 10-11 October. Rather than Loison, Malher and Colbert recrossing the Danube and uniting with Dupont and the others on the north bank as Ney originally requested, Dupont and Baraguey d'Hilliers continued to follow the orders given to them on the day before. Ney wrote Dupont early on 18 vendémiaire (10 October):

> The enemy is gripped by an unprecedented fear. They appear to be retreating towards Biberach, to save themselves by moving into the Tyrol… It is probable that Archduke Ferdinand remains at Ulm with only a weak force in order to act as a rear guard. However, if this is not the case, our preparations and threatening movements will force the enemy commander to emerge from Ulm if he dares to fight.[117]

Orders from Ney to Baraguey d'Hilliers

It was the possibility of this later scenario that made Ney think it wise to unite his corps on the north bank of the Danube. However, because of Murat's directive, no such orders were issued. Instead, Dupont and Baraguey remained on the north bank and were to advance on Ulm without delay. These divisions were supported by General Sahuc's Brigade of dragoons from Bourcier's 4th Dragoon Division.

While some historians have either wondered why Ney left Dupont on the north side of the Danube, or outright blamed the redhead for Dupont's isolated position, it is clear why that marshal's troops did not receive new orders for 11 October. Instead, Ney's letter to Dupont dated 11 October simply summarized the situation and restated the marshal's orders of the day before. Even though Ney told Dupont on the 10th that he believed that the enemy was already on the run towards Biberach, the marshal also was clearly aware of the possibility that the Austrians around Ulm could sortie against his troops on the north bank. It was for that reason that Ney argued to bring the entire 6th Corps onto the north side of the Danube. Murat, at least during the early hours of 10 October, insisted that all troops come over to the south bank. However, owing to the day slipping away by dealing with Ney's continuing objections, Murat sent his written instructions to the commander of 6th Corps that prevented any changes in dispositions. As a result, Dupont marched on 11 October under the same orders he had received the day before because the friction between the two marshals had created a temporary command paralysis. Therefore, with the Danube dividing the divisions of the 6th Corps, Ney's troops kept their relative positions as they resumed their march towards Ulm.

Located on the north bank of the Danube, the fortified place of Ulm was indeed an impressive position. The city was next to the river, with a secession of terraced heights rising up from it towards the northwest. The highest elevation was called the Michelsberg plateau, and it was on those heights and the neighboring Frauenberg plateau that Mack's army was entrenched (for the sake of simplicity,

[116] S.H.A.T., C^2 240.

[117] S.H.A.T., *Journal des opérations du 6e corps.*

the term 'Michelsberg' is intended to include both the Michelsberg and Frauenberg plateaus). Three main roads and one minor one led from Ulm to other points on the north bank. Along the Danube, one major road led south while a minor road followed the river north. Two major roads ascended the Michelsberg heights to lead northwest and north from the city. Alongside each of these roads, the Austrians constructed two redoubts from which their heavy artillery could control the ground. From this dominating terrain, the Austrians could see the surrounding countryside in all directions as the Michelsberg heights dominated not only the marshy plain that comprised the south bank of the Danube, but also the immediately adjoining ground on the north bank.

It was on this north bank terrain that elements of Ney's 6th Corps, reinforced by two regiments of dragoons from Murat's *Corps des Réserves de Cavalerie,* suddenly appeared at the village of Haslach some two miles north of the Austrians encampment on the Michelsberg. Marching south along the road from Albeck were General Dupont and the 1st Infantry Division of 6th Corps, along with Colonel Rouvillois' 1st Hussars and the 15th and 17th Dragoons of General Sahuc's Brigade from the 4th Dragoon Division. The maneuvers over the past several days, conducted by soldiers of the 6th Corps who had not obtained food nor rest, marching in torrents of rain and snow that had fallen almost nonstop, had reduced the number of hardy souls that remained in Dupont's command. When the 1st Infantry Division crossed the Rhine on 26 September, the three infantry regiments that comprised the formation totaled 5,146 combatants present and under arms.[118] When Dupont's infantry formed ranks 15 days later, they numbered 4,105 officers and other ranks—a rate of strategic consumption of just over 20%. Supporting these *fantassins* were artillerists and eight pieces of ordnance. Two 8-pounder guns were manned by a 39-man detachment of horse artillerists, while a 12-pounder cannon, two 8-pounder cannon, two 4-pounder cannon and a 6-inch howitzer formed a six-piece battery served by a full company of foot artillerists that numbered 89 persons.[119] All these artillerists were further supported by 59 personnel of the train of artillery and four *ouvriers*.[120]

Attached to Dupont were three regiments of cavalry. The 1st Hussars were from the 6th Corps Cavalry Brigade, and consisted of three squadrons. When these cavalrymen crossed the Rhine, they numbered 375 officers and other ranks. On 11 October, the numbers of the 1st Hussars had increased to 383, thanks to reinforcements received just days before. The other cavalry regiments marching with Dupont were the 15th and 17th Dragoons totaling some 600 combatants. Therefore, excluding general officers and their staffs, the French force that fought at Haslach-Jungingen numbered 5,275 officers and other ranks, of which 4,105 were infantry, 983 were cavalry, plus 187 artillerists and other support personnel serving eight pieces of ordnance.[121]

Dupont

The leader of these forces was General Pierre Dupont de l'Étang, the commander of Ney's 1st Infantry Division. In 1805, Dupont was considered by many to be one of the army's rising stars. The son of General Pierre-Antoine Dupont-Chaumont, Dupont entered military service in 1784 at the age of 19 as a *sous-lieutenant* with the *légion de Maillebois* in the service of Holland. During the early years of the Revolution, the young Dupont was invariably with the same regiment, or attached to the same headquarters, as his father. He served at the Battles of Tourcoing and Werwicq in 1793. In 1795, at age 30, Dupont was promoted to *général de brigade*. Two years later, Dupont received his advancement in rank

[118] S.H.A.T., C²470.
[119] These were slightly different ordnance assignments then when the division crossed the Rhine. For those details, please see Appendix A.
[120] S.H.A.T., C²482.
[121] S.H.A.T., C²472 and 482.

to *général de division*. During those years, Dupont served in various administrative capacities until being named as chief of staff to Berthier in 1800. Seeing action at Fort Bard and at Marengo, Dupont negotiated the convention of Alexandria, after which he was promoted on 28 August 1800 to the command of the right wing of the *Armée d'Italie.* On Christmas Day of that same year, Dupont with 15,000 men defeated 45,000 Austrians at the Battle of Pozzolo. He was transferred the following year and joined Ney's command in August 1803. Four months later, on 12 December 1803, Dupont was placed in command of the 1st Infantry Division at the camp of Montreuil. Therefore, as Dupont led forward his troops at Haslach-Jungingen, he did so with the confidence of a career soldier who, in 20 years of service, had never tasted defeat.[122]

When Dupont saw the Michelsberg plateau at 1:00 P.M. on 11 October, he was expecting a possible confrontation with the rearguard of the Austrian army. Instead of only a few enemy regiments awaiting the French advance, scouts of the 1st Hussars reported that the enemy was present in great strength. Dupont decided to take a closer look for himself. Riding south along the Ulm-Heidenheim Road that connects Albeck to Ulm, Dupont got an eye full. There on the heights above the city was what must have seemed to Dupont to be Mack's entire host. Although many of Mack's soldiers were not on the Michelsberg but rather deployed on the south bank below Ulm, what the French general did see was well over 20,000 of the enemy, including several regiments of Austrian cavalry.

The sudden appearance of Dupont's command stirred the indolent Austrian cavalry patrols, who took word back to Mack that the army had some unexpected visitors. It was only earlier that morning that General Mack received Colonel Bianchi of Archduke Ferdinand's staff along with FML Gyulai. Bianchi had just come from an inspection of the entrenchments on the Michelsberg, and expressed his concern that if the army was to hold these positions, the works would have to be significantly strengthened. Although Mack dismissed the talk, stating that the French would not dare attack such a strong position, the Austrian general once again changed his mind as to what course the army should follow. By reversing himself from the decision made two days earlier to march forthwith from Ulm along the north bank of the Danube and into Bohemia, Mack once again fell under the spell of Ulm. It was a trance that had long mesmerized the Austrian general. Mack believed that the entrenched camp of Ulm was "the anvil against which the Russian hammer"[123] would destroy Napoleon. Mack told Bianchi and the other officers: "It rains; it snows; the enemy sticks quietly in his camp and we will do the same. We will remain in Ulm, where we are safe."[124] Despite the aura of disaster all around him, Mack remained convinced of the invincibility of the position of Ulm. The general ordered the countryside to be denuded of all foodstuffs and brought into the fortified camp. With the countryside stripped of subsistence, Mack reasoned that the French would be severely handicapped when they arrived in front of Ulm. What's more, Mack's statement to Bianchi strongly suggests that he assumed that the French would not be moving in bad weather—another indication that Mack was fighting an 18th century war against a new, modern army.

Bianchi

However, Mack's attitude abruptly changed after Dupont made his appearance on the Ulm-Heidenheim Road, prompting an Austrian call to arms. While the whitecoated infantry quickly formed ranks as the Austrian cavalry mounted and moved towards the French, Dupont had to make a quick decision. He could either immediately order a withdrawal, or he could stay and fight. If he gave the order to withdraw, Dupont reasoned that such a course would be tantamount to announcing to the Austrians that he was an isolated detachment. If he acted in this manner,

[122] Six, *Dictionnaire biographique*, vol. 1, pp. 404-405.
[123] *K. k. Kriegsarchiv*, *Feldacten* for 1805.
[124] Willbold, *Napoleons Feldzug um Ulm Die Schlacht von Elchingen*, p. 37.

Dupont believed that he would encourage his foe to act more aggressively—a most dangerous possibility considering that the Austrians had an overwhelming numerical superiority. Alternatively, Dupont could deploy his division for battle, hoping that such boldness would cause the Austrians to consider that he might be the advance guard of an entire corps and therefore move against him with caution. With a sense of Gallic élan and audacity, Dupont chose the bold course of action.

The French general gave the orders for his troops to deploy for battle. Since the Ulm-Heidenheim Road passed through Albeck and was his line of communication, Dupont decided to protect this route by anchoring his left flank on the small village of Haslach. The main road passed through Haslach, in front of which Dupont posted his best *ligne* regiment—the 32nd under Colonel Darricau, along with the brigade commander, General Marchand. To the right of the two battalions of the 32nd was the company of foot artillery. Two 4-pounder guns, two 8-pounder guns, one 6-inch howitzer and one 12-pounder were unlimbered across the Ulm-Heidenheim Road. To the right of these pieces were General Rouyer with Colonel Meunier and both battalions of the 9th *Légère*. Deployed as the second line of the division was Colonel Barrois' 96th *Ligne*. The horse artillery and light cavalry protected the left flank of the division. Two 8-pounders manned by the horse artillerists were on a small rise to the left of the 32nd *Ligne*, and served as a link between the infantry and the 1st Hussars who were to the left of the guns. To properly shelter these horsemen until it was time for them to close with the enemy, the light cavalry were positioned in dead ground that offered them protection from Austrian cannon. The right flank of the division was protected by two woods west of Haslach. The smaller of the woods, which was named 'Kleinen Gehr,' was approximately five acres in size and located between Haslach and another small village named Jungingen. Some 650 yards to the north of Kleinen Gehr was the larger wood, called 'Großen Gehr.' The area between the two woods consisted of fields and meadows, and it was this avenue along which any direct movement between the two villages would be conducted. Finally, Dupont posted General Sahuc and his brigade consisting of the 15th and 17th Dragoons behind the 96th *Ligne* to act as the reserves for the French force.[125]

The Kleinen Gehr from the south-east

While these regiments were shaking out for battle, Dupont finished his reconnaissance and realized that the key to his defensive position was his right flank, which offered the Austrians a broad avenue of attack that they could easily traverse. That axis of advance was also the weakness of the French position. The division's right flank rested near the Großen Gehr, but the entire position was untenable unless the French also held the village of Jungingen some 2,200 yards west of Haslach. Between Jungingen and Haslach, a small rivulet and Kleinen Gehr restricted the approach to either village. If the Austrians controlled Jungingen, they could freely direct troops around either the Kleinen Gehr or the Großen Gehr to attack Dupont's right flank or rear as other Austrians assaulted Haslach from the front. Dupont reasoned that he might be able to buy some valuable time by forcing the Austrians to first capture Jungingen before initiating a full-scale attack on Haslach. Also, while busy attempting to capture Jungingen, the Austrian infantry would be susceptible to counterattacks. For Dupont, the danger in posting any troops in Jungingen was that the distance from Haslach to Jungingen was going to make it difficult to properly support any men holding in the latter village. Since Jungingen had to be held in order to maintain the Haslach position, Dupont committed his small command of six battalions, three cavalry regiments and eight pieces of ordnance to a paper-thin defensive line that stretched along an 1.2-mile front when the normal frontage for a division of this size would have been under half a mile, or less. Therefore, in order to give his troops a chance to repulse the

---

[125] S.H.A.T., *Journal des opérations du 6e corps.*

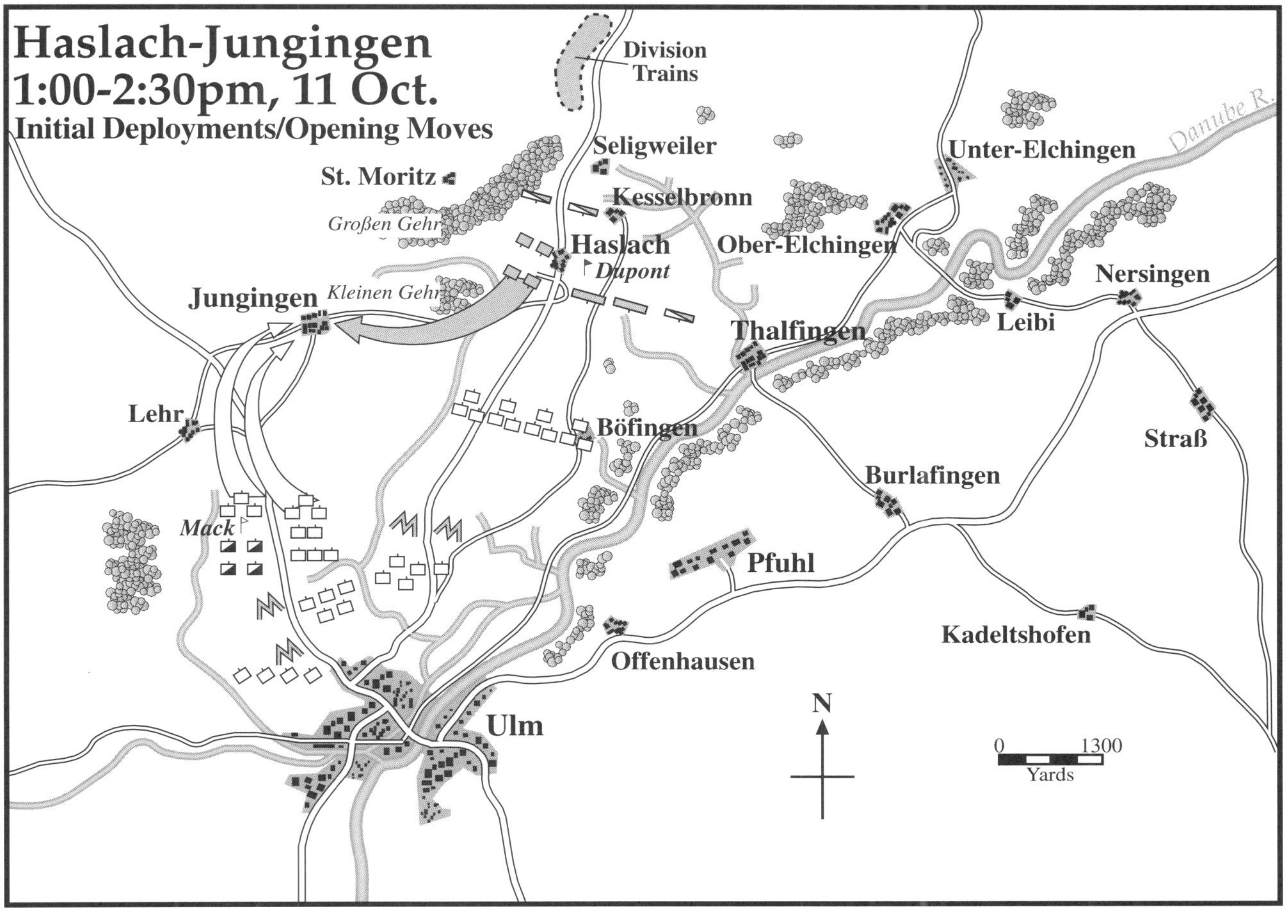

Haslach-Jungingen
1:00-2:30pm, 11 Oct.
Initial Deployments/Opening Moves

Division Trains
Seligweiler
St. Moritz
Großen Gehr
Kesselbronn
Haslach
Dupont
Ober-Elchingen
Unter-Elchingen
Danube R.
Junginen
Kleinen Gehr
Thalfingen
Leibi
Nersingen
Lehr
Böfingen
Straß
Mack
Burlafingen
Pfuhl
Offenhausen
Kadeltshofen
Ulm
N
0 1300
Yards

The village of Junginen today from the south-east

French Officer of Grenadiers

anticipated Austrian attacks and because Jungingen was critical to his position, Dupont decided to employ a version of the strong-point defensive scheme. He ordered the village of Jungingen to be garrisoned with an *ad hoc* battalion of converged élites. To accomplish this, the grenadier and *carabinier* companies from Dupont's six battalions were quickly brought together to form a new battalion and placed under the command of *chef de bataillon* Decouchy from the general's staff and were hustled off to Jungingen. If the Austrians did not properly coordinate their combat arms in trying to expel the garrison of Jungingen, Dupont would not hesitate to commit reinforcements to that front to conduct local counterattacks.

While Dupont was putting up a brave front by deploying his men for battle and sending messengers back to urge General Baraguey d'Hilliers to hurry his division of foot dragoons to Haslach, Mack was wasting no time with his arrangements for the destruction of the unwelcome visitors. From the parapet of one of the redoubts on the Michelsberg, Mack viewed the surrounding countryside. He could not detect any French troop movement along the south bank of the Danube, but could not see if more French were behind Dupont and arriving from the north on the Ulm-Heidenheim Road. With no immediate threat from the south, Mack could dedicate all the troops he needed to the attack on the north bank. The Austrian general had available for battle a total of 11 regiments of infantry, four regiments of cavalry, plus more than 30 pieces of mobile ordnance with more than 100 heavy guns in position on the Michelsberg.[126]

Completing his plans for battle, Mack decided to divide his troops into three columns. Ferdinand and Schwarzenberg would command the two left columns while Riesch and Werneck jointly led the right column. The latter column was closest to the Danube and consisted of seven infantry regiments. In the front line, Riesch and Werneck placed four regiments, each fielding three fusilier battalions for a total of 12 battalions. From right to left were Kolowrat-Krakowsky IR#36, Karl Riese IR#15, Reuss-Plauen IR#17 and Stuart IR#18. In the second line, acting as reserves for the entire Austrian force, were 14 battalions of three regiments, namely: Manfredini IR#12 with four battalions of fusiliers and one battalion of grenadiers, Auersperg IR#24 with four fusilier battalions and one grenadier battalion, plus Erbach IR#42 that had three fusilier battalions and one grenadier battalion. The two left-hand columns under Schwarzenberg and Ferdinand consisted of the infantry from regiments Erzherzog Ludwig IR#8 with three fusilier battalions, Erzherzog Rainer IR#11 with two fusilier battalions, Kaunitz-Rietberg IR#20 with three fusilier battalions[127] and Froon IR#54 fielding two fusilier and one grenadier battalion. Supporting these 11 battalions of infantry were six squadrons from the Cüirassier-Regiment Erzherzog Albert #3, and eight squadrons each from the Cüirassier-Regiment Mack #6, the Chevaulegers-Regiment Latour #4 and the Chevaulegers-Regiment Rosenberg #6. Therefore, Mack's force at Haslach-Jungingen totaled some 23,000 combatants, with the 37 battalions of infantry numbering 20,000 officers and other ranks, the 30 squadrons of cavalry mounting 2,100 people and 900 artillerists and train personnel serving 30 pieces of ordnance. Although Mack enjoyed a significant advantage of numbers and total pieces of ordnance, his only mobile unit was one cavalry battery of six pieces present with the left-hand columns. The remaining 24 guns served as battalion pieces—far fewer than the 74 pieces that were theoretically supposed to support the movements of 37 battalions of infantry. The reason that only 24 battalion guns were ready for action on 11 October was that there simply were not enough healthy horses to pull all the pieces. The remaining guns were left on the Michelsberg.

Baraguey d'Hilliers

[126] *K. k. Kriegsarchiv*, *Feldacten* for 1805.

[127] The battalions of Kaunitz-Rietberg IR#20 were much depleted after Günzburg.

As conceived, Mack's plan of attack would have met with Frederick the Great's approval. The right column under FMLs Count von Werneck and Count von Riesch was to deploy between Örlingen and Böfingen, advance north from the Michelsberg and pin the enemy by attacking him in front of Haslach. Meanwhile, Mack would accompany the two left columns under Archduke Ferdinand and FML Prince Schwarzenberg. These troops, which included all the cavalry on hand, would move north to Jungingen, then wheel into a position facing east from which they would make a Frederician style oblique attack onto the French right flank. If all the Austrian formations could be properly coordinated, Mack reasoned that the French simply did not have enough men to be able to resist such an onslaught.

The battlefield to the east of Junginen: the Kleinen Gehr to the right, the Großen Gehr now hidden in the center by a row of trees lining a railroad that bisects the battlefield

With Mack urging his men on, the two left columns got moving about 2:00 P.M.—long before Werneck and Riesch could get their right column underway. The infantry of the left columns was spearheaded by the three fusilier battalions from Erzherzog Ludwig IR#8 and three fusilier battalions of Kaunitz-Rietberg IR#20. As the Austrians moved towards Jungingen, they were met unexpectedly by an annoying fire from French *tirailleurs* on the edge of the village. These skirmishers were from Decouchy's converged élite battalion that, unknown to the Austrians, had already occupied the village church. Apparently opposed by only skirmishers holding a key village, the two leading Austrian regiments halted, deployed their six battalions into line and advanced into Jungingen, driving the elusive *tirailleurs* before them. As the *tirailleurs* withdrew before the onward moving formed ranks of Austrians, they continued firing into the whitecoated masses. Entering the village, the Austrian battalions soon met the majority of the French élite battalion that had barricaded itself in the church. The church sits today on the same small rise in the middle of Jungingen, dominating the rest of the settlement. When the French *ad hoc* battalion of converged élites moved into this stronghold, sappers from the grenadier and *carabinier* companies fortified the structure by strengthening the doors and making loopholes through which the men could fire. Taking up positions inside the church, the French élites waited while the noise of battle grew louder and louder, finally reaching them shortly after 3:00 P.M. Battalion after Austrian battalion rushed the church in an attempt to gain entrance. Soon, Austrian corpses began to litter the ground as their sacrifice to break into the church proved to be in vain. Unable to demolish the doors, the Austrian infantrymen swirled around the church's stone edifice as the French grenadiers and *carabiniers* poured a deadly fire into the growing masses of assailants.

Ensconced in the village fighting at Jungingen, the Austrian infantry was not aware that the Austrian cavalry had failed to support their movements. Instead of advancing outside the village to protect the infantry's flanks, those in command of the Austrian cavalry chose to hang back, waiting for their comrades to emerge victorious from the village, and thereby resuming the advance against the French right flank. This lack of support would prove to have the direst consequences for the Austrian infantry.

The church at Jungingen as seen today

From his observation point just west of Haslach, Dupont recognized the lack of coordination in the enemy's advance. The absence of Austrian cavalry on the flanks of Jungingen, coupled with the increasing haze of smoke enshrouding the village, was enough to convince him that the Austrians had failed to take the strong point and were ripe for a counterattack. Leaving *général de brigade* Marchand and Colonel Darricau with the 32nd *Ligne* to cover Haslach, Dupont ordered *général de brigade* Rouyer and Colonel Meunier with both battalions of the 9th *Légère* to spearhead the assault. Colonel Barrois and the two battalions of the 96th *Ligne* were to follow in support of the light infantrymen. With each battalion's old Republican flag of the 1802 pattern as well as their national color fluttering above the ranks, the 9th *Légère* hustled past Kleinen Gehr in attack columns. The battalions were abreast with the 1st Battalion on the right and the 2nd Battalion on the left.

Marchand

Turning west towards Jungingen, they used the woods to protect their right flank while the 96th *Ligne* followed in echelon, protecting their left.[128]

Setting the pace for the advance of the 9th *Légère* was *général de brigade* Marie-François Rouyer. Rouyer knew that he was about to execute a counterattack that he and his men had repeatedly trained for in the mock battles at the Channel camp of Montreuil. Joined by his two aides, Captains Débaine and Bonrion, Rouyer and his staff rode along the line waving their swords and haranguing the men in shouts of *"Vive l'Empereur!"* As a young man, Rouyer had served in the Austrian cavalry. With the coming of the Revolution, Rouyer quit the Habsburg army and entered French service as a captain of infantry. Faithfully serving *La Patrie* during the wars of the Revolution, Rouyer was promoted to *général de brigade* on 30 July 1799, and was made a commandant of the *Légion d'Honneur* on 14 June 1804, some seven months after he had reported for duty at Montreuil. During his 21 months in the Channel camp, Rouyer forged a close working relationship with the only regiment of his brigade and their colonel, Meunier. Both Meunier and Rouyer had received their promotions and assignments to Ney's camp in December 1803.[129] The new arrivals became close friends and knew what to expect from each other.

Colonel Claude-Marie Meunier had been a distinguished captain in the *chasseurs à pied* of the Consular Guard when the colonelcy of the 9th *Légère* came open. Accepting the appointment, Meunier proved during the Channel encampment to be an excellent tactician, receiving praise from Rouyer, Dupont and Ney. An exceptional colonel was a must for a regiment as celebrated as the 9th *Légère.* Famous for its exploits in the wars of the French Revolution in the campaigns of 1794, 1795 and 1796, the 9th *demi-brigade légère* reached higher limits of glory on 14 June 1800. It was late in the afternoon of that day that the regiment counterattacked and threw the Austrian line into disorder immediately prior to Kellermann delivering his epic charge—two connected events that turned the Battle of Marengo into one of Napoleon's most famous victories. For this and their previous heroic accomplishments, Bonaparte gave the 9th *Légère* the title *"l'Incomparable."*[130] As the *fantassins* of the 9th *Légère* approached Jungingen, Meunier knew that his men could not afford to stop and fire during a strong point defensive scheme counterattack. Before they moved out, Meunier ordered the light infantrymen to advance with unloaded muskets.

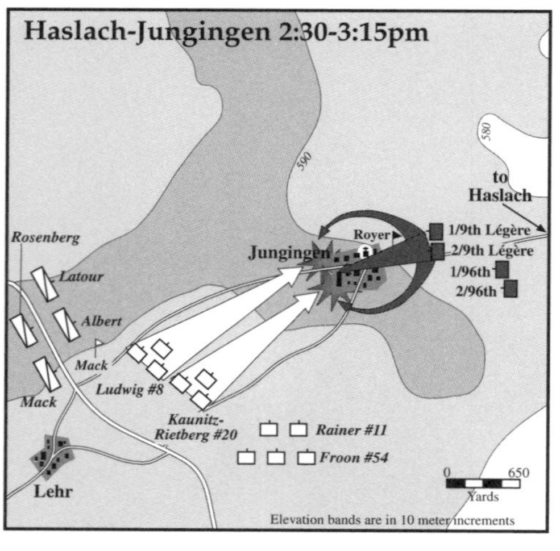

The sudden approach of two French battalions against a force approximately three times their own must have surprised the Austrian commanders. Unable to rapidly redeploy their battalions in order to receive the onrushing French light infantrymen, the Austrians were soon caught inside Jungingen between Decouchy's converged élite battalion holed up in its strong point and the counterattacking light infantry. Even with superior numbers, the disorganized Austrian infantry were no match for an adversary who had practiced time and again this exact scenario. Preventing their escape by blocking their retreat routes from the village and then falling on their prey with the bayonet, the French light infantry first surrounded then cut to pieces the six battalions from Erzherzog Ludwig IR#8 and Kaunitz-Rietberg IR#20. Austrian companies surrendered *en masse* to the 9th *Légère* until more than 2,000 whitecoated infantry were captured by approximately 1,400 Frenchmen (this number includes some of Decouchy's élites who, acting as *tirailleurs*, participated in some of the captures). Colonel Meunier's after-action

---

[128] S.H.A.T., *Journal des opérations du 6e corps.*

[129] Six, *Dictionnaire biographique*, vol. 2, p. 403.

[130] The inscription was prominent on the 1802-pattern flags carried by each battalion of the 9th *Légère*. So proud of their title given them by Bonaparte, the regiment did not retire their 1802-pattern battalion colors when the new national flags with the lozenge design were introduced in 1804. Instead, the battalions carried both pattern flags into the field in 1805, 1806 and into 1807.

The 9th Légère carried their 1801 pattern flag into battle along with the new 1804 lozenge pattern national flag and eagle

report states that the 1st Battalion of the 9th *Légère* netted some 1,200 Austrians in this assault. Once these captives were started off towards Haslach, Rouyer and Meunier repositioned the 9th *Légère* in anticipation of receiving the next Austrian attack.[131]

It was not long in coming. After losing more than 2,000 men from an approximate force of 3,300, the battalions from Erzherzog Ludwig IR#8 and Kaunitz-Rietberg IR#20 were finished for the day. As the panic-stricken survivors who managed to escape from Jungingen streamed back towards Austrian lines, Mack ordered up reinforcements in the form of Erzherzog Rainer IR#11 and Froon IR#54. Leaving the grenadier battalion of Froon in reserve, Archduke Ferdinand took the fusilier battalions of these regiments into the fray. Five times the Austrians charged into Jungingen, pushing the *tirailleurs* before them and capturing all the village except the church. This strong point, tenaciously held by the Decouchy's élites, made it possible for the 9th *Légère* to counterattack each Austrian attempt to carry Jungingen. Despite Austrian numerical superiority in every assault, the well trained and expertly led French light infantry achieved success after success, resetting their defense each time to invite and await the next attack.

The French strong point defensive scheme at Jungingen turned the village into an Austrian slaughter pen, totally consuming Mack's infantry in his two left-hand columns. Austrian losses continued to mount at an alarming rate with the repulse of each assault until Erzherzog Rainer IR#11 and Froon IR#54 had lost over 2,000 men following the repulse of their fifth attack.[132] With the failure of the last attack by Erzherzog Rainer IR#11 and Froon IR#54, it appeared to General Rouyer that only one more Austrian infantry battalion—the grenadiers of Froon—was available to mount another assault against Jungingen. He therefore hastened to start his most recent captives towards the rear before the Austrian cavalry could make its presence felt or another infantry attack was mounted against Jungingen.

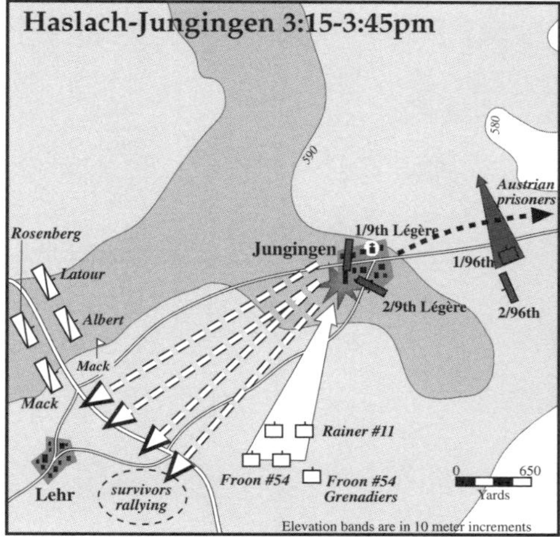

Perhaps it was the steady stream of Austrian prisoners trudging from Jungingen back towards Haslach that finally clued Mack in that his cavalry were needed to support his infantry attacks. Perhaps it was faulty staff work, or the inability of the regimental colonels to work together, that delayed the cavalry from supporting their infantry brothers-in-arms. Whatever the reason, the Austrian horse finally got moving to the north of the Jungingen after the infantry of the left-hand columns had been used up. Swinging around the village, Cüirassier-Regiment Erzherzog Albert #3, Cüirassier-Regiment Mack #6 and Chevaulegers-Regiment Latour #4 thundered towards the bluecoated soldiers. It was on this flank that Colonel Barrois and the 1st Battalion of the 96th *Ligne* had been shifted, leaving the 2nd Battalion of the 96th *Ligne* to guard the flank south of the 9th *Légère* fighting around Jungingen. The 1st Battalion of the 96th was formed in square when the Chevaulegers-Regiment Latour #4 charged, led by General Mack himself. While the Austrian horse did not break Colonel Barrois' 1st Battalion, a French bullet found Mack, wounding the Austrian commander-in-chief, and forcing his retirement from the field. After the repulse of the Latour's, the Austrian cavalry battery was brought into play against the 1st Battalion of the 96th, and the compact French battalion suffered heavily from the discharges of canister.

The movements by so many Austrian horse prompted a response from Dupont. He ordered up General Sahuc and his dragoons, instructing them to charge and relieve the pressure on the 96th. *Général de brigade* Louis-Michel-Antoine Sahuc was one of the oldest officers in the *Grande Armée.* The 50-year-old general had served in the cavalry all his life, passing into semi-retirement following the 1800 campaign. With the establishment of the Empire in May 1804, Sahuc returned to

---

[131] S.H.A.T.,C² 470, *Journal des opérations du 6ᵉ corps.*

[132] S.H.A.T., C² 14.

The Latour Chevauleger break the 15th Dragoons

the active roster and was named brigade commander of the 15th and 17th Dragoons.[133]

As the trumpets blew and the dragoons moved out across the fields and meadows between the Großen Gehr and Kleinen Gehr, Sahuc put the 15th Dragoons in the first line with the 17th Dragoons deployed in echelon behind the 15th. As the French cavalry emerged from the area between the woods, they were charged by Cüirassier-Regiment Erzherzog Albert #3 and Cüirassier-Regiment Mack #6. The two Austrian heavy regiments, under the orders of FML Schwarzenberg, enveloped the 15th, causing the French to withdraw. Following up their victory, the Austrian cavalry then overturned the 17th Dragoons, forcing them to also retire. Both French regiments withdrew to the southwestern edge of the Großen Gehr, quickly reformed and galloped back to renew the struggle.

This time Sahuc formed the brigade in squadrons abreast and was met by the countercharge of the Austrian heavies. Neither side gave way during these movements and soon opponents crashed into each other in a desperate struggle. Greencoated French dragoons intermingled with whitecoated Austrian cüirassiers in a deadly contest of swordplay and carbine fire. The Chevaulegers-Regiment Latour #4 soon added their weight to the contest by charging into this *mêlée*. Thwarted in their earlier attempts to break Barrois' infantry, the Latours took out their frustrations when they swarmed over the flank of the 15th Dragoons. It was the squadron under Waldenburg Schillingsfürst that broke the French cavalry's flank. As the cohesion of the dragoon regiment began coming apart, Schillingsfürst grabbed one of the eagles and its attached standard of the 15th, receiving a bullet from a French carbine as he snatched the prize; he died three days later in Ulm. The charge of the Latour Chevaulegers was too much for the Frenchmen. The 15th Dragoons were driven off in "wild confusion."[134]

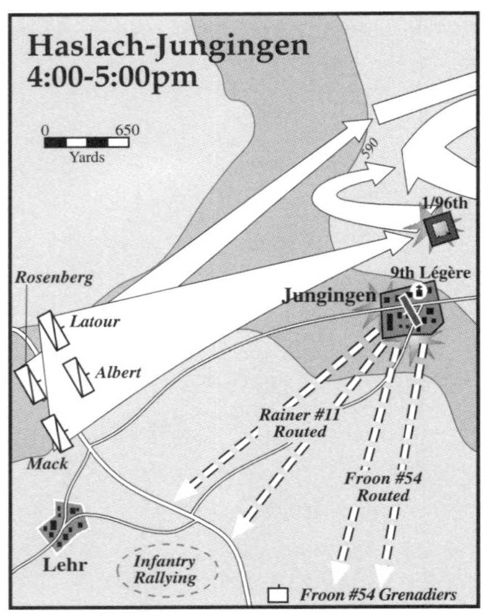

Meanwhile, the 17th Dragoons were suffering key officer casualties. Their colonel, Saint-Dizier, had commanded the regiment for 11 years—at that time the second longest tenure by any colonel in the *Grande Armée*. He had molded the 17th into a rugged outfit, well-trained and stinging from their earlier repulse from a foe who had possessed a superior frontage. They were determined to exact revenge and appeared to have just broken the Mack Cüirassiers when Saint-Dizier suddenly slumped from his saddle, killed by an Austrian bullet.[135] Also falling dead was lieutenant Abel, while *chef d'escadron* Dautrecourt was wounded. With their flank support running away and their colonel down, the 17th Dragoons withdrew. Fortunately for Sahuc, the retrograde movement was conducted without being pursued by the Austrians. Afforded a respite, Sahuc soon rallied the 15th, and ordered both regiments to advance again to support the French infantry that remained in and around Jungingen.

This move, however, was not opposed by the Austrian cavalry. After the 15th Dragoons had been routed, followed by the withdrawal of the 17th Dragoons, the officers of Schwarzenberg's regiments lost control of their men, and the Austrian cavalry spread out over the neighboring plain, rather than pursuing their defeated foe. Passing to the north of the Großen Gehr, the Austrian horse rode far away from the French forces around Jungingen as well as those stationed in front of Haslach. As the Austrian cavalry rode north towards Albeck, they took themselves out of the battle. Upon reaching Albeck, the Austrian cavalry came upon the baggage train of Dupont's Division, as well as that of Baraguey's foot dragoons. Sabering the drivers and ransacking these vehicles, the disorderly Austrian cavalry spent the next hour plundering for meaningless trophies. It was almost 6:00 P.M. when General

Schwarzenberg

[133] Six, *Dictionnaire biographique*, vol. 2, p. 409.

[134] Willbold, *Napoleons Feldzug um Ulm Die Schlacht von Elchingen*, p. 39.

[135] S.H.A.T., dossier Saint-Dizier.

Baraguey d'Hilliers, together with his staff and 60 escort cavalry that he had collected around Albeck, charged and dispersed the looting Austrian horse.[136]

While the French enjoyed—for the most part—great success at Jungingen, they were hard pressed in front of Haslach. It will be remembered that instead of putting Haslach to use as part of a strong point defensive scheme on the French left, Dupont stationed *général de brigade* Marchand and Colonel Darricau with the two battalions of the 32nd *Ligne in front of* Haslach, supported by the 1st Hussars under Colonel Rouvillois and all the division's guns—a force of less than 2,000 combatants and eight pieces of ordnance. *Général de brigade* Jean-Gabriel Marchand had learned his trade as an infantryman while serving under Joubert and Masséna in the *Armée d'Italie*. He had displayed considerable talent leading the 17th *demi-brigade légère* and 11th *demi-brigade de bataille* during Napoleon's epic 1796 and 1797 Italian campaigns. When the Channel camps were formed in 1803, Marchand was selected shortly thereafter to report to Ney at Montreuil. Taking command of the 2nd brigade under Dupont, Marchand had spent over one and one-half years with his soldiers.[137] He knew his men well and what could be expected of them. As he stood with the 32nd *Ligne* of that brigade in front of Haslach on 11 October, Marchand passed the word that French élan would win the day. Although heavily outnumbered, the regiment readied itself to charge the whitecoated horde that was descending upon them.

Arrayed against these French was the Austrian right column under FMLs Werneck and Riesch. Finally getting their regiments underway, the Austrian generals launched an attack three hours after the fighting erupted at Jungingen. Without regard to superior numbers or frontage, Werneck and Riesch used the subtlety of a bludgeon to attack the French in front of Haslach. Forming the units of the column in standard checkerboard fashion with a depth of two battalions, Werneck's and Riesch's command from right to left consisted of Kolowrat-Krakowsky IR#36, Karl Riese IR#15, Reuss-Plauen IR#17 and Stuart IR#18. Without leaving any of these battalions in reserve, the Austrian commanders hurled the weight of their entire column at the French.

As the Austrians came on, the French 1st Hussars attempted to disrupt the enemy's right flank. The light cavalrymen charged Kolowrat-Krakowsky IR#36, compelling two of the regiment's three battalions to fall back. Meanwhile, the foot artillery company poured a devastating fire into Reuss-Plauen IR#17, the crushing canister discharges from the five cannon and one howitzer staggered the Austrian advance. Meanwhile, *général de brigade* Marchand and Colonel Darricau rushed forward with the 32nd *Ligne*, supported by the section of horse artillery. Galloping ahead of the infantry, the 8-pounders unlimbered on the flank of the Austrians and sprayed the whitecoats with canister as the French infantry charged their front. The combination of this one-two punch was simply too much for the men of Karl Riese IR#15. The Austrian regiment recoiled, temporarily losing their two 6-pounder battalion guns to the 32nd *Ligne*.[138]

Following the repulse of this attack, Dupont recalled his troops from outlying Jungingen. They were to quit the defense of that town and make their way to rejoin the rest of the division. However, before Decouchy's converged élites, the 9th *Légère* and 96th *Ligne* could rejoin Marchand and the 32nd *Ligne* in front of Haslach, the Austrians attacked again. Undaunted by their initial repulse at the hands of Marchand and the 32nd, the Austrian officers had quickly reformed the ranks of Karl Riese IR#15 and Reuss-Plauen IR#17 for another attack that got underway about 5:30 P.M. This time the Austrian generals made better use of their

A trophy of war: the Eagle of one of the squadrons of the 15th Dragoons is still in the Army Museum in Vienna

[136] S.H.A.T., *Journal des opérations du 6ᵉ corps.*

[137] Six, *Dictionnaire biographique*, vol. 2, p. 151.

[138] S.H.A.T., *Journal des opérations du 6ᵉ corps.*

To Generals Dupont and Baraguey d' Hilliers
Günzburg, 19th Vendemiaire, Year XIV
(October 11th, 1805)

In compliance with the Emperor's new arrangements, the right wing, upon which the 6th Corps depends, is to be under the orders of His Serene Highness Prince Murat. As it is the formal intention of His Serene Highness to concentrate upon the right bank of the Danube, and parallel to the Iller, all his united force in order to give the enemy battle, who seem determined to defend themselves, only a corps of observation shall remain at Ulm, on the left bank of the Danube. This corps shall be composed of the 1st Battalion of the 9th Light Infantry, and the two last squadrons of the 1st Hussars, lately attached to General Baraguey-d'Hilliers' Division of cavalrie-à-pied. *The detachment shall be commanded by M. Crabbé, my aide-de-camp, to whom I forward particular instructions.*

General Dupont shall therefore immediately quit his position at Albeck, advance with the two first squadrons of the 1st Hussars, and his infantry, which shall be followed by the two regiments of dragoons commanded by General Sahuc, and cross to the right bank of the Danube either by the bridge at Elchingen, or by that at Günzburg. Should the morasses be impractical, this force shall return by Gundelfingen and thence proceed to Günzburg. In either case, the artillery and baggage shall pass by Gundelfingen, and take the lead in the march, by setting out a few hours before the troops.

The Division of General Baraguey-d'Hilliers shall precede the movement of the troops under the command of General Dupont, and shall preserve the same order in the advance of its guns and baggage.

Ney

superior frontage and flanked the French line to the west of Haslach. Rather than have his units enveloped, Marchand had no choice but to conduct a fighting withdrawal while Colonel Rouvillois' 1st Hussars launched charge after repeated charge to help relieve pressure on the infantry and artillery. Slowly falling back along the Ulm-Heidenheim Road, the French contested every inch of ground until darkness settled in before 7:00 P.M.

With nightfall, the fighting came to an end at Haslach-Jungingen. Under the cover of night, Dupont collected his heroic, exhausted survivors and withdrew in good order northward to Albeck. As Dupont quit the field, he took with him all his guns, (the two Austrian guns that had been taken by the 32nd *Ligne* were left on the field), five standards captured by the 9th *Légère* and more than 4,000 Austrian prisoners of war. Most of the captives had been taken in and around Jungingen by *"l'Incomparable"* 9th *Légère*. In addition, the Austrians suffered another 400 killed while more than 1,100 wounded were received into the Austrian hospitals in Ulm the following day.[139] In short, Mack's 23,000-man force had been butchered. In five short hours, no less than 5,500 Austrian combatants—a loss of 24%—had been put out of action by only 5,279 members of the *Grande Armée.*

The price for this victory amounted to 784 Frenchmen from units of the 6th Corps, plus 105 dragoons and an unknown number of artillery train personnel that were cut down by the marauding Austrian cavalry. Within Dupont's infantry, the heroic 9th *Légère* lost 138, including eight wounded officers. The 32nd *Ligne* lost 180, of which two were wounded officers; meanwhile, the 96th *Ligne* suffered 322 killed, wounded and captured. Therefore, Dupont's infantry lost 640 officers and other ranks—a casualty rate of 15.5% of the 4,105 who entered the battle. The 1st Hussars suffered badly. In making repeated charges against infantry prepared to meet their advance, the light horsemen lost 144 troopers out of the 383 that entered the battle, representing a loss of 37.5%.[140] The 15th and 17th Dragoons suffered 105 casualties from their total force of 600, or a casualty rate of 17.5%.[141] Also lost to the Austrian cavalry were 23 wagons along with one precious eagle with attached standard from the 15th Dragoons. Allowing for the felled dragoons as well as the train drivers who had been dispatched by the Austrian horse, Dupont's force of 5,275 lost approximately 1,000 men at Haslach-Jungingen for a casualty rate of almost 19%.

In comparing losses, for every man the French had put out of action they inflicted more than five casualties on the Austrians! This feat becomes especially remarkable when one considers that Dupont's force was outnumbered by a margin of more than four to one. Such accomplishments had to have been done by highly trained troops. The regiment that faced the worst odds during the fighting and inflicted the most damage on the Austrians, the 9th *Légère*, had no less than 13 officers and other ranks receive the coveted *Legion d'Honneur* for their day's work.[142] With men such as these, it is entirely plausible that had Ney been able to secure Murat's permission and move the entirety of the 6th Corps over to the north bank to join up with Dupont on 10 October, Mack's army would have been completely annihilated on the 11th. As it was, the French victory at Haslach-Jungingen serves as a vivid illustration as to how deadly effective the Napoleonic strong point defensive scheme could work. This was especially true when highly-

---

[139] Willbold, *Napoleons Feldzug um Ulm Die Schlacht von Elchingen*, p. 41. Relying on Austrians sources, Willbold is way off the mark insofar as the French casualties are concerned.
[140] S.H.A.T., C^2 16, 482 and *Journal du 6e corps.*
[141] S.H.A.T., C^2 16 and 472.
[142] S.H.A.T., C^2 470. The receipients included *chef de bataillon* Régeau and Adjudant Major Godet of the 1st Battalion.

trained French units were pitted against a foe that did not coordinate movements of all its combat arms.[143]

Two Fateful Days— the 12th and 13th of October

The immediate significance of Dupont's extraordinary performance at Haslach-Jungingen was much more important than the casualties inflicted on Mack's forces. "I have this instant a letter from Prince Murat," Napoleon added as a postscript to a letter dictated to Marshal Soult at 10:00 A.M. on 20 vendémiaire (12 October). "The enemy is at Ulm with 40,000 men. There has been a sortie against Dupont's Division, which standing alone, captured 4,000 prisoners."[144] This news, which reinforced the continued success of French arms, was much needed in order to help counter the effects of the horrendous weather that served to deplete the ranks of Napoleon's army. For those many who remained in ranks, the announcement of Dupont's victory served to further motivate the members of the *Grande Armée* to achieve greater heroics.

While continued stories of victory lifted the hearts and quickened the march pace of the Napoleon's weary soldiers, the tenacity and effectiveness with which the vastly outnumbered French had fought at Haslach-Jungingen, coupled with the disjointed effort made by Austrian arms and the lack of precise information as to the exact whereabouts of the enemy forces, spawned an almost equal and opposite effect in Mack's army. While morale among the Austrian soldiers sank, the latest encounter with the French caused a partial decision-making paralysis, creating in turn a new round of debates at Austrian headquarters as to what course the army should pursue.

Stinging from another costly defeat, their ranks thinned by an opponent whose combat techniques were alien to anything previously encountered, the wounded Mack and his officers faced tough decisions on the night of 11-12 October. In deliberating their next move, the Austrian generals busied themselves with plans that should have been solidified days before. Almost every officer except Mack wanted to move the army either south into the Tyrol or north into Bohemia. But which direction was the best? The French seemed to be everywhere. Their cavalry ably screened the formations of the *Grande Armée*, preventing the Austrian horse from securing vital information. This spelled trouble for those at Austrian headquarters who were used to making decisions based on accurate scouting reports.

Part of the reason for the Austrian cavalry's continued poor showing in scouting, screening and combat were due to the tremendous improvements that the French had achieved during the Boulogne encampment. Despite isolated exceptions such as at Haslach-Jungingen, most 1805 encounters between Austrian and French horsemen had resulted in French successes. Such examples were numerous. In addition to those already mentioned, at Landsberg on 11 October the 26th *Chasseurs à cheval* of Marshal Soult's 4th Corps routed two squadrons of the Cüirassier-Regiment Erzherzog Albert #3, capturing one lieutenant-colonel, two captains, 120 troopers and two 6-pounder cannons.[145] In another series of small

General Dupont to Marshal Ney.
Chabanois, 6 August 1806

Monsieur Le Maréchal,

I have just received your letter in which you ask for further particulars, in reference to the action of the 19th vendemiaire, *concerning the* dragons-à-pied, *commanded by General Baraguey-d'Hilliers. The following is what occurred: On receiving your orders to march upon Ulm, my division began the march and reached Haslach at noon. Having been informed by your instructions that the Division of dragoons was to form in second line behind mine, and support it in case of need, I caused Albeck to be entirely evacuated, and withdrew all the baggage of my division, in order to leave this point free, and avoid all confusion, so that nothing might impede the movement of the Division of dragoons. You are aware,* Monsieur le Maréchal, *that I had scarcely reached Haslach ere I found all the Austrian army prepared for battle, and my division immediately engaged it. Under circumstances so critical, and of which there are but few examples, I despatched orderly upon orderly to General Baraguey, to acquaint him with my situation, and urge him to press his march; but I know not whether these orderlies ever reached him: the fact is, no assistance came.*

I cannot give you any positive information with regard to the hour at which your orders were received by that general; but I believe that the officer of your staff who brought me mine was likewise the bearer of his, and he can therefore give you an exact account of his mission.

I have always thought, Monsieur le Maréchal, *that if your instructions had been executed, and your* corps d'armée *been able to engage, the Austrian army would have been annihilated on that day. The success obtained by my division, and which it owes entirely to the truly extraordinary courage it displayed, only leaves me one regret, that of not having fought under your eye, and in the presence of the Emperor.*

Receive, Monsieur le Maréchal, *the assurance of my respectful sentiments.*

Dupont, General of Division.

---

[143] In his memoirs, Méneval summed up Dupont's remarkable feat thusly: "General Dupont sustained, during the whole day of the 11th, an unequal fight... and by audacious tactics prevented the march of the enemy to Bohemia. Who could then have thought that the career of this general, called to so high a military destiny, would have ended three years later in so deplorable a manner [the capitulation of Baylen]?" *Memoirs of the Baron de Méneval,* vol. 1, p. 390.

[144] Napoléon to Soult, *Correspondance*, number 9379.

[145] S.H.A.T., *Journal des opérations du 4e corps*; 5th Bulletin of the *Grande Armée*, *Correspondance*, number 9380.

actions near Dachau, Marshal Davout's 2nd *Chasseurs à cheval* put to flight the Uhlanen-Regiment Merveldt #1, taking 22 prisoners in the process; then Davout's 1st and 2nd *Chasseurs à cheval* repeatedly engaged and broke a portion of the Hussar-Regiment Blankenstein #6, capturing 60 Austrian troopers.[146] Near Munich, Marshal Bernadotte's advance guard under General Kellermann enjoyed a small success when the enemy invited action. The 4th Hussars and 5th *Chasseurs à cheval* charged and overturned the Hussar-Regiment Liechtenstein #7, capturing one officer and 20 troopers.[147] As one Austrian officer observed: "The enemy has changed [cavalry] tactics. They maneuver in large formations and rapidly bring their numerous squadrons to bear."[148]

The Austrian generals, disappointed by their horsemen's inadequate battlefield performances, became exasperated by the cavalry's failure to provide vital intelligence about the movements of the enemy. What information the Austrian cavalry did manage to gather and forward to general headquarters caused many there to believe that as of 11 October the army was surrounded.

That perception changed in the early morning hours of 12 October. When the Austrian cavalry took themselves out of the fighting at Haslach by disintegrating into a band of undisciplined looters ransacking the French baggage wagons, they made off with the private effects of General Dupont. As the Austrian officers rifled through Dupont's personal possessions, they came across a dispatch that detailed the dispositions of the French army, including the location of the numerous, dispersed supply trains along a line from Stuttgart to Heidenheim to Nördlingen as well as the establishment of a new line of communication back to France. Armed with this information, Mack finally decided that Napoleon was no longer interested in his army; after all, Mack still believed that the position of Ulm was unassailable and that Napoleon had also come to this conclusion. This captured information could only mean, reasoned Mack, that the French army was proceeding east to engage the Russians. Therefore, it was now time to leave Ulm. In order to relocate the army, Mack planned to dispatch a column under FML Werneck to raise havoc with the French supply lines. Werneck's command was to move out of Ulm on the 12th marching swiftly to the northwest, and burn every French supply wagon from Geislingen to Stuttgart. Werneck would then about face and move eastward to Heidenheim, laying waste to every enemy wagon train he came across. With the remainder of the army, Mack would depart Ulm on the 13th, using one division to screen the Danube side flank, and head northeast to Heidenheim where Werneck would rejoin the army. Once reunited, the entire Austrian host would march to Nördlingen and then on into Bohemia.

Austrian Uhlan

When Werneck received Mack's order, the subordinate responded that his men could not depart on the 12th, using the excuse that the troops were too fatigued from the fighting at Haslach-Jungingen, coupled with the fact that they had not had a hot meal since the 10th. When Mack heard this answer, he was furious. "Tell General Werneck," Mack told his chief of staff, "that I will relieve him of command and will personally lead his column to Stuttgart."[149] General Mack soon relented when Colonel Bianchi reported that Werneck's exhausted, hungry troops were just beginning to be fed, and that they could not be ready to move before the morning of 13 October. Faced with officers who were not of a mind to demand that their troops suffer hardships, Mack contemplated changes in his plans while his army sat idle in camp on 12 October.

---

[146] S.H.A.T., *Journal des opérations du 3e corps*; 5th Bulletin of the *Grande Armée*, *Correspondance*, number 9380.
[147] S.H.A.T., C^2 3.
[148] *K. k. Kriegsarchiv*, *Feldacten* for 1805.
[149] David August Schultes, *Chronik von Ulm* (Ulm, 1880).

What course the Austrian general might take was solidified in the evening hours of 12 October when Mack received a dispatch from GM Mecsery. This message disclosed that there were 20,000 to 30,000 French cavalry moving to the west from Weissenhorn and that a large number of French were approaching Memmingen from the east on the Landsberg-Munich road. Within minutes, another report was delivered to Mack from his cavalry scouts northeast of Ulm. The French infantry that had fought at Haslach-Jungingen on 11 October were now isolated at Albeck. Therefore, Mack correctly deduced that the overwhelming majority of the French forces were on the south bank of the Danube, although not as far east as he had hoped. Furthermore, the French cavalry were about to cut his lines of communication with the troops in Memmingen, and with that, threaten the troops under FML Jellachich that were south of Ulm and north of Biberach. This meant that Napoleon was about to eliminate any options Mack might have had of retreating with the entire Austrian army at Ulm into the Tyrol.

Jellachich

After changing column compositions three times during the 12th, Mack finally decided about the troop dispositions he wanted for the relocation of the army. At 2:00 A.M. on 13 October, Mack gave his troops their marching orders. No longer wishing to send a raiding column towards Stuttgart, the Austrians around Ulm were going to evacuate into Bohemia while the troops south of Ulm made for the Tyrol. The latter troops consisted of the column under FML Jellachich. Already below Ulm, the composition of this column would remain unchanged. They were to move along the Iller, destroying all bridges from Oberkirchberg to Memmingen, and then flee into the Tyrol to join Archduke John's forces. If superior numbers of French prevented the retreat along the Iller, then Jellachich was to cut and run towards Biberach and then south into the mountains. Regardless of the route taken, Jellachich and his column were to escape to the Tyrol, join up with the army there, and continue the fight.

Meanwhile, one column under joint command of FMLs Schwarzenberg and Klenau were to hold the south bank approaches to Ulm while two columns under FML Werneck and FML Riesch marched along the north bank to destroy whatever French forces were in the Elchingen-Albeck area and open the way for the army to move towards Heidenheim, and ultimately, Bohemia. Once Werneck and Riesch had cleared the way, the army artillery reserve and baggage train would leave Ulm. The rearguard would comprise of the column under Schwarzenberg and Klenau who would cross over to the north bank and follow the others to safety.

Klenau

Since Werneck was leading the army, his marching orders from Mack were precise:

> It is hereby determined that FML Werneck with half his [column] will move out towards Heidenheim; the other half of his troops will follow 2 to 3 hours later. He should reach Heidenheim today [the 13th], capturing any enemy outposts along the way. The right flank is to be secured, although only few enemy are left on the north bank of the Danube.[150]

Werneck's flank was to be "secured" by the other half of his column—the troops under FML Riesch. Riesch was to move along the north bank towards Elchingen, making certain that the French did not cross the Danube and threaten the right flank of the Austrian army as it moved from Ulm to Heidenheim. Shortly before Riesch moved out, Mack sent him a dispatch, which stated:

> The reserve artillery is to be escorted by a covering force of two squadrons and one battalion from Riesch's [column], and

[150] Willbold, *Napoleons Feldzug um Ulm Die Schlacht von Elchingen*, p. 46.

> will depart at noon on the 13th, go through Albeck to Heidenheim, arriving on the 14th at Nordlingen. The baggage of the army follows the reserve artillery, departing around 4:00 P.M. towards Albeck, where it continues to move all during the night and arrive on the 14th at Heidenheim or as possibly as far as Nordlingen.
>
> FML Riesch provides the covering units as mentioned. With his remaining troops, he will march down the left [north] bank of the Danube, using FML Laudon's men to burn the bridges from Elchingen to Gundelfingen. FML Riesch will then stay overnight around Elchingen, sending a strong detachment to the bridge at Leipheim, continuing tomorrow [the 14th] to Günzburg, destroying all bridges across the Danube. FML Laudon will continue to move along the left bank tomorrow, the 14th, destroying all bridges as far as Donauwörth. FML Riesch will move his headquarters to Günzburg on the 14th while FML Laudon moves his headquarters to Höchstädt. The army's headquarters [of Mack] will tomorrow [the 14th] be at Herbrechtingen.[151]

Mack's order contained a "secret remark" postscript, which added:

> 1. The army moves as one, using Riesch's [column] in the above-mentioned way, namely as an extended flank position along the Danube from which the army extends out in a march parallel to the Danube as circumstances dictate.
>
> 2. Should the enemy be found in large numbers on the left [north] bank of the Danube, it will probably be near Donauwörth as they will be drawn onto Riesch's Column of the army; if this happens, then our troops will move away from the Danube and take up the approaches through the Oberpfalz and then on into Bohemia.[152]

The language of Mack's written instructions reveal that he clearly did not anticipate any serious opposition to his movements until Riesch approached Donauwörth. By then, the general believed that the army would be well on the way to Bohemia where they would join up with Kutuzov's Russians, and with their combined forces, defeat Napoleon.

As Mack dictated these movements, Napoleon had left Augsburg at 11:00 P.M. on 12 October, arriving at Weissenhorn early the next morning. Wanting to ascertain for himself the situation that faced the *Grande Armée*, the Emperor immediately began his personal inspections. In the midst of a blinding storm that combined snow and sleet, Napoleon mounted his horse and rode along the front lines. Discussing the operational situations in front of the 5th, 6th and *Corps des Réserves de Cavalerie* with each of those respective corps commanders, the Emperor found his lieutenants in sharp disagreement.

Murat was still holding onto the belief that all troops should be moved to the south bank of the Danube. Murat's obstinacy in this respect was particularly curious since a captured Austrian dispatch had been brought to him on the 11th that detailed the enemy's dispositions. Rather than acting on this stroke of good luck, Murat merely forwarded the captured document to Imperial headquarters.[153] The captured

---

[151] Willbold, *Napoleons Feldzug um Ulm Die Schlacht von Elchingen*, p. 46.
[152] Willbold, *Napoleons Feldzug um Ulm Die Schlacht von Elchingen*, p. 46.
[153] S.H.A.T., C^2 240.

dispatch, together with Murat's report of the combat at Haslach-Jungingen, reached the Emperor at Augsburg at 10:00 A.M. on 12 October. While Murat had not advised Napoleon of any French troop changes, when Napoleon reached the front lines near Ulm in the early morning hours of 13 October, the Emperor was surprised to learn that his brother-in-law had not shifted any divisions to the north bank in light of the captured document. What's more, the troops under Baraguey d'Hilliers and Bourcier had been recalled by Murat to the south bank, leaving Dupont totally on his own!

The dangerous position in which Dupont had been left was recognized by Lannes and Ney. Both marshals expressed their belief to Napoleon that the enemy would attempt to escape into Bohemia by moving northeast from Ulm, trampling under foot the isolated division of Dupont in the process. During the 12th, Dupont pulled his infantry, along with the 1st Hussars, back to Langenau, while Baraguey's Dismounted Dragoon Division and Bourcier's 4th Dragoon Division had been redirected onto the south side of the Danube on the orders of Marshal Murat. Therefore, in order to prevent Mack's army from fleeing Ulm and destroying Dupont in the process, Lannes and Ney urged the Emperor to shift more troops to the north bank and block the anticipated enemy movement northward.

Napoleon listened to his lieutenants and decided to immediately reestablish communications with Dupont. In order to accomplish this, the Emperor chose the bridge nearest Ulm, that being at Elchingen. This bridge, some six miles northeast of Ulm, was to be captured by the troops nearest the objective—the 6th Corps. Ney's 2nd and 3rd Infantry Divisions, plus the 3rd Hussars and 10th *Chasseurs à cheval* from Auguste de Colbert's 6th Corps light cavalry, all reinforced with Bourcier's 4th Dragoon Division, were to move across the Danube at Elchingen. Once at Elchingen, these troops would link up with Dupont, who was ordered to retrace his steps from Langenau to Albeck to Elchingen. Napoleon wanted Ney to have his men ready to move on the morning of 14 October.

The remainder of Napoleon's plan for the 14th was as follows: while Ney's 6th Corps was surging across the Danube at Elchingen, the 5th Corps under Lannes and the *Corps des Réserves de Cavalerie* under Murat would tighten the stranglehold on the southeast side of Ulm. Meanwhile, Marmont's 2nd Corps at Weissenhorn would move to the Iller and then head north to Ulm, linking up with Lannes' 5th Corps and acting as a link to Soult's 4th Corps. Marshal Soult was directed to mop up any resistance along the line from Memmingen to Biberach. Afterwards, 4th Corps was to march to Ulm and extend the French line to the west of Marmont's command.[154]

As Napoleon was outlining his plans, Mack's Austrians were on the move. According to plan, the first half of FML Count von Riesch's troops struck out from Ulm at 10:00 A.M. on 13 October. They took the minor road that led north from Ulm along the bank of the Danube. The leading half of the column were 7,000 men and six guns belonging to the division under FML Laudon. Laudon's command was subdivided into three brigades. The advance guard was led by Prince Coburg and was comprised of two squadrons from the Hussar-Regiment Blankenstein #6, plus three fusilier battalions and the grenadier battalion from Erzherzog Ludwig Josef IR#8. The center brigade was under the orders of General Genegdegh and consisted of the four fusilier battalions of Karl Riese IR#15, plus the four fusilier battalions of Erzherzog Maximilien IR#35, two squadrons from the Cüirassier-Regiment Hohenzollern #8 and one squadron from Uhlanen-Regiment Schwarzenberg #2. The reserve brigade of Laudon's Division was commanded by General Ulm. This brigade consisted of the grenadier battalions from Froon IR#54 and Josef Coloredo IR#57, plus two fusilier battalions from Froon IR#54 and two

Prince Coburg

[154] S.H.A.T., C^2 3.

squadrons of the Cüirassier-Regiment Hohenzollern #8 under the orders of Colonel Clary.[155]

The march pace by Laudon's troops was torturously slow. Struggling through ankle-deep mud, the men and horses fought the effects of wind-driven sleet and snow. As the accompanying six guns belonging to an Austrian cavalry battery sunk into the Bavarian clay, the Austrians could move no faster than one mile per hour, completing the six mile journey from Ulm to Elchingen in just under six hours.

While Laudon's Austrians approached the outskirts of Elchingen in the late afternoon of 13 October, they unexpectedly came under fire from French troops. The Frenchmen were the 1st Battalion of the 25th *Légère,* protected by Auguste de Colbert's 290 light horsemen from the 3rd Hussars and 10th *Chasseurs à cheval.* This task force, under the leadership of General Marcognet from Malher's 3rd Division of Ney's 6th Corps, had crossed over from the south bank of the Danube and reached Elchingen at 2:00 P.M. After deploying his infantry along the outskirts of the village, Marcognet posted his cavalry to the rear and on the reverse slope of ground on the Danube side of the village. With his troops concealed from any enemy marching from Ulm, Marcognet's troops surprised the Austrians.

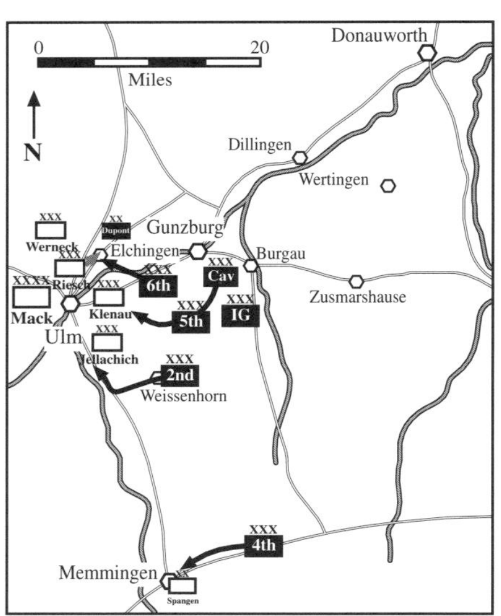

The Austrians are blocked north of the Danube

The presence of these unexpected enemies prompted Laudon to act. He ordered two squadrons of the Cüirassier-Regiment Hohenzollern #8 to clear the French from the village. Although cavalry was ill-suited to village fighting, the cüirassiers dutifully formed columns and charged down the narrow main street of upper Elchingen. As the Austrian horse moved into point-blank range of the French, a *voltigeur* from the 25th *Légère* dropped a captain from his horse—the battle's first fatality. The cüirassiers penetrated into the village only to have their ranks thinned by French *tirailleurs,* who continued to fire from the protection of walls and buildings. However, soon Austrian infantry moved forward to support the cüirassiers, forcing the French to fall back through the village. As the Frenchmen withdrew, they took cover among the walls of the imposing Elchingen convent and shot up the columns of advancing Austrians. The Austrian numbers, however, were too great; the French had no choice but to continue to retreat. While their retrograde movements were covered by Colbert's light horsemen, General Marcognet and the infantry fell back from Elchingen, down the heights and across two bridges, the last one being the southern, main 65-yard-long wooden bridge that spanned the Danube some 1,300 yards from the village. Once at the water's edge, and in order to protect themselves from the overwhelming numbers of Austrians that were milling about the village, Marcognet ordered the shorter northern bridge fired. Despite the intermittent precipitation, the underneath cross timbers ignited easily, and soon the northern Elchingen bridge was burning brilliantly, illuminating the October snowy sky.[156]

Long after this skirmish had reached its conclusion, the second half of Riesch's Column arrived outside Elchingen. Having left Ulm at 2:00 P.M., this portion of Riesch's command was organized similarly to Laudon's Division. It consisted of 8,000 men and eight pieces of ordnance subdivided into three brigades, all under the command of FML von Hessen-Homburg. The advance guard was under General Mescery, consisting of three fusilier and the grenadier battalion from Erbach IR#42, plus two squadrons from Cüirassier-Regiment Erzherzog Franz #2. The center brigade, commanded by General Auersperg, was comprised of eight fusilier battalions—four from Erzherzog Karl IR#3 and four from Auersperg IR#24. With these infantry were one and one-half squadrons from Cüirassier-Regiment Erzherzog Franz #2. General Herrmann led the reserve brigade consisting of two

---

[155] Willbold, *Napoleons Feldzug um Ulm Die Schlacht von Elchingen*, pp. 46-47.
[156] S.H.A.T., *Journal des opérations du 6e corps.*

fusilier battalions from Froon IR#54, the grenadier battalions from Auersperg IR#24 and Erzherzog Karl IR#3, plus two squadrons of Cüirassier-Regiment Erzherzog Franz #2.[157]

Hessen-Homburg's men had an even slower march from Ulm than Laudon's soldiers. Struggling against the effects of the awful roads and harsh weather, Hessen-Homburg's Division labored to reach Elchingen shortly before 10:00 P.M. on 13 October. As these Austrians arrived above the town, they could see the waters of the Danube reflect the lingering flames of the northern Elchingen bridge as the last cross timbers of the bridge were being consumed.

The sounds of gun fire from Elchingen drifted across the Bavarian countryside to Austrian army headquarters some six miles away at Ulm. Mack and the other officers on the Michelsberg could hardly believe their ears. French troops were not expected to be encountered at Elchingen! This unforeseen development played on the morale of the numerous army leaders who were not happy that Mack commanded them in the first place. Their collective mind set was perhaps best summed up in a letter which Archduke Ferdinand wrote that evening to Archduke Charles:

> In a whole book, one could not describe our situation and the madness of Mack. Mack, a complete fool, has through his constant orders to march here and there, has changed plans so often that without striking a blow, the whole army is dissolving before our eyes. His majesty, the Emperor, having given him full power, has placed me in the most unpleasant and desperate situation in the world. Before my very eyes, and under my signature [as titular commander], the army is perishing.[158]

The "unpleasant and desperate situation" of which Ferdinand lamented was, in part, caused by the terrain over which Riesch's troops had to traverse. Writing later on his march from Ulm to Elchingen, Riesch reported:

> The route along the [north] bank of the Danube, which I had to take according to orders, was bad beyond description. The roads had narrow defiles that were flooded, the water coming up to the chest of the horses while the infantry sank to their thighs in water and morass. Movement off the roads was impractical due to large stones that were wedged between thick brush that combined to present an impenetrable landscape, even for infantry. The proof in the futility of attempting to move over this ground was reflected by the loss of the teams of three wagons and one ammunition cart that drowned when they were driven into the high water in the night.[159]

Alternate routes from Ulm to Elchingen were impossible for Riesch, owing to nearby forests that prevented his artillery from accompanying the troops.

Once the fighting had died down at Elchingen on the 13th, Riesch held a conference of war with FML Laudon and the advance guard commander of Hessen-Homburg's Division, GM Mecsery. All three men were aware of Mack's schedule: Riesch's command should have passed through Elchingen and reached Günzburg

---

[157] Willbold, *Napoleons Feldzug um Ulm Die Schlacht von Elchingen*, p. 47.

[158] Archduke Ferdinand, as quoted in Willbold, *Napoleons Feldzug um Ulm Die Schlacht von Elchingen*, p. 49.

[159] Riesch, as quoted in Willbold, *Napoleons Feldzug um Ulm Die Schlacht von Elchingen*, pp. 47-48.

by sundown, having destroyed the Elchingen bridges and the three Günzburg bridges in route. Instead, both divisions of the column were at Elchingen following a snail-like advance from Ulm and an unexpected skirmish with Marcognet's French. In addition, the southern Elchingen bridge was still standing while the northern bridge's piers were usable despite the cross timbers being consumed by the fire. This meant that the structure could be repaired and then be used by the French to move troops over to the north bank of the Danube, if desired. Riesch and his officers discussed whether or not their troops should launch a night assault to complete the destruction of the remaining piers of the northern span as well as the southern Elchingen bridge. The Austrian generals knew that their available manpower vastly outnumbered the French which had previously retreated over the Danube. Despite this critical advantage and the urgency of the situation, Riesch, Laudon and Mecsery decided against a night attack. Their reasoning was simple: an assault following the already exhausting physical demands placed on the men and animals during their march from Ulm would be asking too much. The Austrian generals instead opted to delay the assault until the next day, 14 October; meanwhile, the troops needed to rest. Riesch had his 14,500 soldiers billet with the townspeople while 500 of his officers came to the Elchingen convent for lodging and nocturnal communion.[160] This fateful decision to delay the destruction of the northern portion of the Danube bridge at Elchingen would prove to be the final undoing of Mack's army.

Ney Destroys Riesch—
The Battle of Elchingen

Riesch's decision to hunker down at Elchingen might have been further influenced by three reports. The first was from the local populace, several members of which stated that strong French detachments were already on the north bank of the Danube near Günzburg. Although this information was, in fact, several days old, Riesch had to consider its worth since there had been no scouting reports by his cavalry to either confirm or deny this claim.[161] The second was a message received from FML Werneck, whose column had left Ulm and was west of Riesch near Albeck. Werneck reported that his cavalry scouts had located Dupont's Division at Brenz and, according to the Austrian troopers, the French seemed to number approximately 4,000 men. The third report was a result of one of Napoleon's favorite contrivance—misinformation. On the 12th, the Emperor sent numerous uniformed soldiers across the Danube, with the purpose of being captured by the Austrians and supplying the enemy with lies about the movements and strengths of the *Grande Armée*. Several of these agents of misinformation were rounded up by Laudon's Division during the skirmish at Elchingen on the 13th. The message the prisoners gave their captors was consistent: massive numbers of French formations had crossed over to the north bank from Günzburg to Dillingen.[162] Although these stories were untrue, the misinformation supplied by the French agents helped to attain the effect desired by Napoleon—the Austrian exodus north along the Danube from Ulm had to be reconsidered by its leaders.

Shortly after midnight on 14 October, the high ranking officers of Riesch's command were holding a late-night meeting at the convent of Elchingen. As Generals Riesch, Laudon, Hessen-Homburg, Liechtenstein, Ulm and Herrmann were discussing Mack's "dream of a hostile retreat" and the hoped-for salvation of the army, a messenger arrived from headquarters. In front of his colleagues, Riesch opened and read the latest dispatch from Mack.

---

[160] P. Benedikt Baader, *Chronik von Elchingen*, in the Staatsarchiv, Augsburg.

[161] Baader, *Chronik von Elchingen*.

[162] S.H.A.T., C^2 3.

> Ulm, 13 October 1805, in the evening
>
> My convictions!
>
> Bonaparte stays with the main column headed for Weissenhorn. He has done so because of the great difficulty in crossing the terrain on his way to the Iller which he intends to cross.
>
> A glance at the map shows that it would be nonsense to rush forward after Weissenhorn because you would have to go back after Günzburg and that the Danube presents yet another detour to cross. This way from Günzburg is also difficult to travel due to the nature of the terrain.
>
> What we ought to do then, is to attack him first at Weissenhorn or at least on the day where he attempts to cross the Iller. Perhaps if by tomorrow he has still not crossed, then it presents a great chance, if he has not first taken the turn at Memmingen, that the column which from there is attempting to cross by the left bank of the Iller could be left behind. This would present a favorable opportunity to eliminate or annihilate this part, and if we fail to do so, he would probably think us foolish for not trying.
>
> The column advancing against Memmingen and the one on the left bank of the Danube are watching over his line of retreat. At least we must consider about taking the trouble to block this route of retreat and make it more difficult for him to reach the Rhine. Perhaps by then something will have happened to prevent him from crossing, especially since a Revolution has broken out.[163]

The main street of Elchingen: the abbey is beyond and above the gateway in the center

The consequences of these "convictions" were a whole series of wrong decisions and orders by Mack. The Austrian general mistakenly believed that Napoleon was now retreating back to France. This remarkable assumption was grounded in misinterpretation, misinformation and sheer fantasy. First, the captured documents at Haslach-Jungingen were authentic, but Mack misread their value. Clearly, the dispatches showing Napoleon's re-establishment of his lines of communication had nothing to do with his return to France. The additional reports that were presented to Mack were, in part, from misinformation agents planted by Napoleon. Their stories caused Mack to link what he already chose to believe with the unfounded rumors erroneously reported by his spy, a schoolmaster named Karl Ludwig, that the British had landed at Boulogne and that a counterrevolution had broken out in France. Mack, therefore, chose to combine all these stories in order to come up with a specious campaign hypothesis—the enemy's homeland was in disarray and Napoleon, with the bulk of the *Grande Armée,* was southeast of Ulm at Weissenhorn and heading west in abject misfortune for the Rhine.

This extraordinary deduction caused Mack to direct Schwarzenberg to remain with his column in and around Ulm rather than follow the rest of the army northward. Since the French were believed to be marching home, there was no reason to abandon the position described by Mack as "the key to half of Germany."[164] Meanwhile, Laudon's Division of Riesch's command was to cautiously advance down the Danube. By the time these men reached Nördlingen, the retreat path of

[163] Willbold, *Napoleons Feldzug um Ulm Die Schlacht von Elchingen*, p. 50.
[164] Angeli, 'Ulm und Austerlitz' in *Österreichische Militärische Zeitschrift,* p. 463.

The gatekeeper's house in the abbey grounds

the French to the Rhine would be identified, and Laudon's troops could be redirected to strike out in pursuit. The columns of Werneck and Jellachich would continue to execute the orders previously given to them. While Mack was reveling in his fantasies, he was too far removed from Elchingen, and his "convictions" arrived too late, to affect Riesch's dispositions. The column commander's decision to delay the destruction of the northern Elchingen bridge had already set the stage for the Battle of Elchingen.

The small village of Elchingen sits on a bluff overlooking the Danube. From its dominating position on the north bank, Elchingen commands all the ground from the village south and east to the river. Of the numerous masonry buildings in the settlement, none were as awe-inspiring as the convent. Ironically, this massive, four-story medieval nunnery was no stranger to war. Built in 1128, the imposing cloister had been the site of many battles, most notably its storming during the Thirty Years War. Towards the front of the structure, a bell tower loomed high above the fourth story roof. From the observation point in the tower, one could see the Bavarian countryside some five miles northeasterly to Leipheim and south as far as Weissenhorn, some 10 miles away. This was exactly what Riesch and some of his officers were doing after midnight on 14 October.

Surveying the landscape blown raw by harsh northerly winds that brought sleet and snow during the night, Riesch and the other Austrian generals could easily see the fires of Marcognet's men some three-quarters of a mile away on the south bank of the Danube. While the presence of Marcognet's troops did not pose a threat to his command, what did concern Riesch was the rapidly growing number of fires that kept sprouting up all night in a giant semicircle from Leipheim to Weissenhorn. With the mushrooming number of French fires, especially the large number within two miles of the Danube, Riesch began to seriously doubt Mack's "convictions." Riesch knew that large numbers of the enemy were opposite Elchingen, and if these French were retreating to France, their route was bringing them unexpectedly close to his position.

The camp fires that illuminated the October night as seen by Riesch and his confidants from the tower of the Elchingen convent were those belonging to several corps of the *Grande Armée*. Marmont's 2nd, Lannes' 5th, Murat's Cavalry Reserve and Ney's 6th Corps were all within site of the convent's tower. However, it was the numerous conflagrations closest to Elchingen within a two mile radius of the Danube that heralded the approach of the troops under a French officer who was most eager to come to grips with Riesch's Austrians.

Ney

Michel Ney, the 36-year-old redheaded marshal, was bringing up the remainder of his corps, which consisted of the majority of Mahler's 3rd Infantry Division as well as Loison's 2nd Infantry Division and three regiments of dragoons from the attached 4th Dragoon Division under Bourcier. As Ney and these troops came closer to Elchingen, the members of the 6th Corps staff could see another fire—the one that was burning inside their commanding officer. Ney was seething. In his long and storied career, which had begun at the age of 18 and had already included numerous wounds and distinguished combat performance at a dozen battles while serving under demanding officers, never had Ney endured the verbal abuse that he had suffered a few days previously at the hands of the Emperor's brother-in-law. Although Ney never claimed to be the brightest soldier, he refused to suffer fools easily. This is exactly how he saw Marshal Murat, the recent 'army wing commander' under which Ney had to take orders in the absence of Napoleon. Ney's run-in with Murat had reached its boiling point on 10 October, which led to Dupont having to fight on his own at Haslach-Jungingen on the 11th.

The fearless commander of the 6th Corps could not forget the slanderous insults thrown at him by Murat in their recent altercation. With these words still ringing in his ears, Michel Ney put on his full dress uniform and mounted his horse on the morning of 14 October 1805. Followed by members of his staff, Ney reported

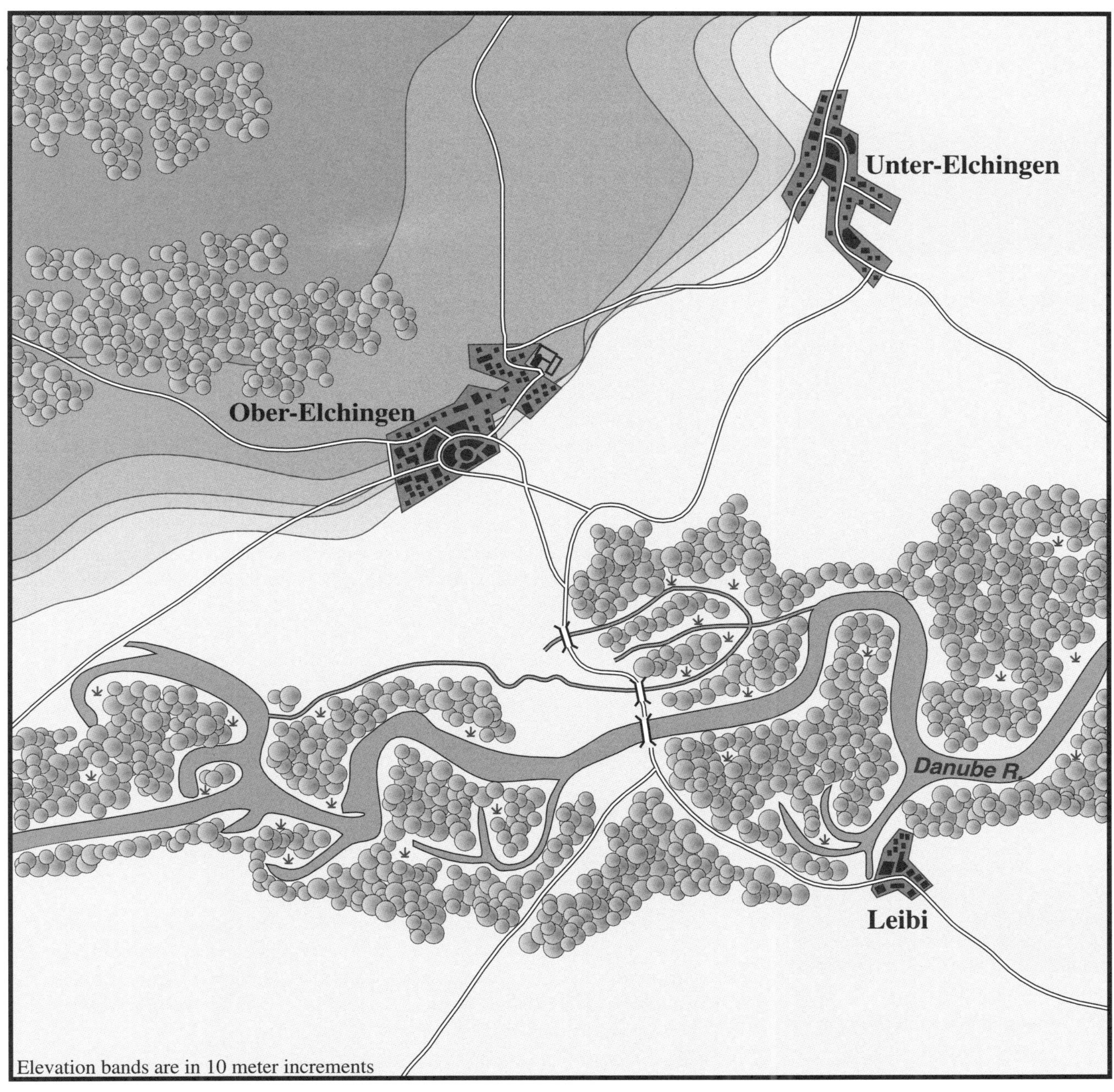

The Battlefield of Elchingen

to Imperial headquarters around 7:30 A.M. The cold rain had stopped before dawn, and the sun shone brightly across the landscape. Puddles of water stood everywhere, and reflected the brilliant uniform colors of Ney and his staff as they rode to meet Napoleon. After receiving the Emperor's final instructions, Ney walked over to Murat. Without hesitating, Ney looked the cavalry commander in the eyes, grabbed his arm and shook it forcibly before Napoleon and the entire Imperial staff, declaring: "Come, Prince; come with me and form your plans in the face of the enemy!"[165] Other than standing motionless, his mouth gaping open in astonishment, Murat did not respond. Facing about, Ney walked to his horse, mounted the steed and rode off with his staff towards the eagerly awaiting French troops massed along the south bank of the Danube. When Ney rode into sight of the soldiers of the 6th Corps, they cheered him by the nickname known throughout the army: *"Rouge Peter! Vive Rouge Peter!"*

Looking down from the abbey towards the Danube

The host of bluecoated French infantry and greencoated French cavalry preparing for battle was described by the chronicler of the Elchingen convent as "a black thundercloud."[166] The troops of which the "black thundercloud" consisted had dressed for the occasion. Overcoats were left with packs that were dropped in preparation for battle. Grenadier and *carabinier* companies attached scarlet plumes to their bearskin headgear. These contrasted with the green plumes tipped in scarlet worn by the *chasseurs* and the yellow-tipped plumes sported by the *voltigeurs* of the 6th *Légère*. Ney and his staff rode along the lines of French soldiers as battalion flags and squadron standards were unfurled against the morning breeze while the massed bands of the 6th Corps struck up *Le Chant du départ.*[167] As the musicians played through the overture and began the first verse, the crisp morning air became filled with a chorus of thousands who joined in the singing of this Republican favorite, which declared, in part:

Tremble, enemies of France,
Kings drunk with blood and pride,
The sovereign people advance,
Tyrants, descend into the grave!

The Republic calls us,
We know how to vanquish, we know how to perish!
For her the French ought to live,
And for her the French ought to die!

Elchingen abbey from the high ground to the east

The resounding, defiant refrains from Ney's soldiers rose from the banks of the Danube, rebounding over the ground that sloped uphill to the village of Elchingen and swirled around Riesch's men who were already standing under arms. The effects that these sights and sounds had on the psyche of the Austrian soldiers and officers were recalled by Riesch:

> The masses of the dark-clad enemy, drawn up in ranks on the south bank, appeared as if they were on parade. While the bands played, their voices proclaimed in unison that they 'knew how to vanquish and knew how to perish,' thus announcing their determination to attack and carry our positions.[168]

---

[165] S.H.A.T., *Journal des opérations du 6e corps;* Thiers, *The History of the Consulate & the Empire of France*, vol. 2, p. 28.
[166] Baader, *Chronik von Elchingen.*
[167] S.H.A.T., *Journal des opérations du 6e corps.*
[168] *K. k. Kriegsarchiv*, *Feldacten* for 1805.

Indeed, the French were not bypassing Elchingen as Riesch had hoped—they were about to attempt to repair the northern bridge, storm across the Danube and attack the village!

To try to defend against this river crossing, Riesch sent out orders for the dispositions of his troops. During the pre-dawn hours of the morning before realizing that he would be attacked, Riesch had dispatched General Mecsery with the Advance Guard of Hessen-Homburg's Division with orders to reconnoiter towards Leipheim and, if possible, burn the bridge located there as well as the other two northward at Günzburg and Reisensburg . It hadn't taken Mecsery long to retrace his steps to Elchingen with the news that he could not risk his small command in a countryside that was swarming with French. What Mecsery had seen from the north bank were Ney's troops moving to their pre-dawn jump-off point opposite the Elchingen bridge on the south bank. The amount of enemy activity was enough to convince Mecsery that he should take his men back to Elchingen posthaste. When Mecsery returned, Riesch ordered him to position his command between lower Elchingen and the Danube in order to cover the left flank of the column. Mecsery deployed his four battalions and two squadrons in two lines facing south. Two battalions of fusiliers from Erbach IR#42 formed the front line and were positioned abreast of one another in column of companies with an interval between the battalions wide enough so that the formations could deploy into line. The second line was formed by another fusilier battalion and the grenadier battalion of the same regiment. The battalions that formed the second line were staggered, or in checkerboard, to the battalions in the front line. Finally, Mecsery divided the two squadrons from Cüirassier-Regiment Erzherzog Franz #2 and positioned one squadron apiece to cover the flanks of the infantry. So deployed, Mecsery was to provide Riesch's flank protection without the benefit of any artillery.

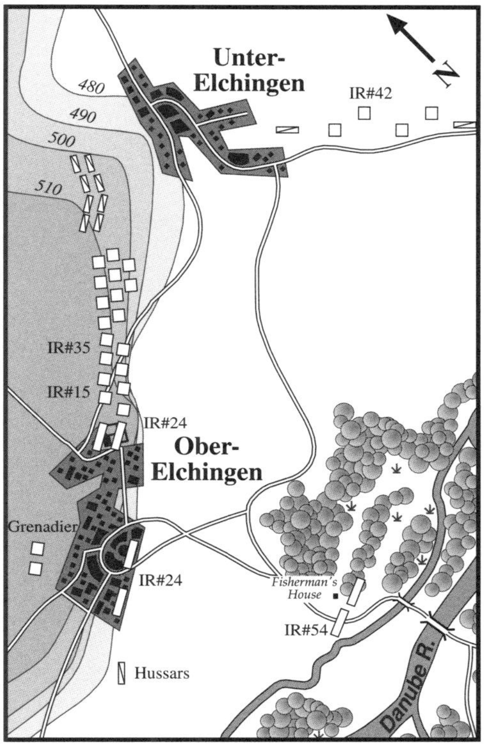

Riesch then ordered the remainder of his troops to be deployed as follows:

1. in the marsh garden and in the village itself—two fusilier battalions of Auersperg IR#24 and their four 6-pounder battalion guns;
2. covering the west side, outside town—one squadron from Hussar-Regiment Blankenstein #6;
3. in the convent and the convent garden—two fusilier battalions of Auersperg IR#24 and two 6-pounder guns;
4. at the south tip of the Großer Forest—two grenadier battalions;
5. plateau on the northeast side of the convent wall—6 battalions;
6. extending past #5 to the north —10 battalions and seven and one-half squadrons of cavalry, supported by one cavalry battery of six pieces;
7. opposite the Danube bridge and at the fisherman's house—two fusilier battalions of Froon IR#54 and two 6-pounder battalion guns; and
8. On the road to Riedheim and Weißinger Höfen under Mecsery and Colonel Biber—three fusilier battalions and one grenadier battalion of Erbach IR#42, plus two squadrons from Cüirassier-Regiment Erzherzog Franz #2.[169]

The Austrian deployment at Elchingen

With his men in position, Riesch had 32 battalions of infantry, 12 and one-half squadrons of cavalry, plus artillerists numbering 15,000 combatants and 14 guns. All units of Riesch's command were significantly understrength; each cavalry squadron averaged only 100 combatants while each infantry battalion averaged 396 officers and other ranks, thanks to heavy casualties previously suffered by some of the units. With this force, Riesch waited for the French to attack.

Across the river, Marshal Ney surveyed the Danube and the ground that lay beyond its waters to Elchingen. Summoning his key subordinates for a conference, Mahler, Loison, Bourcier and Colbert met Ney about 8:00 A.M. due south of the

[169] Willbold, *Napoleons Feldzug um Ulm Die Schlacht von Elchingen*, p. 59.

river on a rise above the river basin. To these men, Ney pointed out the obvious points of the terrain: the meandering water that had carved out a wide river bed which in turn had formed in its course a large island and one small one between the branches; the bed of the Danube, as well as the islands in the middle, where numerous marshes were interspersed with willows and poplar trees; the 65-yard long wooden bridge that spanned the Danube some 1,300 yards from the convent that still connected the south bank with the middle island; the portion of the Danube that separated the middle island from the north bank that was 35 yards wide, and there was the bridge which Marcognet had partially damaged when he ordered it fired during the retreat the previous evening. In addition, the heights of Elchingen were held by a force of Austrians which Marcognet and Colbert estimated to be about 20,000 strong.

With Dupont temporarily separated from the rest of the 6th Corps, Ney's available force at dawn on 14 October 1805 consisted of 14,940 combatants. The 2nd and 3rd Infantry Divisions numbered 12,903 officers and other ranks in 16 battalions, while 290 light cavalrymen of the 6th Corps were with Auguste de Colbert, 835 dragoons in three regiments of General Bourcier's 4th Dragoon Division, plus the various companies of supporting artillery and train personnel attached to these respective formations. All these formations, which exclude Dupont, were supported by 28 pieces of ordnance—six with Mahler and 22 available to support the troops that were to be the first to cross the Danube.[170]

Loison

Since Mahler had fought four days earlier at Günzburg, Ney selected Loison to spearhead the attack. Louis-Henri Loison, the 34-year-old commander of the 2nd Infantry Division, was a prime example of an individual rising quickly because of his talents. From the rank of a lowly private in 1787, Loison rose to become a *général de brigade* in less than eight years. Shortly after his promotion to *général de brigade* in *Armée de Rhin-et-Moselle,* Loison was transferred to Paris. There he met and served under Napoleon Bonaparte, helping to disperse the rebels of 13 vendémiaire with the famous 'whiff of grapeshot.' Following service in 1797 with the *Armée d'Italie*, Loison was transferred to the Swiss front, where he greatly distinguished himself in the 1799 campaign with the *Armée d'Helvétie*. Promoted to *général de division* in October 1799, Loison was transferred to Napoleon's *Armée de Réserve* with which he served during the famed Marengo campaign of 1800. Thoroughly harsh and dissolute, When it was time to select division commanders for the Loison was selected to head the 2nd Infantry Division under Ney at the camp of Montreuil.[171]

Loison's command consisted of eight battalions divided into two brigades, each brigade numbering two regiments, each regiment of two battalions.[172] The 1st Brigade was under the orders of *général de brigade* Eugène-Casimir Villatte, the 35-year-old former aide-de-camp to Bernadotte. His good record during the wars of the Revolution, especially his valuable service while serving under Soult at the Battle of Zürich during the 1799 campaign, was enough to earn him a nomination to command one of Ney's brigades at Montreuil. Villatte's two regiments were good ones. The 6th *Légère* was commanded by Colonel Jean-Grégoire-Barthélemy Rouger de Laplane, who the day before had celebrated his 39th birthday. Laplane had come to Bonaparte's attention during the Egyptian campaign when he was wounded while leading a heroic assault at Acre in May 1799. Following that battle, de Laplane was brought before Bonaparte, who awarded him a sword of honor. In 1805, some six years later, de Laplane was to lead another assault—the attack over the bridge at Elchingen.

---

[170] S.H.A.T., C[2] 472 and 482.

[171] Six, *Dictionnaire biographique*, vol. 2, pp. 128-129.

[172] S.H.A.T., C[2] 482.

The other regiment of Villatte's Brigade was the 39th *Ligne* commanded by Colonel Antoine-Louis Popon de Maucune. At age 33, Popon de Maucune had been an officer in the 39th for one-third of his life. A captain in 1794, rising to *chef de bataillon* in December 1796 following his meritorious conduct at the Battle of Arcole the preceding month, Popon de Maucune became the 39th's regimental commander (termed in the Republican army *chef de brigade)* in 1799. Wounded six times during the wars of the Revolution, three bullets had found Popon de Maucune's left thigh, two of them coming during the attack on Tauffern in March 1799. The repeated injuring of his left thigh resulted in Popon de Maucune developing a noticeable limp. Despite this handicap, Popon de Maucune led the 39th *Ligne* with a confidence and familiarity that came from being in command of the same unit for over six years.[173]

The abbey of Elchingen towers over the battle in this old print

In order for Villatte's Brigade and the remainder of the French to cross the Danube, it was necessary to repair the bridge that connected the middle island with the north bank. Since only the upright piers remained standing following the fire the night before, the cross timbers and flooring of the bridge would have to be reconstructed. Ney ordered Colonel Cazals, the senior engineer officer in 6th Corps, to direct the repair efforts. Only four days earlier at Günzburg, Cazals had taken an Austrian musket ball to his hip while directing repair efforts while under fire at the Günzburg bridge.[174] Cazals had recovered enough to report for duty on the 14th, and Ney did not hesitate to call upon him.

Although there were no engineer companies attached to 6th Corps, Cazals was one of five engineer officers on Ney's staff.[175] Therefore, with just a handful of officers, plus the sappers that were integral to every grenadier and *carabinier* company, Cazals began forming engineering parties from members of one company of *carabiniers* of the 6th *Légère*. While Cazals was organizing these work details, Ney instructed an aide-de-camp of General Loison, Captain Coisel, along with a sapper of the 6th *Légère*, to grab the first plank and rush forward to the piers to begin reconstruction. Coisel and the sapper reached the bank just as the Austrians opened fire around the remote fisherman's house, just under 400 yards away. These troops were two fusilier battalions from Froon IR#54 and two 6-pounder battalion guns. A cannonball from one of these battalion guns struck the sapper, carrying away his leg, and marking the first French casualty of the Battle of Elchingen.[176]

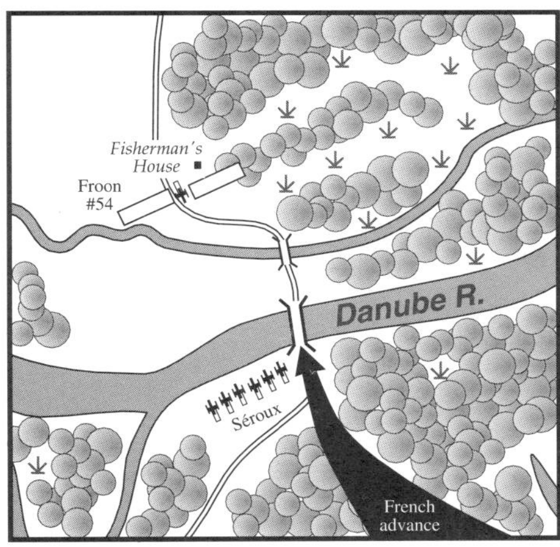

The Action at the bridge over the Danube

The repair work on the bridge was systematic. Planks were placed in the way of joists, then connected from pier to pier, until all but the far northern pier had been connected. The work by Cazals, Coisel and the *carabiniers* had not produced a lasting structure—it was swept away two days later when the Danube flooded—but it was strong enough to be used by all French combat arms for the remainder of the 14th.

To help provide covering fire for the workers, Ney's chief of artillery, the venerable, 63-year-old *général de brigade* Jean-Nicolas Séroux, brought forward two companies of foot artillerists manning a total of 12 pieces of ordnance. Keeping one 12-pounder in reserve, Séroux posted 11 pieces on the west side of the bridge connecting the middle island and the south bank. These 11 pieces consisted of three 12-, five 8-, two 4-pounders and one howitzer. The fire from these guns forced the formed portion of the Austrian infantry battalions around the fisherman's house to seek cover behind the structure and along the edge of the tree line that defined the Danube river bed. A few brave Austrian *tirailleurs* came forward to direct fire against the French workers, but in doing so, exposed themselves to Séroux's guns. Writing in his memoirs that evening, Séroux recalled:

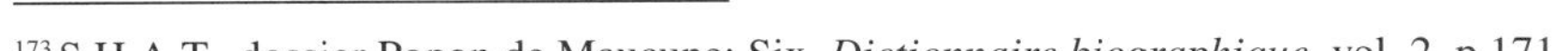

[173] S.H.A.T., dossier Popon de Maucune; Six, *Dictionnaire biographique*, vol. 2, p.171.

[174] S.H.A.T., C² 16.

[175] S.H.A.T., C² 482.

[176] S.H.A.T., C² 16; *Journal des opérations du 6ᵉ corps.*

Austrian Cavalry Battery

> After preparations were made, our artillery opened fire; under the protection of this fire, our troops rushed forward. The few enemy troops who dared to offer resistance were wounded, killed or captured. A brigade of 2nd [Infantry] Division entered the fray by attacking the enemy position at the fisherman's house.
>
> A 4-pounder and a howitzer were taken over the bridge [by a section of horse artillerists] with the 6th *Légère* and directed their fire onto the two enemy guns that had been firing onto the bridge.[177]

Before the bridge's final pier had been connected, an *ad hoc* battalion of converged élites under the command of *chef de bataillon* Michaud of Loison's staff rushed over the nearly completed bridge. Consisting of two companies of *voltigeurs* and one company of *carabiniers* from the 6th *Légère*, plus the two companies of grenadiers from the 39th *Ligne*, Michaud's men ran as far as they could over the newly placed planks, then jumped down into the shallow water before reaching the dry land of the north bank. The members of this converged élite battalion formed a bridgehead behind which the work on the damaged span was completed. Engineer officers supervised the final work on the bridge while Marshal Ney gave orders for the next phase of the battle. In essence, these orders were for General Villatte to place himself at the head of the 39th *Ligne*, cross over the river, and extend the bridgehead to the right, or northeast. Once the 39th was across, Colbert's 150 troopers of the 3rd Hussars along with 140 men and officers of the 10th *Chasseurs à cheval* would follow. The marshal would then cross with the 6th *Légère* and two pieces of ordnance in order to extend the bridgehead northward towards Elchingen. Following Ney would be Roguet's 2nd Brigade of Loison's 2nd Infantry Division, then three regiments of Bourcier's 4th Dragoon Division, and finally, Mahler's 3rd Infantry Division. The ordnance designated by Ney to cross the Danube was limited to six pieces divided into three sections of horse artillery. One section of horse artillery with a 4-pounder cannon and a 6-inch howitzer marched with the 6th *Légère*, while two sections of horse artillery with two 8-pounder guns and two howitzers were assigned to Bourcier's dragoons. With these instructions given, the officers returned to their units.

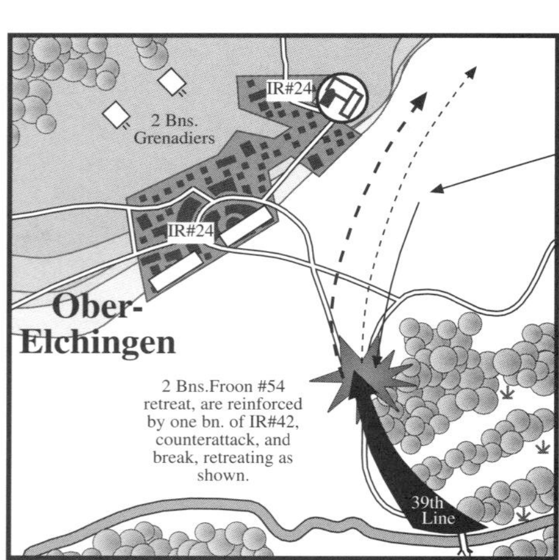

The 1/39th Ligne *defeats IR#54*

General Villatte galloped to the front of the 1st Battalion of the 39th *Ligne* where he found Colonel Antoine-Louis Popon de Maucune. With Villatte's order to advance, Colonel de Maucune turned to *chef de bataillon* Pierre Clavel and harangued his troops. Clavel recalled de Maucune's stirring words: "Men of the 39th! When we crossed the bridge at Arcole, we forever linked our name with the glorious history of the *Armée d'Italie*. Cross with me this bridge of Elchingen, and we will inscribe the name of the 39th with the history of the *Grande Armée!* Forward!"[178] The 1st Battalion of the 39th then rushed over the two spans and onto the north bank to the resounding Gallic battle cry of *"Vive l'Empereur!"*

Once across the Danube, Villatte deployed the 1st Battalion of the 39th in line and took the battalion straight at the two Austrian fusilier battalions from Froon IR#54 and their two 6-pounder guns that were positioned around the fisherman's house. Although possessing superior numbers and frontage, the Austrians were no match for the *élan* and superior leadership of the French. Soon driven from their position, withdrawing northeastward towards the village, the whitecoats were about half way up the slope to Elchingen, when one fusilier battalion of Erbach IR#42 from Mecsery's command arrived as reinforcements. Joining forces, the three Austrian battalions swept back down the hill towards the fisherman's house and the 1st Battalion of the 39th. Villatte, de Maucune and their

---

[177] S.H.A.T., *Journal des opérations du 6ᵉ corps.*

[178] S.H.A.T., *Journal des opérations du 6ᵉ corps.*

men had waited at the fisherman's house for the 2nd Battalion of the 39th *Ligne* to come up. They did this while keeping the 1st Battalion of the 39th stationary and in line until the enemy battalions were spotted. With the Austrian counterattack bearing down on his outnumbered command, Villatte did not hesitate in choosing the audacious course of action—he ordered the battalion to charge. Without time to ascertain the dangers that the superior numbers of Austrians presented, the men of the 1st Battalion of the 39th *Ligne* advanced. Startled to see the blue uniforms coming up the slope for them, the Austrians halted their advance and opened a ragged fire. Most of the bullets from the Austrian volleys sailed harmlessly over the heads of Villatte's men, who continued their charge. Unable to arrest the relentless advance of the 1st Battalion of the 39th, all three Austrian battalions broke and fled back past the northeast side of Elchingen.

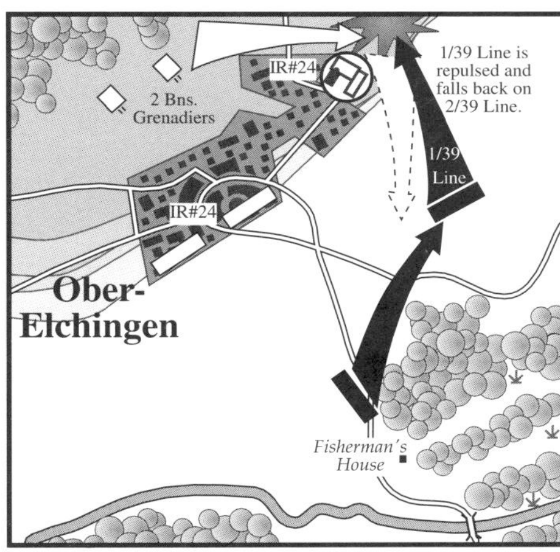

The 1/39th Ligne *is forced to retreat*

With the enemy clearly seen to be on the run, Villatte wasted no time in motioning for the 1st Battalion of the 39th to continue its' advance. As the battalion ascended the slope towards the village in pursuit of the fleeing Austrian infantry, Colonel de Maucune was seen riding along the line waving his sword above his head, shouting exhalations of: *"En avant! En avant!"* The mounted officers preceded the lone unit as they continued their march, passing to the east of the convent and reaching the crest of the hill northeast of town. Once Villatte and his officers reached this position, they saw Riesch's main force of 16 battalions arrayed before them in two lines of battle, along with numerous squadrons protecting the Austrian far left flank. As the 1st Battalion of the 39th crested the hill, the fire from a six-piece Austrian cavalry battery ripped the French ranks. A few moments later, two squadrons from Cüirassier-Regiment Erzherzog Franz #2 came thundering towards Villatte's men. Now under point-blank artillery fire, with overwhelming enemy forces to their front, Villatte ordered the troops to halt. To repulse the approaching Austrian horse, *chef de bataillon* Clavel was ordered to take the right half of the battalion and pull the companies back to form the unit into an L. Once positioned, Clavel's four companies fired a crushing volley into the charging enemy cavalrymen. The cüirassiers recoiled, reformed, and charged again. They moved at only a slow trot over the soggy ground as they approached ground strewn with dead and dying horses and men. This gave the Frenchmen plenty of time to take careful aim with their muskets. Once inside 40 yards, a sheet of flames again erupted from the four companies, dropping many horses and riders, again staggering the Austrian heavy cavalry, forcing them to withdraw.

As the Austrian cüirassiers retreated, three Austrian grenadier battalions were detected advancing towards the 1st Battalion of the 39th. Electing to drive off the French through firepower, the grenadiers halted and commenced a series of volleys. Soon the heavy volume of musketry began to exact a heavy toll on the French. Three company commanders went down with wounds. Other officers and men were falling fast; Villatte had seen enough. He ordered the battalion to start falling back. As his men were slowly retracing their steps back down the slope, the Austrian grenadiers were content in limiting their own advance. They moved forward a few paces, halted and fired, then resumed their advance, halting to fire at the obstinate, withdrawing Frenchmen. By the time the 1st Battalion of the 39th fell back to the fisherman's house, they were met by the 2nd Battalion of the 39th that had finally crossed the bridge, there joined by the two grenadier companies of the 39th that had earlier helped comprise the *ad hoc* élite battalion under *chef de bataillon* Michaud. Under the protection of these troops, the 1st Battalion of the 39th halted and reformed. Together, the battalions of the 39th launched a counterattack of its own. The Austrian grenadier battalions, seeing the growing numbers of French crossing over to the north bank, and themselves isolated below the village, retired to the protection of the reverse slope north of Elchingen as the fighting raged in the streets of the village and around the convent.

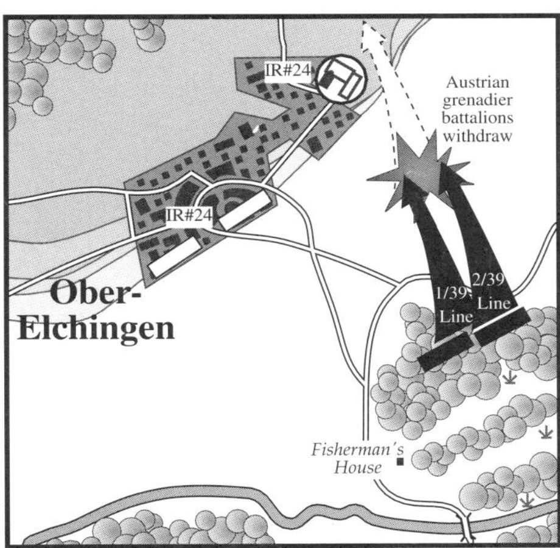

39th Ligne *stops the counterattck of the Austrian grenadiers*

Above, the town of Elchingen as it appears today from across the Danube. Below, the abbey of Elchingen. Ney and the 6th Légère scaled these walls to break into the abbey grounds

While Villatte, Maucune and the 1st Battalion of the 39th were conducting their own mini-battle, Ney had taken both battalions of the 6th *Légère* over the river and collected the élite companies of the regiment that were previously with Michaud. Accompanied by a section of horse artillerists pulling the 4-pounder cannon and a single 6-inch howitzer with them, the 6th *Légère* ascended the slope towards the convent and village. As the regiment approached the top of the hill, the battalions split their march abreast in order to assault different areas. Colonel Laplane, with four chasseur companies and the *voltigeur* company of the 2nd Battalion of the 6th *Légère*, were to attack the marsh garden. Meanwhile, *chef de bataillon* Braun and the three other *chasseur* companies plus the *carabiniers* of the 2nd Battalion of the 6th *Légère*, were to carry the village itself. Placing *chef de bataillon* Groslain and the 1st Battalion of the 6th *Légère* under his direct command along with the two pieces of ordnance, Ney took on the toughest task—attacking the Austrian forces that held the formidable convent and the convent garden.

The 6th Légère *assaults Elchingen*

Marshal Ney, Colonel Laplane and the two battalions of the 6th *Légère* that rushed the Austrian defensive positions in Elchingen and the convent were opposed by the four Austrian fusilier battalions of Auersperg IR#24 and four 6-pounder battalion guns. Normally, four Austrian battalions would have eight 6-pounder cannons as their accompanying battalion artillery. However, owing to the critical shortage of horseflesh and train drivers, the fusilier battalions of Auersperg IR#24 were only able to bring four of the pieces with them on the march from Ulm. These guns had been firing since Ney's men crossed the northern bridge, and had continued as the French light infantrymen, horse artillerists and artillery train personnel struggled up the steep hill to the village. Upon reaching the outskirts of town, the blue uniforms moved through the streets towards the defenders as Austrian canister and musket bullets filled the air. Above the noise of crackling musketry and belching cannon fire were the continual cornet calls made by the French light infantry musicians. Marching close to each battalion's national flag, the horn players' characteristically sharp, piercing calls complemented the shouts of the French officers. Waving swords above their heads, Ney, Laplane and the other mounted officers rode in front of the ranks shouting *"Vive l'Empereur!" Vive la France!"* and *"En avant!"*

French élan was pitted against Austrian numerical superiority and superb defensive positions. Colonel Laplane with *chef de bataillon* Braun drove the enemy from the marsh garden as well as the buildings of Elchingen. The biggest challenge that confronted the 2nd Battalion of the 6th *Légère* was posed by the Austrian companies holding the tavern (known today as "Zur Krone"). In order to take this building, Laplane brought up the 4-pounder after it had assisted Ney's battalion in taking the convent. Letting loose a fire that smashed down the doors of the tavern, the 4-pounder opened the way for the light infantry to rush the defenders.[179]

Laplane took the tavern after Marshal Ney and the 1st Battalion of the 6th *Légère* attacked the two Austrian battalions numbering 1,000 men that formed the defense of the convent and its garden. When the battle began, these Austrians were sheltered along the convent's 1.5 to 1.8 meter-high wall that surrounded the garden. Behind this wall the whitecoats had thrown up makeshift dirt firing steps on which the men lined up in anticipation of the French attack. Once Villatte had disposed of the Austrians around the fisherman's house, *général de brigade* Séroux, on his own initiative, ordered all four of his 12-pounders on the south bank to limber up (one was already limbered in reserve) and moved across the river. Once on the north bank, the artillerists quickly unlimbered their pieces to the left of the repaired bridge and trained the barrels onto the Austrian infantry clearly seen lining

Elchingen's upper gateway from the convent gardens

[179] A. N., 137AP9, No. 385, Ney Papers, "Rapport sur le Bataille d'Elchingen," 14 October 1805.

The walls of Elchingen abbey today

the convent garden wall. Soon cannonballs from these heavy guns crashed into and through the southeast corner of the convent garden wall, tossing stones into the air and crushing the bodies behind. Unable to withstand this direct bombardment from the deadly 12-pounders, the Austrians moved back away from the wall and into the unprotected area of the convent garden.

The fire from Séroux's long range pieces lifted as Ney and the 1st Battalion of the 6th *Légère* completed their advance up the steeply sloping ground. The French horse teams and gunners had a particularly difficult time in dragging the 4-pounder and howitzer up the hill. However, their hard work and determination paid off. These pieces were unlimbered near the convent garden and began pouring fire onto the Austrian infantry through the gaping hole in the southeast corner of the garden wall that had been carved out by the cannonballs of the 12-pounders. Meanwhile, French *tirailleurs* scrambled onto and along the expansive garden wall. French canister and skirmisher fire was returned by volleys from the Austrian battalions in the garden. The fire fight continued for almost half an hour before the Austrian supply of ammunition began running out. Since their munitions carts had been stuck in the mud during the march from Ulm the day before and had not yet reached Elchingen, the Austrians had only the 40 rounds in their cartridge boxes. There was no hope for resupply.[180]

Hunting Horn emblem of the French Light Infantry

As fire slackened from the Austrians in the garden, Ney formed the *carabiniers* of the 1st Battalion of the 6th *Légère* into an assault column and rushed through the opening in the garden wall. In vain, the Austrians tried to stem the French tide. Before they knew what had hit them, Riesch's soldiers were using their rifle butts and bayonets as they were locked in hand-to-hand combat with the *carabiniers* of the 1st Battalion of the 6th *Légère*. The convent chronicle reported that: "The Austrians fought like lions. As they no longer had any powder, they had to defend themselves with bayonets and the butts of their muskets."[181] The tough *carabiniers* went through one Austrian company like a buzz saw, littering the ground with shattered skulls and blood-spattered white uniforms. However, other Austrian companies closed in around the bearskins while the other companies of the 1st Battalion of the 6th *Légère* entered the fray. The leadership, training and tenacity of the light infantrymen were simply too much for the more numerous, but "young, badly educated soldiers"[182] of Auersperg IR#24. The men of these battalions broke and ran back through the courtyard and connecting gate to the massive cloister.

Meanwhile, Ney regrouped his command. Unfazed by the prospects of assaulting the giant structure with only a single battalion, the marshal once again called the *carabiniers* and their sappers to the fore. Rushing towards the convent's main entrance with axes in hand, the engineers went to work at chopping down the doors. Others lent supporting fire against those Austrians who still had ammunition and were shooting back from various openings. The French artillerists sited their pieces and fired into the stained glass windows on the side of the cloister, causing confusion and smoke within the convent . Amidst this action could be heard the unrelenting calls from the 6th *Légère* horn players. While axe work against the convent doors continued, plunging fire from the Austrians in the upper stories of the cloister killed and wounded many Frenchmen. *Chef de bataillon* Groslain went down with a wound, along with three of the battalion's company commanders. Lieutenants Mouroux and Roussel were already dead, while other officers were out of action with wounds from the prior hand-to-hand combat. Although the casualties were heavy, the determination of the men was undaunted. Continuing to exalt the light infantrymen, Ney's leadership inspired fanatical efforts from his soldiers, and soon the doors were broken down, and the light infantry stormed into

Another view of the abbey today

[180] Willbold, *Napoleons Feldzug um Ulm Die Schlacht von Elchingen*, p. 70.
[181] Baader, *Chronik von Elchingen*.
[182] Baader, *Chronik von Elchingen*.

the convent, taking dozens of prisoners who found themselves trapped in the structure with no means of resistance or escape. While the 1st Battalion of the 6th *Légère* had accomplished a feat nothing short of heroic, the severity of the fighting at the convent and garden could only be described as savage. Proof of this lay in the 6th Corps report of captured Austrian arms at the Battle of Elchingen. Of the slightly less than 1,000 Austrian muskets picked up from the area around the convent and its garden following the battle, only 50 were found to be undamaged![183]

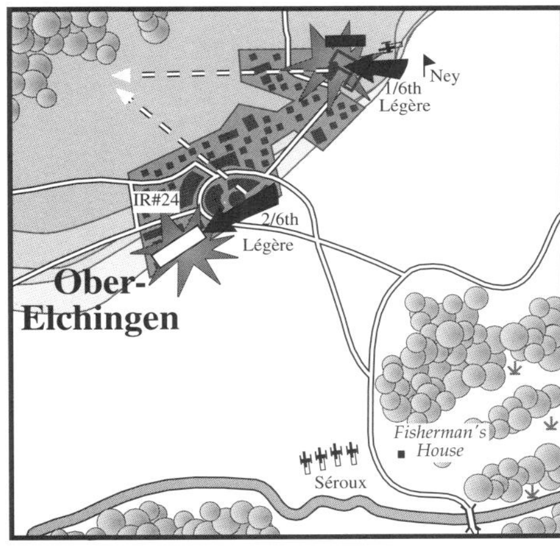

The 6th Légère *takes Elchingen*

Having been driven out of strong defensive positions in the marsh garden, village, convent garden and convent, pitted against French troops that fought as if they were possessed by demons, the surviving Austrians had had enough. The living fled across the open ground west of the village towards the two grenadier battalions stationed outside the Großer Forest. Seeing his men take flight, the Prince Hessen-Homburg rode into their midst in an attempt to stop the rout. It was in vain; the fugitives of the four fusilier battalions of Auersperg IR#24 continued their exodus from the field. In his attempt to stop his fleeing troops, Hessen-Homburg rode too close to the French in the village. Fire from the *voltigeurs* of the 6th *Légère*, who were acting as *tirailleurs*, struck the Prince of Hessen-Homburg as well as Major Kapler of his staff, forcing both to quit the field.[184]

When Ney launched the attack of the 6th *Légère* from the fisherman's house uphill towards Elchingen and the convent, he could not have known the exact positions of the main Austrian force. That information was obtained by Villatte and the 1st Battalion of the 39th *Ligne* while Ney and the light infantry were storming Elchingen. After carrying the village, convent and surrounding areas, Ney ordered Colonel Laplane to post his two battalions along with the 4-pounder and howitzer in order to hold onto their gains. Meanwhile, the marshal rode back down the hill to collect more information on what had happened elsewhere, as well as enemy's exact position and strength.

Ready and waiting for Ney near the fisherman's house were Generals Villatte, Roguet and the rest of the troops comprising Loison's 2nd Division. On the right of these men were the 6th Corps light cavalry under Colbert and three regiments of dragoons from Bourcier's command. Even though Mahler's 3rd Division was preparing to cross the river, the marshal did not want to wait for Mahler and give Riesch a chance to counterattack Laplane's light infantry. Following a brief discussion with Villatte and Colbert (whose troopers had now thoroughly scouted the Austrian line) about the whereabouts of the enemy forces, Ney issued orders for the next phase of the battle. While the 6th *Légère* would hold its position and repulse any attempts to recapture Elchingen, the marshal would accompany General Roguet's fresh brigade, consisting of the 69th and 76th *Ligne* Regiments, ascend the slope and attack the main Austrian force last seen by Villatte to be northeast of town. Roguet's infantry would be supported by Colbert's 3rd Hussars and 10th *Chasseurs à cheval*. Extending further northeastward from Colbert's cavalry would be the 18th and 19th Dragoons supported by two sections of horse artillery from 6th Corps, followed by General Villatte and the 39th *Ligne*. Finally, the 25th Dragoons would form the far right of the French line.

Hessen-Homburg was wounded trying to stop the Austrian rout

Before the attack could start uphill, Ney decided that the Austrian troops on the French far right flank had to be eliminated. The threatening soldiers were Mecsery's Advance Guard of Hessen-Homburg's command, less one fusilier battalion of Erbach IR#42. That battalion had earlier been detached to, and had been defeated along with the two fusilier battalions of Froon IR#54 when they tried to counterattack the 1st Battalion of the 39th *Ligne* around the fisherman's house. Because of losses sustained by prior combat and strategic consumption,

[183] S.H.A.T., *Journal des opérations du 6e corps;* Baader, *Chronik von Elchingen.*
[184] Willbold, *Napoleons Feldzug um Ulm Die Schlacht von Elchingen*, p. 66.

Lefèbvre-Desnouettes

the four battalions and two squadrons of Mescery's Advance Guard had been reduced to approximately 1,800 when the day dawned. With one fusilier battalion of Erbach IR#42 no longer present with the rest of the command, the officers and men present with Mecsery had dropped to less than 1,400. The thinned ranks of the remaining three battalions of Erbach IR#42 contained soldiers who knew they had a hard-fighting reputation to maintain. One of the most solid regiments in Austrian service during the Seven Years War, they were very distinguished under heavy fire at Kolin (1757) and won acclaim at Hochkirch (1758) before being almost annihilated at Torgau (1760).[185] Although IR#42 was destined to win fame in the 1809 Danube campaign, Elchingen must rank as one of the low points in the regiment's history.[186]

To destroy these Austrians, Marshal Ney dispatched his best mounted regiments—the 18th and 19th Dragoons. Passing by the marshal and his staff, the three squadrons of the 18th Dragoons numbered 305 officers and other ranks on the morning of 14 October.[187] Leading the regiment was its colonel—one reason why the 18th had an excellent reputation. Thirty-two-year-old Charles Lefèbvre-Desnouettes was a former aide-de-camp to First Consul Bonaparte during the Marengo Campaign in 1800. The following year, Lefèbvre-Desnouettes served as a squadron commander in the *Gendarmerie d'élite*, and was promoted to the command of the 18th Dragoons on 30 December 1802. Considered the foremost equestrian showman in France, Lefèbvre-Desnouettes used his extensive knowledge of horsemanship to turn the 18th Dragoons into a well-mounted, good-looking, hard-hitting outfit.[188]

Following behind the 18th were the three squadrons of the 19th Dragoons numbering 290 officers and men.[189] One of the few truly good regiments of dragoons during the Revolutionary wars, the 19th distinguished themselves in numerous battles. Nicknamed "Intrepid," the 19th Dragoons were, in 1801, entrusted to the command of Colonel Auguste-Jean-Gabriel Caulaincourt. It proved to be a good match of talent. The new commanding officer was one of the most celebrated dragoon officers in the army. Caulaincourt had once taken a 40-man company of the 1st Dragoons, charged and defeated an Austrian battalion at Vedolago in 1797, capturing 400 men in the process.[190]

Auguste Caulaincourt

Caulaincourt followed Lefèbvre-Desnouettes as their two regiments headed straight for Mecsery's Austrians. Colonel Clary of the Cüirassier-Regiment Hohenzollern #8 spotted the greencoated French cavalry moving towards his position and called for his command to intercept the enemy horsemen. Both squadrons of cüirassiers charged and met the 18th, only to be shattered by Lefèbvre-Desnouettes' dragoons. Lefèbvre-Desnouettes had met the charging cüirassiers with two of his own squadrons and used the third squadron to envelop and break up the Austrian's flank. Once the Austrian heavies were broken, Lefèbvre-Desnouettes turned his attention to Mecsery's infantry.

For whatever reason, the three infantry battalions that remained with Mecsery—two fusilier battalions and the grenadier battalion of Erbach IR#42—had not formed squares in the face of the French cavalry attack. Rather than charging headlong into these infantrymen, Colonel Lefèbvre-Desnouettes swung his regiment to the south and then wheeled his command back to the northwest, thereby moving the 18th onto the left flank of the Austrian battalions. Once in this position, the 18th Dragoons halted while the 19th Dragoons deployed to the Austrian's front

[185] Duffy, *The Army of Maria Theresa,* p. 228.
[186] Scott Bowden and Charles Tarbox, *Armies on the Danube 1809*, p. 165.
[187] S.H.A.T., C^2 472.
[188] Six, *Dictionnaire biographique*, vol. 2, pp. 92-93; S.H.A.T., C^2 3.
[189] S.H.A.T., C^2 472.
[190] Six, *Dictionnaire biographique*, vol. 1, pp. 204-205.

and the two sections of horse artillery unlimbered to the right of the 19th, thereby forming a link between Lefèbvre-Desnouettes and Caulaincourt's commands. Watching activity to his front and left, Mecsery seemed to have become paralyzed. He evidently did not want to form squares and get annihilated by the French artillery. Yet, by not forming his infantry into protective squares, Mecsery invited the dragoons to charge. Rather, he must have decided to wait and change his battalions into square whenever the French cavalry decided to attack.

Without Austrian cavalry to threaten them, and with no opposing artillery in front of them, the French horse artillerists took their two 8-pounders and two 6-inch howitzers to within 200 yards of the Mecsery's infantry, unlimbered and opened a devastating fire with canister. After only a few rounds, the Austrians' view of the field was obscured by the thick smoke of the French horse guns. As a result, they did not see Lefèbvre-Desnouettes and the greencoated troopers on brown horses swooping down on them. The 18th Dragoons struck Mecsery's brigade in the flank, rolling up each battalion in succession and riding down or capturing seven of the 12 companies in these three battalions. Caulaincourt then slipped the leash off his 19th Dragoons, their charge netting 250 prisoners. The terror-stricken survivors of Erbach IR#42 fled to safety by running to the nearest buildings where they found protection against their mounted adversaries.[191]

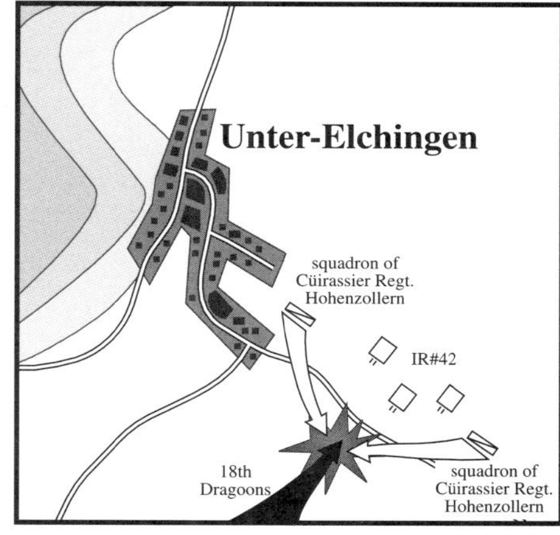

The destruction of IR#42: the 18th Dragoons defeats the protecting cavalry

With the right flank now cleared of Austrian troops, it was about 11:00 A.M. when Ney gave the signal for the rest of the line to advance. The spearhead of this attack was the infantry of Roguet's 2nd Brigade of Loison's 2nd Infantry Division. Moving up the hill, Roguet had positioned his five battalions abreast of each other. Looking from the French position from left to right were the 2nd Battalion of the 69th, the 1st Battalion of the 69th, the 3rd Battalion of the 76th, the 2nd Battalion of the 76th and the 1st Battalion of the 76th. Above each French battalion fluttered the lozenge-designed national colors of the new Empire, while regimental drummers beat out the famous cadence known as the *pas de charge*. Marching alongside the drummers were other regimental musicians, who played the accompanying strains to the French quick cadence.

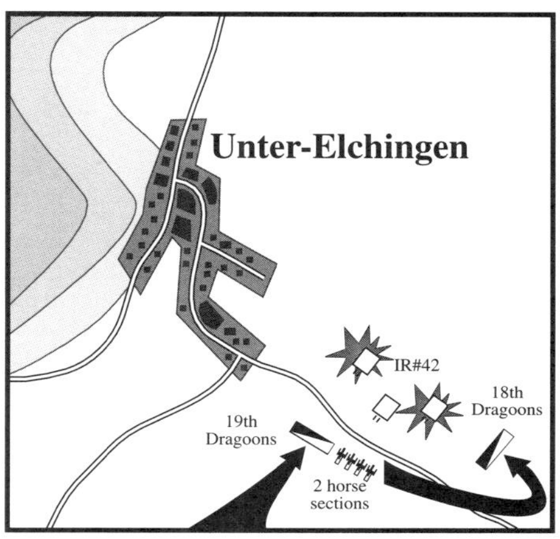

The horse artillery pounds IR#42 while the 18th Dragoons rolls up its flank

The commander of the troops moving to the attack was the 35-year-old *général de brigade* François Roguet. Roguet had been an infantryman for the last 16 years, serving in the *Armée d'Italie* for most of his Revolutionary career. An officer with a reputation of being an exceptional small unit tactician, Roguet found fame with the 33rd *demi-brigade de bataille* before being promoted to *général de brigade* in August 1803. Reporting for duty at Ney's camp at Montreuil in December 1803, Roguet formed a close working relationship with the 69th and 76th *Ligne* regiments.[192] Roguet's colonels were Brun (69th) and Faure-Lajonquière (76th). Forming their battalions into attack columns, Brun and Faure-Lajonquière had each battalion screened by one company of fusiliers that acted as *tirailleurs* during the advance up the Elchingen slope.

Upon reaching the top of the ridge north of the village, the main Austrian line was contacted and the *tirailleurs* of the 69th and 76th opened fire. Meanwhile, both battalions of the 69th and the 2nd and 3rd Battalions of the 76th changed from attack columns to line. Once the quick formation change was accomplished, the brigade resumed the advance and crested the hill as the *tirailleurs* withdrew to the flanks of the formed ranks. The French battalions moved to within 100 yards of the Austrian line that was already ablaze with musketry fire. Halting on Roguet's signal, the 69th and 76th leveled its muskets and fired a deafening and deadly brigade volley. The hail of lead brought down scores of Austrians, whose places were filled by those in the rear ranks. Soon the opposing lines were trading volleys

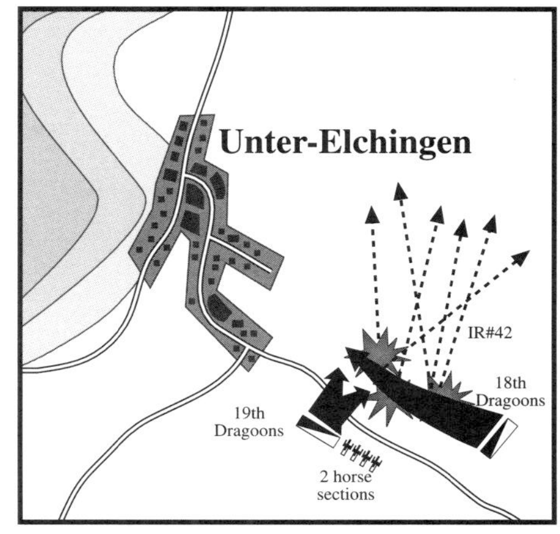

The 19th Dragoons charges to finish off IR#42

[191] S.H.A.T., C^2 3 and 240.

[192] Six, *Dictionnaire biographique*, vol. 2, p. 383; S.H.A.T., C^2 467.

while locked in a heated firefight. To observers on both sides, Roguet's men quickly achieved the upper hand in the exchange of musketry. Riesch recalled:

> They [French] approached to under 100 meters of our line and halted. Suddenly, there was a deafening roar and the bullets from a thousand muskets crashed into our lines and rows of our young soldiers sank dying to the ground. Our men returned fire, but not being fully trained, were not able to achieve the same results.[193]

Roguet described his advance almost identically.

> My brigade moved in attack columns up the hill as if on the parade ground; *tirailleurs* covered our front while the 69th and two battalions of the 76th changed into line. We then dressed ranks and resumed the advance. Once under 100 paces from the enemy line, we opened with such rapid and deadly volleys that our firepower broke the 4,000 Austrian infantry in front of us.[194]

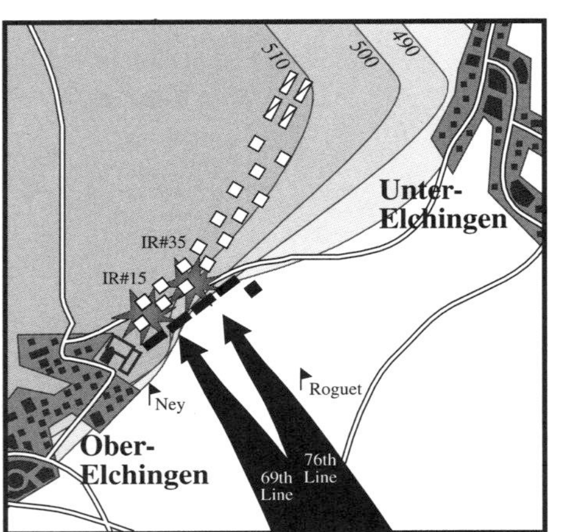

Roguet's brigade attacks the hinge of the Austrian line

Attempting to stand against the fire of Roguet's battalions was the brigade of two regiments of Bohemian infantrymen under *General-Feldwachtmeister* Genegdegh. Deployed in two lines immediately north of the village on the reverse side of the ground sloping towards the Danube, Genegdegh had placed the four fusilier battalions of Erzherzog Maximilien IR#35 on his left with the four fusilier battalions of Karl Riese IR#15 forming his right and were closest to the village. Both regiments were deployed with all battalions in columns of division, with two battalions on the front line with two battalions in the second line. By staggering the front and rear line battalions, the brigade gave the appearance of a mini-checkerboard. GM Genegdegh's command was the link from Elchingen to the rest of Riesch's troops who were deployed further to the north and east. By going straight for Genegdegh's infantry, Ney and Roguet were intent on shattering the hinge on which the Austrian line rested.

The regiment that formed the base of this hinge was Karl Riese IR#15. Three days earlier at Haslach-Jungingen, these Germans had been handled roughly and broken in a sudden charge made by Colonel Darricau and the 32nd *Ligne*. Although the battalions of Karl Riese IR#15 were eventually rallied and returned for the rest of the battle, the experience with the 32nd *Ligne* at Haslach-Jungingen had unnerved them. At Elchingen, instead of being threatened by cold steel, the same Austrian soldiers felt the sting of French lead. During the French advance up the Elchingen slope, the fusiliers of Karl Riese IR#15 stood in ranks while listening to the French drum cadence grow louder and louder. Following a brief exchange of fire with French *tirailleurs,* Roguet's disciplined battalions advanced. The French *fantassins* crested the ridge and poured volley after volley into the men of Karl Riese IR#15. Casualties mounted until the Austrian ranks were depleted of many soldiers and non-commissioned officers. Running short on small arms ammunition, their morale suddenly broke.[195]

The sudden exodus from the field of Karl Riese IR#15 soon left the four battalions of Erzherzog Maximilien IR#35 isolated in the face of Roguet's four

---

[193] S.H.A.T., C² 13.

[194] S.H.A.T., C² 4.

[195] Willbold, *Napoleons Feldzug um Ulm Die Schlacht von Elchingen*, p. 76. Riech's Austrians began their expedition from Ulm with only 40 rounds per man. When the ammunition carts could not get through the flooded countryside, the Austrian infantry knew that resupply was not possible.

battalions. Despite having the same number of battalions, the Austrians of Erzherzog Maximilien IR#35 immediately began to withdraw in an attempt to cover the flight of their comrades. The rupture of the Austrian line immediately north of Elchingen about 1:00 P.M., coupled with the sighting of Mahler's French infantry pouring across the Danube, convinced FML von Riesch to order a withdrawal. As Riesch later told the story: "Our flank was crumbling completely with the enemy in pursuit and more coming to their support. I thought that it was by this time pointless to continue the resistance, so a withdrawal was ordered to towards Thalfingen [Ulm]."[196]

Auguste de Colbert

With the Austrians pulling back, Roguet was quick to order his troops to pursue. Soon the brigade, consisting of four battalions deployed in line and one still in attack column, was advancing after Genegdegh's troops. To the right and rear of Roguet's brigade were the squadrons of Auguste de Colbert. Astride his favorite white horse, Colbert had caught sight of another brigade of Austrians beginning to withdraw to the northwest. Even though the enemy were moving off in square, Colbert sensed confusion in the enemy ranks and ordered his troopers to charge hell-for-leather for the Austrians. Swinging sabers above their heads and trumpets sounding the charge, the troopers shouted at the top of their lungs *"Vive l'Empereur!"* The furious charge by Colbert's light cavalrymen broke two fusilier battalions of Froon IR#54, as well as the grenadier battalion of Auersperg IR#24, capturing in the process General Malachias von Herrmann, *Oberstleutnants* Auerhammer and Colleti, two flags and 1,800 prisoners.[197] The price paid by Colbert's brigade for this triumph amounted to 55 officers and men killed or wounded out of the 150 combatants of the 3rd Hussars; the 10th *Chasseurs à cheval* lost just 20 of its 140 officers and other ranks.[198] Colbert had his horse shot out from under him, but quickly found another and continued to direct his cavalrymen. Detaching enough troopers to watch and escort the prisoners to the rear, Colbert then saw Roguet's brigade being attacked from the north by a squadron from Uhlanen-Regiment Schwarzenberg #2.

It had not been by mistake that Roguet had left the 1st Battalion of the 76th in column to protect the brigade's northern flank. Roguet's men had not advanced 500 yards past Elchingen to the west when the Schwarzenberg uhlans descended upon the brigade's right flank. The formed portion of the 1st Battalion of the 76th quickly changed into square to meet the attack. The uhlans failed to penetrated the square, then swarmed around the bayonets of the *fantassins* until an easier target caught their attention. The widely dispersed *tirailleurs* of the regiment were scurrying to form company squares when the uhlans suddenly galloped towards them. The skirmishers were endangered of being overrun when Colbert and the light cavalry came to their rescue. Seeing the enemy horse moving against Roguet's battle line, Auguste de Colbert ordered the 3rd Hussars and 10th *Chasseurs à cheval* to charge. In his after action report to Marshal Ney, Colbert described his timely intervention: "… I arrived in time to save by a fortunate charge all the *tirailleurs* of the 76th who were about to be cut down by 150 uhlans. Everyone did his part here, and I can assure you, *Monsieur le maréchal,* that if the enemy had not had a reserve, everyone would have been taken, in spite of the inferiority of our number."[199] Colbert and his two regiments overturned the squadron of the Schwarzenberg uhlans during which Colbert killed "at least one"[200] of the enemy. Reforming his regiments once more, the French light horse moved out to the northwest where they rounded up more Austrian prisoners.

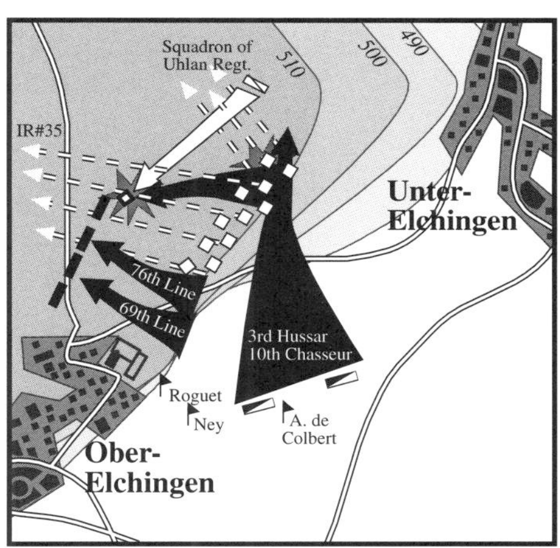

Colbert breaks through and sweeps aside the Schwarzenberg Uhlans

[196] S.H.A.T., C² 13; Willbold, *Napoleons Feldzug um Ulm Die Schlacht von Elchingen*, p. 74.
[197] Jeanne A. Ojala, *Auguste de Colbert* (Salt Lake City, 1979), p. 104.
[198] S.H.A.T., C² 482.
[199] Ojala, *Auguste de Colbert,* pp. 103-104.
[200] Ojala, *Auguste de Colbert,* pp. 103.

As Ney was launching Roguet's brigade up the hill to Elchingen about 11:00 A.M., General Mahler and the 3rd Infantry Division had just begun to cross the bridges over the Danube. These troops had broken camp before dawn on the 14th between Burlafingen and the Danube, about two miles southwest of the Elchingen bridge. They were present on the south bank when the battle began and had waited their turn to cross the rickety rebuilt bridge. By 1:00 P.M., Mahler had completed the passage of the Danube, deployed his entire division, and had advanced his 6,200 men with eight pieces of ordnance to the southwestern side of Elchingen, and cut the Thalfingen Road that directly linked Elchingen with Ulm. This arrival by Mahler had come about the same time that Riesch had ordered his column to quit the battlefield. Requesting instructions from Ney, Mahler received the corps commander's reply: the glory of this day's fight belonged to Loison and the 2nd Infantry Division. They would pursue and finish off the Austrians while Mahler and the 3rd Infantry Division remained in reserve.[201]

Some critics cite Ney's failure to employ the 3rd Infantry Division in a pursuit role as a huge lost opportunity to cut the Austrian escape route to Ulm and bag Riesch's entire command. The marshal's thinking was undoubtedly much more long-term. It was only 1:00 P.M., the battle was seemingly already won and the French cavalry regiments were rounding up prisoners by the thousands. Reports from the north indicated the approach of another Austrian column whose strength was unknown (this was Werneck's command). That Austrian column had, for the moment, been intercepted by Dupont's Division, with the outcome yet to be decided. Marshal Ney therefore decided that Loison's infantry could complete the infantry pursuit while the 6th Corps light cavalry along with the dragoons served as the mounted pursuing forces. By ordering Mahler and the 3rd Infantry Division to stand fast, Ney retained a strategic reserve for the 6th Corps. This was especially important since the 2nd Infantry Division and the 6th Corps light cavalry had lost heavily during the day's fighting. Also, Dupont's 1st Infantry Division had been hurt while destroying the Austrians at Haslach-Jungingen and were reportedly engaged again to the north of Elchingen. Even though Mahler and his troops had fought at Günzburg, they were the only relatively fresh formation of the 6th Corps. Therefore, to keep a reserve in hand should more Austrians appear, Ney prudently ordered that for the time being the 3rd Infantry Division would stay in place. Only after 3:00 P.M., when it became evident to the corps chief that no more Austrians were approaching the field, did Ney authorize Mahler to move out with his division along the river road that led to the southwest and Thalfingen.

Mahler's direct involvement in the battle was certainly not needed. As it turned out, the expertly led troops of Loison, Colbert and the dragoons under Colonels Lefèbvre-Desnouettes and Caulaincourt had been more than a match for Riesch's numerically superior Austrians. As the dispirited Austrians left the vicinity, their discipline began to break down. Officers and non-commissioned officers alike were unable to keep their formations from coming apart. Soon the fugitives from the regiments heavily damaged in the fighting were joined by the dispirited men from formations relatively undamaged during the day. The latter had inexplicably began leaving ranks as they departed the field of Elchingen in ever-increasing haste.[202]

As the defeated and disheartened Austrian survivors fled, the toll of the day's fighting began to be assessed. Of the 15,000 officers and men under Riesch's command to enter the fighting at Elchingen, some 4,000 were killed or wounded. In addition, French commands reported taking 3,000 Austrian prisoners, but did not capture any Austrian ordnance.[203] Interestingly enough, the Austrians admitted

---

[201] A. N., 137AP9, "Rapport sur le Bataille d'Elchingen," 14 October 1805.

[202] P. Birle, *Geschichte des französischen Kriegs von 1805*, Archiv Oberelchingen.

that 4,500 of Riesch's command were either prisoners or missing at Elchingen. The difference was, no doubt, due to the survivors being scattered across the Bavarian landscape, many of which never returned to Austrian ranks. By late in the evening of the 14th, only 2,500 men of Riesch's Column had found their way back to the Austrian lines on the Michelsberg. If counting only the men killed, wounded and captured on 14 October 1805, Riesch lost 8,500 officers and other ranks—or more than 56% of his command. If by counting only the Austrian survivors who returned to Ulm that evening, the losses suffered by Riesch's Column at Elchingen amount to a staggering 83%![204] Regardless of the method chosen to calculate the losses sustained by Riesch's whitecoats, one thing is clear: like the outcomes at Wertingen, Günzburg and Haslach-Jungingen, the Austrians were cut to pieces at the Battle of Elchingen.

After-action reports from the French units engaged at Elchingen establish their losses at 1,589. Among Loison's infantry, General Villatte's brigade had suffered the most casualties. In storming across the bridge, then marching uphill, taking the village, convent garden and convent of Elchingen, the 6th *Légère* had a staggering 60% of its officers put out of action—an unmistakable example of officers 'leading from the front.' Meanwhile, the 39th *Ligne* had six officers wounded. In Roguet's brigade, the 69th took most of the casualties during the fire fight with Genegdegh's brigade. One-third of the 18 company commanders in Colonel Brun's regiment were hit, including one killed. In the same regiment, six lieutenants and sub-lieutenants were either killed or wounded. The 76th suffered the fewest casualties of any regiment in the 2nd Infantry Division, with only one officer wounded. While the 19th and 25th Dragoons lost less than a dozen men and no officers, the 18th Dragoons under Lefèbvre-Desnouettes had one *chef d'escadron* and one captain wounded along with three sub-lieutenants. The French cavalry brigade that suffered the highest percentage losses was that of Colbert. Of the 290 officers and troopers that were in the saddle at the beginning of the battle, only 200 remained at the day's end. In total, the French losses amounted to just under 20% of the slightly more than 8,000 men actually engaged at Elchingen.[205]

These casualties did not include the almost separate combat that took place on the far northern end of the battlefield between Werneck's Column and Dupont's reinforced 1st Infantry Division. Upon hearing the guns at Elchingen, Werneck had turned his ponderous 9,000-man column laden with the army's heavy artillery, and slowly marched the two miles from Albeck to Elchingen in order to come to the assistance of Riesch. As Werneck approached the field, he came in contact with Dupont, who was also coming to the assistance of his countrymen. Dupont had moved south to Elchingen from Brenz through Langenau, and one mile northeast of the village, the opposing commands clashed briefly. In that ensuing fight, the 9th *Légère* and 32nd *Ligne* charged and broke the Austrian infantry while the 96th *Ligne* received in square and repulsed several charges by Austrian cavalry. When the clash ended, both sides withdrew—Werneck towards the northwest and Albeck, while Dupont pulled back to the northeast and Langenau. Casualties were light on both sides. Dupont's forces suffered only two officers wounded—both of them company commanders in *"l'Incomparable"* 9th *Légère*.[206] More important than the casualties were the results: Werneck's Column was turned away by Dupont, and was unable to link up with Riesch, or continue his march back to Ulm. Also, if Austrian morale wasn't already low enough, the outcome of the battle further

---

[203] S.H.A.T., C² 4, 13 and 14; A. N., 137AP9, "Rapport sur le Bataille d'Elchingen," 14 October 1805.

[204] S.H.A.T., C² 16 and 470; Willbold, *Napoleons Feldzug um Ulm Die Schlacht von Elchingen*, p. 76.

[205] S.H.A.T., C² 16, 472 and 482.

[206] S.H.A.T., C² 4 and 16; *Journal des opérations du 6ᵉ corps.*

depressed it to the bottomless depths from which no army could recover.

So ended the battle for which Marshal Ney would later receive his title, *duc d'Elchingen.* Employing only 8,000 of his highly trained and expertly led troops, the redheaded marshal had taken the bit between his teeth and displayed the finest traits of French offensive tactical leadership in directing his troops to an impressive victory. Ney showed that he had both the moral courage and skill to attack a numerically superior enemy who had the considerable advantages of both imposing natural terrain while also being ensconced in strong man-made cover. The marshal knew that with experienced, educated officers directing well-trained troops, he could ask for and get results that others might think to be impossible.[207] If his men could carry such a formidable position as Elchingen against a foe who possessed a numerical superiority of two to one, Ney must have believed that his troops could accomplish anything. The future *duc d'Elchingen* would get to test that theory the very next day against the Austrians holding fortified positions on the Michelsberg plateau.

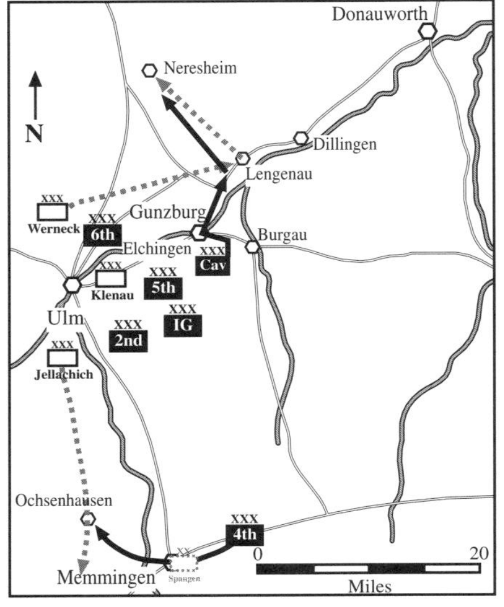

Situation at Ulm as of late 14 October 1805

Murat conducts "The Glorious Ride" as the Encirclement at Ulm is Completed

Johann Sigmund Count von Riesch, the 55-year-old Austrian general in command of the II Column of the Austrian Army of Swabia, may not have realized how, with four times as many battalions and almost twice as many combatants as the French, he could have lost the Battle of Elchingen. Reporting back to General Mack at army headquarters in the late evening hours of 14 October, Riesch's command, once thought to be powerful, had ceased to exist. The pitiful remnants of Riesch's Column returning to the Michelsberg plateau served as a vivid testament to the desperate situation facing Mack's command, and symbolized not only the fate that awaited that Austrian army, but also the utter disaster that had already taken place on the same day far away in Memmingen on the south bank of the Danube.

Marshal Soult and his superbly trained 4th Corps reinforced by the 2nd Dragoon Division under Walther had tramped west from Landsberg towards Memmingen along a road that carried them through a vast pine forest heavily laden with freshly fallen snow. The footsore French soldiers were marching on Memmingen in accordance with the Emperor's instructions to cut the Austrian army's anticipated line of retreat from Ulm to the Tyrol. When Soult's French arrived in front of Memmingen on the 13th, they found the place held by FML Spangen and his division of 5,000 Austrians. Spangen's command consisted of nine battalions supported by nine 3-pounder guns. The infantrymen were the 1st, 3rd and 4th (Fusilier) Battalions of the Galician regiment Czartorisky-Saggusco IR#9, all four fusilier battalions and the battalion of grenadiers from the Moravian regiment Josef Mittrowsky IR#40, plus the 5th, or Grenadier, Battalion from another Galician formation, Beaulieu IR#58. Soult rapidly deployed a covering force around the city while the rest of the 4th Corps pushed past Memmingen and made for the Iller. Soult then called upon Spangen to have his men lay down their arms. With

[207] Ney's victory at Elchingen left a lasting impression on Méneval. Witnessing the battle, Napoleon's private secretary wrote: "I can remember my stupefaction on looking at the sinuous ramparts of the village of Elchingen, rising in an amphitheater above the Danube, surrounded by walled gardens and houses rising above one above the other. These gardens and houses—filled with troops, and from which constant firing proceeded—were topped by the vast buildings of the fortified abbey which was vigorously defended by formidable artillery. Marshal Ney won his title of Duke of Elchingen there, and fully deserved it." *Memoirs of the Baron Méneval,* vol. 1, p. 390.

many times his numbers arrayed against him, and with no help in sight, Spangen agreed to Soult's terms. About the same time that Riesch's troops were hightailing it from Elchingen on the 14th, Spangen's men were going into the bag at Memmingen.

The catch of prisoners at Memmingen was a good haul for Marshal Soult, but they were only a fraction of the larger prize still waiting to be snatched up at Ulm. When Soult arrived before Memmingen, he had already received Napoleon's dispatch of 20 vendémiaire (12 October) anticipating that the forces in Memmingen would prove small and fairly certain that the place was ill-prepared to withstand a siege. The Emperor urged Soult to move "like lightning" for Ulm as what was getting ready to happen there "would prove to be ten times more famous than Marengo."[208] Pushing his advance elements to the west as hard as possible, Soult reached Ochsenhausen on the 14th, barely missing Jellachich's Column as it retreated south to the Tyrol.

The events of the 14th had convinced almost everyone at Austrian army headquarters in Ulm that their position was untenable. FML Abele begged his commander-in-chief to take the remaining forces around Ulm and break out towards the Tyrol. When Abele had finished with pleadings, he described Mack's furious reaction:

> [He] screamed and shouted, behaving in a way that was truly insane. In his fury he advanced on me in a threatening manner, and I feared that I was about to suffer violence at his hands. I backed towards the door with the intention of making my escape, but he came after me and got in the way..."[209]

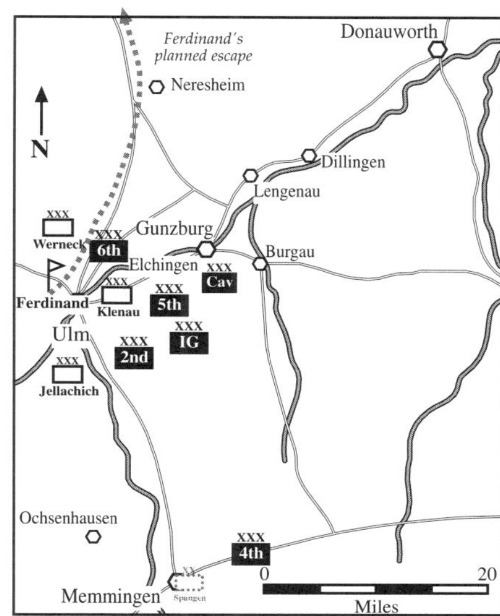

Ferdinand's planned escape route from Ulm

Somewhat regaining his composure, Mack retorted with his old belief: the position of Ulm was impregnable and the army could hold out until the Russians arrived.

Archduke Ferdinand had heard enough. He decided that he was not going to stay in Ulm to await capture. Instead, he declared that he "must deprive the French of the glory of capturing a Habsburg."[210] Together with Prince Schwarzenberg and four other generals, the nobles plotted their escape. They selected 12 squadrons numbering about 2,000 troopers to escort them in the break out from Ulm to the north along the Geislingen road. Galloping out from the Austrian lines at midnight on 14/15 October, swiftly moving past encircling French forces, Ferdinand believed that he could join up with Werneck and slip away into Bohemia. Once arrived in Bohemia, Ferdinand thought that he could move further east, gathering other scattered detachments such as Kienmayer (whose position was not known to the Archduke), and maybe join the Russians on the lower Danube. For Ferdinand, there was one serious problem with his plan: he did not calculate that the French would immediately respond, nor the determination of Murat to swiftly run to ground the Austrian detachment.

The movements of Ferdinand's cavalry were reported to Imperial headquarters. Even though Napoleon was, at this time, unaware as to the exact whereabouts of Werneck's lumbering column that contained the Austrian army's unwieldy baggage and heavy field guns, he ordered Murat to take up the pursuit of Ferdinand while other troops on the north bank were to pin the Austrians to the Ulm position. The troops given Murat to run Ferdinand's Column to ground

---

208 Napoléon to Soult, *Correspondance*, number 9374.

209 Krauss, *1805. Der Feldzug von Ulm*, p. 161.

210 Esposito and Elting, *A Military History and Atlas of the Napoleonic Wars*, text to Map number 50.

consisted of the brigade of *carabiniers* from Nansouty's 1st Heavy Cavalry Division, the *Chasseurs à cheval de la Garde*, the 1st Dragoon Division under Klein, the light cavalry brigade consisting of the 13th and 21st *Chasseurs à cheval* from Lannes' 5th Corps and Oudinot's *Grenadiers de la Réserve*. Along the way, Murat was to pick up Dupont's reinforced command.[211]

Murat pushed his troops with zeal. When firing was heard around Langenau late on the 15th, Klein and his dragoons rode to the sound of the guns to find Werneck's unsupported cavalry battling Dupont's soldiers. The Austrians quickly broke off the action, but Murat's cavalry had discovered what proved to be Werneck's rearguard. When Murat's report reached Napoleon that evening, the Emperor then realized that his lines of communication were exposed, including ammunition trains and the valuable military chest. Murat was ordered to hunt down all Austrians on the north bank.

The 16th dawned with Werneck receiving an order from Ferdinand instructing him to march to Neresheim. Werneck obeyed, only to have his rearguard overwhelmed by Murat's pursuing forces. The resulting clash at Neresheim once again saw the 9th *Légère* of Dupont's Division distinguish itself again, along with the 1st Hussars attached to the same division, the 20th Dragoons of Klein's Division and the *Chasseurs à cheval de la Garde.* During this fight, the 20th Dragoons charged and broke the Palatinal-Hussaren-Regiment #12, with *brigadier* Blondel capturing the Austrian's regimental standard in the process. Another Austrian standard was captured by Colonel Morland's *Chasseurs à cheval de la Garde* when they shattered the Cüirassier-Regiment Mack #6. When the day was over, French forces had captured one Austrian general, two flags and 1,000 men.[212]

The following day, Murat caught up with Werneck's exhausted infantry at Trochtelfingen. Hopelessly outnumbered and demoralized, most of Werneck's infantry were defeated after a short battle on the 17th, in which they laid down their arms. Included in the regiments that surrendered at Trochtelfingen were the remnants of Erbach IR#42. The following day, the Austrian baggage train and heavy artillery were gobbled up between Ellwangen and Oettingen, their clay-laden wheels making it impossible for them to escape Murat's cavalry. Also among the troops that surrender on the 18th were three fusilier battalions as well as the grenadier battalion of Stuart IR#18. Being held prisoners of war did not sit well with many officers and men of that Bohemian regiment. On 19 October, five officers and 300 men of Stuart IR#18 escaped from the prisoner column and made their way to Bohemia.[213]

The pursuit, referred to in the *Grande Armée* as *"La glorieuse chevauchée,"* continued through the 20th. When Murat had concluded the ride, his command had bagged between 12,000 to 13,000 prisoners, 101 pieces of artillery, 500 wagons and carts, 11 flags, seven general officers and the treasury wagons of Mack's army.[214]

The overwhelming success enjoyed by Murat's men against Werneck's Column assisted Ferdinand in making good his escape. While the French were running down and rounding up Werneck's numerous troops and heavy guns, the faster-moving column under Ferdinand was high-tailing it to safety. Ferdinand's Austrians rode north, pushing their horses as hard as they could. They passed through Nördlingen, Nürnberg, Kreussen, Bayreuth and Weissenstadt, arriving in Bohemia on the Eger River at midnight on 22 October 1805. When the cavalrymen of this command reached the city of Eger, they had traveled 229 miles in only eight

---

[211] S.H.A.T., C^2 240.

[212] S.H.A.T., C^2 4.

[213] Willbold, *Napoleons Feldzug um Ulm Die Schlacht von Elchingen*, p. 85.

[214] S.H.A.T., C^2 4, 14, 240 and 470; also, see: Napoléon to Murat, *Correspondance*, numbers 9386, 9387 and 9388. The 101 pieces of captured Austrian ordnance amounted to 14 12-pounders, 38 6-pounders, 19 3-pounders and 30 howitzers.

days, arriving with Archduke Ferdinand, generals Schwarzenberg and Kolowrat-Krakowsky, along with paroled generals Hohenzollern, Dinnersberg and Vogel, some 1,694 cavalrymen, 400 mounted artillerists and 163 artillery train personnel.[215] Turning his command over to FZM Johann Karl Kolowrat, Ferdinand hastened to Vienna to report to Emperor Francis.

What Ferdinand could not carry with him to his master were the details concerning the rapidly deteriorating situation facing the remainder of Mack's army at Ulm. When the 15th dawned under a cold and miserable rain that seemed to depict the morale of the Austrian army, Mack arranged his dispirited troops within their defensive perimeter on the Michelsberg heights. Eight Austrian battalions were positioned in the front line entrenchments. Of these, two were stationed at the brick cottage with two more manning the redoubts (or forts) on the Michelsberg, while the remaining four were deployed along the rest of the works crowning the heights. The utterly demoralized and shattered remnants of Riesch's Column were posted as far away from the front lines as possible by standing just outside the city. Since Schwarzenberg had departed with Ferdinand and 12 squadrons of cavalry, Mack named FML Count Klenau to take command of Schwarzenberg's Column and direct the active defense.[216]

After spending the night of the 14th/15th in Elchingen and listening to all the after-action reports of Ney's battle, Napoleon was determined to press his army's advantage by ordering an assault of the Austrian positions on the Michelsberg. The Emperor reasoned that if these works could be taken, the Austrian army would be totally compromised, forcing Mack to quickly surrender without a formal siege. To obtain a clear view of Ney's assault, Napoleon rode to a nearby hill, escorted by a 25-man detachment of the *Chasseurs à cheval de la Garde* and some members of Napoleon's *Maison Militaire.* Suddenly, an Austrian battery opened fire on the distinguished group. Refusing to retreat under this fire, Napoleon turned to de Ségur and said: "Take my *chasseurs,* and go and bring back some prisoners."[217]

Ségur

Meanwhile, Ney had been given orders to carry the Michelsberg. For the attack, the marshal selected General Malher and his 3rd Infantry Division. Malher had available for action three of his four regiments with the 59th *Ligne* not on the field. To make the assault, Malher arranged the division in two lines. The brigade under *général de brigade* Marcognet formed the leading element, with the two battalions of the 25th *Légère* on the left and two battalions of the 27th *Ligne* on the right. The second, or reserve, line consisted of the reduced brigade under *général de brigade* de Labassée. The general's command consisted of only Colonel de Lamartinière's two battalions of the 50th *Ligne*, the least injured of any regiment in Malher's command. Present at Günzburg, the 50th had lent fire support while the 25th *Légère* attempted to repair the bridge. However, due to positioning, Colonel de Lamartinière's regiment had suffered no officer casualties at that battle.[218]

---

[215] Willbold, *Napoleons Feldzug um Ulm Die Schlacht von Elchingen*, p. 85.

[216] Willbold, *Napoleons Feldzug um Ulm Die Schlacht von Elchingen*, p. 88.

[217] *Memoirs of Ségur,* p. 185; S.H.A.T., C^2 240. The detachment of the "Favored Children" led by Ségur were defeated under the eyes of Napoleon by a squadron of Austrian uhlans. When the detachment of the *Chasseurs à cheval de la Garde* broke and fled, Ségur and one of the brigadiers remained behind in a heroic attempt to stem the Austrian pursuit. Even though the detachment of Guard cavalrymen were outnumbered in the contest, Napoleon was furious with the poor performance of his hand-picked light cavalrymen, and decided to make an example of them. Except for Ségur and the brigadier that fought alongside him, the entire detachment were transferred on 17 October to Murat, who was instructed to draft the entire lot, which included one lieutenant, into the *Corps des Réserves de Cavalerie.*

[218] S.H.A.T., C^2 16; *Journal des opérations du 6e corps;* Martinien, *Tableaux des Officiers Tués et Blessés*, p. 231.

The Michelsberg heights from the north: today the trees hide a substantial fortress built in the 1830s, then it was covered with Austrian earthworks

Following artillery bombardment of 30 minutes, Malher's six battalions began moving up the muddy Michelsberg slope in attack columns at approximately 3:30 P.M. As the bluecoated battalions got closer to Austrian lines, the French artillery fire lifted. General Séroux had been firing his guns against the Austrian works on top of the heights. The cannonballs from the four 12-pounders proved particularly effective since their crews could work efficiently without being subjected to counter battery fire. It will be remembered that the Austrian heavy artillery had been evacuated from Ulm with Werneck, and the 6-pounders that remained in the redoubts and fortified lines did not have the range to duel with Séroux's ordnance. The French heavy guns did noticeable damage to the partially completed works on the Michelsberg. The workmanship on the sector of the line that Malher was attacking had not been good enough to prevent some collapsing due to the rain and snow. When fire from the French ordnance began to hit the timbers, the cover became almost worthless.[219]

Infused by the army's prior success, Malher's men enthusiastically ascended the Michelsberg. Unable to stop the onrushing Frenchmen, the whitecoats were swept off their defending works. The strongest Austrian redoubt fell to Colonel de Lamartinière and his two battalions of the 50th *Ligne*. Storming the fortification in the face of canister fire from numerous 6-pounders, the 50th went up and over the smashed remnants of the redoubt's timbered walls, bayoneting the infantrymen and gunners who resisted. With the Austrian lines broken, Ney rode to the top of the Michelsberg, and together with Malher, had a clear view to Ulm. The French leaders could see a growing crowd of Austrian soldiers apparently without formation and order. As Malher's men were reorganizing themselves following their successful attack, *général de division* Mathieu Dumas, the 2nd *aide-major général de la Grande Armée* and *maréchal des logis* to the Emperor, appeared with orders from Napoleon.[220] The instructions carried by Mathieu Dumas to Ney were simple: suspend your advance long enough for Marshal Lannes to bring up one of his divisions, then continue the attack. Ney, however, believed that he had a fleeting opportunity that would pass if he waited too long. With the Austrian lines broken, Ney wanted to press his advantage, regardless of the numerical odds against him. The redhead's response to Dumas was short: "Tell the Emperor that there is not enough time to await reinforcements. On this day, glory is not to be divided!"[221] He turned his horse and ordered General Malher to resume his division's advance.

Claparède

Ney would have been disappointed if he had waited for Lannes to arrive with one of his divisions. Even though Lannes had persuaded Napoleon to allow him to go to Ney's assistance, the request for action by the fiery commander of the 5th Corps was undoubtedly due to Lannes being anxious for action. Lannes had been present at the end of the combat at Wertingen and had only a small portion of Suchet's 3rd Infantry Division across the Danube and deployed for action when he went to Napoleon with his plea. Returning to his men, Lannes had only *général de brigade* Claparède and the single regiment of his brigade—the 17th *Légère*—waiting for orders. Giving the signal to advance, Lannes, Claparède and their mounted staffs urged on the two battalions of light infantrymen under Colonel Dominique-Honoré-Antoine-Marie Vedel. Quickly ascending the heights and swarming over the Austrians and the three 6-pounder guns in the redoubt closest to the Danube, the French tide reached its crest. The 17th's national colors were clearly visible

---

[219] S.H.A.T., *Journal des opérations du 6e corps;* Willbold, *Napoleons Feldzug um Ulm Die Schlacht von Elchingen*, p. 89. The collapse of the shoody-built works confirmed the observations made by Colonel Bianchi several days earlier.
[220] S.H.A.T., C[2] 4 and 470.
[221] S.H.A.T., *Journal des opérations du 6e corps; Memoirs of Ségur,* pp. 187-188.

from on top of the Austrian bastion as streams of fugitives in whitecoats made for the city.[222]

With the French advancing, Captain Voith of Mack's staff rallied elements of several battalions and, together with units in reserve, formed a quick plan to deal with Ney's and Lannes' battalions. The advance by Malher was checked when the Austrians put up a cohesive front at the Ulm city walls. Meanwhile, five Austrian battalions consisting of all four fusilier battalions and the grenadier battalion of Froon IR#54, were thrown against the isolated 17th *Légère*.[223] The 17th manfully fought to hang on to the ground that they had won. With overwhelming numbers of the whitecoats swirling around them, the light infantrymen finally gave way and recoiled down the heights, leaving the 6-pounders that they had temporarily captured. In addition, the 17th *Légère* left behind some 320 officers and men as prisoners, including Colonel Vedel, while suffering another 157 killed and wounded.[224] These men were, however, freed on the 20th when the Austrian army surrendered.

It was 6:00 P.M. when the last gun shots were being fired as Ney's troops fell back to the top of the Michelsberg. Under a torrential rain, the Austrians gathered within the confines of Ulm. An Austrian eyewitness in Ulm wrote about the situation as it appeared on 15 October 1805:

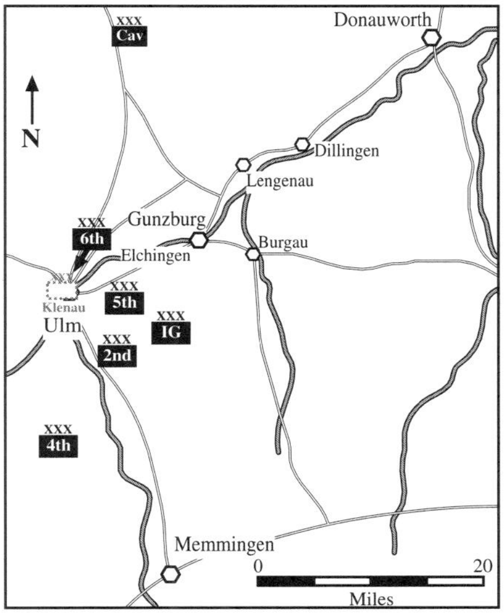

> From the foot of the Michelsberg, over the whole distance of the quiet valley … all the outer entrenchments were in the hands of the enemy by 8 o'clock that evening. From the combat earlier in the day came into the city the wounded; carts and carts, emaciated horses and abandoned guns blocked the streets, preventing communication. All over the city lay hundreds of half-starved Austrian soldiers. Every baker worked only for the military, and each one while under the protection of six to eight grenadiers. The soldiers wore tattered clothes, soaked by rain and snow and many were without shoes. While officers sought the comforts of the taverns, the common soldiers went from house to house begging the citizens for bread. Dead horses lay in the streets along with other filth. The condition of the wounded was far more pitiful still; more than 4,000 crowded the hospitals, from which 15 to 20 died daily.
>
> The misery and deplorable condition, in which so fine an army languished, caused the authorities and the citizens to call for assistance. The general-in-chief von Mack could see from the window of army headquarters this awful situation that caused the partial demoralization of the army.[225]

Ney closes in:
Ulm is virtually under siege

Another writer describing Ulm said:

> The appearance of the city was appalling. Many thousands of men made their quarters on the open streets, where they cooked and slept. Carts and teams were standing everywhere. More

[222] S.H.A.T., *Journal des opérations du 5e corps.* The other heights nearby where taken by Suchet.

[223] Two of the fusilier battalions of Froon IR#54 had been eviscerated at Haslach-Jungingen on 11 October. Also, see: Willbold, *Napoleons Feldzug um Ulm Die Schlacht von Elchingen*, p. 89.

[224] S.H.A.T., C^{2} 16 and 481; *Journal des opérations du 5e corps.*

[225] Willbold, *Napoleons Feldzug um Ulm Die Schlacht von Elchingen*, p. 90.

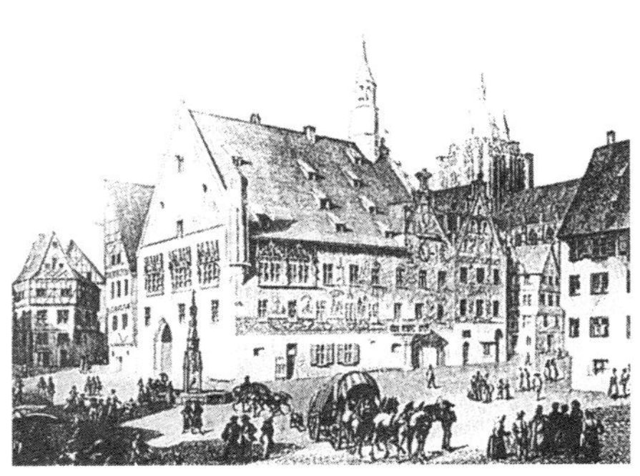

The streets of Ulm in 1805—the famous Cathredral spire has not been completed yet

> than 30 dead horses were littered about, for the gates were shut and they could not be carried away. The whole city was a latrine, permeated with a pestilential stench.[226]

The condition of the survivors in Ulm reflected the Austrian experience throughout the campaign. The various detachments of Mack's army had been humiliated in every engagement, and when it came time for the French army to dash itself to pieces on the "anvil" of Ulm, Marshal Ney, Generals Malher, Marcognet and de Labassée at the head of only six battalions of the 6th Corps, while Claparède and two battalions of the 17th *Légère*, had proved to be enough to carry the famed Michelsberg plateau and forced the Austrian army to retreat into Ulm. The stage was now set for the conclusion of the Ulm campaign.

Napoleon's Strategic Triumph Completed—The Capitulation of Ulm

On 16 October, Napoleon opened a bombardment of the defenseless city, then sent the staff officer Philippe-Paul de Ségur to demand the Austrian surrender. Traveling through a stormy, cold and rain-soaked night, Ségur reached Austrian lines, then was taken blindfolded to Mack's headquarters. Reaching his final destination at 3:00 A.M. on 17 October 1805, Ségur met with Mack. Ségur found the commanding general to be "tall, old and pale."[227]

Mack was in no position to refuse Napoleon's demand, but the Austrian general tried to bargain for some additional time in which he hoped that the long-awaited Russian army might make its appearance. His counter offer to Napoleon was that if an Austro-Russian force large enough to raise the siege did not appear by 25 October, then the Austrian army would be delivered on that day, with the officers free on parole while the men would march back to France and into captivity. Napoleon, in countering Mack's term, granted eight days, beginning with 15 October.[228] When news of the resolution spread through Ulm, Austrian morale completed disintegrated. The rank and file who previously were beggars suddenly turned into bands of marauding thieves. In the meantime, their officers passed the time in taverns, escaping the harsh memories of the campaign with many stiff drinks and soft, willing wenches.[229]

As if nature had seen enough and wanted to hurry the episode to a merciful conclusion, a horrendous storm struck on the night of the 18th, completely outdoing the appalling weather of the previous two weeks. Torrential rains caused the Danube to overflow, and the flood carried away thousands of Austrian corpses that had not yet been buried. "They must have learned in Vienna of the misfortunes of [Mack's] Swabian army," wrote Jean-Baptiste Barrès of the Imperial Guard, "for the bodies were floating down the river like the débris of some wrecked vessel."[230]

That evening, couriers arrived from Marshal Murat, advising Napoleon of the cavalryman's triumph against Werneck. On 19 October Mack was summoned by Napoleon to Imperial headquarters in Elchingen. Informed by the Emperor of Werneck's fate, Mack immediately agreed to surrender Ulm on the following day on two conditions. The first was that Ney's 6th Corps remain immobilized at Ulm until the 25th; the second was that a formal declaration be made stating that the

---

[226] Krauss, *1805. Der Feldzug von Ulm*, p. 477.
[227] *Memoirs of Ségur,* p. 194.
[228] *Memoirs of Ségur,* pp. 198-199.
[229] Krauss, *1805. Der Feldzug von Ulm*, pp. 478-479.
[230] *Memoirs of a French Napoleonic Officer: Jean-Baptiste Barrès,* p. 66.

Russian army was too far away in order to save the Austrian forces at Ulm. Napoleon accepted both conditions.

At 2:00 P.M. on 20 October 1805, with the French corps of Marmont, Soult, Lannes, Ney and the Imperial Guard drawn up on the Michelsberg and forming a vast amphitheater, the Austrian army was delivered into captivity. Marching out of Ulm were seven *Feldmarschall-Leutnants* (FMLs), eight *General-Feldwachtmeisters* (GMs), 51 depleted battalions numbering less than 20,000 combatants, 18 and one-quarter squadrons totaling 3,000 troopers and 273 artillerists with 67 pieces of ordnance, 50 ammunition wagons and numerous baggage vehicles.[231] Add to this number the column under General Jellachich that was overtaken at Dornbirn on 14 November by Marshal Augereau's newly arrived 7th Corps, and the total number of Austrians casualties suffered in the Ulm campaign becomes staggering. Of the 72,000 officers and men that crossed the Inn with Mack at the beginning of hostilities, only FML Kienmeyer's Column had escaped complete destruction. In addition to these men and the few horsemen that escaped from Ulm with Archduke Ferdinand, the total loss for Mack's army came to over 60,000 troops, 192 pieces of ordnance and 90 stands of colors.[232]

Napoleon receives the Austrian standards at Ulm

Such a resounding victory in such a short period of time had never before been witnessed. Napoleon's lightning campaign had been largely an improvised one as the Emperor constantly redirected his commands due to changing circumstances. Despite Napoleon's leadership, the combination of constant forced marches and improvisation, had left the rear areas of the *Grande Armée* littered with stragglers and deserters. Nevertheless, the overwhelming majority of Napoleon's soldiers displayed the tough fabric of which the army was made. It had been the début of history's first modern army in the hands of a Great Captain. For Europe, it was the first blitzkrieg.

"I am the unfortunate General Mack."

[231] S.H.A.T., C[2] 14 and 470. The 67 pieces of captured Austrian ordnance at Ulm consisted of the following: 43 were 6-pounders, 22 were 3-pounders and two howitzers.

[232] S.H.A.T., C[2] 14 and 470. According to the French document in carton C[2] 470 entitled *"État des Bouches à feu, Voitures, Munitions et Principaux effets d'artillerie pris en Allemagne en aus la campagne le au XIV,"* the captured Austrian ordnance totals were detailed throughout this chapter, and were as follows: nine at Wertingen, six at Günzburg, nine at Memmingen, 101 in Murat's *"La glorieuse chevauchée,"* and 67 at Ulm.

PART IV

The Austerlitz Campaign of 1805

Horse Artillery of the Imperial Guard

Chapter VI
"My Eagles Have Never Suffered Dishonor"

"Have them say that the Russians are a nation of barbarians and that their strength lies in their cunning." —Napoleon to Fouche, 30 May 1805, regarding instructions for the press.[1]

Napoleon, Prussia and the Third Coalition

Napoleon's astounding, swift campaign of Ulm produced unexpected complications in foreign relations with Prussia. While the Emperor never seriously thought that Prussia would ally with him against the members of the Third Coalition, he certainly wanted to keep Prussia out of the war until Austria or Russia (or both) could be defeated. In the summer of 1805, as many of the dynastic houses of Europe were mobilizing their armies for yet another war against France, Napoleon sought to politically isolate Prussia and keep her out of the Third Coalition. To accomplish this, the Emperor went to Prussia with an offer. He proposed the territory of Hanover in exchange for the Prussian court acting as mediators between the warring factions. Under conditions set forth by Napoleon—which included the acknowledgment of Holland and Switzerland as republics, recognition of the Kingdom of Italy, acknowledgment of the accession of Piedmont and Genoa to the French Empire as well as free disposal of Parma and Placentia by France—King Frederick William III of Prussia would establish an equilibrium in Europe and, thereby, avoid bloodshed. For this mediation, Prussia would receive Hanover which France had occupied in 1803 after the British broke the Peace of Amiens.[2]

Frederick William III

The proud Prussians had sat out the wars against France for the last 10 years, but desired to expand their kingdom to the west. Napoleon knew that Prussia wanted the fertile northern German territory very badly, and the French Emperor decided to see just how eager the King of Prussia was to pounce on the idea of acquiring Hanover. Frederick William III was a modest and well meaning man, but an intellectual midget and hopelessly irresolute. When Napoleon came calling in the form of his negotiators Duroc and Laforest with the offer of Hanover-for-mediation, Frederick William III could not decide what to do. He wanted to snap up Napoleon's offer, and at the same time save face with the rest of his monarchical contemporaries. The Prussian king's mind was made up for him by his chief minister, Karl August von Hardenberg, who hatched a scheme by which Prussia could hopefully acquire Hanover without appearing to be allied with France.

Hardenberg proposed that Frederick William III announce to the members of the Third Coalition that Prussia was willing to fight France for Hanover, but saw no reason to go to war when equilibrium in Europe could be resolved peaceably. Additionally, Frederick William III would declare that any nation not accepting the terms for equilibrium would find themselves opposed by Prussia, and any nation who was in favor would find an ally in Berlin. Hardenberg hoped that his scheme would have the net effect of gaining the territory Prussia so desperately coveted, and Frederick William III would have the added benefit of playing the role of

---

[1] Léon Lecestre, *Lettres inédites de Napoléon 1er (an VIII-1815)*, 2 volumes (Paris, 1897), vol. 1, p. 51.

[2] Napoléon to Berthier, *Correspondance,* number 6777; Napoléon to Mortier, *Correspondance*, numbers 6809 and 6981.

European peacemaker. Hardenberg reasoned that, due to the fearsome reputation of the Prussian army with the various courts of Europe, the proposition advanced by Prussia would be given serious consideration. This would cause the members of the Third Coalition to think twice before crossing Berlin over this issue.

So mesmerized by the idea of gaining Hanover and with their scheme for acquisition, Hardenberg and Frederick William III misjudged allied reaction, as well as being completely blind to why Napoleon made the offer in the first place. Napoleon's diplomacy was simply nothing more than the old game of 'divide and conquer.' Realistically, the offer of Hanover was bait designed to keep the Prussians on the sidelines until the time came that Napoleon could deal with Frederick William III from a position of strength. In the meantime, the French Emperor knew that he had his hands full with the Russian and Austrian armies.

After receiving the details of the peace initiative from Berlin, it was not at all surprising that the members of the Third Coalition were unanimous in giving it the cold shoulder. To the kings that still clung to the ways of the *ancien régime*, equilibrium in Europe was not going to be on the usurper's terms. Emperor Francis of Austria was opposed to the measure mainly because the Austrian court was receiving huge sums of English gold by putting troops into the field. Additionally, Austria wished to recoup the territorial losses suffered in Italy during the wars of the French Revolution. No one in the English Government could stand to see Bonaparte on the throne of France, let alone allow Holland or Switzerland to be independent, nor see Hanover slip into Prussian hands. Meanwhile, the territorial considerations were the least of the objections raised by Tsar Alexander. Although the Tsar wanted to see French expansion halted, the Saint Petersburg court joined the rest of the Third Coalition members in unanimous opposition to the independence of Holland and Switzerland without some way of being able to later subvert those revolutionary governments and supplant them with a restored monarchy. To put it simply, members of the Third Coalition viewed the French Revolution and its 'product,' Napoleon Bonaparte, as nothing more than a temporary interruption of the rightful rule of kings. These monarchs took the stance that the sooner Napoleon could be disposed of, the sooner the glories of the *ancien régime* could be visited once again upon the peoples of France, Italy, Holland and Switzerland.

Hardenberg

Faced with these strong objections, yet desiring to gain Hanover more than ever, Berlin told Napoleon's negotiators that everything in the equilibrium proposal was going well, except the manner in which the independence of Switzerland and Holland was to be understood and agreed to by all parties. Apart from the fact that the status of the talks was a boldfaced lie, Hardenberg had to find a way to extend the talks in the hopes that something favorable for Prussia could develop. He therefore told Duroc and Laforest that the language in the agreement required by the members of the Third Coalition must permit the enemies of France to effect counterrevolutions in Switzerland and Holland.[3] This was a situation to which Napoleon clearly would not agree. The objections and counter-objections went back and forth until the end of September, by which time the majority of the *Grande Armée* was already across the Rhine. With the opposing armies converging in Italy and Bavaria, negotiations became suspended and Prussia resumed its neutral stance.

Prussian conduct in this matter sent an unmistakable signal to Napoleon confirming what his negotiators already suspected—that the Prussian king was a weakling. If he wasn't, Napoleon asked, then why hadn't he placed the Prussian army on a war footing months ago? Now across the Rhine with his army, Napoleon

[3]S.H.A.T., C^2 13.

knew that, just as he had done in the old school days at Brienne, he was going to have to prove himself to be better than his contemptuous adversaries.

Napoleon wasn't the only one who noted Frederick William III's irresolute personality. Tsar Alexander thought that he could persuade the King of Prussia to join the coalition by first massing Russian armies on his borders, then attempted to intimidate Frederick William III by advising him that he would have to declare for the coalition either out of his own free will or by force if the Tsar ordered his Russian troops to take the shortcut to the Danube by traversing Prussian territory without Prussian permission. However, by such conduct Tsar Alexander pushed Frederick William III too far. The threat of destructive columns of marauding Russians passing through the eastern Prussian territory of Silesia without asking Berlin's permission prompted Frederick William III to place his 80,000 man army on a war footing, and announced that he was willing to use it against the Third Coalition. The thought of being beset by the killing machine crafted by Frederick the Great scared the daylights out of the young Tsar, who requested an audience in Berlin to smooth things over with the Prussian king and to persuade him to join the alliance. The date of that meeting was being negotiated when news arrived that elements of the *Grande Armée* had passed through Ansbach.

When Napoleon directed his corps from their Channel encampments to the Danube, it was not arrogance that caused him to order some of his troops to pass through the Prussian enclave in Franconia known as Ansbach. That province had *not* been included in the treaty of neutrality for Prussia following the wars of the Revolution. The reason for that was simple: Ansbach was surrounded by Bavaria, Württemberg and Austria, and it was understood that *any* army could march through the territory during war, paying for all items requisitioned during their trek. Marshal Kray had done this very thing in 1800 with his Austrian army. Therefore, Napoleon grounded his conduct in this belief that passage across Ansbach was permitted by all, and violation of no treaty.

The French move into Ansbach

Regardless of Napoleon's understandings, the paranoid nobles at the Prussian court felt that foreign troops moving without permission across *any* territory owned by Prussia was nothing less than an act of war. However, before Prussia experienced the Russians ransacking their way through Silesia, but after the French marched through Ansbach, Napoleon's negotiators Duroc and Laforest attempted to gain an audience with the Prussian king in order to convince Frederick William III that the French did not believe that they had done anything wrong.[4]

However, Frederick William III and the Prussian court did not wanted to hear French explanations and apologies; they wanted Hanover. They secretly decided on a new plan whereby the Prussian army would occupy Hanover without the consent of any country. The king believed that the coveted territory could be easily subjugated as it was garrisoned by only a few thousand Frenchmen, most of them locked up in the fortress of Hameln under the command of *général de division* Barbou d'Escourières. The Prussian court members in Berlin schemed to justify this invasion under the "specious pretext of securing themselves against fresh violations of territory… and by such an occupation, Prussia would prevent her own territory from becoming the field of hostile operations."[5] Frederick William III and Hardenberg believed that Napoleon did not wish to also be set upon by the Prussian army. Therefore, without hearing the French explanation for marching across Ansbach, the Prussians put their own proposition to Duroc and Laforest, adding that France should be lucky to be able to resolve the issue at such little cost.

---

[4] Napoléon to the King of Prussia, *Correspondance*, number 9434. Bernadotte and the 1st Corps reached the border of Ansbach on 3 October. Berlin relented about the Russians, who were already crossing Silesia, on 6 October.

[5] Thiers, *The History of the Consulate & the Empire of France*, vol. 2, p. 51.

Meanwhile, the meeting between Tsar Alexander and Frederick William III was set for late October in Berlin. Arriving on the 25th, Alexander's discourse to the Prussian king was simple: you cannot separate yourself from the other legitimate monarchs of Europe; you cannot stand by and watch Napoleon first defeat Austria and Russia, only to turn on you at a later date. If Prussia joined the Third Coalition now and threw her army into the war, Napoleon would surely lose. With the defeat of France, the Tsar assured Frederick William III that Prussia would gain Hanover. The Tsar also advised the Prussian court that he had already written London, explaining that the British must sacrifice their interests in Hanover in order to secure the alliance of Prussia. Finally, the Tsar concluded his argument with the line that it would be honorable for Prussia to gain Hanover as a gift from legitimate monarchs, but it might not be a lasting addition if Prussia was to obtain it from the hands of the usurper.

Then word was received in Berlin and Vienna of Napoleon's triumph at Ulm. The Austrians at once sent an envoy to the Prussian king to join in Alexander's plea for Prussia to declare for the Third Coalition. After much debate between all parties in Berlin, the court members surrounding the Prussian king finally persuaded their sovereign to join the allies. Despite this declaration, Frederick William III was opposed to war against France. He did not believe that with Prussia's accession to the Third Coalition that the combined powers could defeat Napoleon. Instead, he preferred to gain Hanover without going to war. In the end, the overwhelming number of Prussian courtiers in favor of the Third Coalition swayed their king into throwing his lot in with the rest of the 'rightful' European monarchs. Since the Prussian army would not be ready to begin campaigning before the New Year, Frederick William III decided to tell Napoleon that he would try again to act as mediator for a peaceful solution in Europe. As before, Prussia would receive Hanover for the king's services, but the conditions for peace in Europe were a host of new demands stipulated by Prussia, including a new line of demarcation for the Austrian possessions in Lombardy. This meant that if Napoleon accepted, the Kingdom of Italy would be dismembered—something to which Napoleon would never agree. Following the delivery of this message and pressured by his ministers and court nobles, Frederick William III entered into the Third Coalition by meeting with Tsar Alexander in Potsdam on 3 November 1805. To consummate the deal, the monarchs walked into the vault that contained the remains of Frederick the Great. After placing his hand upon Frederick's coffin, Frederick William III supposedly swore eternal friendship and alliance to Tsar Alexander.

The oath over Frederick's tomb

As soon as Duroc learned of the agreement between Frederick William III and Tsar Alexander, known as the Treaty of Potsdam, he returned to Napoleon to make his report. After listening to Duroc's narrative, Napoleon expressed his belief that the Prussian reaction to French troops moving across Ansbach was nothing more than the king bending to the other members of the Third Coalition. The Emperor then sent a strongly worded message to Frederick William III, stating that the changes in the conditions for mediation were unacceptable, and that it was nothing new, nor anything to be feared, to have all of Europe pitted against France. Since Napoleon believed that there was nothing else to lose at this point, he went on to give the Prussian king some old-fashioned Corsican intimidation. The French Emperor advised Frederick William III that his "flags did not know disgrace,"[6] and should Prussian troops violate the borders of Hanover, or join the other allied armies in the field, he would appear at the head of the *Grande Armée* to defeat the Prussians as well as any other enemies.

---

[6] Napoléon to the King of Prussia, *Correspondance*, number 9434.

Once that message was dispatched, the Emperor wrote his assessment of the situation to *général de division* Barbou d'Escourières, commander of the fortress of Hameln in Hanover on 2 brumaire an XIV (24 October 1805):

> I do not know what is getting ready to happen; but whatever be the power, the armies of which shall enter Hanover, should it even be a power that has not declared against me, you will oppose it. Not having sufficient strength to resist an army, shut yourself up in the fortresses, and allow nobody to approach within cannon range of such fortresses. I shall come to the aid of the troops shut up in Hameln. My eagles have never suffered dishonor. I hope that the soldiers which you command will be worthy of their comrades, and above all, that they know how to preserve honor, which is the first and most precious property of nations.
>
> You are not to surrender the place except on an order from me, which shall be carried to you by one of my aides-de-camp.[7]

Examination of the diplomatic relations between France and Prussia during this time period should be viewed as a Napoleonic foreign policy victory. Napoleon had used the prospect of gaining Hanover to effectively neutralize Prussia for several months. During this critical time, the *Grande Armée* dealt a crushing blow to the Third Coalition at Ulm. Some authors have claimed that the French troops traversing Ansbach signify Napoleon's willingness to violate a neutral country and by such action he clumsily pushed Prussia into the war on the side of the Third Coalition. One such example is David Chandler, who states that the French made a monumental mistake by Bernadotte "indifferently violating neutral Prussian territory by marching through Ansbach," and continues his assault on Napoleonic mentality when he argues that: "Bernadotte's insolent violation of Ansbach was the most immediate cause" of the Prussians joining in against Napoleon.[8]

Barbou d'Escourières

To analyze the merit of this argument, one must examine subsequent known military and diplomatic activity or possible diplomatic scenarios. Napoleon's goal was to create conditions that would allow him to defeat his enemies in detail. In order to accomplish the defeat of the Austro-Russian forces without interference of Prussia, Napoleon dangled the prize that he knew Prussia desired. Blinded by excessive pride and seeing himself as the carrier of the mantle of his great-uncle Frederick the Great, Frederick William III took the bait and handled negotiations as poorly as can be imagined. Rather than recognizing the irreconcilable differences between the warring factions and taking steps in the summer of 1805 to either ensure his country's neutrality (i.e., mobilizing his army) or declaring at the outset for the Third Coalition, Frederick William III attempted to gain Hanover by a series of specious machinations, all of which were doomed to fail. Meanwhile, Napoleon cleverly dealt with Prussia, achieving a diplomatic victory to secure a military end. Whatever the significance of French troops passing through Ansbach, there can be no doubt that the Prussian king would have eventually yielded to the overwhelming pressure of his court to side with the allies. By the time Prussia reluctantly joined the alliance, she did not have enough time to mobilize her prized army before the conclusion of the Austerlitz campaign. With Prussia's accession to the Third Coalition successfully delayed, Napoleon focused his attention on defeating posthaste the Allied forces before him in the Danube theater of war.

---

[7] Napoléon to Barbou, *Correspondance*, number 9422.

[8] David Chandler, *The Campaigns of Napoleon* (New York, 1966), p. 392 and p. 403. It is interesting to note that writers like Chandler who condemn the movement of Napoleon's forces across Ansbach never, ever address similiar Allied movements in previous wars.

Kutuzov

"He Seems Unacquainted With the Art of War"—
Kutuzov and the Retreat Onto the North Bank of the Danube

From 12 October until 23 October, Kutuzov remained at the fortress of Braunau on the Inn River. From that stronghold on the Austro-Bavarian border, the Russian general waited over a two-week period to collect the regiments of his scattered army as they straggled in from their labored journey from Teschen. As his numbers slowly grew, Kutuzov anxiously awaited word about events transpiring to the west. As badly as the Austrian Army of Swabia needed the Russians to come to its assistance at Ulm, it seems almost incredible that the last letter received from Mack's command had been penned by Archduke Ferdinand on 8 October. In that dispatch to Kutuzov which reeked with political babble, Ferdinand stated that the Austrian army had 70,000 men "in a good position,"[9] and that he looked forward to joint operations with the Russian's forces. Why Ferdinand—a general that recognized the perils of the Ulm position—did not convey to Kutuzov the urgency in which he and his troops were needed at Ulm to confront the approaching French is unknown. Without a clearly stated appeal for help, Kutuzov found no reason to hurry his army forward to join Mack's forces at the juncture of the Danube and the Iller. Content with building up his supplies and gathering in stragglers along with the extensive artillery and baggage trains, Kutuzov remained immobile despite the suggestions of some Austrians for the Russian army to march to Mack's assistance.

One Austrian officer hoping to see the Russian forces spring into action was FML Maximilian von Merveldt, who was also at Braunau with his column of strategic reserves consisting of the survivors of Kienmayer's troops (originally the easternmost column of Mack's army), three battalions of Deutsch-Banater *Grenz* Regiment #12 and the Hussar-Regiment Hessen-Homburg #4. The 39-year-old Merveldt was born of an old Westphalian family, and had distinguished himself at the head of Austrian cavalry during the Turkish wars, as well as against the French in the wars of the Revolution. Merveldt did particularly well at the Battle of Neerwinden (1793) as well as at other actions in which the Austrians faced the Convention's raw troops. Having been a soldier his entire adult life, and after observing Kutuzov during a number of conferences at Braunau, Merveldt wrote Vienna that while the Muscovite was agreeable enough:

> he seems unacquainted with the art of war, and especially with operations against the French—a very different proposition from campaigning against the Turks. He leaves time and distance completely out of the equation, and is most unwilling to risk his troops. All of this will make it difficult to persuade him to advance.[10]

For a conservative Austrian to write these observations, Merveldt confirmed Kutuzov's ultraconservative nature and outdated visions of war.

Precious days passed at Braunau as Merveldt, Kutuzov and the other allied leaders received news about the combats around Ulm. With each day a new story seemed to float in that was different in detail but consistent in theme: Mack's army was getting the stuffing kicked out of it. On 23 October, Kutuzov finally received some definitive information. General Mack arrived in person to announce the fate of his Swabian army. Whether he wanted to or not, Kutuzov had to make a decision. He had only 27,092 Russians present for duty with approximately 20,000 more

[9] Duffy, *Austerlitz,* p. 54.

[10] Merveldt, as quoted in Angeli, 'Ulm und Austerlitz' in *Mittheilungen des K. K. Kriegs-Archivs,* p. 300.

Austrians that had been scraped together by Merveldt.[11] With these men, Kutuzov knew that he was facing a French army reported to be in excess of 100,000, and that the victors of Ulm would soon be bearing down on him. Despite the urgency of the situation, it took the allied brain trust almost a full week after Kutuzov had learned of Mack's capitulation to call a council of war on 29 October at Wels! Kutuzov conferred with Emperor Francis, Merveldt and other allied generals. The military men were concerned about concentrating their numbers to oppose the French, whereas Emperor Francis was adamant about saving his capital from enemy occupation. A compromise strategy was agreed upon and implemented that day. Kutuzov, recognized as the *de facto* commander of the allied forces in the Danube theater, would conduct a fighting retreat towards Vienna by using the natural defensive barriers of the various tributaries that flowed into the Danube from the south bank. It was hoped that an obstinate delaying action would give Archdukes John and Charles enough time to disengage their armies and march them from the Alps and Italy to Vienna. Once on the Danube, the council planned for the armies of Kutuzov, John and Charles to join forces near Saint Pölten—some 40 miles west of the Austrian capital—give battle and defeat Napoleon.[12]

Merveldt

The importance of Saint Pölten to the allies was obvious to all concerned. It represented the last position in front of Vienna where the Austro-Russian forces could make a stand and still have an escape route to the north bank over the wooden bridge that spanned the Danube at that point near Krems. If the position of Saint Pölten could not be held—and Austrian engineers were supposed to immediately begin to fortify the bridgehead on the south bank at Mautern that would allow the position of Saint Pölten to be contested—allied forces would be compelled to withdraw to the north bank, thereby abandoning Vienna.

While the allies were taking their time piecing together plans for the next step of the campaign, Napoleon had already begun to implement the movements of the *Grande Armée* in order to fulfill his strategic aims. These were twofold. First, the Emperor wished to isolate the remaining Austro-Russian forces on the Danube by preventing them from receiving any reinforcements. This meant that the mountain passes that led into the Danube valley from the Tyrol as well as the route from Italy across the Styrian-Hungarian borders would have to be sealed off. Three days before Kutuzov held the allied conference of war at Wels, Napoleon ordered his forces to seize the vital Tyrolean passes. By capturing these, French forces would choke off the Styrian-Hungarian avenues of approach into the Danube theater. Napoleon selected three corps to sweep the Alpine flank. Marmont and the 2nd Corps (minus Dumonceau's 2nd Infantry Division consisting of troops of the Batavian Republic) would conduct the longest march. They would move into Hungary and Styria, capturing Bruck, Leoben and Graz, thereby denying Charles' army a direct route from Italy to Vienna. Ney, with most of the 6th Corps and part of the Bavarians, would move into the Tyrol and capture Innsbruck. Other Bavarians, with part of Bernadotte's 1st Corps, would move into Salzburg. Once there, Bavarian and French elements would continue south to occupy the crucial mountain passes that Archduke John's army would have to control in order to move to Kutuzov's assistance. Augereau and the 7th Corps would pursue Jellachich into the Vorarlberg, and eliminate any possible Austrian movements towards the French rear areas in Bavaria.[13]

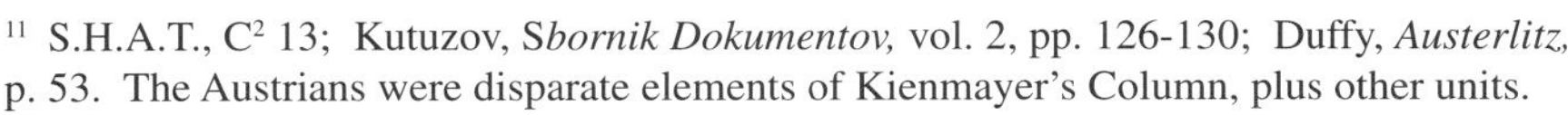

[11] S.H.A.T., C^2 13; Kutuzov, *Sbornik Dokumentov,* vol. 2, pp. 126-130; Duffy, *Austerlitz,* p. 53. The Austrians were disparate elements of Kienmayer's Column, plus other units.

[12] Duffy, *Austerlitz,* p. 55.

[13] S.H.A.T., C^2 5; General Order, *Correspondance*, number 9427. Esposito and Elting, *A Military History and Atlas of the Napoleonic Wars*, illustrate and describe Napoleon's plan in their text and Map number 51.

Napoleon's second strategic aim was his most pressing: he had to destroy the assorted allied forces in the Danube theater before their numbers grew, or before they escaped northward into Moravia. The swift elimination of the enemy formations was the Emperor's top priority, for:

> the fear that the Russians might escape to the north, was the one which dominated Napoleon's thinking throughout the war. No danger was greater for him than the almost inexhaustible resources of the northern powers—of Russia and Prussia. The whole of his campaign in Moravia, and the Battle of Austerlitz itself, was conceived in this persuasion.[14]

From Imperial headquarters then located in Munich, Napoleon gave the *Grande Armée* its marching orders on 25 October.[15] The following day the army moved out. The target of its eastward movement was Kutuzov's Russians which included the remnants of the Austrians last known to be in and around Braunau. "I am maneuvering against the Russian army," Napoleon wrote to his brother Joseph on 5 brumaire (27 October), "which is in position behind the Inn, and strong."[16] The following day, the French were across the Inn, having traversed 45 miles of very muddy countryside in only two days. On the 30th, Napoleon found Kutuzov's former base at Braunau abandoned. The Russians had hastily fled the fortress city the day before, and in doing so had failed to torch the enormous stores of food and munitions—supplies that Napoleon's troops put to immediate use. When the Emperor arrived on the Inn River in the afternoon of the 30th, he penned the following observations to Joseph:

> My Brother, I reached Braunau today. It snows heavily. The Russian army seems frightened by the fate of the Austrians. They have abandoned to me Braunau, one of the keys of Austria, well fortified and full of magazines. We shall see now what this Russian army will do. It has lost its presence of mind. They rob, steal, and outrage everywhere, to the great displeasure of the Austrian people. They look down on the Austrians, who no longer seem to want to fight: by they, I mean the Russian officers; the men are brutes, who do not know an Austrian from a Frenchman.[17]

With the capture of Braunau, Napoleon transformed the place into his forward depot as no time was lost continuing the army's trek eastward in pursuit of the fleeing allies. The French officers of the various corps pushed their men as fast as they could move while Marshal Murat led the way with his cavalry. The horsemen followed the burned, looted and littered trail left by Kutuzov's command. One of Napoleon's aides-de-camp, *général de division* Anne-Jean-Marie-René Savary, noted that following the Russian army was accomplished "easily enough by the stragglers and sick they left behind."[18]

The quickly moving French soon caught up with Kutuzov's rearguard. Clashes began on the 30th when Colonel Louis-Pierre Montbrun's superb 1st *Chasseurs à cheval* of Marshal Davout's corps light cavalry routed the Austrian

---

[14] Captain Paul Claude Alombert-Goget and Jean Lambert Alphonse Colin, *La Campagne de 1805 en Allemagne*, 6 volumes (Paris, 1902-1908), Chapter XXIV, p. 339.

[15] General Order, *Correspondance*, number 9427.

[16] Napoléon to Joseph, *Correspondance,* number 9431.

[17] Napoléon to Joseph, *Correspondance,* number 9437.

[18] *Memoirs of the Duke of Rovigo* (Savary), 2 volumes (London, 1828), vol. 1, p. 103.

Hussar-Regiment Kaiser #1 at Ried. The following day, Davout's cavalry again caught some allies, this time at Lambach near Wels on the Traun River. Montbrun's regiment, along with Colonel Ferdinand-Daniel Marx's 7th Hussars, began at once to torment the four battalions of Austrians that guarded a baggage train. The Austrian units were three battalions of Peterwardeiner *Grenz* #9 and a fusilier battalion of Gyulai IR#60. Carefully selected attacks by the French horse had brought the allied column to a halt, and word was sent to Davout to hurry forward with some infantry. Closer to the gunfire, however, was Prince Bagration, who immediately countermarched to the rescue from Lambach. The Russian general was at the head of two battalions of the 8th *Jaeger*, one company of Russian horse artillery and one squadron of hussars. With none of their own infantry in sight, the French light cavalry let the numerous allied troops leave the field without further incident after inflicting 152 casualties on the Russians and 210 on the Austrians.[19]

The Traun River did not offer the allies what they thought was a favorable defensive line, so they continued their retreat to the Enns River. Holding another council of war on 3 November, Kutuzov declared to those present that the hasty retreat conducted over the preceding four days had so disorganized his army that the men could not turn and fight before reaching a stronger defensive line. It was decided that unless reinforcements reached Kutuzov in time, the army would fall back to the well known defensive position anchored by Saint Pölten on the Traisen River, and then continue the retreat by crossing over to the north bank of the Danube near Krems. Prince Bagration's reinforced column would act as the army's rearguard.

The Austro-Russian forces were starting their withdrawal from the steep banks of the Enns when FML von Merveldt and about 6,000 Austrians suddenly left Kutuzov's command and marched off to the southeast! Remaining with Kutuzov were just four battalions of Austrian *Grenzer* infantry (one battalion of the Peterwardeiner *Grenz* #9 had been ordered back to Stockerau near Vienna) and four regiments of Austrian cavalry. Merveldt had broken off from Kutuzov in response to a directive received from Vienna to march towards Styria with his best troops in order to assist the army under Archduke John. Once Merveldt separated from the main army, he received countermanding orders from Kutuzov. These arrived too late, however, for Merveldt to be able to countermarch to rejoin the Russians. The French were already in hot pursuit and between his Austrians and Kutuzov.[20]

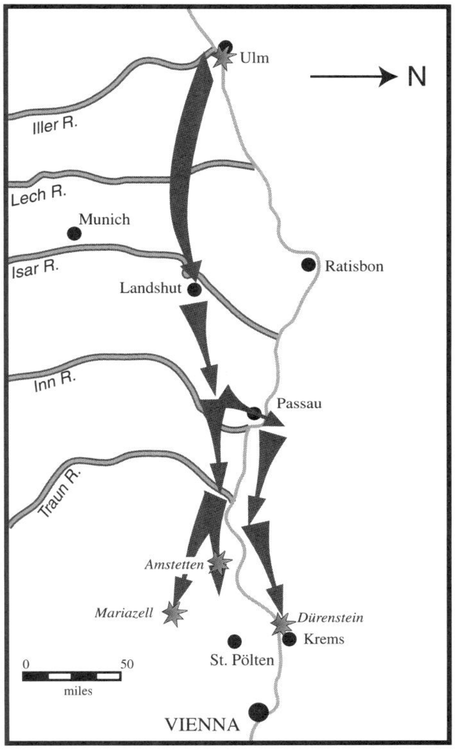

The campaign down the Danube

When the order for the Austrian general to break off from Kutuzov had come from Vienna, little did Merveldt realize that the Habsburg ministers had unwittingly directed his command into the path of Davout's 3rd Corps of the *Grande Armée*. With the French close on his heels, Merveldt realized that speed was of the essence if he and his troops were to escape. However, the inadequacies of the horseflesh taken into the field by the Habsburg army once again compromised its movements. The insufficient number of animals pulling the ordnance and wagons slowed Merveldt's march pace to a dangerously slow crawl. Frantic to escape the pursuing French, the men pitched in alongside the horses "and the grenadiers [from Hoch-und-Deutchmeister IR#4] harnessed themselves to the guns, and dragged them along while the blood was pouring from their feet."[21]

As heroic as this effort was, it proved to be in vain. The leading elements of 3rd Corps caught and destroyed Merveldt's rearguard in one of the Styrian gorges on 6 November. Two days later, Davout's men trapped the main body of the Austrian column at Mariazell. The battle was a short one, despite the fact that the majority of Merveldt's infantry were fine troops. The five battalions (four were fusilier and

---

19 S.H.A.T., C^2 5;, 240 and 472.

20 PRO, FO 7/79, Paget letter of 13 January 1806.

21 PRO, FO 7/79, enclosure in Paget dispatch of 8 November 1805.

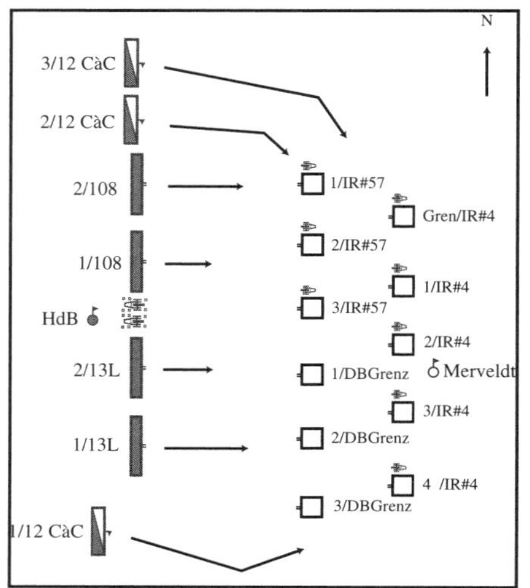

Heudelet de Bierre's attack at Mariazell, 8 November 1805: the French attack used combined arms, coordinating the 12th Chasseurs à cheval and the infantry battalions

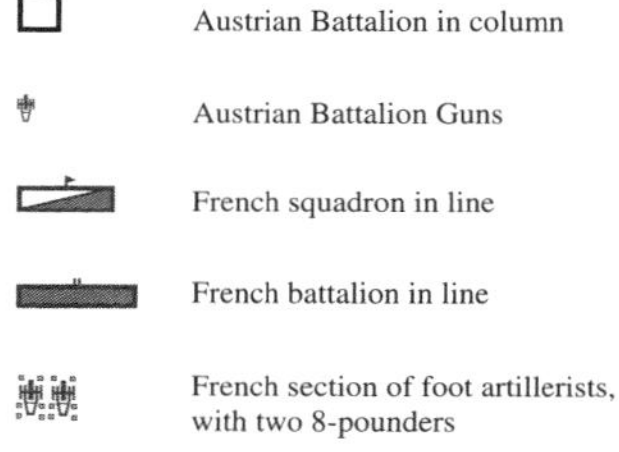

one was grenadier) of Hoch-und-Deutchmeister IR#4 were considered by many in Austrian service to be the army's best. Added to these were three fusilier battalions of one of the better regiments, Josef Coloredo IR#57, as well as three battalions of Deutsch-Banater *Grenz* #12. Despite their excellent reputation, Merveldt's men were hopelessly outnumbered as well as outmatched by the superior combined arms tactics of the Napoleonic troops. Leading the French attack was *général de brigade* Etienne Heudelet de Bierre, the commander of the Advance Guard of the 3rd Corps. Heudelet particularly distinguished himself at Mariazell when he ruptured the Austrian line with a savage, combined arms attack made by the 13th *Légère*, the 108th *Ligne*, the 2nd and the 12th *Chasseurs à cheval.* It took only two short hours for these regiments to tear Merveldt's formations to pieces.[22] Killed or wounded were over 200 Austrians, while 3,000 were captured, along with 16 guns and three stands of colors.[23] One of the colors was captured by sergeant Chevalier of the 108th *Ligne,* who took the Austrian standard after suffering numerous saber wounds.[24] Among the Austrian prisoners were the colonels of Hoch-und-Deutchmeister IR#4 and Josef Coloredo IR#57, along with five battalion commanders.[25] Merveldt escaped the *débâcle,* fleeing into the godforsaken eastern regions of Hungary, accompanied by 2,000 totally demoralized and rag-tag survivors.[26]

While Davout's 3rd Corps was destroying Merveldt on the fields of Mariazell, Napoleon was not allowing Kutuzov any respite. The unexpected detachment of Merveldt's Austrians from his command, followed by Murat's quick pursuit across the Enns at Steyer, had only hastened the Russian general's withdrawal towards Saint Pölten. Kutuzov had never before been confronted by an opponent that moved with the speed of the *Grande Armée*, and the Russian general urged his men to quicken their march.

From the Enns, Kutuzov's army followed two roads through an almost continuous pine forest with the Danube flowing on the north and the foothills of Hungary rising to over 1,200 feet visible to the south. As Kutuzov's troops retreated, they raped, pillaged and plundered the peasants who were unfortunate enough to live in the path of the Russian horde. Following hard on the heels of the marauding Muscovites, the starving French soldiers were hardly sympathetic to the plight of these innocents; they readily took whatever the Russians had passed over.

The roads leading eastward from the cities of Enns and Steyer that were the scene of so much suffering merged into one great road west of the Ips River and the village of Amstetten. The position of Amstetten was one of the few clearings between the Enns and the Traisen where a rearguard could deploy to try to halt its pursuers. It was here that Prince Bagration was ordered to make a stand in order to give Kutuzov's baggage train time to separate itself from the pursuing forces of the advance guard of the *Grande Armée* led by Marshal Murat.

The dashing commander of the French *Corps des Réserves de Cavalerie* was at the head of the two brigades of light cavalry belonging to Lannes' 5th Corps when he and his entourage passed through the forest of Amstetten late in the afternoon of 5 November. Riding with Murat was Louis-François Lejeune, an aide-de-camp to Marshal Berthier, who vividly recalled his impressions of the wooded, winter terrain.

---

[22] 19th Bulletin to the *Grande Armée, Correspondance*, number 9459 and 21st Bulletin to the *Grande Armée, Correspondance*, number 9469.

[23] Adélaïde-Louis de Blocqueville, *Le Maréchal Davout prince d'Eckmühl: correspondance inédite 1790-1815: Pologne, Russie, Hambourg.* (Paris, 1887), pp. 70-74, gives Davout's account of the battle.

[24] S.H.A.T., *Journal des opérations du 3ᵉ corps.*

[25] S.H.A.T., C² 15; 21st Bulletin of the *Grande Armée, Correspondance,* number 9469.

[26] Duffy, *Austerlitz,* p. 58.

> It was cold, and the ground and trees in the Amstetten forest were alike covered with masses of snow, which produced a very remarkable effect on those of us who came from the South of Europe and had never before realized how beautiful nature can be in the winter… I called the attention of Marshal Murat to the beauty of the scene as we rode rapidly beneath the frozen vaults, pursuing a rearguard of cavalry which was fleeing before us, and we were still admiring the grandeur of the northern scene when a break in the forest suddenly revealed a very unexpected sight of a totally different character.[27]

Emerging from the pine forest through a defile, Lejeune, Murat and the others saw stretching across one of the rare clearings, drawn up in two battle lines, a mixed force of Austrians and Russians. In the front line were the four Austrian *Grenzer* battalions along with three regiments of Austrian cavalry. The second line consisted of nine battalions of Russians from the Kiev Grenadiers, Azov Musketeers and 6th *Jaeger*, supported by the Pavlograd Hussars and a company of Russian horse artillery. At their head were Bagration, his staff and a small collection of Austrian officers. Without hesitation and almost instinctively, Murat ordered up his escort squadron that was composed of the élite companies from both the 9th and the 10th Hussars. Drawing his saber, Murat turned to the busby-topped cavaliers and waving his blade above his head, ordered them to charge.

With trumpets blaring, the Marshal of France and 100 hussars rode across the snow-covered fields to attack an enemy force of 6,700 that were deployed and ready for battle. If Murat was thinking that audacity might unnerve and stampede the allied forces, he was very wrong. The charging Frenchmen horsemen were hopelessly outnumbered and enveloped by two regiments of countercharging Austrian cavalry. Murat's escort companies were soon bolting back along the road to the woods, closely followed by the Austrian horse. As Murat, his staff and the exhausted escort squadron arrived back at the opening of the woods where their charge began, they were overtaken by the Hussar-Regiment Hessen-Homburg #4 and the Cüirassier-Regiment Lothringen #7, both led by a colonel on Bagration's staff. Lejeune remembered the terrifying experience:

Bagration

> Our men were swept down, many were taken prisoners, and we ourselves were in danger of being captured. Murat's horse was killed under him, mine fell in the confused rush down the steep path, and I was flung off. I should have been crushed by the onrush before I could get out of the way if I had not flung myself under the shelter of two pieces of cannon which a young officer of artillery, fresh from college, had the presence of mind to place in position in the middle of the path.[28]

The young horse artillery lieutenant was Octave Levasseur, who had brought up and unlimbered his section of 8-pounders. Loading one piece with a double charge of roundshot *and* canister, Levasseur saw:

> gunner Collot reach out with a lighted match to touch off the piece. At the cry of 'Watch out!' our hussars gave way to the right and left into the woods, making a little human embrasure in front of the muzzle. A Russian colonel, covered in gold braid

[27] *Memoirs of Baron Lejeune*, translated by Mrs. Arthur Bell, 2 volumes (New York, 1897), vol. 1, pp. 23-24.
[28] *Memoirs of Baron Lejeune*, vol. 1, pp. 24-25.

> and lace, thundered down on my gunner to sever his arm. The shot discharged, the barrel broke off at the trunnions, and the colonel collapsed... [29]

Lejeune recalled that the discharge of the 8-pounder:

> brought down on our heads the masses of snow in the trees. As if by magic, the squadrons of the enemy disappeared in a cloud of smoke and a storm of snow mixed with great death-dealing icicles that fell from a height of more than 100 feet, crashing upon the helmets of the [Austrian] fugitives with a resounding noise. A sudden panic seized the Austrians, and they took flight. Murat saw this opportunity, returned to the charge, and gave chase to the enemy.[30]

This time Murat's charge succeeded. Following the fleeing Austrian cavalry, the prince led forward the remaining elements of the 9th and 10th Hussars. Animated by the presence of Murat, these light cavalrymen caught and routed the winded Hussar-Regiment Hessen-Homburg #4 along with the Cüirassier-Regiment Lothringen #7. Seeing their comrades put to flight, the Székler *Grenz*-Hussaren-Regiment #11 then charged Murat's troopers. Meeting this attack, the 9th and 10th Hussars quickly enveloped the flanks of the Széklers, thereby overturning the Austrian regiment. Following up this success, Murat led the hussars against Bagration's second line, where they briefly overran the Russian horse artillery battery before withdrawing.[31]

Élite company of the 9th Hussars

While Murat was leading this charge, Marshal Lannes arrived on the field with Oudinot's *Grenadiers de la Réserve* double-timing up the road behind him. The impetus of the French cavalry attack had long since receded when the grenadiers shook out from road columns, fixed bayonets and advanced upon Bagration's line. By the time Oudinot's men reached the enemy position, Lieutenant-General Mikhail Andreivich Miloradovich had doubled back to support Bagration. It was fortunate for Bagration that his fellow countryman had marched to the sound of the guns because it didn't take Oudinot's battalions long to blow through the two battalions of the Broder *Grenz* #7 and then pushed aside the same number of battalions belonging to the Peterwardeiner *Grenz* #9.

After dispersing the *Grenzer* units, Oudinot's men pushed forward to Bagration's second line. The French found out that dealing with the grenadier battalions of the Apsheron and Smolensk Musketeer Regiments was an entirely more difficult matter than tangling with the indifferently-trained *Grenzer* units. Following a fire fight that lasted almost until dusk, the French battalions charged. Oudinot's advancing ranks swept away the four battalions of musketeers, but the two battalions of tough Russian grenadiers stood firm. Opposing ranks of blue and green were soon locked in a vicious *mêlée* that continued until darkness fell about 6:00 P.M. The tenacity of Oudinot's battalions finally forced the Russians from the field after having killed and wounded over 400 of the Tsar's infantry, and capturing almost 700. Added to these were 1,000 Austrian prisoners, most from the Broder *Grenz* #7.[32]

The clash at Amstetten clearly illustrated what well-handled, coordinated French light cavalry could accomplish against superior numbers of allied horsemen,

---

[29] *Souvenirs Militaires d'Octave Levasseur*, (Paris, 1914), p. 40.

[30] *Memoirs of Baron Lejeune*, vol. 1, p. 25.

[31] S.H.A.T., C^2 6.

[32] S.H.A.T., C^2 6; *Journal des opérations du 5e corps.*

and Napoleon gave homage to the 9th and 10th Hussars two days later.[33] More significantly, Amstetten was the first time in the 1805 campaign that the *fantassins* of the *Grande Armée* had been opposed by the Russian infantry. The ferocity of the mitre-capped grenadier battalions impressed many, including the Imperial staff officer Philippe-Paul de Ségur, who remembered that of the Russian prisoners taken at the combat of Amstetten:

> not a single man surrendered willingly; after they had been wounded, disarmed and thrown to the ground they still put up a fight, and even returned to the attack. At the close of the combat the only way we could assemble a few hundred prisoners was to prod them with our bayonets, like a herd of undisciplined animals, and belabor them with the butts of our muskets.[34]

Following Amstetten, the pursuit of Kutuzov's army resumed the next day. For three days, Murat and Lannes pushed their men and horses to the limits of endurance without being able to catch the elusive prey. "The Russians," Marshal Lannes wrote to Napoleon on 17 brumaire (8 November), "fly faster than we are able to pursue them; these miserable beings will not stop a moment even to fight."[35] Marshal Lannes' chief of staff, *général de brigade* Compans added: "The rapidity of our pursuit is forcing the enemy to lose large numbers of stragglers and horses."[36] Arriving before Saint Pölten on 8 November, Lannes and Murat discovered that the adversary had halted and appeared to be preparing to give battle. After passing this information on to Napoleon, Murat was in the process of setting up his headquarters in the castle of Mittrau when his scouts brought him fresh information—two intercepted messages indicated that Kutuzov's army was not going to stand at Saint Pölten, but was instead preparing to cross over to the north bank of the Danube near Krems at the Mautern bridge. Believing that the troops of the 5th Corps and the Cavalry Reserve were insufficient to force a battle at Saint Pölten, and with the Emperor not yet present, Murat sent word for his commander to hurry forward.[37]

Mortier

Napoleon was already in route to Saint Pölten when he received Murat's latest intelligence report. The Emperor was eager to do battle with the Russians and had taken steps several days earlier to give Kutuzov an additional headache by threatening his line of communications. To accomplish this, Napoleon created an *ad hoc* corps that was to operate on the north bank of the Danube. On 6 November, the Emperor selected Marshal Mortier to take charge of this new command. The divisions selected to comprise Mortier's extemporaneous corps were drawn from three different corps of the *Grande Armée.* Two divisions were selected because they were officered by trusted men who had previously served with Mortier. These were: Dumonceau's 3rd Infantry Division consisting of troops of the Batavian Republic (Holland) from Marmont's 2nd Corps; and Gazan's 2nd Infantry Division (augmented by the 4th Dragoons) from Lannes' 5th Corps. In addition to these troops, Mortier was given the victors of Haslach-Jungingen: Dupont's diminutive but superb 1st Infantry Division of Ney's 6th Corps.[38]

With these troops, Mortier was to advance down the north bank, keeping abreast of Murat's advance guard as it pursued Kutuzov's forces along the south bank. If the allies were run to ground and offered battle at Saint Pölten as Napoleon

[33] 20th Bulletin of the *Grande Armée, Correspondance,* number 9463.
[34] *Memoirs of Ségur,* pp. 215-216.
[35] S.H.A.T., C^2 6.
[36] S.H.A.T., *Journal des opérations du 5e corps.*
[37] S.H.A.T., C^2 240.
[38] S.H.A.T., C^2 485.

hoped, Mortier would trap them by swinging his men across Kutuzov's possible routes of escape across the Danube. If the Muscovite crossed the river and attacked Mortier, the Emperor planned to swiftly redirect his other corps to the north bank to join forces with Mortier's command. Regardless of the enemy's course of action, it was Napoleon's intent that Mortier would readily have the support of French troops on the south side of the Danube.

Such a possible large-scale movement of troops across the Danube could only be accomplished by pontoon bridges or numerous boats. Since operations were in a state of fluidity, the best way to shuttle troops from one bank to the other could only be a large flotilla of 250 to 300 boats that Napoleon wished to be assembled in order to accompany the army downstream. The Emperor named *lieutenant de vaisseau* Lostange of the *Bataillon des matelots de la Garde* to coordinate the movement of these boats. For personnel to man the large flotilla, Lostange had not only his 120-man crew of *matelots*, but was empowered by the Emperor to command an assortment of other, dubious sailors. These were supposed to consist of dragoons that did not have horses from the divisions of Klein, Walther and Beaumont (1st, 2nd and 3rd Dragoon Divisions), plus 50 men from each infantry division of Lannes' 5th Corps, as well as 100 men from each regiment of Marmont's 2nd Corps. Theoretically, with such an assembly of boats and men, *lieutenant de vaisseau* Lostange would keep his command ready so that the boats could either ferry men across the river.[39]

Napoleon's extemporaneous plans to support Mortier were ambitious. However, the Emperor forgot, in his driving impatience, the exact whereabouts of Dupont and Dumonceau, and that the delay in their original orders had left them well to the rear.[40] This detail was completely lost on Murat, who proposed to Mortier that he race to Krems and prevent the Russians from crossing the Danube over the Mautern Bridge outside Stein. Furthermore, Murat did not tell Mortier that he was taking the advance guard of the *Grande Armée* and pushing on to Vienna. The cavalryman ordered this move simply for no reason other than to occupy the enemy's capital. By doing this, Murat was leaving Mortier without any immediate south bank support.

Meanwhile, on the north bank, Mortier was moving eastward towards Dürenstein and destiny. Mortier was an ideal subordinate officer, and once given an order he could be trusted to faithfully carry it out. In accordance with Napoleon's and Murat's wishes—which were in agreement with his own desire to come to grips with the Russians—Mortier dutifully advanced down the north bank at the head of only the reinforced division of Gazan, with Dupont's and Dumonceau's Divisions a full day's march behind. The fact that Mortier was in such an exposed position was something that Napoleon did not consider important until the early morning hours of 11 November. The reason for this was that the Emperor was operating under the assumption that the rearguard action at Amstetten was a prelude to a major battle around Saint Pölten on the south bank, or if the allies crossed over to the north bank, help would immediately be available from Murat and Lannes. However, when the Emperor received word from Murat that Kutuzov's army was preparing to withdraw over the Danube, coupled with word from the cavalryman that he was taking his cavalry and Lannes' 5th Corps eastward in a push towards Vienna, thereby leaving Mortier without any immediate support from the south

---

[39] S.H.A.T., C² 7. Later in the campaign, Lostange's rank in shown as *capitaine de frégate*, as shown in: *Tableau de la Grande Armée Dernière quinzaine du mois brumaire an XIV*. Please consult Appendix E.

[40] Rainer Egger, *Das Gefecht bei Dürenstein-Loiben 1805*, volume 3 of the "Militärhistorische Schriftenreihe" series (Vienna, 1986), pp. 10-11; Thiers, *The History of the Consulate & the Empire of France*, vol. 2, p. 63.

bank, Napoleon fired this exasperated response back to Murat at 3:30 A.M.; "The Russians will be able to do what they will with the corps of Marshal Mortier; [he and his men] would not be in the position they are in now if you had executed my orders."[41]

Napoleon's fears were soon justified. By the time the Emperor had written his reprimand to Murat in the early morning hours of 11 November, Kutuzov's forces were already in motion with the intent to crush Mortier. Oddly enough, the decision to counterattack had been forced on Kutuzov by the vigorous pursuit of Napoleon's forces. The French had bounced Kutuzov's troops eastward more quickly than any of the allied generals could have imagined. After losing six precious days at Braunau before ordering the retreat, and being vigorously pursued by a determined foe, Kutuzov had not given the Austrian engineers enough time to construct the planned fortified bridgehead on the south bank anchored by Saint Pölten and extending to Mautern opposite Krems. Without these man-made positions to augment his army's ever-shrinking numbers, and with a French force (Mortier) already detected to be working its way down the north bank threatening his communications, Kutuzov was all but convinced that he would have to pull his army over the Danube. His only hesitation was the Austrian Emperor, who begged Kutuzov not to abandon Vienna to the French. The protestations of Francis II notwithstanding, Kutuzov could not ignore the woeful condition of his army as vividly described by Russian artillery Lieutenant Colonel A. P. Ermolov:

> There were frightful deficiencies in supply, which caused an outbreak of plunder and indiscipline among our force... Most of our regiments were composed of low-grade troops, and we learned to call our vagabonds by the name of 'marauders'—this was the first of our borrowings from the French.[42]

In addition to these breakdowns, Russian troops were beginning to desert at an alarming rate:

> Twenty whole squadrons had escaped across the bridge [at Mautern, near Krems] without authorization, and officers were slipping away from their regiments on the pretense of ill-health... The battalions of *jaeger* were losing men wholesale; even the vigilant efforts of Prince Bagration could not stop the desertions.[43]

With his regiments in such a state of chaos, Kutuzov saw no alternative but to order his seriously depleted and half-demoralized army to seek the protection of the mighty Danube River. When the last of the Muscovites trudged across to the north bank over the rickety wooden bridge at Stein near Krems on 9 November, they set fire to the structure and left:

> throughout Austria terrible traces of their presence. They pillaged, ravaged, even murdered, conducting themselves like real barbarians, and that to such a degree that the French were almost considered as the liberators of the country.[44]

---

[41] S.H.A.T., C^2 7.

[42] *Zapiski A. P. Ermolova,* 2 volumes (Moscow, 1965-1968), vol. 1, p. 13.

[43] Duffy, *Austerlitz,* p. 60; S.H.A.T., C^2 12.

[44] Thiers, *The History of the Consulate & the Empire of France*, vol. 2, p. 63.

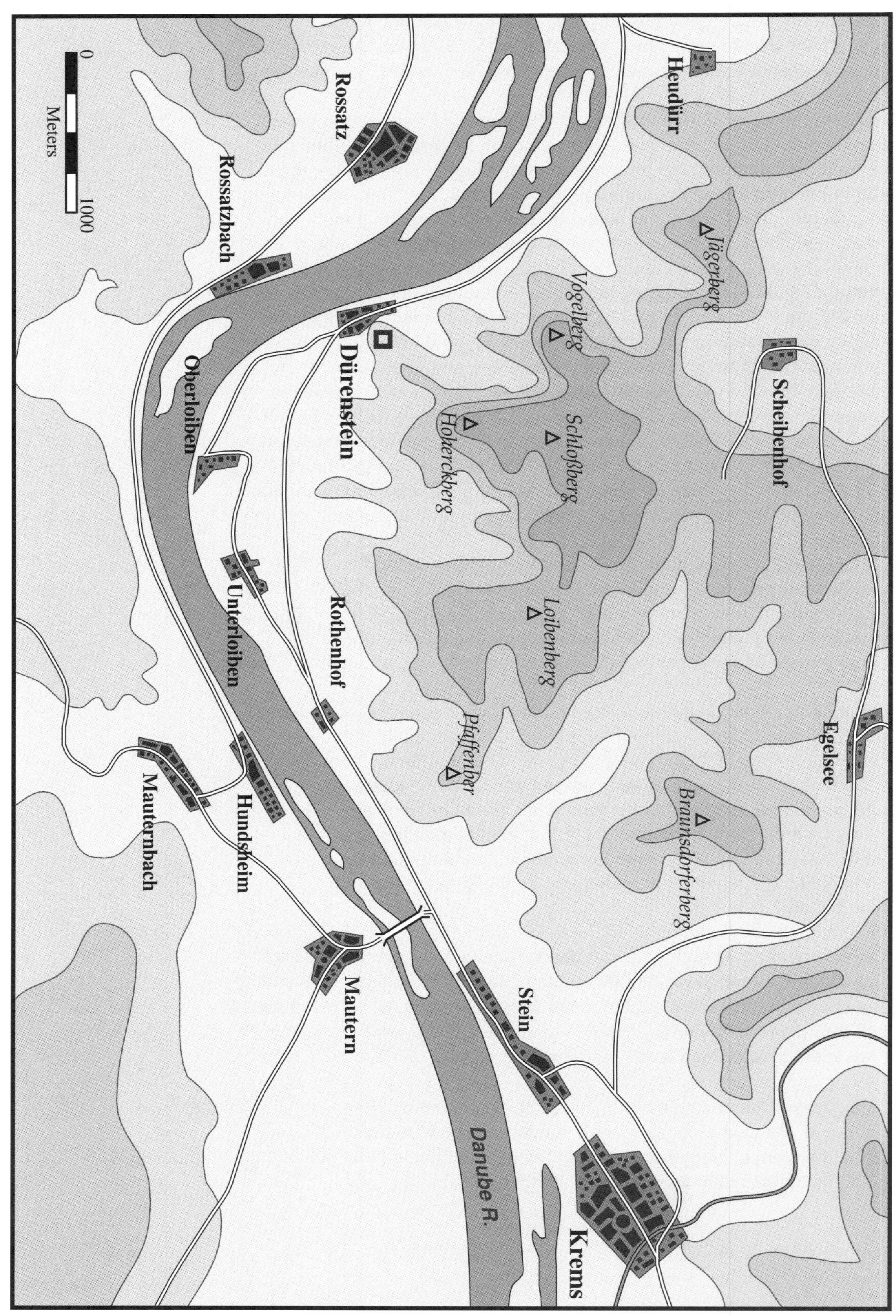

The Battlefield of Dürenstein

"We Must Be Saved or Perish Together"—
Mortier and the Battle of Dürenstein

While the majority of the *Grande Armée* was moving fast in pursuit of the fleeing allies on the south bank of the Danube, the newly formed provisional corps under Mortier found it slower going along the north bank. This was due to the marshal not having a corresponding staff to support his command authority, as well as there being only one road on which his troops could move through the difficult terrain down the north side of the Danube.

As the Danube courses towards Vienna, it turns to the northeast 10 miles past Marbach, bends to the southeast at Weissenkirchen, then turns again to the northeast just past Dürenstein at Loiben. This north bank region of the Danube is characterized by numerous wine-growing valleys that fall off from steeply sloping mountains that rise above a lone road that follows the river near the water's edge. Just off the well-worn path, numerous sand bars extended into the water, while rugged terrain defined the area immediately north of the river. Traveling the road from Weissenkirchen to Dürenstein, the escarpments of the Muglaberg loom across the Danube on the south bank, while a succession of heights tower above the steep rock walls that abut the river road on the north bank. From Weissenkirchen to Dürenstein to Krems, these heights are the Sandlberg, the Jägerberg, the Vogelberg, the Schloßberg, the Hoherechberg, the Loihenberg, the Pfaffenberg and the Braunsdorferberg. When these mountains and the connecting wine growing valleys are full of snow, as they were in the second week of November in 1805, some of the defiles between the heights are closed completely, while others can be traversed only with extreme difficulty. That meant that any force following the river road from Weissenkirchen eastward to Dürenstein and beyond would find it extremely difficult, if not impossible, to reconnoiter beyond the rising ground to the left flank.

Once past the narrow defiles that cut between some of the different heights, a broad plain spreads out to the north of Dürenstein over which the winegrowers of the region had established their vineyards. The different paths from these defiles connected to a main road that led eastward to Krems, near which Kutuzov's army had crossed the Danube. With ice and snow covering the entangled vines of the wine country, and dense forests defining the numerous heights above the vineyards, maneuver in this part of the Danube valley was significantly restricted, especially for cavalry and artillery.

Marshal Mortier led the men of Gazan's Division into this tactical strait jacket on 10 November. While part of their men and most of the ordnance was moving overland along the river road into the village of Dürenstein, Mortier and Gazan transported the 4th *Légère*, the 100th *Ligne* and three guns by boat, disembarking at Dürenstein at 3:00 P.M. on 10 November. The French passed under the ruins of the famous castle where Richard the Lion Heart was once held prisoner by Duke Leopold of Austria. Pushing eastward from Dürenstein, Mortier advanced without first conducting sufficient reconnaissance. Perhaps this was due to the fact that it was never made clear to Mortier whether *général de division* Dominique-Louis-Antoine Klein and his 1st Dragoon Division was under the marshal's control. Without specific orders tying him to Mortier, Klein moved out of contact with the marshal on the 10th, leaving behind with Gazan's infantry only the three squadrons belonging to his worst regiment—the 4th Dragoons. As the French moved through the Dürenstein toward Loiben, the marshal and his men could still see the smoke ascending from the smoldering Mautern Bridge outside the hamlet of Stein near Krems, just over two miles away. Mortier and Gazan reasoned that there could be only one explanation for the allies firing the structure—they had retreated to the north bank.

At this time, Mortier could have used some communication with the south bank. The large number of boats and new sailors that were supposed to have accompanied Mortier's move downstream had not turned up. Instead of the hoped-for massive flotilla ordered by the Emperor, *lieutenant de vaisseau* Lostange had only managed to muster 11 boats—all operated by his 120-man crew of the *matelots*—to assist Mortier and his new command. Without proper liaison with Napoleon, and with Murat gallivanting off to Vienna, Mortier was on his own. His apparent isolation from the rest of the army did little, if anything, to allay the marshal's apprehension about advancing against the enemy. Without adequate knowledge of the ground before him, nor any recent information on enemy forces to his front or left flank, Mortier had been carried away by the "common ardor which prevailed throughout the army [and] thought of nothing but pushing forward to meet the enemy."[45]

The marshal's decision to press on past Dürenstein was also reflective of his personality. The 37-year-old Adolphe-Edouard-Casmir-Joseph Mortier was more than just the tallest of Napoleon's marshals: he was an aggressive soldier with an excellent grasp of tactics who saw the development of action clearly, gave precise orders and never lost his head. He used the combination of his talents and the offensive temperament of his troops to retain the tactical initiative in battle and to keep the adversary off balance.

Gazan

When Mortier was given the command of the *ad hoc* corps of troops on the north bank of the Danube, he left Imperial headquarters to assume his new rôle without the benefit of a large, accompanying staff. Instead, the marshal had only two engineer officers as aides-de-camp and a chief of staff.[46] *Général de brigade* Deo-Gratias-Nicolas Godinot, an old friend of Mortier's from the *Armée d'Helvétie*, was named as the marshal's chief of staff. Fortunately for Mortier, two of his division commanders had also previously served under him: Dumonceau in Hanover in 1803 and Gazan, whom Mortier had commanded in Switzerland. As Mortier's improvised corps made its way down the north side of the Danube, the lead division was commanded by *général de division* Honoré-Théodore-Maxime Gazan. Gazan had been a brigade commander under Mortier in the *Armée d'Helvétie* during the 1799 campaign against Suvórov. Prior to that campaign, Gazan had solidified his reputation as both a gifted tactician and tenacious warrior by forging the 10th *demi-brigade légère* into one of the most feared units in Republican service.[47] When Gazan was reunited with Mortier on the Danube some six years later, they were both eager to face the Russians that they had fought in the wars of the Second Coalition.

Like the generals that led them, the troops that formed Gazan's 2nd Division of the 5th Corps were veteran soldiers. One-third had been in uniform for at least 10 years, and two-thirds had seen action in at least one campaign during the wars of the French Revolution. The 'new' soldiers were those that were too young for the combats of the Revolution, but had been trained with the veterans for the past two years at the Channel camp of Saint-Omer. The good quality of Gazan's troops is reflected by the very few men who fell out of ranks during the march from France to Dürenstein. When Gazan's Division crossed the Rhine in late September, the nine battalions that comprised the 4th *Légère*, 100th *Ligne* and 103rd *Ligne* numbered 5,944 officers and men present and under arms.[48] When parade states were taken one month later on 26 October, these regiments had 5,659 persons present and under arms.[49] On 1 November, Gazan's infantry mustered 5,419

[45] Thiers, *The History of the Consulate & the Empire of France*, vol. 2, p. 64.
[46] S.H.A.T., C[2] 485.
[47] Six, *Dictionnaire biographique*, vol. 1, p. 492.
[48] S.H.A.T., C[2] 470.
[49] S.H.A.T., C[2] 481.

combatants standing in ranks,[50] and increased to 5,529 on 6 November.[51] In addition to these *fantassins*, Gazan had attached some 305 officers and troopers of the 4th Dragoons. In addition, a full company of foot artillerists serving six pieces of ordnance, and a section of horse artillerists handling two 8-pounder guns totaled eight officers and 162 other ranks, all supported by 116 artillery train personnel.[52] Therefore, excluding generals and staff officers, and taking into account some stragglers leaving the ranks between 6 November and the day of the battle, Gazan's command at Dürenstein numbered right around 6,000 officers and men present and under arms. Of the division's eight pieces of ordnance, only two 8-pounders and one howitzer had been brought to Dürenstein by Lostange's boats.[53]

It was about 4:00 P.M. on 10 November when Mortier, Gazan and the advance guard of the division passed through Dürenstein and came upon a small allied rearguard patrol consisting of one Austrian squadron and a Russian grenadier company near Loiben.[54] Mortier sent *général de brigade* Jean-François Graindorge with Colonel Jean-Marie Ritay and the 100th *Ligne* to push back these covering forces. Like so many of Napoleon's officers, Graindorge had learned his trade in the wars of the Revolution. He had been one of the Volunteers of 1791, and received eight wounds fighting the Austrians between 1792 and 1796. Distinguished as a *chef de bataillon* in 1796 and 1797, Graindorge also displayed above average skill as the provisional regimental commander of the 84th *Ligne* during the 1799 campaign against Suvórov's Russians, and was soon thereafter awarded the permanent command of the 36th *Ligne*. After being assigned to Gazan's command in the camp at Saint-Omer when he received his promotion to *général de brigade* in February 1805, Graindorge had trained with his regiments for six months before the campaign began.[55] "It had been six years since our bayonets had vanquished the Russians," Graindorge recalled, "and remembering our past successes, we pressed quickly after the enemy, pushing them past Loiben."[56]

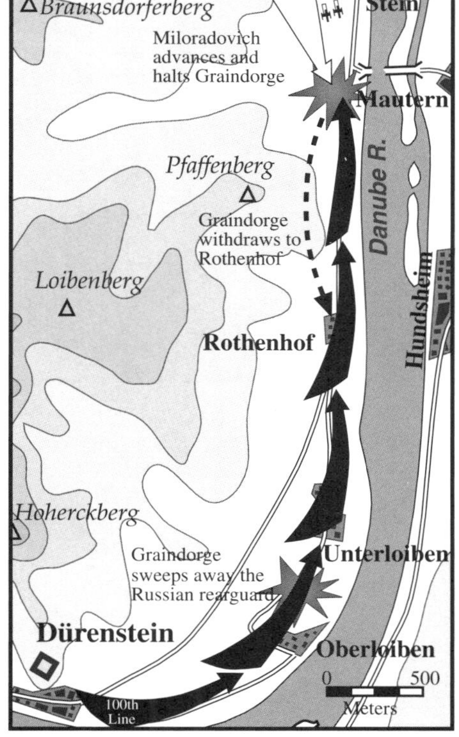

The probe towards Krems, 10 November 1805

At Graindorge's side was Colonel Ritay, another veteran of the Revolutionary wars, and part of the *Armée d'Helvétie* circle who served in the Zürich campaign of 1799. Ritay and Graindorge urged their men eastwards past the tiny establishment of Rothenhof and the rocky cliffs of the Pfaffenberg before finally coming upon the remains of the destroyed Mautern Bridge in the shadow of the Braunsdorferberg only one mile from Krems. It was there that Graindorge's men were met by fire from two Russian 6-pounder guns outside the hamlet of Stein, signalling the advance of a much larger body of Russian troops.

Graindorge's probing attack had stirred the Russian host. Lieutenant-General Miloradovich gathered several colonels, and together with the grenadier battalions of their respective regiments, counterattacked the 100th *Ligne*. The Russians advanced by fire fight and, following a lively exchange, Graindorge decided to pull Ritay's isolated regiment back to Rothenhof.

Shortly before 6:00 P.M., darkness settled over the battlefield and the fighting on the 10th came to an end. Mortier set up his headquarters in Ober Loiben, the

[50] S.H.A.T., C² 485.
[51] S.H.A.T., C² 481.
[52] S.H.A.T., C² 481. On 1 November, the foot artillery company numbered 117 officers and men under arms, while the section of horse artillerists numbered 46 combatants and the train personnel amounted to 108. A separate parade states dated 15 brumaire an XIV (6 November 1805) and signed by Compans, Mortier's chief of staff, show that Gazan's Division had a total of 5,932 officers and men under arms, which excludes the 4th Dragoons. However, since that report does not detail the strengths of the various units within the division, the report that does offer the unit specifics has been cited here.
[53] Please consult Appendix F for the Dürenstein Order of Battle.
[54] Egger, *Das Gefecht bei Dürenstein-Loiben 1805*, p. 13.
[55] Six, *Dictionnaire biographique*, vol. 1, p. 518.
[56] S.H.A.T., C² 8.

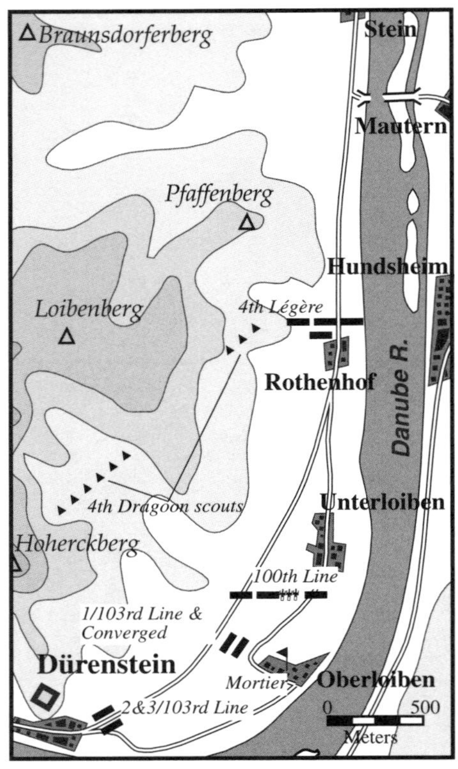

Gazan's division the night before the battle

westernmost portion of Loiben. Nearby was the *compagnie d'élite* of the 4th Dragoons and one battalion of the 103rd *Ligne*, along with an *ad hoc* battalion of converged élites formed with the grenadier and *carabinier* companies of all nine battalions of the division and placed under the command of *chef de bataillon* Tripoul from Gazan's staff. The remainder of the 2nd Brigade, led by *général de brigade* François-Frédéric Campana, consisted of Colonel Eloi-Charlemagne Taupin and his two remaining battalions of the 103rd *Ligne*. These men remained west of Ober Loiben near Dürenstein as the divisional reserve. The marshal then deployed Graindorge's 1st Brigade in two lines east of town in order to cover the river road approach from Krems. The front line consisted of Colonel de Bazancourt and the three battalions of the 4th *Légère*. These troops were positioned near Rothenhof where the flat, river road area was at its narrowest. Meanwhile, Colonel Ritay and the three battalions of the 100th *Ligne*, along with the three pieces of ordnance, formed the second line. The 4th Dragoons—minus the Élite Company serving as Mortier's mounted escort—were thrown out as vedettes to the north to watch the defiles that led between the various heights directly into Dürenstein and Loiben. No troops were posted to watch the gorges that led from the vineyard plains to the river road west of Dürenstein. The reason for this was that General Dupont and his command were known to be bedded down for the night 15 miles to the west in Marbach with the Batavian troops under Dumonceau bivouacked two miles behind Dupont. Mortier also knew that he and Gazan needed support and had therefore ordered both trailing divisions to hurry to Dürenstein on the 11th.

If the scouting reports by the allied cavalry prior to the combat on the 10th had not informed Kutuzov as to the strength and exposed position of the French on the north bank, then all doubt was removed from interrogation of two wounded prisoners taken during that afternoon's fighting. The captives' story was seconded by another member of Mortier's command who was taken prisoner while foraging for food after disembarking from one of the precious boats gathered by *lieutenant de vaisseau* Lostange.[57] The tale told by the French prisoners was consistent and almost too good to be true: encamped only three miles away from Kutuzov's headquarters in Krems were 6,000 Frenchmen, isolated and inviting destruction.

Armed with this information, Kutuzov's chief of staff, FML Heinrich von Schmidt, convinced the Russian general that he *had* to act at once. Before formulating his plan of action, the Russian general reviewed the dispositions and condition of his army. After the completion of the withdrawal over the Danube and the destruction of the Mautern Bridge, most of the Russian army was in and around the villages of Stein and Krems. The hasty retreat from Braunau had worn out men and horses, and Kutuzov had planned to give his troops a badly needed break during 10 and 11 November.

The undernourished animals that labored to pull the army's ordnance were unhitched from their traces while fodder to feed them was confiscated from every house and farm from Krems to Hollabrunn, some 20 miles away to the northeast. East of Krems was the majority of the army consisting of Dokhturov's III, Skepelev's IV and Maltitz's V Columns, while billeted in Krems and Stein were the II Column under Essen and the Advance Guard of Miloradovich. The army's I Column under Bagration extended to the northwest over the wine country to cover that flank. Also placed under Bagration's command were the few Austrians that remained with the army. Two battalions of the Broder *Grenz* #7 and two battalions of Peterwardeiner *Grenz* #9—all terribly weakened from losses suffered at Amstetten and the retreat—were in a brigade commanded by GM von Nostitz-Rieneck. Meanwhile, the Cüirassier-Regiment Nassau-Usingen #5 and the Cüirassier-Regiment Lothringen #7, each with eight squadrons, and the six squadrons of

[57] Lomier, *Le Bataillon des Marins de la Garde*, p. 83.

Hussar-Regiment Hessen-Homburg #4 under FML Hohenlohe completed the Austrian forces that had been roughly handled at Amstetten. (The Székler Hussars that had fought at Amstetten were no longer present as they had been ordered to Vienna.) Kutuzov's staff officers reported on 10 November that only 23,980 Russian regulars remained under arms (see page 293). To this number must be added no more than 2,500 Austrians in the four skeleton-like *Grenzer* battalions and 22 depleted squadrons still marching with Kutuzov. This meant that the 58 battalions (54 of them Russian), 62 squadrons (of which 40 were Russian and excluded the Cossacks) and 14 companies of Russian artillery were woefully understrength. The once proud squadrons that boasted 150 combatants or more now barely mounted 100 men. Meanwhile, the battalions that started the campaign averaging just under 700 people under the banners of the Tsar could only muster between 50% to 60% that strength. Also depleted were the emaciated teams of horses that pulled the army's ordnance and wagons. The shrinking number of underfed animals meant more work for all concerned.[58]

Amidst this disheartened and disintegrating army encamped in and around Krems arrived two messengers looking for Kutuzov. One brought word from Lieutenant-General Rosen that his VI Column of the army would soon make their belated arrival into the theater of war at Teschen, where Kutuzov's main body had camped on 22 September. A second messenger was from Tsar Alexander—he was in route along with General F. W. Buxhöwden's 26,450-man army, plus another 8,500 men of the vaunted Russian Imperial Guard. With Rosen's nine battalions and 10 squadrons, plus the additional forces with Buxhöwden and the Tsar, Kutuzov wanted to remain on the Danube, await these reinforcements and contest any crossing of the river. However, before the whereabouts of Gazan's Frenchmen were known, Kutuzov wanted to rest his weary troops before going into battle.

When 10 November dawned, Kutuzov's starving army spent most of the day ransacking Stein, Krems and the surrounding villages and hamlets in search of food. Horrified townspeople and nearby farmers alike took shelter from the Slavic marauders. The atrocities committed by the Russian troops upon the Austrian populace in and around the Krems area were described by 53-year-old Prince FML Friedrich Karl von Hohenlohe, the commander of the Austrian cavalry. "Dozens of these subhuman creatures would force their way into a house or farm. The Russians either killed or carried off the livestock and foodstuffs; and most households where the Russians entered were left in dishonor."[59] The raping and pillaging finally slacked off in the mid-afternoon when many of the men either returned voluntarily, or were herded back to their units as a result of the firing coming from the direction of the river road; the noise was Graindorge's troops that had pushed back the allied rearguard to Stein. After dark, with the location and strength of the French established, Kutuzov could not let the opportunity pass to destroy Gazan's exposed command—the Russian commander ordered the dispositions for an attack beginning early the next morning.

Troops were reshuffled from the existing columns in order to create six attack columns for the upcoming battle. The designations of the attack columns, the leaders, composition and objectives were set forth by Kutuzov as follows:

I. Column — Lieutenant-General M. A. Miloradovich would attack down the river road from Stein to Loiben. Under his command were 2,500 combatants. These consisted of six battalions of infantry from the

[58] K. k. Kriegsarchiv, *Kriegschronik Österreich-Ungarns.* Militärischer Fürhrer auf den Kriegsschauplätzen der Monarchie, II. "Der südwestliche Kriegsschauplatz im Donauthale und in den österreichischen Alpenländern" (Vienna, 1886).
[59] K. k. Kriegsarchiv, *Kriegschronik Österreich-Ungarns.*

Essen

following regiments: all the battalions (two musketeer and one grenadier) of the Apsheron Musketeer Regiment; the grenadier battalion from the Smolensk Musketeer Regiment; the grenadier battalion from the Little Russia Grenadier Regiment; and the 1st Battalion from the 8th *Jaeger* Regiment. Also attached were two squadrons of the Mariupol Hussar Regiment and four 6-pounder battalion guns.

II. Column — Lieutenant-General D. S. Dokhturov was to march along the plateau road north of the river through the vineyards, then turn his 6,000 men to the south and pass through the defiles to arrive behind Dürenstein. Serving under Dokhturov were 16 battalions of infantry consisting of: all battalions of the Musketeer Regiments Moscow, Yaroslav and Vyatka; the two musketeer battalions from each the Bryansk and Narva Musketeer Regiments; and three battalions from the 6th *Jaeger* Regiment. Attached to the column were two squadrons of the Mariupol Hussars and two 6-pounder battalion guns.

III. Column — Major-General Strik would march with Dokhturov as far as the hamlet of Egelsee, then turn south, and move down the gorge between the Schloßberg and Loihenberg, striking the French in the flank around Dürenstein. Due to the difficult terrain that Strik would traverse, his command consisted only of five battalions of infantry numbering a mere 1,790 effectives. Three battalions (two musketeer and one grenadier) were from the Butyrsk Musketeer Regiment and the 2nd and 3rd Battalions were from the 8th *Jaeger* Regiment.

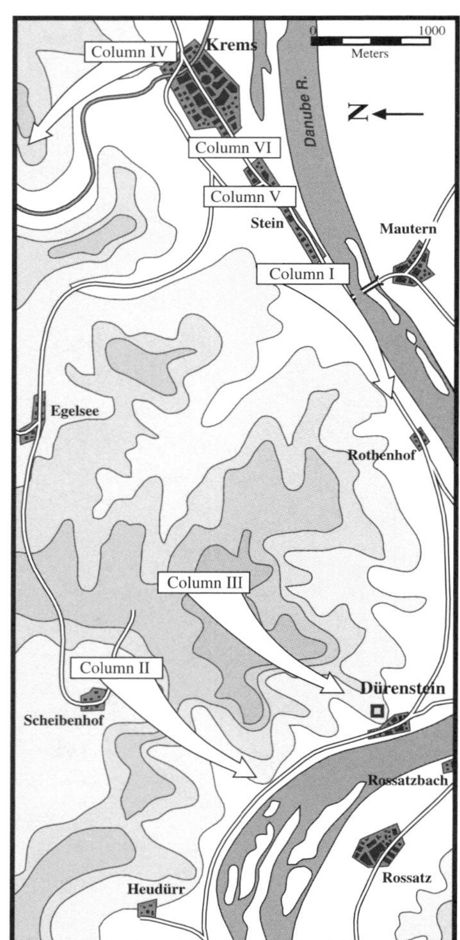

The Russian Plan for Dürenstein

IV. Column — Major-General Prince P. I. Bagration would command 6,000 troops divided into 11 battalions that included all three battalions of the Kiev Grenadier Regiment, all three battalions of the Azov Musketeer Regiment, one battalion of the Podolia Musketeer Regiment, the four Austrian *Grenzer* battalions and all 22 squadrons of Hohenlohe's Austrian cavalry. These troops would deploy along the road from Krems to Zwettl in order to protect the northwestern flank of the army.

V. Column — Lieutenant-General Essen would stand in reserve at Stein. The column consisted of 3,500 men in six battalions and 11 squadrons. Essen's infantry contingent consisted of two musketeer battalions from the Smolensk Musketeer Regiment, the two fusilier battalions from the Little Russia Grenadier Regiment, the grenadier battalions from the Bryansk and the Narva Musketeer Regiments. Essen's cavalry included the five squadrons of the Chernigov Dragoons and the remaining six squadrons of the Mariupol Hussars.

VI. Column — Except for six 6-pounder guns that accompanied the troops under Miloradovich and Dokhturov, all 14 companies of artillery (with 162 pieces of ordnance) served by 3,176 gunners and train personnel would be positioned between Krems and Stein, sighted towards the Danube in order to repulse any attempted French waterborne movement.

Due to the poor condition of the horses in many of the artillery companies, most of these pieces were left in reserve and did not accompany the infantry into the fighting at Dürenstein. Also of great concern was the shaky morale in the Pavlograd Hussars, the Khaznenkov and Sysoev Cossacks. These three regiments totaling 20 squadrons had crossed the Danube earlier without authorization when many of the officers deserted. Without proper supervision, the troopers spread out into the nearby countryside, looting and raping. This chaos drew the attention of Kutuzov's staff, and two such officers spent the 10th and 11th rounding up members of these regiments, replacing bad officers and restoring order.

The converging columns were supposed to arrive about the same time and, in a determined attack, overwhelm the French in and around Dürenstein.[60]

Miloradovich

While Kutuzov was rearranging his regiments and giving orders for the planned destruction of Gazan's men, the French were trying to get some rest while battling the numbing effects of the winter night. "Snow covered the ground, and the cold was biting," one Frenchman wrote. "We maintained our bivouac fires by feeding them with the wooden stakes that supported the vineyards."[61] Shortly before dawn on 11 November, Mortier knew that the day would bring renewed hostilities, and gave the order for the men to drop their packs and overcoats to prepare for action. The marshal also ordered Gazan's artillery commander, *chef de bataillon* St. Loup de Fabvier, to finalize the deployment of the division's three artillery pieces manned by a combination of both foot and horse artillerists. The two 8-pounders and one 6-inch howitzer were unlimbered astride the road in support of the regiment that formed the second line of Graindorge's 1st Brigade—the 100th *Ligne*. The pieces were ready for action when, shortly after 8:00 A.M., the troops under Miloradovich were seen coming up the narrow way.

These Russians had moved out from Stein an hour earlier and thought that they would be attacking about the time that the flanking columns appeared from the north. Marching in dense columns of half-companies, the compact formations made easy targets for the three French light infantry battalions formed in line, who opened a deadly fire "that made the most fearful ravages in their ranks."[62] Passing over the bodies of their fallen comrades, the two serried battalions of grenadiers wearing gray overcoats and tall mitre caps pressed onward and "threw themselves upon [one battalion] of the light infantrymen." The French defended themselves as best they could, but could not keep the overwhelming numbers of the determined giants from closing. The ferocious Russian grenadiers soon were intermingled with bluecoated Frenchmen. "There is no doubt," maintained St. Loup de Fabvier, "that we would have held the [first line] position had all of our guns been present and deployed to support the light infantry."[63]

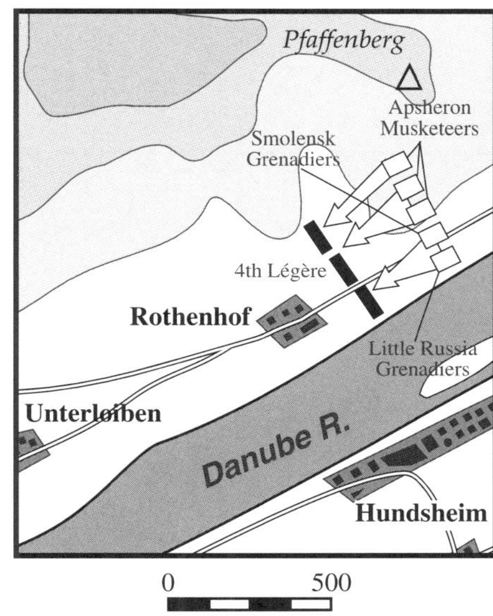

Miloradovich meets the 4th Légère

Posted on a low rise near this *mêlée* were Colonel de Bazancourt and the remaining two of his three understrength battalions of the 4th *Légère*. While the grenadiers from the Smolensk Musketeer Regiment and the grenadiers from the Little Russia Grenadier Regiment faced off against one of his battalions, all three battalions of the Apsheron Musketeer Regiment attacked the remaining two battalions under de Bazancourt. Every charge directed upon the light infantrymen was met with crushing volleys that consumed the leading ranks of the Russian columns. With each repulse, the Apsheron battalions reformed and came on again, and each time the head of their formations crumpled before the deadly fire of the 4th *Légère*. As the blue ranks were mowing down the Apsherons, the Russian grenadiers succeeded in overcoming the other French battalion, thereby exposing the flank of de Bazancourt's two other battalions. The French colonel had no choice but to fall back with his men. They had retired only a short distance when *général de brigade* Graindorge countermanded the order to withdraw. He had sent word to Mortier requesting help, and believed that the narrow defensive line around Rothenhof should be reestablished.[64]

---

[60] Egger, *Das Gefecht bei Dürenstein-Loiben 1805*, pp. 14-15 and 30-31.
[61] Alombert-Goget and Colin, *La Campagne de 1805 en Allemagne*, XXIV, p. 535.
[62] S.H.A.T., C^2 7.
[63] S.H.A.T., C^2 7.
[64] S.H.A.T., C^2 7 and 9.

The church at Dürenstein

Bazancourt obeyed his orders and halted his regiment in the face of the oncoming masses of the enemy that were enveloping his flanks. Stopping the regiment turned out to be a useless sacrifice. The 4th *Légère* was soon surrounded with the Danube to its back. Realizing the hopelessness of the situation, de Bazancourt ordered his men to break out and make their way back to Loiben. The majority of the 1st and 3rd Battalions succeeded in breaking off with the colonel, but the 2nd Battalion was trapped at the water's edge. Although himself wounded, *chef de batallion* Chevillet was determined not to let the unit's sacred eagle and flag fall into Russian hands. After breaking the staff in two, Chevillet cast the eagle and flag into the frigid waters of the Danube; they were never found. Following this last act of defiance, Chevillet and a few comrades then fought their way through the Russian ranks and eventually rejoined de Bazancourt around Ober Loiben.[65]

Graindorge's request for the 100th *Ligne* to advance to the support of the 4th *Légère* had not been carried out at once. The call for help was intended to be delivered to Colonel Ritay by Lieutenant Mignot of Graindorge's staff. Before Mignot could find Ritay, the colonel had received orders to withdraw towards Loiben. These instructions had been relayed to Ritay by Captain Thuillier—one of Mortier's two aides-de-camp. By the time Mortier's aide returned to the marshal with Ritay in tow, Mignot was close behind. These men found Mortier next to the road just northwest of Unter Loiben. *Général de brigade* François-Frédéric Campana was alongside the marshal, and remembered what happened next:

> General Graindorge's aide delivered the request for assistance, which was turned down by the marshal. 'We will not commit any more of our men forward,' he declared. 'We will instead draw the enemy into our defensive positions where our artillery can hit him and we will counterattack and overturn his formations.'[66]

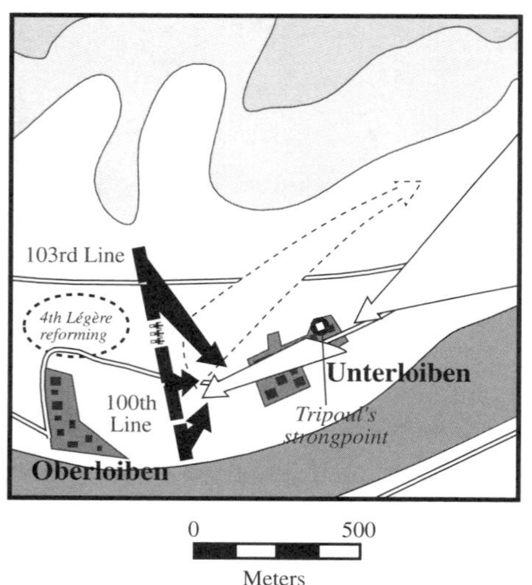

The action around Unter Loiben

Almost as soon as Mortier made this decision, hundreds of fugitives from the 4th *Légère* were seen streaming back towards Loiben. Time was needed to rally these survivors. To provide a covering force for the 4th *Légère*, Ritay then rode off to ready the 100th *Ligne* as the marshal ordered Campana to collect the 103rd *Ligne*, which was standing in deep reserve, and to bring that regiment forward so that his entire brigade could operate together. By doing this, the French totally abandoned the village of Dürenstein in order to fight the Russians east of town.

Mortier then instructed Gazan to quickly set up an improvised strong point in the tiny settlement of Unter Loiben around which the division could conduct a defense. For this task, Tripoul's converged élites were soon hustled off to the hamlet where Gazan directed the bearskins to barricade themselves in one of the masonry buildings on the north edge of the village. Upon entering the structure, the sappers of the grenadier and *carabinier* companies feverishly went to work to strengthen the doors as well as loophole the walls as the sounds of the fighting to the east grew louder.

The rolling fire heard by the French engineers signaled the arrival of Miloradovich's troops that were following de Bazancourt's disorganized survivors fleeing before the Russian advance. Pursuing the 4th *Légère* into the open and level ground east of Unter Loiben, the Russian battalions paused to shake out from the narrow and deep columns that they were forced to employ around Rothenhof. Once the formation changes were completed, Miloradovich ordered his units to

[65] S.H.A.T., C[2] 8.

[66] S.H.A.T., C[2] 7.

resume their advance on Unter Loiben. They arrived outside town just as Gazan was galloping away after giving Tripoul his final instructions to hold fast.

Another view of Dürenstein's church

The Russians passed through the village and by its northern edge as Tripoul's men began shooting up the flanks of Miloradovich's battalions. Before long, some of the Russian formations became disordered. By the time Miloradovich's men were between Unter and Ober Loiben, they were subjected to a murderous fire from the three guns and a coordinated counterattack by five battalions of the 100th and 103rd *Ligne*, directed by *général de brigade* Campana. "The Russians were superior in number but they were encumbered by the size of their greatcoats. Their slow movements gave us a great advantage, and we owed our success to the clumsiness of the enemy and our own speed in the attack."[67] The Frenchmen drove the Russians back past the east edge of town. Then, in keeping with the tactical doctrine of the strong point defensive scheme, Gazan's officers reset their defense in preparation to repulse the next attack. The Russians did not disappoint them. Three times Miloradovich sent his men against Gazan's position. Each time, the Russians stormed into and past the tiny town, pushing the French *tirailleurs* before them and gaining possession of Unter Loiben with the exception of Tripoul's strong point. Once past the few buildings, the Russians threw themselves upon the French line with ferocity, only to have their thinning ranks ripped by blasts of canister from the deadly 8-pounders and 6-inch howitzer. Every attack ended when the Tsar's troops were driven back by the coordinated counterattacks of the 100th and 103rd *Ligne*. Frustrated by Tripoul's strong point, the Russians made an effort to fire the entire hamlet during their last attack. However, after three and one-half hours of this swirling combat, the French, utilizing their makeshift strong point defense around which they conducted an active counterattacking defense, had succeeded in completely eviscerating Miloradovich's command. Of the 2,500 combatants that the Russian general had started the battle, over 900 were killed and wounded. Another 600 of the Tsar's troops had been taken prisoner, including Colonel Denissev, commander of the Little Russia Grenadier Regiment.[68]

The ebb and flow around Unter Loiben had continued until noon. With Unter Loiben on fire and Tripoul's men evacuating their position, Mortier sensed that the Russian attacks had played out and that the time was right to hit hard and drive back for good the weakened battalions of Miloradovich. The marshal gave Gazan new orders: take the rallied elements of de Bazancourt's 4th *Légère*, move across the heights of the Hoherechberg and turn the Russian right flank while the 100th and 103rd *Ligne* attacked their front. Seeking revenge for what had happened to them earlier that day, and with Gazan in front of their ranks, the 4th *Légère* swept up the heights, overunning the 1st Battalion from the 8th *Jaeger* Regiment and capturing in the process 200 *jaeger* along with the four 6-pounder guns attached to Miloradovich's Column.[69] Gazan and Colonel de Bazancourt were taking stock of their catch when General Strik suddenly made his belated appearance with his 2,400 men. These troops consisted of the Butyrsk Musketeer Regiment, the 2nd and 3rd Battalions from the 8th *Jaeger* Regiment and two battalions of the Yaroslav Musketeer Regiment picked up from Dokhturov's Column. Without hesitating, Gazan told the 4th *Légère* to "Follow Me!" The general led the light infantrymen

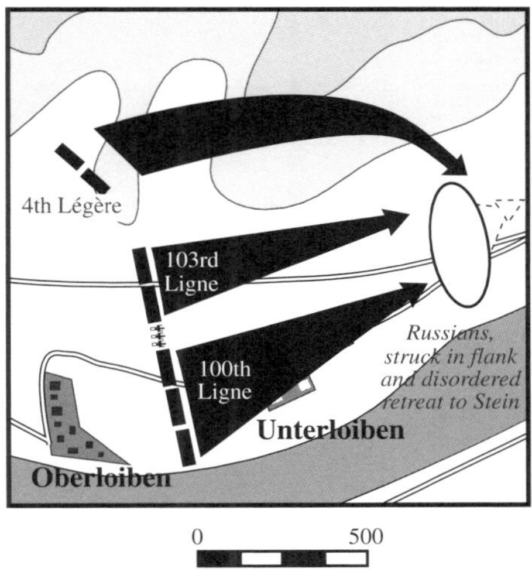

The conclusion of the action around Unter Loiben

[67] Alombert-Goget and Colin, *La Campagne de 1805 en Allemagne*, XXIV, p. 537.

[68] S.H.A.T., C² 8; Colonel Frignet Despréaux, *Le Maréchal Mortier,* 3 volumes (Paris, 1913), vol. 3, pp. 98-103; Captain Paul Claude Alombert-Goget, *Campagne de l'an XIV (1805); Le Corps d'Armée aux Ordres du Maréchal Mortier, Combat de Durrenstein* (Paris, 1897), pp. 106-108; General Serge Andolenko, *Aigles de Napoléon Contre Drapeaux du Tsar* (Paris, 1969), p. 67; Egger, *Das Gefecht bei Dürenstein-Loiben 1805*, p. 18.

[69] S.H.A.T., C² 7 and 15; Alombert-Goget, *Combat de Durrenstein,* p. 108; Alombert-Goget and Colin, *La Campagne de 1805 en Allemagne*, XXIV, pp. 536-538; Despréaux, *Le Maréchal Mortier,* vol. 3, p. 102.

Above and top next page, a panorama of the battlefield as seen from the top of Dürenstein castle.

Left, the Danube at Dürenstein.

Right, Unter Loiben

Below, a view from the floor of the valley, next to the Danube, looking across vineyard stakes to the heights that screened Dokhturov's advance to Dürenstein. Note Dürenstein castle to the far left on the opposite page.

Dokhturov

in an uphill charge that broke Strik's startled *jaeger* battalions. These routed units then panicked the musketeer regiments behind them. Almost as soon as Strik's Column had arrived on the field of battle, it departed in ignominious flight.

Watching his battalions get shredded in their repeated attempts to capture Loiben, then observing Strik's brief engagement, Miloradovich gained a healthy respect for the resiliency of the French troops and their aggressive counterattacking defense. What's more, with Strik's supporting command now driven from the field, with his own right flank now turned, with his guns lost and his battalions shattered, Miloradovich had no choice but to try and disengage from the clutches of Gazan's men.

Meanwhile, Gazan knew what to do against a foe that had reached the end of his staying power. He ordered his men to "keep their bayonets to the enemy's back"[70] and pursued Miloradovich's Russians with vigor. The French soon passed the point next to the river where the 4th *Légère* had been trapped during the morning's fighting, then regained their original position near Rothenhof. The ground was clearly marked by the rows of dead and squirming wounded where the Russians had first engaged the 4th *Légère*. Advancing further eastward while pushing Miloradovich's depleted battalions before them, Gazan's men reached the destroyed Mautern Bridge outside Stein. They halted their counteroffensive just outside range of the massive Russian artillery reserve. Mortier reported that: "By 2:00 P.M., the firing diminished noticeably from all quarters as the affair appeared to be ended entirely. I decided to remain in my new positions until the arrival of Dupont and Dumonceau whom I had given orders to force march to rejoin me."[71]

What Mortier thought to be the end of the action was only the *entre acte*. Unknown to the marshal was the movement of Dokhturov's flanking column that had left Krems at midnight. The Russians had to traverse ice and snow-covered roads, and the men were weakened from not having had a hot meal for the last two days. As a result, Dokhturov's command moved at a torturously slow pace. It took the Russians two hours to march one and one-half miles from Krems to Egelsee. After two more hours they arrived at Rennerkreuz, having labored to move only one more mile.[72]

At Rennerkreuz about 5:00 A.M., Dokhturov split his column into the following four tactical commands: 1) General Gerhardt, with the two battalions of musketeers from the Bryansk Musketeer Regiment, was ordered to move down the valley between the Loihenberg and Scholßberg, protecting the left (east) flank of the column; 2) Dokhturov would lead five battalions. These consisted of all three battalions of the 6th *Jaeger* Regiment and the two musketeer battalions of the Narva Musketeer Regiment, supported by the 200 troopers of the two squadrons of the Mariupol Hussars. This command would move down the valley between the Jägerberg and Vogelberg; 3) FML Heinrich von Schmidt, the army's chief of staff, would advance with six battalions consisting of the entire Vyatka and Moscow Musketeer Regiments. These troops would continue to move to the west through Resch, then turn south through the gap west of the Jägerberg. These troops would provide the right (west) flank protection for the column; and 4) The grenadier and one of the musketeer battalions of the Yaroslav Musketeer Regiment (the remaining musketeer battalion having been sent back to Krems shortly after midnight by Dokhturov because the officers had completely lost control of the unit as it broke ranks and pillaged Egelsee)—were left behind in Egelsee; they joined in with Strik shortly after noon.

Dürenstein Castle today. The name may sound familiar, for Richard the Lionheart was long held captive within its walls on his return from the Crusades.

---

[70] S.H.A.T., C[2] 7.

[71] S.H.A.T., C[2] 7; Despréaux, *Le Maréchal Mortier,* vol. 3, p. 104.

[72] Lieutenant-General Aleksandr Ivanovich Mikhailovsky-Danilevsky, *Relation de la campagne de 1805* (Paris, 1846), pp. 117-118; Egger, *Das Gefecht bei Dürenstein-Loiben 1805*, p. 15.

Dokhturov's four tactical commands eventually separated and continued on their march towards Dürenstein and the Danube. General Gerhardt led his two battalions southward to Scheibenhof, then continued on the southward trek, turning east and arriving at Neudeck about noon. Incredibly, it had taken Gerhardt seven hours to move the one and one-half mile distance from Rennerkreuz to Neudeck! When he arrived at Neudeck, he did so without the regimental ammunition wagons; they had slid off the icy roads in route. The remaining two miles from Neudeck to Dürenstein were covered over the next three hours. Finally reaching the Danube, Gerhardt attacked the French outposts at Dürenstein about 3:30 P.M.

Almost the same time that Gerhardt's two battalions were moving into Dürenstein, Dokhturov reached the Danube some 2,100 yards to the west. About 4:00 P.M., Schmidt's troops—less one battalion of musketeers whose men had collapsed from exhaustion upon reaching Resch—emerged through the snow choked mountain pass west of Dokhturov's five battalions. With the arrival on the Danube, Dokhturov's numbed troops had finally completed their grueling 16-hour march.[73]

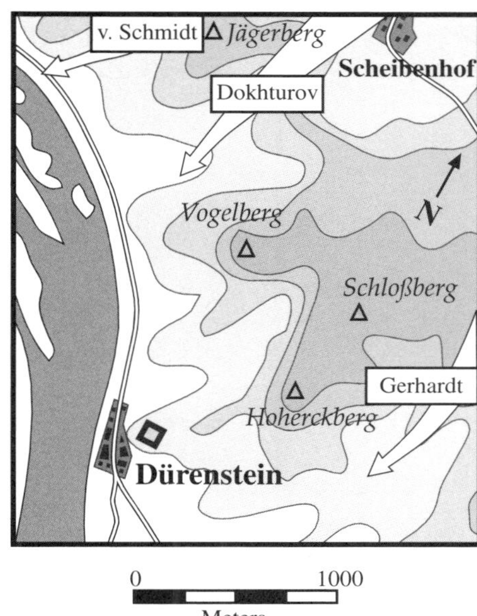

The Russians approach Dürenstein

The Russian's sudden appearance behind French lines and their capture of Dürenstein, while not achieved with celerity, posed the most serious problems for the French. If Gazan's men were unable to breakthrough the blocking Russian forces and march west to link up with reinforcements, they would eventually run out of ammunition and be incapable of further resistance. Riding up to Mortier with news of Dokhturov's presence were the survivors of the 4th Dragoons, including the regimental commander, Colonel Watier de Saint-Alphonse. The humbled officer informed Mortier that his mounted command had been surrounded and mauled by the Mariupol Hussars, and if it had not been for the "courageous resistance of *chef d'escadron* Rozat, who saved the standards of the regiment as well as 24 troopers,"[74] perhaps all would have perished. As it was, Rozat—who in 1814 recalled that the 4th Dragoons of 1805 had been a "miserable regiment"[75]—was one of only 123 officers and men to report for duty after the battle.[76]

The significance of the Russian flanking march and their positions astride the French line of communication was not lost on any officer or man under Mortier. To get out of the predicament, Mortier wanted to break the Russian infantry holding the river road and reestablish communication to the west with Dupont and Dumonceau. The marshal ordered Colonel Watier de Saint-Alphonse to accompany him and the Élite Company of the 4th Dragoons to Dürenstein. At the head of the bearskin cavalrymen, the marshal charged the Russian infantry, but was unable to break their formations. In this close action combat, small arms fire struck and killed Kutuzov's chief of staff, FML von Schmidt. Whether Schmidt was felled by a carbine or pistol shot from the 4th Dragoons, or from Russian 'friendly fire' as whispered in some corners at allied headquarters, Kutuzov's army had lost a valuable officer.[77] Even though Schmidt was down, more of his battalions rushed towards the fighting, forcing Mortier to withdraw to Unter Loiben with his escort. Calling together his senior officers, Mortier had to assess his options at once. Gazan reported that the small arms ammunition for the division was all but exhausted. One company of the 100th *Ligne* had run out of ammunition over an hour ago. The men were using the pause in the fighting to scavenge what cartridges they could find off those who had fallen. Graindorge and Watier de Saint-Alphonse implored their commanding officer to escape by boat, thereby depriving the Russians of capturing

A street scene from Dürenstein today.

[73] Egger, *Das Gefecht bei Dürenstein-Loiben 1805*, pp. 15-16.

[74] S.H.A.T., C^2 7.

[75] Andolenko, *Aigles de Napoléon Contre Drapeaux du Tsar*, p. 72; Alombert-Goget, *Combat de Durrenstein.*

[76] S.H.A.T., C^2 472.

[77] Egger, *Das Gefecht bei Dürenstein-Loiben 1805*, pp. 27-28.

Mortier refuses to abandon his command "No! We must not separate from these brave fellow; we must be saved or perish together!"

a Marshal of France. Campana remembered the marshal's response to this entreatment. "No!" defiantly answered Mortier. "We must not separate from these brave fellows; we must be saved or perish together!"[78] The defiant marshal ordered Gazan to have his division do an about face to the west. They would fight their way back to safety. Mortier could only hope that the sounds of the battle had hastened Dupont towards the fighting. With the marshal leading Gazan's men, and with Dupont believed to be doing the same from the other direction, Mortier was resolved to fight his way out of the trap or die trying.

Mortier's determination was about to be seconded by the officers and troops under Dupont. *Général de division* Dupont de l'Étang had heard the fighting around Dürenstein and knew what to do. Urging on the heroes of Haslach-Jüngingen, Dupont marched his men as fast as they could throughout the morning and early afternoon hours of the 11th. Dupont's Division had already covered 15 miles over treacherous roads from Marbach to Weissenkirchen when the leading elements arrived at the latter village at 4:00 P.M. About this time, Dupont received word from the scouts of the 1st Hussars that there were blocking Russian forces between his men and the fighting. Dupont formed his 4,150 officers and men for battle. The spearhead of the command would be the division's best troops—Colonel Meunier's 9th *Légère* led by *général de brigade* Rouyer. Support for the light infantrymen would be provided by *général de brigade* Marchand with Colonel Darricau and the 32nd *Ligne*. Colonel Barrois' 96th *Ligne*, along with the divisional artillery that was trailing far behind, would be in reserve under the command of Dupont.[79]

As it flows from Weissenkirchen to Dürenstein, the Danube begins to bend to the southeast. That is where the 9th *Légère* came upon the western-most Russians, those being Colonel Bibikov's Vyatka Musketeer Regiment of Schmidt's tactical command from Dokhturov's Column. Bibikov's men caught the full fury of *"l'Incomparable."* The regimental history of the Vyatka Musketeers vividly describes that the "savage bayonet attack" by Colonel Meunier's two battalions of superb light infantrymen "threw the regiment into disorder, and Colonel Bibikov was carried away."[80] Colonel Meunier recalled that "the determination of our men could not be resisted. The charge was led by the *carabiniers*, and almost in an instant, our bayonets completely swept away the leading enemy battalion."[81] The butchered unit was the grenadier battalion of the Vyatka Musketeer Regiment. In addition to the regimental colonel being captured, dead were four officers and 199 men, while only 48 were wounded and another 61 captured.[82] Hundreds more of the Vyatka Musketeers ran northward towards the mountain valleys while another 400 jumped into the dark, icy waters of the Danube in an attempt to escape the unstoppable, deadly meat grinder of the 9th *Légère*. The light infantrymen also captured two standards from the Vyatka Musketeers. One of the blue and purple standards was snatched by Captain Leblanc after he killed the Russian colorguard, while the other was taken by a drummer boy named Drapier of the *carabiniers*. Once again, the 9th *Légère* had "upheld its ferocious reputation and covered itself with glory."[83]

The Viatka Regiment lost two flags to the 9th Légère, one of them a purple and mid-blue version of the older flag pattern

---

[78] S.H.A.T., C² 7; Thiers, *The History of the Consulate & the Empire of France*, vol. 2, p. 64.

[79] S.H.A.T., *Journal des opérations du 6ᵉ corps.* The division had 3,895, plus general officers and staff members, on 7 brumaire (29 October). These numbers increased slightly before the battle as some men previously in hospital returned to ranks. Also, see consult Appendix F.

[80] Andolenko, *Aigles de Napoléon Contre Drapeaux du Tsar*, p. 67.

[81] S.H.A.T., *Journal des opérations du 6ᵉ corps.*

[82] Andolenko, *Aigles de Napoléon Contre Drapeaux du Tsar*, p. 67.

[83] S.H.A.T., *Journal des opérations du 6ᵉ corps;* Andolenko, *Aigles de Napoléon Contre Drapeaux du Tsar*, p. 67.

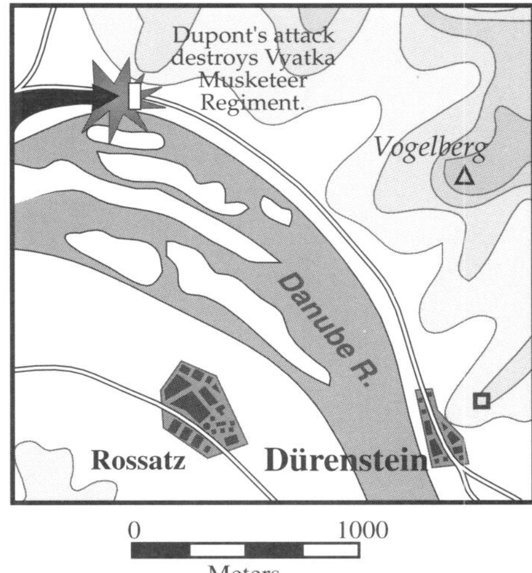

The arrival of Dupont

The savage dusk attack by Dupont's 9th *Légère,* ably supported by the 32nd *Ligne*, shattered Schmidt's hold on the river road west of Dürenstein. Meanwhile, Mortier and Gazan were gathering their men to conduct their own heroics. The trapped division east of Dürenstein needed a unit to spearhead its escape. Major Jean-François Henriod of the 100th *Ligne* offered to lead the grenadiers of his regiment seven abreast down the narrow river road (the companies from Tripoul's converged battalion having since rejoined their parent units). When called to rise to the challenge before them, the soldiers of the 100th shouted that "they would never surrender... and... they were not the [Austrian] soldiers of Ulm."[84] Mortier, Gazan and their staffs were on horseback along with the *compagnie d'élite* of the 4th Dragoons as they rode between the 1st and 2nd Battalions of the 100th *Ligne*. The French launched an unstoppable charge into the cold November night. With sword in hand, the 6-foot, 4-inch Mortier struck an imposing figure, riding high in the saddle on his charger and cutting down Russians with the force of his powerful swing. The marshal "was taller than anyone else, and became a favorite target even in the darkness."[85] The *fantassins* of the 100th *Ligne* followed Mortier, first hacking their way through Gerhardt's two battalions of the Bryansk Musketeers, then carving up the 6th *Jaeger* Regiment before linking up with Dupont's men. Meanwhile, Gazan and the Élite Company of the 4th Dragoons broke free on the Hohereckberg and escaped into the darkness. These mounted Frenchmen soon came across two farmers and persuaded the locals at pistol point to lead them westward past the Russians and to safety.[86]

Many French were not so lucky. Separated from the remainder of their commands, some found their way to the Danube where only three boats were waiting to pick up survivors. One boatload of Frenchmen stayed near the northern bank and successfully rowed upstream to Weissenkirchen and the safety of Dupont's command. Another got too far out into the river where the current swept the boat downstream to Stein where it was blasted out of the water by the Russian artillery. A third boat picked up several officers, including Generals Graindorge and Watier de Saint-Alphonse. As the crew of this boat rowed upstream for Weissenkirchen, the vessel came too close to the shore and got stranded on a sand bar; all aboard were captured by the Russians.

While these waterborne adventures were taking place, many of the survivors of the 4th Dragoons reached safety by following closely behind the 100th *Ligne*. The 3rd Battalion of the 100th *Ligne* escorted 800 Russian prisoners to French lines while the decimated 4th *Légère* proudly lugged one of the four captured 6-pounder guns to Weissenkirchen. The 103rd *Ligne*, however, became separated in the darkness and confusion. Instead of following the 100th *Ligne*, Colonel Taupin and his two battalions veered off course and unsuspectingly ran into Colonel Soulima's Moscow Musketeer Regiment. Until this late hour, the 103rd had suffered relatively few casualties while participating in the strong point defense around Unter Loiben. However, after a few moments of close combat with the Moscow Musketeers, the 103rd lost over 100 officers and men. One of the casualties was *sous-lieutenant* Ferrier, who lost his battalion's eagle and standard when he was killed by Sergeant Nikitine and Private Soloienko of the Moscow Musketeers. When Colonel Soulima returned to army headquarters with his trophy, Kutuzov said: "Colonel, you are very young... I would pay homage to your bravery, but that is only natural for a Russian; so let me salute your skill."[87]

---

[84] S.H.A.T., C^2 7; Despréaux, *Le Maréchal Mortier,* vol. 3, p. 104.

[85] *Memoirs of Ségur*, p. 219.

[86] Egger, *Das Gefecht bei Dürenstein-Loiben 1805*, p. 20.

[87] Andolenko, *Aigles de Napoléon Contre Drapeaux du Tsar*, pp. 67-68.

Soulima's trophy had been the lone bright spot in an otherwise dismal performance by the Russian army. The flanking column under Dokhturov had not kept to the timetable set by Kutuzov, leaving Miloradovich to bear the first half of the battle, while the second half was fought by Dokhturov's men who found themselves trapped between Gazan's and Dupont's French. Even with the advantages of knowing the enemy's position and strength, along with possessing superior numbers, the Russians found Mortier's men to be singularly indigestible.

The size of the Russian force hurled against Mortier has continually been misstated by historians as being 24,000. This reappearing mistake undoubtedly comes from authors either counting the total strength of all columns in Kutuzov's army, regardless of their involvement in the battle, or by assuming that all battalions engaged were at, or close to, full strength. However, only when considering just the columns engaged in the battle does one get a true picture of the odds that Mortier faced, as well as just how badly mauled were the understrength Russian regiments that fought at Dürenstein. The Russian columns that were engaged at Dürenstein—Miloradovich's I, Dokhturov's II, and Strik's III—combined to throw a total of 10,300 officers and men against the French. Of those engaged, the Russians lost a whopping 6,000 combatants—a casualty ratio of more than 58% of those engaged! Miloradovich's I Column was horribly butchered, suffering no less than 1,800 killed, wounded and captured of the 2,500 men that had started the battle. Strik lost another 600—most of them missing among the snow covered hills and valleys. Dokhturov had suffered a minimum of 1,900 casualties, with majority of the losses experienced by the Vyatka and Bryansk Musketeer Regiments, and by the 6th *Jaeger*. Losses by the three columns included two colonels and 800 prisoners taken on the 11th, to which must be added some 1,700 to 2,000 fugitives that were scattered into the mountains—few rejoined their units. Of the Russian wounded, some 1,200 were captured on the 14th when the French occupied the field hospitals that had been hastily set up, then abandoned, in Stein and Krems. In addition, two Russian flags were taken by the 9th *Légère*, while the 4th *Légère* came away with one of the 6-pounder guns that accompanied Miloradovich's Column.[88] Dokhturov was not able to bring his two guns into action; they had been left behind on the snow-choked roads, and one of those was abandoned after the battle.

Because the battle had been fought in two distinct phases, the Russians never outnumbered their worthy opponents. In the first phase of the battle, the majority of the fighting was shouldered by Miloradovich's men. These 2,500 were all but used up when Strik's battalions made their brief and inglorious appearance. After Dokhturov finally arrived behind French lines at Dürenstein, his 5,000 men (three of his original 16 battalions did not arrive with him on the Danube) unexpectedly became sandwiched between two fires—Gazan and his remaining 4,000 men to the east and Dupont's hard-charging 2,377 men of the 9th *Légère* and 32nd *Ligne* to the west. Had the converging Russian columns been able to attack Gazan or arrive on the Danube at the same time, there is little doubt that the French division would have perished. However, the weakened Tsarist battalions, the horrible weather, the almost impassable roads, the quality of the opposition and Kutuzov's unrealistic timetable—characteristic of the Russian general that FML Maximilian von Merveldt earlier described as being "unacquainted with the art of war"—all contributed to the Russian defeat.

Outnumbered but not outfought, the French had won a dramatic tactical triumph. Mortier's keen tactical skill was never better illustrated than at Dürenstein. He was seconded by excellent officers such as Gazan, and by tenacious veteran troops who flawlessly implemented an improvised strong point defensive scheme to produce another battlefield triumph for Napoleon's military machine. The price of victory was, however, bought dearly by Gazan's Division. Parade states taken

[88] S.H.A.T., C^2 470.

four days after Dürenstein on 15 November reveal that Gazan's command had 3,848 officers and men present and under arms, with another 829 in hospitals and 1,227 acknowledged to be lost as prisoners of war. Trapped against the Danube, the 4th *Légère* had suffered the most, including the loss of 788 as prisoners. The 100th *Ligne* had lost 175 men as prisoners, while the 103rd listed 167 captured, along with 97 of the 4th Dragoons.[89] When those present on 15 November are compared to the 6,000 that entered the battle (excluding general staff members), Gazan's Division suffered 2,152 casualties at Dürenstein—a loss of approximately 36%. In addition to the killed, wounded and captured, two precious eagles and standards were lost, along with Generals Graindorge and Watier de Saint-Alphonse. Surviving the battle, Gazan's chief of artillery, St. Loup de Fabvier, believed that "the 8-pounders rendered the most effective service."[90] Entering the battle as night was falling, Dupont's heroic troops suffered only 106 casualties of the 2,377 engaged, or a loss of a mere 4%.[91]

Berthier wrote Mortier from Saint Pölten on 21 brumaire (12 November):

> Your aide-de-camp arrived here at 3:00 P.M., as the Emperor had been waiting impatiently to hear the report of your engagement. If the Russians remain in the position where they are, or if they advance on the Inn, their army is lost. As for you, form the body of your corps of observation on the left bank [of the Danube]. The Emperor is extremely satisfied with the brave conduct of the troops, as well as your good bearing.[92]

Two days later, Mortier reoccupied Dürenstein and resumed his march against Kutuzov. The pursuit continued until 18 November. From the 15th through the 18th, the marshal's troops collected 132 more Russian prisoners. Finally, the depleted divisions of Gazan and Dupont were ordered to Vienna by Napoleon for some sorely needed rest and regrouping. The end of the pursuit by Gazan and Dupont on the 18th closed the book on Mortier's struggle against Kutuzov. For all the bravery displayed by several of the Russian regiments, Dürenstein was yet another example that clearly illustrated the superior fighting power of Napoleon's legions.

The Capture of Vienna and the Pursuit Into Moravia

Just when Kutuzov thought he had a golden opportunity to deal the Napoleon's forces a defeat, his plan of battle miscarried and his troops suffered a humiliating reverse at Dürenstein. As bad as the news of this thrashing was, it could not compare to the utterly disastrous announcement that the French had captured intact the Tabor Bridge at Vienna, thereby exposing the Russian line of retreat into Moravia. Kutuzov might have been very reluctant to commit his troops to an attack, but he did not flinch at ordering a hasty retreat. The Russian general authorized the immediate evacuation of Krems and directed the army northward towards Hollabrunn and then Brünn, the capital of Moravia, where he expected to join forces with Rosen, Buxhöwden and the Tsar.

---

[89] S.H.A.T., *Tableau de la Grande Armée Dernière quinzaine du mois brumaire an XIV*, "Situation au 24 brumaire an XIV (15 November 1805);" Also see: S.H.A.T., C^2 485 .
[90] S.H.A.T., C^2 7.
[91] S.H.A.T., *Tableau de la Grande Armée Dernière quinzaine du mois brumaire an XIV*, "Situation au 24 brumaire an XIV (15 November 1805)."
[92] Berthier to Mortier, *Correspondance,* number 9471.

Gros' famous portrait of Murat

The Russian general's decision to withdraw posthaste from the Danube came after receiving word that an inconceivable event had occurred. Murat had galloped eastward at the head of his own *Corps des Réserves de Cavalerie* as well as two infantry divisions and the light cavalry comprising Lannes' 5th Corps, reaching Vienna on 12 November. While Murat's decision to march on Vienna theoretically endangered Mortier, the fact was that there were not enough boats available on 11 November to ferry the troops under Murat and Lannes across the Danube to support Mortier's isolated command.

Upon Murat's arrival in Vienna, the cavalryman found out that the Austrians had declared their capital an open city, but the principal bridge over the Danube had not been destroyed. The Austrians had always displayed an odd tendency not to destroy bridges on a timely basis. It cost them dearly at Lodi and again at Arcole in 1796, but those incidents pale in comparison to the utter imbecility displayed at the Tabor Bridge.

The Tabor Bridge was not a vision of engineering beauty, nor was it what most people envision as a bridge. Instead, it was:

> a series of rickety wooden structures and connecting causeways, which carried the main road across the thickly wooded islands and myriad channels immediately north of the city. The last span stretched for no less than 550 yards from the large Wolsau island to the north bank at Spitz.[93]

A company of artillery commanded the northern exit of the bridge, "and the timbers were strewn with straw, firewood and charges of gunpowder ready for immediate ignition."[94] Deployed opposite the Tabor Bridge on the north bank was the Austrian Reserve Corps under the command of FML Prince Auersperg. The 55-year-old Austrian general had not seen action for 12 years, but had been hurriedly called out of retirement as the most qualified candidate to command a motley assortment of 17 battalions and 30 squadrons that guarded Kutuzov's retreat route to Brünn. Alongside Auersperg was the ancient but hardy warrior, the 70-year-old FML Michael von Kienmayer, who a month earlier had commanded the easternmost column of Mack's army during the Ulm campaign. Kienmayer had been successful in escaping with the majority of his command the pincers of the *Grande Armée* in October, and he now stood on the north bank of the Danube with Auersperg as the French marched into their capital.

Murat fools the Austrians, while French grenadiers cross the bridge

Murat immediately sent couriers to Napoleon with word that the Tabor Bridge was still intact. Napoleon had no sooner issued his rebuke to Murat (not the only one for that marshal in the 1805 campaign) for galloping ahead and occupying an undefended Vienna, than the Emperor sent his trusted aide-de-camp, *général de brigade* Henri-Gatien Bertrand to Murat with orders to capture the vital Tabor Bridge by any means possible—and it was by those ground rules that Murat intended to carry out the Imperial wishes.[95]

It was 11:00 A.M. on 13 November when a large group of mounted French officers arrived at the southern end of the Tabor Bridge ahead of Oudinot's *Grenadiers de la Réserve*. Leading the entourage was Napoleon's 38-year-old brother-in-law, Prince Joachim Murat. The son of a Gascon innkeeper and one of 12 children, Murat had been a cavalryman his entire career, joining the mounted arm in 1787. In October 1795, it was Murat— then a major—who brought the cannon with which Bonaparte delivered the famous "whiff of grapeshot" and

[93] Duffy, *Austerlitz*, p. 63.

[94] Duffy, *Austerlitz*, p. 63.

[95] Napoléon to Murat, *Correspondance,* number 9472.

Another view of Murat's coup at the Tabor bridge

dispersed the rebels of 13th vendémiaire, thus saving the Convention. From that day, his destiny was attached in some way to Napoleon. Serving in the first Italian campaign in 1796 as a *général de brigade*, Murat gained invaluable experience and then established himself as France's premier cavalry general by his brilliant conduct during the Egyptian campaign of 1799. Murat was promoted to *général de division* late that year and then installed as the commander of the Consular Guards in December 1799. Shortly thereafter, Murat was introduced to Napoleon's youngest sister, Caroline. The attractive, petite and ambitious Caroline found the black-haired, dark-eyed, five-foot six-inch Murat desirable. He instantly fell under her spell, and only one month later, in January 1800, the 33-year-old cavalryman married the 18-year-old temptress. Leaving his young bride after only four months, Murat again distinguished himself at the Battle of Marengo on 14 June 1800. His performances in Egypt and at Marengo, plus his Imperial family connection, earned him the command of the *Corps des Réserves de Cavalerie* as well as the distinction of being the head of the advance guard of the *Grande Armée*.[96]

Murat was in front of the mounted French officers as they presented themselves to *Oberst* Gabriel Geringer von Oedenburg of the Székler *Grenz*-Hussaren-Regiment #11, the man in charge of the southern post of the Tabor Bridge. Geringer had been the colonel of the Széklers since 1801, but his training had not prepared him for the unexpected encounter with Murat. The marshal announced to dark blue uniformed Geringer that he had come with glorious news—an armistice had brought an end to hostilities! Baffled, Geringer mounted his horse and hurriedly rode away to advise Auersperg. As the hussar was galloping across the long spans that connected the various islands, trailing were Murat and a host of French officers while the grenadier battalions under Oudinot hurried behind them. Finally arriving at the southern end of the *main* span soon after Geringer had passed, the French officers momentarily startled the Austrians that guarded this post. One Austrian artillery officer picked up a match and was on his way to light a fuse to set fire to the structure when he was stopped by Colonel Dode de la Brunerie, an engineering officer who served as Bertrand's aide-de-camp. As soon as Bertrand saw the charges on the bridge, he ordered them removed.

While Bertrand and Dode were supervising the dismantling of the charges on the main span of the Tabor Bridge, the rest of the mounted entourage pressed forward. Marshal Murat and his chief of staff, *général de division* Auguste-Daniel Belliard, along with Marshal Lannes and his staff, galloped across the 550-yard-long span, waving their hats at the Austrian gunners on the northern bank. The French marshals and their staffs soon got amongst the Austrian artillerists about the same time Oudinot's grenadiers came into view from the wooded islets. Lannes, Murat and the others prevented any fire onto the grenadiers by telling the Austrians that an armistice had been signed, a peace was being negotiated and that they had come to see their commanding general. Auersperg soon appeared at the bridge, dumbfounded at what Geringer had told him. Auersperg found that his artillerists were disarmed, the Austrian ordnance pointed inland and manned by French grenadiers, with the rest of Oudinot's Division pouring across the bridge. Murat audaciously informed Auersperg that because of the armistice, he would allow the Austrians near the bridge to withdraw, but insisted on holding the guns of river battery. Incredibly, the Gascon's bombast worked! Auersperg rode back to his headquarters, scarcely able to comprehend what had happened. Once there, he dispatched three messengers by three different routes to warn Kutuzov that the French were across the Danube.[97]

Napoleon receives the keys of Vienna

---

[96] Six, *Dictionnaire biographique*, vol. 2, pp. 242-243.

[97] Duffy, *Austerlitz*, p. 64; Thiers, *The History of the Consulate & the Empire of France*, vol. 2, pp. 65-66.

The Palace at Schönbrunn

The loss of the Tabor Bridge was disastrous for the allies on several counts. First, the immediate result was that it exposed Kutuzov's army to destruction. If the French conducted a rapid march from Vienna, coupled with a vigorous pursuit from Krems, they could stop the retreat of the Russians and cut them off before reaching Brünn and their expected reinforcements. This is exactly what Napoleon planned in his *manœuvre sur Hollabrunn.* Second, the loss of the Danube as a geographical barrier eliminated any possibility for the Russians and Austrians on the north side to sandwich Napoleon's forces between themselves and the Austrian armies of John and Charles. The army of Archduke John—already reeling from defeats suffered in the Tyrol—and the main Austrian army under Archduke Charles that was withdrawing from Italy in order to cover John's retreat, were slowly making their way to the theater of operations. Finally, the way that the Austrians were duped into losing the bridge only exacerbated the problem of cooperation between the allied powers. Emperor Francis believed that the episode was "all the more hurtful since this stupid and unpardonable blunder has destroyed the whole trust of my allies at a single stroke."[98]

The capture of Vienna was also of considerable military importance for Napoleon because the vast magazines and store houses near the Austrian capital at Stockerau were seized intact. Tens of thousands of muskets, hundreds of cannon, tons of powder, ammunition and food suddenly fell into French hands. With such a windfall, Napoleon only had to have shoes and overcoats forwarded from France. It seems as though the Austrian court had given priority to removing the governmental archives rather than the means of war with which Napoleon would put to his own good use. Also taken at Stockerau was one battalion of the Peterwardeiner *Grenz* Regiment #9. When Lannes moved his corps through the stockpiled city, he repeated the same story used on the Austrians to capture the Tabor Bridge. This time the marshal tricked the battalion commander of the Peterwardeiner *Grenz* #9, Major Theodor von Milotinovich, and the entire unit went into the bag.[99]

With good fortune abounding, Napoleon staged a ceremonial arrival in Vienna the same day that Murat was capturing the Tabor Bridge. Adorned in their dress uniforms, many replete with plumed headgear, the soldiers of the *Grande Armée* who entered Vienna marched behind their regimental bands as the musicians played continuous repeats from the opening strains of *"La Victoire est à nous."* The Emperor found the Viennese to be civil, courteous and greatly restrained towards himself, while at the same time totally contemptible of the savage Russians. "We and the French are the children of the Romans," the Austrians said. "The Russians are the children of the Tartars. We prefer a thousand times such enemies as the French to such allies as the Russians."[100] The French officers toured the city, mingled with the populace, attended the Opera where Mozart's 'The Magic Flute' was playing, or found other entertainment with the local ladies. Napoleon took up temporary residence in the magnificent, opulent halls of the Schönbrunn palace, appointed administrative specialist *général de division* Henri Clarke as military governor and made plans for the *manœuvre sur Hollabrunn*—the destruction of Kutuzov's forces by cutting off their line of retreat to Brünn at the village of Hollabrunn.[101]

The French Army enters Vienna

---

[98] Angeli, 'Ulm und Austerlitz,' *Mittheilungen des K. k. Kriuegsarchiv (Vienna, 1878),* p. 337.

[99] S.H.A.T., *Journal des opérations du 5e corps.*

[100] Thiers, *The History of the Consulate & the Empire of France*, vol. 2, p. 66.

[101] Berthier to Bernadotte, *Correspondance,* numbers 9474 and 9491; Napoléon to Berthier, *Correspondance*, number 9478; Napoléon to Murat, *Correspondance*, number 9479; Napoléon to Lannes, *Correspondance*, number 9481; and Napoléon to Murat, *Correspondance*, numbers 9482 and 9493.

Bagration Sacrifices the Rearguard at Hollabrunn and Schöngrabern

As Napoleon was further developing his plan to force Kutuzov into a major battle, a messenger from Auersperg found the Russian general and relayed to him word of the bloodless capture of the Tabor Bridge. There was no time to lose if the Russian army was to be saved; Kutuzov evacuated Krems on the 13th. The following day, another courier brought a letter from Francis explaining clearly the precarious situation of Kutuzov's little army. The Russian general claimed that the news of the capture of the Tabor Bridge:

> completely altered my plan. I had intended to defend the passage of the Danube and await our reinforcements... Now I had to hasten my march through Hollabrunn so as to evade combat with the vastly superior forces of the enemy.[102]

From Krems, the retreat route for Kutuzov's army ran northeastward to Hollabrunn, converging at that town with the road that led southward to Vienna, only 30 miles away. The Tsarist units trudged over the frozen, dreadful Moravian countryside, losing stragglers, worn out animals and broken down vehicles along the way.

It took Kutuzov's army two days to complete the 20-mile journey from Krems to Hollabrunn. As they passed through the latter village on the 15th, the leading elements of the pursuing French approached the same city on the road from Vienna. Continuing another three miles northward, the Russians arrived at the small, ramshackle village of Schöngrabern. A narrow creek cut across the terrain about 650 yards north of town, and from there northward for another 900 yards was a vast vineyard until another creek ran roughly parallel to the first. Just north of the second stream, the vineyards continued up to a low ridge. From this subtle rise, guns could command the ground as far south as Schöngrabern, some 2,000 yards away. Prince Bagration believed that this ground was about as strong a defensive position as one could find in the gently rolling countryside. The terrain offered little in the way of cover from small arms fire, and if fired on by artillery, there was even more of a risk for the troops than being in the open since the numerous vineyard stakes would splinter when hit by solid iron shot or exploding howitzer shells. The strength of the position, however, outweighed these worrisome shortcomings. The low ridge, coupled with the ground falling off southward to Schöngrabern, would make it easy for cannon shot and licorne shell to bounce towards French lines, thereby effectively increasing the range of the Russian ordnance while having the opposite effect on the longer range French pieces. Also, it offered a depth in places of up to 1,000 yards of entangling vineyards that provided excellent protection from Murat's overwhelming numbers of cavalry. After studying the ground, Bagration went to Kutuzov with a proposition. Bagration suggested that he deploy a rearguard of 6,800 men among and north of the vineyard stakes in order to make a stand and allow the remainder of the army to escape from the pursuing French forces. Kutuzov was willing to try anything to get the faster moving French off his back long enough to save his remaining baggage, artillery and munitions trains; he readily consented to Bagration's plan.

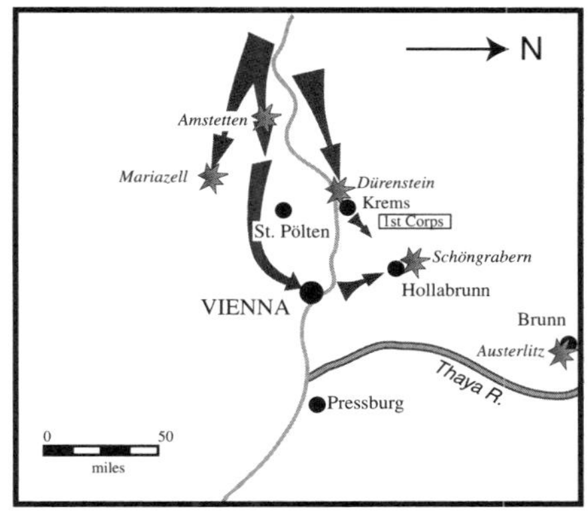

The manœuvre sur Hollabrunn

The pursuing forces under Murat, Lannes and Soult were not supposed to have been the only French closing in on Kutuzov's Russians. The Emperor's *manœuvre sur Hollabrunn* called for Bernadotte to ferry his corps across the Danube and place his troops in front of Mortier's depleted divisions. With Bernadotte and his fresh 1st Corps quickly marching from the west supported by Mortier, and with the corps of Murat, Lannes and Soult closing from the south, the Emperor reasoned

[102] *Kutuzov. Sbornik*, vol. 2, p. 352.

that the Russians would be run to ground and sandwiched at Hollabrunn between the converging elements of the *Grande Armée*. Success of Napoleon's plan absolutely depended on Bernadotte not dragging his feet but rather sticking to the Imperial timetable. However, the Emperor found that his marshal was not up to the task. The shortage of boats available to ferry troops across the Danube could have been overcome if the dawdling Bernadotte had not shown complete indifference in supervising the crossing. That absence of energy and urgency, followed by a lackadaisical march pace once the troops crossed the Danube, resulted in Bernadotte having the 1st Corps a full day's march behind Napoleon's schedule. Instead of five French corps converging on Hollabrunn from two different directions on the 15th, only Murat, Lannes and Soult were running down the Russians along the road from Vienna. On their march northward from the occupied Austrian capital, part of Murat's light cavalry screen under *général de brigade* Milhaud overtook Kienmayer's Austrian rearguard on the 14th. Easily scattering the covering infantry and cavalry forces, Milhaud seized 30 cannon, dozens of ammunition carts and 600 men.[103]

While news of this capture was welcomed by Napoleon, disturbing information was also received at the Schönbrunn on the whereabouts of 1st Corps. Bernadotte was not going to rendezvous as planned with Murat, Lannes and Soult. Bernadotte's case of the 'slows' angered the Emperor, and he showed his displeasure in a letter penned that afternoon to his brother Joseph:

Milhaud

> I maneuver today against the Russian army, and have not been satisfied with Bernadotte; perhaps the fault is in his health.
>
> When I let him enter Munich and Salzburg, and enjoy the glory of these great expeditions without his having to fire a gun or to endure any of the fatiguing services of the army, I had a right to expect that he would now not be lacking in activity nor zeal. He has lost me a day, and on a day may depend the destiny of the world. Not a man of the Russian army would have escaped me. I hope that he will atone himself tomorrow by a more active movement.[104]

The Emperor did not hide his feelings from the commander of 1st Corps. In a scorching letter also written on 15 November, the Emperor's secretary told Bernadotte:

> The Emperor, *Monsieur le Maréchal*, is very displeased that, in this moment where Prince Murat and Marshals Lannes and Soult are to fight two days out of Vienna, you are not where you should be north of the Danube; your soldiers will be sorry not to have shared all the glory of this campaign. When my officer of the headquarters staff returns, the Emperor hopes that all your troops will be in pursuit of the Russians...[105]

As Napoleon was venting his disappointment with Bernadotte, little did the Emperor know that his brother-in-law was in the process of pulling one of the most unintelligent acts of the war.

---

[103] Napoléon to Murat, *Correspondance*, number 9482; 23rd Bulletin of the *Grande Armée*, *Corrspondance,* number 9483.
[104] Napoléon to Joseph, *The Confidential Correspondence of Napoleon Bonaparte with His Brother Joseph*, vol. 1, number 96.
[105] Le secrétaire d'État, par ordre de l'Empereur to Bernadotte, *Correspondance*, number 9491.

Prince Murat arrived at Hollabrunn early on the 15th at the head of three divisions of his cavalry corps. Hotfooting behind his horsemen were Marshal Lannes with Oudinot's grenadiers, followed by the remainder of the 5th Corps with Soult's entire 4th Corps bringing up the rear. Preceding all these forces were five French light cavalry regiments led by native Corsican *général de brigade* Horace-François-Bastien Sébastiani de la Porta. Like so many men hailing from that Mediterranean island, Sébastiani was a small man possessing a handsome face, dark eyes and long, curly dark hair. General Roguet described Sébastiani as a man "distinguished by his refined nature, with the elegance and manners of a great lord."[106] Griois painted a picture of the Corsican in a similar manner while adding an important aspect of his character:

> He [Sébastiani] was an aimable man, spiritual, with an agreeable exterior. His manners, whose softness touched almost everyone who came in contact with him, contrasted sharply to the brutal personality of General Nansouty. Always brave, he went dutifully into battle, but lacked the ability to issue firm orders while also having a reputation about not being happy while at war (thus, his nickname in the army was 'General Surprise').[107]

Sébastiani

Sébastiani's permanent command in the 1805 campaign was the 1st Brigade of the 2nd Dragoon Division under Walther.[108] That assignment was temporarily changed when Murat needed a hard-riding officer to command his *ad hoc* Advance Guard consisting of the 9th and 10th Hussars, plus the 13th and 21st *Chasseurs à cheval* from Lannes' 5th Corps and Colonel Montbrun's 1st *Chasseurs à cheval* from Davout's 3rd Corps.[109] However, light cavalry generals who were proven go-getters were few in 1805, and the best—Kellermann (the younger)—already had a divisional command. Because the constraints of time and distance would not make it feasible to get Kellermann and his four superb regiments of light horse to the front in time, Murat received instead (at Napoleon's suggestion) the capable but easygoing Sébastiani. The Corsican took command of the Advance Guard and rode into Hollabrunn the day before his 33rd birthday.

First to meet the French around Hollabrunn were the Austrian troops under GM Johann Neponuck von Nostitz-Rieneck. The 37-year-old Nostitz was a distinguished veteran of the wars of the French Revolution, and had with him six squadrons of one of the best regiments in Austrian service—Hussar-Regiment Hessen-Homburg #4. In addition, Nostitz commanded a handful of men that represented the pitiful remnants of two battalions of the Peterwardeiner *Grenz* Regiment #9. Forced to give ground between Hollabrunn and Schöngrabern in the face of Sébastiani's skillfully conducted flanking movements, Nostitz recalled that "the enemy advanced in strength and with purpose up the road from Vienna, and at the same time they sent word to me that they wanted to parley with the commander of the rearguard."[110]

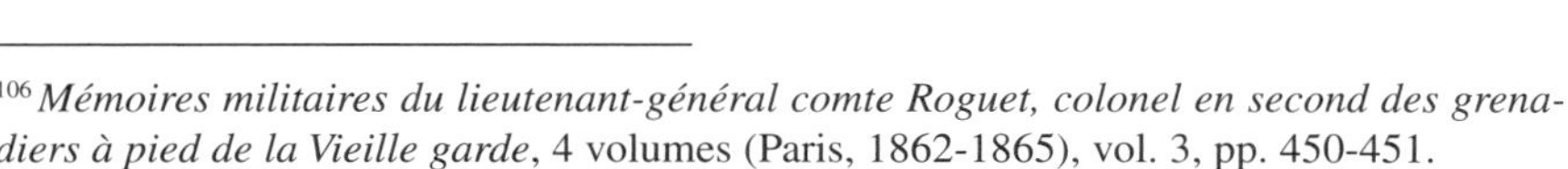

[106] *Mémoires militaires du lieutenant-général comte Roguet, colonel en second des grenadiers à pied de la Vieille garde*, 4 volumes (Paris, 1862-1865), vol. 3, pp. 450-451.

[107] *Mémoires du général Griois (1792-1822)*, 2 volumes (Paris, 1902), vol. 2, p. 312.

[108] S.H.A.T., C² 470 and 472.

[109] S.H.A.T., C² 481. Compans' parade states report of the 5th Corps dated 24 brumaire an XIV (15 November 1805) very clearly states that all four of the light cavalry regiments of 5th Corps were detached for service with the Advance Guard of the Army Wing. Further, C² 476 confirms that Colonel Montbrun's 1st *Chasseurs à cheval* were specifically requested to join the Advance Guard for the *manœuvre sur Hollabrunn* .

[110] K. k. Kriegsarchiv,Johann Baptist Schels,"Biographie des Grafen Johann Nepomuk von Nostitz-Rieneck, k. k. Feldmarschalleutnant," in: *Österreichische Militärische Zeitschrift* (Vienna, 1843), volume 1.

The officer that had been dispatched to Nostitz under a flag of truce was *chef d'escadron* Lameth of Murat's staff. The young officer was a member of the extensive Lameth military family, most of whom had fled France after the Coup of 18 brumaire. Lameth's appointment to Murat's staff was part of Napoleon's attempt to convince *émigrés* that they could return to and serve their native country. Lameth's mission was one that he must have seen as an opportunity for him to display his value to the Emperor's brother-in-law as well as his refined and courtly manner. Once within sight of Schöngrabern, Lameth, Murat and the rest of the staff caught a glimpse what they believed to be the entire Russian army. Indeed, the Frenchmen saw from a distance the massive trains of Kutuzov's army as they sprawled across the countryside and cleared the small village on their way north to Brünn. Hoping to dupe the Russians into halting their retreat and thereby allowing Lannes and Soult time to bring up their corps, Belliard, the chief of staff of the Cavalry Reserve, recalled that Murat sent Lameth with a proposal for a cease fire, "now that the French and the Austrians were observing an armistice."[111]

Receiving Lameth was Prince Peter Ivanovich Bagration. To the 40-year-old Georgian whose imposing physique, thick black hair and dark eyes conveyed every portion of his being as that of a thoroughly professional soldier, the story born by Murat's messenger was simply not believable. Why would an opponent wear out horses in a pursuit if an armistice was at hand? With all his experience gained from fighting the Turks from 1787 through 1791, and against the French with Suvórov in 1799, Bagration sensed that something was amiss. Rather than dismiss Lameth, Bagration decided to convey the fantastical story to his army commander. To an experienced campaigner who knew his army was in trouble and needed to buy every precious minute of time in an attempt to save it from the pursuing forces, Kutuzov saw Murat's proposal as a double-edged sword. The Russian general, with his "peculiarly Byzantine cunning," decided "to repay the deceitful French in their own coin."[112]

Wintzingerode

Kutuzov elected to dispatch two men who he believed would be perfect for conducting negotiations. These were the Tsar's most aggressive and arrogant aides-de-camp, General-Adjutants Baron Wintzingerode and Prince Dolgoruky. Kutuzov gave these men instructions to discuss terms, flatter Murat, and do whatever else they could do in order to gain time while the main body of the army continued to retreat. The young sycophants of the Tsar had a relish for this mission. They believed themselves to be superior to any upstart that was in the service of the usurper, and were eager to outsmart the French. With that attitude, the Russians carried themselves with the arrogance customary to officers of the *ancien régime.* Returning with staff officer Lameth, General-Adjutants Wintzingerode and Dolgoruky were brought before Murat. The pomposity of the two Romanovs evidently did not register with the social climbing cavalryman. Murat—whose aides-de-camp were already enveloping him in an almost monarchial atmosphere by constantly referring to him as 'His Serene Highness' rather than his military rank—had an ego that was played like a Stradivarius by Wintzingerode and Dolgoruky.[113] However, to a modest yet intelligent soldier who had risen from a Volunteer of 1791 to become Murat's chief of staff, *général de division* Auguste-Daniel Belliard found the Russian emissaries to be:

> contemptuous beyond all belief. Their speech and their mannerisms were such as if they had come to discuss terms of our capitulation, while it was their army that had been driven

[111] S.H.A.T., C^2 240.

[112] K. k. Kriegsarchiv, F.A., *Tagebuch:* Deutschland 1805, XIII, p. 59.

[113] K. k. Kriegsarchiv, F.A., *Tagebuch:* Deutschland 1805, XIII, p. 182.

> back over 50 leagues [150 miles] and was on the verge of destruction.[114]

The tongue-in-cheek flatteries made by Wintzingerode and Dolgoruky that were perceived as unabashed insults by Belliard were lapped up by the vainglorious Murat as sincere compliments. Before the suspicious Belliard knew it, Murat had concluded an armistice. The provisions of the cease fire included that the French were to advance no further into Moravia and that a four-hour notice was to be given of any renewed hostilities. The armistice was to be ratified by Napoleon and Kutuzov.[115] However, as the wily Kutuzov explained to Tsar Alexander, he did "not have the slightest intention of accepting the terms [of the armistice]. The army meanwhile continued to retreat and thus gained two marches on the French."[116]

When 16 November dawned, news of Murat's unauthorized action reached Napoleon, who was still at the Schönbrunn. The Emperor immediately realized that his lieutenant had been deceived. Dictating a scathing reprimand to Murat, Napoleon selected one of his aides-de-camp, *général de brigade* Jean-Léonor-François Lemarois, to personally deliver the *billet* and to order him and the other marshals to immediately attack the enemy. It was after noon when Murat broke open the Imperial seal and read:

> Schönbrunn, 25 brumaire an XIV (16 November 1805) at 8 o'clock in the morning
>
> My Cousin, it is impossible for me to find words to express my displeasure. You command only my advance guard, and you have no right to conclude an armistice without my order. You have made me lose the fruits of a campaign. Break the armistice instantly, and march upon the enemy. You will declare to him that the Russian general who signed the convention had no right to do so; and that no one but the Tsar of Russia possesses such a right.
>
> Still, however, if the Tsar of Russia would ratify this convention, I would ratify it: but it is only a trick. March! Destroy the Russian army; you are in a position to take its baggage and artillery. The aide-de-camp of the Tsar of Russia is an ass. Officers are nothing without powers; this one has none. The Austrians suffered the humiliation of being duped out of the passage of the bridge of Vienna; you have let yourself be duped by an aide-de-camp of the Tsar.[117]

Lemarois

As Murat was reading Napoleon's communiqué, across the field Bagration was passing the time "in a state of justifiable anxiety." As the able Russian general later wrote: "With my small numbers I remained in the face of a superior enemy, alone and without support, and awaiting the attack at any minute."[118] About 1:00 P.M., Bagration received a messenger from Lannes advising him of the attack order just received from Napoleon (through the Imperial aide-de-camp Lemarois) and that hostilities would commence in four hours. The Russian general immediately made final preparations for battle.

---

[114] S.H.A.T., C² 240.
[115] K. k. Kriegsarchiv, F.A., Deutschland 1805, XI, p. 73.
[116] *Kutuzov. Sbornik*, vol. 2, p. 171.
[117] Napoléon to Murat, *Correspondance*, number 9497.
[118] *Kutuzov. Sbornik*, vol. 2, p. 164.

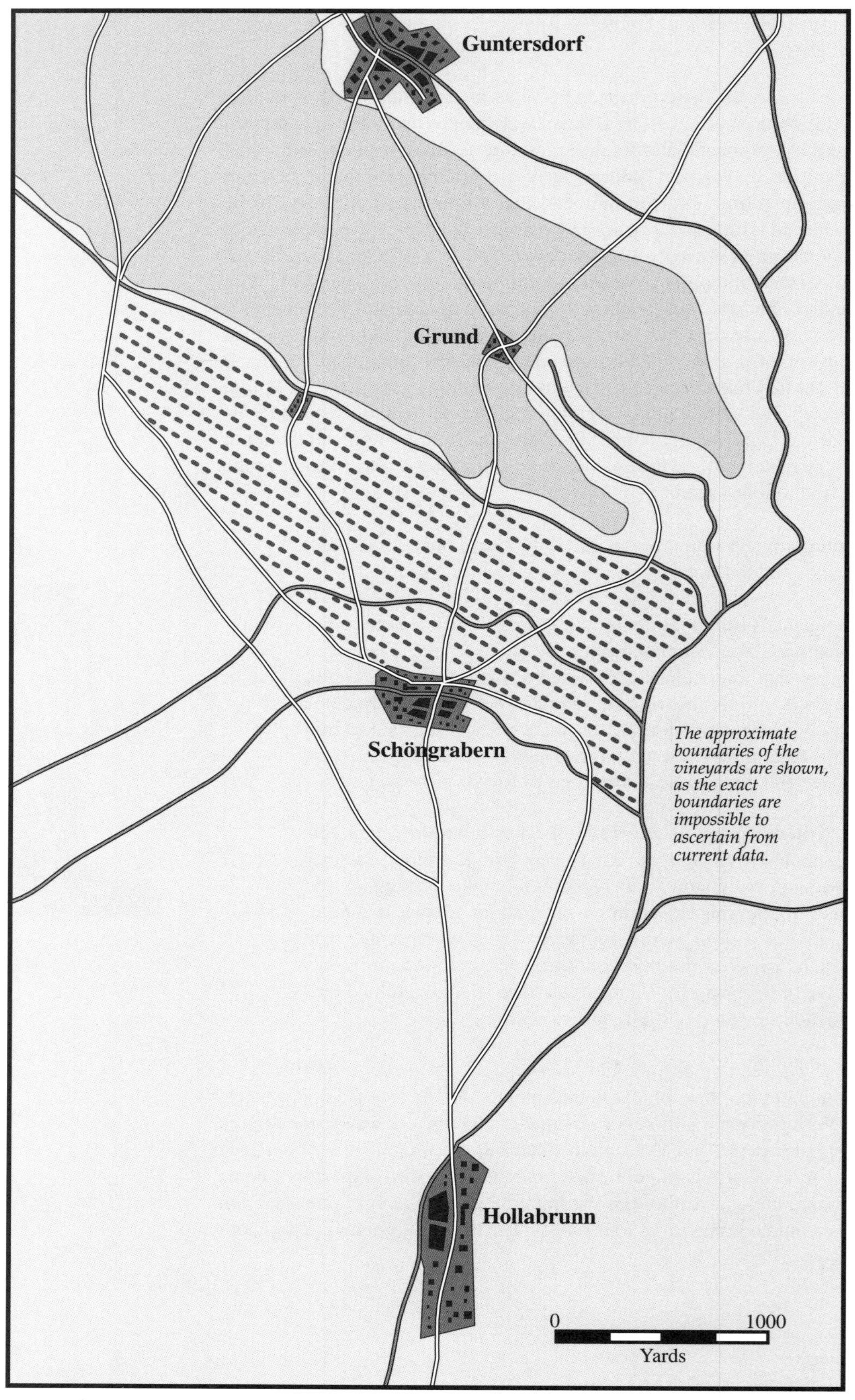

The Battlefield of Schöngrabern

Bagration's command at Schöngrabern consisted of approximately 6,800 Russian regulars in 17 weakened battalions, 15 smallish squadrons of cavalry and one company of artillerists serving 12 pieces of ordnance. In addition to these forces, Bagration also had six squadrons of Austrian cavalry and the survivors of two battalions of the Peterwardeiner *Grenz* Regiment #9. Bagration's understrengthed units represented more than one-third of the regulars still under arms in Kutuzov's ever-shrinking army as of 15 November. The infantry contingent of the rearguard consisted of the entire regiments (three battalions each) of the Kiev Grenadiers, Little Russia Grenadiers, Azov Musketeers, Podolia Musketeers and the 6th *Jaeger;* and the grenadier battalions from the Narva and Novgorod Musketeer Regiments. The Russian cavalry consisted of five squadrons of the Chernigov Dragoons and 10 squadrons of the Pavlograd Hussars, while the Austrian cavalry consisted of the six squadrons of the Hussar-Regiment Hessen-Homburg #4. Bagration's ordnance amounted to a lone company of light foot artillery from the 4th Artillery Regiment under the command of Major Bogoslavski, consisting of eight 6-pounder guns and four 10-pounder licornes. Owing to a lack of horseflesh, battalion guns were not deployed with Bagration's rearguard. Finally, two regiments of Cossacks—the Sysoev and the Khaznenkov—were attached to the rearguard.

Assuming that each squadron of cavalry mustered a strength of 90—about 10% less than they had averaged at Dürenstein a week before—Bagration's regular cavalry numbered about 1,350. After adding another 250 for each Cossack regiment, and Bagration's total mounted contingent comes to 1,850. The artillery company, including supporting train personnel, could not have mustered more than 150. Not counting the Cossacks, this leaves 5,300 infantry serving in 17 battalions, or an average battalion strength of only 311. After taking into account the casualties suffered at Dürenstein as well as projecting the same strategic consumption rate suffered by the Tsar's battalions since leaving Braunau, the 5,300 infantrymen with Bagration at Schöngrabern is as close an estimate as possible. More importantly, these strengths represent almost 20% less than what the average Russian battalion mustered on 10 November at Krems, the day before the Battle of Dürenstein.[119]

The view today of Schöngrabern from the rear of the Russian position looking west. The vineyards are all gone.

[119] Sources that list Bagration's rearguard to be stronger than 6,800 fail to closely analyze the strategic consumption of Kutuzov's army, and simply assume that the battalions and squadrons were much stronger than they really were.

Comparison of Strengths for Kutuzov's Army

Theoretical, or "Paper Strength," Compared to Actual Strength

What's the difference between "paper strength" when compared to those troops who are present and under arms? Consider the following:

Before leaving camp at Radziwilow on 25 August, Kutuzov's army took parade states, which meant that every unit formed up "on parade," and a head count was made of all those present and under arms. The following are a few examples between the theoretical strength of the Russian units and their actual strength. Keep in mind, these strengths are before the regiments began campaigning. Once on the move, the numbers of men with the colors would shrink due to men falling out of ranks for any number of reasons. When combatants no longer remained in ranks due to reasons not associated with battle, their departure was defined as "strategic consumption."

This chart is one example of why theoretical troop establishments were just that—theoretical.

	# (bns/) (sqds)	Theoretical establishment	Under arms at the beginning of campaign	% of theoretical strength that are actually under arms
Azov Musketeer Regiment	(3)	2,451	2,247	92%
Butyrsk Musketeer Regiment	(3)	2,451	2,152	88%
Narva Musketeer Regiment	(3)	2,451	2,159	88%
Podolia Musketeer Regiment	(3)	2,451	1,989	81%
Galicia Musketeer Regiment	(3)	2,451	1,820	74%
Kiev Grenadier Regiment	(3)	2,451	2,096	85%
Little Russia Grenadier Regiment	(3)	2,451	2,095	85%
6th *Jaeger* Regiment	(3)	1,584	1,495	94%
8th *Jaeger* Regiment	(3)	1,584	1,748	110% *
Pavlograd Hussar Regiment #2	(10)	1,889	1,486	79%
Mariupol Hussar Regiment #3	(10)	1,889	1,738	92%
Leib-*Cuirassier* "Tsar" aka "Kaiser"	(5)	1,054	886	84%
Saint Petersburg Dragoon Regt. #13	(5)	1,054	845	80%
Tver Dragoon Regiment #4	(5)	1,054	710	67%
Kutuzov's entire infantry & cavalry complement—54 battalions & 40 sqdns		50,378 **	42,434 **	84% **

Therefore, when the Tsar and his ministers *hoped* for Kutuzov's army to be 50,000 strong (see Chapter 4), those estimates were made based on theoretical establishments.

* The 8th *Jaeger* is the only regiment in Kutuzov's army to start the campaign with a larger than authorized establishment. However, after the march to Braunau, the average battalion strength of the 8th was almost identical to the battalions of the 6th *Jaeger* (see next page). This strongly suggests that while the 8th may have started with more men, those less-than-hardy souls soon fell out of ranks.

** Excludes artillery, specialist troops and Cossacks.

Compiled from S.H.A.T., C[2] 13 and regimental histories in the Russian Archives, Saint Petersburg.

Comparison of Strengths for Kutuzov's Army for the Period 25 August to 25 November 1805

The Russian Army—General of Infantry Mikhail Ilariónovich Goleníchtchev Kutuzov

Totals are for Russian formations only, and include officers Strengths shown are those present & under arms	# (bns/) (sqds)	Advance 25 Aug. Radziwi	Advance 23 Oct. Braunau	Retreat 10 Nov. Krems	Retreat 25 Nov. Olmütz	% casualties & strategic consumption suffered during this period
I. Column— Major-General Prince Bagration						
Kiev Grenadier Regiment	(3)	2,096	1,667	1,577	716	66%
Azov Musketeer Regiment	(3)	2,247	1,433	1,290	591	86%
6th *Jaeger* Regiment	(3)	1,495	1,137	911	364	76%
Pavlograd Hussar Regiment #2	(10)	1,486	1,198	1,058	722	51%
II. Column— Lieutenant-General von Essen II						
Little Russia Grenadier Regiment	(3)	2,095	1,739	1,591	1,011	52%
Apsheron Musketeer Regiment	(3)	2,049	1,434	1,309	410	80%
Smolensk Musketeer Regiment	(3)	2,091	1,247	1,098	685	67%
Chernigov Dragoon Regiment #3	(5)	785	572	458	366	53%
III. Column— Lieutenant-General Dokhturov						
Butyrsk Musketeer Regiment	(3)	2,152	1,305	1,220	864	60%
Moscow Musketeer Regiment	(3)	1,993	1,397	1,276	882	56%
8th *Jaeger* Regiment, 1st Battalion	(1)	484	397	319	79	84%
Mariupol Hussar Regiment #3	(10)	1,738	1,376	1,117	712	59%
IV. Column— Lieutenant-General Skepelov						
Novgorod Musketeer Regiment	(3)	1,947	1,208	962	769	61%
Narva Musketeer Regiment	(3)	2,159	1,163	963	731	67%
Podolia Musketeer Regiment	(3)	1,989	1,258	1,102	509	74%
V. Column— Lieutenant-General von Maltitz						
Vyatka Musketeer Regiment	(3)	2,090	1,359	1,187	379	82%
Bryansk Musketeer Regiment	(3)	2,046	1,287	1,130	829	61%
Yaroslav Musketeer Regiment	(3)	1,977	1,178	999	754	62%
8th *Jaeger* Regiment, 2nd & 3rd Bns	(2)	1,264	788	570	333	74%
Leib-*Cuirassier* "Tsar's" aka "Kaiser"	(5)	886	739	667	566	37%
VI. Column— Lieutenant-General von Rosen						
(diverted towards the Turkish border, then countermarched to rejoin the army)						
New Ingermanland Musketeer Regiment	(3)	2,013	—	—	1,903	5%
Vladimir Musketeer Regiment	(3)	1,977	—	—	1,901	4%
Galicia Musketeer Regiment	(3)	1,820	—	—	1,564	19%
Saint Petersburg Dragoon Regt. #13	(5)	845	—	—	800	5%
Tver Dragoon Regiment #4	(5)	710	—	—	632	11%
Artillery—						
14 artillery companies—168 pieces		3,971	3,210	3,176	2,900	27%
Battalion artillery pieces were drawn from the above mentioned companies.						
Total infantry battalions (54)						
Total cavalry squadrons (40)						
Army Totals*		46,405	27,092	23,980	21,972 **	53%

* Totals exclude staff, equipage and Cossacks.
** If the returns of the VI. Column are excluded, the 25 November 1805 strength of the army is only 15,172!

Compiled from S.H.A.T., C[2] 13 and regimental histories in the Russian Archives, Saint Petersburg.

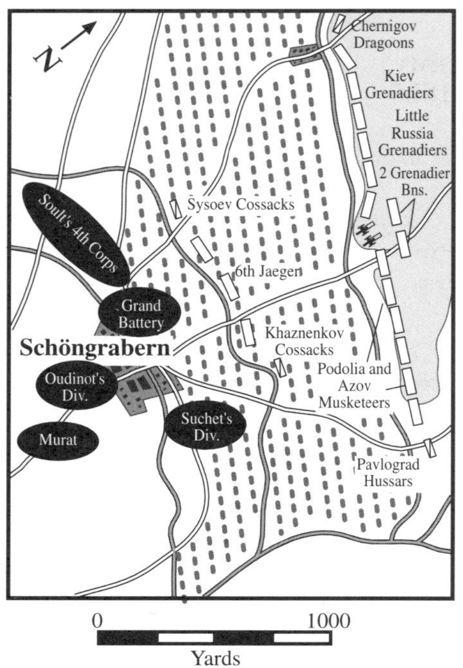

The Russian deployment at Schöngrabern

The church at Schöngrabern today

Prince Bagration deployed his forces in two lines. The small front line was positioned in the middle of the vineyards south of the second creek about 1,000 yards in front of the main battle line. Placed as to act as a breakwater to absorb the initial brunt of the French attack, the troops in Bagration's first line consisted of his most expendable troops—the three battalions of the 6th *Jaeger* that had suffered moderate casualties at Dürenstein, along with the revived Sysoev and Khaznenkov Cossacks—all under the command of General Ulanius. The second, or main, battleline was on the low ridge in front of the second creek and anchored in the center by Major Bogoslavski's company of artillery. Looking south towards the French lines, to the right (or west) of the artillery were the Little Russia and Kiev Grenadier Regiments under the personal leadership of Prince Bagration. After an opening wide enough to allow the *jaeger* to fall back and take their position in the second line, the Chernigov Dragoons formed the far right. To the left (or east) of the ordnance were the regiments of the Podolia Musketeers and Azov Musketeers under the orders of General Selikov. On the left of the Azov Musketeers were the squadrons of the Pavlograd Hussars. Positioned immediately behind the company of artillery were the grenadier battalions from the Narva and the Novgorod Musketeer Regiments. Once these deployments were made, Nostitz was allowed to withdraw his woefully depleted Austrians before the battle began.[120]

Looking north towards the Russians, the French shook out for battle with Soult's 4th Corps to the left of Schöngrabern. Lannes positioned Oudinot's *Grenadiers de la Réserve* immediately on the south edge of the village and Suchet's Division to the right of town. Murat placed his three divisions of horse—Walther's 2nd Dragoon Division along with Nansouty and d'Hautpoul's divisions of heavy cavalry—in reserve behind Oudinot. Even though the ground was very gently rolling, the French artillery officers recognized that the ever-present vineyards made it impossible for their ordnance to move forward with the infantry. Therefore, the French from 4th and 5th Corps concentrated their companies of artillery into an extemporaneous grand battery just north of Schöngrabern. When they unlimbered, the pieces were about 800 yards away from Ulanius' *jaeger* and Cossacks, but 1,800 yards from the center of Bagration's main line.[121]

With the expiration of the four hours' notice to resume hostilities, the battle began at 5:00 P.M. with barely 30 minutes of daylight remaining. The muzzles of the French artillery erupted in deafening roars and sheets of flaming smoke. Concentrating their fire onto Bagration's forward elements, the French artillery crews hammered the three battalions of the 6th *Jaeger* and the two regiments of Cossacks. For almost one-half hour, the French poured a hail of deadly shot and shell into these front line Russians. Meanwhile, Major Bogoslavski's artillery at the north end of the field directed a counter battery fire over the heads of General Ulanius' men. Most of the shells from the Russian licornes intended for the French artillery bounced through and exploded instead amongst the frame structures of Schöngrabern. It was not long before the village church and 60 flimsy houses were set on fire. This conflagration forced Oudinot to move his grenadier battalions around to the east side of the village while Murat had little trouble with his generals moving their terrified horses away from the burning buildings. The artillery train also found it necessary to reposition to the west of town. As the last rays of light yielded to the November night, the burning buildings of Schöngrabern lighted the battlefield. The huge bonfire silhouetted the French artillerists as they served their pieces and the battalions of French infantry that were moving to the attack across the vast vineyards.

[120] Ernst von Kwiatkowski, "Die Kämpfe bei Schöngrabern und Oberhollabrunn 1805 und 1809," in *Mitteilungen des k. k. Archivs für Niederösterreich* (Vienna, 1908), vol. 1; Rainer Egger, *Das Gefecht bei Hollabrunn und Schöngrabern 1805* (Vienna, 1982), p. 16.
[121] S.H.A.T., *Journal des opérations du 4e corps; Journal des opérations du 5e corps.*

Before the French could reach the position held by General Ulanius and his troops, Bagration authorized the withdrawal of the battered front line units. As previously planned, the 6th *Jaeger* fell back to a position on the right of Kiev Grenadier Regiment while the Sysoev and Khaznenkov Cossacks scattered in order to move through the vineyards and take up positions on the far flanks.

Oudinot

The first of the advancing French regiments to get underway were from Lannes' 5th Corps under the command of *général de division* Nicolas-Charles Oudinot. From the time Oudinot first volunteered for military service in 1784 at the age of 17 with the *Régiment du Médoc*, until the combat at Schöngrabern on 16 November 1805, he had already suffered no less than 14 wounds. Greatly distinguished in numerous battles and considered an excellent tactician by his peers, Oudinot seemed to be the perfect division commander for the soldiers that made up the élite *Grenadiers de la Réserve.* The men enthusiastically liked Oudinot, calling the 38-year-old general "their father."[122]

The 10 battalions in Oudinot's Division were divided into three brigades. The 1st Brigade consisted of the four battalions of the 1st and 2nd Grenadier Regiments (see Chapter I for regimental organizational details) while the 2nd Brigade was composed of the same number of battalions from the 3rd and 4th Grenadier Regiments. The 3rd Brigade had only two battalions from the 5th Grenadier Regiment. For the attack at Schöngrabern, Oudinot deployed his division in three checkerboard lines. The 3rd Brigade formed the front line, followed by the 1st Brigade in the second line, while the 2nd Brigade formed the third line. All battalions deployed in attack columns with intervals between the battalions to allow the passage of lines by brigade. Moving forward with his men, Oudinot and his mounted staff rode between the 1st and 2nd Brigades.[123]

The strength of Oudinot's 10 battalions on 8 September 1805—more than two weeks before the division crossed the Rhine—amounted to 251 officers and 6,970 other ranks.[124] By the time the division reached Hollabrunn on 15 November, the numbers of these battalions had been reduced to 199 officers and 5,264 other ranks, while 399 officers and other ranks comprised the artillerists and supporting personnel that rounded out the division.[125] Therefore, 10 weeks of campaigning and two engagements at Wertingen and Amstetten had already claimed about a quarter of Oudinot's command.

Oudinot's Deployment at Schöngrabern

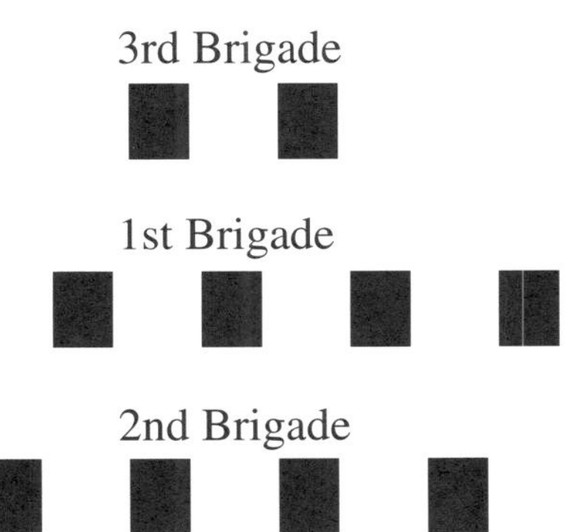

The losses already suffered in the campaign had done little, if anything at all, to damper the élan of Oudinot's troops. The grenadier battalions eagerly marched through the vineyards past the position vacated by Ulanius' troops. Stepping over the killed and maimed bodies of the 6th *Jaeger,* Oudinot's men marched to the beat of the *pas de charge* while the wind instrument musicians struck up their familiar accompanying strains. As Oudinot's battalions moved relentlessly closer to Bagration's main line, the gigantic flames of the Schöngrabern inferno illuminated the fields before them while the sounds of French drums and flutes could be heard alternately between the deafening discharges of the cannon.[126] The Russian artillery crews of eight of the 12 pieces, apparently transfixed by the blaze caused by their counter battery fire 'overs,' maintained their fire against the French artillery in front of the village. The remaining four cannon switched their fire onto Oudinot's

[122] Gaston Stiegler, *Le Maréchal Oudinot; Duc de Reggio d'après les Souvenirs Inédits de la Maréchale* (Paris, 1898), p. 33.
[123] S.H.A.T., *Journal des opérations du 5ᵉ corps.*
[124] S.H.A.T., C² 481.
[125] S.H.A.T.,C² 481. The strength of Oudinot's Division had increased since 6 November, thanks to the rest granted after the capture of Vienna. For comparison, see the *Tableau de la Grande Armée Dernière quinzaine du mois brumaire an XIV,* "Situation au 15 brumaire an XIV (6 November 1805)" in Appendix E.
[126] S.H.A.T., *Journal des opérations du 5ᵉ corps.*

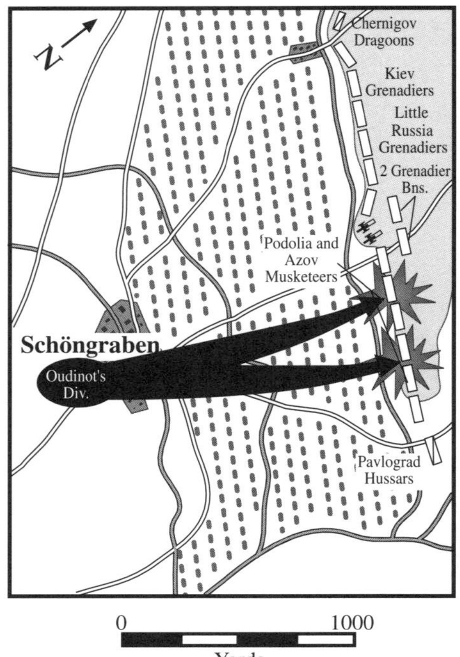

Oudinot's attack

advancing ranks. Meanwhile, to the west of Schöngrabern, Soult got some of his troops moving cautiously forward into the vineyards.

Holding the left side of Bagration's line were General Selikov and the six battalions belonging to the Podolia and Azov Musketeer Regiments. Positioned immediately east of the artillery, Selikov's men had been standing under arms since early that afternoon without any water rations. By the time darkness fell, the sulfuric smoke of the nearby Russian ordnance had dehydrated the lips and burned the eyes of so many in Selikov's command that he heard constant clamoring for relief. What Selikov should have taken care of long before the French attack began he now felt compelled to authorize. Even though Oudinot's battalions were bearing down upon him, the Russian general allowed numerous runners to go to the nearby stream to fetch water for the rest of the battalions. When the water bearers returned, they were mobbed by inexperienced and suffering soldiers who broke ranks for a drink. Amidst this chaos, Oudinot's disciplined battalions were completing the one and one-half mile march from their start positions to Bagration's main line, and struck the disorganized regiments under Selikov. The French grenadiers wasted no time in pressing their advantage. The initial success enjoyed by Oudinot's leading regiment—the 5th—prompted the general to feed the other brigades into the fight in order to envelop both of Selikov's flanks. Soon, Selikov's entire command was being pushed from three sides, but instead of breaking ranks, the cornered Russians stiffened and the opponents grappled in a savage hand-to-hand struggle.[127]

The scope of this contest quickly expanded as Lannes and Bagration fed more troops into the fight. Exchanges of point-blank musketry alternated with charge and countercharge. Oudinot, among his grenadiers, was shot through the thigh, but refused to leave the field and continued to give orders until the end of the battle. Also, Suchet's Division became embroiled in the *mêlée* and the 40th *Ligne* lost one of its eagles and attached battalion flag.[128] Outside the vineyards, part of Sébastiani's light cavalry tangled indecisively with the Pavlograd Hussars.

Meanwhile, Soult's *fantassins* found the vineyards on the west side of the field more difficult to negotiate than did Lannes' troops. As a result, participation by the 4th Corps was minimal. Only *général de division* Legrand, commander of the 3rd Infantry Division of Soult's corps, pushed his command into the right side of Bagration's line. It was there that the 3rd *Ligne* got locked up in a desperate struggle with the Kiev Grenadier Regiment. In this hand-to-hand combat, *chef de bataillon* Horiot of the 3rd *Ligne* saw his battalion's eagle and flag repeatedly fall to the ground when three different standard bearers went down with wounds. In his after-action report, Horiot recalled that following the fall of the third standard bearer, the precious emblem of the unit was about to fall into the hands of the Russians when:

> *fourrier* Daigrond rushed and seized the eagle of the battalion, and without retreating and all alone, held it over his head. Numerous enemies tried to take it from him, but swinging with a superhuman vigor the eagle and the standard like a giant club, Daigrond stunned or killed all the Russians that came within his reach.[129]

---

[127] *Zapiski A. P. Ermolova,* vol. 1, pp. 22-26.

[128] S.H.A.T., *Journal des opérations du 4e corps;* Charrié, *Drapeaux & Étendards de la Révolution et de l'Empire*, p. 208.

[129] S.H.A.T., *Journal des opérations du 4e corps;* Bourgue, *Historique du 3e régiment d'infanterie* (Paris, 1894), p. 257.

Bagration sensed that the time had come to withdraw, and ordered a fighting retreat. Although the combat was desperate, he managed to keep out of the fight his last reserve consisting of the Little Russia Grenadier Regiment. As the Russians slowly drew back, they came across the hamlet of Grund. Hundreds of Bagration's weakened and wounded eagerly sought shelter in the rickety frame houses, but their respite was very brief. When the French advance reached Grund, the resulting fighting caught the frame structures of the small village on fire.

> Many [soldiers], wounded in the legs or otherwise severely injured, were burned alive in the ruins. Some had endeavored to escape by crawling on the ground, but the fire had pursued them into the streets, and one might see thousands [*sic*] of poor fellows half reduced to ashes; some of them were even still breathing. The corpses of the men and horses killed in the fight had also been roasted, so that from the unhappy town emanating a horrible and sickening odor of roasted flesh, perceptible at some leagues' distance.[130]

About 11:00 P.M. on that freezing night, the Russians were finally able to disengage from the bitter and confused fighting. The valor and sacrifice made by the men under Bagration's command were clearly seen in the fields illuminated by the fires from Schöngrabern and Grund. Of the 6,800 regulars comprising Bagration's rearguard that began the battle, some 3,139—or 46% of the entire force, and 57% of those engaged—were lost. A large number of the Russians lay dead—more than 1,200. Many of those were from two of the three battalions of the 6th *Jaeger* that were pummeled by the French artillery, and from Selikov's unfortunate regiments. In addition to these losses, 1,448 Russians were captured, including two officers and 366 men from the Azov Musketeers and two officers and 297 men from the Podolia Musketeers.[131] Also taken by the French were four 6-pounder cannon. The remaining eight pieces of Major Bogoslavski's artillery were able to limber and escape into the night, no doubt inspiring Tolstoy's *War and Peace* Schöngrabern episode with Captain Tushin.[132]

French losses, often quoted at 2,000, were only slightly over 1,200. More than half of those killed, wounded and captured belonged to Oudinot's Division. Including the commanding general and two of his aides-de-camp—*chefs d'escadron* Demangeot and Lamotte—Oudinot's *Grenadiers de la Réserve* had 22 officers and 645 other ranks listed as casualties. Marshal Lannes had one of his aides-de-camp wounded along with two other officers on the staff of 5th Corps. Among the units of 4th Corps, the 3rd *Ligne* Regiment absorbed most of the losses. Overall, two French officers and 50 men were captured by the Russians, along with one eagle and attached battalion color from the 40th *Ligne*. If counting all units in the divisions of Oudinot, Suchet and Legrand as those being engaged, the French lost 5% of the 20,661 people that entered the fighting at Schöngrabern.[133]

---

[130] *Memoirs of Baron de Marbot,* vol. 1, p. 185.

[131] By totaling returns from the individual regimental histories, the losses come to this figure. Rainer Egger, *Das Gefecht bei Hollabrunn und Schöngrabern 1805* (Vienna, 1982), p. 17 is very close when he states 3,000 casualties. Andolenko, *Aigles de Napoléon Contre Drapeaux du Tsar*, p. 69, accurately states the number of prisoners lost by the Azov and Podolia Musketeers. Therefore, the often quoted Russian casualty figure of 2,402 is too low. On the other hand, Napoleon's 26th Bulletin of the *Grande Armée*, *Correspondance,* number 9510, overstates the Russian losses at 2,000 killed and wounded with another 2,000 prisoners.

[132] Tolstoy, *War and Peace*, pp. 219-229.

[133] S.H.A.T., C^2 16, 477 and 481.

The sacrifice made by Prince Bagration's rearguard had bought the remainder of Kutuzov's army the two precious marches it needed to pass the dangerous road junctions at Etzelsdorf and Pohrlitz in order to reach Brünn. When Bagration rejoined Kutuzov on 18 November, the army commander embraced the Georgian, proclaiming: "I shall not ask about your losses. You are alive, and that is enough for me."[134]

Bagration's return with about 3,600 men was just one of several significant reinforcements to reach Kutuzov's tiny army. The day after Schöngrabern, FML Prince Johann Josef von Liechtenstein joined up with Kutuzov, bringing with him a bouillabaisse of 9,400 Austrians that had been scraped together from every possible source in the Danube theater.[135] Following close behind were some more Austrians—most of which were depot troops. With the reinforcements from Liechtenstein, and after the reunion of Bagration, the strength of Kutuzov's troubled army swelled to slightly more than 25,000.

Continuing to retreat, the allies passed through Brünn, the capital of Moravia, on 18 November. Leaving the city and all its supplies to Napoleon, Kutuzov met up with the leading elements of Buxhöwden's army the following day at Wischau. Still withdrawing northeastward, Kutuzov picked up the remainder of Buxhöwden's troops at Prossnitz on 21 and 22 November. Buxhöwden's 30 battalions numbering 18,050 infantrymen, along with 30 squadrons mounting 3,000 troopers, 2,400 artillerists and specialist troops accompanied by six regiments of 3,000 pillaging Cossacks, boosted Kutuzov's army to 51,450. Also arriving was Lieutenant-General Rosen and the VI Column belonging to Kutuzov's original army. Utilizing an exceptionally slow march pace, Rosen had managed to keep together 6,800 of the 7,365 men with which he had started the campaign. With Rosen's addition, the army total was now 58,250.[136] Having been with Kutuzov throughout the campaign, artillery Lieutenant Colonel A. P. Ermolov noted that:

> the forces coming from Russia were completely fresh and in splendid order. Our army, on the contrary, had been ruined by perpetual hardship, and broken down by the lack of supplies and the foul weather of late autumn. The troops' uniforms had been destroyed by the conditions in the bivouacs, and their footwear had almost ceased to exist. Even our commanders were arrayed in ill-assorted, almost comic attire.[137]

Even more so than from the weather and losses, morale sank in Kutuzov's army from the constant brutalizing of the men by many of the officers. The most barbaric was General Alexei Andreevich Arakcheev, the Inspector General of Artillery. During the retreat from Braunau, this demented man killed officers and men alike. When a few of the artillerists from Miloradovich's Column returned without their guns following the Battle of Dürenstein, Arakcheev flew into a rage. He personally scalped the men by pulling out their hair by the handful. Following the Battle at Schöngrabern, the insatiable inspector general made further examples

---

[134] Mikhailovsky-Danilevsky, *Relation de la campagne de 1805,* p. 131.

[135] K. k. Kriegsarchiv, F.A., *Tagebuch:* Deutschland 1805, XI; Duffy, *Austerlitz,* p. 68.

[136] An exhaustive compilation of the regimental histories yields this figure, which is substantially less than other writers. It seems as though the higher numbers of troops in Kutuzov's army, repeated in innumerable works, never take into consideration the strategic consumption suffered by the Russian forces, deducting instead only battle casualties from the theoretical troop strengths at the beginning of the campaign. Even Stutterheim, who joined the Combined Russian and Austrian Army prior to Austerlitz, couched his estimates in careful language.

[137] *Zapiski A. P. Ermolova,* vol. 1, p. 29.

of officers and men who had lost their four guns during the fighting. Having two lieutenants buried alive up to their necks and left to die, Arakcheev then killed several gunners by beating them to death with the flat of his sword. A week later, when Arakcheev thought two of his officers were being insolent, he drew his saber and cut their heads off.[138] With such reprisals waiting for any officer or man who lost his guns in battle or did not please Arakcheev, it is little wonder why most Russian artillerists preferred to die at their pieces rather than to survive the battle without them.

Arriving on the 25th at the camp of Olmütz some 45 miles northeast of Brünn was the Russian Imperial Guard numbering some 8,500 combatants under arms. Austrian GM Stutterheim saw these men, and recalled that "after a long and forced march from Saint Petersburg, this fine body of men was in the best order."[139] Therefore, by 25 November, all the major allied formations in Moravia had joined the Tsar and Emperor Francis at Olmütz. Excluding artillerists, train drivers and specialists, the Combined Russian and Austrian Army mustered only 66,089 infantry and cavalry. If including the artillerists and other speciality troops, the combined allied forces numbered almost 71,800. With his regiments now united, the supremely confident Tsar Alexander and his zealous young courtiers were eager to humiliate Napoleon. The Russian nobles at once began to plan the battle to send the usurper, along with his *Grande Armée,* running back to France in ignominious defeat. That dream, however, was to be shattered on a rolling, windblown battlefield known as Austerlitz.

[138] S.H.A.T., C^2 10 and 240; Following Schöngrabern, the French light cavalry of 5th Corps came upon the two artillery lieutenants, buried up to their necks and dead from exposure. What had happened to them and by whose hand, as well as the other episode mentioned here, were explained by other Russian artillery officers captured at Austerlitz. In his very sympathetic biography of *Arakcheev: Grand Vizier of the Russian Empire*, Michael Jenkins quotes Lieutenant Zhirkevich of the Guard Artillery Battalion, who described Arakcheev thusly: "I had heard many disagreeable things about him and in general little good of him. But I spent three years under his command and can speak dispassionately of him. His honorable and ardent devotion to the throne [Alexander] and to the country, his naturally penetrating mind, which was, however, completely uneducated… were the main features of his character. But his tremendous pride, self-reliance and self-assurance made him frequently rancorous and vindictive."

[139] *A Detailed Account of the Battle of Austerlitz, by the Austrian Major-General Stutterheim* (London, 1807), p. 33.

Above, Oudinot's Grenadiers attack at Schöngrabern

Below, Schöngrabern from the east

Chapter VII
"Examine this terrain carefully. We shall fight on it."

"A common French soldier is more interested in winning a battle than is a Russian officer." —Napoleon[1]

Napoleon Chooses His Ground

Napoleon spent 14, 15 and most of 16 November at the Schönbrunn, administering the extensive affairs of state as well as those of the *Grande Armée*. During this time, he received word of Marshal Ney's successful campaign against Archduke John in the Tyrol, which sent the Austrian survivors running southeastward into Carinthia.[2] The Emperor also learned of the Battle of Caldiero fought in Italy on 29-30 October, where Marshal Masséna's *Armée d'Italie* had been repulsed by Archduke Charles' numerically superior forces. Meanwhile, Archduke Charles sent word to Vienna on his whereabouts and his plans to reunite with what remained of Archduke John's Tyrolian army. Charles never knew that his courier was intercepted on the afternoon of 15 November. The communiqué captured by Colonel Marx's 7th Hussars of Marshal Davout's 3rd Corps was forwarded to Napoleon, giving the Emperor definitive information as to the whereabouts of the Austrians. The combined forces of John and Charles were headed for Marburg in southeastern Carinthia, more than 160 miles south of Vienna. Since Ney and Marmont's corps were between these Austrians and the rest of the allies in Moravia and upper Bohemia, and with Masséna's troops supposedly pursuing the enemy from the west, Napoleon knew that he could focus all his attention on destroying Kutuzov's army.

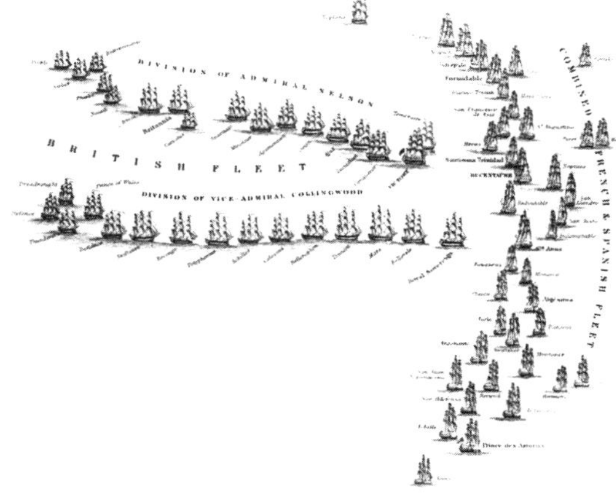

The Battle of Trafalgar

Late in the afternoon of 16 November, the Emperor and his Imperial staff left the palace of the Schönbrunn, escorted by Marshal Bessières and the Imperial Guard. They moved through Vienna and northward into the countryside, leaving the scenic and majestic city behind. As night fell, the Imperial entourage saw the northern horizon aglow. The flames from the burning tinderbox structures of Schöngrabern and Grund indicated to Napoleon that Murat had finally attacked the Russians north of Hollabrunn.

Eager to arrive at the front to regain personal direction of the army, the Emperor's attention was temporarily diverted when a courier from Paris intercepted the Imperial personage with a message about developments far away from the *Grande Armée*. The dispatch was from Admiral Decrès who had written Napoleon with news that the Combined French and Spanish Fleets under Admiral Villeneuve had met with utter disaster at Cape Trafalgar off the southwestern coast of Spain on 21 October. Apart from the staggering losses suffered by the Spanish navy, Napoleon learned that of the 18 French ships in Villeneuve's force, half were sunk or captured. One of Napoleon's private secretaries, Claude-François de Méneval, recalled that the ramifications of the news of the naval defeat were instantly recognized by the Emperor as he expressed his belief "that the only resource now

---

[1] Jean Antoine Chaptel, comte de Chanteloup, *Mes Souvenirs sur Napoléon* (Paris, 1893), p. 297.

[2] Frieda Bauer, *Die Kämpfe um die Pässe Strub, Scharnitz und Leutasch 1805* (Vienna, 1987), gives a good account of this campaign.

left to him was the execution of a vast continental blockade, and the extraordinary measures which would complete its effectiveness."[3] The implementation of the blockade was something that Napoleon would tackle after the continental foes had been defeated in 1807.

Meanwhile, the Emperor's immediate problem had to do with the allied forces that continued to fall back further northeastward into Moravia. While on the way to the front, the Emperor often came across different formations of the *Grande Armée*. Every time Napoleon met his troops, Jean-Baptiste Barrès of the *Chasseurs à pied de la Garde* recalled that the men:

> halted to give him military honors and salute him... All the corps of the army did the same unless otherwise ordered. Often, at these unpremeditated reviews, the Emperor complimented regiments which had distinguished themselves in a recent action, filled gaps by promotion, and distributed decorations. This was a fortuitous happening which was eagerly awaited, and the desires of many were satisfied in this way.[4]

Napoleon joined the advance guard of his army early on the 17th as it entered the important supply center of Znaïm on the Thaya River. Once at Znaïm, it became evident to Napoleon that what he had feared most had happened—Kutuzov's army had escaped.

With the prey beyond his clutches, Napoleon decided to rest, resupply and reorganize the weary *Grande Armée* before again going into battle. The center of this reorganization would be the fortified city of Brünn.[5] Like the other important towns given up by the retreating allies, the capital of Moravia proved to be another major supply depôt. Packed with food, footwear and other provisions that were left to the French by the retreating allies, Brünn was a perfect forward base for the French army.[6] On the 20th, Napoleon arrived outside the city, where the clergy and municipal officials "came out in all their finery to present the keys of the gates to the conqueror."[7]

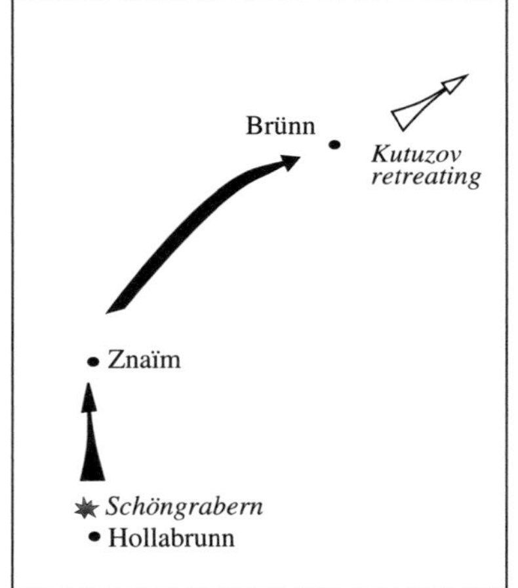

Kutuzov retreated from Znaïm and Brünn before the Grande Armée *arrived*

The appearance of the French army was also warmly greeted by the average citizens, who saw the French as their liberators from the barbaric Russians. The Imperial Guard and Oudinot's grenadiers were billeted in Brünn, where they found comfortable accommodations and ample food. What's more, one captain in Oudinot's division of grenadiers found the females of Brünn to be "extremely pretty women, who were gotten up in the most tasteful and tempting way."[8] The remaining units of 5th Corps and all of 4th Corps along with the *Corps des Réserves de Cavalerie* camped just outside the city or on the barren countryside to the north and east of Brünn. These men had far less to eat and wretched quarters, which caused a renewed outbreak of French marauding.

Since the capitulation of Ulm, Napoleon had been fighting another battle—the march conduct of his army. The rapid movements over desolate, enemy countryside ravaged by the retreating Russians had made it impossible for the French to requisition supplies. Regiments that had marched from the Channel to the Rhine without losing a man now shrank daily due to the departure of hungry stragglers. The barren countryside was only one contributing factor in the French

[3] *Memoirs of the Baron de Méneval,* vol. 1, p. 392.
[4] *Memoirs of a French Napoleonic Officer: Jean-Baptiste Barrès, Chasseur of the Imperial Guard,* pp. 71-72.
[5] Napoleon to Barbé-Marbois, *Correspondance,* number 9515.
[6] 28th Bulletin of the *Grande Armée, Correspondance,* number 9513.
[7] Duffy, *Austerlitz,* p. 70.
[8] *Journal du Général Fantin des Odoards* (Paris, 1895), p. 69.

rear areas being littered with men no longer with the colors. Bad weather and the resulting muddy roads took its toll on people and horses alike that were needed with the army around Brünn. To attempt to correct this problem, Napoleon issued a series of orders that gave instructions to his subordinates as to how they should round up and deal with the individuals that "dishonor themselves by all sorts of excesses."[9] On 4 frimaire (25 November) Napoleon's Order of the Day authorized "five mobile columns" to sweep the French rear. The Emperor instructed the commanders of these columns that "every straggler who, under the pretext of fatigue, leaves his corps for marauding, shall be arrested, tried by one of the military commissions, and executed on the spot."[10] The other men taken into custody—stragglers on their way to rejoin the army—were forwarded without delay to their respective units.

As important as securing the rear areas and forwarding to the army those loiterers otherwise fit for service was, Napoleon had to turn his foremost attention to the perilous position of the different corps needed to fight the next battle. The Emperor had already come to realize that he could not keep pushing his army ever eastward in a relentless pursuit of the enemy. While the allied forces only ran in front of a French advance, the Emperor thought that perhaps the Russians and Austrians might be tempted to turn and attack. Napoleon reasoned that if the allies thought the French to be vulnerable and committed themselves to an offensive, their clumsiness in the attack would betray them. This maladroitness was, in part, due to their lack of coordination between regiments as well as the other handicaps associated with *ad hoc* columns of *ancien régime* armies. Such an occurrence would provide the *Grande Armée* with the opportunity to use its greater command flexibility to counterattack and destroy the allied army in a single stroke.

In preparation for this decisive battle, Napoleon began carefully reconnoitering the ground east of Brünn as far as Wischau, which was half way to the allied army camp at Olmütz. However, it was ground closer to Brünn that caught Napoleon's keen eye. As the Emperor looked over the terrain to the west of the village of Austerlitz, he began to imagine the action unfolding. If he let the allies occupy the Pratzen heights and positioned the *Grande Armée* in such a way that invited the allies to attack him, Napoleon reasoned that the Russians and Austrians would see this as weakness on his part, and would therefore not hesitate in committing themselves to the offensive. As the allied forces moved off the Pratzen Plateau into the low-lying areas of the Goldbach and Bosenitz brooks, they would unknowingly be moving into Napoleon's killing ground. Once the allies were in this compromising position, the Emperor would launch his coordinated counterattacks from the undulating plains west of the streams. Napoleon believed that the result would be an overwhelming French victory. "Examine this terrain carefully," he told the Imperial staff. "We shall fight on it."[11]

Alexander Decides to Fight Napoleon

To Tsar Alexander, there was never any doubt as to his purpose for war. The glories of being the one to defeat Napoleon, using the Russian influence to wipe out the gangrene of the French Revolution and to restore the Bourbons to their rightful throne were all part of Alexander's fantasy world. The reverses suffered

---

[9] S.H.A.T., C^2 12; General Staff—Order of the Day, 16 brumaire an XIV (7 November 1805), *Unpublished Correspondence of Napoleon I*, vol. 1, number 214.

[10] S.H.A.T., C^2 12; Order of the Day, 4 frimaire an XIV (25 November 1805), *Unpublished Correspondence of Napoleon I*, vol. 1, number 214.

[11] Relation Officielle de la Bataille d'Austerlitz, *Correspondance,* number 10032; *Memoirs of Ségur*, p. 230.

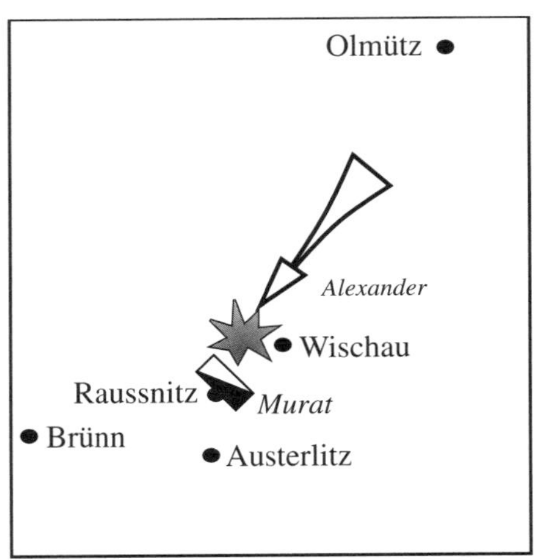

Alexander's cavalry reconnaissance to Russnitz

by Kutuzov's army after the fall of Ulm were easily explainable, thought Alexander and his sycophants. To blame were incompetent, distrustful Austrians who allowed their army around Ulm to be defeated in detail, and then let the French capture the strategic Tabor Bridge in Vienna. If that wasn't bad enough, the Austrian hosts were constantly complaining about the excesses of the Tsar's troops upon their populace. Clearly, thought the Russian courtiers, the imbecilic Austrians failed not only to appreciate the contributions of the Russian war effort, but did not know *how* to fight.

With that type of contemptuous air permeating Russian headquarters, the Tsar joined his staff in accompanying a large body of cavalry to the road junction of Raussnitz east of Brünn and north of Austerlitz on 20 November. General-Adjutant Prince Dolgoruky had convinced the Tsar that a reconnaissance in force was needed to push back the French cavalry outposts, and that his presence with the troops would double their fortitude; victory would surely follow. That sort of thing was just what the narcissistic Alexander loved to hear. He mounted his horse and rode to the front behind the Russian cavalry as they pushed westward from Olmütz in search of French mounted patrols.

As hoped, the 6,000 Russian cavalry found a fight. Astride the Olmütz Road were two divisions of French cavalry under the overall command of Marshal Murat. On the point were the first two of the three brigades from the 2nd Dragoon Division under *général de division* Walther (the 13th and 22nd Dragoon Regiments were not present). The lead brigade—once again under the direction of *général de brigade* Horace-François-Bastien Sébastiani de la Porta following his stint as Murat's advance guard commander during the *manœuvre sur Hollabrunn*—was almost immediately engulfed by the tidal wave of Russian cavalry that came thundering down the Olmütz Road. During this action, Colonel Bourdon of the 11th Dragoons was mortally wounded attempting to stem the Russian tide, and the standard bearer of the 1st Squadron was killed, with the eagle and standard falling into Russian hands.[12] The trophy was taken by private Dimitri Tchoumakov of the Saint Petersburg Dragoons, who presented it to the elated Tsar.[13]

At the opposite end of the line, Captain Matheret of the *compagnie d'élite* of the 9th Hussars saw something that made his blood boil. The eagle and attached standard of the 3rd Squadron, 11th Dragoons, was seized by another group of Russian horsemen, who then held the trophy over their head in jubilation. Captain Matheret immediately ordered the Élite Company of the 9th Hussars to move to the attack:

> and at the head of the company, Matheret and his men charged a force of 300 Cossacks and one squadron of Russian hussars… They stopped the progress of the enemy, took many prisoners and recaptured the eagle and standard.[14]

Élite company of the 9th Hussars

The impetus of the Russian attack had forced Walther's four regiments of dragoons to fall back in disorder when Murat arrived on the scene. The Prince rode at the head of reinforcements in the form of d'Hautpoul's 2nd Heavy Cavalry Division. Murat ordered that the four *cuirassiers* regiments deploy in squadrons abreast, and soon d'Hautpoul's troopers charged into the midst of the swarming Russian host. Although outnumbered, the French *cuirassiers* used their superior swordsmanship and tactics to arrest the advance of the Russian cavalry. For almost an hour, d'Hautpoul's armored cavalrymen kept the issue in doubt. The ebb and flow of repeated charge and countercharge had the effect of exhausting the men

[12] S.H.A.T., C^2 16.

[13] Andolenko, *Aigles de Napoléon Contre Drapeaux du Tsar*, pp. 74-75.

[14] S.H.A.T., dossier Matheret.

and the animals. Both sides were reaching enervation when Marshal Bessières galloped onto the field with six fresh squadrons of the magnificent cavalry of the Imperial Guard. Deploying three squadrons of the *Grenadiers à cheval de la Garde* along with two squadrons of the *Chasseurs à cheval de la Garde* in the first line, and keeping one squadron of the "Favored Children" in the second line as a reserve, Bessières launched the charge that broke the Russian cavalry and sealed the French minor tactical victory.

Chasseur à cheval *of the Imperial Guard charging at Raussnitz*

Dead were 200 Russian *cuirassiers* and dragoons, while 100 horses had been captured by the French. Despite these losses, the mood at allied headquarters was optimistic. In addition to the prized eagle and standard that was being admired by the Tsar, the Russians came away with 100 prisoners, most of them dragoons from Walther's Division.[15] Even though Murat had cleared the Olmütz Road of the Russian cavalry, Prince Dolgoruky and Baron Wintzingerode saw the combat at Raussnitz as a Russian victory. They told Alexander that this clash was proof enough that the Russian army, inspired by the presence of its Tsar, would crush the French. This blather was seconded by other young and inexperienced officers, who joined in by pleading with Alexander to commit to an offensive that would surely result in the ruination of the usurper and his army.

With an ego that was inflated beyond measure, the vainglorious Tsar returned to allied headquarters at Olmütz. It was evident to all present that Alexander and his inner circle were bubbling with enthusiasm; they could not wait to fight a major battle against Napoleon. Looking for complete acceptance of the idea in attacking the French among the numerous generals from both his own country and Austria, Alexander called for a council of war that was held on 24 November. With Buxhöwden's forces now in camp and with the Russian Imperial Guard due to complete its arrival the next day, Alexander first asked his generals for a state of the army. Although morale had improved with the appearance of these reinforcements, the additional troops only speeded up the rate in which the Olmütz area was picked clean of all foodstuff. Furthermore, Austrian and Russian logistical officers reported that there was no subsistence to be found from anywhere around Olmütz south to the Danube. The country was denuded of food as if a horde of locusts had passed through. Also, the Austrian cavalry generals eager to replace their lame horses learned from their purchasing agents the distressing news that the Russians had already stolen every horse worth riding from Moravia southward into Hungary. Finally, allied cavalry scouts could not penetrate the covering French cavalry screen in order to ascertain the size of the French forces around Brünn. Even a sortie led by Prince Bagration failed to brush aside Murat's cloud of horsemen.[16]

An adversary whose strength could not be ascertained, and a countryside stripped of food and horseflesh, gave Kutuzov sufficient grounds to recommend to the Tsar that the Combined Russian and Austrian Army withdraw further eastward into the unforaged territory of the Carpathian Mountains. Kutuzov pointed out that such a retreat would not only help feed the army, but it would also give the allied cavalry a better chance to determine French strength should Napoleon follow. Such a withdrawal would also buy extra time for Archduke Charles to move northward from Marburg and give the Prussians more time to complete the mobilization of their army. In short, Kutuzov wanted to play for time. Several other the generals who had fought the French during the retreat from Braunau supported Kutuzov's proposal. Not surprisingly, generals Bagration, Dokhturov and Miloradovich were among the most vocal supporters of Kutuzov. After all, they were the ones that had experienced the fighting prowess of the new French

French dragoon trumpeter sounding the charge

[15] S.H.A.T., C[2] 16.

[16] S.H.A.T., C[2] 240; Esposito and Elting, *A Military History and Atlas of the Napoleonic Wars*, text to Map number 53.

army, and were not eager to tangle with the *Grande Armée* again until every advantage could be mustered. Furthermore, Kutuzov's proposed course of action was supported by Langeron as well as the Tsar's foreign advisory, Prince Adam George Czartoryski.[17]

Such a stratagem was not the audacious course of action that glory-seeking Alexander and his cocky, young colleagues were seeking. Besides, Kutuzov's proposal *did* ignore the rapidly deteriorating condition of the army and its animals. With no replacements on the way to make good the considerable losses already suffered in the campaign, the units of the army could only get weaker. Bivouacked around Olmütz, the Austrian and Russian regiments—especially those fatigued and starving soldiers of Kutuzov's army that had remained with the colors since the opening of hostilities—were being ravaged by disease. If battle was postponed, argued Wintzingerode, Dolgoruky and many other officers, the army might never again be as strong. Besides, counseled the Russian courtiers, why should the Tsar expect Archduke Charles to be able to fight his way into the theater of war. The Russians had already seen what they considered to be the lack of fighting skill displayed by their brothers-in-arms. If French forces were between Charles and the combined allied army at Olmütz—and everyone at allied headquarters knew they were—there was no reason to doubt that Charles himself might be destroyed, thereby releasing *all* French forces, including the *Armée d'Italie,* northward into Moravia. Furthermore, the sudden halt around Brünn by the French and their apparent inactivity gave further encouragement to those in favor of immediate action.

Adding his voice to the young officers that surrounded Alexander was Austrian staff officer GM Weyrother. Weyrother had guided the Russian army on their march from Radziwilow to Braunau, and had recently taken the position as Kutuzov's chief of staff after the previous officer to hold that post, FML Heinrich von Schmidt, had been killed in action at Dürenstein. As the one Austrian at allied headquarters to whom the Tsar listened, Weyrother was also one of the biggest sycophants. Maybe that was why Alexander gave him the time of day, a courtesy that the Tsar did not extend to any other Austrian other than Emperor Francis. What can be said with relative certainty is that Weyrother suppressed any of his instincts and opinions that did not conform to those held by Alexander. Weyrother clearly did not have "that confidence in himself which could enable him to give advice at headquarters, where the greatest degree of wisdom was requisite."[18] The Austrian general did, however, confirm what Kutuzov had already said: the army could not stay around Olmütz owing to the scarcity of supplies. What did not make sense—and is proof that Weyrother's "single ambition was to give practical effect to the Tsar's fantasies"[19]—was the Austrian's suggestion that the allied supply problems could be solved by advancing westward towards Brünn. The subsistence around that area had long since been eaten up.

Alexander was not paying attention to any potential difficulties. He fed on the optimistic arrogance of his entourage and the euphoria of thinking about defeating Napoleon. Deciding against Kutuzov's delaying course of action, the Tsar believed that the time was right to commit the allied forces to a counteroffensive, even though no one in the allied camp knew exactly where the French were, or in what strength. Watching the Tsar come to this conclusion, General Langeron remembered that Alexander "seemed to be confident of a victory that would place him at one stroke above the man who as yet had no equal, let

---

[17] Duffy, *Austerlitz*, pp. 72-73; Esposito and Elting, *A Military History and Atlas of the Napoleonic Wars*, text to Map number 53.
[18] Stutterheim, *A Detailed Account of the Battle of Austerlitz*, p. 36.
[19] Duffy, *Austerlitz*, p. 73.

alone a rival on the battlefield."[20] Even though Emperor Francis of Austria was in attendance, he "believed that it was beneath his dignity to oppose the will and resolve of Alexander."[21] When Kutuzov asked Alexander what his intentions were concerning the movements of the army, the Tsar brusquely replied: "That is none of *your* business."[22] Kutuzov then "withdrew into himself and virtually contracted out of the war."[23] Therefore, on 24 November 1805, the control of the Combined Russian and Austrian Army passed from Kutuzov to Tsar Alexander I. Orders would be written by Count Lieven of Alexander's personal staff, and communicated to the other senior officers by another egomanical Russian courtier, General-Adjutant Prince Volkonsky. The Tsar and his advisors decided that the army would break camp at Olmütz and move against the French last known to be in and around Brünn. Meanwhile, Archduke Ferdinand with about 9,000 Austrians would march southward from Prague in Bohemia in an attempt to block the enemy's potential line of retreat.[24]

The Tsar then instructed Weyrother to draw up an explanation of the allied strategy, and that it be distributed among the generals. In his *Journal,* Weyrother wrote on 24 November that his fellow officers were to maneuver as one, since:

> we shall attempt to turn the enemy's right flank, and take up a position which will threaten his communications with Vienna, thereby forcing him to abandon Brünn without a fight and retire behind the Thaya. If this... movement does not produce the desired effect, we shall exploit the advantages of our own position and superior forces and launch a decisive attack against his right flank, which will drive him from his ground and throw him back on the Znaïm Road. Subsequently, we will send strong raiding detachments racing ahead of our left wing, and in concert with the column of Archduke Ferdinand, who is advancing on Iglau, we will compel the enemy to retreat through the roadless mountains above Krems.[25]

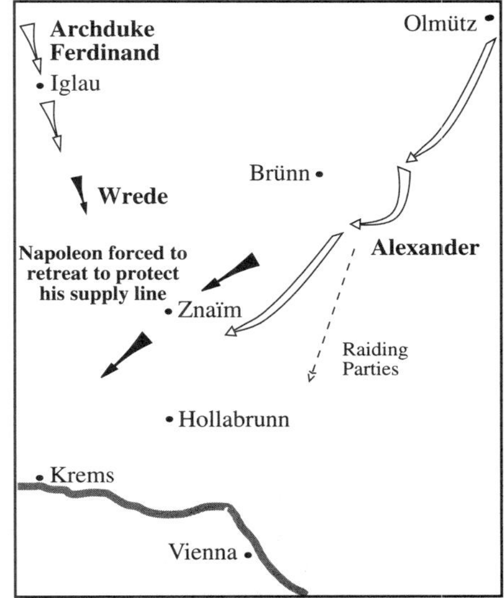

Weyrother's planned advance to Brünn

The fact that Alexander did not know the exact strength or location of Napoleon's forces before authorizing Weyrother to complete the *Disposition* for the army's movement speaks volumes about the Tsar's military talents. What's more, Alexander ordered the army to move out on 25 November after two day's rations had been gathered. That proved to be impossible owing to the lack of provisions in the Olmütz area. Therefore, the army remained motionless on the 25th, which then carried over to the 26th as well because "when *that* day came, some of the generals had not sufficiently studied their dispositions; and thus, another day was lost."[26] Despite all that had already happened in the 1805 campaign, certain allied generals just didn't understand that they were involved in a new type of warfare that demanded their complete attention.

Finally, at 8:00 A.M. on 27 November, the allied host moved forward. Screened by the advance guard under Bagration which did not move the first day, the army

---

[20] Anon. *Austerlitz Raconté par les Témoins de la Bataille des Trois Empereurs* (Geneva, 1969), p. 147.
[21] Duffy, *Austerlitz*, p. 73.
[22] Russian General Staff, *Stoletie Voennogo Ministerstva* (Saint Petersburg, 1902-1913), part 2, p. 179.
[23] Duffy, *Austerlitz*, p. 73.
[24] Esposito and Elting, *A Military History and Atlas of the Napoleonic Wars*, see Map number 53 and accompanying text.
[25] K. k. Kriegsarchiv, F.A. Weyrother, *Tagebuch:* Deutschland 1805.
[26] Stutterheim, *A Detailed Account of the Battle of Austerlitz*, pp. 40-41.

marched westward in five columns along five parallel roads across a five mile front, numbered in order from the north. The first two columns were to the north of the Olmütz Road, with the third marching along the highway, while the fourth and fifth were south of the road. The Russian Imperial Guard formed the reserve and followed behind the front five columns.

As typical with armies of the *ancien régime*, the Combined Russian and Austrian Army had been reorganized for this offensive. Regiments formerly of Kutuzov's army were combined with those of Buxhöwden, as well as with the various Austrian units. Excluding artillerists, the allied army that marched to Austerlitz numbered only 66,089 officers and other ranks present and under arms. Once those serving the guns were included, the Combined Russian and Austrian Army at Austerlitz numbered 72,789—significantly fewer than the 85,000 or more so often repeated in seemingly countless secondary sources (see Appendix I). These combatants were supported by 318 pieces of ordnance, of which 170 served in the capacity of battalion guns.[27]

It took four hours before the lumbering columns had moved 10 miles to come abreast of Bagration's command at Prödlitz. The movement was screened by swarms of allied cavalry, who carefully felt their way westward, looking for the French. Shortly after noon on the 27th, the allies stopped their march in order to make camp with no reported sightings of Napoleonic forces.

Resuming their march on the 28th, the allies continued westward, running into Murat's picket line around the village of Wischau. Once contact was made with the French cavalry by Bagration's advance guard, General-Adjutant Prince Dolgoruky sent for the Tsar. Alexander rode forward to see Dolgoruky capture Wischau. It took the General-Adjutant more than two hours for his troops, consisting of one battalion of the 6th *Jaeger* and the entire regiment of the Pskov Musketeers to wrest the village from 104 Frenchmen.[28] After evicting these French from Wischau, the Russian troops advanced to the heights around Raussnitz, where the sharp cavalry action had been fought eight days earlier. The day's minor success further bolstered the ego of Dolgoruky and the other hangers-on surrounding the Tsar. Officers like the levelheaded Ermolov were far from impressed with the day's developments. He believed that:

Haugwitz

> the importance of the affair was greatly exaggerated, and Prince Bagration, as a shrewd kind of man, attributed the success to Prince Dolgoruky. This courtier had the complete confidence of the Tsar, and Bagration knew that he might prove useful to him.[29]

Napoleon Gathers His Eagles and Deceives the Allies

Napoleon had hoped that his sudden lack of activity would help draw out the allied forces, but he had no idea that his bait would be so quickly taken. Sometime after midday on 28 November, as the Emperor was talking to the Prussian envoy Haugwitz in Brünn about dispatches concerning the recently mobilized Prussian army moving towards the Bohemian border, a series of reports began to arrive with news that Murat's picket line was being driven in. Napoleon believed that

---

[27] österreichischen Kriegsarchiv, Vienna (K.A., F.A. Deutschland 1805); C[2] 13, *Archives du Service Historique de l'État-Major de l'Armée de Terre,* (S.H.A.T.), VINCENNES, and numerous regimental historiesin the Russian Archives, Saint Petersburg. These numbers are a result of lengthy and painstaking research, which are detailed in Appendix I.

[28] "Relation Officielle de la Bataille d'Austerlitz," *Correspondance,* number 10032.

[29] *Zapiski A. P. Ermolova,* vol. 1, p. 30.

something was afoot, and that he had no time to lose. Quickly dismissing Haugwitz, the Emperor then ordered his aide-de-camp, *général de division* Anne-Jean-Marie-Rene Savary, to ride to allied headquarters on the pretense of requesting an interview with Tsar Alexander. Savary's real mission, however, was to observe the enemy's camp and return with his best educated estimate as to their intentions.[30]

Napoleon then began sending out a flurry of orders designed to concentrate the army east of Brünn in anticipation of a great battle. To *général de division* Caffarelli, commander of the 1st Infantry Division of Davout's 3rd Corps, who was a day's march south of Brünn at the road junction of Pohrlitz, the Emperor transmitted the following order through Marshal Berthier at 7:00 P.M.

> It is ordered that General Caffarelli will prepare his division to ready arms and make sure to have proper supplies of cartridges; there will be a great battle. The general will speak to the *généraux de brigade* and to the colonels, and will put the division in motion at 1:00 A.M. tomorrow morning. The division will march *en guerre,* without stragglers, and with its artillery, and without any kind of baggage; it will be present at 6:30 A.M. tomorrow at Brünn, and will continue on the road to Olmütz. The general will send to the Emperor an aide-de-camp in order to receive the orders as to what position the division will occupy. It is probable that by 8:00 A.M. the action will already be vigorously underway.[31]

The following hour, the Emperor's chief of staff sent a separate message to Marshal Bernadotte, whose French divisions were encamped about 30 miles to the west of Brünn. The reader will note the precise words used by Berthier on Napoleon's behalf, which left the Emperor's worrisome lieutenant no room for interpretation, nor allowed Bernadotte any excuse to delay the implementation of the Imperial directive.

> It is ordered that Marshal Bernadotte will promptly take the most direct route in sending his advance guard to Brünn; it is ordered that, without losing a moment, the marshal will place himself in step with his troops in order to arrive at Brünn at the earliest possible moment.
>
> The marshal will send to me his aides-de-camp, to advise me of the successive arrival of his troops, so I can advise them of the positions that they will occupy on the other side of Brünn.
>
> The marshal will warn the Bavarians [Wrede's Division] of these movements, in the event that they have to maneuver in light of these pressing circumstances.
>
> Marshal Bernadotte will warn his corps that there will be a battle on the other side of Brünn, tomorrow or after; the corps will put its guns in order and will have proper supplies of cartridges; the artillery will march *en guerre*, and the corps will take whatever bread it can.[32]

7 Frimaire, Year XIV
To The Marshal commanding 3rd Corps

It appears certain, Monsieur Marshal, that we will have a major battle tomorrow or the next day in the vicinity of Brünn.

His Majesty orders that you should leave immediately with your two divisions nad by forced marches arrive at Brünn as quickly as possible.

Here are Berthier's instructions to a trusted lieutenant, Marshal Davout. Notice the difference between these instructions and those issued to Bernadotte.

In addition to the orders for Bernadotte, Napoleon had Berthier instruct Marshal Mortier to hold Vienna with the depleted divisions of Dupont and Gazan, along with the Batavian troops under Dumonceau. The latter division was southwest of Vienna, and was ordered to join Mortier at once in the Austrian capital. Marmont

[30] *Memoirs of the Duke of Rovigo* (Savary), vol. 1, pp. 112-128.

[31] Napoléon to Caffarelli, *Correspondance,* number 9530.

[32] Napoléon to Bernadotte, *Correspondance,* number 9531.

was ordered to keep his 2nd Corps in readiness to move northward, while Soult's 4th Corps and Murat's cavalry were authorized to fall back closer to Brünn to the west side of the Goldbach and Bosenitz Brooks. The Emperor also had Berthier send the following message to Marshal Davout:

> It appears certain, Marshal, that we will have a large battle tomorrow or the next day on the other side of Brünn. His Majesty orders that you should leave immediately with your two divisions [Friant and Gudin] and by forced marches arrive at Brünn as quickly as possible.[33]

When the Imperial messenger arrived at Davout's headquarters in Vienna at 3:00 P.M. on 29 November, the marshal was 40 miles away in Pressburg by previous orders from Napoleon. Davout's chief of staff, *général de brigade* Daultanne, forwarded copies of the Emperor's dispatch to divisional commanders Friant and Gudin. Friant was in Vienna with the 2nd Infantry Division of 3rd Corps when his copy of the order was received at 8:00 P.M.[34] Friant and his men were on the march within 90 minutes. They moved all night and all the next day, picking up Bourcier's 4th Dragoon Division north of Vienna. The two divisions arrived at Nikolsburg on the evening of the 30th after Friant had covered a distance of 45 miles. Friant's exhausted men had little trouble sleeping that night. The following day, they stirred from their slumbers and marched another 25 miles. Both Friant and Bourcier's divisions arrived at the Raigern Abbey seven miles south of Brünn at 7:00 P.M. on 1 December, thereby completing their remarkable 70 mile march to Austerlitz in under 48 hours![35] Gudin's 3rd Infantry Division and most of Klein's 1st Dragoon Division did not arrive in time for the battle as they had to come from Pressburg. Therefore, Marshal Davout went into action at Austerlitz with only Friant's 2nd Infantry Division, Colonel Arrighi de Casanova's 1st Dragoon Regiment that was independently attached to 3rd Corps from Klein's 1st Dragoon Divisions and Bourcier's mounted command. Since Caffarelli's infantry of Davout's corps were already in the vicinity of Brünn on the 28th, they were temporarily attached to Marshal Lannes' 5th Corps.

Gudin

While Friant and Bourcier were conducting their forced march to Austerlitz, Napoleon was again carefully reconnoitering the ground on which he expected to fight. The Emperor did this as Murat, Lannes and Soult pulled back their corps from Austerlitz to the brooks west of the Pratzen Plateau. According to the order given by Napoleon following a meeting with the three marshals at the Posortiz Post House on the evening of 28 November (see page 341), these corps performed this retrograde movement by forming a giant checkerboard five miles wide (the width of the advancing allied forces), with cavalry covering the movements of the infantry. "I was no less struck by the novelty than by the magnificence of the spectacle," recalled *général de brigade* Thiébault of Soult's 4th Corps. "The two [infantry] corps executed this movement in squares, checker-wise, reminded Morand of the marches in Egypt amid immovable swarms of Mameluks."[36]

---

[33] Louis N. Davout, *Opérations du 3e Corps, 1806-1807. Rapport du maréchal Davout, duc d'Auerstadt,* edited by Général Léopold Davout (Paris, 1896). Hereafter cited as: *Opérations du 3e Corps.* Berthier to Davout, p. v.

[34] John G. Gallaher, *The Iron Marshal, A Biography of Louis N. Davout* (Carbondale, 1976), pp. 104-105. Because it did not take five hours for a Napoleonic corps chief of staff to generate orders, Daultanne must have first sent a courier to, and then received word back from, Davout before giving Friant his marching orders.

[35] Davout, *Opérations du 3e Corps,* p. v-vi.

[36] *The Memoirs of Baron Thiébault,* translated and condensed by Arthur John Butler, 2 volumes (New York, 1896), vol. 2, p. 147.

From his study of the ground, from his vivid recollections of how arrogant the Russian aides had conducted themselves during the campaign, and after observing the allied columns continually shift position to the south of the Olmütz Road throughout the 30th—often watching the Russians and Austrians from beyond his outermost cavalry pickets—Napoleon concluded that the enemy army was going to attack his center or his right, or southern flank, with the intent of driving his army away from Vienna. Such a move, if successful, would in the minds of the allied generals, force the French to retreat into hostile country and remove them from their last *known* established line of supply and communication that ran along the line Brünn—Vienna—Braunau—Augsburg—Ulm—Strasbourg. To counter this move, Napoleon ordered Davout to take up defensive positions on the vital southern flank. Assisting Davout on that flank would be Legrand's 3rd Infantry Division of the 4th Corps, along with the 4th Corps' Light Cavalry Division. Occupying the center and linking the southern front with the northern flank were the 1st and 2nd Infantry Divisions of Soult's 4th Corps. The remainder of the *Grande Armée*, including the commands of Lannes, Bernadotte, Murat and the Imperial Guard, were all stacked up along and on the south side of the Olmütz Road in order to readily reinforce the center or launch a counterattack. By the time that Friant and Bourcier arrived on the evening of 1 December 1805, Napoleon had the equivalent of 10 divisions of infantry and nine divisions of cavalry totaling 74,595 officers and men under arms, supported by 139 pieces of mobile ordnance and another 18 guns of position (see Appendix H).[37]

During the afternoon of 30 November as both armies were making preparations for an epic battle, the facade of negotiations continued. Savary returned to French lines with none other than General-Adjutant Prince Dolgoruky who was escorted by a detachment of Cossacks of the Russian Imperial Guard. The Emperor and his staff rode out to meet them. When Napoleon caught sight of Dolgoruky, he and his staff dismounted in the no man's land that was beyond the range of French guns or outpost line. The Emperor then walked towards Dolgoruky without escort. The Russian, whose claim to distinction was that he loved women as much as he hated the French, then saw for the first time the man that he and the Tsar held in such contempt. Napoleon's costume could have only reinforced Dolgoruky's feelings. Wearing a simple, gray greatcoat over a green, white and red uniform of a colonel of the *Chasseurs à cheval de la Garde* topped with black cocked hat displaying the French red, white and blue cockade, the Emperor's outer wardrobe reflected none of the importance of his rank. What's more, Napoleon put on his best act to appear to be a deeply worried man. Cordial small talk continued for about 10 minutes without anyone in the Imperial staff being able to hear all that was being said. What was evident to those who saw the meeting was the increasing arrogance of Dolgoruky, who comported himself as a Russian noble would talk to a lowly serf. Finally, raising his voice for all to hear, Dolgoruky announced: "Here are the Tsar's terms for equilibrium in Europe. If France desires immediate peace, she must give up Italy. If she continues to war unsuccessfully, she will be required to relinquish Belgium, Savoy and Piedmont." These conditions, put to Napoleon in the most forceful and demanding way, brought the Corsican's blood to an instant boiling point. "What, Belgium too?" replied Napoleon ironically. "Why—here we are in Moravia. You wouldn't get Brussels if you were on Montmartre! Withdraw; go and tell your master that I am not in the habit of being trifled with in this way. Withdraw this very moment!"[38]

Savary

---

[37] C² 470, 472, 474, 476, 477 and 481, *Archives du Service Historique de l'État-Major de l'Armée de Terre,* (S.H.A.T.), VINCENNES, plus the *Journaux des opération* of the various corps.

[38] *Memoirs of Ségur*, pp. 232-233; *Memoirs of the Duke of Rovigo* (Savary), vol. 1, pp.127-128.

The Tsar's adjutant returned to allied headquarters in the most excitable frame of mind. "Napoleon draws back!" Dolgoruky exclaimed to the Tsar. "He is in full retreat; it is necessary to fall upon and crush him!"[39] The picture painted by Dolgoruky was seconded by the army's cavalry scouts. The troopers reported that the French were withdrawing because, except for cavalry patrols, they had abandoned the local dominating feature of terrain—the Pratzen Plateau. Wanting to occupy these heights as soon as possible, five allied columns advanced onto the eastern-most portions of the Pratzen Plateau between 3:00 P.M. on 30 November and 2:00 A.M. on 1 December.[40] Meanwhile, Archduke Constantine and the Russian Imperial Guard followed the five columns and remained in reserve immediately west of the village of Austerlitz behind the Twaroschna River. Meanwhile, to the north, Bagration's command straddled the Olmütz Road.

Battle Plans and Final Dispositions

After Napoleon spoke to Dolgoruky, Savary rejoined the Emperor along the outpost line. Napoleon spoke freely to Savary about the way Dolgoruky had insulted him and France with the Tsar's insane demands. As the Emperor was venting his frustrations, they walked by a sentry belonging to the *carabiniers* of the 17th *Légère*. Savary remembered that the man wearing the bearskin was:

> an old soldier, and overheard him; and being at ease, he had his musket between his legs, and was filling his pipe. Napoleon, as he passed close to him, glanced up and said, 'Those Russian bastards fancy they have nothing to do but to swallow us up!' The old soldier immediately joined in the conversation. 'Oh no! That won't be such an easy job—we'll stick ourselves right across.'
>
> This repartee made the Emperor laugh; resuming a serene look, he mounted his horse, and returned to his headquarters.[41]

Once back at his military headquarters, Napoleon paced back and forth with his hands clasped behind his back—the Emperor's trademark that he was in deep thought.[42] Napoleon then sent for his marshals and advised them that they and the Imperial staff would tour the battlefield together. The Imperial entourage mounted up about 11:00 A.M. on 30 November, and followed the Emperor from headquarters to their first stop—the rounded hill on the northern side of the Olmütz Road. This high ground, dubbed by the veterans of the Egyptian campaign as "the Santon" because it reminded them of the tombs of the Moslem saints, was the anchor on which the French left rested. Garrisoned by one battalion of the 17th *Légère*, the Santon bristled with 18 Austrian 3-pounder cannon. These had been captured at Stockerau along with ample supplies of the small-caliber ammunition. Brought to the front, the Austrian ordnance and munitions had been hauled by hand up the steep slope to the summit of the Santon and manned by personnel from the army's *Grand Parc d'Artillerie*. Napoleon pointed out the 3-pounders to the marshals, and declared "if these pieces get off 50 rounds at short range I am quite happy for

---

[39] Thiers, *The History of the Consulate & the Empire of France*, vol. 2, p. 73.

[40] Esposito and Elting, *A Military History and Atlas of the Napoleonic Wars*, text to Map number 54.

[41] *Memoirs of the Duke of Rovigo* (Savary), vol. 1, p. 129.

[42] *Souvenirs Diplomatiques et Miltaires du Général Thiard* (Paris, 1805), p. 213.

the Austrians to get them back—they will have earned them. Besides, the guns are really theirs."[43]

Napoleon and the collection of high-ranking officers then turned south and rode along the western and central portions of the Pratzen that was still patrolled by French cavalry. Ascending to the summit, the Emperor, his staff and his marshals gazed eastward and took in an amazing sight. Extending through the valley to the village of Austerlitz was the allied host "still milling about in some confusion"[44] but already beginning to move towards the Pratzen. Everything the allies were doing further convinced Napoleon that the Russians and Austrians were going to attack his center in the area of Kobelnitz. With the glittering masses of the enemy before them, Napoleon told the marshals and the Imperial staff:

> I could certainly stop the Russians here, if I held on to this fine position; but that would be just an ordinary battle. I prefer to abandon this ground to them and draw back my right. If they then dare to descend from the heights to take me in my flank, they will surely be beaten without hope of recovery.[45]

The Emperor then explained to his attentive audience the further details for his planned battle of annihilation.

> Once the enemy were fully committed in the Goldbach valley, [Napoleon] intended to fall on the flanks and rear of their salient. Approaching from the southwest, Davout and the 3rd Corps would take the host in the left flank; more important still, the mass of the main army was to debouch from the Santon area to the north, and sweep over the Pratzen plateau… [46]

The Emperor and the Imperial entourage then returned to headquarters for further discussion. By nightfall on 30 November, Napoleon had received one of Bernadotte's aides-de-camp, advising that all the divisions of 1st Corps—less Karl Philipp von Wrede's Bavarians that were left to the northwest to act as troops of observation—had reached the gates of Brünn. Marshal Davout arrived soon thereafter with news that Friant's infantry and the attached dragoon division under Bourcier would be on the field the next day. Napoleon ordered them to march for Turas in anticipation of the allied attack upon his center. With all formations assigned their positions, Napoleon went to work on issuing a proclamation for the army.

While the French knew where they were to deploy, things were different on the other side of the hill. By midday on 1 December, the unwieldy allied columns were shuffling about after being horrible entangled. It will be remembered that when the allies broke camp to begin their westward movement, the numbered columns of the army were arranged from north to south, with the I Column being the furthermost north. The columns became jumbled when headquarters decided to change the relative positions of march order with I Column being the southern most body of troops. Unable to completely shake out before nightfall, instead of the five columns being abreast of each other, only the first three were positioned correctly. Austrian staff work had been less than precise, but when coupled with officers who had not worked together, the result was an awful traffic jam. The IV and V Columns were nowhere close to their assigned positions, let alone allowing

[43] *Souvenirs Diplomatiques et Miltaires du Général Thiard,* p. 201.

[44] Duffy, *Austerlitz*, p. 80.

[45] *Memoirs of Ségur*, pp. 235-236.

[46] Duffy, *Austerlitz*, p. 80.

time for the troops to reconnoiter the ground over which they were to attack. Only Kienmayer's Austrian cavalry on the extreme southern end of the battlefield probed French positions near Tellnitz. Nevertheless, the movements of the allies had brought them unknowingly close to the French that were in the defiles west of the Pratzen. Located from north to south, these defiles were Schlappanitz, Sokolnitz and Tellnitz. With the advantages of terrain, and with a self-professed moral superiority, Tsar Alexander was determined to attack and destroy Napoleon's forces the next day.

Acting chief of staff for the Combined Russian and Austrian Army, GM Weyrother, drew up the battle plans. Despite the proximity of the rival armies, the allied battle plans were drawn up with the most imperfect knowledge about the French positions. These were verbally delivered to the allied general officers at the staff meeting held at a peasant's house in the small hamlet of Krzenowitz two miles west of Austerlitz shortly after midnight on 2 December. The scene was described in detail by General Langeron.

> General Weyrother came into the room. He had an immense map, showing the area of Brünn and Austerlitz in the greatest precision and detail. He spread it over a large table, and read his dispositions to us in a loud voice, and with a boastful manner which betrayed smug self-satisfaction. He might have been a schoolmaster reading a lesson to his pupils, though he was far from being a good teacher. We had found Kutuzov half asleep in a chair when we arrived at his house, and by the time we prepared to leave he had dozed off completely. Buxhöwden was standing. He listened to what was being said, though it must have gone in one ear and out the other. Miloradovich spoke not a word. Prebyshevsky kept in the background, and only Dokhturov examined the map with any attention.[47]

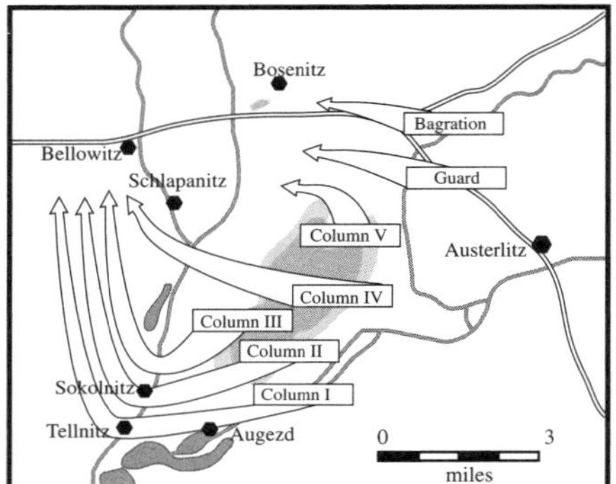

Weyrother's Plan

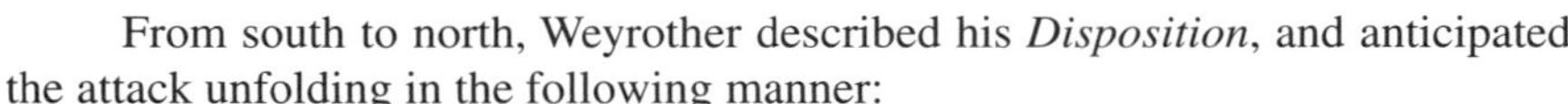

From south to north, Weyrother described his *Disposition*, and anticipated the attack unfolding in the following manner:

(Please consult Appendix I for the complete, detailed Allied Order of Battle at Austerlitz).

> Advance Guard of the I Column—FML M. Kienmayer—with five battalions of Grenz infantry, three companies of pioneers, elements of five regiments of Austrian cavalry and two regiments of Cossacks, supported by two Austrian 6-pounder cavalry batteries with a total of 12 pieces of ordnance, all totaling 4,935 officers and other ranks excluding artillerists—would brush against the Salschan Pond, cover the left flank of the infantry of I. Column and force the lower Goldbach.

> I Column—Lieutenant-General D. S. Dokhturov—with 21 battalions of Russian infantry, two and one-half squadrons of Cossacks, one company of pioneers, supported by 40 battalion guns and 24 pieces in two Russian 6-pounder position batteries, totaling 7,752 plus artillerists—would attack towards Tellnitz, sweep across the Goldbach Brook, turn the enemy's extreme right, then move north towards the Turas Wood and the hamlet of Latain near the Olmütz Road.

> II Column—Lieutenant-General A. Langeron—with 17 battalions of Russian infantry, two squadrons of cavalry and one squadron of Cossacks, plus one company of pioneers, supported by 30 battalion guns, totaling 10,283 people

[47] Anon. *Austerlitz Raconté par les Témoins de la Bataille des Trois Empereurs*, p. 126.

excluding artillerists—would advance on the right flank of Dokhturov, cross the Goldbach, driving the French between Tellnitz and Sokolnitz, and help Dokhturov break the French right flank before driving northwestward.

III Column—Lieutenant-General I. Y. Prebyshevsky—with 18 battalions of Russian infantry, one company of pioneers, supported by 30 battalion guns, totaling 5,448 combatants excluding artillerists—would advance on Langeron's right, cross the Goldbach between Sokolnitz and Kobelnitz Pond, carry Sokolnitz Castle and pheasantry before turning to join the I and II Columns in their drive north against the French flank.

IV Column—Under joint command of Lieutenant-General M. A. Miloradovich and FZM J. K. Kolowrat—with 12 battalions of Russians and 16 battalions of Austrians, two companies of Vienna *jaeger,* two squadrons of cavalry, two companies of pioneers, 76 pieces of ordnance of which 52 were battalion guns, two Austrian 12-pounder position batteries totaling 12 pieces and one Russian 12-pounder battery with 12 pieces, with a total effective strength of 12,099 excluding artillerists—the column would advance on the right of Prebyshevsky. Passing by the north of Kobelnitz, the column would cross the Goldbach then swing north towards Schlappanitz.

V Column—FML J. J. Liechtenstein—with 50 squadrons of cavalry, 11 and one-half squadrons of Cossacks, supported by 24 pieces of ordnance, of which six were in one Austrian cavalry battery and 18 more were in one and one-half Russian horse artillery batteries, totaling 4,622 combatants excluding artillerists—would move north to Blasowitz, then turn to the west, forming the link between the IV. Column and the Advance Guard.

Advance Guard of the Army—Major-General Prince P. I. Bagration—with 15 battalions of Russian infantry, 33 squadrons of cavalry, 15 squadrons of Cossacks, supported by 18 battalion guns, two Austrian 6-pounder cavalry batteries and one Russian 6-pounder horse artillery battery for a total ordnance count of 42 pieces, and 11,750 officers and other ranks under arms excluding artillerists—would initially stand fast, "but as soon as Prince Bagration observes the advance of our left wing, he must attack on his own account and throw back the extreme left wing of the enemy, which by then will be giving way. He must strive to unite with the remaining columns of our army."

Reserve—Grand Duke Constantine—with the Russian Imperial Guard consisting of 10 battalions of infantry, 17 squadrons of cavalry, one company of pioneers, supported by four batteries of Russian Guard artillery fielding 40 pieces of ordnance, with 8,500 combatants under arms that included some 400 artillerists—would advance behind Liechtenstein ready to support either the IV or V Columns, as well as the Advance Guard.[48]

Excluding artillerists, train personnel and specialists, the Combined Russian and Austrian Army fielded 64,989 officers and men under arms on the morning of 2 December 1805. Excluding the various staffs at army headquarters and with the different columns, but including the 7,800 specialists and those serving the ordnance, the total came to 72,789.[49]

---

[48] K. k. Kriegsarchiv, F.A. Weyrother, *Disposition:* Deutschland 1805, XII.

[49] österreichischen Kriegsarchiv, Vienna (K.A., F.A. Deutschland 1805); C² 13, *Archives du Service Historique de l'État-Major de l'Armée de Terre,* (S.H.A.T.), VINCENNES, and numerous regimental historiesin the Russian Archives, Saint Petersburg.

To summarize, Weyrother proposed a giant flanking movement by which the bulk of the army would cross the Goldbach along a three mile front. Once across the stream and after driving in the French right flank, Columns I through IV would pivot northward and drive for the Olmütz Road while Bagration pressured the enemy from the east. The V Column and the Russian Imperial Guard would support the advance as was necessary. It was hoped that the combination of this attack would "overthrow and pursue"[50] the *Grande Armée*, forcing it to retreat into the foothills of Moravian Switzerland. Once this happened, Weyrother announced, Napoleon would be finished and the campaign won.

Weyrother's *Disposition*, so much maligned by most historians as being nothing more than a worthless piece of fantasy authored by someone still entrenched in the *ancien régime*, did have several favorable points as well as serious flaws. On the positive side, the *Disposition* set forth in understandable terms ('understandable' being a relative term—what was understandable to an Austrian was not grasped by many Russians) the grand tactical situation, clearly defined areas of operation and objectives for each column as well as for the army as a whole, and instructed the commanders on what were the coordinating guidelines between columns. One must give Weyrother his due on those points. However, the flaws of the plan were legion. Nowhere in the *Disposition* were there contingencies for the French doing anything other than what the allies wanted them to do—that being to stand mindlessly and motionless on the defensive, providing the allied army with a series of static targets. No thought was given of the French putting up a fight along the Goldbach. "The valley between Tellnitz and Sokolnitz was to be passed with rapidity,"[51] the Austrian general proclaimed. Additionally, Weyrother assumed that the French would allow his columns to freely traverse the valley and streams before putting up a defense. Similarly, the Austrian general made no allowance for the French launching any counterattacks. Weyrother also assumed that the columns would conduct their attacks "with celerity and vigor."[52] Weyrother also misjudged just how slow the allied staff would work in transmitting the orders to the column commanders. Finally, the Austrian general assumed that his plan could be comprehended by all the Russian officers.

Napoleon questions prisoners before Austerlitz

The reaction from Russian officers differed widely. After receiving his copy, Prince Bagration told his staff: "I do not see why I should stand idly by, and watch the enemy send reinforcements from their left wing to our right."[53] Always one to want to jump into the thick of things, Bagration did not object to the attack once the army had committed itself to an offensive after leaving Olmütz; he only wished to get into the action sooner. Langeron, the French *émigré* who knew his former countrymen's fondness for movement, supposedly warned Weyrother of the possibility of the French launching a counterattack. However, the Tsar's General-Adjutants Dolgoruky and Wintzingerode drowned out such dissident talk. "We're not just going to win a battle," Dolgoruky shot back at Langeron. "The battle is *already* won." Wintzingerode then added: "We must surround the French army and force it to lay down its arms—the army and its Emperor."[54] Miloradovich and Dokhturov were worried about their men being able to move more easily than they had done at Dürenstein, when the troops went into action wearing their backpacks which was contrary to the normal Russian practice. After a brief discussion, it was recommended that the allied infantry would drop packs before falling into ranks the next morning.

---

[50] K. k. Kriegsarchiv, F.A. Weyrother, *Disposition:* Deutschland 1805, XII.

[51] K. k. Kriegsarchiv, F.A. Weyrother, *Disposition:* Deutschland 1805, XII.

[52] K. k. Kriegsarchiv, F.A. Weyrother, *Disposition:* Deutschland 1805, XII.

[53] T. Bernhardi, *Denkwürdigkeiten aus dem Leben des Kaiserlich Russischen Generals... von Toll,* 4 parts (Leipzig, 1865), vol. 1, p. 177.

[54] K. k. Kriegsarchiv, F.A. Weyrother, *Disposition:* Deutschland 1805, XII.

A far more typical Russian response to Weyrother's *Disposition* was that honestly admitted to by artillery Lieutenant-Colonel Ermolov.

> I saw General-Adjutant Uvarov return with the plans written on several sheets, crowded with difficult names of villages, lakes, streams, and distances and heights. We were not permitted to make a copy, for the plan had to be read by a good many commanders, and there were very few copies available. I must confess that when I heard it read out loud, I understood very little of what it intended.[55]

Earlier in the evening, Ermolov had seen another sight that had made a lasting impression. The artillerist remembered that he saw Prince Dolgoruky and another staff officer riding along Bagration's line. Dolgoruky was reconnoitering the front because he was convinced that the French were going to retreat, and was afraid that the French army would try to escape during the night. Therefore, he wanted to be the first to detect the enemy's anticipated withdrawal. Joining these officers and peering into the darkness, Ermolov:

> could see a few enemy fires, which seemed to indicate the line of their advanced pickets. Everything was silent in the direction of the hostile army, and we were nearly all convinced that the enemy were retreating. At about midnight, fires suddenly blazed into life across the foot of the heights on which we were standing, and we could see their bivouacs extending across a wide stretch of ground. Obviously, the enemy were not bothering to conceal their retreat, or so it seemed to many of us.[56]

Above and below, two portrayals of the French army's torchlight homage to Napoleon on the eve of Austerlitz

The numerous French torches that lit the night were for Napoleon's nocturnal visit to his front lines—hardly symbols of a demoralized and retreating army. The Emperor had earlier stirred from his quarters and made his way to be among his men. To the simple, hardly souls that bore the thousands of lights that flickered around the familiar figure in the grey greatcoat, the Emperor was their nation visible in person. His strength was characterized by an almost unshakable Olympian calm that radiated an authentic aura of confidence and majesty. The soldiers of the *Grande Armée* admired and loved this uncompromising man. They had total faith in the Emperor's generalship, and believed that, under his direction, anything was possible. In return, Napoleon knew the fatigues and deprivations suffered by his veteran soldiers since the start of the campaign; he could sense their strength of resolve and knew that men such as these expected nothing less than total victory. Whenever Napoleon was among them, he always found the words to stir their emotions. While the torch lights blazed, the soldiers gave their repeated and resounding Gallic cry: *"Vive l'Empereur!"*[57]

This famous torchlight procession came after an intensive day of preparation for battle. Napoleon had been on and off horseback throughout most of the daylight hours of 1 December:

> inspecting the army in person, regiment by regiment. He spoke to the troops, inspected each company of guns and horse artillery, and gave instructions to all the officers and gunners. Then he

[55] *Zapiski A. P. Ermolova,* vol. 1, p. 33.
[56] *Zapiski A. P. Ermolova,* vol. 1, p. 32.
[57] *Memoirs of Ségur*, pp. 244-245; *Memoirs of Baron Lejeune*, vol. 1, p. 28.

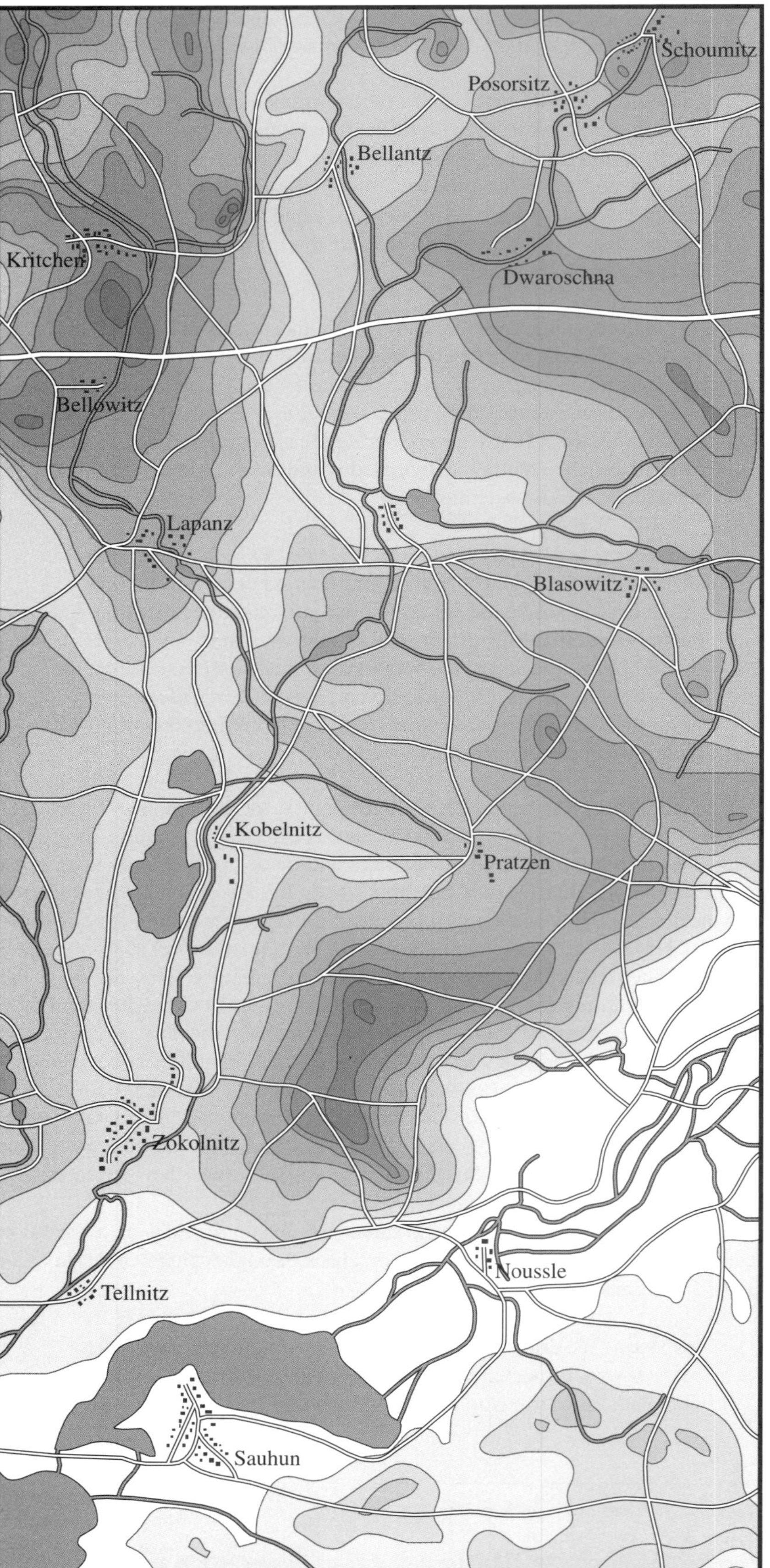

The Battlefield of Austerlitz

> went to the field hospitals and inspected arrangements for the transportation of the wounded.[58]

Raffet's picture of Napoleon the night before Austerlitz

The Emperor did this while his proclamation to the army was being typeset and printed by the mobile Imperial press. Copies were then distributed that evening to the colonels of the regiments, who then passed the sheets to the company commanders, who read Napoleon's words to the men by the light of the camp fires:

> Soldiers, the Russian army is before you, come to avenge the Austrians at Ulm. These are the same battalions that you beat at Hollabrunn, and the same which you have constantly pursued without respite until now.
>
> The positions that we occupy are formidable; and, while the enemy are marching to turn my right, they will present their flank.
>
> Soldiers, I shall direct your battalions in person. I shall keep out of range if you succeed, with your usual bravery in throwing the enemy lines into disorder and confusion. But if victory should at any time seem doubtful, you will see your Emperor exposing himself in the front line. We cannot afford to let victory slip from our grasp on a day like this when the honor of the French infantry and the whole nation is at stake.
>
> Under the pretext of carrying away the wounded, let no one leave the ranks, and let everyone be convinced that we must beat these hirelings of England, who are animated with such a bitter hatred against our nation.
>
> This victory will finish the campaign, and we shall be able to take up our winter quarters, where we shall be joined by new armies forming in France; and then the peace which I shall make will be worthy of my people, of you, and of myself.[59]

Encouraged by the proclamation of their Emperor, one of the *grenadiers à pied* of the Imperial Guard stepped up to Napoleon and uttered a few words that summarized the mood of the entire *Grande Armée:*

> Sire, you will not have to expose yourself. I promise you, on behalf of the grenadiers of the army—you will have to fight only with your eyes. Tomorrow we are going to bring you the flags and the artillery of the Russian army as a present for the anniversary of your coronation.[60]

---

[58] *Memoirs of the Duke of Rovigo* (Savary), vol. 1, p. 131.
[59] S.H.A.T., C^2 12.
[60] Aubry, *Napoleon: Soldier and Emperor*, p. 153.

Napoleon at Austerlitz

Chapter VIII
"It is Impossible to Make a Good Omelet Without Breaking a Great Many Eggs!" *The Epic Battle of Austerlitz*

"The whole art of war consists in a well-reasoned and extremely circumspect defensive, followed by rapid and audacious [counter]attack." —Napoleon

"The transition from the defensive to the offensive is one of the most delicate operations in war." —Napoleon[1]

Opening Moves of the Armies

At 6:00 A.M. on Monday morning, 2 December 1805, a cold, thick fog blanketed the Moravian countryside before the first rays from the sun began to crest the horizon. The early morning darkness found the soldiers of the *Grande Armée* shouldering their weapons, saddling their horses, and making their way to assembly areas. Once there, many of the infantrymen from the various corps dropped their packs, and made sure that the three or four cartridge packets, each containing 15 rounds, were in their pouch and ready for the day, along with a canteen of water. Napoleon meanwhile took a hurried breakfast along with his staff members while standing outside Imperial headquarters on Zuran Hill near the Olmütz Road. Finishing the light meal, the Emperor was buckling on his sword as he looked to his Imperial aides-de-camp and confidently said: "Now, gentlemen, let us go and begin a great day!"[2]

Napoleon at his command post surrounded by his Chasseur escort

The Imperial aides quickly moved outside, mounted their horses and dashed off to fetch all the corps commanders except Davout, who was at far-away Raigern Abbey. The Imperial aides soon returned to Zuran Hill with the marshals and one of their own aides-de-camp. Dismounting from their horses, these men gathering around Napoleon. Ségur remembered the assemblage of talented, brilliantly uniformed personalities as one of the most unforgettable sights of his life.[3] To these officers, the Emperor set forth his battle plan, modified one last time based on fresh information received during the night: Davout, with the infantry of Friant and Bourcier's dragoons, would advance and hold the lower crossings of the Goldbach—the French far right flank—rather than be brought to Turas; Soult would hold the middle-to-lower Goldbach with the infantry division of Legrand and the 4th Corps light cavalry until Davout arrived; once Davout was on the field, Legrand would compress his frontage towards the middle Goldbach and protect Davout's left; the remaining two infantry divisions of 4th Corps (Saint Hilaire and Vandamme) were to form their battalions in attack columns in the low, foggy area west of the Bosenitz Stream from which they could rapidly advance upon the Pratzen Plateau, counterattack and overturn the enemy formations; Bernadotte with two infantry divisions of 1st Corps would wait in reserve until ordered into action; the Imperial Guard and Oudinot's *Grenadiers de la Réserve* would form the army's élite reserve; Lannes would wait until the enemy was fully

---

1 *The Military Maxims of Napoleon,* p. 62.
2 *Memoirs of Ségur*, p. 245.
3 *Memoirs of Ségur*, p. 246.

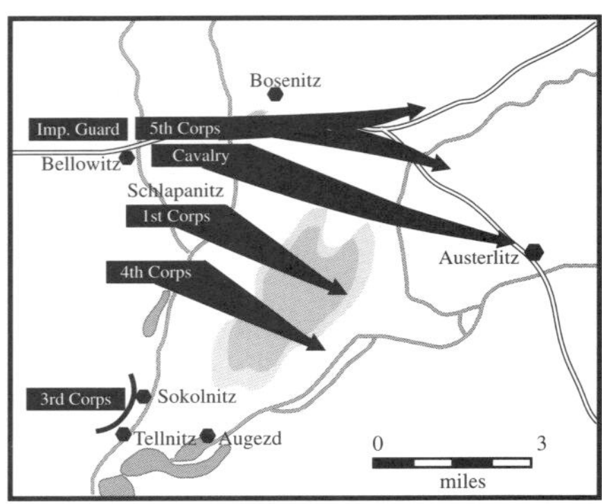

The French Plan

engaged, then deliver a crucial attack designed to clear the Brünn-Olmütz Road and cut off the enemy army from its base at Olmütz; meanwhile, Murat and his cavalry corps would initially serve as the link between Lannes and Soult. When committed to action, the cavalry would operate in the intervals between, and on the flanks of, the infantry divisions. The defensive posture of the *Grande Armée* would draw the enemy into the trap from which their formations would be overturned, their lines of communication severed and the surviving fugitives scattered into the hinterland of eastern Moravia.[4] The Emperor then concluded the conference about 7:30 A.M. with these words: "In half-an-hour, the entire line will be on fire!"[5]

With these final instructions, Napoleon dispatched each of the marshals except Soult with the command "Go!" Ségur noticed that when it came time for Napoleon to send Bernadotte on his way, the Emperor's voice instantly turned to a "dry and imperious tone."[6] Each marshal saluted in turn, walked briskly away, remounted his horse and returned to his respective corps. As the marshals departed, they did so without the aides-de-camp that accompanied them to Imperial headquarters—these staff officers remained behind to help carry orders back to their respective corps commander when the time came.

Near Zuran Hill, the bands of the Imperial Guard were playing a mellow, operatic air that wasn't martial enough for Napoleon. Turning to Bessières, the Emperor asked of the marshal's bandsmen, "Have they forgotten *Le Chant du départ?*"[7] A few words from Bessières, and Drum Major Gebauer immediately struck up the strains that tugged on the Revolutionary heartstrings of the army. Thousands soon joined in singing the declaration that included the immortal line: "We know how to vanquish, we know how to perish!" Thiard, Count de Bissy, a former *émigré* who witnessed the outpouring of emotion, believed that the singing was indicative of the army's "enthusiasm for its chief and devotion to the cause."[8]

From the Zuran Hill, Napoleon maintained control by using his aides

As the French were making final preparations for action at their assembly areas, first light found most of the columns of the Combined Russian and Austrian Army in a state of considerable confusion. Most of the disorder had been caused by Liechtenstein's errant cavalry column. They had spent the night much further to the south than Weyrother had planned. Liechtenstein realized this in early hours of the morning, and ordered his horsemen to move to the right. Once underway, the cavalry cut through Langeron's II Column, thereby delaying the march of the rear portion of this command. The chain reaction caused by Liechtenstein having to reposition his column, and Langeron having to halt his march, had the effect of forcing in turn the joint-commanders of the IV Column, Miloradovich and Kolowrat, to stop their movement until the traffic jam had cleared.

Watching with a sense of self-resignation as the allied soldiers of the II, IV and V Columns were untangling themselves, Kutuzov noted that even though the battalions had been under arms for more than an hour, for some inexplicable reason the officers had yet to order the men to load their muskets. Kutuzov did not intervene, but merely observed some of the troops on which the day's battle would depend. In the IV Column, the general took note of the pitiful remnants of the 12 Russian battalions under Miloradovich that numbered a mere 2,875 officers and other ranks—an average of only 240 combatants per battalion! Alongside these worn-out Russians were 15 battalions of Austrians, many of which were the 6th

---

[4] "Dispositions Générales," *Correspondance*, number 9535, were Napoleon's dispositions for the army issued at 8:00 P.M. on 1 December. These were verbally modified at the early morning conference on 2 December as described here.

[5] *Memoirs of Ségur*, p. 247.

[6] *Memoirs of Ségur*, p. 248.

[7] Lachouque and Brown, *The Anatomy of Glory—Napoleon and his Guard,* p. 61.

[8] *Souvenirs Diplomatiques et Miltaires du Général Thiard,* p. 227.

Tsar Alexander I

Battalions, or depot units, of the various regiments. "Perhaps the war-weary old Muscovite was reflecting on the apparent uselessness of his troops"[9] when Emperors Francis and Alexander rode through the mist and appeared before Kutuzov as the sun was continuing its slow ascent shortly after 8:00 A.M. Not seeing the troops in motion as expected, Alexander initiated one of the more notable exchanges in military history.

> "Mikhail Ilariónovich! Why haven't you begun your advance?"
>
> "Your Highness," replied Kutuzov. "I am waiting for all the columns of the army to get into position."
>
> "But we are not on the Empress' Meadow, where we do not begin a parade until all the regiments are formed up!"
>
> "Your Highness! If I have not begun, it is because we are not on parade, and not on the Empress' Meadow, Sire. However, if such be Your Highness' order."[10]

So it was that following a delay of more than an hour and one-half, the entirety of the I through V Columns were finally moving off the Pratzen and towards French lines. Because of the *ad hoc* nature of the columns, coupled with the woefully inadequate and unsophisticated staffs, the allied commanders of the various columns had to use cavalrymen borrowed from units attached to their column to act as scouts and as messengers. However, the III Column had no cavalry whatsoever, while the IV Column had only two squadrons of Austrian cavalry. Wanting Russian cavalry with whom to communicate:

> General Miloradovich begged the commander of a regiment for just 20 hussars to convey vital messages. Thus, the columns advanced in false security. Wide intervals yawned between the battalions, for we *assumed* they would deploy into line of battle on the approach of the enemy.[11]

As these gangling, uncoordinated allied columns made their way westward in expectation of crossing the Goldbach Stream unopposed, they were about to find out that very little was going to unfold according to Weyrother's plan.

Kienmayer

Action on the Lower Goldbach—
The Initial Clash at Tellnitz

The lower Goldbach valley was rumbling with the noise of battle by the time all the milling allied columns had vacated the Pratzen. Not part of the confusion were the troops of the Advance Guard of I Column under FML Michael von Kienmayer. They had spent the night closest to the French and were the first to get under way between 7:00 and 8:00 A.M. Briskly moving over the ground they had reconnoitered the night before, Kienmayer's mounted scouts soon reached the vicinity of Tellnitz shortly before 8:00 A.M. The small village was located on the eastward side of the Goldbach between the brook and a low hill. The buildings of Tellnitz intermingled with the numerous orchards and vineyards, and the vegetation extended eastward onto the hill.

---

[9] Duffy, *Austerlitz,* p. 103.

[10] Mikhailovsky-Danilevsky, *Relation de la campagne de 1805*, p. 181-182.

[11] *Zapiski A. P. Ermolova,* vol. 1, p. 33-34.

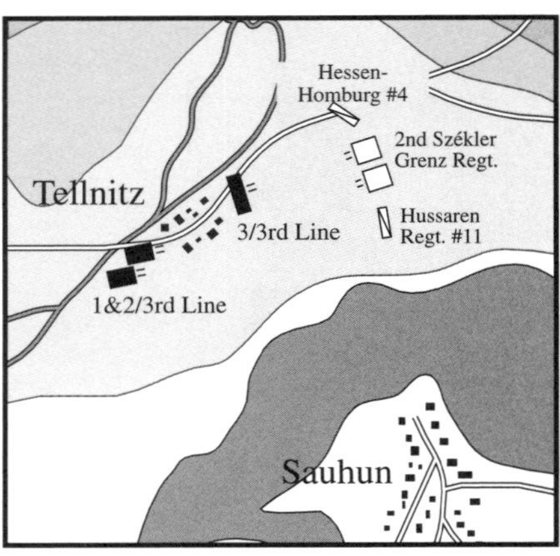

The initial contact at Tellnitz

Advancing to closely scout this position was one squadron from the Hussar-Regiment Hessen-Homburg #4. The horsemen detected only a few companies of French infantry deployed on the hill in front of Tellnitz, while the village and surrounding orchards and vineyards swarmed with *tirailleurs*. Behind the village to the south and on the western side of the Goldbach were French light cavalry. The information was relayed to Kienmayer, who instantly ordered an attack to clear the village and open the way for the main body of the I Column to force the Goldbach. *General-Feldwachtmeister* Carneville came up with the 2nd Székler *Grenz* Regiment #15, and he pushed these 'border troops' against the French infantry on the hill. Meanwhile, the Székler *Grenz*-Hussaren-Regiment #11 and the Hussar-Regiment Hessen-Homburg #4 were posted on the southern and northern flanks of the infantry respectively in order to protect the troops on foot from any French cavalry counterattacks.[12]

As Carneville and the 2nd Széklers pushed their way into the vineyards on the hill in front of Tellnitz, they came in contact with the 3rd *Ligne*, commanded by Colonel Laurent Schobert. At age 42, Schobert was one of the older colonels in the *Grande Armée,* and considered to have been a 'late bloomer' insofar as his military talents were concerned. Serving throughout the Revolution, Schobert was a company commander for four years in the *Garde du Directoire/Garde des Consuls* before serving at Marengo. He then quickly rose in rank from *chef de bataillon*, to major, to colonel in a 16 month span. In February 1805, Schobert had the confidence of Napoleon to succeed the talented Mouton as the commander of the 3rd *Ligne*.[13]

Schobert's command was the only infantry regiment of 4th Corps to take the field in 1805 with three war battalions. When the 3rd crossed the Rhine, the battalions fielded 2,049 officers and other ranks.[14] On 7 November, the regiment still had 1,888 in ranks. However, after the march into Moravia and the brief fight at Schöngrabern, the three battalions of the 3rd *Ligne*—which alone comprised the 2nd Brigade of Legrand's Division—mustered 80 officers and 1,564 other ranks combatants at Austerlitz.[15] Schobert deployed his regiment without the supervision of his 48-year-old brigade commander. That 'older man,' *général de brigade* Jean-Baptiste-Michel Féry, had missed the training at the Channel camps, and had only assumed command of the brigade on 23 October 1805. Perhaps that is why he took no active role in the battle, giving Schobert a free hand with the deployments and movements of the 3rd *Ligne*.[16]

French Engineer

To defend Tellnitz, Schobert positioned his troops in a variant of the strong point defensive doctrine. The seven fusilier companies of the 3rd Battalion were deployed in line formation among the vineyards and in front of a ditch on the hill immediately east, or in front, of town. On their flanks extending back into the village were the regiment's *tirailleurs*, consisting of three companies of *voltigeurs*, along with two companies of fusiliers from each of the 1st and 2nd Battalions. Waiting inside the village at the church in the town's square were the converged grenadiers of the 3rd *Ligne*. Busy fortifying the church were the 16 engineers of the regiment, resplendent in their custom uniforms that had been authorized by Schobert consisting of sky blue coats with scarlet lapels, collars, turnbacks and epaulettes. Like the grenadiers of the regiment, the sappers of the 3rd *Ligne* wore bearskin headgear. While these men worked, the 1st and 2nd Battalions stood in

[12] Stutterheim, *A Detailed Account of the Battle of Austerlitz*, p. 83.

[13] Six, *Dictionnaire biographique*, vol. 2, p. 436.

[14] S.H.A.T., C^2 470.

[15] S.H.A.T., *Tableau de la Grande Armée Dernière quinzaine du mois brumaire an XIV*, "Situation au 16 brumaire an XIV (7 November 1805)," C^2 477 and *Journal des opérations du 4e corps.*

[16] S.H.A.T., dossier Féry.

reserve to the west of town, each with their remaining six companies of fusiliers deployed in attack columns.[17]

When GM Carneville advanced on Tellnitz, he initially committed only one of the two available battalions of the 2nd Székler *Grenz* Regiment #15. The 1st Battalion advanced straight into the deployed fusiliers of the 3rd Battalion of the 3rd *Ligne*. When the French muskets erupted, the ranks of the browncoated 2nd Széklers were soon shredded by the murderous volleys which caused the *Grenzer* battalion to fall back. Carneville then threw both *Grenzer* battalions of the 2nd Széklers against the hill while the hussars advanced to cover their flanks. Coming closer to the maze of vineyards than was necessary, both regiments of hussars "suffered severely"[18] from the French *tirailleurs* lining the defensive position. Meanwhile, for the second time, the 3rd Battalion of the 3rd *Ligne* held its ground, pouring a deadly fire into their foes who had advanced with reckless courage. In less than 20 minutes, the *Grenzer* battalions of the 2nd Széklers were cut to pieces. After the first two assaults, the 1st Battalion of the 2nd Székler *Grenz* Regiment #15 had lost more than half its strength. Despite these horrendous casualties, both battalions were rallied by GM Stutterheim, who then led the regiment in a third attack.[19]

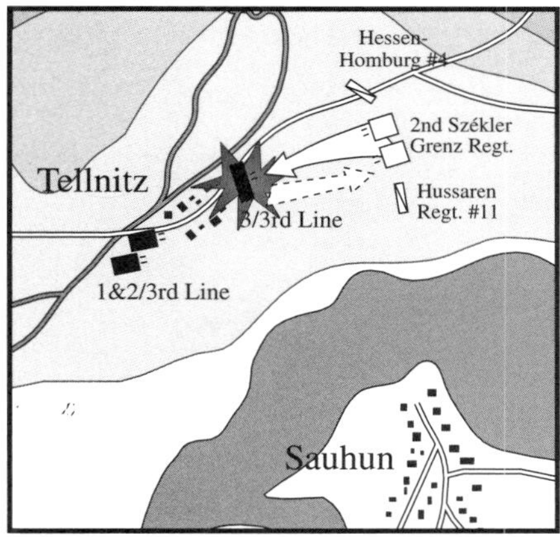

Carneville's first attack

As Stutterheim was advancing with the 2nd Széklers, Kienmayer instructed Carneville to take the remainder of his infantry against Tellnitz. Stutterheim was coming to grips with the obstinate 3rd Battalion of the 3rd *Ligne* when Carneville got moving with the two battalions of the 1st Székler *Grenz* Regiment #14 and one battalion of the Broder *Grenz* Regiment #7. These whitecoated *Grenzer* battalions[20] tipped the scales for the fight on the hill, forcing the 3rd Battalion of the 3rd *Ligne* to fall back into and through Tellnitz. All five Austrian battalions then advanced in mutual support of one another as best they could, fighting not only the swarms of French *tirailleurs*, but also the difficult, closed terrain. Eager to repay the French for their previous losses, Stutterheim and the 2nd Széklers advanced faster than Carneville and his three battalions. Once Stutterheim succeeded in penetrating to the eastern outskirts of the village, Schobert sensed that the time was right to launch a counterattack. Because Austrian cavalry were protecting the flanks of the *Grenzer* battalions, Schobert could not flank his adversaries, but instead had to send his counterstrike through the village. The 1st and 2nd Battalions of the 3rd *Ligne* moved briskly forward, fell upon and crushed the disorganized battalions of the 2nd Széklers. The routed regiment fled past the other three *Grenzer* battalions led by Carneville. With fugitives fleeing all around him, Carneville ordered his formations to stay within the protection of the vineyards on the hill east of town. He then sent an urgent message to Kienmayer requesting reinforcements. Kienmayer had no more infantry battalions in his Advance Guard of the I Column, and forwarded Carneville's plea to Dokhturov.

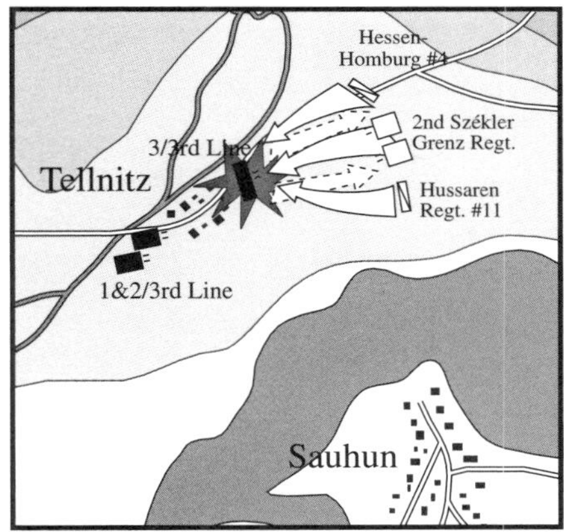

Carneville's second attack

With the third repulse of the 2nd Székler *Grenz* Regiment #15 in a little more than an hour, the first phase of the fight for Tellnitz had come to a close. Stutterheim noticed that the 2nd Széklers had all but ceased to exist, having lost two-thirds of its 1,100 officers and men![21] Including the losses suffered by the other formations under Kienmayer, the Austrians had already suffered almost 1,000 casualties while the French 3rd *Ligne* had thus far lost less than 300.[22] In spite of

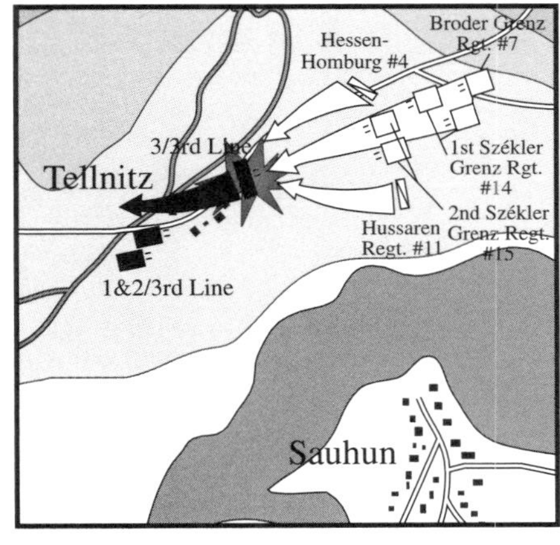

Carneville's third attack takes Tellnitz

[17] S.H.A.T., C² 10; *Journal des opérations du 4e corps.*

[18] Stutterheim, *A Detailed Account of the Battle of Austerlitz*, p. 83.

[19] Stutterheim, *A Detailed Account of the Battle of Austerlitz*, pp. 83-84.

[20] Some *Grenzer* regiments had white coats while others had brown coats. For a complete list, see: Scott Bowden and Charles Tarbox, *Armies on the Danube 1809*, p. 30.

[21] Stutterheim, *A Detailed Account of the Battle of Austerlitz*, pp. 84-85.

[22] S.H.A.T., C² 16.

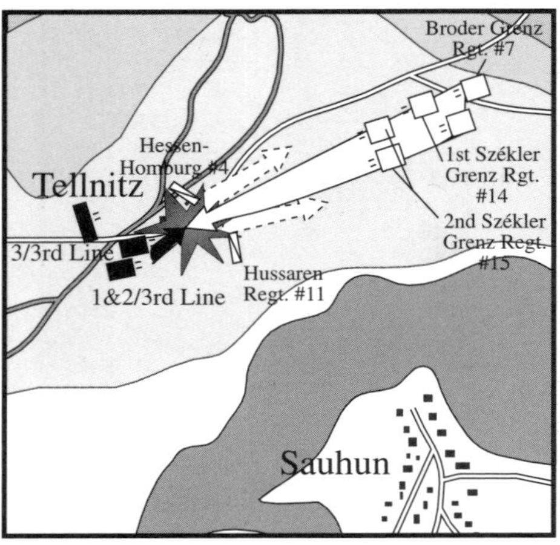

Schobert's second attack

the initial success enjoyed by Schobert's regiment, long columns of greenclad troops moving towards Tellnitz signaled to the French colonel that allied reinforcements were at hand.

The new arrivals were the regiments of the I Column under Dokhturov, which were accompanied by the overall commander of Columns I, II and III—Lieutenant-General F. W. Buxhöwden. Since Buxhöwden was riding with Dokhturov, the senior officer responded when Kienmayer's request for infantry reinforcements at Tellnitz was received. Buxhöwden immediately authorized the only light troops with the I Column—a single battalion of the 7th *Jaeger* Regiment—to advance to support the *Grenzers*. Once the Russian *jaeger* battalion reached the hill, they joined in with Carneville's infantry in a renewed attack on Tellnitz.[23]

The attack made by the combined Austro-Russian troops was opposed only by French *tirailleurs*. Upon seeing the approach of Dokhturov's overwhelming numbers, Schobert had wisely repositioned all three battalions of his regiment—as well as the grenadiers occupying the church—to the west side of the Goldbach, leaving only the *tirailleurs* in Tellnitz as a covering force. Therefore, most of the surviving 1,200 *fantassins* of the 3rd *Ligne* had been evacuated from Tellnitz when the three *Grenzer* battalions and the single battalion from the 7th *Jaeger* pushed the *tirailleurs* out of the village. However, the allied troops did not press onward after the 3rd *Ligne*, undoubtably due to the presence of Margaron's 1,161 French light cavalry and horse artillerists with five 8-pounder guns that had been repositioned to the northwest between Sokolnitz and Tellnitz. Securing the latter village, Buxhöwden rode forward to check out his prize, then returned to the hill outside the eastern part of Tellnitz. As Buxhöwden maneuvered his horse around the numerous bodies of the 2nd Széklers, he soon reached the top of the hill in order to get a better view of his II and III Columns as they came into line.

The Fight Intensifies Along the Goldbach—
Action From Tellnitz to Sokolnitz

Peering northward through the patchy fog that obscured his view towards Sokolnitz, Buxhöwden was anxious for his other columns under Langeron and Prebyshevsky to come abreast of the column headed by Dokhturov. Once in position, all these commands would cross the Goldbach in force and turn the French right flank. Meanwhile, the forces that Buxhöwden was accompanying had already reached their first objective. After the capture of Tellnitz, Kienmayer and Dokhturov were bringing up the remainder of their troops when they were suddenly confronted with additional French forces hurrying to the assistance of the 3rd *Ligne*.

The French reinforcements were some of the footsore infantry of Friant and the dragoons of Bourcier that were part of Marshal Davout's command. The marshal's forces had broken camp at the abbey of Raigern at 5:00 A.M. on 2 December after their epic march from Vienna. The marathon had significantly reduced the hardy souls that remained in ranks. For example, the infantry regiments that marched in Friant's Division had numbered 6,887 officers and other ranks on 5 November.[24] These formations arrived at Austerlitz with 3,200 effectives. With artillerists included, the entire division's strength, excluding the 1st Dragoons, was no more than 3,300.[25] These men began moving northward to take up their position around Turas as ordered by Napoleon the day before.

---

[23] Stutterheim, *A Detailed Account of the Battle of Austerlitz*, pp. 85-86.

[24] S.H.A.T., *Tableau de la Grande Armée Dernière quinzaine du mois brumaire an XIV*, "Situation au 14 brumaire an XIV (5 November 1805)."

[25] Davout, *Opérations du 3e Corps*, p. vi.

However, while on the march, Davout received two messages. The first was from Napoleon, ordering him to make for Sokolnitz instead of Turas. Once at Sokolnitz, he was to hold the right flank of the army. Immediately altering his troops' course of march, Davout then received an urgent message from *général de brigade* Pierre Margaron, commander of the Light Cavalry Division of 4th Corps. The light cavalry general knew of Davout's arrival the day before, and wanted to advise him of his findings. Margaron explained that while the allied troops had yet to appear front of Sokolnitz, there was serious trouble further south. "The enemy is present in great strength at Tellnitz," Margaron wrote to the marshal. "Without assistance, the infantry [3rd *Ligne*] will be crushed."[26] Responding to the plea for help, Davout again altered the march direction for some of his command. The marshal instructed Friant to send one brigade to Tellnitz, along with the dragoons under Bourcier. The remaining troops of Friant, including the 1st Dragoons, would follow the division general and marshal towards Sokolnitz.[27]

Davout

Leading these troops was Louis-Nicholas Davout, the marshal commanding the 3rd Corps of the *Grande Armée*. When Davout rode onto the field of Austerlitz, it was the first time since the Egyptian campaign of 1798-1799 that he had commanded troops in a major battle.[28] Further, Davout was only a *général de brigade* of cavalry when he had last fought under the eyes of Napoleon at Aboukir on 25 July 1799. Perhaps that is why so many in the army raised their eyebrows in wonderment when, in 1804, Davout was named to the marshalate. However, during the years between Egypt and the 1805 war, Davout had demonstrated an unequaled ability among the various generals of the army as a meticulous organizer and efficient administrator. A convinced Republican, the 35-year-old Davout was not exactly an Adonis. At five-foot nine-inches tall, the marshal had a medium build and was nearsighted, which forced him to tie a pair of combat spectacles around his balding head.[29]

Davout made up for his physical shortcomings in other areas. Endorsed by his friend and patron—the famed General Louis Desaix—Davout was upheld as an officer of unequaled merit. Following Desaix's death at Marengo, Davout continued to prove that the confidence placed in him by Desaix was justified. His splendid performance at the camp of Bruges was reflected in the superb level of training and discipline in his regiments, and Napoleon believed that he saw in Davout a rare trait—a man that excelled in detailed management as well as intuitive battlefield direction. As a result, Napoleon rewarded Davout with a baton. Davout had fulfilled part of that confidence by handling the 3rd Corps from the Channel to Moravia with flawless skill. However, Austerlitz was to be his battlefield proving ground as Napoleon's "Iron Marshal."

Friant

Riding alongside Davout was his hyperactive, 47-year-old brother-in-law, *général de division* Louis Friant. The general got his start as a private in the old Royal Army in 1781. Declaring for the Revolution in 1789, Friant was confirmed as a *général de brigade* by 1795, having held the provisional rank since the previous year. Friant was transferred to the *Armée d'Italie* in January of 1797, after which he commanded a brigade in Bernadotte's Division. Friant was unimpressed with

26 S.H.A.T., *Journal des opérations du 4e corps.*

27 Davout to Berthier, *Correspondance Davout*, volume 1, numbers 123, 126 and 128 contain Davout's after-action reports of Austerlitz, hereafter referred to as Austerlitz after-action reports; Also, see Adélaïde-Louis de Blocqueville, *Le Maréchal Davout prince d'Eckmühl: raconté par les siens et par lui-même*, 4 volumes (Paris, 1879-1880), vol. 2, pp. 192-193.

28 While acting as commander of the light cavalry of the *Armée d'Italie*, Davout did participate in the engagement near Monzambano on 25-26 December 1800.

29 Marie-Théodore Gueilly, comte de Rumigny, *Souvenirs du général comte de Rumigny* (Paris, 1921), pp. 51-52.

Tellnitz church

his superior officer and described Bernadotte as a "swaggering bravado, more interested with intrigue than in the welfare of his men." [30] In 1799, the highly-regarded Friant was named as a brigade commander in Desaix's Division of the *Armée d'Orient,* distinguishing himself in the battles of the Egyptian campaign. Upon his return to France in 1801 as a *général de division*, Friant was named as *Inspecteur général d'infanterie*, a position he ably held until being assigned to the Channel camp at Bruges.[31] There united with Davout, Friant spent the next two years forging his command into what arguably became the finest line division on the face of the earth—the 2nd Infantry Division of the legendary 3rd Corps of the *Grande Armée*.

Friant's men answered reveille in the darkness of the early morning hours of 2 December and fell into ranks about 5:30 A.M. Following two changes of direction, the division was bearing down on Tellnitz about 9:00 A.M. As the men got closer to the fighting, Corporal Jean-Pierre Blaise of the 108th *Ligne* remembered that:

> we heard a tremendous exchange of musketry between the Russians and the 3rd *Ligne*, and we began to encounter a great number of wounded from the latter regiment. At this moment they made us double time forward. Thus I was prevented from biting into a leg of goose which I had ready on top of my knapsack. I had intended to eat it there and then, knowing full well that I would scarcely have the leisure later in the day.[32]

As one brigade of Friant's troops hustled to the assistance of the hard-pressed 3rd *Ligne*, the thick fog hid their movements until they were close to the village. The infantrymen halted just long enough to drop packs, straighten ranks and catch their collective breath before suddenly emerging from the haze. Leading the way for these French was *général de brigade* Etienne Heudelet de Bierre. An aggressive officer who had proven skills, both throughout the wars of the Revolution as well as at the camp of Bruges, Heudelet was described by Bourcier as an officer "of morals and public-spiritedness without equal; as for his military talents, all reports said that he had whatever was necessary to fill the functions of his rank."[33] Commanding the Advance Guard of the entire 3rd Corps during the march to Vienna, Heudelet had engaged and destroyed Merveldt's Austrians at Mariazell on 8 November. Moving north from Vienna into Moravia with Friant, Heudelet's command at Austerlitz consisted of the two battalions of the 108th *Ligne* and the companies of *voltigeurs* from the 15th *Légère*. Together at Austerlitz, these formed the 3rd Brigade of Friant's 2nd Infantry Division. On 5 November, the two battalions of the 108th *Ligne* numbered 1,728 officers and other ranks present and under arms. Following their fight at Mariazell and the march to Vienna, the regiment numbered 1,637 on 28 November. However, after the force march from Vienna, the regiment could not have gone into the fighting on the southern end of the battlefield of Austerlitz with more than 800 effectives. Add to this number the two depleted companies of *voltigeurs* from the 15th *Légère*, and Heudelet's brigade at the start of the battle was close to 900 combatants.[34]

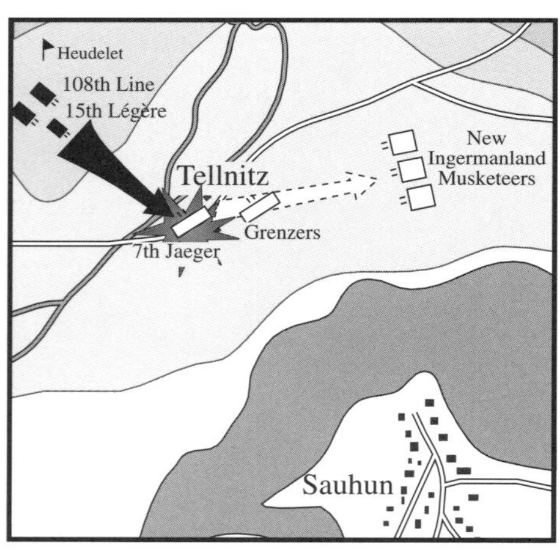

Heudelet's arrival

Kienmayer's Austrians were first to see Heudelet's onrushing *fantassins*. The two 6-pounder Austrian cavalry batteries of the Advance Guard of the I Column

[30] S.H.A.T., dossier Friant.
[31] Six, *Dictionnaire biographique*, vol. 1, p. 471.
[32] Fairon and Heuse, *Lettres de Grognards*, p. 105.
[33] *Général* Bourcier, "Sabretache" 1936, p. 45.
[34] S.H.A.T., *Tableau de la Grande Armée Dernière quinzaine du mois brumaire an XIV*, "Situation au 14 brumaire an XIV (5 November 1805)" and C² 476.

immediately opened fire, and the smoke from these 12 pieces, "together with the continuous fire of musketry, made such a cloud of smoke that you could not see beyond a few paces."[35] The dim worked to the advantage of the French as they quickly approached Tellnitz. Heudelet ordered his troops to recapture the village at the point of the bayonet, and the 108th *Ligne* formed in attack columns, preceded by the *voltigeurs* of the 15th *Légère,* crossed the Goldbach and rushed the town from the north. Unable to ascertain what was advancing against them, the single battalion of the Russian 7th *Jaeger* from Dokhturov's I Column that were holding Tellnitz were facing west when they got flanked and routed by Heudelet's command.

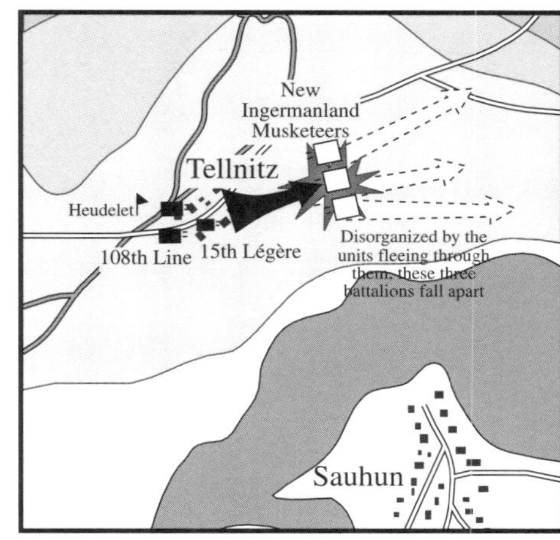

The New Ingermanland Regiment is broken

The French were quick to follow up on their success, and pressed forward, driving the fugitives of the 7th *Jaeger* before them. Heudelet's troops then rolled up one *Grenzer* battalion of Carneville as well, and soon two battalions of allies were fleeing eastward from Tellnitz. Major-General Lewis, commanding the leading brigade of Dokhturov's I Column, ordered up the three battalions of the New Ingermanland Musketeer Regiment as support. This regiment had been part of Rosen's Column of Kutuzov's original army, and therefore had missed the battles preceding Austerlitz. The regiment's two battalions of musketeers and one of grenadiers took 1,903 officers and men into their 1805 baptism of fire. However, before the New Ingermanland battalions could come to grips with the French, their formations were thrown "into confusion"[36] by the panicked survivors from the *Grenzer* and 7th *Jaeger* battalions. This disorganization proved costly, as the 108th *Ligne* burst upon the musketeer regiment and, within a matter of a few minutes, cut down over 200 of the Russians. During this brief *mêlée,* grenadiers Mauzy and Pront of the 108th *Ligne* distinguished themselves by each capturing an enemy standard. Marshal Davout saw the action and reported that Mauzy single-handedly "killed several Russians, then charged into the middle of a large body of the enemy, and seized their flag," while Pront "snatched one flag of the enemy."[37] Both men were rewarded by being decorated as *chevaliers* in the *Légion d'Honneur.* Indeed, their valor was indicative of the intense pressure applied by the diminutive but tenacious battalions of 108th *Ligne* which turned the numerically superior but disorganized New Ingermanland Musketeer Regiment into a dissolving mob.

Having shattered five allied battalions that hours earlier had counted almost 3,000 effectives, along with the capturing of two standards by the 108th *Ligne,* only fueled the adrenaline-charged assault by Heudelet's outnumbered men. Rather than halt on the vine-covered hill east of Tellnitz that afforded protection against allied cavalry, Heudelet pushed the fire-eaters of the 108th *Ligne* eastward in search of more victims. Meanwhile, the *voltigeurs* of the 15th *Légère* remained behind among the vineyards around the village.

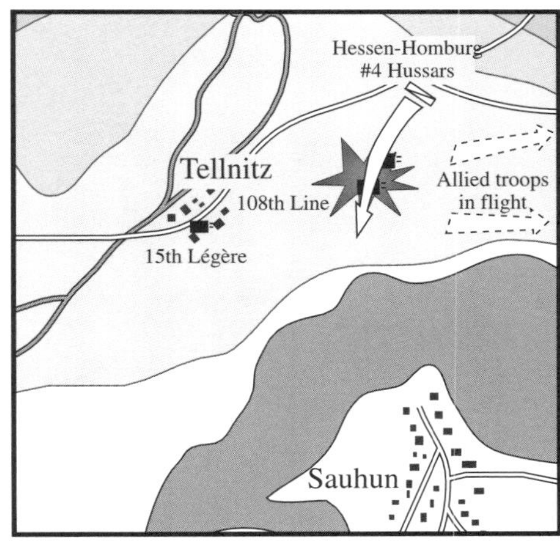

The Hessen-Homburg Hussars ride down the 108th Ligne

The advancing *fantassins* were "seen by Colonel Baron Mohr, commander of the Hessen-Homburg Hussars, which were standing in reserve. He immediately launched an attack … "[38] The charge led by Mohr, was laid into the 108th *Ligne* with the greatest of vigor. Evidently, the hussars mistook the French line troops for Bavarians, whom they hated for not joining with them in the Third Coalition. After a few minutes, the 360 determined troopers of the Hussar-Regiment Hessen-Homburg #4 proved to be more than a match for the over zealous French infantry. The hussars broke up the ranks of infantry and cut the proud 108th *Ligne* to pieces, killing or wounding over 300, including eight of the infantry regiment's 18 company

[35] K. k. Kriegsarchiv, F.A., Deutschland 1805, *Kurzgefasste Beschreibung der in dem Feldzug 1805 … Ausfürhrlichen Relation der am 2 ten Dezember, 1805…*, hereafter referred to as *Ausführliche Relation der am 2 ten Dezember, 1805.*

[36] Stutterheim, *A Detailed Account of the Battle of Austerlitz*, p. 87.

[37] Andolenko, *Aigles de Napoléon Contre Drapeaux du Tsar*, p. 80.

[38] K. k. Kriegsarchiv, F.A., *Ausführliche Relation der am 2 ten Dezember, 1805.*

Bourcier

commanders.[39] Managing to save their own standards and eagles, as well as the previously captured trophies, the survivors of the 108th *Ligne* ran pell-mell for the safety of the Tellnitz vineyards. Even when they reached relative safety, the bluecoated troops continued to move westward. Making their way through the town, Heudelet's men retraced their steps northward towards the position where they had dropped packs and began their charge. Meanwhile, the *voltigeurs* of the 15th *Légère* fell back from Tellnitz to cover the retreat.

As the 108th *Ligne* fled along the Goldbach and then across the meadows west of the brook, they suddenly came upon the 1st Battalion of the 26th *Légère* from Legrand's Division. The light infantrymen were withdrawing to the southwest from the nearby village of Sokolnitz when, in the fog and smoke of the low ground near the brook, they mistook the 108th for an onrushing enemy force. The light infantry began pouring volleys into Heudelet's men until Captain Livadot of the 108th grabbed a battalion's eagle and standard, waving it frantically at the 1st Battalion of the 26th *Légère*. The familiar Napoleonic emblem was soon recognized, and the 26th ceased fire. The recoiling 108th *Ligne* resumed its retreat to Turas, where Heudelet finally rallied the exhausted remnants of his depleted command.

Meanwhile, the fog had lifted to the south in and around Tellnitz. Now able to get a clear picture of the forces arrayed against him on the west bank of the Goldbach, Dokhturov saw the 1st Dragoons as well as Bourcier's 4th Dragoon Division deployed about 1,000 yards west of the brook. Alongside these cavalry could be seen a few pieces of ordnance, while deployed near the horse was the 3rd *Ligne*. Even though French resistance in this sector looked very weak, Dokhturov decided to bring up the brigade of Major-General Urusov before crossing the Goldbach. He deployed these troops in two lines while the broken battalions of Lewis' command were being rallied. Dokhturov also brought up his two 6-pounder foot batteries and had them unlimber on the unobstructed portion of the hill east of Tellnitz. These 24 pieces soon belched forth their discharges to provide a covering fire for Kienmayer, who pushed his cavalry across the Goldbach. Following Kienmayer, the cavalry brigades of Stutterheim and Prince Moritz Josef Liechtenstein splashed across the muddy brook and deployed in squadrons abreast on the west side while their own cavalry batteries unlimbered near the Goldbach on the east bank. As these cavalry and guns were getting into position, Dokhturov pushed the Yaroslav Musketeer Regiment belonging to Lewis' brigade into Tellnitz. The regiment's six battalion guns were positioned so their fire could sweep the northside road approaches into town.[40]

Anatole de Montesquiou

When Davout sent Heudelet's brigade towards Tellnitz, the marshal also dispatched one of his aides-de-camp to watch and oversee the action. This was the marshal's youngest—and arguably most intelligent—aide-de-camp, *sous-lieutenant* Anatole de Montesquiou. Having witnessed Heudelet's attack and repulse, then noticing the allied deployments and subsequent artillery bombardment, Montesquiou took the initiative and responded to these developments by ordering Bourcier, then Colonel Schobert, and finally Colonel Arrighi de Casanova to pull their commands back a few hundred yards to the Sokolnitz Brook. Thus, in another example of Napoleon's system of command whereby aides-de-camp carried with them the embodiment of authority of their commanding officer, *sous-lieutenant* Anatole de Montesquiou was giving the orders to officers that far outranked him. Bourcier was only too glad to oblige, and in so doing, arranged his cavalry brigades in several angles whereby they could pounce upon and flank any allied advance. Colonels Schobert and Arrighi de Casanova followed suit. By repositioning further to the west, Montesquiou took the French dragoons and infantry out of range of

---

[39] S.H.A.T., C[2] 10 and 16; A. Martinien, *Tableaux des Officiers Tués et Blessés,* p. 329.

[40] Stutterheim, *A Detailed Account of the Battle of Austerlitz,* pp. 87-88.

the Russian and Austrian 6-pounder guns and accompanying howitzers or licornes in and around Tellnitz. However, the increased distance did not have the same effect for the two French 8-pounders and the single howitzer of the one-half horse artillery company attached to Bourcier's Division. Beyond effective range of the enemy's guns, the French horse artillerists demonstrated the value of their longer-ranged weapons by opening a bombardment onto the exposed Austrian cavalry on the west side of the Goldbach.[41]

Not wanting to see his idle cavalry take casualties from the French artillery, Kienmayer requested permission for the Advance Guard of the I Column, as well as the main body of the I Column, to either expand the bridgehead over the Goldbach with a major attack, or pull the cavalry back out of range of the French 8-pounders. However, Kienmayer's request was refused by an inebriated Buxhöwden. As commander of the first three columns, Buxhöwden wanted to keep the bridgehead over the Goldbach as is and the troops of Kienmayer and Dokhturov were instructed to stay at Tellnitz until word came that the II and III Columns had captured the village and castle of Sokolnitz.

The fighting spreads to Sokolnitz

The Initial Struggle for Sokolnitz

The contest for Tellnitz was only a skirmish compared to the savage fighting at Sokolnitz. The outer portions of these neighboring villages were separated by a distance of 1,200 yards, but the comparison in the intensity of the fighting at the separate locations placed them worlds apart. Situated to the north of Tellnitz along the Goldbach Brook, the village of Sokolnitz crowned the western, muddy bank. The village consisted of sturdy structures that lined two roads and formed a 'T' on the north side of town. About 400 yards north of the village was the castle of Sokolnitz. An imposing two-story country house with large, surrounding masonry barns, the entire castle area included an expansive area of more than 100 yards back towards the south that was enclosed by high walls.

Following the Goldbach further north, the stream ran through a massive game park known as the pheasantry. With perimeter dimensions of 580 yards east and west by 800 yards north and south, the pheasantry was a mass of trees and bushes bordered by a low, brick wall.

From the northern wall of the pheasantry to the southern-most building of Tellnitz, the two-mile stretch along the Goldbach was initially held only by Margaron's light cavalry and a few battalions of Legrand's infantry. *Général de division* Claude-Juste-Alexandre Legrand, the 43-year-old commander of the 3rd Infantry Division of Marshal Soult's 4th Corps, had to have been one of the luckiest officers in French uniform. Never wounded in combat despite seeing action in an almost endless succession of battles throughout the wars of the Revolution, Legrand had been a soldier since his enlistment in the regiment *Dauphin* at age 15. He rose through the ranks to become a *général de brigade* in 1793, and a *général de division* in 1799. Legrand's distinguished service record earned him the command of the 3rd Infantry Division at the Channel camp of Saint-Omer in 1803, and during the following two years, Legrand molded his division.[42]

Legrand

From his field headquarters four miles away at Kobelnitz, Legrand could hear the sounds of battle echoing through the early morning fog from the direction of Tellnitz. Within a few minutes, one of the general's aide-de-camp returned to headquarters with news that the noise was from the direction of Tellnitz. The

---

[41] S.H.A.T., C^2 18; dossier Montesquiou. The bright, young Montesquiou's performance under Davout earned him a promotion and, eventually, a spot in Napoleon's Military Household as one of the Emperor's *Officiers d'Ordonnance.*

[42] Six, *Dictionnaire biographique*, vol. 2, p. 98; S.H.A.T., C^2 223 and 459.

messenger was Legrand's son who held the rank of captain. The younger Legrand told his father that the 3rd *Ligne* was under heavy pressure at Tellnitz, and that since the only other infantry at that moment along the Goldbach were the battalions of the *Tirailleurs du Pô* and the *Tirailleurs corses*, he should come at once with reinforcements. Legrand immediately took his son's advice. First, he went to *général de brigade* Levasseur, and ordered him to take the four battalions (two battalions of the 18th *Ligne*, two battalions of the 75th *Ligne*) of the division's 3rd Brigade and head for the pheasantry to anchor the north end of the Sokolnitz position. Then Legrand turned to *général de brigade* Merle and, together with their staffs, headed south to the most threatened sector of the field with a section of foot artillerists and two 8-pounders in tow along with the two battalions of the 26th *Légère*.

At the head of the 26th *Légère* was 38-year-old Colonel François-René Pouget. Elected captain in a battalion of Volunteers of 1791, Pouget served throughout the wars of the Revolution. He had risen to the rank of major in the 62nd *Ligne* when, in February 1805, Napoleon selected him to be the new colonel of the 26th *Légère*.[43] The position had come open after the regiment's former colonel, Félix Baciocchi, had been promoted. In the six months that followed, Pouget impressed his superiors, especially Marshal Soult. "Colonel Pouget puts his regiment through drills with celerity and exactitude," Soult wrote on 18 thermidor (6 August). "The 26th *Légère* is one of the best regiments in camp."[44]

Another reason for the solid character of the 26th *Légère* was its high percentage of veteran soldiers and officers that combined to form the heart and soul of the unit. Of the 1,587 officers and other ranks that were present and under arms on 7 November 1805, some 835 members had been in uniform between 10 and 15 years. Most of these were still with the colors on 30 November, when the head count of those present was 1,564. What's more, 92% of the officers and NCOs had been in uniform at least 10 years.[45] Even with a core of veteran soldiers possessing excellent longevity, the mettle of this veteran regiment was soon to be severely tested.

As the 26th moved south, then crested the hill north of the pheasantry, a gentle breeze began to blow, and a brilliant sunlight began to clear the fog off the higher points of the battlefield, exposing a powerful enemy force pouring down the Pratzen Plateau and heading for the village of Sokolnitz. Legrand, Merle, and Pouget halted their march long enough to get a good look at the adversary through the dissipating mist. The French officers could identify "more than a dozen greencoated battalions of the Tsar above which their distinctive flags fluttered in the morning breeze."[46] There wasn't a moment to lose if Sokolnitz along with its castle and pheasantry were to be contested. Since the village was the point that was immediately threatened, Pouget led the 1,564 members of the 26th *Légère* forward into the town. Double-timing into position, the light infantrymen found the remainder of the 1st Brigade consisting of 340 combatants of the *Tirailleurs du Pô* and 519 members of the *Tirailleurs corses* already fanned out along their front in skirmish order. Not having enough time to set up a strong point defense, Pouget swung his 1st Battalion into position along the road that ran through the village in a north-south direction. Pouget then had these men shake out into line formation while the 2nd Battalion of the 26th *Légère* followed Merle.

Merle

The stocky, prematurely gray-haired, 39-year-old *général de brigade* Pierre-Hugues-Victoire Merle was not a flashy officer. Rather than a long combat career,

---

[43] Six, *Dictionnaire biographique*, vol. 2, p. 328.

[44] S.H.A.T., C^2 223.

[45] S.H.A.T., *Tableau de la Grande Armée Dernière quinzaine du mois brumaire an XIV*, "Situation au 16 brumaire an XIV (7 November 1805)" and C^2 477.

[46] S.H.A.T., *Journal des opérations du 4e corps.*

Merle had served capably in many posts, and his exceptional handling of the military department of Marengo earned him a command at Soult's camp of Saint-Omer in 1803. As Merle approached the Sokolnitz castle, he realized that the entirety of his tiny command could not be committed forward in defense of that place. The general instead dispatched three companies as *tirailleurs* to contest the castle grounds. The remaining six companies of the 2nd Battalion of the 26th were formed alongside the detachment of foot artillerists from the 16th Company of the 5th *Artillerie Regiment à pied* which served two 8-pounders that had already been unlimbered on the rising ground to the west of the castle.

The time was 8:30 A.M., and the 1st Battalion of the 26th *Légère* had been in Sokolnitz for just a few minutes when the leading Russian troops of the II Column under Langeron pulled up in front of the village. The commander of this allied column was Lieutenant-General Andrault de Langeron. The 42-year-old French *émigré* was at the head of 17 battalions of infantry, two squadrons of the Saint Petersburg Dragoons, one squadron of Cossacks and a company of pioneers supported by 30 battalion guns. These 10,283 officers and other ranks were supposed to pass the Goldbach below Sokolnitz. However, in their delayed march off the Pratzen, the column had instead veered off course and headed straight for Sokolnitz. The Russians were able to cross the brook with their battalion guns, and once in front of the village, Langeron anxiously looked to the north, but could not see any evidence of the arrival of Prebyshevsky's III Column. What's more, with no messengers communicating between the columns, Langeron did not know how much longer, or where, Prebyshevsky and his men would show. Langeron therefore decided to halt his advance east of town, deploy his men and cannon of Olsuvev's Brigade, and blow the 26th *Légère* out of Sokolnitz. The Russian battalions and ordnance soon swept Sokolnitz with a hail of musketry and canister. The storm of lead and iron was described by Colonel Pouget, whose horse became terrified:

> by the bullets as they whistled around its ears and between its legs, preventing me from going to where I knew I was needed. Major Brillat offered me his own horse, which I eagerly accepted. At the instant I dismounted, I was engulfed in a shower of earth and pebbles, which flew into my face with such force that I was covered in blood and almost blinded.[47]

Langeron continued to pummel Sokolnitz until after 9:00 A.M. when Prebyshevsky's III Column began to arrive on the scene. The 18 battalions of infantry, one company of pioneer and 30 battalion guns had labored to cross a series of plowed fields on their way from the Pratzen. Approaching the fire fight in front of the village, Prebyshevsky discovered that French troops were already at the castle and their *tirailleurs* covering the pheasantry. After detaching one battalion of the 7th *Jaeger* to cover the column's right flank, Prebyshevsky ordered the remainder of his 5,448 combatants to "form dense columns by companies and regiments, so as to facilitate whatever movements might prove necessary."[48]

Langeron

By 9:30 A.M., the regiments in Prebyshevsky's and Langeron's columns were moving forward to clear Sokolnitz village and the castle. After changing formation for the assault, Prebyshevsky's troops moved in first. Leading the way was the brigade under Major-General Müller III with the two battalions of the 7th *Jaeger* and all three battalions of the Galicia Musketeer Regiment. As they slogged across the muddy banks of the Goldbach north of where Langeron's men had crossed,

[47] *Souvenirs de Guerre du Général Baron Pouget* (Paris, 1895), pp. 71-72.

[48] Prebyshevsky to Tsar Alexander, 11 July 1806, as quoted in *Kutuzov. Sbornik Dokumentov*, vol. 2, p. 269.

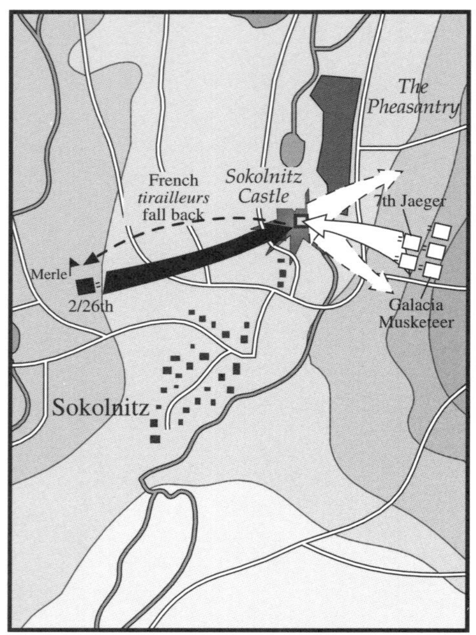

The counterattack of the 2/26th Ligne

their legs sinking into knee-deep mud, these Russians were forced to leave their battalion guns on the east bank. Even without supporting artillery fire, these Russians pushed aside the few *tirailleurs* of the 2nd Battalion of the 26th *Légère* that were trying to defend the castle. The French skirmishers fell back to the hill where the remaining six companies of the battalion were deployed in line and waiting under the covering fire of the two 8-pounders. These guns sprayed their deadly canister into Müller's battalions which were already disorganized from their clearing the castle. One of the blasts felled Müller, who was then captured along with his aide-de-camp, Lieutenant Sobersewsky, when the French light infantry counterattacked. That counterstroke came when Merle, sensing that the moment was right, drew his saber and gave the order for his small command to charge. The surge by the 2nd Battalion of the 26th *Légère* overturned the 7th *Jaeger* and then tore through the Galicia Musketeers, routing all five battalions. During the counterattack, Sergeant Baylin and Corporal Lebout of the 26th distinguished themselves when each man captured one of the Galicia Musketeer's six colors.[49]

With Müller captured and his brigade in shambles, more Russians were needed to deal with the 2nd Battalion of the 26th *Légère* around Sokolnitz castle. As Prebyshevsky rode among the fugitives in an attempt to rally the broken formations, Major-General Strik led the skeleton-like battalions of the Butyrsk and Narva Musketeer Regiments into the fray. The strengths of these regiments reflected the heavy losses they had suffered heavily during the earlier phase of the campaign. The three battalions of the Butyrsk Musketeers came onto the field of Austerlitz with only 864 officers and other ranks—an average of only 288 combatants per battalion. However, the strength of the Narva Musketeers was worse, with only 731 people under arms, making for an average battalion strength of a mere 244! Although their battalions were small, Strik and his colonels better coordinated their advance. As a result, there were simply too many Russians for the 2nd Battalion of the 26th *Légère* to handle. Moving through the castle grounds, the six battalions threw the French light infantry back onto the hill, where Merle rallied the battalion behind the protective fire of the two 8-pounders.

While this mini-battle was going on, Langeron managed to get some of his troops to cease firing and resume their advance into the village of Sokolnitz. Nine battalions under the 30-year-old Major-General Olsuvev—two from the 8th *Jaeger,* three each from the Viborg and the Perm Musketeer Regiments, plus the grenadier battalion of the Kursk Musketeers—almost 4,400 troops in all—rolled into Sokolnitz, there opposed by Colonel Pouget and the 1st Battalion of the 26th *Légère*. The combined five battalions of the 8th *Jaeger* and the Viborg Musketeers ran into Pouget's waiting troops. Outnumbered and their flanks enveloped, the 1st Battalion of the 26th put up a tenacious fight before being forced to fall back to the south. While these light infantrymen were pulling away from Sokolnitz, they collided with the retreating 108th *Ligne* of Heudelet's brigade (see page 330). Meanwhile, the three battalions of Perm and the grenadier battalion from Kursk charged from a easterly direction, swept over the northern half of town, then turned north towards the 2nd Battalion of the 26th *Légère*. Suddenly, Merle found himself and his men sandwiched between the converging brigades under Olsuvev and Strik. Consequently, the French general ordered his command to fall back. Most of the light infantry escaped the closing trap, but the crews of 8-pounders could not limber and move their pieces before the masses of Russians—their battalions noticeably disorganized after moving through Sokolnitz—were upon them. The artillerists therefore temporarily abandoned their pieces. Strik's command occupied the hill, while Olsuvev's battalions returned to the village.

Olsuvev

By 10:00 A.M., some 90 minutes after Langeron's troops had first appeared in front of Sokolnitz, the Russians had finally cleared the village and castle areas.

---

[49] S.H.A.T., *Journal des opérations du 4ᵉ corps.*

The delaying action of Pouget, Merle and their men had been heroic. With only two battalions of the 26th *Légère* and supporting gunners with their two 8-pounders, the French had kept the Russians under Langeron and Prebyshevsky jammed in the Goldbach valley. This was especially remarkable when one considers that the entirety of the II and III Columns outnumbered the French by a margin of 10 to one!

Lochet

Friant's Counterattack at Sokolnitz

If Langeron or Prebyshevsky thought that the fighting for Sokolnitz was over with the ouster of the 26th *Légère*, they were very mistaken. Shortly after 10:00 A.M., Friant arrived on the scene with his 1st and 2nd Brigades under the commands of *généraux de brigade* Kister and Lochet, respectively. Seeing the survivors of the 26th *Légère* recoiling away from the village and castle, Friant wasted no time in ordering his command to counterattack the enemy. Thrown into action first was the 2nd Brigade, commanded by 38-year-old Pierre-Charles Lochet. The native of Châlons-sur-Marne joined the army at age 17 when he was a fusilier in the regiment *La Reine*. Within two years, Lochet had been accepted into the grenadier company. In 1791, he was named as company commander in the 2nd Battalion of *Volontaires de la Marne* and had performed well in the turbulent Republican *Armée du Nord*. Lochet was then promoted to *chef de bataillon* in 1794 and his soldierly qualities earned him the command of the 94th *demi-brigade de bataille* in 1796. Following duty under Soult in 1799 and under Molitor in 1800, during which he served with distinction at a number of battles, Lochet was promoted to *général de brigade* in 1803. Hand-picked to serve under the expert tactician Friant, Lochet spent the next two years at the camp of Bruges.[50] Lochet impressed his fellow officers with his grenadier-like toughness, enthusiasm and iron discipline. While at the camp of Bruges, the stern taskmaster Davout found Lochet to be "an exceptional officer in every respect."[51]

As Lochet bore down on the village of Sokolnitz, the general led forward the finest regiment of Friant's Division—the 48th *Ligne*. Experienced, superbly drilled and disciplined, the 48th was undoubtedly one of the most fanatic Republican outfits in the *Grande Armée*. The descendent of the old Royal army's *Régiment Artois*, the soldiers of the unit had joined the rioters at Rennes on 17 July 1789 to the cries of "Long Live the Third Estate!"[52] Many of these men were still in uniform in 1805, when the 48th boasted some 33 men with more than 15 years of service, while another 758 had been in uniform between 10 to 15 years. Therefore, of the 1,365 officers and other ranks that were present before the 48th *Ligne* left Vienna on 29 November, almost 58% had fought in and survived the wars of the Revolution.[53] Following a review on 1 fructidor an XIII (19 August 1805), *Inspecteur aux revues* Brunek noted that "many officers and NCOs of the 48th still wear modified Republican uniforms or have memorabilia attached to their coats and hats."[54] Following their forced march from Vienna, it is estimated that 800 members of this superb regiment arrived on the field of Austerlitz.

Barbanègre

The commanding officer of the 48th *Ligne* was 33-year-old Colonel Joseph Barbanègre. A former *chef de bataillon* in the *Grenadiers à pied de la Garde,* Barbanègre shared his men's Republican zeal. When Barbanègre was named by Napoleon as the colonel of the 48th, the new regimental commander directed that

[50] Six, *Dictionnaire biographique*, vol. 1, p. 471.
[51] S.H.A.T., C^2 213.
[52] Bertraud, *The Army of the French Revolution*, p. 25.
[53] S.H.A.T., C^2 477.
[54] S.H.A.T., C^2 477.

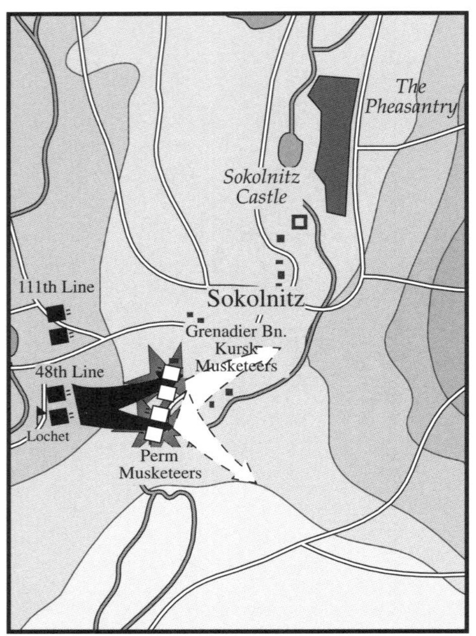

Barbanègre's attack

the musicians be clothed "only in our national colors." In addition, Barbanègre ordered Drum Major LaFontaine (whose brother was a company commander in the same regiment) to have the regiment's 24-piece band "play *Le Chant du Départ* every morning." [55] Barbanègre was, however, much more than an enthusiastic revolutionary and accomplished officer. "He was an imposing physical specimen, commanding a distinguished military bearing, coupled with an amiable personality. He conversed in a most favorable manner, giving the impression of an élite officer."[56] Another described Barbanègre similarly: "Complementing his character as an élite officer, he was wonderful in the role of a courtier, and these qualities therefore greatly pleased the Emperor." [57]

Barbanègre and Lochet led the two battalions of the 48th *Ligne* in a furious counterattack. Formed in line of battle, moving across the ground west of town as the regimental bands played *Le Chant du Départ*, the 48th swept forward. Despite being heavily outnumbered, the bold French attack overran the three battalions of the Perm Musketeers and the grenadier battalion of the Kursk Musketeers, then moved into the village where the 1st Battalion of the 26th *Légère* had previously deployed. During the attack, three *voltigeurs* of the 48th distinguished themselves. Privates Parent and Hubert each captured one color from the Perm Musketeers, while Private Halluin single-handedly killed the entire crew of one of Perm's battalion guns, then claimed the prize. All three men were decorated with the *Légion d'Honneur* after the battle. Also taken in the assault were the other five battalion guns belonging to the Perm Musketeers.[58]

Following up the deadly thrust of the 48th *Ligne* was the other regiment of Lochet's brigade—the 111th *Ligne* under Colonel Gay. On 5 November, the two battalions of the 111th numbered 58 officers and 1,664 other ranks present and under arms. Following the combat at Mariazell, and then the march to Vienna, the 111th was down to 1,440 people with the colors by 28 November.[59] The forced march to Austerlitz is estimated to have reduced the regiment to approximately 700 present and under arms.

Colonel Gay and his depleted battalions deployed into line and swung into action on the left flank of the 48th, charging the other battalions of Olsuvev's command that were mingling about the west side of Sokolnitz. As Gay and his 700 men went into action against approximately three times their numbers that consisted of the two battalions of the 8th *Jaeger* and the three battalions of the Viborg Musketeers, Friant recalled how the 111th promptly dispatched the adversaries. In his after-action report, Friant recalled that Gay's men drove back the "huge mass of leaderless men who were advancing in disorder and uttering horrible cries."[60] Lochet's counterattack, expertly officered and skillfully delivered by an élite force of 1,600 men, tore to pieces the Russian battalions that an hour earlier had numbered 4,700 combatants. Watching his brigade general deliver the deadly riposte, Friant recalled that "no officer was as beautiful in combat" [61] as Lochet.

[55] S.H.A.T., C[2] 1.

[56] Everts, "Sabretache" 1901, notes for p. 622.

[57] Everts, "Sabretache" 1901, p. 691.

[58] S.H.A.T., C[2] 21; Davout to Berthier, *Correspondance Davout*, vol. 1, Austerlitz after-action reports.

[59] S.H.A.T., *Tableau de la Grande Armée Dernière quinzaine du mois brumaire an XIV*, "Situation au 14 brumaire an XIV (5 November 1805)" and C[2] 476.

[60] Friant to Davout, 12 frimaire an XIV (3 December 1805), *Correspondance Davout,* vol. 1, p. 215.

[61] S.H.A.T., dossier Lochet.

Above, the massive barn and granary of Sokolnitz

Below, the eastern wall of the pheasantry today. The lighter patches are said to be where the walls were pulled down to create gun positions.

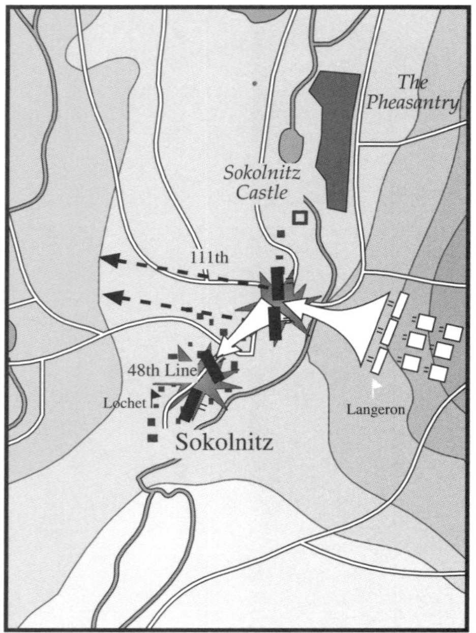

Langeron drives back the 111th Ligne

As the broken battalions of Olsuvev ran back across the Goldbach, Langeron rode into their midst and rallied their formations. Once that was accomplished, Langeron threw the entirety of the nine rallied battalions against the northern portion of Sokolnitz. The numerous Russians first encountered Colonel Gay's 111th *Ligne*. Outnumbered and their northern flank enveloped, Gay's men were driven back through Sokolnitz. Once past the western edge of town, Sergeant-Major Combet decided that his unit had retreated far enough. Carrying the eagle and standard of the 1st Battalion, he stopped and began waving it defiantly over his head. Serving as the rallying point for the rest of the battalion, the men reformed. Combet then walked 20 paces in front of the 1st Battalion of the 111th, halted and stoically waited for the Russians to come after him.

Rather than pursuing the 111th, Olsuvev screened the northwestern approach into Sokolnitz with the 8th *Jaeger* and the grenadier battalion of the Kursk Musketeers. The Russian general then took his five other battalions, wheeled them to the left and attacked Lochet, Barbanègre and the 48th *Ligne* that were holding the southern portion of Sokolnitz village. For 45 minutes, the two battalions of the 48th *Ligne* fended off these Russians. During the intense fighting Lochet had four horses shot out from underneath him and *chef de bataillon* Bourdon-Lacombe went down with a wound. The 48th was hanging on for dear life when assistance arrived in the form of Kister's 1st Brigade, which Friant had kept in reserve. Rushing forward on the orders of Friant, the first regiment of the brigade to contact the Russians were the troops of the 15th *Légère* under Colonel Jean-Charles Desailly. A distinguished light infantry officer since early in the wars of the Revolution, Desailly had been the colonel of the 15th since 1799. Owing to the fact that his battalions contributed companies to the *Grenadiers de la Réserve,* Desailly's small command numbered 813 officers and other ranks on 5 November, and upon leaving Vienna, the regiment's two battalions mustered only 754 combatants.[62] After deducting those who dropped out on the forced march from Vienna, and the detachment of the regiment's *voltigeurs* to Heudelet, the number of men Desailly brought onto the field of Austerlitz could not have numbered more than 300.

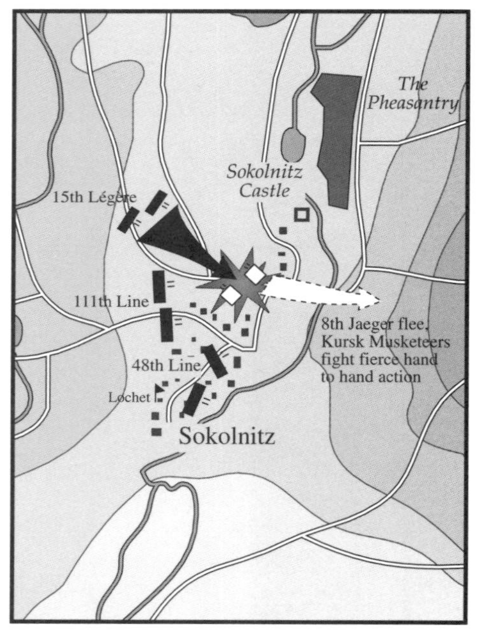

The attack of the 15th Légère

Deploying into line his two tiny battalions consisting of 12 depleted companies, Desailly struck the northwest angle of Sokolnitz. Ready and waiting to resist these French were what remained of the 8th *Jaeger*, along with the grenadier battalion from the Kursk Musketeer Regiment. Desailly's light infantrymen quickly blew through the *jaeger*, who scattered and ran towards the friendly east bank of the Goldbach. Not budging, however, were the grenadiers of Kursk. They countercharged the 15th *Légère*, and both commands were soon locked in hand-to-hand combat on the west edge of town. Eleven of the 15th *Légère's* 12 company commanders were wounded in this fierce struggle, along with *chef de bataillon* Dulong, Major Geither and a dozen other officers.[63] Marshal Davout was close enough to the action to see what followed. Both eagle/standard-bearers of the 15th, Sergeant-Majors Broudes and Deschamps, struggled to "defend their eagles against several Russian NCOs and grenadiers who were doing their level best to seize them. These two heroes each knocked down a number of the enemy by the weight of their eagles, and thus managed to save these standards for their regiment."[64]

To the left of the 15th *Légère*, Kister's other regiment—the last reserve of Friant's Division—was committed to action. That regiment was the 33rd *Ligne* under the command of Colonel Saint Raymond. The two battalions of the regiment

---

[62] S.H.A.T., *Tableau de la Grande Armée Dernière quinzaine du mois brumaire an XIV*, "Situation au 14 brumaire an XIV (5 November 1805)" and C² 476.

[63] S.H.A.T., C² 16.

[64] Davout to Berthier, *Correspondance Davout*, vol. 1, Austerlitz after-action reports.

had numbered 56 officers and 1,307 other ranks present and under arms on 5 November, and had left Vienna with 1,214 under the colors.[65] When Saint Raymond marched his battalions onto the field at Austerlitz, those still under the eagles could not have counted more than 500. Deploying these combatants into line, the 33rd went straight for the Russians under Strik that had earlier forced Merle and the 2nd Battalion of the 26th *Légère* to withdraw from the hill west of the Sokolnitz castle. It will be remembered that Strik had six depleted battalions of the Butyrsk and Narva Musketeer Regiments. These formations, which began the day with a combined strength of 1,595, had not suffered many casualties thus far in the battle. That, however, was about to change dramatically. Even though his command was outnumbered three to one, Saint Raymond tore into the Russians. The sudden attack made by the 33rd shook the fragile psyche of the Tsar's troops, and they fell back towards the castle. Without support, Saint Raymond could not follow up his victory, but halted his men to await the Russian response. That was not long in coming. Strik soon halted his retreating men and turned their battalions around. Seeing the approach of the superior numbers of the enemy, Saint Raymond did not want to let his heavily outnumbered command get caught in a fire fight. Consequently, he immediately ordered his regiment to advance once again. As the drummers beat the *pas de charge*, the 33rd *Ligne* collided with Strik's battalions. Riding from danger spot to danger spot, Davout watched Saint Raymond's men charge the Russian host. Describing the assault of the 33rd *Ligne,* Davout wrote that "their courage approached a storm's fury."[66] Blue and greencoated troops collided in a life-and-death struggle. Fighting through the enemy battalions, Corporal Villain of the 33rd *Ligne* captured one flag of the Butyrsk Musketeers before the Russians broke and ran. Meanwhile, on the far left of the regiment's line, Captain Belin, company commander of the *voltigeurs* of the 2nd Battalion, was inspiring his company's own heroics. The company was facing north, protecting the left flank of the regiment when they were suddenly engulfed by a battalion of musketeers from the Narva regiment. Instead of fleeing, Belin and his *voltigeurs* stood their ground, knowing that if they broke the entire regiment would be flanked. Outnumbered nine to one, the *voltigeurs* fought as men possessed. In his after-action report, Davout recalled the astounding feat. "Captain Belin killed seven Russians before being wounded several times. The entire company fought like the heroes that they are, struggling against ten times the numbers of the enemy. Not only did they hold, but later returned to the attack, the drummers beating the *pas de charge*."[67]

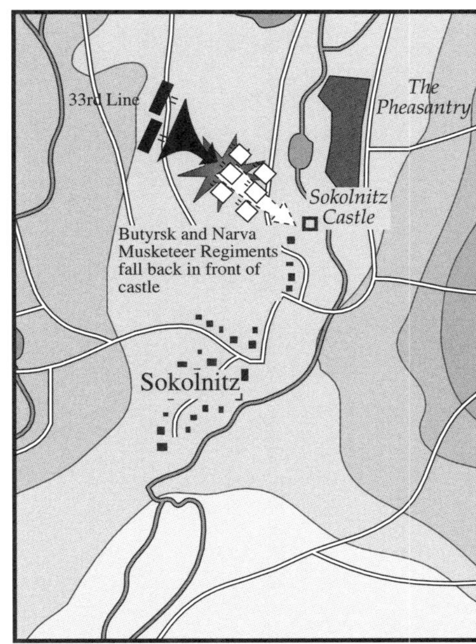

The 33rd Ligne *is committed*

The Russians in front of Sokolnitz and its castle would rally and return to the attack a few more times. Each assault was less powerful than the one it succeeded. Despite their superior numbers, the Russians of the II Column could never recapture the southern portion of the village from the 48th *Ligne,* nor could those of the III Column break through the nine pieces of artillery and the well coordinated, but diminutive battalions of the 111th *Ligne*, 15th *Légère,* 33rd *Ligne* and the rallied elements of the 26th *Légère* that held onto the ground between the center of the village and Sokolnitz Castle. With Langeron's and Prebyshevsky's columns stalled out along the Goldbach, Buxhöwden refused to give Dokhturov and Kienmayer the go ahead to resume their advance from Tellnitz. Therefore, from the pheasantry south to Tellnitz, the Napoleonic forces had accomplished a major feat. With slightly more than 6,700 infantry, plus the supporting use of a few regiments of cavalry, all of which were ably backed by a grand total of 19 pieces of ordnance, the French had completely ground to a halt Buxhöwden's first

Sokolnitz castle today

[65] S.H.A.T., *Tableau de la Grande Armée Dernière quinzaine du mois brumaire an XIV*, "Situation au 14 brumaire an XIV (5 November 1805)" and C^2 476.
[66] Davout to Berthier, *Correspondance Davout*, vol. 1, Austerlitz after-action reports.
[67] Davout to Berthier, *Correspondance Davout*, vol. 1, Austerlitz after-action reports.

three columns. Despite hurling more than 24,000 troops supported by 84 pieces of ordnance at Napoleon's tenacious forces along the Goldbach Brook (not all of Langeron's or Prebyshevsky's troops had been committed to action), the allies suffered significantly heavier casualties and many more numerous tactical reverses than they inflicted.

Those results did not bode well for the remainder of the Combined Russian and Austrian Army that had yet to engage the *Grande Armée*. The remaining allied forces would not enjoy the same numeric superiority on the other parts of the battlefield. Since portions of Napoleon's forces that were outnumbered three to one had stopped Buxhöwden, then what was going to happen on the other parts of the far-flung field of Austerlitz, where the odds were much more even? That answer was soon to be delivered with an exclamation mark by the bluecoated troops quickly moving from west to east, already crossing the Goldbach and ascending the Pratzen Plateau.

Action on the Pratzen Plateau—
The Fight to Control the Center of the Battlefield

When we left Napoleon after the conclusion of the morning conference, he had dismissed all his marshals except for Soult. The commander of 4th Corps was kept by the Emperor's side, as they watched and waited for the allied forces to clear the Pratzen Plateau. Ségur recalled that:

> During this time the rising sun was obscured by heavy mists which seemed to the Russians to favor their flank movement forwards to their left; but on the contrary the fog veiled our attack... It was not yet 8:00 A.M. and silence and darkness were still reining over the rest of the line when, beginning with the heights, the sun suddenly breaking through this thick fog, revealed to our sight the Pratzen Plateau growing empty of troops from the flank march of the enemy's columns. As for us who had remained in the ravine which defines the foot of this plateau, the smoke of the bivouacs and the vapors which, heavier at this point than elsewhere, still hung around, concealing from the eyes of the Russians our center deployed in columns and ready for the attack.[68]

Soult

As the fabled sun of Austerlitz burned off the morning haze, Napoleon *believed* that all the allied troops had moved off the Pratzen, just as he had predicted. The Emperor then gave the signal and sent Soult on his way. Followed by his aides-de-camp, the marshal rode quickly to the infantry divisions of Saint-Hilaire and Vandamme, both of which were formed in attack columns and awaiting orders.

Nicolas-Jean de Dieu Soult, the 36-year-old commander of the 4th Corps, was a highly regarded drill master and administrator. A man who had risen from the ranks to become a Marshal of France, Soult was the cornerstone on which the encampment of Boulogne was built. His natural flair for administration, his passion for drill, his interest in further developing the battlefield doctrines of the army, all led him to the forefront in the tactical molding of the *Grande Armée*. From the Channel camp of Saint-Omer, Soult's mock battles shook the coastline, while under his watchful eye the officers and men of the future 4th Corps were the first to improve upon the existing drill *Règlement du 1er août 1791*. With the codification

[68] *Memoirs of Ségur*, pp. 248-249.

that became known as the *Ordonnance du 12 pluviôse an XIII* (also referred to as the *Ordonnance du 1er février 1805),* Napoleonic infantry would use what some officers loosely referred to as "Soult's 1805 *Ordonnance"* throughout the remainder of the Napoleonic era.

Despite his valuable contributions at the Boulogne encampment, despite his high rank and the honors that accorded his position, despite the confidence placed in him by his commander-in-chief with the reins of the largest corps of the *Grande Armée,* Soult did not possess the qualities of character to make him a great general, or even a good comrade. A man who should have been comfortable enough with himself and his self-worth to work amiably with fellow officers was instead a selfish, jealous, petty and intractable soul that carried a grudge without hope of forgiveness. His haughty manner, combined with a bad habit of never looking people in the eye when talking to them, made Soult a hard person to know, and even more difficult with whom to communicate. A brave man on the battlefield (no one could have been anything less and still be named into the marshalate), Soult nevertheless had another serious personality flaw that turned him into a childish coward when it came to owning up to responsibility. This is no better illustrated than a few days before Austerlitz.

On the evening of 28 November, Soult was visiting Murat at the cavalryman's headquarters located at the Posoritz Post House along the Olmütz Road. From recently captured Russian prisoners, it was known that the allied army had received substantial reinforcements, and that the Russian and Austrians now outnumbered the French troops that were positioned immediately east of Brünn. Soult believed that, in light of the disparity of forces, it was the better part of valor to call for a retreat. After a few minutes, Murat was won over to this line of thinking, but the two marshals were at a loss as to *how* they should put their beliefs before the Emperor. Soult felt that they should solicit the aid of Marshal Jean Lannes. Lannes, whose plain spoken honesty in the presence of Napoleon was already legendary, was one of the reasons that caused him to be the Emperor's favorite marshal. And it was Lannes who, at that moment, suddenly rode up to the post house as if he was an answer to a prayer. In less than 10 minutes, Soult's forceful oratory persuaded the open-minded Lannes that it would be prudent to put these thoughts on paper and present them to the Emperor as the opinions of the three marshals. Without stopping to think that Napoleon might already be calling in reinforcements, Lannes agreed to write the letter. With the other two marshals watching smugly, Lannes sat down at a table and began putting pen to paper when none other than Napoleon unexpectedly arrived. *Chef d'escadron* Jacques-Gervais Subervie, Lannes' senior aide-de-camp, recalled what happened next. Following the exchange of greetings, the Emperor waded right into a conversation.

Lannes

"Well, gentlemen, we are pretty comfortable here," Napoleon said confidently after coming from his headquarters in Brünn following his issuance of the various dispatches summoning Bernadotte and Davout to the future battlefield.

"We do not think so," quickly answered Lannes, "and I was writing to Your Majesty to that effect." Without replying, Napoleon snatched up the incomplete letter and read it. Upon finishing, the Emperor looked at his favorite lieutenant and queried:

"What! You, Lannes advise retreat? This is the first time that this has ever happened. Was this your idea?"

"No, Sire."

"If not, then whose was it."

"All of ours, Sire."

"All of yours?... And you, Marshal Soult?"

"In whatever way Your Majesty employs the 4th Corps, it will account for itself with twice its number." Soult's cowardly and evasive answer sent Lannes into orbit, who angrily gave a rejoinder.

Shako Plate of a Napoleonic Officer

"Sire, I have not been here a quarter of an hour, and I know nothing about our position other than what these gentlemen have told me. My opinion was founded and formed solely on their statements, just as it was their request that I write you. Marshal Soult's answer is that of a dirty sneak. I consider it as an insult, and I will have satisfaction for it." Soult then tried to explain away his answer, which Lannes would have none of, and the two men continued their heated argument. Meanwhile, Napoleon had tuned out the bickering, paced up and down the room for a few moments and then turned to his lieutenants and said, "I, too, think a retreat is necessary." Napoleon then ordered Subervie to fetch Marshal Berthier, who was himself was just arriving at the post house. As Berthier walked in, Napoleon dismissed his marshals and then dictated the order for the army to withdraw across the Pratzen to the lower terrain west of the Goldbach.[69]

Lannes returned to his headquarters, and sent a challenge to Soult. When Lannes' old friend and instructor, Colonel Pierre-Charles Pouzet, heard of the incident, he did not hesitate to go the marshal's headquarters, offering himself as Lannes' second, even though it was Soult under which Pouzet served! However, Soult did not reply. During the next few days, anytime the commanders of the 4th and 5th Corps got close to each other, the tension was so strong that the staff members around them could cut the air with a knife. Finally, on the morning of the battle, Lannes noticed that Soult arrived for the meeting at Imperial headquarters without wearing his sword. Unable to resist watching a coward squirm with uneasiness, Lannes walked up to Soult and in front of all present, said to the commander of 4th Corps:

"I thought you had a sword. I have been waiting for you."

"We have more important matters to attend to today," Soult said coldly, shrugging his shoulders while refusing to look directly at Lannes.

"You are a miserable creature!" retorted Lannes.[70] Soult then turned and walked away.

Soult's initial objections as put forth to Murat and Lannes and without knowledge of Napoleon calling in the outlying troops, evidently did affect final dispositions for the Battle of Austerlitz. Without a doubt, Napoleon finalized his general plan of battle while pacing the floor at the post house during the argument between Lannes and Soult. However, the minor withdrawal from the Pratzen that Napoleon ordered was not the retreat Soult was seeking when he first talked to Murat and then to Lannes. What's more, Soult's answer given to the Emperor, especially after his fellow marshal had attempted to cover for him, speaks volumes about his character. Therefore, it is not surprising that the cordial relationship between Soult and Lannes ended at the Posoritz Post House a few days before the Battle of Austerlitz; the two marshals would never be on speaking terms again.

Couronne de Fer

With the Lannes feud lurking somewhere in the back of his mind, Soult rode up to his ready-and-waiting infantry under Vandamme and Saint-Hilaire. These men had been under arms already for five hours, a situation that hardly pleased anyone serving under Soult. "It was a ridiculous order," *général de brigade* Thiébault candidly admitted, "for military dawn did not occur till nearly 8:00 A.M., and no risk would have been run by letting the men have another three hours' rest."[71] Nevertheless, Soult's orders had been obeyed, and the divisions had long since fallen in ranks when the marshal made his appearance. Soult knew his men well, and addressed each regiment in turn. Going from Vandamme's Division to Saint-Hilaire's, Soult came upon the vaunted 10th *Légère*. The men had just finished

[69] S.H.A.T., C² 10; Thiébault draws on this account for his version in *The Memoirs of Baron Thiébault,* vol. 2, pp. 146-147.

[70] S.H.A.T., C² 10; Thiébault draws on this account for his version in *The Memoirs of Baron Thiébault,* vol. 2, p. 153.

[71] *The Memoirs of Baron Thiébault,* vol. 2, pp. 152-153.

their third round of potent brandy and were in the most eager of spirits to come to grips with the enemy when Soult asked them: "Do you remember how you beat the Russians in Switzerland?" A reply quickly came back: "Nobody's likely to forget it today!"[72]

The 10th *Légère* was acknowledged by many officers to be one of the best units in the *Grande Armée*. On 24 floréal an XIII (14 May 1805), the drill expertise of the 10th was described by their division commander, Saint-Hilaire, as being "magnificent… Colonel Pouzet's unit is the finest of the division."[73] Morand also noted earlier in the year that: "Pouzet and his command continue to perform exceptionally well… [they] present the finest look of any regiment in camp."[74]

The legacy of this excellent regiment started in 1788 with the formation of the 10th *bataillon de Chasseurs du Gévaudan.* Its nomenclature was changed in 1791 to the 10th *bataillon légère,* then to the 10th *demi-brigade légère* in 1795, and finally to a regimental designation in 1803. Under the command of Gazan, the regiment had covered itself with glory in the 1800 campaign. In one battle, Gazan had led two battalions of the regiment as they stormed and captured a village against the fire of 12 Austrian guns and an infantry force three times their size.[75] In 1803, command of the regiment passed to one of the army's outstanding infantry officers, Colonel Pierre-Charles Pouzet. A former *chef de bataillon* in the *Grenadiers à pied de la Garde*, the 39-year-old Pouzet was arguably the most accomplished unit instructor in the *Grande Armée*, and the 10th *Légère* mirrored the colonel's precision. This was also reflected in the regiment losing virtually no one through strategic consumption. Crossing the Rhine on 25 September with 1,542 people present, the two battalions of the regiment numbered 1,478 officers and other ranks with the colors on 7 November. Owing to the return of some previously detached soldiers, the strength of the 10th *Légère* at Austerlitz was 1,488 present and under arms. Of these combatants, some 594, or 40% of the men, had been in uniform at least 10 years. Therefore, after marching across Bavarian and Moravia over more than a two month period which included horrendous weather, the 10th *Légère* had lost only 54 men.[76]

Two different portraits of Morand, the top being a far more flattering image of this talented general

Pouzet's superb regiment further benefited from the organizational structure of Saint-Hilaire's Division. Like many other divisions of the *Grande Armée*, there was only one regiment constituting the 1st Brigade. The commander of the brigade was 34-year-old *général de brigade* Charles-Antonie-Louis-Alexis Morand. A man of short stature, with a noticeably small head and an enormously large Gallic nose, Morand's physical appearance must not have inspired many ladies. However, to his subordinates and superiors alike, Morand's looks had nothing to do with his status as one of the army's gifted tacticians.

Like countless other officers, Morand's career had been launched by the Revolution. First coming to the attention of Bonaparte during the Egyptian campaign, Morand served as the commander of the 88th *demi-brigade de bataille* in Desaix's Division. His flawless and outstanding combat performances in the numerous battles of that campaign earned him a promotion to *général de brigade* in 1800. When the Channel camps were established, Napoleon called for Morand to report to Saint-Omer in late August 1803.[77] By the time they marched off to war

[72] A. Pétiet, *Souvenirs Militaires de l'Histoire Contemporaine* (Paris, 1844), p. 28.
[73] S.H.A.T., C² 201.
[74] S.H.A.T., C² 192.
[75] S.H.A.T., *Historique du 10ᵉ régiment d'infanterie légère.*
[76] S.H.A.T., C² 470; *Tableau de la Grande Armée Dernière quinzaine du mois brumaire an XIV*, "Situation au 16 brumaire an XIV (7 November 1805)," C² 477 and *Journal des opérations du 4ᵉ corps.*
[77] Six, *Dictionnaire biographique*, vol. 2, pp. 223-224.

Saint-Hilaire

Side View of Thiébault in his Republican uniform

two years later, Morand enjoyed a close, working relationship with Pouzet and his light infantrymen.

The remainder of Saint-Hilaire's Division was composed of two brigades under *généraux de brigade* Thiébault and Varé. Thiébault commanded the 2nd Brigade, consisting of the 14th and 36th *Ligne,* while Varé lead the 3rd Brigade with the regiments of the 43rd and 55th *Ligne.* These brigades, as well as that under Morand, formed the 1st Infantry Division of the 4th Corps. The commanding officer of the division, 39-year-old Louis-Vincent-Joseph Le Blond Saint-Hilaire, was the very embodiment of a model Napoleonic general. His remarkable talents, his bravery and spirit, his utter devotion to his sovereign, earned him the respect of his men as well as his subordinate and superior officers. Pierre Berthezène, who would become the colonel of the 10th *Légère* in February 1807 and served under Saint-Hilaire until the division general's death in the Danube Campaign of 1809, put it succinctly when he described Saint-Hilaire as "the finest division commander on the face of the earth."[78]

With Marshal Soult's order to advance, Saint-Hilaire relayed orders to his brigade generals. Morand was to seize the plateau south of the village of Pratzen (some refer to the village as Pratze—without the 'n'), while Thiébault was to attack the village proper, and then rejoin with the 1st Brigade on the plateau, "towards which Saint-Hilaire proceeded simultaneously with Morand."[79] The artillerists of the 12th Company of the 5th *Artillerie Regiment à pied* that was serving two 8-pounders, two 4-pounders and two 6-inch howitzers, was to divide into half-company strengths. The three most valuable pieces—two 8-pounders and one howitzer—marched with Morand's brigade while the remaining howitzer and two 4-pounders were attached to Thiébault. Another detachment of foot artillerists serving two 8-pounder guns also advanced with Saint-Hilaire and the 1st and 2nd Brigades. Meanwhile, the 3rd Brigade under Varé, "was to follow General Vandamme's movement and take orders from him."[80] With Varé detached, Saint-Hilaire and the 1st and 2nd Brigades—these men still carrying their packs—quickly moved across the Goldbach and swept the southern bank of the eastern fork of the Goldbach below the slopes of the Pratzen Plateau. As these brigades made their trek eastwards, they formed a broad arrow-looking formation with Morand's two battalions in front, followed by Thiébault's four battalions.

As the men were moving along the brook towards the Pratzen, two of Saint-Hilaire's staff members returned with their reports. The village appeared deserted, but there was a lot of enemy activity on the plateau to the south. Responding to this fresh information, Saint-Hilaire rode over to Thiébault and advised the brigade general that the village of Pratzen was *likely* to be held only by enemy pickets. Therefore, the division general believed it was prudent for Thiébault to send a force sufficient to sweep the place, keeping the remainder of his brigade available to support Morand should he run into trouble; Thiébault readily complied.[81]

The commander of Saint-Hilaire's 2nd Brigade was Paul-Charles-François-Adrien-Henri Dieudonné Thiébault. Twenty-two years of age when he joined the army as one of the Volunteers of 1792, Thiébault saw extensive service in the light infantry during the Revolution. Following his transfer to Paris, Thiébault first came to Napoleon's attention in 1795 when the two men found themselves on the same side in putting down the rebellion of 13 vendémiaire (the "Whiff of

---

[78] S.H.A.T., dossier Saint-Hilaire; also see: Général Baron Pierre Berthezène, *Souvenirs militaires de la République et de l'Empire*, 2 volumes (Paris, 1855), vol. 1, p. 212; in *Memoirs of Baron Lejeune*, vol. 1, p. 281, Lejeune describes Saint-Hilaire as: "the pride of the army, as remarkable for his wit as for his military talents."

[79] *The Memoirs of Baron Thiébault,* vol. 2, p. 159.

[80] *The Memoirs of Baron Thiébault,* vol. 2, p. 159.

[81] *The Memoirs of Baron Thiébault,* vol. 2, p. 159.

Grapeshot"). Later transferred to the *Armée d'Italie*, seeing action at Rivoli, then followed by service under the renowned light infantry general, Philibert-Guillaume Duhèsme, the self-confident Thiébault was characterized by one contemporary as a "man of spirit and merit that does not have the modesty to hide it."[82] General Desaix described Thiébault as a "man of esteem, possessing a large, good-looking physique, with a long nose and simple manners."[83] Thiébault's hollow cheeks and ever-present bloodshot eyes gave those who saw him a chilling indication of the killer instinct that he possessed, and a clue as to why the enemies of France called him by his sinister nickname—'The Butcher General.'

Thiébault, shown here in his uniform of a général de division

Following Saint-Hilaire's instructions, Thiébault briefly halted his brigade, then instructed Colonel Mazas to take the 1st Battalion of the 1,551-man 14th *Ligne*,[84] and clear the village of Pratzen. After deploying, and in contrast to established tactical doctrine, Mazas led the 1st Battalion of the 14th towards Pratzen with all nine companies in line, with no *tirailleurs* preceding the formed ranks. The detachment of foot artillerists from the 16th Company, serving two 8-pounders accompanied Mazas. Meanwhile, Thiébault followed at a respectable distance with his remaining three battalions still in attack columns with the half-company of artillery in support.

What no Frenchman then knew was the extent of allied activity on the Pratzen. While the two brigades that remained under Saint-Hilaire were moving eastwards, the Austro-Russian IV Column was already positioning itself squarely across the Frenchmen's path. The allied troops had been warned of the approaching bluecoated soldiers by Major C. F. Toll of the Tsar's staff. He had been leading the way for the IV Column when, having passed through the village of Pratzen, he spied some troops moving to the west. He initially assumed that these were the rear elements of Prebyshevsky's III Column. However, moving closer he suddenly came under fire from Morand's 10th *Légère*. Toll galloped back to give his warning to Lieutenant-General Mikhail Andreivich Miloradovich, co-commander of the IV Column. Of the 12,099 officers and other ranks that composed the IV Column at Austerlitz, the Russian general only had readily at hand Lieutenant-Colonel Monakhtin's 750 combatants in three very weak battalions and two understrength squadrons that made up the column's so-called Advance Guard. Miloradovich immediately sent forward one of the musketeer battalions from the Novgorod Musketeer Regiment, along with their two battalion pieces, to hold the area south of the village, while another musketeer battalion of the same regiment, along with their two pieces of ordnance, were hustled through town and posted on the west side of town. Once there, they lay flat on the bank of the stream while the two battalion guns attached to this unit were kept in a shallow depression near the men and out of sight from any French approaching from the west. The reserve of this Advance Guard, a single musketeer battalion from the Apsheron Musketeer Regiment that numbered only 137 officers and other ranks, was positioned to the rear and between the Novograd battalions along with the handful of troopers from two squadrons of the Austrian Dragoons-Regiment Erzherzog Johann #1.

Miloradovich

The curly brown haired 35-year-old Miloradovich was a proud officer and eager to avenge the humiliating thrashing he and his command had suffered at Dürenstein in November. Knowing that the Tsar was watching, Miloradovich wasn't going to miss this chance to impress his sovereign. Waving his sword over his head, then sheathing the blade and drawing two silver pistols, firing them into the air, Miloradovich:

---

82 Stanislas-Cécile comte de Girardin, *Mémoires, journal et souvenirs de S. de Girardin*, 2 volumes (Paris, 1829), vol. 2, p. 555.

83 Desaix, "Journal de voyage," as quoted in Pigeard, *L'Armée Napoléonienne*, p. 128.

84 S.H.A.T., C^2 477.

The smoke from the burning village of Pratzen could be seen from afar

> was mounted on a splendid English horse… He galloped back and forth along the front, maintaining a loud voice amid all the sounds of battle. He yelled, swore and grumbled at the soldiers, and always positioned himself between them and the enemy.[85]

The news of the oncoming French was rushed to the Tsar and his staff, who were on the high ground of the Staré Vinohrady (literally, 'Old Vineyards') about a mile northeast of the village of Pratzen. About the time the messenger was panting up to the Imperial entourage, Alexander and the others could see for themselves what trouble was afoot. In the clearing light of day, arrayed in front of them all along the central and northern sections of the battlefield, were seen large bodies of French troops advancing eastwards. This was not what the Tsar had in mind and something had to be done at once. One of the officers on the Staré Vinohrady, Austrian Colonel Maximilian Baron Wimpfen, spoke up for all to hear, suggesting "that our most important objective must be to win the heights to the left of Pratze [village] and occupy them as rapidly as possible."[86] Neither the Tsar nor his adjutants disputed this observation, and with a nod of the head, Alexander gave Kutuzov the go-ahead to issue appropriate orders. The Russian general then directed the IV Column to split in two. Austrian FZM Johann Karl Kolowrat-Krakowsky, the 57-year-old co-commander of the IV Column, was instructed to take the Austrian infantry brigades under GM Rottermund and GM Jurczik, head south below Pratzen village, and gain the heights of the Pratzen Plateau. Meanwhile, the Russian contingent of the IV Column would commit to a defense around the village of Pratzen. These troops moved with deliberation, and many of the Austrian battalions were especially slow in their evolutions owing to the fact that they were depot formations. However, the French were far enough away that the formation change was complete before contact was made.

As Kolowrat and Miloradovich were busy deploying their battalions, the French were moving up the Pratzen. It will be remembered that Colonel Mazas at the head of the 1st Battalion of the 14th *Ligne,* along with a detachment of artillerists with two 8-pounders, had gone ahead of Thiébault and the rest of 2nd Brigade. As Mazas was approaching Pratzen, Thiébault described what followed. The Novgorod battalion that had earlier passed through the village and had gone to ground were lying in wait for the French. The Russians suddenly:

> sprang up just when Mazas, marching in line, found himself checked by the very wide ravine before the village, and poured such a murderous fire almost point-blank into him that in their surprise and alarm the entire 1st Battalion of the 14th broke and fled. How an officer with his experience of war could have fallen into such an ambush for want of sending forward some vedettes to reconnoiter the ravine and find the Russians, I do not know.[87]

Just about this time, the main body of Miloradovich's infantry came into action, led by Major-Generals G. M. Berg and S. Ya. Repninsky. The only unit opposing these Russians was the section of 8-pounders that had accompanied Mazas. Seeing two prizes waiting to be taken, the grenadier battalion of the Apsheron Musketeer Regiment, along with the three battalions of the Little Russia Grenadier Regiment—a total for all four battalions of only 1,148 combatants—charged the isolated guns. The crewmen put up a furious resistance, firing the canister-loaded

[85] Alombert-Goget and Colin, *La Campagne de 1805 en Allemagne*, XXVI, p. 531.
[86] K. k. Kriegsarchiv, F.A., *Ausführliche Relation der am 2 ten Dezember, 1805.*
[87] *The Memoirs of Baron Thiébault,* vol. 2, p. 160.

pieces as fast as they could. Each blast cut a swath through the ranks of the oncoming Russians, and for a short while, the artillerists' efforts paid off. Despite the advantages of frontage and numbers, the four Russian battalions could not get through the hail of lead in order to close with the 8-pounders. Exhorting his men for another try, Captain Morozov of the Little Russia Grenadiers (commanding in place of Colonel Denissev, who was captured at Dürenstein), led the battalions forward once again. This time the Russian attack succeeded and the artillerists were driven off.[88]

The Russians had little time to enjoy their success because Thiébault was soon on the scene to restore order. The French general recalled that:

> there was no time to waste on reprimands, so I rode forward, calling on Mazas to rally his battalion. Then, having dismounted and ordered the 36th to march on the village and force their way in, I set off, crying, *"Vive L'Empereur!"* and charging at the head of the 2nd Battalion of the 14th, which deployed [into line] as it ran, I flung myself into the ravine where my horse could not have gotten down, attacked the Russians with the bayonets, and routed them, avenging on them the losses of the 1st Battalion.[89]

While Thiébault and the 2nd Battalion of the 14th swept over one of the musketeer battalions of the Novgorod, the two battalions of the 36th *Ligne*, numbering 1,643 officers and other ranks and led by Colonel Houdar de Lamotte, quickly deployed into line.[90] Once the formation change was completed, the regimental band struck up Jean-François Le Sueur's *Marche pour grand orchestre en sol majeur*. In 1807, Le Sueur would use this same tune as the march in his opéra entitled *Le Triomphe de Trajan*, but on this December day it heralded the advance of Napoleonic infantry.[91] With martial music fortifying their souls and with Houdar de Lamotte riding up and down the lines of the battalions and inspiring their visual senses, the 36th *Ligne* launched a memorable charge. The targets for the 36th were the four battalions under Major-Generals G. M. Berg and S. Ya. Repninsky that had just captured the two 8-pounders. The Russian generals had halted their formations in order to wait for the rest of the brigade to deploy. However, the remaining five battalions under Major-General Wodniansky were to the rear when the 36th suddenly emerged from the smoke.

The 36th *Ligne* was a fine regiment. It had been crafted to be such by Graindorge during the past six years. In February 1805, following Graindorge's promotion to *général de brigade*, the command of the regiment passed to Houdar de Lamotte. Having marched from the English Channel to Moravia without engaging in any major battles, Houdar de Lamotte, along with the other officers and men of the regiment, were anxious for action. In a sudden release of emotion following months of anticipation, the 36th *Ligne* burst upon the Russians like a torrent. Within minutes, Houdar de Lamotte's men utterly shattered the Little Russia Grenadier Regiment, wounding Captain Morozov in the process. When Major-General Berg tried to rally the regiment by taking one of the colors and calling for the men to stand with him, he too was wounded and then taken prisoner.[92]

---

[88] Pravikov, *Petit historique du 10e grenadiers Petite Russe* (Morchansk, 1889), p.43.

[89] *The Memoirs of Baron Thiébault,* vol. 2, p. 160.

[90] S.H.A.T., C^2 477; *The Memoirs of Baron Thiébault,* vol. 2, p. 161.

[91] *Messe du Sacre de Napoléon 1er,* program notes by Jean Mongredien (Koch/Schwann, 1996). According to Captain Hippolyte de Mauduit, the *Triomphe de Trajan* was the preferred march of the Old Guard Grenadiers. See: Fallou, *La Garde Impériale 1804-1815,* p. 98.

[92] S.H.A.T., C^2 15 and 470.

Once the 36th finished with the Little Russia Grenadier Regiment, they routed the grenadier battalion of the Apsheron Musketeer Regiment, wounded Major-General Repninsky and recaptured the 8-pounders. The remaining musketeer battalion of the Novgorod regiment had no intention of being chewed up by the 36th *Ligne*. Seeing their comrades put to flight, the 256 officers and men of that musketeer battalion suddenly broke ranks and ran, leaving the two squadrons from the Dragoons-Regiment Erzherzog Johann #1 to cover their flight.

The fugitives of the five battalions ran northeastward, where they were met by Alexander who was riding down from the Staré Vinohrady. The Tsar rode into their midst and tried to rally the routed formations. Despite the Imperial exhortations, the substantial losses suffered earlier in the campaign, plus the sudden and violent attack by the 36th *Ligne*, had simply obliterated these units. As the fugitives ran by the Tsar, Kutuzov tried to stay their flight, only to meet with the same result. During his attempt at rallying the Little Russia Grenadier Regiment, Kutuzov was grazed in the cheek by a musket shot from a soldier of the 36th. With blood streaming from his face, Kutuzov was soon visited by Dr. James Wylie, the Tsar's physician. "Would you thank His Highness," Kutuzov told Wylie, "and assure him that I am not badly wounded." Then pointing to the advancing French under Houdar de Lamotte, Kutuzov added, "that is where we are really hurt!"[93] Failing to rally his men, Kutuzov then made off to the south towards Kolowrat's Austrians.

The Austrian contingent of the IV Column was facing west and beginning to advance, when further south on the Pratzen, another allied formation appeared. It was the infantry contingent of the second half of Langeron's II Column, whose march had been delayed due to Liechtenstein's cavalry cutting through earlier in the morning. The troops of this contingent consisted of six battalions—three from the Fanagoria Grenadier Regiment and three from the Ryazan Musketeer Regiment—under the command of Major-General I. S. M. Kamensky I. The Fanagoria Grenadiers were a veteran outfit, and the grenadier battalion of the regiment one of the army's fiercest. The three battalions were led by capable officers and knowledgeable NCOs. In contrast, the Ryazan Musketeers were mostly new troops with equally inexperienced officers and NCOs. Leading these troops, Kamensky was following Langeron's leading brigade under Olsuvev, and had yet to reach the Goldbach Brook, when he saw to the north Morand's 10th *Légère* rolling over the Pratzen. On his own initiative, Kamensky ordered his two regiments to wheel northward, and he led them up the slope to attack the French light infantry. To oppose these Russians, Morand had only two battalions totaling 1,488 officers and men, supported by three pieces of ordnance. Morand gave the order, and Pouzet deployed his two battalions of the 10th *Légère* into line. As the blue uniformed troops quickly shook out from their attack columns, they readied themselves to take on a force that had three times their number of battalions, two and one-half times their number of men and four times the number of guns.

Kamensky I

With these superior forces, Kamensky advanced his brigade in battalion columns, with the Fanagoria Grenadiers comprising the right half of his command and the Ryazan Musketeers his left half. The capable Kamensky sent his musketeer battalion on the far left end of the line to envelope the 10th *Légère* while the remainder of his command marched straight ahead. Faced with these movements, Morand and Pouzet had no choice but to have their men give ground. As the French light infantry fell back, they fired periodic volleys while the crews of the two 8-pounders and the one howitzer manhandled their pieces to the rear. Once the artillerists had retired a few paces with the guns, the crews fired their pieces in order to cover the withdrawal of the infantry. Therefore, infantry and artillery

[93] Mikhailovsky-Danilevsky, *Relation de la campagne de 1805*, p. 184.

provided covering fire for the other as they withdrew in the face of superior numbers.

These capable retrograde movements bought Morand, Pouzet and the 10th *Légère* enough time for help to arrive. The light infantrymen were about to be flanked on their right when Saint-Hilaire suddenly appeared. The division commander was riding in front of Colonel Mazas and the rallied 1st Battalion of the 14th *Ligne*. Bringing on these *fantassins* at the dead run, Saint-Hilaire inserted them on the threatened right flank of the 10th *Légère*, forcing the Russian musketeer battalion to withdraw and thereby temporarily stabilized the situation.[94]

Meanwhile, Thiébault recalled the 36th *Ligne* following their impressive charge against Berg and Repninsky. Having the 36th fall in alongside the 2nd Battalion of the 14th *Ligne,* Thiébault had these three battalions change formation from line into attack column, and then hustled the units southward towards Morand and Pouzet's hard-pressed troops. Thiébault pulled up with his command on the left side of the 10th *Légère* with the intent of counterattacking Kamensky's six battalions, when Thiébault saw:

> four regiments in close order marching towards us from the direction of Krzenowitz [due east]; that is, on our left flank and in the rear of Morand's line. On seeing them, I halted the three battalions I had with me, and, being at once rejoined by Saint-Hilaire, we examined the approaching masses through our field-glasses, but could see nothing to show that they were the enemy. Soon, however, we heard their bands, and presently an officer from them, having come within shouting distance, called out: 'Do not fire; we are Bavarians.'[95]

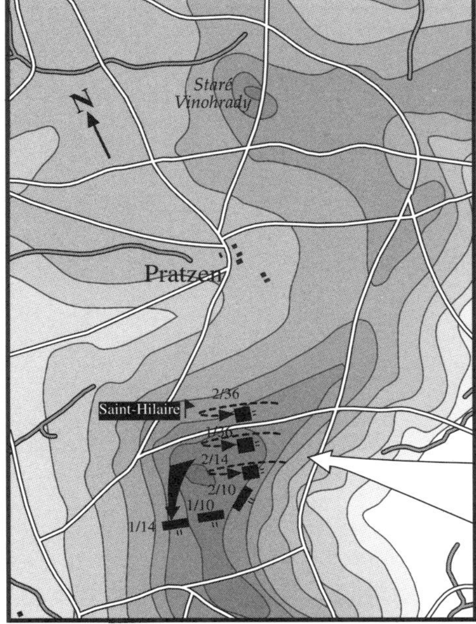

Saint-Hilaire's Division prepares for the Russian counterattack

Turning to Thiébault, Saint-Hilaire asked:

> 'What are we going to do?' 'General,' I answered, with a sharpness I could not repress, 'these Bavarians look to me very suspicious, and the officer, who did not venture close to us, looks still more so.' 'Would you run the risk of firing on the Emperor's allies?' asked Saint-Hilaire. [To which Thiébault retorted] 'And how do you suppose that allies of the Emperor are marching on us?' In fact, we could not make out either Bavarian uniforms or their commander.[96]

With the end of that conversation, both Thiébault and Saint-Hilaire noted that Marshal Soult was nowhere to be seen. Something had to be done at once. Saint-Hilaire authorized Thiébault to take precautionary measures in the event it was a ruse. Thiébault described his deployments:

> I ordered the 36th to deploy [into line] with all speed, resting on Morand's regiment so as to form the pivot about with I might maneuver, and placed the 2nd Battalion of the 14th in column on the left of my line, so as to have a mass which I could oppose, if necessary, to those advancing towards us, and a force with which I could, without disturbing my line, meet any cavalry or other troops that might try to surround us.
>
> Morand was using three guns belonging to the division, so I placed the other three between the two battalions of the 36th;

[94] *The Memoirs of Baron Thiébault,* vol. 2, p. 160.
[95] *The Memoirs of Baron Thiébault,* vol. 2, pp. 160-161.
[96] *The Memoirs of Baron Thiébault,* vol. 2, p. 161.

> but just then *chef de bataillon* Fontenay brought us six 12-pounders [the reserve artillery company of 4th Corps] by order of the Emperor, who judged how serious our position was getting. These I placed, three and three, on each wing of the 36th; and with my line thus bristling at three points, I masked my guns with squads of infantry and galloped off at full speed to reconnoiter the newcomers. Morand, who had thought quite as seriously as I of the four regiments, had taken the same step, and we met half-way between them and my line. Just as Morand came up to me, an officer belonging to those regiments was joined by one who I saw come from Kamensky's brigade. They talked for a minute, and then each went quickly back to whence he came.[97]

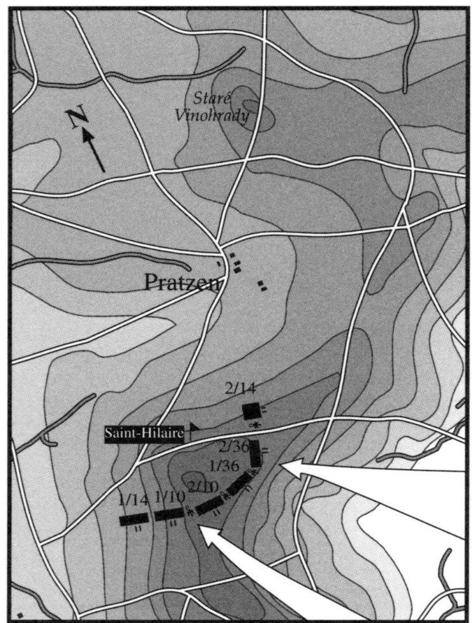

The Austrian of Jurczik and Rottermund join the Russian attack on Saint-Hilaire

With all doubts removed as to who these troops were, Morand and Thiébault readied their commands for an attack that would come from two directions. Thiébault ordered *chef de bataillon* Fontenay to double-load the 12-pounders with grape and roundshot and have them sighted to fire at a distance of 30 to 40 yards. He meanwhile instructed his infantrymen to be sure that they took aim at the enemy's cross belts and be ready to fire on the signal.

The hostile infantry approaching Thiébault were over 8,000 Austrians in two brigades under GMs Rottermund and Jurczik. Of the 16 infantry battalions that made up these brigades, almost half were depot, or the 6th, battalions of their respective regiments. The appearance and military bearing of these formations were summed up by members of the Austrian general staff:

> Judging by the composition of these forces, you would have put very little reliance on them. The men were drawn from the two extremes of military uselessness—namely invalids, and the totally untrained recruits of the 6th [depot] Battalions.[98]

The hopes of many allied generals to turn back Saint-Hilaire's two brigades on the Pratzen Plateau rested on the shoulders of these unpromising soldiers. As the whitecoated battalions under Rottermund and Jurczik approached the thinly held French line, a large number of Austrian and Russian officers, including Weyrother and Kutuzov, arrived on the scene to inspire and urge on the Austrian troops. The Austrian soldiers marched from east to west, and as they continued to move closer to Thiébault's silent line, the French general:

> let the formidable masses approach to the appointed distance, and then my nine pieces of ordnance abruptly unmasked, and my whole line poured in one of the most destructive fires ever seen... My satisfaction may be imagined when I saw every round tear square holes through these regiments until they fled in mobs of fugitives before my three battalions. I had not lost a man, and if I had had a brigade of cavalry at my disposal, not one of my assailants would have escaped.[99]

---

[97] *The Memoirs of Baron Thiébault,* vol. 2, p. 161. Fontenay was the commander of the artillery for Saint-Hilaire's Division. See S.H.A.T., C² 477; *Tableau de la Grande Armée Dernière quinzaine du mois brumaire an XIV*, "Situation au 16 brumaire an XIV (7 November 1805)," and *Journal des opérations du 4ᵉ corps.*

[98] K. k. Kriegsarchiv, F.A., *Ausführliche Relation der am 2 ten Dezember, 1805.*

[99] *The Memoirs of Baron Thiébault,* vol. 2, p. 162.

As the Austrian brigades of Rottermund and Jurczik were being obliterated by Thiébault, the Russian attack against Morand, Pouzet and the 10th *Légère* also stalled out. Unable to dislodge Morand's obstinate troops, and with their supporting Austrian attack all but vaporized, Kamensky's troops began falling back. The retrograde movement was soon seized upon by Saint-Hilaire. Wanting to capitalize on the confusion within the enemy's ranks, the division commander quickly relayed orders to his brigade generals for a counterstrike. The message was then passed along to colonels and battalion commanders, and soon the six French battalions of Morand and Thiébault were brought into a straight line heading south, where they immediately launched a charge that first collapsed the Ryazan Musketeers and then pushed back the Fanagoria Grenadiers. The French attack captured the artillery belonging to two Russian battalions that were "already harnessed [limbered]."[100]

The timely and spirited counterattack by Saint-Hilaire's regiments had momentarily cleared the southern half of the Pratzen of all allied resistance. Halting their men, Saint-Hilaire, Morand and Thiébault surveyed the landscape for much needed reinforcements if their breakthrough was to be supported. Marshal Soult was still nowhere to be seen, nor was there any sight of an Imperial aide-de-camp with news from Napoleon. In his searching the horizon for help, Thiébault remembered the chilling feeling that "it was with a certain anxiety that we became convinced of our isolation."[101] What made the position even more frightening for the French was that they had advanced beyond the canister range of their supporting artillery, which had not limbered and moved forward to support the infantry. The reason for the pieces not advancing was probably due to the deep, clay mud that made ordnance movement extremely difficult.

Out of close support range of their ordnance, the French watched Kamensky's troops rallied and reform their battalions. Soon the Fanagoria Grenadiers and the Ryazan Musketeers were joined by elements of the horribly depleted, but still game, Austrian regiments, whose formations had somehow been rallied by the superhuman efforts of Weyrother, Jurczik and other members of the Austrian brass. With these allied forces coalescing, Saint-Hilaire's unsupported French infantry were themselves now in an exposed position and ripe for destruction. The precarious situation of Saint-Hilaire's men had not gone unnoticed by the allies. Not wanting to wait for the French to receive reinforcements, the Austrians believed that:

> only a general attack with the bayonet could decide the possession of the [Pratzen] summit… To this end the Austrian infantry and Kamensky's brigade joined up, and launched an attack on a wide front. The Russians came on with their usual battle cries, but the French met them with a powerful and sustained musketry fire, which worked to deadly effect in the compact ranks of the allied infantry. The impetus of the first onrush was reduced to a slow advance, supported by musketry. However, the courage of the troops was hardened by the exhortations and personal example of the generals and all the other staff officers. Thus, the heroic Russian brigade and the attached Austrians… were led to the summit of the [Pratzen] heights.[102]

The Austrian generals must have realized the urgency of the situation, for they exposed themselves to French fire in a rare show of bravado. In this all-out effort, GM Jurczik—a Czech by birth—fell severely wounded while Weyrother had his horse shot out from under him. Of the single battalion from Reuss-Greitz

---

[100] *The Memoirs of Baron Thiébault,* vol. 2, p. 163.
[101] *The Memoirs of Baron Thiébault,* vol. 2, p. 163.
[102] K. k. Kriegsarchiv, F.A., *Ausführliche Relation der am 2 ten Dezember, 1805.*

Volkonsky

IR#55, 12 officers were wounded and captured, including two company commanders and Major Ransan, the unit commander.[103] While these Austrians were sacrificing themselves, the Russians were also putting forth a supreme effort. General-Adjutant Prince Volkonsky, Tsar Alexander's future chief of staff, led the Fanagoria Grenadiers into a hail of musket balls. Three times the mitre-wearing fusiliers and grenadiers of Fanagoria charged, only to be repulsed by the equally determined French, who "made a dreadful carnage in the compact ranks of the Russians."[104]

However, the weight of the allied attack was forcing Saint-Hilaire and his brigadier generals to conduct a slow, fighting withdrawal. By giving ground towards their guns, the French were also buying more time between enemy assaults. Thiébault said that every time he and Morand met after Austerlitz, they always recalled their tenuous situation at the epic battle. "I have seen plenty of fighting," Morand would say, "and I was lucky enough since the time of the Army of Egypt to be present at all the great battles fought by the Emperor; but I never saw anything like our position there."[105] The condition of the division was perhaps best reflected by *chef de batallion* Perrier of the 36th *Ligne.* His tunic had been blown off and his shredded shirt was soaked red with blood; however, he was wild with rage, riding up and down the lines of his battalion waving his sword and encouraging his men. Finally, two more musket balls pierced his body and he fell to the ground; he was lucky to survive.[106] Believing that the regiment had retreated far enough, *adjudant-major* Labadie of the 36th *Ligne* grabbed the eagle and standard of one of the battalions, and waving it above his head, shouted: "Soldiers! Here is your line of battle!"[107] Two company commanders, Captains Raoul and Duhil, were armed with muskets and stood alongside Labadie to meet the fury of the allied assault. For the next 20 minutes, the incessant series of allied attacks failed to dislodge Saint-Hilaire's determined men.[108] The French division commander then called on Morand, Thiébault and the regimental colonels to discuss their options. Once all these senior officers had reported to Saint-Hilaire, the general said: "This is becoming unbearable, and I propose, gentlemen, that we should take up some position to our rear which we can defend."[109] The division commander had barely finished the sentence, when Colonel Pouzet of the 10th *Légère*, who was behind the brigade commanders, dug his spurs into his horse, sprang in between Morand and Thiébault, and blurted out:

> 'Retire, general? If we take one more pace to the rear, we are done for. There is only one way to get out of this with honor, and that is, to put our heads down and go at everything in front of us; and, above all, not allow the enemy time to count our numbers.'[110]

Saint-Hilaire yielded to the opinion of the old drill-master, and sending his officers back to their commands, told them to ready their battalions for a counterstrike.

However, before the French could get moving, the Ryazan Musketeers and the Fanagoria Grenadiers returned with another series of furious assaults. Each

---

[103] K. k. Kriegsarchiv, F.A., *Ausführliche Relation der am 2 ten Dezember, 1805;* Stutterheim, *A Detailed Account of the Battle of Austerlitz*, pp. 105-106.
[104] Stutterheim, *A Detailed Account of the Battle of Austerlitz*, p. 105.
[105] *The Memoirs of Baron Thiébault,* vol. 2, p. 164.
[106] S.H.A.T., C² 16 and 470; Martinien, *Tableaux des Officiers Tués et Blessés*, p. 202.
[107] S.H.A.T., *Journal des opérations du 4ᵉ corps.*
[108] *The Memoirs of Baron Thiébault,* vol. 2, p. 164.
[109] *The Memoirs of Baron Thiébault,* vol. 2, p. 164.
[110] *The Memoirs of Baron Thiébault,* vol. 2, p. 164.

regiment delivered its attack separate from the other as the Russians hurled themselves against Saint-Hilaire's men for another half hour.[111] During these repeated charges and advances by fire, Colonel Mazas of the 14th *Ligne* was killed, while Saint-Hilaire, Morand, and Colonel Houdar de Lamotte of the 36th *Ligne* were all wounded, and Thiébault had two horses shot out from under him. Of the six French battalion commanders, three were wounded while Simonin of the 10th *Légère* was killed. The carnage swept through the company ranks as well. Twenty one of the 54 company commanders were rendered *hors de combat.*[112] Despite the blood-letting, the stubborn French battalions refused to break. Finally, with their supply of small arms ammunition all but exhausted and with a significant number of their men down, Kamensky's men had shot their bolt. With the fire from the Russian formations slacking off noticeably, and with their own supply of cartridges almost out, the French officers sensed that the time was right to order their own line to sweep forward in a counterattack. Colonel Pouzet quickly rode over to Saint-Hilaire:

"General, we must advance with the bayonet, or we are lost."

"Yes—forward!" responded Saint Hilaire.[113]

With drums and trumpets sounding the advance, Saint-Hilaire's line swept forward. The six Russian battalions were not about to stand if they had nothing to shoot; most of those who were not wounded broke ranks and ran at the approach of Saint-Hilaire's formations. Kamensky, however, refused to retreat and was captured along with six guns belonging to three of his battalions. In this counterthrust, *chasseur* Corporal Jacot and *carabinier* Charpentier, both of the 10th *Légère*, each captured a flag of the Ryazan Musketeers, thus earning promotions as well as being awarded the *Legion d'Honneur.*[114]

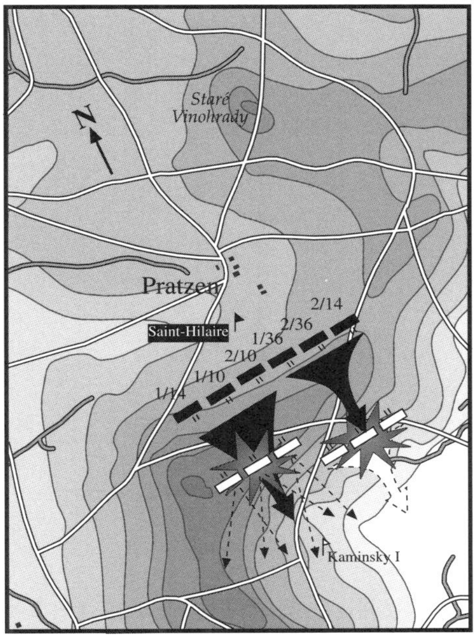

Finally, the crisis and denouement of the struggle between these opposing infantry in this mini-battle on the southern half of the Pratzen graphically reflects the brutality of war. Every time the French had encountered the Russian infantry prior to Austerlitz at the combats of Amstetten, Dürenstein and Schöngrabern, the Tsarist soldiers had displayed a consistent tendency not to surrender if they were still physically capable of resistance. Time and again during the battles earlier in the campaign, wounded Russians that had been passed over and presumed by the French to conduct themselves as prisoners of war in accordance with the traditional European code of honor, would almost always take up arms and start firing into the back of the unsuspecting French. Such eastern barbarity, no doubt a symptom of many bitter wars against the ruthless Turks, prompted the strongest possible countermeasures by the officers and men of the *Grande Armée*. Prior to Austerlitz, it was ordered that only those Russian soldiers asking for quarter were to be spared. Therefore, whenever Morand and Thiébault's battalions advanced against the greencoated adversaries, the French made sure that no wounded Russians remained alive behind their lines. The final counterattack delivered by Saint-Hilaire's *fantassins* was especially savage; other than for the brigade commander, no quarter was given to *any* member of the Ryazan Musketeers nor to most of the Fanagoria Grenadiers. When the Battle of Austerlitz was over, not a single Russian prisoner from the Ryazan Musketeers was in French hands.[115]

As savage and heroic as Saint-Hilaire's men had been, the Russians under Kamensky had fought with near-equal courage and tenacity. Thiébault recalled that: "In those terrible shocks, whole battalions [*sic*] of Russians were killed without

Saint-Hilaire's division wins the Pratzen heights

[111] *The Memoirs of Baron Thiébault,* vol. 2, p. 165.

[112] S.H.A.T., C^2 16 and 470; Note that Martinien, *Tableaux des Officiers Tués et Blessés*, pp. 148, 202 and 412 lists only 18 company commanders killed or wounded.

[113] S.H.A.T., *Journal des opérations du 4e corps.*

[114] S.H.A.T., *Historique du 10e régiment d'infanterie légère.*

[115] S.H.A.T., C^2 15 and 470.

a man leaving his rank, and their corpses lay in the same alignment as their parent battalions."[116] Undoubtedly, the heavy casualties suffered by the two Russian regiments had given Thiébault the impression of whole battalions disintegrating. Of the 3,800 officers and men of the Ryazan Musketeers and the Fanagoria Grenadiers that started the battle, almost 1,200—or 31%—spilled their blood into the Moravian earth. Indeed, these six Russian battalions—formations that had missed the earlier phase of the campaign—only broke when they no longer had the ammunition to continue the fight. The Ryazan Musketeers and Fanagoria Grenadiers did honor to their names, but simply did not have the means to continue the struggle against the six superbly led French battalions that they faced.

While the sounds of battle coming from the Pratzen intermingled with the noise from the rest of the field, making it hard for anyone to determine by hearing alone exactly what was going on, one of Kamensky's aides found Langeron, and told the column commander that the French were on the high ground. Langeron at once left his position in front of Sokolnitz and rode towards the plateau, reaching Kamensky's regiments while they were still hotly engaged with Saint-Hilaire's men. Langeron found Kamensky's battalions replying to the scourge of French musketry "with a slow and inaccurate fire,"[117] and the column commander remembered that his:

> troops had fought for almost two hours, which is all the more admirable when you consider that they were unaccustomed to warfare, that they had been attacked by surprise in the rear, and that they must have been shrinking from the noise of the cannon, which many of them must have heard for the first time.[118]

Recognizing that reinforcements for Kamensky's battalions were needed at once, Langeron rode back down to the Goldbach. On the east side of the brook he found the two unengaged musketeer battalions of the Kursk Musketeer Regiment. Ordering these two formations to follow him, Langeron marched the men up the south slope of the Pratzen, arriving after Kamensky's regiments had finally broken. Without any other supporting troops, the two musketeer battalions of Kursk—about 1,050 officers and men—immediately attracted the attention of not only Saint-Hilaire, but also a newly arrived brigade of 4th Corps.

The only uncommitted infantry of Legrand's 3rd Infantry Division of Soult's corps was the 3rd Brigade under *général de brigade* Victor Levasseur. The 33-year-old Levasseur had given up his study of medicine to enter the army as one of Volunteers of 1792. A protégé of the famous Republican General Kléber, Levasseur had risen quickly in the turbulent wars of the French Revolution, becoming a *général de brigade* in 1800. Levasseur missed most of the encampment of Boulogne, arriving at Saint-Omer in March 1805. However, when the campaign began, Levasseur was given command of the brigade which at that time consisted of 18th *Ligne* and 75th *Ligne* and the *Tirailleurs corses*. The two *ligne* regiments, each with two battalions, had crossed the Rhine in late September with 1,604 and 1,895 respectively, present and under arms.[119] On 7 November, the 18th numbered 1,507 with the colors, while the 75th had 1,532.[120] At Austerlitz, the 18th *Ligne* brought 1,402 officers and men onto the field, while the 75th *Ligne*, owing to the return to

[116] *The Memoirs of Baron Thiébault,* vol. 2, p. 165.
[117] Duffy, *Austerlitz,* p. 119.
[118] Alombert-Goget and Colin, *La Campagne de 1805 en Allemagne*, XXVI, p. 529.
[119] S.H.A.T., C^2 470.
[120] S.H.A.T., *Tableau de la Grande Armée Dernière quinzaine du mois brumaire an XIV*, "Situation au 16 brumaire an XIV (7 November 1805)."

ranks of many previously detached, had 1,688 with the eagles.[121] The *Tirailleurs corses,* commanded by Colonel Philippe-Antoine Ornano, had 427 officers and other ranks at Austerlitz, down from the 766 that crossed the Rhine and the 635 that were in ranks on 7 November.[122] However, before the great battle, the *Tirailleurs corses* were transferred to the 1st Brigade and served along side the *Tirailleurs du Pô* under the orders of Merle.

Ornano, shown here later in the Empire in the uniform of a général de division

Of the men who commanded the regiments in Levasseur's brigade, Colonel Jean-Baptiste-Ambroise Ravier of the 18th *Ligne* struck the most imposing figure. Astride his brown horse *"Foudre,"* Ravier—like the other members of the *Grande Armée*—wore his dress uniform for battle, replete with gold laced bicorne topped by a red, white and blue plume. The colonel, as well as his officers and men, had a particular fondness for the national-colored plumes; all officers of company grade or higher, as well as the regiment's musicians, sported the tricolor attachments.

Perhaps it was the 18th's exposure to the American Continental Army that fueled its fascination with *Liberté, Egalité et Fraternité*, and the red, white and blue. Created as the *Régiment Gatenois* in 1776, their distinguished conduct under Rochambeau during the American Revolution earned them a name change to *Royal-Auvergne*. Whatever the reason may be, the 18th *Ligne* was a striking and unmistakable regiment with their sea of national color plumes. Even the regimental band's "Jingling Johnny" had one of these attachments on top of his instrument.[123] The waves of red, white and blue plumes were eminently suitable to the 18th—they were one of the celebrated regiments of Bonaparte's *Armée d'Italie*, and had won further glory in the Egyptian campaign.

Like the 18th *Ligne*, the 75th had won fame at Caldiero in Bonaparte's First Italian Campaign of 1796-97. In 1805, the 75th *Ligne* was commanded by Colonel François L'Huillier de Hoff. One of the older colonels in the *Grande Armée*, L'Huillier was 46 years of age when he led his men onto the field of Austerlitz. He had been a soldier in the Royal Army before the Revolution, and had been the colonel of the 75th since 1800, and therefore present in the camp of Saint-Omer from 1803 until the beginning of the 1805 war.[124] As the 75th marched into action, L'Huillier's 24 regimental bandsmen, clothed in scarlet coats, white waistcoats, blue pants and all trimmed in gold lace, had been converged with the 24 band members of the 18th, who sported dark blue coats with light blue facings and cuffs, and their bicornes topped with red, white and blue plumes. Jacques Ledraps, the 26-year-old Drum Major of the 75th, led the massed brigade bands up the Pratzen as they played Napoleonic France's defining march, Joseph David Buhl's *"La Victoire est à nous."*[125]

Levasseur's brigade hit the Kursk Musketeers in the flank while Saint-Hilaire's brigades smashed into the Russians along their front. As a result of this deadly combined attack, the two battalions of the Kursk Musketeers were crushed within minutes. Of the 1,050 officers and men that comprised these two battalions, more than two-thirds were cut down by the French assault, and the Russians lost all four of their colors, as well as all four pieces that composed their battalion ordnance. One of the colors was captured by fusilier Noblé of the 75th *Ligne* after he single-handedly bayoneted six Russians![126]

---

[121] S.H.A.T., C² 477.

[122] S.H.A.T., C² 470; *Tableau de la Grande Armée Dernière quinzaine du mois brumaire an XIV*, "Situation au 16 brumaire an XIV (7 November 1805)," and C² 477.

[123] S.H.A.T., *Journal des opérations du 4ᵉ corps;* Commandant E.-L. Buocquoy, *L'Infanterie de Ligne et L'Infanterie Légère* (Paris, 1979), pp. 204-207.

[124] Six, *Dictionnaire biographique*, vol. 2, p. 122.

[125] S.H.A.T., *Journal des opérations du 4ᵉ corps.*

[126] S.H.A.T., C² 20.

Besides the white standard carried by the grenadier battalion, the Podolia Musketeers lost four other standards at Austerlitz, like this pink and white one.

As the terror-stricken survivors of the two Kursk Musketeer battalions were fleeing before their assailants, the Podolia Musketeer Regiment from Prebyshevsky's III Column arrived on the scene. This regiment had suffered horribly during the retreat from Braunau, and brought only 509 officers and other ranks onto the field in its three battalions. The reduced formations of the Podolia regiment were no match for Levasseur's four battalions that numbered more than six times that of the Russians. Levasseur wasted no time in taking full advantage of the opportunity before him. Ordering a brigade charge, the French overwhelmed the Podolia Musketeers, captured the regiment's white color from the grenadier battalion, and pushed the survivors back down the Pratzen to the walls of the pheasantry. By the time the Podolia survivors jumped over the wall and ran into the preserve, some 250 officers and men—almost half of those that had gone into action—had been either killed or wounded.[127]

Hanging back from this bloodletting, Langeron had escaped injury, while the slightly wounded Kutuzov was about to leave the battle. With the breaking of the last Russian battalions on the lower Pratzen, Kutuzov decided to retire with the survivors of Kamensky's brigade, unable to see what transpired thereafter "since my location for the rest of that day did not permit me to personally see what was happening on the field."[128]

Meanwhile, riding back down the slope towards Sokolnitz, Langeron could see no more reserves available; the rest of his and Prebyshevsky's commands were already faced off against the French west of Sokolnitz village and the castle. Langeron therefore decided to head south in search of Buxhöwden, to ask him what they should do. Finding Buxhöwden still riveted to the hill east of Tellnitz that had long ago been cleared by the troops of Dokhturov's I Column, Langeron described the appearance of his superior:

> His face was flushed, and it seemed to me that he was [drunk and] no longer in possession of his faculties. I told him what had happened on the Pratzen, and that we had been turned and about to be surrounded by the enemy. He replied rather rudely: 'My dear general, you appear to see enemies all over the place.' I was disrespectful enough to answer: 'And you, *monsieur le comte*, are in no state to see the enemy anywhere!'[129]

Buxhöwden

Buxhöwden's refusal to listen to Langeron, or to find out what was going on and give orders accordingly, is partial proof of his profound contempt for Langeron, who Buxhöwden saw as an *émigré* poltroon. By choosing to claim martial indignation and do nothing, Buxhöwden doomed the remainder of the I, II and III Columns to certain destruction. With the Pratzen irreversibly lost, along with most of the battalion artillery of Langeron's II Column, and with the French swinging down from the north to envelope the allied troops south and west of the plateau, the rest of Buxhöwden's command was now in a trap whose door would continue to close tighter with each passing minute.

As Saint-Hilaire was clearing the Pratzen plateau south of the village of Pratzen, Soult's remaining infantry division was apparently conquering the northern end of the heights, including the vine-covered spur known as the Staré Vinohrady. These Frenchmen were the 2nd Infantry Division of 4th Corps, commanded by Dominique-Joseph-René Vandamme. A highly intelligent, quick-witted and energetic officer of considerable merit, the 35-year-old Vandamme had received much of his training from the capable infantry generals Gouvion-Saint-Cyr and

---

[127] S.H.A.T., *Journal des opérations du 4e corps.*

[128] *Kutuzov. Sbornik*, vol. 2, p. 265.

[129] Alombert-Goget and Colin, *La Campagne de 1805 en Allemagne*, XXVII, p. 381.

Vandamme

Duhèsme. Vandamme was also a devoted follower of Napoleon and a strict disciplinarian who took great pains to care for his men. What's more, Vandamme wanted and demanded that his officers and men hate the enemies of France as much as he did. This is no better illustrated than the general's comment made on 4 floréal an XII (24 April 1804):

> Discipline and the quick execution of orders on the battlefield are necessary, but I demand more. All members of my division must have instilled in them a sense of savage brutality that will harden them in combat, save their lives and destroy the enemies of our country.[130]

During the two year encampment of Boulogne, Vandamme built his killing machine with several fine regiments.

The single regiment that formed the 1st Brigade of Vandamme's Division was the 24th *Légère* under Colonel Bernard PouCourailly. A 30-year-old former battalion commander in the *Garde des Consuls*, Pourailly had crossed the Rhine with 1,504 people in the regiment's two battalions.[131] By 7 November, the 24th *Légère* fielded 1,310 officers and men under arms, and brought 1,291 onto the field at Austerlitz.[132] The brigade commander of the 24th *Légère* was 44-year-old *général de brigade* Joseph-François-Ignace-Maximilien Schiner. Schiner had started his military career as a sous-lieutenant in the *Régiment suisse de Courten* in 1780. He distinguished himself throughout the Revolutionary wars, and had received multiple wounds at Salzburg in 1800, after which he was promoted to général de brigade. Present throughout the Channel encampments, Schiner and was transferred to Vandamme's command in June, 1805.[133]

Two regiments formed the 2nd Brigade of Vandamme's Division—the 4th *Ligne* and the 28th *Ligne*. The 4th was another one of the regiments from Bonaparte's *Armée d'Italie,* having crossed the bridge with the young general at Arcole. Although the colonelcy of the 4th *Ligne* belonged to Napoleon's older brother, Joseph, the regiment was commanded in the field in 1805 by Joseph's second in command, Major Auguste-Julien Bigarré. An officer of competence, Bigarré rose slowly in rank from a Volunteer of 1791 to a company commander in the *Garde des Consuls* by 1802. Promoted to major, the 30-year-old Bigarré joined the 4th *Ligne* in the camp of Saint-Omer in February 1805. During the six months that followed, Bigarré seemed to make substantial progress in his own training. Following an inspection in early August, the outspoken Vandamme paid the major a back-handed compliment by describing him as: "a capable officer who is finding out what it is like to command more than a company of ceremonial troops."[134] When the 4th crossed the Rhine in late September, the two battalions numbered 1,889 officers and other ranks under arms.[135] On 7 November, those present with the colors had only dropped slightly to 1,822.[136] When Bigarré led the 4th *Ligne* up the slopes of the Pratzen, there were 1,658 officers and other ranks with the eagles.[137]

Bigarré

[130] S.H.A.T., C[2] 192.
[131] S.H.A.T., C[2] 470.
[132] S.H.A.T., *Tableau de la Grande Armée Dernière quinzaine du mois brumaire an XIV*, "Situation au 16 brumaire an XIV (7 November 1805)," and C[2] 477.
[133] Six, *Dictionnaire biographique*, vol. 2, pp. 434-435.
[134] S.H.A.T., C[2] 459.
[135] S.H.A.T., C[2] 470.
[136] S.H.A.T., *Tableau de la Grande Armée Dernière quinzaine du mois brumaire an XIV*, "Situation au 16 brumaire an XIV (7 November 1805)."
[137] S.H.A.T., C[2] 477.

The unit that formed part of the same brigade with the 4th was 28th *Ligne*, commanded by 46-year-old Colonel Jean-Georges Edighoffen. Like many other regimental commanders under Vandamme, Edighoffen's climb up the professional ladder had taken him through the wars of the Revolution and into the ranks of the *Garde des Consuls*. After serving a year as a *chef de bataillon* in the prestigious regiment, Edighoffen was promoted to colonel of the 28th *Ligne* and reported to the camp of Saint-Omer in March 1804.[138] Bonaparte selected Edighoffen to command a regiment that had covered itself with glory in two epic battles of 1800. Following Marengo, the First Consul said: "I do not know braver men than these of the 28th. In reward, they will be in the front line in the next battle." Almost six months later on 3 December at the Battle of Hohenlinden, the 28th was instrumental in the French victory, repulsing waves of Austrian cavalry and infantry. These heroics caused Bonaparte to say: "I will never forget the service that the brave 28th has rendered to the Homeland."[139] As they crossed the Rhine on 26 September, the two battalions of the 28th *Ligne* numbered 1,730 people present and under arms;[140] on 7 November, the regiment had 1,636 combatants with the colors, and Edighoffen brought with him some 1,599 onto the field at Austerlitz.[141]

The brigadier general in command of the 2nd Brigade of Vandamme's Division was Claude-François Férey. Thirty-four-years-old at the time of Austerlitz, Férey was an accomplished light infantry officer, having served throughout the wars of the Revolution, rising to command the 24th *demi-brigade légère* in the famed 1800 Marengo campaign. Like so many other regimental commanders of note, Férey was elevated to *général de brigade* and ordered to report to the camp of Saint-Omer in August 1803. During the next two years, Férey made favorable impressions on his peers. Colonel Edighoffen described Férey as "a strict, but fair superior officer, who demands excellence, which is nothing more than what he himself is willing to give." The normally sharp-tongued Vandamme complimented Férey "as an officer of high merit, who handles his brigade with smoothness."[142]

Like the 2nd Brigade, the 3rd Brigade of Vandamme's Division consisted of two regiments of *ligne* infantry. Numerically, the first regiment of the brigade was the 46th *Ligne*. Commanded by Colonel Guillaume Latrille de Lorencez, the 32-year-old veteran of the Revolutionary wars and protégé of Marshal Augereau, Latrille de Lorencez took command of the regiment in February 1805. Like the other regiments of the division, the 46th fielded two war battalions for the 1805 campaign. When the 46th *Ligne* crossed the Rhine, the total number of persons with the colors numbered 1,733.[143] On 7 November, the number present with the eagles had shrunk to 1,559, and the regiment fought at Austerlitz with 1,350 officers and other ranks.[144] The sappers, musicians and other members of the regiment's so-called 'head of the column' sported the typical dark blue national coat with sky-blue collars, cuffs and facings trimmed in scarlet. Wearing their dress uniforms, the sappers, along with the drummers of the grenadier companies, had scarlet plumes, with sky-blue tips. As the regiment ascended the Pratzen, Latrille de Lorencez remembered that "the brilliant plumes of the grenadiers and the band members contrasted sharply against the almost lifeless ground of the Moravian countryside."[145]

---

[138] Six, *Dictionnaire biographique*, vol. 1, pp. 421-422.

[139] S.H.A.T., copy of Simond, *Historique du 28e régiment d'infanterie* (Rouen, 1889).

[140] S.H.A.T., C^2 470.

[141] S.H.A.T., *Tableau de la Grande Armée Dernière quinzaine du mois brumaire an XIV*, "Situation au 16 brumaire an XIV (7 November 1805)," and C^2 477.

[142] S.H.A.T., C^2 459.

[143] S.H.A.T., C^2 470.

[144] S.H.A.T., *Tableau de la Grande Armée Dernière quinzaine du mois brumaire an XIV*, "Situation au 16 brumaire an XIV (7 November 1805)," and C^2 477.

[145] S.H.A.T., C^2 19.

Alongside the band of the 46th were another, larger group of musicians wearing dark blue coats trimmed in yellow collars, cuffs, lapels and epaulettes. The 36 members of this band were from one of the most celebrated regiments in French service—the 57th *Ligne*. Present with the *Armée d'Italie* during Bonaparte's First Italian Campaign in 1796-97, then with the *Armée du Rhin* in 1800, the 57th was envied throughout the army for its greatly distinguished combat record. At La Favorite, the 57th decisively threw back the repeated assaults of 7,000 Austrian infantry and a regiment of hussars. At Ancône, the regiment had attacked and defeated a much larger enemy force, capturing more than 2,000 Austrians. At Moskirch, the 57th withstood a torrent of lead to stop superior numbers of the enemy, while at Höhenlinden, the regiment defeated a numerically superior force of Hungarians, thus insuring the French victory. So ferocious was the spirit of the regiment, and so tenacious was their fighting technique, that *both* the French and the Austrian armies referred to the 57th as "*La Terrible!*"[146]

The colonel of this lionized regiment was Jean-Pierre-Antoine Rey, a 38-year-old career soldier that had fought in Bonaparte's *Armée d'Italie,* and who had greatly distinguished himself in the ranks of the 51st *demi-brigade de bataille* at the Battle of Arcole. It was during that immortal crossing of the Arcole bridge, when Bonaparte seized the colors of the 51st and led the men across the span, that Rey's company was the first to rush across the river and break the Austrians defending the opposite bank. Rey's heroics of that moment were never lost on Napoleon. After Rey had proven himself on other battlefields and in administrative duties under Davout, Napoleon believed that Rey had been properly steeled to command the army's best regiment. In August 1803, Rey was promoted to colonel of the renowned 57th.[147] The regiment's two battalions had crossed the Rhine in late September with 1,854 people present and under arms.[148] By 7 November, that number had been reduced by only 83.[149] When the 57th marched up the Pratzen on 2 December, there were 1,743 battle-hardened souls in ranks.[150]

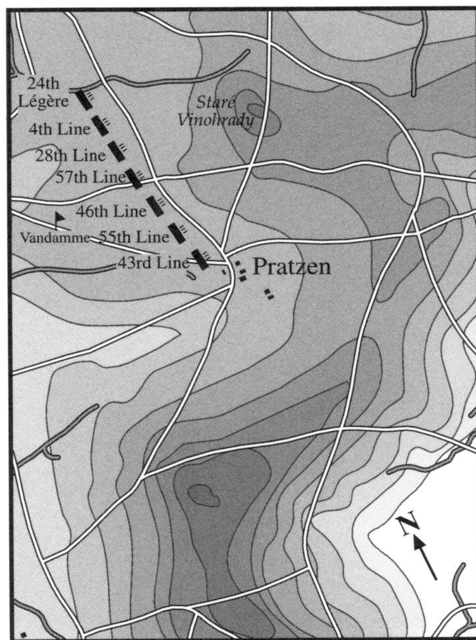

The advance of Vandamme's division

The *général de brigade* entrusted to command the excellent regiments of Vandamme's 3rd Brigade was Jacques-Lazare de Savettier de Candras. Rising in rank from a Volunteer of 1792 to *chef de bataillon* in the 4th *demi-brigade de bataille* in early 1796, Candras served in Augereau's Division during Bonaparte's First Italian Campaign. Wounded twice in a heroic but failed attempt to dislodge the Austrians at Caldiero on 11 November, Candras had made a lasting impression on Bonaparte. Following service in the *Armée du Rhin* during the 1800 campaign, Napoleon selected the brave officer he had seen at Caldiero to command one of Vandamme's brigades in the camp of Saint-Omer.[151]

Crossing the Bosenitz Brook and ascending the broad Pratzen Plateau, and with his staff members returning to report that there were two, widely separated bodies of enemy troops before them on the heights, Vandamme decided to expand his division's frontage. He ordered *général de brigade* Schiner to take his 24th *Légère* and occupy the left of the division's line. *Général de brigade* Férey, with the 4th and 28th *Ligne*, would be next in line from left to right, with *général de brigade* Candras and the 57th and 46th continuing the sequence. Finally, 39-year-old *général de brigade* Louis-Prix Varé, attached from Saint-Hilaire's Division, completed Vandamme's enlarged command by forming the right of the line with

---

[146] The title was first given to the 57th by Bonaparte in 1797.
[147] Six, *Dictionnaire biographique*, vol. 2, pp. 361-362.
[148] S.H.A.T., C² 470.
[149] S.H.A.T., *Tableau de la Grande Armée Dernière quinzaine du mois brumaire an XIV*, "Situation au 16 brumaire an XIV (7 November 1805)."
[150] S.H.A.T., C² 477.
[151] Six, *Dictionnaire biographique*, vol. 1, p. 188.

his two regiments—the 55th and 43rd *Ligne*. Varé had been a dragoon in the old Royalist army before his transfer and promotion to *sous-lieutenant* in the *Garde Nationale de Versailles* in 1789. With the coming of the Revolution, Varé joined the Republicans and was named as one of the battalion commanders of the Volunteers of 1791. He ably served as *chef de brigade* (regimental commander) of the 43rd and then the 54th *demi-brigade de bataille* from 1794 through 1803.[152] Augereau thought highly of Varé, describing him as "intelligent and extremely competent."[153] Augereau employed him in the Channel encampment of Bayonne and Brest. Once the 1805 campaign was underway, and with Saint-Hilaire needing another brigade general, Varé was ordered to leave his command under Desjardin in Augereau's 7th Corps and report for duty with Saint-Hilaire. On the morning of Austerlitz, with Varé's additional units operating with his division, Vandamme brought all his regiments into line abreast and rode in front of these 14 battalions. As the reinforced division rolled forward, the division's foot artillery marched with the right half of the command. A full company of six pieces—two 8-pounders, two 4-pounders and two 6-inch howitzers—moved between the 57th and the 46th, while another detachment manning two 8-pounders was between the 46th and the 55th *Ligne*.

With these dispositions completed, Vandamme's 2nd Infantry Division passed to the north of the village of Pratzen, but only after the 55th on the end of the line had encountered a battalion of the 7th *Jaeger* that Prebyshevshy had dropped off to cover his right flank; the greencoated infantry withdrew posthaste when the 55th delivered volley fire by battalions. Following this brief delay, the division marched another half mile before coming upon the only two cohesive bodies of allied troops then occupying the northern half of the Pratzen. These were: the yet to be engaged five battalions of Russians from the IV Column under Miloradovich holding the area south of the Staré Vinohrady; and the northern-most group consisting of all six battalions of the Salzburg IR#23, complete with battalion artillery and sitting on the Staré Vinohrady. The whitecoated regiment with red facings had earlier occupied the far right of Kolowrat's line when it had advanced against Thiébault's brigade. Since these battalions overlapped the northern end of Thiébault's French, they barely escaped the carnage visited upon the other formations in that doomed attack. When the remainder of the Austrians vanished in front of Thiébault, Salzburg IR#23 was withdrawn northward to the high ground, there deployed among the vineyards and readied to meet the French onslaught.

However, before Schiner's and Férey's brigades could get into position to attack the Austrians holding the Staré Vinohrady, Candras' brigade came upon the remaining Russians of IV Column. Major-General Wodniansky was on horseback in front of five battalions that comprised his remaining command. Except for the grenadiers of Novgorod Musketeer Regiment who were almost too few to bother counting, the other formations of the brigade had previously been shattered by the charge of Houdar de Lamotte's 36th *Ligne* in and around the village of Pratzen. Furthermore, the five battalions that Wodniansky had ready for action were formations that had suffered very heavy losses from the earlier marches and battles of the campaign. They had been with Kutuzov since August, and their strengths reflected the heavy strategic consumption and battle casualties that were common among the regiments of Kutuzov's army. This is no better illustrated than in the strengths of the grenadier battalion from the Novgorod Musketeers, and one musketeer battalion from the Apsheron Musketeers, numbering a mere 256 and 137 effectives, respectively! Finally, all three battalions of the Smolensk Musketeer Regiment brought onto the field of Austerlitz a total of 685 officers and other

[152] Six, *Dictionnaire biographique*, vol. 2, p. 532.
[153] S.H.A.T., C[2] 214.

ranks.[154] Therefore, with 1,078 combatants supported by 10 battalion guns, Wodniansky faced an attack by Candras' four superb French battalions numbering 3,093 effectives, backed up by eight pieces of ordnance.

Candras' brigade came on "with every battalion deployed [in line of battle], with the 46th on the right and the 57th to their left." Once the frontage and strength of Wodniansky's Russians had been determined by French scouts, the 57th *Ligne* halted as "six pieces of the division's artillery unlimbered and opened a covering fire on the Russian line." Meanwhile, "the 46th moved in echelon to the right with the section of 8-pounders still limbered and moving with them."[155] The maneuver by Latrille de Lorencez's regiment was intended to envelop and turn the Russian line, and as they came closer to the greencoated formations, they attracted the full attention of every Russian gun that could be brought to bear. Before moving within small arms fire range of the Russians, Latrille de Lorencez "redirected the battalions to bring them once again into line abreast."[156] Once this was accomplished and the two French battalions came within musket range, the Russian line erupted with both canister fire and small arms fire. Scores of men were dropping from each battalion of the 46th as Colonel Latrille de Lorencez pushed his men closer and closer to the enemy line. The advance continued:

> until we were almost 60 paces from the enemy line. Once there the command was given, the two [8-pounder] cannon were unlimbered, and together with leveled muskets of my regiment, we delivered a devastating fire that consumed the Russians. With a shout of '*Vive l'Empereur!*' the regiment resumed the advance and passed over the débris of the enemy.[157]

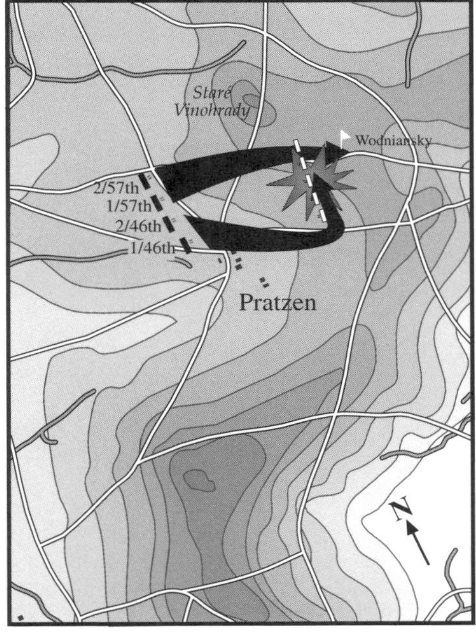

Wodniansky's command is overwhelmed

The charge of the 46th was seconded by an attack from the 57th as well. Rey's battalions took a few rounds from the Russian battalion artillery before the gunners fled as their parent battalions broke and ran in order to avoid the closing nutcracker of the 46th and 57th *Ligne*. The disciplined and highly coordinated French regiments had simply been too much for Wodniansky's smaller command. The outnumbered and outmatched Russians collapsed like a house of cards, managing to save their flags but leaving most of their guns to the onrushing French. The 46th and 57th pursued as fast as they could, not offering quarter to any Russian that they came upon. Like the mini-battle between Saint-Hilaire's men and Kamensky's brigade, Vandamme's French were not interested in taking prisoners from Wodniansky's formations; the wounded Russians were bayoneted on the spot.

With the quick elimination of Wodniansky's five weak battalions of Russians, the only allied troops still clinging to the Pratzen were the six Austrian battalions of the Salzburg IR#23 standing motionless on the Staré Vinohrady. As the left half of Vandamme's Division approached this high ground, the French were opposed by 3,044 members and 12 battalion guns of the Salzburg IR#23, who were all that remained of Miloradovich and Kolowrat's joint command. This was less than 25% of the 12,099 soldiers and just about 15% of the 76 pieces of ordnance that only three hours earlier had moved to the attack.

The apparent strength of the Austrian regiment and the potentially formidable position which it occupied did not deter Colonel Pourailly from testing the mettle of the opposition. The colonel deployed four companies of each battalion of the

---

[154] Maksoutov, *Historique du 25ᵉ régiment d'infanterie Smolensk [Musketeers]* (Saint Petersburg, 1901).
[155] S.H.A.T., C² 21.
[156] S.H.A.T., C² 21.
[157] S.H.A.T., C² 21.

24th *Légère* as *tirailleurs* and went straight for the Austrians. The French skirmishers took advantage of terrain and worked their way to within 80 paces of the Austrian line, peppering the whitecoated formations with musketry. Under this masking fire, the other companies of the 24th were fed into the fight, each breaking down into *tirailleurs* and working their way around each flank of the Austrian line. For more than half an hour, the exchange of musketry continued. The *tirailleurs* of the 24th *Légère* fired into the formed ranks of Salzburg IR#23, who volley fired back against the swarms of individual targets in blue. To make matters worse, the inexperienced commander of the Austrian regiment had deployed his battalions on the geographical crest of the Staré Vinohrady rather than slightly forward on the military crest. As a result, the faulty placement made it extremely difficult for the Austrians to punish Pourailly's units, while affording the French *tirailleurs* every advantage of the vine entangled ground. Even with the benefit of cover, the *tirailleurs* alone could not force the Austrians off the high ground. Word then came from Vandamme to pull back, and Schiner passed the order along to Pourailly; the 24th withdrew.

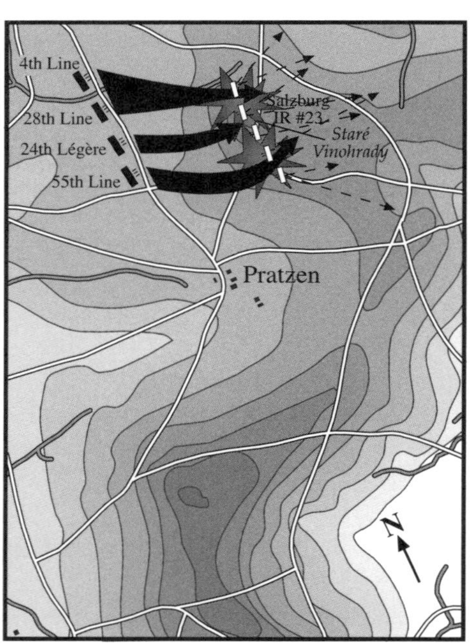

IR#23 is defeated

The reason for disengaging the 24th *Légère* was that Vandamme wanted to organize a new attack. Bringing up reinforcements in the form of Férey's brigade (4th and 28th *Ligne*) and the 55th *Ligne* from Varé's command, Vandamme then put in a coordinated assault. The French attack had the 24th *Légère* in the center with the 4th and 28th *Ligne* on their left and the 55th *Ligne* to the right. The eight battalions—all in line formation—swept forward, led by three brigadier generals. The units moved eastward until it was time for the flanking battalions to wheel in from the north and south against the flanks of the Austrian line. For a few minutes, the Salzburg IR#23 kept up a good fire, and the battalion guns exacted a heavy toll from the ranks of the 24th *Légère* and the 55th *Ligne.* Taking this punishment, the French held their fire until they were "within 80 paces of the enemy line, when the battalions, already in line, halted and began pouring a series of deadly volleys into their ranks."[158] Austrian fire immediately slacken noticeably. A combination of the well-led French units unleashing a torrent of lead, the heavy casualties suffered by the whitecoats in a short period of time, combined with a lack of thorough training and the exhaustion of their limited small arms ammunition (only 40 rounds per man), spelled doom for the Austrians on the Staré Vinohrady. Within a few minutes, the battalions of Salzburg IR#23 came apart. Miloradovich saw the Austrian struggle to retain the heights, and wrote the day after the battle that:

> until then the troops had put up a stubborn fight. However, the cumulative effect of the catastrophic situation [of the IV Column], their own exhaustion, the lack of cartridges, the disadvantageous lie of the land, and the enemy fire which came in from every side, all made them give way in disorder.[159]

With the defeat of the Salzburg IR#23, the Pratzen Plateau had been temporarily cleared of all allied forces, and with it the annihilation of the center of the Combined Russian and Austrian Army. Since the IV Column of the allied army was destroyed, and with Buxhöwden's three columns stalled or partially crippled, the only forces that remained intact were the forces on the northern end of the battlefield under Prince Bagration and the reserves of the Russian Imperial Guard positioned just east of the Pratzen Plateau. It was the latter forces that were determined to recapture the Pratzen and save the battle for the Tsar.

---

[158] S.H.A.T., C² 20.

[159] *Kutuzov. Sbornik*, vol. 2, p. 231.

The Counterattack and Defeat of the Russian Imperial Guard

As the allied army was coming apart and its commanders struggling to meet the changing circumstances of battle, Napoleon was calmly, yet intensely, following the course of the fighting. From his position on top of Zuran Hill with his staff and military household surrounding him, the Emperor could see the entire field to the summit of the Pratzen. Throughout the morning, couriers and aides-de-camp galloped to and from this simple field headquarters. These men provided Napoleon with information as to the details of the fighting, then returned to the front with the Emperor's instructions. Before each new directive was issued, Napoleon would consult his order log maintained by the members of Marshal Berthier's staff which contained the last order entry and troop condition for each brigade and division. Thus, Napoleon always had immediate access to the latest information.

When the Emperor saw Vandamme's troops storming up the Staré Vinohrady some time after 11:00 A.M., Napoleon decided that it was time to relocate his headquarters closer to the front. In concert with this movement, Napoleon wanted all formations then in reserve to advance as well. The aides from the various commands were given the appropriate instructions to carry back to their superior officers. Lieutenant Lebrun from Bernadotte's staff was at Imperial headquarters and charged by the Emperor to go back to Bernadotte and have the 1st Corps advance on his left. Suspecting Bernadotte's reluctance to promptly move out, Napoleon waited for Lebrun's departure, then called for one of his own Imperial aides-de-camp. Ségur vividly remembered that the Emperor:

> distrusted this marshal and sent me to repeat his orders to him, and to watch how they were carried out.
>
> When I arrived, I found Bernadotte on foot at the head of his infantry, agitated and uneasy, expecting from his soldiers a calmness of which he did not set them the example. This anxiety was not, it is true, devoid of reason; pointing out to me the formidable masses of cavalry which were gathering in front of him, he complained somewhat too loudly that he had not a single squadron to oppose them, [the light cavalry of 1st Corps having been detached to serve under Murat for the battle] and beseeched me so earnestly to go and beg Napoleon to send some cavalry to his aid that [even though not under attack], I was not able to resist his entreaties, and undertook to convey them to the Emperor. Napoleon answered with some impatience: 'Why, he knows very well that I have none to spare!'[160]

As Napoleon had suspected, it was only under protest that Bernadotte advanced with his two infantry divisions. That feeling held by the marshal was not shared by his troops. So far unengaged in any battles of the campaign, the *fantassins* of the 1st Corps were anxious for combat and showed their enthusiasm as they marched by Zuran Hill. Jean-Baptiste Barrès of the *Chasseurs à pied de la Garde* recalled how 1st Corps passed by Zuran Hill on the way to the front.

> Passing to the right and left of the little hill, saluting, shouting '*Vive l'Empereur!*' and hoisting their headgear on the points of their bayonets, swords and sabers, Marshal Bernadotte at their

[160] *Memoirs of Ségur*, pp. 250-251.

1st Corps Divisional Deployment

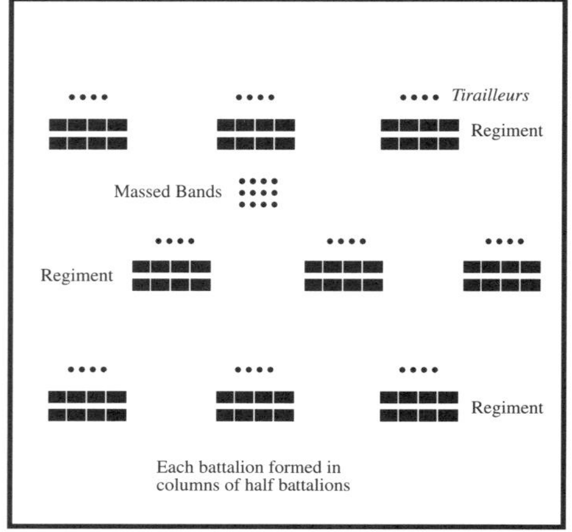

> head, bearing his hat aloft in the like manner, and all to the sound of drums and music.[161]

Adjudant-commandant Maurice-Etienne Gérard, Bernadotte's premier aide-de-camp, had similar recollections of how the infantrymen of the 1st Corps could not contain their excitement, as well as the formation in which the battalions advanced.

> We passed by the Emperor waving our hats and shouting '*Vive l'Empereur!*' Each division advanced in three lines, with each battalion formed by columns of half battalion, and in the middle were the massed regimental bands playing the *"Chant du départ."*[162]

Like the soldiers of 1st Corps, the officers and men of the *Grenadiers de la Réserve* and the French Imperial Guard also had no hesitation in their forward movements. Jean-Baptiste Barrès described the advance of the remaining reserves:

> After the 1st Corps had passed we began to move. The reserve consisted of [16] picked battalions, [four] being of the Imperial Guard, [two] of the Italian Royal Guard, and 10 of the *Grenadiers de la Réserve*. Behind us marched the cavalry of the Guard. The picked battalions were in close column formation by divisions. This formidable reserve marched in line of battle, with full dress uniforms and bearskins, plumes fluttering in the wind, with eagles and standards uncased, proudly pointing the way to victory. In this order we crossed the plain and ascended the [Pratzen] heights to the cries of '*Vive l'Empereur!*'[163]

As the four reserve infantry divisions and the cavalry of the Imperial Guard were moving onto the Pratzen, the bands of the Imperial Guard played a series of stirring marches, and Coignet, a *Grenadier à pied de la Garde*, remembered how the music of the Guardsmen "was enough to galvanize a paralytic."[164]

While Napoleon and the reserve formations were crossing the field amidst this pomp and spectacle, over two miles away east of the village of Blasowitz, Russian Grand Duke Constantine Pavlovich was leading the Russian Imperial Guard westward towards the sounds of battle. Younger brother to Tsar Alexander, the 26-year-old Constantine shared a few similar physical features with his sibling, including a rounded face, red hair and a protruding brow. However, apart from the obvious genetic features that all the Romanovs seemed to possess, the Grand Duke had none of the good looks, intelligence and wit of the Tsar. Instead, Constantine had gotten all of the family's bad genes. His face had several odd bumps, his hands could pass for those of a gorilla, his walk was unrefined and his wild eyes reflected the depths of his disturbed, violent personality. Twice already Constantine:

Grand Duke Constantine

> had strangled valets who had failed to do his bidding fast enough.
>
> Interminable nights had seen him prostrated before icons, begging with sobs to be forgiven for the debaucheries into which he had plunged himself since the morning.[165]

---

[161] *Memoirs of a French Napoleonic Officer: Jean-Baptiste Barrès,* p. 75.
[162] S.H.A.T., C^2 22.
[163] *Memoirs of a French Napoleonic Officer: Jean-Baptiste Barrès,* pp. 75-76.
[164] *Les Cahiers du Capitaine Coignet*, pp. 472-473
[165] Claude Manceron, *Austerlitz: The Story of a Battle* (New York, 1966), p. 274.

With no more qualifications to command other than his birthright, Constantine rode into battle in his immaculate white uniform trimmed in gold with a black helmet of the *Chevalier Garde* astride his black steed.

The units that composed Constantine's command were the Russian Imperial Guard. At Austerlitz, the Tsar's gilded phalanx consisted of 10 battalions of infantry, 17 squadrons of cavalry, one company of pioneers and 40 pieces of ordnance. At nominal establishment, these Guard formations were supposed to have numbered over 10,500 officers and men. However, no more than 8,500 were present and under arms on 2 December 1805.[166] The majority of those not with the colors were sick, suffering from various effects of syphilis that ravaged the ranks of the Russian élite. Those that marched towards the battle front were huge, formidable looking soldiers, nevertheless. As their flags fluttered in the breeze while their bands played, the Russian Imperial Guard battalions were readily identifiable as the sun reflected off the smartly aligned ranks of bayonets and tall, distinctive headgear.

The Tsar's prized formations advanced in the four lines as ordered by Constantine. The first line consisted of four Guard Fusilier battalions, two each of the Semenovsky and Preobrazhensky regiments, while the second line consisted of two Guard Fusilier battalions from the Izmailovsky Regiment and the battalion of Guard *Jaeger*. The cavalry of the Guard formed a staggered third line. Finally, the fourth line was in deep reserve. It consisted of the three Guard Grenadier battalions, one each from the Semenovsky, Preobrazhensky and Izmailovsky Guard Regiments. Because these grenadier battalions served together, they were the so-called Guard Grenadier Regiment.[167]

Sometime after 9:30 A.M., Constantine realized that he needed to occupy Blasowitz. The Grand Duke ordered the battalion of his Guard *Jaeger* to hustle off to secure the village; they were supported by a half-battery (5 pieces) of Russian Guard Horse Artillery. Shortly thereafter, a battalion of Guard Fusiliers from the Semenovsky Regiment was dispatched as reinforcements. These parade-ground formations became embroiled in a small mini-battle of their own. Before the Russian Guardsmen knew it, they were torn to pieces by elements of Caffarelli's Division attached to Lannes' 5th Corps (see page 404).

Following the Grand Duke's detachment of those two battalions, a courier from Miloradovich arrived, briefly explaining that there was big trouble on the Pratzen and imploring Constantine to send help at once. The Tsar's brother responded by ordering Colonel Khrapovitsky of the Izmailovsky Regiment to take one of his two Guard Fusilier battalions and see what he could do. The colonel and his battalion were led westward by the messenger, arriving about the time that the six battalions of Salzburg IR#23 were being mauled and broken by Vandamme's regiments. The subsequent flight of the Salzburg regiment carried its survivors directly into the ranks of Colonel Khrapovitsky's battalion. Through a combination of disorder in their ranks caused by the fleeing Austrians, coupled with the threatening advances of many French battalions, Khrapovitsky and his Guard Fusiliers were caught up in the retreat and withdrew in confusion without firing a shot. Therefore, Constantine had bled off in piecemeal fashion three of his seven leading battalions, only to have them either smashed or routed from the field.

These reverses illuminated two things to Constantine. First, it must have dawned on him that he had no real idea of what was going on. The messenger from Miloradovich gave no information as to where the French were or in what strength. Second, what Constantine *did* know was that his forces were the only allied troops in the right center of the field, because the troops that the Guardsmen were supposed to be following—the IV Column—were now in headlong retreat.

Russian Guards Deployment

Guard Fusilier Battalions of Semenovsky and Preobrazhensky Regiments

Two Guard Fusilier Battalions of the Izmailovsky Regiment and Guard *Jaeger*

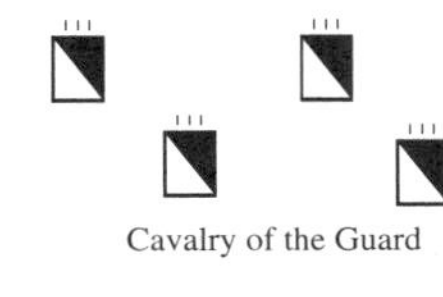

Cavalry of the Guard

Guard Grenadier Battalions, one from Semenovsky, Preobrazhensky, and IzmailovskyRegiments

[166] Stutterheim, *A Detailed Account of the Battle of Austerlitz*, p. 33.

[167] Please refer to Chapter II, footnote 28.

Austrian Cüirassiers

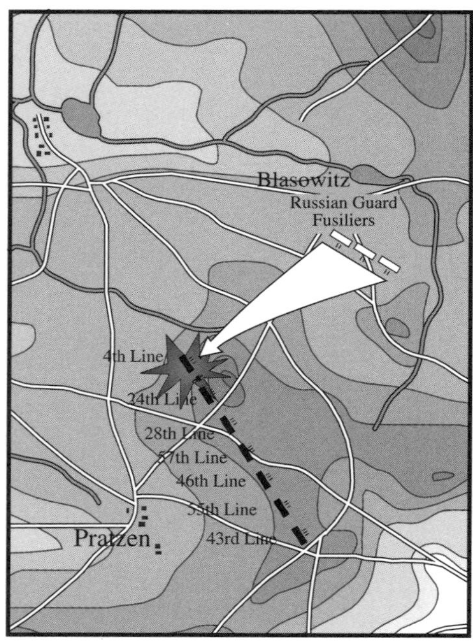

Vandamme's division meets the Russian Imperial Guard

Instead of receiving some orders from the Tsar and his staff, the inexperienced Grand Duke was suddenly on his own. Constantine had little choice but to order his remaining units to retire behind the Raussnitz stream where he hoped to try to establish some semblance of a line with rallied elements of the IV Column. By 11:30 A.M., Constantine's retrograde movement was being implemented. To protect his right flank, the Grand Duke decided to put to use a battery of Austrian 12-pounders that had started the battle as the reserve artillery for the IV Column, but had not been involved with the earlier reverses suffered by the infantry of that column. Constantine ordered Captain Zocchi to unlimber his battery of six heavy pieces facing north on the high ground above the upper Raussnitz where it bends to an east-west direction. To support this ordnance, the rallied elements of the Guard *Jaeger* Battalion, along with the Guard Hussars, were thrown out in a screen facing west.[168]

These adjustments in the line gave some much needed cover to the Austrian cavalry division under FML Friedrich Karl Prince Hohenlohe-Ingelfingen. The 53-year-old cüirassier general, a veteran of the Turkish wars as well as the wars of the French Revolution, knew that cavalry were not meant to simply occupy ground. He had kept his regiments of horse which numbered less than 1,200 people out of harm's way, maneuvering them from one area of dead ground to another, waiting for the moment that he could order them into action. When Constantine established his newly formed line along the north-south axis of the upper Raussnitz, Hohenlohe moved his three cüirassier regiments—Kaiser #1, Nassau-Usingen #5 and Lothringen #7—around and positioned them behind and on the flanks of the Russian Imperial Guard.[169]

From his position atop the Staré Vinohrady, Vandamme had watched Constantine and Hohenlohe conduct these defensive alignments. Recognizing the opportunity in front of him, and since several divisions of reinforcements were now headed his way, the fiery Vandamme decided to resume his own division's advance over the eastward prolongation of the vine covered Staré Vinohrady towards Constantine's position. Although only Schiner's and Férey's brigades were at hand along with six of the division's eight pieces of ordnance—Candras' brigade was still too far south and Varé's men from Saint-Hilaire were on their way back to their own division at the request of Saint-Hilaire—Vandamme wanted to occupy the extensive vineyards that were located on the northern slopes of the Staré Vinohrady. Once his infantry were thoroughly ensconced in this cover, Vandamme realized that he would be greatly protected against cavalry attack as well as in position to resume the advance when reinforcements arrived.

Seeing Vandamme's six battalions move down the slopes towards the vineyards, Constantine felt that he must somehow contest the French move. Therefore, the Grand Duke ordered that the Guard *Jaeger* Battalion and the Guard Hussar Regiment leave their covering positions on the north flank and move for the vineyards. Meanwhile, the remaining battalion of Guard Fusiliers from the Semenovsky Regiment, and both Guard Fusilier battalions from the Preobrazhensky Regiment would form the front line. The second battalion of Guard Fusiliers from the Izmailovsky Regiment, along with the other regiments of Guard cavalry positioned to protect both flanks, were to form a second line. Hohenlohe's Austrian cüirassiers would form the third line and cover the flanks of the Russian Guard cavalry.

As the Guard *Jaeger* and Guard Hussars moved forward, they arrived too late to prevent Major Bigarré and the two battalions of the 4th *Ligne* from entering the vineyards. Marching in line formation, the 4th moved eastward as the *jaeger* entered the vineyard from the north while the hussars halted outside the stakes and

[168] K. k. Kriegsarchiv, F.A., *Ausführliche Relation der am 2 ten Dezember, 1805.*
[169] K. k. Kriegsarchiv, F.A., *Ausführliche Relation der am 2 ten Dezember, 1805.*

watched the action. Soon the 2nd Battalion of the 4th *Ligne* and the Russian Guard *Jaeger* Battalion were engaged in a lively fire fight. It did not take long for the French volleys to take their toll, forcing the *jaeger* to fall back. Unable to stem the French tide with just the *jaeger* and hussars, Constantine decided to launch an all-out counterattack, even though the three battalions of Guard Grenadiers were too far to the rear to participate.

The three Guard Fusilier battalions in the front line were ordered into action without further delay. Led by two generals, the mustachioed giants sporting tall distinctive headgear, advanced steadily up the slope in line formation, then executed a charge into the vineyards at the double-quick over the last 300 paces, screaming at the top of their voices 'Hurrah!' The 1st Battalion of the 4th *Ligne* met the charge with a series of disciplined, deadly volleys that ripped the Russian ranks. Despite the casualties suffered from French small arms fire, despite their own fatigue from having run a long distance, and despite the disorder in their ranks from quickly moving through the vineyards, the three Guard Fusilier battalions pressed on, enveloped both flanks of the 1st Battalion of the 4th *Ligne,* and broke the French at the bayonet point. As the 1st Battalion of the 4th was recoiling, the 2nd Battalion of the 4th *Ligne* fell back to the protection of a company of artillery that was moving down the rows of stakes. Upon hearing that the enemy was approaching, the pieces were immediately unlimbered. The targets for the guns soon showed themselves. Following up their victory over the 1st Battalion of the 4th, the Russian Guardsmen had pushed on, but their disordered battalions were checked by the murderous fire of the 2nd Battalion of the 4th *Ligne* and the canister fire from six pieces of ordnance under the command of *chef de bataillon* Degemes. The three Guard Fusilier battalions fell back to the eastern edge of the vineyard to regroup.[170]

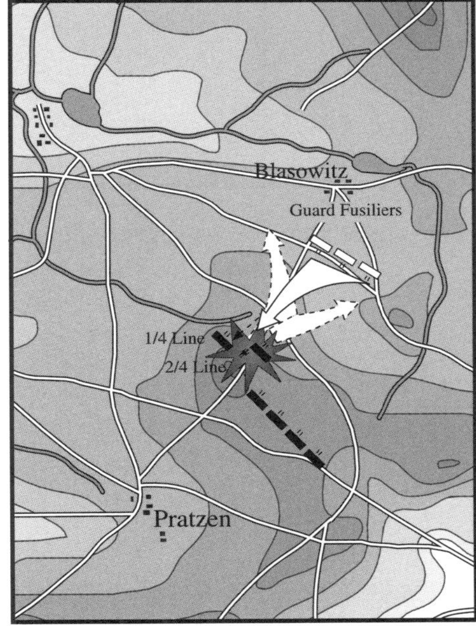

The 4th Ligne *repels the infantry of the Russian Imperial Guard*

Major Bigarré had just rallied the 1st Battalion of the 4th *Ligne* along the northwestern edge of the vineyard. Witnessing the repulse of the three Russian Guard Fusilier battalions at the hands of the 2nd Battalion of the 4th and the artillery, rode back to see Vandamme. The major found the division general sitting on an overturned cart above the vineyard, surrounded by his aides-de-camp, all anxiously peering eastward through the smoke. They had spotted another column of enemy troops approaching the hotly-contested vineyard. Vandamme told one of his aides, Captain Seron, to ride forward and find out who was closing on them. After issuing this order, Vandamme told Bigarré to go with Seron and deploy his regiment as necessary. Reaching the eastern edge of the Pratzen just above the vineyards, Seron and Bigarré saw what must have appeared to them to be masses of cavalry coming on at a trot in column of squadrons.

As Seron galloped back to report this to Vandamme, Bigarré spurred his horse to the 1st Battalion of the 4th *Ligne* and ordered the unit to form square. The battalion was still in the protective cover of the vineyard and had completed its formation change when the Russian cavalry reined in approximately 200 yards from the French infantry. Deploying from column of squadrons to squadrons abreast, the leading regiment was the Russian Garde du Corps *Cuirassier* Regiment led by Colonel Count Ojarovsky I and Colonel Olenine. Mounting 800 officers and other ranks, the five squadrons of the regiment were supported by a half battery of five pieces from the Russian Guard Horse Artillery that unlimbered and opened with a canister fire onto the 1st Battalion of the 4th *Ligne*. The compact square made a splendid target for the Russian artillerists, and each discharge seemed to exact some casualties. One blast from the Russian pieces killed the eagle-bearer. However, the symbol of the battalion was then quickly picked up and carried by another.

[170] S.H.A.T., *Journal des opérations du 4ᵉ corps.*

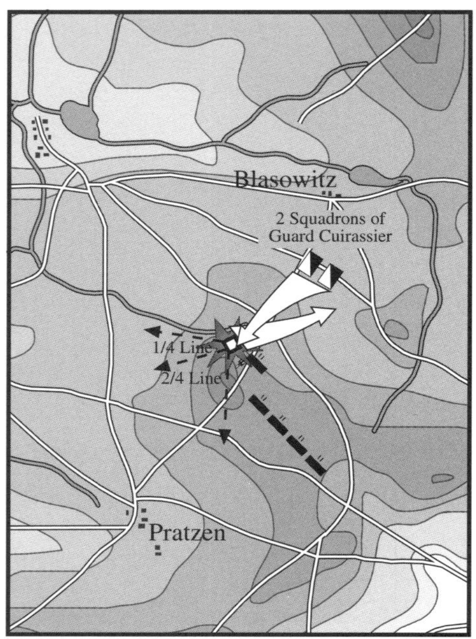

The Garde du Corps breaks the square of the 1st battalion, 4th Ligne

Meanwhile, after listening to Seron's report, Vandamme wasted no time in telling his aide to ride at once to Colonel Pourailly and order the 24th *Légère* to march to the aid of their brothers-in-arms. Before the light infantrymen could move into within supporting distance of the 1st Battalion of the 4th *Ligne*, the Garde du Corps commenced their attack to Constantine's cry of: "For God, the Tsar and Russia!"[171] Fortunately for the Russian cavalry, the rows of the vineyard ran in an east-west direction, allowing the horsemen to easily move down the rows of the vineyard stakes against the French battalion. Committing only two of their five squadrons in this attack, the ranks of the Garde du Corps became partially disordered as they galloped through the vineyard. The 1st Squadron was led by Colonel Ojarovsky, and were within 30 paces of the French when the facing sides of the square erupted in a sheet of flames. The crushing volley issued at point-blank range by the 1st Battalion of the 4th staggered the 1st Squadron, preventing them from closing. However, before the French could reload, the 2nd Squadron of the Gardes du Corps were upon them. Led by Lieutenant Khmelev, the 3rd Company [the 2nd Squadron was composed of the 3rd and 4th Companies of the regiment] penetrated the ranks of the *fantassins*, destroying the cohesion of the battalion. In the brief *mêlée* that followed, a savage fight for the eagle and standard of the 1st Battalion of the 4th *Ligne* ensued. At this time of the battle, the precious emblem of the battalion was being carried by Sergeant-Major Saint-Cyr. This NCO had picked up the eagle after the battalion's second standard bearer of the day had been shot dead only moments earlier. Fighting tenaciously, and after receiving 12 wounds about his arms and head, Saint-Cyr was finally overcome by three Garde du Corps troopers named Elie Omeltchenko, Zacharie Lazounov and Théodore Ouchakov. As Saint-Cyr fell to the ground covered in blood and gore, he joined *chef de bataillon* Guye and 10 other officers of the battalion that were already wounded. With the 1st Battalion of the 4th *Ligne* totally dissolving, the 2nd Squadron of the Gardes du Corps turned around and passed back over the wreckage towards their lines, sabering as many French as they could. The Russian Guard cavalrymen withdrew with the eagle-standard of the 1st Battalion of the 4th *Ligne*—the only trophy gained by the allies at Austerlitz—leaving behind the gruesome evidence of a battalion that had been overrun by cavalry. Some 200 men of Bigarré's command had been killed or wounded.[172]

The first two squadrons of the Garde du Corps were drawing off to the east as Colonel Pourailly arrived with his two battalions of the 24th *Légère*. Both battalions marched in line formation, pushing into the vineyard past the hysterical fugitives of the 1st Battalion of the 4th *Ligne*. The light infantrymen soon found out that the vineyard's layout offered little protection from determined heavy cavalry moving down the rows of stakes. No sooner had the blue uniformed troops of the 24th *Légère* made their way into the vineyard than the remaining three squadrons of the Garde du Corps were unleashed against them. As the Russian horse came hell-for-leather, the French light infantry issued an effective volley, but it failed to stop the Russian charge. Coming through the fire, the white uniformed cavalrymen on large horses were soon hacking their way through the thin, three-rank deep blue line. French officers and men alike fell by the dozens. Of the 60 officers of the 24th *Légère* that went into action, *chef de bataillon* Kuhn was wounded, as were 11 of 18 company commanders and 17 other officers.[173] Also, a desperate fight for the eagles of the 24th ensued. Despite receiving five severe wounds, Sergeant-

The standard of the 4th Ligne

---

[171] Duffy, *Austerlitz,* p. 135; Manceron, *Austerlitz: The Story of a Battle,* p. 274.

[172] S.H.A.T., *Journal des opérations du 4ᵉ corps;* and *Historique du 4ᵉ régiment d'infanterie,* p. 47; Colonel Stackelberg, *Un siècle et demi de la Garde du Corps* (Saint Petersburg, 1881), p. 21; S.H.A.T., C^2 16 and 470.

[173] S.H.A.T., C^2 16 and 470.

Major Barjeot fought off the Russian horsemen by wildly swinging the eagle-standard of his battalion like a giant club.[174]

It was about this time that Napoleon and the Imperial staff finished their ascent up the Staré Vinohrady, only to see a horde of dark-clothed infantry streaming towards them. "What on earth is that?" asked Napoleon. "Your Majesty," answered Marshal Berthier, "what a splendid crowd of prisoners they are bringing back for you!"[175] However, the mob was soon discovered to be part of the 1st Battalion of the 4th *Ligne* that had been overrun by the Garde du Corps. As the infantrymen ran by, they kept looking back over their shoulders to see if they were being pursued by the Russian horse. Then on horseback next to the Emperor, Marshal Bessières turned to his aide-de-camp, Major César de Laville, and said: "Laville, we are going to have a cavalry engagement." Laville did not question Bessières then, but:

> the evening after the battle I asked him how he [Bessières] had guessed so correctly that a cavalry engagement was imminent. He replied: 'Because the retreating soldiers kept looking back. When infantry retires before infantry, they never turn their heads.'[176]

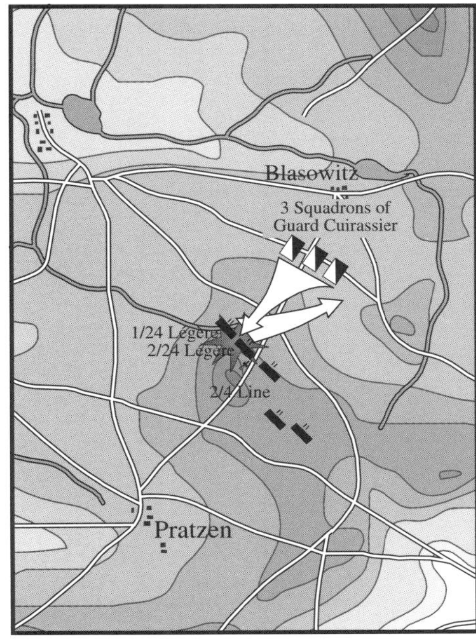

The 24th Légère *tries to stop the Russian Guard Cavalry*

So panicked were these unfortunate soldiers, that their flight could not be stopped by any member of the Imperial entourage, including Napoleon. The men were used to giving a salutation to their leader whenever they saw him, and flying past him faster than ever, they panted out in an almost mechanical way "*'Vive l'Empereur!'* Napoleon smiled pitifully; then with a disgusted gesture he said to us: 'Let them go.'"[177]

Napoleon then looked for Marshal Bessières, the commander of the Imperial Guard, to rectify the situation. Jean-Baptiste Bessières, 37 years of age at the battle, was a well-educated, enterprising man. He was the family's eldest son, and according to the Bessières' household tradition, was supposed to study to be a surgeon. However, after obtaining a secondary education at the college of Saint-Michel of Cahors during which time he proved himself to be an excellent student, economic hardships prevented Bessières from attending medical school. Nevertheless, he began learning medicine under a cousin who was a doctor, while at the same time earning a living as a barber. The Revolution interrupted this unusual education, and Bessières then joined the 22nd *Chasseurs à cheval.* The trooper rose in rank, and at the Battle of Millesimo and again at Lodi, Bessières distinguished himself under the eyes of Bonaparte. Such conduct, plus his friendly connection with Murat who he had met at Saint-Michel of Cahors, was rewarded with the command of the Mounted Guides, a picked bodyguard for Bonaparte that would become part of the Consular Guard and later the famous *Chasseurs à cheval de la Garde*. Bessières was part of the Egyptian expedition, and participated unhesitatingly in the coup of 18 brumaire. At Marengo on 14 June 1800, Bessières played a key role in the battle, first by covering the retreat of the French right under Lannes, and later by participating in the counterattack that won the battle. His valuable service and loyalty to Napoleon earned him a marshal's baton in 1804, then command of the Imperial Guard.[178] More than an excellent cavalry leader, Bessières was a handsome man with long and hanging hair, a well-

Bessières

---

[174] Andolenko, *Aigles de Napoléon Contre Drapeaux du Tsar*, p. 110.
[175] *Mémoirs du Général Comte de Saint-Chamans* (Paris, 1896), pp. 25-26.
[176] Lachouque and Brown, *The Anatomy of Glory*, p. 64.
[177] *Memoirs of Ségur*, p. 252.
[178] Six, *Dictionnaire biographique*, vol. 1, p. 94.

One of the most famous cavalry charges in history was immortalized in this painting by Myrbach. General Rapp (in the middle distance) leads forward two duty squadrons of Chasseurs à cheval de la Garde *and the company of* Mameluks *(foreground). Heavily outnumbered, these French cavalrymen stabilized the situation in the center, setting the stage for the decisive charge of the duty squadron of the* Grenadiers à cheval de la Garde.

Rugendas' painting of Austerlitz. Napoleon observes the Chasseurs à cheval *and* Mameluks *charge in the center, while the village of Pratzen burns to center right.*

proportioned athletic body, lots of common sense, a well-rounded personality with social graces to match. Bessières seemed to know every man in the Guard by name, and his good-natured personality favorably impressed everyone. Napoleon may have said it the best: "Bessières has many civilian qualities which I welcome in military men."[179]

It was the military talents of Bessières that Napoleon was looking to about 1:00 P.M. on the field of Austerlitz. The marshal had at his disposal the finest cavalry regiments in the *Grande Armée*—the *Chasseurs à cheval de la Garde* and the *Grenadiers à cheval de la Garde.* These two regiments, which totaled eight and one-half squadrons, were divided into three formations. The first was the regiment of *Chasseurs à cheval* which had two of its four squadrons operating as the 'parent' unit under its commanding officer, Colonel Morland. The second was the *Grenadiers à cheval* under *général de brigade* Michel Ordener, which operated at Austerlitz with three of its squadrons.

As was the custom in the army, the regiments of Guard cavalry contributed squadrons to form the daily mounted bodyguard for the Emperor. At Austerlitz, these so-called 'duty squadrons' comprised the third formation of Guard cavalry, and consisted of a total of three and one-half squadrons—two from the *Chasseurs à cheval*, including one squadron commanded by *chef d'escadron* Camille Borghèse, Napoleon's brother-in-law (the husband of Pauline Bonaparte), one from the *Grenadiers à cheval* and the company of *Mameluks*.

Including regiment staffs, as well as those persons detached and in hospitals, the eight and one-half squadrons under Bessières had a total effective strength of over 1,700. However, counting only those officers and other ranks that were in the saddle and on the field of battle, the Guard cavalry formations were considerably understrength. The four squadrons of the *Chasseurs à cheval* mounted only 375 officers and other ranks at Austerlitz—another 373 people of the regiment were strung out in detachments from Strasbourg to Vienna. The company of *Mameluks* at Austerlitz mounted only six officers and 42 other ranks—far below their authorized establishment. Finally, the four squadrons in the *Grenadiers à cheval* mounted 706 officers and other ranks at Austerlitz, with another 248 not present because they were also detached from the regiment. The remaining cavalry regiment of the Imperial Guard, the *Gendarmie d'élite,* were all detached after 21 November and were not on the field at Austerlitz. Therefore, the total French Imperial Guard cavalry force present at Austerlitz numbered 1,129 officers and other ranks.[180]

With these cavalry from which to choose, Bessières immediately committed the formations under Morland and Ordener. Morland rode with the first two squadrons of the *Chasseurs à cheval,* which were supported on his right by Ordener's three squadrons of *Grenadiers à cheval.* Colonel Doguereau with two companies (16 pieces) of *Volante*—the Imperial Guard Horse Artillery—moved forward with the two regiments.[181]

The five squadrons consisting of Colonel Morland's "Favored Children" and Ordener's "Gods" hit the three squadrons of the Gardes du Corps like a whirlwind. The Russians were already disordered from the combined effects of the terrain and battling the 24th *Légère*, and their line was quickly enveloped and overturned by the French Guard cavalry. Ordener's formidable troopers also captured from the Gardes du Corps the raspberry-colored standard of their 5th

An officer of the "favored children" of the Imperial Guard

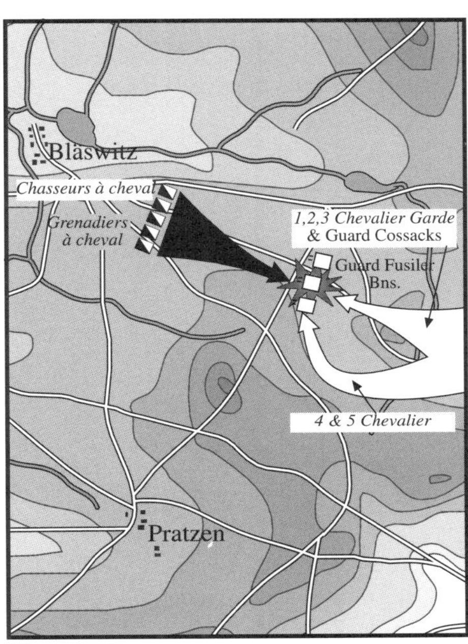

The French Guard Cavalry counterattacks

Morland

[179] Georges Blond, *La Grande Armée,* translated by Marshall May (London, 1995), p. 76.
[180] S.H.A.T., C[2] 470.
[181] Each company of *Volante* fielded eight pieces of ordnance in 1805, which was different from any other campaign during the Napoleonic wars. See Chapter I and Appendix J for further details.

Grenadier à cheval
of the Imperial Guard

Squadron.[182] Following up this victory, the French Guard cavalry continued their charge deeper into the vineyards, attacking the three Guard Fusilier battalions from the Semenovsky and Preobrazhensky Regiments that had earlier tangled with the 4th *Ligne*. The French cavalry hacked with their sabers and fired their pistols into the Russian ranks as the guns of Doguereau's horse artillerists ripped the greencoated ranks; the infantrymen fought back with musketry and battalion guns, but with little effect. Definitely on the worst end of this exchange, the battalion from the Semenovsky Regiment seemed to suffer the most as they were unmercifully sabered by Ordener's "Gods." However, despite the uneven contest, the Russian Guard battalions refused to break. Hanging on with all their grit, the giant infantrymen lasted long enough for Constantine to commit to action his redcoated Guard Cossacks as well as the *Chevalier Garde*. These seven squadrons rode forward in three formations: the 1st, 2nd and 3rd Squadrons of the *Chevalier Garde* were in the lead, with both squadrons of the Guard Cossacks in echelon to the left and the 4th and 5th Squadrons of the *Chevalier Garde* in reserve.

The two leading waves of the Russian horse rode straight into the vineyard and engaged Morland's *Chasseurs à cheval* who were themselves engaged in hand-to-hand combat against the two Preobrazhensky Guard Fusilier battalions. Meanwhile, the last line consisting of the 4th and 5th Squadrons of the *Chevalier Garde*, peeled off to the left, halted briefly to reposition themselves and then spurred their horses on and slammed into the flank of Ordener's *Grenadiers à cheval*. The timely arrival by the fresh formations of the *Chevalier Garde* and Guard Cossacks momentarily swung the balance of the action to the Russians, and temporarily saved their infantry brothers-in-arms.

From his position on the Staré Vinohrady, Napoleon saw the mass of humanity and horseflesh intermingled in the huge *mêlée*. Such disorder was not to his liking, and Napoleon turned to one of his Imperial aide-de-camp, *général de brigade* Jean Rapp, saying: "General, there is a mess there; go and put it right."[183] By ordering Rapp forward, Napoleon authorized the use of his last mounted reserve in the area—the duty squadrons of the Guard and the remaining half-company of *Volante*. Jean Rapp, the stocky, 34-year-old Alsatian had been in the cavalry his entire career. Enlisting as a trooper in the *chasseurs à cheval* in 1788, Rapp rose in rank and reputation, and by 1797 he was named aide-de-camp to Desaix. After serving in Egypt and at Marengo, Rapp organized the company of *Mameluks* for the Imperial Guard, and it was with this formation that the general spearheaded his attack at Austerlitz. Leaving the duty squadron of the *Grenadiers à cheval* in reserve, the general advanced with the two duty squadrons of *Chasseurs à cheval* and the company of *Mameluks*—a force of about 236 officers and men. Rapp recalled what followed:

> I took off at a gallop; the enemy cavalry was sabering our soldiers. A short distance to the rear, we could see masses of infantry and cavalry which formed their reserve. The enemy broke contact and rushed against me; four pieces of their artillery arrived at

Ordener, the same man who arrested the duc d'Enghien, led the Grenadiers à cheval *at Austerlitz*

[182] There are dozens of conflicting accounts of what Russian Guard cavalry standards were taken, and when, by the French Guard cavalry. As a sampling of the wide variations, Fantin des Odoards, *Journal* (Paris, 1895), pp. 72-73, states that the French Guard cavalry took two standards from the Gardes du Corps. Meanwhile, Stackelberg, *Un siècle et demi de la Garde du Corps,* p. 216, dismisses the fact that any flags were taken from the regiment at Austerlitz. However, if Stackelberg's account was true, then the regiment would not have been missing the standards of the 1st and 5th squadrons at the end of campaign! When the regiment returned to Saint Peterburg, the director of the arsenal noted that only the 2nd, 3rd and 4th squadron standards were returned.

[183] Blond and May, *La Grande Armée,* p. 77.

> the gallop and unlimbered in battery. I advanced in good order; on my left was the brave Colonel Morland, and General Dallemagne (Dahlmann) to my right. We charged the artillery and captured it, and in the same onslaught we overturned the enemy cavalry, which had received our charge at the halt; they broke under the shock and fled in disorder.[184]

One of the "Gods" takes on a Russian Guardsman

Astride their beautiful Arabian horses, the nimble *Mameluks* "proved murderously effective."[185] Wielding their exotic weapons, "they could sever a head with a single blow of their curved sabers, and with their sharp-edged stirrups they cut into the soldiers' backs."[186] Though only a small company in strength, the *Mameluks* demonstrated that they were clearly superior warriors to the Tsar's prized outfit. Hitting the 3rd Squadron of the *Chevalier Garde*, the *Mameluks* went through the enemy like a buzz saw. Trooper Moustapha cut the head off the Russian squadron standard bearer and claimed the trophy for which he was awarded the *Légion d'Honneur*.[187]

However, the charge of *Mameluks* and the two duty squadrons of *Chasseurs à cheval* soon bogged down; there were simply too many Russian horsemen. Napoleon responded by ordering into action the 176 combatants in the remaining duty squadron drawn from the *Grenadiers à cheval.* These large warriors in bearskin headgear, riding magnificent 16-hand-high black horses, were the consummate veteran troopers. Hand picked for their distinguished prior combat performance, led by officers and NCOs who were the best in the French mounted service, the *Grenadiers à cheval* lived for moments like this. Rapp remembered how the finest cavalry in the world:

> came to my support at the same moment as reserves arrived to support the Russian Guard. The shock was terrific. The [Russian] infantry did not dare fire since we were all jumbled together, fighting hand-to-hand.[188]

Arriving at the same time as did the duty squadron of the *Grenadiers à cheval* were the Russians reserves consisting of the 1st and 2nd Squadrons of the Gardes du Corps—the formations that had earlier overrun the 1st Battalion of the 4th *Ligne*. Counting the commitment of the last squadron of the "Gods," the cavalry of the French Imperial Guard was still outnumbered by the Russian Guard cavalry by a margin of at least two to one. In a contest pitting both sides best horsemen, the troopers fought heroically. Some squadrons would break off, retired slightly to the rear to reform and charge again into the *mêlée*.

Drouet d'Erlon in later years

To the right rear of this action advanced the 2nd Infantry Division of Bernadotte's 1st Corps. The division was commanded by *général de division* Jean-Baptiste Drouet, later known as the Count d'Erlon. Like so many other French officers, the 40-year-old Drouet had risen from the ranks during the wars of the French Revolution. Considered a competent and intelligent officer, Drouet earned his promotion to division command following his distinguished service in the Hohenlinden campaign of 1800. Austerlitz was his first battle as a division commander, and as his command advanced towards the enemy, Drouet had deployed his 5,786 infantrymen in columns of half battalions—each battalion formed on a frontage of four companies (two divisions wide) with a depth of two companies

---

[184]Commandant Henry Lachouque, *La Garde Impériale* (Paris, 1982), p. 85.

[185]Duffy, *Austerlitz,* p. 137.

[186]*Les Cahiers du Capitaine Coignet*, p. 473.

[187]S.H.A.T., dossier Moustapha.

[188]Lachouque, *La Garde Impériale*, p. 85.

(six files). Each battalion used one of their companies as *tirailleurs* to precede the remaining formed companies.[189]

Drouet arranged his division in three lines, each line consisting of three battalions belonging to the same regiment. The first two lines consisted of the brigade under the command of Bernard-Georges-François Frère. The 41-year-old Frère had served under Augereau in Bonaparte's *Armée d'Italie* in the 1796-97 campaign, and in 1800 was the commander of the *Grenadiers à pied de la Garde des Consuls* before receiving his promotion to *général de brigade*.[190] Frère commanded the 1st Brigade, which consisted of the 94th and 95th *Ligne*. Frère formed his brigade of six battalions in checkerboard formation with the three battalions of the 94th *Ligne* numbering 1,814 combatants in front under the command of Jean-Nicolas Razout, with the three battalions of the 95th *Ligne* fielding a strength of 1,903 people under Colonel Marc-Nicolas-Louis Pécheux in the second line.[191]

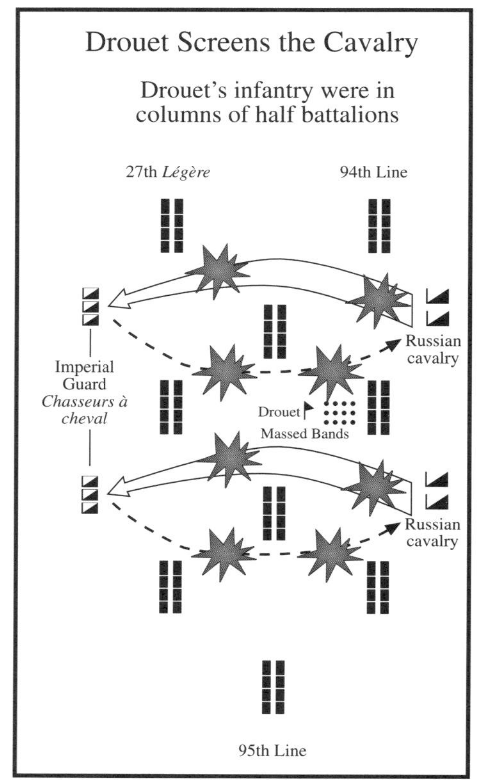

Forty-two-year-old *général de brigade* François-Jean Werlé commanded the 2nd Brigade. The only regiment of Werlé's command was the 27th *Légère* under Colonel Jean-Baptiste Charnotet. The 27th *Légère* was positioned as the division's third line, and brought three battalions onto the field at Austerlitz numbering 2,069 officers and other ranks. The division's two companies of artillery with 229 combatants and 10 pieces of ordnance moved with Werlé and the light infantrymen.[192]

The appearance of Drouet's command was a welcome sight for the French Guard cavalry. Using Drouet's battalions as a shield, squadrons of tiring French horsemen withdrew from the cavalry *mêlée*, moved past Drouet's battalions and halted behind the infantrymen in order to rest the animals and troopers before spurring their formations back into action. At one point, some Russian cavalry tried to attack a group of "Favored Children" that were reforming to the rear of Drouet's command. The Russian horse charged through the wide intervals between Drouet's battalions, taking fire from the wide columns of half battalions as they moved by. After the Russian cavalry passed the ranks of the bluecoated infantry, they were met by carbine fire from the troopers of *Chasseurs à cheval* who had received the charge while standing. Winded by their prior combat, disorganized when they came upon the French Guard *Chasseurs à cheval*, and then unexpectedly blasted by point-blank fire from the leveled carbines of the busby-topped troopers, these Russian squadrons broke and fled. On their return towards friendly lines, the Russian squadrons were further punished by fire from Drouet's formations.

Meanwhile, the superior quality of the French cavalry was becoming more apparent with each passing minute. Although heavily outnumbered, the French horsemen began pushing back their counterparts. Excellent French swordsmanship and discipline became too much for the Tsar's noblemen; their squadrons began coming apart. In this *mêlée*, the "Gods" captured the standard of the 1st Squadron of the Garde du Corps. The Russians lost more and more troopers as the French Guard cavalry pressed relentlessly onward, increasing their advantages which they had worked so hard to achieve.

The superiority of the French horsemen was nowhere more graphically apparent than in the struggle between the squadrons of the "Gods" and the *Chevalier Garde*. Napoleon's prized heavy cavalry regiment dealt the *Chevalier Garde* a particularly horrible defeat. The *Chevalier Garde*:

---

[189] S.H.A.T., C^2 22 and 474.
[190] Six, *Dictionnaire biographique*, vol. 1, p. 468.
[191] S.H.A.T., *Tableau de la Grande Armée Dernière quinzaine du mois brumaire an XIV*, "Situation au 18 brumaire an XIV (9 November 1805)" and C^2 474.
[192] S.H.A.T., C^2 474.

composed of the most notable young men of the Russian nobility, lost heavily, because the swagger in which they had indulged against the French having come to the ears of our soldiers, these, especially the *Grenadiers à cheval*, attacked the Russians with fury, skewering them with their enormous swords while crying out: 'We will give the ladies of Saint Petersburg something to cry about!'[193]

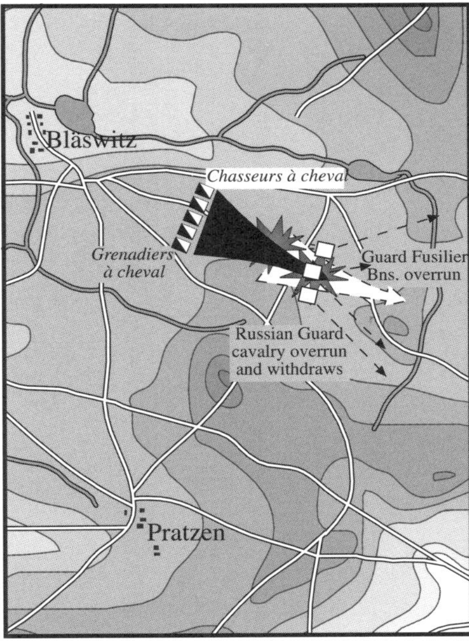

The French Guard Cavalry defeats their Russian counterparts and go on to defeat the Russian Guard Infantry

After disposing of the Tsar's most prestigious horsemen, the French Guard cavalry continued to press onward, charging with a vengeance into the ranks of the nearby Russian Guard infantry. With their supporting formations of cavalry now gone, and with the French Guard cavalry hacking through their formations, the Russian Guard infantry broke and ran (the Guard Grenadier Regiment was not included in this slaughter as they were still far to the rear). As the formations of the Russian Guard came apart, their survivors fled eastward past the village of Krzenowitz, and continued the rout through Austerlitz. No doubt, Bernadotte was aware of the victory earned by the French Imperial Guard Cavalry. Rather than pursue and utterly destroy this fleeing rabble, Bernadotte, true to his character, ordered Drouet to halt his division on the heights above Krzenowitz. About a half mile to the north and lagging far behind Drouet's advance, was *général de division* Oliver Macoux Rivaud de la Raffinière with his 5,266 combatants and 12 guns of the 1st Infantry Division of the 1st Corps.[194] Although these men had not fired a shot during the entire campaign, they were not allowed to engage the reeling allies.

Therefore, Bernadotte pulled in the reins of his command when the only thing that opposed him were Hohenlohe's three regiments of Austrian cüirassiers as well as a few battalions of Russians. Regrettably for the French army, Bernadotte was not a man to take more than 11,000 infantry and 22 guns and try to advance against what at that time was no more than 3,300 enemy—800 exhausted Austrian horsemen and the 2,300 Russians in three battalions of the Guard Grenadier Regiment, supported by its' six battalion pieces and a full company of Guard heavy artillery.[195] There can be not doubt that a golden opportunity to trap and utterly destroy the rudderless hordes of the Russian Imperial Guard slipped through Bernadotte's fingers. The Emperor's aide-de-camp, Savary, said that Napoleon was "astonished" to find out about Bernadotte's timid behavior, considering the general course of the battle.

> Had Marshal Bernadotte's Division [Drouet] continued marching another half hour, instead of halting in its position [above Krzenowitz], it would have been across the road from Austerlitz to Ozeitsch, by which the right wing of the Russian army was retreating. By stopping that movement, we would have completed the destruction of the latter.[196]

Rapp returns to present his trophies to Napoleon

While Bernadotte was reining in his command, Rapp and the other officers were returning to Napoleon on the Staré Vinohrady shortly after 1:30 P.M. with captives and trophies. One of the prisoners was Colonel Prince Repnin, commander of the 4th Squadron of the *Chevalier Gardes*. Nine other officers belonging to the

---

[193] *Memoirs of Baron de Marbot,* vol. 1, p. 199.

[194] S.H.A.T., C[2] 474.

[195] Duffy, *Austerlitz,* p. 138, states that only the Austrian cüirassiers were there to cover the fleeing Russian Imperial Guard. However, he omits the Guard Grenadier Regiment, their battalion artillery and the supporting 12-pounder battery that were also in reserve and not yet comitted to action.

[196] *Memoirs of the Duke of Rovigo* (Savary), vol. 1, p. 135.

Chasseur à cheval
of the Imperial Guard

Russian Guard cavalry regiments were also captured, along with one standards belonging to the *Chevalier Gardes* and another taken from the Guard Cossacks.[197]

After receiving these prisoners and trophies, Napoleon rode forward to the scene of the Guard's combat on the Pratzen. Perhaps nowhere else was the superior fighting power of the *Grande Armée* more vividly displayed than where the Emperor's best units had weighed into the finest that the Russians had to offer. The ground where the duty squadron of the "Gods" hit the *Chevalier Garde* was marked by a whole rank of dead bodies from Alexander's young and unfortunate regiment.[198] Fighting the "Favored Children," the *Mameluks* and the "Gods," the *Chevalier Garde* suffered a total of 36 officers *hors de combat,* along with 200 troopers killed or wounded. Further to the east, the earth was covered with the bodies from the Russian Guard infantry. One eyewitness remembered that "whole companies were heaped in bloody piles along their original alignments"[199] where they had been hit and sabered unmercifully by the *Grenadiers à cheval.* Philippe de Ségur, one of Napoleon's aides-de-camp, described the scene almost identically.

> A whole row of Alexander's unfortunate young Gardes du Corps lying on the ground with their death wounds in front, encumbered the spot where this terrible encounter had taken place. Other lines of dead and wounded, with the knapsacks of the infantry, (which it is the Russian custom to deposit on the ground at their feet before entering combat) indicated the other positions where the infantry of the enemy's Guard had succumbed... [200]

Mameluk

The "Gods" had paid an astonishing low price for the awful carnage that they had visited upon the Russian Imperial Guard cavalry and infantry. Only six officers of Napoleon's superb heavy cavalry regiment had been wounded, while only three troopers were killed and 18 others were wounded. The heaviest losses sustained by the *Grenadiers à cheval* were among their horses; they lost 99 due to wounds and fatigue.[201] The light cavalry of the French Imperial Guard had paid a higher price. The "Favored Children" mourned the loss of Colonel Morland and Captain Thervay, both of whom were killed in action, along with eight troopers and 153 horses. In addition, 18 officers were wounded as well as 57 other ranks.[202] For their important role in the fighting and for all the damage they inflicted, the ferocious *Mameluks* did not lose a single combatant![203] Indeed, Napoleon's Imperial Guard cavalry had proved the difference between truly élite combat veterans as opposed to parade ground troops selected solely for their physical size or their noble birth.

[197] Andolenko, *Aigles de Napoléon Contre Drapeaux du Tsar*, pp. 103-106.
[198] *Memoirs of Ségur*, pp. 253-254.
[199] Pétiet, *Souvenirs Militaires de l'Histoire Contemporaine,* p. 32;
[200] *Memoirs of Ségur*, pp. 253-254. Several French eyewitnesses mention the rows of Russian backpacks taken during the course of the battle.
[201] S.H.A.T., C^2 16 and 470.
[202] S.H.A.T., C^2 16 and 470.
[203] S.H.A.T., C^2 16 and 470.

The Final Destruction of Buxhöwden's First Three Columns

While "the litter of corpses and wreckage on the Pratzen testified to the defeat of the allied IV Column and Russian Imperial Guard,"[204] Napoleon was seeking the complete destruction of the other allied formations. To the north, Lannes and Murat were locked in a separate combat against Bagration and Liechtenstein, while to the south of the Staré Vinohrady and still engaged along the Goldbach the Emperor could see the yawning flanks and rear of the allied I, II and III Columns. The changing circumstances of battle caused Napoleon to immediately alter his plan. The wide sweeping encirclement from the far left designed to entrap the entire allied army that had been planned by Napoleon the evening before was no longer feasible. The Emperor seized the moment and decided to wheel his units already on the conquered Pratzen Plateau towards the south in a smaller version of the encirclement in order to fall upon the exposed enemy formations. Napoleon dictated orders directly to the division generals: Saint-Hilaire and Vandamme were to take their divisions, conduct a right wheel at once and attack the allied troops south of the Pratzen. After quickly conferring with each other by going over their plan of maneuver, Saint-Hilaire and Vandamme got their men moving shortly after 2:00 P.M. Meanwhile, Imperial orders also reached General Legrand, instructing him to support the movements of Saint-Hilaire, while General Beaumont with his 3rd Dragoon Division would follow in support. Other formations directed southward were Oudinot's 5,123-man *Grenadiers de la Réserve* and Bessières' 5,208 members of the French Imperial Guard.[205]

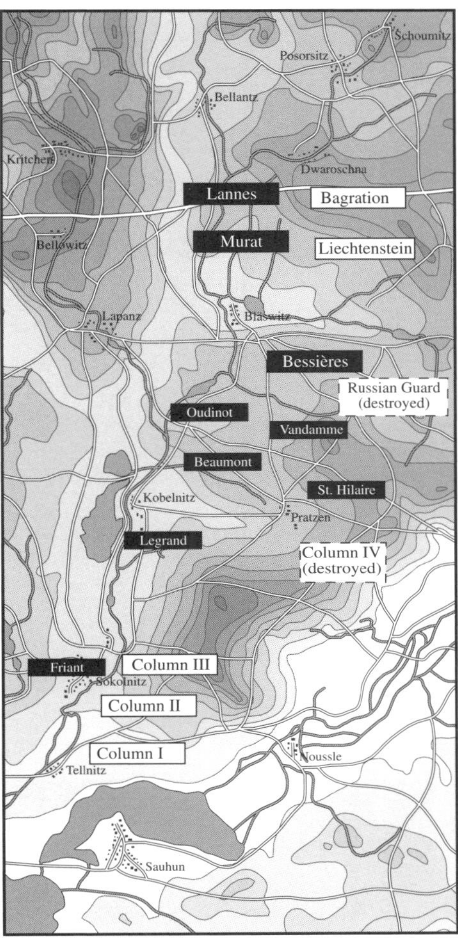

By 2 P.M. the French are ready to exploit their victory on the Pratzen Heights

As the new French attack began to get underway, the brigades of Schiner and Férey marched with Vandamme and made for the steep southern edge of the Pratzen Plateau that overlooked any possible allied retreat from the Goldbach further south to the village of Augezd. Meanwhile, Candras' brigade from Vandamme's Division supported the movements of Saint-Hilaire's Division. These troops passed to the south of the village of Pratzen, then wheeled westward and descended off the Pratzen Plateau towards Sokolnitz. Levasseur's 3rd Brigade of Legrand's Division swung into line on the right flank of Saint-Hilaire, while Generals Legrand, Merle and Féry brought the 26th *Légère* and the rallied 3rd *Ligne* into line north of the Sokolnitz complex to further extend Saint-Hilaire's flank.

About the same time that the French forces were rolling down off the Pratzen, Marshal Davout launched an attack with his redoubtable troops. After repositioning the 33rd *Ligne*, Davout sent this regiment against the western salient of the village of Sokolnitz. Meanwhile, the 48th *Ligne* attacked and expanded its foothold on the southern edge of town. Further north around the Sokolnitz castle, the 15th *Légère* and the 111th *Ligne*, operating as *tirailleurs en grande bande,* swarmed over the grounds, tormenting the Russian defenders.

While Langeron and Prebyshevsky were fighting off Davout's infantry, the worst possible news came to the Russian generals: French forces were bearing down on them from the Pratzen. With their men already locked in combat, with their supply of small arms ammunition all but exhausted, the Russians were now becoming totally enveloped by the troops spearheaded by Saint-Hilaire and Vandamme. Both Langeron and Prebyshevsky knew the battle was lost. Langeron took the remnants of the 8th *Jaeger* and Viborg Musketeers and headed south to escape Saint-Hilaire. Meanwhile, the Perm Musketeers from Langeron's II Column and the two battalions of the 7th *Jaeger* from Prebyshevsky's III Column were separated from the rest of their commands and holed up in the castle of Sokolnitz. Saint-Hilaire ordered Thiébault to carry the castle with his brigade, while the other

[204] Duffy, *Austerlitz,* p. 140.
[205] S.H.A.T., C^2 481 and 470.

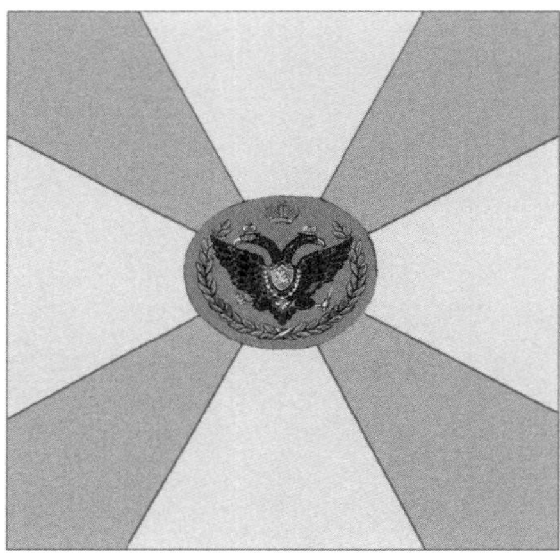

The Perm Musketeer Regiment lost this yellow and green standard after their last stand at Sokolnitz

brigades of the division mopped up the enemy resistance from the pheasantry south to the village. Thiébault recalled that:

> the Russians who were on the flanks of the château offered little resistance, but those who held the castle and its outbuildings made a desperate defense. Avenues, stables, barns—everything served them for shelter, and everywhere they fought until the last extremity. A great massacre took place there. All had to be vanquished, man by man... I can claim on that day, proved to me the truth of the saying that it is easier to kill six Russian soldiers than to conquer one.[206]

While at the head of the 36th *Ligne*, Thiébault was wounded when separate discharges of canister from two Russian battalion guns bruised his breast-bone in two places, went through his collar-bone and smashed his shoulder. The general was lucky to survive because 20 men behind him were killed by the same blasts. The regiment pressed forward and fell upon the Russian gunners with a vengeance, killing the entire crew.[207]

Another group of Russians—the remaining units of Prebyshevsky's III Column—were cut off in and around the pheasantry with their commanding officer. Not wanting to surrender, Prebyshevsky decided that his only course of action was to break out of the trap and move northeastward towards the last known position of the IV Column. He hoped that somewhere east of Kobelnitz the columns would join forces. While moving to find the IV Column, Prebyshevsky's command was continually assailed from the flanks and rear. The southern flank was menaced by the 10th *Légère*, 18th and 75th *Ligne,* along with the *Tirailleurs corses*, while the rear of the Russians was assailed by the 36th *Ligne,* and the northern flank attacked by part of Oudinot's grenadiers. In addition to the volleys of musketry, discharges of canister from the French artillery swept Prebyshevsky's ranks. The retreating Russians kept up their fire as long as their dwindling supplies of cartridges lasted. However, around the frozen pond of upper Kobelnitz, their ammunition finally gave out. Unable to respond to the incessant punishment inflicted by the French, the strain became too much for the Russian battalions. No amount of shouting from the generals or other officers could keep men in ranks if they had no means of defending themselves. As a result, the Russians threw down their muskets in order to run faster. The plight of the III Column was described in Prebyshevsky in his after-action report to Tsar Alexander.

Another of Prebyshevsky's regiments, the Azov Musketeers lost this brown and pink standard and two others when they were trapped at Sokolnitz

> We had endured the most intense fire for eight *[sic]* hours and our casualties were heavy. One of my subordinate commanders had been killed, another wounded and the rest were reduced to confusion by the vicious salvoes of canister which came in from three sides. We ran out of small arms ammunition and we had no hope of support. With all of this we fought on against the enemy to the limit of our strength, according to the loyalty we owe to Your Imperial Highness.[208]

The French infantry were close to taking Prebyshevsky and his men prisoner when Colonel Jean-Baptiste Franceschi-Delonne, at the head of the Élite Company of the 8th Hussars, suddenly charged into the Russian ranks and compelled them to surrender. The survivors of the allied III Column "surrendered without more

[206] *The Memoirs of Baron Thiébault,* vol. 2, p. 167.
[207] *The Memoirs of Baron Thiébault,* vol. 2, p. 168.
[208] *Kutuzov. Sbornik*, vol. 2, p. 268.

ado to a handful of hussars."[209] Taken by Franceschi's 8th Hussars were four generals including Prebyshevsky, Müller III, Selekhov and Strik, along with two colonels (one of which was Prince Tibersky of the Narva Musketeers), some majors, 60 other officers and about 2,500 men.[210]

Lejeune, one of Marshal Berthier's aides-de-camp, was returning from Davout to make a report to Imperial headquarters when he had a memorable encounter. Riding with Lejeune was *adjudant-major* Louis-Charles-Barthélemy Sopransi and 20 troopers of the 1st Dragoons. These men came across a group of Russian soldiers from the Narva Musketeer Regiment that had been separated from the rest of Prebyshevsky's Column. The French noticed an allied general in a simple, white uniform blackened with powder stains standing in front of the greencoated infantrymen. The Russians:

> tried to bare our passage, but we pushed right through them and wounded the general in the arm, while Sopransi seized the bridle of his horse. We dragged him along with us to our own lines. I asked him his name, and he replied: 'I am the Baron Wimpfen.'[211]

The Narva Musketeer Regiment lost two blue and orange standards of an older pattern

Thus, the second highest-ranking officer of the allied III Column had been captured.

As Prebyshevsky's III Column was being hunted down and rounded up, Vandamme and Beaumont halted at the Chapel of Saint Anthony in advance of their divisions. They were soon joined by Soult, Napoleon and the Imperial staff. Peering southward, the French commanders saw the village of Augezd, "which offered the only apparent path of retreat for the allies as they flooded from right to left across the darkening plain."[212] South of Augezd stretched two large expanses of ice covered with snow—the frozen ponds of Satschan and Menitz. The French officers realized that the sooner Augezd could be captured, the more allied prisoners would be taken. Soult then issued another order—his first in several hours—when he told Vandamme to seal off the escape route.[213]

Vandamme hurried forward his infantry that had just completed their march from the Staré Vinohrady and appeared on the southern edge of the Pratzen where they deployed for action outside canister range of the enemy's artillery. Vandamme's divisional artillery arrived soon thereafter, unlimbered and began firing on the allies below. Under this covering fire, Colonel Edighoffen and the 1st Battalion of the 28th *Ligne* marched down the slope to the east of Augezd and cut the road that led to Hostieradek. Meanwhile, the 2nd Battalion of the 28th, along with the 4th *Ligne* and the 24th *Légère* were led forward by Vandamme, Schiner and Férey past the Chapel of Saint Anthony, saluting Napoleon with cries of "*Vive l'Empereur!*" These five battalions descended on the village of Augezd "like a torrent,"[214] sweeping away the diminutive 8th *Jaeger* and capturing its commanding officer, Colonel Sulima.[215]

With the retreat route directly to the east now closed to the allies, what remained of Langeron's II Column and the commands of Kienmayer and Dokhturov now faced irrevocable annihilation. The only way to save some of the men was to form a determined rearguard to buy as much time as possible while the rest of the troops escaped. Dokhturov and Kienmayer held a hurried conference. They decided

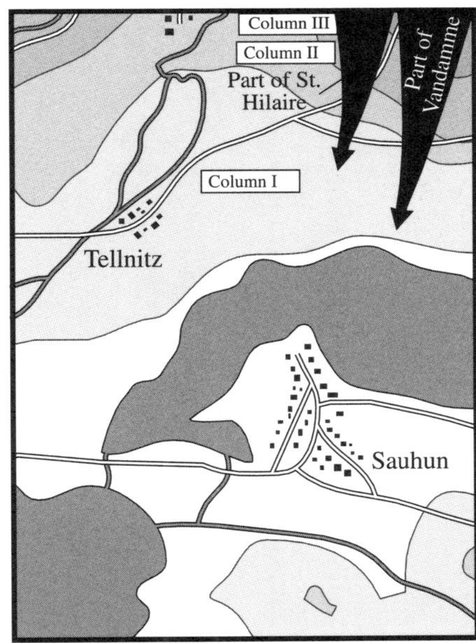

Saint-Hilaire and Vandamme close on the Allied escape route

[209] Pétiet, *Souvenirs Militaires de l'Histoire Contemporaine,* p. 33.

[210] S.H.A.T., C^2 15 and 470.

[211] *Memoirs of Baron Lejeune*, vol. 1, pp. 31-32.

[212] Duffy, *Austerlitz,* p. 144.

[213] S.H.A.T., C^2 25.

[214] Stutterheim, *A Detailed Account of the Battle of Austerlitz*, p. 121.

[215] S.H.A.T., *Journal des opérations du 4e corps;* C^2 15 and 470.

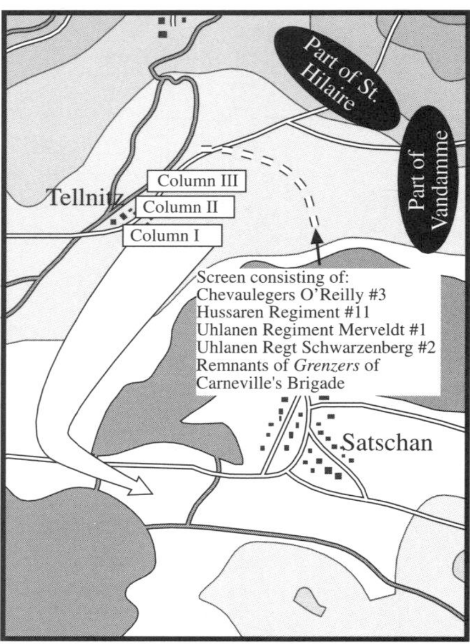

The Allies try to cover their retreat

to immediately pull their men out of Tellnitz and head south to safety. The Chevaulegers-Regiment O'Reilly #3, the Székler *Grenz*-Hussaren-Regiment #11, the small detachments from Uhlanen-Regiment Merveldt #1 and Uhlanen-Regiment Schwarzenberg #2, together with one of their two cavalry batteries, along with what remained of the *Grenzer* battalions from Carneville's Brigade, would form the screen behind which the rest of the I Column would retreat. The generals designated that their escape path lay across the frozen ponds, or the narrow stretch of land between them. To secure the retreat route on the eastern side of the ponds, the Hussar-Regiment Hessen-Homburg #4 was dispatched to watch and intercept any French movement which might issue from Augezd.

As the Austrian cavalry and infantry formed their protective umbrella, they were joined by the Sysoev and Melentev Cossack Regiments. The other troops of I Column retreated:

> in a single column, breaking off in succession from the left wing, and retired [from Tellnitz] along the narrow spur of land between the village of Tellnitz and the Satschan pond. The troops maintained good order, even though they were under a continuous fire of musketry and canister... The O'Reilly Chevaulegers drove back the pursuing enemy cavalry, and kept up an accurate fire with its cavalry battery, silencing several French guns; the regiment's action covered the retreat of the infantry, which was carried out in good order over the Satschan pond and further onwards to Neudorf.[216]

The French cavalry that the Chevaulegers-Regiment O'Reilly #3 drove back before retiring across the Satschen Pond were elements of the 3rd Dragoon Division under the command of *général de division* Marc-Antoine Bonin Beaumont de la Boninière. The 42-year-old Beaumont had been in the cavalry his entire military career, serving as colonel of the 9th and then the 5th Dragoons during the wars of the French Revolution before being promoted to *général de brigade* in 1795. Transferred to the *Armée d'Italie* in 1796, Beaumont came to Bonaparte's attention early in the First Italian Campaign. During the next four years, Beaumont commanded different cavalry brigades and divisions before being promoted to *général de division* in December 1802.[217]

Beaumont de la Boninière

Beaumont was a capable enough officer to be entrusted with one of the Emperor's divisions of cavalry, but he was saddled with two uneven brigade commanders with equally uneven regiments of dragoons. The brigade commanders, Charles-Joseph Boyé and Nicolas-Joseph Scalfort, aged 43 and 53 respectively, had never shown any exceptional qualities that would point them towards higher command. They had taken part in the opening combat at Wertingen (see Chapter V), and now had an opportunity to fight under the eyes of the Emperor. Of the six regiments which comprised their two brigades, the 21st Dragoons were unquestionably the best. Commanded by 30-year-old Colonel Jean-Baptiste-Charles-René-Joseph du Mas de Polart, the 21st brought three squadrons totaling 285 officers and other ranks onto the field at Austerlitz.[218] Of these, 83 had seen at least 10 years service, while 57 others had been in uniform over 15 years. Furthermore, the reputation of the 21st Dragoons was held in so high esteem that the 61 members of the regiment's Élite Company served during part of the campaign

---

[216] K. k. Kriegsarchiv, F.A., *Ausführliche Relation der am 2 ten Dezember, 1805.*
[217] Six, *Dictionnaire biographique*, vol. 1, pp. 67-68.
[218] S.H.A.T., *Tableau de la Grande Armée Dernière quinzaine du mois brumaire an XIV*, "Situation au 30 brumaire an XIV (21 November 1805);" C^2 470 and 473.

as either mounted *gendarmes* at Napoleon's headquarters, or as Marshal Davout's mounted escort. Therefore, it was with this excellent core of veteran soldiers that the 21st was posted as the divisional reserve. The remainder of Scalfort's Brigade, the 9th and 16th Dragoons numbering 539 combatants, formed the division's second line. Meanwhile, the 814 members of the 5th, 8th and 12th Dragoons under Boyé formed the first line.[219]

Beaumont had given permission for Boyé to launch his command against the withdrawing allied troops. Moving forward in columns of squadrons, the three regiments of French dragoons were countercharged by the Chevaulegers-Regiment O'Reilly #3, which had deployed in squadrons abreast. With a frontage wider than the French, the single Austrian regiment was able to envelop the flanks and defeat Boyé's dragoons. While this action was taking place, the 9th and 16th Dragoons had been standing under the fire of an Austrian cavalry battery. Amidst the explosions of howitzer shells and bouncing cannonballs, Scalfort could see Boyé was in trouble and ordered in the 9th and 16th forward in order to help extricate their comrades. However, these two regiments became engaged before they could properly deploy, and their flanks were also enveloped and the formations broken by the excellent regiment of Austrian horse.

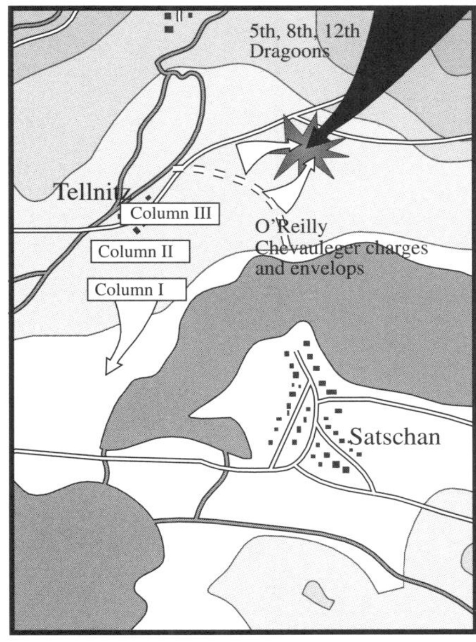

The O'Reilly Chevauleger halts Beaumont's dragoons

Relentlessly pursuing the five regiments of defeated French dragoons, the O'Reilly Chevaulegers—in their white coats trimmed in red, and riding brown horses—had shot their bolt. With exhausted men and horses, with their ranks disordered, the O'Reillys were ripe for a counterstrike. Seeing the oncoming Austrians, Colonel du Mas de Polart realized that he had to save the situation. Never one to shy away from an adversary, the colonel—who had commanded the regiment almost four years—gave the signal to charge and led his 21st Dragoons forward. Although the French regiment was only half the size and therefore occupied about half the width of the O'Reilly Chevaulegers, the veterans of the 21st had no trouble in scattering the blown Austrian horse, thus saving the rest of the division.

Napoleon saw Mas de Polart and the 21st Dragoons save the rest of the 3rd Dragoon Division. Despite the heroics of the 21st Dragoons, the minor setback by the 3rd Dragoon Division put the Emperor:

> in an evil temper. He caught sight of [a colonel] who had accompanied the division. 'Go back there,' said the Emperor, 'and tell the general in command from me that he is no bloody good![220]

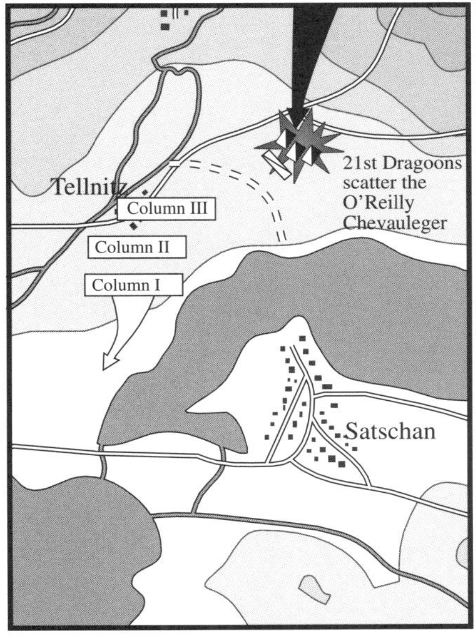

The 21st Dragoons finally drive off the O'Reilly Chevaulegers

Turning to his Imperial staff, Napoleon then ordered General Gardane to go take command of the dragoons, charge at their head and break the enemy resistance. Gardane rode off to Beaumont, who was rallying his regiments behind the protection of Mas de Polart's 21st Dragoons and the division's half-company of horse artillery. By this time, the French horse guns had attracted the fire of not only the Austrian cavalry battery, but perhaps as many as 20 other Russian pieces under the command of Colonel Sievers. The weight of the allied fire soon silenced the three French horse guns, which prompted the O'Reillys—now reformed since their repulse at the hands of the 21st Dragoons—to advance once again. As the whitecoated cavalry came on, the dragoons suddenly peeled away, unmasking a company of the Imperial Guard *Volante* that Napoleon had ordered up to help stabilize Beaumont's front. The superb artillerists poured a deadly canister fire onto the ranks of the O'Reilly

---

[219] S.H.A.T., *Tableau de la Grande Armée Dernière quinzaine du mois brumaire an XIV*, "Situation au 30 brumaire an XIV (21 November 1805);" C^2 470 and 473.

[220] *Mémoirs du Général Comte de Saint-Chamans,* p. 27.

Chevaulegers that staggered their formation, forcing them to retire to the south of Tellnitz. Meanwhile, the surviving 2,000 members of the Advance Guard of the I Column reached the village of Satschan by way of the narrow strip of land that divided the ponds.[221]

As Kienmayer was extricating his command with professionalism, Buxhöwden displayed much less ability in his handling of the Russian survivors of the I and II Columns. The overall commander of the I, II and III Columns had an order from Kutuzov to save what he could. Evidently, Buxhöwden was only concerned with himself. Leaving his men and general officers to fend for themselves, Buxhöwden and his staff were the first to reach the relative safety of the south bank as they shamelessly bolted across the rickety Satschan Pond Bridge that was just below Augezd. Some of the Russian guns followed next, but their weight was too much for the bridge. Breaking through the planks, some equipment became stuck fast. About this same time, one of the ammunition carts was struck by a French shell from one of the howitzers of the Imperial Guard *Volante*, exploding into the afternoon sky. With this retreat path now closed, the remaining troops on the north bank of the ponds faced a cruel choice: try to escape or surrender. A couple of cavalry regiments ventured to run the gauntlet between Augezd and the ponds, and galloped by under a hail of canister fire from the Horse Artillery of the Italian Guard and *Volante* gunners. Meanwhile, a few of the remaining Russian artillerists abandoned their pieces on the north bank, but most of them simply unlimbered their guns and heroically sacrificed themselves by continuing to fire until being overrun by the French. Many Russian infantrymen broke ranks and streamed across the ice in an attempt to save themselves as the French Imperial Guard *Volante* fired on them.

Eye-witnesses differ on what happened to the Russians that chanced to flee across on the frozen ponds. Imperial aide-de-camp Philippe-Paul de Ségur was with the Emperor when Napoleon saw that the:

> white and glistening mirror become suddenly black with the scattered multitude of fugitives, who had risked themselves on the dangerous foothold which gave way beneath their feet under the indentation of our pitiless bullets. From the heights [Chapel of Saint Anthony] where he had remained, the Emperor saw this and exclaimed: 'It is Aboukir!'[222]

Napoleon then dispatched Ségur to help lead a charge against the Russian survivors on the north bank. Ségur first passed by the dragoons of Beaumont as they fell back after another unsuccessful charge—this one a try at closing with the Russian ordnance that was still operational. Joining with Vandamme's infantry as they descended on the Russian artillery trapped on the north bank, Ségur remembered that the Russian gunners "waited for us steadfastly until we were almost upon their pieces, then discharged them at us point at blank range so that my face was scorched by the flame issued from one of them."[223] Once these and many other guns were captured, Ségur noticed that one of the battalions of the 24th *Légère* had been:

> reduced to 150 men; and on my exclamation at the sight of so small a number, Vandamme replied: 'Yes, indeed; it is impossible

[221] Stutterheim, *A Detailed Account of the Battle of Austerlitz*, pp. 124-125; *Memoirs of Ségur*, p. 255.
[222] *Memoirs of Ségur*, p. 255
[223] *Memoirs of Ségur*, p. 256

> to make a good omelet without breaking a great many eggs!'[224]

After cutting his way through those who still resisted, Ségur took pity on the soldiers who were struggling to save themselves in the freezing water.

> Some of us even held out a helping hand to these drowning men. As I passed by, I pulled out a Cossack from the frozen water. Little did I then think that the following year, after first taking part in the conquest of Naples and the Calabrias, then in that of Prussia, very far from these lakes I should meet him again, and that, wounded myself, and a prisoner in the middle of Poland, I should be recognized and saved in my turn by this Tartar![225]

Ségur's view is seconded by Captain Louis-François Lejeune, and aide-de-camp to Marshal Berthier. Lejeune was also at the scene, and saw the trapped Russian infantry on the north bank:

> finally imagined that their only chance of safety was to try and cross the icy ponds dividing them from the other side. A few men, indeed, might have got over safely; but when a number had reached the middle of the pond, the ice began to crack beneath their weight. They paused, and the troops behind them pushed on, and soon some 6,000 men collected in a dense crowd on the swaying slippery ice. There was a pause, and then in the brief space of a couple of minutes the whole mass with arms and baggage disappeared beneath the broken-up ice, not one man escaping or even appearing again at the top of the water. We looked down upon the churning, rippling waves produced by the struggles of so many human creatures swallowed up so suddenly, and a thrill of horror ran through us all. Very soon the fractured ice, broken up by the useless efforts of those beneath it, sank again into repose, the clouds were once more reflected on its gleaming surface, and we knew that it was over.[226]

Another French eyewitness in the *Chasseurs à pied* of Napoleon's Imperial Guard, described the scene as follows:

> Coming to the slope that overlooks the lakes I fell out of ranks for a moment, and was thus able to observe, in the plain, the terrible struggle engaged between the 4th Corps and the portion of the Russian army facing it, having the lakes at its rear. This last deadly movement was terrible. Imagine 12,000 to 15,000 men fleeing at the top of their speed over thin ice and suddenly falling in, almost to a man!
>
> What a grievous and melancholy spectacle, but what a triumph for the victors! Our arrival at the lakes was saluted by a score of cannon-shot [Colonel Sievers' Russian guns], which

---

[224] *Memoirs of Ségur*, p. 256. It might have seemed to Ségur that one battalion was reduced to only 150, because the 1,564 members of the two battalions of the 26th *Légère* lost 54 killed and 262 wounded at the battle—right at 20% casualties. Whatever the numeric strength of the battalion witnessed by Ségur, the quote by Vandamme is illustrative of the fierce combat on the Pratzen that had been experienced by his division.

[225] *Memoirs of Ségur*, p. 256.

[226] *Memoirs of Baron Lejeune*, vol. 1, p. 32.

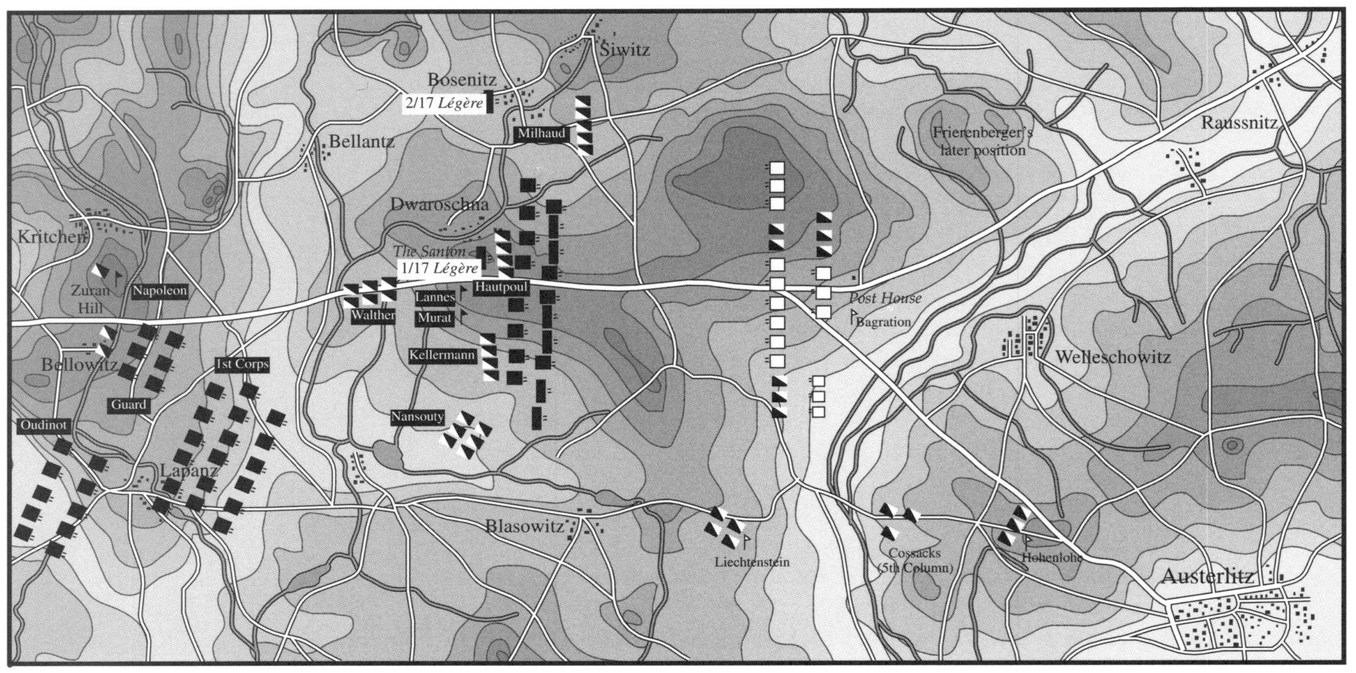

Above, the northern part of the battlefield

Below, the gentle slope of the Pratzen Heights seen from Sokolnitz

> did us no great harm. The artillery of the Guard very soon extinguished this fire and itself proceeded to fire with incomparable briskness upon the ice, in order to shatter it and render it incapable of supporting the weight of men.[227]

Whatever the number of allied soldiers that perished in the lakes, the official Austrian report on the battle does not specifically mention what happened to the men that crossed the ice of the Satschan Pond, but does offer details about what had happened on the Menitz Pond:

> The mass of men retreating over the ice of the Satschan Pond attracted the fire of the enemy cannon on the chapel hill at Augezd to the area of the causeway. An ammunition cart on the causeway was struck by a howitzer shell and blew up, provoking a jam among the pieces which were travelling behind. Some of the artillery of the column was therefore left on the field, and part of the infantry now made their retreat across the ice of the Menitz Pond; luckily the surface was frozen so hard that it bore the weight of the mass of troops without breaking. Just two men and a few of the horses fell through. Their bodies were found afterwards, when the ponds were drained.[228]

The firmness of the Menitz Pond was also confirmed by the Count of Comeau, an *émigré* officially in Bavarian service that was at Imperial headquarters and close enough to see the débâcle. Comeau did not think that the depth of the water was a concern; he saw Russians swimming around the edges of the pond, and that "even if a few platoons paddled in the water, it was not deep enough to have drowned them."[229]

As the last allied survivors disappeared to the south, thousands of prisoners were being rounded up on the north bank. Many Frenchmen who had up until this point fought the battle with a 'no quarter' mentality, suddenly took pity on the enemy as entire companies of beaten and exhausted Russians surrendered *en masse*. Thiard remembered that once "the Emperor gave the order to cease fire … we managed to save the men on the banks."[230] One of the final members of the Combined Russian and Austrian Army to leave this frightful scene was General Langeron. "I had already seen some battles lost," the commander of the II Column said, "but I never had an idea of such a defeat."[231] Mercifully for the allies, the fighting on this part of the field was over. However, there was still firing on the north end of the battlefield, where Lannes and Murat were waging their own battle against Liechtenstein and Bagration.

Fighting on the Northern Flank—
The Opening Moves

Just to the west of the Posoritz Post House, deployed mostly to the north of the Brünn-Olmütz Road, was the Advance Guard of the Combined Russian and Austrian Army under Prince Bagration. From these positions, the Russian general and his men could hear the early morning sounds of the battle rumbling along the

[227] *Memoirs of a French Napoleonic Officer: Jean-Baptiste Barrès,* pp. 76-77.
[228] K. k. Kriegsarchiv, F.A., *Ausführliche Relation der am 2 ten Dezember, 1805.*
[229] Baron de Comeau, *Souvenirs des Guerres d'Allemagne* (Paris, 1900), p. 231.
[230] *Souvenirs Diplomatiques et Miltaires du Général Thiard,* p. 239.
[231] Thiers, *The History of the Consulate & the Empire of France*, vol. 2, p. 82.

The view east from the Napoleon's command post on Zuran Hill. The Santon is visible as the isolated hill to the left

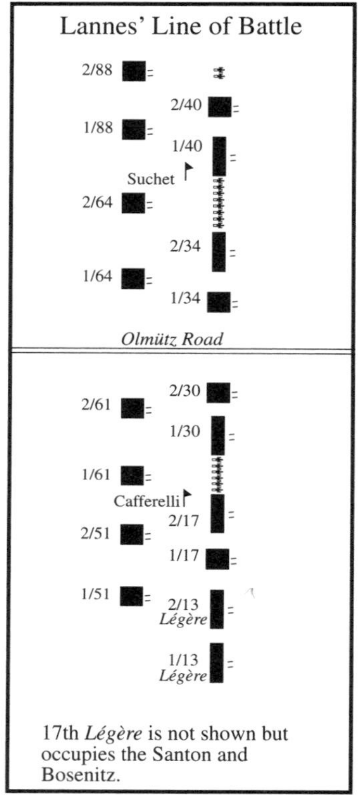

Left and right, the opposing orders of battle

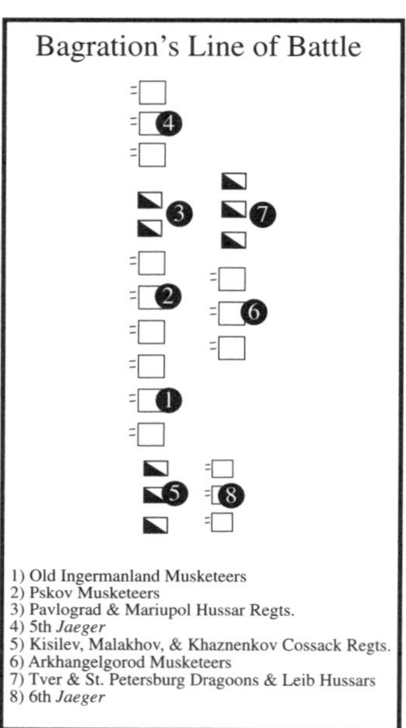

The Santon seen from the south

Goldbach. As the noise of the fighting moved closer, signaling that the combat had escalated to encompass the Pratzen Plateau, then came rebounding off the northern end of the high ground around the Staré Vinohrady, Bagration sensed that it was time to send his troops into action. After ordering his infantry to take off their heavy packs because it was not good for the men to carry that "embarrassing weight in the struggle," Bagration rode along the lines, shouting encouragement to his troops: "You will get the French backpacks; they are full of gold!"[232]

Having completed his inspirational ride, Bagration ordered his units to move out forward shortly before 10:00 A.M., the troops deployed in two lines. The center of the Advance Guard was anchored by Bagration's three regiments of musketeers, with two regiments in the front line astride the Olmütz Road, while the third regiment and the formidable battle cavalry comprised the second line. The hussars completed the units in the first line, with the extremities of both flanks covered by the expendable regiments of *jaeger* whose extended deployments would not interfere with the serious battle work to be performed by the musketeer and cavalry regiments.

Bagration's Advance Guard was a mixture of regiments from Kutuzov's and Buxhöwden's armies. Of the 11,750 officers and other ranks that comprised Bagration's command, some 5,934—slightly more than half—were in the nine battalions that consisted of the Arkhangelgorod, Old Ingermanland and Pskov Musketeer Regiments. The latter two regiments formed the first line, with the former regiment in the second line. The remaining infantry under Bagration were two *jaeger* regiments. The unscathed 5th *Jaeger* had arrived with Buxhöwden, its three battalions numbering 1,440 officers and other ranks. They were deployed on the far right flank of Bagration's first line. By contrast, the number of combatants present in the three battalions of the 6th *Jaeger* reflected the hardships, losses through strategic consumption and grievous battle casualties that had been suffered by the regiments of Kutuzov's army. Following their engagement at Amstetten, after suffering heavy casualties at Dürenstein and then being pounded by French artillery fire at Schöngrabern, the 6th *Jaeger* was beyond being used up—the pitiful remnants of a regiment's three battalions fielded only 364 people at Austerlitz—an average of 121 combatants per battalion! Bagration positioned the survivors of the 6th *Jaeger* on the far left flank of the Advance Guard, sheltered between the small hamlets of Holubitz and Krug and screened by the dubious Kiselev, Malakhov and Khaznenkov Cossack Regiments. The remainder of Bagration's command consisted of the Prince's regular cavalry: the Pavlograd and Mariupol Hussar Regiments, deployed to the right of the Pskov Musketeers, while the Tver and Saint Petersburg Dragoons along with the Leib-*Cuirassier* ("Tsar's") formed to the right of the Arkhangelgorod Musketeers. When the battle began, Bagration had 30 pieces of ordnance supporting his command. These consisted of 18 battalion guns and one company of Russian horse artillery with 12 pieces. When the battle was almost over, two Austrian cavalry batteries totaling 12 pieces arrived from Olmütz. Although these newly-arrived batteries could not make up for the 16 guns already lost, they did increase the number of ordnance that fought under Bagration at some point in the battle to a total of 42 pieces.[233]

To the left of Bagration's command there yawned a wide gap of a mile to the northern slopes of the Staré Vinohrady. This open ground was supposed to have been filled by Liechtenstein's small V Column consisting of only four brigades of cavalry. The troops of that Austrian general had been delayed in their march due to poor staff work that had incorrectly positioned the column the night before

---

[232] *Memoirs of Baron Lejeune*, vol. 1, p. 29.

[233] Russian strengths compiled from various regimental histories in the Russian Archives, Saint Petersburg; also, details on Austrian batteries in: K. k. Kriegsarchiv, F.A., *Ausführliche Relation der am 2 ten Dezember, 1805.*

Liechtenstein

(see page 322). In order to get his horsemen correctly positioned as soon as possible, FML Johann Josef Liechtenstein had sent his two brigades of Russian cavalry ahead of the two brigades of Austrian cavalry.[234]

The 45-year-old Liechtenstein had fought with distinction in the Turkish wars of 1789-1790 as well as throughout the wars of the French Revolution. With this considerable experience, he was the most capable allied officer available to lead a column composed entirely of cavalry. Of the 4,622 officers and other ranks that comprised the 10 regiments of Liechtenstein's command, over half the combatants were in two Russian regiments—the Grand Duke Constantine Uhlans and the Elisabetgrad Hussars. Both units had recently arrived as part of Buxhöwden's army, and the large regiment of 950 uhlans formed their own brigade under General Shepelev. Although the hussars were brigaded with the Chernigov and Kharkov Dragoon Regiments that fielded 366 and 500 combatants respectively, that organization existed only on paper; the 950-man Elisabetgrad Hussars operated completely independently from the dragoons or any other regiment. Bringing up the rear of the V Column was the Austrian contingent consisting of two brigades. The Cüirassier-Regiment Kaiser #1 numbering 566 officers and other ranks in eight squadrons formed one of the brigades, while the Cüirassier-Regiment Nassau-Usingen #5 and the Cüirassier-Regiment Lothringen #7, each fielding only six squadrons, brought about 300 combatants per regiment onto the field. Imperfectly rounding out Liechtenstein's regiments of horse were three regiments of Cossacks totaling 690 combatants. The artillery support for Liechtenstein's cavalry consisted of one Austrian cavalry battery of six guns and one and one-half Russian horse artillery companies of 18 cannon and licornes, making for a total of 24 pieces of ordnance.[235]

A mile to the west of Bagration's and Liechtenstein's forces were two French corps under Marshals Murat and Lannes. Straddling the Olmütz Road was the 5th Corps of the *Grande Armée* under Jean Lannes. Probably a more accurate way to describe the 5th Corps at Austerlitz would be to say that Jean Lannes had with him only one of his three infantry divisions (the 3rd), which was reinforced with the 1st Infantry Division from 3rd Corps plus the 2nd Dragoon Division under Walther temporarily attached from Murat's Reserve Cavalry Corps. It was those three divisions that Lannes commanded on that December day.[236]

Walther

What had happened to the other divisions of 5th Corps not being under the command of Lannes was a combination of factors. The 1st Infantry Division consisting of the *Grenadiers de la Réserve*, had been detached to augment the army's reserve and served at Austerlitz alongside the Imperial Guard. Meanwhile, the 2nd Infantry Division of the 5th Corps, Gazan's victorious yet heavily damaged command that had won at Dürenstein, was still licking its wounds in Vienna. Finally, in a continuation of the command arrangement seen from Amstetten to Schöngrabern, the light cavalry of 5th Corps continued to be detached from Lannes in order to serve with the *Corps des Réserves de Cavalerie* under Murat. In exchange for the detachment of the 5th Corps Light Cavalry, Lannes was given the 2nd Dragoon Division from Murat's command. In summation, with three of his four

[234] K. k. Kriegsarchiv, F.A., *Ausführliche Relation der am 2 ten Dezember, 1805.* Stutterheim, *A Detailed Account of the Battle of Austerlitz*, pp. 92-93.

[235] Russian strengths compiled from various regimental histories in the Russian Archives, Saint Petersburg; also, details on the Austrians in: K. k. Kriegsarchiv, F.A., *Ausführliche Relation der am 2 ten Dezember, 1805;* Stutterheim, *A Detailed Account of the Battle of Austerlitz*, pp. 44-45.

[236] S.H.A.T., C[2] 481, *État de Situation du 5e Corps de la Grande Armée aux ordres de Monsieur le Maréchal Lannes, à l'épogue du 13 frimaire an 14, avec le Detail des pertes éprouvées a la Bataille d'Austerlitz*, hereafter referred to as: *État de Situation du 5e Corps a la Bataille d'Austerlitz.*

divisions either not present or detached to serve under other marshals, Lannes had only one of his own divisions plus temporary authority over two other divisions.[237]

The infantry division assigned to serve under Lannes from Davout's 3rd Corps was under the command of 39-year-old *général de division* Marie-François-Auguste Caffarelli du Falga. Caffarelli earned his hard-fighting reputation in the wars of the French Revolution, being promoted to *général de division* in February 1805. Named to Napoleon's *Maison Militaire* in August in the capacity of an Imperial aide-de-camp, Caffarelli received his division command assignment when *général de division* Baptiste-Pierre-François Bisson, the commander of Davout's 1st Infantry Division, was seriously wounded during the crossing of the Traun River at Lambach on 1 November.[238]

Caffarelli

Like almost every infantry division of the *Grande Armée,* Caffarelli's command consisted of three brigades. *Général de brigade* Joseph-Laurent Demont, a relatively ancient officer for the *Grande Armée* at age 58, commanded the 1st Brigade which consisted of the 17th and 30th *Ligne.* At Austerlitz, these regiments each fielded two battalions with a strength of 1,561 and 1,011, respectively.[239] Jean-Louis Debilly, the 42-year-old *général de brigade* in command of the 2nd Brigade, led the 51st *Ligne* with 1,214 combatants and 61st *Ligne* with 1,175 officers and other ranks.[240] The 3rd Brigade was headed by *général de brigade* Georges-Henri Eppler, a 45-year-old officer who led the most veteran regiment outside the Imperial Guard, the 13th *Légère.* Of the 1,240 officers and other ranks in the two battalions of the 13th *Légère* that were under the colors at Austerlitz, some 918—or 74% of the regiment—had at least 10 years of service in the French army![241]

The artillery support for Caffarelli's Division consisted of one company each of foot artillerists and train personnel totaling 169 persons that served four 8-pounder guns and two 6-inch howitzers. In addition to these specialists, there were the division's 17 staff personnel, which brought Caffarelli's command to a total of 6,387 officers and other ranks present and under arms at Austerlitz.[242]

The other body of infantry commanded by Lannes at Austerlitz was the 3rd Infantry Division of the marshal's own 5th Corps. This division was commanded by 35-year-old *général de division* Louis-Gabriel Suchet. An officer of solid military talents who did his duty without flamboyance, Suchet served as a *chef de bataillon* in the 18th *demi-brigade de bataille* in Bonaparte's *Armée d'Italie,* seeing action at the famous battles of Lodi, Castiglione, Bassano, Arcole and Rivoli. Following his wounding at Newmarkt in April 1797, Suchet was promoted to the regimental commander of the 18th later that year. Beginning in 1798, Suchet served in various capacities over the next three years in *Armée d'Italie* as well as in the *Armée d'Helvétie,* including chief of staff to General Brune in Switzerland. Promoted to *général de brigade* in March 1798 and to *général de division* in 1799, Suchet performed brilliantly in the 1800 campaign and was named as *Inspecteur général d'infanterie* in 1801.[243]

Suchet

When the marshalate was formed in 1804 and the initial members named, Suchet was disappointed that he was not named as a Marshal of France. This, however, was somewhat of an unrealistic reaction from a man who, among other things, had been closely connected to the traitorous Moreau, had never been a member of Napoleon's inner circle, had always maintained a rather critical attitude

[237] S.H.A.T., C² 481, *État de Situation du 5ᵉ Corps a la Bataille d'Austerlitz.*
[238] S.H.A.T., dossier Caffarelli.
[239] S.H.A.T., C² 481, *État de Situation du 5ᵉ Corps a la Bataille d'Austerlitz.*
[240] S.H.A.T., C² 481, *État de Situation du 5ᵉ Corps a la Bataille d'Austerlitz.*
[241] S.H.A.T., C² 481, *État de Situation du 5ᵉ Corps a la Bataille d'Austerlitz; Journal des opérations du 5ᵉ corps.*
[242] S.H.A.T., C² 481, *État de Situation du 5ᵉ Corps a la Bataille d'Austerlitz.*
[243] Six, *Dictionnaire biographique*, vol. 2, pp. 481-482.

Above, the spoils of victory are presented to Napoleon

Below, a guns sits on the north side of the Santon today as a memorial

towards the Corsican and yet relentlessly fawned over Josephine—all details which could not have escaped Napoleon's attention. However, Suchet's disappointment at not being named a marshal turned to resentment a year later when, in August of 1805, he was assigned to command the 4th Infantry Division of the newly formed 4th Corps, and placed under his former colleague, Soult. Suchet clearly believed that his unswerving loyalty to *la Patrie* and his superior combat record when compared to Soult, was more deserving.[244] Certainly, Suchet was an intelligent, brave and experienced divisional commander. In Napoleon's last review of Suchet's Division before Austerlitz, the general performed flawlessly. When asked by the Emperor, Suchet knew the average age of the soldiers in every regiment as well as the effective strength of every company of every battalion of every regiment, which bears witness to the depth and detail of knowledge that was expected of a division commander in the *Grande Armée*.[245]

However, there was another side of Suchet that was widely whispered throughout Paris. Former Director La Reveillière-Lepeaux described Suchet as "a very insolent soldier and one of the most shameless plunderers." While there is no doubt that Suchet made himself a rich man during his service with the *Armée d'Helvétie*, his plundering did not retard his advancement. It was instead Suchet's high-handed personality that did not sit well with others, especially Marshal Soult who was cut from much the same cloth. Suchet's reluctance to serve under Soult was appeased when Suchet's Division was transferred to Lannes on 5 vendémiaire (27 September) and renamed the 3rd Infantry Division of the 5th Corps.[246]

Claparède

Suchet was fortunate to have under his command a truly fine collection of troops and officers that included Michel-Marie Claparède. Handsome and personable, honest and professional in manner, coolly confident and brave under fire, yet unpretentious and completely without vanity regardless of the honors heaped upon him, Claparède was a valued officer and generally liked throughout the army.[247] Thirty-five years old at Austerlitz, Claparède had volunteered for service in 1793 and had spent much of the wars of the French Revolution in the light infantry. In 1802-03 and in 1805, Claparède had two tours of duty in the Caribbean, the latter one as commander of the infantry forces that had been transported by Admiral Missiessy (see page 163). Upon his return to Rochefort on 22 March, Claparède was soon thereafter transferred to the Channel encampment where his good service record and knowledge of waterborne activities earned him a spot in Oudinot's *Grenadiers de la Réserve*. However, once the Ulm campaign got underway, Claparède was transferred to Suchet's command to lead the division's 1st Brigade consisting of one regiment—the 17th *Légère*. The 17th was one of the oldest regiments in French service, its lineage going back to 1671 as *Le Royal-Italien*. As members of the *Armée d'Italie*, the 17th *Légère* participated in the battles of Mondovi, Lodi, Lonato, Castiglione and Rivoli. What was already an excellent light infantry regiment became even better as a result of the 1803-1805 Channel encampment. This was vividly demonstrated in Colonel Vedel's assault against the Ulm fortifications on 15 October 1805 (see page 242). There were 1,373 of these eager soldiers in the regiment's two battalions on the morning of 2 December 1805.[248] The 1st Battalion marched to it's battle start position with all the musicians of the regiment—resplendent in their powder blue coats with contrasting scarlet lapels, collars and cuffs while sporting red, white and blue

---

[244] F. Rousseau, *La carrière du maréchal Suchet, duc d'Albufera* (Paris, 1898), p. 44.
[245] S.H.A.T., C[2] 481.
[246] S.H.A.T., *Journal des opérations du 5e corps.*
[247] *Général* Raymond-Aimery-Philippe-Joseph de Montesquiou-Fézensac, *Souvenirs militaires* (Paris, 1863), p. 500.
[248] S.H.A.T., C[2] 481, *État de Situation du 5e Corps a la Bataille d'Austerlitz.*

Valhubert

plumes—playing Buhl's *"La Victoire est à nous."*

Suchet's 2nd Brigade was under the leadership of *général de brigade* Nicolas-Léonard Bagert Beker. It was an oddity that a cavalry general was given command of a brigade of infantry, but that is precisely what happened in August 1805. After many years of serving in the mounted arm, Beker was commanding the Department of Puy-de-Dôme when he was called to the *Grande Armée* and placed under Suchet. The division commander was not amused. "The Emperor has assigned to me an administrative cavalry general to lead my splendid soldiers," Suchet wrote Lannes on 18 vendémiaire (10 October). "Colonel Dumoustier is far more qualified to lead the brigade than this man."[249]

Pierre Dumoustier, the 34-year-old colonel of the 34th *Ligne*, was an accomplished soldier who commanded one of the most seasoned regiments in the *Grande Armée*. Created in 1775 as *Savoie-Carignan*, the regiment became known as *Angoulême* in 1785, and could trace its combat glory during the wars of the Revolution to Jourdan's victory at Fleurus in 1794. (Interestingly enough, the last great battle fought by the 34th during the Napoleonic wars would be on that same field called Ligny in June 1815). Within the two battalions of the 34th to fight at Austerlitz, of the 1,615 officers and other ranks that were present, some 759 had at least 10 years of service.[250]

Brigaded with Dumoustier's 34th was the 40th *Ligne* under Colonel François-Marie-Guillaume Legendre d'Harvesse. The 39-year-old colonel was one of the most fanatic Republicans in the service, having gotten a taste of *Liberté, Egalité et Fraternité* during his brief visit to America in 1791. As such, Legendre d'Harvesse was given command of the 40th, which had descended from the famed *Soissonnais* Regiment that had served under Rochambeau in America. Of the 1,149 officers and men in the ranks of the 40th *Ligne* at Austerlitz, seven men had witnessed Cornwallis' surrender at Yorktown.[251] The spirit of freedom that sparked these men's minds, as well as countless other Frenchmen who were present in America in the early 1780s, served to help continue to motivate this regiment some 24 years later. This was clearly illustrated in the words of the 5th Corps' *Inspecteur aux revues* Buhot. "Everything reflects the regiment's dedication to the Nation by its colonel, officers and men," Buhot wrote shortly after an inspection on 15 brumaire (6 November). "The plumes and streamers of the officers and musicians are the national colors [red, white and blue], and Colonel Legendre d'Harvesse swears that if it were possible, so would be the underwear of the regiment."[252]

Curial

The 3rd Brigade of Suchet's Division was under the leadership of Jean-Marie-Mellon-Roger Valhubert. The 41-year-old *général de brigade* began his military service as a Volunteer of 1791, rising through the ranks to be the commander of the 28th *demi-brigade de bataille* in 1797. As that regiment's commander, Valhubert led his men in the immortal 1800 campaign, and his conduct at Montebello, Marengo and Pozzolo during that year earned favorable comments from many officers. Friant was among those who held Valhubert in high regard and expressed this view in an 1802 letter. Friant believed that Valhubert was: "A distinguished officer who possessed the rarest merits of combined good sense and military knowledge."[253]

The regiments with which Valhubert had worked for two years in the camp

---

249 S.H.A.T., C² 4.

250 S.H.A.T., C² 481, *État de Situation du 5ᵉ Corps a la Bataille d'Austerlitz*; *Journal des opérations du 5ᵉ corps.*

251 S.H.A.T., C² 481, *État de Situation du 5ᵉ Corps a la Bataille d'Austerlitz*; *Journal des opérations du 5ᵉ corps.*

252 S.H.A.T., *Tableau de la Grande Armée Dernière quinzaine du mois brumaire an XIV*, "Situation au 15 brumaire an XIV (6 November 1805)."

253 S.H.A.T., C² 206.

of Saint-Omer were the 64th and 88th *Ligne*. Both regiments had served in Bonaparte's *Armée d'Italie*, with the 64th having the better combat record. However, once in the Channel encampment, the 88th was forged into "an excellent regiment"[254] by its hard-fighting new colonel, 31-year-old Philibert-Jean-Baptiste-François Curial, along with the new battalion commanders, one of which was a fire-eater named Pierre-Jacques-Etienne Cambronne. On 2 December 1805, the two battalions of the 64th fielded 1,052 officers and other ranks, while the same number of battalions in the 88th brought 1,428 people onto the battlefield.[255]

Cambronne

The ordnance for Suchet's Division consisted of 10 pieces served by 240 artillerists and artillery train personnel. Two 8-pounders were manned by one detachment of foot artillerists while another full company manned eight pieces—two 12-pounders, four 8-pounders and two 4-pounders. Including the divisional staff numbering 20 officers, Suchet's Division at Austerlitz totaled 6,877 personnel.[256]

Attached to Lannes at Austerlitz was the 2nd Dragoon Division under the direction of *général de division* Frédéric-Henri Walther. A cavalryman since his enlistment in 1781, Walther had a long and distinguished career during the wars of the French Revolution, serving under divisional commanders Augereau, Alexander Dumas, Gouvion-Saint-Cyr, Ney, Souham, Klein and Soult. Following his promotion to *général de division* in August 1803, Walther reported to Davout's camp at Bruges. Over the next two years and under the strict supervision of Davout, Walther turned his six regiments into the finest dragoon division in the army, the clash at Raussnitz on 20 November notwithstanding.

The 1st Brigade was commanded by Sébastiani and consisted of the 3rd and 6th Dragoons. The 2nd Brigade was led by 45-year-old *général de brigade* Mansuy-Dominique Roget de Belloguet and was composed of the 10th and 11th Dragoons. The 3rd Brigade was under the leadership of *général de brigade* André-Joseph Boussart. This 47-year-old officer had under his orders the 13th and 22nd Dragoons. When Sébastiani was not with the division during the *manœuvre sur Hollabrunn*, the six regiments were equally divided into two brigades. However, the familiar three brigade arrangement reappeared shortly after the occupation of Brünn. Because of losses suffered through strategic consumption and at actions such as Schöngrabern and Raussnitz, Walther's dragoon regiments were very weak at Austerlitz. The three squadrons fielded by each regiment only totaled the following combatants: the 3rd with 177; the 6th with 150; the 10th with 207; the 11th with 196; the 13th with 269 and the 22nd with 134. Additionally, the division had a half-company of horse artillery attached; the two 8-pounders and one 6-inch howitzer were manned by 89 artillerists and artillery train personnel. Therefore, Walther's 2nd Dragoon Division brought a total of 1,222 combatants to the battle—significantly fewer than the 1,534 persons present before the action at Raussnitz and very different from the more than 2,100 combatants of the division that had crossed the Rhine in late September![257]

Sébastiani de la Porta

The divisions under Lannes were placed by the marshal astride the Olmütz Road. Suchet was positioned on the north side of the road with Beker's 2nd Brigade consisting of the 34th and 40th in the front line and Valhubert's 3rd Brigade with the 64th and 88th *Ligne* in the second line. The 1st Brigade under Claparède with the 17th *Légère* was deployed to cover the division's left flank. The 2nd Battalion of this light infantry regiment provided the infantry garrison for the Santon that bristled with 18 captured Austrian 3-pounders. The 1st Battalion of the 17th *Légère* covered its front and northern flank with *tirailleurs* while the formed portion of

[254] S.H.A.T., C^2 192.

[255] S.H.A.T., C^2 481, *État de Situation du 5e Corps a la Bataille d'Austerlitz.*

[256] S.H.A.T., C^2 481, *État de Situation du 5e Corps a la Bataille d'Austerlitz.*

[257] S.H.A.T., C^2 481, *État de Situation du 5e Corps a la Bataille d'Austerlitz.* and C^2 470.

the battalion was positioned immediately behind the small settlement of Bosenitz, thereby using the structures to shield its ranks from the enemy. The division under Caffarelli was deployed on the south side of the Olmütz Road in a manner similar to that of Suchet's command. The two brigades of *ligne* infantry formed two lines with the 17th and 30th in front and the 51st and 61st in the second line. The remaining brigade, consisting of the single regiment of light infantry—the 13th—screened the division's right flank. The divisional artillery units were deployed to support the front-line regiments. Meanwhile, Lannes placed Walther's dragoons one-half mile behind the infantry in reserve just south of the Olmütz Road across from the Santon.

The marshal commanding the 5th Corps was Jean Lannes. Like Napoleon, he was a second son and a fighter by instinct. However, even more so than the Emperor, Lannes was a self-made man. Undoubtedly, this was among the reasons that Napoleon respected him so much. Thirty-six-years-old at the time of Austerlitz, Lannes had never been given the chance to attend high school; his Gascon father had not thought enough of him to give him that opportunity. Undaunted by the prospects of self-learning, Lannes struggled to obtain a meager education administered by his older brother, who was a priest, and courageously completed his education with results that astonished Napoleon. Like most self-educated men, Lannes was unrefined around the edges. However, beneath his roughhewn exterior was strength of character with an honest heart and a soul of a pure warrior, unafraid of anything or anybody.

The Revolution gave Lannes countless opportunities to prove himself and earn promotions. In Bonaparte's *Armée d'Italie*, Lannes consistently showed his fierce Gallic heritage, fearlessly proving himself and his handling of troops under fire at Dego, Piacenza, Fombio, Lodi and Bassano. After the latter battle, Augereau requested a promotion for Lannes because of his "most striking examples of bravery."[258] However, it was the Battle of Arcole on 15 November 1796 that forever fused the personal bond between Lannes and Bonaparte. In that famous battle, Lannes was hit twice by Austrian small arms fire and had been taken to the rear by medical personnel. While his arm was being bandaged and put in a sling, Lannes received word of continued French failures to storm the Austrian position. Refusing to stay with the wounded in an ambulance, Lannes remounted his horse and returned to the fighting. Just as he rode up the front, Lannes saw Bonaparte caught up in the latest failed charge and subsequent retreat of a French column. Bonaparte's horse slipped off a dike, dumping the rider into the swamp. As the army commander's aides struggled to protect Bonaparte from the closing Austrian counterattack, Lannes quickly went to the head of some nearby troops and gave the command "Follow Me!" Taking a third bullet while in front of their ranks, Lannes was the hero of the day. He provided the necessary leadership in an audacious assault that drove back the Austrians, turned the tide of the battle and saved Bonaparte's life.

With a combination of his irrepressible personality, his conduct at Arcole, and his active role in Bonaparte's coup of 18 brumaire, Lannes could address Napoleon as no other man dared. Most often, when in large company, Lannes adhered to proper etiquette by addressing Napoleon as 'Sire' or 'Your Majesty.' At other times, especially when there were only a few people within ear shot, Lannes addressed Napoleon simply as '*tu*.' The *tutoyer* phrase was reciprocated by Napoleon "which he generally did to those generals to whom he wished to show a certain preference."[259] The handsome and honest Lannes had more than Napoleon's friendship; he possessed an indomitable spirit and charisma that galvanized ordinary soldiers into heroes. Lannes could almost will his men to either carry a seemingly

---

[258] S.H.A.T., dossier Lannes.

[259] Louis-Antoine Fauvelet de Bourrienne, as quoted in Blond, *La Grande Armée,* p. 71.

impregnable position or hold out against overwhelming odds. This unconquerable resolve is no better illustrated than Lannes' spectacular victory at Montebello on 9 June 1800 when he assaulted a fortified hill held by an Austrian force twice the size of his own. He won more laurels on the field of Marengo, and three months after that battle the successful general married the rich and beautiful Louise Guéhénuc. She bore Lannes five children; the first was named Napoleon to which the First Consul and Josephine were godparents. Following a successful stint as minister plenipotentiary to Portugal for three years, Lannes returned to France in November 1804, some six months after being named to the marshalate. Given command of the troops that became the 5th Corps of the *Grande Armée*, Lannes proved himself in the combats leading up to 2 December 1805 to be an extremely capable and aggressive corps commander. Austerlitz would provide Lannes with a stage on which he was to further demonstrate his considerable military talents.

The Battle of Montebello

Protecting the flanks of 5th Corps was Murat's *Corps des Réserves de Cavalerie*. Marshal Murat had four and one-half divisions of cavalry under his command at Austerlitz. These consisted of the formidable 1st and 2nd Heavy Cavalry Divisions from his own corps, along with the light cavalry divisions from 1st and 5th Corps plus a separate light cavalry brigade. The 1st and 2nd Heavy Cavalry Divisions, under the command of Nansouty and d'Hautpoul, respectively, totaled 10 regiments with a strength of 2,961 officers and other ranks present and under arms. Nansouty's command had six regiments—four were *cuirassiers* and the other two were the fearsome *carabiniers*—while d'Hautpoul led four regiments of *cuirassiers*.[260] The two and one-half divisions of light cavalry under Murat's orders numbered 2,863 officers and troopers in 10 regiments of which five were hussars and five were *chasseurs à cheval*.[261] Of these light cavalry, only the division from 1st Corps under the orders of Kellermann had horse artillery attached. Kellermann's ordnance consisted of six Hanoverian pieces—two 6-pounders, two 3-pounders and two 5.3-inch howitzers.[262]

As with all heavy cavalry or dragoon divisions, the 1st and 2nd Heavy Cavalry Divisions each had a half-company of horse artillery attached, with each half-company consisting of two 8-pounder cannon and one 6-inch howitzer. While there were four dragoon divisions in Murat's corps, three were on the field of Austerlitz, but none operated directly under Murat's orders on that day. Therefore, the formations directed by Murat at Austerlitz consisted of 20 regiments of horse numbering 5,824 sabers, plus 12 pieces of ordnance served by 314 artillerists and train personnel.[263]

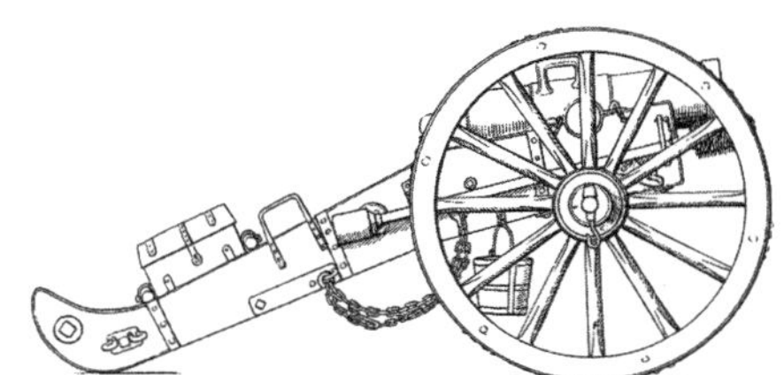

French 6-inch howitzer

Murat positioned three brigades of light cavalry on the left, or northern flank, of Lannes. Two brigades of these troopers were the 5th Corps light cavalry under the orders of *général de brigade* Anne-François-Charles Treillard. The 9th and 10th Hussars along with the 13th and 21st *Chasseurs à cheval* totaled 986 officers and other ranks, and these regiments had seen constant action since the opening of the Ulm campaign. Deployed next to Treillard's horsemen was the independent Light Cavalry Brigade under *général de brigade* Edouard-Jean-Baptiste Milhaud. Milhaud's regiments were the 16th and 22nd *Chasseurs à cheval* mounting a total of 610 combatants. To the right, or southern, flank of Lannes, Murat positioned the Light Cavalry Division of 1st Corps under *général de division* François-Etienne Kellermann. These four splendid regiments—the 2nd, 4th and 5th Hussars and the 5th *Chasseurs à cheval*—totaled 1,267 sabers, and were commanded by arguably the finest cavalry general in French uniform.[264] The 35-

---

[260] S.H.A.T., C² 472.
[261] S.H.A.T., C² 470, 472, 474 and 481.
[262] S.H.A.T., C² 474.
[263] S.H.A.T., C² 470, 472, 474 and 481.

Kellermann, shown here in a flattering portrait

year-old Kellermann (often called Kellermann the younger) was the son of Marshal Kellermann, the hero of Valmy who had saved France from the Prussians in 1792. The younger Kellermann served with distinction in Bonaparte's 1st and 2nd Italian Campaigns, and was responsible for one of the most famous and decisive cavalry charges in history. At the Battle of Marengo on 14 June 1800, Kellermann won everlasting fame when, at the head of only 200 French cavalry, he compelled some 6,000 Austrians to lay down their arms or flee, and helped to dramatically alter the course of the day's fighting.

Like his father, Kellermann the younger was confident, brave, skillful and resourceful. However, in personal mannerisms he was also brash, outspoken and one of those rare men who was not intimidated by Napoleon. These traits were no better illustrated than the 5 December 1804 fête held at the Tuilleries the evening after Napoleon had distributed the eagles to the army and three days after Napoleon's coronation as Emperor. During the course of the celebration, Kellermann and Napoleon were standing almost back-to-back but each engaged in separate conversations. As a lull in the conversation came over the group which included Kellermann, the general overheard Napoleon talk about Marengo and his destiny. With that, Kellermann whirled around and plunged into the conversation. "Sire, I too will never forget Marengo and how I made it possible for you to be wearing the crown."[265]

If Kellermann's impetuous personality did not help his career, his looks were even more of a liability. Because western society places so much emphasis on a person's physical appearance, many of Kellermann's contemporaries—including those who called him 'the ugliest man in the French army'—believed that he was never made a marshal due to his unflattering image. Regardless of the reason that the younger Kellermann was not a member of the marshalate, nobody doubted his instinctive talents to lead cavalry. It was after 9:00 A.M. when Kellermann heard the firing along the other portions of the field grow louder and louder. Finally, the battle came to the northern end of the field when Liechtenstein's late arriving V Column came thundering over the northern end of the Pratzen Plateau to support Bagration.

Action Between the French and Russian Cavalry

Liechtenstein led the 4,556 members of the Russian cavalry brigades of V Column past the northeastern edge of Blasowitz, then halted them between that village and the small settlement of Krug. The one and one-half batteries of Russian horse artillery set up in front of the cavalry, and these 18 pieces began a bombardment onto the French who were about 900 yards away. Meanwhile, FML Hohenlohe was following this part of the column with his 1,166 Austrian heavy

---

[264] Marmont was one of Kellermann's biggest admirers. The French marshal wrote: "During those 25 years of warfare [French Revolution and Napoleonic wars], only three men in the French army really understood how to lead and control massed cavalry: Kellermann, Montbrun, Lasalle."

[265] S.H.A.T., dossier Kellermann. In a letter to Lasalle, Kellermann, writing shortly after Marengo, said: "Would you believe, my friend, that Bonaparte has not made me a *général de division*? I who have just placed the crown upon his head!" Napoleon was well aware of Kellermann's pivotal rôle at Marengo, and on 4 July 1800, the First Consul gave Kellermann his promotion. Also, in the portrait of Bonaparte as First Consul which was painted by Antoine de la Gros, Bonaparte authorized the inclusion of Kellermann's famous charge in the scrolls of paper on his desk. However, his frequent impolitic utterances about Marengo cost the cavalryman dearly. For example, when, after a successful campaign like those of 1805, Napoleon would pay out millions of francs in donations to his senior officers, Kellermann would receive no such sum.

cavalry and the six pieces belonging to an Austrian cavalry battery. Hohenlohe pealed off Cüirassier-Regiment Lothringen #7 to guard the far left of the column and watch the movements taking place below the Staré Vinohrady. He then halted Cüirassier-Regiment Kaiser #1 and Cüirassier-Regiment Nassau-Usingen #5, supported by the Austrian cavalry battery, east of Blasowitz in order to wait for some friendly infantry to come up to occupy the village. About the same time that the Russian Guard *Jaeger* Battalion was hustling towards Blasowitz, Liechtenstein decided to launch his Russian regiments straight into the French that were now advancing eastward astride the Olmütz Road. The Russian horse charged pell-mell into the teeth of the French infantry, who coolly received the charge without changing formation.

In keeping with the accustomed way to deploy infantry divisions, Lannes had his *ligne* units draw up in two echelons, each line consisting of the regiments of one brigade. The front line battalions of Suchet and Caffarelli consisted of a closed attack column guarding each flank with the remaining battalions in between deployed in line formation. This mixed order was a 'linked regiments' formation that gave the battalions in line solid protection on both flanks, as well as providing the units in closed attack column greater security against any allied cavalry sorties. Supporting the front line was the artillery of each division as well as the *tirailleurs* from the battalions. The second line consisted of closed attack columns positioned between the intervals of the units in front. Finally, the *légère* regiment in each division was positioned to cover one of the far flanks of the first line. Meanwhile, the French cavalry had deployed each regiment in column of squadrons.

As the Russian horse bore down on their targets, the French infantry and cavalry stood fast and leveled their small arms while the artillerists in blue stood to their artillery pieces with port-fires lit. Suddenly, the entire French line erupted in sheets of flame and smoke. The official Austrian account of the battle described the volcano of French "canister, murderously supported by the musketry of the enemy foot and the carbines of their cavalry"[266] as simply too much for the Russian cavalry. Unable to close with the French line, the Russian horsemen recoiled. As these horsemen began peeling away, Lannes sent his senior aide-de-camp, *chef d'escadron* Subervie, with a message for Murat. "These numerous enemy cavalry remind the marshal of the battles of Egypt," Subervie told the commander of the *Corps des Réserves de Cavalerie*. "The marshal believes that we can not have empty cartridge boxes when it is time to engage the enemy infantry."[267] Murat's chief of staff, *général de division* Belliard, remembered that Murat agreed with this opinion and immediately turned to his aide-de-camp, *chef d'escadron* Exelmans, with orders for Kellermann: "The general will precede the advance of the infantry by taking his light cavalry and dispersing the enemy horse."[268] With this order from Exelmans, Kellermann immediately had his regiments sling their smoking carbines and move out. The Russians had long since scattered when Kellermann's light cavalry, each brigade marching abreast of the other and every regiment formed in column by squadrons, began to rein in about 600 yards in front of Caffarelli's troops.

The repositioning of Kellermann's Division was of no immediate concern to Russian cavalry generals Uvarov and Essen; they were busy rallying their regiments for another try at the French line. While these allied cavalry were being reorganized, the Russian horse artillery opened an oblique fire onto Kellermann's light cavalrymen. Meanwhile, six Cossack regiments swarmed over the countryside, masking the Russian advance up the Olmütz Road and also obscuring Kellermann's view of Uvarov and Essen, who were near Krug. It seems as though all the Russian

Subervie, in later years

[266] K. k. Kriegsarchiv, F.A., *Ausführliche Relation der am 2 ten Dezember, 1805.*
[267] S.H.A.T., *Journal des opérations du 5e corps.*
[268] S.H.A.T., C^2 240.

regiments in V Column had been reformed when the commander of one of the brigades, Major-General Essen, launched a second charge. Essen selected Major-General Müller-Zakomelsky and his gigantic regiment of the Grand Duke Constantine Uhlans to advance from the area around the southwest side of the settlement of Krug, and attack Kellermann's exposed horsemen. Ordering to the attack his 10 squadrons that before the battle numbered 950 men, Müller-Zakomelsky headed straight for the French light cavalry's right flank. The sudden movement of this large body of cavalry armed with lances and pointed against the southern flank of his division gave Kellermann no options. He immediately shouted the command: *"Changement de front en arrière sur le premier escadron de la deuxième brigade!"*[269] Kellermann's regiments smartly turned and withdrew posthaste along the Olmütz Road in the gap between Suchet and Caffarelli's infantry.

No sooner had Kellermann's regiments withdrawn to safety, than Müller-Zakomelsky's galloping uhlans arrived on the scene and tried to close with Caffarelli's *fantassins*. The uhlans were met by "a rolling fire at point blank range."[270] Due to the shallow angle that the uhlans had in approaching the French line, the constant, deadly fire from the infantry and artillerists had the effect of deflecting, rather than arresting, the impetus of the charging Russians. "They rampaged along the front of the infantry divisions of Caffarelli and Suchet from one end to the other, meeting fire all the way, and finally disappeared along the highway."[271] As the uhlans finally drew off to the east to reform behind Bagration's lines, they left behind a staggering number of casualties. Littering the ground were 400 dead and wounded men of the Grand Duke Constantine Uhlans. General Essen rode away, but was seriously wounded. The unhorsed Müller-Zakomelsky was taken prisoner rather than killed on the spot, no doubt thanks to his distinctive general's white uniform with red and gold trim. Other members of the uhlans that were wounded in front of the French line were not as fortunate; the Russian cavalrymen were bayoneted by French infantry as the bluecoated troops passed over the wreckage of Müller-Zakomelsky's regiment.[272]

With the uhlans now driven off, Kellermann advanced past Caffarelli once again. Detecting the Chernigov Dragoons, Kharkov Dragoons and the Elisabetgrad Hussars moving up from Krug, Kellermann wheeled his command facing southwest to meet the oncoming Russians. For this advance, Kellermann had his four regiments in echelon formation from left to right. The left, leading regiment was the 4th Hussars, followed next the 2nd Hussars, then the 5th Hussars and finally the 5th *Chasseurs à cheval.* The 280 officers and troopers of the 4th Hussars, led by Colonel André Burthe, were the first to get into this fight. As the red and blue uniformed hussars clashed with the greencoated dragoons, the Russians quickly got the upper hand, thanks to the fact that the two regiments of dragoons numbered 866 effectives and that they enveloped the flanks of the 4th, forcing the French light cavalrymen to break off. During this sword play and carbine fire, Burthe's horse was killed and the colonel was taken captive.[273]

However, the temporary loss of the 4th Hussars from his division did not prevent Kellermann from continuing the fight. He knew that the situation could be quickly restored by a spirited thrust from his three remaining regiments. Sending the next two regiments in echelon—the 2nd and the 5th Hussars—straight for the Russians, Kellermann then advanced his right-most regiment onto the left flank of the Russian brigade, then swung that regiment—the 5th *Chasseurs à cheval*—into the side of the Elisabetgrad Hussars. The three squadrons of the 5th *Chasseurs à*

---

[269] Picard, *La Cavalerie dans Les Guerres de la Révolution et de l'Empire*, vol. 1, p. 311.
[270] Duffy, *Austerlitz,* p. 124.
[271] Duffy, *Austerlitz,* p. 124.
[272] S.H.A.T., C² 15 and 470.
[273] S.H.A.T., C² 16.

cheval numbering 317 officers and troopers were rolling up the 10 squadrons of 950 Russian hussars when the dragoons under Sébastiani arrived to lend their assistance. Earlier, Lannes had sent one of his aides-de-camp, young Captain Bessières, to General Walther with orders for him to support Kellermann with one of his brigades. Walther dispatched Sébastiani with instructions to swing behind and past the right flank of Caffarelli, thereby giving support to Kellermann's right. After Sébastiani brought his two regiments into line while approaching the *mêlée*, he directed the 327 members of the 3rd and 6th Dragoons into the rear of the already enveloped Russian brigade. With Sébastiani's dragoons crashing into the back of Uvarov's horsemen, the Russian brigade broke. Farther away from the French envelopment than the other two regiments, the Chernigov Dragoons escaped without losing any prisoners. The next regiment in line, the Kharkov Dragoons, had one officer and 41 troopers captured. However, it was the Elisabetgrad Hussars that suffered the most. Charged from the front by Kellermann's hussars, their flank driven in by the 5th *Chasseurs à cheval,* then finally assailed from the rear by Sébastiani's dragoons, the Elisabetgrad Hussars lost 134 killed and wounded plus two officers and 140 troopers captured—an extraordinary loss (over 28% of the regiment's beginning strength of 950) for a single cavalry engagement.[274]

As soon as arrangements were made to escort the Russian prisoners from the area, Kellermann quickly rallied his three regiments on hand and deployed them in squadrons abreast. Then, pointing the way, Kellermann directed his horsemen to charge and take the one and one-half batteries of Russian horse artillery located southwest of Krug. The crews of these 18 pieces had decided to keep their ordnance unlimbered during the cavalry *mêlée* and now suddenly found themselves unsupported as Kellermann's light cavalry bore down upon them. Through the smoke of the discharges from the 6-pounder guns and 10-pounder licornes the French hussars and *chasseurs à cheval* emerged at the full gallop. Arriving at the guns, Kellermann's troopers sabered some of the gunners who had not sought safety. Colonel Claude-Louis Corbineau, the commander of the 5th *Chasseurs à cheval*, was determined to come away with trophies. He ordered a detachment of the regiment to quickly mount some Russian limbers and these troopers drove three of the captured Russian cannon back to French lines.[275]

After the mauling of Uvarov's brigade and the accompanying half-company of horse artillery (the full company of artillerists under Ermolov that also supported Uvarov had somehow escaped heavy losses during this charge), Kellermann quickly reformed his division. The light cavalry troopers were regrouping while Sébastiani's dragoons faced eastward towards Bagration's advancing troops, thereby providing Kellermann's regiments with a covering screen. Kellermann had no sooner readied his horsemen for the next round of action when Bagration slipped the leash on his reserve cavalry. Thundering towards the French in squadrons abreast were, from north to south, the 480 combatants of the Saint-Petersburg Dragoons, the 566 officers and other ranks of the Leib-*Cuirassier* ("Tsar") and 632 effectives in the Tver Dragoons. The sudden appearance of these fresh regiments, fully deployed and coming straight for his command, convinced Kellermann that discretion was the better part of valor. With Sébastiani still covering his command, Kellermann ordered his light cavalry to withdraw to a position behind Caffarelli's infantry. "At this juncture you could appreciate just how much military training and experience can affect the course of an action," wrote the eyewitness Thiard. As Kellermann's horsemen wheeled about, "the troops of Caffarelli's Division… opened up their intervals as coolly as if they had been on a parade ground. As soon as Kellermann's

---

[274] S.H.A.T., C^2 470.

[275] S.H.A.T., C^2 10; Picard, *La Cavalerie dans Les Guerres de la Révolution et de l'Empire*, vol. 1, p. 312.

cavalry passed through they closed up again."[276] Sébastiani then broke off as well, and moved around Caffarelli's southern flank as Caffarelli's men "opened fire on the enemy,"[277] throwing back their charge.

The latest Russian attempts to defeat the French cavalry had not gone unnoticed by Marshal Murat, who was preparing the strongest possible response. Because of overtaxing command responsibilities placed upon him earlier in the campaign which thrust him into an unfamiliar role as an army wing commander, and since the resulting demands placed on Murat were outside his modest intellectual capabilities, coupled with the resulting criticisms leveled against him by Napoleon in connection to the premature occupation of Vienna and by the hoax played on him at Schöngrabern, Murat had often been embarrassed in 1805. However, at Austerlitz, circumstances were vastly different. With the Emperor on the field and with only cavalry and their supporting horse artillery under his orders, Murat was in his element. It was in this environment that the man called 'The Thunderbolt' knew perhaps better than any other human being how to direct large bodies of horse in order to overwhelm and devastate an opponent.

Bringing up his two divisions of superb heavy cavalry to join in the fighting with the other horsemen on the northern end of the battlefield, Murat was determined to clear Lannes' front of the bothersome presence of allied cavalry. As soon as Kellermann had reformed his division once again—this time in two lines with the 5th *Chasseurs à cheval* and 2nd Hussars in the first line, while the 4th and 5th Hussars were in the second line—Murat sent his aides-de-camp spurring across the Moravian countryside with orders to advance. Kellermann emerged again through the protective shield of Caffarelli's infantry, followed by Walther's entire division of dragoons. Meanwhile, Nansouty and d'Hautpoul were to swing their superb heavy cavalry around Caffarelli's right. Nansouty brought his six regiments alongside the southern flank of the infantry while d'Hautpoul followed.

While all the shifting of French formations was going on, the Russians were likewise realigning their regiments. The brigade from Bagration's command that earlier had caused Kellermann to seek the safety of his infantry brothers-in-arms had been pulled back, and was currently in front of the musketeer regiments of the Advance Guard which straddled the Olmütz Road. Meanwhile, Uvarov had managed to rally two of his three shattered regiments between Krug and Blasowitz. The survivors of the Chernigov Dragoons as well as those of the badly damaged Elisabetgrad Hussars were brought alongside the southern flank of the Tver Dragoons, and it was on the rolling ground between the two hamlets that Uvarov halted his regiments. Meanwhile, Bagration's Russian horse artillery came forward, unlimbered its 12 pieces and began firing on the advancing French cavalry.

Uvarov

The shot and shell from the Russian horse artillery tore through the French light cavalry. Kellermann was not about to let his regiments get shot up by enemy artillery fire; sending word to Murat of his desire to charge, Murat gave him the go-ahead. As Kellermann moved out, Murat and his staff galloped forward to a position in front of Walther's dragoons and ordered them advance in support of Kellermann. Before long, Murat, his staff, and the two divisions of French cavalry—which at this point in the battle could not have numbered more than 2,300 sabers—were mixing it up along the Olmütz Road with five regiments of Russian cavalry. These Russians had started the battle with 3,544 troopers and must have had at least 3,300 when Kellermann and Walther reached their line.

Both sides were fighting as if they were men possessed, but the élite 5th *Chasseurs à cheval* were too much for the Tver Dragoons. Colonel Corbineau's troopers broke the regiment of Russian horse, then followed up their victory by

[276] *Souvenirs Diplomatiques et Miltaires du Général Thiard,* p. 228-229.
[277] *Souvenirs Diplomatiques et Miltaires du Général Thiard,* p. 229.

attacking a portion of the first line of Russian infantry just north of the Olmütz Road consisting of the Pskov Musketeer Regiment. These infantrymen were advancing to the attack behind their cavalry screen when Corbineau's *chasseurs* suddenly came out of the smoke and jumped on the left-hand battalion of the regiment. Hardly able to issue one ragged volley in defense of themselves, the musketeer battalion became unexpectedly embroiled in a hand-to-hand fight with the French light horsemen. *Général de division* Auguste-Daniel Belliard, Murat's chief of staff, saw Corbineau's charge. "The brave Corbineau took a flag in the middle of one enemy battalion," Belliard wrote in his after-action report, "at the same moment when the colonel was wounded."[278] In a letter written to his son, Corbineau related the circumstances of him capturing the prize.

> The charge of my regiment broke up the advance of the Russian infantry, making it possible for the cavalry to overturn the infantry. I had fallen into the ranks of the Russian infantry at the moment when I seized one flag. I took it by pulling it out of the hands of the colorguard.[279]

According to Belliard, the colonel was saved by Trooper Tassu "who rescued the colonel and the captured flag."[280] Nearby, Belliard also saw two brigadiers from the 5th *Chasseurs à cheval* named Fortier and Legendre cut down the other members of the Russian colorguard and made off with the remaining flag of the same battalion.[281]

While the 5th *Chasseurs à cheval* were busy slicing up one battalion of the Pskov Musketeers, the Tver Dragoons had not taken long to rally their ranks, and they charged back into the fray. This Russian attack forced the already fatigued and disorganized 5th *Chasseurs à cheval* to withdraw. Meanwhile, *général de brigade* Joseph-Denis Picard sent the other regiment of his brigade—the 4th Hussars—to cover the retrograde movement of the 5th *Chasseurs à cheval*. Since the 4th Hussars were outnumbered two to one by the Tver Dragoons, it wasn't long before both flanks of the 4th Hussars were enveloped. With their flanks driven in, the 4th recoiled. However, their place in the line was soon filled when Colonel François-Xavier de Schwarz and his regiment of the 5th Hussars. A former Badener who had served in the Bavarian army, Schwarz gave the signal for his troopers to charge to the relief of the embattled 4th. Even though the 5th Hussars were also outnumbered about two to one, their arrival at the front temporarily restored the situation.

At this point, with two of his four regiments withdrawn from the fight and attempting to rally, Kellermann knew that his remaining two regiments would soon reach the end of their endurance. Seeing Sébastiani standing in reserve, Kellermann decided to break off with his command in order to rally the entire division behind the dragoons. Meanwhile, Murat and his staff were previously tied down in swordplay along the line, yet managed to extricate themselves and ride back towards French lines in order to assess the progress of the cavalry battle. When the marshal saw Kellermann removing his division from the fight, and with the remaining and outnumbered brigades under Walther manfully hanging on against the also tiring regiments of Russian horse, Murat sensed it was time for the *coup de grâce*. Orders were sent from the curly-haired marshal in the brilliant uniform and a tigerskin over his saddle to division commanders Nansouty and d'Hautpoul; these men were to bring their formidable divisions forward at once.

Uvarov

---

278 S.H.A.T., C^2 240.
279 "Sabretache" 1895, p. 299.
280 S.H.A.T., C^2 240.
281 S.H.A.T., C^2 240.

Nansouty

Both heavy cavalry division commanders differed significantly from their flamboyant corps chief. The 37-year-old Etienne-Marie-Antoine Champion Nansouty was born of the Bordeaux aristocracy. A slender man of great integrity, meticulous, well educated and intelligent,[282] Nansouty was the Colonel of the 9th Cavalry by the time he was 25. A *général de brigade* in 1799, over the next five years Nansouty served with such notables as Saint-Cyr, Ney, Gudin and Mortier.[283] In 1805, *général de division* Nansouty was in command of the most important cavalry division of the line in the *Grande Armée*. He had been around big horses and heavy cavalry regiments his entire life; his men were always well trained and cared for. Despite these good traits, Nansouty was very much a nobleman cut from the mold of the *ancien régime.* Silent by nature, Nansouty was virtually mute in combat. However, it was his caustic personality that irritated subordinates and superiors alike. That aspect of Nansouty's personality was completely devoid of any élan and rendered him "incapable of making one of those unexpected maneuvers of war that decide a lot of battles."[284]

Unlike Nansouty, the other heavy cavalry division commander, Jean-Joseph-Ange d'Hautpoul, had come from a simple Gascon family. Rising in rank despite a poor education, by the time of Austerlitz the 51-year-old d'Hautpoul had been a *général de division* for more than 10 years, serving with distinction throughout the wars of the Revolution. What's more, d'Hautpoul had received a well deserved reputation for being one of the most capricious and arbitrary officers in the army. He judged his regimental colonels by their spit and polish rather than by the more important matters of horsemanship and training. Laure Permon Junot, who was the leader of Napoleonic court society, later known as the duchess d'Abrantès and the wife of *général de division* Jean-Andoche Junot, perhaps best summed up d'Hautpoul: "He was a man of excellent quality, handsome but with a negligible education. He was so vain that it is impossible to describe him other than by saying that the stories are absurd."[285]

d'Hautpol

As Nansouty's and d'Hautpoul's Divisions heavy cavalry moved forward, Murat led with Nansouty's regiments while keeping d'Hautpoul's in reserve. Riding to meet the advancing French were the Elisabetgrad Hussars and the Chernigov Dragoons from Uvarov's brigade of Liechtenstein's V Column, along with the Tver Dragoons from Bagration's command. Nansouty caught sight of the Russians and decided to lead his attack with his best units—the 1st and 2nd *Carabiniers.* Nansouty ordered the big men wearing the tall bearskin headgear and riding black horses to charge the Tver Dragoons. The 471 officers and other ranks comprising both regiments of *carabiniers* moved forward "with such precision and coordination that you might have thought they were drilling in front of an inspector general."[286] The Tver Dragoons crumbled immediately in front of the charge of the *carabiniers.* By the time that Uvarov arrived on the scene with the Elisabetgrad Hussars and the Chernigov Dragoons, the *carabiniers* had wheeled in a southeasterly direction to meet them. Although outnumbered approximately three to one, the unarmored *carabiniers* crashed into the Russian horse and were holding their own when Nansouty fed into the *mêlée* the 2nd and 3rd *Cuirassiers.* These 596 armored horsemen thundered forward and overthrew the Chernigov Dragoons as well as a portion of the Elisabetgrad Hussars. The remaining part of the Russian hussar

---

[282] *Mémoires du général Griois,* vol. 2, p. 283.
[283] Six, *Dictionnaire biographique*, vol. 2, p. 249.
[284] Ameil, "Sabretache" 1907, p. 658.
[285] Laure Junot, duchesse d'Abrantès, *Mémoires de Mme la duchesse d'Abrantès ou souvenirs historiques sur Napoléon, la Révolution, le Directoire, le Consulat, l'Empire et la Restauration*, 10 volumes (Paris, 1893), vol. 3, p. 265.
[286] Alombert-Goget and Colin, *La Campagne de 1805 en Allemagne*, XXVI, p. 543.

regiment was being pushed back by the 3rd *Cuirassiers* when Nansouty spotted some more Russian cavalry moving towards the fight. Even though Nansouty still had two regiments of *cuirassiers* in reserve, the extremely conservative general did not wish to commit all his regiments to the action against an enemy of unknown strength and quality. He therefore ordered the recall to be sounded.

As the French heavy horse disengaged and withdrew to a position behind and to the west of Caffarelli's infantry, the Kharkov Dragoons—finally rallied following their earlier defeat at the hands of Kellermann's light cavalry and Sébastiani's dragoons—attacked what they thought was the exposed southern flank of Caffarelli. Positioned on the far right of the division was the 13th *Légère* under the command of Colonel Castex. The 13th had been formed in 1791 from the companies of the old *Gardes Françaises* that had been poured into the *Garde Nationale de Paris*, and the regimental muster rolls reflected that a large number of veteran soldiers still remained in the ranks. Of the 1,240 people of the 13th *Légère* that were on the field at Austerlitz, 885 had been in the French army between 10 and 15 years. Thirty-three other members of Colonel Castex's command had longer terms of service, including 12 people that had been in the army for 25 years![287]

The 13th Légère *repels the Kharkov Dragoons*

With almost three-quarters of his regiment composed of a solid core of veteran soldiers, and with a much wider frontage than the oncoming horsemen, it is little wonder that instead of forming square, Castex coolly kept his two battalions standing side-by-side in line to receive the enemy. Closer and closer the dragoons came, their horses moving in an ever-escalating gait and the troopers wildly screaming 'Hurrah!' The sight of 400 charging Russian dragoons might have unnerved a foe like the Turkish infantry, but it certainly did not frighten Castex and the expertly trained, experienced 13th *Légère*. Unflinching, Castex waited until the Russians were in point-blank range, then giving the order to fire, saw the enemy horsemen disappear into a hail of lead and a cloud of smoke. Although it is highly unlikely that "one out of four horsemen"[288] were brought down by the regimental volley as claimed by Caffarelli, what is certain is that the fire of the 13th *Légère* stopped the charge and turned back the Kharkov Dragoons. Once again, Caffarelli's troops had easily repulsed a Russian cavalry charge by remaining in line rather than by forming square.

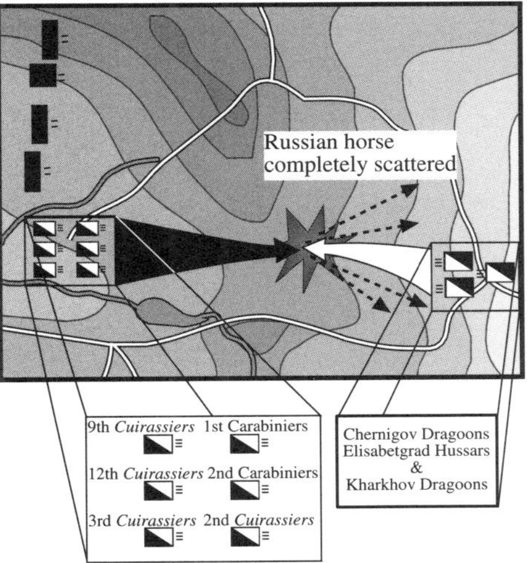

Nansouty advances

The respite given by Caffarelli's unshakable infantry had afforded Nansouty the opportunity to reform his division. Once this was accomplished, the *cuirassier* general gave the order for his regiments to advance in column of companies (half-squadrons). Once past the *fantassins*, Nansouty widened each regiment into column of squadrons and deployed the division in two battle lines. The 1st and 2nd *Carabiniers* along with the 2nd *Cuirassiers* were in the front line while the 3rd, 9th and 12th *Cuirassiers* formed the second line. In this configuration, the 1st and 3rd Brigades (1st and 2nd *Carabiniers* and 9th and 12th *Cuirassiers*, respectively) formed their regiments abreast of one another. Meanwhile, the 2nd and 3rd *Cuirassiers* of the 2nd Brigade were formed with one regiment behind the other.[289] Nansouty's half-company of horse artillery moved alongside the regiments in the first line, then unlimbered and began firing onto the advancing Russian horse.

These oncoming cavalry were the resilient Elisabetgrad Hussars and the Chernigov Dragoons from Uvarov's over-used brigade. Apart from these regiments, Liechtenstein had still uncommitted to battle all three regiments of Austrian heavy cavalry and their supporting cavalry battery. However, these forces were well to the rear on the orders of the column commander. What's more, the heavily-damaged

---

[287] S.H.A.T., C² 481, *État de Situation du 5ᵉ Corps a la Bataille d'Austerlitz*.

[288] S.H.A.T., C² 10.

[289] S.H.A.T., C² 240; Picard, *La Cavalerie dans Les Guerres de la Révolution et de l'Empire*, vol. 1, p. 315.

Grand Duke Constantine Uhlans were still unaccounted for, while hanging back on their own volition were three regiments of Cossacks. Therefore, only the formations under Uvarov were available to oppose Nansouty's advance. The French cavalry general directed his division along the ground in between the villages of Krug and Blasowitz, there finding the weakened regiments of Russian cavalry. Uvarov's regiments had already gamely fought virtually unsupported for almost 90 minutes, and were no match for Nansouty's coordinated attack delivered by six regiments of rested, heavy cavalry. The Elisabetgrad Hussars, Chernigov Dragoons and Kharkov Dragoons were all quickly overturned and scattered, not to return for the rest of the battle.

Lannes Presses His Offensive

Once the Russian cavalry on the south side of the Olmütz Road had finally been dispersed, Lannes ordered Caffarelli to send some of his men to capture the village of Blasowitz. Caffarelli immediately dispatched the 13th *Légère* and the 51st *Ligne* to secure that place. Colonel Castex's light infantrymen led the way, with two companies from each battalion acting as *tirailleurs* in advance of the formed troops. Once in front of Blasowitz, the 13th ran into the Russian Guard *Jaeger* Battalion. The French *tirailleurs* were unable to dislodge the *jaeger* from the village, so Colonel Castex led the 1st Battalion in a charge to evict the Russians. Arriving in front of the village, Castex was struck by a musket ball in the forehead and was instantly killed.[290] When word got back to the 2nd Battalion about the death of their colonel, the men could not be restrained. Charging forward into the village under a hail of musket balls to avenge the death of Castex, the 2nd Battalion was soon joined by their comrades in the 1st Battalion. Within minutes, the entire 13th *Légère* routed the Russian Guard *Jaeger* Battalion from Blasowitz, then overpowered the nearby half-battery of Russian Guard Horse Artillery. These artillerists, not wishing to find out what Arakcheev would have in store for them should they lose their guns and not their lives, contested to their death the capture of their five pieces. Meanwhile, as the Russian Guard *Jaeger* survivors were fleeing from the village, they were overtaken and virtually annihilated by the 2nd Battalion of the 51st *Ligne*. This formation had been directed by Colonel Bonnet d'Honnières to take up a position north of Blasowitz. As a result of this excellent placement, these Frenchmen were in a position to intercept and destroy the disorganized gaggle of retreating *jaeger* when they hurriedly fled the village.

Just as the Russian Guard *Jaeger* and supporting Guard Horse Artillery were being destroyed, a battalion of Guard Fusiliers from the Semenovsky Regiment arrived. Without hesitating, the French turned their full attention to this unsupported formation. Before the giant Guardsmen knew it, their front and flanks were being shot up by the *tirailleurs* of the 13th *Légère* and 51st *Ligne*. Unable to respond to the clouds of French skirmishers, the Semenovsky battalion began falling back towards the rest of the Russian Imperial Guard.

By this time, Vandamme had cleared the Austrian Salzburg IR#23 off the Staré Vinohrady and had positioned some of his divisional artillery on that high ground. When the French guns opened a destructive fire onto the Austrian cüirassiers, Hohenlohe decided to move against the heights with his three regiments of cüirassiers and supporting cavalry battery. The Austrian horse had not advanced very far before they became entangled in the ever-present vineyards. Once encumbered among the vines, their movement all but stopped, the cüirassiers became almost static targets for the expert gunlayers of the French artillery. The Austrian heavy cavalry regiments were raked unmercifully by Vandamme's guns,

---

[290] S.H.A.T., C^2 16.

giving Hohenlohe no alternative but to order his troopers to withdraw to the northeast.[291]

Meanwhile, another cavalry duel was taking place along the Olmütz Road between the combined divisions of Kellermann and Walther against four of Bagration's regiments of horse—two of dragoons, one *cuirassier* and the Pavlograd Hussars. The coordination between French formations quickly gained the upper hand. Kellermann's light cavalry, supported by Walther's dragoons, temporarily broke up the Russian cavalry and finally cleared the way for the Lannes to deal with Bagration's infantry.

North of the Olmütz Road, Prince Bagration had sent the 5th *Jaeger* along with the Mariupol Hussars and the Khaznenkov Cossacks on a wide movement designed to attack the French northern, or left, flank from an oblique angle while the main infantry force astride the highway assailed Lannes' front. The 5th *Jaeger*, with the Mariupol Hussars split into two battle groups following behind and on their flanks, and the Cossacks swarming about, pushed past Siwitz, then turned south and headed for Bosenitz and the Santon which anchored the French left. Lannes had posted pickets from the 17th *Légère* in the vineyards north of Bosenitz, and they quickly retired in the face of the advancing Russians. According to the official Austrian account of the battle:

> The French outposts were overthrown in short order, and only the artillery fire from the enemy left wing [the Santon] prevented the fugitives from being totally wiped out by the Cossacks and the Mariupol Hussars, which came hurrying up. *Jaeger* and Cossacks pressed into Bosenitz itself... [292]

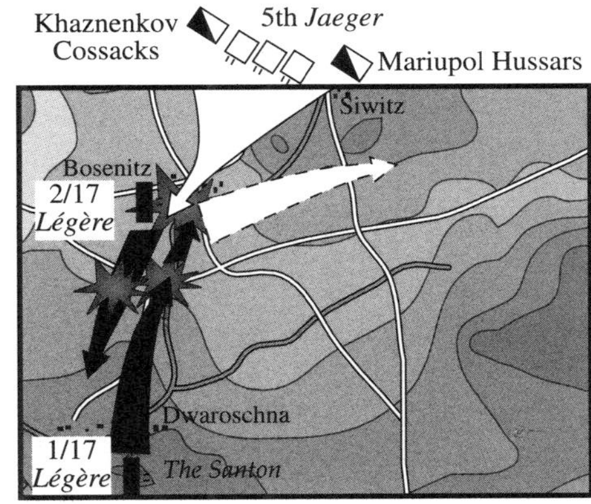

The 5th Jaeger *attacks toward the Santon*

Of the three battalions in the 5th *Jaeger*, two of them were thrown at Bosenitz to clear out the covering French *tirailleurs*. Once these skirmishers had been pushed back, the first formed French troops were discovered deployed behind the hamlet. These men belonged to the 1st Battalion of the 17th *Légère* with Colonel Vedel and General Claparède at their side. Assessing the isolated position of his small command, Claparède ordered the battalion to fall back in order to gain the protective gun fire of the Santon. The 1st Battalion of the 17th *Légère* retired as the Russians pressed hard in attempts to break them. The Mariupol Hussars charged repeatedly, but the isolated battalion formed square and repulsed each charge. The 1st Battalion of the 17th *Légère* then reached the bottom of the Santon while the fire of the 18 captured Austrian 3-pounders on the summit was directed at the oncoming masses of the 5th *Jaeger*, to which were added a fusillade of musketry from the 2nd Battalion of the 17th *Légère*. It did not take the officers and men of the 5th *Jaeger* long to figure out that they had become engaged in a fire fight that they could not win; they fell back out of canister range of the numerous 3-pounders. Once this retrograde movement was detected by Claparède, he ordered the 2nd Battalion of the 17th *Légère* to charge. The battalion descended from the Santon and swept away the three battalions of the 5th *Jaeger*, recapturing Bosenitz in the process. The pursuit was then taken up by the light cavalry under Treillard and Milhaud. The coordinated attacks by these hussars and *chasseurs à cheval* first overturned the Mariupol Hussars, then chased the fugitives of the 5th *Jaeger* and their supporting Cossacks from the valley of Siwitz.

French légère, *by Philippoteaux*

Meanwhile, with his front now cleared of menacing cavalry, Lannes ordered a general advance. Caffarelli kept his same axis of march along the south side of

---

291 K. k. Kriegsarchiv, F.A., *Ausführliche Relation der am 2 ten Dezember, 1805.*

292 K. k. Kriegsarchiv, F.A., *Ausführliche Relation der am 2 ten Dezember, 1805.*

Quiot du Passage

the highway in an easterly direction with the intent of linking up with the 13th *Légère* and 51st *Ligne* which had previously been sent to clear Blasowitz. On the north side of the road, Suchet also moved his division eastward. Marching at almost at a parade ground pace, the French could see three regiments of musketeers that composed Bagration's main force. As the two divisions of French *fantassins* moved closer to Bagration's lines, some 30 allied guns suddenly erupted in a deafening roar, raining a hail of shot and shell onto Lannes' soldiers. Although 18 of the Russian pieces were attached to the nine battalions in the musketeer regiments, and these fired straight into the French formations, the remaining ordnance belonged to a Russian horse artillery battery (12 pieces) and they hammered the bluecoated lines from an oblique angle from the northeast. The cannonballs from this horse artillery unit bounced into the French battalions down their files, tearing through flesh and blood at an alarming rate. Within a matter of minutes, some 400 Frenchmen were rendered *hors de combat*, including a section of drummers in the 30th *Ligne* and *général de brigade* Valhubert, commander of the 3rd Brigade under Suchet.[293] When the general went down with his thigh shattered by a cannonball, he refused to be carried away. Remembering the Emperor's instructions to the army, Valhubert said: "Remain at your posts. I can die just as well by myself. If one man falls, we do not have to lose six."[294]

Instinctively, Lannes was drawn to the focal point of the battle. He rode to the front of his infantry and shouted orders to three of his aides-de-camp to collect all the available artillery attached to Suchet and Caffarelli, except for one foot artillery detachment of Suchet consisting of two 8-pounders already in position covering that division's northern flank. When *chef d'escadron* Subervie and *chef de bataillon* Quiot du Passage returned along with Captain Bessières, they had in tow three companies of foot artillerists with 15 pieces of ordnance. These companies had manned 18 pieces at the start of the battle, but three guns had already been put out of action from Russian artillery fire. When the French artillerists arrived along the Olmütz Road, they found Lannes flushed from battle. The marshal was on horseback with his collar unbuttoned and his blue woolen tunic trimmed in gold already partially blackened from powder stains. Moreover, Lannes' hat was already blown off and he had dirt covering his hair and face, barely making it possible to see that he had not shaved for two days.

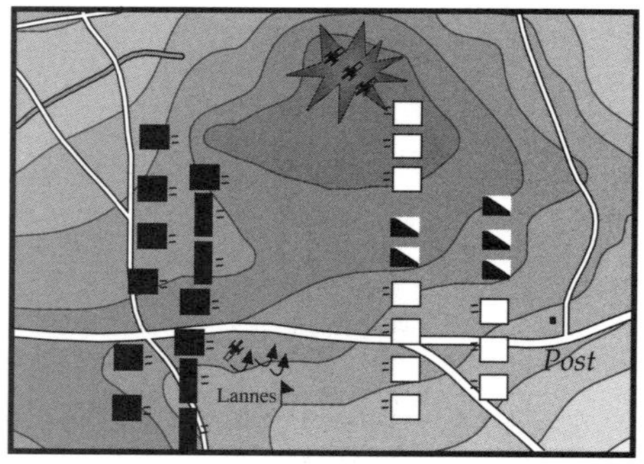

The French artillery conduct a moving counterbattery against the Russian guns

When the limbered pieces pulled up, Lannes personally positioned the ordnance on the south side of the highway and instructed the crews that after firing each round, they would limber the smoking pieces and move them to a new location, keeping their distance from the Russian horse artillery on the north side of Bagration's line. In this way, the French would make it more difficult for the less-skilled Russian gunlayers to get a fix on their position as well as reach the French with their shorter-ranged ordnance. Lannes ordered his artillery to silence the Russian line horse battery, and for the next quarter of an hour the French artillerists put on a display of superior counter battery fire skills. After each discharge, the French crews would limber their pieces, move to a new location, unlimber, load and fire. The Russian crews shot back at the constantly moving French targets, but without success. It did not take long before the expertly trained French crews manning the heavier 12- and 8-pounders overpowered the lighter Russian 6-pounder guns and accompanying 10-pounder licornes. Perhaps at no other time in the 1805 campaign were the superior crews and range of the French ordnance more evident than during these exchanges of artillery fire. The punishment became too much for the Russian horse artillerists. After losing a few pieces and several horse teams, they limbered their remaining pieces and withdrew.[295]

---

[293] These were the majority of the casualties suffered by the division at the battle.
[294] Thiers, *The History of the Consulate & the Empire of France*, vol. 2, p. 80.
[295] S.H.A.T., *Journal des opérations du 5e corps.*

The Posoritz Post House

With the silencing of the Russian horse battery, Lannes once again signaled for his command to resume the offensive. The French artillery supported the infantry advance as Caffarelli was directed to exploit the success enjoyed by his regiments at Blasowitz, sweep forward and clear the hamlets of Krug and Holubitz. Meanwhile, Suchet and the cavalry would deal with Bagration's main force that was still on the north side of the highway. Suchet forged ahead with all his battalions now deployed in line of battle. As they moved closer to Bagration's infantry, the 18 battalion guns attached to the Arkhangelgorod, Old Ingermanland and Pskov Musketeer Regiments spewed forth a hail of canister that put the splendid infantry of the 34th and 40th *Ligne* to their severest test of the battle. However, Colonel Dumoustier's and Colonel Legendre d'Harvesse's troops were some of the finest in the *Grande Armée*. Suchet reported:

> Drawn up in lines, our infantry withstood the canister fire with total composure, filling in the files as soon as they had been struck down. The Emperor's order was carried out to the letter, and for perhaps the first time in this war, most of the wounded made their way to the dressing stations unaided.[296]

During this time, rallied regiments of Russian cavalry dashed out to attack Suchet's front line infantry, only to be halted by French musketry and canister fire, then counterattacked and driven off by Kellermann's or Walther's horsemen. Perhaps at no other time during the Battle of Austerlitz were the workings of the opposing armies more starkly contrasted than during this fight on the north side of the Olmütz Road. While the French combat arms worked to provide mutual support for one another, the Russians lacked total coordination between not only combat arms, but between regiments as well. Watching his countrymen in action, Ermolov vividly recalled that:

> our cavalry, like the rest of our forces, acted mostly on its own initiative, without any attempt at mutual support. Therefore, from one wing to another our forces came into actions by detachments, and one after another our forces became disordered, overthrown and chased off the field.[297]

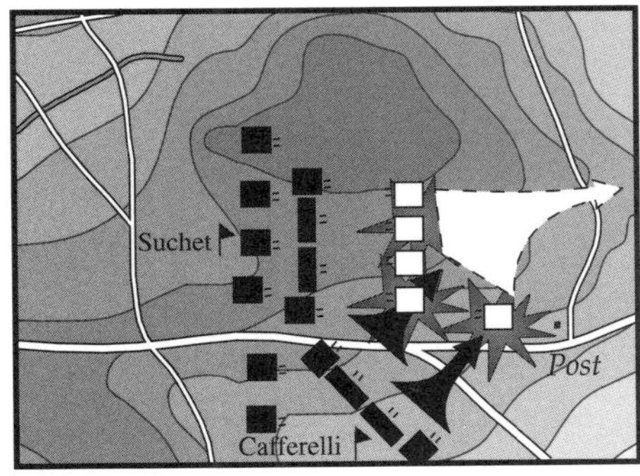

Caffarelli flanks Bagration's infantry

Following the repulse of every charge made by these Russian cavalry, the line of French infantry resumed its advance, passing over the latest killed and wounded Russian cavalrymen. These disabled horsemen of the Tsar did not possess the same determination to continue resistance like some of their infantry brothers-in-arms. Once the French came upon them, most of the horsemen held their hands above their head, even if wounded and lying on the ground. The Russian cavalrymen would cry out for mercy, and from these men the French readily accepted their surrender.

Meanwhile, Caffarelli had moved his division past Suchet sometime after noon. He then swept General Ulanius, the 6th *Jaeger* and various squadrons of spent cavalry and Cossacks from Krug. Upon seeing the exposed southern flank of Bagration's infantry, Caffarelli ordered *général de brigade* Demont to take his two regiments—the 17th and 30th *Ligne*—and swing north across the highway, supporting Suchet by moving northward against the Russian infantry and cutting off their retreat route. However, the pressure already applied against Bagration's

[296] Alombert-Goget and Colin, *La Campagne de 1805 en Allemagne*, XXVI, p. 543.
[297] *Zapiski A. P. Ermolova,* vol. 1, p. 36.

The black flag of the Arkhangelgorod Musketeers captured by the 5th Cuirassiers

line by Suchet and the cavalry was too much for the greencoated formations. As the Russians began falling back, they were periodically assailed by French cavalry. One charge made by the 5th *Cuirassiers* from d'Hautpoul's Division broke a battalion square of the Arkhangelgorod Musketeers and captured most of the unit. In that charge, Belliard saw *chef d'escadron* Jacquemin of the 5th *Cuirassiers* capture one of the flags of the Arkhangelgorod Musketeers.[298]

Assailed frontally by infantry and cavalry, and with more French now moving against his southern flank with the obvious intent to cut off his retreat path towards Olmütz, Bagration now knew that the battle was lost. The only thing that remained for the Prince was to extricate as much of his command as quickly as possible. Ordering the withdrawal, Bagration and the Russians fell back as fast as they could, pursued every step of the way by the formations urged forward by Lannes and Murat. Attempts to stem the French tide were made by exhausted regiments of Russian horse. However, the masses of tightly controlled French dragoons and light cavalry simply overwhelmed each disjointed sortie made by the Russian cavalry. Bagration's command was driven eastward past the Posoritz Post House where one of the final cavalry actions took place. During this *mêlée*, General Sébastiani was hit by a Russian bullet while in front of his brigade of dragoons.[299] Most of the Russian cavalry finally broke off and fled, leaving their surviving infantry comrades to take the full brunt of the French heavy cavalry and infantry. Not too far away, Lannes was pushing on his *fantassins* and driving the Russian infantry from the field in ever-increasing disorder. Meanwhile, Murat's *carabiniers* and *cuirassiers* carved up the Pavlograd Hussars that made a final, heroic and self-sacrificing attempt to cover the infantry's retreat.

As the troops under Lannes and Murat advanced, they came to the jump off area where early that morning Bagration's infantry had dropped their backpacks.

Meissonier painted Cuirassiers *at Austerlitz waiting for orders*

> Ten thousand [*sic*] haversacks ranged in rows fell into our possession; but our booty, vast as it appeared, was only 10,000 [*sic*] little black boxes or rather triptych reliquaries, each containing an image of Saint Christopher carrying the infant Christ above the waters, with an equal number of pieces of black bread made from straw and bran rather than barley or wheat. Such was the sacred and simple baggage of the Russians![300]

This final attack by the French captured 16 Russian pieces of ordnance while leaving 2,000 of Bagration's soldiers dead and wounded on the field and hundreds more captured.

Bagration was hurriedly trying to rally what remained of his shattered command when Austrian Major Frierenberger arrived from Olmütz with two fresh Austrian cavalry batteries totaling 12 pieces of ordnance.

> These guns reached Raussnitz at the moment when fugitives came pouring back to confirm the frightful news of various disasters experienced by the army. The commander [Frierenberger] pushed his train along the Brünn highway [Olmütz Road], and, although he had no real covering force, he positioned the guns on the most advantageous site on the high ground to the right of Welleschowitz.[301]

---

[298] S.H.A.T., C² 240.
[299] S.H.A.T., C² 16 and 470.
[300] *Memoirs of Baron Lejeune*, vol. 1, p. 30.
[301] K. k. Kriegsarchiv, F.A., *Ausführliche Relation der am 2 ten Dezember, 1805.*

Above, the memorial on the Pratzen Heights today. Below, Austerlitz Castle

Bagration began reforming his shattered regiments under the cover of these fresh batteries as the spent troops under Lannes and Murat had their pursuit halted by the "extraordinary"[302] fire of Frierenberger's 12 Austrian pieces. The thousands of fresh troops in Rivaud de la Raffinière's Division of 1st Corps could have taken up where Lannes and Murat stopped, but Bernadotte refused to display any initiative and Rivaud's Division remained inactive. Meanwhile, Hohenlohe's Austrian cüirassiers were dispersed by Kellermann's tireless light cavalry during which Captain Braun of the 2nd Hussars captured one of the Austrian standards.[303] Further to the south, stranded against the western side of the Raussnitz stream, were the surviving units of Uvarov's brigade from Liechtenstein's V Column. These soldiers were crowded around the isolated bridges over which they could escape the oncoming victorious French army. Ermolov's Russian horse artillery battery was still with Uvarov when the pursuing French charged. Ermolov, writing in his honest and even-handed manner, described the hellish scene:

> Our losses were greatly increased when we crowded against an extremely boggy stream [Raussnitz], which could be passed only by a few bridges. Our fugitive cavalry tried to get across by wading, and many of the men and horses were drowned. I was abandoned by the regiment to which I was attached, but unlimbered my battery in the hopes of holding off the enemy, who were pursuing our horse. I extricated one gun from the press of our own cavalry, but was only able to get off a few rounds before the enemy rode over us and captured the piece. My men were cut down in the process and I myself was taken prisoner. Survivors of Uvarov's command, standing at the bridges, now had time to appreciate that it had been fleeing from only a small force of the French, and that the main enemy force was still positioned on the [Pratzen] heights, not having ventured into the valley. Our pursuers were then put to flight or destroyed. So it was that I was freed from my brief captivity, when a dangerously short distance from the French lines. I rejoined the remnants of my shattered battery, and found the rest of Uvarov's command milling about in disorder at the foot of the little hill where the Tsar was standing... hardly anyone remained of his retinue. His facial features were lined with deep sorrow, and his eyes were full of tears.[304]

Finale

The Tsar had only his private surgeon, Dr. James Wylie, and his groom Iene remaining with him. Dismounting from his horse, Alexander sat down beneath a tree and buried his head in his hands. At the urging of a passing staff officer, the Tsar got back on his horse and rode past the village of Austerlitz to the small hamlet of Hodiegitz where he found Kutuzov. Following a brief conference, Alexander got back on a horse (there were no carriages to be had) and rode through the rain for seven miles until he came to Urchitz. Taken there to a peasant's hut, the Tsar drank a mixture of opium and wine, then collapsed into an exhausted sleep on a pile of straw.

---

[302] K. k. Kriegsarchiv, F.A., *Ausführliche Relation der am 2 ten Dezember, 1805.*
[303] S.H.A.T., C^2 240.
[304] *Zapiski A. P. Ermolova,* vol. 1, pp. 36-37.

On the other side of the field, the French celebrated their stupendous victory. Bands played *"La Victoire est à nous"* over and over again until the Moravian hills echoed the Napoleonic refrain. Men recalled the events of the day while others dropped on the field in exhaustion. Meanwhile:

> the Emperor came back in the evening along the whole line where the different regiments of the army had fought. It was already dark: he had recommended silence to all who accompanied him, that he might hear the cries of the wounded; he immediately went to the spot where they were, dismounted, and ordered a glass of brandy be given them from the canteen which always followed him... the duty squadron passed the whole night stripping the cloaks from the Russian dead, for the purpose of covering the wounded. Napoleon ordered a large fire to be kindled near each of them... and did not retire til... they were all in the hospital. These brave men heaped him with blessings, which found the way to his heart much better than all the flatteries of courtiers. It was thus that Napoleon won the affection of his soldiers, who knew that when they suffered, it was not his fault; and therefore they never spared themselves in his service.[305]

About 10:00 P.M., Napoleon and his staff completed their ride over the war torn ground, arriving at the Posoritz Post House, the location of the famous 28 November meeting between the Emperor and his marshals (see page 341). The tiny two-room structure was already being used as a Russian dressing station when the wet and exhausted Imperial entourage entered and began warming themselves in front of a fire. Standing before the flames, his soaked clothes steaming from the heat, Napoleon began to dictate his proclamation to the army. He partially finished the dictation before choosing to complete the address the following day:

> Soldiers, I am pleased with you! You have this day at Austerlitz realized all I expected of your bravery. You have covered your eagles with immortal glory. In less than four hours, you have cut to shreds and routed an army of 100,000 men [*sic*], commanded by the Emperors of Russia and Austria. The enemy that escaped your bayonets have drowned in the lakes... Soldiers, when I have accomplished everything that is necessary for the happiness and prosperity of your land, I shall lead you back to France. There you will be the objects of my most tender care. My people will greet you with joy, and it will be enough for you to say 'I was at the Battle of Austerlitz,' and they will reply 'There stands a hero!'[306]

---

[305] *Memoirs of the Duke of Rovigo* (Savary), vol. 1, p. 136.
[306] Napoléon to the Army, *Correspondance,* number 9537.

The fruits of victory are displayed after the Battle of Austerlitz

Chapter IX
"I Give Myself Only Half the Credit"— Napoleon and a Judgement of the Immortal Ulm-Austerlitz Campaigns of 1805

> *"I give myself only half the credit for the battles I have won, and a general gets enough credit when he is named at all, for the fact is that a battle is won by the army.* —Napoleon[1]

The Aftermath of Austerlitz

The Moravian landscape reflected the débris and carnage of a Napoleonic battle. Several eye witnesses stated that it seemed as though everywhere one looked, the number of lifeless Russian and Austrian bodies lying prostrate on the ground outnumbered the French dead by a multiple of at least five or six to one. The losses suffered by the Combined Russian and Austrian Army at Austerlitz were staggering. The total allied losses on 2 December 1805 amounted to 28,900, or slightly less than a whopping 40% of the 72,789 Russian and Austrian soldiers that entered the fighting. Of these, some 7,000 allied soldiers were dead, almost 10% of those who began the day under arms. And if one counts just prisoners taken by Napoleon's forces, the Combined Russian and Austrian Army lost more than 15% of those who went into action.

Dealing with the aftermath

Breaking down the casualties by nationality, the Russian killed, wounded and captured, excluding the Russian Imperial Guard save the *Chevalier Garde*, came to 23,502. Of these, 19,886 were in the infantry and cavalry, while 3,616 were in the artillery.[2] Add to the 23,502 figure the casualties suffered by the Russian Imperial Guard, which included six officers and 90 other ranks captured, and losses for the Russians can be placed at 25,400. Of this total loss, all the Russian formations—including the Guard—had 9,423 people captured, of which 320 were officers and 9,103 were other ranks.[3] Therefore, if one backs out the number of Russian captives, this leaves some 15,977 of the Tsar's soldiers either killed or wounded. Considering the savage nature of the battle, especially on the Pratzen Plateau where almost no prisoners were taken, the author estimates that the number of Russian dead at Austerlitz had to come to at least 6,400; this represents more than 11% of the Russian combatants—an extraordinarily high percentage of the Russian troops engaged.

Meanwhile, the Austrians lost about 3,500 officers and men at Austerlitz, of which 1,669 were made prisoner.[4] The Austrian captives included 39 officers and 1,630 other ranks, a quarter of which were from the Salzburg IR#23, the last defenders of the Pratzen.[5] The remaining Austrian casualties amounted to 600 dead and 1,231 wounded.[6]

The allies also suffered extraordinarily heavy losses of artillery and mobile equipment. Kienmayer managed to save his pieces of the Advance Guard of the I

---

[1] Gourgaud, *Sainte Hélène: Journal,* vol. 2, p. 425.
[2] Kutuzov, *Sbornik Dokumentov,* vol. 2, pp. 235-236.
[3] S.H.A.T., C^2 15 and 470.
[4] S.H.A.T., C^2 15 and 470.
[5] S.H.A.T., C^2 470.
[6] S.H.A.T., C^2 13 and 470.

Column, but all the other major commands suffered significant losses in materiel. Of the 60 pieces of Russian ordnance that supported the II and III Columns, not a single tube was brought out of the fight. Add to this number the artillery lost by the I, IV and V Columns, the Russian Imperial Guard and Bagration's Advance Guard, the Combined Russian and Austrian Army lost 183 pieces of the 318 tubes that were at the battle—a loss of almost 58%. Of the 183 pieces that were captured by the French, 149 were Russian and 34 were Austrian.[7] Also taken were 45 standards and over 400 caissons and wagons.[8]

Naturally, the units that composed the I, II and III Columns had suffered the most. Within Dokhturov's I Column, the New Ingermanland Musketeers typified the losses suffered by Russian units on the southern end of the field. Entering the battle with 1,903 people, the regiment lost 70 officers and 947 men—a casualty rate of 53%.[9] In Langeron's II Column, the Kursk Musketeers entered the battle with 1,600 combatants. In addition to their 526 killed and wounded, the regiment lost 705 officers and men as prisoners, for a total loss of 1,231, or about 77% casualties.[10] Some Russian regiments had all but ceased to exist. Consider the case of the Butyrsk Musketeers from Prebyshevsky's III Column. This regiment broke camp at Radziwilow on 25 August with 2,152 officers and men under the colors. After combat casualties and strategic consumption, the three battalions of the Butyrsk Musketeers entered the fighting at Austerlitz with only 864 of all ranks; only 269 returned to Russia![11] Fighting on the northern end of the battlefield, the Arkhangelgorod Musketeers began the day with 1,978 officers and other ranks; they lost 1,631—more than 82% of the regiment.[12]

Regardless of the column in which they fought, the regiments of Russian *jaeger* fared poorly as well. For example, of the 1,736 members that comprised the nine woefully understrength battalions of the 6th, 7th and 8th *Jaeger,* some 986 officers and other ranks were captured at Austerlitz.[13]

Larrey

In butchering the allied army, the *Grande Armée* escaped with an extraordinarily light casualty list. Napoleon's army suffered a total of 8,279 killed and wounded, of which thousands of slightly wounded had already been released from the hospitals six days after the battle. As of 8 December 1805, the medical staffs at the 21 hospitals that had been established to treat the French wounded—except the members of the Imperial Guard that were all cared for at Larrey's hospital—had only 2,476 officers and men still under their care. Of these, 2,167 were ordinary soldiers, while the other 309 were officers.[14] Immediately after the battle, Larrey treated 87 wounded Guardsmen, of which six officers and 18 troopers were from the *Grenadiers à cheval* and 65 officers and men were from the *Chasseurs à cheval.*[15] This total number of 2,563 wounded remaining in the hospitals as of 8 December is significantly fewer than the 6,991 listed as wounded the day after the battle. Therefore, it is clear that 4,428 of the men declared as wounded the day

---

[7] S.H.A.T., C² 470. The French report dated 30 frimaire an XIV (21 December 1805) is very exact about the number and caliber of allied pieces captured at Austerlitz. Of the 149 captured pieces of Russian ordnance, 26 were 12-pounders, 70 were 6-pounders, 14 were 18-pounder licornes and 39 were 10-pounder licornes. The 34 pieces of captured Austrian ordnance consisted of one 12-pounder cannon, 22 6-pounders, the lone 3-pounder that participated in the battle and 10 howitzers.

[8] S.H.A.T., C² 9, 10 and 470.

[9] Andolenko, *Aigles de Napoléon Contre Drapeaux du Tsar*, p. 96.

[10] S.H.A.T., C² 470; Andolenko, *Aigles de Napoléon Contre Drapeaux du Tsar*, p. 94.

[11] Andolenko, *Aigles de Napoléon Contre Drapeaux du Tsar*, p. 100.

[12] S.H.A.T., C² 470; Nicolaiev, *Historique du 17e régiment d'infanterie Arkhangelgorod* (Saint Petersburg, 1900), p. 254.

[13] S.H.A.T., C² 15 and 470.

[14] S.H.A.T., C² 16 and 470.

[15] S.H.A.T., C² 16 and 470.

after the fight had either been patched up and sent back to their units or had died. Whatever the case may be, almost two-thirds of those wounded at Austerlitz were no longer in the hospitals on 8 December. Add to the number of wounded the 1,288 French killed in action, of which only two were from the "Gods" and 19 more from the "Favored Children." There were also 573 French captured during the battle, with these men being returned to the *Grande Armée* shortly thereafter. When considering that Napoleon had 74,595 combatants at Austerlitz, the *Grande Armée* therefore suffered slightly more than 11% casualties. If one counts only the 1,288 French dead, coupled with the 2,653 wounded still in hospitals on 8 December, and assuming that one half of the other wounded had already recovered just days after the battle, the percentage losses suffered by Napoleon's forces drops to only 8%!

Invariably, the divisions of the *Grande Armée* which bore the brunt of the fighting shouldered the majority of the casualties. Based on the casualty returns the day after the epic confrontation, the highest percentage losses were suffered by Friant's Division of Davout's 3rd Corps. Of the 3,300 officers and men that made the series of forced marches from Vienna to participate in the battle, some 1,318 were rendered *hors de combat*—a loss of 40%.[16] In the two divisions that carried the Pratzen Plateau, Vandamme lost 1,182 out of 8,213, or 14% of his people; meanwhile, Saint-Hilaire counted 1,798 casualties from the 7,890 officers and men that he took into action, or almost 23% of his command.[17]

In mauling Bagration's Advance Guard, Lannes had suffered relatively light casualties. Suchet's Division, which began the day with 6,877 under arms, lost only 5 officers and 115 men killed in action, while another 38 officers and 632 men were wounded. Therefore, Suchet suffered only 790 casualties, or just above 11% of his command.[18] For all the fighting his command saw, Caffarelli lost fewer men than Suchet. Incredibly, only one officer of the division was killed in action—Colonel Castex of the 13th *Légère*. The colonel was joined by some 98 men of the division who were also killed.[19] In addition, Caffarelli's Division lost 25 officers and 623 men wounded, plus one man taken prisoner from the 13th *Légère*.[20] Therefore, Caffarelli had a total casualty count of 748, or slightly more than 11% of those who went into action. Also part of Lannes' command during the battle, the 2nd Dragoon Division under Walther suffered just over 10% losses. Of the 1,222 officers and men of the division to enter the fighting, some 129 were lost, including 22 troopers of the 10th Dragoons taken prisoner.[21] Not surprisingly, Kellermann's ever-present division of light cavalry took more losses than any other mounted command in Napoleon's army. Including staff, artillerists and train personnel, Kellermann's command at Austerlitz numbered 1,442 combatants, of which 126 were killed and 152 were wounded. The extraordinary high percentage of killed to wounded reflects the punishment taken at the hands of the Russian horse artillery. Nevertheless, the 278 casualties suffered by Kellermann represents

The wounded are carried away

[16] S.H.A.T., C[2] 476; Davout, *Opérations du 3e Corps,* p. vi; F. G. Hourtoulle, *Davout; le terrible* (Paris, 1975), p. 120. The breakdown of casualties for 3rd Corps troops were as follows: 17 officers killed and 57 wounded; 207 *sous-officiers* and soldiers killed while 963 were wounded. In addition, casualties among Bourcier's dragoons amounted to 35 killed in action with another 41 wounded.

[17] S.H.A.T., C[2] 16, 470 and 477.

[18] S.H.A.T., C[2] 481.

[19] S.H.A.T., C[2] 481; Martinien, *Tableaux des Officiers Tués et Blessés*, p. 421, also shows sous-lieutenant Deruet as killed in action. However, I have used "État de Situation du 5e Corps de la Grande Armée" dated two days after the battle and signed by Compans, who was Lannes' chief of staff.

[20] S.H.A.T., C[2] 481.

[21] S.H.A.T., C[2] 481.

not only the most casualties suffered by any cavalry division of the *Grande Armée*, but also represents the highest percentage losses by any French cavalry command that went into action—more than 19%.[22]

At the other end of the spectrum among the commands that were supposed to have been in the fighting were Bernadotte's divisions of infantry. Although Drouet's Division took 17 killed and 190 wounded, Rivaud de la Raffinière's Division lost only three killed and 11 wounded.[23] Perhaps one of the most remarkable statistics of the battle surrounds the *Mameluks* of the French Imperial Guard. For all the death and destruction the company of *Mameluks* wrought on the Russian *Chevalier Garde*, not one single man of the six officers and 42 troopers was either killed, wounded or captured![24]

* *

Tsar Alexander and Emperor Francis met at noon on 3 December to discuss what to do next. The choices were few. About 15,000 reinforcements were due to arrive any day (Merveldt with 4,000 Austrian survivors of the action at Mariazell and elsewhere arrived on the 4th, while Essen and 11,000 Russians were two days behind). Even with these reinforcements, the allied army was totally lacking in horses, ordnance and supplies in the event some generals wanted to continue a campaign that the soldiers already knew was lost. Not surprisingly, morale was at an all time low. Austerlitz had even broken Alexander's will to fight. With the 5th Corps of the *Grande Armée* sitting across the road to Olmütz, the Tsar wasted no time in ordering that the remnants of his army to immediately withdraw along the only retreat route left open, that being deeper into Hungary by crossing the March River at Göding. By withdrawing in this manner before negotiations had been made, Alexander doomed the Austrians. Francis was bitter, and wrote: "After the battle, Tsar Alexander strongly urged the total withdrawal of the Russian forces, if he did not actually demand it. This decision deprived us of support that we badly needed, now that we had to bargain for peace."[25]

Gudin

Meanwhile, Murat sent back a mistaken report that the Russians were returning to the Olmütz Road, which caused Napoleon to respond by sending off to the northeast Lannes' 5th Corps and Murat's Cavalry Reserve. When this turned out to be a wild goose chase, Napoleon redirected the army's pursuit towards Göding. Soult was supposed to lead on the morning of the 4th, but he was so slow in moving that Davout and the 3rd Corps spearheaded the drive, led by the recently arrived infantry division under Gudin as well as the light cavalry of the 3rd Corps and the dragoon division under Klein.[26] By 3:00 P.M., the hard-marching troops under Davout had overtaken the allied forces in and around the Göding Bridge over the March. As the French drew up for an attack, Merveldt sent one of his colonels to tell the French marshal that an armistice was already in place as a result of a meeting between Napoleon and Francis. Davout did not believe the tale, and sent the colonel back to Merveldt with word that the allies better get ready to catch French cannonballs. The Austrian soon returned with a letter from Kutuzov swearing to the armistice and a penciled note of confirmation from the Tsar: both testaments were bald-faced lies. At 2:00 P.M. that afternoon, Napoleon and Francis had met to discuss the terms of an armistice that had been requested by Francis and

[22] S.H.A.T., C^2 16 and 472.
[23] S.H.A.T., C^2 16 and 474.
[24] S.H.A.T., C^2 16 and 470.
[25] Angeli, 'Ulm und Austerlitz' in *Mittheilungen des K. K. Kriegs-Archivs,* p. 360.
[26] Gudin and Klein were only one day's march from the field when Austerlitz was fought.

that was agreed to take effect on the 5th and to be "extended to the Russians on condition that they withdrew to their own territory." However, with a note in hand from Kutuzov that was also seconded and signed by the Tsar himself, Davout halted his advance and did not attack the allies at Göding. Therefore, "wily old monarchical Europe won the last trick in the game of fraud and bluff which began at the Vienna [Tabor] bridge three weeks before."[27]

A suppliant Francis seeks peace

The armistice came as a great relief to Wrede and his division of Bavarians that were falling back on Brünn. They had been driven out of Iglau on 5 December by Archduke Ferdinand's Austrians. Elsewhere, the numerous allied diversionary attacks that were supposed to take place across the continent either dissipated quickly, or failed to materialize as planned. The electrifying news of Austerlitz swept over Europe, spelling the end to the Third Coalition.

Napoleon used the next three weeks to strengthen and re-equip his army. The arsenals of Vienna were emptied of 2,951 cannon and 100,000 muskets that were forwarded to various points of the new French Empire.[28] While Napoleon was negotiating peace terms with Austria, he concluded a deal with the Prussian Foreign Minister Haugwitz (Treaty of Schönbrünn) of 15 December 1805, whereby Prussia received Hanover, but had to cede Ansbach to Bavaria as well as the two tiny Rhineland principalities of Cleves and Neufchâtel to France. Further, Prussia agreed that France could have a free hand in southern Germany and Italy.[29]

Austria grudgingly accepted Napoleon's terms with the Treaty of Pressburg that was signed on 27 December 1805. Napoleon obtained minor territorial areas for his German allies of Württemberg and Baden, while for Bavaria, the Emperor forced Austria to cede the Tyrol and other minor enclaves. For the Kingdom of Italy, Napoleon wrested from Francis the territories of Dalmatia, Friaul, Istria and Venetia. Finally, for the seriously depleted French treasury, Napoleon obtained a sum of 50 million francs from the defeated Austrians.[30]

Returning to France after a campaign of three months, the French Empire now:

> carried to those limits which it never ought to have passed, a dazzling glory added to her arms, public and private credit miraculously re-established, new prospects of repose and prosperity opened to the nation, under a powerful government.[31]

Haugwitz

Napoleon crossed the Rhine and rode onto to Paris to the continued shouts of *"Vive l'Empereur!"* Perhaps the importance of Austerlitz to France and to Napoleon was best summed up by French historian M. A. Thiers:

> It was a return again to Marengo. Austerlitz was, in fact, that for the Empire which Marengo had been for the Consulate. Marengo

[27] Duffy, *Austerlitz,* p. 154.

[28] C[2] 470. Among the vast haul of Austrian field ordnance taken were: 326 12-pounders, 398 6-pounders, 554 3-pounders and more than 200 howitzers. The remainder of the captured Austrian ordnance were siege guns and mortars.

[29] Connelly, Parker, Becker and Burton, *Historical Dictionary of Napoleonic France, 1799-1815*, p. 437; Thiers, *The History of the Consulate & the Empire of France*, vol. 2, p. 90.

[30] Thiers, *The History of the Consulate & the Empire of France*, vol. 2, p. 92; Duffy, *Austerlitz,* p. 162, states that the treaty was accepted on 27 December; Connelly, Parker, Becker and Burton, *Historical Dictionary of Napoleonic France, 1799-1815*, pp. 403-404 state that the treaty was signed on 26 December. For an in-depth analysis of the negotiations between Napoleon, Prussia and Austria, consult Thiers' *The History of the Consulate & the Empire of France*, vol. 2, pp. 85-92, and Paul Schroeder, *The Transformation of European Politics 1763-1848* (Oxford, 1994), pp. 257-286.

[31] Thiers, *The History of the Consulate & the Empire of France*, vol. 2, p. 92. Also see Schroeder's *The Transformation of European Politics 1763-1848*, pp. 257-286.

> had confirmed the Consular power in the hand of Napoleon; Austerlitz fixed the Imperial crown upon his head. Marengo had made France pass in one day from a threatened position to one which was tranquil and great; Austerlitz, in crushing in one day a formidable coalition, did not produce a less important result.[32]

* *

Historical Analysis and the Ulm-Austerlitz Campaigns in Perspective

Any evaluation of the Ulm-Austerlitz campaigns of 1805 must include a look at all the major personalities as well as the armies, including their strengths and weaknesses.

Archduke Charles

The Allies

The Austrians, drawn into the Third Coalition by the British and Russians, were the biggest losers of the 1805 war. Ceding sizable territories, population and wealth as a result of the Treaty of Pressburg, the humiliation of 1805 ultimately drove the Austrian military establishment into many much needed reforms. However, the blame for Austria's disastrous outcome in 1805 can be assessed all the way from the head of state to the lowliest soldier. Emperor Francis I proved to be an ignorant participant in war. A man whose knowledge in war only minutely compared to his interests in the arts, Francis had nevertheless been eager for another war designed to defeat Napoleon Bonaparte—the 'product' of the French Revolution—and also punish to the country that murdered his sister, Marie Antoinette. However, beyond these genuine interests, Francis simply was not capable of leading a warring nation, and as a result, he depended on his generals for results.

Of the Austrian generals that participated in the 1805 war, the most capable was Archduke Charles, commander of the Austrian Army of Italy. Although only a minor character in this study, Charles had to call off his cautious offensive in Italy when his strategic northern flank collapsed with Mack's surrender at Ulm, followed by Archduke John's sound thrashing in the Tyrol. Charles handled his army, which was numerically superior to Masséna's *Armée d'Italie*, with competence, which is significantly more than what one can say of how John or Mack performed.

Archduke John, younger brother of Charles and also a minor figure in this work, tried to stem the advance of the Napoleonic forces into the Tyrol, only to have his dispersed forces defeated at Strub, Scharnitz and Leutasch. These battles in the Tyrol, which also featured fighting between Austrian and Bavarian forces, along with Charles' operations in Italy, are worthy of a separate study.

Within the confines of the battles in the Danube theater, extending into Moravia and to Austerlitz, solid evaluations and conclusions may be drawn on the performance of the Austrian army and its leaders of 1805. Apart from the faceless, bureaucratic direction and sometimes interference from the *Hofkriegsrat* that

---

[32] Thiers, *The History of the Consulate & the Empire of France*, vol. 2, pp. 92-93. Also see Schroeder's *The Transformation of European Politics 1763-1848*, pp. 257-286.

resulted in such embarrassing moves as Merveldt's separation from Kutuzov early in the Austerlitz campaign, the fighting along the Danube was Mack's war. The decision to march the army westward through then-neutral Bavaria in order to occupy Ulm, followed by a blind adherence to a plan that was based solely on the supposed strength of the position of that legendary city and which did nothing more than transfix his army at the juncture of the Iller and Danube, were strategic failings of Mack. Once the opposing armies came to grips, Mack's ever-constant and unrealistic shifting of objectives, while all the time being tied to holding onto Ulm, was perhaps best summed up by Archduke Ferdinand, who wrote on 13 October:

> In a whole book, one could not describe our situation and the madness of Mack. Mack, a complete fool, has through his constant orders to march here and there, has changed plans so often that without striking a blow, the whole army is dissolving before our eyes.[33]

It can, therefore, be accurately stated that Mack was thinking in terms of 18th century warfare while pitted against a foe that was far more advanced in every aspect of operational warfare.

Archduke Ferdinand

Mack's failings as an army commander were seconded by the numerous shortcomings of most of the senior Austrian officers that led the different columns. The performance of Riesch, Schwarzenberg, and Werneck all seemed to reflect a sense of continually being in slow motion. No doubt, a large part of these officers' seemingly poor combat performances must stem from the lack of an efficient staff. However, none of these senior officers displayed any inkling of inspired leadership in an attempt to overcome the many difficulties that the army faced due to a combination of Mack's decisions and the tactical methodology under which the Austrian army operated. These collective shortcomings are no better illustrated than that of Riesch at Elchingen. Ordered on a mission by his superior who hadn't a clue as to where the French really were, coming in contact with a small patrol that he pushed out of Elchingen late on the 13 October, observing that the northern span over the Danube was still usable when it was his mission to destroy posthaste all such bridges, faced with horrendous weather and related march delays from Ulm, Riesch passed up the fleeting opportunity to complete the destruction of the remains of the northern bridge, which would have secured his command from a direct assault on the 14th. Believing that his troops were already completely used up from their march from Ulm, Riesch—who saw the growing number of French campfires on the eastern side of the Danube during the night—should have realized the urgency of the situation and literally driven his men into action. Whether Riesch believed that he could not ask his troops to do any more that day, or whether he believed that any attempt by the French to carry Elchingen the next day could be repulsed by his troops, Riesch's decision to remain idle on the evening of 13-14 October seems to typify the mind set of the column commanders of the Austrian army.

If any Austrian general in the Danube theater seemed to exhibit some operational common sense, it was young Archduke Ferdinand. His recognition of the avenues that the French would use in their advance towards Ulm, coupled with his competent handling of his *ad hoc* command during the Austerlitz campaign, earn him the highest marks of any Austrian general serving outside Italy. However, the princeling had only limited battle experience. This is no better illustrated than in Ferdinand's less than ideal handling of the infantry in the attack on Jungingen

[33] Archduke Ferdinand, as quoted in Willbold, *Napoleons Feldzug um Ulm Die Schlacht von Elchingen*, p. 49.

during the Battle of Haslach-Jungingen on 11 October as his repeated assaults were cut to pieces by Dupont's infantry. Six weeks later, Ferdinand looked good in the maneuver on Iglau during the Austerlitz campaign when he was pitted against the energetic but overrated Bavarian general, Karl Philipp Wrede.

If any Austrian general in this study displayed any hint of tactical expertise in the 1805 war, it was FML Kienmayer. His handling of the Advance Guard of the I Column at Austerlitz was about as good a tactical performance as any Austrian general displayed. However, neither Kienmayer nor any other Austrian general gave any hint of being able to coordinate for very long the movements and attacks of multiple regiments. This complete lack of battlefield sophistication was a trademark of the armies of the *ancien régime* and something that the Austrian army began to address after 1805.

Among the different Austrian combat arms we have seen in this study, the artillery displayed the most competence. Major Frierenberger's two cavalry batteries that arrived after noon along the Olmütz Road during the Battle of Austerlitz, providing the firepower necessary to stem the French tide on the northern flank, arguably saved Bagration and the Advance Guard of the Combined Russian and Austrian Army. However, opportunities such as Frierenberger's at Austerlitz were too few in 1805. The army was still married to the idea of battalion artillery which greatly dissipated the hitting power of the arm. Also, the shortage of draft horses and transport personnel significantly affected the deployment of the otherwise well served Austrian artillery arm. The lack of transport drivers and draft horses that severely limited the Austrian ordnance deployment and mobility during 1805 was something else that was going to be corrected before the army went off to war in 1809.

In contradistinction to the artillery, the Austrian cavalry's performance varied from uneven to pitiful. It is hard to imagine any cavalry bungling its security mission worse than the Austrian cavalry did before Ulm. Just how badly the Austrian cavalry was screening and scouting for Mack's army is no more clearly illustrated than on 11 October, when Dupont's isolated command, never seeing an Austrian horseman, stumbled onto Mack's army that was hunkered down on the Michelsberg outside Ulm. If the Austrian cavalry had been doing its job, Dupont would have been discovered much earlier somewhere north of Haslach, thus making it possible for events of that memorable day to unfold much differently. On the battlefield, the Austrian regiments of horse performed unevenly. This was due, in part, to the insistence of the officers, at least early in the Ulm campaign, of subdividing the regiments into two-squadron tactical operational entities. It might have made some sense to deploy in such a manner if the two-squadron units could have been properly coordinated. As it was, these smaller uncoordinated commands were swallowed whole and digested easily by the highly coordinated and tactically sophisticated regiments and multi-regimental cavalry formations of the *Grande Armée.* When not betrayed by its leaders or by its antiquated tactical doctrine, Austrian cavalry regiments that kept their squadrons together on the field of battle did perform admirably. Without a doubt, the finest Austrian cavalry in the theater of war were the Chevaulegers-Regiment Latour #4 who upheld their excellent fighting reputation at Haslach-Jungingen, as well as the Chevaulegers-Regiment O'Reilly #3 who demonstrated their mettle at Austerlitz.

Austrian chevauleger in camp

If the Austrian artillery performed well within the limitations of their restricted deployment while the cavalry were generally uneven, then the Austrian infantry performance in 1805 can be judged as heroic on rare occasions, mediocre on most, and poor on many. If the majority of infantry regiments did not have their ranks filled with large numbers of out-of-shape men returning from a lengthy furlough, then they were combined with young and completely inexperienced soldiers. While these troops could fight like tigers, as they did in the garden of the Elchingen convent, they could not come close to matching the French formations in experience, maturity, tactical flexibility and cadre leadership. Furthermore, if some of those in the Austrian military establishment questioned the combat dedication of the *Grenzer* battalions, they only had to look at the blood-soaked ground in front of Tellnitz to see that they were every bit as brave and as competently led as any formations in Austrian service to see action during the Ulm or Austerlitz campaigns.

The Ulm-Austerlitz campaigns also revealed the organizational weaknesses of the Mack reforms, most especially the lack-luster combat performance of the new Grenadier battalions as well as the unacceptable achievements of the four-company infantry battalions. When compared to the larger, nine-company French battalion, the Mack four-company battalion—with the companies invariably understrength—simply had nothing to recommend itself given the fact that it was extremely difficult for the commanders to effectively coordinate multi-battalion maneuvers. After 1805, the Austrians would return to the familiar six-company battalion establishment, although a few converged grenadier battalions in 1809 and 1813 employed only four instead of six companies.

Austrian infantry in the 1805 helmets

Furthermore, the Austrian infantry that participated in the Ulm-Austerlitz campaigns were seemingly always running short on small arms ammunition. At Elchingen, the Austrian soldiers under Riesch entered the fighting with only 40 rounds of ammunition and no prospects of resupply. When Marshal Ney led the assault of the 6th *Légère* into town, the conscripts of Auersperg IR#24 ran out of ammunition during its defense of the Elchingen convent. When that happened, they were overcome by the better led, crack troops of the 6th *Légère.* Similarly, during the fighting for the Staré Vinohrady on northern end of the Pratzen plateau at Austerlitz, the small arms ammunition for the Salzburg IR#23 ran out, hastening the defeat of that regiment. Like the Austrians at Elchingen, the shortages of small arms ammunition at Austerlitz can be attributed to the inadequate preparations for war, which led to an insufficient number of horses and mobile equipment that were necessary to fully mobilize the army.

Finally, the Austrian 1805 experience vis-à-vis the conduct of the Russian soldiers was simply horrendous. The raping and pillaging by the Tsar's troops convinced the ruling nobles in Vienna that they never again wanted to see Russian troops in their country. After 1805, the Austrian and Russians would again be allies against Napoleon, but the Russians would assist by operating in territory outside the Habsburg Empire.

The Russians, of course, believed that it was nothing out of the ordinary to completely wreck a town as they passed nearby. Certainly, the Russian army treated the hamlets and peasants of Great Russia with greater respect than they did foreign cities and populations. However, even in Russia, when the army went on maneuvers in an area, the householders were forced from their property, only to return later to find their homes "wrecked and plundered as completely as if in the time of the Nogai Tartar raids."[34] If the Russians acknowledge that they treated their own in such a manner, we can therefore accept the statements by various Austrians concerning the conduct of the Russians while in Bavaria, Austria and Moravia previously quoted in this work as being accurate. The wreckage, raped and suffering left in the wake of the Tsar's forces were the closest thing to a barbarian invasion that early 19th century western Europeans could imagine.

Apart from the horrendous conduct off the battlefield by the Russian army as a whole, their involvement in the 1805 war in central Europe provides the student of history with an opportunity to further explore the effectiveness of the Tsar's forces in combat. While the battlefield strengths of the 1805 Russian army can be noted with admiration, its overall downfall was rooted in the trappings and failures of an armed force still steeped in the traditions of the *ancien régime*. First on the list of offenders must be Tsar Alexander I. Convinced of his messianic mission to

[34] A. M. Turgenev, as quoted in Duffy, *Russia's Military Way to the West,* p. 130.

save Europe's ruling houses, defeat Napoleon and turn back the clock of time, Alexander played the role of a meddling dilettante. Alexander was easily swayed by inexperienced counselors who were more interested in feeding his immense ego than with the realities of warfare, and the cumulative effect resulted in the army being committed to battle at Austerlitz—an engagement in which the entire Russian army *could* have been completely and utterly annihilated. This, following Kutuzov's escape after Hollabrunn, was when the army should have been handled with utmost circumspection. Instead, the Tsar and his young courtiers only compounded the problems facing the allies by forcing the Battle of Austerlitz. Without a doubt, the Russian nobles foolishly held not only Napoleon and the *Grande Armée* in complete contempt, but had a similar, low opinion of their Austrian allies. This self-proclaimed superiority compromised the allied chances of victory, thereby viciously rebounding on Alexander, his advisors and his army.

Among the Russian generals to see action in 1805, the one who deserves the most attention is Kutuzov. Like so many generals that were pitted against Napoleon, Kutuzov entered the 1805 war ill-prepared to met the Great Captain. Within a matter of weeks, Kutuzov got a crash course on how the Emperor waged modern warfare, as well as seeing for the first time the fighting capabilities of the new French army—both experiences being entirely different than those Kutuzov had previously met in fighting the Turks. It might be reasonable to assume that any appreciation that Kutuzov developed on the fighting capabilities of Napoleon, the French army in general and its leaders, could not have begun to be assimilated until his army was thoroughly thrashed at Dürenstein, and must have been further developed by the utterly disastrous Austerlitz experience. Some may therefore see Kutuzov's appreciation of his foe, which led to a proposed Fabian strategy prior to Austerlitz, finally become implemented when he was thrust back into command of the main Russian armies during the 1812 campaign.

Kutuzov

However, closer examination of Kutuzov and his method of waging war in 1805 show that he was a general neither skilled in maneuvers for offensive warfare, nor one with the power or ability to keep his army supplied, both of which spelled disaster in central Europe. From the opening of the 1805 campaign up until the time that the Russian army reached Braunau, Kutuzov's forces suffered horribly from strategic consumption due to the army's complete lack of a proper commissariat system. The problem of supply only became exacerbated when the Russians were forced to conduct a hasty retreat in order to escape the pursuing French forces following the capitulation of Mack's army at Ulm. Evidently, Kutuzov did not make the connection between the army's virtually non-existent system of supply and his subsequent plans of operation as demonstrated by his battle plan for Dürenstein, a methodology that was described by Merveldt as being:

> unacquainted with the art of war, and especially with operations against the French—a very different proposition from campaigning against the Turks. He leaves time and distance completely out of the equation, and is most unwilling to risk his troops. All of this will make it difficult to persuade him to advance.[35]

True to Merveldt's words, when Kutuzov did commit himself to an attack, as he did at Dürenstein, his plan did not incorporate the effects of the weather into his equation and the effort failed. Also, prior to Kutuzov's army going into action, the composition of the various columns of the army were rearranged—an unmistakable trademark of an *ancien régime* army. Kutuzov did, however, have

---

[35] Merveldt, as quoted in Angeli, 'Ulm und Austerlitz' in *Mittheilungen des K. K. Kbiegs-Archivs,* p. 300.

enough individual cunning to dupe Murat at Hollabrunn. Further, some might view Kutuzov as the wise head who suggested a Fabian strategy in order to buy time until the spring of 1806 when the Prussia could bring her prized army into the field. However, rather than seeing Kutuzov's proposed course of action as a prudent decision that was only part of a long-term plan that would be shifted into a bold offensive stroke at a later date, Kutuzov's push for a Fabian solution can more likely be attributed to a simpler explanation—it was the only thing he knew to do against the French. It was sheer coincidence that Kutuzov's proposal to retreat prior to Austerlitz was probably the best strategy for the allies. However, in the kaleidoscope of changing events that would have been brought about by such a move (had Tsar Alexander been willing to accept Kutuzov's plan), one should never forget the extremely limited capabilities of the cumbersome and greatly weakened Russian forces to resume the offensive, their virtual absence of a supply system, as well as Kutuzov's complete lack of aptitude in offensive warfare. Despite his eventual place in history for his role during the 1812 war, it is clear that the 1805 campaigns exposed Kutuzov for not being near the equal of his mentor, Suvórov.

Among the various Russian senior officers, it is difficult to find much good in the performances of Buxhöwden, Prebyshevsky and Constantine. Undoubtably, the worst of the three was Buxhöwden. We see him at Austerlitz as a drunken, aloof commander, unable or unwilling to redirect his columns from their prearranged plans when they became endangered from the French advance on the Pratzen. As a result, Buxhöwden doomed the majority of the I, II and III Columns. How a man with so little military talent could have held such an important position in a major, setpiece battle speaks volumes about the qualifying process of officers in the Russian army.

Buxhöwden

Buxhöwden was born in Estonia and had advanced himself by marrying an illegitimate daughter of Catherine the Great. During the 1805 war, Buxhöwden seemed to be continually inebriated and paid no attention to his duties, choosing instead to indulge himself in other interests. His character, along with a description of the baggage train that accompanied this Russian officer, are no better described than by a parish priest of Kutscherau, where Buxhöwden had established his headquarters. The priest saw Buxhöwden to be:

> a man of extreme conceit and pride, while also, if I am not mistaken, of very little education... The French went to great lengths to become acquainted with the lay of the land by obtaining maps. Buxhöwden, on the contrary, carried about him a train of hunting dogs and [prostitutes]. The whole took up 11 coaches and as many carts, whereby the entire space of the vicarage was taken up with the quantity of riding horses for himself, his generals and servants, and the vast quantity of his sentries, which came to no less than 96 animals, with 139 attendant personnel.[36]

Also cut from this mold were Prebyshevsky and Constantine. Both men credited their rank solely to their birthright and both failed miserably in their 1805 command positions. Certainly, some of their failings must be attributed to the regimental army system, whereby the individual regimental commanders had almost no experience in coordinating movements with each other. However, since Constantine was the Tsar's brother, his position as commander of the Russian Imperial Guard was secure, no matter how poorly he performed in battle.

The best of the middle-ranking Russian generals were Bagration, Dokhturov, Langeron and Miloradovich. If one tries to rank these four men, undoubtedly the

[36] C. Janetschek, *Die Schlacht bei Austerlitz* (Brünn, 1898), pp. 39-40.

Langeron

weakest performance was turned in by Miloradovich. While he put his attack in at Dürenstein with determination, he was simply beaten by better generals using superior battle tactics implemented by more highly trained troops. At Austerlitz, Miloradovich did not keep his very weak Russian battalions together. As a result, he and his command were swept away.

The next higher up on the list would be the *émigré* Langeron. Unable to completely capture the village of Sokolnitz from some superb French troops, Langeron found his command permanently split when Kamensky correctly judged the dangers facing Langeron's troops, and moved his brigade against Saint-Hilaire's French that had suddenly seized the Pratzen and were moving against the flank of II Column. It might have been interesting to see if, or just how long, Langeron would have taken in finally seizing Sokolnitz had there been no French on the Pratzen. In any event, Langeron would have to answer a barrage of harsh criticism from other Russian officers for his failure to seize the village of Sokolnitz, and prove himself on many other battlefields, before the Tsar finally restored him to favor.

Continuing up the grading ladder, we find Dokhturov. He was given the toughest assignment at Dürenstein, where he brought his troops into action after completing a torturous 16-hour march. Dokhturov would have probably succeeded in keeping Mortier cut off at Dürenstein if it had not been for the intervention and rescue by Dupont's élite infantry. At Austerlitz, Dokhturov handled his I Column with about as much competence as was possible in the Russian army. When, towards the battle's end, he had to save his command, Dokhturov exhibited a cool head and skill.

Finally, the remaining officer of these middle-ranking generals to be evaluated was undoubtedly the best—Bagration. He is the only senior Russian officer to emerge from the Austerlitz campaign with his reputation enhanced. That conclusion is certainly grounded in solid facts. While his successful stand at Schöngrabern may be more attributed to a combination of good fortune, Kutuzov's cunning and Murat's gullibility than his own battlefield prowess, Bagration did exhibit some tactical skill and a lot of tenacity both at Schöngrabern and at Austerlitz. At the latter battle, his infantry and cavalry advanced in a disjointed manner, which can be attributed to the regimental army mentality. At the end of the day, when his troops were being driven from the field in ever increasing disorder and with most of his guns lost, Bagration was saved by the timely arrival of two Austrian cavalry batteries that provided the covering fire behind which he rallied his defeated regiments. Despite being driven back with heavily losses, Bagration ended Austerlitz with his battered Advance Guard still intact after having engaged superior numbers of French commanded by excellent Napoleonic corps and divisional leaders. Further, he had thwarted—at least for one day—the French attempts to get across the road to Olmütz which, if successful, would have cut off the allies from their base of operations. For that reason alone, Bagration's reputation as a capable, hard-fighting combat officer justifiably grew.

Dokhturov

When considering the low-ranking generals of the Russian army—those men who typically commanded brigades—the one which turned in the best performance of the 1805 war was Kamensky I. At Austerlitz, he pivoted his brigade from in front of Sokolnitz and quickly moved it northward to confront the majority of Saint Hilaire's Division. Kamensky succeeded in keeping his regiments together and, as a result, gave the brigades of Morand and Thiébault all they wanted. Indeed, Kamensky's inspirational leadership and excellent direction of his troops was seconded by the troops under his command. The resulting savage combat between Kamensky's Russians and Saint-Hilaire's Frenchmen stands as the most desperate fighting to take place at Austerlitz, as well as one of the most brutal during the Napoleonic wars.

The 1805 war also provides an opportunity to evaluate the three Russian combat arms. The Russian cavalry had several bright moments at the various combats leading up to the Battle of Austerlitz. However, at the great battle, the Tsar's horsemen were repeatedly handled and disposed of by better coordinated French formations. This was never better illustrated than by the mini-battles between the French light cavalry and dragoons against the Russian horse of Bagration and Uvarov, as well as the confrontation between the cavalry of the Russian Imperial Guard and that of the French Imperial Guard. In the former fight, the French overcame the Russians—most notably the tenacious Elisabetgrad Hussars and Chernigov Dragoons—through coordinated divisional and brigade evolutions. The latter fight exposed the Russian Guard cavalry—who enjoyed a numerical superiority of two-to-one over the French Guard cavalry—for the parade ground troops that they were. Truly, the Russian Imperial Guard cavalry were "the noblest cavalry in Europe and the worst led." [37]

Like their cavalry brothers-in-arms, the Russian Imperial Guard infantry performed at a level that belie their title. Statuesque and brave, the formations of Russian Guard infantry could not best the *ligne* and *légère* units of Napoleon's army, let alone the units of the French Imperial Guard. The outcome of the fighting on the Pratzen did prove one critical point when it came to troop terminology: formations that carried the 'guard' title without corresponding combat experience and leadership were nothing more than ceremonial troops.

Insofar as the remainder of the Russian infantry were concerned, most of the regiments of musketeers and *jaeger* were handled unimaginatively by their officers. This lack of tactical flexibility was due to a combination of poorly trained officers and NCOs, coupled with a large percentage of conscripts that filled the ranks. Surgeon Larrey of the French Imperial Guard noted the inflexible tactics employed by the Russians at Austerlitz.

> The Muscovite hordes threw themselves with blood-curdling yells on our advance guard. They [Russians] believed themselves certain of victory for they had left their packs and greatcoats at their bivouacs. Their attack was spirited, but they did not realize that courage alone never won a war; tactics were essential.[38]

Russian Guardsmen

Not surprisingly, the regiments of *jaeger* did not excel in combat, although the spirited attack by the 5th *Jaeger* against Lannes' northern flank at Austerlitz showed some promise of future good deeds. Meanwhile, the 6th and 8th *Jaeger* had been chewed up so badly at Dürenstein and Schöngrabern that they were incapable of achieving even modest goals by the time they arrived on the field of Austerlitz. The 1805 war demonstrated that it was going to take years and a superior officer dedicated to their improvement before the Russian *jaeger* were to become a force to be reckoned with on the Napoleonic battlefield.

As with the *jaeger*, some regiments of musketeers performed much better than others. It is difficult to find a performance better than that of the Ryazan Musketeers at Austerlitz. At the other end of the spectrum, the Novgorod Musketeers were singled out by Kutuzov in his after-action report to Tsar Alexander. "Two battalions of the Novgorod Musketeers ran away without offering the slightest

[37] Frederick E. Smith, *Waterloo* (London, 1970), p. 134. Based on the screenplay by H. A. L. Craig for the movie *Waterloo*, Smith takes this line directly from the movie's script. The quote comes from Kellermann, who is at Napoleon's side, and comments about the charging Scots Greys. While this line makes for great cinema, I believe that it is far more accurate in describing the Russian Guard cavalry.

[38] Robert G. Richardson, *Larrey: Surgeon to Napoleon's Imperial Guard* (London, 1974), p. 98.

Russian Grenadiers

resistance, which spread fear and panic among the whole [IV] column."[39] While Kutuzov's statement was not entirely accurate (his reports rarely were, because one battalion of the Novgorod Musketeers had surprised and routed the 1st Battalion of the 14th *Ligne* before they were in turn put to flight), it is indicative of the fragility of the regiments within Kutuzov's army that had already suffered heavy battle casualties and strategic consumption prior to Austerlitz. What one does often see in 1805, however, is the Russian regimental colonel personally leading the grenadier battalion of his respective musketeer or grenadier regiment. In this manner, he could make sure that his best troops got into action where and when he wanted. Many times, the grenadier battalion of the musketeer regiments provided a valuable and reliable unit of troops, personally led by the regimental colonel.

If the combats of the Austerlitz campaign showed the grenadier battalions of the different musketeer regiments to be respectable combat units, then the Russian grenadier regiments proved themselves the most formidable opponents for the French. This was especially true if the ranks of the grenadier regiments had not already been significantly thinned by losses. The tenacity of the Russian grenadier regiments is no better illustrated than the heroic fight put up by the Kiev Grenadiers at Schöngrabern and the Fanagoria Grenadiers at Austerlitz. Certainly, it is no surprise that the French came out of their 1805 experience believing that the regiments of Russian grenadiers were their most dangerous opponents.

Being a feared battlefield force was certainly not the case for the Russian artillery in 1805. With the majority of its pieces dispersed as battalion artillery, there just wasn't enough concentration of firepower to influence the outcome of any action. Moreover, when the parent battalion moved across ground that the guns could not traverse, as was the case at some places along the lower Goldbach, the battalion pieces had to be left behind, and were therefore unable to fulfill their close fire support mission. On the other hand, the Russians got favorable results when they sensibly kept entire artillery companies together, like Major Bogoslavski's company of 6-pounders at Schöngrabern, or the companies of well-directed Russian horse artillery involved in the fighting on the northern flank at Austerlitz. However, once all the pieces necessary for battalion support were allocated, there simply were not enough guns and licornes remaining for the deployment of many company sized batteries. This is graphically illustrated by the Battle of Austerlitz. Of the total of 246 pieces of ordnance fielded by the Russians on 2 December 1805, some 160 pieces, or about two-thirds, were employed as battalion artillery. The remaining 86 cannon and licornes were employed in only seven and one-half companies spread out along a seven mile front. With such a wide dispersion of the companies, there can be little wonder as to why the Russian artillery had a minimal effect on the outcome of the battle. In addition to being unable to influence the course of the fighting, by the Russians deploying their companies in such a dispersed fashion, they made it easier for the coordinated French formations to overrun and capture their pieces. In summary, the employment of the Tsar's artillery is indicative of the operation of the 1805 Russian army as a whole; it was a force still tied to the philosophies of the *ancien régime*, and it fell woefully short when pitted against Napoleon and history's first modern army.

Models of Russian guns

The Grande Armée

In contradistinction to many allied formations, the units that composed the *Grande Armée* of 1805 generally acquitted themselves very well on the different battlefields, which was consistent with their combat experience, maturity and training. The numerous instances in which the regiments of Napoleon's army

[39] Kutuzov, *Sbornik Dokumentov,* vol. 2, p. 265.

repeatedly displayed their superiority in battle, already detailed in the previous chapters and often against odds that would have otherwise influenced the outcome of the fighting if the French troops involved had been of lesser caliber, are almost too numerous to recount again in this section. However, a few of these instances richly deserve a retelling.

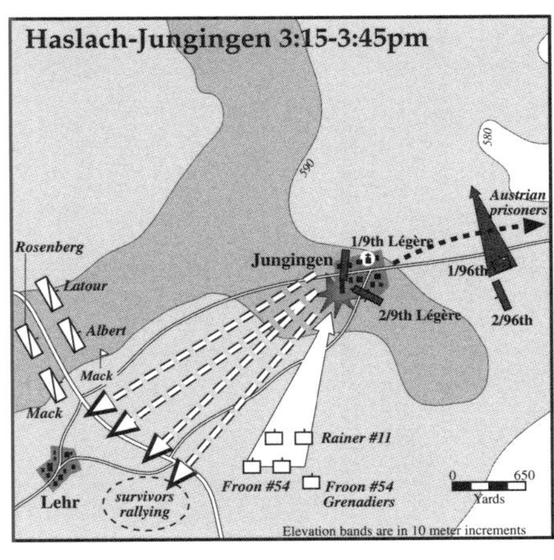

Insofar as the battles fought by detachments of the *Grande Armée* are concerned, Dupont's stand at Haslach-Jungingen on 11 October during the campaign of Ulm is the most remarkable. Isolated and outnumbered over four to one, Dupont and his command employed the strong point defensive scheme to inflict an astounding defeat on Mack's Austrians. Three days later at Elchingen, Marshal Ney led his troops to an impressive victory over a numerical superior Austrian force that had impressive advantages of both terrain and man-made cover. Almost a month later at Dürenstein, Marshal Mortier pulled off another admirable victory with Gazan's Division—this time against superior numbers of Russians—and greatly aided by Dupont's superb, hard-charging *fantassins*.

As impressive as these feats were, which are seconded by numerous smaller combats during both the Ulm and Austerlitz campaigns, we are drawn to Austerlitz for deeper analysis. The only major battle which the *Grande Armée* fought during the 1805 war was on this Moravian field, and it is from the events of that battle that one can draw many conclusions about Napoleon's army as a whole. Austerlitz displayed on a large scale what the smaller battles had already shown—that the French formations were tactically flexible and very well officered. All along the expansive Austerlitz battlefront, the French demonstrated the value of units composed of a high percentage of veteran soldiers with extremely capable officers and NCOs. On the southern part of the field along the Goldbach, inferior numbers of French succeeded in bottling up the weight of the Combined Russian and Austrian Army. Meanwhile, other areas of the field in which the French had relatively equal or superior numbers required only brief clashes for the bluecoated troops to disperse the allied formations. However, along the lower Goldbach, as well as on the Pratzen and on the northern flank, there were many near-run miniature battles. It took all the cool direction of Davout and Friant, along with the charismatic leadership of Lochet leading the superb combat soldiers of 3rd Corps, to successfully storm back into and hold Sokolnitz against Langeron's Russians. It took all the savvy of their drill field experiences of the Channel camp of Saint-Omer for the officers and men of Saint-Hilaire's Division to repulse the savage allied counterattacks and keep possession of the middle-to-lower Pratzen Plateau. It took experience in brigade and divisional attacks for Vandamme and his command to efficiently conquer the upper Pratzen and the Staré Vinohrady. Finally, it was solid experience and cooperation between infantry and cavalry that saw the divisions under Murat and Lannes work together so smoothly on the northern end of Austerlitz.

The close-knit and coordinated workings of the *Grande Armée* from corps command to the smallest tactical level are testaments to the immeasurable value of the Camp of Boulogne. The two years that the French army spent training along the English Channel helped enormously to carry them to victory in 1805, 1806 and 1807. The familiarity between officers and their commands, the tactical evolutions and refinement of doctrine, molded many veteran formations into élite outfits. The results of this is perhaps best reflected in how the infantry of Napoleon's army reacted when charged by enemy cavalry. If a battalion was relatively isolated when charged by enemy horse—as was the 1st Battalion of the 4th *Ligne* at Austerlitz—or was at the end of a line and attacked from the flank, as witnessed by the 1st Battalion of the 76th *Ligne* at Elchingen, the unit under attack would form square in an attempt to repulse the cavalry. However, if the French battalions had other friendly formations nearby that effectively secured their flanks—such as the entire deployed divisions of Suchet, Caffarelli and Drouet at Austerlitz—or if there

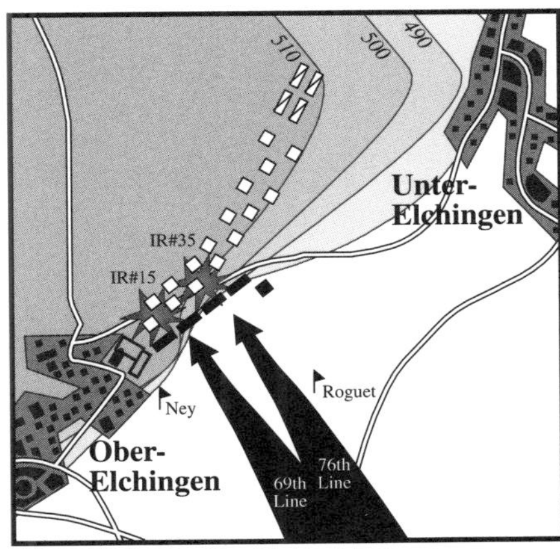

The 76th Ligne *attacks at Elchingen*

were at least two battalions of well-trained troops that had confidence in their abilities to withstand a charge of enemy horse, as seen by the 13th *Légère* at Austerlitz, the Napoleonic infantry would almost always receive the enemy cavalry charge in the formation in which they were already deployed. This apparent disdain exhibited by the French for the opposition's horse on many occasions, is the mark of a professional army in philosophy and implementation.

These admirable qualities shown on the battlefield does not, by any means, suggest that the *Grande Armée* was a perfect instrument of war. Off the battlefield, the army managed to keep an overall low rate of strategic consumption early in the Ulm campaign, despite the fact that the army's commissariat system was no where close to being fully developed to the Emperor's satisfaction. However, as the campaign dragged on, strategic consumption increased. Any positives about this aspect of the 1805 army was that the maturity level of Napoleon's soldiers was further reflected by one other aspect—the men returning to ranks after a temporary absence. This was seen when the army marched deeper into enemy territory following Mack's capitulation at Ulm and many formations began losing some men to straggling and marauding. However upset Napoleon was when he saw the disorder in the rear of his 1805 army and took steps to get the men back to their units, these problems were nothing compared to the chaos and devastation wrought by the plague of marauders that permanently left the inexperienced and poorly officered *Grande Armée* of 1813. Of the soldiers that slipped away from their formations during the Ulm-Austerlitz campaigns, most of them did so only temporarily. Many hurriedly returned to ranks after Napoleon's Order of the Day of 4 frimaire (25 November) announced that "every straggler who, under the pretext of fatigue, leaves his corps for marauding, shall be arrested, tried by one of the military commissions, and executed on the spot."[40]

The 1802 pattern flag the 9th Légère *carried into battle in addition to the regulation 1804 lozenge pattern flag*

Among the numerous formations of Napoleon's army, certain units from the infantry and cavalry combat arms deserve special mention. No infantry regiment in the 1805 *Grande Armée* outfought *"l'Incomparable"* 9th *Légère*. Their superb performance against the Austrians at Haslach-Jungingen, followed by their brief and effective charge at Elchingen, capped of by their vicious bayonet attack against the Russians at Dürenstein that broke Dokhturov's hold on the river road and thereby saved Marshal Mortier's embattled command, were the epic actions of which legends were made. In January 1806, when reflecting on the Ulm-Austerlitz campaigns just recently completed, Colonel Meunier estimated that his regiment of light infantry killed, wounded or captured more than 6,100 of the enemy, while also taking five Austrian flags at Haslach-Jungingen and two Russian standards from the Vyatka Musketeers at Dürenstein![41] For the 9th *Légère,* the campaigns of 1805 added only more luster to their already scintillating reputation. If based on combat performance alone, the officers and men of the 9th *Légère* proved themselves to be the finest infantry outfit in the *Grande Armée*.

Also deserving of special mention are the officers and men of Friant's Division. These infantrymen (along with Bourcier's dragoons) arrived at the Raigern Abbey seven miles south of Brünn at 7:00 P.M. on 1 December, thereby completing a remarkable 70 mile march from Vienna to Austerlitz in under 48 hours! Following this singularly impressive feat, these *fantassins* went into action with only a few hours of rest and punished the Russians in and around Sokolnitz and Tellnitz. The combination of the Herculean march, followed by an inspired and tactically expert display against superior numbers of enemy troops, makes the accomplishments of Friant's Division at Austerlitz one of the greatest feat of arms during the Napoleonic wars.

---

[40] S.H.A.T., C^2 12; Order of the Day, 4 frimaire an XIV (25 November 1805), *Unpublished Correspondence of Napoleon I*, vol. 1, number 220.
[41] S.H.A.T., *Journal des opérations du 6e corps.*

In the cavalry arm, many regiments had memorable days, including the 3rd Hussars and 10th *Chasseurs à cheval,* under Auguste de Colbert at Elchingen, plus Lefèbvre-Desnouettes' 18th Dragoons at Elchingen, as well as Corbineau's 5th *Chasseurs à cheval* and the brigade of *carabiniers* at Austerlitz. However, no regiment comported itself as brilliantly as did the *Grenadiers à cheval de la Garde* at Austerlitz. The decisive charge of the "Gods," especially the destruction inflicted by the duty squadron, against the troops of the Russian Imperial Guard while suffering only two dozen casualties, speaks volumes about their combat effectiveness and why they were unquestionably Napoleon's most formidable cavalry regiment. Also, one cannot mention the decisive charge of the French Imperial Guard cavalry at Austerlitz without also drawing special attention to the *Mameluks.* Although only a company in strength, these ferocious warriors sliced to shreds the 3rd Squadron of the *Chevalier Garde.* At the other end of the spectrum were many regiments of Dragoons that performed poorly in 1805. Without a doubt, the worst performance were turned in by the 4th Dragoons at Dürenstein, as well as the 5th, 8th, 12th and 16th Dragoons at Austerlitz. Also, the dragoons that dismounted to fight at Wertingen did not impress those who saw them in action. The 1805 experience let the French cavalry generals know that they still had a lot of work ahead of them to bring most of the dragoon regiments up to the excellent standards already exhibited by the line light cavalry as well as the *cuirassiers, carabiniers* and the Imperial Guard.

The Grenadiers à cheval *of the Imperial Guard charge at Austerlitz*

The artillery of the *Grande Armée* gave an overall superb performance in 1805. The companies were extremely well officered, the guns made very mobile by excellent horse teams and train personnel. Among the many examples illustrating this point are the pieces that supported the men of the 6th *Légère* in their assault up the steep slope of Elchingen, as well as the horse artillery sections that supported the infantry divisions in the favorable outcomes at Haslach-Jungingen and Dürenstein. The battles of 1805 led further weight to Marmont's pre-campaign recommendation to increase the establishment of the horse artillery whereby every infantry division, in addition to its foot artillery, would be supported by a full company of horse artillery. Meanwhile, the pieces repeatedly proved to be superior to those antiquated guns used by the Austrians and to the new ordnance system of the Russians. The 1805 experience repeatedly demonstrated the value of the longer ranged, hard hitting 8-pounder as opposed to the lighter 6-pounder pieces employed by the allies. This was especially true when those 8-pounders were in the hands of the élite French line horse artillerists or the Imperial Guard. Indeed, the campaigns of 1805 only made those who championed the 8-pounder all the more convinced of its superiority and even more resentful about its scheduled, impending 'retirement' in favor of the new 6-pounder of the System Year XI.

The officers of the *Grande Armée* also offer fertile ground for analysis. All courageous under fire, the infantry regimental commanders provided, with very few exceptions, the tactical leadership and élan which the Emperor demanded. They knew their soldiers well and wielded their battalions efficiently. As a whole, the cavalry colonels also did well in 1805, although clearly certain colonels did elevate the performance of their troops. Among the regiments of the cavalry of the line, the French *cuirassier* officers proved that their regiments were superior to any of the allied heavy cavalry while the commanders of the French light cavalry also acquitted themselves well in 1805. They effectively maneuvered and fought their squadrons, regiments and brigades.

If any officers in the French line cavalry were thought to be a collective disappointment in 1805, it was those within the dragoons. Except for a few regiments such as the 18th, 19th and 21st Dragoons—all of which consisted of a core of highly seasoned troopers and commanded by expert colonels—the rest projected only a marginal battlefield presence. The highest level of effectiveness that was exhibited by most dragoon regiments was seemingly traced not to the regimental colonels, but to coordinated, multi-regimental maneuvers, such as those displayed by Sébastiani's Brigade at Austerlitz. Furthermore, those in command of the foot dragoons did little to impress anyone by their action at Wertingen. Most dragoon officers were eager to mount all the foot troopers, although it would take one more campaign before enough quality horses were available.

Many of the brigadier generals in the *Grande Armée*, were expert tacticians. Some of the best performances turned in during 1805 were by de Labassée at Günzburg, Roguet at Elchingen and several generals at Austerlitz, including Merle and Claparède. However, the best combat performances by brigadier generals must include Rouyer at Haslach-Jungingen, along with Morand, Thiébault and Lochet at Austerlitz.

One of the greatest strengths of the *Grande Armée* was the collective talent of the division commanders, several of which deserve special praise for their accomplishments in the 1805 war. These include Dupont at Haslach-Jungingen and Gazan at Dürenstein. At Austerlitz, several division commanders furthered their reputations. The heroic stand of both Legrand's and Friant's heavily outnumbered divisions on the lower Goldbach, which were highlighted by vicious, local counterattacks, deserve high marks. Caffarelli's performance on the north end of the field was also impressive. Meanwhile, Saint-Hilaire's conquest of the middle-to-lower Pratzen was the hardest fought combat in 1805, and Vandamme superbly handled his division in taking the upper Pratzen.

Bernadotte

The best division commander was Kellermann. His fight on the northern end of the Austerlitz battlefield was arguably the finest tactical handling of cavalry by any leader at any battle during the Napoleonic wars. Kellermann always had his regiments under control and moving in concert. And when one regiment broke, as did the 4th Hussars at one point in the battle, Kellermann kept his head and used his remaining three regiments to envelop and overturned the enemy horse. By wielding his nimble light cavalry in a succession of complicated maneuvers and charges, Kellermann masterfully engaged and defeated vastly superior numbers of allied troops.

The performance of the corps commanders of the *Grande Armée* varied greatly. In ranking the corps commanders from worst to best, undoubtedly the worst was Marshal Bernadotte. The timid commander of the 1st Corps failed utterly in his mission at the *manœuvre sur Hollabrunn,* while his conduct at Austerlitz was contemptible. At the great battle, Bernadotte had to be pressured into action by Ségur—one of Napoleon's Imperial aides-de-camp—and when one of Bernadotte's infantry division commanders (Drouet) succeeded in helping defeat the Russian Imperial Guard, the marshal elected to halt his advance rather than press on to the village of Austerlitz and cut off the allied forces on the northern end of field. For Bernadotte to call off the march of 1st Corps, especially when Drouet had only been briefly engaged while the other division under Rivaud de la Raffinière had not fired a shot, was simply inexcusable. Therefore, instead of the certain ruin of Bagration and Liechtenstein, the allies on the northern end of the field had the good fortune that Bernadotte was exactly at the right place at the right time in order to effectively avert their complete destruction.[42]

Apart from Bernadotte, the biggest disappointment as a combat corps commander was Soult. The superb drillmaster of the Camp of Boulogne could organize and march his corps with consummate skill and admirable efficiency, but his conduct in battle left much to be desired. While Soult did nothing to influence or drive his men into action at Schöngrabern when he committed only one infantry

[42] Vandamme, who was in favor of exterminating every allied soldier on the battlefield, was not amused by any show of magnanimity. Vandamme's prophetic words would ring true: "To spare them [the allies] today is to have them in Paris six years from now." Eight years later, the allies entered Paris.

division to the dusk attack, it is the Battle of Austerlitz that exposed the commander of 4th Corps for what he really was—a superb organizer and drillmaster who no longer possessed the motivation to expose his person anywhere near the front lines in order to effectively lead a Napoleonic corps in battle. Giving the devil his due, Soult cannot be criticized at Austerlitz for the latitude he allowed Legrand and Margaron to wage their own fight in order to hold on to the middle and lower Goldbach. That was exactly the way a corps chief was supposed to let his detached subordinates operate within the confines of their mission. Instead, it was Soult's distant management of the divisions that were supposed to be under his immediate watch—Vandamme and Saint-Hilaire—that invites a harsh critique.

The capture of the Pratzen, so crucial to Napoleon's modified plan to overturn and destroy the allies, entrusted to the corps commander who had been the Emperor's chief architect in training the *Grande Armée*, should have prompted Soult to follow as closely as possible the progress of the battle. Had he done so, he would have been able to make the battle an even more impressive victory by requesting reinforcements from Napoleon when warranted. Make no mistake about it, that time came when Saint-Hilaire's infantry were fighting for their lives on the Pratzen against seemingly overwhelming numbers of allied troops. However, Soult was nowhere around and the only help that Saint-Hilaire received was the reserve artillery company consisting of six 12-pounders that had been ordered forward, thanks to one of Napoleon's Imperial aides-de-camp. By not closely following the fighting of his divisions and by not keeping a firm handle on the course of the battle on the Pratzen Plateau, Soult failed to fulfill the basic role of a corps commander while also jeopardizing Saint-Hilaire's embattled command.

In spite of his own inaction, Soult nevertheless believed that he should have received a title 'Duke of Austerlitz.' For Soult to make such a fraudulent claim, especially after doing nothing that a corps commander should have done during the most critical phase of the battle, was entirely consistent with his manipulative character.

Soult

Soult's battlefield management at Austerlitz has never been better summarized than that done by Thiébault. The *général de brigade* in Saint-Hilaire's Division wrote:

> In spite of the critical position in which Saint-Hilaire's troops were for the space of three hours, Marshal Soult never appeared either to direct them in case of need, to encourage them by his presence, or to judge if it was necessary to reinforce them... Marshal Soult had fulfilled none of the functions of a soldier or shared the danger of any of the men of his corps... Thus it is clear that Marshal Soult took no personal part in the Battle of Austerlitz [for] we did not once see the marshal, whose business was to have been constantly going from one to another of his divisions, to stop them, to back up the generals. I can still hear the exclamations which 10 times burst from each of us: 'What! No news of the marshal? And is he not going to turn up?'[43]

If it were not for two facts, Thiébault's comments might have to be used with some caution. First, Thiébault was a participant in the desperate fighting on the Pratzen, and his personal experience cannot be dismissed. Moreover, what makes Thiébault's powerful charges virtually indisputable concerning Soult being nowhere close to the fighting, nor sending any new orders or reinforcements during

[43] *The Memoirs of Baron Thiébault*, vol. 2, p. 178. Thiébault is a difficult source, because he had nothing good to say about anyone. But Austerlitz was the greatest of his career, and is the most most valuable part of his memoirs.

the critical phase of the battle, is that his story is corroborated by another officer of 4th Corps—Captain Henri-Catherine-Baltazard Vincent. Vincent, who in 1805 was officially was an aide-de-camp to *général de brigade* Ferrey, spent the entire day at Soult's side. Before the battle began, Vincent was sent by Vandamme (Ferrey's division commander) to Soult in order to "act as a messenger for any new orders from the corps commander to that division." Following Soult's addressing of the troops, Vincent clearly remembered that he remained with Soult, "never being asked to carry a single new order to my division [Vandamme], nor remembering the marshal ever issuing any new directives to the division under Saint-Hilaire."[44] Indeed, after Soult gave Vandamme the orders to carry the Pratzen, the next time the 4th Corps chief issued a directive was again to Vandamme when the two men met hours later just south of the Chapel of Saint Anthony. That verbal order was for Vandamme to carry Augezd and cut off the allied retreat route on the north side of the Satschan Pond.

Despite these two eyewitnesses, some English historians have found it fashionable to support Soult's fraudulent claim. They point to Soult and cry out in righteous indignation that by the Emperor denying the marshal a title that included the name 'Austerlitz,' Soult became an injured party in Napoleon's never-ending quest for self-aggrandizement. The English authors posit that Napoleon recognized the commander of the 4th Corps as "the *premier manœuvrier* in Europe" and that Soult "was deprived of the Austerlitz title simply because Napoleon wished to reserve that particular laurel to himself."[45] This raises an interesting question: why do these English historians support this imposture? It is known through eyewitness testimony that any assertion Soult may have made about his role in the Austerlitz victory is disingenuous. Therefore, any attempt to build up Soult's battlefield reputation as one of Napoleonic France's greatest leaders so his later defeat at the hands of the Duke of Wellington can seem to be an all the more brilliant feat of arms, while also doubling as a way to denigrate Napoleon, is as clumsy as it is transparent as it is inaccurate. Napoleon's 1805 compliment about Soult being "the *premier manœuvrier* in Europe" was directed towards Soult's magnificent accomplishments at the Channel encampment, rather than to any battlefield prowess. Indeed, Soult's contemporary and subordinate officer, General Thiébault, remains the best possible response to those Johnny-come-lately supporters of the calculating and egomaniacal Soult. Thiébault accurately summed up the entire matter when he said:

Marmont

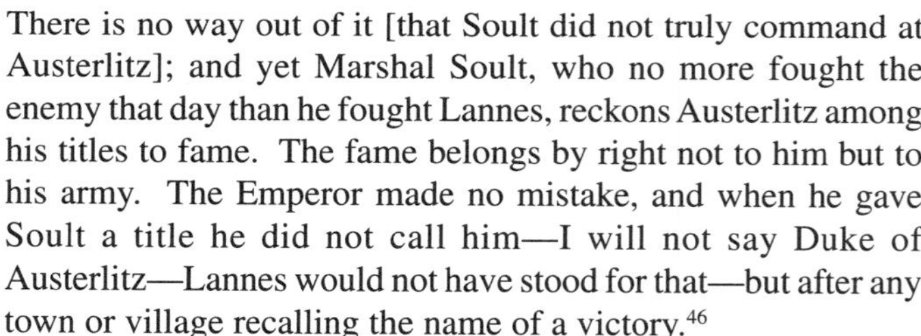

> There is no way out of it [that Soult did not truly command at Austerlitz]; and yet Marshal Soult, who no more fought the enemy that day than he fought Lannes, reckons Austerlitz among his titles to fame. The fame belongs by right not to him but to his army. The Emperor made no mistake, and when he gave Soult a title he did not call him—I will not say Duke of Austerlitz—Lannes would not have stood for that—but after any town or village recalling the name of a victory.[46]

The commander of the 2nd Corps, Marmont, did a lot of marching and little fighting during the Ulm-Austerlitz campaigns. This was due to a combination of

---

44 S.H.A.T., C^{2} 25.

45 Paddy Griffith, "King Nicolas," in *Napoleon's Marshals*, p. 466. David Chandler is of the same opinion. In his book, *On the Napoleonic Wars* (London, 1994), p. 127, Chandler maintains that: "When, in 1808, consideration was being given to suitable ducal titles for award to the Marshalate, Soult suggested that his might be 'Duke of Austerlitz.' The idea was abruptly rejected... Austerlitz was one title that Napoleon was determined not to award—but keep for himself."

46 *The Memoirs of Baron Thiébault*, vol. 2, p. 179.

fate and the Emperor's design. Had Mack acted differently and either bolted for Vienna or the Tyrol, Marmont and the 2nd Corps would have been in the middle of the fighting. Also, had the Tsar listened to Kutuzov, and the allied army withdrew into the Carpathian Mountains thereby extending the campaign into the spring of 1806, Marmont would have seen significant action south of Vienna against Archduke Charles. However, fate dictated otherwise. The 1805 experience showed that Marmont handled his corps with competence, giving Napoleon no reason to regret his position as the only 1805 corps commander that was not a member of the marshalate.

Ney, as painted by Gros

Similar to Marmont was Augereau. Arriving late in the theater of operations following a long march from Brest and only rarely mentioned in this study, Augereau and his 7th Corps gobbled up the last remnants of Mack's army when he cornered Jellachich in the Vorarlberg in mid-November. The circumstances of the 1805 war had not placed excessive demands on the marshal, who handled the small 7th Corps with efficiency.

The performance of both Marshals Mortier and Ney were crucial to Napoleon's success in the 1805 war. It is difficult to find fault with how Ney handled his corps, either in an operational sense, or while under fire. His victory at Elchingen demonstrated how crack troops, when led by expert tacticians, could accomplish what many would deem a very difficult assignment. Indeed, Ney's title as the Duke of Elchingen was well deserved. Following the capitulation of Ulm, Ney was ordered into the Tyrol, where he and his corps—reinforced with some Bavarians—thoroughly broke up Archduke John's forces. Therefore, 1805 enhanced Ney's reputation as an intelligent, quality corps commander.

Mortier also deserves praise for his role in the 1805 war. Appointed in early November to command an *ad hoc* corps on the north bank of the Danube, Mortier handled his semi-independent command well and accomplished his mission with competence. This is especially impressive considering that he had virtually no staff and no cavalry. What's more, had Mortier not been as excellent a tactician as he proved to be at Dürenstein, the course of events in the Danube valley would have been dramatically altered.

Within the context of performing his duties as a corps commander, Murat performed very well in 1805. His handling of the cavalry during the approach to Ulm, as well as *"La glorieuse chevauchée"* that ran down Werneck's column and the pursuit into Moravia, all showed that Murat could handle large cavalry formations with competence that was far above average. At Austerlitz, Murat handled his cavalry divisions extremely well, working with Lannes to defeat Liechtenstein and Bagration. In stark contradistinction, when Murat was asked to perform in a role above that of a corps commander, he failed miserably. Therefore, Murat's performance in 1805 should have sent an unmistakable signal to Napoleon about the pronounced limitations of his brother-in-law.

Without a doubt, the best performances by Napoleonic corps commanders in 1805 were turned in by Davout and Lannes. As the commander of the 3rd Corps, Davout handled his troops as flawlessly as one can imagine. Whether it was his march to the Rhine and subsequent envelopment of Mack's army, or his pursuit of the allies across Austria, or his Herculean march from Vienna to Austerlitz, or his battlefield management at the great battle, or his pursuit after Austerlitz, Davout always kept a close handle on the soldiers of the 3rd Corps. His conduct in 1805 serves as a model example of administrative diligence and masterful battlefield competence.

Certainly an equal to Davout in most aspects, and arguably a better combat commander than the marshal who led the 3rd Corps, was Lannes. Except for Murat, the commander of the 5th Corps fought in more engagements in 1805 than any other corps commander of the *Grande Armée*. At each combat, Lannes performed with the highest efficiency and unrestrained enthusiasm—characteristics of his personality that were, in turn, transferred to the officers and men of his command. In short, Lannes displayed every characteristic important in an outstanding commander of an army's vanguard.

Although fighting far less than Lannes, thanks largely to the fact that his command was usually near the Imperial personage, Marshal Bessières also did very well in 1805. While his role at the head of the small Imperial Guard was limited, he nevertheless proved to be an extremely able commanding officer for the best troops in the *Grande Armée*.

Napoleon, His Army and His Foes— *A Final Assessment of 1805 and Austerlitz*

For Napoleon as well as every man in French uniform, the outcome of the Ulm-Austerlitz campaigns of 1805 represented the greatest satisfaction and justification of everything for which the *Grande Armée* had been training since the establishment of the Channel camps in 1803. The French army which marched across the Rhine to triumph time and again against superior numbers of Austrians and Russians was no longer a highly motivated, but unevenly trained Republican force led by mostly capable officers as seen in the last war; it was instead a highly motivated, expertly trained killing machine led by hand-picked officers. Beginning with the Peace of Amiens, Napoleon made the most of his opportunity to weed out any deadwood in French service and molded the rest into an army that would bear his personal stamp. Through the use of the Channel encampments, Napoleon and his lieutenants forged an instrument of war that, within the context of all that was accomplished in 1805, 1806 and 1807, can rightly be proclaimed as one of the greatest armies of history.

On the allied side, Alexander was not willing to give the French their due. After all, according to the logic of that 'legitimate' monarch, what had happened in 1805 was simply an aberration. To cover up the real causes for defeat, the Tsar instructed Kutuzov to write a relation about the campaign to counter any French publicity. Kutuzov's subsequent history misstated almost every fact. According to the Russian general, the Russian army had fought gloriously and had won more fame in 1805; however, the reasons for the over all allied defeat could always be laid at the feet of the incompetent Austrians. What's more, Kutuzov pronounced that the Tsar's army triumphed at Dürenstein and Schöngrabern while brilliantly making a 'march manœuvre' from Braunau to Moravia. Finally, Kutuzov stated that allied losses at Austerlitz were under 12,000 and any guns that had to be left behind were because of mistakes of the Austrian guides.[47]

What had been won and lost on the bloody fields of Austria and Moravia was not so quickly measured as Kutuzov and the Tsar might have imagined. Judging solely the 10 hours of desperate combat fought at Austerlitz on a purely tactical level, for example, the *Grande Armée* could justly claim one of the most impressive victories of the 19th century. Napoleon's army had eviscerated a foe far superior in ordnance and inflicted more than three times as many casualties than it suffered. In the Austerlitz campaign as a whole, French combat losses came to some 12,000, against an allied total, including prisoners, of more than 47,000. If one combines the Ulm and the Austerlitz campaigns, the magnitude of Napoleon's triumph becomes even more pronounced. French combat losses from Wertingen to Austerlitz

---

[47] Kutuzov's *Relation* can be read, along with Napoleon's response, in: "Relation Officielle de la Bataille d'Austerlitz," *Correspondance*, number 10032.

came to almost 16,000, whereas the allied total, including prisoners, was more than a whopping 113,000 along with 3,653 pieces of ordnance![48]

Such a disparity in casualties cannot be minimized by any serious student of military history. The campaigns of 1805 vividly demonstrated that the *Grande Armée* and its commanders had elevated warfare to a new level, and at this new level they waged war with a vengeance. Before the Battle of Austerlitz, Napoleon had rated his men the best soldiers in the world, and that December day gave him no reason to think less of them. From one end of the lengthy Moravian battlefield to the other, from the Santon to Tellnitz, Napoleon's soldiers had "maneuvered with coolness and precision, fought with courage, and executed [their] bold movements with admirable concert."[49]

Moreover, the French were given the leadership their courage deserved. While criticism can deservedly be leveled against Napoleon for elevating Murat to a position of army wing commander during the Ulm campaign and again during the pursuit to Vienna—a position far above the cavalryman's intellectual capabilities—at Austerlitz, except for Bernadotte not pressing his advantage, and except for Napoleon not making sure that the 1st Corps cut off the allied forces on the northern end of the field, as well as Soult not keeping close enough supervision on his attacking divisions, the severest military critic would be hard pressed to find fault with the way the French high command conducted the battle. Napoleon's assessment of allied intentions, and his subsequent dispositions of the *Grande Armée*, coupled with his plan of battle and modifications to that plan once the battle was joined, was nothing short of masterful. Had Napoleon known all that we know now of the allied plans and forces, it is difficult to see how he could have been more wisely disposed. Once the battle was joined, the Emperor was able to modify his wide sweeping maneuver and implement a smaller version that began on the Pratzen and pivoted southward. Ten days before the actual conflict, the Emperor had eyed this piece of terrain, and had used it as the centerpiece of his planned destruction of the allied army. Napoleon's plan of battle predicted that the allies would vacate the Pratzen on their way to attack his center or right flank, and by such a maneuver, would open up themselves to destruction. While Napoleon's plan did not unfold perfectly, few leaders in history have come as close to calling their own shot in a great battle. Furthermore, the officers and troops that executed these maneuvers did so in the belief that Napoleon was the greatest soldier of the age, and that they could accomplish anything while under his leadership.

Yet for all the battlefield triumphs by the *Grande Armée* in 1805, Napoleon had not won a lasting peace. At Austerlitz, the French Emperor believed that by suckering the unwieldy allied forces into battle, he could deliver a knockout blow from which they would never recover. That judgment was only half right. The allied army of the Austerlitz campaign was less-skilled than his own, but they were not Mack's dispirited Austrian army of the Ulm campaign. In fighting courage the allied soldiers who stood in the rearguards at Amstetten and Schöngrabern, or who had attacked at Dürenstein or who had clung to the Pratzen Plateau at the Battle of Austerlitz until their last round of ammunition was exhausted, proved themselves *in selected instances* to be the equal of the French they faced. It would be the particular tragedy of the men of the Combined Russian and Austrian Army that they seldom got the generals their courage deserved. With only very few

---

[48] C[2] 13, 16 and 470. Insofar as loss of ordnance is concerned, the allies were devastated by the 1805 war. The *Grande Armée* captured 154 pieces of the 1805 pattern Russian ordnance. These new guns and licornes were then taken to firing ranges for testing and study by Napoleon's artillery officers. Meanwhile, the Austrians lost 3,499 pieces of ordnance in the 1805 war, including hundreds of siege guns and mortars.

[49] Stutterheim, *A Detailed Account of the Battle of Austerlitz*, p. 36.

conspicuous exceptions such as Kamensky I and Bagration, that courage was betrayed by the privileged officers of the Romanov and Habsburg dynasties, most notably by Kutuzov as well as Tsar Alexander himself.

More than any other individual in allied uniform, it was the Tsar—who assumed command of the combined allied forces several days before Austerlitz—who betrayed his own men. With the exception of selected battles in the Peninsula which saw Spanish generals commanding, on no other Napoleonic battlefield did a commanding general violate so many of the established principles of the art of war. Tsar Alexander failed to employ his cavalry usefully to establish the whereabouts and strength of the French army or to protect his different columns that were to deliver the main blows against Napoleon. As a result, Alexander learned nothing of his foe and was surprised. Throughout the day, when it became apparent that all was not going according to plan, Alexander made no attempt to modify the allied battle plan. Whether this was due to the Tsar becoming flustered or due to the abysmal allied army staff being too slow and inflexible to change orders, the result was that Alexander retained no flexibility. That lack of flexibility was also reflected in the allied columns that maneuvered without coordination or mutual support.

And however poorly some of his lieutenants served him, most notably Buxhöwden and Prebyshevsky, the Tsar shrank from his paramount responsibility—to command. Rather than take an active role in the operations and supervise his various columns, Alexander repeatedly played the idle spectator at Austerlitz by letting his column commanders fight their own battles. And when Kienmayer and Dokhturov cleared Tellnitz and established a foothold across the Goldbach, while Miloradovich became embroiled in the struggle on the Pratzen, Alexander in no way tried to intervene the way an army commander should. In return for his indecisiveness, the entire allied attack stalled and was enveloped by Napoleon's counterattack: irrevocable defeat soon followed. Even if the first phase of the allied plan had succeeded and the Goldbach crossed, the idea of turning north and thereby cutting the French off from Vienna was nothing short of delusional. Nevertheless, by doing *nothing*, Alexander merely contributed to the allied defeat. And when the campaign was over, with his defeated army trudging eastward while his dreams of glory and conquest were in abject disarray, Alexander had the gall to say that his Russian officers had been "betrayed by cowardly Austrians who also contaminated the ignorant peasants that were the common soldiers of our army."[50] There is little doubt that Tsar Alexander never appreciated what it took to be an army commander, nor the manner of men he had with him.

That opinion about the men was also held by Kutuzov. When the toadies around the Tsar tried to shift the blame for the lost battle towards the one-eyed general, Kutuzov responded in kind by diverting attention away from himself and claiming that it was the Austrians, Prebyshevsky (the commander of the III Column) and the Novgorod Musketeers, who "ran away without offering the slightest resistance, which spread fear and panic among the whole [IV] column"[51] that gave the French the advantage.

It is no little irony that, unlike Tsar Alexander and Kutuzov, Napoleon held the rank and file Russians of Austerlitz in high esteem. Although the French Emperor had no use for the far too many slothful Russian officers whose uninspired leadership led in large measure to the lackluster performance of the Tsar's army, Napoleon did recognize and appreciate the qualities of the common Russian soldier. Comparing the Russian troops of 1805 to those of 1812, Napoleon was of the

---

[50] S.H.A.T., C^2 13.

[51] Kutuzov, S*bornik Dokumentov,* vol. 2, p. 265.

opinion that "the Russian army which fought at Austerlitz would not have lost the battle of Borodino."[52]

At that, he could have been right. In 1805, the manpower in all the armies of Europe was of a more mature and highly-trained quality than the masses of more youthful, conscripted soldiers that formed the majority of the armies that fought in 1812. Certainly, the *Grande Armée* that crossed the Niemen River in June of 1812 was nothing more than a shadow of the superb *Grande Armée* with which Napoleon had crossed the Rhine in 1805 and that he led to victory through 1807. And the Tsar's 1812 forces, though still a relic of the *ancien régime*, had made definite strides to improve organization and command, but were still not the battlefield equals to the 1812 *Grande Armée*. Nevertheless, like the French, the Russian soldiers of 1812 were not as good as their 1805 counterparts. Still, with all the manpower and superior numbers of ordnance that was available to him, the Tsar and his firebrands could have been victorious in 1805 if they had been fighting another army and another commanding general.

Had the Tsar been leading his host against troops that had not spent two years in the Channel encampments and generals that had not been steeled under the watchful eye of Napoleon, Alexander might have won the glorious victory he predicted. In the Danube theater of war, Napoleon was the commander of his own army, and there was little chance that those who still warred according to the ways of the *ancien régime* were going to defeat the Great Captain at the head of history's first modern army. This was especially true at Austerlitz, where the armies where relatively equal in numbers, but the qualitative difference was so great that Alexander's basic premise of engaging and defeating Napoleon was therefore almost impossible.

With all the mistakes Napoleon ever made, with all the limitations of his combative character and the limitations imposed by his incessant need to become an accepted member of the European family of rulers, as a military leader at Austerlitz his performance must rank him, if on that battle alone, as one of the greatest warriors of all the ages.

In him, such genius as was inherent in France's archaic and tumultuous civilization was brought to full bloom in those last days of November and the early days of December, in him the self-made man of the Revolution assumed his own place among the immortals of history. As Rossbach illustrated the weakness in the generals of France of a bygone era, Austerlitz clearly showed the strength of the French army when unbetrayed by its leaders. It was this fusion of military talent and devotion to country, coupled with the genius of one man, that forever made the inseparable bond between the *Grande Armée* and Napoleon.

---

[52] Mikhailovsky-Danilevsky, *Relation de la campagne de 1805*, p. 216.

NAPOLEON and AUSTERLITZ

APPENDICES

SITUATION of the *GRANDE ARMÉE*

On or About the Time of the Crossing of the Rhine 4 vendémiaire an XIV (26 September 1805)

His Majesty
The Emperor Napoleon I, commanding in person

The Emperor's Military Household
Général de division Duroc, Grand Marshal of the Palace
Général de division Caulaincourt, Grand Equerry

Aides-de-Camp to His Majesty:
Général de division Caffarelli
Général de division Junot
Général de division Savary
Général de brigade Bertrand
Général de brigade Lemarois
Général de brigade Mouton
Général de brigade Rapp
Colonel Lebrun

* *

Suite de l'État-major
The Imperial Staff
Major-Général of the Army—Marshal Berthier

General Officers Attached to the Major Général
Général de brigade Pannetier
Général de brigade Reille

Assistant Chief of Staff—Chief of the General Staff
Général de division Andréossy

Assistant Chief of Staff—*Maréchal des Logis*
Général de division Mathieu Dumas
Général de brigade Sauson, Chief of the Topographical Service

Artillery
Général de division Songis, Commander of the Artillery
Général de brigade Pernetti, Chief of Staff
Colonel Sénarmont, Assistant Chief of Staff

Engineers
Général de division Marescot, Commander of the Engineers
Colonel Matel, Chief of Staff
Chef de bataillon Decaux, General Director of the Park

General Administration of the Army
Staff consisted of five personnel.

Administrative Services
Inspector general and chief medical officer: Costé
Inspector general and chief surgeon: Percy
Inspector general and chief pharmacist: Parmentier
Plus 13 other personnel.

Attached to Imperial Headquarters
22nd *Chasseurs à cheval* (3 squadrons)

IMPERIAL GUARD
Strengths as of 8 vendémiaire an XIV (30 September 1805) Upon Crossing the Rhine at Strasbourg

Marshal Bessières
Général de brigade Roussel, Chief of Staff (in route)
Colonel Couin, commanding the artillery
Corps headquarters staff—16 personnel

	Bns/Sqdns	All Ranks Present & Under Arms
Infantry of the Imperial Guard		
1st Brigade: *Général de brigade* Hulin		
Regiment of *Grenadiers à pied* of the Imperial Guard	(2)	1,635
2nd Brigade: *Général de brigade* Soulès		
Regiment of *Chasseurs à pied* of the Imperial Guard	(2)	1,602
3rd Brigade—Regiment of the Royal Italian Guard: Colonel Lecchi		
Battalion of *Grenadiers à pied* and		
Battalion of *Chasseurs à pied* of the Royal Italian Guard	(2)	897
Cavalry of the Imperial Guard		
1st Brigade: *Général de brigade* Ordener		
Regiment of *Grenadiers à cheval* of the Imperial Guard	(4)	740
2nd Brigade: Colonel Morland		
Regiment of *Chasseurs à cheval* of the Imperial Guard	(4)	631
Company of *Mameluks* of the Imperial Guard	(½)	63
3rd Brigade: *Général de division* Savary		
Regiment of *Gendarmerie d'élite* of the Imperial Guard	(2)	203
Artillery of the Imperial Guard—		
1st and 2nd Companies of Horse Artillery (*Volante*) of the Imperial Guard		
Company of Horse Artillery of the Royal Italian Guard, one company		
Each of the above three horse artillery companies had identical ordnance, consisting of:		
Four 8-pdr. guns, two 4-pdr. guns and two 6-inch howitzers—total of eight pieces of ordnance in each company.		
All the artillerists from the three companies totaled		286
Train of the Imperial Guard Artillery		181
Flying Ambulance of the Guard (Larrey)		27
Total strength of all artillerists and supporting personnel for the entire Imperial Guard—		494
Imperial Guard Totals, excluding staffs—		
Infantry	6	4,134
Cavalry	10 ½	1,637
Artillerists and supporting personnel, number of companies	5	494
Total Present and Under Arms		6,265 and 24 pieces of ordnance
Total number of horses with the Imperial Guard		2,107
Total number of personnel in rear areas, in route to join up with their respective units		846
Total of personnel in hospitals		N/A
Total effectives—all personnel, excluding general officers & staffs		7,111 and 24 pieces of ordnance

1st CORPS
Strengths as of 8 vendémiaire an XIV (30 September 1805) Upon Arrival at Würzburg

Marshal Bernadotte

Général de division Victor-Léopold Berthier, Chief of Staff
Général de division Jean-Baptiste Eblé, commanding the artillery
Colonel Morio, commanding the engineers
Corps headquarters staff—33 personnel

	Bns/Sqdns	All Ranks Present & Under Arms
1st Infantry Division—*Général de division* Rivaud de la Raffinière		
Division headquarters staff—16 personnel		
1st Brigade: *Général de brigade* Dumoulin		
8th Regiment of the *Ligne*	(3)	1,900
2nd Brigade: *Général de brigade* Pacthod		
45th Regiment of the *Ligne*	(3)	1,822
54th Regiment of the *Ligne*	(3)	1,937
Division artillery and train:		
8th Regiment of Foot Artillery, one company consisting of:		
Four 3-pounders and one 5.3-inch howitzer—total of five pieces of ordnance.		
3rd Regiment of Horse Artillery, one company consisting of:		
Four 6-pounders and one 5.3-inch howitzer—total of five pieces of ordnance.		
2nd Battalion, Train of Artillery, two companies		
2nd Infantry Division—*Général de division* Drouet		
Division headquarters staff—19 personnel		
1st Brigade: *Général de brigade* Frere		
27th *Légère* Infantry Regiment	(3)	2,069
2nd Brigade: *Général de brigade* Werlé		
94th Regiment of the *Ligne*	(3)	1,947
95th Regiment of the *Ligne*	(3)	2,161
Division artillery and train:		
8th Regiment of Foot Artillery, one company consisting of:		
Five 3-pounders and one 5.3-inch howitzer—total of six pieces of ordnance.		
3rd Regiment of Horse Artillery, one company consisting of:		
Five 6-pounders and one 5.3-inch howitzer—total of six pieces of ordnance.		
2nd Battalion, Train of Artillery, two companies		
1st Corps Light Cavalry Division—*Général de division* Kellermann		
Corps cavalry division staff—19 personnel		
1st Brigade: *Général de brigade* Van Marisy		
2nd Hussars	(3)	430
5th Hussars	(3)	355
2nd Brigade: *Général de brigade* Picard		
4th Hussars	(3)	444
5th *Chasseurs à cheval*	(3)	436
Division artillery and train:		
1st Company, 3rd Regiment of Horse Artillery, consisting of:		
Two 6-pounders, two 3-pounders and two 5.3-inch howitzers—total of six pieces of ordnance.		
2nd Battalion, Train of Artillery, one company		
1st Corps Artillery Reserve—		
Corps artillery reserve staff—7 personnel		
8th Regiment of Foot Artillery, one company, with:		
Four 12-pounder guns—total of four pieces of ordnance.		
3rd Regiment of Horse Artillery, one company, with:		
Two 6-pounders, two 3-pounders and two 5.3-inch howitzers—total of six pieces of ordnance.		
2nd Battalion, Train of Artillery, two companies		
Pontonniers, one company and *Ouvriers* of the Artillery, ½ company		
Total strength of all artillerists and supporting personnel for the entire 1st Corps—		1,166
1st Corps Totals, excluding staffs—		
Infantry	18	11,836
Cavalry	12	1,665
Artillerists and supporting personnel, number of companies	14 ½	1,166
Total Present and Under Arms		14,667 and 38 pieces of ordnance
Total number of horses with the 1st Corps		3,442
Total number of personnel in rear areas		702
Total of personnel in hospitals		1,550
Total effectives—all personnel, excluding general officers & staffs		16,919 and 38 pieces of ordnance

2nd CORPS
Strengths as of 1 vendémiaire an XIV (23 September 1805)
Upon Arrival on the Rhine

Général de division Marmont

Général de division Vignolle, Chief of Staff
Général de brigade Tirlet, commanding the artillery
Colonel Somis, commanding the engineers
Corps headquarters staff—39 personnel

	Bns/Sqdns	All Ranks Present & Under Arms
1st Infantry Division—*Général de division* Boudet		
Division headquarters staff—15 personnel		
1st Brigade: *Général de brigade* Dessaix		
18th *Légère* Infantry Regiment	(2)	1,476
2nd Brigade: *Général de brigade* Soyez		
11th Regiment of the *Ligne*	(3)	2.199
35th Regiment of the *Ligne*	(2)	1,626
2nd Infantry Division—*Général de division* Grouchy		
Division headquarters staff—15 personnel		
1st Brigade: *Général de brigade* Lacroix		
84th Regiment of the *Ligne*	(3)	2,045
92nd Regiment of the *Ligne*	(3)	2,345
2nd Brigade: *Général de brigade* Delzona		
8th Batavian Regiment of the *Ligne*	(2)	1,003
3rd Infantry Division—*Général de division* Dumonceau		
Division headquarters staff—17 personnel		
1st Brigade: *Général de brigade* Van Heldring		
1st and 2nd Batavian *Légère* Infantry Regiments (1 Bn each)	(2)	1,154
1st Batavian Regiment of the *Ligne*	(2)	1,183
2nd Batavian Regiment of the *Ligne*	(2)	1,018
2nd Brigade: *Général de brigade* Van Hadel		
Régiment de Waldeck	(2)	1,064
6th Batavian Regiment of the *Ligne*	(2)	1,144
2nd Corps Light Cavalry Division—*Général de division* Lacoste		
Corps cavalry division staff—11 personnel		
1st Brigade: *Général de brigade* —		
6th Hussars	(3)	512
8th *Chasseurs à cheval*	(3)	414
2nd Brigade: *Général de brigade* Quaita		
2nd Batavian Light Dragoons	(2)	364
Batavian Hussars	(2)	390
2nd Corps Artillery —		
Corps artillery reserve staff—7 personnel		
8th Regiment of French Foot Artillery, four companies		352
Batavian Foot Artillery, five companies		491
Batavian Horse Artillery, one company		108
7th Battalion, French Train of Artillery, six companies		453
Batavian Train of Artillery, four companies		266
Batavian *Pontonniers*, detachment		30
French *Ouvriers* of the Artillery, one company		72
4th French Engineer Battalion, 7th company		88
Batavian Engineers, one company		85
French Miners, one company		80
Batavian Miners, one company		75
Total strength of all artillerists and supporting personnel for the entire 2nd Corps—		2,100
2nd Corps Totals, excluding staffs—		
Infantry	25	16,257
Cavalry	10	1,680
Artillerists and supporting personnel, number of companies	25 +	2,100
Total Present and Under Arms		20,037 and 26 pieces of ordnance
Total number of horses with the 2nd Corps		2,789
Total number of personnel in rear areas		392
Total of personnel in hospitals		1,712
Total effectives—all personnel, excluding general officers & staff		22,141 and 26 pieces of ordnance

3rd CORPS
Strengths as of 1 vendémiaire an XIV (23 September 1805)

Marshal Davout

Général de brigade Fournier de Loysonville Daultane, Chief of Staff
Général de division Sorbier, commanding the artillery
Général de brigade Andreossy, commanding the engineers
Corps headquarters staff—39 personnel

	Bns/Sqdns	All Ranks Present & Under Arms
1st Infantry Division—*Général de division* Bisson		
Division headquarters staff—19 personnel		
1st Brigade: *Général de brigade* Demont		
13th *Légère* Infantry Regiment	(2)	1,629
2nd Brigade: *Général de brigade* Debilly		
17th Regiment of the *Ligne*	(2)	1,817
30th Regiment of the *Ligne*	(2)	1,570
3rd Brigade: *Général de brigade* Eppler		
51st Regiment of the *Ligne*	(2)	1,648
61st Regiment of the *Ligne*	(2)	1,550
2nd Infantry Division—*Général de division* Friant		
Division headquarters staff—20 personnel		
1st Brigade: *Général de brigade* Heudelet		
15th *Légère* Infantry Regiment*	(2)	905 *
33rd Regiment of the *Ligne*	(2)	1,689
2nd Brigade: *Général de brigade* Lochet		
48th Regiment of the *Ligne*	(2)	1,522
111th Regiment of the *Ligne*	(2)	1,778
3rd Brigade: *Général de brigade* Grandeau		
108th Regiment of the *Ligne*	(2)	1,567
*Six companies of the 15th *Légère* were detached from the regiment and formed the 2nd Battalion, 5th Regiment of the Grenadiers *de la Réserve* in 5th Corps.		
3rd Infantry Division—*Général de division* Gudin		
Division headquarters staff—13 personnel		
1st Brigade: *Général de brigade* Petit		
12th Regiment of the *Ligne*	(2)	1,583
21st Regiment of the *Ligne*	(2)	1,792
2nd Brigade: *Général de brigade* Gauthier		
25th Regiment of the *Ligne*	(2)	1,750
85th Regiment of the *Ligne*	(2)	1,603
3rd Corps Light Cavalry Division—*Général de brigade* Viallanes		
Corps cavalry division staff—11 personnel		
1st Brigade: *Général de brigade* —		
1st *Chasseurs à cheval*	(3)	380
7th Hussars	(3)	324
2nd Brigade: *Général de brigade* —		
2nd *Chasseurs à cheval*	(3)	331
12th *Chasseurs à cheval*	(3)	513
3rd Corps Artillery —		
Corps artillery reserve staff—13 personnel		
7th Regiment of French Foot Artillery, 1st, 2nd, 3rd, 4th, 14th & 15th cos.		380
5th Regiment of French Horse Artillery, 5th company		90
1st and 2nd Battalions, French Train of Artillery, five companies		485
French *Pontonniers*, detachment		43
French *Ouvriers* of the Artillery and Armorers		50
French Engineers and Miners, two companies		162
Total strength of all artillerists and supporting personnel—3rd Corps		1,210
3rd Corps Totals, excluding staffs—		
Infantry	28	22,403
Cavalry	12	1,548
Artillerists and supporting personnel, number of companies	13	1,210
Total Present and Under Arms		25,161 and 48 pieces of ordnance
Total number of horses with the 3rd Corps		2,093
Total number of personnel in rear areas		1,282
Total of personnel in hospitals		1,573
Total effectives—all personnel, excluding general officers & staffs		28,016 and 48 pieces of ordnance

4th CORPS
Strengths as of 1 vendémiaire an XIV
(23 September 1805)

Marshal Soult

Général de division Salligny, Chief of Staff
Général de brigade Lariboissière, commanding the artillery
Colonel Poitevin, commanding the engineers
Corps headquarters staff—40 personnel

	Bns/Sqdns	All Ranks Present & Under Arms	
1st Infantry Division—*Général de division* Saint Hilaire			
Division headquarters staff—22 personnel			
1st Brigade: *Général de brigade* Morand			
10th *Légère* Infantry Regiment	(2)	1,542	
2nd Brigade: *Général de brigade* Thiébault			
14th Regiment of the *Ligne*	(2)	1,764	
36th Regiment of the *Ligne*	(2)	1,780	
3rd Brigade: *Général de brigade* Waré			
43rd Regiment of the *Ligne*	(2)	1,766	
55th Regiment of the *Ligne*	(2)	1,752	
2nd Infantry Division—*Général de division* Vandamme			
Division headquarters staff—22 personnel			
1st Brigade: *Général de brigade* Schiner			
24th *Légère* Infantry Regiment	(2)	1,504	
2nd Brigade: *Général de brigade* Férey			
4th Regiment of the *Ligne*	(2)	1,889	
28th Regiment of the *Ligne*	(2)	1,730	
3rd Brigade: *Général de brigade* Candras			
46th Regiment of the *Ligne*	(2)	1,733	
57th Regiment of the *Ligne*	(2)	1,854	
3rd Infantry Division—*Général de division* Legrand			
Division headquarters staff—21 personnel			
1st Brigade: *Général de brigade* Merle			
26th *Légère* Infantry Regiment	(2)	1,732	
Tirailleurs du Pô	(1)	722	
2nd Brigade: *Général de brigade* Lavasseur			
18th Regiment of the *Ligne*	(2)	1,604	
75th Regiment of the *Ligne*	(2)	1,895	
Tirailleurs corses	(1)	766	
3rd Brigade: *Général de brigade* Féry			
3rd Regiment of the *Ligne*	(3)	2,049	
4th Corps Light Cavalry Division—*Général de brigade* Margaron			
Corps cavalry division staff—9 personnel			
1st Brigade: *Général de brigade* Margaron			
8th Hussars	(3)	443	
11th *Chasseurs à cheval*	(4)	633	
26th *Chasseurs à cheval*	(3)	405	
Part of this division, the 16th *Chasseurs à cheval*, did not cross the Rhine until 22 vendémiaire (14 October). When they did, they had:	(4)	575	men with 500 horses
4th Corps Artillery —			
Corps artillery reserve staff—9 personnel			
5th Regiment of French Foot Artillery, six companies		579	
5th Regiment of French Horse Artillery, 5th company		92	
1st and 2nd Battalions, French Train of Artillery, six companies		450	
French *Ouvriers* of the Artillery, 1/2 company		46	
French Engineers, one company		62	
Total strength of all artillerists and supporting personnel—4th Corps		1,230	
4th Corps Totals, excluding staffs—			
Infantry	31	25,087	
Cavalry	10	1,481	
Artillerists and supporting personnel, number of companies	14 ½	1,230	
Total Present and Under Arms		27,798	and 36 pieces of ordnance
Total number of horses with the 4th Corps		1,946	
Total number of personnel in rear areas		927	plus the 16th *Chasseurs à cheval*
Total of personnel in hospitals		1,393	
Total effectives—all personnel, excluding general officers & staffs		30,118	and 36 pieces of ordnance

5th CORPS
Strengths as of 1 vendémiaire an XIV
(23 September 1805)

Marshal Lannes

Général de brigade Compans, Chief of Staff
Général de brigade Foucher de Careil, commanding the artillery
Colonel Kirgener, commanding the engineers
Corps headquarters staff—20 personnel

	Bns/Sqdns	All Ranks Present & Under Arms
1st Infantry Division (*Grenadiers de la Réserve*)—*Général de division* Oudinot		
Division headquarters staff—23 personnel		
1st Brigade: *Général de brigade* Laplanche-Morthières		
1st Grenadier Regiment		
1st *bataillon d'élite* from the 13th *Ligne*	(1)	684
2nd *bataillon d'élite* from the 58th *Ligne*	(1)	747
2nd Grenadier Regiment		
1st *bataillon d'élite* from the 9th *Ligne*	(1)	662
2nd *bataillon d'élite* from the 81st *Ligne*	(1)	692
2nd Brigade: *Général de brigade* Dupas		
3rd Grenadier Regiment		
1st *bataillon d'élite* from the 2nd *Légère*	(1)	702
2nd *bataillon d'élite* from the 3rd *Légère*	(1)	744
4th Grenadier Regiment		
1st *bataillon d'élite* from the 28th *Légère*	(1)	719
2nd *bataillon d'élite* from the 31st *Légère*	(1)	717
3rd Brigade: *Général de brigade* Ruffin		
5th Grenadier Regiment		
1st *bataillon d'élite* from the 12th *Légère*	(1)	682
2nd *bataillon d'élite* from the 15th *Légère*	(1)	699
2nd Infantry Division—*Général de division* Gazan		
Division headquarters staff—16 personnel		
1st Brigade: *Général de brigade* Graindorge		
4th *Légère* Infantry Regiment	(3)	1,732
58th Regiment of the *Ligne*	(2)	1,000
2nd Brigade: *Général de brigade* Campana		
100th Regiment of the *Ligne*	(3)	2,068
103rd Regiment of the *Ligne*	(3)	2,144
3rd Infantry Division—*Général de division* Suchet		
Suchet's Division was transferred to Marshal Lannes' 5th Corps on 5 vendémiaire (27 September).		
Division headquarters staff—23 personnel		
1st Brigade: Général *de brigade* Claparède (joined the division on 18 vendémiaire (10 October)		
17th *Légère* Infantry Regiment	(2)	1,857
2nd Brigade: *Général de brigade* Beker		
34th Regiment of the *Ligne*	(3)	2,250
40th Regiment of the *Ligne*	(2)	1,670
3rd Brigade: *Général de brigade* Valhubert		
64th Regiment of the *Ligne*	(2)	1,675
88th Regiment of the *Ligne*	(2)	1,702
5th Corps Light Cavalry Division—*Général de brigade* Fauconnet		
Corps cavalry division staff—12 personnel		
1st Brigade: *Général de brigade* Treillard		
9th Hussars	(3)	344
10th Hussars	(3)	335
2nd Brigade: *Général de brigade* Fauconnet		
13th *Chasseurs à cheval*	(3)	339
21st *Chasseurs à cheval*	(3)	331
5th Corps Artillery —		
Corps artillery reserve staff—5 personnel		
1st Regiment of French Foot Artillery, four companies		393
5th Regiment of French Horse Artillery, 2nd company		100
5th Battalion, French Train of Artillery, five companies		240
French *Pontonniers*, 1/2 company		45
French *Ouvriers* of the Artillery, 1/2 of the 1st Company		49
2nd French Engineer Battalion, four companies		283
French Miners, one company		84
Total strength of all artillerists and supporting personnel—5th Corps		1,194

5th Corps Totals, excluding staffs—

Infantry	32	23,146	
Cavalry	12	1,349	
Artillerists and supporting personnel, number of companies	16	1,194	
Total Present and Under Arms		25,689	and 34 pieces of ordnance
Total number of horses with the 5th Corps		1,861	
Total number of personnel in rear areas		565	
Total of personnel in hospitals		1,262	
Total effectives—all personnel, excluding general officers & staffs		27,516	and 34 pieces of ordnance

6th CORPS
Strengths as of 1 vendémiaire an XIV (23 September 1805)

Marshal Ney

Général de brigade Dutaillis, Chief of Staff
Général de brigade Séroux, commanding the artillery
Colonel Cazals, commanding the engineers
Corps headquarters staff—47 personnel

1st Infantry Division—*Général de division* Dupont

Division headquarters staff—18 personnel

	Bns/Sqdns	All Ranks Present & Under Arms
1st Brigade: *Général de brigade* Rouyer		
9th *Légère* Infantry Regiment	(2)	1,763
2nd Brigade: *Général de brigade* Marchand		
32nd Regiment of the *Ligne*	(2)	1,662
96th Regiment of the *Ligne*	(2)	1,721

Division Artillery—
One section of horse artillerists serving one 4-pounder and one 6-inch howitzer—total of two pieces.
One company of foot artillerists serving one 12-pounder, four 8-pounders and one 4-pounder—total of six pieces.

2nd Infantry Division—*Général de division* Loison

Division headquarters staff—14 personnel

1st Brigade: *Général de brigade* Villatte		
6th *Légère* Infantry Regiment	(2)	1,742
39th Regiment of the *Ligne*	(2)	1,646
2nd Brigade: *Général de brigade* Rouget		
69th Regiment of the *Ligne*	(2)	1,716
76th Regiment of the *Ligne*	(3)	1,795

Division Artillery—
One section of horse artillerists serving one 4-pounder and one 6-inch howitzer—total of two pieces.
One company of foot artillerists serving one 12-pounder, four 8-pounders and one 4-pounder—total of six pieces.

3rd Infantry Division—*Général de division* Malher

Division headquarters staff—15 personnel

1st Brigade: *Général de brigade* Marcognet		
25th *Légère* Infantry Regiment	(3)	2,023
27th Regiment of the *Ligne*	(2)	1,828
2nd Brigade: *Général de brigade* Labassée		
50th Regiment of the *Ligne*	(2)	1,714
59th Regiment of the *Ligne*	(2)	1,504

Division Artillery—
One section of horse artillerists serving one 4-pounder and one 6-inch howitzer—total of two pieces.
One company of foot artillerists serving one 12-pounder, four 8-pounders and one 4-pounder—total of six pieces.

6th Corps Light Cavalry Division—*Général de division* Tilly

Corps cavalry division staff—6 personnel

1st Brigade: *Général de brigade* Duprès		
1st Hussars	(3)	375
3rd Hussars	(3)	342
10th *Chasseurs à cheval*	(3)	354

6th Corps Artillery —

Corps artillery reserve staff—8 personnel

1st Regiment of French Foot Artillery, total of all five companies 468
Two companies of foot artillerists were in the 6th Corps Reserve. These gunners manned the following:
Three 12-pounders, six 8-pounders and three 6-inch howitzers—total of 12 pieces of ordnance.

2nd Regiment of French Horse Artillery, 1st company 94
This company was sub-divided into three sections, one section serving with each one of the 6th Corps' Infantry Divisions.

3rd and 5th Battalions, French Train of Artillery, six companies		412
French *Pontonniers*, ½ company		45
French *Ouvriers* of the Artillery, ½ of the 4th Company		46
Total strength of all artillerists and supporting personnel—6th Corps	1,065	

6th Corps Totals, excluding staffs—

Infantry	24	19,114	
Cavalry	9	1,071	
Artillerists and supporting personnel, number of companies	16	1,065	
Total Present and Under Arms		21,250	and 36 pieces of ordnance
Total number of horses with the 6th Corps		1,780	
Total number of personnel in rear areas		323	
Total of personnel in hospitals		1,508	
Total effectives—all personnel, excluding general officers & staffs		23,081	and 36 pieces of ordnance

7th CORPS
Strengths as of 1 brumaire an XIV (23 October 1805)
The 7th Corps crossed the Rhine on the 1st through 4th brumaire

Marshal Augereau

Général de brigade Donzelot, Chief of Staff
Général de division Dorsner, commanding the artillery
Colonel Lagastine, commanding the engineers
Corps headquarters staff—46 personnel

	Bns/Sqdns	All Ranks Present & Under Arms
1st Infantry Division—*Général de division* Desjardins		
Division headquarters staff—20 personnel		
1st Brigade: *Général de brigade* Lapissè		
16th *Légère* Infantry Regiment	(3)	2,382
2nd Brigade: *Général de brigade* Lamarque		
44th Regiment of the *Ligne*	(2)	1,355
105th Regiment of the *Ligne*	(2)	1,578
2nd Infantry Division—*Général de division* Maurice Mathieu		
Division headquarters staff—16 personnel		
1st Brigade: *Général de brigade* Sarut		
7th *Légère* Infantry Regiment	(2)	2,094
63rd Regiment of the *Ligne*	(2)	1,337
2nd Brigade: *Général de brigade* Sarazin		
24th Regiment of the *Ligne*	(3)	1,966
7th Corps Light Cavalry —Colonel Lagrange et de Fourilles		
7th *Chasseurs à cheval*	(4)	452

Throughout the 1805 campaigns, the 7th *Chasseurs à cheval* were officially attached to either the 2nd Infantry Division (until early November), or the 1st Infantry Division. Please also consult Appendix E.

7th Corps Artillery —

Corps artillery reserve staff—8 personnel	
3rd Regiment of French Foot Artillery, four companies	334
6th Regiment of French Horse Artillery, 5th company	90
8th Battalion, French Train of Artillery, six companies	544
French Miners, 7th Company	89
French *Ouvriers* of the Artillery, 1/2 of the 6th Company	69
4th Battalion of French Engineers, 2nd and 4th Companies	157
Total strength of all artillerists and supporting personnel for the entire 7th Corps—	1,283

7th Corps Totals, excluding staffs—

Infantry	14	10,712	
Cavalry	4	452	
Artillerists and supporting personnel, number of companies	14 ½	1,283	
Total Present and Under Arms		12,447	and 24 pieces of ordnance
Total number of horses with the 7th Corps		1,184	
Total number of personnel in rear areas		466	
Total of personnel in hospitals		968	
Total effectives—all personnel, excluding general officers & staffs		13,881	and 24 pieces of ordnance

Corps des Réserves de Cavalerie
Strengths as of 1 vendémiaire an XIV (23 September 1805)

Marshal Murat

Général de division Belliard, Chief of Staff
Général de brigade Hanicque, commanding the artillery
Colonel Hayelle, commanding the engineers
Corps headquarters staff—38 personnel

	Bns/Sqdns	All Ranks Present & Under Arms
1st Heavy Cavalry Division—*Général de division* Nansouty		
Division headquarters staff—16 personnel		
1st Brigade: *Général de brigade* Piston		
1st Regiment of *Carabiniers*	(3)	478
2nd Regiment of *Carabiniers*	(3)	575
2nd Brigade: *Général de brigade* La Houssaye		
2nd Regiment of *Cuirassiers*	(3)	532
9th Regiment of *Cuirassiers*	(3)	513
3rd Brigade: *Général de brigade* Saint-Germain		
3rd Regiment of *Cuirassiers*	(3)	520
12th Regiment of *Cuirassiers*	(3)	590
2nd Heavy Cavalry Division—*Général de division* d'Hautpoul		
Division headquarters staff—15 personnel		
1st Brigade: Colonel Noirot		
1st Regiment of *Cuirassiers*	(3)	407
5th Regiment of *Cuirassiers*	(3)	480
2nd Brigade: *Général de brigade* Saint-Sulpice		
10th Regiment of *Cuirassiers*	(3)	406
11th Regiment of *Cuirassiers*	(3)	420
1st Dragoon Division—*Général de division* Klein		
Division headquarters staff—15 personnel		
1st Brigade: *Général de brigade* Senerols		
1st Regiment of Dragoons	(3)	374
2nd Regiment of Dragoons	(3)	410
2nd Brigade: *Général de brigade* Lasalle		
4th Regiment of Dragoons	(3)	396
20th Regiment of Dragoons	(3)	413
3rd Brigade: *Général de brigade* Milet		
14th Regiment of Dragoons	(3)	342
26th Regiment of Dragoons	(3)	554
2nd Dragoon Division—*Général de division* Walther		
Division headquarters staff—20 personnel		
1st Brigade: *Général de brigade* Sébastiani de la Porta		
3rd Regiment of Dragoons	(3)	343
6th Regiment of Dragoons	(3)	245
2nd Brigade: *Général de brigade* Roget de Belloguet		
10th Regiment of Dragoons	(3)	308
11th Regiment of Dragoons	(3)	339
3rd Brigade: *Général de brigade* Boussart		
13th Regiment of Dragoons	(3)	350
22nd Regiment of Dragoons	(3)	648
3rd Dragoon Division—*Général de division* Beaumont		
Division headquarters staff—12 personnel		
1st Brigade: *Général de brigade* Boyé		
5th Regiment of Dragoons	(3)	429
8th Regiment of Dragoons	(3)	341
2nd Brigade: *Général de brigade* Scalfort		
9th Regiment of Dragoons	(3)	365
12th Regiment of Dragoons	(3)	365
3rd Brigade: *Général de brigade* Milhaud		
16th Regiment of Dragoons	(3)	345
21st Regiment of Dragoons	(3)	435
4th Dragoon Division—*Général de division* Bourcier		
Division headquarters staff—17 personnel		
1st Brigade: *Général de brigade* Sahuc*	Bns/Sqdns	All Ranks Present & Under Arms
15th Regiment of Dragoons	(3)	322
17th Regiment of Dragoons	(3)	351

2nd Brigade: *Général de brigade* Laplanche*		
18th Regiment of Dragoons	(3)	359
19th Regiment of Dragoons	(3)	458
3rd Brigade: *Général de brigade* Verdière		
25th Regiment of Dragoons	(3)	664
27th Regiment of Dragoons	(3)	366

*Laplanche and Sahuc switched brigade commands before crossing the Rhine. This shows each general at the head of his respective brigade after the switch.

Division of *Dragons à pied*—*Général de division* Baraguey d'Hilliers
Strengths as of 4 vendémiaire an XIV (26 September)—These troops were without horses and were utilized as infantry.

Division headquarters staff—16 personnel		
1st Brigade: *Général de brigade* Lesuire		
1st Regiment of *Dragons à pied*	(2)	1,170
2nd Regiment of *Dragons à pied*	(2)	1,468
2nd Brigade: *Général de brigade* Brouard		
3rd Regiment of *Dragons à pied*	(2)	1,770
4th Regiment of *Dragons à pied*	(2)	1,097

***Corps des Réserves de Cavalerie* Artillery —**

Corps artillery reserve staff—7 personnel	
1st Regiment of French Foot Artillery, two companies	185
These two companies were attached to the *Dragons à pied* and totaled the following ordnance: two 12-pounders, four 8-pounders, two 4-pounders and two 6-inch howitzers—total 10 pieces.	
2nd & 6th Regiments of French Horse Artillery, three companies	285
These three companies were each divided into six half-companies. One half-company was attached to each division of cavalry. Every half-company had identical ordnance composition, which was: two 8-pounder guns and one 6-inch howitzer, for a total of three pieces per half-company—total 18 pieces.	
2nd Battalion, French Train of Artillery, six companies	534
Total strength of all artillerists and supporting personnel for the entire *Corps des Réserves de Cavalerie* —	1,002

***Corps des Réserves de Cavalerie* Totals, excluding staffs—**

Infantry (*Dragons à pied*)	8	5,505	
Cavalry	102	14,443	
Artillerists and supporting personnel, number of companies	11	1,002	
Total Present and Under Arms		20,950	and 28 pieces of ordnance
Total number of horses with the Reserve Artillery		14,163	
Total number of personnel in rear areas		526	
Total of personnel in hospitals		371	
Total effectives—all personnel, excluding general officers & staffs		21,847	and 28 pieces of ordnance

Grand Parc d'Artillerie

Strengths as of 8 vendémiaire an XIV (30 September 1805)

Colonel Vermot, Director

Grand Parc d'Artillerie headquarters staff—19 personnel

Grand Parc d'Artillerie	All Ranks Present & Under Arms
French Foot Artillery, 12 companies	1,145
French Horse Artillery, three companies	221
The 15 companies of artillerists manned the following ordnance: Eighteen 12-pounders, twenty-two 8-pounders, eight 4-pounders and eight 6-inch howitzers—total 56 pieces.	
French *Pontonniers*, three companies	280
French *Ouvriers* of the Artillery, two companies	188
French Armorers, 1/2 company	45
French Train of Artillery, 18 companies	1,418
French Train of *Ouvriers* of the Artillery, ½ company	52
Total strength of all artillerists and supporting personnel for the entire *Grand Parc d'Artillerie*—	3,349

***Grand Parc d'Artillerie* Totals, excluding staffs—**

Artillerists and supporting personnel, number of companies	39	3,349	
Total Present and Under Arms		3,349	and 56 pieces of ordnance
Total number of horses with the *Grand Parc*		1,965	
Total number of personnel in rear areas		N/A	
Total of personnel in hospitals		N/A	
Total effectives—all personnel, excluding general officers & staffs		3,349	and 56 pieces of ordnance

RECAPITULATION of the *GRANDE ARMÉE* Upon Crossing the Rhine

Formation	Infantry Battalions	Cavalry Sqd./Regiments	Guns	Total Present— Infantry	Cavalry	All Arms*
Suite de l'État-major	-0-	3 / 1	-0-		NA	NA
Imperial Guard	6	10½ / 3	24	4,134	1,637	6,265
1st Corps	18	12 / 4	34	11,836	1,665	14,667
2nd Corps	25	10 / 4	26	16,257	1,680	20,037
3rd Corps	28	12 / 4	48	22,403	1,548	25,161
4th Corps	31	10 / 3	36	25,087	1,481	27,798
5th Corps	32	12 / 4	34	23,146	1,349	25,689
6th Corps	24	9 / 3	36	19,114	1,071	21,250
7th Corps	14	4 / 1	24	10,712	452	12,447
Réserves de Cavalerie	8	102 / 34	28	5,505	14,443	8,778
Grand Parc d'Artillerie	-0-	-0-	56	-0-	-0-	3,349
Excluding staffs, artillerists and supporting personnel— Totals for the Army	186	184½ / 61	346	138,194	25,326	163,520
*Excluding staffs, but including artillerists and supporting personnel— Totals for the Army	186	184½ / 61	346	138,194	25,326	177,613 *

*This number includes 14,093 artillerists, engineers and other personnel that were present and serving as support troops. The total number of horses as mounts for the cavalry, for the horse artillery and for the train of artillery was 33,330; this number excludes the 22nd *Chasseurs à cheval* at Imperial headquarters, troops on the way to join the army, all horses for staff and headquarters personnel, as well as all horses in the General Administration and Administrative Services.

Source: C2 470, *Archives du Service Historique de l'État-Major de l'Armée de Terre,* (S.H.A.T.), VINCENNES: "Composition de la *Grande Armée* au moment ou elle a passé le Rhin pour la Campagne d'Autriche," and *Journal des opérations du 6e corps.*

Composition of the Artillery in the *Grande Armée* as of September 1805

(Consult Specific Orders of Battle in Other Appendices for More Details)

Poundage of Guns and Number in each Corps

Corps Designation	3*/ 4 pdrs.	6 pdrs.*	8 pdrs.	12 pdrs.	Howitzers	Total in Corps
Imperial Guard	- / 6	-	12		6	24
1st Corps	13* / -	13 *	-	4 **	8 *	38
2nd Corps	- / 6	-	12	4	4	26
3rd Corps	- / 8	-	24	8	8	48
4th Corps	- / 6	-	18	6	6	36
5th Corps	- / 6	-	18	4	6	34
6th Corps	- / 6	-	18	6	6	36
7th Corps	- / 4	-	12	4	4	24
Réserves de Cavalerie	- / 2	-	16	2	8	28
Grand Parc d'Artillerie	- / 8	-	22	18	8	56
Totals for the Army	13* / 52	13 *	152	56	64	350

*The 3- and 6-pounders were Hanoverian ordnance, as were the 5.3-inch howitzers that were part of these companies of 1st Corps.

**The four 12-pounders were of French origin.

Source: C2 470, *Archives du Service Historique de l'État-Major de l'Armée de Terre,* (S.H.A.T.), VINCENNES: "État du Matériel de l'Artillerie de la *Grande Armée*," 22 fructidor an XIII (9 September 1805), plus the *Journaux des opération* of the various corps. Totals adjusted based on Suchet's transfer to 5th Corps on 5 vendémiaire (27 September).

SITUATION of the Bavarian Troops that joined the *GRANDE ARMÉE*

30 vendémiaire an XIV (22 October 1805)

The Bavarian Army under the Orders of
General-Leutnant von Deroi and General-Leutnant Baron von Wrede
Headquarters Staff: 10 personnel

Bavarian Army—Brigades are shown as they were organized on 22 October 1805.		
1st Brigade: General-Major Minneri	Bns/Sqdns	All Ranks Present & Under Arms
1st Infantry Regiment *Leib Gardes*	(2)	1,360
2nd Infantry Regiment *Kronprinz*	(2)	1,302
1st Light Infantry Battalion *Metzen*	(1)	656
1st Dragoon Regiment *Minucci*	(3)	220
2nd Brigade: General-Major Marsigli		
4th Infantry Regiment *Salern*	(2)	1,348
5th Infantry Regiment *Preysing*	(2)	1,364
5th Light Infantry Battalion *LaMotte*	(1)	854
2nd Dragoon Regiment *Taxis*	(3½)	294
3rd Brigade: General-Major Count Mezzanelli		
3rd Infantry Regiment *Prinz Karl*	(2)	1,366
7th Infantry Regiment	(2)	1,363
2nd Light Infantry Battalion *Vincenti*	(1)	674
1st Chevaulegers Regiment *Kronprinz*	(3)	280
4th Brigade: General-Major Baron Karg		
6th Infantry Regiment *Herzog Wilhelm*	(2)	1,378
13th Infantry Regiment	(2)	1,374
3rd Light Infantry Battalion *Preysing*	(1)	680
2nd Chevaulegers Regiment *König*	(4)	310
5th Brigade: General-Major Count Minucci		
8th Infantry Regiment *Herzog Pius*	(2)	1,330
12th Infantry Regiment *Löwenstein*	(2)	1,308
4th Light Infantry Battalion *Stengel*	(1)	673
3rd Chevaulegers Regiment Lei*ningen*	(3)	306
6th Brigade: General-Major von Siebein		
9th Infantry Regiment *Ysenburg*	(2)	1,252
10th Infantry Regiment *Junker*	(2)	1,340
6th Light Infantry Battalion *Steinbach*	(1)	630
4th Chevaulegers Regiment *Bubenhofen*	(4)	298
Artillery of the Bavarian Army—		
1st and 2nd Companies of Bavarian Foot Artillery		
Each of the foot artillerist companies had identical ordnance, consisting of:		
four 12-pounder guns and two howitzers—total of six pieces of ordnance in each company—12 total pieces.		
Company of Bavarian Horse Artillery, consisting of:		
four 6-pounder guns and two howitzers—total of six pieces of ordnance in the horse artillery company.		
All the artillerists from the three companies totaled		407
Infantry Regimental Artillery: Twenty-four 6-pounder guns were in the field—two pieces with each of the 12 regiments of infantry.		
Total strength of all artillerists and supporting personnel for the entire Bavarian Army—		407
Bavarian Army Totals, excluding staffs—		
Infantry	30	20,252
Cavalry	20 ½	1,708
Artillerists and supporting personnel	3	407
Total Present and Under Arms		22,367 and 42 pieces of ordnance
Total of horses with the artillery and train		1,891
Total number of personnel in rear areas, in route to join up with their respective units in one horse artillery company with 6 guns.		
Total of personnel in hospitals		N/A
Total effectives—all personnel, excluding general officers & staffs		22,367 and 42 pieces of ordnance

RECAPITULATION of the Bavarian Troops that joined the *GRANDE ARMÉE*

Formation	Infantry Battalions	Cavalry Sqd./Regiments	Guns	Total Present— Infantry	Cavalry	All Arms
Suite de l'État-major	-0-	0 / 0	-0-	NA	NA	10
1st Brigade	5	3 / 1	4	3,318	220	3,538
2nd Brigade	5	3½ / 1	4	3,566	294	3,860
3rd Brigade	5	3 / 1	4	3,403	280	3,683
4th Brigade	5	4 / 1	4	3,432	310	3,742
5th Brigade	5	3 / 1	4	3,311	306	3,617
6th Brigade	5	4 / 1	4	3,222	298	3,520
Artillery	-0-	0 / 0	18	-0-	-0-	407
Excluding artillerists, staff and supporting personnel— Totals—Bavarian Army	30	20½ / 6	42	20,252	1,708	21,960
*Including artillerists, staff and supporting personnel— Totals—Bavarian Army	30	20½ / 6	42	20,252	1,708	22,377 *

*This number includes 407 artillerists that were present and serving as support troops. One company of horse artillerists with six pieces of ordnance were not present. For those who were present and under arms, the total number of horses as mounts for the cavalry was 1,888; the number of horses present for the officers in the infantry totaled 159. Both these totals exclude all horses for staff and headquarters personnel, as well as all horses in the General Administration and Administrative Services.

The six brigades were equally divided in order to create two divisions, one under Deroi and the other under Wrede.
Note: The cavalry regiments were not fully mobilized, as each regiment at full strength was supposed to have four squadrons.

Source: C^2 470, *Archives du Service Historique de l'État-Major de l'Armée de Terre,* (S.H.A.T.), VINCENNES: "État des Bavaroise sous les ordres du Lieutenant Général de Deroy & le Lieutenant Général Baron de Wrede, Munich le 22 Octobre 1805." An earlier and separate document entitled: "État effectif des troupes fournies par L'Electeur de Bavière. A Bamberg, le 2 Octobre 1805," simply lists all the units in the army at their respective maximum theoretical strengths, which totaled 24,405 officers and other ranks. Therefore, in order to present the most accurate strengths of the Bavarian Army, the author has used the 22 October return, which provides an accurate head count closest to 12 September 1805, the day that Bavaria's Elector, Maximilian-Joseph, declared for Napoleonic France.

SITUATION of the FRENCH TROOPS at the Battle of Haslach—Jungingen

11 October 1805

1st Infantry Division (from Marshal Ney's 6th Corps)—*Général de division* Dupont			
Division headquarters staff—8 personnel			
1st Brigade: *Général de brigade* Rouyer	Bns/Sqdns	Officers-Other ranks	Present & Under Arms
9th *Légère*, Colonel Meunier			
1st and 2nd battalions	(2)	58	1,200
2nd Brigade: *Général de brigade* Marchand			
32nd *Ligne*, Colonel Darricau			
1st and 2nd battalions	(2)	57	1,333
96th *Ligne*, Colonel Barrois			
1st and 2nd battalions	(2)	54	1,403
Divisional artillery and train:			
Detachment from the 2nd Horse Artillery Regiment, consisting of: Two 8-pounder guns—total of 2 pieces of ordnance.		1	38
Company from the 1st Foot Artillery Regiment, consisting of: One 12-pounder gun, two 8-pounder guns, two 4-pounder guns, and one 6-inch howitzer—total of 6 pieces of ordnance.		4	85
Detachments from two companies of artillery train personnel		1	58
Attached to the division:			
1st Hussars, Colonel Rouvillois	(3)	21	362
from the 4th Dragoon Division(-)			
1st Brigade: *Général de brigade* Sahuc			
15th Dragoons, Colonel Barthélémy	(3)	22	261
17th Dragoons, Colonel Saint-Dizier	(3)	23	294

French totals at Haslach-Jungingen, excluding general officers and their staffs:		
Infantry	(6)	4,105
Cavalry	(9)	983
Artillerists and train personnel serving eight pieces of ordnance		187
Total:		5,275

Source: C[2] 470, 473,482 and *Journal des opérations du 6e Corps*;
Archives du Service Historique de l'État-Major de l'Armée de Terre, (S.H.A.T.), VINCENNES.

SITUATION of the AUSTRIAN TROOPS at the Battle of Haslach—Jungingen

11 October 1805

THE AUSTRIAN ARMY OF SWABIA

Feldmarschall-Leutnant (FML) Freiherr Karl Mack von Leiberich

The Right Column—FML Riesch and FML Werneck

Troops in the Front Line:	Bns/Sqdns	Notes
Karl Riese IR#15	(3)	All three were fusilier battalions
Reuss-Plauen IR#17	(3)	All three were fusilier battalions
Stuart IR#18	(3)	All three were fusilier battalions
Kolowrat-Krakowsky IR#36	(3)	All three were fusilier battalions

These troops were supported by 24 battalion guns. These pieces were all 6-pounder cannon, with two such guns attached to each battalion, thereby acting as battalion ordnance.

Troops in the Second Line, in Reserve: (not engaged)		
Manfredini IR#12	(5)	Four fusilier battalions and one grenadier battalion
Auersperg IR#24	(5)	Four fusilier battalions and one grenadier battalion
Erbach IR#42	(4)	Three fusilier battalions and one grenadier battalion

The Left-Hand Columns—Erzherzog Ferdinand and FML Schwarzenberg

Left-Hand Column I: The Infantry—Erzherzog Ferdinand		
Erzherzog Ludwig IR#8	(3)	All three were fusilier battalions
Erzherzog Rainer IR#11	(2)	Both were fusilier battalions
Kaunitz-Rietberg IR#20	(3)	All three were fusilier battalions and had suffered heavy casualties at Günzburg.
Froon IR#54	(3)	Two fusilier battalions and one grenadier battalion

These infantry formations did not have any battalion guns in this battle.

Left-Hand Column II: The Cavalry—FML Schwarzenberg		
Cüirassier-Regiment Albert #3	(6)	Two squadrons were on detached duty, and two others had suffered heavy casualties at Wertingen on 8 October.
Cüirassier-Regiment Mack #6	(8)	
Chevaulegers-Regiment Latour #4	(8)	Two squadrons had suffered heavy losses at Wertingen.
Chevaulegers-Regiment Rosenberg #6	(8)	

Artillery Attached to the Left-Hand Columns:
One cavalry Battery was attached to Schwarzenberg's command, and consisted of:
Four 6-pounder guns and two 7-pounder howitzers—total of six pieces of ordnance.

Austrian Army totals at Haslach-Jungingen	Bns/Sqdns	Present and Under Arms
Infantry	37	20,000
Cavalry	30	2,100
Artillerists and train personnel serving 30 pieces of ordnance		900
Total:		23,000

Source: österreichischen Kriegsarchiv, Vienna (K.A., F.A. Deutschland 1805).

SITUATION of the FRENCH TROOPS at the Battle of Elchingen

14 October 1805

6th CORPS
Strengths as of 21 vendémiaire an XIV
(13 October 1805)

Marshal Ney
Général de brigade Dutaillis, Chief of Staff
Général de brigade Séroux, commanding the artillery
Colonel Cazals, commanding the engineers
Corps headquarters staff—43 personnel

	Bns/Sqdns	All Ranks Present & Under Arms
1st Infantry Division—*Général de division* Dupont		
Division headquarters staff—15 personnel		
1st Brigade: *Général de brigade* Rouyer		
9th *Légère* Infantry Regiment	(2)	1,120
2nd Brigade: *Général de brigade* Marchand		
32nd Regiment of the *Ligne*	(2)	1,210
96th Regiment of the *Ligne*	(2)	1,135
Attached: 1st Hussars	(3)	239
Division Artillery—		191
One section of horse artillerists serving two 8-pounders—total of two pieces of ordnance.		
One company of foot artillerists serving one 12-pounder, two 8-pounders, two 4-pounders and one 6-inch howitzer—total of eight pieces of ordnance.		
2nd Infantry Division—*Général de division* Loison		
Division headquarters staff—11 personnel		
1st Brigade: *Général de brigade* Villatte		
6th *Légère* Infantry Regiment	(2)	1,728
39th Regiment of the *Ligne*	(2)	1,633
2nd Brigade: *Général de brigade* Rouget		
69th Regiment of the *Ligne*	(2)	1,698
76th Regiment of the *Ligne*	(3)	1,789
Division Artillery—		89
One section of horse artillerists serving one 4-pounder and one 6-inch howitzer—total of two pieces.		
One company of foot artillerists serving three 8-pounders and one 6-inch howitzer—total of four pieces.		
3rd Infantry Division—*Général de division* Malher		
Division headquarters staff—12 personnel		
1st Brigade: *Général de brigade* Marcognet		
25th *Légère* Infantry Regiment	(3)	1,540
27th Regiment of the *Ligne*	(2)	1,347
2nd Brigade: *Général de brigade* Labassée		
50th Regiment of the *Ligne*	(2)	1,547
59th Regiment of the *Ligne*	(2)	1,621
Division Artillery—		65
One company of foot artillerists serving one 12-pounder, four 8-pounders and one 4-pounder—total of six pieces.		
6th Corps Light Cavalry Division—Colonel Auguste de Colbert		
1st Hussars—detached; with Dupont's 1st Infantry Division		
3rd Hussars	(3)	150
10th *Chasseurs à cheval*	(3)	140
6th Corps Artillery —		
Corps artillery reserve staff—7 personnel		
1st Regiment of French Foot Artillery, total of four companies		331
Two companies of foot artillerists were in the 6th Corps Reserve. These gunners manned the following: Four 12-pounders, five 8-pounders, two 4-pounders and one 6-inch howitzer—total of 12 pieces of ordnance.		
2nd Regiment of French Horse Artillery, two sections of the 1st company		65
This company was sub-divided into three sections; one section was serving with Dupont and the remaining two operated together at Elchingen. These two sections manned two 8-pounders and two 6-inch howitzers—total of four pieces.		

3rd & 5th Battalions, French Train of Artillery, five companies		289
Gendarmerie		50
French *Ouvriers* of the Artillery, 1/4 of the 4th Company		19
Total strength of all artillerists and supporting personnel—6th Corps		1,099

4th Dragoon Division(-)

2nd Brigade:: *Général de brigade* Laplanche	Bns/Sqdns	All Ranks Present & Under Arms
18th Regiment of Dragoons	(3)	305
19th Regiment of Dragoons	(3)	290
25th Regiment of Dragoons	(3)	240

Note: *Général de brigade Verdière*, who commanded the 3rd Brigade of this division as it crossed the Rhine, was detached on 16 vendémiaire (8 October) to command the heavy cavalry depot in Harburg. When this occurred, the division's command structure was modified into two brigades of three regiments per brigade.

French totals at Elchingen, excluding staffs—

Infantry	24	16,368	
Cavalry	18	1,364	
Artillerists and supporting personnel, number of companies	12	1,099	
Total Present and Under Arms		18,831	and 36 pieces of ordnance
Total of horses with the artillery and train		N/A	
Total number of personnel in rear areas		N/A	
Total of personnel in hospitals		N/A	
Total effectives—all personnel, excluding general officers & staffs		18,831	and 36 pieces of ordnance

Of this total, Dupont's Division numbered 3,895. Therefore, Marshal Ney had an available force of 14,940 with which to begin the battle.

Source: C[2] 470, 473,482 and *Journal des opérations du 6e Corps*, *Archives du Service Historique de l'État-Major de l'Armée de Terre,* (S.H.A.T.), VINCENNES.

SITUATION of the AUSTRIAN TROOPS at the Battle of Elchingen

14 October 1805

Detachment from the THE AUSTRIAN ARMY OF SWABIA, consisting of the II Column Strengths as of 12 October 1805

FML Count von Riesch

Laudon's Division—FML von Laudon

Advance Guard: GM Prince Coburg	Bns/Sqdns	Notes
Erzherzog Ludwig IR#8	(4)	Three were fusilier battalions and had suffered extremely heavy casualties at Haslach-Jungingen; the remaining battalion was the grenadier battalion.
Hussar-Regiment Blankenstein #6	(2)	
Center Brigade: GM Genegdegh		
Karl Riese IR#15	(4)	All four were fusilier battalions, three of which had been engaged at Haslach-Jungingen.
Erzherzog Maximilien IR#35	(4)	All four were fusilier battalions
Cüirassier-Regiment Hohenzollern #8	(2)	
Uhlanen-Regiment Schwarzenberg #2	(1)	
Reserve Brigade: GM Ulm		
Froon IR#54	(3)	Two were fusilier battalions, and one was grenadier. The two fusilier battalions were cut to pieces at Haslach-Jungingen, while the grenadier battalion was only lightly engaged at Haslach-Jungingen.
Josef Colloredo IR#57	(1)	This unit was the regiment's grenadier battalion.
Cüirassier-Regiment Hohenzollern #8	(2)	

Division Artillery: One cavalry battery, consisting of: four 6-pounder guns and two howitzers—total of six pieces of ordnance. There were no battalion guns present with Laudon's Division.

Hessen-Homburg's Division—FML von Hessen-Homburg

Advance Guard: GM GM Mescery	Bns/Sqdns	Notes
Erbach IR#42	(4)	Three fusilier battalions and one grenadier battalion
Cüirassier-Regiment Erzherzog Franz #2	(2)	
Center Brigade: GM Auersperg		
Erzherzog Karl IR#3	(4)	Three were fusilier battalions and one was grenadier; the regiment had been engaged at Günzburg.
Auersperg IR#24	(4)	All four were fusilier battalions.
Cüirassier-Regiment Erzherzog Franz #2	(1½)	
Reserve Brigade: GM Hermann		
Froon IR#54	(2)	Both were fusilier battalions, and these that had not been engaged at Haslach-Jungingen.
Erzherzog Karl IR#3	(1)	This unit was the grenadier battalion.
Auersperg IR#24	(1)	This unit was the grenadier battalion.
Cüirassier-Regiment Erzherzog Franz #2	(2)	

Division Artillery: Battalion guns only, consisting of 6-pounder guns—total of eight pieces of ordnance. Six of these guns were battalion artillery for the fusilier battalions of Auresperg IR#24, and the remaining two guns were battalion ordnance for Froon IR#54.

Consult Chapter V for further details. Obviously, the number of guns present was nothing close to the two pieces per battalion that that were theoretically supposed to support the infantry—further proof that theoretical establishments were just that.

Austrian Army totals at Elchingen	Bns/Sqdns	Present and Under Arms
Infantry	32	13,300
Cavalry	12 ½	1,250
Artillerists and train personnel serving 14 pieces of ordnance		450
Total:		15,000

Source: österreichischen Kriegsarchiv, Vienna (K.A., F.A. Deutschland 1805).

SITUATION of the *GRANDE ARMÉE*

during the last 15 days of brumaire an XIV (5 through 21 November 1805)

His Majesty

The Emperor Napoleon I, commanding in person

The Emperor's Military Household

Général de division Duroc, Grand Marshal of the Palace
Général de division Caulaincourt, Grand Equerry

Aides-de-Camp to His Majesty:
Général de division Caffarelli du Falga—detached to 3rd Corps
Général de division Junot
Général de division Savary
Général de brigade Bertrand
Général de brigade Lemarois
Général de brigade Mouton
Général de brigade Rapp
Colonel Lebrun

* *

État Major Général
Major Général

Major-Général of the Army—Marshal Berthier, Minister of War

Aides-de-Camp to Marshal Berthier:
Chef d'escadron Girardin
Capitaine Colbert
Capitaine Lejeune
Lieutenant Périgord
Lieutenant LeGrange
Lieutenant Armand Périgord

General Officers Attached to the Major Général

Général de brigade Pannetier
Général de brigade Reille
Général de brigade René
and four aides-de-camp, including Reille's son, who had a rank of lieutenant.

Other Officers Attached to the Major Général

Adjudant commandant LeCamus
Adjudant commandant Dalton

Adjoints to LeCamus and Dalton
Capitaine Simonier
Capitaine Falkowski
Capitaine Mahon
Capitaine LeVaillans
Capitaine de Piré
Capitaine Montholon
Capitaine Destermeaux
Capitaine Tricard
Lieutenant Saraire
Lieutenant Longuerue

Sous Inspecteur aux Revues Duhesme
Colonel du Génie Vallongue
Capitaine de frégate Lostange, commanding the flotilla on the Danube

Extra Officers Attached to the Major Général

Chef de bataillon Desnoyers
Chef de bataillon Blein
Chef de bataillon Parigots
Chef de bataillon Bailly de Monthion
Chef de bataillon Mergès
Chef de bataillon Dalvimar
Chef de bataillon Desnoyers

Suite de l'État Major Général

Officers and Auxiliary Troops In the Service of the Major Général

Bavarian Officers: *Major* Pocci, *Major* DeAubert
Württemberg Officers: *General-Major* von Geismar, *Leutnant* von Spitzemberg
Baden Officer: Grolman, *aide-de-camp to the Grossherzog*
Polish Officers: Colonel Adamistowski, *Chef de bataillon* Junger

Military Administration of the Army

Daru, *Intendant Général of the Army*
Ordonnateur en chef Joinville
plus, a staff of six commissioners

Administrative Services

Chief Baker: LePayen
Chief of Procuring Beef: Mamignard
Chief Forager: Giguet
Chief Surgeon: Poussielgue
Chief of the Ambulance Service: LeGendre
Chief of Military Equipage: Sorlet
Postmaster: Juliac
Chief Printer: Levraux
Telegraph Director: Chappe
Colonel Wolff, Chief Sanitary Officer
Philippe, Assistant Sanitary Officer

Escort Troops

Élite Company, 21st Regiment of Dragoons
Mounted Gendarmes (61 officers and other ranks)
3rd Company, 2nd Battalion of French Engineers

Assistant Chief of Staff—Chief of the General Staff

Général de division Andréossy
Andréossy had three *généraux de brigade,* six *adjudant commandants*, and 24 other officers on his staff.

Assistant Chief of Staff—*Maréchal des Logis*

Général de division Mathieu Dumas
Général de brigade Sauson, Chief of the Topographical Service, plus 16 other officers

Other Officers Attached to the Assistant Chiefs of Staff—

Five colonels and nine *chefs de bataillon*

Artillery

Général de division Songis, Commander of the Artillery
Général de brigade Pernetti, Chief of Staff
Colonel Sénarmont, Assistant Chief of Staff,
plus a staff of 11 other officers

Engineers

Général de division Marescot, Commander of the Engineers
Major Birot Ducoudsary, Chief of Staff
Chef de bataillon Rouzier, General Director of the Engineers in Augsburg,
plus a staff of 12 ofther officers

General Administration of the Army

Intendant Général

Pétiet, Intendant Général,
plus a staff of four commissioners

Administrative Services

Inspector general and chief medical officer: Costé
Inspector general and chief surgeon: Percy
Inspector general and chief pharmacist: Parmentier
Plus eight other personnel.

Attached to the General Staff, Intendent Général

Mounted Gendarmes (40 officers & other ranks)

Administration of Troop Revues

Inspecteur en chef aux Revues Villemanry, plus a staff of four

Total Number of Personnel at Imperial Headquarters—

282, which does not include
The Emperor's Military Houshold, the
Élite Company of the 21st Regiment of Dragoons and the
3rd Company, 2nd Battalion of French Engineers

IMPERIAL GUARD
Strengths as of 30 brumaire an XIV
(21 November 1805)

Marshal Bessières

Général de brigade Roussel, Chief of Staff
Colonel Couin, commanding the artillery
Corps headquarters staff—16 personnel

	Bns/Sqdns	All Ranks Present & Under Arms	
Infantry of the Imperial Guard			
1st Brigade: *Général de brigade* Hulin			
Regiment of *Grenadiers à pied* of the Imperial Guard	(2)	1,549	
2nd Brigade: *Général de brigade* Soulès			
Regiment of *Chasseurs à pied* of the Imperial Guard	(2)	1,281	
3rd Brigade—Regiment of the Royal Italian Guard: Colonel Lecchi			
Battalion of *Grenadiers à pied* and			
Battalion of *Chasseurs à pied* of the Royal Italian Guard	(2)	589	
Cavalry of the Imperial Guard			
1st Brigade: *Général de brigade* Ordener			
Regiment of *Grenadiers à cheval* of the Imperial Guard	(4)	628	
2nd Brigade: Colonel Morland			
Regiment of *Chasseurs à cheval* of the Imperial Guard	(4)	331	
Company of *Mameluks* of the Imperial Guard	(½)	48	
3rd Brigade: *Général de division* Savary			
Regiment of *Gendarmerie d'élite* of the Imperial Guard	(2)	203	
Artillery of the Imperial Guard—			
1st and 2nd Companies of Horse Artillery (*Volante*) of the Imperial Guard			
Company of Horse Artillery of the Royal Italian Guard, one company			
Each of the above three horse artillery companies had identical ordnance, consisting of:			
Four 8-pounders, two 4-pounders and two 6-inch howitzers—			
total of eight pieces of ordnance in each company= 24 total pieces.			
All the artillerists from the three companies totaled		283	
Train of the Imperial Guard Artillery		241	
Flying Ambulance of the Guard (Larrey)			Not available
Total strength of all artillerists and supporting personnel			
for the entire Imperial Guard—		524	
Imperial Guard Totals—			
Infantry	6	3,419	
Cavalry	10 ½	1,210	
Artillerists and supporting personnel, number of companies	5	524	
Total Present and Under Arms		5,153	and 24 pieces of ordnance
Total number of horses with the Imperial Guard	3,100*		
Total number of personnel in rear areas,			
including detachments and personnel in hospitals		1,952	
Total of personnel in hospitals		N/A	
Total effectives—all personnel, including general officers & staffs		7,121	and 24 pieces of ordnance

*Almost 700 of these horses were with officers and men who were detached and currently not present with the main body.

1st CORPS
Strengths as of 18 brumaire an XIV (9 November 1805)

Marshal Bernadotte

Général de division Victor-Léopold Berthier, Chief of Staff
Général de division Jean-Baptiste Eblé, commanding the artillery
Colonel Morio, commanding the engineers
Corps headquarters staff—34 personnel

	Bns/Sqdns	All Ranks Present & Under Arms
Advance Guard of the 1st Corps—*Général de division* Kellermann		
Advance Guard headquarters staff—17 personnel		
1st Brigade: *Général de brigade* Frere		
27th *Légère* Infantry Regiment	(3)	2,041
2nd Brigade: *Général de brigade* Picard		
4th Hussars	(3)	501
5th *Chasseurs à cheval*	(3)	489
Advance Guard artillery and train:		
1st Company, 3rd Regiment of Horse Artillery, with:		79
Two 6-pounders, two 3-pounders and two 5.3-inch howitzers—total of six pieces of ordnance.		
8th Company, 2nd Battalion of French Engineers		61
2nd Battalion, Train of Artillery, one company		78
1st Infantry Division—*Général de division* Rivaud de la Raffinière		
Division headquarters staff—14 personnel		
1st Brigade: *Général de brigade* Dumoulin		
8th Regiment of the *Ligne*	(3)	1,835
2nd Brigade: *Général de brigade* Pacthod		
45th Regiment of the *Ligne*	(3)	1,613
54th Regiment of the *Ligne*	(3)	1,509
Division artillery and train:		
8th Regiment of Foot Artillery, one company consisting of:		56
Four 3-pounders and one 5.3-inch howitzer—total of five pieces of ordnance		
3rd Regiment of Horse Artillery, one company consisting of:		77
Four 6-pounders and one 5.3-inch howitzer—total of five pieces of ordnance		
2nd Battalion, Train of Artillery, two companies		127
2nd Infantry Division—*Général de division* Drouet		
Division headquarters staff—17 personnel		
1st Brigade: *Général de brigade* Van Marisy		
2nd Hussars	(3)	491
5th Hussars	(3)	385
2nd Brigade: *Général de brigade* Werlé		
94th Regiment of the *Ligne*	(3)	1,858
95th Regiment of the *Ligne*	(3)	2,100
Division artillery and train:		
8th Regiment of Foot Artillery, one company consisting of:		55
Five 3-pounders and one 5.3-inch howitzer—total of six pieces of ordnance		
3rd Regiment of Horse Artillery, one company consisting of:		85
Five 6-pounders and one 5.3-inch howitzer—total of six pieces of ordnance		
2nd Battalion, Train of Artillery, two companies		171
Advance Guard of the Bavarian Army—General-Leutnant Baron von Wrede		
Bavarian Advance Guard headquarters staff—Numbers not available		
1st Brigade: Major General Minneri		
5th Infantry Regiment *Preysing*	(2)	1,317
7th Infantry Regiment	(2)	1,378
1st Light Infantry Battalion *Metzen*	(1)	687
1st Chevaulegers Regiment *Kronprinz*	(4)	207
1st Dragoon Regiment *Minucci*	(4)	232
5th Brigade: Major General Count Minucci		
8th Infantry Regiment *Herzog Pius*	(2)	1,282
12th Infantry Regiment *Löwenstein*	(2)	1,286
4th Light Infantry Battalion *Stengel*	(1)	590
3rd Chevaulegers Regiment *Leningen*	(4)	227
Company of Bavarian Horse Artillery, consisting of:		169
Four 6-pounder guns and two howitzers—total of six pieces of ordnance		
Infantry Regimental Artillery: Eight 6-pounder guns attached, with two guns supporting each of the four infantry regiments.		

1st Corps Artillery Reserve—

Corps artillery reserve staff—5 personnel			
8th Regiment of Foot Artillery, one company—personnel only		154	
3rd Regiment of Horse Artillery, one company		85	
Only the above horse artillery company had ordnance, with:			
Four 6-pounders and two 5.3-inch howitzers—total of six pieces of ordnance.			
2nd Battalion, Train of Artillery, two companies		236	
Pontonniers, one company and *Ouvriers* of the Artillery, ½ company		124	
Total strength of artillerists and supporting personnel in the 1st Corps Artillery Reserve—		599	

1st Corps Totals—

French Infantry	18	10,956	
French Cavalry	12	1,866	
French artillerists and supporting personnel, # of companies	14 ½	1,388	
Total French Present and Under Arms		14,210	and 34 pieces of ordnance
Bavarian Infantry	10	6,540	
Bavarian Cavalry	12	666	
Bavarian artillerists and supporting personnel, # of companies	1	169	
Total Bavarians Present and Under Arms		7,375	and 14 pieces of ordnance
Total French and Bavarians Present and Under Arms		21,585	and 48 pieces of ordnance
Total number of horses with the 1st Corps	3,948		
Total number of personnel in rear areas, including detachments and personnel in hospitals		1,937	
Total effectives—all personnel, including general officers & staffs		23,522	and 48 pieces of ordnance

2nd CORPS
Strengths as of 18 brumaire an XIV (9 November 1805)

***Général de division* Marmont**

Général de division Vignolle, Chief of Staff
Général de brigade Tirlet, commanding the artillery
Colonel Somis, commanding the engineers
Corps headquarters staff—38 personnel

	Bns/Sqdns	All Ranks Present & Under Arms
1st Infantry Division—*Général de division* Boudet		
Division headquarters staff—18 personnel		
1st Brigade: *Général de brigade* Dessaix		
18th *Légère* Infantry Regiment	(2)	1,440
2nd Brigade: *Général de brigade* Soyez		
11th Regiment of the *Ligne*	(3)	1,929
35th Regiment of the *Ligne*	(2)	1,450
Division artillery and train:		
8th Regiment of French Foot Artillery, 3rd Company and one-half of the 9th Company		119
7th Battalion, French Train of Artillery, one company		134
2nd Infantry Division—*Général de division* Grouchy		
Division headquarters staff—17 personnel		
1st Brigade: *Général de brigade* Lacroix		
84th Regiment of the *Ligne*	(3)	1,949
92nd Regiment of the *Ligne*	(3)	2,203
2nd Brigade: *Général de brigade* Delzona		
8th Batavian Regiment of the *Ligne*	(2)	310
Division artillery and train:		
8th Regiment of French Foot Artillery, 4th Company and one-half of the 9th Company		96
7th Battalion, French Train of Artillery, one company		146
3rd Infantry Division—*Général de division* Dumonceau—detached to Marshal Mortier		
2nd Corps Light Cavalry Division—*Général de division* Lacoste		
Corps cavalry division staff—6 personnel		
1st Brigade: *Général de brigade* —		
6th Hussars	(3)	426
8th *Chasseurs à cheval*	(3)	452
2nd Brigade: *Général de brigade* Quaita		
Batavian Light Dragoons	(2)	227
Batavian Hussars	(2)	123
2nd Corps Artillery Reserve—		
Corps artillery reserve staff—12 personnel		
8th Regiment of French Foot Artillery, 7th Company		75
7th Battalion, French Train of Artillery, 4th, 5th & 6th Companies		192
7th Battalion, French Train of Artillery, *Ouvriers*		19
French *Ouvriers* of the Artillery, 8th Company		39
2nd Regiment of Batavian Foot Artillery, 1st Company		77
2nd Regiment of Batavian Foot Artillery, 4th Company		83
Batavian Horse Artillery, 1st Company		110
Batavian Train of Artillery, one company		48
Batavian *Pontonniers*, detachment		21
2nd French Engineer Battalion, 1st Company		71
Total strength of all artillerists and supporting personnel for the 2nd Corps Artillery Reserve—		2,100
2nd Corps Totals—		
Infantry	15	9,281
Cavalry	10	1,228
Artillerists and supporting personnel, number of companies	15 +	736
Total Present and Under Arms		11,245 and 18 pieces of ordnance
Total number of horses with the 2nd Corps	2,550	
Total number of personnel in rear areas, including detachments and personnel in hospitals		2,872
Total effectives—all personnel, including general officers & staffs		14,208 and 18 pieces of ordnance

3rd CORPS
Strengths as of 14 brumaire an XIV (5 November 1805)

Marshal Davout

Général de brigade Fournier de Loysonville Daultane, Chief of Staff
Général de division Sorbier, commanding the artillery
Général de brigade Andreossy, commanding the engineers
Corps headquarters staff—46 personnel

	Bns/Sqdns	All Ranks Present & Under Arms
Advance Guard of the 3rd Corps—*Général de brigade* Heudelet		
Advance Guard headquarters staff—12 personnel		
1st Brigade: *Général de brigade* Eppler		
13th *Légère* Infantry Regiment	(2)	1,619
108th Regiment of the *Ligne*	(2)	1,728
2nd Brigade: *Général de brigade* —		
2nd *Chasseurs à cheval*	(3)	290
12th *Chasseurs à cheval*	(3)	293
Advance Guard artillery and train:		
7th Regiment of Foot Artillery, detachment		30
1st Battalion, Train of Artillery, detachment		22
1st Infantry Division—*Général de division* Caffarelli du Falga		
Division headquarters staff—20 personnel		
2nd Brigade: *Général de brigade* Debilly		
17th Regiment of the *Ligne*	(2)	1,514
30th Regiment of the *Ligne*	(2)	1,253
3rd Brigade: *Général de brigade* Demont		
51st Regiment of the *Ligne*	(2)	1,300
61st Regiment of the *Ligne*	(2)	1,280
Division artillery and train:		
7th Regiment of Foot Artillery, one company		73
1st Battalion, Train of Artillery, one company		85
2nd Infantry Division—*Général de division* Friant		
Division headquarters staff—21 personnel		
1st Brigade: *Général de brigade* Kister		
15th *Légère* Infantry Regiment*	(2)	813 *
2nd Brigade: *Général de brigade* Lochet		
48th Regiment of the *Ligne*	(2)	1,261
111th Regiment of the *Ligne*	(2)	1,722
3rd Brigade: *Général de brigade* Grandeau		
33rd Regiment of the *Ligne*	(2)	1,363
Division artillery and train:		
7th Regiment of Foot Artillery, one company		88
1st Battalion, Train of Artillery, one company		98
*Six companies of the 15th *Légère* were detached from the regiment and formed the 2nd Battalion, 5th Regiment of the *Grenadiers de la Réserve* in 5th Corps.		
3rd Infantry Division—*Général de division* Gudin		
Division headquarters staff—20 personnel		
1st Brigade: *Général de brigade* Petit		
12th Regiment of the *Ligne*	(2)	1,430
21st Regiment of the *Ligne*	(2)	1,619
2nd Brigade: *Général de brigade* Gauthier		
25th Regiment of the *Ligne*	(2)	1,565
85th Regiment of the *Ligne*	(2)	1,473
Division artillery and train:		
7th Regiment of Foot Artillery, one company		87
1st Battalion, Train of Artillery, one company		98
3rd Corps Light Cavalry Division—*Général de brigade* Viallanes		
Corps cavalry division staff—4 personnel		
1st Brigade: *Général de brigade* —		
1st *Chasseurs à cheval*	(3)	275
7th Hussars	(3)	457

3rd Corps Artillery Reserve—

Corps artillery reserve staff—5 personnel			
7th Regiment of French Foot Artillery, 21/2 companies		175	
5th Regiment of French Horse Artillery, 5th company		89	
1st and 2nd Battalions, French Train of Artillery, 21/2 companies		192	
French *Pontonniers*, detachment		43	
French *Ouvriers* of the Artillery		26	
French Engineers, one company		70	
Total strength of all artillerists and supporting personnel for the 3rd Corps Artillery Reserve—		552	

3rd Corps Totals—

Infantry	28	19,940	
Cavalry	12	1,315	
Artillerists and supporting personnel, number of companies	13	1,133	
Total Present and Under Arms		22,388	and 48 pieces of ordnance
Total number of horses with the 3rd Corps	2,559		
Total number of personnel in rear areas, including detachments and personnel in hospitals		4,873	
Total effectives—all personnel, including general officers & staffs		27,380	and 48 pieces of ordnance

4th CORPS
Strengths as of 16 brumaire an XIV (7 November 1805)

Marshal Soult

Général de division Salligny, Chief of Staff
Général de brigade Lariboissière, commanding the artillery
Colonel Poitevin, commanding the engineers
Corps headquarters staff—42 personnel

	Bns/Sqdns	All Ranks Present & Under Arms
1st Infantry Division—*Général de division* Saint Hilaire		
Division headquarters staff—21 personnel		
1st Brigade: *Général de brigade* Morand		
10th *Légère* Infantry Regiment	(2)	1,478
2nd Brigade: *Général de brigade* Thiébault		
14th Regiment of the *Ligne*	(2)	1,589
36th Regiment of the *Ligne*	(2)	1,643
3rd Brigade: *Général de brigade* Waré		
43rd Regiment of the *Ligne*	(2)	1,687
55th Regiment of the *Ligne*	(2)	1,714
Division artillery and train:		
5th Regiment of Foot Artillery, 12th Company		98
5th Regiment of Foot Artillery, detachment of the 16th Company		22
1st Battalion, Train of Artillery, one company		108
2nd Battalion of French Engineers, 9th Company		47
2nd Infantry Division—*Général de division* Vandamme		
Division headquarters staff—23 personnel		
1st Brigade: *Général de brigade* Schiner		
24th *Légère* Infantry Regiment	(2)	1,310
2nd Brigade: *Général de brigade* Férey		
4th Regiment of the *Ligne*	(2)	1,822
28th Regiment of the *Ligne*	(2)	1,636
3rd Brigade: *Général de brigade* Candras		
46th Regiment of the *Ligne*	(2)	1,559
57th Regiment of the *Ligne*	(2)	1,771
Division artillery and train:		
5th Regiment of Foot Artillery, 13th Company		95
5th Regiment of Foot Artillery, detachment of the 16th Company		22
2nd Battalion, Train of Artillery, one company		132
3rd Infantry Division—*Général de division* Legrand		
Division headquarters staff—20 personnel		
1st Brigade: *Général de brigade* Merle		
26th *Légère* Infantry Regiment	(2)	1,587
Tirailleurs du Pô	(1)	547
2nd Brigade: *Général de brigade* Lavasseur		
18th Regiment of the *Ligne*	(2)	1,507
75th Regiment of the *Ligne*	(2)	1,532
Tirailleurs corses	(1)	635
3rd Brigade: *Général de brigade* Féry		
3rd Regiment of the *Ligne*	(3)	1,888
Division artillery and train:		
5th Regiment of Foot Artillery, 14th Company		94
5th Regiment of Foot Artillery, detachment of the 16th Company		22
3rd Battalion, Train of Artillery, one company		101
4th Corps Light Cavalry Division—*Général de brigade* Margaron		
Corps cavalry division staff—7 personnel		
1st Brigade: *Général de brigade* Margaron		
8th Hussars	(3)	276
11th *Chasseurs à cheval*	(4)	317
26th *Chasseurs à cheval*	(3)	331
Division artillery and train:		
5th Regiment of Horse Artillery, 4th Company		91
3rd Battalion, Train of Artillery, one company		52

4th Corps Artillery Reserve—

Corps artillery reserve staff—5 personnel			
5th Regiment of Foot Artillery, 17th and 18th Companies		199	
1st Battalion, Train of Artillery, one company		56	
French *Ouvriers* of the Artillery, ½ company		46	
French Armorers, detachment		12	
Total strength of all personnel—4th Corps Artillery Reserve		313	

4th Corps Totals—

Infantry	31	23,905	
Cavalry	10	924	
Artillerists and supporting personnel, number of companies	14 ½	1,197	
Total Present and Under Arms		26,026	and 36 pieces of ordnance
Total number of horses with the 4th Corps	1,932		
Total number of personnel in rear areas, including detachments and personnel in hospitals		4,661	
Total effectives—all personnel, including general officers & staffs		30,805	and 36 pieces of ordnance

5th CORPS
Strengths as of 15 brumaire an XIV (6 November 1805)

Marshal Lannes

Général de brigade Compans, Chief of Staff
Général de brigade Foucher de Careil, commanding the artillery
Colonel Kirgener, commanding the engineers
Corps headquarters staff—20 personnel

	Bns/Sqdns	All Ranks Present & Under Arms
1st Infantry Division (*Grenadiers de la Réserve*)—*Général de division* Oudinot		
Division headquarters staff—22 personnel		
1st Brigade: *Général de brigade* Laplanche-Morthières		
1st Grenadier Regiment		
1st *bataillon d'élite* from the 13th *Ligne*	(1)	596
2nd *bataillon d'élite* from the 58th *Ligne*	(1)	652
2nd Grenadier Regiment		
1st *bataillon d'élite* from the 9th *Ligne*	(1)	569
2nd *bataillon d'élite* from the 81st *Ligne*	(1)	684
2nd Brigade: *Général de brigade* Dupas		
3rd Grenadier Regiment		
1st *bataillon d'élite* from the 2nd *Légère*	(1)	495
2nd *bataillon d'élite* from the 3rd *Légère*	(1)	517
4th Grenadier Regiment		
1st *bataillon d'élite* from the 28th *Légère*	(1)	447
2nd *bataillon d'élite* from the 31st *Légère*	(1)	392
3rd Brigade: *Général de brigade* Ruffin		
5th Grenadier Regiment		
1st *bataillon d'élite* from the 12th *Légère*	(1)	492
2nd *bataillon d'élite* from the 15th *Légère*	(1)	493
Division artillery and train:		
1st Company, 1st Regiment of Foot Artillery, and Detachment of the 4th Company, 5th Regiment of Horse Art—all artillerists		171
5th Battalion, Train of Artillery, two companies		191
2nd French Engineer Battalion, 2nd Company		72
2nd Infantry Division—*Général de division* Gazan—detached to Marshal Mortier		
3rd Infantry Division—*Général de division* Suchet		
Division headquarters staff—23 personnel		
1st Brigade: *Général de brigade* Claparède		
17th *Légère* Infantry Regiment	(2)	1,457
2nd Brigade: *Général de brigade* Beker		
34th Regiment of the *Ligne*	(3)	1,270
40th Regiment of the *Ligne*	(2)	1,394
3rd Brigade: *Général de brigade* Valhubert		
64th Regiment of the *Ligne*	(2)	1,016
88th Regiment of the *Ligne*	(2)	1,602
Division artillery and train:		
5th Regiment of Foot Artillery, one company		125
3rd Battalion, Train of Artillery, one company		113
5th Corps Light Cavalry Division—*Général de brigade* Fauconnet		
Corps cavalry division staff—11 personnel		
1st Brigade: *Général de brigade* Treillard		
9th Hussars	(3)	231
10th Hussars	(3)	261
2nd Brigade: *Général de brigade* Fauconnet		
13th *Chasseurs à cheval*	(3)	259
21st *Chasseurs à cheval*	(3)	235
5th Corps Totals—		
Infantry	21	12,076
Cavalry	12	986
Artillerists and supporting personnel, number of companies	7	672
Total Present and Under Arms		13,734 and 24 pieces of ordnance
Total number of horses with the 5th Corps	1,867	
Total number of personnel in rear areas, including detachments and personnel in hospitals		4,662
Total effectives—all personnel, including general officers & staffs		18,472 and 24 pieces of ordnance

6th CORPS
Strengths as of 15 brumaire an XIV (6 November 1805)

Marshal Ney

Général de brigade Dutaillis, Chief of Staff
Général de brigade Séroux, commanding the artillery
Colonel Cazals, commanding the engineers
Corps headquarters staff—45 personnel

1st Infantry Division—*Général de division* Dupont—detached to Marshal Mortier

	Bns/Sqdns	All Ranks Present & Under Arms
2nd Infantry Division—*Général de division* Loison		
Division headquarters staff—14 personnel		
1st Brigade: *Général de brigade* Villate		
6th *Légère* Infantry Regiment	(2)	1,700
39th Regiment of the *Ligne*	(2)	1,600
2nd Brigade: *Général de brigade* Rouget		
69th Regiment of the *Ligne*	(2)	1,317
76th Regiment of the *Ligne*	(3)	1,616
3rd Infantry Division—*Général de division* Malher		
Division headquarters staff—15 personnel		
1st Brigade: *Général de brigade* Marcognet		
25th *Légère* Infantry Regiment	(3)	1,329
27th Regiment of the *Ligne*	(2)	1,543
2nd Brigade: *Général de brigade* Labassée		
50th Regiment of the *Ligne*	(2)	1,158
59th Regiment of the *Ligne*	(2)	1,450
6th Corps Light Cavalry Division—*Général de division* Tilly		
Corps cavalry division staff—5 personnel		
1st Brigade: *Général de brigade* Duprès		
1st Hussars, detachment	(-)	20
3rd Hussars	(3)	202
10th *Chasseurs à cheval*	(3)	157
6th Corps Artillery Reserve—		
Corps artillery reserve staff—Return not available		
1st Regiment of French Foot Artillery, 9th, 10th & 11th Companies		241
2nd Regiment of French Horse Artillery, detachment from 1st Company		42
3rd & 5th Battalions, French Train of Artillery, four companies, and detachments of two others		255
Detachment of French Infantry soldiers,		71
French *Ouvriers* of the Artillery, 1/2 of the 4th Company		12
Total strength of all personnel—6th Corps Artillery Reserve		621
6th Corps Totals—		
Infantry	18	11,713
Cavalry	6	379
Artillerists and supporting personnel, number of companies	8 +	621
Total Present and Under Arms		12,713 and 28 pieces of ordnance
Total number of horses with the 6th Corps	1,432	
Total number of personnel in rear areas, including detachments and personnel in hospitals		3,957
Total effectives—all personnel, including general officers & staffs		16,749 and 28 pieces of ordnance

7th CORPS
Strengths as of 4 brumaire an XIV (26 October 1805)

Marshal Augereau

Général de brigade Donzelot, Chief of Staff
Général de division Dorsner, commanding the artillery
Colonel Lagastine, commanding the engineers
Corps headquarters staff—46 personnel

	Bns/Sqdns	All Ranks Present & Under Arms
1st Infantry Division—*Général de division* Desjardins		
Division headquarters staff—21 personnel		
1st Brigade: *Général de brigade* Lapissè		
16th *Légère* Infantry Regiment	(3)	2,056
2nd Brigade: *Général de brigade* Lamarque		
44th Regiment of the *Ligne*	(2)	1,199
105th Regiment of the *Ligne*	(2)	1,595
Attached:		
7th *Chasseurs à cheval*	(4)	584
2nd Infantry Division—*Général de division* Maurice Mathieu		
Division headquarters staff—19 personnel		
1st Brigade: *Général de brigade* Sarut		
7th *Légère* Infantry Regiment	(2)	2,181
63rd Regiment of the *Ligne*	(2)	1,364
2nd Brigade: *Général de brigade* Sarazin		
24th Regiment of the *Ligne*	(3)	2,100
7th Corps Artillery Reserve—		
Corps artillery reserve staff—6 personnel		
3rd Regiment of French Foot Artillery, 2nd, 3rd, 4th & 5th Cos.		247
6th Regiment of French Horse Artillery, 5th company		76
8th Battalion, French Train of Artillery, 1st through 6th Companies		478
French Miners, detachment of the 7th Company		52
French *Ouvriers* of the Artillery, ½ of the 6th Company		53
4th Battalion of French Engineers, 2nd and 4th Companies		165
Total strength of all artillerists and supporting personnel for the entire 7th Corps—		1,071
7th Corps Totals—		
Infantry	14	10,495
Cavalry	4	584
Artillerists and supporting personnel, number of companies	14 ½	1,071
Total Present and Under Arms		12,150 and 24 pieces of ordnance
Total number of horses with the 7th Corps	1,137	
Total number of personnel in rear areas, including detachments and personnel in hospitals		1,509
Total effectives—all personnel, including general officers & staffs		13,751 and 24 pieces of ordnance

PROVISIONAL CORPS
Strengths as of 24 brumaire an XIV (15 November 1805)

Marshal Mortier
Général de brigade Godinot, Chief of Staff
Corps headquarters staff—4 personnel

	Bns/Sqdns	All Ranks Present & Under Arms	
1st Infantry Division (from 6th Corps)—*Général de division* Dupont			
Division headquarters staff—19 personnel			
1st Brigade: *Général de brigade* Rouyer			
9th *Légère* Infantry Regiment	(2)	1,162	
2nd Brigade: *Général de brigade* Marchand			
32nd Regiment of the *Ligne*	(2)	1,109	
96th Regiment of the *Ligne*	(2)	1,326	
Attached:			
1st Hussars	(3)	238	
Division Artillery and Train—			
Detachment of the 2nd Regiment of Horse Artillery, with		38	
Two 8-pounder guns—total of two pieces			
1st Regiment of Foot Artillery, one company, serving		91	
Two 4-pounders and four 6-inch howitzers—total of six pieces.			
3rd Battalion, Train of Artillery, one company and *ouvriers*		86	
2nd Infantry Division (from the 5th Corps)—*Général de division* Gazan			
Division headquarters staff—16 personnel			
1st Brigade: *Général de brigade* Graindorge			
4th *Légère* Infantry Regiment	(3)	458	
58th Regiment of the Ligne	(2)		detached—at Braunau
2nd Brigade: *Général de brigade* Campana			
100th Regiment of the *Ligne*	(3)	1,519	
103rd Regiment of the *Ligne*	(3)	1,492	
Attached:			
4th Regiment of Dragoons	(3)	108	
Division Artillery and Train—			
Detachment of Horse Artillery, with		46	
Two 8-pounder guns—total of two pieces			
Foot Artillery, one company, serving		91	
Two 12-pounders, four 8-pounders, two 4-pounders and two 6-inch howitzers—total of 10 pieces.			
Train of Artillery, one company		108	
3rd Infantry Division (from 2nd Corps)— *Général de division* Dumonceau			
Division headquarters staff—22 personnel			
1st Brigade: *Général de brigade* Van Heldring			
1st and 2nd Batavian *Légère* Infantry Regiments (1 Bn each)	(2)	860	
1st Batavian Regiment of the *Ligne*	(2)		detached
2nd Batavian Regiment of the *Ligne*	(2)	699	
2nd Brigade: *Général de brigade* Van Hadel			
Régiment de Waldeck	(2)	828	
6th Batavian Regiment of the *Ligne*	(2)	884	
Attached:			
2nd Batavian Light Dragoons	(2)	230	
Division Artillery and Train, with:			
Six 4-pounders and two howitzers—total of eight pieces of ordnance			detached
Provisional Corps Totals—			
Infantry	23	10,337	
Cavalry	8	576	
Artillerists and supporting personnel, number of companies	4 ⅔	486	
Total Present and Under Arms		11,399	and 26 pieces of ordnance
Total number of horses with the Provisional Corps	1,047		
Total number of personnel in rear areas, including detachments and personnel in hospitals		7,443	
Total effectives—all personnel, including general officers & staffs		18,903	and 26 pieces of ordnance

Corps des Réserves de Cavalerie
Strengths as of 30 brumaire an XIV (21 November 1805)

Marshal Murat

Général de division Belliard, Chief of Staff
Général de brigade Hanicque, commanding the artillery
Colonel Hayelle, commanding the engineers
Corps headquarters staff—35 personnel

	Bns/Sqdns	All Ranks Present & Under Arms
1st Heavy Cavalry Division—*Général de division* Nansouty		
Division headquarters staff—17 personnel		
1st Brigade: *Général de brigade* Piston		
1st Regiment of *Carabiniers*	(3)	232
2nd Regiment of *Carabiniers*	(3)	239
2nd Brigade: *Général de brigade* La Houssaye		
1st Regiment of *Cuirassiers*	(3)	350
2nd Regiment of *Cuirassiers*	(3)	305
3rd Brigade: *Général de brigade* Saint-Germain		
3rd Regiment of *Cuirassiers*	(3)	291
5th Regiment of *Cuirassiers*	(3)	335
2nd Heavy Cavalry Division—*Général de division* d'Hautpoul		
Division headquarters staff—13 personnel		
1st Brigade: Colonel Noirot		
9th Regiment of *Cuirassiers*	(3)	318
12th Regiment of *Cuirassiers*	(3)	298
2nd Brigade: *Général de brigade* Saint-Sulpice		
10th Regiment of *Cuirassiers*	(3)	260
11th Regiment of *Cuirassiers*	(3)	333
1st Dragoon Division—*Général de division* Klein		
Division headquarters staff—15 personnel		
1st Brigade: *Général de brigade* Senerols		
1st Regiment of Dragoons	(3)	321
2nd Regiment of Dragoons	(3)	253
2nd Brigade: *Général de brigade* Lasalle		
4th Regiment of Dragoons	(3)	319
20th Regiment of Dragoons	(3)	283
3rd Brigade: *Général de brigade* Milet		
14th Regiment of Dragoons	(3)	257
26th Regiment of Dragoons	(3)	360
2nd Dragoon Division—*Général de division* Walther		
Division headquarters staff—18 personnel		
1st Brigade: *Général de brigade* Sébastiani de la Porta		
3rd Regiment of Dragoons	(3)	258
6th Regiment of Dragoons	(3)	284
2nd Brigade: *Général de brigade* Roget de Belloguet		
10th Regiment of Dragoons	(3)	225
11th Regiment of Dragoons	(3)	347
3rd Brigade: *Général de brigade* Boussart		
13th Regiment of Dragoons	(3)	268
22nd Regiment of Dragoons	(3)	152
3rd Dragoon Division—*Général de division* Beaumont		
Division headquarters staff—12 personnel		
1st Brigade: *Général de brigade* Boyé		
5th Regiment of Dragoons	(3)	234
8th Regiment of Dragoons	(3)	289
2nd Brigade: *Général de brigade* Scalfort		
9th Regiment of Dragoons	(3)	297
12th Regiment of Dragoons	(3)	291
3rd Brigade: *Général de brigade* Milhaud		
16th Regiment of Dragoons	(3)	242
21st Regiment of Dragoons	(2½)	240

	Bns/Sqdns	All Ranks Present & Under Arms
4th Dragoon Division—*Général de division* Bourcier		
Division headquarters staff—18 personnel		
1st Brigade: *Général de brigade* Sahuc		
15th Regiment of Dragoons	(3)	227
17th Regiment of Dragoons	(3)	290
27th Regiment of Dragoons	(3)	214
2nd Brigade: *Général de brigade* Laplanche		
18th Regiment of Dragoons	(3)	279
19th Regiment of Dragoons	(3)	266
25th Regiment of Dragoons	(3)	220
Division of *Dragons à pied*—*Général de division* Baraguey d'Hilliers		
These troops were without horses and were utilized as infantry.		
Division headquarters staff—16 personnel		
1st Brigade: *Général de brigade* Lesuire		
1st Regiment of *Dragons à pied*	(2)	963
2nd Regiment of *Dragons à pied*	(2)	1,004
2nd Brigade: *Général de brigade* Brouard		
3rd Regiment of *Dragons à pied*	(2)	1,241
4th Regiment of *Dragons à pied*	(2)	795
Light Cavalry Brigade—*Général de brigade* Milhaud		
Brigade headquarters staff—11 personnel		
1st Brigade: *Général de brigade* Milhaud		
16th *Chasseurs à cheval*	(3)	338
22nd *Chasseurs à cheval*	(3)	272

***Corps des Réserves de Cavalerie* Artillery —**

Corps artillery reserve staff—6 personnel	
1st Regiment of French Foot Artillery, two companies	138
These two companies were attached to the *Dragons à pied* and totaled the following ordnance: Two 12-pounders, four 8-pounders, two 4-pounders and two 6-inch howitzers—total 10 pieces.	
2nd & 6th Regiments of French Horse Artillery, three companies	158
These three companies were each divided into six half-companies. One half-company was attached to each division of cavalry. Every half-company had identical ordnance composition, which was: Two 8-pounder guns and one 6-inch howitzer, for a total of three pieces per half-company—total 18 pieces.	
2nd Battalion, French Train of Artillery, three companies	158
2nd Battalion of French Engineers, 7th Company	52
Total strength of all artillerists and supporting personnel for the entire *Corps des Réserves de Cavalerie* —	506

***Corps des Réserves de Cavalerie* Totals—**

Infantry (*Dragons à pied*)	8	4,003	
Cavalry	107 ½	9,987	
Artillerists and supporting personnel, number of companies	9	506	
Total Present and Under Arms		14,496	and 28 pieces of ordnance
Total number of horses with the Cavalry Reserve	13,208		
Total number of personnel in rear areas, including detachments and personnel in hospitals		6,106	
Total effectives—all personnel, including general officers & staffs		20,746	and 28 pieces of ordnance

Note: In double-checking the accuracy of the return, the author noted that an error was made in bringing forward the totals of the 3rd Dragoon Division. The numbers shown above reflect the author's corrections to the original document.

Grand Parc d'Artillerie
Strengths as of 11 brumaire an XIV (2 November 1805)

Colonel Vermot, Director

Grand Parc d'Artillerie headquarters staff—32 personnel

Grand Parc d'Artillerie

	Companies	All Ranks Present & Under Arms
French Foot Artillery, 12 companies		1,050
French Horse Artillery, four companies		260
The 16 companies of artillerists manned the following French ordnance: Seventeen 12-pounders, thirty-seven 8-pounders, thirteen 4-pounders and nineteen 6-inch howitzers—total 86 pieces.		
Also available for use were the following captured Austrian ordnance: Seven 12-pounders, forty-four 6-pounders, thirty-one 3-pounders, fourteen howitzers and two garrison howitzers—total 98 pieces.		
1st Battalion, French *Pontonnier*s, three companies		280
French *Ouvriers* of the Artillery, two companies		210
French Armorers, ½ company		45
French Train of Artillery, 20 companies		1,959
French Train of *Ouvriers* of the Artillery, ½ company		28
Total strength of all artillerists and supporting personnel for the entire *Grand Parc d'Artillerie*—		3,832

***Grand Parc d'Artillerie* Totals—**

Artillerists and supporting personnel, number of companies	42	3,832
Total Present and Under Arms		3,832 and 184 pieces of ordnance
Total number of horses with the Grand Park	1,965	
Total number of personnel in rear areas		N/A
Total of personnel in hospitals		N/A
Total effectives—all personnel, including general officers & staffs		3,864 and 184 pieces of ordnance

ALLIED TROOPS EMPLOYED AS GARRISONS IN THE REAR AREAS OF THE ARMY
Strengths as of 12 brumaire an XIV (3 November 1805)

Württemberg Division—*Général de division* Baron de Séeger—in Braunau	Bns/Sqdns	All Ranks Present & Under Arms
Baron Hügel, Chief of Staff		
Division headquarters staff—11 personnel		
1st Brigade: *Général de brigade* von Lilienberg		
Infantry Regiment *Prinz Paul*	(1)	590
Infantry Regiment *von Seckendorf*	(1)	600
Infantry Regiment *von Lilienberg*	(1)	590
2nd Brigade: Colonel von Roman		
Jäger Battalion *König*	(1)	320
Jäger Battalion *von Neuffer*	(1)	329
Light Infantry Battalion *von Scheler*	(1)	442
König Chevaulegers	(1)	102
Division artillery and train:		
Württemberg Horse Artillery, one-half company		46
Württemberg Foot Artillery, one-half company		52
The artillerists manned the following pieces, with:		
Six 6-pounder guns and two 7-pounder howitzers—total of eight pieces of ordnance.		
Württemberg Train of Artillery		62
Health and Sanitary Officers		5
Württemberg Division Totals—		
Division Staff	-	11
Infantry	6	2,871
Cavalry	1	102
Artillerists and supporting personnel, number of companies	1 ½	165
Total Present and Under Arms		3,149 and 8 pieces of ordnance
Total number of horses with the Würtembergers	257	
Total number of personnel detached in rear areas		183
Total number of personnel in route to join the division		2,500
Total effectives—all personnel, including general officers & staffs		5,832 and 8 pieces of ordnance

(Also, please see Appendix J).

Baden Brigade—*Général de brigade* de Harranth—in Augsburg		
Brigade headquarters staff—3 personnel		
1st Brigade: *Général de brigade* de Harranth		
1st Regiment *Grossherzog*, 1st Battalion	(1)	435
1st Regiment *Grossherzog*, 2nd Battalion	(1)	529
2nd Regiment *Erbgrossherzog*, 1st Battalion	(1)	456
2nd Regiment *Erbgrossherzog*, 2nd Battalion	(1)	397
Jäger Battalion de Lingg	(1)	339
Hussars	(-)	24
Baden Foot Artillery Company		141
All personnel, number of battalions or squadrons	5	
Total Present and Under Arms		2,321 and 8 pieces of ordnance

1st Division of the Bavarian Army—General-Leutnant Baron von Deroi

Bavarian Division headquarters staff—Numbers not available		
2nd Brigade: General-Major Marsigli		
1st Infantry Regiment *Leib Gardes*	(2)	1,398
2nd Infantry Regiment *Kronprinz*	(2)	1,398
5th Light Infantry Battalion *LaMotte*	(1)	706
2nd Dragoon Regiment *Taxis*	(4)	479
3rd Brigade: General-Major Count Mezzanelli		
3rd Infantry Regiment *Prinz Karl*	(2)	1,398
4th Infantry Regiment *Salern*	(2)	1,398
2nd Light Infantry Battalion *Vincenti*	(1)	706
4th Brigade: General-Major Baron Karg		
6th Infantry Regiment *Herzog Wilhelm*	(2)	1,398
13th Infantry Regiment	(2)	1,398
3rd Light Infantry Battalion *Preysing*	(1)	706
2nd Chevaulegers *König*	(4)	469
6th Brigade: General-Major von Siebein		
9th Infantry Regiment *Ysenburg*	(2)	1,398
10th Infantry Regiment *Junker*	(2)	1,398
6th Light Infantry Battalion *Steinbach*	(1)	706
4th Chevaulegers Regiment *Bubenhofen*	(4)	449

Division Artillery and Train:
1st and 2nd Companies of Bavarian Foot Artillery
Each of the foot artillerist companies had identical ordnance, consisting of:
Four 12-pounder guns and two howitzers—
total of six pieces of ordnance in each company—12 total pieces.
Company of Bavarian Horse Artillery, with:
Four 6-pounder guns and two howitzers—
total of six pieces of ordnance in the horse artillery company.
All the artillerists from the three companies totaled 440

Infantry Regimental Artillery: Sixteen 6-pounder guns were in the field—two pieces with each of the eight regiments of infantry.

Bavarian Division Totals—

Infantry	20	14,008
Cavalry	12	1,397
Artillerists and supporting personnel, number of companies	3	440
Total Present and Under Arms		15,845 and 34 pieces of ordnance
Total number of horses with the Bavarian Division	1,130	
Total number of personnel detached in rear areas		—0—
Total number of personnel in hospitals		—0—
Total effectives—all personnel, including general officers		15,850 and 34 pieces of ordnance

Note: The composition of the Bavarian brigades changed several times during the 1805 war. For example, compare the details shown in Appendix B with the Bavarian returns in this appendix (including those attached to 1st Corps and those shown above). Further, the troops that were dispatched into the Tyrol and fought alongside Ney's 6th Corps are shown as follows:

Bavarian Army Forces Dispatched to operate in the Tyrol during November under General-Leutnant Baron von Deroi

	Bns/Sqdns
1st Brigade: General-Major Minneri	
1st Infantry Regiment *Leib Gardes*	(2)
2nd Infantry Regiment *Kronprinz*	(2)
1st Light Infantry Battalion *Metzen*	(1)
1st Dragoon Regiment *Minucci*	(2)
2nd Brigade: General-Major Marsigli	
4th Infantry Regiment *Salern*	(2)
5th Infantry Regiment *Preysing*	(2)
3rd Light Infantry Battalion *Preysing*	(1)
2nd Dragoon Regiment *Taxis*	(3)
3rd Brigade: General-Major Count Mezzanelli	
3rd Infantry Regiment *Prinz Karl*	(2)
7th Infantry Regiment	(2)
5th Light Infantry Battalion *LaMotte*	(1)
1st Chevaulegers Regiment *Kronprinz*	(2)

Artillery: Twelve 6-pounder regimental guns—two per regiment; and
two companies of artillerists with a total of 12 pieces of ordnance.
Total number of ordnance in force was 24 pieces.

RECAPITULATION of the *GRANDE ARMÉE*
during the last 15 days of brumaire an XIV (5 through 21 November 1805)

Formation	Infantry Battalions	Cavalry Sqd./Regiments	Guns	Total Present— Infantry	Cavalry	All Arms
Suite de l'État-major	-0-	½ / -	-0-	-0-	-0-	282 *
IMPERIAL GUARD	6	10½ / 3	24	3,419	1,210	5,153
1st CORPS**	28	24 / 4	48	17,496	2,532	21,585
2nd CORPS	15	10 / 4	18	9,281	1,228	11,245
3rd CORPS	28	12 / 4	48	19,940	1,315	22,388
4th CORPS	31	10 / 3	36	23,905	924	26,026
5th CORPS	21	12 / 4	24	12,076	986	13,734
6th CORPS	18	6 / 2	28	11,713	379	12,713
7th CORPS	14	4 / 1	24	10,495	584	12,150
PROVISIONAL CORPS	23	8 / 3	26	10,337	576	11,399
RÉSERVES de Cavalerie	8	107½ / 36	28	4,003	9,987	14,496
Grand Parc d'Artillerie	-0-	-0-	184	-0-	-0-	3,864
Allied Troops as Garrisons						
Württembergers	6	1 / 1	8	2,871	102	3,149
Badeners	5	-0-	8	2,156	24	2,321
Bavarians***	20	12 / 3	34	14,008	1,397	15,845
Including all artillerists and support personnel, general officers and staff personnel— Totals for the Army	223	217½ / 68	538	141,700	21,244	176,350

* Excludes the Élite Company of the 21st Dragoons and the 3rd Company, 2nd Battalion of French Engineers who were attached to Imperial Headquarters, as well as Napoleon's Military Household.
** Includes the Advance Guard of the Bavarian Army under Wrede.
*** These were Deroi's Division, part of which participated in the Tyrolian Campaign with Ney's 6th Corps.

ıncluding all personnel detached, in hospitals and in route to join their respective units, the total number of combatants for the *Grande Armée* comes to 219,596 officers and other ranks. The total number of horses as mounts for the cavalry, for the horse artillery and for the train of artillery was 37,579; this number excludes the Élite Company of the 21st Dragoons at Imperial headquarters, troops on the way to join the army, all horses for staff and headquarters personnel, as well as all horses in the General Administration and Administrative Services.

Source: C[2] 470 and "*Tableau de la Grande Armée Dernière quinzaine du mois brumaire an XIV,*" *Archives du Service Historique de l'État-Major de l'Armée de Terre,* (S.H.A.T.), VINCENNES.

Composition of the Artillery in the *Grande Armée* as of November 1805
(Consult Specific Orders of Battle in Other Appendices for More Details)

Poundage of Guns and Number in each Corps

Corps Designation	3* / 4 pdrs.	6 pdrs.*	8 pdrs.	12 pdrs.	Howitzers	Total in Corps
Imperial Guard	- / 6	-	12	-	6	24
1st Corps	11* / -	27 *	-	-	10 *	48
2nd Corps	- / -	-	12	4	2	18
3rd Corps	- / 8	-	24	8	8	48
4th Corps	- / 6	-	18	6	6	36
5th Corps	- / 4	-	14	2	4	24
6th Corps	- / 4	-	16	6	2	28
7th Corps	- / 4	-	12	4	4	24
Provisonal Corps	- / 10	-	6	2	8	26
Réserves de Cavalerie	- / 2	-	16	2	8	28
Grand Parc d'Artillerie	31 / 13	44	37	24	35	184
Württembergers	- / -	6	-	-	2	8
Badeners	- / -	6	-	-	2	8
Deroi's Bavarians	- / -	20	-	8	6	34
Totals for the Army	44 / 57	101	167	66	103	538

*All these 3-pounders and 15 of the 6-pounders were Hanoverian ordnance, as were eight 5.3-inch howitzers that were part of the French artillery companies of 1st Corps. The remainder of the 6-pounders and the two other howitzers were Bavarian ordnance in a Bavarian horse artillery company with Wrede.

Source: C[2] 470, 472, 474, 475, 476, 477, 481, 482, 483, 484 and "*Tableau de la Grande Armée Dernière quinzaine du mois brumaire an XIV,*" *Archives du Service Historique de l'État-Major de l'Armée de Terre,* (S.H.A.T.), VINCENNES, plus the *Journaux des opération* of the various corps.

SITUATION of the FRENCH TROOPS at the Battle of Dürenstein

10-11 November 1805

PROVISIONAL CORPS
Marshal Mortier
Général de brigade Godinot, Chief of Staff
Corps headquarters staff—4 personnel

2nd Infantry Division (from the 5th Corps)—*Général de division* Gazan
Strengths as of 15 brumaire an XIV (6 November 1805)

	Bns/Sqdns	All Ranks Present & Under Arms	
Division headquarters staff—16 personnel			
1st Brigade: *Général de brigade* Graindorge			
4th *Légère* Infantry Regiment	(3)	1,518	
58th Regiment of the Ligne	(2)		detached—at Braunau
2nd Brigade: *Général de brigade* Campana			
100th Regiment of the *Ligne*	(3)	1,973	
103rd Regiment of the *Ligne*	(3)	2,038	
Attached:			
4th Regiment of Dragoons	(3)	305	
Division Artillery—		170	
Horse Artillery, detachment,			
Serving two 8-pounder guns—total of two pieces.			
Foot Artillery, one company, serving			
Two 12-pounders, four 8-pounders, two 4-pounders and two 6-inch howitzers—total of 10 pieces.			
Note: Only two 8-pounders and one howitzer were brought to Dürenstein and participated in the battle.			
Train of Artillery, one company		116	

1st Infantry Division (from 6th Corps)—*Général de division* Dupont
This division arrived late in the afternoon of 11 November 1805.
Strengths as of 7 brumaire an XIV (29 October 1805)

	Bns/Sqdns	All Ranks Present & Under Arms
Division headquarters staff—19 personnel		
1st Brigade: *Général de brigade* Rouyer		
9th *Légère* Infantry Regiment	(2)	1,120
2nd Brigade: *Général de brigade* Marchand		
32nd Regiment of the *Ligne*	(2)	1,210
96th Regiment of the *Ligne*	(2)	1,135
Attached:		
1st Hussars	(3)	239
Division Artillery and Train—		
2nd Regiment of Horse Artillery, detachment,		39
Serving two 8-pounder guns—total of two pieces.		
1st Regiment of Foot Artillery, one company, serving		89
Two 4-pounders and four 6-inch howitzers—total of six pieces.		
Ouvriers of Artillery		4
Train of Artillery		59

Note: *Journal des opérations du 6ᵉ corps* states that the combined strength of the 9th *Légère* and the 32nd Regiment of the *Ligne* at the Battle of Dürenstein was 2,377.

3rd Infantry Division (from 2nd Corps)— *Général de division* Dumonceau
Marching behind Dupont, this division was not engaged in the fighting at Dürenstein.
Consult Appendix E for composition and strengths as of 24 brumaire an XIV (15 November 1805).

Provisional Corps Totals Present in the vincinity of Dürenstein (excludes Dumonceau's Division)—

Infantry	15	9,041	
Cavalry	6	544	
Artillerists and supporting personnel, number of companies	22/3	477	
Total Present and Under Arms, excluding general officers and staffs		10,062	and 18 pieces of ordnance

Source: C² 475, 481, 482 and *Journal des opérations du 6ᵉ Corps, Archives du Service Historique de l'État-Major de l'Armée de Terre,* (S.H.A.T.), VINCENNES.

SITUATION of the RUSSIAN ARMY at the Battle of Dürenstein

10-11 November 1805

THE RUSSIANARMY
Strengths as of 10 November 1805
General of Infantry Kutuzov

Unit	Bns/Sqdns	Notes
I. Column—Lieutenant-General Miloradovich		
Apsheron Musketeer Regiment	(3)	Two musketeer battalions and one grenadier battalion.
Smolensk Musketeer Regiment	(1)	This was the regiment's Grenadier Battalion.
Little Russia Grenadier Regiment	(1)	This was the regiment's Grenadier Battalion.
8th *Jaeger* Regiment	(1)	This was the regiment's 1st Battalion.
Mariupol Hussar Regiment #3	(2)	
Attached: Four 6-pounder battalion guns.		
		I. Column strength was 2,500 combatants.
II. Column—Lieutenant-General Dokhturov		
Moscow Musketeer Regiment	(3)	Two musketeer battalions and one grenadier battalion.
Yaroslav Musketeer Regiment	(3)	Two musketeer battalions and one grenadier battalion.
Vyatka Musketeer Regiment	(3)	Two musketeer battalions and one grenadier battalion.
Bryansk Musketeer Regiment	(2)	Two musketeer battalions.
Narva Musketeer Regiment	(2)	Two musketeer battalions.
6th *Jaeger* Regiment	(3)	
Mariupol Hussar Regiment #3	(2)	
Attached: Two 6-pounder battalion guns		
		II. Column strength was 6,000 combatants.
III. Column—Major-General Strik		
Butyrsk Musketeer Regiment	(3)	Two musketeer battalions and one grenadier battalion.
8th *Jaeger* Regiment	(2)	These were the regiment's 2nd and 3rd Battalions.
		III. Column strength was 1,790 combatants.
IV. Column—Major-General Prince Bagration		
Kiev Grenadier Regiment	(3)	Two fusilier battalions and one grenadier battalion.
Azov Musketeer Regiment	(3)	Two musketeer battalions and one grenadier battalion.
Podolia Musketeer Regiment	(1)	This was the regiment's Grenadier Battalion.
Austrian Infantry Brigade: GM Count Nostitz-Rieneck		
Broder *Grenz* #7	(2)	
Peterwardeiner *Grenz* #9	(2)	
Austrian Cavalry Brigade: GM Prince Hohenlohe		
Cüirassier-Regiment Nassau-Usingen #5	(8)	
Cüirassier-Regiment Lothringen #7	(8)	
Hussar-Regiment Hessen-Homburg #4	(6)	
		IV. Column strength was 6,000 combatants.
V. Column—Lieutenant-General Essen		
Little Russia Grenadier Regiment	(2)	Two fusilier battalions.
Smolensk Musketeer Regiment	(2)	Two musketeer battalions.
Bryansk Musketeer Regiment	(1)	This was the regiment's Grenadier Battalion.
Narva Musketeer Regiment	(1)	This was the regiment's Grenadier Battalion.
Chernigov Dragoon Regiment #3	(5)	
Mariupol Hussar Regiment #3	(6)	
		V. Column strength was 3,500 combatants.
VI. Column (Army Reserves)—		
Podolia Musketeer Regiment	(2)	These two musketeer battalions were not in good morale.
Novgorod Musketeer Regiment	(3)	In good morale as part of the army reserve.
Leib-*Cuirassier* "Tsar's" (Kaiser)	(5)	In good morale as part of the army reserve.
Pavlograd Hussar Regiment #2	(10)	The regiment was not in good morale.
Khaznenkov Cossack Regiment	(5)	The regiment was not in good morale.
Sysoev Cossack Regiment	(5)	The regiment was not in good morale.
Remainder of all 14 artillery companies with a total of 162 pieces of ordnance.		
		VI. Column strength, excluding all units not in good morale (because they were not available for parade states, much less ready for action), was 3,176 artillerists and train personnel, plus 667 in the Leib-*Cuirassiers*.

*This was the total for all Russian artillerists and train personnel in the army.

Russian Army totals at Dürenstein— **Troops available and in good morale**	Bns/Sqdns	Present and Under Arms
Russian Infantry	43	16,769
Austrian Infantry	4	
Russian Cavalry	20	2,242
Austrian Cavalry	22	
Artillerists and train personnel in 14 companies		3,176
Total: Russians Present and Available		22,187
Total: Austrians Present and Available		2,500

Source: österreichischen Kriegsarchiv, Vienna (K.A., F.A. Deutschland 1805); C[2] 13, *Archives du Service Historique de l'État-Major de l'Armée de Terre,* (S.H.A.T.), VINCENNES and numerous regimental histories.

SITUATION of the FRENCH TROOPS during the *manœuvre sur Hollabrunn* and the Battle of Schöngrabern

16 November 1805

Wing of the *Grande Armée*

Marshal Prince Murat, Lieutenant of the Emperor, Commanding in the Absence of His Majesty Napoleon

Advance Guard of the Army Wing—*Général de brigade* Sébastiani		
Advance Guard staff—12 personnel		
1st Brigade: *Général de brigade* Treillard	Bns/Sqdns	All Ranks Present & Under Arms
9th Hussars	(3)	231
10th Hussars	(3)	261
1st *Chasseurs à cheval*	(3)	275
2nd Brigade: *Général de brigade* Fauconnet		
13th *Chasseurs à cheval*	(3)	259
21st *Chasseurs à cheval*	(3)	235

4th CORPS

Strengths as of 16 brumaire an XIV (7 November 1805)

Marshal Soult

Général de division Salligny, Chief of Staff
Général de brigade Lariboissière, commanding the artillery
Colonel Poitevin, commanding the engineers
Corps headquarters staff—42 personnel

1st Infantry Division—*Général de division* Saint Hilaire		
Division headquarters staff—21 personnel		
1st Brigade: *Général de brigade* Morand	Bns/Sqdns	All Ranks Present & Under Arms
10th *Légère* Infantry Regiment	(2)	1,478
2nd Brigade: *Général de brigade* Thiébault		
14th Regiment of the *Ligne*	(2)	1,589
36th Regiment of the *Ligne*	(2)	1,643
3rd Brigade: *Général de brigade* Waré		
43rd Regiment of the *Ligne*	(2)	1,687
55th Regiment of the *Ligne*	(2)	1,714
Division artillery and train:		
5th Regiment of Foot Artillery, 12th Company		98
5th Regiment of Foot Artillery, detachment of the 16th Company		22
1st Battalion, Train of Artillery, one company		108
2nd Battalion of French Engineers, 9th Company		47
2nd Infantry Division—*Général de division* Vandamme		
Division headquarters staff—23 personnel		
1st Brigade: *Général de brigade* Schiner		
24th *Légère* Infantry Regiment	(2)	1,310
2nd Brigade: *Général de brigade* Férey		
4th Regiment of the *Ligne*	(2)	1,822
28th Regiment of the *Ligne*	(2)	1,636
3rd Brigade: *Général de brigade* Candras		
46th Regiment of the *Ligne*	(2)	1,559
57th Regiment of the *Ligne*	(2)	1,771
Division artillery and train:		
5th Regiment of Foot Artillery, 13th Company		95
5th Regiment of Foot Artillery, detachment of the 16th Company		22
2nd Battalion, Train of Artillery, one company		132

3rd Infantry Division—*Général de division* Legrand		
Division headquarters staff—20 personnel		
1st Brigade: *Général de brigade* Merle		
26th *Légère* Infantry Regiment	(2)	1,587
Tirailleurs du Pô	(1)	547
2nd Brigade: *Général de brigade* Lavasseur		
18th Regiment of the *Ligne*	(2)	1,507
75th Regiment of the *Ligne*	(2)	1,532
Tirailleurs corses	(1)	635
3rd Brigade: *Général de brigade* Féry		
3rd Regiment of the *Ligne*	(3)	1,888
Division artillery and train:		
5th Regiment of Foot Artillery, 14th Company		94
5th Regiment of Foot Artillery, detachment of the 16th Company		22
3rd Battalion, Train of Artillery, one company		101
4th Corps Light Cavalry Division—*Général de brigade* Margaron		
Corps cavalry division staff—7 personnel		
1st Brigade: *Général de brigade* Margaron		
8th Hussars	(3)	276
11th *Chasseurs à cheval*	(4)	317
26th *Chasseurs à cheval*	(3)	331
Division artillery and train:		
5th Regiment of Horse Artillery, 4th Company		91
3rd Battalion, Train of Artillery, one company		52
4th Corps Artillery Reserve—		
Corps artillery reserve staff—5 personnel		
5th Regiment of Foot Artillery, 17th and 18th Companies		199
1st Battalion, Train of Artillery, one company		56
French Ouvriers of the Artillery, 1/2 company		46
French Armorers, detachment		12
Total strength of all personnel—4th Corps Artillery Reserve		313
4th Corps Totals—		
Staffs		118
Infantry	31	23,905
Cavalry	10	924
Artillerists and supporting personnel, number of companies	14 ½	1,197
Total Present and Under Arms, including general officers and staff		26,144 and 36 pieces of ordnance

5th CORPS(-)
Strengths as of 24 brumaire an XIV (15 November 1805)

Marshal Lannes

Général de brigade Compans, Chief of Staff
Général de brigade Foucher de Careil, commanding the artillery
Colonel Kirgener, commanding the engineers
Corps headquarters staff—16 personnel

	Bns/Sqdns	All Ranks Present & Under Arms	
1st Infantry Division (*Grenadiers de la Réserve*)—*Général de division* Oudinot			
Division headquarters staff—22 personnel			
1st Brigade: *Général de brigade* Laplanche-Morthières			
1st Grenadier Regiment			
1st *bataillon d'élite* from the 13th *Ligne*	(1)	611	
2nd *bataillon d'élite* from the 58th *Ligne*	(1)	659	
2nd Grenadier Regiment			
1st *bataillon d'élite* from the 9th *Ligne*	(1)	584	
2nd *bataillon d'élite* from the 81st *Ligne*	(1)	695	
2nd Brigade: *Général de brigade* Dupas			
3rd Grenadier Regiment			
1st *bataillon d'élite* from the 2nd *Légère*	(1)	509	
2nd *bataillon d'élite* from the 3rd *Légère*	(1)	522	
4th Grenadier Regiment			
1st *bataillon d'élite* from the 28th *Légère*	(1)	459	
2nd *bataillon d'élite* from the 31st *Légère*	(1)	396	
3rd Brigade: *Général de brigade* Ruffin			
5th Grenadier Regiment			
1st *bataillon d'élite* from the 12th *Légère*	(1)	498	
2nd *bataillon d'élite* from the 15th *Légère*	(1)	497	
Division artillery and train:			
5th Regiment of Foot Artillery, one company, and			
5th Regiment of Horse Artillery, one company—all artillerists		158	
Train of Artillery, two companies		170	
2nd French Engineer Battalion, 2nd Company		71	
2nd Infantry Division—*Général de division* Gazan—detached to Marshal Mortier			
3rd Infantry Division—*Général de division* Suchet			
Division headquarters staff—23 personnel			
1st Brigade: *Général de brigade* Claparède			
17th *Légère* Infantry Regiment	(2)	1,461	
2nd Brigade: *Général de brigade* Beker			
34th Regiment of the *Ligne*	(3)	1,279	
40th Regiment of the *Ligne*	(2)	1,404	
3rd Brigade: *Général de brigade* Valhubert			
64th Regiment of the *Ligne*	(2)	1,020	
88th Regiment of the *Ligne*	(2)	1,606	
Division artillery and train:			
5th Regiment of Foot Artillery, one company		115	
3rd Battalion, Train of Artillery, one company		101	
5th Corps Light Cavalry Division—*Général de brigade* Fauconnet			
Corps cavalry division staff—11 personnel			with the Advance Guard
1st Brigade: *Général de brigade* Treillard			
9th Hussars	(3)		with the Advance Guard
10th Hussars	(3)		with the Advance Guard
2nd Brigade: *Général de brigade* Fauconnet			
13th *Chasseurs à cheval*	(3)		with the Advance Guard
21st *Chasseurs à cheval*	(3)		with the Advance Guard
5th Corps Totals—			
Staff		61	
Infantry	21	12,200	
Cavalry	-0-		detached
Artillerists and supporting personnel, number of companies	7	615	
Total Present and Under Arms, including general officers and staff		12,876	and 24 pieces of ordnance

Corps des Réserves de Cavalerie (-)
Strengths as of 30 brumaire an XIV (21 November 1805)

Marshal Murat

Général de division Belliard, Chief of Staff
Général de brigade Hanicque, commanding the artillery
Colonel Hayelle, commanding the engineers
Corps headquarters staff—35 personnel

1st Heavy Cavalry Division—*Général de division* Nansouty		
Division headquarters staff—17 personnel		
1st Brigade: *Général de brigade* Piston	Bns/Sqdns	All Ranks Present & Under Arms
1st Regiment of *Carabiniers*	(3)	232
2nd Regiment of *Carabiniers*	(3)	239
2nd Brigade: *Général de brigade* La Houssaye		
1st Regiment of *Cuirassiers*	(3)	350
2nd Regiment of *Cuirassiers*	(3)	305
3rd Brigade: *Général de brigade* Saint-Germain		
3rd Regiment of *Cuirassiers*	(3)	291
5th Regiment of *Cuirassiers*	(3)	335
2nd Heavy Cavalry Division—*Général de division* d'Hautpoul		
Division headquarters staff—13 personnel		
1st Brigade: Colonel Noirot		
9th Regiment of *Cuirassiers*	(3)	318
12th Regiment of *Cuirassiers*	(3)	298
2nd Brigade: *Général de brigade* Saint-Sulpice		
10th Regiment of *Cuirassiers*	(3)	260
11th Regiment of *Cuirassiers*	(3)	333
1st Dragoon Division—*Général de division* Klein—not present; operating to the west with Mortier		
2nd Dragoon Division—*Général de division* Walther		
Division headquarters staff—18 personnel		
1st Brigade: not operational as *Général de brigade* Sébastiani de la Porta was detached to the Advance Guard.		
2nd Brigade: *Général de brigade* Roget de Belloguet		
10th Regiment of Dragoons	(3)	225
11th Regiment of Dragoons	(3)	347
3rd Regiment of Dragoons	(3)	258
3rd Brigade: *Général de brigade* Boussart		
13th Regiment of Dragoons	(3)	268
22nd Regiment of Dragoons	(3)	152
6th Regiment of Dragoons	(3)	284
3rd Dragoon Division—*Général de division* Beaumont—not present; operating to the southeast with Davout.		
4th Dragoon Division—*Général de division* Bourcier—not present; operating to the southwest.		
Division of *Dragons à pied*—not present; operating to the west.		
Light Cavalry Brigade—*Général de brigade* Milhaud		
Brigade headquarters staff—11 personnel		
1st Brigade: *Général de brigade* Milhaud		
16th *Chasseurs à cheval*	(3)	338
22nd *Chasseurs à cheval*	(3)	272

Corps des Réserves de Cavalerie Artillery —

Corps artillery reserve staff—6 personnel
French Horse Artillery, 11/2 companies
These one and one-half companies were each divided into three half-companies. One half-company was attached to each division of cavalry. Every half-company had identical ordnance composition, which was: two 8-pounder guns and one 6-inch howitzer, for a total of three pieces per half-company—total nine pieces.
2nd Battalion, French Train of Artillery, 1½ companies
2nd Battalion of French Engineers, 7th Company

Total strength of all artillerists and supporting personnel for the present formations of *Corps des Réserves de Cavalerie* —		320
Corps des Réserves de Cavalerie Totals—		
Staff		100
Cavalry	54	5,105
Artillerists and supporting personnel, number of companies	4	320
Total Present and Under Arms, including officers and staff		5,525 and 9 pieces of ordnance

Wing of the *Grande Armée;* Total Present at Schöngrabern—			
General officers and staffs		279	
Infantry	52	36,105	
Cavalry	79	7,290	
Artillerists and supporting personnel, number of companies	25½	2,132	
Total Present and Under Arms, including general officers and staffs		45,806	and 69 pieces of ordnance

RECAPITULATION of the Wing of the *GRANDE ARMÉE* under the command of Marshal Prince Murat during the *manœuvre sur Hollabrunn* and Battle of Schöngrabern (16 November 1805)

Formation	Infantry Battalions	Cavalry Sqd./Regiments	Guns	Total Present— Infantry	Cavalry	All Arms
Suite de l'État-major (All Staffs)				279		
ADVANCE GUARD	-0-	15 / 5	-0-	-0-	1,261	1,261
4th CORPS	31	10 / 3	36	23,905	924	26,026
5th CORPS (-)	21	*	24	12,200	*	12,815
RÉSERVES de Cavalerie(-)		54 / 18	9	-0-	5,105	5,425
Including all artillerists and support personnel, general officers and staff personnel— Totals for the Army	52	79 / 26	69	36,105	7,290	45,806

* All the light cavalry of 5th Corps, as well as the 1st *Chasseurs à cheval* of the 3rd Corps, were detached from their parent corps for service with the Advance Guard.

Source: C² 472, 477, 481 and "*Tableau de la Grande Armée Dernière quinzaine du mois brumaire an XIV,*" *Archives du Service Historique de l'État-Major de l'Armée de Terre,* (S.H.A.T.), VINCENNES.

Composition of the Artillery of the Wing of the *Grande Armée* during the *manœuvre sur Hollabrunn* and Battle of Schöngrabern (16 November 1805)

Poundage of Guns and Number in each Corps

Corps Designation	4 pdrs.	6 pdrs.	8 pdrs.	12 pdrs.	Howitzers	Total in Corps
ADVANCE GUARD	-	-	-	-	-	-0-
4th CORPS	6	-	18	6	6	36
5th CORPS(-)	4	-	14	2	4	24
RÉSERVES de Cavalerie(-)	-	-	6	-	3	9
Totals for the Army	10	-	38	8	13	69

Source: C² 472, 477, 481 and "*Tableau de la Grande Armée Dernière quinzaine du mois brumaire an XIV,*" *Archives du Service Historique de l'État-Major de l'Armée de Terre,* (S.H.A.T.), VINCENNES; plus the *Journaux des opération du 5ᵉ and 6ᵉ corps.*

SITUATION of the RUSSIAN ARMY at the Battle of Schöngrabern

16 November 1805

REAR GUARD of the THE RUSSIAN ARMY
Major-General Prince Bagration

The Front Line—Major-General Ulanius

	Bns/Sqdns	Notes/Strengths
6th *Jaeger* Regiment	(3)	800
Khaznenkov Cossack Regiment	(5)	250
Sysoev Cossack Regiment	(5)	250
Front Line strength=		800 regulars & 500 Cossacks.

The Main Line—

Right Side—Grenadier Brigade: Major-General Prince Bagration		
Little Russia Grenadier Regiment	(3)	Two musketeer bns. and one grenadier bn.
Kiev Grenadier Regiment	(3)	Two musketeer bns. and one grenadier bn.
Center—		
Narva Musketeer Regiment	(1)	This was the regiment's Grenadier Battalion.
Novgorod Musketeer Regiment	(1)	This was the regiment's Grenadier Battalion.
Major Bogoslavski's Line Light Foot Company of Artillery		Eight 6-pounders and four 10-pounder licornes.
Left Side—Musketeer Brigade: Major-General Selikov		
Azov Musketeer Regiment	(3)	Two musketeer bns. and one grenadier bn.
Podolia Musketeer Regiment	(3)	Two musketeer bns. and one grenadier bn.
Cavalry Brigade:		
Chernigov Dragoon Regiment #3	(5)	Deployed to cover the far right flank.
Pavlograd Hussar Regiment #2	(10)	Deployed to cover the far left flank.
Main Line strength was		6,000 regulars.

Not in Condition to Fight and Withdrawn into Reserve—GM Count Nostitz-Rieneck

Austrian Troops:		
Peterwardeiner *Grenz* #9 Infantry Regiment	(2)	These battalions were very, very weak.
Hussar-Regiment Hessen-Homburg #4	(6)	400

Russian Rearguard Totals at Schöngrabern—

	Bns/Sqdns	Present and Under Arms
Russian Infantry	17	5,300
Russian Regular Cavalry	15	1,350
Artillerists and train personnel in one company		150
Total: Russians Regulars Present and Under Arms		6,800
Russian Cossacks Present		500

Source: österreichischen Kriegsarchiv, Vienna (K.A., F.A. Deutschland 1805); C[2] 13, *Archives du Service Historique de l'État-Major de l'Armée de Terre,* (S.H.A.T.), VINCENNES and numerous regimental histories.

SITUATION of the *GRANDE ARMÉE* at the Battle of Austerlitz

2 December 1805

His Majesty

The Emperor Napoleon I, commanding in person

The Emperor's Military Household

Général de division Duroc, Grand Marshal of the Palace,
with the *Grenadiers de la Réserve*
Général de division Caulaincourt, Grand Equerry

Aides-de-Camp to His Majesty:
Général de division Caffarrelli du Falga—detached to 3rd Corps
Général de division Junot
Général de division Savary
Général de brigade Bertrand
Général de brigade Gardane
Général de brigade Lemarois
Général de brigade Mouton
Général de brigade Rapp
Colonel Lebrun

* *

État Major Général

Major Général

Major-Général of the Army—Marshal Berthier, Minister of War

Aides-de-Camp to Marshal Berthier:
Chef d'escadron Girardin
Capitaine Colbert
Capitaine Lejeune
Lieutenant Périgord
Lieutenant LeGrange
Lieutenant Armand Périgord

General Officers Attached to the Major Général

Général de brigade Pannetier
Général de brigade Reille
Général de brigade René
and four aides-de-camp, including Reille's son, who had a rank of lieutenant.

Other Officers Attached to the Major Général

Adjudant commandant LeCamus
Adjudant commandant Dalton

Adjoints to LeCamus and Dalton
Capitaine Simonier
Capitaine Falkowski
Capitaine Mahon
Capitaine LeVaillans
Capitaine de Piré
Capitaine Montholon
Capitaine Destermeaux
Capitaine Tricard
Lieutenant Saraire
Lieutenant Longuerue

Sous Inspecteur aux Revues Duhesme
Colonel du Génie Vallongue
Capitaine de frégate Lostange

Extra Officers Attached to the Major Général

Chef de bataillon Desnoyers
Chef de bataillon Blein
Chef de bataillon Parigots
Chef de bataillon Bailly de Monthion
Chef de bataillon Mergès
Chef de bataillon Dalvimar
Chef de bataillon Desnoyers

Suite de l'État Major Général

Officers and Auxiliary Troops In the Service of the Major Général

Bavarian Officers: *Major* Pocci, *Major* DeAubert
Württemberg Officers: *General-Major* von Geismar, *Leutnant* von Spitzemberg
Baden Officer: Grolman, *aide-de-camp to the Grossherzog*
Polish Officers: Colonel Adamistowski, *Chef de bataillon* Junger

Military Administration of the Army

Daru, *Intendant Général of the Army*
Ordonnateur en chef Joinville
plus, a staff of six commissioners

Administrative Services

Chief Baker: LePayen
Chief of Procuring Beef: Mamignard
Chief Forager: Giguet
Chief Surgeon: Poussielgue
Chief of the Ambulance Service LeGendre
Chief of Military Equipage: Sorlet
Postmaster: Juliac
Chief Printer: Levraux
Telegraph Director: Chappe
Colonel Wolff, Chief Sanitary Officer
Philippe, Assistant Sanitary Officer

Escort Troops

Mounted Gendarmes (61 officers and other ranks)
3rd Company, 2nd Battalion of French Engineers

Assistant Chief of Staff—
Chief of the General Staff

Général de division Andréossy
Andréossy had three *généraux de brigade,*
six *adjudant commandants*, and 24 other officers on his staff.

Assistant Chief of Staff—*Maréchal des Logis*

Général de division Mathieu Dumas
Général de brigade Sauson, Chief of the Topographical Service, plus 16 other officers

Other Officers Attached to the Assistant Chiefs of Staff—

Five colonels and nine *chefs de bataillon*

Artillery

Général de division Songis, Commander of the Artillery
Général de brigade Pernetti, Chief of Staff
Colonel Sénarmont, Assistant Chief of Staff,
plus a staff of 11 other officers

Engineers

Général de division Marescot, Commander of the Engineers
Major Birot Ducoudsary, Chief of Staff
Chef de bataillon Rouzier, General Director of the Engineers in Augsburg,
plus a staff of 12 ofther officers

General Administration of the Army

Intendant Général

Pétiet, Intendant Général,
plus a staff of four commissioners

Administrative Services

Inspector general and chief medical officer: Costé
Inspector general and chief surgeon: Percy
Inspector general and chief pharmacist: Parmentier
Plus eight other personnel.

Attached to the General Staff, Intendent Général

Mounted Gendarmes (40 officers & other ranks)

Administration of Troop Reviews

Inspecteur en chef aux Revues Villemanry, plus a staff of four

Total Number of Personnel at Imperial Headquarters—

282, which does not include
The Emperor's Military Household, and the
3rd Company, 2nd Battalion of French Engineers

IMPERIAL GUARD
Strengths as of 10 frimaire an XIV (1 December 1805)

Marshal Bessières

Général de brigade Roussel, Chief of Staff
Colonel Couin, commanding the artillery
Corps headquarters staff—16 personnel

	Bns/Sqdns	All Ranks Present & Under Arms at Austerlitz	
Infantry of the Imperial Guard			
1st Brigade: *Général de brigade* Hulin			
Regiment of *Grenadiers à pied* of the Imperial Guard	(2)	1,519	
2nd Brigade: *Général de brigade* Soulès			
Regiment of *Chasseurs à pied* of the Imperial Guard	(2)	1,613	
3rd Brigade—Regiment of the Royal Italian Guard: Colonel Lecchi			
Battalion of *Grenadiers à pied* and			
Battalion of *Chasseurs à pied* of the Royal Italian Guard	(2)	753	
Cavalry of the Imperial Guard			
1st Brigade: *Général de brigade* Ordener			
Regiment of *Grenadiers à cheval* of the Imperial Guard	(4)	706	
2nd Brigade: Colonel Morland			
Regiment of *Chasseurs à cheval* of the Imperial Guard	(4)	375	
Company of *Mameluks* of the Imperial Guard	(½)	48	
3rd Brigade: *Général de division* Savary			
Regiment of *Gendarmerie d'élite* of the Imperial Guard	(2)		detached—in Brünn
Artillery of the Imperial Guard—			
1st and 2nd Companies of Horse Artillery (*Volante)* of the Imperial Guard			
Company of Horse Artillery of the Royal Italian Guard, one company			
Each of the above three horse artillery companies had identical ordnance, consisting of: Four 8-pounders, two 4-pounders and two 6-inch howitzers—eight pieces of ordnance in each company—total of 24 pieces.			
All the artillerists from the three companies totaled		283	
Train of the Imperial Guard Artillery		257	
Matelots (Marins) of the Guard		120	
Flying Ambulance of the Guard (Larrey)			Not available
Total strength of all artillerists and supporting personnel for the entire Imperial Guard—		660	
Imperial Guard Totals—			
Staff		16	
Infantry	6	3,885	
Cavalry	8 ½	1,129	
Artillerists and supporting personnel, number of companies	6	660	
Total Present and Under Arms, including general officers and staff		5,690	and 24 pieces of ordnance
Total number of horses with the Imperial Guard	3,320*		
Total number of personnel in rear areas, including detachments and other absentees		1,258	
Total of personnel in hospitals		419	
Total effectives—all personnel, including general officers & staffs		7,367	and 24 pieces of ordnance

*Does not include the 821 horses belonging to detached troops who were not present with the main body.

in Reserve
alongside the Imperial Guard—
from the 5th CORPS:

1st Infantry Division (*Grenadiers de la Réserve*)—*Général de division* Oudinot* and *Général de division* Duroc*
Strengths as of 1 frimaire an XIV (22 November 1805)

	Bns/Sqdns	All Ranks Present & Under Arms at Austerlitz
Division headquarters staff—22 personnel		
1st Brigade: *Général de brigade* Laplanche-Morthières		
1st Grenadier Regiment		
1st *bataillon d'élite* from the 13th *Ligne*	(1)	340
2nd *bataillon d'élite* from the 58th *Ligne*	(1)	422
2nd Grenadier Regiment		
1st *bataillon d'élite* from the 9th *Ligne*	(1)	499
2nd *bataillon d'élite* from the 81st *Ligne*	(1)	526
2nd Brigade: *Général de brigade* Dupas		
3rd Grenadier Regiment		
1st *bataillon d'élite* from the 2nd *Légère*	(1)	399
2nd *bataillon d'élite* from the 3rd *Légère*	(1)	542
4th Grenadier Regiment		
1st *bataillon d'élite* from the 28th *Légère*	(1)	425
2nd *bataillon d'élite* from the 31st *Légère*	(1)	432
3rd Brigade: *Général de brigade* Ruffin		
5th Grenadier Regiment		
1st *bataillon d'élite* from the 12th *Légère*	(1)	538
2nd *bataillon d'élite* from the 15th *Légère*	(1)	532
Division artillery and train:		
1st Company, 1st Regiment of Foot Artillery, with Four 8-pounders and two 4-pounders—total of six pieces of ordnance		104
Detachment of the 4th Company, 5th Regiment of Horse Artillery, with Two 8-pounder guns—total of two pieces of ordnance		28
5th Battalion, Train of Artillery, two companies		174
2nd French Engineer Battalion, 2nd Company		33

Grenadiers de la Réserve Totals—		
Staff		22
Infantry	10	4,655
Artillerists and supporting personnel, number of companies	4 ⅓	339
Total Present and Under Arms at Austerlitz		5,016 and 8 pieces of ordnance
Total number of horses with the *Grenadiers de la Réserve*	328	
Total number of personnel in rear areas, including detachments and other absentees		1,488
Total of personnel in hospitals		1,697
Total effectives—all personnel		8,201 and 8 pieces of ordnance

*Due to the wounding Oudinot at the Battle of Schöngrabern (Hollabrunn), Napoleon decided to split the command of this division at Austerlitz. Oudinot commanded the 2nd and 3rd Brigades, while Duroc commanded the 1st Brigade.

1st CORPS
Strengths as of 10 frimaire an XIV (1 December 1805)

Marshal Bernadotte

Général de division Victor-Léopold Berthier, Chief of Staff
Général de division Jean-Baptiste Eblé, commanding the artillery
Colonel Morio, commanding the engineers
Corps headquarters staff—34 personnel

	Bns/Sqdns	All Ranks Present & Under Arms at Austerlitz
Advance Guard of the 1st Corps*—		
1st Brigade: *Général de brigade* Frere		
27th *Légère* Infantry Regiment	(3)	2,069
1st Infantry Division—*Général de division* Rivaud de la Raffinière		
Division headquarters staff—14 personnel		
1st Brigade: *Général de brigade* Dumoulin		
8th Regiment of the *Ligne*	(3)	1,858
2nd Brigade: *Général de brigade* Pacthod		
45th Regiment of the *Ligne*	(3)	1,603
54th Regiment of the *Ligne*	(3)	1,614
Division artillery:		111
1st Company, 8th Regiment of Foot Artillery, with:		
Four 3-pounders and one 5.3-inch howitzer—total of five pieces of ordnance.		
2nd Company, 3rd Regiment of Horse Artillery, with:		
Four 6-pounders and one 5.3-inch howitzer—total of five pieces of ordnance.		
2nd Battalion, Train of Artillery, 1½ companies		80
2nd Infantry Division—*Général de division* Drouet		
Division headquarters staff—17 personnel		
1st Brigade: detached—serving as Advance Guard of the 1st Corps		
2nd Brigade: *Général de brigade* Werlé		
94th Regiment of the *Ligne*	(3)	1,814
95th Regiment of the *Ligne*	(3)	1,903
Division artillery—all artillerists total:		118
2nd Company, 8th Regiment of Foot Artillery, with:		
Five 3-pounders and one 5.3-inch howitzer—total of six pieces of ordnance.		
3rd Company, 3rd Regiment of Horse Artillery, with		
Five 6-pounders and one 5.3-inch howitzer—total of six pieces of ordnance.		
2nd Battalion, Train of Artillery, 1½ companies		111
1st Corps Light Cavalry Division—*Général de division* Kellermann—detached to the *Corps des Réserves de Cavalerie*		
1st Corps Artillery Reserve—detached for service with Wrede's Bavarians		
1st Corps Totals—		
Staff		65
Infantry	18	10,861
French artillerists and supporting personnel, # of companies	5	420
Total Present and Under Arms at Austerlitz		11,346 and 22 pieces of ordnance

* The Advance Guard operated at Austerlitz as part of its' parent 2nd Division.

3rd CORPS
Strengths as of 8 frimaire an XIV (29 November 1805)
followed by estimated strengths upon arrival on the battlefield of Austerlitz

Marshal Davout

Général de brigade Fournier de Loysonville Daultane, Chief of Staff
Général de division Sorbier, commanding the artillery
Général de brigade Andreossy, commanding the engineers
Corps headquarters staff—46 personnel

1st Infantry Division—*Général de division* Caffarelli du Falga—detached to 5th Corps

2nd Infantry Division—*Général de division* Friant

Division headquarters staff—21 personnel		
1st Brigade: *Général de brigade* Kister	Bns/Sqdns	All Ranks Present & Under Arms at Austerlitz
15th *Légère* Infantry Regiment, less *Voltigeurs**	(2)	628 / 300
33rd Regiment of the *Ligne*	(2)	1,214 / 500
2nd Brigade: *Général de brigade* Lochet		
48th Regiment of the *Ligne*	(2)	1,365 / 800
111th Regiment of the *Ligne*	(2)	1,440 / 700
3rd Brigade: *Général de brigade* Heudelet		
Voltigeurs of the 15th *Légère* Infantry Regiment*	(-)	126 / 70
108th Regiment of the *Ligne*	(2)	1,637 / 800
Division artillery and train:		186 / 130

2nd Company, 7th Regiment of Foot Artillery, consisting of:
Four 8-pounder guns and two 6-inch howitzers—total of six pieces.
Half-company of the 1st Company, 5th Regiment of Horse Artillery, with
Two 8-pounder guns and one 6-inch howitzer—total of three pieces.
1st Battalion, Train of Artillery, one company
*Six companies of the 15th *Légère* were detached from the regiment and formed the 2nd Battalion, 5th Regiment of the *Grenadiers de la Réserve* in 5th Corps.

Attached from the *Corps des Réserves de Cavalerie*: from the 4th Dragoon Division

1st Regiment of Dragoons	(3)	321 / 120

3rd Infantry Division—*Général de division* Gudin—not present—in route

3rd Corps Light Cavalry Division—*Général de brigade* Viallanes—not present—in route

3rd Corps Artillery Reserve—not present—in route

Attached from the *Corps des Réserves de Cavalerie*: 4th Dragoon Division—*Général de division* Bourcier

Division headquarters staff—17 personnel		
1st Brigade: *Général de brigade* Sahuc	Bns/Sqdns	All Ranks Present & Under Arms / at Austerlitz
15th Regiment of Dragoons	(3)	227 / 90
17th Regiment of Dragoons	(3)	290 / 120
2nd Brigade: *Général de brigade* Laplanche		
18th Regiment of Dragoons	(3)	279 / 150
19th Regiment of Dragoons	(3)	266 / 160
3rd Brigade: *Général de brigade* Verdière		
25th Regiment of Dragoons	(3)	220 / 100
27th Regiment of Dragoons	(3)	214 / 90
Division artillery and train:		82 / 60

Detachment of the 3rd Company, 2nd Regiment of Horse Artillery,
Two 8-pounder guns and one 6-inch howitzer—total of three pieces.

Note: *Général de brigade* Verdière, who commanded the 3rd Brigade of this division as it crossed the Rhine, was detached on 16 vendémiaire (8 October) to command the heavy cavalry depot in Harburg. When this occurred, the division's command structure was modified into two brigades of three regiments per brigade. General Verdière joined the division in time for the Battle of Austerlitz.

3rd Corps Totals—

Staff		84
(Infantry—upon leaving Vienna)	10	(6,410)
Infantry—at Austerlitz	10	3,200
(Attached Cavalry—before the forced march)	21	(1,817)
Attached Cavalry—at Austerlitz	21	830
Artillerists and supporting personnel, number of companies	2	190
Total Present and Under Arms at Austerlitz		4,304 and 12 pieces of ordnance

4th CORPS
Strengths as of 10 frimaire an XIV (1 December 1805)

Marshal Soult

Général de division Salligny, Chief of Staff
Général de brigade Lariboissière, commanding the artillery
Colonel Poitevin, commanding the engineers
Corps headquarters staff—42 personnel

	Bns/Sqdns	All Ranks Present & Under Arms at Austerlitz
1st Infantry Division—*Général de division* Saint Hilaire		
Division headquarters staff—20 personnel		
1st Brigade: *Général de brigade* Morand		
10th *Légère* Infantry Regiment	(2)	1,488
2nd Brigade: *Général de brigade* Thiébault		
14th Regiment of the *Ligne*	(2)	1,551
36th Regiment of the *Ligne*	(2)	1,643
3rd Brigade: *Général de brigade* Waré—operating under Vandamme during the Battle of Austerlitz		
43rd Regiment of the *Ligne*	(2)	1,598
55th Regiment of the *Ligne*	(2)	1,658
Division artillery and train:		
12th Company, 5th Regiment of Foot Artillery, with		98
Two 8-pounders, two 4-pounders and two 6-inch howitzers—total of six pieces of ordnance		
Detachment of the 16th Company, 5th Regiment of Foot Artillery, with		22
Two 8-pounder guns—total of two pieces of ordnance		
1st Battalion, Train of Artillery, one company		132
2nd Battalion of French Engineers, 9th Company		47
2nd Infantry Division—*Général de division* Vandamme		
Division headquarters staff—22 personnel		
1st Brigade: *Général de brigade* Schiner		
24th *Légère* Infantry Regiment	(2)	1,291
2nd Brigade: *Général de brigade* Ferrey		
4th Regiment of the *Ligne*	(2)	1,658
28th Regiment of the *Ligne*	(2)	1,599
3rd Brigade: *Général de brigade* Candras		
46th Regiment of the *Ligne*	(2)	1,350
57th Regiment of the *Ligne*	(2)	1,743
Division artillery and train:		
13th Company, 5th Regiment of Foot Artillery, with		95
Two 8-pounders, two 4-pounders and two 6-inch howitzers—total of six pieces of ordnance		
Detachment of the 16th Company, 5th Regiment of Foot Artillery, with		22
Two 8-pounder guns—total of two pieces of ordnance		
2nd Battalion, Train of Artillery, one company		132
3rd Infantry Division—*Général de division* Legrand		
Division headquarters staff—21 personnel		
1st Brigade: *Général de brigade* Merle		
26th *Légère* Infantry Regiment	(2)	1,564
Tirailleurs du Pô	(1)	340 *
Tirailleurs corses	(1)	519
2nd Brigade: *Général de brigade* Féry		
3rd Regiment of the *Ligne*	(3)	1,644
3rd Brigade: *Général de brigade* Lavasseur		
18th Regiment of the *Ligne*	(2)	1,402
75th Regiment of the *Ligne*	(2)	1,688
Division artillery and train		
14th Company, 5th Regiment of Foot Artillery, with		94
Two 8-pounders, two 4-pounders and two 6-inch howitzers—total of six pieces of ordnance		
Detachment of the 16th Company, 5th Regiment of Foot Artillery, with		22
Two 8-pounder guns—total of two pieces of ordnance		
3rd Battalion, Train of Artillery, one company		101

* The *Tirailleurs du Pô* had only 308 people present on 1 frimaire (22 November), and recovered some of their detached personnel before the battle.

	Bns/Sqdns	All Ranks Present & Under Arms at Austerlitz	
4th Corps Light Cavalry Division—*Général de brigade* Margaron			
Corps cavalry division staff—5 personnel			
1st Brigade: *Général de brigade* Margaron			
8th Hussars	(3)	359	
11th *Chasseurs à cheval*	(4)	343	
26th *Chasseurs à cheval*	(3)	316	
Division artillery and train:			
4th Company, 5th Regiment of Horse Artillery, with		91	
Five 8-pounder guns—total of five pieces of ordnance			
3rd Battalion, Train of Artillery, one company		52	
Attached from the *Corps des Réserves de Cavalerie*: 3rd Dragoon Division—*Général de division* Beaumont			
Division headquarters staff—12 personnel			
1st Brigade: *Général de brigade* Boyé			
5th Regiment of Dragoons	(3)	234	
8th Regiment of Dragoons	(3)	289	
2nd Brigade: *Général de brigade* Scalfort			
9th Regiment of Dragoons	(3)	297	
12th Regiment of Dragoons	(3)	291	
3rd Brigade: *Général de brigade* Milhaud			
16th Regiment of Dragoons	(3)	242	
21st Regiment of Dragoons	(3)	285	
Division artillery and train:			
Detachment of the 3rd Company, 2nd Regiment of Horse Art., with		42	
Two 8-pounder guns and one 6-inch howitzer—total of three pieces of ordnance			
Detachment, Train of Artillery		46	
4th Corps Artillery Reserve—			
Corps artillery reserve staff—2 personnel			
17th and 18th Companies, 5th Regiment of Foot Artillery, manning		154	
Six 12-pounder guns—total of six pieces of ordnance			
1st Battalion, Train of Artillery, two companies		233	
French *Ouvriers* of the Artillery, 1/2 company		26	
Total strength of all personnel—4th Corps Artillery Reserve		413	
4th Corps Totals—			
Staff		112	
Infantry	31	22,736	
Cavalry	28	2,656	
Artillerists and supporting personnel, number of companies	14 ½	1,321	
Total Present and Under Arms at Austerlitz		26,825	and 38 pieces of ordnance

5th CORPS
Strengths as of 11 frimaire an XIV (2 December 1805)

Marshal Lannes

Général de brigade Compans, Chief of Staff
Général de brigade Foucher de Careil, commanding the artillery
Colonel Kirgener, commanding the engineers
Corps headquarters staff—20 personnel

1st Infantry Division (*Grenadiers de la Réserve*)—*Général de division* Oudinot—detached to the Army Reserve

2nd Infantry Division—*Général de division* Gazan—not present—detached to Marshal Mortier in Vienna

3rd Infantry Division—*Général de division* Suchet

	Bns/Sqdns	All Ranks Present & Under Arms at Austerlitz
Division headquarters staff—20 personnel		
1st Brigade: *Général de brigade* Claparède		
17th *Légère* Infantry Regiment	(2)	1,373
2nd Brigade: *Général de brigade* Beker		
34th Regiment of the *Ligne*	(3)	1,615
40th Regiment of the *Ligne*	(2)	1,149
3rd Brigade: *Général de brigade* Valhubert		
64th Regiment of the *Ligne*	(2)	1,052
88th Regiment of the *Ligne*	(2)	1,428
Division artillery and train:		
15th Company, 5th Regiment of Foot Artillery, with		61
Two 12-pounders, four 8-pounders and two 4-pounders—total of eight pieces of ordnance		
Detachment of the 16th Company, 5th Regiment of Foot Artillery, with		22
Two 8-pounder guns—total of two pieces of ordnance		
Detachment of the 5th Company, 1st Regiment of Foot Artillery, with		28
Two 8-pounders and two 6-inch howitzers—total of four pieces of ordnance		
3rd Battalion, Train of Artillery, two companies		129

Attached from 3rd Corps: 1st Infantry Division—*Général de division* Caffarelli du Falga

	Bns/Sqdns	All Ranks Present & Under Arms at Austerlitz
Division headquarters staff—17 personnel		
1st Brigade: *Général de brigade* Demont		
17th Regiment of the *Ligne*	(2)	1,561
30th Regiment of the *Ligne*	(2)	1,011
2nd Brigade: *Général de brigade* Debilly		
51st Regiment of the *Ligne*	(2)	1,214
61st Regiment of the *Ligne*	(2)	1,175
3rd Brigade: *Général de brigade* Eppler		
13th *Légère* Infantry Regiment	(2)	1,240
Division artillery and train:		
1st Company, 7th Regiment of Foot Artillery, with		77
Four 8-pounders and two 6-inch howitzers—total of six pieces of ordnance		
1st Battalion, Train of Artillery, one company		92

5th Corps Light Cavalry Division—*Général de brigade* Fauconnet—detached to the *Corps des Réserves de Cavalerie*

Attached from the *Corps des Réserves de Cavalerie*: 2nd Dragoon Division—*Général de division* Walther

	Bns/Sqdns	All Ranks Present & Under Arms at Austerlitz
Division headquarters staff—19 personnel		
1st Brigade: *Général de brigade* Sébastiani de la Porta		
3rd Regiment of Dragoons	(3)	177
6th Regiment of Dragoons	(3)	150
2nd Brigade: *Général de brigade* Roget de Belloguet		
10th Regiment of Dragoons	(3)	207
11th Regiment of Dragoons	(3)	196
3rd Brigade: *Général de brigade* Boussart		
13th Regiment of Dragoons	(3)	269
22nd Regiment of Dragoons	(3)	134
Division artillery and train:		
Detachment of the 2nd Company, 2nd Regiment of Horse Art., with		41
Two 8-pounders and one 6-inch howitzer—total of three pieces of ordnance		
Detachment, Train of Artillery		48

5th Corps Totals—

Staff		76
Infantry	21	12,818
Cavalry	18	1,133
Artillerists and supporting personnel, number of companies	7 ½	498
Total Present and Under Arms at Austerlitz		14,525 and 23 pieces of ordnance

Corps des Réserves de Cavalerie
Strengths as of 10 frimaire an XIV (1 December 1805)

Marshal Murat

Général de division Belliard, Chief of Staff
Général de brigade Hanicque, commanding the artillery
Colonel Hayelle, commanding the engineers
Corps headquarters staff—35 personnel

	Bns/Sqdns	All Ranks Present & Under Arms at Austerlitz
1st Heavy Cavalry Division—*Général de division* Nansouty		
Division headquarters staff—17 personnel		
1st Brigade: *Général de brigade* Piston		
1st Regiment of *Carabiniers*	(3)	205
2nd Regiment of *Carabiniers*	(3)	181
2nd Brigade: *Général de brigade* La Houssaye		
2nd Regiment of *Cuirassiers*	(3)	304
9th Regiment of *Cuirassiers*	(3)	280
3rd Brigade: *Général de brigade* Saint-Germain		
3rd Regiment of *Cuirassiers*	(3)	333
12th Regiment of *Cuirassiers*	(3)	277
Detachment of the 4th Company, 2nd Regiment of Horse Art., with:		44
Two 8-pounder guns and one 6-inch howitzer—total of three pieces of ordnance		
Detachment, Train of Artillery		48
2nd Heavy Cavalry Division—*Général de division* d'Hautpoul		
Division headquarters staff—14 personnel		
1st Brigade: Colonel Noirot		
1st Regiment of *Cuirassiers*	(3)	388
5th Regiment of *Cuirassiers*	(3)	375
2nd Brigade: *Général de brigade* Saint-Sulpice		
10th Regiment of *Cuirassiers*	(3)	254
11th Regiment of *Cuirassiers*	(3)	327
Detachment of the 4th Company, 2nd Regiment of Horse Art., with:		42
Two 8-pounder guns and one 6-inch howitzer—total of three pieces of ordnance		
Detachment, Train of Artillery		41
1st Dragoon Division—*Général de division* Klein—not present—detached to 3rd Corps—in route		
2nd Dragoon Division—*Général de division* Walther—detached to 5th Corps		
3rd Dragoon Division—*Général de division* Beaumont—detached to 4th Corps		
4th Dragoon Division—*Général de division* Bourcier—detached to 3rdCorps		
Light Cavalry Brigade—*Général de brigade* Milhaud		
Brigade headquarters staff—4 personnel		
1st Brigade: *Général de brigade* Milhaud		
16th *Chasseurs à cheval*	(3)	338
22nd *Chasseurs à cheval*	(3)	272
Attached from 1st Corps: 1st Corps Light Cavalry Division—*Général de division* Kellermann		
Division headquarters staff—18 personnel		
1st Brigade: *Général de brigade* Van Marisy		
2nd Hussars	(3)	328
5th Hussars	(3)	342
2nd Brigade: *Général de brigade* Picard		
4th Hussars	(3)	280
5th *Chasseurs à cheval*	(3)	317
Division artillery and train:		
1st Company, 3rd Regiment of Horse Artillery, with		79
Two 6-pounders, two 3-pounders and two 5.3-inch howitzers—total of six pieces of ordnance		
2nd Battalion, Train of Artillery, one company		78
Attached from 5th Corps: 5th Corps Light Cavalry Division—*Général de brigade* Fauconnet		
Corps cavalry division staff—8 personnel		
1st Brigade: *Général de brigade* Treillard		
9th Hussars	(3)	233
10th Hussars	(3)	261
2nd Brigade: *Général de brigade* Fauconnet		
13th *Chasseurs à cheval*	(3)	259
21st *Chasseurs à cheval*	(3)	256

	Companies	All Ranks Present & Under Arms	
***Corps des Réserves de Cavalerie* Artillery —**			
Corps artillery reserve staff—6 personnel			
2nd Battalion of French Engineers, 7th Company		52	
***Corps des Réserves de Cavalerie* Totals—**			
Cavalry	60	5,810	
Artillerists and supporting personnel, number of companies	4 ⅓	384	
Total Present and Under Arms at Austerlitz		6,194	and 12 pieces of ordnance

Grand Parc d'Artillerie (-)
Strengths as of 10 frimaire an XIV (1 December 1805)

***Grand Parc d'Artillerie*—deployed on the hill known as "The Santon"**	Companies	All Ranks Present & Under Arms	
16th, 17th and 18th Companies, 7th Regiment of Foot Artillery, with		230	
Eighteen captured Austrian 3-pounder guns as "batteries of position"—total of 18 pieces of ordnance			
2nd and 3rd Companies, *Ouvriers* of the Artillery		60	
4th Company, 8th Battalion of Train of Artillery		95	
French Train of *Ouvriers* of the Artillery, 1/2 company		28	
Total strength of all artillerists and supporting personnel for the *Grand Parc d'Artillerie*—		413	
***Grand Parc d'Artillerie* Totals—**			
Artillerists and supporting personnel, number of companies	7 ½	413	
Total Present and Under Arms at Austerlitz		413	and 18 pieces of ordnance

* *

RECAPITULATION
of the
GRANDE ARMÉE
at the Battle of Austerlitz
2 December 1805

Formation	Infantry Battalions	Cavalry Sqd./Regiments	Guns	Infantry	Cavalry	Total Present—All Arms
Suite de l'État-major	-0-	-0-	-0-	-0-	-0-	282*
IMPERIAL GUARD	6	8 1/2 / 2	24	3,885	1,129	5,690
Grenadiers de la Réserve	10	-0-	8	4,655	-0-	5,016
1st CORPS	18	-0-	22	10,861	-0-	11,346
3rd CORPS	10	21 / 7	12	3,200	830	4,304
4th CORPS	31	28 / 9	38	22,736	2,656	26,825
5th CORPS	21	18 / 6	23	12,818	1,133	14,525
RÉSERVES de Cavalerie	-0-	60 / 20	12	-0-	5,810	6,194
Grand Parc d'Artillerie	-0-	-0-	18	-0-	-0-	413
Including all artillerists and support personnel, general officers and staff personnel— Totals for the Army	96	135 1/2 / 44	157	58,155	11,558	74,595

* Excludes the 3rd Company, 2nd Battalion of French Engineers who were attached to Imperial Headquarters, as well as Napoleon's Military Household.

Source: C[2] 470, 472, 474, 476, 477 and 481, *Archives du Service Historique de l'État-Major de l'Armée de Terre,* (S.H.A.T.), VINCENNES, plus the *Journaux des opération* of the various corps.

Composition of the Artillery in the *Grande Armée* at the Battle of Austerlitz

Poundage of Guns and Number in each Corps

Corps Designation	3*/ 4 pdrs.	6 pdrs.*	8 pdrs.	12 pdrs.	Howitzers	Total in Corps
IMPERIAL GUARD	- /6	-	12	-	6	24
Grenadiers de la Réserve	- /2	-	6	-	-	8
1st CORPS	9* / -	9*	-	-	4 *	22
3rd CORPS	- / -	-	8	-	4	12
4th CORPS	- /6	-	19	6	7	38
5th CORPS	- /2	-	14	2	5	23
RÉSERVES de Cavalerie	- /2*	2*	4		4 *	12
Grand Parc d'Artillerie	18** / -	-	-	-	-	18
Totals—Mobile Ordnance	9 /18	11	63	8	30	139
Totals—Ordnance of Position	18** / -	-	-	-	-	18
Totals—All Pieces	27 /18	11	63	8	30	157

*All these 3-pounders and 6-pounders were Hanoverian ordnance, as were two 5.3-inch howitzers that were part of the French artillery companies of 1st Corps.

** These 3-pounders were captured Austrian ordnance that were positioned on "The Santon."

Source: C^2 470, 472, 474, 476, 477 and 481, *Archives du Service Historique de l'État-Major de l'Armée de Terre,* (S.H.A.T.), VINCENNES, plus the *Journaux des opération* of the various corps.

SITUATION of the COMBINED RUSSIAN AND AUSTRIAN ARMY at the Battle of Austerlitz

2 December 1805 (Strengths as of 27 November 1805)

The Tsar
Alexander I, commanding in person

Aides-de-Camp to the Tsar
General-Adjutant Dolgoruky
General-Adjutant Prince Volkonsky
General-Adjutant Wintzingerode

Nominal Commander-in-chief
General of Infantry Mikhail Ilariónovich Goleníchtchev Kutuzov

General-Feldwachtmeister (GM) Weyrother, Chief of Staff

Commander of the Austrian Contingent
Feldmarschall-Leutnant (FML) Prince Johann von Liechtenstein, with
The Emperor Francis II of Austria, also present

Escort for the Imperial Entourage:
Austrian Cüirassier-Regiment Kaiser #1, two squadrons

Commander of the First Three Columns
Lieutenant-General Buxhöwden

ADVANCE GUARD OF THE I. COLUMN
***Feldmarschall-Leutnant* (FML) Kienmayer**

	Bns/Sqdns	Present and Under Arms	
1st Brigade: *General-Feldwachtmeister* (GM) Carneville			
Broder *Grenz* #7 Infantry Regiment	(1)	350	These were survivors from two battalions.
1st Székler *Grenz* #14 Infantry Regiment	(2)	1,000	
2nd Székler *Grenz* #15 Infantry Regiment	(2)	1,100	
Austrian Pioneers, three companies	(-)	250	
2nd Brigade: GM Stutterheim			
Chevaulegers-Regiment O'Reilly #3	(8)	700	
Uhlanen-Regiment Merveldt #1	(¼)	25	
Two Austrian Cavalry Batteries, each with:			
Four 6-pounder guns and two howitzers—total of 12 pieces of ordnance.			
3rd Brigade: GM Count Nostitz-Rieneck			
Hussaren-Regiment Hessen-Homburg #4	(6)	360	
Uhlanen-Regiment Schwarzenberg #2	(½)	50	
4th Brigade: GM Prince Moritz Liechtenstein			
Székler-Grenz-Hussaren-Regiment #11	(8)	600	
Attached:			
Sysoev Cossack Regiment	(5)	200	
Melentev Cossack Regiment	(5)	300	
Totals of the Advance Guard of the I. Column, excluding artillerists		4,935	with 12 pieces of ordnance.

I. COLUMN—Lieutenant-General Dokhturov

1st Brigade: Major-General Lewis	Bns/Sqdns	Present and Under Arms	
7th *Jaeger* Regiment	(1)	470	This was the regiment's 1st Battalion.
New Ingermanland Musketeer Regiment	(3)	1,773	Two musketeer bns. and one grenadier bn.
2nd Brigade: Major-General Urasov			
Yaroslav Musketeer Regiment	(2)	754	One musketeer bn. and one grenadier bn.*
Vladimir Musketeer Regiment	(3)	1,649	Two musketeer bns. and one grenadier bn.
Bryansk Musketeer Regiment	(3)	829	Two musketeer bns. and one grenadier bn.
3rd Brigade:			
Vyatka Musketeer Regiment	(3)	379	Two musketeer bns. and one grenadier bn.
Kiev Grenadier Regiment	(3)	716	Two fusilier bns. and one grenadier bn.
Moscow Musketeer Regiment	(3)	882	Two musketeer bns. and one grenadier bn.
Attached:			
Denisov Cossack Regiment	(5)	210	
Russian pioneers, one company	(-)	90	

Column Artillery:

40 pieces of either 6-pounder guns or 10-pounder licornes serving as battalion ordnance for the 20 battalions in the musketeer and grenadier regiments.

Two Russian line heavy foot companies, each with:

Four medium 12-pounder guns, four light 12-pounder guns and four 18-pounder licornes—total of 24 pieces.

Totals of the I. Column, excluding artillerists 7,752 with 64 pieces of ordnance.

* Due to prior severe losses, the two musketeer battalions of this regiment were converged to form one operational battalion.

II. COLUMN—Lieutenant-General Langeron

1st Brigade: Major-General Olsuvev			
8th *Jaeger* Regiment	(2)	333	These were the 2nd and 3rd Battalions.
Viborg Musketeer Regiment	(3)	1,881	Two musketeer bns. and one grenadier bn.
Kursk Musketeer Regiment	(3)	1,908	Two musketeer bns. and one grenadier bn.
Perm Musketeer Regiment	(3)	1,911	Two musketeer bns. and one grenadier bn.
2nd Brigade: Major-General Kamensky I			
Fanagoria Grenadier Regiment	(3)	2,017	Two fusilier bns. and one grenadier bn.
Ryazan Musketeer Regiment	(3)	1,783	Two musketeer bns. and one grenadier bn.
Attached:			
Saint Petersburg Dragoons	(2)	320	
Isayev Cossack Regiment	(1)	40	
Russian pioneers, one company	(-)	90	

Column Artillery:

30 pieces of either 6-pounder guns or 10-pounder licornes serving as battalion ordnance for the 15 battalions in the musketeer and grenadier regiments.

Totals of the II. Column, excluding artillerists 10,283 combatants with 30 pieces of ordnance.

III. COLUMN—Lieutenant-General Prebyshevsky

1st Brigade: Major-General Müller III			
7th *Jaeger* Regiment	(2)	1,020	The regiment's 2nd and 3rd Battalions.
Galicia Musketeer Regiment	(3)	1,564	Two musketeer bns. and one grenadier bn.
2nd Brigade: Major-General Strik			
Butyrsk Musketeer Regiment	(3)	864	Two musketeer bns. and one grenadier bn.
Narva Musketeer Regiment	(3)	731	Two musketeer bns. and one grenadier bn.
3rd Brigade: Major-General Loshakov			
8th *Jaeger* Regiment	(1)	79	This was the 1st Battalion.
Azov Musketeer Regiment	(3)	591	Two musketeer bns. and one grenadier bn.
Podolia Musketeer Regiment	(3)	509	Two musketeer bns. and one grenadier bn.
Attached:			
Russian pioneers, one company	(-)	90	

Column Artillery:

30 pieces of either 6-pounder guns or 10-pounder licornes serving as battalion ordnance for the 15 battalions in the musketeer regiments.

Totals of the III. Column, excluding artillerists 5,448 with 30 pieces of ordnance.

IV. COLUMN—Lieutenant-General Miloradovich and *Feldzeugmeister* (FZM) Kolowrat

Advance Guard: Lieutenant-Colonel Monakhtin	Bns/Sqdns	Present and Under Arms	
Apsheron Musketeer Regiment	(1)	137	This was a musketeer battalion.
Novgorod Musketeer Regiment	(2)	513	One musketeer bn. and one grenadier bn.
Dragoons-Regiment Erzherzog Johann #1	(2)	100	
1st Brigade: Major-General Berg			
Novgorod Musketeer Regiment	(1)	256	One musketeer battalion.
Little Russia Grenadier Regiment	(3)	1,011	Two fusilier bns. and one grenadier bn.
2nd Brigade: Major-General Repninsky			
Apsheron Musketeer Regiment	(2)	273	One musketeer bn. and one grenadier bn.
Smolensk Musketeer Regiment	(3)	685	One musketeer bn. and one grenadier bn.
Austrian Infantry Brigade: GM Rottermund			
Salzburg IR#23	(6)	3,044	All battalions of the regiment were present..
Kaunitz-Rietberg IR#20	(1)	500	This was the 6th (depot) Battalion.
Auersperg IR#24	(1)	400	This was the 6th (depot) Battalion.
Austrian Infantry Brigade: GM Jurczik			
Kaiser Franz II IR#1	(1)	600	This was the 6th (depot) Battalion.
Czartorisky-Saggusco IR#9	(1)	600	This was the 6th (depot) Battalion.
Lindenau IR#29	(1)	500	This was the 4th Battalion.
Württemberg IR#38	(1)	600	This was the 3rd Battalion.
Josef Mittrowsky IR#40	(1)	600	This was the 6th (depot) Battalion.
Kerpen IR#49	(1)	700	This was the 6th (depot) Battalion.
Reuss-Greitz IR#55	(1)	600	This was the 6th (depot) Battalion.
Beaulieu IR#58	(1)	600	This was the 3rd Battalion.
Vienna Jäger, two companies	(-)	200	
Austrian pioneers, two companies	(-)	180	

Column Artillery:

Battalion pieces—

24 pieces of either 6-pounder guns or 10-pounder licornes serving as Russian battalion ordnance for the 12 battalions in the musketeer and grenadier regiments.

28 pieces of 3- and 6-pounder guns serving as battalion ordnance for the Austrian battalions. Note: not every Austrian battalion fielded battalion guns.

Field artillery—

One Russian line heavy foot company, with: Four medium 12-pounder guns, four light 12-pounder guns, and four 18-pounder licornes—total of 12 pieces of ordnance.

Two Austrian 12-pounder position batteries, each with: Four 12-pounder guns and two howitzers—total of 12 pieces.

Totals of the IV. Column, excluding artillerists — 12,099 combatants with 76 pieces of ordnance.

V. COLUMN—*Feldmarschall-Leutnant* (FML) Prince Johann von Liechtenstein

Austrian Cavalry—*Feldmarschall-Leutnant* (FML) Prince Hohenlohe

1st Brigade: GM Caramelli			
Cüirassier-Regiment Nassau-Usingen #5	(6)	300	
Cüirassier-Regiment Lothringen #7	(6)	300	
2nd Brigade: GM Weber			
Cüirassier-Regiment Kaiser #1	(6)	425	Two squadrons at Army HQ. 566 for all eight squadrons of the regiment.

Austrian Artillery:

One Austrian cavalry battery, with: Four 6-pounder guns and two howitzers—total of 6 pieces of ordnance.

Russian Cavalry—Lieutenant-Generals von Essen II and Skepelov

1st Brigade: Major-General Penitzki		
Grand Duke Constantine Uhlan Regiment #3	(10)	950
2nd Brigade: General-Adjutant Uvarov		
Elisabetgrad Hussar Regiment #5	(10)	950
Kharkov Dragoon Regiment #2	(5)	500
Chernigov Dragoon Regiment #3	(5)	366
Attached:		
Denisov Cossack Regiment	(21/2)	150
Gordeev Cossack Regiment	(5)	300
Isayev Cossack Regiment	(4)	240

Russian Artillery:

One Russian line horse artillery company, with: Six light 6-pounders and six 10-pounder licornes—total of 12 pieces.

One-half Russian line horse artillery company, with: Six light 6-pounders—total of six pieces.

Totals of the V. Column, excluding artillerists — 4,622 combatants with 24 pieces of ordnance.

ADVANCE GUARD OF THE ARMY—Major-General Prince Bagration

	Bns/Sqdns	Present and Under Arms
1st Brigade: Major-General Dolgoruky		
5th *Jaeger* Regiment	(3)	1,440
6th *Jaeger* Regiment	(3)	364
2nd Brigade: Major-General Kamensky II		
Arkhangelgorod Musketeer Regiment	(3)	1,947
3rd Brigade: Major-General Engelhardt		
Old Ingermanland Musketeer Regiment	(3)	2,009
Pskov Musketeer Regiment	(3)	1,978
4th Brigade: Major-General Wittgenstein		
Pavlograd Hussar Regiment #2	(10)	722
Mariupol Hussar Regiment #3	(10)	712
5th Brigade: Major-General Voropaitzki		
Leib-*Cuirassier* "Tsar's" (Kaiser)	(5)	566
Tver Dragoon Regiment #4	(5)	632
Saint Petersburg Dragoon Regiment #13	(3)	480
Attached: Major-General Chaplits		
Khaznenkov Cossack Regiment	(5)	300
Kiselev Cossack Regiment	(5)	300
Malakhov Cossack Regiment	(5)	300

Column Artillery:

Battalion pieces—

18 pieces of either 6-pounder guns or 10-pounder licornes serving as Russian battalion ordnance for the nine battalions in the three musketeer regiments.

Field artillery—

One Russian line horse artillery company, with: Six light 6-pounder guns and six 10-pounder licornes—total of 12 pieces of ordnance.

Two Austrian cavalry batteries, each with: Four 6-pounder guns and two howitzers—total of 12 pieces of ordnance. These two Austrian batteries were not on the field when the battle start, but arrived from Olmütz during the afternoon.

Totals of the Advance Guard of the Army, excluding artillerists 11,750 combatants with 42* pieces of ordnance.
* This is the total for the battle. Bagration began the fight with 30 pieces of ordnance, the two Austrian batteries arriving later.

RUSSIAN IMPERIAL GUARD—Grand Duke Constantine

INFANTRY OF THE RUSSIAN IMPERIAL GUARD—Lieutenant-General Maliutin

1st Brigade: Major-General Depreradovich I			
Preobrazhensky Imperial Guard Regiment #1	(2)	1,000	Two fusilier battalions.
Semenovsky Imperial Guard Regiment #2	(2)	1,000	Two fusilier battalions.
Izmailovsky Imperial Guard Regiment #3	(2)	1,000	Two fusilier battalions.
Guard *Jaeger* Battalion	(1)	500	
2nd Brigade: Major-General Lobanov			
Imperial Guard Grenadier Regiment	(3)	1,900	Three grenadier battalions.
Imperial Guard Pioneers, one company	(-)	100	

CAVALRY OF THE RUSSIAN IMPERIAL GUARD—Lieutenant-General Kologrivov

1st Brigade: Major-General Jankovich		
Imperial Guard Hussar Regiment	(5)	800
Imperial Guard Cossack Regiment	(2)	300
2nd Brigade: Major-General Depreradovich II		
Chevalier Garde Regiment	(5)	700
Gardes du Corps (Horse Guards) Regiment	(5)	800
Artillery of the Imperial Guard:		400

Battalion pieces—

20 pieces of either 6-pounder guns or 10-pounder licornes serving as Russian battalion ordnance for the ten battalions in the three Guard regiments, the Guard Grenadiers, and the Guard *Jaeger*. These 20 pieces were broken down from two Russian Guard Light Foot Companies, each of which had five medium 6-pounders and five 10-pounder licornes.

Field artillery—

One Russian Guard Horse Artillery Company, with: Five light 6-pounder guns and five 10-pounder licornes—total of 10 pieces of ordnance.

One Russian Guard Heavy Foot Company, with: Four medium 12-pounders, two light 12-pounders and four 18-pounder licornes—total of 10 pieces of ordnance.

Totals of the Russian Imperial Guard, including artillerists 8,500 combatants with 40 pieces of ordnance.

RECAPITULATION of the COMBINED RUSSIAN AND AUSTRIAN ARMY at the Battle of Austerlitz 2 December 1805

Formation	Infantry Battalions	Cavalry** Sqd./Regiments	Guns	Infantry	Cavalry**	Total Present— All Arms	
Army Headquarters	-0-	2 / -	-0-	-0-	-0-	NA	*
Adv. Gd. of I. Column	5	32¾ / 7	12	2,450	2,235	4,935	***
I. Column	21	5 / 1	64	7,452	210	7,752	***
II. Column	17	3 / -	30	9,833	360	10,283	***
III. Column	18	0	30	5,358	-0-	5,448	***
IV. Column	30	2 / -	76	11,619	100	12,099	***
V. Column	-0-	59½ / 10	24	-0-	4,622	4,622	***
ADV GD of the Army	15	48 / 8	42	7,738	4,012	11,750	***
IMPERIAL GUARD	10	17 / 4	40	5,400	2,600	8,500	****
Including all artillerists and support personnel, but excluding general officers and staff personnel—							
Totals for the Army	116	169¼ / 30	318	49,850	14,139	72,789	

* The two squadrons of the Austrian Cüirassier-Regiment Kaiser #1 were at army headquarters as escort for the Imperial entourage. All squadrons for this regiment are included in the V. Column totals.
** Includes both regular cavalry and Cossacks.
*** Includes pioneers, but excludes artillerists.
**** Imperial Guard totals includes pioneers and artillerists.

Source: österreichischen Kriegsarchiv, Vienna (K.A., F.A. Deutschland 1805); C² 13, *Archives du Service Historique de l'État-Major de l'Armée de Terre,* (S.H.A.T.), VINCENNES; and numerous regimental histories in the Russian Archives, Saint Petersburg.

Composition of the Artillery in the COMBINED RUSSIAN AND AUSTRIAN ARMY at the Battle of Austerlitz

Poundage of Guns and Number in each Column

Column Designation	6 pdrs.*	Howitzers	10-pdr. L	12 pdrs.	18-pdr. L	Total in Corps
Adv. Gd of the I. Column	8	4	-	-	-	12
I. Column	26	-	14	16	8	64
II. Column	20	-	10	-	-	30
III. Column	20	-	10	-	-	30
IV. Column	44	4	8	16	4	76
V. Column	16	2	6	-	-	24
Adv. Guard of the Army	26	4	12	-		42
IMPERIAL GUARD	15	-	15	6	4	40
Totals—All Ordnance	175	14	75	38	16	318

Ordnance Designation	6 pdrs.*	Howitzers	10-pdr. L	12 pdrs.	18-pdr. L	Total by Usage
Totals—Battalion pieces	116	-	56	-	-	172
Totals—in field companies	59	14	19	38	16	146
Totals—All Pieces	175	14	75	38	16	318

*One of the Austrian battalion guns was a 3-pounder. This piece has been included here in the 6-pounder totals.

Summary by Nationality—
COMBINED RUSSIAN AND AUSTRIAN ARMY
at the Battle of Austerlitz

Troop Nationality and Type	Bns/Sqdns	Present and Under Arms
Russian Infantry	95	38,656
Russian Regular Cavalry	82	8,798
Russian Cossacks	42 ½	2,340
Russian Pioneers		370
Total for Russians, excluding artillerists		50,164
Austrian Infantry	21	11,194
Austrian Cavalry	42 ¾	3,001
Austrian Pioneers and Jäger		630
Total for Austrians, excluding artillerists		14,825
Artillerists and train personnel		7,800
Total: Combined Russian and Austrian Army—Present and Available		72,789

Source: österreichischen Kriegsarchiv, Vienna (K.A., F.A. Deutschland 1805);
C^2 13, *Archives du Service Historique de l'État-Major de l'Armée de Terre,* (S.H.A.T.), VINCENNES and numerous regimental histories in the Russian Archives, Saint Petersburg.

General Comments on Allied Troop Strengths at Austerlitz

For almost 200 years, allied troops strengths at the Battle of Austerlitz have been overestimated. While a separate chapter could be devoted to the origin and continued perpetuation of the familiar estimated number of 85,000 or more Russians and Austrians that were present on 2 December 1805, the author—as with his 1983 work *Armies at Waterloo*—chose to go back to the army archives and regimental histories to validate the number of troops actually present and under arms at Austerlitz.

The reasoning for such an approach is obvious. No matter how many times one sees the same number of allied troops repeated in innumerable secondary sources, nothing can possibly be more accurate than the empirical reports held in various army archives. Through painstaking reconstruction using the Austrian, Russian and French army archival sources, the number of allied troops that were present at Austerlitz as detailed in this appendix were far less than what has previously been believed. Perhaps what is most revealing about this laborious methodology, is how the author saw the strengths of Kutuzov's army dwindle at an alarming rate through battle casualties and strategic consumption. From the time this Russian army started the campaign, through its advance to Braunau, its subsequent retreat from that place, including the battles at Amstetten, Dürenstein and Schöngrabern, until its reorganization at Olmütz, Kutuzov lost over 60% of his men (see the chart in Chapter VI). Higher estimates of the regiments that began the campaign under Kutuzov fail to allow for the significant casualties and numerous stragglers that conspired to eviscerate this general's army from the beginning of the campaign until the time of the great battle. It is of no small importance that the venerable Christopher Duffy, writing in his study, *Austerlitz*, states that the oft-repeated numbers of allied troops supposedly present at the Battle of Austerlitz represents an "over-optimistic nominal establishment"[1] of those forces.

The less than previously accepted numbers of Russians and Austrians also helps to explain to some degree the magnitude of Napoleon's greatest victory. When one considers the impressive victories won by significantly outnumbered French forces at Haslach-Jungingen, Elchingen and Dürenstein, it is little wonder that the outcome of Austerlitz, where the highly-trained *Grande Armée* actually outnumbered the Combined Russian and Allied Army, was as impressive as it turned out to be.

[1] Duffy, *Austerlitz*, p. 96.

SITUATION of Selected Formations of the *GRANDE ARMÉE*

in December 1805

IMPERIAL GUARD
Strengths as of 1 nivôse an XIV (22 December 1805)

Marshal Bessières
Général de brigade Roussel, Chief of Staff
Colonel Couin, commanding the artillery
Corps headquarters staff—15 personnel

	Bns/Sqdns	All Ranks Present & Under Arms	
Infantry of the Imperial Guard			
1st Brigade: *Général de brigade* Hulin			
Regiment of *Grenadiers à pied* of the Imperial Guard	(2)	1,648	
2nd Brigade: *Général de brigade* Soulès			
Regiment of *Chasseurs à pied* of the Imperial Guard	(2)	1,679	
3rd Brigade—Regiment of the Royal Italian Guard: Colonel Lecchi			
Battalion of *Grenadiers à pied* and			
Battalion of *Chasseurs à pied* of the Royal Italian Guard	(2)		detached; in Münich
Cavalry of the Imperial Guard			
1st Brigade: *Général de brigade* Ordener			
Regiment of *Grenadiers à cheval* of the Imperial Guard	(4)	629	
2nd Brigade: Colonel Morland			
Regiment of *Chasseurs à cheval* of the Imperial Guard	(4)	394	
Company of *Mameluks* of the Imperial Guard	(½)	48	
3rd Brigade: *Général de division* Savary			
Regiment of *Gendarmerie d'élite* of the Imperial Guard	(2)		detached

Artillery of the Imperial Guard—

1st, 2nd and 3rd Companies of Horse Artillery (*Volante)* of the Imperial Guard
Each of the above three horse artillery companies had identical ordnance, consisting of:
Three 8-pounders, two 4-pounder and one 6-inch howitzers—total of six pieces of ordnance in each company= 18 pieces.
Company of Horse Artillery of the Royal Italian Guard, one company, consisting of:
Three 8-pounders and two 4-pounders and one 6-inch howitzer—total of six pieces of ordnance.
Two line foot companies from the *Grand Parc d'Artillerie*, attached as reserve artillery and consisting of:
Six 12-pounders, two 4-pounders and four 6-inch howitzers—total of 12 pieces of ordnance.

All the artillerists from the three *Volante* companies totaled—		254	
Train of the Imperial Guard Artillery		332	
Matelots (Marins) of the Guard		117	
Flying Ambulance of the Guard (Larrey)			Not available
Total strength of all artillerists and supporting personnel for the entire Imperial Guard—		703	
Imperial Guard Totals—			
Staff		15	
Infantry	6	3,327	
Cavalry	8 ½	1,071	
Artillerists and supporting personnel, number of companies	4	703	
Total Present and Under Arms		5,116	and 36 pieces of ordnance
Total number of horses with the Imperial Guard	4,203 *		
Total number of personnel in rear areas, including detachments and personnel in hospitals		820	
Total of personnel in hospitals		283	
Total effectives—all personnel, including general officers & staffs		6,219	and 36 pieces of ordnance

*Some 752 of these horses were with officers and men who were detached and currently not present with the main body.

3rd CORPS
Strengths as of 1 nivôse an XIV (22 December 1805)

Marshal Davout

Général de brigade Fournier de Loysonville Daultane, Chief of Staff
Général de division Sorbier, commanding the artillery
Général de brigade Andreossy, commanding the engineers
Corps headquarters staff—33 personnel

	Bns/Sqdns	All Ranks Present & Under Arms	
1st Infantry Division—*Général de division* Caffarelli du Falga—detached to 5th Corps			
2nd Infantry Division—*Général de division* Friant			
Division headquarters staff—22 personnel			
1st Brigade: *Général de brigade* Kister			
15th *Légère* Infantry Regiment*	(2)	812*	
2nd Brigade: *Général de brigade* Lochet			
48th Regiment of the *Ligne*	(2)	1,221	
111th Regiment of the *Ligne*	(2)	1,390	
3rd Brigade: *Général de brigade* Grandeau			
33rd Regiment of the *Ligne*	(2)	981	
Division artillery and train:			
7th Regiment of Foot Artillery, one company		105	
1st Battalion, Train of Artillery, one company		109	
Ouvriers of Artillery		2	
*Six companies of the 15th *Légère* were detached from the regiment and formed the 2nd Battalion, 5th Regiment of the *Grenadiers de la Réserve* in 5th Corps.			
3rd Infantry Division—*Général de division* Gudin			
Division headquarters staff—18 personnel			
1st Brigade: *Général de brigade* Petit			
12th Regiment of the *Ligne*	(2)	1,557	
21st Regiment of the *Ligne*	(2)	1,852	
2nd Brigade: *Général de brigade* Gauthier			
25th Regiment of the *Ligne*	(2)	1,695	
85th Regiment of the *Ligne*	(2)	1,749	
Division artillery and train:			
7th Regiment of Foot Artillery, one company		103	
1st Battalion, Train of Artillery, one company		124	
Attached: One company of the 2nd *Chasseurs à cheval*		57	
3rd Corps Light Cavalry Division—*Général de brigade* Viallanes			
Corps cavalry division staff—4 personnel			
1st Brigade: *Général de brigade* —			
1st *Chasseurs à cheval*	(3)	531	
2nd *Chasseurs à cheval,* less one company with 3rd Inf. Div.	(3)	481	
12th *Chasseurs à cheval*	(3)	548	
7th Hussars	(3)	477	
3rd Corps Artillery Reserve—			
Corps artillery reserve staff—16 personnel			
7th Regiment of French Foot Artillery, 21/2 companies		182	
5th Regiment of French Horse Artillery, 5th company		89	
1st and 2nd Battalions, French Train of Artillery, 21/2 companies		191	
Ouvriers of the Artillery		14	
French Engineers, one company		78	
Total strength of all artillerists and supporting personnel for the 3rd Corps Artillery Reserve—		554	
3rd Corps Totals—			
Staff		93	
Infantry	16	11,257	
Cavalry	12	2,094	
Artillerists and supporting personnel, number of companies	13	997	
Total Present and Under Arms		14,441	and 31 pieces of ordnance
Total number of horses with the 3rd Corps	2,689		
Total number of detached personnel in rear areas		1,467	
Total number of personnel in hospitals		1,823	
Total effectives—all personnel, including general officers & staffs		17,731	and 31 pieces of ordnance

4th CORPS
Strengths as of 16 frimaire an XIV (7 December 1805)

Marshal Soult

Général de division Salligny, Chief of Staff
Général de brigade Lariboissière, commanding the artillery
Colonel Poitevin, commanding the engineers
Corps headquarters staff—28 personnel

	Bns/Sqdns	All Ranks Present & Under Arms
1st Infantry Division—*Général de division* Saint Hilaire		
Division headquarters staff—20 personnel		
1st Brigade: *Général de brigade* Morand		
10th *Légère* Infantry Regiment	(2)	1,121
2nd Brigade: *Général de brigade* Thiébault		
14th Regiment of the *Ligne*	(2)	1,386
36th Regiment of the *Ligne*	(2)	1,048
3rd Brigade: *Général de brigade* Waré		
43rd Regiment of the *Ligne*	(2)	1,130
55th Regiment of the *Ligne*	(2)	1,205
Division artillery and train:		
5th Regiment of Foot Artillery, 12th Company		98
5th Regiment of Foot Artillery, detachment of the 16th Company		22
1st Battalion, Train of Artillery, one company		132
2nd Battalion of French Engineers, 9th Company		47
2nd Infantry Division—*Général de division* Vandamme		
Division headquarters staff—22 personnel		
1st Brigade: *Général de brigade* Schiner		
24th *Légère* Infantry Regiment	(2)	658
2nd Brigade: *Général de brigade* Ferrey		
4th Regiment of the *Ligne*	(2)	1,704
28th Regiment of the *Ligne*	(2)	1,509
3rd Brigade: *Général de brigade* Candras		
46th Regiment of the *Ligne*	(2)	1,234
57th Regiment of the *Ligne*	(2)	1,743
Division artillery and train:		
5th Regiment of Foot Artillery, 13th Company		95
5th Regiment of Foot Artillery, detachment of the 16th Company		22
2nd Battalion, Train of Artillery, one company		132
3rd Infantry Division—*Général de division* Legrand		
Division headquarters staff—20 personnel		
1st Brigade: *Général de brigade* Merle		
26th *Légère* Infantry Regiment	(2)	1,210
Tirailleurs du Pô	(1)	361
Tirailleurs corses	(1)	409
2nd Brigade: *Général de brigade* Lavasseur		
18th Regiment of the *Ligne*	(2)	1,189
75th Regiment of the *Ligne*	(2)	1,756
3rd Brigade: *Général de brigade* Féry		
3rd Regiment of the *Ligne*	(3)	1,364
Division artillery and train:		
5th Regiment of Foot Artillery, 14th Company		94
5th Regiment of Foot Artillery, detachment of the 16th Company		22
3rd Battalion, Train of Artillery, one company		101
4th Corps Light Cavalry Division—*Général de brigade* Margaron		
Corps cavalry division staff—5 personnel		
1st Brigade: *Général de brigade* Margaron		
8th Hussars	(3)	345
11th *Chasseurs à cheval*	(4)	337
26th *Chasseurs à cheval*	(3)	310
Division artillery and train:		
5th Regiment of Horse Artillery, 4th Company		91
3rd Battalion, Train of Artillery, one company		52

4th Corps Artillery Reserve—			
Corps artillery reserve staff—2 personnel			
5th Regiment of Foot Artillery, 17th and 18th Companies		144	
1st Battalion, Train of Artillery, two companies		229	
Ouvriers of the Artillery, 1/4 company		23	
Total strength of all personnel—4th Corps Artillery Reserve		396	
4th Corps Totals—			
Staff	97		
Infantry	31	19,027	
Cavalry	10	992	
Artillerists and supporting personnel, number of companies	14 ¼	1,304	
Total Present and Under Arms		21,434	and 57 pieces of ordnance
Total number of horses with the 4th Corps		2,557	
Total number of detached personnel in rear areas		2,236	
Total number of personnel in hospitals		6,362	
Total effectives—all personnel, including general officers & staffs		30,032	and 57 pieces of ordnance

5th CORPS
Strengths as of 1 nivôse an XIV (22 December 1805)

Marshal Mortier, commanding in place of Marshal Lannes

Général de brigade Compans, Chief of Staff
Général de brigade Foucher de Careil, commanding the artillery
Colonel Kirgener, commanding the engineers
Corps headquarters staff—25 personnel

	Bns/Sqdns	All Ranks Present & Under Arms
1st Infantry Division (*Grenadiers de la Réserve*)—*Général de division* Oudinot—detached to the Army Reserve		
2nd Infantry Division—*Général de division* Gazan—not present—detached and in Vienna		
3rd Infantry Division—*Général de division* Suchet		
Division headquarters staff—included in total		
1st Brigade: *Général de brigade* Claparède		
17th *Légère* Infantry Regiment	(2)	
2nd Brigade: *Général de brigade* Beker		
34th Regiment of the *Ligne*	(3)	
40th Regiment of the *Ligne*	(2)	
3rd Brigade: *Général de brigade* Valhubert		
64th Regiment of the *Ligne*	(2)	
88th Regiment of the *Ligne*	(2)	
Division artillery and train:		
15th Company, 5th Regiment of Foot Artillery		
Detachment of the 16th Company, 5th Regiment of Foot Artillery		
Detachment of the 5th Company, 1st Regiment of Foot Artillery		
3rd Battalion, Train of Artillery, two companies		
Total Present and Under Arms for Suchet's 3rd Division—		7,652
Attached from 3rd Corps: 1st Infantry Division—*Général de division* Caffarelli du Falga		
Division headquarters staff—included in total		
1st Brigade: *Général de brigade* Demont		
17th Regiment of the *Ligne*	(2)	
30th Regiment of the *Ligne*	(2)	
2nd Brigade: *Général de brigade* Debilly		
51st Regiment of the *Ligne*	(2)	
61st Regiment of the *Ligne*	(2)	
3rd Brigade: *Général de brigade* Eppler		
13th *Légère* Infantry Regiment	(2)	
Division artillery and train:		
1st Company, 7th Regiment of Foot Artillery, with		
1st Battalion, Train of Artillery, one company		
Total Present and Under Arms for Caffarelli's Division—		6,923
5th Corps Light Cavalry Division—*Général de brigade* Fauconnet		
Corps cavalry division staff—included in total		
1st Brigade: *Général de brigade* Treillard		
9th Hussars	(3)	
10th Hussars	(3)	
2nd Brigade: *Général de brigade* Fauconnet		
13th *Chasseurs à cheval*	(3)	
21st *Chasseurs à cheval*	(3)	
Total Present and Under Arms for 5th Corps Light Cavalry—		1,160
5th Corps Artillery Reserve —		
Corps artillery reserve staff—included in total		
Artillerists, two foot companies and one horse company		240
5th Battalion, French Train of Artillery, five companies		203
French Engineers, one company		46
Total Present and Under Arms for 5th Corps Reserve Artillery		489

Attached from the *Corps des Réserves de Cavalerie*: 2nd Dragoon Division—*Général de division* Walther

Division headquarters staff—included in total		
1st Brigade: *Général de brigade* Sébastiani de la Porta		
3rd Regiment of Dragoons	(3)	
6th Regiment of Dragoons	(3)	
2nd Brigade: *Général de brigade* Roget de Belloguet		
10th Regiment of Dragoons	(3)	
11th Regiment of Dragoons	(3)	
3rd Brigade: *Général de brigade* Boussart		
13th Regiment of Dragoons	(3)	
22nd Regiment of Dragoons	(3)	
Division artillery and train:		
Detachment of the 2nd Company, 2nd Regiment of Horse Art., with Two 8-pounders and one 6-inch howitzer—total of three pieces of ordnance		
Detachment, Train of Artillery		
Total Present and Under Arms for Walther's 2nd Dragoon Division—		3,183

5th Corps Totals—

Corps HQ Staff		25
Infantry Divisions Totals	21	14,575
Cavalry Divisions Totals	30	4,343
Artillery Reserve Totals		489
Total Present and Under Arms		19,432 and 31 pieces of ordnance

6th CORPS
Strengths as of 15 frimaire an XIV (6 December 1805)

Marshal Ney
Général de brigade Dutaillis, Chief of Staff
Général de brigade Séroux, commanding the artillery
Colonel Cazals, commanding the engineers
Corps headquarters staff—38 personnel

	Bns/Sqdns	All Ranks Present & Under Arms
1st Infantry Division—*Général de division* Dupont—detached to Marshal Mortier		
2nd Infantry Division—*Général de division* Loison		
Division headquarters staff—13 personnel		
1st Brigade: *Général de brigade* Villate		
6th *Légère* Infantry Regiment	(2)	1,523
39th Regiment of the *Ligne*	(2)	1,475
2nd Brigade: *Général de brigade* Rouget		
69th Regiment of the *Ligne*	(2)	1,417
76th Regiment of the *Ligne*	(3)	2,215
3rd Infantry Division—*Général de division* Malher		
Division headquarters staff—13 personnel		
1st Brigade: *Général de brigade* Marcognet		
25th *Légère* Infantry Regiment	(3)	1,346
27th Regiment of the *Ligne*	(2)	1,544
2nd Brigade: *Général de brigade* Labassée		
50th Regiment of the *Ligne*	(2)	1,581
59th Regiment of the *Ligne*	(2)	1,549
6th Corps Light Cavalry Division—*Général de division* Tilly		
Corps cavalry division staff—7 personnel		
1st Brigade: *Général de brigade* Duprès		
1st Hussars, detached—with Dupont		
3rd Hussars	(3)	389
10th *Chasseurs à cheval*	(3)	490
Mounted Gendarmes		49
6th Corps Artillery Reserve—		
Corps artillery reserve staff—10 personnel		
1st Regiment of French Foot Artillery, 9th, 10th, 11th & 12th Cos		339
2nd Regiment of French Horse Artillery, detachment from 1st Company		41
3rd & 5th Battalions, French Train of Artillery, four companies, and detachments of two others		354
Ouvriers of the Artillery, 1/2 of the 4th Company		21
Total strength of all personnel—6th Corps Artillery Reserve		755
6th Corps Totals—		
Staff		81
Infantry	18	12,650
Cavalry	6	928
Artillerists and supporting personnel, number of companies	8 +	755
Total Present and Under Arms		14,414 and 30 pieces of ordnance*
Total number of horses with the 6th Corps	1,948	
Total number of detached personnel in rear areas		960
Total number of personnel in hospitals		2,417
Total effectives—all personnel, including general officers & staffs		17,791 and 30 pieces of ordnance*

*The 30 pieces listed above were of French origin. Inspection notes on the 1er nivôse an XIV parade states mention that Artillery Reserve of 6th Corps also had 12 Austrian pieces, consisting of four 6-pounders, four 3-pounders and two howitzers.

7th CORPS
Strengths as of 15 frimaire an XIV (6 December 1805)

Marshal Augereau

Général de brigade Donzelot, Chief of Staff
Général de division Dorsner, commanding the artillery
Colonel Lagastine, commanding the engineers
Corps headquarters staff—33 personnel

	Bns/Sqdns	All Ranks Present & Under Arms	
1st Infantry Division—*Général de division* Desjardins			
Division headquarters staff—20 personnel			
1st Brigade: *Général de brigade* Lapissè			
16th *Légère* Infantry Regiment	(3)	2,372	
2nd Brigade: *Général de brigade* Lamarque			
44th Regiment of the *Ligne*	(2)	1,359	
105th Regiment of the *Ligne*	(2)	1,523	
Division Artillery:			
4th Company, 3rd Regiment of Foot Artillery		99	
1st and 2nd Companies, 8th Battalion, Train of Artillery		184	
2nd Company, 4th Battalion of Engineers		83	
Detachment, Equipment Train		21	
Attached			
7th *Chasseurs à cheval,* 2nd Squadron	(1)	102	
2nd Infantry Division—*Général de division* Maurice Mathieu			
Division headquarters staff—18 personnel			
1st Brigade: *Général de brigade* Sarut			
7th *Légère* Infantry Regiment	(2)	2,044	
63rd Regiment of the *Ligne*	(2)	1,336	
2nd Brigade: *Général de brigade* Sarazin			
24th Regiment of the *Ligne*	(3)	2,115	
4th Company, 4th Battalion of Engineers		84	
Division Artillery:			
3rd Company, 3rd Regiment of Foot Artillery		100	
3rd and 4th Cos., 8th Battalion, Train of Artillery		168	
Attached			
7th *Chasseurs à cheval,* 3rd Squadron	(1)	152	
7th Corps Artillery Reserve—			
Corps artillery reserve staff—3 personnel			
3rd Regiment of French Foot Artillery, 2nd & 5th Cos.			detached
6th Regiment of French Horse Artillery, 5th company		96	
8th Battalion, French Train of Artillery, 5th and 6th Companies			detached
Attached:			
7th *Chasseurs à cheval,* 1st Squadron (4th Sqdrn. detached)	(1)	163	
Mounted Gendarmes		24	
7th Corps Totals—			
Staff		74	
Infantry	14	10,749	
Cavalry and Mounted Gendarmes	3	441	
Artillerists and supporting personnel, number of companies	7 ½	835	
Total Present and Under Arms		12,099	and 28 pieces of ordnance
Total number of horses with the 7th Corps	1,640		
Total number of personnel in rear areas, including detachments and personnel in hospitals		755	
Total effectives—all personnel, including general officers & staffs		12,854	and 28 pieces of ordnance

PROVISIONAL CORPS
Strengths as of 15 frimaire an XIV (6 December 1805)

Marshal Mortier
Général de brigade Godinot, Chief of Staff
Corps headquarters staff—4 personnel

	Bns/Sqdns	All Ranks Present & Under Arms	
1st Infantry Division (from 6th Corps)—*Général de division* Dupont			
Division headquarters staff—16 personnel			
1st Brigade: *Général de brigade* Rouyer			
9th *Légère* Infantry Regiment	(2)	1,212	
2nd Brigade: *Général de brigade* Marchand			
32nd Regiment of the *Ligne*	(2)	1,142	
96th Regiment of the *Ligne*	(2)	1,157	
Attached:			
1st Hussars	(3)	272	
Division Artillery and Train—			
Detachment of the 2nd Regiment of Horse Artillery, with Two 8-pounder guns—total of two pieces		39	
1st Regiment of Foot Artillery, one company, serving Two 4-pounders and four 6-inch howitzers—total of six pieces.		85	
3rd Battalion, Train of Artillery, one company and *ouvriers*		111	
Ouvriers of Artillery		4	
Mounted Gendarmes		5	
2nd Infantry Division (from the 5th Corps)—*Général de division* Gazan			
Division headquarters staff—12 personnel			
1st Brigade: *Général de brigade* Graindorge			
4th *Légère* Infantry Regiment	(3)	766	
58th Regiment of the Ligne	(2)		detached—at Braunau
2nd Brigade: *Général de brigade* Campana			
100th Regiment of the *Ligne*	(3)	1,589	
103rd Regiment of the *Ligne*	(3)	1,712	
Attached:			
4th Regiment of Dragoons	(3)	278	
Division Artillery and Train—			
Detachment of Horse Artillery, with Two 8-pounder guns—total of two pieces		40	
Foot Artillery, one company, serving Two 12-pounders, four 8-pounders, two 4-pounders and one 6-inch howitzers —total of nine pieces of ordnance		120	
Train of Artillery, one company		113	
Ouvriers of Artillery		5	
3rd Infantry Division (from 2nd Corps)— *Général de division* Dumonceau			
Division headquarters staff—22 personnel			
1st Brigade: *Général de brigade* Van Heldring			
1st Batavian *Légère* Infantry Regiment	(1)	481	
2nd Batavian *Légère* Infantry Regiment	(1)	329	
1st Batavian Regiment of the *Ligne*	(2)	717	
2nd Batavian Regiment of the *Ligne*	(2)	697	
2nd Brigade: *Général de brigade* Van Hadel			
Régiment de Waldeck	(2)	670	
6th Batavian Regiment of the *Ligne*	(2)		detached
Attached:			
Detachment, 1st Batavian Light Dragoons	(-)	54	
Division Artillery and Train: Three 8-pounders, one 4-pounder and one howitzer—total of five pieces of ordnance		289	
Provisional Corps Totals—			
Staff	54		
Infantry	23	9,802	
Cavalry	6	604	
Artillerists and supporting personnel, number of companies	6⅔	811	
Total Present and Under Arms		11,271	and 24 pieces of ordnance
Total number of horses with the Provisional Corps	1,047		
Total number of detached personnel in rear areas		646	
Total number of personnel in hospitals		3,115	
Total effectives—all personnel, including general officers & staffs		15,032	and 24 pieces of ordnance

Grand Parc d'Artillerie
Strengths as of 1 nivôse an XIV (21 December 1805)

Colonel Vermot, Director
Grand Parc d'Artillerie headquarters staff—32 personnel

Grand Parc d'Artillerie	Companies	All Ranks Present & Under Arms
French Foot Artillery, 11 companies		
French Horse Artillery, two companies		
The 13 companies of artillerists manned the following French ordnance:		
Forty-four 12-pounders, 161 8-pounders, 60 4-pounders and 63 6-inch howitzers—total 328 pieces.		
Also available for use were hundreds of captured Austrian pieces.		
1st Battalion, French *Pontonnier*s, three companies		
French Ouvriers of the Artillery, two companies		
French Armorers, 1/2 company		
French Train of Artillery, 18 companies		
French Train of Ouvriers of the Artillery, 1/2 company		
Total strength of all artillerists and supporting personnel for the entire *Grand Parc d'Artillerie*—		3,533
***Grand Parc d'Artillerie* Totals—**		
Artillerists and supporting personnel, number of companies	37	3,533
Total Present and Under Arms		3,533 and 328 French pieces of ordnance
Total number of horses with the Grand Park	2,692	
Total number of personnel in rear areas		N/A
Total of personnel in hospitals		N/A
Total effectives—all personnel, including general officers & staffs		3,533 and 328 French pieces of ordnance

ALLIED TROOPS EMPLOYED AS GARRISONS IN THE REAR AREAS OF THE ARMY
Strengths as of 1 nivôse an XIV (22 December 1805)

Württemberg Division—*Général de division* Baron de Séeger—in Linz

	Bns/Sqdns	All Ranks Present & Under Arms
Baron Hügel, Chief of Staff		
Division headquarters staff—10 personnel		
1st Brigade: *Général de brigade* von Seckendorff		
Infantry Regiment *Prinz Paul*	(1)	258
Infantry Regiment *Kronprinz*	(1)	549
Infantry Regiment *Herzog Wilhelm*	(1)	568
2nd Brigade: *Général de brigade* von Lilienberg		
Infantry Regiment *von Seckendorf*	(1)	564
Infantry Regiment *von Lilienberg*	(1)	311
3rd Brigade: Colonel von Roman		
Jäger Battalion *König*	(1)	161 *
Jäger Battalion *von Neuffer*	(1)	153 *
Light Infantry Battalion *von Scheler*	(1)	438
Light Infantry Battalion *Neubronn*	(1)	183 *
*Each of these battalions had entire companies detached from the parent battalion.		
Attached:		
König Chevaulegers	(4)	358
Division artillery and train:		
Württemberg Horse Artillery, one company		122
Württemberg Foot Artillery, one company		88
Württemberg Artillerists—Parc de Reserve		63
The artillerists manned the following pieces, with:		
Twelve 6-pounder guns and ten 7-pounder howitzers—total of 22 pieces of ordnance.		

Württemberg Division Totals—

Division Staff	-	10
Infantry	9	3,185
Cavalry	4	358
Artillerists and supporting personnel, number of companies	3	273
Total Present and Under Arms		3,826 and 22 pieces of ordnance
Total number of horses with the Würtembergers	670	
Total number of personnel detached and in rear areas		1,794
Total number of personnel in hospitals		110
Total effectives—all personnel, including general officers & staffs		5,730 and 22 pieces of ordnance
(Also, please see Appendix E.)		

Baden Brigade—*Général de brigade* de Harranth—in Donauwörth

Brigade headquarters staff—6 personnel		
1st Brigade: *Général de brigade* de Harranth		
1st Regiment *Grossherzog*, 1st Battalion	(1)	
1st Regiment *Grossherzog*, 2nd Battalion	(1)	
2nd Regiment *Erbgrossherzog*, 1st Battalion	(1)	
2nd Regiment *Erbgrossherzog*, 2nd Battalion	(1)	
Jäger Battalion de Lingg	(1)	
Hussars	(-)	
Baden Foot Artillery Company		
All personnel, number of battalions or squadrons	5	
Total Present and Under Arms		2,206 and 8 pieces of ordnance
(Also, please see Appendix E.)		

THE BAVARIAN ARMY
Strengths as of 13 frimaire an XIV (4 December 1805)

	Bns/Sqdns	All Ranks Present & Under Arms
Advance Guard of the Bavarian Army—General-Leutnant Baron von Wrede		
Bavarian Advance Guard headquarters staff—Numbers not available		
1st Brigade: Major General Minneri		
5th Infantry Regiment *Preysing*	(2)	1,317
7th Infantry Regiment	(2)	1,272
1st Light Infantry Battalion *Metzen*	(1)	577
1st Chevaulegers Regiment *Kronprinz*	(4)	209
1st Dragoon Regiment *Minucci*	(4)	233
5th Brigade: Major General Count Minucci		
8th Infantry Regiment *Herzog Pius*	(2)	1,262
12th Infantry Regiment *Löwenstein*	(2)	1,273
4th Light Infantry Battalion *Stengel*	(1)	583
3rd Chevaulegers Regiment *Leiningen*	(4)	222
Company of Bavarian Horse Artillery, consisting of:		169
Four 6-pounder guns and two howitzers—total of six pieces of ordnance		
Infantry Regimental Artillery: Eight 6-pounder guns attached, with two guns supporting each of the four infantry regiments.		
1st Division of the Bavarian Army—General-Leutnant Baron von Deroi		
Bavarian Division headquarters staff—Numbers not available		
2nd Brigade: General-Major Marsigli		
1st Infantry Regiment *Leib Gardes*	(2)	1,307
2nd Infantry Regiment *Kronprinz*	(2)	1,276
2nd Light Infantry Battalion *Vincenti*	(1)	638
2nd Chevaulegers *König*	(4)	318
3rd Brigade: General-Major Count Mezzanelli		
3rd Infantry Regiment *Prinz Karl*	(2)	1,280
4th Infantry Regiment *Salern*	(2)	1,280
9th Infantry Regiment *Ysenburg*	(2)	1,280
10th Infantry Regiment *Junker*	(2)	1,280
13th Infantry Regiment	(2)	1,280
3rd Light Infantry Battalion *Preysing*	(1)	640
4th Chevaulegers Regiment *Bubenhofen*	(4)	370
4th Brigade: General-Major von Siebein		
6th Infantry Regiment *Herzog Wilhelm*	(2)	1,270
5th Light Infantry Battalion *LaMotte*	(1)	640
6th Light Infantry Battalion *Steinbach*	(1)	640
2nd Dragoon Regiment *Taxis*	(4)	318
Division Artillery and Train:		
1st and 2nd Companies of Bavarian Foot Artillery		
Each of the foot artillerist companies had identical ordnance, consisting of:		
Four 12-pounder guns and two howitzers—total of six pieces of ordnance in each company—12 total pieces.		
Company of Bavarian Horse Artillery, with:		
Four 6-pounder guns and two howitzers		
—total of six pieces of ordnance in the horse artillery company.		
All the artillerists from the three companies totaled		440
Infantry Regimental Artillery: Sixteen 6-pounder guns were in the field		
—two pieces with each of the eight regiments of infantry.		
Bavarian Army Totals—		
Infantry	30	19,095
Cavalry	24	1,670
Artillerists and supporting personnel, number of companies	4	609
Total Present and Under Arms		21,374 and 48 pieces of ordnance

Note: The composition of the Bavarian brigades changed several times during the 1805 war. For example, compare the details shown in Appendices B and E with the Bavarian returns in this appendix.

RECAPITULATION of Selected Formations of the *GRANDE ARMÉE* in December 1805

Formation	Infantry Battalions	Cavalry Sqd./Regiments	Guns	Infantry	Cavalry	Total Present— All Arms*
IMPERIAL GUARD	4	8½ / 2	24	3,327	1,071	5,116
3rd CORPS	16	12 / 4	31	11,257	2,094	14,441
4th CORPS	31	10 / 3	57	19,027	992	21,434
5th CORPS	21	30 / 10	31	14,575	4,343	19,432
6th CORPS	18	6 / 2	30	12,650	928	14,414
7th CORPS	14	3 / 1	28	10,749	441	12,099
PROVISIONAL CORPS	23	8 / 3	24	9,802	604	11,271
Grand Parc d'Artillerie	-0-	-0-	328	-0-	-0-	3,533
Württembergers	9	4 / 1	22	3,185	358	3,826
Badeners	5	-0-	8			2,206
Bavarians	30	24 / 6	48	19,095	1,670	21,374

*Includes all artillerists and support personnel, but does not include detached personnel, or those in hospitals.

Source: C[2] 470, 476, 477, 481, 482, 483, 484 and 485, *Archives du Service Historique de l'État-Major de l'Armée de Terre,* (S.H.A.T.), VINCENNES.

Composition of the Artillery in the entire *Grande Armée* on 1er nivôse an XIV (21 December 1805)

Poundage of Guns and Number in each Corps

Corps Designation	3 / 4 pdrs.	6 pdrs.	8 pdrs.	12 pdrs.	Howitzers	Total in Corps
IMPERIAL GUARD	- / 10	-	12	6	8	36
1st CORPS	12* / -	12*	-	2	6	32
2nd CORPS	- / 6	-	16	-	8	30
3rd CORPS	- / 6	-	14	6	5	31
4th CORPS	- / 8	-	32	8	9	57
5th CORPS	- / 6	6	12	6	1	31
6th CORPS	- / 6	-	16	6	2	30 **
7th CORPS	- / 5	-	15	-	8	28
PROVISIONAL CORPS	- / 5	-	11	2	6	24
RÉSERVES de Cavalerie	- / -	2	12	-	7	21
Grand Parc d'Artillerie	- / 60	-	161	44	63	328 ***
Württembergers	- / -	12	-	-	10	22
Badeners	- / -	6	-	-	2	8
Bavarians	- / -	32	-	8	8	48
Totals for the Army	12* / 112	70	301	88	143	726

* All these 3-and 6-pounders were Hanoverian ordnance.

** These were French pieces. There were also a total of 12 Austrian pieces in the 6th Corps Artillery Reserve, consisting of four 6-pounders, four 3-pounders and four howitzers.

*** Only the French ordnance in the *Grand Parc d'Artillerie* are listed in this return.

Source: C[2] 470, 472, 474, 475, 476, 477, 481, 482, 483, and 484, *Archives du Service Historique de l'État-Major de l'Armée de Terre,* (S.H.A.T.), VINCENNES.

The Hours of Dawn during the Austerlitz Campaign

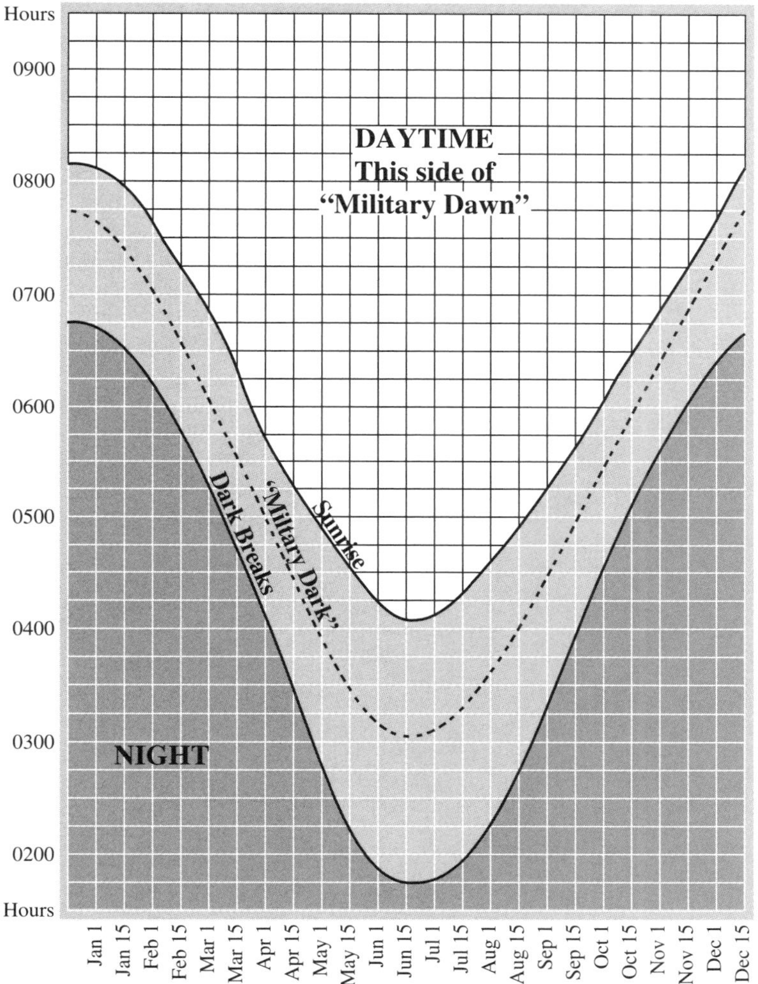

The time of dawn has been calculated for the latitude of Brunn.

The Hours of Dawn during the Austerlitz Campaign

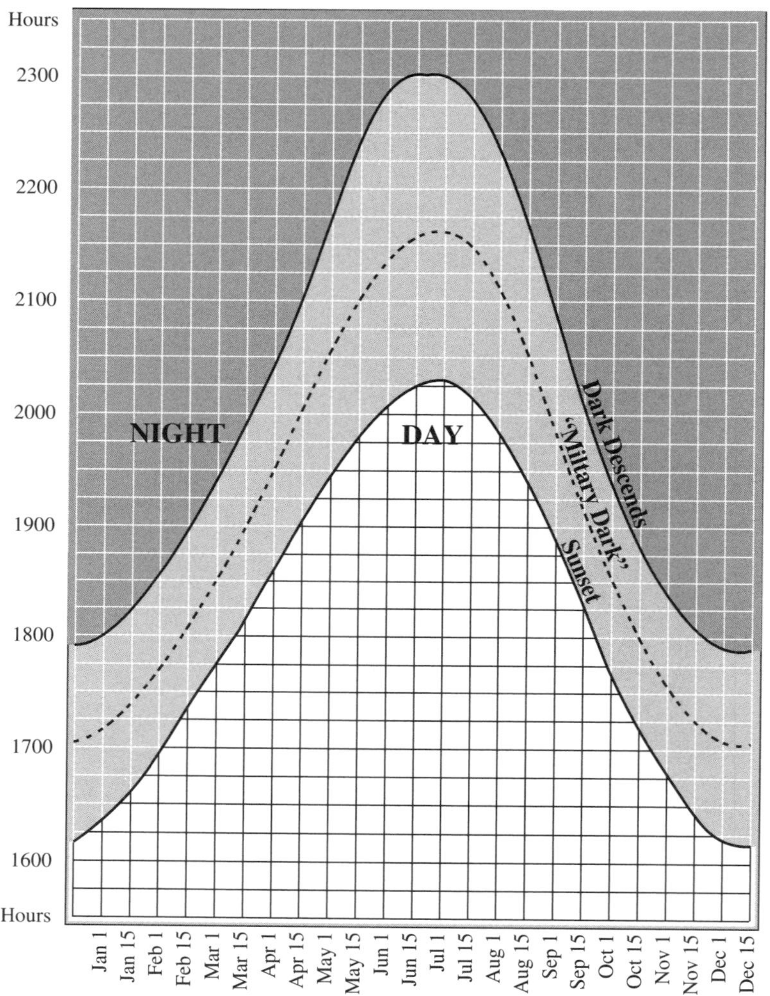

The time of dusk has been calculated for the latitude of Brunn.

SELECT BIBLIOGRAPHY

Archival Sources

The *Archives du Service historique de l'état-major de l'armée* at the Château de Vincennes (S.H.A.T.) proved the principal source of manuscript material for *Napoleon and Austerlitz.* The contents from 193 different cartons at S.H.A.T., totaling thousands of pieces of correspondence and troop returns, were utilized by the author. Among the most helpful cartons that contained the general correspondence of the *Grande Armée* of 1805 included C^2 1 through 10, plus other documents found in cartons from C^2 18 through 24, and 201, plus documents in C^3 5, C^4 4 and 5 that dealt with the *Armée d'Italie* and Eugène's communiques with Napoleon. Other cartons contained specific correspondence from various Napoleonic military and civil officials during 1805. Among those many which were used included the "Orders of the Day" for the *Grande Armée* (C^2 11, 12 and 241), the extensive *Registres* of correspondence that dealt with the Channel encampments and Hanover that included C^2 12, 191, 192, 193, 194, 212, 213, 214, 218, 223 and 235, 236, 237, and C^{17} 159, 160 and 163. The details on the training, organization and development of the troops in the Channel encampments spanned dozens of cartons. The *Registre* of General Belliard found in C^2 240 was also consulted often, as were the valuable cartons C^2 13 through 17 that detailed the allied forces, prisoners taken at Ulm and Austerlitz, along with details on Frenchmen killed, wounded and captured in the 1805 war. Many cartons in the "X" series containing organizational details were of great help, as were the "2w" and "4w" series cartons that dealt with the artillery. Also, carton C^2 470 contained the organization details of the early French Empire as seen at the end of Chapter I. Finally, the various "Situations" (detailing officers and men present and under arms, detached, in hospitals, etc.) of the *Grande Armée* during the 1805 war were taken from S.H.A.T., using the various *Journaux des opérations* of the different corps, plus the following cartons: C^2 470, 472, 474, 475, 476, 477, 479, 481, 482, 483, 484, 485 and 724.

Also, of important use were:

Archives Nationale, Paris, that included several cartons in the "AF IV" series on personnel and *matériel* of artillery, as were the "AP" series that included the Ney Papers.

Kriegsgeschichtlichen Abteilung des k. und k. Kriegsarchiv, Vienna. Most often consulted were: *Feldacten*; *Tagebuch: Deutschland 1805*; Weyrother's *Disposition*; Adolf Beer's *Österreich und Rußland in den Jahren 1804 und 1805*; *Ausführliche Relation der am 2 ten Dezember, 1805*; O. Regele, "Karl Freiherr von Mack und Johann Ludwig Graf Cobenzl. Ihre Rolleim Kriegsjahr 1805." *Mittheilungen des Österreichischen Staatsarchivs.*

P. Benedikt Baader's *Chronik von Elchingen* in the Staatsarchiv, Augsburg.

P. Birle's *Geschichte des französischen Krieges von 1805.* Archiv Oberelchingen.

P. Baumgartner's *Chronik von Thalfingen.* Archiv Thalfingen.

Public Records Office (PRO), Foreign Office Papers (FOP), London.

Voenno-Istoritjeskij Musej Artillerij, Insjenernich Woisk i Woisk Swjasi (Military Museum of Artillery, Pioneers and Signal troops), Saint Petersburg.

Vorontsov, Semen R. "Zapiski S. R. Vorontsov o Russkom Voiske, Predstavlennaya Imperatoru Aleksandru Palvlovichu v 1802 godu," *Arkiv Knyazya Vorontsova.* 40 Volumes. Moscow 1870-1895.

Official Histories and Regulations

Journal Militaire.

Instruction concernant les manœuvres de la cavalerie légère (Year VII).

Règlement concernant l'exercise et les manœuvre de l'infanterie du 1er août 1791.

Règlement concernant le service intérieur des troupes à cheval du 24 juin 1792.

Ordonnance concernant l'exercise et manœuvres de l'infanterie du 12e pluviôse an XIII, simplified and renamed *Le système de discipline et manœuvres d'infanterie formant les bases de tactiques modernes* and adopted throughout the Empire for drill use by the National Guard formations.

Ordonnance provisoire du 1er vendémiaire an XIII.

Bellegarde, General der Cavalerie Heinrich von. *Erstes Feld-Manoeuvre bei Aviano den May 1805. Annahme, Wechselseitige Lagen Beyder Armeen, und Ihre Absichten.* Vienna, 1805.

Davout, Louis N. *Opérations du 3e Corps, 1806-1807. Rapport du maréchal Davout, duc d'Auerstadt.* Edited by Général Léopold Davout. Paris, 1896.

Ministere de la Marine. *Historique de L'Artillerie de la Marine.* Paris, 1889.

Russian General Staff. *Stoletie Voennogo Ministerstva.* Saint Petersburg, 1902-1913.

Memoirs and Correspondence

Abrantès, Laure Junot, duchesse d'. *Mémoires de Mme. la duchesse d'Abrantès ou souvenirs historiques sur Napoléon, la Révolution, le Directoire, le Consulat, l'Empire et la Restauration.* 10 volumes. Paris, 1893.

Ameil, General Auguste Jean Joseph Gilbert. *Notes et Documents.* In the *Sabretache* 1906 and 1907.

Aubry, Joseph Thomas. *Souvenirs du 12e chasseurs (1799-1815).* Paris, 1889.

Barrès, Jean-Baptiste. *Memoirs of a French Napoleonic Officer: Jean-Baptiste Barrès, Chasseurs of the Imperial Guard.* Translated by Bernard Miall. London, 1925.

Beaucour, Fernand Émile. *Lettres, Décisions et Actes de Napoléon à Pont-de-Briques (An VI/1798 - An XII/1804).* Levallois, 1979.

Belliard, Augustin Daniel. *Mémoires du comte Belliard.* Paris, 1842.

Bigarré, Auguste. *Mémoires du général Bigarré, aide de camp du roi Joseph.* Paris, 1893.

Berthezène. General Baron Pierre. *Souvenirs militaires de la République et de l'Empire.* 2 volumes. Paris, 1855.

Blocqueville, Adélaïde-Louis de. *Le Maréchal Davout prince d'Eckmühl: correspondance inédite 1790-1815: Pologne, Russie, Hambourg.* Paris, 1887.

Bourrienne, M. de. *Mémoires de Bourrienne.* 10 volumes. Paris, 1829.

Buckingham and Chandos, Duke of. *Memoirs of the Courts and Cabinets of George III.* London, 1835.

Chaptal, Jean Antoine, comte de Chanteloup. *Mes Souvenirs sur Napoléon.* Paris, 1893.

Coignet, Jean-Roch. *Les Cashiers du Capitaine Coignet (1799-1815).* Paris, 1883.

Comeau, Baron de. *Souvenirs des Guerres d'Allemagne.* Paris, 1900.

Czartoryski, Prince. *Mémoires du Prince Czartoryski.* Paris, 1887.

Gallina, J. "Suggestions for the Drill and Evolutions of Foot," *Beiträge zur Geschichte des österreichischen Heerwesens.* Volume 1, *Der Zeitraum von 1757-1814.* Vienna 1872.

Gourgaud, Gaspard. *Sainte Hélène: Journal inédit de 1815 à 1818.* 2 volumes. Paris, no date.

Griois, General L. *Mémoires.* 2 volumes. Paris, 1909.

Davout, Louis N. *Correspondance du maréchal Davout prince d'Ekmühl: ses commandements, son ministère, 1801-15.* Edited by Charles de Mazade. 4 volumes. Paris, 1885.

d'Hautpoul, Armand. *Souvenirs sur la Révolution, l'Empire et la Restauration.* Paris, 1904.

Ermolov, A. P. *Zapiski A. P. Ermolova.* 2 volumes. Moscow, 1965-1968.

Fairon, E. and H. Heusse. *Lettres des grognards.* Paris, 1936.

Fantin des Odoards, General. *Journal du Général Fantin des Odoards.* Paris, 1895.

Fézensac, Général Raymond-Aimery-Philippe-Joseph de Montesquiou. *Souvenirs militaires.* Paris, 1863.

Girardin, Stanislas-Cécile comte de. *Mémoires, journal et souvenirs de S. de Girardin.* 2 volumes. Paris, 1829.

Griois, General. *Mémoires du général Griois (1792-1822).* 2 volumes. Paris, 1902.

Las Cases, Emmanuel. *Mémorial de Saint Hélène*. 9 volumes. Paris, 1897.

Kutuzov, Mikhail Ilariónovich Golenichtchev. *M. I. Kutuzov. Sbornik Dokumentov*. 5 volumes. Moscow, 1950-1956.

Langeron, Andrault comte de. *Mémoires du comte Langeron: Austerlitz, campagne de Russe, bataille de Paris.* Revue Rétrospective, 1895.

Lecestre, Léon. *Lettres inédites de Napoléon 1er (an VII-1815)*. 2 volumes. Paris, 1897.

Levasseur, Octave. *Souvenirs Militaires d'Octave Levasseu, officier d'artillerie, aide-de-camp du maréchal Ney, publiés par le commandant Beslay.* Paris, 1914.

Lejeune, General Baron. *Memoirs of Baron Lejeune*. Translated and edited by Mrs. Arthur Bell. 2 volumes. New York, 1897.

Lhomel, G. de. *Documents pour servir à l'Histoire de Montreuil-sur-Mer de 1789 à 1830.* 2 parts. Paris, 1965.

Napoleon I, Emperor. *Correspondance de Napoléon 1er*. 32 volumes. Paris, 1858-1870.

Napoleon I, Emperor. *Supplément à la Correspondance de Napoléon, Lettres Curieuses Omises par le Comité de Publication, Rectifications.* Edited by Albert DuCasse. Paris, 1887.

Napoleon I, Emperor. *Unpublished Correspondence of Napoleon I.* Edited by Ernest Picard. 5 volumes. New York, 1913.

Napoleon I, Emperor. *Lettres, Décisions et Actes de Napoléon à Pont-de-Briques (An VI/1798 - An XI/1804).* Compiled by Fernand Émile Beaucour. Levallois, 1979.

Napoleon I, Emperor. *The Confidential Correspondence of Napoleon Bonaparte with His Brother Joseph.* 2 volumes. London, 1855.

Napoleon I, Emperor. *The Military Maxims of Napoleon.* Translated by George C. D'Aguilar. London, 1901.

Marbot, Baron M. de. *Memoirs of Baron de Marbot.* Translated by Arthur J. Butler. 2 volumes. Paris, 1893.

Marmont, Auguste F. L. V. *Mémoires du Marechal Marmont, Duc de Raguse.* 9 volumes. Paris, 1857.

Malmesbury, The Earl of. *Diaries and Correspondence.* London, 1844.

Méneval, Claude-François, Baron de. *Memoirs of the Baron de Méneval.* Translated by His Grandson, Baron Napoleon Joseph de Méneval. 2 volumes. New York, 1894.

Montholon, Charles Tristan. *Histoire de la captivité de Saint-Hélène*. 2 volumes. Brussels, 1846.

Murat, Joachim. *Lettres et documents pour servir à l'histoire de Joachim Murat.* 8 volumes. Paris, 1909-1914.

Ney, Marshal Michel. *Memoirs of Marshal Ney: Published by His Family.* 2 volumes. London, 1834.

Oudinot, Nicolas Charles, Duc de Reggio. *Memoirs of Marshal Oudinot Duc de Reggio. Compiled from the Hitherto Unpublished Souvenirs of the Duchesse de Reggio.* Edited by Gaston Steigler, translated by Alexander Teixeira de Mattos. London, 1896.

Ney, Michel Louis Félix. *Military Studies.* Translated by G. H. Caunter. London, 1833.

Pétiet, A. *Souvenirs Militaires de l'Histoire Contemporaine.* Paris, 1844.

Pouget, General Baron. *Souvenirs de Guerre du Général Baron Pouget.* Paris, 1895.

Puraye, Jean. *Mémoires du Général Comte François Dumonceau, 1790-1881.* Brussels, 1958.

Rapp, General Jean. *Mémoires du Général Rapp, aide de camp de Napoléon.* 2 volumes. Paris, 1821.

Roguet, General. *Mémoires militaires du lieutenant-général comte Roguet, colonel en second des grenadiers à pied de la Vielle garde.* 4 volumes. Paris, 1862-1865.

Rumigny, Marie-Théodore Gueilly, comte de. *Souvenirs du général comte de Rumigny.* Paris, 1921.

Saint-Chamans, Alfred-Romand-Robert de. *Mémoires du général comte de Saint-Chamans, ancien aide-de-camp du maréchal Soult (1802-1823).* Paris, 1896.

Savary, General A.J.M.R., Duc de Rovigo. *Memoirs of the Duke of Rovigo.* English edition, 3 volumes. London, 1828.

Ségur, Philippe de. *An Aide-de-camp of Napoleon.* Translated by H.A. Patchett-Martin. London, 1895.

Schultes, David August. *Chronik von Ulm.* Ulm, 1880.

Thiard. General. *Souvenirs Diplomatiques et Militaires du Général Thiard.* Paris, 1805.

Thiébault, Baron. *The Memoirs of Baron Thiébault.* 2 volumes. Translated and condensed by Arthur John Butler, New York, 1896.

Secondary Works

Anon. *Austerlitz Raconté par les Témoins de la Bataille des Trois Empereurs.* Geneva, 1969.

Alombert-Goget, Captain Paul Claude, and Jean-Lambert-Alphonse Colin. *La Campagne de 1805 en Allemagne.* 6 volumes. Paris, 1902-1908.

Alombert-Goget, Captain Paul Claude. *Campagne de l'an XIV, Le corps d'armée aux ordres du maréchal Mortier. Combat de Durrenstein.* Paris, 1897.

Angeli, Moritz Elder von. "Ulm and Austerlitz. Studie auf Grund Archivalische Quellen ueber den Feldzug 1805 in Deutschland." *Österreichische Militärische Zeitschrift.* Vienna, 1877-1878.

Andolenko, General Serge. *Aigles de Napoléon Contre Drapeaux du Tsar 1799, 1805-1807, 1812-1814.* Paris, 1969.

Andolenko, General Serge. *Histoire de l'Armée Russe.* Paris, 1967.

Alexander, John T. *Catherine the Great.* Oxford, 1989.

Aubry, Octave. *Napoleon: Soldier and Emperor.* Translated by Arthur Livingston. New York, 1938.

Azan, Paul. *Du Rhin à Ulm.* Paris, 1909.

Bauer, Frieda. *Die Kämpfe um die Pässe Strub, Scharnitz und Leutasch 1805.* Vienna, 1987.

Bennett, Geoffrey. *The Battle of Trafalgar.* Annapolis, 1977.

Bergerot, Bernard. *Daru. Intendant général de la Grande Armée.* Paris, 1991.

Bernhardi, T. *Denkwürdigkeiten aus dem Leben des Kaisel. Russ. Generals . . . von Toll.* 4 parts. Leipzig, 1865.

Bertraud, Jean-Paul. *The Army of the French Revolution.* Translated by R. R. Palmer. Princeton, 1988.

Blond, Georges. *La Grande Armée.* Translated by Marshall May. London, 1995.

Bogdanovitch, Ivanovich. *Histoire de la Russe sous Alexandre Ier.* 6 volumes. Saint Petersburg, 1869-1871.

Bonnal, Henri. *La Vie militaire du Maréchal Ney, duc d'Elchingen, prince de la Moskowa.* Paris, 1911.

Bonnal, Henri. *L'Ésprit de la Guerre Moderne, de Rosbach à Ulm et la manœuvre d'Iena.* 2 volumes. Paris, 1903-1904.

Bottet, Captain Maurice. *Napoléon aux camps de Boulogne. La côte de fer et les flottilles.* Paris, 1914.

Boulay de la Meurthe, A. *Les dernières années du duc d'Enghien.* Paris, 1886.

Bourgue. *Historique du 3e régiment d'infanterie.* Paris, 1894.

Bowden, Scott. *Armies at Waterloo.* Arlington, 1983.

Bowden, Scott and Tarbox, Charles. *Armies on the Danube 1809*, revised and expanded edition. Chicago, 1989.

Bowden, Scott. *Napoleon's Grande Armée of 1813.* Chicago, 1990.

Bowden, Scott. "The 1812 French Uniform Myth." *Empires, Eagles & Lions.* July/August, 1993.

Bremond d'Ars, Théophile-Charles. *Historique du 21e régiment de chasseurs à cheval, 1792-1814.* Paris, 1903.

Bressonnet, Pascal. *Études Tactiques sur la Campagne de 1806.* Paris, 1909.

Buat, Edmond. *L'artillerie de campagne; son Histoire—son Évolution—son État Actuel.* Paris, 1911.

Bucquoy, Cdt. E.-L. *L'Infanterie de Ligne et L'Infanterie Légère.* In the series *Les Uniformes du Premier Empire.* 7 volumes. Paris, 1986.

Camon, H. *La Bataille Napoléonienne.* Paris, 1899.

Camon, H. *Les campagnes de la Grande Armée par un officier de la Vielle garde.* 3 volumes. Paris, 1856-1857.

Camon, H. *Quand et comment Napoléon a conçu son système de bataille.* Paris, 1935.

Camon, H. *La guerre Napoléonienne–Précis des campagnes.* 2 volumes. Paris, 1925.

Campana, Ignace Raphaël. *L'artillerie de campagne, 1792-1901.* Paris, 1901.

Chandler, David. *The Campaigns of Napoleon.* New York, 1966.

Chardigny, Louis. *Les maréchaux de Napoléon.* Paris, 1946.

Chatelle, Albert. *Napoléon et la Légion d'honneur au camp de Boulogne 1801-1805.* Paris, 1956.

Chapuisat, E. *La Suisse et la Révolution française.* Geneva, 1945.

Charrie, Pierre. *Drapeaux et Étendards de la Révolution et de l'Empire.* Paris, 1982.

Clermont, Paul de. *Le soleil d'Austerlitz, 1800-1815.* Paris, 1934.
Colin, Jean-Lambert-Alphonse. "La surprise des ponts de Vienne en 1805, Austerlitz, et la question des étangs d'Austerlitz." *Revue d'Histoire.* 1905, 1907 and 1908.
Connelly, Owen, Harold T. Parker, Peter W. Becker and June K. Burton. *Historical Dictionary of Napoleonic France, 1799-1815.* Westport, 1985.
Connelly, Owen. *Blundering to Glory: Napoleon's Military Campaigns.* Wilmington, 1987.
Cognazzo, J. *Freymüthige Beytrag zur Geschichte des österreichischen Militairdienstes.* Frankfort and Leipzig, 1789.
Courcelles, Jean-Baptiste-Pierre Jullien. *Dictionnaire historique et biographique des généraux français depuis le XIème siècle, jusqu' à 1820.* Paris, 1820-1823.
Coutanceau, H. H. Lepus and Clément La Jonquière. *La campagne de 1794 à l'armée du Nord.* 2 parts. Paris, 1903-1908.
Criste, Oskar. *Erzherzog Carl von Österreich.* 3 volumes. Vienna-Leipzig, 1912.
Criste, Oskar. *Feldmarschall Johannes Fürst von Liechtenstein.* Vienna, 1905.
Cronin, Vincent. *Napoleon Bonaparte: An Intimate Biography.* New York, 1972.
Dechamps, J. "La rupture de la Paix d'Amiens: Comment elle fut préparée." *Revue des Études napoléoniennes.* 1939.
Derselbe. *Die Schlacht bei Austerlitz am 2. 12. 1805.* Vienna, 1912.
Detaille, Edouard. *L'Armée Française.* New York, 1992.
Deutsch, Harold C. *The Genesis of Napoleonic Imperialism.* Philadelphia, 1975.
Dodge, Theodore Ayrault. *Hannibal.* 2 volumes. New York, 1891.
Dodge, Theodore Ayrault. *Napoleon: A History of the Art of War from the Beginning of the French Revolution to the End of the 18th Century. With a Detailed Account of the Wars of the French Revolution.* 4 volumes. New York, 1904-1907.
Dolleczek, A. *Geschichte des österreichischen Artillerie.* Vienna, 1887.
Dolleczek, A. *Monographie der k. und k. österrung blanken und Handfeurwaffen.* Vienna, 1896.
Duffy, Christopher. *Austerlitz.* London and Hamden, 1977.
Duffy, Christopher. *The Army of Maria Theresa.* New York, 1977.
Duffy, Christopher. *Russia's Military Way to the West.* London, 1981.
Egger, Rainer. *Das Gefecht bei Dürenstein-Loiben 1805.* Vienna, 1986.
Egger, Rainer. *Das Gefecht bei Hollabrunn und Schöngrabern 1805.* Vienna, 1974.
Elting, John R. *Swords Around A Throne.* New York, 1988.
Epstein, Robert M. *Prince Eugene at War: 1809.* Arlington, 1984.
Esposito, Brig. General Vincent J. and Elting, Colonel John Robert. *A Military History and Atlas of the Napoleonic Wars.* New York, 1968.
Esterházy de Gallantha, J. *Regulament und unumänderlich-gebräuchliche Observations-Puncten.* Gavi, 1747.
Fallou, Louis. *La Garde Impériale.* Paris, 1975 reprint of 1901 original.
Favé, General. *Études sur le passé et l'avenir de l'artillerie.* 5 volumes. Paris, 1871.
Fortescue, John W. *British Statesmen of the Great War 1793-1814.* Oxford, 1911.
Gallaher, John G. *The Iron Marshal.* Carbondale, 1976.
Griffith, Paddy. "King Nicolas." *Napoleon's Marshals.* Edited by David Chandler. New York, 1987.
Guibert, Jacques-Antoine-Hypolite de. *Essai général de tactique.* 2 volumes. London, 1773.
Hollander, O. *Les Drapeaux des Demi-Brigades d'Infanterie de 1794 à 1804.* Paris, 1913.
Hourtoulle, F.-G. *Davout; le terrible.* Paris, 1975.
Hourtoulle, F.-G. *Ney; le brave des braves.* Paris, 1981.
Jany, Curt. "Der Russische Soldat im Felde 1806." *Das Kasket.* Berlin and Vienna, 1925.
Janetschek, C. *Die Schlacht bei Austerlitz.* Brünn, 1898.
Jenkins, Michael. *Arakcheev: Grand Vizier of the Russian Empire.* London, 1969.
Job (Jacques Onfroy de Bréville). *Bonaparte.* Paris, 1975.
Johnson, David. *Napoleon's Cavalry and its Leaders.* New York, 1978.
Junkelmann, Marcus. *Napoleon und Bayern.* Regensburg, 1985.
Kennett, Lee. *The French Armies in the Seven Years' War.* Durham, 1967.
Khrestiachitsky. *Historique des Cosaques de la Garde.* Saint Peterburg, 1913.
Krauss, Generalmajor Alfred. *1805. Der Feldzug von Ulm.* Vienna, 1912.
Krestovsky. *Historique des Cosques de la Garde.* Saint Petersburg, 1876.
Lachouque, Commandant Henry. Translated by Anne Brown. *The Anatomy of Glory.* New

York, 1961.

Lachouque, Commandant Henry. *La Garde Impériale.* Paris, 1982.

Lachouque, Commandant Henry. *Napoléon à Austerlitz.* Paris, 1961.

Lauerma, Matti. *L'artillerie de campagne française pendant les guerres de la Révolution.* Helsinki, 1956.

Léonard, Emile G. *L'armée et ses problèmes au XVIII*[e] *siècle.* Paris, 1958.

Loeffler, E. von. *Das Treffen bei Elchingen und die Katastrophe von Ulm im Jahre 1805.* Ulm, 1904.

Lomier, D. *Le Bataillon des Marins de la Garde 1803-1815.* Paris, 1991 reprint of the 1905 original.

Lynn, John A. *Bayonets of the Republic.* Urbana, 1984.

Lynn, John A. "Toward an Army of Honor: The Moral Evolution of the French Army, 1789-1815," *French Historical Studies* 16 (Spring, 1989).

Lyons, Martyn. *Napoleon Bonaparte and the Legacy of the French Revolution.* New York, 1994.

Maccunn, F. J. *The Contemporary English View of Napoleon.* London, 1914.

Maksoutov. *Historique du 25*[e] *régiment d'infanterie Smolensk [Musketeers].* Saint Petersburg, 1901.

Manceron. Claude. *Austerlitz: The Story of a Battle.* Translated by George Unwin. New York, 1966.

Markham, Felix. *Napoleon.* New York, 1963.

Martinien, A. *Tableaux par Corps et par Batailles des Officiers Tués et Blessés Pendant les Guerres de l'Empire (1805-1815).* Paris, 1899.

Mayerhoffer von Vedropolje, Eberhard. *1805. Der Krieg der 3. Koalition gegen Frankreich (in Süddeutschland, Österreich u. Oberitalien).* Vienna, 1905.

Mercer, Cavalie. *Journal of the Waterloo Campaign.* New York, 1969 reprint from the London, 1870 edition.

Michiels, René and Raymond Perciaux. *Au soleil d'Austerlitz: l'apogée de l'Empire.* Geneva, 1974.

Mikhailovsky-Danilevsky, Lieutenant-General Aleksandr Ivanovich. *Relation de la campagne de 1805.* Paris, 1846.

Mikhailovsky-Danilevsky, Lieutenant-General Aleksandr Ivanovich. *Vie du Feld-Maréchal Koutouzoff, traduit du russe par A. Fizelier.* Paris, 1860.

Muller, P. *L'Espionnage Militaire sous Napoléon 1*[er]. Paris, 1896.

Müller and Brünn. *Geschichte der Bayern Armee.* Munich, 1903.

Müller and Brünn. *Organisation der Koeniglich-Bayerischen Armee, 1806-1906.* Munich, 1906.

Napoleon III. *History of Julius Caesar.* 2 volumes. New York, 1866.

Nicolaiev. *Historique du 17*[e] *régiment d'infanterie Arkhangelgorod [Musketeers].* Saint Petersburg, 1900.

Nicolay, Fernand. *Napoleon at the Boulogne Camp.* Translated by Georgina L. Davis. New York, 1907.

Nosworthy, Brent. *With Musket, Cannon and Sword: Battle Tactics of Napoleon and His Enemies.* New York, 1996.

Ojala, Jeanne A. *Auguste de Colbert: Aristocratic Survival in an Era of Upheaval 1793-1809.* Salt Lake City, 1979.

Oman, Sir Charles. *Wellington's Army.* London, 1913.

Pantchoulidzev. *Histoire des Chevaliers-Gardes.* Saint Petersburg, 1912.

Parker, Harold T. *Three Napoleonic Battles.* Durham, 1944.

Parker, Harold T. "Napoleon and the Values of the French Army: The Early Phases." *Proceedings of the Annual Meeting of the Western Society for French History.* 18 (November, 1990).

Parker, Harold T. "Why did Napoleon Invade Russia? A Study in Motivation, Personality & Social Structure." *Proceedings 1989, Consortium on Revolutionary Europe 1750-1850.* Edited by Donald D. Horward and John C. Horgan. Tallahassee, 1990.

Parkinson, J. *A Tour of Russia, Siberia and the Crimea 1792-1794.* London, 1971.

Picard, Commandant L. *La Cavalerie dans les guerre de la Révolution et de l'Empire.* 2 volumes. Saumur, 1895–1896.

Pigeard, Alain. *L'Armée Napoléonienne 1804-1815.* Paris, 1993.

Pigeard, Alain. *Les étoiles de Napoléon: Maréchaux, Amiraux & Généraux 1792-1815.* Paris, 1996.

Pimlott, John L. "Friendship's Choice." *Napoleon's Marshals.* Edited by David Chandler. New York, 1987.

Pravikov. *Petit historique du 10e grenadiers Petite Russe.* Morchansk, 1889.

Quennevat, Jean-Claude. *Atlas de la Grande Armée.* Paris-Brussels, 1966.

Quimby, Robert S. *The Background of Napoleonic Warfare.* New York, 1957.

Quintin, D & B. *Dictionnaire d'colonels de Napoléon.* Paris, 1996.

Regnault, General Jean. *Les aigles impériales et la drapeau tricolore 1804–1815.* Paris, 1967.

Reitzenstein, J. Freiherr von. *Das Geschützwesen und die Artillerie in den Landen Braunschweig und Hannover.* Leipzig, 1900.

Richardson, Robert G. *Larrey: Surgeon to Napoleon's Imperial Guard.* London, 1974.

Rivollet, Georges. *Général de bataille Charles Antoine Louis Morand, généraux Friant et Gudin du 3e Corps de la Grande Armée.* Paris, 1863.

Rothenberg, Gunther E. *Napoleon's Great Adversaries.* London, 1982.

Rousset, Camille. *Les volontaires, 1791-1794.* Paris, 1892.

Rüstow, W. *Der Krieg von 1805 in Deutschland und Italien.* Frauenfeld, 1853.

Saxe, Marshal Maurice de. *My Reveries on the Art of War.* Translated by T. R. Phillips. Harrisburg, 1940.

Schimmer, Karl August. *Dis französischen Invasionen in Österreich und die Franzosen in Wien in den Jahren 1805 und 1809.* Vienna, 1846.

Schönhals, Carl von. *Der Krieg in Deutschland.* Vienna, 1873.

Schroeder, Paul W. *The Transformation of European Politics 1763-1848.* Oxford, 1994.

Seton-Watson, Hugh. *The Russian Empire 1801-1917.* Oxford, 1967.

Simond. *Historique du 28e régiment d'infanterie.* Rouen, 1889.

Six, Georges. *Le Dictionnaire biographique des généraux et amiraux de la Révolution et de l'Empire.* edited by. George Saffroy. 2 volumes. Paris, 1934.

Six, Georges. *Les généraux de la Révolution et de l'Empire.* Paris, 1947.

Smith, Frederick E. *Waterloo.* London, 1970.

Smirnov. *Historique du 65e régiment d'infanterie Moscow.* Warsaw, 1890.

Stackelberg, Colonel. *Un siècle et demi de la Garde du Corps.* Saint Petersburg, 1881.

Stiegler, Gaston. *Le Maréchal Oudinot; Duc de Reggio d'après les Souvenirs Inédits de la Maréchale.* Paris, 1898.

Stocklaska, Walter. *Die Schlacht bei Austerlitz.* Brünn, 1905.

Stutterheim, Major-General. *A Detailed Account of the Battle of Austerlitz, by the Austrian Major-General Stutterheim.* London, 1807.

Suvórov, Generalissimo Aleksandr Vasil'evich. *Nauke pobezhdat (Art of Victory).* Moscow, 1806.

Suvórov, Generalissimo Aleksandr Vasil'evich. *Dokumenty.* 4 volumes. Moscow, 1949-1953.

Stein, F. von. *Geschichte des Russischen Heeres vom Ursprunge desselben bis zur Thronbesteigung des Kaisers Nikolai I. Pavlovich.* 2 volumes. Hanover, 1885.

Talandier, Jean. *Relation de la bataille de Durrenstein.* Strasbourg, 1835.

Thiers, M. Adolphe. *History of the Consulate and the Empire of France Under Napoleon.* Translated by D. Forbes Campbell and H. W. Herbert. 5 volumes. Philadelphia, 1875.

Thiry, Jean. *Ulm, Trafalgar, Austerlitz.* Paris, 1962.

Tolstoy, Leo. *War and Peace.* New York, 1978.

Tranie, Jean & Juan-Carlos Carmignani. *Napoléon et la Russie, les années victorieuses 1805-1807.* Paris, 1980.

Tulard, Jean, editor. *Dictionnaire Napoléon.* Paris, 1987.

Vachée, Le Commandant. *Etude du caractère militaire du maréchal Davout.* Paris, 1907.

Veynante, Commandant Jean-Claude. *Histoire de la tactique de l'infanterie française.* Paris-Limoges, 1892.

Willbold, Franz. *Napoleons Feldzug um Ulm Die Schlacht von Elchingen 14 Oktober 1805.* Ulm, 1987.

Willing, Paul. *Napoléon et ses Soldats l'Apogée de la Gloire 1804-1809.* Paris, 1977.

Wilson, Sir Robert. *Brief Remarks on the Character and COmposition of the Russian Army and a Sketch of the Campaigns in Poland in the Years 1806 and 1807.* London, 1810.

Wilson, Sir Robert. *History of the British Expedition to Egypt.* 18 January 1803 edition of *The Times.*

Wintle, Justin. *The Dictionary of War Quotations.* New York, 1989.

Wolf, François-Stanislas-Arthur. *Historique du 10e régiment de chasseurs à cheval depuis sa création jusqu'en 1890.* Paris, 1890.

Wrede, Major Alphons Freiherrn von. *Geschichte der k. und k. Wehrmacht. Die Regimenter, Corps, Branchen und Anstalten von 1618 bis Ende des XIX. Jahrhunderts.* 5 volumes. Vienna 1898-1905.

Zweguintzow, W. *L'Armée Russe.* 4 parts. Paris, 1973.

NAPOLEON AND AUSTERLITZ

Book and dust jacket design by Scott Bowden
Maps by David McElhannon
Thanks to Dave Waxtel for the use of the picture on this page from Quantum Printing's edition of Detaille's book, *L'Armée Française*

Composed in Times Roman PS
Printed by Print Systems, Inc. of Grand Rapids, Michigan, USA on 60# Smooth Husky Offset

"Information for the General Staff"—Detaille's look at the 1805 Campaign